# TRANSFORMATIVE CONSUMER RESEARCH
## FOR PERSONAL AND COLLECTIVE WELL-BEING

# TRANSFORMATIVE CONSUMER RESEARCH
## FOR PERSONAL AND COLLECTIVE WELL-BEING

Edited by

**David Glen Mick**
University of Virginia

**Simone Pettigrew**
University of Western Australia

**Cornelia Pechmann**
University of California, Irvine

**Julie L. Ozanne**
Virginia Tech

Routledge
Taylor & Francis Group

LONDON AND NEW YORK

First published 2012 by Routledge

2 Park Square, Milton Park, Abingdon, Oxfordshire OX14 4RN
52 Vanderbilt Avenue, New York, NY 10017

*Routledge is an imprint of the Taylor & Francis Group, an informa business*

First issued in paperback 2019

ISBN: 978-1-84872-852-3 (hbk)
ISBN: 978-0-367-86482-3 (pbk)

*To all researchers dedicated to improving well-being*

# Contents

# Foreword

## Consuming and Evolving

Like it or not, we are all consumers. Life is only possible because of consuming; every life-form must take in energy—sunshine, water, and minerals—to survive and reproduce. Humans are no different from plants or other animals in this respect. In fact, our species has developed into a superconsuming life-form. It can be said that what made us human—what allowed us to build pyramids and cathedrals, write symphonies, and develop scientific theories—is precisely the fact that we have been able to stimulate an upward spiraling demand for new knowledge, new artifacts, and new lifestyles.

Of course, like any strength pursued too far, our inclination to never be satisfied with what we have—our desire for more powerful technologies and more coddling lifestyles—has its dark side. Just over 50 years ago, the social philosopher Hannah Arendt (1958) warned us with impeccable farsightedness that our species, left clueless as to what it should do or aspire to do, was in danger of "consuming the world" out of listless boredom (p. 133). Year by year, her dystopic vision seems increasingly prophetic.

Is the doom of the human race to eat up the resources needed to keep alive the spark of life on this planet? The possibility is not too far-fetched, especially as the entire population of the earth is slipping into a daydream in which it is entitled to a life of effortlessness and waste formerly open only to nabobs, high priests, and other potentates. Almost 3,000 years ago, Emperor Mu Wang of China (ca. 985–907 BCE) paid a handsome salary to an engineer who was supposedly capable of building a self-propelled chariot, possibly one that could also fly. Yet, all the treasures of the Orient could not succeed in fulfilling the emperor's dream, one that any able-bodied person with no credit and no cash can now fulfill. What will happen to all of us when the present 1.3 billion Chinese are able to attain what eluded Mu Wang?

Yet, the doom is not foreordained. We have learned in the past decades that what will happen in the future is increasingly the function of human choice. Whereas past generations could resign themselves to blame the will of gods or demons or emperors, we are getting to realize that, by and large, it is our own choices today that will determine what tomorrow will bring. Biological evolution has been shaped in the past by external events, including ecological changes, variations in prey–predator ratios, and competition between phenotypes that were more or less adapted to the natural environment. After the first tools were developed around 12,000 years ago, human societies exploded into the plethora of things that became the bedrock of the first urban revolutions. Ever since, the future of humankind has been increasingly determined by cultural, rather than biological, evolution.

The gods that people worshipped, the languages they spoke, the weapons they forged, the kind of families they lived among, and the rulers they endured were all chosen or permitted by themselves—our ancestors. Most of the time they did not do so consciously, but rather, they followed the cultural script of their society. As the British biologist Richard Dawkins pointed out, it is the memes transmitted from one generation to the next, rather than the genes we carry in our chromosomes, that increasingly shape our future (Dawkins, 1976). In other words, we have come to realize that the responsibility for the future of the world is in our own hands. What kind of a world do we want to make and consume?

The act of *consuming*, which can be defined as the breaking down of natural or manmade structures to satisfy biological or cultural urges, is among the farthest reaching of human activities. What food we eat, what house we buy, what car we drive, and what leisure we engage in as neighbors, parents, or coworkers—these all have impacts on how the world will be a generation hence. Consuming is one of the most selective forces in determining which memes will survive, reproduce, and be transmitted into the future.

It has been in the interest of a capitalist economy to try exempting consumption from close analysis. In a free-market economy, citizens should be allowed, encouraged, or even required to consume. I remember driving home across the United States the day after the September 11 attacks, listening to the radio, as one politician after another exhorted listeners to go out and buy that car or refrigerator they had been contemplating, so our enemies would know that America was unflinching in its values and goals. The resolve to consume was framed as a sign of heroic vitality. Alas, our enemies were probably rejoicing upon hearing such messages. Who would fear a nation whose response to attack is, "Go forth and buy a refrigerator"? How do you explain to the rest of the world that in our society, you get flagged as a bad financial risk if you use your credit cards sparingly and do not go into debt? What recourse does the person in the street have when our eminent economists calculate societal well-being by lumping production vital to human welfare with the manufacture of land mines, toxic waste, tobacco, and other "goods" that will make our lives, and those of our descendants, increasingly miserable?

Given the biases resulting from a mindless worship of the invisible hand over a laissez-faire market, the responsibility for finding ways to understand the benefits and pitfalls of consuming falls on the shoulders of independent scholars. It is a serious task, one that would not be exaggerated to call a life-or-death quest, on par with cancer or climate research. The task, in short, is to make clearer how consumer behavior can help or impair human and planetary evolution.

All of us should cast a grateful optimism toward the scholars in the field of consumer research who have taken up this responsibility with the formation of a transformative agenda, by examining more closely how consumer behavior impacts personal and collective well-being. I take *transformative* in this context to mean that consumer behavior can be directed either by past habits and genetic instructions that might well destroy life on earth or by a vision based on knowledge that will transform human life on the planet from a self-inflicting disease into a self-enhancing growth. In other words, these researchers have chosen the task of helping consumer behavior become a selective factor in shaping the future that we can proudly leave as a heritage to our children and theirs.

The current volume is a significant stride in that direction. After the four opening chapters, which frame the conceptual approach of the book, the chapters that follow deal with some of the momentous issues that are involved in this difficult transformative task. They range from the socioeconomical context of consuming, the evolution of new technologies, the influence of materialism on the environment, and the effects of consumption on health (e.g., obesity, substance addictions) to considerations of debt versus saving and the neuroscience of consumption. The volume then closes with a series of upbeat chapters on topics such as sharing, resilience, and practical wisdom.

It is on these last themes that I would like to expand. As a psychologist, I have come to believe that one of the main forces in cultural evolution is the selective effect of human choice driven by enchantment and other positive experiences. In other words, we choose to support those things, persons, or procedures that we think will provide us with the greatest return—not necessarily in any material sense, but in terms of the quality of experience they may afford. The early mechanically powered technologies, like the waterwheels invented over 2 millennia ago in the Near East to turn millstones that ground grain, were greeted by poets as wonderful devices, making the lives of women easier and freer. That technology, like many more coming on its heels, spread rapidly, because it was a harbinger of a happier life—one in which women did not have to wake up before dawn to turn wheat into flour by grinding kernels between stones for hours so the family could have breakfast.

At Bell Labs, where the first transistor was developed by John Bardeen and his colleagues, the new discovery was treated as an interesting but ineffectual piece of technology. Its rights were subsequently sold for nearly nothing to Sony, where Masao Ibuka realized the transistor's potential for making radios small enough for people to carry around. He bet insightfully on the expectation that millions of people might appreciate listening to music as they walked among impersonal and noisy metropolitan crowds, and he was not disappointed. Consider, too, that cars were used at first for long-distance rallies, not useful, personal transportation. Additionally, the success of computers was due at least as much to their primitive electronic games as to their potential for helping people communicate with each other or balance their household budget.

The lesson I draw from these reflections is that if we wish to change consumer behavior in line with a positive evolutionary trend, then we need to find ways to provide alternatives to consumption that are as rewarding as consumption often promises to be. We know now that accumulating material goods, including money, is not a very powerful enhancer of the quality of life (e.g., Csikszentmihalyi, 1999; Kasser, 2003; Sheldon & McGregor, 2000), but perception is what counts. Emerging from a past of scarcity, people have come to equate happiness with possessions and the ability to get more. At the same time, contemporary societies have lost much of their abilities to design or find rewards in nonmaterial things. The transistor was a remarkable invention, but it also facilitated some arguably cheerless outcomes. Many Andean shepherds, for instance, put away their panpipes and *quenas* (flutes) in favor of Walkman radios. Slowly, the belief has spread that only the consumption of things, especially new things, can make a life worth living.

So, the challenge I see as the most pressing is to find forms of activity that are as interesting, exciting, and attractive as those we can buy at the store and then passively consume. Or at least, the challenge is to think of making commodities for the market that not only offer a temporary buzz or relaxation but also are in line with consciously selected, scientifically justified evolutionary goals. The present volume should serve as the first map for this transformative, evolutionary journey.

## REFERENCES

Arendt, H. (1958). *The human condition*. Chicago: University of Chicago Press.
Csikszentmihalyi, M. (1999). If we are so rich, why aren't we happy? *American Psychologist, 54*, 821–827.
Dawkins, R. (1976). *The selfish gene*. New York: Oxford University Press.
Kasser, T. (2003). *The high price of materialism*. Boston: MIT Press.
Sheldon, K. M., & McGregor, H. (2000). Extrinsic value orientation and the tragedy of the commons. *Journal of Personality, 68*, 383–411.

**Mihaly Csikszentmihalyi**
*Claremont Graduate University*

# Preface

The academic field of consumer research has evolved over the years into a radiant yet deficient prism. Its multihued insights have long served executives in making their organizations and businesses more competitive and more profitable. It has also frequently served scholars themselves in seeking breakthroughs on theories of marketing, buying, and consuming. Occasionally, it has also served policy makers in protecting the populace from deceits and hazards in the marketplace. However, scarcely has it directly served the well-being of consumers, families, communities, and their environments.

There are many reasons for these trends. Some have to do with the nature of capitalism and the needs of corporations, as well as the lucrative consulting opportunities therein. Some reasons have to do with the norms and standards of academic settings with respect to the familiar pressures of "publish or perish," which are attended by objectives among the most prestigious journals to accept only the more conceptually abstract and empirically sophisticated work. These sorts of reasons, and many others, have combined to tamp down the fortitude of those consumer scholars who otherwise wish they could turn their talents to doing research that might make a more direct, if not bigger, positive impact on the quality of everyday life.

Nonetheless, changes are occurring that demand and facilitate a renaissance of consumer research that focuses intently on well-being. The influence of consumption on the global natural environment is perhaps foremost. Severe economic imbalances are another, leading to political and social tensions that are threatening peace and security. Mounting household debt and addictions to various consumer products and activities are also experienced by millions of people. Additionally, handheld computers and the Internet now provide an unfathomable array of information and interaction venues for consumers to ply their needs and desires.

Aside from ecological, socioeconomic, and technological developments, the academic field of consumer research has matured to the point where new scholars are training to be more capable than their predecessors at mitigating the debatable trade-off between the relevance of their work and the rigor of their research designs. New journals have also appeared, and established ones are expanding their objectives and scopes, to encourage a wider range of ideas and findings that could enhance quality of life for all beings affected by the escalation of worldwide consumption practices.

Following along these parallel paths, the present book is the first of its kind to rise out of a broad movement called Transformative Consumer Research (TCR). As we discuss in the opening chapter, TCR has emerged from the coalescing of international experts in consumer behavior who are dedicated to understanding and improving well-being and join together professionally through the Association for Consumer Research (see Chapter 1 in this volume for more details on TCR and the Association). Our goals in developing this book were to fortify the mission and foundations of TCR and display and amplify its value for the present and the future. Thus, we set out to recruit authorities in consumer behavior to write chapters that overview many of the urgent contemporary issues of well-being, including the state of current knowledge and trends about those issues. We also exhorted these authorities to reach for new insights and recommendations that are both stirring and practicable for researchers as well as consumers and their guardians.

Part I, "Declaring and Projecting Transformative Consumer Research," begins the book by laying out TCR's historical fundamentals, some themes and ambitions for its future, and advice on how to optimize its overall success. Part II, "Economic and Social Issues," focuses on the challenges and best practices of doing TCR in developing economies and subsistence markets, and in more advanced commercial contexts, where poverty, discrimination, and injustice are still too commonplace. Part III, "Technological Edges," addresses a series of questions about well-being related to accessibility, social capital, online communities, and virtual lives surrounding the Internet. Materialism and the environment serve as the motif for Part IV, "Materialism and the Environment." These chapters place a heavy emphasis on the centrality of human values in matters of well-being as pertaining to acquiring, consuming, and disposing, while also expounding on the meanings and requirements for contentment and survival through sustainable consumption behaviors.

Health and consumer finances make up Part V, "Enhancing Health," and Part VI, "Consumer Finances," offering chapters covering key subdomains of those large topic areas. The discussions range from childhood obesity, nutritional labeling, tobacco, alcohol, and sexually transmitted diseases to financial planning, retirement saving, and the abuse of credit cards. Part VII, "Other Risky Behaviors and At-Risk Consumers," a general category section on additional risky consumption and at-risk consumers, follows. Compulsive buying, gambling, pornography, visually impaired consumers, and elderly consumers are among the subjects focused on. Part VIII, "Family Matters," concentrates on two essential family-level topics in well-being, namely parenting young consumers and creating family time in consumption activities. The book concludes with Part IX, "Enriching Behaviors and Virtues," which brings together chapters on sharing, resiliency, and the prospects of practical consumer wisdom.

Naturally, given the breadth of consumer behaviors in daily life across varied regions and nations of the world, it was not possible to cover every topic of importance in this inaugural volume on TCR. The Epilogue by Lehmann and Hill particularly helps identify several of the topical spaces of consumption and well-being that the present book was unable to fill. Their discussion, and the elaborations on future research that other authors undertake in their respective chapters, sketches the blueprint for new and expanded content in subsequent volumes on TCR.

The intended audience for this first volume on TCR is primarily academic researchers, policy makers, and executives who have strong interests in consumer behavior and well-being. We hope the book serves as a plentiful resource of ideas and guidelines for relevant, innovative research, governmental initiatives, and corporate social responsibility strategies. It may also serve as a textbook for graduate courses in consumer behavior or marketing, policy making, and ethics. Consumers could also readily find several chapters that convey immediate and useful suggestions on quality of life.

It may seem incongruous that consumers are not the foremost audience for this initial volume on TCR. However, as much as TCR is meant to focus intensively on the actualities of well-being in consumers' lives, for TCR to mature and have long-lasting positive influences, the academy of TCR scholars requires syntheses of prior research and detailed priority setting in terms of the unsolved challenges and new opportunities they face with respect to theories, methods, and topics pertinent to well-being, and how to reach their audiences most effectively. We believe that this book begins to meet those prerequisites.

On a sad note, during the development of the book, we lost to an abrupt death one of our most renowned authors, Martin Fishbein. A highly influential social psychologist, he spent a large portion of the last 30 years of his distinguished career working on health promotion, including the public policy challenge of reducing sexually transmitted infections (for more details on his contributions, see the "In Memoriam" essay by Cohen, Ajzen, & Albarracin, 2010). We appreciate the efforts of his coauthor, Susan Middlestadt, to complete their chapter here.

Several people assisted us tremendously in bringing this book to culmination. First, we thank the Board of Directors of the Association for Consumer Research for supporting the development of TCR in many lasting ways. We also benefited from early discussions with our Association for Consumer Research colleagues Mike Solomon and Curt Haugtvedt, both experienced book editors who together helped us establish the right priorities and strategies for a smoother voyage toward an appealing outcome. In addition, we offer our heartfelt gratitude to Anne Duffy and Robert Sims of the Taylor & Francis Group as well as Matt Baker of Cadmus Communications, who supported us in establishing the vision for the book, ensuring the style and quality of the chapters, and fashioning the final manuscript into its handsome form. We also thank Mihaly Csikszentmihalyi for preparing an incisive and receptive Foreword. Above all, we express our respectful appreciation to all the authors of the chapters herein and the reviewers who commented on first drafts, all of whom worked hard and expeditiously to complete their contributions on schedule. Last, we thank our respective university homes that have provided us with the encouragement and resources to bring to greater realization our commitment to TCR.

## REFERENCE

Cohen, J., Ajzen, I., & Albarracin, D. (2010). In memoriam: Martin Fishbein. *Journal of Consumer Research*, *36*(5), iii–iv.

**David Glen Mick**

**Simone Pettigrew**

**Cornelia Pechmann**

**Julie L. Ozanne**

# Editors

**David Glen Mick** is the Robert Hill Carter Professor of Marketing at the University of Virginia's McIntire School of Commerce. His research has centered on the nature and role of meaning in consumer behavior, across topics such as advertising rhetoric, gift-giving, materialism, customer satisfaction, and technological products. His recent work has focused on practical wisdom in executive leadership and consumer behavior. David has edited four prior books and authored several dozen articles, conference papers, and book chapters. His work has won several scholarly awards, including Best Paper from the *Journal of Consumer Research* (1989) and the Maynard Award from the *Journal of Marketing* (1999). He has also been invited to conduct seminars at universities worldwide, including Oxford University, the Stockholm School of Economics, Harvard University, and Stanford University. David is a fellow in the Society for Consumer Psychology, former editor of the *Journal of Consumer Research*, and past president of the Association for Consumer Research.

**Simone Pettigrew** is Professor of Marketing at the University of Western Australia's Business School. Her primary research interest is consumer education and empowerment, particularly in the areas of physical and mental health. Her research has focused on vulnerable populations such as children, the elderly, and low-income families. She is the founder and editor of the *Journal of Research for Consumers* (http://www.jrconsumers.com), a Web-based journal that caters to both academic and consumer audiences. Simone has won numerous competitive grants from Australian and international funding organizations and is a regular reviewer for the Australian Research Council. She has published more than 100 articles, book chapters, and refereed conference papers. Her work has been featured in a variety of journals, including *Marketing Theory*, *Annals of Tourism Research*, *Pediatric Exercise Science*, *Food Quality and Preference*, *Aging and Mental Health*, and *Australian Psychologist*. She is also a coauthor of the top-selling Australasian textbook *Consumer Behaviour: Implications for Marketing Strategy* (2007, McGraw-Hill).

**Cornelia (Connie) Pechmann** is Professor of Marketing at the University of California at Irvine. Her research focuses on tobacco-related advertising and antidrug advertising. She received the Pollay Prize for Research in the Public Interest in 2009 and the Best Article award in 2005 from the *Journal of Consumer Research*. Connie has received grants amounting to $1.5 million to study adolescents' responses to pro- and antismoking advertising as well as product placements in television and films. Her research has led directly to the use of antismoking ads on movie DVDs. She has published more than 70 articles, reports, and conference proceedings, appearing in top journals such as the *Journal of Consumer Research*, *Journal of Marketing Research*, *Journal of Marketing*, *Journal of Consumer Psychology*, and *Journal of Public Policy & Marketing*. Media citing her research have included *The Wall Street Journal*, *The New York Times*, *The Washington Post*, and *USA Today*.

**Julie L. Ozanne** is the Sonny Merryman Professor of Marketing at Virginia Tech's Pamplin College of Business. In 2006, she was named the Ferber Award winner by the *Journal of Consumer Research* for best article, based on a dissertation for which she was the head advisor. She was also recognized as the best reviewer of 2007 by the *Journal of Public Policy & Marketing*. Julie specializes in alternative methodologies for the study of social problems, such as interpretive, critical, participatory, and community action research methods. She also examines the problems of the poor and the low literate, as well as new forms of sustainable exchange. Her scholarship has appeared in the *Journal of Consumer Research, Journal of Public Policy & Marketing, Journal of International Business Studies,* and *Journal of Marketing Management,* among other outlets. She is an editorial review board member for the *Journal of Consumer Research* and *Journal of Public Policy & Marketing.*

# Contributors

**Julie M. Albright**
Department of Sociology
University of Southern California
Los Angeles, California

**Alan R. Andreasen**
McDonough School of Business
Georgetown University
Washington, District of Columbia

**Stacey Menzel Baker**
Department of Management and Marketing
University of Wyoming
Laramie, Wyoming

**Russell Belk**
Schulich School of Business
York University
Toronto, Ontario, Canada

**Frank-Martin Belz**
Brewery and Food Industry Management
Technische Universität München
Munich, Germany

**Shlomo Benartzi**
Anderson School of Management
University of California at Los Angeles
Los Angeles, California

**Anthony Biglan**
Promise Neighborhoods Research Consortium
Oregon Research Institute
Eugene, Oregon

**Lisa E. Bolton**
Department of Marketing
Pennsylvania State University
University Park, Pennsylvania

**James E. Burroughs**
McIntire School of Commerce
University of Virginia
Charlottesville, Virginia

**Eugene Y. Chan**
Rotman School of Management
University of Toronto
Toronto, Ontario, Canada

**Amar Cheema**
McIntire School of Commerce
University of Virginia
Charlottesville, Virginia

**Christine Cody**
Promise Neighborhoods Research Consortium
Oregon Research Institute
Eugene, Oregon

**June Cotte**
Richard Ivey School of Business
University of Western Ontario
London, Ontario, Canada

**Cynthia E. Cryder**
Olin Business School
Washington University
Saint Louis, Missouri

**Mihaly Csikszentmihalyi**
Claremont Graduate University
Claremont, California

**Susan Dobscha**
Bentley University
Waltham, Massachusetts

**Amber M. Epp**
Department of Marketing
University of Wisconsin–Madison
Madison, Wisconsin

**Ronald J. Faber**
School of Journalism & Mass
  Communication
University of Minnesota
Minneapolis, Minnesota

**Andrés Barrios Fajardo**
Facultad de Administración
Universidad de los Andes
Bogotá, Colombia

**Eileen Fischer**
Schulich School of Business
York University
Toronto, Ontario, Canada

**Martin Fishbein (deceased)**
Annenberg School for Communication
University of Pennsylvania
Philadelphia, Pennsylvania

**Stephanie Geiger-Oneto**
Department of Management and Marketing
University of Wyoming
Laramie, Wyoming

**Marvin E. Goldberg**
Department of Marketing
Pennsylvania State University
University Park, Pennsylvania
and
University of Arizona
Tucson, Arizona

**Sonya A. Grier**
Kogod School of Business
American University
Washington, District of Columbia

**Joel W. Grube**
Prevention Research Center
Pacific Institute for Research and Evaluation
Berkeley, California

**Klaus G. Grunert**
MAPP Centre for Research on Customer
  Relations in the Food Sector
Aarhus University
Aarhus, Denmark

**Geraldine Rosa Henderson**
Department of Advertising
University of Texas at Austin
Austin, Texas

**Ronald Paul Hill**
School of Business
Villanova University
Villanova, Pennsylvania

**Donna L. Hoffman**
Department of Management and
  Marketing
University of California, Riverside
Riverside, California

**Punam Anand Keller**
Tuck School of Business
Dartmouth College
Hanover, New Hampshire

**William Kilbourne**
Department of Marketing
Clemson University
Clemson, South Carolina

**Robert V. Kozinets**
Schulich School of Business
York University
Toronto, Ontario, Canada

**Kathryn A. LaTour**
Department of Tourism and Convention
    Administration
University of Nevada, Las Vegas
Las Vegas, Nevada

**Donald R. Lehmann**
Graduate School of Business
Columbia University
New York, New York

**Ab Litt**
Graduate School of Business
Stanford University
Stanford, California

**Rosa Llamas**
School of Business
University of León
León, Spain

**George Loewenstein**
Department of Social and Decision Sciences
Carnegie Mellon University
Pittsburgh, Pennsylvania

**Annamaria Lusardi**
Department of Economics
Dartmouth College
Hanover, New Hampshire

**Salvatore R. Maddi**
Department of Psychology and Social
    Behavior
University of California, Irvine
Irvine, California

**Marlys Mason**
Department of Marketing
Oklahoma State University
Stillwater, Oklahoma

**Pierre McDonagh**
Business School
Dublin City University
Dublin, Ireland

**David Glen Mick**
McIntire School of Commerce
University of Virginia
Charlottesville, Virginia

**Susan E. Middlestadt**
Department of Applied Health Science
Indiana University
Bloomington, Indiana

**John Mittelstaedt**
Department of Marketing
Clemson University
Clemson, South Carolina

**Elizabeth S. Moore**
Department of Marketing
University of Notre Dame
Notre Dame, Indiana

**George Moschis**
Department of Marketing
Georgia State University
Atlanta, Georgia

**Thomas P. Novak**
Department of Management and
    Marketing
University of California, Riverside
Riverside, California

**Julie L. Ozanne**
Department of Marketing
Virginia Polytechnic Institute and State
    University
Blacksburg, Virginia

**Cornelia (Connie) Pechmann**
Paul Merage School of Business
University of California, Irvine
Irvine, California

**Simone Pettigrew**
UWA Business School
University of Western Australia
Perth, Western Australia, Australia

**Dante M. Pirouz**
Richard Ivey School of Business
University of Western Ontario
London, Ontario, Canada

**Alessandro Previtero**
Richard Ivey School of Business
University of Western Ontario
London, Ontario, Canada

**Linda L. Price**
Department of Marketing
University of Arizona
Tucson, Arizona

**Ronald J. Prinz**
Parenting and Family Research Center
University of South Carolina
Columbia, South Carolina

**Andrea Prothero**
School of Business
University College Dublin
Blackrock, County Dublin, Ireland

**Monique M. Raats**
Food, Consumer Behaviour and Health
    Research Centre
University of Surrey
Guilford, Surrey, United Kingdom
and
Business School
Korea University
Seoul, Korea

**Aric Rindfleisch**
Department of Marketing
University of Wisconsin–Madison
Madison, Wisconsin

**José Antonio Rosa**
Department of Management and Marketing
University of Wyoming
Laramie, Wyoming

**Barry Schwartz**
Department of Psychology
Swarthmore College
Swarthmore, Pennsylvania

**Stanley J. Shapiro**
Faculty of Business Administration
Simon Fraser University
Burnaby, British Columbia, Canada

**Baba Shiv**
Graduate School of Business
Stanford University
Stanford, California

**Clifford J. Shultz, II**
School of Business Administration
Loyola University Chicago
Chicago, Illinois

**M. Joseph Sirgy**
Department of Marketing
Virginia Polytechnic Institute and State
    University
Blacksburg, Virginia

**Dilip Soman**
Rotman School of Management
University of Toronto
Toronto, Ontario, Canada

**Madhu Viswanathan**
Department of Business Administration
University of Illinois at Urbana-Champaign
Champaign, Illinois

**Kathleen D. Vohs**
Department of Marketing
University of Minnesota
Minneapolis, Minnesota

**Brian Wansink**
Cornell Food and Brand Lab
Cornell University
Ithaca, New York

**Jerome D. Williams**
Management & Global Business Department
Rutgers University
Newark and New Brunswick, New Jersey

# Reviewers

The editors thank the following individuals for providing insightful commentaries on the first drafts of the authors' chapters.

**Aaron Ahuvia**
University of Michigan–Dearborn

**Alan Andreasen**
Georgetown University

**Stacey Baker**
University of Wyoming

**Gary Bamossy**
Georgetown University

**Paul Bartone**
National Defense University (USA)

**Russell Belk**
York University, Canada

**Paul Bloom**
Duke University

**David Boush**
University of Oregon

**James Burroughs**
University of Virginia

**Edward Castronova**
Indiana University

**Dipankar Chakravarti**
Johns Hopkins University

**Pierre Chandon**
INSEAD, France

**Amar Cheema**
University of Virginia

**Helena Christensen**
Australian National University, Australia

**Joel Cohen**
University of Florida

**Andy Crane**
York University, Canada

**David Crockett**
University of South Carolina

**Edith Davidson**
Auburn University

**Susan Dobscha**
Bentley University

**Kent Drummond**
University of Wyoming

**Meme Drumwright**
University of Texas at Austin

**Karen Finlay**
University of Guelph, Canada

**Fuat Firat**
University of Texas–Pan American

**Eileen Fischer**
York University

**James Fitchett**
University of Leicester, United Kingdom

**Susan Fournier**
Boston University

**Shane Frederick**
Yale University

**James Gentry**
University of Nebraska–Lincoln

**Marvin Goldberg**
Pennsylvania State University and University of Arizona

**Gerald Gorn**
Hong Kong University of Science and Technology, Hong Kong

**Anne-Marie Hakstian**
Salem State University

**Richard Harvey**
San Francisco State University

**Manoj Hastak**
American University

**Gerard Hastings**
University of Stirling, United Kingdom

**William Hedgcock**
University of Iowa

**Andrea Hemetsberger**
University of Innsbruck, Austria

**Geraldine Henderson**
University of Texas at Austin

**Ronald Hill**
Villanova University

**Wilhelm Hofmann**
University of Würzburg, Germany

**Elif Izbek-Bilgin**
University of Michigan–Dearborn

**James Jaccard**
Florida International University

**Punam Keller**
Dartmouth College

**Patricia Kohl**
Washington University in Saint Louis

**Shiriki Kumanyika**
University of Pennsylvania

**Peggy Sue Loroz**
Gonzaga University

**Susan Love**
California State University–Northridge

**Nicholas Lurie**
Georgia Tech University

**Richard Lutz**
University of Florida

**Debbie MacInnis**
University of Southern California

**Kevin Malotte**
California State University–Long Beach

**Anil Mathur**
Hofstra University

**Pierre McDonagh**
Dublin City University, Ireland

**Peter McGraw**
University of Colorado

**Sue McGregor**
Mount Saint Vincent University, Canada

**John Mittelstaedt**
Clemson University

**Jeff Murray**
University of Arkansas

**Nathan Novemsky**
Yale University

**Cele Otnes**
University of Illinois at Urbana-Champaign

**Collin Payne**
New Mexico State University

**Christopher Peterson**
University of Michigan

**Mark Peterson**
University of Wyoming

**Ratti Ratneshwar**
University of Missouri

**Marsha Richins**
University of Missouri

**Scott Rick**
University of Michigan

**Nancy Ridgway**
University of Richmond

**Aric Rindfleisch**
University of Wisconsin–Madison

**James Roberts**
Baylor University

**Deborah Roedder-John**
University of Minnesota

**Dennis Rook**
University of Southern California

**José Rosa**
University of Wyoming

**Michael Rothschild**
University of Wisconsin–Madison

**Julie Ruth**
Rutgers University

**Hope Jensen Schau**
University of Arizona

**Ann Schlosser**
University of Washington

**Clifford Schultz, II**
Loyola University Chicago

**Maura Scott**
University of Kentucky

**Joseph Slade**
Ohio University

**Jack Soll**
Duke University

**Michael Solomon**
Saint Joseph's University, Philadelphia

**Dilip Soman**
University of Toronto, Canada

**Nguyen Dinh Tho**
University of Economics, Vietnam

**Hans van Trijp**
Wageningen University, Netherlands

**Richard Varey**
University of Waikato, New Zealand

**Alladi Venkatesh**
University of California–Irvine

**Madhu Viswanathan**
University of Illinois at Urbana-Champaign

**Monica Wadhwa**
INSEAD, France

**Dmitri Williams**
University of Southern California

**Nancy Wong**
University of Wisconsin–Madison

**Carolyn Yoon**
University of Michigan

# I

## *DECLARING AND PROJECTING TRANSFORMATIVE CONSUMER RESEARCH*

# 1

# Origins, Qualities, and Envisionments of Transformative Consumer Research

DAVID GLEN MICK, SIMONE PETTIGREW,
CORNELIA PECHMANN, AND JULIE L. OZANNE

For millennia, humans have asked themselves, what is the good life? Answers to this perplexing question cannot be developed in any detail without reference to personal and collective consumption behaviors. Without consumption—at least at the basic level of air, water, food, and shelter—life ceases. Tragically, millions of people today in developing economies still face uncertain survival because they lack some or all of these necessities (Worldwatch Institute, 2004). At the same time, consumption in economically vigorous regions has increased in volume and variety to such degrees that living, thriving, suffering, and dying are more interdependently connected to the acquiring, owning, and disposing of products than in any other historical era (see, e.g., Csikszentmihalyi, 2000; Schor & Holt, 2000; Speth, 2008). Consumption now facilitates a myriad of purposes and consequences, from nourishment, contentment, and achievement to gluttony, disfranchisement, and destruction.

In response to the exponential growth of global consumption, numerous governmental and nongovernmental organizations have arisen to support consumers, societies, and the earth. The governmental efforts include a wide range of country- and region-specific agencies that oversee public welfare in such areas as agriculture, product safety, merchandising, and advertising. For example, the Food and Drug Administration (FDA) is the oldest comprehensive consumer protection agency in the U.S. federal government. Although not formally known as the FDA until 1931, its regulatory functions trace back to 1906 with the passage of the Pure Food and Drugs Act, which prohibited interstate commerce in adulterated and misbranded food and drugs.

Among the oldest of the relevant nongovernmental organizations is the National Consumers League (NCL), founded in the United States in 1899. The NCL has sought throughout the years to protect workers in their employment conditions and safeguard consumers in terms of product use. Shortly afterward, the International Federation of Home Economics was founded in Switzerland in 1908 to address food nutrition, housing, textiles, and home management, among other topics. A year later, the American Home Economics Association was established and has since become known as the American Association of Family and Consumer Sciences. A decade hence (1919), Stuart Chase and Frederick Schlink founded Consumers' Research (now defunct) and began publishing comparative tests of branded products, analyses of advertising claims, and so forth. Then, in 1936, Arthur Kallet, Colston Warne, and a few others established Consumers Union and began publishing *Consumer Reports*. This publication remains today as one of the most circulated and consulted sources of consumer product information, especially in the United States. The staff of Consumers Union also seeks to influence laws and regulations on issues such as telecommunications, car and food safety, health care, financial services, and energy.

More pro-consumer organizations appeared during the second half of the 20th century. For instance, in 1953, the American Council on Consumer Interests grew out of the Consumers Union to focus on consumer policy research and education. Soon afterward on the global scene, Consumers International (formerly the International Organization of Consumer Unions) was founded in 1960 and now includes over 220 member organizations in 115 countries. It focuses on consumer rights, consumer safety, and sustainability. In 1962, the Bureau Européen des Unions de Consommateurs was created to represent consumer organizations from 6 European nations, expanding eventually to cover 30 European nations. A few years later, the Consumer Federation of America began operations to advance pro-consumer policies and educate on consumer issues. Additionally, in 1974, the Worldwatch Institute was established to conduct interdisciplinary research specifically on consumption and ecology, including climate change, natural resources, and population growth.

Several journals also began to publish research on the welfare of consumers, societies, and the earth. Among the first was the *Journal of Consumer Affairs*, inaugurated in 1967 by the American Council on Consumer Interests. Other publications followed, each with similar foci but varying emphases, including the *International Journal of Consumer Studies* (1977, originally known as the *Journal of Consumer Studies and Home Economics*), *Journal of Consumer Policy* (1977), *Journal of Public Policy & Marketing* (1981), and *Journal of Macromarketing* (1981). Produced through the Illinois Consumer Education Association, the *Journal of Consumer Education* also began publishing in 1983 to facilitate communication about consumer education among researchers, educators, and practitioners. With the growth of the Internet, the *Journal of Research for Consumers* was founded in Australia in 2001 as a free, Web-based resource of scholarly consumer studies that are simultaneously summarized in laypersons' language for public audiences (Pettigrew, 2001). Many other journals from diverse fields also periodically publish special issues and individual articles on consumer and earthly welfare (see, e.g., the October 2008 issue of the *Journal of Consumer Research*).

Of course, the number of books over the years that have taken pro-consumer perspectives is large, and the variety is wide. To mention one that is now dated, but grew to have iconic status, is Ralph Nader's (1965) *Unsafe at Any Speed: The Designed-In Dangers of the American Automobile*, which analyzed and detailed the reluctance of car manufacturers to invest in more safety features as new designs were developed. As a more recent example, the marketing field has seen the rise of its own community of vocal scholars who write and edit books from the tradition of critical theory. These researchers scrutinize social institutions and deconstruct their roles in the international consumption system, with the goal of motivating positive social change (e.g., Tadajewski & Maclaran, 2009).

Our summary here of organizations, activism, and research on behalf of consumers and the environment they inhabit has been unavoidably selective and brief. A comprehensive history has yet to be constructed. However, several excellent articles, books, and book chapters have focused on additional and different components of these developments, including Andreasen, Goldberg, and Sirgy (Chapter 2 of this volume), Cohen (2010), Hilton (2008), McGregor (2010), Speth (2008), and Wilkie and Moore (2003). More details can also be found on the websites of relevant nongovernmental and governmental organizations, and in editorials from related academic journals.

Taking these activities as a whole, it is apparent that interests in consumption and quality of life have ebbed and flowed over time, depending on many factors, including the booms and busts of global and regional economics, developments in geopolitics and governmental leadership, and evolutions in science and education. Inevitably, this complex arena is fragmented, since different organizations and researchers have often worked independently on similar as well as different issues, and often used disparate research paradigms, theories, and methods. Although many sources of outstanding programs and insights on behalf of consumers and the planet exist, they tend to reside in disconnected silos of institutes, agencies, associations, and publication outlets. To date, there have been few efforts to coordinate research and organizations on behalf of well-being.

The book you are holding has grown out of recent and exciting developments at the Association for Consumer Research (ACR), from a movement known as Transformative Consumer Research (TCR). This volume on TCR is part of the long tradition of organizations and research outlined above that aims to support consumers, societies, and the environment. With its broad scope of topics, paradigms, and distinguished authors, this book seeks to fill gaps and overcome some of the fragmentation and separation that characterize the field of consumer research in the essential domain of well-being.

## THE ASSOCIATION FOR CONSUMER RESEARCH (ACR) AND TRANSFORMATIVE CONSUMER RESEARCH (TCR)

ACR began in 1969 and has grown into one of the largest international organizations of highly trained scholars who focus on consumer behavior. Several of its founders perceived the association's mission as centering on consumer problems and orchestrating "the natural talents of academia, government, and industry so as to enhance consumer welfare" (Kernan, 1979, p. 1). The earliest ACR conferences involved academics as well as executives from consumer-oversight organizations, such as the FDA and the Consumers Union. In 1974, the association served as a founding sponsor of the *Journal of Consumer Research*, which, in its initial years, included articles on subjects such as energy and conservation, consumer credit and debt, consumer education, product safety, nutrition, poverty, and elderly consumers.

Eventually, both ACR and the *Journal of Consumer Research* put less emphasis on research that could benefit consumers and the environment. Part of this change in the 1980s and 1990s was due to a new surge of faith in capitalism, as corporations and people worldwide became more engrossed in the profits and pleasures of consumption rather than concerned with quality of life as a function of consumption. Concurrently, ACR and the *Journal of Consumer Research* turned more strictly to making theoretical and methodological advancements, due to the growing influence of the cognitive/information-processing paradigm in experimental psychology, with its focus on human memory and attitudes for revealing the processes underlying consumer judgments and choice. Around the same time, there also began the rise and maturation of a sociocultural orientation to consumer behavior. Consumer culture theory, as it is now called, draws heavily from anthropology, sociology, and the humanities to provide more macro and experiential perspectives in consumer research, including underappreciated qualitative methods, while maintaining a strong focus on theoretical advances (Arnould & Thompson, 2005).

The advent of the 21st century brought ruptures that spurred reconsiderations of the aforementioned paradigms and practices. The United States underwent an immense economic downturn that spread throughout the world; large corporations such as Enron and Tyco were destroyed or severely damaged by their own rogue executives; and political and religious extremists attacked the United States, England, Spain, Indonesia, and other countries, partly as an ideological declaration against the perceived hegemony of Western capitalism and its defenders. Also, scientific evidence continued to mount regarding the disturbing effects of consumer behaviors on the earth's ecology, reaching a new vista through Al Gore's film *An Inconvenient Truth* (2006) and his subsequent receipt of the 2007 Nobel Peace Prize. In addition, new health studies elevated concerns about the overconsumption of unhealthy foods and the growth of tobacco consumption in developing parts of the world. As a result of these and other trends, debates intensified about capitalism and materialism, religion and consumption, immigration and discrimination, economic growth and environmental sustainability, and the continuation of abject poverty in many regions despite a dynamic global economy.

Voices within ACR and scholarship within the *Journal of Consumer Research* began to call for a rebirth of research on well-being and the ethics of consumption (see, e.g., Adkins & Ozanne, 2005b; Bazerman, 2001; Bernthal, Crockett, & Rose, 2005; Borgmann, 2000; Csikszentmihalyi, 2000; Denzin, 2001; Henry, 2005; Khare & Inman, 2006; Pechmann & Knight, 2002; Thompson, 2005; Wansink & van Ittersum, 2003). David Mick's (2006) presidential address before ACR sought to channel these concerns and aspirations into TCR, through which he challenged the association to take greater leadership. Founded within ACR, TCR strives to encourage, support, and publicize research that benefits quality of life for all beings engaged in or affected by consumption trends and practices across the world.

In the next section, six defining qualities and commitments of TCR are highlighted (see Figure 1.1). Then, each of the four coeditors of this book develops an envisionment of TCR that represents a more nuanced understanding of its tenets and their role in guiding the future of TCR.

## SIX CORE QUALITIES AND COMMITMENTS OF TCR

### To Improve Well-Being

Although TCR is a dynamic and evolving program of research, six core commitments serve to anchor this endeavor. First, the normative goal of TCR is to improve well-being, which is a state of flourishing that involves health, happiness, and prosperity. McGregor and Goldsmith (1998) identified seven dimensions of well-being: emotional, social, economic, physical, spiritual, environmental, and political (for a similar taxonomy, see Stiglitz, Sen, & Fitoussi, 2009; see also Andreasen, Goldberg, & Sirgy, Chapter 2 of this volume; Burroughs & Rindfleisch, Chapter 12 of this volume). TCR concentrates on the problems and opportunities that surround one or more of the different dimensions of well-being, and thus, TCR has a pragmatic and concrete orientation at its base. In

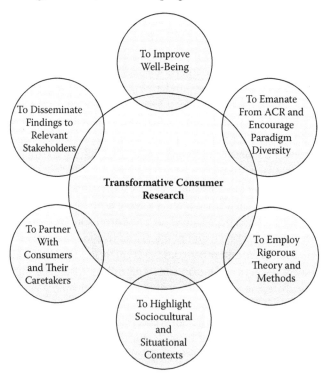

**Figure 1.1**  The six core qualities and commitments of Transformative Consumer Research.

David Mick's following envisionment, he philosophically grounds this focus by seeking to move beyond the mere accumulation of knowledge toward the more ambitious goal of seeking practical wisdom.

Although the emphasis on the goal of improving well-being provides TCR with a firm motivational foundation, this goal is not without significant challenges. Over 6 billion people cannot all individually maximize their well-being without considering the needs of others and even the very survival of the planet (see also Burroughs & Rindfleisch, Chapter 12 of this volume; Kilbourne & Mittelstaedt, Chapter 14 of this volume). Achieving widespread well-being will inevitably require respectful civic exchange and democratic deliberation on how the individual and collective dimensions of well-being can be met (see, e.g., Kozinets, Belz, & McDonagh, Chapter 10 of this volume; McGregor, 2010). Therefore, TCR seeks to improve well-being while maximizing social justice and the fair allocation of opportunities and resources. Meeting such a challenge will require open-mindedness, compassion, and the best scientific research.

## To Emanate From ACR and Encourage Paradigm Diversity

Second, TCR emanates uniquely from ACR. With more than 4 decades of substantial progress in understanding the intricacies of consumer behavior, and with a revitalized dedication to human and earthly welfare, ACR has a distinctive capacity to guide and support consumer research on well-being toward its finest manifestations. This opportunity for TCR within ACR is spread widely across the globe as the association has been from its beginning an international organization, with regular conferences now held in North America, Europe, Latin America, and the Asia–Pacific region. Also, consistent with ACR's long commitment to fostering diverse research traditions, TCR is intended to serve as a large tent and a unifying juncture. Consumer researchers from all backgrounds and perspectives are needed to accomplish a shared mission to protect and improve well-being. TCR recognizes, welcomes, and endorses the plurality of theories, methods, levels of analyses, and paradigms needed to understand and positively influence well-being. TCR does not favor any particular paradigm, theory, or method over others in the absence of knowing the focus of the research, its challenges, and its intended audience and uses (see Anderson, 1986, for a justification of this approach). In Julie L. Ozanne's subsequent envisionment, she explores how different paths exist for research aimed at social change, depending on the intended audience and anticipated use of the research (see also Ozanne & Fischer, Chapter 4 of this volume; Wansink, Chapter 3 of this volume).

## To Employ Rigorous Theory and Methods

Third, TCR promotes the meticulous application of theory and methods to achieve its mission and goals. Strong theory and methods should be neither depreciated nor traded off as a result of TCR's pragmatism. Rigorous theory and methods are more likely to optimize applied goals successfully than less rigorous theory and methods. In fact, rigor and relevance can readily go hand in hand (Lehmann, 2003; see also Lehmann & Hill, Chapter 33 of this volume; Wansink, Chapter 3 of this volume). Potent theory can provide for richer, more penetrating insights on everyday consumer behavior and well-being, while sound methods lead to more trustworthy conclusions, implications, and advice. In Connie Pechmann's forthcoming envisionment, she probes the trials and opportunities of theoretical contributions in TCR and offers some detailed cogent advice.

## To Highlight Sociocultural and Situational Contexts

Fourth, TCR highlights the sociocultural context or situational embedding of the well-being problem or opportunity. The life world of consumers must be kept in clear focus if the research is to maximize its meaningfulness, relevance, and usefulness. This focus does not mean that all TCR must be anthropological or sociological, but it does mean that TCR seeks to work on those problems that are perceived by consumers to be most pressing, and it seeks to learn and develop solutions within the proximal conditions in which consumption and well-being are mutually influential. Physical and environmental factors, family and social settings, and other situational dimensions are elemental to well-being and consumption and cannot be expediently ignored or bracketed away without compromising the raison d'être of TCR. Indeed, TCR's emphasis on context can also improve theory building and theory extending, as Connie Pechmann discusses in her following envisionment.

## To Partner With Consumers and Their Caretakers

Fifth, given the goal to do meaningful and relevant research, TCR endorses a new role and image for consumer researchers as advocates for, and close partners with, consumers. Scholars of TCR seek to engender insights that directly translate into new capabilities and behaviors that support well-being. These researchers are neither solitary scientists nor lofty intellectuals in pursuit of basic, theoretical, methodological, or empirical breakthroughs per se. Instead, they are committed to a role of public servant (for further discussion and variations on this viewpoint, see Andreasen, Goldberg, & Sirgy, Chapter 2 of this volume; Lehmann & Hill, Chapter 33 of this volume; Ozanne & Fischer, Chapter 4 of this volume; Wansink, Chapter 3 of this volume). TCR investigators pursue straightforward insights about consumer behaviors that can potentially make life healthier, safer, and more rewarding.

## To Disseminate Findings to Relevant Stakeholders

Sixth, TCR is planned and executed with an objective to share its insights with consumers, policy makers, or anyone else who is likely to benefit from learning and using the research results. From the start of their work, transformative consumer researchers are concerned not only with design and implementation but also with how they will communicate the findings effectively (see also Wansink, Chapter 3 of this volume). Moreover, TCR must be proffered in usable forms, and many researchers will need to roll up their sleeves and work side by side with consumers to ensure that the research outcomes are both pertinent and intelligible to them. In the final envisionment, Simone Pettigrew offers several insights on how TCR communication efforts can be customized for intended audiences.

## FOUR ENVISIONMENTS FOR TCR

In light of these defining qualities and commitments of TCR, we turn now to articulating four envisionments on its behalf (see Figure 1.2) that foreshadow the chapters in this volume and look beyond to the horizon on which the next generation of TCR scholars is now emerging. Taken together, the envisionments represent our personal faith and hope in the development of TCR. In the first envisionment, David Mick appraises the role of practical wisdom for establishing a philosophy of science in TCR.

### Philosophical Roots: Beyond Knowledge to Wisdom

In the 1980s and 1990s, ardent debates about philosophy of science took place at ACR and in the *Journal of Consumer Research* (e.g., Anderson, 1983, 1986; Hudson & Ozanne, 1988; Hunt, 1991). The natures of theory, method, and truth were contended, including whether the preeminent goal of consumer research should be explanation or understanding. Holbrook (1985) particularly criticized consumer researchers for overemphasizing the production of managerially relevant insights, rather than developing an independent field to pursue knowledge of consumption for its own sake,

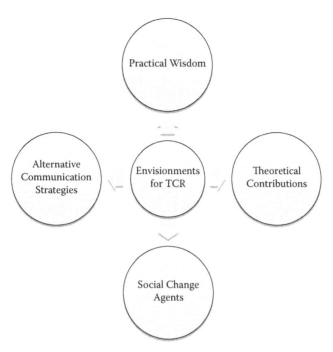

**Figure 1.2**    Four envisionments for Transformative Consumer Research.

but few were asking whether consumer researchers should be producing insights for improving quality of life. Then, and subsequently, an emphasis on foundational knowledge, as explanation or understanding, gained wide support across the field.

Today, the single-minded search for basic knowledge across scientific fields has come under sharp attack. Cynicism and anxieties have arisen across the world because of the massive amounts of money being spent on science of questionable benefit (much of it coming from tax sources) and due to the exploitation of some innovations that have led to weapons of mass destruction, ecological degradation, and so on (see, e.g., Cialdini, 2009; Maxwell, 2002; Winston, 2005). A comparable scenario can be found in the growing distrust of corporations (see, e.g., Fournier, Dobscha, & Mick, 1998; Mick, 2007). Many marketers, for instance, draw from knowledge advancements in social science and consumer research to construct pricing tactics, packaging, promotions, and retail store layouts that take advantage of human biases and unconscious tendencies, among them being cognitive heuristics, social jealousies and fears, fantasies and hopes, and impulsivities and addictions.

Two intrepid scholars, Nicholas Maxwell (1984, 2002, 2008) and Bent Flyvbjerg (2001), have railed against the pursuit of knowledge in the absence of open and vigorous dialogue about society's needs and priorities. Both scholars take as their starting point Aristotle's notion of *phronesis*, translated from Greek as "practical wisdom." Their elaborations on practical wisdom offer stimulating and opportune guidance for the development and success of TCR.

In his treatise *Nicomachean Ethics*, Aristotle (350 BC/1999) describes practical wisdom as developing plans and solutions that are well reasoned and capable of action in regard to matters that are good or bad for humanity. Linking this conceptualization to his ambitions for phronetic social science, Bent Flyvbjerg (2001) has written that "The purpose of social science is not to develop theory, but to contribute to society's practical rationality in elucidating where we are, where we want to go, and what is desirable according to diverse sets of values and interests" (p. 167). He has extended the Aristotelian view of social science by drawing from Michel Foucault's work to add an additional question: Who gains and who loses, and by which mechanisms of power, when it comes to understanding what to value as well as what solutions to consider and assess for solving societal problems? Flyvbjerg illustrates his approach to practical wisdom in social science by reviewing his involvement in regional and urban planning in Denmark, and also through brief summaries of work by Foucault, Pierre Bourdieu, Robert Putnam, Naomi Wolf, and Paul Rabinow, among others.

Nicholas Maxwell (1984, 2002, 2008) has spent the bulk of his philosophic career arguing vociferously for redirecting and revitalizing scientific and academic research according to Aristotle's practical wisdom. Maxwell (1984, p. 66) has maintained that standard empiricism in science—which, in his view, obsessively seeks explanatory truth—has produced a cornucopia of disunified findings, with little prethought of their usefulness or application. Science spends too much time, in his view, on problems of knowledge rather than problems of living. Maxwell has advanced what he calls aim-oriented empiricism that pursues, first and foremost, valuable truth. The principle task of such inquiry is the application of reason to the enhancement of practical wisdom. This wisdom, he asserts,

> includes knowledge and understanding but goes beyond them in also including: the desire and active striving of what is of value, the ability to see what is of value, actually and potentially, in the circumstances of life, the ability to experience value, the capacity to help realize what is of value for oneself and others, the capacity to help solve those problems of living that arise in connection with attempts to realize what is of value, [and] the capacity to use and develop knowledge, technology and understanding as needed for the realization of value. (p. 66)

Two rules, according to Maxwell (1984, p. 67), are essential to any science focused on rational problem-solving in the spirit of practical wisdom: (1) to communicate, and improve the communication of, the problems to be remedied, and (2) to propose and critically evaluate potential solutions. His writings expand on these themes in numerous ways, drawing connections to education, technology, the environment, and, periodically, economics and consumption. Maxwell's practical scientific wisdom has gained increased attention in recent years, as discussed by Iredale (2008) and Maxwell (2009). These efforts have circled around new funding initiatives as well as new institutes, centers, and so forth.

The history of consumer research has been dominated by standard empiricism and by priorities of basic fact-finding and theory testing that Flyvbjerb and Maxwell assail in the physical and social sciences (see also Kilbourne & Mittelstaedt, Chapter 14 of this volume, regarding dominant paradigms). The daunting problems and fulfilling opportunities of consumption across the world call out for a new era of enlightenment in the philosophy of science in consumer research. This new era stands to be actualized, in part, through practical wisdom as a bedrock of TCR. Accomplishing this will require some bold changes in the doctrine and practices of consumer research as we know it today. Although hardly exhaustive, the following are some of the directions we must ponder and implement for wiser consumer research and behavior in the service of well-being: First, we should newly consider, to whom are consumer researchers most responsible for their work and their legacies? Who *really* should own our research and its findings, if not the human societies and ecologies where well-being is substantiated or compromised by worldwide consumption? Second, we should convene a summit of leading consumer researchers, activists, and policy makers, from multiple disciplines and perspectives, to establish a mission, philosophy, and list of priorities that can guide the consumer research field toward the production of aim-oriented insights of timely and recognizable use. Consumers must also be welcomed into this discourse to articulate their values and goals for setting the top priorities in the evolution of consumer research in the 21st century.

Third, and based on these prior efforts, we need to establish in greater depth and detail what consumers and policy makers most need to know that will directly and materially help them construct homes, societies, and ecologies where lives are flourishing in the context of consumption. Fourth, we must similarly consider how consumer researchers can engage businesses in general, and marketers in particular, to influence in authentic and positive ways the development and success of TCR. The Internet via social media provides various opportunities to achieve such egalitarian dialogues in ways never before available.

Fifth, we should seek ways to reinvigorate a range of conversations among journal editors and their policy boards on philosophy of science, to clarify and promote the meaning, value, and application of practical wisdom in consumer research. Finally, we must revisit the design of doctoral programs in consumer research in terms of TCR (Mari, 2008). We need to make upcoming scholars more knowledgeable about the nature of science via practical wisdom, versus historical or standard views of science. We need also to consider how these younger scholars can be encouraged and rewarded for conducting consumer research that is founded on a pursuit of practical wisdom.

TCR must be a devoted engagement with consumers and the world we all inhabit to address problems and opportunities of well-being in a manner that speaks of shared values, empathy, immediacy, and usefulness. Aristotle's practical wisdom is a profound and fertile concept on which TCR can build its future.

In the next envisionment, Connie Pechmann explores the need and opportunity for theory contributions within the TCR program and offers several concrete recommendations. Even though TCR is substantively driven—focusing steadily on consumer behavior and well-being—the development and advancement of theory remain crucial to TCR's mission and success.

## Making Theoretical Contributions Through TCR

Some consumer researchers may be concerned that TCR will be consistently prone to making limited theoretical contributions. Because TCR is committed to addressing specific problems or opportunities of well-being, researchers may be skeptical that TCR can contribute new theoretical or conceptual knowledge that is not subject specific, and they may be doubtful that it can have an impact both within and across disciplines. Most consumer researchers at top research universities have a strong allegiance to academic principles and values, and primarily seek to make theoretical contributions. These researchers are evaluated on this basis as well. For them, TCR's potential weakness in terms of making theoretical contributions may not completely offset its potential impacts on well-being, however large those impacts might be. Therefore, TCR may not appear to be a viable research path for them.

In his 1981 ACR presidential address, Jerry Olson (1982) pleaded for more theory development in consumer behavior. He defined theory as "abstract conceptualizations that represent the phenomenon" (p. vii) and "a basic requirement for a science" (p. v). ACR presidents before and after have made similar pleas, and the field has followed accordingly. Thought leaders who serve as journal editors have also continued to reinforce a theoretical orientation (e.g., Erdem, 2010).

Unfortunately, between scholars focusing on theory development and those focusing on substantive quality-of-life issues, a chasm opened several years ago and remains quite discernible. Twenty-six years ago, a seminal book (Brinberg & McGath, 1985) and article (Brinberg & Hirschman, 1986) solidified the dichotomy between theory building and real-world relevance, while emphasizing that both are necessary and important. Subsequently, in her 1995 ACR presidential address, Alice Tybout (1995) stated that it was a myth that "a well-designed study will provide theoretical insight and will allow generalization of the effects observed to a real-world situation of interest" (p. 1). She opined that, in reality, "theory testing and generalization typically imply different choices regarding the subjects, the setting, and the selection of independent and dependent variables" (p. 1). Thus, she argued, "a particular study should give clear priority to one of these goals" (p. 1). Over time, many academics have taken sides in terms of valuing one research orientation over the other, in what seems to be viewed as a zero-sum game. To the extent that there is limited journal space, and faculty positions, this perspective is certainly reasonable.

As previously emphasized, scholars of TCR start by addressing substantive problems or opportunities of well-being rather than theory contributions per se. In fact, some TCR builds on a highly substantive-oriented research paradigm known as program development and evaluation (Wansink, Chapter 3 of this volume), which itself is underpinned by educational theory. A few TCR scholars have received formal training in program development and evaluation (Pichert, Hanson, & Pechmann, 1985), a field with its own graduate programs (e.g., Vanderbilt University's Community Research and Action Program), journals (e.g., Sage's *Evaluation and the Health Professions*), and how-to books (e.g., Timmreck, 2003). Similarly, the *Journal of Marketing* encourages and publishes program evaluations and other large-scale field studies (see, e.g., Andrews, Netemeyer, Burton, Moberg, & Christiansen, 2004). Consumer researchers who conduct program evaluations typically are guided by theory, but they may use several theories that they view as complementary, and they use these theories as means to an end (e.g., to solve a problem) rather than as ends in themselves (e.g., to build theory or demonstrate that one theory is superior to another).

The program development and evaluation paradigm has a pragmatic action orientation that fits TCR's mission very well (Wansink, Chapter 3 of this volume). However, it cannot be the sole or even the favored research approach for TCR scholars, because this would be too constraining and would reinforce the stereotype that TCR cannot build theory. In our view, many more scholars of TCR should seek to make theory contributions, in addition to addressing substantive issues; otherwise, many groundbreaking and valuable insights—both practical and theoretical—may never be realized. It is highly challenging to be both substantively and theoretically focused, and it is sometimes necessary to prioritize one aim over the other when making decisions about research participants and methods (Brinberg & Hirschman, 1986; Brinberg & McGrath, 1985). Theory may not be the first priority for many TCR scholars, but this does not mean that theory contributions are unattainable or incompatible with TCR. Sometimes theory contributions are eminently achievable through TCR, especially if creative and careful research designs are utilized.

One approach to generating theoretical insights is to adopt interpretive or qualitative research methods (for a thorough volume on these techniques, see Belk, 2007), which lend themselves to theory development by nature of their flexible, incisive, and boundary-spanning capabilities. For a recent example, consider that consumer researchers have focused considerably over the years on the positive aspects of gift-giving. Marcoux's (2009) recent ethnography, however, offers a surprising and decidedly different perspective that unpacks detrimental implications for well-being within the gift economy. His work provides new insights on the humiliation, oppression, and subjection that occur on the dark side of gift-giving.

A different approach to building theory is through quantitative hypothesis testing, which primarily involves controlled lab or field experiments. However, regardless of a chosen method, we believe that transformative consumer researchers who seek to build theory need to look beyond the substantive problem they are addressing and reconceptualize the problem at a more abstract level. Furthermore, we believe that these researchers should envision the possible theoretical contributions up front and build in appropriate mechanisms to ensure these contributions are realized. In our experience, this process involves four crucial steps, which are discussed below. Our examples focus on quantitative studies, but the principles are broadly applicable.

### Step 1: Conceptualize the Substantive Problem at a Higher Level of Abstraction

Imagine that TCR investigators reach out to, or are approached by, a community group to identify an important, substantive problem. In one actual example, members of the entertainment community (i.e., writers, directors) asked TCR scholars if television shows for youth can convey antismoking messages without being counterproductive (Pechmann & Wang, 2010). Members of the community were concerned that television shows with plots about youth and smoking might convey the wrong normative message: that a lot of (attractive) youth smoke. These entertainment experts also asked if they should air an antismoking public-service announcement at the end of the television show to reinforce the health message, or if the subtle messages embedded within the show were sufficient or even preferable.

Once TCR scholars have identified the substantive research questions, in order to begin to build theory, they should reconceptualize the issues at a more general or abstract level. Antismoking messages in television shows primarily convey reference group information about peer group norms (Bearden & Etzel, 1982; Cialdini, Reno, & Kallgren, 1990). Moreover, these normative messages are not overt or even conspicuous, and as a result, viewers may lack knowledge about the sponsor's persuasive intent (Friestad & Wright, 1994, 1995). Hence, in this example, the TCR investigators formulated the following theory-based research questions: What combinations of normative reference group messages are effective or ineffective in preventing youth drug use, and does persuasion knowledge moderate these message effects?

### Step 2: Find a Match to Existing Constructs and Theory

Next, to build theory, TCR scholars should conduct an extensive literature review to identify the constructs or concepts that are most related to their research questions and identify relevant theory about how the constructs are interrelated and the effects they produce. This literature review is essential, because new theories are built almost always on prior theories (e.g., regulatory focus theory; see Higgins, 1997), which is how theoretical knowledge grows incrementally. Returning to our earlier example (Pechmann & Wang, 2010), the TCR investigators identified reference group theory in marketing (Bearden & Etzel, 1982; Park & Lessig, 1977) and the focus theory of normative conduct in psychology (Cialdini et al., 1990) as most relevant for predicting the effects of a television show with antismoking messages. The investigators also identified persuasion knowledge theory in marketing (Campbell & Kirmani, 2000; Friestad & Wright, 1994, 1995) as most useful for predicting the effects of an antismoking public-service announcement after the show.

Consistent with the core philosophy of TCR, literature reviews should be multidisciplinary. Once the research questions are conceptualized at a higher level of abstraction, researchers are likely to find that various disciplines offer useful insights. TCR scholars are also likely to discover that each discipline has focused on a different set of constructs or conceptualizations, or even different theories, related to the substantive phenomenon of interest. For parsimony, we recommend that TCR scholars focus on the constructs and theories that best match their research questions. Trying to include an exhaustive list of theories could actually diffuse the theoretical contributions.

### Step 3: Develop Hypotheses to Build Theory and Verify Theoretical Contributions

TCR investigators should next develop research hypotheses that incorporate the most relevant constructs and theory from their literature reviews. Then, they should ask themselves, if these hypotheses are supported, will the research make a major theoretical contribution? The researchers should verify that the expected findings (i.e., affirmative hypotheses tests) will build theory by identifying extensions, refinements, and/or qualifications, rather than merely supporting the theory as currently formulated.

Identifying hypotheses that will actually build theory can be very challenging. TCR scholars may discover that, even if the research hypotheses are fully supported, they will only replicate past findings, albeit in a new context; hence, there will be no noteworthy theoretical contributions. If past research is already extensive, as is often the case, it may be infeasible to make any theoretical contributions. However, past research may be more limited in its scope or more inconsistent than it first appears. Researchers working in the same area (e.g., on regulatory focus theory) tend to use very similar methods in order to ensure that past results are replicated; in fact, this is often a necessary first step to making additional contributions. This approach to research generates systematic, step-by-step, incremental contributions, but it limits the contexts and domains that are examined.

Researchers who are substantively driven often examine new contexts and domains, and/or use new methods, and this novelty can yield significant theoretical contributions. In our earlier example (Pechmann & Wang, 2010), the TCR investigators examined antismoking television shows that contained complex—but realistic—configurations of normative messages about what most people do, what attractive people do, and what people should do to avoid disapproval (with respect to smoking). As a result, the research contributed to both reference group theory (Bearden & Etzel, 1982; Park & Lessig, 1977) and the focus theory of normative conduct (Cialdini et al., 1990) by examining the relative impact of each normative message type on persuasion. Additionally, the TCR investigators examined television shows with antismoking messages that some viewers would find highly counterattitudinal (e.g., smokers). Thus, the research also contributed to persuasion knowledge theory (Friestad & Wright, 1994, 1995) by examining attitudinal congruence as a moderator of persuasion knowledge effects.

### Step 4: Directly Test Hypotheses and Emphasize Theoretical Contributions

In this final step, TCR scholars who seek to build theory should measure their key constructs in the studies they are conducting and directly test their theory-driven hypotheses. If the prior steps have been successfully completed and the hypotheses are supported (e.g., the desired significance level is attained and the effect size is adequate), there will be a theoretical contribution. This theoretical contribution should be explicitly stated in the write-up, including in the title and abstract; that is, it should strongly influence the paper's positioning. A possible concern about emphasizing the theoretical contributions is that the substantive contributions will inevitably be deprioritized, making it more difficult for the broader community to understand and use the research results. However, in our experience, practitioners, consumers, and policy makers will usually understand the paper's substantive insights, which will not be undermined by the theoretical contributions. The pragmatic insights can also be communicated through additional essays and reports in varied outlets.

Some prominent academics in consumer behavior have argued that studies with realistic settings, subjects, and/or stimuli cannot build theory because they are too messy, which obscures the true causal relationships among the variables (e.g., Tybout, 1995). However, mounting empirical evidence suggests otherwise; for example, several studies have shown the same effects in the controlled lab and the relatively uncontrolled field, indicating that valid theory can be developed in either setting. Davis and Pechmann (2010), for instance, recently found that structured social group activity (e.g., involvement in sports or clubs) is a protective factor that reduces youths' consumption of junk food; however, this protective factor is undermined by fast food restaurants that are near schools. The researchers replicated these effects in both the lab and the field, and contributed to construal level theory by demonstrating how perceptions of construal level are affected by social group activity. In summary, although it is demanding to conduct substantively driven TCR that builds theory, it most certainly can be done.

In the following two sections, challenges and opportunities that extend beyond the community of TCR scholars are explored. To achieve the goal of improving well-being, transformative consumer researchers need to interact with an array of social change agents, as elaborated next by Julie L. Ozanne.

### Engaging With Agents of Social Change Through TCR

Many academic researchers produce studies strictly for the academic community and do not consider the impact of their work beyond measuring how much their work is cited by other academics.

Yet, the paramount mission of TCR is to produce research that leads to greater well-being. Although no one knows definitively how to produce research that will lead to positive social change, some research paths may be more fruitful than others. Therefore, TCR is committed to encouraging a spectrum of alternative paths for improving consumer and earthly welfare and systematically assessing the success and sustainability of these efforts for affecting real social change. In this section, we explore five potential directions for those scholars who seek to make an impact through revelatory research, policy research, participatory research, coalition research, and incendiary research. These approaches link to different agents of change. Revelatory and incendiary research seek to inspire widespread social interest and involvement, policy research aligns with key political decision makers, participatory research partners with those people who are affected by the social problem, and coalition research works with organizations committed to alleviating the social problem.

*Revelatory Research*

Research with a purpose to unveil hidden or little known social problems can improve well-being by revealing these problems, seeking their deeper understanding, and attracting public attention and resources. Revelatory research often draws its inspiration from at-risk groups, such as the poor, the disenfranchised, and the very young or old, who lack the voice and resources to make their needs widely known. For example, Hill and Stamey's (1990) work on the homeless highlighted the consumption practices and coping strategies of a marginal group in society that is far too often ignored.

Although such topics may be studied in other fields, consumer researchers can bring a different theoretical lens and offer unique insights. For example, one problem concealed from public view is the mistreatment of elderly women by their caregivers. Whereas significant insights can be brought to bear by a gerontologist who might examine the ongoing physical neglect and abuse, consumer researchers might also highlight the dispossession of sacred objects and the subsequent assault on elderly women's identity as self-defining objects are taken and then given away or sold.

Revelatory research can have impact by delving thoroughly into the phenomenon to offer an insider's perspective on problems that are concealed from view, such as compulsive shopping. In-depth interviews and case studies, for example, might provide research findings that could be used to put a face on the problem and inspire social action (on the topic of compulsive buying, e.g., see Hirschman, 1992; O'Guinn & Faber, 1989). Alternatively, quantitative methods, such as surveys, might document the prevalence of the problem as well as the special needs of the group (e.g., O'Guinn & Faber, 1989). Ultimately, the power of revelatory research increases as qualitative and quantitative findings are used to develop theoretical insights that help consumers better understand their social problems and potential solutions.

*Policy Research*

Within the field of consumer research, a long tradition exists of researchers who seek to understand and inform public policy (e.g., Gorn & Goldberg, 1982; Pechmann & Ratneshwar, 1994). Through laws and regulations, governments exert a significant impact on the well-being of citizens. Thus, transformative consumer researchers can seek social change by conducting studies to inform policy dialogues through examining problems that might need greater governmental oversight and protection (e.g., the consumption of violent video games, underage patronage of hookah or smoking bars) or to assess the efficacy of existing policies (e.g., the ability of health warnings on product labels to compel positive behavioral changes). The path of policy research often assumes that a division of labor exists, with researchers generating relevant results that are used by politicians or pro-consumer groups to influence laws and regulations. However, consumer researchers can and do take a more active role by testifying before legislative bodies or working as government consultants.

The goal of policy research is to work from within the existing political system to gradually improve it. Researchers leverage their scientific credibility and expert status to generate authoritative research. These researchers, therefore, often employ research tools that have the greatest popular legitimacy, such as large-scale surveys using representative samples, or experiments in controlled laboratory conditions. Skepticism of the presumed superiority of such scientific methods has been well voiced within the academy (see, e.g., Anderson, 1983, 1986). Yet, policy makers and the public tend to give greater weight to quantitative forms of research, believing these to be more exacting and reliable than subjective forms. Nevertheless, we would not want to discount the potential power of other methods to capture the human condition and the political imagination, including those that are humanistic and interpretive (Holbrook & O'Shaughnessy, 1988). For example, the poignant photographs of Roy Stryker during the Great Depression had a significant influence on public policies regulating farming (Stryker, 1977).

*Participatory Research*

While revelatory researchers seek to do research *for* the benefit of at-risk and disadvantaged groups, participatory researchers seek also to do research *with* these groups (Ozanne & Saatcioglu, 2008). Participatory research is called by many names (e.g., action research, collaborative research, community action research), but, regardless of the name, this type of research assumes that the act of doing research is a powerful and empowering act. Thus, those people who are being researched become collaborators in the research process. Individuals, groups, and communities who engage in collaborative research exert significant influence on the research itself and gain beneficial learning experiences as they define the problem to be examined, select the methods to be employed, gather and analyze the data, generate potential solutions, and implement and evaluate programs of social change.

For instance, Ozanne and Anderson (2010) worked with a range of community partners to examine consumption and health care practices in an economically poor community with a 23% rate of diabetes. Community research partners included medical practitioners, professors and local students at a community college, and a local health advocacy group. Iterative and participative data collection revealed that past health programs and recommendations often had a poor cultural fit when they ignored the community members' desire for experiential and family-based learning or the importance of food as a symbolic marker of community membership. As such, the community partners used this research to guide the creation of a promotora or local health worker program at the local community college. The community stakeholders believed that a program housed and run by a local organization would be most feasible. In addition, the local health care workers could work with local families to generate culturally appropriate interventions, such as altering local dishes to be healthier and devising exercise plans that are responsive to the opportunities and obstacles found within the community.

While the benefits of participatory research for the participants are well documented (Schultz et al., 2003), a participatory turn in research could yield significant benefits for TCR, in particular, and for consumer research in general. Yadav's (2010) recent longitudinal study of the marketing and consumer research field has documented a decline of new conceptual work, suggesting that the field's emphasis on testing and extending existing theories continues to be well entrenched. Participatory research could be theoretically generative as we explore perspectives that may be unlike our own, as we work from the bottom up using contextually grounded observations, and as we engage empathetically with those people who are enmeshed in a given social problem. Moreover, when the findings are fed back to the community and acted on, participatory research can generate additional theoretical findings. For example, Hondagneu-Sotelo (1996) used participatory research with domestic workers to develop an intervention in which novellas were created to portray situations in which these women can be at risk. While evaluating these materials, she discovered new theoretical insights about how domestic work is more dynamic and more evolving than it originally appeared, and she also unveiled a new hierarchy of domestic labor.

*Coalition Research*

Some researchers become thoroughly committed to a social issue or marginalized group, and as a result, they decide to build an ongoing relationship with the relevant individuals, group, or organization to engage in additional research and assist them further. Such a coalition could arise through work with university-sponsored centers, nonprofit organizations, or even for-profit firms. It takes considerable time for researchers to develop relationships suffused with integrity and respect among their informants and organizations in the field. However, efficiencies and value in future research can be garnered by developing and maintaining long-term partnerships, such as ongoing access to data collection sites, and perhaps to more sensitive data, given that these ongoing relationships are based on greater trust. In addition, an investment in such a partnership may allow for the development of a richer understanding of the evolving social problem as it accrues over time.

For example, DeBerry-Spence (2010) created a successful social enterprise in Ghana called the MASAZI Visitor and Welcome Centre. She hoped to help increase the success of local subsistence vendors of arts and crafts by facilitating longer and more positive buyer–seller interactions. She has continued to use this site to conduct research on subsistence markets and leverage insights gained through her extensive contacts while working in this social enterprise.

*Incendiary Research*

A relatively small group of researchers write cogently and accessibly on important social issues, and, as such, their ideas are widely read and disseminated to the public. For example, Michael Pollan (e.g., 2008, 2009) writes best-selling books on the politics of food consumption and has translated important research ideas for a much wider audience than would be read by any journal article. Traditionally, the dissemination of our research ideas beyond the academy has not been important, but the growing attention to journals' impact factors suggests that expectations may be changing. For example, the *Journal of Consumer Research* has initiated public relations strategies for attaining increased media coverage of its most revealing and edifying scholarship, and the results suggest that these efforts have been quite successful (see http://www.jcr.wisc.edu).

TCR would itself benefit from more consumer researchers adopting the role of the public intellectual and seeking to spread their findings across public domains. Clearly, a different skill set is needed to write for mainstream consumers. Whereas academic writing is often obscurant, public writing needs to be crisp, creative, and stirring (see also Wansink, Chapter 3 of this volume, for discussion of his own related efforts).

Arguably, the goal of the public intellectual should be to write incendiary research, which should be passionate and inspiring. As Agger (2006) suggested, the public intellectual should write "agitationally, to enlighten, edify, engage, and energize" (p. 209). New knowledge is likely to be most transformative when it migrates out of narrow academic circles to be considered, debated, and acted on by the general public.

Consistent with the goal to partner with agents of social change, transformative consumer researchers need to disseminate their findings in the most effective and emerging new media forms. In the next section, Simone Pettigrew further details the needs and opportunities for communicating TCR insights to various stakeholders for greater consumer resolve and well-being.

### Communicating TCR: Beyond Information to Empowerment

As we have stressed, a primary objective of TCR is the timely and effective dissemination of research outputs to enhance consumer, societal, and earthly welfare. In the past, academic consumer researchers have emphasized the communication of their findings among themselves, with an assumed trickle-on effect to textbooks and industry publications. This practice fails to provide an adequate research-dissemination template to achieve the most basic mission of TCR, that is, to promote well-being. Instead, alternative communication strategies are required.

The TCR mandate—to share our insights with all those who could benefit—expands the audience scope to include consumers, consumer organizations, public policy makers, nonprofit organizations, industry representatives, and the media. Although some forward-thinking consumer researchers have previously suggested the need to include these audiences in our research-dissemination strategies (e.g., Bazerman, 2001; Thøgersen, 2005; Wansink, Chapter 3 of this volume), this practice is uncommon, and we lack the guiding principles for how it can be achieved.

Each research audience represents a different assortment of communication needs and challenges. For example, while informing consumer organizations and policy makers of research outcomes is relatively straightforward because of their smaller numbers and greater accessibility as compared to other audiences, close attention still needs to be given to the quantity and nature of information provided, and to the manner in which that information should be best packaged to maximize usefulness for particular recipients. Similarly, communicating TCR outputs to industry representatives entails careful consideration of how the information can be positioned to highlight the long-term merits of the research outcomes to organizations that adopt a pro-consumer/pro-society stance. In the case of the media as an audience for TCR, information is typically conveyed with the hope and expectation that the information will be forwarded in some manner to the public, such as inclusion in news and current affairs programs, lifestyle magazines, and even story lines in television shows (see, e.g., Sandlin, 2007). The broad range of available media vehicles underscores the need to build enduring relationships with the media to facilitate continuing access and actively ensure that the style and format of the research results provided are appropriate for the targeted outlet.

Communicating directly with consumers is relatively more difficult because it involves (a) targeting groups of consumers according to their need for and interest in the particular results being reported, (b) identifying multiple information channels that supply access to these groups, and (c) garnering consumers' attention amid the numerous other sound bites competing for their interest as they cope with the manifold complexities of daily life. In addition, it is important for research findings to be conveyed using minimal jargon, contextualized in relation to previous knowledge to allow individuals to understand the relative contribution of the new information, and translated into recommendations that are meaningful and feasible for consumers. Those of us who have researched in the area of consumer health, for example, are well accustomed to consumers' complaints about the piecemeal dissemination of research findings that are perceived in isolation to be competing, if not contradictory. Providing a more integrated and holistic approach to information dissemination represents an enormous challenge that will make new demands on our intellect and creativity.

The ideal approach is likely to be a multiaudience strategy that incorporates communications plans for all these target audiences to maximize the likelihood that the benefits of new research will translate into outcomes that enhance consumers' lives. Such an approach will require much greater attention to results dissemination than now exists among consumer researchers, and it constitutes a daunting prospect. However, there are examples of this approach outside of the TCR academia that can serve as useful guides.

For illustration, the New South Wales branch of the Australian Cancer Council (CCNSW) is a nonprofit organization that regularly undertakes consumer-focused research with the aim of improving the health of Australians. The organization actively communicates significant findings to multiple stakeholders to increase the likelihood that the research outputs will translate into constructive policies and practices. A recent example is its investigation of food labeling practices. This topic was selected for attention because the federal government was in the process of launching a review of food labeling laws in Australia. In order to have a voice in this debate, CCNSW designed and administered a detailed study that compared consumers' preferences for different visual representations of the major nutrients contained within foods, and consumers' relative abilities to understand the various representations. The results were published in the academic literature (Kelly et al., 2009) and in a consumer-friendly report (Kelly, Hughes, Chapman, Dixon, & King, 2008) that was distributed to government ministers, health agencies, research centers, seniors' groups, food manufacturers, food retailers, and international organizations that are known for their interest in food and nutrition issues (e.g., the International Obesity Taskforce). In addition, the report was made available on the CCNSW website (http://www.cancercouncil.com.au), where it could be accessed on demand by thousands of consumers. Media releases issued by CCNSW successfully generated coverage in metropolitan and regional media, drawing attention to the study and directing consumers to the online report. This comprehensive strategy provides an admirable model for members of the TCR movement to consider and emulate when developing their own research-dissemination plans.

A further issue is the nature of the information to be communicated. Motives for consumer education have typically stemmed from a desire to increase the efficiency of the market and remove the need for additional regulation (Fast, Vosburgh, & Frisbee, 1989; Howells, 2005; Langrehr & Mason, 1977). As a result of this orientation, there has been an emphasis in consumer education on topics such as budgeting, use of credit, complaint mechanisms, and consumers' legal rights. Information delivery has taken place largely in secondary school classrooms, often only reaching students who enroll in home economics courses (Benn, 2002; Lipstreu, 1949). If alternative methods of consumer education are developed, there is the potential to introduce more individuals to a broader range of concepts that could increase their consumer agency by offering greater insight into the consumption process. For instance, Bazerman (2001) has noted that previous efforts to encourage consumers to be more rational in their buying decisions have failed to acknowledge the reality that consumers are surrounded by marketplace actors who aim to induce them to behave irrationally. Explicitly sensitizing consumers to this state of affairs and informing them of metacognitive processes relating to persuasion may assist them to cope better in commercial environments (Wright, 2002). However, we lack any detailed understanding of the extent to which consumers can be trained in such matters and how best to implement this training (Wathieu et al., 2002). This is a crucial area for future dialogue and research within the TCR field.

Recently, there have also been increasing calls for consumer educators to deliver greater awareness of the consumer/citizen nexus (Adkins & Ozanne, 2005a; Benn, 2002, 2004; McGregor, 2005, 2008). These authors generally argue that providing consumers with information does not necessarily lead to their empowerment. Instead, consumer education should also assist people to evoke better decision processes that can have positive individual, social, and ecological outcomes, while also ensuring that people are aware of their legal rights and available methods of redress (Bannister, 1983).

In addition, consumers could be encouraged to appreciate the social interests served by existing market structures and consumer policies, and question the power imbalances that limit their knowledge and agency (Adkins & Ozanne, 2005a; McGregor, 2005). This approach would focus on assisting consumers to attain a global citizenship perspective that promotes conscious consumption as an alternative to the mass consumption of cheap consumer goods that inevitably results in oppressive conditions for those in low-wage economies (McGregor, 2008). Consumers are thus considered empowered not only when they have access to desired goods and services, but also when they are adequately informed and motivated to make decisions that have laudable social consequences beyond the satisfaction of their personal needs and desires (see also Mick & Schwartz, Chapter 32 of this volume; Thøgersen, 2005). Once again, the challenge in TCR will be to identify effective means of conveying these complex ideas to consumers in a manner that they will find comprehensible and implementable in their lives.

Effective communication with consumers requires constant adaptation to the changing patterns of their information-gathering activities. The increasing extent to which consumers are "networked" has important implications for those attempting to disseminate their research findings at a societal level. Moreover, with enormous amounts of information readily available through the Internet, it is not sufficient to rely on the one-way information flows that have traditionally characterized academics' interactions with the world beyond their research designs.

Instead, Repo, Timonen, and Zilliacus (2009) have recommended that, rather than trying to control information flows to and between consumers, a priority should be to facilitate these flows. They noted that information search costs have substantially declined since the advent of the Internet, especially as a result of consumers' willingness to share their experiences with others through social media that serve to build a communal knowledge base. Information is available in real time and in large quantities, which can make it more reliable and useful than the more static information typically provided by companies and policy makers (Kozinets et al., Chapter 10 of this volume; Shankar, Cherrier, & Canniford, 2006). It is in this context that consumer researchers seeking to disseminate their findings will need to (a) determine whether the most effective course of action is to embed their findings in conversations that consumers are already conducting among themselves, (b) incorporate their findings into formal consumer education classes being delivered in schools and adult education programs, (c) attempt to obtain coverage for their findings in the mass media, or (d) create a combination of these and other approaches.

Consumer research that is truly transformative in its ability to enhance well-being will need to acknowledge the limitations of the patriarchal approach that has typified our interactions with research audiences in the past. Instead, a more inclusive and egalitarian approach that explicitly recognizes the consumer/citizen nexus and all of its implications will be required to facilitate effective engagement (Jocz & Quelch, 2008). These efforts need to occur within a rapidly evolving information environment that offers new but uncertain prospects for meaningful, mutually beneficial interaction. Rising to this challenge will be a difficult, yet ultimately rewarding, task for transformative consumer researchers.

## CONCLUSION

The Worldwatch Institute and the Commission on the Measurement of Economic Performance and Social Progress have both argued that the nature and extent of the "good life" can no longer be principally judged according to a criterion of wealth or gross domestic product. Instead, the predominant standard must shift to well-being (Stiglitz et al., 2009; Worldwatch Institute, 2004). Today, it is commonly recognized that, in the march of human and earthly history, well-being has become fundamentally and intricately conjoined with the acquiring, consuming, and disposing of goods and services.

In this opening chapter, we have provided an overview of the development and chief characteristics of a recent movement emerging from the Association for Consumer Research, namely Transformative Consumer Research, whose goals are to encourage, guide, and foster a new generation of consumer research on well-being that is conceptually rich, methodologically sound, and pragmatically influential. This first volume on TCR addresses a wide spectrum of the prevalent problems and opportunities of consumer behaviors that pertain to varied dimensions of well-being. The authors we recruited to write these authoritative chapters are among the most knowledgeable and distinguished of all consumer researchers. We thank them for their steadfast efforts, on the complex and momentous calling we share through this inaugural book on TCR, on behalf of millions of consumers and their caretakers worldwide.

At a 2009 conference on TCR, keynote speaker Marc Mathieu (2009) spoke of the inspiration he felt while listening to the numerous scholars who had gathered to present and discuss their latest insights. He closed his remarks by suggesting—half in jest but fully in truth—that TCR might consider revising its name to Tremendously Courageous Research. We agree, and we believe that the chapters that compose this book bear the fruit and the future of that tribute.

## REFERENCES

Adkins, N. R., & Ozanne, J. L. (2005a). Critical consumer education: Empowering the low-literate consumer. *Journal of Macromarketing, 25*(2), 153–162.

Adkins, N. R., & Ozanne, J. L. (2005b). The low literate consumer. *Journal of Consumer Research, 32*(1), 93–105.

Agger, B. (2006). *Critical social theories.* Boulder, CO: Paradigm.

Anderson, P. F. (1983). Marketing, scientific progress, and scientific method. *Journal of Marketing, 47*(Fall), 18–31.

Anderson, P. F. (1986). On method in consumer research: A critical relativist perspective. *Journal of Consumer Research, 13*(2), 155–173.

Andrews, J. C., Netemeyer, R. G., Burton, S., Moberg, D. P., & Christiansen, A. (2004). Understanding adolescent intentions to smoke: An examination of relationships among social influence, prior trial behavior, and antitobacco campaign advertising. *Journal of Marketing, 68*(3), 110–123.

Aristotle. (1999). *Nicomachean ethics* (M. Ostwald, Trans.). Upper Saddle River, NJ: Prentice Hall. (Original work published 350 BC)

Arnould, E., & Thompson, C. J. (2005). Consumer culture theory (CCT): Twenty years of research. *Journal of Consumer Research, 31*(4), 868–882.

Bannister, R. (1983). A classification of concepts in consumer education. *NASSP Bulletin, 67*, 10–15.

Bazerman, M. H. (2001). Consumer research for consumers. *Journal of Consumer Research, 27*, 499–504.

Bearden, W. O., & Etzel, M. J. (1982). Reference group influence on product and brand purchase decisions. *Journal of Consumer Research, 9*(2), 183–194.

Belk, R. W. (Ed.). (2007). *Handbook of qualitative research methods in marketing.* Northhampton, MA: Edward Elgar.

Bender, L., Burns, S. Z., David, L. (Producers), & Guggenheim, D. (Director). (2006). *An inconvenient truth* [Motion picture]. United States: Paramount Classics.

Benn, J. (2002). Consumer education: Educational considerations and perspectives. *International Journal of Consumer Studies, 26*, 169–177.

Benn, J. (2004). Consumer education between "consumership" and citizenship: Experiences from studies of young people. *International Journal of Consumer Studies, 28*, 108–116.

Bernthal, M. J., Crockett, D., & Rose, R. L. (2005). Credit cards as lifestyle facilitators. *Journal of Consumer Research, 32*(1), 130–145.

Borgmann, A. (2000). The moral complexion of consumption. *Journal of Consumer Research, 26*(4), 418–422.

Brinberg, D., & Hirschman, E. C. (1986). Multiple orientations for the conduct of marketing research: An analysis of the academic/practitioner distinction. *Journal of Marketing, 50*(4), 161–173.

Brinberg, D., & McGrath, J. E. (1985). *Validity and the research process.* Beverly Hills, CA: Sage.

Campbell, M. C., & Kirmani, A. (2000). Consumers' use of persuasion knowledge: The effects of accessibility and cognitive capacity on perceptions of an influence agent. *Journal of Consumer Research, 27*(1), 69–83.

Cialdini, R. B. (2009). We have to break up. *Perspectives on Psychological Science, 4*(1), 5–6.

Cialdini, R. B., Reno, R. R., & Kallgren, C. A. (1990). A focus theory of normative conduct: Recycling the concept of norms to reduce littering in public places. *Journal of Personality and Social Psychology, 58*(6), 1015–1026.

Cohen, L. (2010). Is it time for another round of consumer protection? The lessons of twentieth century U.S. history. *Journal of Consumer Affairs, 44*(Spring), 234–247.

Csikszentmihalyi, M. (2000). The costs and benefits of consuming. *Journal of Consumer Research, 27*(2), 267–272.

Davis, B., & Pechmann, C. (2010). *Structured group activity, proximity to fast food, and unhealthy consumption.* Unpublished manuscript, Baylor University, Waco, TX.

DeBerry-Spence, B. (2010). Making theory and practice in subsistence markets: An analytic autoethnography of MASAZI in Accra, Ghana. *Journal of Business Research, 63*(6), 608–616.

Denzin, N. K. (2001). The seventh moment: Qualitative inquiry and the practices of a more radical consumer research. *Journal of Consumer Research, 28*(2), 324–330.

Erdem, T. (2010). Spanning the boundaries. *Journal of Marketing Research, 47*(1), 1–2.

Faber, R. J., & O'Guinn, T. (1992). A clinical screener for compulsive buying. *Journal of Consumer Research, 19*(3), 459–469.

Fast, J., Vosburgh, R. E., & Frisbee, W. R. (1989). The effects of consumer education on consumer search. *Journal of Consumer Affairs, 23*(1), 65–90.

Flyvbjerg, B. (2001). *Making social science matter: Why social inquiry fails and how it can succeed again* (S. Sampson, Trans.). New York: Cambridge University Press.

Fournier, S., Dobscha, S., & Mick, D. G. (1998). Preventing the premature death of relationship marketing. *Harvard Business Review,* January–February, 42–51.

Friestad, M., & Wright, P. (1994). The persuasion knowledge model: How people cope with persuasion attempts. *Journal of Consumer Research, 21*(1), 1–31.

Friestad, M., & Wright, P. (1995). Persuasion knowledge: Lay people's and researchers' beliefs about the psychology of advertising. *Journal of Consumer Research, 22*(1), 62–74.

Gorn, G. J., & Goldberg, M. E. (1982). Behavioral evidence of the effects of televised food messages on children. *Journal of Consumer Research, 9,* 200–205.

Henry, P. C. (2005). Social class, market situation, and consumers: Metaphors of (dis)empowerment. *Journal of Consumer Research, 31*(4), 766–778.

Higgins, E. T. (1997). Beyond pleasure and pain. *American Psychologist, 52*(12), 1280–1300.

Hill, R. P., & Stamey, M. (1990). The homeless in America: An examination of possessions and consumption behaviors. *Journal of Consumer Research, 17,* 303–321.

Hilton, M. (2008). *Prosperity for all: Consumer activism in an era of globalization.* Ithaca, NY: Cornell University Press.

Hirschman, E. C. (1992). The consciousness of addiction: Toward a general theory of compulsive consumption. *Journal of Consumer Research, 19*(2), 155–179.

Holbrook, M. B. (1985). Why business is bad for consumer research: The three bears revisited. In E. C. Hirschman & M. B. Holbrook (Eds.), *Advances in consumer research* (Vol. 12, pp. 145–156). Provo, UT: Association for Consumer Research.

Holbrook, M. B., & O'Shaughnessy, J. (1988). On the scientific status of consumer research and the need for an interpretive approach to studying consumption behavior. *Journal of Consumer Research, 15*(3), 398–402.

Hondagneu-Sotelo, P. (1996). Immigrant women and paid domestic work: Research, theory, and activism. In H. Gottfried (Ed.), *Feminism and social change* (pp. 105–122). Chicago: University of Illinois Press.

Howells, G. (2005). The potential and limits of consumer empowerment information. *Journal of Law and Society, 32*(3), 349–370.

Hudson, L. A., & Ozanne, J. L. (1988). Alternative ways of seeking knowledge in consumer research. *Journal of Consumer Research, 14*(4), 508–521.

Hunt, S. C. (1991). Positivism and paradigm dominance in consumer research: Toward critical pluralism and rapprochement. *Journal of Consumer Research, 18*(1), 32–44.

Iredale, M. (2008). From knowledge-inquiry to wisdom-inquiry: Is the revolution underway? In R. Barnett & N. Maxwell (Eds.), *Wisdom in the university* (pp. 21–33). London: Routledge.

Jocz, K. E., & Quelch, J. A. (2008). An exploration of marketing's impacts on society: A perspective linked to democracy. *Journal of Public Policy & Marketing, 27*(2), 202–206.

Kelly, B., Hughes, C., Chapman, K., Dixon, H., & King, L. (2008). *Front-of-pack food labeling: Traffic light labeling gets the green light.* Sydney, Australia: Cancer Council.

Kelly, B., Hughes, C., Chapman, K., Louie, J. C. Y., Dixon, H., Crawford, J., et al. (2009). Consumer testing of the acceptability and effectiveness of front-of-pack food labelling systems for the Australian grocery market. *Health Promotion International, 24*(2), 120–129.

Kernan, J. B. (1979). Presidential address: Consumer research and the public purpose. In W. L. Wilkie (Ed.), *Advances in consumer research* (Vol. 6, pp. 1–2). Ann Arbor, MI: Association for Consumer Research.

Khare, A., & Inman, J. J. (2006). Habitual behavior in American eating patterns: The role of meal occasions. *Journal of Consumer Research, 32*(4), 567–575.

Langrehr, F. W., & Mason, J. B. (1977). The development and implementation of the concept of consumer education. *Journal of Consumer Affairs, 11*(2), 63–79.

Lehmann, D. R. (2003). The relevance of rigor. *Marketing Science Institute Reports* (No. 03-105), 83–91.

Lipstreu, O. (1949). Consumer education: Modern style. *The School Review, 57*(2), 101–103.

Marcoux, J. S. (2009). Escaping the gift economy. *Journal of Consumer Research, 36*(December), 671–685.

Mari, C. (2008). Doctoral education and transformative consumer research. *Journal of Marketing Education, 30*(1), 5–11.

Mathieu, M. (2009, June). Keynote address at the Second Biennial Conference on Transformative Consumer Research, Villanova University, Villanova, PA.

Maxwell, N. (1984). *From knowledge to wisdom: A revolution in the aims and methods of science.* Oxford, England: Basil Blackwell.

Maxwell, N. (2002). Is science neurotic? *Metaphilosophy, 33*(3), 1036–1068.

Maxwell, N. (2008). From knowledge to wisdom: The need for an academic revolution. In R. Barnett & N. Maxwell (Eds.), *Wisdom in the university* (pp. 1–19). London: Routledge.

Maxwell, N. (2009, June). Are universities undergoing an intellectual revolution? *Oxford Magazine, 290,* 13–16.

McGregor, S. (2005). Sustainable consumer empowerment through critical consumer education: A typology of consumer education approaches. *International Journal of Consumer Studies, 29*(5), 437–447.

McGregor, S. (2008). Ideological maps of consumer education. *International Journal of Consumer Studies, 32,* 545–552.

McGregor, S. (2010). *Consumer education as a site of political resistance: 50 years of conceptual evolutions.* Seabright, NS, Canada: McGregor Consulting Group. Retrieved March 20, 2010, from http://www.consultmcgregor.com

McGregor, S. L. T., & Goldsmith, E. B. (1998). Expanding our understanding of quality of life, standard of living, and well-being. *Journal of Family and Consumer Sciences, 90*(2), 2–6.

Mick, D. G. (2006). Meaning and mattering through transformative consumer research. In C. Pechmann & L. L. Price (Eds.), *Advances in consumer research* (Vol. 33, pp. 1–4). Provo, UT: Association for Consumer Research.

Mick, D. G. (2007). The end(s) of marketing and the neglect of moral responsibility by the American Marketing Association. *Journal of Public Policy & Marketing, 26*(2), 289–292.

Nader, R. (1965). *Unsafe at any speed: The designed-in dangers of the American automobile.* New York: Grossman.

O'Guinn, T. C., & Faber, R. J. (1989). Compulsive buying: A phenomenological exploration. *Journal of Consumer Research, 16*(2), 147–157.

Olson, J. C. (1982). Presidential address 1981: Toward a science of consumer behavior. In A. Mitchell (Ed.), *Advances in consumer research* (Vol. 9, pp. v–x). Ann Arbor, MI: Association for Consumer Research.

Ozanne, J. L., & Anderson, L. (2010). Community action research. *Journal of Public Policy & Marketing, 29*(1), 123–137.

Ozanne, J. L., & Saatcioglu, B. (2008). Participatory action research. *Journal of Consumer Research, 35,* 423–439.

Park, C. W., & Lessig, V. P. (1977). Students and housewives: Differences in susceptibility to reference group influence. *Journal of Consumer Research, 4*(2), 102–110.

Pechmann, C., & Knight, S. J. (2002). An experimental investigation of the joint effects of advertising and peers on adolescents' beliefs and intentions about cigarette consumption. *Journal of Consumer Research, 29*(1), 5–19.

Pechmann, C., & Ratneshwar, S. (1994). The effects of antismoking and cigarette advertising on young adolescents' perceptions of peers who smoke. *Journal of Consumer Research, 21,* 236–252.

Pechmann, C., & Wang, L. (2010). Effects of indirectly and directly competing reference group messages and persuasion knowledge: Implications for educational placements. *Journal of Marketing Research, 47*(1), 134–145.

Pettigrew, S. (2001). Why a journal of research for consumers? *Journal of Research for Consumers, 1.* Retrieved December 20, 2010, from http://www.jrconsumers.com.

Pichert, J. W., Hanson, S. L., & Pechmann, C. A. (1985). A system for assessing use of patients' time. *Evaluation & the Health Professions, 8*(1), 39–54.

Pollan, M. (2008). *In defense of food: An eater's manifesto*. New York: Penguin.

Pollan, M. (2009). *Food rules: An eater's manual*. New York: Penguin.

Repo, P., Timonen, P., & Zilliacus, K. (2009). Alternative regulatory cases challenging consumer policy. *Journal of Consumer Policy, 32*, 289–301.

Sandlin, J. A. (2007). Netnography as a consumer education research tool. *International Journal of Consumer Studies, 31*, 288–294.

Schor, J. B., & Holt, D. B. (Eds.). (2000). *The consumer society reader*. New York: New Press.

Schulz, A. J., Israel, B. A., Parker, E. A., Lockett, M., Hill, Y. R., & Willis, R. (2003). Engaging women in community based participatory research for health. In M. Minkler & N. Wallerstein (Eds.), *Community based participatory research for health* (pp. 293–315). San Francisco: Jossey-Bass.

Shankar, A., Cherrier, H., & Canniford, R. (2006). Consumer empowerment: A Foucauldian interpretation. *European Journal of Marketing, 40*(9/10), 1013–1030.

Speth, J. G. (2008). *A bridge at the edge of the world*. New Haven, CT: Yale University Press.

Stiglitz, J. E., Sen, A., & Fitoussi, J. (2009). *Report by the Commission on the Measurement of Economic Performance and Social Progress*. Retrieved March 20, 2010, from http://www.stiglitz-sen-fitoussi.fr

Stryker, F. J. (1977). *Portrait of a decade: Roy Stryker and the development of documentary photography in the thirties*. New York: Da Capo.

Tadajewski, M., & Maclaran, P. (Eds.). (2009). *Critical marketing studies* (Vols. 1–3). London: Sage.

Thøgersen, J. (2005). How may consumer policy empower consumers for sustainable lifestyles? *Journal of Consumer Policy, 28*, 143–178.

Thompson, C. J. (2005). Consumer risk perceptions in a community of reflexive doubt. *Journal of Consumer Research, 32*(2), 235–248.

Timmreck, T. C. (2003). *Planning, program development, and evaluation: A handbook for health promotion, aging and health services*. Sudbury, MA: Jones & Bartlett.

Tybout, A. M. (1995). Presidential address: The value of theory in consumer research. In F. R. Kardes & M. Sujan (Eds.), *Advances in consumer research* (Vol. 22, pp. 1–8). Provo, UT: Association for Consumer Research.

Wansink, B., & van Ittersum, K. (2003). Bottoms up! The influence of elongation on pouring and consumption volume. *Journal of Consumer Research, 30*(3), 455–463.

Wathieu, L., Brenner, L., Carmon, Z., Chattopadhyay, A., Wertenbroch, K., Drolet, A., et al. (2002). Consumer control and empowerment: A primer. *Marketing Letters, 13*(3), 297–305.

Wilkie, W. L., & Moore, E. S. (2003). Scholarly development in marketing: Exploring the "4 eras" of thought development. *Journal of Public Policy & Marketing, 22*(2), 116–146.

Winston, R. (2005, September). *Who owns the science and what is the role for the scientist in the future?* Presidential address at the annual meeting of the British Association Festival of Science, Dublin, Ireland. Retrieved January 23, 2010, from http://www.britishscienceassociation.org/web/News/FestivalNews/_FestivalNews2005/_BAPresidentialAddress2005.htm

Worldwatch Institute. (2004). *State of the world 2004: Richer, fatter, and not much happier—a special focus on the consumer society*. Washington, DC: Author.

Wright, P. (2002). Marketplace metacognition and social intelligence. *Journal of Consumer Research, 28*, 677–682.

Yadav, M. S. (2010). The decline of conceptual articles and implications for knowledge development. *Journal of Marketing, 74*, 1–19.

# 2

# Foundational Research on Consumer Welfare
## Opportunities for a Transformative Consumer Research Agenda

Alan R. Andreasen, Marvin E. Goldberg, and M. Joseph Sirgy

As scholars seek to contribute to improving consumer welfare throughout the world through future research and writing, a valuable exercise is to review a selection of the earliest work in what we might call the new social conscience of marketing. The purpose of this chapter is to conduct such a selective review to serve three distinct purposes. First and most fundamentally, it is to alert present-day scholars to significant past work on particular topics. Second, it is to describe the approaches used and some of the principal findings. Last, it is to reflect on such work and offer what the authors see as implications for present-day scholars considering working in, or near to, the particular domain. Such implications may highlight unresolved issues that have present-day relevance and/or identify methodological challenges requiring new theory or conceptual development.

The chapter's overview necessarily reflects both the experience and approaches of the three authors. It is thereby selective in its topics and, perhaps, subjective in its treatment. We have, however, sought to provide citations to some of the most central works that can then be used by others for further bibliographic explorations.

The chapter is divided into three major parts. The first part provides a historical and motivational overview of the research on consumer welfare. The second part (in two subsections) highlights consumer welfare research related to vulnerable consumers, specifically the young and old. The third part focuses on research in consumer welfare guided by the quality-of-life (QOL) concept, the purpose of which is to motivate future research using theoretical concepts from the growing field of QOL studies.

Throughout the chapter, we make a distinction between what we and others have called the "dark side" and "bright side" of marketing's social impact. Dark side considerations reflect the fact that a range of marketing strategies and tactics have the potential—and often the reality—of negatively impacting the welfare of consumers and/or the broader societies which they inhabit. These impacts can include outright deception, promotion of undesirable values and behaviors, and neglect of societies' most vulnerable target audiences. Bright side considerations focus on the ways in which marketing practices can improve individuals' lives and the social world they inhabit. Much of the latter work is subsumed under the broad label of *social marketing*.

## THE AWAKENING OF MARKETING'S SOCIAL CONSCIENCE

The discipline of marketing as a field of study is well over a century old. Wilkie and Moore (2003) have partitioned the field's historical progress into "four eras" of thought development. During Era I (1900–1920), the dominant paradigm was economic efficiency: Does the marketing system provide society with the goods it needs at fair prices? Critics in this period raised questions about the economic and social value of marketing tools, such as advertising and selling, and the efficiency and fairness of distribution systems. Was advertising wasteful and personal selling too intrusive and subject to abuses? In Era II (1920–1950), criticism escalated and took the form of a "consumer movement" that contributed to the creation and/or strengthening of a number of the major consumer protection laws and institutions like the Food and Drug Administration and the Federal Trade Commission (FTC), under which the market operates today (Gaedeke & Etcheson, 1972). During the period, the federal government's role in regulating markets grew. In the main, however, the focus continued to be on marketer behavior, particularly issues of fairness and efficiency in competition, fair pricing, and advertising deception.

Era III (1950–1980) featured immense growth in the marketplace and in the contributions of marketing scholarship. Of relevance to the present chapter is the fact that the era was marked by two fundamental shifts in orientation. First, the focus of marketing research and teaching shifted from an approach that might be described as "above the fray" in describing marketing activities and how they worked, assessing the goodness and badness of market systems, and offering recommendations for better performance in the system. Era III saw a shift to an approach that focused on helping managers become better decision makers and better marketers, which had an important impact on the study of consumers.

For the first two thirds of this period, there was no distinct field called *consumer behavior*. However, by the late 1960s, the growing managerial focus required that the study of consumers shift from a descriptive emphasis on "socio-demographic profiles, income levels and geographic spread … [to drawing] much more heavily from behavioral science concepts applied to marketing" (Myers, Massy, & Greyser, 1980, p. 92). Contributing to this in particular were several publications: Gerald Zaltman's (1965) collection *Marketing: Contributions From the Behavioral Sciences*, Kassarjian and Robertson's (1968) collection *Perspectives in Consumer Behavior*, and Howard and Sheth's (1969) pioneering attempt at a comprehensive framework, *The Theory of Buyer Behavior*. Significantly, the first consumer behavior textbook appeared in 1968 (Engel, Kollat, & Blackwell, 1968), and the Association for Consumer Research was brought to life at an informal meeting at Ohio State University in 1969.

The middle of this era also witnessed two sets of events that dramatically affected the interests and careers of a subset of those faculty members who called themselves *consumer behavior scholars*. The first of these was external to the field and comprised a major escalation of social unrest. The Vietnam War energized many citizens and many students and faculty on many college campuses to become actively involved in social criticism and seek broad objectives of social betterment and personal fulfillment. Marches, rallies, and protests on college campuses became common occurrences,* and marketing scholars were among those protesting!

The second influence had more direct relevance to the field. It was the urban riots of the late 1960s. The burning, looting, and trashing of retail establishments in what were then called *urban ghettos* made it abundantly clear to scholars and citizens alike that members of a major segment of America's economic underclass, African Americans, were frustrated and angry about how they were treated, especially in the marketplace (Andreasen, 1975; Myers, 1997). These two influences

---

* The first author found tear gas wafting into his classroom during a memorable class session during this period.

dramatically increased the need for careful investigation and potential suggestions for remediation. Many members of the early cohort of consumer scholars took up this challenge.

The desire of consumer scholars to study the social impacts of managerial behavior was given a significant boost from another landmark event in the late 1960s that fundamentally changed the outer bounds of what was thought of as the proper domain of "marketing." Philip Kotler and his Northwestern University colleagues Sid Levy and Gerald Zaltman proposed that the borders of the marketing discipline be extended in future to encompass applications beyond the narrow confines of the private sector. This paradigm shift gave permission to scholars to look at "consumer" behaviors that were of interest to nonprofit organizations and government agencies that wanted to generate greater arts attendance, blood donations, and voting. Their expansive perspective also prompted others to begin looking at the potential for using consumer and marketing models and frameworks to address important world social problems that could be linked to consumer behavior, such as smoking, family planning, and child survival. The latter field of interest and application became known as social marketing (Kotler & Zaltman, 1971).

These broad sets of events in Era III provoked not only scholarly attention but also scholarly passion—passion that was no doubt fueled by the emotional environment of post-Vietnam college campuses. Along one pathway, a significant cadre of consumer behavior researchers focused their interests on issues raised during the urban riots. As noted above, these interests were labeled by Senator Warren Magnuson and coauthor Jean Carper (1968), and later Elizabeth Hirschman (1991), as "the dark side of the marketplace." The focus of this line of investigation was on highlighting and then righting wrongs within marketing systems and reforming unethical practices of marketers, particularly in urban inner cities. Leading scholars in consumer behavior admitted that "marketing's maturity [is] coupled with growing consciousness within the marketing community that basic societal problems can often be characterized as mass consumption/exchange problems" (Sheth & Wright, 1974, p. 1).

At the same time, a different—although sometimes overlapping—group of scholars became interested in what might be called the *bright side of marketing*, in which the potential for important consumer research was identified by Kotler, Levy, and Zaltman. The major foci of this cohort were understanding and suggesting remedies for what have been called *problem behaviors* on the part of citizens around the world (e.g., having too many children, not getting proper immunizations, practicing unsafe sex, smoking) and how marketing approaches could be used to change or prevent such behaviors from occurring in future. We shall consider each side of this early interest in the social side of marketing behavior in turn.

## Marketing's Dark Side

The urban riots in the United States in the late 1960s and early 1970s revealed a range of issues that became a key interest of a small, but significant, set of consumer researchers. Their interest was piqued by a particularly dramatic feature of the riots, namely, the fact that much of the damage that occurred was to the stores and service businesses that served the very same rioters in their own communities. Sturdivant (1968) reported that "of more than 600 buildings damaged by looting and fire, over 95 per cent were retail stores" (p. 131).

Why was that? As marketing scholars turned their attention to this subject, they discovered that some of the key issues had already been addressed by a sociologist, David Caplovitz (1963), who asked, "Do the poor pay more?" (cf. Richards, 1966). Caplovitz carried out extensive interviews in urban "ghettoes" (as they were called then) and concluded that the poor suffered major exploitation. As Andreasen summarized in 1975, Caplovitz found that the poor "with astonishing frequency were charged outrageous prices and unconscionable interest rates and sold unneeded, misrepresented and shoddy merchandise" (p. 13). Caplovitz found that their marketplace attempts at survival often led consumers to use various forms of credit that involved exorbitant rates of interest and eventual repossessions. Purchases intended to improve poor consumers' lives then often had the compounding effect of causing loss of employment that only worsened their situation. In a follow-up book in 1974, Caplovitz looked specifically at this problem by studying debtors in default to catalog the negative impacts not only on spending power and employment but also on the affected families' marriages and health (as cited in Andreasen & Cady, 1973).

Fortunately, a small set of marketing scholars also became interested in these issues and engaged in a range of carefully contrived field studies. One group, led by Marcus Alexis, had already investigated the consumption behavior of African Americans, using economic databases to understand how race, combined with retail structure, affected their welfare (Alexis, 1962; Bullock, 1961). These early studies were followed by more careful attention to Black–White differences in expenditure patterns and product and brand usage as the basis for both understanding problematic behaviors and setting the groundwork for what became great interest in the aggregate spending power of this audience (Alexis, 1962; Gensch & Staelin, 1972; Gibson, 1969; Hiltz, 1971).

Guidance for some of this work was found in Frederick Sturdivant's (1968) landmark piece in the *Harvard Business Review* titled "Better Deal for Ghetto Shoppers." He reported field research in Los Angeles that revealed that both African American and Mexican ghetto areas suffered from "the prevalence of small, inefficient, uneconomical units" (p. 132). He also laid the problems of inner-city consumers to a "tendency on the part of many stores to prey on an undereducated and relatively immobile population with high-pressure, unethical methods" (p. 132). Proposed solutions included increases in minority-owned businesses and in the skills of inner-city marketers. A 1970 American Marketing Association–sponsored symposium sought to energize further focus on these problems (Andreasen, 1972). Attending this symposium were a significant number of the marketing field's major scholars of the era.

Alexis again was instrumental in following up Sturdivant's work with a stream of carefully designed research in this era. With colleagues at the University of Rochester, he, like many other researchers at the time, looked at food shopping behavior in inner-city versus non–inner-city neighborhoods (Haines, Simon, & Alexis, 1971). This stream of research routinely found that a major problem faced by the poor and minorities in their neighborhoods was that they had fewer chain store alternatives. The poor paid more simply because there were very few lower-priced supermarkets and discount outlets in their areas (U.S. Department of Agriculture, 1968). Similar results were found in investigations by Cox (1969), Andreasen (1971), Berry (1972), Sexton (1971), Goodman (1972), Marcus (1969), and Dixon and McLaughlin (1969). A number of these studies concluded, as Sturdivant did, that a major source of disadvantage was a market structure operated by managers with limited skills and absentee ownership. It was not the case, as many community activists thought, that supermarkets, for example, charged more for merchandise in poor communities or engaged in disreputable practices like off-loading stale products and poor produce in poor areas.

Other scholars used data from hearings at government commissions to explore Caplovitz's claim of high levels of exploitation of poor and minorities (Andreasen & Upah, 1979). These studies identified the tactics typically used by devious merchants, particularly in the use of credit contracts to further impoverish these target audiences. The upshot of this close attention, fueled by antigovernment protests of the late 1960s and early 1970s, was more regulation, more laws, closer monitoring, and more funding for regulatory agencies (Day & Brandt, 1974).

In terms of marketing scholarship, academics produced collections of readings during this period that focused on dark side issues (Sturdivant, 1968; Wish & Gamble, 1971). Andreasen (1975) produced a summary of much of the work, not limited to racial minorities but including challenges facing ethnic minorities and others with specific market handicaps. Many years later, Alwitt and Donley (1996) produced an updated look at low-income consumers and reached many of the same conclusions as the earlier studies, suggesting that not much had changed in the intervening years to improve the lot of disadvantaged consumers.

One bright side outcome of the focus on minority consumers was D. Parke Gibson's (1969) book *The $30 Billion Negro*, which sought to bring the attention of private-sector marketers to the significant potential in minority markets. Academics sought to contribute to this increased attention by exploring differences in consumption patterns across racial groups, particularly between Blacks and Whites. Building on early work by Sterner and Mauritz (1943) and others, Alexis (1962) and Bauer, Cunningham, and Wortzel (1965) found differences in allocations across various consumption categories. Bauer et al. found little differences in spending for necessities, lower spending on labor-saving devices and luxury goods, and more spending on furniture. Other findings were that Blacks used newspapers less than Whites for shopping, more often shopped locally, and engaged in less comparison shopping. They were much more sensitive to their treatment in stores, especially stores that were White-owned. They also exhibited preferences for well-known national brands, which was seen as a particular attraction to mainstream marketers.

Early studies also found differences in saving rates and allocations across many budget categories (Galenson, 1972). Hypotheses for such differences were offered in four broad categories (Andreasen 1975, p. 74):

1. The lack-of-assets hypothesis that Blacks were handicapped by the absence of past savings (e.g., in the form of home ownership)
2. The lack-of-credit hypothesis that Blacks obtained less credit because of their lower asset base and because of discrimination (e.g., redlining)
3. The permanent income hypothesis that White consumers had better future income prospects and could spend against it
4. The relative income hypothesis that differences (e.g., in savings rates) can be explained not by absolute income but by one's position in the income distribution for one's racial group

Prior research by Brady and Friedman (1947) and a classic work by Duesenbury (1949) argued that the last hypothesis best explained differences across races in savings behavior.

Other topics of concern to those making interracial comparisons involved credit use. Hiltz (1971), for example, found that Blacks had less knowledge about credit and paid higher interest rates than Whites. Blacks also had higher levels of debt, but only if they lived outside of poverty areas. The latter was one causal factor in Caplovitz's (1974) research, which found that not only did Blacks default more than Whites, but also that the causes were more likely to be overextension and not job instability, as some had thought.

The recommendations that flowed from this broad set of studies can be partitioned into five categories. First are strategies to simply increase the income and assets of the poor. In the 1960s and 1970s, this led to discussions of income supplement programs and a guaranteed income. It also contributed a major element to efforts to eliminate (or, at least, reduce) racial discrimination, as it affected one's ability to both build income (due to job discrimination) and build assets (due to redlining). Third, many strategies advocated improving the retail and service structures in poor and minority marketplaces, such as subsidizing supermarkets, training and funding minority entrepreneurs, and so on. The fourth approach was to clamp down on marketers' unconscionable behavior, for example, exorbitant credit terms and product and service deception. Finally, many conservative critics argued for a fifth approach of simply creating programs and structures that would help the poor and minorities better fend for themselves.

In the main, interest in disadvantaged consumers declined in the late 1970s without having much lasting impact on either consumer problems or marketing scholarship. This has important implications for the future of Transformative Consumer Research (TCR). First of all, as Andreasen noted in 1978, the "ghetto marketing life cycle" began to decline after barely 5 years of concentrated work. As noted above, this was particularly disappointing in that, at the outset of the period, many of today's leading marketing scholars were involved in addressing the issues surfaced by the riots and the "power to the people" ethos of the Vietnam War protests. These scholars included George Day, David Aaker, Ray Bauer, Marcus Alexis, Leonard Berry, Steven Greyser, George Haines, Harold Kassarjian, and Richard Staelin.

In our view, a major problem causing many to migrate away from the topic area was that much of the published work was descriptive in character. To the extent that analyses involved consumer behavior theories, these were drawn largely from economics or the researchers' own speculations. Further, major issues surrounding the question of whether the poor pay more were resolved early on and the proposed remedies around inner-city market development, consumer education, and the policing of marketers' behavior were rather obvious and needed little research support. The rhetoric around both problems and solutions was also often phlegmatic and frequently led to challenges to research that were based on ideology ("That can't be true") rather than careful analysis. As a result, many of our best marketing scholars moved on. Urban challenges also declined in interest in other intellectual fields as well, indirectly supporting the view of future Senator Daniel Patrick Moynihan, who famously advised the Richard Nixon administration that the government should pull back from trying to solve urban problems for a period of "benign neglect" that would encourage a cooling off of extremists on both sides.

One domain in which significant research did emerge and continues today as a secondary result of concerns about the poor and minorities was in the area of advertising regulation. The political environment in the United States under Presidents Nixon and Ford supported increased interest in regulation and remediating mechanisms rather than direct subsidies. The FTC grew in importance as a vehicle for consumer protection. Under progressive leaders such as Mary Gardiner Jones, the commission for the first time made room in its headquarters for marketing academics who took leaves to be in residence for a period of time to conduct significant research that then found its way into our major journals (FTC, 1968). Over the years, these scholars-on-leave—Bill Wilkie, Michael Mazis, Gary Ford, and over 25 others—generated a large number of studies that advanced our understanding of fundamental consumer behavior (Murphy & Wilkie, 1990).

Because commissioners of the FTC wanted to understand how people could be deceived and what could be done about it, there was particular interest in studies that scholars conducted on perception and information processing (Johnson & Russo, 1984), consumer search behavior (Ratchford, 1982), and the apprehension and misapprehension of advertising content (Jacoby & Hoyer, 1989). This line of research necessitated attention to attitude theories and the ability of intentions to predict behavior, a point to which we shall return below.

While attention was being paid to government-led protection regimes, another thread of research focused on the possibility of consumer self-help. Sparked by Ralph Nader's book *Unsafe at Any Speed*, this research stream focused on dissatisfied consumers and tried to understand who they were and what they did about their dissatisfaction (Hunt, 1977). Nader's Center for Research in the Public Interest sponsored one of the earliest studies on the topic seeking to identify "problem" product and service categories and the characteristics of consumer complainers (Andreasen & Best, 1977a, 1977b). The research on consumer self-help ultimately led to the emergence of a burgeoning commercial business category generating consumer ratings of offerings in a wide range of product and service categories (initially the J.D. Power and Associates automobile ratings). After several conferences on the topic in the early 1980s, a new scholarly journal emerged in 1988, edited by H. Keith Hunt, called the *Journal of Consumer Satisfaction, Dissatisfaction & Complaining Behavior.*

Marketing's Bright Side

Undoubtedly, the urban riots, Vietnam War protests, and other elements of social upheaval in the late 1960s and 1970s had a parallel effect on marketing scholars, who asked themselves whether they should only be studying and teaching concepts and tools that will help make private-sector marketers richer. Could marketing concepts help child welfare organizations, international health programs, charities, or government social agencies be more effective? Can marketing—and, by implication, creative thinking about marketing—have impacts on major social problems such as rapid population growth or low rates of child survival in developing countries?

As noted earlier, the early academic champions of this view were found at Northwestern University. Philip Kotler and Sidney Levy (1969) began what turned out to be a major shift in the way marketing is conceived by publishing an article in the *Journal of Marketing* called "Broadening the Concept of Marketing." They argued,

> Every organization performs marketing-like activities whether or not they are recognized as such … marketing is a pervasive activity that goes considerably beyond the selling of toothpaste, soap and steel. Political contests remind us that candidates are marketed as well as soap; student recruitment in colleges reminds us that higher education is marketed; and fundraising reminds us that "causes" are marketed…. [Yet, no] attempt is made to examine whether the principles of "good" marketing in traditional product areas are transferable to the marketing of services, persons, and ideas. (p. 11)

Two years later, Kotler and Zaltman (1971) focused on a particular set of applications that they termed *social marketing*.

Expanding marketing's purview was not without its critics, who argued that marketing was a field that required "markets" and that social and nonprofit marketing risked distracting scholars from what is or was essential to the field (Bartels, 1974; Luck, 1969, 1974). However, these caveats did not deter a growing number of scholars, both senior and junior, to seek out academic and consulting opportunities in the expanded domain. Mainstream consumer research over the decades has helped strengthen many nonprofit organizations that provide medical and social services, performing arts, and education. However, our focus here is on what scholars in the social marketing domain label as *problem behaviors*. This focus is well captured by a 1995 definition: "Social marketing is the application of commercial marketing concepts and tools to influence the voluntary behavior of target audiences to improve their lives or the society of which they are a part" (Andreasen, 1994, p. 109).

It is not surprising that some of the very first applications to social marketing of basic concepts like segmentation and the four Ps (i.e., product, price, place, promotion) were in applications not greatly different from private-sector marketing in that they emphasized products and services and the conventional four Ps. The iconic pioneering application was in the field of family planning, in which the "problem behavior" was simply couples having too many children, a challenge that concerned governments, nongovernmental organizations, and, of course, the mothers who found themselves physically debilitated, their children increasingly sickly, and their households falling deeper into poverty due to having too many children with too few years between them.

The earliest social marketing contraceptive campaigns found considerable untapped demand. It was found that nongovernmental contraceptive marketing programs could be successful if one applied clever branding and packaging, priced condoms and pills at very low levels (but not zero), paid careful attention to ensuring reliable distribution, and carried out imaginative promotions that reached villagers through the radio, posters, and town meetings. Numerous nongovernmental organizations and international agencies were able to *sell* contraceptive products that had been available for free in the health services throughout Southeast Asia and Africa. The impact of such programs over the following decades has been a dramatic decrease in population growth almost everywhere (Harvey, 1999).

Yet, in most respects, these campaigns were relatively straightforward from a marketing perspective, in that they applied well-accepted and tested private-sector concepts and tools to product marketing. Despite this simple use of basic commercial tools here, other applications in much of social marketing's early history caused critics and many would-be practitioners to think that it was basically *social advertising*. This perception led many of those trained in health promotion and health education to claim that social marketing was just putting new labels on things they had always done and was nothing new. But customer research in the early family planning programs found that, in many cases, *distribution*, not advertising or promotion, was crucial. Women could become positively disposed toward using contraceptive products, particularly the contraceptive pill, if they were guaranteed a regular source of supply. Marketing researchers learned that, if the products were not reliably available, women would not begin to use the products. Women simply had to feel that, because they could not afford to stock up, they could be sure that their next cycle of pills would always be available when the current one ran out and the family could afford one more cycle. Distribution was so important that it prompted partnerships with private-sector marketers, such as Unilever and Brooke Bond Tea Company, which already had the capability of bringing products to the most remote and barely accessible regions. These were essential to early programs like the Nirodh marketing program in India (Harvey, 1999). Pricing was also critical, in that strategists had to figure out price points such that they were affordable by very poor people but signaled that the items were valuable—reliable, easy to use, and prestigious—as compared to what were often the very same products given out for free at public health centers.

Success in family planning led many of the pioneering social marketing organizations to then focus on what came to be called *child survival programs* (Rasmuson, Seidel, Smith, & Booth, 1988). It was well-known that a depressingly large number of children in the developing world died each year from maladies that we are able to prevent in the Western world, including measles, upper respiratory infections, and the particularly troublesome simple diarrhea. Children who were routinely weakened by diseases and had fragile constitutions often caught simple colds or food poisoning that produced diarrhea. Their systems had precious little in the way of protective electrolytes, so the diarrhea simply drained them of these vital elements. Frail children oftentimes died within hours.

Mothers were desperate. They tried traditional methods to no avail. What was needed was not promotion telling them they had a problem but low-cost *products* that would replace critical chemistry. Fortunately, such products were available in the form of oral rehydration therapies. All an ailing child really needed was a concoction of 1 liter of water, 8 teaspoons of sugar, and 1 teaspoon of salt. Initially, social marketing programs focused on training mothers in the skills of preparing this solution themselves. However, over time and given that mothers might get the formula wrong, it became clear that prepackaged solutions would be the preferred method. Distribution, packaging, and, in some cases, branding then became important to campaign success. Andreasen and Kotler (2003, p. 343) cited a range of successes in Honduras, the Gambia, Egypt, Bangladesh, Colombia, Indonesia, and Swaziland, and similar positive findings were reported by Victora, Bryce, Fontaine, and Monasch (2000).

Social marketing was also gaining a toehold in the United States, as commercial advertising and public relations organizations saw opportunities for using their marketing skills to win government contracts that sought to influence important social behaviors, particularly in the area of health. A pioneer in this regard was Porter Novelli, which secured a contract with the National Institutes of Health to address the significant problems associated with high blood pressure. In the 1970s, Americans were unware that high blood pressure could lead to stroke, heart attacks, and death. The National High Blood Pressure Education Program campaign is one of the major success stories for social marketing. Data from surveillance studies over time have shown that age-adjusted mortality rates from stroke have declined over 60% since the early 1970s when the campaign started (Chobanian et al., 2003).

On the academic side, early writings about social marketing were relatively speculative. The first National Conference on Social Marketing was held at the University of Illinois in 1972 and attracted a range of the field's most active and prominent scholars who explored ways in which marketing concepts and tools could apply to social problems. In the volume arising from this workshop (Sheth & Wright, 1974), chapters focused on key research areas:

- Louis P. Bucklin and James M. Carmen, "Vertical Market Structure Theory and the Health Care Delivery System" (with commentary by Louis W. Stern and Frederick D. Sturdivant)
- Ivan Ross, "Application of Consumer Information to Public Policy Decisions"
- Gerald Zaltman, "Strategies for Diffusing Innovations"
- Peter L. Wright, "On the Application of Persuasion Theory in Social Marketing"

Application areas discussed at the conference included malnutrition (Jagdish Sheth and Seymour Sudman), education (Philip Kotler and Bernard Dubois), birth control (Julian Simon), health care (Philip Burger), and the environment (Norman Kangun).

Advances in Theory

Mid-level and micro-level social marketing research during this period confronted a major challenge because of the unique characteristics of the behaviors being studied. Bloom and Novelli (1981) highlighted many of the unique challenges these applications raised when compared with private-sector marketing ventures. Social marketing campaigns had the following features:

- There were less good secondary data about target audiences.
- Valid, reliable primary data were harder to collect.
- Research budgets were extremely limited or constricted by donors who preferred direct program activity.
- There was often a bias against segmentation ("We have to help everyone!").
- Target audiences were often those most negatively disposed toward the behavior (not just indifferent).
- There was less flexibility in tailoring products or offerings (e.g., vasectomies, clean needles, intrauterine devices) to meet what is learned about target audience perceptions and motivations.
- Intermediaries were more difficult to recruit or control.
- Paid advertising was often impossible to use because of cost and/or funder bias against it, and had to appear as public-service announcements, which often were run at odd hours, if at all.
- Organizational staff and (typically) senior management of programs that would implement social marketing campaigns usually did not understand or appreciate marketing.
- Effectiveness was difficult to measure, for example, where there was often no observable marker that would signal that one had achieved behavioral outcomes (e.g., not smoking, not using drugs).

All of these characteristics provide important research challenges for future scholars of TCR. Two other research problems were revealed in early applications were: (1) Benefits were hard to portray when they constituted an expectation (promise?) of outcomes that would take place many years in the future (e.g., a longer, healthier life) or when they were, in fact, the expectation (promise?) of the nonoccurrence of an outcome, such as not having a stroke or breast cancer, and (2) desired outcomes required repeated behaviors into the future, where marketers may have no way of reinforcing behaviors (as they might in the private sector).

A consequence of many of these unique characteristics was the positive effect of early researchers focusing on the challenge of measuring and tracking target audiences' *intentions* to behave. Fortunately, general theories of individual choice and behavior were being developed in mainstream marketing writing and research by Howard and Sheth (1969), Nicosia (1966), and Bettman (1979). A specific focus in the 1970s and 1980s was on attitude theory (Lutz 1975, 1977), which had direct relevance to social marketing. The general approach was seeing products and services as attitude objects that target audiences evaluated in terms of a set of attributes, each of which had its own importance weight. These components, when measured, would then comprise the target audience's attitude toward a product or brand, or simply a behavior. Attitudes were conceived as a multiattribute phenomenon with three components: cognitive, affective, and conative. The latter was typically called *intentions*. A similar focus on attitude models was also gripping the field of health promotion. Because the majority (perhaps 80%) of social marketing applications then (and now) were in the area of health, social marketing scholars sought out this literature and discovered not only similar interests but also new models that had not migrated to commercial marketing scholarship and practice.

Initially, private-sector marketing scholarship focused on the relationships between beliefs about product and service offerings and customers' likely choice. A major advance in the way attitudes were conceived was proposed by psychologists Martin Fishbein and Icek Ajzen (1975), who posited that, in addition to beliefs about a specific behavioral opportunity, intentions were strongly linked to the influence of others. These influences were the perceptions of what others wanted the target individual to do with a weighting factor added to reflect the degree to which the individual is likely to follow what these others recommend. Their approach was labeled the theory of reasoned action.

The next major development in the quest to predict intentions reflected the work of Albert Bandura (1977), whose social learning theory had as its major emphasis the extent to which individuals learn from role models. His contribution to attitude research was to propose that behavioral intentions and, thus, behaviors were not solely driven by attitudes toward the object of the behavior and toward significant others who may express behavioral preferences. He also argued that whether someone is likely to carry out a behavior—and, by implication, whether one has high or low intentions to do so—depends on what Bandura called the individual's sense of self-efficacy. This cognitive element had two components: perceptions of the likelihood that one can actually carry out the behavior and perceptions of whether the behavior will actually achieve the goal sought. Ajzen (1991) took up this concept in a revised version of the theory of reasoned action by adding a self-efficacy component and calling the new framework the theory of planned behavior.

When social marketers turned to the health promotion literature for insights into how this discipline handled the problem, they discovered theorists who focused on narrower subsets of specific beliefs. The first of these was Rosenstock's (1974) health belief model, which focused on individuals' personal assessments of their lifestyles, demographics, and behaviors, and the extent to which these made them susceptible to a negative health outcome. These beliefs were then weighted by the extent to which the individuals believed they were vulnerable to the negative health outcome and the perceived severity of the outcome. A further consideration in the health belief model is Bandura's second self-efficacy component, whether the individual believes that moderating his or her behavior will have a positive impact. The prospect of achieving a good outcome and the likelihood that there will be low personal barriers to making it happen lead to a high probability for action.

A related model that has continued to receive much attention from consumer behavior researchers (Pechmann, Zhao, Goldberg, & Reibling, 2003) is Ronald Rogers's (1975) protection motivation theory, which originated from work on fear appeals and is similar to the approaches of Rosenstock and Bandura. Rogers posited that individuals respond to threats based on two factors: a threat appraisal and a coping appraisal. Threat appraisals involve assessing the perceived severity of a harmful event and the probability it will occur if the individual takes no action. Coping appraisals mirror Bandura's concept of self-efficacy and include an appraisal of the effectiveness of the contemplated behavior and the individual's ability to actually carry it out. In a later formulation, Rogers (1983) postulated that individuals also considered the cost of the proposed response and forgone benefits of the existing behavior that would be abandoned.

A key question in all of this work for health promotion scholars was whether intentions actually predicted behavior, which has also been a consistent concern of marketing scholars. A recent meta-analysis by Webb and Sheeran (2006) addressed this issue by analyzing 47 experimental studies of the linkage between intentions as formulated in various theories and resulting behavior change. Eighty-one percent of the health promotion studies were grounded in one of the four models described above. The most commonly used two theories (29%) were Fishbein and Ajzen's theory of reasoned action and the modification in Ajzen's theory of planned behavior, followed by Bandura's social learning theory (21%), Rogers's protection motivation theory (18%), and Rosenstock's health belief model (13%). Webb and Sheeran concluded the following:

> A medium-to-large sized change in intention generated only a small-to-medium change in behavior. Findings also showed that intentions have less impact on behavior when participants lack control over the behavior, when there is potential for social reaction and when circumstances of the performance are conducive to habit formation. Thus, this review suggests that intentional control of behavior is a great deal more limited than previous analyses of correlational studies have indicated. (p. 262)

All of the early models focused on factors that potentially influence intentions, such as beliefs and personal appraisals. However, scholars were not unmindful of other factors that could also influence beliefs and weightings directly. These potential modifiers were recently summarized by Fishbein and Cappella (2006) as six sets of background factors: (1) past behavior, (2) demographics and culture, (3) attitudes toward targets (i.e., stereotypes, stigma), (4) personality, moods, and emotions, (5) other individual difference variables (e.g., perceived risk), and (6) exposure to interventions and media.

An interesting approach to the potential role of past behavior was Bagozzi and Warshaw's (1990) theory of trying. Health behavior researchers often treated the belief–behavior linkage as a single step. Prochaska and DiClemente's (1983) transtheoretical theory of change considered behaviors as taking place only after an often complex process involving a series of steps over time (Prochaska, DiClemente, & Norcross, 1992; Prochaska & Velicer, 1997). This approach recognized that, with respect to what marketers label as high-involvement behaviors, people do not go from being unaware or disinterested to carrying out a socially or personally desirable behavior that may, in fact, save their lives. These researchers proposed that people pass through six possible stages: precontemplation, contemplation, preparation, action, maintenance, and termination.

The principal insights of this approach were twofold. First, marketers should concentrate not just on getting target audiences to the desired end state but also on moving them to the next stage from wherever they are currently. This insight, in turn, provides a useful approach to segmentation. The second insight was that the appropriate marketing tools will differ in each stage. In the precontemplation stage, a principal focus will be on communication, whereas the contemplation stage will center on responses to insights gained about how target audiences think about the behavioral option, often using one of the models described above. In the preparation and action stages, more attention would be paid to making the behaviors *possible*, while the maintenance stage focus must be on reinforcement mechanisms that prevent defections from the desired outcome. The latter turned out to be a significant problem for the National High Blood Pressure Education Program mentioned earlier, 20 years after its beginnings, when it was discovered that many individuals with high blood pressure had dropped prevention behaviors (i.e., stopped watching their diet, exercising, and taking their high blood pressure medicine). The campaign had to reallocate a significant proportion of its budget to addressing this challenge. Indeed, the attention to the maintenance stage was often lacking in many programs that were counted as successes because they simply got people started on a desirable behavior. In the high blood pressure case, a challenge not uncommon in social marketing was that the desired outcome had no visible or sensory signals. Unlike stopping smoking, after which one breathes better, has more endurance, and so on, lowered blood pressure produces no such noticeable, rewarding outcomes.

The final theoretical model frequently consulted in early social marketing campaigns was Everett Rogers's (1995) classic work on innovation adoption. Marketing planners sought to adapt Rogers's findings on the characteristics of innovators and/or the characteristics of innovations more likely to be adapted to social behaviors. This focus often led social marketing researchers to look carefully at "doer–nondoer" contrasts. By studying individuals in each group otherwise matched on demographic and other lifestyle factors, researchers often could discern actionable triggers that were missing in the nondoers' lives or environments.

Besides exploring micro-level models of behavior, many social marketing researchers involved in large-scale programs turned for insights to the range of significant large-scale health care interventions conducted in the United States and elsewhere in the past 30 years. The majority of these interventions involved efforts to reduce deaths by heart attacks, especially among men. The campaigns were typically community trials over many years with target cities matched to control cities that were presumably uncontaminated by the interventions. An early example was the Stanford Five-City Project in the 1980s, which was carried on over 5 years to reduce cardiovascular risk (Farquhar et al., 1990). With the goal of behavior change, the project's principal form of marketing was an emphasis on communication approaches, including television and radio spots, classes, and contests. In a recent assessment of the project, Robert Hornik (2002) admitted that analysis was "messy," but noted that "a reader disposed to take a skeptical view would conclude that the effects of the program were either small or not established" (p. 2).

Hornik (2002) also looked at three other major multicity projects focusing on heart attacks: the Minnesota Heart Health Program (Jacobs et al., 1986), the Pawtucket Heart Health Program (Lefebvre & Flora, 1988)—both patterned on the Stanford approach—and the North Karelia (Finland) Project (Puska et al., 1985). According to Hornik, although the two U.S. programs had some effects, "neither program show[ed] a consistent pattern of pro-treatment city effects" (p. 3). He did conclude that the COMMIT antismoking campaign showed some positive outcomes (COMMIT Research Group, 1991), as did the early years of the North Karelia Project. Useful reviews of these projects, which are largely based on communications, and a range of others are available in *Public Health Communication: Evidence for Behavior Change* (Hornik, 2002).

## VULNERABLE CONSUMERS: YOUTH

Two age segments, youth and older adults, have each been found to have important information-processing deficits, which have drawn the attention of researchers in an effort to both understand the deficits and consider how their negative consequences might be redressed. At root, the commonality across these two groups is deficiencies in the "executive functioning" of the brain, which has been variously described for one or both of these groups by John and Cole (1986); Moses and Baldwin (2005); Yoon, Cole, and Lee (2009); and Goldberg (2008b) and is elaborated on below. A significant aspect of this discussion is the extent to which some marketers have sought to take advantage of these vulnerabilities through the dark side of marketing, and how these negative effects can be mitigated, if not eliminated, by strategies drawn from the bright side of marketing. This section addresses these issues with respect to youth, and the subsequent section focuses on older adults.

### Early Years: 3–7-Year-Olds

Early research, largely in the 1970s, focused primarily on television advertising as it expanded its reach. The research determined that children below 7 years of age were unaware of the persuasive intent of advertising and the profit motive that guided advertisers. As such, these children could not understand or describe the true difference between commercials and programs (Palmer & McDowell, 1979; Ward, 1972). In a seminal piece, Roedder (1981) labeled these younger children as "limited processors." The obvious conclusion was that they were particularly vulnerable to advertising. Although 70% of 4-year-olds could distinguish between programming and commercials, 90% of them did not understand the difference between the two (Butter, Popovich, Stackhouse, & Garner, 1981). It is only by age 7 or 8 that children recognize that the intent of commercials is to sell and represents something other than "friendly advice" (Robertson & Rossiter, 1974; Ward, Wackman, & Wartella, 1977).

### Tweens: 8–12-Year-Olds

While the research in the 1970s led to relative convergence regarding the potential impact of advertising on very young children, considerable differences emerged as to how children ages 8–12 were affected. Initial findings suggested that these children, in response to direct survey questions, understood both the selling intent of commercials as well as advertisers' motives, and they reported that they trusted commercials less and less as they grew older (Robertson & Rossiter, 1974; Ward et al., 1977). In one study, the percentage of children understanding the persuasive intent of advertising rose from 53% in first grade to 87% in third grade and 99% in fifth grade (Robertson & Rossiter, 1974). Commensurate with this change, children were found to trust and like commercials less as they aged (Robertson & Rossiter, 1974; Rossiter & Robertson, 1974). This was initially taken by some to represent a cognitive defense for the children that would protect them in the face of advertising. However, through experimental research, others documented that advertising did, in fact, influence children of this age. Offered an opportunity to win a toy by solving a complex puzzle, children exposed to a commercial for the toy worked considerably longer than those who were not exposed to the commercial (Goldberg & Gorn, 1974; Gorn & Goldberg, 1977). The children's actual behavior in the face of advertising was clearly at odds with their stated survey responses.

Later research resolved this apparent paradox. As Wright, Friestad, and Boush (2005) explained, the key distinction was "knowledge in mind" versus "knowledge in use." As noted above, 8–12-year-old children are aware that advertising's intent is to sell, that advertising could deceive and should not necessarily be trusted, and that they needed to be wary of the advertiser's motives. However, as Brucks, Armstrong, and Goldberg (1988) found, this knowledge did not necessarily serve as a cognitive defense. In an experiment they conducted, the children could not access or use their general knowledge as it related to advertising unless it was (a) buttressed by an educational training film that went into specific strategies and tactics used by advertisers, *and* (b) this more specific knowledge was cued shortly before the children watched television commercials. When the children watched the commercials after seeing only the training film, they generated relatively few counterarguments indicative of a cognitive defense. It was primarily when the training film was *combined* with a last-minute cue that the children not only appeared to access the information they had gained but also generated a significant number of counterarguments. With these types of findings in mind, this age group has appropriately been labeled "cued processors" (Roedder, 1981).

## Adolescents

It is only by age 12 and beyond that children can spontaneously call on their knowledge of advertising as a cognitive defense as they watch advertising. Youths at this stage were labeled "strategic processors" (Roedder, 1981). At least theoretically, adolescents can process advertising in as vigilant and effective a manner as adults. Unfortunately, reality is more complex. First, the evidence is mixed as to how much more vigilant adolescents are with regard to advertising targeted at them. Roedder, Sternthal, and Calder (1983) found that 9-year-olds, but not 13-year-olds, were induced to disregard their strong, preestablished preference hierarchy once they had seen a commercial for what earlier had been described as a much less preferred option. However, a study by Ross et al. (1984) found that 14-year-olds were no less influenced by the irrelevancies in an ad for a toy racing car than were younger children.

While the emphasis in the Roedder (1981) tripartite model and other comparable cognitive approaches has been on what young people perceive, understand, and remember, as John (1999) noted, the hedonic value of a product suggested by a commercial can override the presumed vigilance of adolescents as well as younger children. But more than that, the imagery and symbolic value establish an emotional allure for the product, especially for adolescents. In addition, as discussed below, the advertiser's ability to tap into powerful adolescent motives can offset the ostensible cognitive defense represented by adolescents' knowledge of advertising (Goldberg, 2008a).

Importantly, the Roedder (1981) tripartite model described above assumes that adolescents typically process advertising or other information under circumstances of calm, "cold cognition." However, the adolescent reality is such that information is often processed under circumstances of emotionally charged "hot cognition." This process is elucidated in an insightful article by Pechmann, Levine, Loughlin, and Leslie (2005). The executive control portion of the adolescent brain (i.e., the prefrontal cortex) has not developed sufficiently in adolescence to exert cognitive control over emotions or impulsive responses to the environment. Citing Spear (2000), Pechmann et al. wrote, "This immature executive control is believed to underlie the greater risk-taking behavior and novelty seeking that is a hallmark of adolescence" (p. 205). While there are individual differences among adolescents, reckless behavior may be more the norm than the exception (Maggs, Almeida, & Galambos, 1995; Moffitt, 1993; Trimpop, Kerr, & Kirkcaldy, 1999).

Added to this impairment is the finding that adolescents are in a negative mood more often than adults or younger children; they experience more frequent and more intense negative emotions, fewer positive emotions, and greater emotional volatility (Larson & Richards, 1994; Larson, Moneta, Richards, & Wilson, 2002). Adolescents seek to repair their negative emotions, including anger, depression, and anxiety, by engaging in short-term pleasures that may relieve their distress. Their high negative affect constrains their cognitive processing resources. Guided by their impulsivity and sensation-seeking, they are at higher risk with regard to behaviors such as smoking, drinking, illicit drug use, gambling, reckless driving, unwanted pregnancies, and, as recognized more recently, obesity. This is a far cry from the cold cognition assumed to guide vigilant adolescents in their exposure to advertising.

## Remedies Related to Information Processing and Advertising

### 3–7-Year-Olds

Given the evident vulnerability of these young children, an active debate in the 1970s culminated in an FTC proposal to ban advertising aimed at children under 8. Subsequently, in an antiregulatory climate, the proposal was defeated. The advertising industry created a self-regulatory body, the Children's Advertising Review Unit (2009), that developed some basic safeguards for children under 8, including ensuring that commercials were not embedded within program content (see http://www.caru.org).

### 8–12-Year-Olds

As noted above, a central part of the 1970s debate was the question as to whether 8–12-year-old children were sufficiently vulnerable to advertising that they needed some form of protection. In fact, the primary reason given by the FTC when it rejected a proposal to eliminate advertising directed at children was that this age group was a good deal less vulnerable and did not need this special protection. Since the commercial audience data then available grouped all children 12 and under together, the FTC concluded that there was no workable solution that would limit advertising constraints to those who were 7 and under.

While First Amendment rights in the United States likely preclude this remedy, in the Canadian province of Quebec, the debate during the 1970s led to the elimination of advertising directed at children. The law resulted in a "natural experiment" that provided an opportunity to examine the effects on Quebec children of advertising versus eliminating advertising. The law eliminated it on Quebec television stations but not on American stations originating from northern New York and Vermont that were available to Quebec viewers. A study assessed the effects of the law on English- and French-speaking children in Montreal and concluded that the law had an impact on French-speaking children who were held captive by their language to Quebec television stations but not on English-speaking children whose viewing patterns and exposure to advertising on American stations continued unchanged after the law was passed. The French-speaking children failed to learn about new toys in the marketplace and had fewer children's (i.e., sugared) cereals in their homes as compared to the English-speaking children (steps were taken to rule out a cultural explanation for the noted differences). This comparison documents the continuing impact that television advertising had on the English-speaking children, just as the curtailment of such advertising had a clear effect on the French-speaking children (Goldberg, 1990).

Another solution might be to use the Brucks et al. (1988) intervention model. Educational training films are available to schools and parents, which could be viewed as part of a more extensive remedy: training children to be more media literate and, in particular, schooling them in "persuasion knowledge" (a term coined by Friestad & Wright, 1994, and discussed below). However, following the Brucks et al. findings, at least for 8–12-year-olds, a last-minute cue would also be needed.

### Adolescents

Whereas a last-minute cue appears to be necessary for the utilization of persuasion knowledge by 8–12-year-olds (Brucks et al., 1988), adolescents are not necessarily subject to the same constraint. Following Friestad and Wright (1994), Goldberg, Niedermeier, Bechtel, and Gorn (2006) structured an intervention that helped adolescents develop persuasion (or process) knowledge to produce effective coping skills for dealing with alcohol advertising. As Friestad and Wright explained, as long as consumers remain naive to the scripted nature of advertising, they are more trusting of the communications. Once they gain persuasion knowledge, the understanding that someone is using a particular tactic to influence them is fundamentally off-putting. As a result, their subsequent response is guided both cognitively and emotionally. The Goldberg et al. intervention, consisting of five 50-minute lessons, also included a consideration of topic (or substantive) knowledge and agent (or source) knowledge.

The intervention first focused on advertising "myths" (e.g., alcohol is an essential part of any party) and hooks (e.g., fun, sex appeal, music, celebrities, humor). Associative learning was labeled *rub-off*, and students were shown how advertising hooks were used to rub off onto advertised alcoholic beverages to alter attitudes toward the products. To address the misperception that drinking is the norm, the intervention made clear that the vast majority of alcohol is consumed by a small minority of people. Students were encouraged to counterargue with liquor ads by getting them to understand how they naturally used the phrase "Yes, but" when they sought to counter a request of their parents or others. Armed with these and other concepts, the students were asked to locate a magazine ad for an alcoholic beverage and structure a counteradvertisement.

Relative to the students who did not receive the intervention, test group students demonstrated heightened persuasion knowledge regarding alcohol advertising. This knowledge was especially pronounced for students who had prior experience with alcohol. Students subject to the intervention developed heightened persuasion-coping behaviors; specifically, they reported that they would be more vigilant and counterargue more when exposed to alcohol advertising in the future. Their responses also reflected more critical attitudes toward alcohol advertising and advertisers. Among those who had drunk alcohol, students subject to the intervention were significantly less likely to indicate that they would drink in the future. In closing these remarks, we also direct the reader to Pechmann, Biglan, Grube, and Cody (Chapter 17 of this volume) for additional research and detailed discussion about adolescents and alcohol.

### An Example From the Dark Side: Tobacco Advertising and Promotion

In a mid-1990s study, nearly 9 in 10 adults (89%) ages 30–39 who smoked indicated that they started before age 18, and more than 6 in 10 (62%) were smoking before age 16. Over half (53%) were smoking daily by age 18 and over three quarters (77%) by age 20 (Lynch & Bonnie, 1994; USDHHS, 1994). Given these statistics, smoking initiation is rightly viewed as an adolescent problem (see also Pechmann, Biglan, Grube, & Cody, Chapter 17 of this volume).

Over the last 15 years, four consensus documents have concluded that tobacco advertising and promotion has a causal relationship with youth smoking (Food and Drug Administration, 1996; Lynch & Bonnie, 1994; National Cancer Institute, 2008; USDHHS, 1994). The most recent is a monograph by the National Cancer Institute (2008) titled *The Role of Media in Promoting and Reducing Tobacco Use*, which concluded,

> The total weight of evidence from multiple types of studies, conducted by investigators from different disciplines, using data from many countries, *demonstrates a causal relationship* between tobacco advertising and promotion and increased tobacco use as manifested by increased smoking initiation and increased per capita tobacco consumption in the population. (p. 16)

An examination of the powerful motives that are tapped by tobacco advertising suggests why these campaigns have been so effective and why adolescents' knowledge of the advertising process provides so little protection.

### *The Issue of Individuation*

Adolescents are motivated to separate from their parents, take increasing responsibility for their actions, and make independent decisions. This motivation is utilized in advertising for Marlboro, the brand smoked by over half (52%) of adolescent smokers today ("Cigarette Brand Preference," 2009): "The Marlboro cowboy symbolizes the ability to make your own decisions … he represents the ability to make a choice and a decision" (Bowling & Taylor, 1976).

## The Desire to Grow Up and Become an Adult

Adolescents look up to and aspire to be like the young, attractive models in cigarette ads. Research has shown that it is more effective to use young-looking adults in cigarette advertising than same-age peers as models for the adolescent audience (Pechmann, Pirouz, & Pezzuti, 2009).

## The Desire to Be Accepted by Peers

Adolescents' level of conformity peaks around ninth grade (i.e., 14–15-year-olds; Berndt, 1979). With their relatively weak sense of self and correspondingly shaky self-confidence, adolescents seek props that will help them gain acceptance by their peers (Lynch & Bonnie, 1994). Tobacco advertising has associated positive imagery with various tobacco brands and, in so doing, has provided such a prop for adolescents. These associations include stereotypical images of smokers, such as cool, macho, social, and popular. Following adolescents across a one-year span, one study showed that when an adolescent's self-image was more closely aligned with these images, he or she was almost twice as likely to become a smoker (Aloise-Young, Hennigan, & Graham, 1996).

Heavy exposure to cigarette advertising creates a perception that smoking is more prevalent than it actually is. Adolescents who are more exposed to magazine advertising for cigarettes estimate a higher prevalence of cigarette smoking among their peers (Botvin, Goldberg, Botvin, & Dusenbury, 1993). Overestimation of the number of peers who smoke is a strong risk factor leading to smoking (Chassin, Presson, Sherman, Corty, & Olshavsky, 1984; Leventhal, Glynn, & Fleming, 1987).

Currently, the focus of tobacco promotion is on convenience stores, where 60% of cigarettes are sold. Three out of four teenagers shop at a convenience store at least once a week, staying an average of 10 minutes per visit, which is twice as long as adults; one third of teenagers shop in a convenience store at least two or three times a week (Chanil, 2002). One study indicated that stores where middle school students shopped most frequently had three times the amount of marketing materials and significantly more shelf space devoted to the three cigarette brands most popular among these students and their friends (Henriksen, Feighery, Schleicher, Haladjian, & Fortmann, 2004). Relatedly, another study showed that when stores near schools featured Marlboro in their advertising and promotions, students from the nearby schools tended to prefer Marlboro, and when the stores featured Camels, the students preferred Camels (Wakefield, Ruel, Chaloupka, Slater, & Kaufman, 2002).

## Remedies Related to Tobacco Consumption

Over time, greater restrictions have been placed on tobacco advertising in general and to some extent on tobacco advertising directed at children. Television and radio advertising were eliminated altogether in 1970. In 1998, the Tobacco Master Settlement Agreement (National Association of Attorneys General, n.d.) between the tobacco industry and 46 states' attorneys general resulted in the elimination of billboard advertising for tobacco and some constraints on tobacco advertising in magazines read by substantial numbers of youths (for a summary of the agreement, see http://www.ag.ca.gov/tobacco/resources/msasumm.htm).

Recent legislation giving the Food and Drug Administration power to regulate tobacco and tobacco advertising will permit only "tombstone" advertising: black-and-white with text only, no imagery ("Text of H.R. 1256," 2009). How effective this step would be in reducing the appeal of cigarettes for adolescents is an important empirical question. The legislation will also eliminate tobacco advertising and promotion at many convenience stores by ruling out advertising within 1000 feet of schools. Several tobacco companies, including R. J. Reynolds and Lorillard, have filed a lawsuit challenging the constitutionality of aspects of the legislation (Kesmodel, Etter, & Mundy, 2009). The advertising industry has considered doing the same (Thomaselli, 2009).

Under the rubric of media literacy (closely akin to persuasion knowledge), Austin, Pinkleton, Hust, and Cohen (2005) sought to increase youth's vigilance with regard to tobacco advertising and promotion. The approach they took was intended to "help young people develop critical viewing skills necessary to resist the appeals advertisers use to make tobacco tempting … [by getting young people] to develop logic-based defenses against the emotional appeals of [tobacco advertising's] persuasive messages" (p. 77). Compared to a control group, high school students subject to this intervention demonstrated (a) a greater skepticism toward persuasive media messages, (b) a heightened ability to counter tobacco advertising and promotional efforts, and (c) a lesser inclination to smoke if offered a cigarette by a peer.

The American Legacy's "Truth" campaign, a national antitobacco campaign targeting adolescents, has been successful in contributing to a drop in smoking levels for this age group. Smoking prevalence (in the last 30 days) among 12th graders dropped from a high of 36.5% in 1997 to 20.4% in 2008 (Johnston, O'Malley, Bachman, & Schulenberg, 2009). In an incisive study, Farrelly, Davis, Haviland, Messeri, and Healton (2005) concluded that 22% of this reduction was due to the Truth campaign. A central theme of the campaign has been to increase youths' persuasion knowledge by pointing to the tobacco companies' strategies in developing the sophisticated advertising campaigns that have been so effective in inducing adolescents to smoke (Sly, Trapido, & Ray, 2002; http://www.legacyforhealth.org). As discussed below, further development and assessment of these types of interventions would appear well warranted.

### A Second Example: The Impact of Food Advertising and Promotion on Youth's Food Intake

Youth obesity has become a major health issue in the United States and globally (see Grier & Moore, Chapter 15 of this volume, for a detailed discussion). One third of children in the United States are obese and another third overweight; about one third of children will end up with diabetes and the various problems associated with that disease (Ogden et al., 2006). Marketing has been implicated as contributing to this problem (see, e.g., McGinnis, Gootman, & Kraak, 2006; Nestle, 2002).

#### Advertising

Comprehensive and critical content analyses of the available data have attempted to provide a more solid footing for the overall conclusions that have been drawn regarding advertising's effects on youth and their food-related attitudes and behaviors (Hastings et al., 2003; McGinnis et al., 2006). Relying in particular on Hastings et al. (2003), the UK Office of Communications (Ofcom, 2007) found that "advertising had a modest, direct effect on children's food choices and a larger but unquantifiable indirect effect on children's food preferences, consumption and behaviour" (para. 6). In an even more comprehensive analysis, the Institute of Medicine (McGinnis et al., 2006) concluded that for children ages 2–11 (but not adolescents ages 12–18), there is considerable evidence that television advertising influences food and beverage preferences, purchase requests, and short-term consumption patterns. By contrast, evidence regarding the impact of television advertising on "usual dietary intake" and level of obesity is far more tentative. The typical reliance on correlational studies linking levels of exposure to television advertising and obesity makes it impossible to rule out alternative explanations, such as the increased sedentary behavior associated with television viewing. Moreover, given the covariation between levels of television viewing and sedentary behavior, any effort to experimentally manipulate one without affecting the other would be difficult, if not impossible.

#### In-Store Promotions

As indicated above, children spend a considerable amount of time in convenience stores. A study of unplanned or impulse purchases, as a percentage of total sales for selected categories at convenience stores (by both adults and youths), indicated that sweet snacks (52%), candy/gum/mints (40%), and salty snacks (38%) were the three highest categories (POPAI, 2002a, 2002b). Convenience stores are the heaviest users of in-store point-of-purchase promotions (POPAI, 1992). These in-store programs, together with the prominent positioning of products such as sodas, sweets, and candy, likely have much to do with their level of success in convenience stores.

Remedies Related to Food Advertising and Promotion to Youth

In the United States, the remedy taken to date has been a self-regulatory one, with 15 leading food processors and retailers (e.g., Kraft, Kellogg's, McDonald's, Coca-Cola, PepsiCo) agreeing to take actions to reduce the amount of advertising targeting children and improve the healthfulness of the foods that are advertised to them (Children's Food and Beverage Advertising Initiative, 2008). Recent research has noted a decrease in the level of advertising for sweet snacks and carbonated, sweetened beverages targeting youths. At the same time, however, restaurant advertising targeting both children and adolescents has increased (Rudd Report, 2010). By contrast, the United Kingdom has passed legislation outlawing the advertising of foods to children. The Quebec natural experiment referred to above and field experiments (Gorn & Goldberg, 1982) have indicated that eliminating food advertising directed at children can result in significant changes in their food selections. The impact of smaller changes, such as those associated with the self-regulations described above, remains to be tested. Research is underway to test the effectiveness of other, lesser steps that are being attempted in various U.S. cities (e.g., New York, Seattle), such as listing calories on menu boards in fast-food restaurants and on the menus of chain restaurants (Bassett et al., 2008). This tactic has now been mandated by federal health care legislation in the United States for restaurants with more than 20 outlets (as part of the Health Care and Education Reconciliation Act of 2010, Pub.L. 111-152).

Unsurprisingly, researchers have noted that the taste of food products is the most important factor guiding the food preferences and choices of children, adolescents, and adults (Neumark-Sztainer, Wall, Perry, & Story, 2003). However, there is clear research evidence that, to some extent at least, "taste" is a function of how products are labeled, packaged, and advertised. One experiment found that 3–5-year-old children thought that foods and beverages (including baby carrots, milk, and juice) in McDonald's packaging tasted better than when the same foods were presented in unbranded packaging (Robinson, Borzekowski, & Matheson, 2007).

In a field experiment with adults, the same lunch meals sold in a cafeteria were labeled differently on different days. For example, one such meal was identified as "succulent Italian seafood filet" on some days and merely "seafood filet" on others. Those who bought and ate the foods when they were described in an embellished way reported that the foods were more appealing to the eye and tasted significantly better, and the individuals felt fuller and more satisfied after eating the meal (Wansink, van Ittersum, & Painter, 2005). Although there are limits to this approach, it represents one way of enhancing the appeal of healthier foods for young people and bears further testing. Similarly, healthier foods can be positioned via effective advertising that is appealing to youth (Goldberg & Gunasti, 2007).

## VULNERABLE CONSUMERS: OLDER ADULTS

As with young children, older adults have limitations with regard to speed of information processing, use of memory strategies, and specific knowledge regarding important aspects of their environment (John & Cole, 1986). Age-related limitations in processing capacity typically accelerate for adults in their 70s and beyond (Park et al., 2002). Excellent reviews of these declines and the contexts in which they may have greater or lesser consequences for well-being can be found in Pettigrew and Moschis (Chapter 27 of this volume) and Yoon et al. (2009). Older adults increasingly encounter problems with tasks that draw on working memory—the processing of small amounts of information for short periods of time as they read, listen, problem-solve, and think (Moscovitch & Winocur, 1995). There is a slowdown in processing speed (Salthouse, 1996). Further, executive functions that involve shifting between different task goals, updating the contents of working memory, and inhibiting inappropriate responses become increasingly impaired (Hedden & Yoon, 2006).

One consequence of these impairments is a heightened susceptibility to persuasion. For example, people over the age of 60 account for 26% of telemarketing fraud and represent 60% of the victims in categories such as prizes and sweepstakes (Goldberg, 2008b). Other financial scams that target older adults include funerals and burial plots, living trusts and annuity sales, and predatory lending (Finberg, 2003).

A very different issue that confronts older adults is ageism. A content analysis of the manner in which older adults are portrayed in the media suggested a set of stereotypes, including sick, feeble, infirm, deaf, and confused; perhaps still worse, older adults are often not portrayed in media at all (AARP, 1998). Relatedly, health care providers and others often lapse into a patronizing, condescending manner of speech, labeled *elderspeak*, when interacting with older adults (e.g., "How are we feeling today, sweetie?"; Kemper, Ferrell, Harden, Finter-Urczyk, & Billington, 1998).

Research has shown that those older adults who internalize these perceptions and stereotypes can find their health quite adversely affected. In an impressive multimethod research program, Levy (2003) demonstrated through experimental, longitudinal, and cross-cultural research that older adults who hold a less positive self-image of themselves (or a less positive view of aging when they were middle-aged) perform more poorly on memory tests, have higher levels of cardiovascular stress, show physical deterioration as evidenced in a slower walk and shakier handwriting, have poorer functional health, and live significantly shorter lives.

## Remedies for Older Adults in Marketing Contexts

In addition to many state consumer laws, two federal laws provide protections with regard to the prize and sweepstakes scams referred to above. The Telemarketing Sales Rule prohibits many fraudulent telemarketing practices, among which are disclosure requirements about the odds of winning and how the participants may participate without buying or paying anything. The Deceptive Mail Prevention and Enforcement Act serves to regulate written solicitations. Among other issues, the law prohibits claims that you are a winner unless you have actually won a prize (for a review of both federal and California laws that aim to protect older adults, see Finberg, 2003).

Despite the existing array of federal and state laws aimed at protecting the elderly, both the Office of Community Oriented Policing Services of the U.S. Department of Justice (Johnson, 2004) and Finberg (2003) have concluded that the legal approach to protecting older adults is unlikely to be effective, since (a) the laws are rarely invoked; (b) even if invoked, significant relief is difficult to come by; and (c) largely as a result of (a) and (b), the laws are unlikely to have a deterrent effect. Both the Office of Community Oriented Policing Services (Johnson, 2004) and Finberg (2003) have recommended an educational, rather than a legal, approach in attempting to protect older adults against common financial scams.

Just as persuasion knowledge represents an educational route to make youth more vigilant and less susceptible to advertising, a similar approach also appears to be effective with older adults. As noted above, Campbell and Kirmani (2000) found that experimentally reducing the cognitive capacity of subjects (by otherwise distracting them) led them to evaluate a salesperson as more sincere than did those with greater cognitive capacity (not distracted). These results suggest that given older adults' limitations in cognitive capacity and processing, it is important to increase their awareness of salespeople's motives and more broadly increase their level of persuasion knowledge. Another reason to adopt this strategy is that the older adult age cohort has a higher level of perceived trustworthiness of others relative to younger age cohorts (Davis & Smith, 1983).

Gaeth and Heath (1987) assessed a training program intended to increase critical thinking and persuasion knowledge among older adults and acquaint them with some of the more common misleading advertising techniques. The program succeeded in reducing older adults' susceptibility to inferentially misleading advertising statements. This approach takes on increased significance given the finding that older adults have heightened susceptibility to the "truth" effect—recalling a false but familiar claim as true (Skurnik, Yoon, Park, & Schwarz, 2005). Of course, a key role of advertising is to increase a product's familiarity.

In a recent book, Boush, Friestad, and Wright (2009) reviewed six field experiments sponsored by the AARP (2003) that were aimed at heightening older adults' vigilance vis-à-vis telephone scams. In each study, the treatment group received a "training" phone call lasting from 5 to 15 minutes. The control group received a phone call that raised irrelevant matters. Interestingly, the subjects were older adults, whom the FBI had determined were listed as "hot prospects" by financial scam artists. Subsequent to the intervention, the subjects received a phone call from people trained by the researchers to operate as "scammers," pitching fraudulent rare coin investments or charity donations. In most of the studies, the interventions were effective in significantly reducing the percentage of older adults who succumbed to the fraudulent appeal relative to those in the control group. Boush et al. highlighted some of the factors that were critical to the self-protection training intervention: (a) The older adult was convinced that he or she was vulnerable to the scams described, (b) the coaching explained the scam effectively, (c) the training involved an active-skills/rehearsal component, and (d) overall, self-efficacy beliefs and competency skills were developed.

### Further Research on Developing Persuasion Knowledge Among Youth and Older Adults: Drawing on the Bright Side of Marketing

Public policy remedies that involve regulating or legislating constraints on advertising and promotion practices may be necessary and useful. However, they also can be controversial and more or less difficult to implement, depending on the political climate at the time. For this reason, the development of persuasion knowledge programs for both youth and older adults can be a useful complementary strategy.

To date, persuasion knowledge interventions and media literacy interventions, as referred to above, have taken a predominantly cognitive approach, focusing on knowledge and literacy. As Austin et al. (2005) stated, "It is important for young people to develop *logic-based defenses* against the emotional appeals of persuasive messages" (p. 77). In part, this knowledge has been intended to give young people a sense of self-efficacy, a concept developed by Bandura (1977), as described earlier. Yet, also as noted above, Friestad and Wright (1994) have suggested that once people gain persuasion knowledge, there is an off-putting or negative emotional response to the persuasive attempt as well. This emotional response can be used as the basis of a motivational component that might augment the more cognitive approach described to this point. Specifically, "reactance," a concept developed by Brehm (1966) and Brehm and Brehm (1981), might be generated.

According to reactance theory, individuals who view their freedom as threatened, for example, by persuasive messages, will be motivated to reestablish their autonomy. If people construe a persuasive message to be a threat to their attitudinal freedom, they will try to reassert their freedom by maintaining their original opinion or changing their opinion in opposition to the position advocated by the message (Eagly & Chaiken, 1993). Thus, youths and older adults who come to understand advertisers' tactics and motives may come to view the advertisers' efforts as a restriction of their options. To the extent they do, their reactions might be one of reactance (or, more colloquially, *push-back*). As noted above, this approach is a significant element of the highly successful national antitobacco Truth campaign.

Very little research, if any, has been done to assess the separate cognitive and motivational components of reactions to such interventions as described in the studies above. In fact, at least some of the dependent measures used in these studies tend to confound the two. In the same way, a scale measuring "smoking media literacy" also confounds both the cognitive and motivational components of their reactions (Primack et al., 2006). Efforts to decompose the two might benefit from a scale that measures psychological reactance, although the scale is not specific to situations involving advertising and advertisers (Hong & Page, 1989).

*Research Issues Unique to Youth*

Just how young children might be before they can benefit from elements of persuasion knowledge is a researchable issue. For example, at what age might parents effectively advise children that those people on the television screen who are telling them to buy toys, cereals, and fast foods are "strangers" and should be treated with the caution all strangers are treated? Of course, this approach is subject to the criticism that it creates general mistrust among children.

As noted above, for 8–12-year-olds, developing persuasion knowledge programs appears to be a necessary but insufficient condition. A last-minute "reminder" cue is also required for children to use the persuasion knowledge they may have learned earlier. Working parents can hardly sit by their children every minute they are watching television to provide a reminder, and this is even more true for all the new media to which children are increasingly exposed. However, at least for television, there is a model that was attempted for a few years in the 1980s. At the time, the small Group W network of television stations had a brief message that preceded each commercial break. The message told children that they were about to watch some commercials, that they had to watch these in a different way from the program they were watching, and that they might not need some of the things advertised. There is a need for research to test whether (a) broader persuasion knowledge programs, perhaps as delivered within a school context, and (b) reminder television messages and cues would be effective in heightening children's vigilance as they processed commercials. From a public policy perspective, the mandated presence of such reminder messages and cues could be considered a minimal requirement as long as children continue to be the targets of heavy commercial fare.

Much persuasion research has focused on the nature of the persuasive message. With the exception of level of involvement (Petty & Cacioppo, 1979; Petty, Cacioppo, & Schumann, 1983), little attention has been paid to the state of the individual receiving a persuasive message. An issue relatively unique to adolescents is the difficulty in persuading them, given their level of emotionality and impulsivity. One approach that might be tested is to (temporarily) reduce adolescents' emotionality and impulsivity just prior to delivering a persuasive health-oriented message (e.g., antialcohol, antitobacco, antidrugs) in the hope of making them more receptive to the message. Given that there is considerable literature linking relaxation exercise as well as aerobic exercise to a reduction in levels of anxiety (Altchiler & Motta, 1994; Borkovec & Costello, 1993; Broman-Fulks et al., 2004; Kim, 2005; Petruzzello, 1995; Salmon, 2001; Steptoe et al., 1989), it seems plausible that the same approaches would temporarily calm the adolescents, reducing levels of emotionality and impulsivity. To the extent that adolescents were relaxed, calmer, and on a more even and positive emotional keel, they might be more inclined to listen to a persuasive message without actively counterarguing and so be more effectively won over by that message.

*Research Issues Unique to Older Adults*

There is a need to build on the various approaches described earlier in order to create and evaluate broad persuasion knowledge programs for older adults. Beyond that, it should be noted that those who seek to improve media literacy have considered issues beyond advertising, such as the representation of gender and minorities in television programming (for a recent review, see Bergsma & Carney, 2008). A valuable extension of this perspective would involve a consideration of both ageism in the media and elderspeak among health care providers and others. Heightening awareness and vigilance regarding the distortions represented by both, and their possible consequences, could be an effective strategy in restoring a stronger sense of self to many older adults. As Levy's (2003) research has suggested, this would contribute to improved health-related outcomes for older adults.

## QUALITY OF LIFE: CONSUMER WELL-BEING, HAPPINESS, AND LIFE SATISFACTION

TCR is obviously not limited to addressing the issues of consumer vulnerability in relation to specific segments of the population (e.g., very young and old consumers). More broadly, consumer welfare research focuses on how marketing institutions affect the quality of life (QOL) of people through the marketplace (i.e., their role as consumers). This research has interested many consumer researchers and macromarketers. These scholars focus on understanding the construct of consumer well-being (CWB), capturing its indicators through reliable and valid measures, and mapping out its antecedents and consequences. CWB research supports professional, industry, governmental, and consumer advocacy organizations by advocating and setting CWB policies and standards, training personnel in developing and implementing marketing programs to enhance CWB, and monitoring CWB contributions to society.

This section provides an overview of CWB research, with more emphasis on recent work in an effort to motivate future research. Specifically, much of the research in CWB can be categorized in terms of five theoretical perspectives: (1) consumer sovereignty, (2) nonmaleficence, (3) stakeholder theory, (4) social justice, and (5) QOL. For an overview of these CWB research programs and a discussion of their ethical and public policy implications, consult Sirgy (2008). We will concentrate here on providing an overview of CWB research related to QOL.

QOL is a theoretical notion well accepted by many social scientists as an ethics theory (Lane, 2000; Lee & Sirgy, 2005; Nussbaum & Sen, 1993; Sirgy, 2001; Sirgy et al., 2006). The central tenet of QOL theory is the enhancement of human development. Human development (i.e., QOL) is a societal goal that governments seek to meet at the national, community, and individual levels. QOL researchers traditionally capture the concept through subjective and objective indicators. Subjective indicators of QOL are typically in the form of measuring overall happiness, perceived QOL, life satisfaction, or subjective well-being (e.g., Meadow, Mentzer, Rahtz, & Sirgy, 1992; Sirgy, 2002; Sirgy & Lee, 2006; Sirgy et al., 1995a, 1995b). Objective indicators, in contrast, typically capture economic, social, and environmental well-being based on expert assessment (e.g., Hagerty et al., 2001; Sirgy & Lee, 2006). The pursuit of QOL is well recognized as an important end goal. Government institutions develop public policy and design intervention programs to enhance QOL (e.g., Sirgy, Samli, & Meadow, 1982).

There are many programs of research in CWB guided by the theoretical notion of human development or QOL, the goal of which is to demonstrate the impact of some facet of the marketplace on QOL. The basic premise is that a marketplace facet contributes positively and negatively to the consumer's overall sense of well-being (i.e., life satisfaction, perceived QOL, overall happiness, subjective well-being) and/or consumers' actual well-being (i.e., objective indicators of economic, social, and environmental well-being). Examples of consumer research guided by the

QOL concept include research on materialism, compulsive consumption, consumption equity, specific consumer populations, consumption life cycle, consumer–life satisfaction, perceived QOL impact of a product, need satisfaction, and goals related to subjective well-being (Sirgy, Lee, & Rahtz, 2007).

### QOL Research Related to the Dark Side of Consumer Welfare

Just as it guided discussion in our previous sections, the distinction between dark side and bright side topics surrounding consumer welfare also helps categorize much of the research on QOL. Specifically, QOL research on materialism, compulsive shopping, and consumption equity can be considered as the dark side, whereas QOL research dealing with specific consumer populations, consumption life cycle, consumer–life satisfaction, perceived QOL impact of a product, need satisfaction, and goals related to subjective well-being represent the bright side of consumer welfare.

#### Research on Materialism and QOL

Russell Belk (1984) has long defined *materialism* as "the importance a consumer attaches to worldly possessions. At the highest levels of materialism, such possessions assume a central place in a person's life and are believed to provide the greatest source of satisfaction and dissatisfaction in life" (p. 291). Materialistic people believe that the continued acquisition of possessions will lead to greater happiness and satisfaction in life and that lack of possessions will lead to dissatisfaction in life. Contrary to lay beliefs, research has shown the opposite. In other words, life dissatisfaction, not satisfaction, is the result of a materialistic orientation (e.g., Belk, 1984, 1985; Burroughs & Rindfleisch, 2002; Dawson & Bamossy, 1991; Keng, Jung, Jiuan, & Wirtz, 2000; La Barbera & Gurhan-Canli, 1997; Richins, 1987, 2004; Richins & Dawson, 1992). To reiterate, research has demonstrated a negative correlation between materialism and life satisfaction (for literature reviews, see Larsen, Sirgy, & Wright, 1999; Wright & Larsen, 1993).

There are at least two explanations to account for the negative relationship between materialism and life satisfaction: a top-down theory and a bottom-up theory of subjective well-being. QOL researchers have consistently used these two theories to explain the determinants of life satisfaction (for a review of this literature, see Diener, 1984; Diener, Suh, Lucas, & Smith, 1999; for an alternative, more evolutionary, and neurological perspective, see Burroughs & Rindfleisch, Chapter 12 of this volume). The top-down theory of subjective well-being states that life satisfaction is influenced by personality or dispositional factors (e.g., self-esteem, alienation, optimism, pessimism, neuroticism). In contrast, the bottom-up theory argues that life satisfaction is influenced by situational factors (e.g., standard of living, job, family, leisure, neighborhood, community). Based on the top-down theory, Belk (1985) suggested that materialistic people are usually possessive, nongenerous, and envious. These dispositional factors reflect a tendency to experience negative emotions. That is, negative affect related to dispositional materialism may spill over (top-down) to influence life satisfaction; thus, materialism influences life satisfaction in a negative way.

The bottom-up theory states that life satisfaction is greatly influenced by life domain evaluations. Specifically, positive and negative affect are invested in life domains capturing certain types of emotional experiences, which in turn influences one's sense of well-being in various life domains (e.g., sense of well-being in family life, leisure life, love life, work life, social life, and spiritual life). One important life domain is material life (or standard of living). The material life domain houses emotional reactions related to material possessions, household income, savings, investment, and other material resources related to personal wealth. In this vein, life satisfaction judgments are directly influenced by how one feels about important life domains such as material life.

Empirically, Sirgy, Lee, Kosenko, et al. (1998) were able to demonstrate that the negative relationship between materialism and life satisfaction can be explained by the mediation of evaluation of standard of living. Specifically, their study found that materialistic people are less satisfied with their material possessions and, in turn, less satisfied with life than nonmaterialistic people. Furthermore, Sirgy, Lee, Larsen, et al. (1998) showed that product satisfaction does impact life satisfaction as moderated by materialism. That is, those who are highly materialistic were found to experience a greater spillover between product satisfaction and life satisfaction.

Yet, another explanation of the negative relationship between materialism and life satisfaction was provided by Sirgy (1998), who proposed that materialistic people have inflated expectations of their standard of living, whereas nonmaterialistic people have realistic expectations. He elaborated on various types of expectation and how materialistic people (compared to nonmaterialistic people) use these expectations. Six types of expectations were delineated: (1) their ideal view of standard of living, (2) what they feel they deserve in terms of financial resources, (3) what they need to maintain a certain lifestyle, (4) what they have predicted all along in attaining a certain level of personal wealth, (5) how far they have achieved in relation to what they had in the past, and (6) how much personal wealth they were able to amass based on their ability (i.e., their educational background, inheritance, socioeconomic status, etc.).

Materialistic people tend to make more frequent evaluations of their standard of living using these six types of expectations. The greater the frequency of their evaluations, the more likely they are to make negative ones. Also, materialistic people tend to make standard of living evaluations using ideal-, deserve-, and need-based expectations than nonmaterialistic people. The negative affect generated from negative evaluations of their standard of living spills over to judgments of life overall, making materialistic people feel dissatisfied with life. In contrast, the nonmaterialistic tend to evaluate their standard of living using predictive, past-, and ability-based expectations. The nature of these expectations is likely to generate more feelings of satisfaction than dissatisfaction in relation to standard of living.

### Research on Compulsive Consumption and QOL

Compulsive consumption is consumption behavior that is addictive or beyond the control of the consumer (see also Faber & Vohs, Chapter 22 of this volume; Litt, Pirouz, & Shiv, Chapter 25 of this volume). Motivated by stress, anxiety, boredom, or depression, some people consume products in ways that are unhealthy. Research has shown that many factors affect compulsive consumption, such as personality and family structure. Personality-wise, research has shown that there are two types of compulsive consumers: distressed and sociopathic (Hirschman, 1992; Hoch & Loewenstein, 1991). Distressed compulsives have feelings of self-doubt, incompetence, and personal inadequacy. They are not good at managing stress, so they resort to behaviors that reduce stress temporarily and reduce their overall QOL in the long run, such as shopping beyond one's financial means, overeating, abusing drugs, and engaging in sexual promiscuity. Distressed compulsive consumers feel guilty and regretful after their actions. In contrast, sociopathic compulsive consumers are motivated by sensation-seeking and do not feel remorse or guilt over their actions. Many compulsive consumers are cross-addicted, having more than one addiction (Natataajan & Goff, 1992).

There is some evidence suggesting that family structure plays an important role in fostering compulsive consumption (e.g., Rindfleisch, Burroughs, & Denton, 1997; Roberts, Manolis, & Tanner, 2003; Roberts & Tanner, 2005). For example, one study found that adolescents from divorced families are more likely to engage in compulsive shopping than adolescents from nondivorced families. The explanation is that adolescents are likely to deal with the stress of the divorce-situational ramifications by shopping.

Much research has focused on one form of compulsive consumer behavior, namely, compulsive shopping (e.g., Faber & Vohs, Chapter 22 of this volume; Kwak, Zinkhan, & Crask, 2003; Mowen & Spears, 1999; O'Guinn & Faber, 1989; Roberts & Jones, 2001; Kwak, Zinkhan, & Dominick, 2002). People who buy compulsively are reported to have low self-esteem and tend to be prone to fantasy. They are motivated not by the product acquired but by the process of acquiring it. The adverse QOL consequences related to compulsive shopping include stress, frustration, loss of one's sense of control, financial debt, and ensuing family conflict.

### Research on Consumption Equity and QOL

The United Nations Development Programme uses a variety of indicators and data to compare countries and world regions in their state of consumption (Fukuda-Parr, 2003). The goal is to identity and measure inequities in the consumption of goods and services that meet basic needs (cf. Hill, Felice, & Ainscough, 2007). In the area of marketing and development, consumption equity research focuses on marketing solutions to alleviate poverty in the Third World (e.g., Chakravati, 2006; Kotler & Roberto, 1989; Kotler, Roberto, & Leisner, 2006; Rosa, Geiger-Oneto, & Fajardo, Chapter 7 of this volume; Shultz, 1997; Shultz & Shapiro, Chapter 6 of this volume; Viswanathan, Chapter 5 of this volume).

Related to consumption equity is research that focuses on inequities between men and women in consumption opportunities. For example, Hill and Dhanda (2004) examined the relationship between a country's level of technological achievement and gender equity. They concluded that countries should develop policies that promote technological achievement because technological advancement serves to reduce gender inequity.

There is also consumer research related to inequity issues of poor consumers in that the poor pay more for consumer goods and services. This type of research focuses on the cost of living. Measures such as the consumer price index have been used to guide public policies related to government entitlement programs designed to assist the poor (e.g., Hobijin & Lagokos, 2003; Samli, 2003). For example, by using consumer price index data, Samli (2003) was able to demonstrate that lower income bracket consumers do indeed spend more money on consumer goods and services than do upper income consumers. This research has important public policy implications (e.g., adjustments to entitlement programs are based on changes in the Consumer Price Index but do not take into effect the fact that the poor pay more). More research on the poor and their consumption behavior has been conducted by the United Nations (Fukuda-Parr, 2003) and the World Bank (2000).

## QOL Research Related to the Bright Side of Consumer Welfare

Research on QOL related to the bright side of consumer welfare includes specific consumer populations, consumption life cycle, consumer–life satisfaction, perceived QOL impact of a product, need satisfaction, and goals related to subjective well-being.

### Research on Specific Consumer Populations and QOL

Much research in CWB has focused on the elderly to assist these consumers in using goods and services most likely to enhance their QOL. Note that the focus is not treating this market segment as vulnerable. Instead, the focus is to understand older adults' needs and design specific goods and services that meet these needs, and ultimately enhance their QOL. For example, CWB has been conducted to investigate the QOL impact of the Internet on elderly consumers (e.g., Eastman & Iyer, 2005), new age technologies (e.g., Sherman, Schiffman, & Mathur, 2001), nostalgia products (e.g., Goulding, 1999), consumer market interactions (e.g., Kang & Ridgway, 1996), retailing and shopping within a given community (Meadow & Sirgy, 2008), and product innovations (e.g., Lunsford & Burnett, 1992).

*Research on the Consumption Life Cycle and QOL*

The concept of the consumption life cycle refers to the various stages or types of marketplace experiences that consumers have with goods and services. The experiences involve shopping (product acquisition), preparation (product assembly for personal use), use (product consumption), possession (product ownership), maintenance (product service and repair), and disposal (the selling, trading in, or actual junking of the product). Much CWB research has focused on how satisfaction with any one or combination of these marketplace experiences over an aggregation of goods and services contribute to life satisfaction (e.g., Lee, Sirgy, Larsen, & Wright, 2002; Leelakulthanit, Day, & Walters, 1991; Sirgy, Lee, Grzeskowiak, et al., 2008). The same concept of consumption life cycle has been used in other product-specific contexts, such as housing (e.g., Grzeskowiak, Sirgy, Lee, & Claiborne, 2006), mobile phones (e.g., Sirgy, Lee, Kamra, & Tidwell, 2008), and clothing (e.g., Marshall & Meiselman, 2006).

*Research on Consumer–Life Satisfaction*

As previously indicated, much research in CWB has been conducted using bottom-up spillover theory, which involves the notions of a satisfaction hierarchy and that positive and negative affect spill over from concrete events to specific life domains (e.g., work life, leisure life, family life, social life, love life) and overall life. Thus, events occurring in a given life domain may affect life satisfaction through a bottom-up spillover of affect (Diener, 1984; Sirgy, 2002). A segment of this research focuses on the extent to which consumption satisfaction with a particular product category influences life satisfaction. For example, in health care, Rahtz and Sirgy (2000); Rahtz, Sirgy, and Lee (2004); Sirgy, Mentzer, Rahtz, and Meadow (1991); and Sirgy, Hansen, and Littlefield (1994) have developed models that show how patient satisfaction with various medical services can affect patient life satisfaction through the impact of these services on patients' sense of well-being in various life domains (e.g., health life, community life, work life).

Similarly, in relation to travel and tourism, Neal and her colleagues (Neal, Sirgy, & Uysal, 1999, 2004; Neal, Uysal, & Sirgy, 2007) were able to show that satisfaction with travel and tourism services can affect life satisfaction through the mediation of leisure well-being. In other words, satisfaction with travel and tourism services contributes positively to the sense of well-being in leisure life, which in turn spills over to life satisfaction. Similar models were constructed and tested in other settings, such as college campus programs and services (Sirgy, Grzeskowiak, & Rahtz, 2007); various business, government, and nonprofit services located in a given community (e.g., Grzeskowiak, Sirgy, & Widgery, 2003; Sirgy & Cornwell, 2001; Sirgy, Rahtz, Cicic, & Underwood, 2000); and neighborhood amenities (e.g., Sirgy & Cornwell, 2002).

*Research on Perceived QOL Impact of a Product*

An inherent premise of bottom-up spillover theory is the notion that consumption of a product affects overall sense of well-being through its perceived impact on various life domains. For example, Sirgy, Lee, and Bae (2006) developed a measure of Internet well-being based on the concept of perceived QOL impact of the Internet on consumers of the Internet. This perception of perceived QOL impact, in turn, was conceptualized as determined by consumers' perceptions of the Internet in various life domains, such as consumer life, work life, leisure life, social life, community life, and sensual life. In turn, the perception of impact of the Internet in a given life domain (e.g., leisure life) is determined by perceptions of benefits and costs of the Internet in that domain.

Sirgy, Lee, Kamra, and Tidwell (2007) conducted a study that described the use of mobile communications in contributing to the QOL of customers. The major construct of their model was perceived QOL impact of cell phone use. They hypothesized that perceived QOL impact of cell phones is determined by consumer perceptions of the impact of the cell phone in various life domains, such as social life, leisure life, family life, education life, health and safety, love life, work life, and financial life. In turn, the perception of impact of the cell phone in a given life domain (e.g., social life, leisure life) is determined by perceptions of benefits and costs of the cell phone within that domain.

Grzeskowiak and Sirgy (2007) also equated CWB with perceived impact of a product on QOL. Specifically, they were able to empirically demonstrate that the perceived impact of coffee consumption on QOL can be predicted by brand loyalty and brand-community belongingness. The effect of brand loyalty on perceived impact of coffee consumption was moderated by self-image congruence in that the effect was more evident in relation to consumers who experienced a greater match between the image of a typical patron of the coffee shop and their own self-image than those who did not experience that match. Furthermore, the effect of brand-community belongingness was moderated by consumption recency in that the effect was more evident for consumers who have recently patronized the coffee shop than those who have not.

### Research on Need Satisfaction and QOL

One conceptualization of QOL involves the humanistic notion of need satisfaction based on Maslow's concept of hierarchy of needs (e.g., Sirgy, 1986; Sirgy et al., 1995a). The idea is simple: The more likely a product satisfies a variety of developmental needs (i.e., biological, safety, social, esteem, self-actualization, intellectual, and aesthetic needs), the more likely it will be that this product may enhance the consumer's sense of well-being (i.e., QOL). The more needs (varied in terms of the hierarchy of needs) a product satisfies the consumer population, the greater the QOL impact of that product on that population. The needs hierarchy perspective has been used by a number of researchers in and outside of marketing. Examples include application to nursing care services (e.g., Jones, 1992), personal transportation (e.g., Sirgy, Lee, & Kressman, 2006), internal marketing (e.g., Lee, Singapakdi, & Sirgy, 2007; Sirgy, Efraty, Siegel, & Lee, 2001), and housing (e.g., Annison, 2000).

### Research on Goals Related to Subjective Well-Being

There is much research on goal theory of subjective well-being in QOL studies (for a review of this literature, see Diener, 1984; Diener et al., 1999; Sirgy, 2002). The major thrust of this research involves the notion that the setting of meaningful goals and the attainment of such goals provide the greatest amount of satisfaction that ultimately plays an important role in life satisfaction (or subjective well-being). For example, Sirgy (2010) used much of the research published in QOL studies using goal theory to develop a foundation of a theory to explain how leisure travel plays an important role in life satisfaction of tourists. The extent to which tourists select positive and value-laden goals (e.g., intrinsic goals, autonomous goals, approach goals, goals related to growth needs), the more likely it will be that the attainment of these goals would induce much positive affect that spills over to life satisfaction. The extent to which tourists select positive and value-laden goals that have a high expectancy of attainment (i.e., goals that are realistic), the more likely it will be that the attainment of these goals would induce much positive affect that spills over to life satisfaction. The extent to which tourists develop successful plans to implement positive, value-laden, and realistic goals, the more likely it will be that the attainment of these goals would induce positive affect that spills over to life satisfaction. The extent to which tourists develop successful strategies to savor goal attainment, the more likely it will be that the positive affect experienced through goal attainment would play a significant role in life satisfaction (Sirgy, 2006).

Implications Regarding Consumer Research Related to QOL

Addressing first some of the dark side topics in consumer welfare, research on materialism and QOL should guide the formulation of public policy. For example, policies and programs should be designed to discourage consumers from purchasing a product guided strictly by status and prestige. Consumers should spend wisely by shopping around and comparing brands based on quality, safety, and price savings. Policies and programs should be designed to discourage consumers from using acquisition, consumption, and possession of consumer goods as a means to happiness and fulfillment in life. Much research has been done on materialism using correlational research. We know much about the antecedents and QOL consequences of materialism. It is time to move beyond correlational research and demonstrate causality. We need to test many of the correlational findings using well-designed experiments.

With respect to research on compulsive consumption, public policies can be formulated to help compulsive consumers combat unhealthy compulsive behaviors, ranging from cigarette smoking to compulsive shopping. Future research should focus on identifying situational triggers that prompt compulsive consumption and help identify situational cues that may counter these triggers. Such research may help develop specific public policy programs to reduce compulsive consumption.

Research on consumption equity has significant public policy implications. For example, the research conducted by the United Nations Development Programme to identify and measure inequities in the consumption of basic goods and services guides the formulation of public policy to reduce consumption inequities among the developed and developing countries. Research related to gender equity is designed to reduce resource inequities between males and females, research related to the poor is designed to reduce disparities between the affluent and the poor in entitlement programs, and so on. This area of research is ripe for a surge. Future research should explore the effectiveness of specific policies and programs designed to reduce consumption disparities among various population groups (e.g., male vs. females, developed vs. developing geographic regions within a country and between countries, affluent consumers vs. the poor, minority consumers vs. nonminority ones).

We turn now to the implications of QOL research on bright side topics. Research on elderly consumers, for example, is useful in directing professional and industry associations in setting standards and developing training programs to help their members develop and market goods and services that can enhance QOL of the elderly. By the same token, the same research assists government agencies in setting policies that can encourage business development and marketing of goods and services that can enhance QOL of older adults. Future research should explore how new technologies, products, and services affect the QOL of the elderly and other consumer age groups, such as children, adolescents, and middle-aged consumers. Of course, similar research can focus on other consumer populations related to a variety of demographic variables, such as income, race and ethnicity, marital status, education, and age cohorts.

In regard to research related to the consumption life cycle, the goal here is to develop community- and organizational-level policies designed to promote the specific type of marketplace experience shown to contribute to life satisfaction or QOL. At the community level, public policy promotes programs designed to maximize consumer satisfaction with various marketplace experiences in the local area. Such experiences contribute to community well-being and overall life satisfaction of the community residents. At the organizational level, public policy is designed to encourage specific industries (e.g., housing, transportation) develop and market their products in ways to maximize consumer satisfaction with the purchase, use, ownership, maintenance, and disposal of the product. Industry associations can also play an important role in the development and implementation of these policies (Sirgy & Lee, 2008). Future research should focus on specific formulations of public policy and test their QOL effectiveness as they are implemented through community organizations, government agencies, and industry associations.

The public policy implications of CWB research related to consumer–life satisfaction may be evident. Once a relationship between consumer satisfaction with a certain facet of the marketplace and life satisfaction is mapped out, then industry associations could develop specific policies and programs to maximize consumer satisfaction with that facet. Specifically, CWB performance measures can be guided by this type of research to gauge the effectiveness of certain industries (e.g., health care, travel and tourism, transportation, telecommunications, housing) in enhancing the QOL of customer populations. Future research should focus on further developing CWB performance measures of emerging high-tech industries guided by the consumer–life satisfaction approach.

CWB research on the perceived QOL impact of a product also has many implications for government agencies, consumer advocacy groups, and industry associations. Similar to the consumer–life satisfaction approach, CWB performance measures can be designed to gauge the effectiveness of certain industries (e.g., Internet, mobile communications, coffee shops) through the extent to which consumers perceive significant QOL impact of the product. Future research should explore further the underlying antecedents of certain products and services on consumers' perceptions of QOL impact, as well as mediators and moderators related to the perceived QOL impact.

The needs satisfaction approach is equally useful in guiding the formulation of public policy. Industry and public policy officials specialized in certain institutional sectors (e.g., nursing care, personal transportation, housing) can use the needs satisfaction approach to formulate public policies and design programs that would encourage the business sector to develop and market goods and services to meet the full spectrum of human development needs in target populations. Future research is encouraged to develop performance metrics related to additional major product categories based on the needs satisfaction approach, such as public transportation, telecommunications, pharmaceuticals, information technology, and housing.

CWB research related to goal theory can assist marketers in designing programs that help consumers select positive and value-laden goals and goals that are more likely to be attained. Attainment of these should enhance consumers' QOL. Marketers also can help consumers attain their selected positive, value-laden, and realistic goals through programs designed to implement the selected goals. Marketers can also enhance consumers' QOL by helping consumers savor the positive affect induced from goal attainment. Future research should formally test the QOL effectiveness of specific types of marketing programs that reflect consumers' goal setting, implementation, and attainment.

## CONCLUSION

Throughout the chapter, we have made the distinction between dark side and bright side topics for scholarship that comes under the broad rubric of TCR. The dark side invites research that reflects the fact that marketing practice does, under certain conditions, impact consumers and society adversely. This adversity may be in the form of failing to provide consumers with accurate marketplace information to help them choose high-quality products at low prices, promoting undesirable or unhealthy behaviors such as cigarette smoking, or neglecting societies' most vulnerable target consumers, such as children and the poor. The bright side invites research that links marketing practices with increments of QOL of individual consumers or the social world they inhabit. In other words, marketing designed to enhance CWB typically involves two goals related to the dark and bright sides of TCR.

The TCR goal for dark side topics is to suggest social programs or policies that may serve to minimize the negative effects of marketing practices on CWB and society at large. In contrast, the TCR goal for bright side topics is to suggest marketing strategies and practices that can enhance the positive experience of the marketplace, thus enhancing the QOL of consumers (see Layton & Grossbart, 2006; Mick, Bateman, & Lutz, 2009; Sirgy, 1991, 1996; Sirgy & Lee, 1996). Thus, in our view, TCR should guide businesses' marketing to improve the well-being of customers (i.e., decrease negative impact and increase positive impact) while also preserving the well-being of the firms' other stakeholders. In sum, TCR can push the frontiers of research to decrease externalities of the marketing system on consumers and society at large while enhancing CWB in measurable ways. As such, TCR can play a strategic role in bringing together diverse disciplines in service of these goals. TCR is, in essence, an amalgam of research in consumer sciences, marketing, business ethics, environmental sciences, industrial ecology, and so forth that serves consumer welfare and society at large.

We have sought to demonstrate that consumer welfare can be achieved through advances in research in social marketing, research that focuses on consumer vulnerabilities and their remedies, and research guided by QOL. We hope readers of this chapter will be motivated to conduct TCR as guided by the various principles we have discussed throughout.

## REFERENCES

AARP. (1998). *You and advertising: A few words about advertising and AARP's acceptance policies.* Lakewood, CA: Author.

AARP. (2003). *Off the hook: Reducing participation in telemarketing fraud.* Washington, DC: Author.

Ajzen, I. (1991). The theory of planned behavior: Some unresolved issues. *Organizational Behavior and Human Decision Processes,* 179–211.

Alexis, M. (1962). Some Negro–White differences in consumption. *American Journal of Economics and Sociology, 21*(January), 11–28.

Aloise-Young, P. A., Hennigan, K. M., & Graham, J. W. (1996). Role of the self-image and smoker stereotype in smoking onset during early adolescence: A longitudinal study. *Health Psychology, 15*(6), 494–497.

Altchiler, L., & Motta, R. (1994). Effects of aerobic and nonaerobic exercise on anxiety, absenteeism, and job satisfaction. *Journal of Clinical Psychology, 50*(6), 829–840.

Alwitt, L. F., & Donley, T. D. (1996). *Low income consumer: Adjusting the balance of exchange.* Thousand Oaks, CA: Sage.

American Legacy Foundation. n.d. Retrieved August 16, 2009, from http://www.legacyforhealth.org

Andreasen, A. R. (1971). *Inner city business: A case study of Buffalo, New York.* New York: Praeger.

Andreasen, A. R. (Ed.). (1972). *Improving inner city marketing.* Chicago: American Marketing Association.

Andreasen, A. R. (1975). *The disadvantaged consumer.* New York: Free Press.

Andreasen, A. R. (1978). The ghetto marketing life cycle: A case of underachievement. *Journal of Marketing Research, 15,* 20–28.

Andreasen, A. R. (1994). Social marketing: Definition and domain. *Journal of Marketing and Public Policy, 13*(1), 108–114.

Andreasen, A. R., & Best, A. (1977a). Consumers complain: Does business respond? *Harvard Business Review, 55*(4), 93–101.

Andreasen, A. R., & Best, A. (1977b). Consumer response to unsatisfactory purchases: A survey of perceiving defects, voicing complaints, and obtaining redress. *Law & Society Review, 11*(4), 701–742.

Andreasen, A. R., & Cady, J. F. (1973). Price levels, price practices and price discrimination in the retail market for prescription drugs. *Journal of Consumer Affairs, 9,* 33–38.

Andreasen, A. R., & Kotler, P. (2003). *Strategic marketing for nonprofit organizations* (6th ed.). Upper Saddle River, NJ: Prentice Hall.

Andreasen, A. R., & Kotler, P. (2008). *Strategic marketing for nonprofit organizations* (7th ed.). Upper Saddle River, NJ: Prentice Hall.

Andreasen, A. R., & Upah, G. D. (1979). Regulation and the disadvantaged: The case of the creditors' remedies rule. *Journal of Marketing, 43*(2), 75–83.

Annison, J. E. (2000). Towards a clearer understanding of the meaning of a "home." *Journal of Intellectual and Developmental Disability, 25*(4), 251–262.

Austin, E. W., Pinkleton, B. E., Hust, S. J., & Cohen, M. (2005). Evaluation of an American Legacy Foundation/ Washington State Department of Health media literacy pilot study. *Health Communication, 18*(1), 75–95.

Bagozzi, R. P., & Warshaw, P. (1990). Trying to consume. *Journal of Consumer Research, 17*, 127–140.

Bandura, A. (1977). Self-efficacy: Toward a unifying theory of behavior change. *Psychological Review, 84*, 191–215.

Bartels, R. (1974). The identity crisis in marketing. *Journal of Marketing, 38*, 73–76.

Bassett, M. T., Dumanovsky, T., Huang, C., Silver, L. D., Young, C., & Nonas, C., et al. (2008). Purchasing behavior and calorie information at fast-food chains in New York City, 2007. *American Journal of Public Health, 98*(8), 1457–1459.

Bauer, R. A., Cunningham, S. M., & Wortzel, L. H. (1965). The marketing dilemma of Negroes. *Journal of Marketing, 29*(July), 1–6.

Belch, G. E., & Belch, M. A. (2004). *Advertising and promotion: An integrated marketing communications perspective* (6th ed.). Boston: McGraw-Hill/Irwin.

Belk, R. W. (1984). Three scales to measure constructs related to materialism: Reliability, validity, and relationships to measures of happiness. In T. Kinnear (Ed.), *Advances in consumer research* (Vol. 11, pp. 291–297). Ann Arbor, MI: Association for Consumer Research.

Belk, R. W. (1985). Materialism: Trait aspects of living in the material world. *Journal of Consumer Research, 12*(December), 265–280.

Bergsma, L. J., & Carney, M. E. (2008). Effectiveness of health-promotion media literacy education: A systematic review. *Health Education Research, 23*(3), 522–542.

Berndt, T. (1979). Developmental changes in conformity to peers and parents. *Developmental Psychology, 15*(6), 608–616.

Berry, L. L. (1972). The low-income marketing system: An overview. *Journal of Retailing, 48*(Summer), 44–63, 90.

Bettman, J. R. (1979). *An information processing theory of consumer choice.* Reading, MA: Addison-Wesley.

Bloom, P. N., & Novelli, W. D. (1981). Problems and challenges in social marketing. *Journal of Marketing, 45*(2), 79–88.

Botvin, G. J., Goldberg, C. J., Botvin, E. M., & Dusenbury, L. (1993). Smoking behavior of adolescents exposed to cigarette advertising. *Public Health Reports, 108*(2), 217–224.

Borkovec, T. D., & Costello, E. (1993). Efficacy of applied relaxation and cognitive-behavioral therapy in the treatment of generalized anxiety disorder. *Journal of Consulting and Clinical Psychology, 61*(4), 611–619.

Boush, D. M., Friestad, M., & Wright, P. (2009). *Deception in the marketplace.* New York: Routledge.

Bowling, J. C., & Taylor, P. (1976, August 16). Philip Morris. On *This week* [Interview]. London: Thames Broadcasting Co. Bates No. 1002410318-1002410351.

Brady, D. S., & Friedman, R. D. (1947). Savings and the income distribution. In Conference on Research in Income and Wealth (Ed.), *Studies in income and wealth* (Vol. 10, pp. 247–265). Cambridge, MA: UMI.

Brehm, J. W. (1966). *A theory of psychological reactance.* New York: Academic Press.

Brehm, S. S., & Brehm, J. W. (1981). *Psychological reactance: A theory of freedom and control.* New York: Academic Press.

Broman-Fulks, J. J., Berman, M. E., Rabian, B. A., & Webster, M. J. (2004). Effects of aerobic exercise on anxiety sensitivity. *Behaviour Research and Therapy, 42*, 125–136.

Brucks, M., Armstrong, G. M., & Goldberg, M. E. (1988). Children's use of cognitive defenses against television advertising: A cognitive response approach. *Journal of Consumer Research, 14*(March), 471–482.

Bullock, H. A. (1961). Consumer motivations in black and white—I and II. *Harvard Business Review, 39*(May/ June), 89–104.

Burroughs, J. E., & Rindfleisch, A. (2002). Materialism and well-being: A conflicting value perspectives. *Journal of Consumer Research, 29*(December), 348–370.

Butter, E. J., Popovich, P. M., Stackhouse, R. H., & Garner, R. K. (1981). Discrimination of television programs and commercials by preschool children. *Journal of Advertising Research, 21*(April), 53–56.

Campbell, M. C., & Kirmani, A. (2000). Consumers' use of persuasion knowledge: The effects of accessibility and cognitive capacity on perceptions of an influence agent. *Journal of Consumer Research, 27*(June), 69–83.

Caplovitz, D. (1967). *The poor pay more.* New York: Free Press.

Caplovitz, D. (1974). *Consumers in trouble: A study of debtors in default.* New York: Free Press.

Chakravati, D. (2006). Voices unheard: The psychology of consumption in poverty and development. *Journal of Consumer Psychology, 16*(4), 363–376.

Chanil, D. (2002). Profile of the convenience store customer. *Convenience Store News, 11*(February), 54–70.

Chassin, L., Presson, C. C., Sherman, S. J., Corty, E., & Olshavsky, R. W. (1984). Predicting the onset of cigarette smoking in adolescents: A longitudinal study. *Journal of Applied Social Psychology, 14*(3), 224–243.

Children's Advertising Review Unit. (2009). Retrieved February 24, 2009, from http://www.caru.org

Children's Food and Beverage Advertising Initiative. (2008). *Changing the landscape of food and beverage advertising: The children's food and beverage advertising initiative in action.* Retrieved August 16, 2009, from http://www.bbb.org/us/childrens-food-beverage-initiative/

Chobanian, A. V., Bakris, G. L., Black, H. R., Cushman, W. C., Green, L. A., Izzo, J. L., Jr., et al. (2003). Seventh report of the Joint National Committee on Prevention, Detection, Evaluation, and Treatment of High Blood Pressure. *Hypertension, 42*, 1206–1252.

Cigarette brand preference among middle and high school students who are established smokers—United States, 2004 and 2006. (2009). *Morbidity & Mortality Weekly Report, 58*(5), 112–115. Retrieved October 12, 2010, from http://www.cdc.gov/mmwr/preview/mmwrhtml/mm5805a3.htm

COMMIT Research Group. (1991). Community Intervention Trial for Smoking Cessation (COMMIT): Summary of design and intervention. *Journal of the National Cancer Institute, 83*(22), 1620–1628.

Cox, W. E., Jr. (1969). A commercial structure model for a depressed neighborhood. *Journal of Marketing, 33*(3), 1–9.

Davis, J. A., & Smith, T. W. (1983). *General social survey cumulative file, 1972–1982.* Ann Arbor, MI: Inter-University Consortium for Political and Social Research.

Dawson, S., & Bamossy, G. (1991). If we are what we have, what are we when we don't have? An exploratory study of materialism among expatriate-Americans. *Journal of Social Behavior and Personality, 6*(6), 363–384.

Day, G. S., & Brandt, W. K. (1974). Consumer research and the evaluation of information disclosure requirements: The case of truth in lending. *Journal of Consumer Research, 1*(1), 21–32.

Diener, E. (1984). Subjective well-being. *Psychological Bulletin, 95*(3), 542–575.

Diener, E., Suh, E. M., Lucas, R. E., & Smith, H. L. (1999). Subjective well-being: Three decades of research. *Psychological Bulletin, 125*, 276–302.

Dixon, D. F., & McLaughlin, D. J., Jr. (1969). Do the inner city poor pay more for food? *Economic and Business Bulletin, 20*(Spring), 6–12.

Duesenbury, J. S. (1949). *Income, saving and the theory of consumer behavior.* Cambridge, MA: Harvard University Press.

Eagly, A. H., & Chaiken, S. (1993). *The psychology of attitudes.* Fort Worth, TX: Harcourt Brace.

Eastman, J. K., & Iyer, R. (2005). The impact of cognitive age on Internet use of the elderly: An introduction to the public policy. *International Journal of Consumer Studies, 29*(2), 125.

Engel, J. F., Kollat, D. T., & Blackwell, R. D. (1968). *Consumer behavior.* New York: Holt, Rinehart & Winston.

Farquhar, J. W., Fortmann, S. P., Flora, J. A., Taylor, B., Haskell, W. I., Williams, P. T., et al. (1990). Effects of communitywide education on cardiovascular disease risk factors: The Stanford Five-City Project. *Journal of the American Medical Association, 264*(3), 359–365.

Farrelly, M. C., Davis, K. C., Haviland, L., Messeri, P., & Healton, C. G. (2005). Evidence of a dose–response relationship between "truth" antismoking ads and youth smoking prevalence. *American Journal of Public Health, 95*(3), 425–429.

Federal Trade Commission. (1968). *Economic report on installment credit and retail sates practices of District of Columbia retailers.* Washington, DC: U.S. Government Printing Office.

Finberg, J. (2003). Financial abuse of the elderly in California. *Loyola of Los Angeles Law Review, 36*(2), 667–691.

Fishbein, M., & Ajzen, I. (1975). *Belief, attitude, intention and behavior.* Reading, MA: Addison-Wesley.

Fishbein, M., & Cappella, J. N. (2006). The role of theory in developing effective health communications. *Journal of Communications, 56*, S1–S17.

Food and Drug Administration. (1996). Regulations restricting the sale and distribution of cigarettes and smokeless tobacco to protect children and adolescents: Final rule. *Federal Register, 168*(61), 44396–44618.

Friestad, M., & Wright, P. (1994). The persuasion knowledge model: How people cope with persuasion attempts. *Journal of Consumer Research, 21*(1), 1–31.

Fukuda-Parr, S. (Ed.). (2003). *Human Development Report 2003: Millennium development goals: A compact among nations to end human poverty.* New York: Oxford University Press.

Gaedeke, R. M., & Etcheson, W. (1972). *Consumerism: Viewpoints from business, government and the public interest.* San Francisco: Canfield Press.

Gaeth, G. J., & Heath, T. B. (1987). The cognitive processing of misleading advertising in young and old adults. *Journal of Consumer Research, 14*(June), 43–54.

Galenson, M. (1972). Do blacks save more? *American Economic Review, 62*(March), 211–216.

Gensch, D. H., & Staelin, R. (1972). The appeal of buying black. *Journal of Marketing Research, 9*(May), 141–148.

Gibson, D. P. (1969). *The $30 billion Negro.* New York: Macmillan.

Goldberg, M. E. (1990). A quasi-experiment assessing the effectiveness of TV advertising directed to children. *Journal of Marketing Research, 27*(November), 445–454.

Goldberg, M. E. (2008a). Assessing the relationship between tobacco advertising and promotion and adolescent smoking behavior: Convergent evidence. In C. P. Haugtvedt, P. M. Herr, & F. R. Kardes (Eds.), *Handbook of consumer psychology* (pp. 933–958). Mahwah, NJ: Erlbaum.

Goldberg, M. E. (2008b). Consumer decision making and aging: Current knowledge and future directions: A commentary from a public policy/marketing perspective. *Journal of Consumer Psychology, 19*(1), 28–39.

Goldberg, M. E., & Gorn, G. J. (1974). Children's reactions to television advertising: An experimental approach. *Journal of Consumer Research, 1*(September), 69–75.

Goldberg, M. E., & Gunasti, K. (2007). Creating an environment in which youths are encouraged to eat a healthier diet. *Journal of Public Policy & Marketing, 26*(2), 162–181.

Goldberg, M. E., Niedermeier, K. E., Bechtel, L. J., & Gorn, G. J. (2006). Heightening adolescent vigilance toward alcohol advertising to forestall alcohol use. *Journal of Public Policy & Marketing, 25*(2), 147–159.

Goodman, C. (1972). Do the poor pay more? *Journal of Marketing, 32*(January), 18–24.

Goodman, C., & Goldberg, M. E. (1982). Behavioral evidence of the effects of televised food messages on children. *Journal of Consumer Research, 9*(September), 200–205.

Gorn, G. J., & Goldberg, M. E. (1977). The impact of television advertising on children from low income families. *Journal of Consumer Research, 4*(September), 86–88.

Gorn, G. J., & Goldberg, M. E. (1982). Behavioral evidence of the effect of televised food messages on children. *Journal of Consumer Research, 9*, 200–205.

Goulding, C. (1999). Heritage, nostalgia, and the "grey" consumer. *Journal of Marketing Practices, 5*(6–8), 177.

Grzeskowiak, S., & Sirgy, M. J. (2007). Consumer well-being (CWB): The effects of self-image congruence, brand community belongingness, brand loyalty, and consumption recency. *Applied Research in Quality of Life, 2*(4), 289–304.

Grzeskowiak, S., Sirgy, M. J., Lee, D., & Claiborne, C. B. (2006). Housing well-being: Developing and validating a measure. *Social Indicators Research, 79*, 503–541.

Grzeskowiak, S., Sirgy, M. J., & Widgery, R. (2003). Residents' satisfaction with community services: Predictors and outcomes. *Journal of Regional Analysis and Policy, 33*(2), 1–36.

Hagerty, M. R., Cummins, R., Ferriss, A. L., Land, K., Michalos, A., Peterson, M., et al. (2001). Quality-of-life indexes for national policy: Review and agenda for research. *Social Indicators Research, 55*(1), 1–96.

Haines, G. H., Jr., Simon, L. S., & Alexis, M. (1971). The dynamics of commercial structure in central city areas. *Journal of Marketing, 35*(April), 10–18.

Harvey, P. D. (1999). *Let every child be wanted: How social marketing is revolutionizing contraceptive use around the world.* Westport, CT: Auburn House.

Hastings, G., Stead, M., McDermott, L., Forsyth, A., MacKintosh, A. M., Rayner, M., et al. (2003). *Review of research on the effects of food promotion to children.* Glasgow, Scotland: Food Standards Agency. Retrieved August 16, 2009, from http://www.food.gov.uk/multimedia/pdfs/foodpromotiontochildren1.pdf

Health Care and Education Reconciliation Act of 2010, Pub.L. 111-152. http://www.gpo.gov/fdsys/pkg/PLAW-111publ152/content-detail.html, 124 Stat. 1029. (2010).

Hedden, T., & Yoon, C. (2006). Individual differences in executive processing predict susceptibility to interference in verbal working memory. *Neuropsychology, 20*(5), 511–528.

Henriksen, L., Feighery, E. C., Schleicher, N. C., Haladjian, H. H., & Fortmann, S. P. (2004). Reaching youth at the point of sale: Cigarette marketing is more prevalent in stores where adolescents shop frequently. *Tobacco Control, 13*, 315–318.

Henriksen, L., Flora, J. A., Feighery, E., & Fortmann, S. P. (2002). Effects on youth of exposure to retail tobacco advertising. *Journal of Applied Social Psychology, 32*(9), 1771–1789.

Hill, R. P., & Dhanda, K. K. (2004). Globalization and technological achievement: Implications for macromarketing and the digital divide. *Journal of Macromarketing, 24*(2), 147–155.

Hill, R. P., Felice, W. F., & Ainscough, T. (2007). International human rights and consumer quality of life: An ethical perspective. *Journal of Macromarketing, 27*, 370–379.

Hiltz, S. R. (1971). Black and White in the consumer financial system. *American Journal of Sociology*, *76*(May), 987–998.

Hirschman, E. C. (1991). Presidential address: Secular mortality and the dark side of consumer behavior; or how semiotics saved my life. In E. C. Hirschman, M. R. Solomon, & R. Holman (Eds.), *Advances in Consumer Research* (Vol. 18, pp. 1–4). Provo, UT: Association for Consumer Research.

Hirschman, E. C. (1992). The consciousness of addiction: Toward a general theory of compulsive consumption. *Journal of Consumer Research*, *19*, 155–179.

Hobijin, B., & Lagokos, D. (2003). Social security and the consumer price index for the elderly. *Current Issues in Economics and Finance*, *9*(5), 1–6.

Hoch, S. J., & Loewenstein, G. F. (1991). Time-inconsistent preferences and consumer self-control. *Journal of Consumer Research*, *17*(March), 492–507.

Hong, S., & Page, S. (1989). A psychological reactance scale: Development, factor structure and reliability. *Psychological Reports*, *64*, 1323–1326.

Hornik, R. (Ed.). (2002). *Public health communication: Evidence for behavior change*. Mahwah, NJ: Erlbaum.

Hosch, S. J., & Loewenstein, G. F. (1991). Time-inconsistent preferences and consumer self-control. *Journal of Consumer Research*, *17*, 492–507.

Howard, J. A., & Sheth, J. N. (1969). *The theory of buyer behavior*. New York: John Wiley.

Hunt, H. (1977). Conceptualization and measurement of consumer satisfaction and dissatisfaction, marketing science institute. *Journal of Retailing*, *76*(3), 309–322.

Indian Institute of Management. (1965). Proposals for family planning promotion: A marketing plan. *Studies in Family Planning*, *1*(6), 7–12.

Jacobs, D. R., Luepker, R. V., Mittlemark, M. B., Folsom, A. R., Pirei, P., Mascioli, S., et al. (1986). Community-wide prevention strategies: Evaluation design of the Minnesota Heart Health Program. *Journal of Chronic Disease*, *39*(2), 775–788.

Jacoby, J., & Hoyer, W. D. (1989). The comprehension/miscomprehension of print communication: Selected findings. *Journal of Consumer Research*, *15*(March), 434–443.

John, D. R. (1999). Consumer socialization of children: A retrospective look at twenty-five years of research. *Journal of Consumer Research*, *26*(December), 183–213.

John, D. R., & Cole, C. A. (1986). Age differences in information processing: Understanding deficits in young and elderly consumers. *Journal of Consumer Research*, *13*(December), 297–315.

Johnson, E. J., & Russo, J. E. (1984). Product familiarity and learning. *Journal of Consumer Research*, *11*(1), 542–550.

Johnson, K. D. (2004). *Financial crimes against the elderly* (Problem-Oriented Guides for Police, Problem-Specific Guides Series No. 20). Washington, DC: U.S. Department of Justice, Office of Community Oriented Policing Services.

Johnston, L. D., O'Malley, P. M., Bachman, J. G., & Schulenberg, J. E. (2009). *Monitoring the future: National results on adolescent drug use* (NIH Publication No. 09-7401). Bethesda, MD: National Institute on Drug Abuse.

Jones, G. M. M. (1992). A nursing model for the care of the elderly. In G. M. M. Jones & B. M. L. Miesen (Eds.), *Care-giving in dementia. Vol. 1: Research and applications*. New York: Tavistock/Routledge.

Kang, Y., & Ridgway, N. M. (1996). The importance of consumer market interactions as a form of social support for elderly's consumers. *Journal of Public Policy & Marketing*, *15*(1), 108–118.

Kassarjian, H. H., & Robertson, T. S. (1968). *Perspectives in consumer behavior*. Glenview, IL: Scott, Foresman.

Kemper, S., Ferrell, P., Harden, T., Finter-Urczyk, A., & Billington, C. (1998). Use of elderspeak by young and older adults to impaired and unimpaired listeners. *Aging, Neuropsychology and Cognition*, *5*(1), 43–55.

Keng, K. A., Jung, K., Jiuan, T. S., & Wirtz, J. (2000). The influence of materialistic inclination on values, life satisfaction, and aspirations: An empirical analysis. *Social Indicators Research*, *49*(March), 317–333.

Kesmodel, D., Etter, L., & Mundy, A. (2009, September 2). Tobacco giants challenge law. *The Wall Street Journal*, p. A31.

Kim, H. (2005). Effects of a relaxation breathing exercise on anxiety, depression, and leukocyte in hemopoietic stem cell transplantation patients. *Cancer Nursing*, *28*(1), 79–83.

Kotler, P., & Levy, S. J. (1969). Broadening the concept of marketing. *Journal of Marketing*, *33*, 10–15.

Kotler, P., & Roberto, E. (1989). *Social marketing: Strategies for changing public behavior*. New York: Free Press.

Kotler, P., Roberto, N., & Leisner, T. (2006). Alleviating poverty: A macro/micro marketing perspective. *Journal of Macromarketing*, *26*(2), 233–239.

Kotler, P., & Zaltman, G. (1971). Social marketing: An approach to planned social change. *Journal of Marketing*, *35*(July), 3–12.

Kwak, H., Zinkhan, G. M., & Crask, M. R. (2003). Diagnostic screener for compulsive buying: Applications to the USA and South Korea. *Journal of Consumer Affairs, 37*, 161–171.

Kwak, H., Zinkhan, G. M., & Dominick, J. R. (2002). The moderating role of gender and compulsive buying tendencies in the cultivation effects of TV shows and TV advertising: A cross-cultural study between the U.S. and South Korea. *Media Psychology, 4*, 77–111.

La Barbera, P. A., & Gurhan-Canli, Z. (1997). The role of materialism, religiosity, and demographics in subjective well-being. *Psychology & Marketing, 14*(1), 71–97.

Lane, R. E. (2000). *The loss of happiness in market democracies.* New Haven, CT: Yale University Press.

Larsen, V., Sirgy, M. J., & Wright, N. D. (1999). Materialism: The construct, measures, antecedents, and consequences. *Academy of Marketing Studies Journal, 3*(2), 75–107.

Larson, R., Moneta, G., Richards, M. H., & Wilson, S. (2002). Continuity, stability, and change in daily emotional experience across adolescence. *Child Development, 73*(4), 1151–1165.

Larson, R., & Richards, M. H. (1994). *Divergent realities: The emotional lives of mothers, fathers and adolescents.* New York: Basic Books.

Layton, R. A., & Grossbart, S. (2006). Macromarketing: Past, present, and future. *Journal of Macromarketing, 26*, 193–213.

Lee, D., Singapakdi, A., & Sirgy, M. J. (2007). Further validation of a need-based quality-of-work-life (QWL) measure: Evidence from marketing practitioners. *Applied Research in Quality of Life, 2*(4), 273–287.

Lee, D., & Sirgy, M. J. (2005). *Well-being marketing: Theory, research, and applications.* Seoul, Korea: Pakyoungsa.

Lee, D., Sirgy, M. J., Larsen, V., & Wright, N. D. (2002). Developing a subjective measure of consumer well-being. *Journal of Macromarketing, 22*(2), 158–169.

Leelakulthanit, O., Day, R., & Walters, R. (1991). Investigating the relationship between marketing and overall satisfaction with life in a developing country. *Journal of Macromarketing, 11*(1), 3–23.

Lefebvre, R. C., & Flora, J. A. (1988). Social marketing and public health intervention. *Health Education Quarterly, 15*(3), 299–315.

Leventhal, H., Glynn, K., & Fleming, R. (1987). Is the smoking decision an "informed choice"? *Journal of the American Medical Association, 24*(257), 3373–3376.

Levy, B. (2003). Mind matters: Cognitive and physical effects of aging self-stereotypes. *The Journals of Gerontology, 58B*(4), P203–P215.

Luck, D. J. (1969). Broadening the concept of marketing: Too far. *Journal of Marketing, 33*(3), 53–55.

Luck, D. J. (1974). Social marketing: Confusion compounded. *Journal of Marketing, 38*, 70–72.

Lunsford, D. A., & Burnett, M. A. (1992). Marketing product innovations to the elderly: Understanding. *Journal of Consumer Marketing, 9*(4), 53–64.

Lutz, R. J. (1975). Changing brand attitudes through modification of cognitive structure. *Journal of Consumer Research, 1*, 49–59.

Lutz, R. J. (1977). An experimental investigation of causal relations among cognitions, affect, and behavioral intention. *Journal of Consumer Research, 3*, 197–208.

Lynch, B. S., & Bonnie, R. J. (1994). *Growing up tobacco free: Preventing nicotine addiction in children and youths.* Washington, DC: National Academies Press.

Maggs, J. L., Almeida, D. M., & Galambos, N. L. (1995). Risky business: The paradoxical meaning of problem behavior for young adolescents. *Journal of Early Adolescence, 15*(3), 344–362.

Magnuson, W. G., & Carper, J. (1968). *The dark side of the marketplace: The plight of the American consumer.* Englewood Cliffs, NJ: Prentice Hall.

Marcus, B. H. (1969). Similarity of ghetto and non-ghetto food costs. *Journal of Marketing Research, 6*(August), 365–368.

Marshall, D. W., & Meiselman, H. L. (2006). Limited choice: An exploratory study into issue items and soldier subjective well-being. *Journal of Macromarketing, 26*(June), 59–76.

McGinnis, J. M., Gootman, J. A., & Kraak, V. A. (Eds.). (2006). *Food marketing to children and youth: Threat or opportunity?* Washington, DC: National Academies Press.

Meadow, L., Mentzer, J. T., Rahtz, D. R., & Sirgy, M. J. (1992). A life satisfaction measure based on judgment theory. *Social Indicators Research, 26*(1), 23–59.

Meadow, L., & Sirgy, M. J. (2008). Developing a measure that captures elderly's well-being in local marketplace transactions. *Applied Research in Quality of Life, 3*(1), 63–80.

Mick, D. G., Bateman, T. S., & Lutz, R. J. (2009). Exploring the pinnacle of human virtues as a central link from micromarketing to macromarketing. *Journal of Macromarketing, 29*(2), 98–118.

Moffitt, T. E. (1993). Adolescence-limited and life-course persistent antisocial behavior: A developmental taxonomy. *Psychological Review, 100*(4), 674–701.

Morgan, M. (1984). Heavy television viewing and perceived quality of life. *Journalism Quarterly, 61*(Autumn), 499–504.

Moscovitch, M., & Winocur, G. (1995). Frontal lobes, memory, and aging. *Annals of the New York Academy of Sciences, 769*(December), 119–150.

Moses, L. J., & Baldwin, D. A. (2005). What can the study of cognitive development reveal about children's ability to appreciate and cope with advertising? *Journal of Public Policy & Marketing, 24*(Fall), 186–201.

Mowen, J. C., & Spears, N. (1999). Understanding compulsive buying among college students. *Journal of Consumer Psychology, 8*(4), 407–430.

Murphy, P. E., & Wilkie, W. L. (Eds.). (1990). *The future for marketing and advertising regulation: The Federal Trade Commission in the 1990s.* Notre Dame, IN: University of Notre Dame Press.

Myers, D. J. (1997). Racial rioting in the 1960s: An event history analysis of local conditions. *American Sociological Review, 62,* 94–112.

Myers, J. G., Massy, W. G., & Greyser, S. A. (1980). *Marketing research and knowledge development.* Englewood Cliffs, NJ: Prentice Hall.

Natataajan, R., & Goff, B. G. (1992). Manifestations of compulsiveness in the consumer-marketplace domain. *Psychology and Marketing, 9,* 31–44.

National Association of Attorneys General. (n.d.). *Tobacco Master Settlement Agreement summary.* Retrieved August 16, 2009, from http://www.ag.ca.gov/tobacco/resources/msasumm.htm

National Cancer Institute. (2008). *The role of media in promoting and reducing tobacco use* (Tobacco Control Monograph No. 19, NIH Publication No. 07-6242). Bethesda MD: U.S. Department of Health and Human Services, National Institutes of Health, National Cancer Institute.

Neal, J., Sirgy, M. J., & Uysal, M. (1999). The role of satisfaction with leisure travel/tourism services and experiences in satisfaction with leisure life and overall life. *Journal of Business Research, 44*(March), 153–163.

Neal, J., Sirgy, M. J., & Uysal, M. (2004). Measuring the effect of tourism services on travelers' quality of life: Further validation. *Social Indicators Research, 69,* 243–277.

Neal, J., Uysal, M., & Sirgy, M. J. (2007). The effect of tourism services on travelers' quality of life. *Journal of Travel Research, 46,* 154–163.

Nestle, M. (2002). *Food politics: How the food industry influences nutrition and health.* Berkeley: University of California Press.

Neumark-Sztainer, D., Wall, M., Perry, C., & Story, M. (2003). Correlates of fruit and vegetable intake among adolescents: Findings from Project EAT. *Preventive Medicine, 37*(3), 198–208.

Nicosia, F. N. (1966). *Consumer decision processes.* Englewood Cliffs, NJ: Prentice Hall.

Nussbaum, M., & Sen, A. (Eds.). (1993). *The quality of life.* Oxford, England: Clarendon Press.

Ofcom. (2007, February 22). *Television advertising of food and drink products to children: Final statement.* Retrieved August 16, 2009, from http://www.ofcom.org.uk/consult/condocs/foodads_new/statement/

Ogden, C. L., Carroll, M. D., Curtin, L. R., McDowell, M. A., Tabak, C. J., & Flegal, K. M. (2006). Prevalence of overweight and obesity in the United States, 1999–2004. *Journal of the American Medical Association, 295*(13), 1549–1554.

O'Guinn, T. C., & Faber, R. J. (1989). Compulsive buying: A phenomenological exploration. *Journal of Consumer Research, 16,* 147–157.

Palmer, E. L., & McDowell, C. N. (1979). Program/commercial separators in children's television programming. *Journal of Communication, 29*(Summer), 197–201.

Park, D. C., Lautenschlager, G., Hedden, T., Davidson, N., Smith, A. D., & Smith, P. K. (2002). Models of visuospatial and verbal memory across the adult life span. *Psychology and Aging, 17*(2), 299–320.

Pechmann, C., Levine, L., Loughlin, S., & Leslie, F. (2005). Impulsive and self-conscious: Adolescents' vulnerability to advertising and promotion. *Journal of Public Policy & Marketing, 24*(2), 202–221.

Pechmann, C., Pirouz, D., & Pezzuti, T. (2009, October). *Symbolic interactionism and adolescent reactions to cigarette advertisements.* Paper presented at the annual conference of the Association for Consumer Research, Pittsburgh, PA.

Pechmann, C., Zhao, G., Goldberg, M. E., & Reibling, E. T. (2003). What to convey in antismoking advertisements for adolescents: The use of protection motivation theory to identify effective message themes. *Journal of Marketing, 67,* 1–18.

Petruzzello, S. J. (1995). Anxiety reduction following exercise: Methodological artifact or "real" phenomenon? *Journal of Sport & Exercise Psychology, 17,* 105–111.

Petty, R. E., & Cacioppo, J. T. (1979). Issue involvement can increase or decrease persuasion by enhancing message-relevant cognitive responses. *Journal of Personality and Social Psychology, 37*, 1915–1926.

Petty, R. E., Cacioppo, J. T., & Schumann, D. (1983). Central and peripheral routes to advertising effectiveness: The moderating role of involvement. *Journal of Consumer Research, 10*, 135–146.

POPAI. (1992). *The point-of-purchase advertising industry fact book.* Washington, DC: Author.

POPAI. (2002a). *In-store advertising becomes a measured medium: Convenience channel study.* Englewood, NJ: Author.

POPAI. (2002b, April 19). *P-O-P measures up: Convenience channel study: Introduction and consumer insights.* PowerPoint presentation by D. Blatt, developed for GlobalShop 10th anniversary.

Primack, B. A., Gold, M. A., Switzer, G. E., Hobbs, R., Land, S. R., & Fine, M. J. (2006). Development and validation of a smoking media literacy scale for adolescents. *Archives of Pediatrics & Adolescent Medicine, 160*(4), 369–374.

Prochaska, J. O., & DiClemente, C. C. (1983). Stages and processes of self-change of smoking: Toward an integrative model of change. *Journal of Consulting and Clinical Psychology, 51*, 390–395.

Prochaska, J. O., DiClemente, C. C., & Norcross, J. C. (1992). In search of how people change: Applications to addictive behaviors. *American Psychologist, 47*(9), 1102–1114.

Prochaska, J. O., & Velicer, W. F. (1997). The transtheoretical model of health behavior change. *American Journal of Health Promotion, 12*, 38–48.

Puska, O., Toumilehto, J., Salonen, J., Neittaanmaki, L., Maki, J., & Virtamo, J. (1985). The community based strategy to prevent heart disease: Conclusions of the ten years of the North Karelia Project. *Annual Review of Public Health, 6*, 147–191.

Rahtz, D., & Sirgy, M. J. (2000). Marketing of healthcare within a community: A quality-of-life needs assessment model and method. *Journal of Business Research, 49*, 165–176.

Rahtz, D., Sirgy, M. J., & Lee, D. (2004). Further validation and extension of the quality-of-life/community healthcare model and measures. *Social Indicators Research, 69*(2), 167–198.

Rasmuson, M. R., Seidel, R. E., Smith, W. A., & Booth, E. M. (1988). *Communication for child survival.* Washington, DC: Academy of Educational Development.

Ratchford, B. T. (1982). Cost-benefit models of measuring consumer choice and information seeking behavior. *Management Science, 28*(2), 197–212.

Richards, L. C. (1966). Consumer practices of the poor. In L. M. Irelan (Ed.), *Low income life styles.* Washington, DC: U.S. Department of Health, Education and Welfare.

Richins, M. L. (1987). Media materialism and human happiness. In M. Wallendorf & P. Anderson (Eds.), *Advances in consumer research* (Vol. 14, pp. 352–356). Ann Arbor, MI: Association for Consumer Research.

Richins, M. L. (2004). The material values scale: Measurement properties and development of a short form. *Journal of Consumer Research, 31*(1), 209–219.

Richins, M. L., & Dawson, S. (1992). A consumer values orientation for materialism and its measurement: Scale development and validation. *Journal of Consumer Research, 19*(3), 303–316.

Rindfleisch, A., Burroughs, J. E., & Denton, F. (1997). Family structure, materialism, and compulsive consumption. *Journal of Consumer Research, 23*, 312–325.

Roberts, J. A., & Jones, E. (2001). Money attitudes, credit card use, and compulsive buying among American college students. *Journal of Consumer Affairs, 35*, 213–240.

Roberts, J. A., Manolis, C., & Tanner, J. F., Jr. (2003). Family structure, materialism, and compulsive consumption: A reinquiry and extension. *Journal of the Academy of Marketing Science, 31*, 300–311.

Roberts, J. A., & Tanner, J. F., Jr. (2005). Materialism and family structure-stress relation. *Journal of Consumer Psychology, 15*(2), 183–190.

Robertson, T. S., & Rossiter, J. R. (1974). Children and commercial persuasion: An attribution theory analysis. *Journal of Consumer Research, 1*(June), 13–20.

Robinson, T. N., Borzekowski, D. L., & Matheson, D. M. (2007). Effects of fast food branding on young children's taste preferences. *Archives of Pediatrics & Adolescent Medicine, 161*(8), 792–797.

Roedder, D. L. (1981). Age differences in children's responses to television advertising: An information processing approach. *Journal of Consumer Research, 8*(September), 144–153.

Roedder, D. L., Sternthal, B., & Calder, B. J. (1983). Attitude behavior consistency in children's responses to television advertising. *Journal of Marketing Research, 10*(November), 337–349.

Rogers, E. M. (1995). *Diffusion of innovations* (4th ed.). New York: Free Press.

Rogers, R. W. (1975). A protection motivation theory of fear appeals and attitude change. *Journal of Psychology, 91*, 93–111.

Rogers, R. W. (1983). Cognitive and physiological processes in fear appeals and attitude change: A revised theory of protection motivation. In J. Cacioppo & R. E. Petty (Eds.), *Social psychophysiology* (pp. 153–176). New York: Guilford.

Rosenstock, I. M. (1974). Historical origins of the health belief model. *Health Education Monographs, 15,* 328–335.

Ross, R. P., Campbell, T., Wright, J. C., Huston, A. C., Rice, M. L., & Turk, P. (1984). When celebrities talk, children listen: An experimental analysis of children's responses to TV ads with celebrity endorsement. *Journal of Applied Developmental Psychology, 5,* 185–202.

Rossiter, J., & Robertson, T. S. (1974). Children's TV commercials: Testing the defenses. *Journal of Communication, 24*(Autumn), 137–144.

Rudd Report. (2010). *Trends in television food advertising: Progress in reducing unhealthy marketing to young people?* New Haven, CT: Rudd Center for Food Policy & Obesity. Retrieved January 4, 2010, from http://www.yaleruddcenter.org/resources/upload/docs/what/reports/RuddReport_TVFoodAdvertising_2.10.pdf

Salmon, P. (2001). Effects of physical exercise on anxiety, depression, and sensitivity to stress: A unifying theory. *Clinical Psychology Review, 21*(1), 33–61.

Salthouse, T. A. (1996). The processing-speed theory of adult age differences in cognition. *Psychological Review, 103*(3), 403–428.

Samli, A. C. (2003). The consumer price index and consumer well-being: Developing a fair measure. *Journal of Macromarketing, 23*(December), 105–111.

Sexton, D. E., Jr. (1971). Comparing the costs of food to Blacks and to Whites: A survey. *Journal of Marketing, 35*(July), 40–47.

Sherman, E., Schiffman, L. G., & Mathur, A. (2001). The influence of gender on the new-age elderly's consumption orientation. *Psychology and Marketing, 18*(10), 1073.

Sheth, J. N., & Wright, P. L. (Eds.). (1974). *Marketing analysis for societal problems.* Champaign: University of Illinois.

Shultz, C. J., II. (1997). Improving life quality for the destitute: Contributions from multiple-method fieldwork in war-ravaged transition economies. *Journal of Macromarketing, 17,* 56–67.

Sirgy, M. J. (1986). A quality of life theory derived from Maslow's developmental perspective: 'Quality' is related to progressive satisfaction of a hierarchy of needs, lower order and higher. *The American Journal of Economics and Sociology, 45*(July), 329–342.

Sirgy, M. J. (1991). Can business and government help enhance the quality of life (QOL) of workers and consumers? *Journal of Business Research, 22*(June), 327–334.

Sirgy, M. J. (1996). Strategic marketing planning guided by the quality-of-life (QOL) concept. *Journal of Business Ethics, 15*(March), 241–259.

Sirgy, M. J. (1998). Materialism and quality of life. *Social Indicators Research, 43,* 227–260.

Sirgy, M. J. (2001). *Handbook of quality-of-life research: An ethical marketing perspective.* Dordecht, the Netherlands: Kluwer Academic.

Sirgy, M. J. (2002). *The psychology of quality of life.* Dordecht, the Netherlands: Kluwer Academic.

Sirgy, M. J. (2006). Developing a conceptual framework of employee well-being (EWB) by applying goal concepts and findings from personality-social psychology. *Applied Research in Quality of Life, 1,* 7–38.

Sirgy, M. J. (2008). Ethics and public policy implications of consumer well-being (CWB) research. *Journal of Public Policy & Marketing, 27*(2), 207–212.

Sirgy, M. J. (2010). Toward a quality-of-life theory of leisure travel satisfaction. *Journal of Travel Research, 49*(2), 246–260.

Sirgy, M. J., Cole, D., Kosenko, R., Meadow, H. L., Rahtz, D., Cicic, M., et al. (1995a). Developing a life satisfaction measure based on need hierarchy theory. In M. J. Sirgy & A. C. Samli (Eds.), *New dimensions of marketing/quality-of-life research* (pp. 3–26). Westport, CT: Greenwood Press.

Sirgy, M. J., Cole, D., Kosenko, R., Meadow, H. L., Rahtz, D., Cicic, M., et al. (1995b). Judgment type life satisfaction measure: Further validation. *Social Indicators Research, 34,* 237–259.

Sirgy, M. J., & Cornwell, T. (2001). Further validation of the Sirgy et al.'s measure of community quality of life. *Social Indicators Research, 56,* 125–143.

Sirgy, M. J., & Cornwell, T. (2002). How neighborhood features affect quality of life. *Social Indicators Research, 59,* 79–114.

Sirgy, M. J., Efraty, D., Siegel, P., & Lee, D. (2001). A new measure of quality-of-work life (QWL) based on need satisfaction and spillover theories. *Social Indicators Research, 55*(September), 241–302.

Sirgy, M. J., Grzeskowiak, S., & Rahtz, D. (2007). Quality of college life (QCL) of students: Developing and validating a measure. *Social Indicators Research, 80*(2), 343–360.

Sirgy, M. J., Hansen, D., & Littlefield, J. E. (1994). Does hospital satisfaction affect life satisfaction? *Journal of Macromarketing, 14*(Fall), 36–46.

Sirgy, M. J., & Lee, D. (1996). Setting socially responsible marketing objectives: A quality-of-life approach. *European Journal of Marketing, 30*(2), 20–27.

Sirgy, M. J., & Lee, D. (2006). Macro measures of consumer well-being (CWB): A critical analysis and a research agenda. *Journal of Macromarketing, 26*(1), 27–44.

Sirgy, M. J., & Lee, D. (2008). Well-being marketing: An ethical philosophy for consumer goods firms. *Journal of Business Ethics, 77*(4), 377–403.

Sirgy, M. J., Lee, D., & Bae, J. (2006). Developing a measure of Internet well-being: Nomological (predictive) validation. *Social Indicators Research, 78*(2), 205–249.

Sirgy, M. J., Lee, D., Grzeskowiak, S., Chebat, J., Herrmann, A., Hassan, S., et al. (2008). An extension and further validation of a community-based consumer well-being measure. *Journal of Macromarketing, 28*(3), 243–257.

Sirgy, M. J., Lee, D., Kamra, K., & Tidwell, J. (2007). Developing and validating a measure of consumer well-being in relation to cell phone use. *Applied Research in Quality of Life, 2*(2), 95–124.

Sirgy, M. J., Lee, D., Kamra, K., & Tidwell, J. (2008). What determines perceived quality-of-life impact of mobile phones? A model based on the consumption life cycle. *Applied Research in Quality of Life, 3*(4), 251–268.

Sirgy, M. J., Lee, D., Kosenko, R., Meadow, H. L., Rahtz, D., Cicic, M., et al. (1998). Does television viewership play a role in the perception of quality of life? *Journal of Advertising, 27*(1), 125–142.

Sirgy, M. J., Lee, D., & Kressman, F. (2006). A need-based measure of consumer well being in relation to personal transportation: A nomological validation. *Social Indicators Research, 79*, 337–367.

Sirgy, M. J., Lee, D., Larsen, V., & Wright, N. (1998). Satisfaction with material possessions and general well-being: The role of materialism. *Journal of Consumer Satisfaction/Dissatisfaction and Complaint Behavior, 11*, 103–118.

Sirgy, M. J., Lee, D., & Rahtz, D. (2007). Research in consumer well-being (CWB): An overview of the field and introduction to the special issue. *Journal of Macromarketing, 27*(4), 341–349.

Sirgy, M. J., Mentzer, J. T., Rahtz, D. R., & Meadow, H. L. (1991). Satisfaction with healthcare services consumption and life satisfaction among the elderly. *Journal of Macromarketing, 11*(1), 24–39.

Sirgy, M. J., Michalos, A. C., Ferriss, A. L., Easterlin, R., Patrick, D., & Pavot, W. (2006). The quality-of-life (QOL) research movement: Past, present, and future. *Social Indicators Research, 76*(3), 343–466.

Sirgy, M. J., Rahtz, D., Cicic, M., & Underwood, R. (2000). A method for assessing residents' satisfaction with community-based services: A quality-of-life perspective. *Social Indicators Research, 49*, 279–316.

Sirgy, M. J., Samli, A. C., & Meadow, H. L. (1982). The interface between quality of life and marketing: A theoretical framework. *Journal of Public Policy & Marketing, 1*, 69–84.

Skurnik, I., Yoon, C., Park, D. C., & Schwarz, N. (2005). How warnings become recommendations: Paradoxical effects of warnings on beliefs of older consumers. *Journal of Consumer Research, 31*(March), 713–724.

Sly, D. F., Trapido, E., & Ray, S. (2002). Evidence of the dose effects of an anti-tobacco counteradvertising campaign. *Preventive Medicine, 35*, 511–518.

Spear, L. P. (2000). The adolescent brain and age-related behavioral manifestations. *Neuroscience & Biobehavioral Reviews, 24*(4), 417–463.

Steptoe, A., Edwards, S., Moses, J., & Mathews, A. (1989). The effects of exercise training on mood and perceived coping ability in anxious adults from the general population. *Journal of Psychosomatic Research, 33*(5), 537–547.

Sterner, R., & Mauritz, E. (with Epstein, L., Winston, E., et. al.). (1943). *The Negro's share.* New York: Harper & Brothers.

Sturdivant, F. D. (1968). Better deal for ghetto shoppers. *Harvard Business Review, 46*(2), 130–139.

Text of H.R. 1256: Family Smoking Prevention and Tobacco Control Act. (2009). Retrieved August 16, 2009, from http://www.govtrack.us/congress/billtext.xpd?bill=h111-1256

Thomaselli, R. (2009, June 16). ANA mounts suit to block tobacco legislation. *Advertising Age*, p. 1.

Trimpop, R. M., Kerr, J. H., & Kirkcaldy, B. D. (1999). Comparing personality constructs of risk-taking behavior. *Personality and Individual Differences, 26*(2), 237–254.

U.S. Department of Agriculture. (1968). *Comparison of prices paid for selected foods in chain stores in high and low income areas in six cities.* Washington, DC: U.S. Government Printing Office.

U.S. Department of Health and Human Services. (1994). *Preventing tobacco use among young people: A report of the Surgeon General.* Washington, DC: Author.

Victora, C., Bryce, J., Fontaine, O., & Monasch, R. (2000). Reducing deaths from diarrhoea through oral rehydration therapy. *Bulletin of the World Health Organization, 78*(10), 1246–1255.

Wakefield, M., Ruel, E. E., Chaloupka, F. J., Slater, S., & Kaufman, N. J. (2002). Association of point-of-purchase tobacco advertising and promotions with choice of usual brand among teenage smokers. *Journal of Health Communication, 7*, 113–121.

Wansink, B., van Ittersum, K., & Painter, J. E. (2005). How descriptive food names bias sensory perceptions in restaurants. *Food Quality and Preference, 16*(5), 393–400.

Ward, S. (1972). Children's reactions to commercials. *Journal of Advertising Research, 12*(April), 37–45.

Ward, S., Wackman, D. B., & Wartella, E. (1977). *How children learn to buy.* Beverly Hills, CA: Sage.

Webb, T. L., & Sheeran, P. (2006). Does changing behavioral intentions engender behavior change? A meta-analysis of the experimental evidence. *Psychological Bulletin, 132*(2), 249–268.

Wilkie, W. L., & Moore, E. S. (2003). Scholarly research in marketing: Exploring the "4 eras" of thought development. *Journal of Public Policy & Marketing, 22*(2), 116–146.

Wish, J. R., & Gamble, S. H. (1971). *Marketing and social issues: An action reader.* New York: John Wiley & Sons.

World Bank. (2000). *World development report 2000/2001: Attacking poverty.* New York: Oxford University Press.

Wright, N. D., & Larsen, V. (1993). Materialism and life satisfaction: A meta-analysis. *Journal of Consumer Satisfaction, Dissatisfaction & Complaining Behavior, 6*, 158–165.

Wright, P., Friestad, M., & Boush, D. M. (2005). The development of marketplace persuasion knowledge in children, adolescents, and young adults. *Journal of Public Policy & Marketing, 24*(2), 222–233.

Yoon, C., Cole, C. A., & Lee, M. P. (2009). Consumer decision making and aging: Current knowledge and future directions. *Journal of Consumer Psychology, 19*(1), 2–16.

Zaltman, G. (1965). *Marketing: Contributions from the behavioral sciences.* New York: Harcourt, Brace & World.

# 3

# *Activism Research*
## Designing Transformative Lab and Field Studies

Brian Wansink

Transformational research is often identified by its results. It transforms thinking and behavior, and it can happen without the researcher even intending for it to happen. Academia is ripe with examples of researchers who published a paper that they saw as "no big deal" but that went on to transform a field. Milgram's (1963) work on compliance to authority has influenced the human subject regulations of every institutional review board. The work of Evans, Gonnella, Marcynyszyn, Gentile, and Salpekar (2005) on childhood memories has changed the weight given to long-term recall testimonies in child abuse trials. Pechmann and Shih's (1999) work on tobacco use in films led to inoculation trailers on DVDs that depict smoking. Although research can transform regardless of the original intent of the researcher, most academics seldom have a direct influence on non-academics (Hill, 1995).

But activism research is different because of its intention. It starts with the intention that the final product, if it evolves as expected, will change the behavior of a target population. Activism research translates the qualitative associations of participatory action research (Ozanne & Saatcioglu, 2008) into an approach more understandable for mainstream empirical researchers. Activism research focuses on actionable, solution-oriented variables that will initiate, clarify, or balance a critical debate (Dash, 1999). The results are then aggressively disseminated with the purpose of changing behavior among targeted stakeholders, which could range from changing the way Congress votes on a bill to changing harmful habits of pregnant drug users. Activism research involves being a behavioral engineer (cf. Association of University Technology Managers, 2007, 2008a, 2008b, 2009).

When it comes to changing behavior, most academics are bred to believe we are the first step in a chain of events. That is, we publish our insight, and we assume it might make it into a textbook, which makes it into a classroom, where it influences a student, who eventually influences others (Shimp, 1994). This view may assume too much, may be self-serving, and could lead an insight to die in a journal (Murray & Ozanne, 2009).

This chapter emphasizes how we can think about engineering our research so it has the best potential to transform. It then shows how to enlist outreach partners who can make it transform. The chapter ends with some insights and distinctions that have separated successful from less successful attempts at activism research. These mini–case studies and illustrations are intended to help motivate and guide readers in taking small reinforcing steps toward Transformative Consumer Research.

## FROM ACTION RESEARCH TO ACTIVISM RESEARCH

Before discussing the features of activism research, it is important to understand the tradition from which it came. Shortly after the end of World War II, the social psychologist Kurt Lewin (1951) was credited with coining the term *action research*. His contention was that "research needs to help people solve a problem" (p. 207). Using allusions to social management and social engineering, Lewin contended that research that produces nothing but academic papers and books will not suffice. His ivory tower concerns (as interpreted in Figure 3.1) underscored that there was a tremendous opportunity to influence the world that was being lost because of academic isolation.

Lewin's Action Research

Lewin's (1951) approach involved a spiral of steps, each involving a cycle of "planning, action and fact-finding about the result of the action" (p. 206). The action (and the ideas referred to below) can be what experimentalists might consider hypotheses.

A fundamental premise of action research is that it commences with an interest in the problems of a group, community, or organization. Its purpose is to help people extend their understanding of their situation and resolve problems that confront them (Greenwood & Levin, 1998). As noted by Stringer (2007), action research is (a) democratic (it enables the participation of all people), (b) equitable (it acknowledges people's equality of worth), (c) liberating (it provides freedom from oppressive, debilitating conditions), and (d) life enhancing (it enables the expression of people's full human potential). Interest in action research declined during the 1960s, because it was too strongly associated with radical political activism and had lost the vision that it could also be quantitatively scientific (Ferreyra, 2006; Noffke, 1997). In recent years, action research has begun to regain credibility with qualitative researchers in the areas of community-based participatory action research and as a form of practice oriented to the improvement of education (Coleman & Lumby, 1999; Larkins, 2009).

**Figure 3.1**   One view toward participatory action research and its counterpart. (From Kneebone, S., & Wadsworth, Y., What is participatory action research? *Action Research International*, 1998. With permission.)

This process has been summarized as working through three basic phases (Stringer 2007):

1. *Look*—Build a picture and gather information; while evaluating, define and describe the problem to be investigated and the context in which it is set.
2. *Think*—Analyze and interpret the situation; examine areas of success and any deficiencies, issues, or problems.
3. *Act*—Resolve issues and problems; act to formulate solutions to any problems.

The basic phases are similar to the process mentioned in most marketing research studies (Aaker, Kyman, Day, & Leone, 2009). The more detailed steps generally associated with action research include the following (McNiff, 2002): (1) start with a problem or issue; (2) explore possible solutions (plan); (3) select one solution and act on it; (4) discuss, think, and learn (monitor); (5) evaluate the solution (did it solve the issue or problem?); and (6) repeat until the problem is solved. For researchers, there is an insistence that action research must be collaborative and entail group work (Predota, 2009; Pullman, 2009). Figure 3.2 illustrates action research in the context of improving the motivation of students in a school literacy context.

In contrast to traditional, well-structured approaches to research, action research can often appear poorly structured to experimental researchers (Kidd & Kral, 2005; Martí & Villasante, 2009). There is a general idea of a problem but not always a clear notion of what the key independent variables will be and what their predicted relationship will be to the key outcome variables. Indeed, the initial discovery process is likely to strike traditional researchers as being atheoretical and ad hoc (McNiff, 2008; Small, 1995).

## Action Research Versus Activism Research

Part of the resurging interest in qualitative action research is due to how it repeatedly focuses on embedding the researcher into the community he or she is studying. To underscore the importance to this even further, *participant action research* (Ozanne & Saatcioglu, 2008) has been coined to emphasize how critical the context and the stakeholders are in defining a research question and one's research approach.

Participant action research has long been found in problem-solving contexts that are often investigated in the academic domains of education, counseling, and agriculture (Minkler, 2000), yet it has been much less widely embraced in experimental studies in consumer behavior (Mick, 2006). This may be partly due to its costs, such as its inconvenience, and a misunderstanding of the value it can bring. Yet, it may simply be because many experimental researchers do not understand how to conduct this research. For instance, the most vivid examples of participant action research are political in nature and from either qualitative studies or dated field studies (Stahl & Shdaimah, 2008). To a hard-core experimentalist, some of these examples could be politically off-putting, and their methods might be dismissed as confounded or overdetermined, which would understandably leave many experimental researchers to question how or whether it was even worth making their research action-oriented. Their sharply defined constructs and surgical-like tools might appear to be out of place and even unwelcome.

To some experimentalists, action research can appear to be iterative, largely qualitative, applied research that does not seek to provide a general solution outside the setting in which it is conducted. Yet this is the exact reason why activism research holds such promise for experimentalists who wish to focus on actively having an impact in the day-to-day world as well as in the literature. In contrast to action research, activism research provides a path that experimentalists (as well as qualitative researchers) can use to approach problems deterministically, conceptualize them rigorously, and answer them using the methodologies that have made them experts.

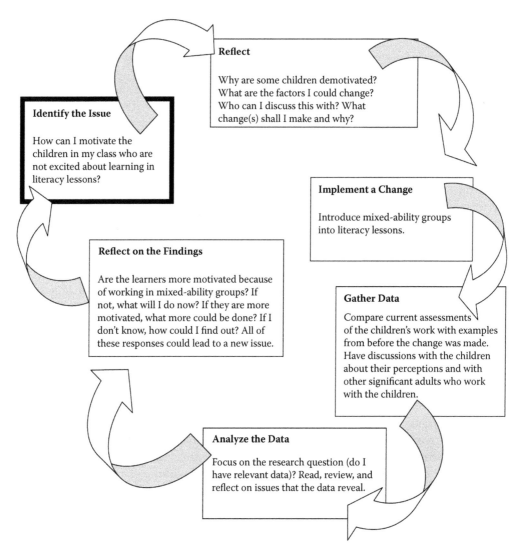

**Figure 3.2**   The qualitative nature of participatory action research in a school literacy context. (Modified from Hurford, D., & Read, A., *The Qualitative Nature of Participatory Action Research in a School Literacy Context*, Qualifications and Curriculum Authority/University of Cumbria Co-Development Initiative, 2003. With permission.)

## FROM ACTIVISM RESEARCH TO TRANSFORMATION

Are experimentalists inflexible and artificial in the way they conceptualize, constrain, and test their theories? Often, they are. This is precisely why their work has the potential to transform. Activism research is a vehicle to do so.

### Operationalizing Activism Research

Intentions are different from results. Whereas transformational research is research that *has* made a difference, activism research is research the authors *intend* to make a difference before they even begin. It starts with the intention that the final product—should it evolve as planned—will change the behavior of a target population. There are four components to activism research: (1) it investigates actionable solutions, (2) it stimulates, clarifies, or balances a debate, (3) it focuses on changing behavior, and (4) it is aggressively disseminated. Figure 3.3 illustrates different examples of these components, which are explained in more detail below.

*Activism Research Investigates Actionable Solutions*

One criticism of action research is that it is too practical and too focused on "Monday morning" problems instead of on contributing to a larger body of theory or understanding. This criticism is understandable. Many doctoral programs in the social sciences train scholars to think in terms of broad, generalizable constructs (e.g., self-efficacy, the need for cognition) and distinctions (e.g., individualistic vs. collectivistic, prevention-focused vs. promotion-focused). This leaves scholars well trained to conceptualize generalizable research problems and write rigorous, highly cited papers. Yet, the blessing of this training is also its curse.

Because the constructs and theories we often strive to develop are general, they are often *too* general to be well suited to activism research. This extends Merton's (1968) notion of middle-range theories. For example, it is less actionable to think in terms of a "prevention-focused" segment than to think in terms of cancer survivors or diabetics. It is less actionable to think in terms of a collectivist population than to think of non–English-speaking immigrants struggling to assimilate. Good activism research is conceptually rigorous, but it operationalizes constructs in actionable, targetable, solution-oriented ways (cf. Lynch, Netemeyer, Spiller, & Zammit, 2010).

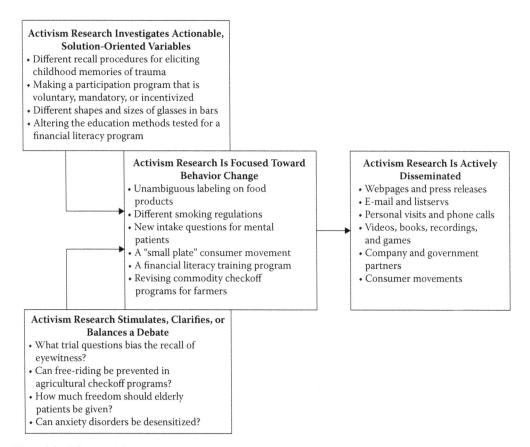

**Figure 3.3**  A framework for activism research.

### Activism Research Stimulates, Clarifies, or Balances a Debate

Whereas action research solves problems that might be specific to one situation, activism research intends to solve problems that are more generalizable in theory or in the evidence they provide. One way this can be done is to aim at a solution that attempts to solve the Monday morning problems in a way that initiates, clarifies, or balances a larger debate. Indeed, most social, heath, and political issues involve debates between differing positions (e.g., prochoice vs. right to life) or about resource allocations (such as how much time, money, or energy should be spent on welfare, the homeless, or environmental cleanup; see Keller & Lusardi, Chapter 21 of this volume; Prinz, Chapter 28 of this volume). Such debates often have assumptions or overlooked issues that can be introduced, proven, clarified, or made more vivid through research. In other cases, activism research can slow down a bandwagon effect. For instance, Young and Nestle's (2002) work slowed down the "personal responsibility" bandwagon of obesity by showing that the industry trend of supersizing portions has made it increasingly easy for consumers to overeat.

Yet, actionable solutions can also lead to useful theories. Consider the gap in the budgeting and spending literature as to whether people know how much they are spending as they shop. This gap has ramifications for budgeting and spending theories; activism research can develop a theory for this gap by identifying key variables, how they are related, who is most affected, and so on (van Ittersum, Pennings, & Wansink, 2010).

### Activism Research Focuses on Changing Behavior

"It would be interesting to know …" is perhaps the most overused prefacing comment made in research seminars. Most people believe they do interesting research, because it is a subject they are curious about or a puzzle they find challenging enough to solve and publish. Activism research begins with "It would be *useful* to know …." Its focus is on how the research will eventually be used to change behavior, which could lead to the passing of a state law on health care, or increased participation in an employer savings plan. Other targeted behaviors could include decreases in AIDS infections, malnutrition, smoking, burglaries, alcoholism, car accidents, recidivism, or loan defaults (Fishbein & Middlestadt, Chapter 18 of this volume; Viswanathan, Chapter 5 of this volume).

A remarkable example of this is the work of the development economist Esther Duflo, who won the 2010 John Bates Clark Medal. To examine different solutions for reducing poverty around the world, she uses field experiments employing randomized trials to examine how microfinance, education, economic assistance, and pricing influence wealth development and equality. Because another of her transforming notions is to teach and empower village leaders to conduct their own experiments, hundreds of randomized trials are being conducted at any given time.

### Activism Research Is Aggressively Disseminated

The "publish it and they will come" approach works better in theory than in practice. In a world of 140-character electronic messages, it is unlikely that a journal article will directly impact decision makers whose behavior we wish to change. Different research has different gatekeepers and different channels. This might mean presenting at companies and conventions, starting a blog and a website, sending a direct-mail campaign to legislators, or visiting with congressional staffers. These efforts can be either top-down or bottom-up. When the research suggesting a tax on sugared beverages failed to get traction on the national level, some researchers began campaigning state governments, in order to develop a state-level proof of concept.

It has often been stated that there is nothing more practical than a great theory. If a researcher develops a theory that is robust, versatile, and compelling, this may be true. Unfortunately, many of our theories are "hothouse" theories. Like hothouse flowers that can only live and grow under

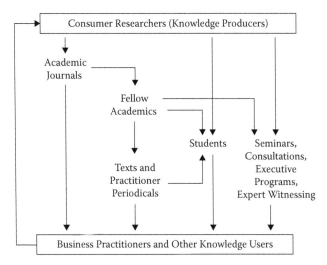

**Figure 3.4** A 1994 view of how academic research passively trickles down to users. (From Shimp, T., Presidential address: Academic Appalachia and the discipline of consumer research. In D. R. John & C. Allen (Eds.), *Advances in Consumer Research* (Vol. 21, pp. 1–7), Association for Consumer Research, Provo, UT, 1994. With permission.)

carefully controlled conditions (such as the lighting, temperature, and humidity of a greenhouse), the same is true with many of our theories. That is, we often test them with homogeneous undergraduates in an artificial lab context, where we ask them about an artificial scenario, and their decision or behavior involves circling a number on a questionnaire or pressing a key on a keyboard. When it comes to having a practical impact, it is difficult to see how many of these hothouse theories could guide a person to confidently make the leap from theory to practice. Activism research starts off with the end—changing behavior—in mind. The researcher may not know exactly what behavior should change in what way when the project begins, but the research starts with an additional purpose than simply being academically interesting.

Moving From Passive to Active Research

Terry Shimp's (1994) presidential address for the Association for Consumer Research focused on how research influences society. His framework (see Figure 3.4) illustrated that research is produced and disseminated through consulting, teaching, and textbooks. In this manner, research findings—if they are useful—will eventually find their way into influencing the lives of others.

Although this was a bold thought in 1994, its passive approach did not move our research impact far enough, fast enough. At the time, however, Shimp's address was well received. It gave researchers two reassurances that they wanted to believe: (1) our research findings will eventually be recognized and have a wide-ranging impact we cannot begin to imagine, and (2) we do not have to do anything for this to happen. We are not experiencing an evolution.

In 1994, our academic community believed that it was enough for our thoughts to move from articles to books to students to practice. That was a start, but we have now evolved to realize that we can have a bigger and more immediate impact (Mick, 2006). Activism research argues for a more intentional, more direct, more aggressive path to transformation.

## DESIGNING RESEARCH TO TRANSFORM

What makes research transformative is how it is used. Yet we cannot always predict how research is going to be used when we start a project. At that point, we do not even know what results to expect. How, then, do we conduct research that is intended to transform? Consider these five steps: (1) visualize transformation; (2) ask the right question; (3) answer the right question with a clear, practical answer; (4) collect cool data in the right context; and (5) disseminate the findings to the right actors.

### Visualize Transformation

If transforming behavior is an end goal, it is important to be able to take the time to visualize how this *might* happen, even if we do not yet know the results. Three questions can be useful in helping accomplish this:

1. What very specific person should use these results (e.g., drug abuse counselors at colleges, directors or trainers at homeless shelters, parents of preschool children)?
2. What might be their one-sentence takeaway of this research?
3. What would make this research most memorable, relevant, worthy of word-of-mouth transmission, and compelling to this person?

To make this more clear, consider the following example (Parmar, 2007). Suppose researchers have a working hypothesis that people pour more liquid into short, wide glasses than tall, narrow glasses of the same volume (see Wansink & van Ittersum, 2003). Before conducting that research, the researchers might answer these abbreviated questions in the following way:

1. Who should use this? Procurement (purchasing) officers for national casual dining restaurant chains such as T.G.I. Friday's, Olive Garden, and Chili's would be interested in the research results.
2. What is their one-sentence takeaway? "We can save 30% in alcohol costs by switching to highball glasses instead of tumblers."
3. What would make this compelling? Real bartenders in real bars in a real city (e.g., Philadelphia), who pour the four most commonly poured drinks into the most common glass sizes.

Visualizing possible answers to these three questions—even though the results of the study are not yet known—will direct the research design to be most potentially impactful. The answers can suggest a new context, a different population, or overlooked independent variables (see also McDonagh, Dobscha, & Prothero, Chapter 13 of this volume; Soman, Cheema, & Chan, Chapter 20 of this volume). Starting off with an intention to eventually transform behavior is the first step in activism research, because it helps a researcher shape the right research question.

### Ask the Right Question

In casual conversations with social scientists over the years, there appear to be three common sources they use to develop their research questions: the literature, personal experiences, and immersion and engagement within a consumer context. Basing one's research question on the literature is perhaps most common (Sheth & Sisodia, 2005), because it aligns with doctoral training. We read the literature looking for gaps and potential mediators and moderators that might apply to well-cited findings. These well-cited findings provide an great starting point for the literature, theory, and methods needed to answer this new question.

Other researchers use their own personal experiences to generate their research questions (see Levy, 1996). This has led them to investigate questions such as those related to impulsiveness, product cults, overconsumption, and postpurchase regret. In some cases, answering the question is more of a personal matter to the researcher than it is a general issue relevant to others. Whereas the resulting answers can be interesting and relevant to others, that was not necessarily the intent when initially framing the question. Too often, the resulting answers have a degree of academic interest, but they can be too stylized, not intended to change behavior, or not disseminated to any particular stakeholder other than a journal.

The third approach to developing research questions involves immersion and engagement within a consumer context (Whyte, 1991). Being immersed in the consumer context enables these researchers to learn directly from people as to what problems are most troubling to them. Consumer contexts can include AIDS care facilities, homeless shelters, grocery stores, blood banks, bars, and nursing homes. It is in these contexts and with this knowledge that the appropriate research question can emerge, be appropriately framed, and eventually be answered.

For instance, consider the question of how people track their grocery bill as they shop (this is an ongoing concern for the one sixth of Americans who live paycheck to paycheck). This is an abstract, academic question for those of us who are not on a budget or do not do the shopping for our families. Because of a research project we were conducting in this area, it was important to understand how families on food budgets shopped beyond what they say in focus groups or what we observed in stores. To better grasp their struggle, I persuaded my five-person family to limit ourselves to $458/month in food to mirror the food stamp benefits that the federal government allocates to a family of four with one minimum wage ($7.25/hour) earner. For the 30 days of June, I did all the grocery shopping and cooking (instead of my wife), and we saved all food receipts, including those for school lunches, fast food, and soft drinks ($389.52 total). Some of the resulting insights led to revised survey questions, a reorganized paper, and a repositioning of the findings to be more useful for dollar-counting family shoppers (van Ittersum, Pennings, & Wansink, 2010).

The additional power of questions borne from immersion in these contexts is that their solution may be more relevant and actionable. Having spent time with consumers also enables researchers to determine which of the potential independent variables (such as illustrated in Figure 3.3) will be the ones most practical and actionable to study. This immersion also gives a researcher the language necessary to describe the problem and the interventions in a way that is most sensible. In this manner, what might otherwise be referred to as a *restricted debit card* in a school lunch study turns into an *anything but dessert card*, and a *large-sized dosage applicator* in a liquid medicine study becomes a *tablespoon* (Wansink & van Ittersum, 2010).

An analogue in the business-to-business context of marketing is that of customer visits (McQuarrie, 1993), which are an important business-to-business market research technique involving on-site team visitations. In one of the most basic forms of a customer visit, managers and engineers leave their offices and travel to the customer's place of business. They interview buyers and users and tour the work site. In a program of customer visits, a dozen or more visits are planned and conducted systematically. There are four primary advantages to customer visits (McQuarrie, 1993):

1. They generate better information on what customers really want.
2. They develop a common vision, shared across the organization, on what customers expect.
3. They build closer relations with customers.
4. They generate greater commitment by all functional areas to satisfying customer needs.

There are additional benefits to immersion and engagement within the context. First, the research question is more likely to address a real problem suggested by experience than an academic problem suggested by the literature. Second, the independent variables being examined are most likely to be actionable and relevant. Third, the way in which the research is carried out is more likely to be realistic. Fourth, the language used in communicating the research will be relevant and actionable.

In a commentary in the *Journal of Consumer Research*, Max Bazerman (2001) criticized consumer behavior researchers for focusing on issues that are small problems—or no problems at all—for consumers. He contended that the big questions that influence consumer welfare, such as saving, budgeting, investing, and medical decision making, are dwarfed in our literature in favor of research focusing on small, inconsequential decisions, preference formations, and similarly minor behaviors. His challenge was to focus on the real problems that are most bewildering to real people. He provided two suggestions in deciding the topics that could most help change lives: (1) determine what is most important and challenging to consumers, and (2) recognize that these decisions are seldom made in isolation. Decisions are made with input from salespeople, agents, spouses, and friends. Research and the advice that follow need to reflect these realities.

Yet, the professional priority for a researcher is that the research must be publishable. A piece of research that solves a real problem but cannot be published in an esteemed journal may be less impactful than it would be otherwise. Bazerman suggested that after the problem is identified, researchers should apply existing research models and extend the literature by identifying biases unique to or exacerbated by the consumer context. The problem-solving should not occur in a vacuum, but instead it should be associated with existing models and theories that can be modified by the realities of the situation.

### Answer the Right Question With a Clear, Practical Answer

Past writings on participatory action research (Ozanne & Saatcioglu, 2008) have focused on how research needs to be actionable and relevant. For this to be so, research should be born from engagement with the target audience. It should involve real problems that suggest research questions with potentially clear, actionable solutions.

Each fall at Cornell, I teach an interdisciplinary PhD course called "Advanced Consumer Research." One of the last assignments for the course is titled "Crafting a Classic Paper." Each student identifies a professor whose research he or she admires and interviews that professor about the paper he or she wrote that had the most transformative impact outside of academia. The professor is also asked to speculate why it had impact and what made it different from the favorite paper he or she wrote that was pretty much ignored. These papers come from a wide range of fields, including consumer research, food science, sociology, medicine, anthropology, community nutrition, education, sociology, psychology, and industrial and labor relations. Among these papers, there were a surprising number of consistencies that are instructive to activism research.

Some of these consistencies are uncontrollable, like winning an award or being a lead article in a journal. However, three of the similarities were controllable: (1) the researchers answered the right question with a simple, clear, and practical answer; (2) they collected data in the right context; and (3) about half of them published their paper in a journal in which they typically did not publish. The first two similarities are consistent with Ozanne and Saatcioglu's (2008) emphasis on participation. In these cases, participation occurred in both framing the right question and collecting the right data. Without participation, the question could have been theoretically relevant but practically irrelevant. Without participation, the data collection could have been tightly controlled (e.g., in a lab, on a computer) but unconvincing.

Designing potentially transformative research entails asking the right question, which may not be the one our training would suggest. Whereas academic journals are interested in interactions and answering "why," potentially transformative questions may be more focused on main effects and answering "whether" or "how." There are ways to carefully accommodate both.

Most of these transforming papers investigated important conceptual issues, but they did so with a practical end in sight (see Table 3.1 for examples). The researchers conceptualized their constructs in a way that suggested simple changes that could be made. In many cases, the questions that were answered were not ones at the center of an existing debate. They were often new questions that had not been earlier identified, and they underscored a new "main effect" that had not been previously considered. Much of the world is driven by main effects: Donating time or money makes people feel better, resolving conflict increases productivity, empowering a disadvantaged person increases the likelihood of employment, positive after-school role models reduce gang activity, and so on.

While the world cares about main effects, academics often focus on interactions, mediation, or counterintuitive findings that are idiosyncratic to a narrow set of circumstances. In tackling the question of after-school role models and gang activity, we might focus on psychological factors, such as how the need for cognition or individualism might moderate this relationship (instead of trying to identify easily segmentable demographic variables). Or, we might focus on factors that might mediate effectiveness, such as locus of control and self-efficacy.

In the end, we may have a publishable article, but our focus on interactions or mediations could very easily obscure the real impact that a clear, compelling finding could have otherwise have had

**Table 3.1**    Illustrations of Classic Transformative Studies

| Critical Question | The Answer | Key Variables | Context (C) and Target (T) | Impact |
|---|---|---|---|---|
| What questions bias or lead eyewitnesses in jury trials?[a] | Questions that directly asked about or indirectly implied the presence of a nonexistent object led to erroneous recall one week later. | • The recalled existence of nonexistent objects<br>• The presence or absence of cued questions directly or indirectly asking about the nonexistent objects | • C: Subjects shown films of traffic accidents and crimes, then questioned a week later<br>• T: Attorneys and judges | • Led to revised questioning protocols of witnesses<br>• Has been used by therapists to more accurately elicit repressed memories of child abuse |
| How can we improve the happiness of nursing home patients?[b] | Giving people the perception of increased responsibility increases happiness, involvement, and activity level. | • Choices made by you or us<br>• Ratings of happiness and involvement | • C: Patients in an upscale nursing home<br>• T: Nursing home administrators and staff | • The death rate in the increased-responsibility group half as high over the next 18 months<br>• Altered the training of nursing home staff |
| How can neuroses be desensitized?[c] | Reducing phobias can be accomplished by putting patients in relaxed states and describing situations involving the phobia, and measuring their responses on a regular basis. | • No exposure to the actual phobia necessary in treatment<br>• Relaxation before describing the scenarios critical | • C: Actual patients with debilitating phobias (e.g., of heights, public speaking, animals, small places)<br>• T: Psychologists and therapists | • Now considered the treatment of choice for anxiety disorders |

[a] From "Leading Questions and the Eyewitness Report," by E. F. Loftus, 1975, *Cognitive Psychology, 7*, pp. 560–572.
[b] From "The Effects of Choice and Enhanced Personal Responsiblity for the Aged: A Field Experiment in an Institutional Setting," by E. J. Langer and J. Rodin, 1976, *Journal of Personality and Social Psychology, 34*, pp. 191–198.
[c] From "The Systematic Desensitization Treatment of Neuroses," by J. Wolpe, 1961, *Journal of Nervous and Mental Disease, 132*, pp. 180–203.

on the world of counseling and after-school programming. As was once said by the distinguished Cambridge economist W. Brian Reddaway, "Better to be rough and relevant than to be precise and irrelevant" (Singh, 2009, p. 314). As a result, the powerful focus that positive after-school role models could have on reducing gang activity could be lost (see also Firat, 2001).

Our focus on these subtleties—instead of focusing on the research question—might often come at the expense of discovering and underscoring the main effect that could make a transformational difference. It is not uncommon for researchers to find the narrow context in which a phenomenon does not work and then focus on that context. Yet, not starting with the right context can lead us down the road to irrelevance. A common problem with academics is not that we miss seeing the forest because of the trees. We miss seeing the trees because we are focused on the bark. Becoming immersed in the context not only helps us move to a more immediately relevant question but also provides a context for collecting compelling data.

### Collect Cool Data in the Right Context

The crucial characteristic of the classic papers the students examined involved the context of data collection or the method of analysis. One study involved analyzing the wage discrepancies between men and women longitudinally instead of cross-sectionally. The analyses showed different results and were used to help equalize wages. In another instance, labor union activity was analyzed in the context of alcohol abuse. The results showed a much greater reliance on alcohol in some unions than others, and it altered the way health care negotiations were approached (Sonnenstuhl, 1997).

The "right" data are contextually rich. They are compelling and difficult to dismiss as irrelevant. These are exactly the type of data that many researchers do not want to collect. Most highly productive social scientists, especially psychologists, are experts at undergraduate lab studies, computer lab studies, complex modeling exercises, or short-term trials involving begrudging sophomores who need the extra credit (Sears, 1986). When deciding to become academics, it was probably not so they could negotiate and conduct studies in restaurants, soup kitchens, AIDS care facilities, homeless shelters, grocery stores, movie theaters, blood banks, bars, and nursing homes. Yet, this is where the right contextually rich, or "cool," data hide. They are data from real people in real situations who are being observed, coded, measured, and dispassionately analyzed and reported.

Contextually rich data are difficult to collect. It can be difficult to get institutional review board approval to collect the data. It can be logistically complicated to staff and set up the studies, debrief participants, and analyze data that are disordered, incomplete, or miscoded because of the chaos that surrounded the study. Yet, contextually rich data can capture imaginations. Cool results from cool data can suddenly make science relevant to unsuspecting groups of people (Wansink, 2006), and they can almost always be published, eventually.

Yet, even the right question answered in a practical way with data from the right context may not seem important when being read by a gatekeeping reviewer. It becomes our responsibility to be starkly clear about the specific problem, why it is a problem, for whom it is a problem, and the size of the problem. This can be calculated in dollars spent, number of people influenced, volume consumed, hours spent, time lost, or so forth.

### Disseminate Your Findings to the Right Actors

Who makes research transformational? Academics read it and build on the theory or findings, but they are rarely the ones who act on it and make it transformational. The people who make it transformational are the actors to whom it is directed. They are the drug abuse counselors at colleges, the directors or trainers at homeless shelters, the parents with preschool children, the people receiving federal food assistance, and so on.

Here is the good news: If we do the previous four steps right (visualize transformation, ask the right question, clearly answer it, and collect cool, contextual data), the story writes itself. The problem and our recommended solution will quickly be seen as relevant, interesting, and useful. Yet, simply getting widespread exposure for a finding—however interesting—may not be what makes it transformable. Who was on the cover of *Time* magazine last week? Most of us never saw it, and the rest of us cannot remember who it was. Media exposure is surprisingly ephemeral.

Blasting all consumers with our findings is not likely to result in transformation. As we become more focused, however, we can better aim our findings at the people who can have the biggest referred impact (see also Mick, Pettigrew, Pechmann, & Ozanne, Chapter 1 of this volume). A study was mentioned earlier that showed people pouring more alcohol into wider glasses than narrower glasses. These findings could be targeted at a number of users: people who drink mixed alcoholic beverages and do not want to overimbibe, alcohol abuse counselors, bar owners, or the corporate procurement officers of casual dining restaurant chains, such as T.G.I. Friday's, Olive Garden, and Chili's. It was believed that the biggest potential impact would be in targeting the research design and findings toward the procurement officers of these national chains. They would be clearly financially motivated to change, they could be easily pinpointed, and they could be personally visited and potentially persuaded. Interestingly, perhaps the most effective way to disseminate findings to the right actors is also the most ignored. Nothing focuses the dissemination of findings better than a sponsoring partner.

## THE POWER OF PARTNERS

Whereas "too many cooks spoil the broth," it is also said that "many hands make light work." In academia, as in other industrialized Western cultures, individualism is often admired more than partnerships. Despite this bias, the right partner can be the engine that funds, facilitates, implements, or helps disseminate our ideas and findings.

### No Programs Without Partners

Much of academic life is solitary. We learn to collect our own data, do our own debriefings, run our own analysis, write our own papers, and suffer alone from its initial rejection. Seeking an external partner is a strange, seemingly unnecessary notion for most scholars. The value of such a partnership is just not obvious. However, trying to disseminate research that has potentially transforming insights almost always necessitates a partner. These partners can be a granting agency, the government, companies, nonprofit groups, or consumers.

Let us consider four types of partners: funding, facilitating, implementation, and dissemination. These involve four different roles that partners can take, and they can often overlap. Funding partners provide or help underwrite a project or to support a researcher with a new idea. They can include government agencies (e.g., National Institutes of Health), private foundations (e.g., Russell Sage Foundation, Pew Charitable Trust), companies, family trust funds, and individual donors. Facilitating partners aid the research process by helping collect data or providing data. Implementation partners help make the intervention work in its target population. Dissemination partners are information multipliers that help make sure the research is used in a way that changes behavior.

Having to sell a potential partner on the idea of joining with you on a project has its benefits. It sharpens one's focus and vision of the project, it sharpens the anticipated end results, and it sharpens the benefits of the research itself. If we cannot find a partner that is equally passionate about our project, it may simply be because the project lacks the correct focus and precision. Yet, it could also be because no one really cares about the problem we are trying to solve. In either case, it would be good to know where a project stands. The results could lead to a sharpened focus and value, or it could lead a researcher to move on to another more fruitful plan.

## Two Ends of the Partnership Continuum

From the 1960s through today, academics have enjoyed a rich, comfortable life. For the most part, academics have been expected to be decent teachers, decent department citizens, and regular publishers in decent journals. Other than that, they could follow their own idiosyncratic research muse in whatever way they wanted. In the past 50 years, there has been a wide continuum along which two extremes have emerged: the solo scholar versus "Professor, Inc." The solo scholar often sees research topics as puzzles to elegantly solve and cleverly position for publication. His or her office is remote, and the door is closed. With the exception of an occasional doctoral student, interactions with outside research influences are minimal. The solo scholar's research problems are insulated from the real problems of others. Solo scholars often solve academic puzzles in ways that can be elegant and clever to colleagues but inaccessible and irrelevant to anyone else.

At the other extreme is Professor, Inc. This person surrounds him- or herself with a fully equipped squad of students and missionary-zealed staff who view academic journal articles as only one objective of their well-focused mission. Unfortunately, this multidimensional strategy—and their zeal—makes them an easy target for collegiate criticism. One example is the late University of Wisconsin–trained history professor Stephen Ambrose, who focused on putting a face on the Greatest Generation (World War II veterans) and honoring them in their last years. In addition to writing classic articles, his team at the University of New Orleans produced books (e.g., *Citizen Soldiers* [1987], *The Wild Blue* [2001], *Pegasus Bridge* [1985]), an HBO miniseries (*Band of Brothers* [Spielberg, Hanks, Smith, Jendresen, & Ambrose, 2001]), European and Pacific battlefield tours, and a $425 million World War II museum in New Orleans. These efforts contributed to critics describing him as a "sloppy researcher," "fallen academic," and "greedy popularizer" ("Ambrose, Inc.," 2004, pp. 1–2). If activism research involves changing behavior, it is notable when a history professor succeeds at it so well. Besides helping raise $425 million for a museum, Ambrose's work stimulated living history exhibits at other museums, recollection recordings at libraries, the publishing of nearly forgotten memoirs, and countless rekindled relationships with a misunderstood or underappreciated parent (Goldstein, 2002).

Academia is evolving, and it is unclear whether the future of academia will tilt more toward one extreme than the other. Professor, Inc. represents one type of research activist, and certainly one with legitimate faults. Indeed, many colleagues did find numerous faults with Ambrose, but it is difficult to fault his effectiveness in making the difference he sought. One of the most notable lessons was how he accomplished this, namely, by finding partners for each of his projects. These partners included high-profile directors (Steven Spielberg and Tom Hanks), politicians (Bob Dole and George McGovern), companies (Chrysler and IBM), and governments (Louisiana and New Orleans).

## Forming Partnerships With Policy Makers

More than 30 years ago, Dyer and Shimp (1977) outlined three suggestions for how to make research more impactful. Their suggestions could not be more relevant to Transformative Consumer Research.

### 1. Person-to-Person Contact Is Critical

In any research investigation, it is fundamentally important to interact with the user at the problem formulation and research design stages. This personal contact is even more important in the public policy area. Many successful activism researchers tailor their studies to the needs of the consumer or other decision makers. This requires the research to have a forward and other orientation.

The perfect research study has little or no value unless the individual sees its value and its fit with their needs (cf. Wilkie & Gardner, 1974).

### 2. Timing Is Critical

Much of the research done to date on public policy issues, for example, has been done *after* the case has been settled or the policy or program set in motion. It provides less of a diagnosis and prescription than it does an autopsy. Most research will have a much greater impact if it is conducted before the policy maker or decision maker is committed to a position. One source of delay for research is the journal process. Many scholars are hesitant to show their results and do not begin implementing their findings until their papers are published. In many ways, this renders the research much less relevant and potentially less transformational. There are numerous examples of researchers who have conducted research and published their findings as a white paper or on the Internet long before it was eventually submitted for publication. In this way, the results could have an immediate impact.

### 3. Communicating Before and After the Project Begins

Many government agencies, such as the U.S. Department of Agriculture (USDA), Federal Trade Commission, and Food and Drug Administration, have public comment periods when they welcome insights and comments. Dyer and Shimp (1977) recommended a strategy of "priming the pump" to generate policy maker attention to research findings. Sending copies of study results to concerned industry offices, writing press releases, and contacting consumer organizations can be critical. The wider the dissemination of study results, the more assured a researcher would be of his or her study's consideration by policy makers or other relevant target groups (Mick, 2004).

Partnerships can take many forms with many different stakeholders. Some partnerships can be made in defining the right question and collecting the right data. Another set of partnerships can be useful in helping disseminate the data. As an example, the USDA sponsored a study to examine how payment systems, such as using debit cards, influenced the types of foods high school students purchased. It showed that debit cards led students to eat less of the healthy foods and more of the less healthy foods. It also showed that restricting what debit cards could be used for (healthier foods) and still allowing other foods to be purchased with cash provided students a win-win result for both the nutrition of students and the profitability of the lunchroom (Wansink, Just, & Payne, 2011). While the relevant researchers and policy makers at the USDA were partners in initiating and eventually disseminating the research findings, five different sets of high school principals, food service directors, meal staff, and students were partners in helping determine the right questions to ask and collecting the right field data.

## ACTIVISM ADVICE FOR THE UNTENURED AND TENURED

A notable academic once told me, "We're not in this business to write 10 papers; we're in it to write 100." If we break this down over a 40-year career, publishing two and a half papers a year sounds like it should be doable. Then, why does it happen so seldom?

### Untenured Faculty: Keep the Fire Burning

If one starts with a burning desire to conduct activism research as a PhD student, the biggest danger to "waiting until I have tenure" is that the fire will burn out before anything happens. Activism research can be difficult to publish in the preeminent journals. Elite top-10 universities want to see five to seven top publications by tenure time, and it would be nearly impossible for them to all be activism research (Mari, 2008). In fact, the vast majority of PhDs will never publish in these journals, and most of the rest will do so only once (Keith, Layne, Babchuk, & Johnson, 2002).

Most of us do not start out as professors at Yale, Stanford, or the University of Chicago. But we do start out at a school where we have the choice to pursue activism research if we wish. The overall goal in our early years is to do the research that keeps our spark alive and the fire burning in our belly. Here are some thoughts on how to manage this.

### Choose Research You'll Do When It's Dark Outside

Although this sounds metaphorical, it is literal. A brilliantly productive academic once told me, "Everything I ever did that has made the difference in my life, I did while other people were sleeping." Assuming he was not referring to his lectures, this is a testament to believing that your research is so important that it is worth working on at 11:00 p.m. or at 6:00 a.m. For some, transformative research in a context that is close to them can inspire this "working when it's dark" mentality more than they would be inspired by writing an article for which they had no passion.

### Answer the Question, Then Find the Journal

If a person has an important question and answers it compellingly, the paper will find a great home. Too often, however, scholars first target a journal (e.g., "Let's write a paper for the *Journal of Personality and Social Psychology*"), *then* start the research process. This can unnaturally constrain and bias the research question, context, and independent variables in a way that makes them irrelevant for practically focused decision makers. Starting with and answering the right question can give the right insight, even if you have to do an add-on study to make it worthy for that preeminent journal after the paper is otherwise finished.

### Team Up With a Senior Scholar

If this senior scholar is academically productive, he or she can greatly increase the likelihood that your work together will get into a respected journal. When approaching this person, you need to clearly demonstrate what your value would be to the project and their overprogrammed schedule. Being prepared to do 80% of the legwork is a good start. Additionally, the right person can be a valuable confidant and advocate as you grow and move through the field.

### Think of a Portfolio of Target Journals

Write and submit to a variety of journals where you think your ideas will have the biggest impact. Even if these journals are not all preeminent journals, this strategy has three advantages: (1) it extends your ideas to multiple audiences; (2) the publications still count toward tenure, except at the most elite institutions; and (3) it keeps you in the game, keeps you motivated, and sharpens your skills as a researcher. (My first 11 submissions to preeminent journals were rejected, but the skills I developed by publishing these articles in specialty journals enabled some of the next submissions to get in). Without some early publication victories, even at specialty journals, it is easy to become discouraged and let the fire die out.

### Leverage the Hidden Synergies of Activism Research

Grant money, interdisciplinary collaboration, media exposure, and outreach (especially at land-grant schools) are all much easier to obtain for a person doing activism research. They help build your research capacity and broaden its impact. The hurdle of tenure is measured with a rubber ruler. This is an unspoken secret at many schools. While the quality and quantity of publications matters, the relative measure of quality and quantity can be stretched up for some people and scrunched down for others. Grant money, interdisciplinary collaboration, media exposure, and outreach can scrunch down the ruler to measure the tenure hurdle as high enough.

*Research What You Want, and the Job Will Follow*

Many of us professors are academic migrant workers. We start at one school, and we keep moving until we find a school where the match is a synergistic fit. Finding the right fit has to do with a lot of obvious factors, but a very important one for an activism researcher is being at a place that appreciates our work and offers the promise of synergy. If our activism research interests stay closeted, it is doubtful that we will ever find that ideal department or that it will find us.

Another danger to "waiting until I have tenure" before we start activism research is that the fire in our bellies will burn out. After our dissertation and our "sure bet" articles are rejected, some of us will begin to distance ourselves from the "research game," calling it irrelevant and an "insider's club." We will invest more in the immediate returns of teaching or consulting. After one or two moves, we will settle into a comfortable school, continuing to work on earlier interests and unpublished data sets. Comfortable as it may be, it is far removed from the impassioned Indiana Jones-like research drama we once imagined our professor life would be.

Tenured Faculty: Finding a New Spark

By the time a professor has tenure at a research university, he or she has become successful at collecting data, managing research assistants, and publishing certain types of research (Miller, 1969; Zimbardo, 2004). Yet, despite one's successful publication record, such a person would not be reading this chapter or this book if they were not considering a way to expand their impact. The good news is that moving toward activism research may not require an overhaul of one's methodological skills or having to learn an unrelated set of theories. However, it may require "tooling up" on the perplexing questions in an applied context and understanding what can or cannot be realistically done by the consumers or decision makers in that context. Here is how that could be done.

*Broaden Your View of "Acceptable" Journals*

Focusing only on preeminent journals can prevent one from trying to answer the most critical questions in a specific context. Also, a portfolio of articles in different types of journals broadens the academic market for your ideas. Recall that when we asked academics about their most transformative impact outside of academia (i.e., "crafting the classic paper"), about half claimed it was published in a journal in which they had not previously published.

*Attend Unfamiliar Conferences*

Although reading unfamiliar journals is valuable, going to unfamiliar conferences in your applied context area is even more useful. These conferences are forums for a wider range of topics and questions that are more relevant to the context and the decision makers in the field. Although you will be the unknown person at the party, it can be liberating not to attend the same types of conference sessions you usually would.

*Find Nonacademic Partners*

Partners can facilitate or disseminate the research on the right question in the right context (Pechmann & Knight, 2002). In some cases, a senior professor can add legitimacy and inspiration that go beyond the mutual project of interest.

*Don't Delegate the Fieldwork*

Part of the power of activism research is being embedded in a context that makes the research more relevant and compelling. A tendency of senior professors is to ask research assistants to do the fieldwork, interviews, and data collection and be the main contact person with the research partners. This often results in noisy data and seldom (if ever) results in valuable serendipitous insights. Even the best trained graduate students and research assistants are inexperienced with making real-time decisions about adjustments in an experimental method, for example. Their judgment calls about an unexpected debriefing glitch, a broken piece of equipment, or an unruly participant will seldom be the judgment call you would have made. Furthermore, their hypothesis-driven mission can lead to a tunnel vision that prevents them from seeing an unanticipated—but far more interesting—pattern of results that a more experienced researcher might recognize.

Moving outside the circle of influence that made one successful is difficult for most academics. With a new journal or a new partner, it means building our credibility from scratch. With new conferences, it is even more difficult. It is humbling to see how little influence most of us have outside our field. Yet, this may also indicate how little we have to lose by moving toward activism research.

## CONCLUSION: "WHAT'S YOUR BIGGEST REGRET?"

In 2002, while a marketing professor at the University of Illinois at Urbana-Champaign, I was asked to be one of two faculty speakers at the annual spring meeting of the university's Business Advisory Committee. What excited me most was the other faculty speaker, one of the most notable economists at the university. He occupied a rare niche at the intersection of economics, real estate, finance, and law. He was widely published and widely influential, and people—even his economist colleagues—often spoke of him in awe. He had won numerous awards, and the rumor was that he was one of the most highly paid faculty in the business school. This year was his retirement year, and his speech would perhaps be his "last waltz" in front of a group like this. His talk was brilliant, and we got to know each other throughout the day and at the closing reception.

On the rainy 4-hour drive home, we sat next to each other in the back of the plush chartered bus. I asked him which of his many accomplishments he was most proud of and which had the most impact. At one point, however, I also asked a question that was not met with the same warmth and candor. I asked, "In light of all of the remarkable things you've accomplished so far in your career, what's your biggest professional regret?" Silence. Then, he eventually said, "I don't have any regrets. If I had to do it again, I would do everything pretty much the same way." After another seemingly long pause, he said (I am paraphrasing),

> Well, maybe I have one regret. My work lies at the intersection of four areas: economics, finance, real estate, and law. I have a very complete picture of how these interact and how they influence everything from real estate prices in ghettos to land speculation prices in the middle of nowhere. The problem is that I'm the only one who sees the big picture. Some of my papers are published in econ journals and finance journals, while others are published in real estate journals and law reviews. Nobody else sees the big picture, because they only read one type of journal.

I asked, "Would it be easier for people to see the big picture if you were to write a book that pulled all of this together? That way, everything would be in one place, and you could connect all the dots." He chuckled and immediately dismissed this: "I don't know about *marketing*, but in economics, they don't reward books."

After 45 years of research, here was a person who was retiring with one needless regret. Yet, what he let get in his way was how he would be rewarded or whether a colleague might think he was dumbing down his research for the amateurs. I could not think of anything to say. It seemed to me that writing a book would have been a potentially transforming project. At the very least, it would have started out as activism research. It would have focused on solution-oriented variables, and it would have clarified a series of debates. Given his career-long focus in this area, I suspect that he would have aggressively disseminated the work and that it would have ultimately changed behavior. It could have become transforming.

The metaphor that is relevant for us, however, is not necessarily a book. It is any project that might ratchet up our level of influence. It is any project that may not be rewarded with the respect of the "professor next door," but it is that which we think is critically important. In fact, it might be actively derided. That's what happened to a number of metaphorical books. It happened to Carl Sagan's award-winning *Cosmos* (Andorfer & McCain, 1980) series on PBS, to Gary Becker's famous *Business Week* columns, to Steven Levitt's *Freakonomics* (Levitt & Dubner, 2005), to Paul Krugman's *New York Times* columns, to Richard Posner's federal judge appointment, and to Stephen Ambrose's National World War II Museum.

The unwritten book can be a useful metaphor for us. For many of us, there is at least one metaphorical book that would take our ideas to a new level of influence. It might be starting a website and blog, presenting research in front of a House subcommittee in order to propose a law, making class modules for science teachers, writing a review article in a related field, or starting a new class and turning the notes into a book. Transforming behavior is what many of us dream of doing. But, it cannot be guaranteed. Yet, when we start with an activism research mind-set, we start leaving fewer things to chance.

I remember another topic that I discussed with that eminent economics professor back in 2002. It was how quickly he said that his research years had passed. He said that after he graduated with his PhD, he blinked and had tenure; he blinked again and had an endowed chair; he blinked again and was riding with me on what he called "my retirement bus." The idea of starting a career of activism research when "the time is right" could disappear in a blink of an eye.

## ACKNOWLEDGMENTS

Special thanks are extended to Pierre Chandon, Koert van Ittersum, Collin R. Payne, Sibylle Kranz, Marc Rockmore, Jenny Lee, and Brennan Davis for their help on earlier drafts of this chapter.

## REFERENCES

Aaker, D. A., Kyman, V., Day, G. S., & Leone, R. (2009). *Marketing research* (10th ed.). Hoboken, NJ: Wiley.

Ambrose, Inc. (2004, August 20). *The Wall Street Journal*, pp. 1–2.

Ambrose, S. E. (1985). *Pegasus Bridge: June 6, 1944*. New York: Simon & Schuster.

Ambrose, S. E. (1997). *Citizen soldiers: The U.S. Army from the Normandy beaches to the Bulge to the surrender of Germany, June 7, 1944–May 7, 1945*. New York: Simon & Schuster.

Ambrose, S. E. (2001). *The wild blue: The men and boys who flew the B-24s over Germany*. New York: Simon & Schuster.

Andorfer, G., & McCain, R. (Producers). (1980). *Cosmos: A personal voyage* [Television series]. Arlington, VA: Public Broadcasting Service.

Arnould, E. J., & Thompson, C. J. (2005). Consumer culture theory (CCT): Twenty years of research. *Journal of Consumer Research, 31*(4), 868–882.

Association of University Technology Managers. (2007). *Building a stronger economy: Profiles of 25 companies rooted in academic research*. Deerfield, IL: Author.

Association of University Technology Managers. (2008a). *Technology transfer works: 100 innovations from academic research to real-world applications*. Deerfield, IL: Author.

Association of University Technology Managers. (2008b). *The art of collaboration: The relationships that bring academic innovations to the marketplace*. Deerfield, IL: Author.

Association of University Technology Managers. (2009). *Innovations from academic research that positively impact global health*. Deerfield, IL: Author.

Bazerman, M. H. (2001). Consumer research for consumers. *Journal of Consumer Research, 27*(4), 499–504.

Chandon, P., & Wansink, B. (2007a). Is obesity caused by calorie underestimation? A psychophysical model of fast-food meal size estimation. *Journal of Marketing Research, 44*(1), 84–99.

Chandon, P., & Wansink, B. (2007b). The biasing health halos of fast food restaurant health claims: Lower calorie estimates and higher side-dish consumption intentions. *Journal of Consumer Research, 34*(3), 301–314.

Coleman, M., & Lumby, J. (1999). The significance of site-based practitioner researcher in educational management. In D. Middlewood, M. Coleman, & J. Lumby (Eds.), *Practitioner research in education: Making a difference* (pp. 1–20). London: Paul Chapman.

Dash, D. P. (1999). Current debates in action research. *Systemic Practice and Action Research, 12*(5), 457–492.

Deighton, J. (2005). From the editor-elect. *Journal of Consumer Research, 32*(1), 245–247.

Dyer, R. F., & Shimp, T. A. (1977). Enhancing the role of marketing-research in public-policy decision-making. *Journal of Marketing, 41*(1), 63–67.

Evans, G. W., Gonnella, C., Marcynyszyn, L. A., Gentile, L., & Salpekar, N. (2005). The role of chaos in poverty and children's socioemotional adjustment. *Psychological Science, 16*(7), 560–565.

Ferreyra, C. (2006). Practicality, positionality, and emancipation: Reflections on participatory action research with a watershed partnership. *Systemic Practice and Action Research, 19*(6), 577–598.

Firat, A. F. (2001). Consumer research for (the benefit of) consumers. *Journal of Research for Consumers, 1*(May). Retrieved October 13, 2010, from http://www.jrconsumers.com/Consumer_Articles/issue_1

Goldstein, R. (2002, October 14). Stephen Ambrose, historian who fueled new interest in World War II, dies at 66. *The New York Times.* Retrieved October 13, 2010, from http://www.nytimes.com/2002/10/14/arts/stephen-ambrose-historian-who-fueled-new-interest-in-world-war-ii-dies-at-66.html?scp=1&sq=Stephen%20Ambrose,%20historian%20who%20fueled%20new%20interest%20in%20World%20War%20II&st=cse

Greenwood, D. J., & Levin M. (1998). *Introduction to action research: Social research for social change.* Thousand Oaks, CA: Sage.

Henriques, G. R. (2005). Toward a useful mass movement. *Journal of Clinical Psychology, 61*(1), 121–139.

Hill, R. P. (1995). Researching sensitive topics in marketing: The special case of vulnerable populations. *Journal of Public Policy & Marketing, 14*(1), 143–148.

Hurford, D., & Read, A. (2003). *The qualitative nature of participatory action research in a school literacy context.* Classroom instructional materials from the Qualifications and Curriculum Authority/University of Cumbria Co-Development Initiative, University of Cambria, Australia.

Keith, B., Layne, J. S., Babchuk, N., & Johnson, K. (2002). Scientific achievement: Sex status, organizational environments, and the testing of publication on scholarship outcomes. *Social Forces, 80*(4), 1253–1282.

Kernan, J. B. (1979). Presidential address: Consumer research and the public purpose. In W. L. Wilkie (Ed.), *Advances in consumer research* (Vol. 6, pp. 1–2). Ann Arbor, MI: Association for Consumer Research.

Kidd, S. A., & Kral, M. J. (2005). Practicing participatory action research. *Journal of Counseling Psychology, 52*(2), 187–195.

Kneebone, S., & Wadsworth, Y. (1998). What is participatory action research? *Action Research International.* Retrieved September 3, 2007, from http://www.research-for-real.co.uk/resources.asp

Langer, E. J., & Rodin, J. (1976). The effects of choice and enhanced personal responsiblity for the aged: A field experiment in an institutional setting. *Journal of Personality and Social Psychology, 34*, 191–198.

Larkins, C. (2009). Research for action: Cross-national perspectives on connecting knowledge policy and practice for children. *International Social Work, 52*(6), 843–845.

Levy, S. J. (1996). Stalking the amphisbaena. *Journal of Consumer Research, 23*(December), 163–176.

Lewin, K. (1951). Psychological ecology. In D. Cartwright (Ed.), *Field theory in social science* (pp. 170–187). New York: Harper & Row.

Levitt, S. D., & Dubner, S. J. (2005). *Freakonomics: A rogue economist explores the hidden side of everything.* New York: William Morrow.

Loftus, E. F. (1975). Leading questions and the eyewitness report. *Cognitive Psychology, 7*, 560–572.

Lynch, J. G., Netemeyer, R. G., Spiller, S. A., & Zammit, A. (2010). A generalizable scale of propensity to plan: The long and the short of planning for time and for money. *Journal of Consumer Research, 37*(1), 108–128.

Mari, C. (2008). Doctoral education and transformative consumer research. *Journal of Marketing Education, 30*(1), 5–11.

Martí, J., & Villasante, T. R. (2009). Quality in action research: Reflections for second-order inquiry. *Systemic Practice and Action Research, 22*(5), 383–396.

McNiff, J. (2002). *Action research for professional development: Concise advice for new action researchers* (3rd ed.). New York: Vantage.

McNiff, J. (2008). The significance of "I" in educational research and the responsibility of intellectuals. *South African Journal of Education, 28*, 351–364.

McQuarrie, E. J. (1993). *Customer visits: Building a better market focus.* Newbury Park, CA: Sage.

Merton, R. K. (1968). *Social theory and social structure.* New York: Free Press.

Mick, D. G. (2004). *For consumers: Steps toward transformative consumer research.* Retrieved December 14, 2010, from http://acrwebsite.org/Carlo_Mari_JME_Education_and_TCR.pdf

Mick, D. G. (2006). Meaning and mattering through transformative consumer research. In C. Pechmann & L. L. Price (Eds.), *Advances in consumer research* (Vol. 33, pp. 1–9). Provo, UT: Association for Consumer Research.

Milgram, S. (1963). Behavioral study of obedience. *Journal of Abnormal and Social Psychology, 67,* 371–378.

Miller, G. A. (1969). Psychology as a means of promoting human welfare. *American Psychologist, 24*(11), 1063–1075.

Minkler, M. (2000). Using participatory action research to build healthy communities. *Public Health Reports, 115*(2/3), 191–197.

Murray, J. B., & Ozanne, J. L. (2009). The critical participant. *Journal of Marketing Management, 25*(7/8), 835–841.

Murray, J. B., Ozanne, J. L., & Shapiro, J. M. (1994). Revitalizing the critical imagination: Unleashing the crouched tiger. *Journal of Consumer Research, 21*(3), 559–565.

Nelson, A., Colleen, H., & Michael, R. (2009). Connecting people, participation and place via action research: Why? How? *Area, 41*(3), 364–367.

Noffke, S. E. (1997). Professional, personal, and political dimensions of action research. *Review of Research in Education, 22,* 305–343.

Ozanne, J. L., & Saatcioglu, B. (2008). Participatory action research. *Journal of Consumer Research, 35*(3), 423–439.

Parker, I. (2010, May 17). The poverty lab: Transforming development economics, one experiment at a time. *The New Yorker,* 79–89.

Parmar, N. (2007, July). 10 things your bartender won't tell you. *Smart Money,* pp. 31–32.

Pechmann, C., & Knight, S. J. (2002). An experimental investigation of the joint effects of advertising and peers on adolescents' beliefs and intentions about cigarette consumption. *Journal of Consumer Research, 29*(1), 5–19.

Pechmann, C., & Shih, C. F. (1999). Smoking scenes in movies and antismoking advertisements before movies: Effects on youth. *Journal of Marketing, 63,* 1–13.

Predota, E. (2009). Participatory action research approaches and methods: Connecting people, participation and place. *Geography, 94,* 223–225.

Pullmann, M. D. (2009). Participatory research in systems of care for children's mental health. *American Journal of Community Psychology, 44*(1/2), 43–53.

Rick, S., Small, D. A., & Finkel, E. (in press). Fatal (fiscal) attraction: Spendthrifts and tightwads in marriage. *Journal of Marketing Research.*

Rolls, B. J., Morris, E. L., & Roe, L. S. (2002). Portion size of food affects energy intake in normal-weight and overweight men and women. *American Journal of Clinical Nutrition, 76,* 1207–1213.

Schachter, S., & Rodin, J. (1974). *Obese humans and rats.* Hillsdale, NJ: Erlbaum.

Sears, D. O. (1986). College sophomores in the laboratory: Influences of a narrow database on psychology's view of human nature. *Journal of Personality and Social Psychology, 51,* 515–530.

Seligman, M. E. P., & Csikszentmihalyi, M. (2000). Positive psychology. *American Psychologist, 55*(1), 5–14.

Sheth, J. N., & Sisodia, R. S. (2005). A dangerous divergence: Marketing and society. *Journal of Public Policy & Marketing, 24,* 160–162.

Shimp, T. A. (1994). Presidential address: Academic Appalachia and the discipline of consumer research. In D. R. John & C. Allen (Eds.), *Advances in consumer research* (Vol. 21, pp. 1–7). Provo, UT: Association for Consumer Research.

Singh, A. (2009). Better to be rough and relevant than to be precise and irrelevant: Reddaway's legacy to economics. *Cambridge Journal of Economics, 33,* 363–379.

Small, S. A. (1995). Action-oriented research: models and methods. *Journal of Marriage and Family, 57,* 941–955.

Sonnenstuhl, W. J. (1997). Working sober: The transformation of an occupational drinking culture. *Journal of Studies on Alcohol, 58*(2), 211–219.

Spielberg, S., Hanks, T., Smith, P., Jendresen, E., & Ambrose, S. (Producers). (2001). *Band of brothers* [Television miniseries]. New York: Home Box Office.

Stahl, R., & Shdaimah, C. (2008). Collaboration between community advocates and academic researchers: Scientific advocacy or political research? *British Journal of Social Work, 38*(8), 1610–1629.

Stringer, E. T. (2007). *Action research: A handbook for practitioners* (3rd ed.). Newbury Park, CA: Sage.

van der Riet, M. (2008). Participatory research and the philosophy of social science: Beyond the moral imperative. *Qualitative Inquiry, 14*(4), 546–565.

van Ittersum, K., Pennings, J. M. E., & Wansink, B. (2010). Trying harder and doing worse: How grocery shoppers track in-store spending. *Journal of Marketing, 74*(2), 90–104.

Wansink, B. (2005). *Marketing nutrition: Soy, functional foods, biotechnology, and obesity.* Champaign: University of Illinois Press.

Wansink, B. (2006). *Mindless eating: Why we eat more than we think.* New York: Bantam Dell.

Wansink, B., Just, D. R., & Payne, C. R. (2011). *The behavioral economics of healthier school lunch payment systems.* Unpublished manuscript.

Wansink, B., & Payne, C. R. (2009). The *Joy of Cooking* too much: 70 years of calorie increases in classic recipes. *Annals of Internal Medicine, 150,* 291–292.

Wansink, B., & van Ittersum, K. (2003). Bottoms up! The influence of elongation and pouring on consumption volume. *Journal of Consumer Research, 30*(3), 455–463.

Whyte, W. F. (1991). *Participatory action research* (Sage focus ed.). Newbury Park, CA: Sage.

Wilkie, W. L., & Gardner, D. M. (1974). The role of marketing research in public policy decision making. *Journal of Marketing, 38*(1), 38–47.

Wolpe, J. (1961). The systematic desensitization treatment of neuroses. *Journal of Nervous and Mental Disease, 132,* 180–203.

Young, L., & Nestle, M. (2002). The contribution of expanding portion sizes to the US obesity epidemic. *American Journal of Public Health, 92,* 246–249.

Zimbardo, P. G. (2004). Does psychology make a significant difference in our lives? *American Psychologist, 59*(5), 339–351.

# 4

# Sensitizing Principles and Practices Central to Social Change Methodologies

JULIE L. OZANNE AND EILEEN FISCHER

The purpose of this chapter is to identify the central shared *sensitizing principles* that guide research methodologies seeking the goal of social change and to illuminate the range of methodological techniques developed to put these principles into practice. Transformative Consumer Research (TCR) seeks to improve consumer well-being, which will require a broader range of methodological tools aimed at social transformation. Although many traditions of social change research exist, we take our inspiration from three methodological approaches that share many common principles: feminism (Bristor & Fischer, 1993; Fonow & Cook, 1991), participatory action research (Ozanne & Saatcioglu, 2008; Reason & Bradbury, 2006), and indigenous research (Denzin, Lincoln, & Smith, 2008; Harrison, 2002; Smith, 1999).

We use the term *methodology* to evoke a broad theory of how research should be done as well as the specific data gathering techniques or methods of analysis employed. We use the term sensitizing principles to describe convergent clusters of epistemological and ethical beliefs and assumptions that inform social change methodologies. To illustrate these principles, we draw on examples from all three research traditions. We then offer specific recommendations for doing TCR (Mick, 2006).

The historical focus of feminist research was on women, although more recent forms of feminisms explore the intersection of race, class, gender, and other categories that entail different experiences of marginalization (Bristor & Fischer, 1993; Glen, 1985; Peñaloza, 2000). Although myriad distinctions and divergences exist in feminist thought, the shared concern of feminist scholars is to create more equitable social structures and open up opportunities for those subjugated by patriarchal elements in societies. Participatory action research emerged out of efforts to study and improve the lot of people in economically less developed nations who were living in abject poverty (Hall, 1981); the broad goal of action research is to improve the lives of people who face significant challenges to their economic or social well-being (Reason & Bradbury, 2006). Recent work on "indigenous" methodologies arose in response to the long history of native peoples being constrained by various forms of colonialism (Denzin et al., 2008; Smith, 1999). This indigenous research approach is focused on improving the life of native peoples and often uses methodological techniques that are attuned to and based on their cultural practices (Denzin et al., 2008).

Researchers within each of these dynamic traditions have learned some difficult lessons as they have struggled to do research aimed at improving the well-being of those groups who have been marginalized in various ways. In this chapter, we seek to help transformative consumer researchers leverage these hard-won insights. In the sections that follow, we distill these lessons into a series of sensitizing principles, which are informed by ideology and ethical considerations, as well as by epistemological considerations. Each principle has implications for preferred methodological practices. A few of the research techniques we describe originate within one specific tradition or another; our focus, however, is on principles and methodological practices that are common across the various types of social change research that can inform TCR.

In brief, the first sensitizing principle common to all three traditions is that research should lead to greater social justice for and empowerment of marginalized groups (see also Baker & Mason, Chapter 26 of this volume; Viswanathan, Chapter 5 of this volume; Williams & Henderson, Chapter 8 of this volume). Researchers within social change traditions are hopeful that social scientists can improve individual and societal well-being by foregrounding the experiences of marginal groups and, through research, attempting to address the problems that are most pervasive for members of these groups. This commitment arises, in part, because so many social groups have been excluded from the process of knowledge production and have benefited unevenly at best from the fruits of scientific research.

The second sensitizing principle is that research should be reflexive. The premises behind this principle are that the process of knowledge production is influenced by power relations that are often tacit and that researchers must be vigilant in identifying whose interests are and are not served, and what power relations are preserved by questions that are asked and the manner in which answers are sought (see also Mick, Pettigrew, Pechmann, & Ozanne, Chapter 1 of this volume). Because a commitment to social change is the first principle, researchers in these traditions must be ever-vigilant that they conduct research in a manner that shares power between researchers and those being researched. In order to do so, reflexivity is required.

A third sensitizing principle is that research must take into account intersectionality, the notion of which reflects an understanding that members of marginalized groups are rarely homogeneous. Instead, within any group, there are likely to be distinguishable subgroups whose experiences are contingent on their being at the intersection of more than one marginalized category. Rather than glossing over differences among members of a larger marginalized group, committed social change researchers use various strategies to explore the similarities and differences between those who experience intersecting marginalizations. These researchers use these insights to destabilize universalistic knowledge claims and to attempt to identify implications of social change research for those who are more disadvantaged, or differently disadvantaged, by their position in a marginalized group (see also Andreasen, Goldberg, & Sirgy, Chapter 2 of this volume). Behind this principle lies a commitment to ensuring that research does not reinforce subordination among some of the people that it seeks to help.

The final sensitizing principle is that researchers should engage with the stakeholders of research. This engagement can be expressed in varying ways, but many social change researchers go beyond merely conducting research to proactively seeking ways to implement changes. Sometimes deeper forms of engagement, such as political activism, become part of social change research (Hesse-Biber, Leavy, & Yaiser, 2004; Reason & Bradbury, 2006; Smith, 1999). This commitment is very consistent with activism research (see Wansink, Chapter 3 of this volume). As we shall discover later, each of these principles offers important guidance for TCR scholars.

As we explore each of these principles, we proffer a range of specific methods that help enact the principles, along with examples from one or more of the social change research traditions on which we are drawing. We wish to reinforce two points before proceeding, however, to put what follows in context and guide readers in their interpretation. First, while we have distilled several principles of social change research, it would misrepresent the state of such research if we implied that all researchers with a social change agenda adhere to each of these principles with equal intensity in each and every piece of research they undertake, as there are sometimes difficult trade-offs among the principles. Our second caveat concerns existing practices among consumer researchers with interests in social change. In the following pages, we seek not to suggest that existing research approaches have nothing to offer transformative consumer researchers, but rather to expand awareness of challenges that face would-be researchers, and the range of methodological options for consumer researchers who want to engage in transformative research. We call for plural methods, which is consistent with the ethos of each of these social change traditions and the desire for a cacophony of voices and a wide range of flexible research instruments. This call is also consistent with a TCR approach, as explicated in the introductory chapter of this book. Table 4.1 provides an overview of the discussion that follows.

## SENSITIZING PRINCIPLES

### Principle 1: Research Should Promote Social Justice for and Empowerment of Marginalized Groups[*]

Traditions of social change research share a perspective that we associate with Enlightenment beliefs in the possibility of positive change: Just as researchers inspired by Enlightenment worldviews believed that social progress was desirable and possible, so too are social change researchers optimistic that their work can contribute to creating a more just society in which currently marginalized people come to face fewer obstacles and enjoy greater empowerment. In short, like TCR researchers, social change researchers are committed to improving social life through their research; their goal is to better somehow the conditions faced by members of marginalized groups.

In contrast to Enlightenment thinkers who put their faith in the power of reason and believed that researcher objectivity was possible and desirable, many contemporary change researchers challenge the notion that "objective" data are possible to obtain. To the extent that objectivity is achievable, they question whether objectivity alone will be sufficient to inform researchers about what problems are paramount for marginalized groups and what solutions might be workable. The Enlightenment's dualism between reason and emotion, and between objective and subjective knowledge (e.g., Bristor & Fischer, 1993), are challenged by social change researchers who have come to understand that if research is to benefit members of marginalized groups, it must take into account subjective, emotion-laden data that help researchers and those people who are the subjects of research to better understand their lived experiences and the factors that contribute to their relative lack of power or access to needed resources (e.g., Fonow & Cook, 1991). These approaches draw inspiration from the Romantic tradition that affirms the importance that emotions play in our social lives and assumes that researchers' passionate engagement with social problems can be a driver of social change. Clearly, TCR investigators are passionate about their engagement with a number of marginalized consumer groups, such as the poor, the stigmatized, and the at-risk.

Given this principle, methods that simultaneously contribute to consciousness-raising and gathering information about lived experiences are critical. Chief among these methods are alternatives to conventional structured or semistructured interviews. Feminist, action, and indigenous researchers have often found that traditional tools for eliciting information from informants work poorly for many marginal groups. For example, early feminist researchers found that formal interview methods created a separation between the researcher and the women studied, which created an obstacle for scholars struggling to build sufficient trust, so women would share their experiences. Moreover, traditional interviews did little to evoke the kinds of reflections that led subjects of research to a greater awareness of the factors that contributed to their lack of power or dissatisfaction with current conditions. Likewise, participatory action researchers realized that written surveys were not viable among people with little formal education (Chambers, 1997). Similarly,

---

[*] This principle does not negate the value of social change research done in marketing that uses the scientific method (e.g., Pechmann & Ratneshwar, 1994). Rather, it suggests that a necessary complement to research premised on traditional scientific methods is research that seeks to give voice to the lived experiences of people in marginalized groups.

**Table 4.1**    Overview of Sensitizing Principles and Implications

| Principle | Rationale | General Approaches | Specific Techniques |
|---|---|---|---|
| Research should promote social justice for and empowerment of marginalized groups. | • Research that strives solely for objectivity and rationality may reinforce the very marginalization it seeks to alleviate.<br>• A necessary complement to traditional scientific methods are methods that give voice to the subjective lived experiences of marginalized groups. | • Methods adapted to the knowledge and practices of marginalized groups<br>• Methods that aid in consciousness-raising | • Oral histories and storytelling<br>• Social mapping, seasonal calendars, photovoice, and other methods that entail visual images<br>• Indigenizing |
| Researchers should be reflexive. | • The micropolitics of knowledge production means that powerful interests shape research.<br>• Reflexivity is required to address the possibility that researchers unwittingly reinforce marginalization through the questions they ask or the way they pursue and produce answers to these questions. | • Sensitivity to origins of research questions and answers<br>• Openness to reframing of research questions<br>• Democratization of research process | • Gathering and analyzing historical data<br>• Open-ended data collection and analysis techniques: unstructured interviewing and follow-up interviewing; testimony and fishbowl technique<br>• Research findings represented in a way that reveals researchers' potential biases and assumptions |
| Researchers should address intersectionality. | • Marginalized groups may have diverse experiences.<br>• Intersecting sources of marginalization must be acknowledged to avoid misrepresentation and overly simplistic analyses. | • Intracategorical<br>• Intercategorical | • Ethnographic case studies, comparative ethnographic case studies, and econometric analyses of macrodata |
| Researchers should engage with research stakeholders. | • To bring about change, researchers must feel a personal stake in their research, not a dispassionate distance. | • Raising issues through reporting research<br>• Taking action to make changes happen | • Telenovelas, songs, puppetry, and dance<br>• Action plans, interventions, and participatory drama |

indigenous scholars became aware that traditional research approaches to data collection frequently privileged Western conceptualizations, such as notions of space, time, individual boundaries, or ideas of progress.

To overcome the limits of formal structured or semistructured interviews, a particularly popular technique utilized by diverse social change scholars is creating oral histories. All cultures have developed ways of organizing, representing, and preserving important cultural insights and knowledge. One of the oldest and most widespread forms is firsthand accounts of people's life stories in the form of oral histories. Such life narratives explore the experiences of ordinary people who are often lost or overlooked, such as the stories of women and elders (Smith, 1999). In consumer research, Elliot and Davies (2006) use oral histories of women born in the early part of the 20th century to recover women's views on frugality that have been ignored. Although the researcher and storyteller cocreate oral histories or life stories in dialogue, the storyteller decides which life events are shared and explored (Reinharz, 1992). Oral histories can, if analyzed with sensitivity, provide insight into the tacit cultural categories that might otherwise be forgotten or lost. Within traditional societies, oral histories provide connections between the past and the future (Smith, 1999). Thus, oral histories are critical data gathering techniques for giving marginalized people the opportunity to tell their stories by leveraging existing modes of communication, giving considerable control to the research participant and allowing local cultural understandings to unfold (Ozanne & Anderson, in press).

Social change researchers also develop alternatives to the dominant verbal means of data collection. When informants, such as subsistence farmers, lack literacy skills, it is possible to use a range of visual techniques suited to the perceptual frames and communication styles that are habitual for those people whose input is sought. One such technique, developed among low-literate farmers, involves mapping: Groups of farmers cocreate visual maps of community resources or problems. Another example of a visual tool for data collection in this setting is seasonal calendars. Appropriate to the project at hand, these calendars allow community members to share patterns of crop rotation, market demands for crops, patterns of weather, and so forth (Roos & Mohatle, 1998). Such seasonal maps have also been useful in exploring social problems, such as the seasonal patterns of diseases and illnesses (see Mukherjee, 1993, for the range of methods). Other kinds of visual mapping approaches have been developed for other social issues. For example, body maps are often helpful in understanding the social construction of people's bodies, sexuality, and illnesses (Cornwall, 1992).

Other visually oriented methods entail photography. For example, Photovoice takes its inspiration from documentary photography and the catalytic power of images to arouse people. This action research method is often used with groups, such as women, children, the poor, and the handicapped, to help members articulate their needs to each other as well as to people who control resources (Wang, 2003). Cameras are given to the research participants, who are encouraged to document their lives and capture domains of action that may be off-limits to outsiders or to record seemingly mundane tasks that may have deeper meaning (Wang, Morrel-Samuels, Hutchison, Bell, & Pestronk, 2004). Photovoice works even when groups have little formal education or cannot read and write but can use the photos of their life to capture important insights.

Photos can further be analyzed and discussed within community venues wherein the photographer and the community members select sets of photos for public display and discussion, thus increasing the chances that issues of shared concern to group members are highlighted. Photos can also sensitize the researcher to differences that arise within social groups. When they have been presented to community leaders, such techniques provide an insight into the overlooked perspectives of impoverished groups and have inspired social and policy change, such as the provision of increased financial resources to group members by politicians (Wang, Burris, & Ping, 1996). Similarly, visual techniques are used in consumer research to evoke richer and more emotive data (Zaltman, 2003; Zaltman & Coulter, 1995).

The theme that unites this category of techniques is that they avoid a primary emphasis on obtaining spoken or written answers to closed-ended questions. Modes of communication that fit more closely with informants' regular practices can allow both questions and insights into understandings to emerge, rather than formed and shaped primarily through the cultural prism of the researcher (Chambers, 1997).

"Indigenizing" is an additional method that has been used in light of the principle that research should reflect the concerns and promote the interests of marginalized groups. Indigenizing is a technique that arose among those studying native peoples who feared that their very culture was at risk of being lost. This method leverages cultural repositories of knowledge, such as mythology, legend, and folkways. For example, rather than assuming that indigenous spirituality is primitive and based on superstition, people interrogate traditional rituals and legends and beliefs to probe the understandings they reveal of what is important and why it is important (Smith, 1999).

### Principle 2: Researchers Should Be Reflexive[*]

Social change theorists hold that, in order for research to have the impact they desire (discussed in regard to the first sensitizing principle), it is essential that research be reflexive. Reflexivity has multiple meanings. One of the earliest meanings associated with the term was simply that research-ers should reflect on, examine critically, and explore analytically the nature of the research pro-cess. A second implication of the term was that people who were subjects of research should also be encouraged to reflect on the meanings of phenomena or experiences under investigation (e.g., Fonow & Cook, 1991). Today, the term *reflexivity* also refers to the need for scholars to attempt to understand how their own social locations affect the research they produce and the agendas and assumptions that have shaped their disciplines as sites of knowledge production (Fonow & Cook, 2005). What unites these varied meanings is the understanding that research is inevitably and inescapably perspectival and political. Researchers, other stakeholders in the research process, and the scholarly fields in which research takes place are all influenced by tacit assumptions and agen-das that must be acknowledged to the extent possible if desirable social change is to be achieved. Reflexivity is required in order to achieve consciousness-raising on the parts of all stakeholders in research projects.

It is important for TCR scholars to engage in such reflection, so the questions that are asked and the answers that are developed can serve to relieve marginalization rather than reinforce it. Foucault (1972), in his analysis of the microprocesses of power, has skillfully shown that what gets counted as knowledge is determined within social discourses that are shaped by hidden interests. Thus, as social change researchers discover all too frequently, the interests of marginal peoples are often ignored in the very framing of research questions and/or topics of investigation. For example, much of women's work involves unpaid labor in the private domain; it remained both invisible and undervalued until feminist researchers began to focus on the phenomenon of unpaid work as a topic worthy of investigation and ask questions about how it could and should be valued (DeVault, 1991). Similarly, agricultural researchers often ignored the productive practices, like mixed crop-ping, that poor local farmers had employed successfully for generations in their pursuit of sustain-able solutions. Instead of asking questions about the efficacy of traditional practices, experts tended to conduct research on technological solutions that were based on large-scale farming techniques but were unsustainable and unsuitable (Chambers, 1989).

Insights from indigenous research offer the most dramatic examples of the necessity of inter-rogating the very questions that are deemed relevant. Smith (1999, p. 90) pointed out that native peoples were framed as "the indigenous problem" to be solved by controlling rebellion, physically containing groups on reservations, and seeking solutions to the tribes' cultural and moral deficits. Thus, indigenous peoples' very existence was deemed problematic by the early researchers who studied them. In an increasingly global marketplace, a wide range of diverse stakeholder interests need to be considered within a TCR agenda.

---

[*] Following the principle of reflexivity, we would like to recognize that, as authors, we are both senior women scholars with lives of considerable economic and educational privilege. The authors both entered the academy when women were a small minority, and this experience of relative marginality informs our analysis. Our firsthand experiences of being challenged in the questions we wanted to ask and the methodologies we preferred clearly affected our desire to have an academy that is tolerant of alternative approaches. This chapter is motivated by our desire to carve out and defend a space in the academy where researchers can engage in research that explicitly seeks to be socially relevant and impactful.

In response to the principle that research should be reflexive, one method of vital importance for social change researchers is historical research. Historical research, based on archival data of various kinds, can help unearth the origins of current conditions that structure the lived experiences of marginalized groups. Historical methods can help shed light on how groups come to be marginalized and how that marginalization comes to be so taken for granted that it sometimes seems invisible and inevitable. For instance, Terry (1999), a feminist scholar, uses historical medical texts, scientific reports, psychiatric case studies, statistical accounts, legal cases, legislative debates, and published first-person accounts of homosexuality to show the material effects of these contradictory discourses on the constitution of women's and men's homosexual identities. Her methods, reliant on texts from different genres, allow her to see how individuals in the marginalized category accept, transform, and/or resist experts' accounts of who they are.

Historical studies of marginalized groups are particularly critical for peoples whose histories were constructed by someone else. For instance, feminists use historical research not only to correct a past record that included few women but also to allow women to identify with assertive women of the past (Reinharz, 1992). Action and indigenous researchers also seek out alternative histories to challenge a record written by those in power, such as colonial invaders. These researchers also engage in a critical rereading of colonial accounts of history. Smith (1999), for example, discussed how indigenous peoples have developed variants of historical methodologies in response to their need to lay claim to land, resources, and basic rights. Relying on historical research of families, tribes, and nations, indigenous researchers have created historical accounts of land claims and social injustices. These histories are written both for formal governmental hearings and to document shared tribal experiences. Smith (1999) argued that "*re*writing and *re*righting our position in history" empowers indigenous people to fight against colonizing forces that sought to destroy their culture (p. 28).

Historical methods are particularly useful for uncovering the perspectives that privilege certain research questions and silence others. Bhavnani (2004) argued that scientific knowledge is social in nature but that a historical analysis of the origins of this knowledge can help us understand why researchers asked a specific question at a particular historical moment. For example, why were 19th-century researchers preoccupied with racial differences? And what inspired them to use craniometry to see how many marbles fit into skulls varying by race and gender (Gould, 1981)? Adopting a historical approach reveals who raised the research questions and the kinds of interests that led certain facts to be interpreted in particular ways.

Historical research can thus lead to the reframing of research questions asked by transformative researchers. For example, the problem of alcoholism might be framed as an individual consumption addiction, and research questions would focus on preventing or curing individuals' addictions. Alternatively, alcoholism might be reframed as a coping behavior by a people who have lost control and self-determination (Smith, 1999). On this framing, research questions would focus at a more macrolevel on how to create conditions that promote self-control and self-determination among groups in which alcoholism has been a coping mechanism.

Social change theorists also practice reflexivity and maintain a stance of openness to reframing research questions by democratizing the research process, which, in effect, means involving research subjects throughout the research process from problem identification, design of the study, analysis of the findings, and the creation of findings, including an implementable change program (Reason & Bradbury, 2006). The act of doing research is viewed as important for people who are the subjects of the research to become aware of their ability to act in their own interests and assert their agency (Ozanne & Saatcioglu, 2008).

A key to democratizing the research process is using data collection and analysis methods that reduce power differences between the researcher and the researched and allow informants to shape the research process. For instance, social change scholars may use informal conversations rather than formal research interviews. By avoiding a standard open-ended question format to explore a priori domains, less structured conversations can allow differences among informants and avoid the tendency for the researcher's taken-for-granted assumptions to shape the research questions and findings (Reinharz, 1992). Free-flowing social interactions not only have the potential to develop intimacy and rapport that can lead to greater insights for the interviewer, but also they can lead to more insights for the interviewee (DeVault, 1990). In some cases, interview techniques may include self-disclosure on the part of the researcher in response to queries on the part of the informant (e.g., Oakley, 1981). This approach stands in sharp contrast to the traditional image of the social scientist as an objective and removed observer, but serves to underscore the point that the research participant is in a position of equal power and can cocreate not only the direction of the interview but also the course of the research project.

A related technique that helps ensure that the research participant shares power in the research process is providing opportunities for informants to give feedback on what the researcher believes she is discovering so that the informant can correct mistakes or offer elaboration (Reinharz, 1992). This entails repeated interviews in which researchers share initial and updated insights and gather whatever feedback informants are willing to share. As Brueggerman (1996) has noted, however, it is important for social change researchers to recognize limits to subjects' willingness to be enlisted as research collaborators; she cautioned that researchers should not "unequivocally assume that [subjects] want to be involved, to collaborate, to respond, to co-construct" (p. 33). This reticence may be significant among some indigenous groups if past research has adversely affected them. Nevertheless, TCR scholars need to consider how participation and feedback from those groups examined can help flatten the distribution of power in the relationship.

Data collection methods that follow the cultural practices of the groups studied can be appropriate alternatives to democratizing the research process. An indigenous method that fits well here is the practice of giving testimony that is a formal and structured oral presentation of evidence about a painful past event. Within the cultural context, such testimony is assumed to be given under oath while the audience listens and gives witness. The speaker has considerable power to structure and control the testimony. "While the listener may ask questions, testimonies structure the responses, silencing certain types of questions and formalizing others" (Smith, 1999, p. 144). This example suggests that TCR scholars can interrogate the cultural resources of a community for culturally appropriate forms of expression that are more democratic.

Other methods that integrate data collection with knowledge dissemination can also ensure that the research process is empowering. Feminist action researchers developed a fishbowl technique to manage democratic dialogue on sexual topics that were culturally sensitive in Zambia (Gordon, 2004). People were asked for the questions that they would like to ask the opposite sex on matters of sexual intimacy and safe sex practices. A facilitator then posed these questions to women who were sitting together in an inner circle while men listened without speaking in an outer circle; the positions were then reversed. Typically, men verbally dominate in social settings, so this technique managed these power dynamics by giving both genders the opportunity to both speak and be heard. Safer and more satisfying sex was reported in a follow-up study (Gordon & Cornwall, 2004).

A final methodological practice that is inspired by the principle of reflective research concerns the representation of research findings. Given the importance of attention to the agendas and assumptions that shape research questions and the answers that are offered, social change scholars frequently endeavor to make their own roles in the research process as transparent as possible and ensure that the voices of informants are not ultimately subjugated to those of the researchers. This entails seeking modes of representation that reveal something about the researcher as well as the researched. For example, in their book on women with HIV, Lather and Smithies (1997), through a novel writing approach, attempted to expose both their own points of view as scholars and the outcome of the collaborative research process in which they engaged. In one section of their book, they included extracts from interview transcripts on the top half of the page and sections from the authors' research journals on the bottom half. They also juxtaposed poetry created by one of their research subjects with statistics from the Centers for Disease Control. Further, they used drawings to illustrate some of their overarching themes. Their goal was to highlight their role as coconstructors of the research rather than experts whose knowledge and insight exceeded that of those they studied. Such forms of representation were also used to reveal as much as possible about their own assumptions and biases that informed the way they pursued their project. In general, social change researchers seek to ensure that subjects' voices are heard, that their own potential sources of bias are acknowledged, and that concerns and trade-offs that surface before and during a research project are identified and discussed within the research report so that the micropolitics of their research are not hidden from view.

### Principle 3: Researchers Should Address Intersectionality

Research with a social change agenda, however well-intentioned, runs the risk of essentializing a given category of marginalized peoples. That is, social change research can all too readily perpetuate the idea that members of marginalized groups possess homogeneous and static identities, share common issues, and will benefit equally from a given intervention. In attempting to alleviate oppressive conditions of a broadly defined marginalized group, an ever-present risk exists of overlooking subgroups whose experiences and issues differ due to intersecting sources of marginalization. Thus, the third principle that permeates much social change research is that it should attempt to address intersectionality, which can be defined as "the relationships among multiple dimensions and modalities of social relations and subject formations" (McCall, 2005, p. 1771).

Black feminists have been at the forefront in sensitizing researchers to the need of addressing intersectionality (see, e.g., hooks, 1982). Although early feminism introduced the complicated notion of gender as an analytic category in analysis, a focus on women's experiences versus those of men tended to overlook the often vast differences between the experiences of, and problems faced by, White women and women of color. Equally, the experiences and issues of Black women cannot be assumed to be homogeneous: For example, the marginalization suffered by lower class Black women differs in degree and kind from that experienced by middle-class Black women. Of course, issues of intersectionality are not faced only by feminists. Indigenous researchers, for example, must be sensitive to the different issues and problems faced, for example, by the South African Blacks, the Sioux of South Dakota, and the Maori of Aotearoa (Kincheloe & Steinberg, 2008).

One generic strategy for addressing intersectionality has been labeled the *intracategorical approach*. To deal with considerable complexities raised by a recognition of the heterogeneity within a broadly defined marginalized category, this approach tends to focus analytic attention either on a single social group at a neglected point of intersection of multiple dominant categories or on a particular social setting. The method best suited to an intracategorical approach is an ethnographic case study of a group defined either by the multiple marginalized categories in which they are situated or by the geographically defined social setting they inhabit. By using ethnographic techniques of observation and extended immersion in the field, researchers focus on people at the intersection of single dimensions of multiple categories rather than on the full range of dimensions. For example, to understand issues at the intersection of gender, race, and social class categories, Hondagneu-Sotelo (2001) studied Latina domestic workers. Her approach is intracategorical in that she does not study non-Latinas, nor does she study affluent Latinas or men. However, as is typical for intracategorical case studies, she compares the experiences and issues of those she studies with a group that has been the subject of previous studies: earlier generations of African American domestic workers.

Crenshaw (1991) has similarly studied Black female victims of domestic violence and compared her findings with results from earlier studies of White female victims of domestic violence. The ethnographic case study approach is particularly well suited to addressing intersectionality, because it allows the researcher to remain open to documenting differences among those who are members of the same intersectional group or social setting rather than constraining them to represent all members of the group as sharing the same lived experiences and confronting the same issues. Moreover, ethnographic case studies can focus on the experiences and issues of the focal group as the current outcome of a socially constructed process that is experienced, reproduced, and resisted: They can avoid essentialization and highlight the possibility for change.

A second approach that attempts to deal with intersectionality can be described as intercategorical, the main goal of which is to compare and contrast the inequities facing subgroups. Like the intracategorical approach, it treats the grouping categories as provisional in acknowledgment of the fact that they are sociohistorically constructed and that relationships among these socially constructed groups are not static. Unlike the intracategorical approach, the intercategorical approach explicitly looks, within the scope of a single study, at contrasting subgroups that are hypothesized to have different experiences. Whereas single-group studies drill down to examine one intersection of a subset of dimensions of multiple categories, multigroup studies analyze the intersection of a range of dimensions of multiple categories. For example, if race is one marginalized category of interest, then Whites, Hispanics, and Blacks might be compared, and if social class is a second category of interest, then working and middle classes could also be compared.

Both qualitative and quantitative methods have been harnessed for use within an intracategorical approach. Among qualitative methods, comparative ethnographic case studies of two groups that contrast along a major category of marginalization are common. For example, Blum (1999) compared beliefs and practices associated with breast-feeding among Black working-class women versus White working-class women. Pardo (1998) compared community activism among Mexican American women in working-class and middle-class communities. A primary quantitative method used to explore complex intersections of marginalized categories is econometric analysis of macrolevel data that examines interaction effects or multilevel models.

For example, McCall (2001a, 2001b) used econometric analysis of demographic data to examine earning inequalities among subgroups classified according to race, class, and gender. Her goal was to determine which groups had benefited from shifts away from a manufacturing-based economy. Her findings indicated that patterns of inequality differed across urban regions with different bases of employment. For example, heavily unionized blue-collar cities experiencing deindustrialization (e.g., Detroit) exhibited relatively minimal class and racial wage inequality among employed men but considerable class inequality among employed women, as well as high inequality between men and women. In contrast, a postindustrial city such as Dallas exhibited more class and racial inequality than gender inequality. She also found that gender inequality was higher among the college-educated than the non–college-educated in Dallas, whereas the reverse was true in Detroit. Her findings make clear that bases of economic inequality are multiple, conflicting, and complex and illustrate how econometric methods can facilitate an investigation of intersecting sources of marginalization. They also help illustrate that without sensitivity to intersectionality, social change researchers are hampered in the pursuit of their objectives.

### Principle 4: Researchers Should Engage With Research Stakeholders

By definition, marginalized people are not benefiting equitably from the current social and political arrangements. Hence, social change theorists see the status quo as implicated in current oppressive structures. They seek greater equity and justice both by raising consciousness among members of marginalized groups and by changing social relationships, processes, practices, and institutions.

Discussing a particular tradition of social change research, Fuller stated, "Some folk do research for the sake of doing research while black folk do research to save the lives of black children" (as cited in Denzin et al., 2008, p. 92). Similarly, Smith (1999) argued that indigenous peoples' main task is to increase their rates of surviving disease, diminish their vulnerability to war with colonists, reduce the loss of tribal lands, reverse unjust public policies, and arrest the destruction of their languages and cultures. Likewise, social change theorists study domestic violence in order to stop it, poverty-reduction policies to increase fairness, and indigenous peoples' relationship to geographic place to challenge practices that threaten environmental sustainability. In short, the final sensitizing principle animating social change research is a belief in researcher engagement and attachment with a change agenda.

The nature of the social change researchers' engagement with research subjects and the researchers' attachment to the issues they face is often captured by the words used to describe their research relationships. Terms commonly used include *research partnership* (Reason & Bradbury, 2006), *a passionate and sympathetic relationship* (Smith, 1999), and *a collaborative altruistic relationship* (Bishop, 2008). In using such terms, scholars reflect their belief that exemplary social change research requires researchers to feel they have a stake in the questions asked and the solutions forged (Errante, 2004). Thus, researchers are guided by sympathetic and empathetic understandings for the pain and injustice faced by those people they study to seek greater engagement.

Clearly, this is a principle of animating social change shared by TCR scholars who seek to do research to improve consumer well-being. Social change theorists offer a range of options for inciting social change that can inform the TCR agenda. This engagement and attachment sometimes, but not always, leads to scholarly output versus direct social or political action by the researcher. Some social change researchers believe that by studying the often invisible social problems of marginalized people or identifying social contradictions, their research can incite social change; these researchers are engaged with and attached to their research subjects and the questions that matter to them, but they feel their role is to raise awareness without attempting to intervene directly on behalf of those they study. Other researchers believe that social action is integral to their research and take an active role in lobbying for and attempting to shape and implement changes. Researchers who adhere to this view feel it is inappropriate to extract or mine insights related to the experiences of marginalized groups while leaving social injustices and suffering in place (Madison, 2008). These researchers often indicate their engagement by labeling their research as moral and ethical (Denzin & Lincoln, 2008), engaged research and living inquiry (Gordon, 2001), or liberatory research (Harrison, 2002). Thus, TCR investigators can engage in social change directly or indirectly.

Among social change researchers whose form of engagement and attachment entails social action, a range of methodological practices exist. Community action researchers, for example, begin the research project by studying only those problems that local people have deemed as important (Reason & Bradbury, 2006). Given that the goal is social change, local capacities and community resources are identified, so they can be eventually leveraged in solutions that can be sustainable. The sample used is shaped by those people who are affected, motivated, or willing to participate. When the social problem is communitywide, the research process needs to include those stakeholders and community groups who would need to be involved in implementing an effective solution. These partnerships help ensure that research findings can include an action plan to resolve the problem that is implementable and can be evaluated for success. Thus, in collaboration with those affected by the problem, developing a program of action is an essential part of an action research project (Ozanne & Saatcioglu, 2008). The indigenous method of intervening for social change is similar in practice: Rather than going "into the field" to do research, much indigenous research is community-based research that seeks to improve the lives of locals (Smith, 1999).

Participatory drama is another method developed by social change researchers whose goal is implementing change and is based on Boal's work (1979). In his *Theater of the Oppressed*, actors do not work from a script, but instead engage the audience dynamically within the play itself. Actors role-play scenarios to educate the audience on the focal topic, such as a social problem, but rather than offering finished and scripted performances, the audience is invited to interrogate and discuss characters, situations, and outcomes of the drama. The ultimate goal is to get the audience to reflect and act on the social issues explored in the drama (Boal, 1995). Such drama-based methods have, for example, been used in Kenya to bring about an AIDS intervention for teens. Short scenes from the life of a young man infected with AIDS were acted out, then teenagers engaged the issues in dialogue (Chamberlain, Chillery, Ogolla, & Wandera, 1995). Other methods used by social change researchers seeking to ensure that their research has immediate local impact include using art and local cultural forms to educate stakeholders about research findings and motivate social change. Examples include crafting telenovelas (Nariman, 1993), songs (Lewis, 2001), puppetry, and dance (Mohapatra, 2000).

## IMPLICATIONS OF THE SENSITIZING CHANGE PRINCIPLES TO METHODOLOGIES FOR TCR

Having discussed both sensitizing principles and related methods from three traditions of social change research, we now consider the implications for consumer researchers with a transformative agenda. First, however, we want to acknowledge that examples of many of the methods that we linked to each principle are found in extant consumer research that may or may not be transformational in intent. For example, Chaplin and John (2007) used pictures in the form of collages to explore the perspectives of children, consistent with the visual methods previously discussed. As another example, Belk (1992) used historical archival materials in his study of Mormons moving their possessions.

We make three observations here. First, it is entirely possible to use the methods discussed above without them being linked to a social change agenda. It is only when the methods are informed by the sensitizing principles that we would expect research with transformative potential to result. Second, the methods that were linked to each sensitizing principle need not be used to the exclusion of other, more traditional methods. Combining techniques highlighted above with traditional techniques can result in research with transformative potential, so long as the researchers are attuned to the sensitizing principles. Third, it is nearly always the case that research with a transformative agenda will generate multiple "products," some of which take the form of written texts, and some of which do not.

The sensitizing principles listed above tend to inform research projects as a whole but may be more or less readily apparent in any given written text that is produced. Particularly when texts are published in journals that require contributions to focus on theory building or theory testing, the role of sensitizing principles may be difficult to discern. Thus, although it is not always possible, when reading a given text produced in the course of a research project with a change agenda to see how the sensitizing principles may have informed that particular product of the project, those seeking to understand transformative research should consider how the principles may inform projects as a whole. Next, we offer seven recommendations for a TCR agenda based on our analysis of these sensitizing principles.

### Go Looking for Trouble

Transformative consumer researchers cannot assume that social injustices (i.e., trouble) will come looking for them. They have to go looking for trouble. Consistent with feminist, action, and indigenous research, TCR should seek opportunities in the form of problems faced by, or opportunities for, improving the well-being of those people who are not benefiting from the current social and economic arrangements. By being vigilant in looking for social injustices and by striving to see the world through the eyes of the poor, the vulnerable, and the forgotten, transformative consumer researchers should affirm the pursuit of social justice as a central and defining value.

## Mix It Up

Transformative consumer researchers need to be eclectic in their use of methods by developing a broad range of tools to deal with diverse social problems and social change agendas. For example, it is problematic to study low-literate consumers in a controlled laboratory context in a university setting. Educational settings were often the central site where low-literate consumers first experienced the painful stigma of low literacy. Moreover, low-literate consumers cope by actively controlling their shopping setting and leveraging personal and social resources (Adkins & Ozanne, 2005). Thus, in the case of low literates, the laboratory context will likely change the very phenomenon that it seeks to understand. For other purposes, however, methods that afford control and comparison are ideal. For example, a controlled study that examines the efficacy of different message formats for antismoking appeals to teenagers would be appropriate both for studying the phenomenon (Pechmann, Zhao, Goldberg, & Reibling, 2003) and creating arguments that would be likely to influence public policy makers' decisions.

Mixed methods will, in fact, often be required through the course of a single project (Ozanne & Anderson, 2010). For example, when examining social problems that are hidden, such as low literacy or violence against women, oral histories and case studies are generally most useful for putting a face on issues, raising awareness, and encouraging community dialogue. Such consciousness-raising methodologies that shine light on the problem can later give way to quantitative methods. For example, after initial qualitative research, quantitative methods, such as surveys, can help assess the prevalence and severity of a problem. At later stages in such a project, alternate methods may again be appropriate. For instance, one problem facing literacy programs is the lack of tutors. Negative stereotypes of low literates might be dispelled among potential volunteer tutors through the use of qualitative case studies that present low literates as mothers and fathers who share common hopes and dreams. The inherent complexity of real social problems means that transformative consumer researchers must be nimble in applying the most relevant methodological tool for the problem at hand given the emerging requirements of a program of social change research.

## Stay a While

Social problems are complex and deeply embedded in specific sociohistorical contexts affecting groups differently and implicating a range of stakeholders. No one study will be definitive, and ongoing programmatic research is typically needed. Transformative consumer researchers will often need to make a long-term commitment to study a social issue. Andreasen's (1975, 2002) work on poverty is exemplary in this regard. Equally, researchers may require a long-term commitment to study a specific group. Hill's research on the homeless (Hill, 2001; Hill & Stamey, 1990) typifies this approach.

As an added complication, some social groups are suspicious of outsiders or are overstudied. In such cases, significant time investments will be needed to develop rapport and trust (Adkins & Ozanne, 2005). Moreover, if ongoing social change interventions arise from TCR, then extended time will be needed in the field to implement interventions and assess the potential long-term impact of these interventions on consumer well-being.

## Make New Friends

Multiperson research teams offer a number of advantages for doing TCR and are ideally composed of people with different methodological and substantive expertise and varying points of view.

Incorporating members of the group being studied into the research team helps achieve this goal and adhere to the sensitizing principles. A diversity of perspectives, methods training, and context or issue expertise can be leveraged to make the research more reflexive and less systematically biased toward any one perspective or set of interests. Teams typically provide a richer understanding of the social problem. The benefits of diverse teams are similarly appreciated in activist research (Wansink, Chapter 3 of this volume).

For example, in a study of diabetes, not only consumer and health researchers were involved but also people from within the community, such as health workers, policy makers, and members of the affected group (Ozanne & Anderson, 2010). Consumer researchers have a particular expertise in understanding the good reasons that people have for engaging in behaviors even when these behaviors may be unhealthy. Obviously, people suffering from diabetes have important insights into the lived experience of being diabetic. Health practitioners often stress following medically prescribed regimes, which may ignore the daily constraints faced by the people studied. Yet, these health experts may have important insights into the epidemiology of the health problem, which could go unrealized were they not part of the research team. Local stakeholders, such as policy makers, can bring further assets to such a project, as they may have access to important resources and insights on barriers to the implementation of possible policy initiatives. The team approach allows these multiple perspectives and complementary assets to be deployed.

Thus, it makes sense to "make new friends" in order to bring together a diverse and effective research team. Together, they can share such tasks as engaging local community groups in the process, doing the research, disseminating the research findings to those affected, and developing educational and intervention programs. While a team approach means that no single person is expected to possess all the necessary skills (Stoecker 2003), it also increases the complexity of the challenges that transformational consumer researchers face. Sherry (2006) offered a helpful examination of the synergistic capabilities that may arise in an ethnographic research team and advice for managing team dynamics. Management of teams is likely to be even more challenging—and more critical—in TCR projects, given the varied skills and perspectives that team members (ideally) have and the many separate tasks involved when social change projects are initiated, implemented, and monitored over an extended period of time. Thus, for TCR projects, strong team management skills are likely to be needed.

Go With the Flow

As transformative consumer researchers expand their contact with social problems and social groups, opportunities will emerge to create and experiment with new methods that arise in situ. Rather than viewing methods as a reified set of procedures, we need to reconceptualize our methods as an open-ended set of dynamic tools to be used for varying purposes.

One possibility is that researchers can use old methods in new ways. For example, a deliberative focus group is a method based on the traditional marketing research tool of focus groups. The twist is that participants are first provided with cutting-edge scientific findings about the social issue at hand before the focus group begins, and this knowledge informs discussions (Ozanne, Corus, & Saatcioglu, 2009). Another possibility is that new methods can be invented. For example, some feminist researchers use systematic examination and reflection on experiences that they go through unexpectedly, such as having a mastectomy or experiencing menopause, as a research method (Reinharz, 1992). Finally, cultural categories and practices can be used to shape new and old methods. For example, as we do more TCR in collective societies, we will need more methods that are based on a collective ethos (Steenkamp, 2005), such as group diaries and community capacity inventories.

The reflexive researcher should critically examine how the methods employed shape the questions asked and are influenced by power relations. Different methods invite different groups to participate and allow different realities to emerge. A consumer food diary may facilitate the participation of those people who are less socially skilled, whereas a dialogical method, such as a focus group, will likely privilege those people who are more verbally skilled. All methodological decisions involve trade-offs. The important point here is to excavate deeply to unearth both the advantages and limitations of each method and to be creative in adapting methods so as to achieve the transformational objectives of the project.

## Shout It Out

Many consumer researchers strive primarily to work within the current reward system to engage in rigorous research and publish this research in the best possible publication outlets in which other academics will read their work. But, if we are serious about the *transformative* part of TCR, we need to do more. Social change will not arise if we continue to talk only among ourselves. We need at least some transformative consumer researchers to reach out and disseminate their findings to relevant stakeholders within the communities where we do our research and to those beyond these communities who can benefit from the research. Wansink's (2006) *Mindless Eating* offers one potential dissemination model; he distilled years of his and colleagues' research on the psychology of eating into an engaging book with popular appeal. At minimum, transformative consumer researchers will need to develop a healthy relationship with their university public relations department. However, effective dissemination will likely need to leverage local forms of cultural communication, ranging from texting technologically wired teens to developing songs and jingles for groups who are less literate (see also Mick et al., Chapter 1 of this volume).

## Be Prepared to Get Changed

Finally, we offer a cautionary piece of advice: Be prepared to be profoundly changed. Based on our own research, as well as discussions with many researchers who have studied pressing social problems or marginalized groups, most researchers are personally transformed (see also Viswanathan, Chapter 5 of this volume). When faced with the hardships experienced by marginalized people, one appreciates one's rich life in which so much is taken for granted: good shelter, physical safety, free education for children, access to health care, an abundance of food and material wealth, and the opportunity to be heard. When faced with the courage demonstrated by people who confront daily adversities, one is humbled. When exposed to the resilience and hopefulness of people who do so much with so little, one is filled with admiration.

At the professional level, researchers engaging in transformative projects become increasingly sensitive to the ethical issues surrounding our use of data. They think twice about mining, extracting, and poaching data from groups who are already marginalized. Additionally, some researchers start to feel committed to giving back something to the people and communities who have shared their insights and understanding. The beauty—and sometimes the beast—of a TCR agenda is that notions of what matters are expanded beyond the creation of academic articles. To the surprise of conventionally trained researchers, the dissemination of research with a goal of improving the well-being of less fortunate people may become not just possible but also paramount.

## ACKNOWLEDGMENTS

The authors deeply appreciate the helpful suggestions made by Stacey Baker, Susan Dobscha, Jeff Murray, and Mark Tadajewski.

## REFERENCES

Adkins, N. R., & Ozanne, J. L. (2005). The low literate consumer. *Journal of Consumer Research, 32*, 93–105.

Andreasen, A. (1975). *The disadvantaged consumer*. New York: Free Press.

Andreasen, A. (2002). Marketing social marketing in the social change marketplace. *Journal of Public Policy & Marketing, 21*, 3–13.

Belk, R. (1992). Moving possessions: An analysis based on personal documents from the 1847–1869 Mormon migration. *Journal of Consumer Research, 19*, 339–361.

Bhavnani, K. (2004). Tracing the contours: Feminist research and feminist objectivity. In S. N. Hesse-Biber & M. L. Yaiser (Eds.), *Feminist perspectives on social research* (pp. 65–77). New York: Oxford University Press.

Bishop, R. (2008). Te kotahitanga: Kaupapa Maori in mainstream classrooms. In N. K. Denzin, Y. S. Lincoln, & L. T. Smith (Eds.), *Handbook of critical and indigenous research* (pp. 439–458). Los Angeles: Sage.

Blum, L. (1999). *At breast: Ideologies of breastfeeding and motherhood in the contemporary United States*. Boston: Beacon.

Boal, A. (1979). *Theater of the oppressed*. New York: Urizen Books.

Boal, A. (1995). *The rainbow of desire: The Boal method of theatre and therapy*. New York: Routledge.

Bristor, J., & Fischer, E. (1993). Feminist thought: Implications for consumer research. *Journal of Consumer Research, 19*, 518–536.

Brueggermann, B. J. (1996). Still-life: Representations and silences in the participant-observer role. In P. Mortensen & G. Kirsch (Eds.), *Ethics and representation in qualitative studies of literacy* (pp. 17–39). Urbana, IL: National Council of Teachers of English.

Chamberlain, R., Chillery, M., Ogolla, L., & Wandera, O. (1995). Participatory educational theatre for HIV/AIDS awareness in Kenya. *PLA Notes, 23*, 69–74.

Chambers, R. (1989). *Farmer first: Farmer innovation and agricultural research*. London: Intermediate Technology.

Chambers, R. (1997). *Whose reality counts? Putting the first last*. London: Intermediate Technology.

Chaplin, L. N., & John, D. R. (2007). Growing up in a material world: Age differences in materialism in children and adolescents. *Journal of Consumer Research, 34*, 480–493.

Cornwall, A. (1992). Body mapping in health RRA/PRA. *RRA Notes, 16*, 69–76.

Crenshaw, K. (1991). Mapping the margins: Intersectionality, identity politics, and violence against women of color. *Stanford Law Review, 43*, 1241–1279.

Denzin, N. K., & Lincoln, Y. S. (2008). Introduction: Critical methodologies and indigenous inquiry. In N. K. Denzin, Y. S. Lincoln, & L. T. Smith (Eds.), *Handbook of critical and indigenous research* (pp. 1–20). Los Angeles: Sage.

Denzin, N. K., Lincoln, Y. S., & Smith, L. T. (Eds.). (2008). *Handbook of critical and indigenous methodologies*. Los Angeles: Sage.

DeVault, M. L. (1990). Talking and listening from women's standpoint: Feminist strategies for interviewing and analysis. *Social Problems, 37*, 701–721.

DeVault, M. L. (1991). *Feeding the family: The social organization of caring as gendered work*. Chicago: University of Chicago Press.

Elliot, R., & Davies, A. (2006). Using oral history methods in consumer research. In R. W. Belk (Ed.), *Handbook of qualitative research methods in marketing* (pp. 244–254). Northampton, MA: Edward Elgar.

Errante, A. (2004). But sometimes you're not part of the story: Oral histories and ways of remembering and telling. In S. N. Hesse-Biber & M. L. Yaiser (Eds.), *Feminist perspectives on social research* (pp. 411–434). New York: Oxford University Press.

Fonow, M., & Cook, J. (1991). *Beyond methodology: Feminist scholarship as lived research*. Bloomington: Indiana University Press.

Fonow, M., & Cook, J. (2005). Feminist methodology: New applications in the academy and public policy. *Signs, 30*, 2211–2286.

Foucault, M. (1972). *The archaeology of knowledge* (A. Sheridan Smith, Trans.). New York: Pantheon.

Glen, E. N. (1985). Racial ethnic women's labor: The intersection of gender, race, and class oppression. *Review of Radical Political Economics, 17*, 86–108.

Gordon, G. (2001). Transforming lives: Toward bicultural competence. In P. Reason & H. Bradbury (Eds.), *Handbook of action research* (pp. 243–252). Thousand Oaks, CA: Sage.

Gordon, G. (2004). Fishbowl. *Participatory Learning and Action, 50*, 200–201.

Gordon, G., & Cornwall, A. (2004). Participation in sexual and reproductive well-being and rights. *Participatory Learning and Action, 50*, 73–80.

Gould, S. J. (1981). *The mismeasure of man*. New York: W.W. Norton.

Hall, B. (1981). Participatory research, popular knowledge and power: A personal reflection. *Convergence, 14,* 6–17.

Harrison, F. V. (2002). *Decolonizing anthropology*. Washington, DC: American Anthropological Association.

Hesse-Biber, S. N., Leavy, N. P., & Yaiser, M. L. (2004). Feminist approaches to research as a process: Reconceptualizing epistemology, methodology, and method. In S. N. Hesse-Biber & M. L.Yaiser (Eds.), *Feminist perspectives on social research* (pp. 3–26). New York: Oxford University Press.

Hill, R. P. (2001). Surviving in a material world: Evidence from ethnographic consumer research on people in poverty. *Journal of Contemporary Ethnography, 30,* 364–391.

Hill, R. P., & Stamey, M. (1990). The homeless in America: An examination of possessions and consumption behaviors. *Journal of Consumer Research, 17,* 303–321.

Hondagneu-Sotelo, P. (2001). *Doméstica: Immigrant workers cleaning and caring in the shadows of affluence*. Berkeley: University of California Press.

hooks, b. (1982). *Ain't I a woman: Black women and feminism*. Boston: South End Press.

Kincheloe, J. L., & Steinberg, S. R. (2008). Indigenous knowledges in education: Complexities, dangers, and profound benefits. In N. K. Denzin, Y. S. Lincoln, & L. T. Smith (Eds.), *Handbook of critical and indigenous methodologies* (pp. 135–156). Los Angeles: Sage.

Lather, P., & Smithies, C. (1997). *Troubling the angels: Women living with HIV/AIDS*. Boulder, CO: Westview.

Lewis, H. M. (2001). Participatory research and education for social change: Highlander research and education center. In P. Reason & H. Bradbury (Eds.), *Handbook of action research* (pp. 262–268). Thousand Oaks, CA: Sage.

Madison, D. S. (2008). Narrative poetics and performative interventions. In N. K. Denzin, Y. S. Lincoln, & L. T. Smith (Eds.), *Handbook of critical and indigenous research* (pp. 391–406). Los Angeles: Sage.

McCall, L. (2001a). *Complex inequality: Gender, class and race in the new economy*. New York: Routledge.

McCall, L. (2001b). Sources of racial wage inequality in metropolitan labor markets: Racial, ethnic and gender differences. *American Sociological Review, 66*(4), 520–542.

McCall, L. (2005). The complexity of intersectionality. *Signs, 30,* 1771–1800.

Mick, D. G. (2006). Meaning and mattering through transformative consumer research. In C. Pechmann & L. Price (Eds.), *Advances in consumer research* (Vol. 33, pp. 1–4). Provo, UT: Association for Consumer Research.

Mohapatra, A. K. (2000). Pre-election voters' awareness campaign in Rajasthan—a journey. *PLA Notes, 39*(October), 53–58.

Mukherjee, N. (1993). *Participatory rural appraisal: Methodology and applications*. New Delhi, India: Concept.

Nariman, H. N. (1993). *Soap operas for social change*. Westport, CT: Praeger.

Oakley, A. (1981). Interviewing women: A contradiction in terms. In H. Roberts (Ed.), *Doing feminist research* (pp. 30–61). Boston: Routledge & Kegan Paul.

Ozanne, J. L., & Anderson, L. (2010). Community action research. *Journal of Public Policy & Marketing, 29*(1), 123–137.

Ozanne, J. L., & Anderson, L. (in press). Action research in consumer culture. In L. Peñaloza, N. Toulouse, & L. Visconti (Eds.), *Marketing management: A cultural perspective*. London: Routledge.

Ozanne, J. L., Corus, C., & Saatcioglu, B. (2009). The philosophy and methods of deliberative democracy: Implications for public policy and marketing. *Journal of Public Policy & Marketing, 28,* 29–40.

Ozanne, J. L., & Saatcioglu, B. (2008). Participatory action research. *Journal of Consumer Research, 35,* 423–439.

Pardo, M. S. (1998). *Mexican American women activists: Identity and resistance in two Los Angeles communities*. Philadelphia: Temple University Press.

Pechmann, C., & Ratneshwar, S. (1994). The effects of antismoking and cigarette advertising on young adolescents' perceptions of peers who smoke. *Journal of Consumer Research, 21,* 236–252.

Pechmann, C., Zhao, G., Goldberg, M. E., & Reibling, E. T. (2003). What to convey in antismoking advertisements for adolescents: The use of protection motivation theory to identify effective message themes. *Journal of Marketing, 67,* 1–18.

Peñaloza, L. (2000). Have we come a long way, baby? Negotiating a more multicultural feminism in the marketing academy in the USA. In M. Catterall, P. Maclaran, & L. Stevens (Eds.), *Marketing and feminism* (pp. 39–56). New York: Routledge.

Reason, P., & Bradbury, H. (2006). Introduction: Inquiry and participation in search of a world worthy of human aspiration. In P. Reason & H. Bradbury (Eds.), *Handbook of action research* (pp. 1–14). Thousand Oaks, CA: Sage.

Reinharz, S. (1992). *Feminist methods in social research.* New York: Oxford University Press.

Roos, M., & Mohatle, M. (1998). Investigating local markets using PRA. *Participatory Learning and Action, 33,* 45–53.

Sherry, J. F. (2006). Fielding ethnographic teams: Strategy, implementation and evaluation. In R. W. Belk (Ed.), *Handbook of qualitative research methods in marketing* (pp. 268–276). Northampton, MA: Edward Elgar.

Smith, L. T. (1999). *Decolonizing methodologies: Research and indigenous peoples.* New York: Zed Books.

Steenkamp, J. E. M. (2005). Moving out of the U.S. silo: A call to arms for conducting international marketing research. *Journal of Marketing, 69,* 6–8.

Stoecker, R. (2003). Are academics irrelevant? Approaches and roles for scholars in community-based participatory research. In M. Minkler & N. Wallerstein (Eds.), *Community-based participatory research for health* (pp. 98–112). San Francisco: Jossey-Bass.

Terry, J. (1999). *An American obsession: Science, medicine and homosexuality in American society.* Chicago: University of Chicago Press.

Wang, C. (2003). Using photovoice as a participatory assessment and issue selection tool: A case study with the homeless in Ann Arbor. In M. Minkler & N. Wallerstein (Eds.), *Community-based participatory research for health* (pp. 179–200). San Francisco: Jossey-Bass.

Wang, C., Burris, M. A., & Ping, X. Y. (1996). Chinese village women as visual anthropologists: A participatory approach to reaching policymakers. *Social Science & Medicine, 42,* 1391–1400.

Wang, C., Morrel-Samuels, S., Hutchison, P. M., Bell, L., & Pestronk, R. M. (2004). Flint photovoice: Community building among youths, adults, and policymakers. *American Journal of Public Health, 94,* 911–913.

Wansink, B. (2006). *Mindless eating: Why we eat more than we think.* New York: Bantam Dell.

Zaltman, G. (2003). *How customers think: Essential insights into the mind of the market.* Boston: Harvard Business School Press.

Zaltman, G., & Coulter, R. H. (1995). Seeing the voice of the customer: Metaphor-based advertising research. *Journal of Advertising Research, 35,* 35–51.

# II

## ECONOMIC AND SOCIAL ISSUES

# 5

# Conducting Transformative Consumer Research
## Lessons Learned in Moving From Basic Research to Transformative Impact in Subsistence Marketplaces

Madhu Viswanathan

This chapter is set in the context of low-literate, low-income consumer behavior in the United States as well as buyer, seller, and marketplace behavior in subsistence marketplaces in India. It is based on the synergies that have developed between research, teaching, and social initiatives through the academic Subsistence Marketplaces Initiative (http://www.business.illinois .edu/subsistence) and a nonprofit initiative, the Marketplace Literacy Project (http://www .marketplaceliteracy.org; Viswanathan & Sridharan, 2009). Whereas much of the consumer research and related research in the social sciences has focused on literate, relatively resource-rich settings, our goal in embarking on this program many years ago was to examine consumer behavior across literacy and resource barriers.

In contrast to macrolevel economic approaches or midlevel business strategy approaches, such as the base of the pyramid model (Prahalad, 2005), our approach begins at the microlevel, starting with individuals, consumers, entrepreneurs, and communities and studying them in their own right. We coined the term *subsistence marketplaces* to reflect our determination to understand these preexisting marketplaces in their own right and view them not just as markets to sell into but also as individuals and communities to learn from (Viswanathan & Rosa, 2007). Our primary goal was—and is—to understand and enable these marketplaces to be sustainable along multiple dimensions: economic, ecological, and social.

Following a brief overview of our work, this chapter focuses primarily on the lessons learned in moving from basic research to applications designed to create transformational impact. These lessons comprise such topics as designing research methods for Transformative Consumer Research (TCR), making the important transition from research to transformational impact, and benefiting from the feedback loop between practice and research. I conclude with a brief discussion of the nature of TCR and review the previous literature in relevant areas, such as action research, which provides additional helpful perspectives.

## A SUMMARY OF OUR JOURNEY TO DATE

Our work began with the study of low-literate consumer behavior in the United States, using a variety of methods and working with students at adult education centers (Viswanathan, Rosa, & Harris, 2005). Striking here was the lack of work in this area across disciplines, particularly regarding such issues as marketplace interactions and decision making. This was less true at the macro or societal level—where, in fact, numerous studies examine literacy rates—but it was strikingly true at the level of consumer-behavior phenomena. (See Figure 5.1 for a timeline of research, social, and teaching initiatives.)

In the United States, working with the Cooperative Extension Program at the University of Illinois, we developed educational materials that were user-friendly for low-literate audiences and, at the same time, reflected the reality they faced during shopping trips (Viswanathan & Gau, 2005). We did so by listening to clients and teachers and observing teacher–client interactions. We then moved into a phase of using our big picture understanding in the United States to seek in-depth insight into specific issues, for example, through experimental studies of nutritional labeling for

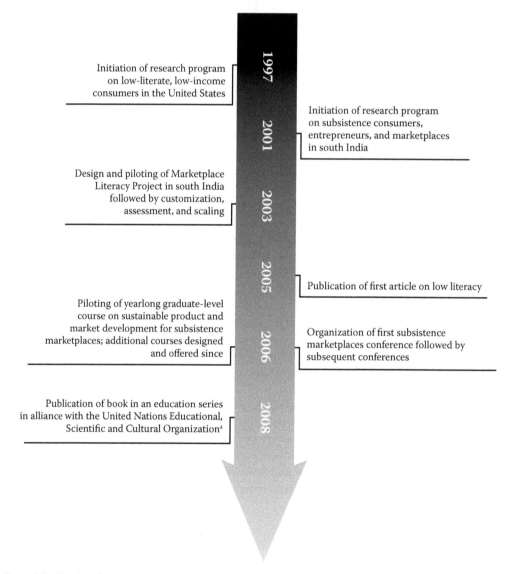

**Figure 5.1** Timeline of research, social, and teaching initiatives.
[a] *Enabling Consumer and Entrepreneurial Literacy in Subsistence Marketplaces*, by M. Viswanathan, S. Gajendiran, and R. Venkatesan, 2008, Dordrecht, the Netherlands: Springer.

low-literate consumers, and of literacy and consumer memory (Viswanathan, Hastak, & Gau, 2009; Viswanathan, Torelli, Xia, & Gau, 2009).

A few years after launching our program in the United States, we expanded our research to subsistence marketplaces in India, where I built a small team consisting of two core members who had grown up in the contexts we were studying and had extensive experience in community development. As we listened and learned during the early Indian research phase, the idea of an extended engagement with an educational program on consumer and entrepreneurial literacy, which we came to call *marketplace literacy*, took preliminary shape. Ultimately, it led to the creation of a nonprofit dubbed the Marketplace Literacy Project.

As the name implies, our focus was not on basic literacy. Rather, it was on what we now describe as a socioculturally embedded form of marketplace literacy, one that is a necessity in an intensely one-to-one interactional environment. Similarly, we focused not so much on concrete vocational skills, but rather on *know-how* in running a business and *know-why* to adapt to changing circumstances (e.g., why be customer-oriented, why choose a business, how and why value chains work). Although we certainly turned up numerous programs focusing on vocational skills, our search for programs on know-how was relatively unsuccessful and programs with the starting point of know-why appeared to be nonexistent. These were the gaps that we set out to fill.

For example, to make these distinctions more concrete, a poor woman who knows how to cook may decide to start a food shop where she lives. We aim to help her engage in broader kinds of thinking, which may involve know-how (e.g., in designing and promoting products) or know-why, which comprises the kinds of variations (e.g., home delivery, selling ingredients to hotels) that may help her adapt to changing circumstances. We hope that by thinking in these ways, individuals will be able to function better as consumers, entrepreneurs, or subsistence consumer-merchants (Viswanathan, Rosa, & Ruth, 2010).

We have noted elsewhere that the overarching goals of the Marketplace Literacy Project are to concretize, localize, and *social*ize the learning experience (Viswanathan, Sridharan, Gau, & Ritchie, 2009). By socialization, we mean enabling learning through social interactions between participants, as they usually possess such skills irrespective of low levels of literacy and income. This three-part perspective infuses every element of the project.

Once we had several years of experience on the ground in India, we began documenting and assessing the project. The iterative documentation, editing, and fine-tuning process that ensued over the course of several years culminated in a book that describes the project and its implications for different sectors of society (Viswanathan, Gajendiran, & Venkatesan, 2008a; see also Viswanathan, Gajendiran, & Venkatesan, 2008b), recently published in an education series in alliance with the United Nations Educational, Scientific and Cultural Organization.

Meanwhile, we continued to offer our programs in an increasingly broad variety of settings and configurations. For example, we developed a daylong marketplace and consumer literacy program and a 2-day entrepreneurial literacy program. These and similar experiments were conducted in cooperation with community-based organizations, such as local women's groups, in a given locality. Our approach was (and is) problem centered, rather than program centered, emphasizing a customized approach to creating educational programs rather than using our existing program as a hammer as we look for nails. We emphasized know-why—again, to enable individuals to learn and adapt to the changing marketplace—and treated buyers and sellers as two sides of the same coin. Finally, and most recently, we began seeking ways to scale the project. We are convinced that, given sufficient commitment and customization, our programs are highly effective, which encourages us to push for broader reach and more impact. This scaling effort is ongoing.

We also continue to work on multiple levels. Our approach in India—again, based on previous learnings in the United States—was to operate at the microlevel as we moved through different communities during the development and customization phase. Those impacts were almost entirely local, but we also continued to work at the macrolevel, partnering with larger organizations whose impact is felt over a far broader base. Each approach informs and supports the other. Individual communities are our platforms for change; we need to stay in close touch with them to develop a holistic understanding of the issues they face and to get ongoing feedback on our educational programs and their impact. This helps us paint the big picture, which, in turn, lends rigor and system to our local efforts. In parallel, similar to our progression in the United States, research has grown from big picture understanding to specific projects encompassing experimental, survey, and qualitative approaches (Chaturvedi, Chiu, & Viswanathan, 2009; Viswanathan et al., 2010).

## LESSONS ABOUT METHODOLOGICAL ISSUES

### Develop Diverse Skills Through Local Partnerships

TCR brings together in-depth theory and practical realities. Therefore, its methods have to be designed to achieve this ambitious goal. In venturing into the arena of low-literate consumer behavior in the United States, it was unclear how we were going to move forward (i.e., research methods, samples, etc.) or even what we expected to find. Obviously, this was not a discrete research project with a circumscribed outcome; rather, our goal was to understand and educate ourselves as a first step, a process that I now readily describe as immersion.

We began by attending a required training session to serve as volunteer tutors at the local adult education center, and we subsequently tutored students and observed classroom activities. This required reaching out to the staff at the adult education center, communicating to them about our objectives, and—drawing on their expertise—emphasizing the need to build relationships with organizations. The classes at the adult education center were roughly divided into three grade-equivalent levels: 0–4, 5–8, and 9–12. Although we observed a range of classes, we began by interviewing students in levels 5–12 and teachers from all levels. We used unstructured approaches, essentially aiming to learn in different ways. (Clearly, with low-literate participants, tools such as surveys did not seem to hold much potential, at least as a starting point.) We were more cautious with students in the 0–4 level; we spent more than a year building rapport with them before attempting to interview them, a delay that, in retrospect, may have been unnecessary. In those intervening months, we interacted with these students in classroom settings and observed them on group shopping trips. Over time, as we tried to disentangle literacy from related issues, we moved to studying comparison groups through in-depth interviews, including literate but poor individuals and students of English as a second language at adult education centers.

Although unearthing the stories of all of these individuals was a slow process, and one that took me well out of my comfort zone—that is, conducting experiments with U.S. students in a campus setting—it was more than worth the effort. Above all, I found myself learning about the many things that I take for granted as a result of my literacy. In many ways, my educational level made me least qualified to study those with low levels of literacy; it was difficult for me to unlearn what I already knew and see the world as they saw it. In retrospect, it is clear that our focus was still one of developing the big picture, that is, understanding this realm in a broad way. Going into parts of the picture in greater depth, and expanding our methodological toolkit, would come later.

Driving our methodological approach was the need to accumulate a diverse set of skills, through working with organizations in the field, and develop our research team's own skills, through activities like volunteer training and tutoring. One point of satisfaction and pride is that we have developed relationships with teachers and staff that continue to this day. Central to building such relationships, I believe, has been our practice of informing our partners of our research goals—and doing so on a regular basis. Their goals and ours, without exception, are well aligned; we all seek to improve the lives of low-literate, low-income consumers. The currency that sustains these relationships is not money but, rather, a shared sense of purpose and a habit of sustained communication about the research, its anticipated outcomes, and the social initiatives that might grow out of those outcomes.

This collaborative approach has been duplicated in our work in India. That work initially was construed by our team somewhat narrowly; we saw ourselves simply as studying low-literate consumer behavior in a different setting. It soon expanded in new directions to comprise research on subsistence consumers, entrepreneurs (or consumer-merchants), and marketplaces.

My initial contact in India was a large nongovernmental organization, an employee of which was recommended to assist me on a part-time basis with interviews. We began with in-depth interviews in neighborhoods where my associate had worked with families on a variety of initiatives, and our research method evolved as I began to understand the constraints under which we would operate and also the limits on what feasibly could be implemented. My associate, who had grown up in the same subsistence contexts we studied, spoke little English but was fluent in the native language and had worked with the communities we studied. More than anything else, my goal was to listen and learn in a relatively bottom-up way, without specific research goals and the associated in-depth study of the relevant literature. Again in retrospect, this was well suited for my larger objectives of creating a broad program of research and social initiatives, with the goal of educating myself being the first step. It would be less well suited for the researchers at the stage of their careers where time is scarce and during which it is important to be both grounded in the phenomenon and have an understanding of the theoretical lenses that can be applied to make the research more efficient.

To sum up, our interviews were sincere conversations, nothing more and nothing less. Growing up in India as part of the middle class meant that I had some understanding of the culture, but a sustained study of people who live in subsistence was, for me, an eye-opening experience. In a sense, all that we do begins and ends with the generosity of people in sharing their life experiences and thereby educating us. Participants generously opened up their lives to us, often relating the saddest of circumstances with deep emotions. I thereby gained a window into a previously unknown world, one that was resource poor but network rich, in which the people survived through their ability to communicate orally. These social connections offered individuals a stepping stone to learn and develop skills, but—as it turned out—there were significant downsides as well.

We soon realized that to take our research to the next level, we needed a trained team on the ground. I therefore hired my part-time associate and another person, both of whom had employment (at the nongovernmental organization mentioned above) that was coming to an end. They had grown up in the cultural contexts we studied and spent decades in community development. The fact that they did not possess a business background has been, in my view, an advantage, because it has helped us jointly approach projects without preconceptions and honestly assess our progress. Also important was our decision, early on, to view the field team as partners rather than simply data collectors. They do serve multiple important functions, a fact that needs to be recognized. Their role as cultural brokers within communities, for example, has been highlighted in the literature (Molyneaux et al., 2009).

In these settings, the support of local organizations, such as nongovernmental organizations and community-based organizations, is vital. As noted elsewhere, such organizations tend to have a deep understanding of local communities and can facilitate research and other initiatives in a number of ways (Molyneaux et al., 2009). A note of caution should be sounded here, however: Conducting the kinds of research described herein requires a trained team, one that a given nongovernmental organization may not be able to field or may not have the capacity to share. Thus, a central methodological lesson is that TCR can examine complex social phenomena, but these efforts require diverse skills best embodied by teams of researchers, field workers, and alliances with indigenous organizations.

We design and adapt methods in the field and implement them through an array of relationships on the ground. Developing and nurturing relationships are paramount as well. Understanding capabilities *and* limitations in these relationships is also essential in this regard. The conceptual understanding of research is an important area in which communication with the field team is critical, an issue highlighted in the literature (Molyneaux et al., 2009). A key challenge is to communicate about the nature of academic research and the need for abstract understanding. Training through means such as role-playing is important in administering data collection procedures.

Language is another arena in which understanding capabilities and limitations is critical. We try to adhere closely to the original statements made by our research participants, but this is not always a simple task. Of the two core members of my team, the junior associate is learning English, while the senior associate has moderate oral and written English skills. The process of translation has involved transcription work in Tamil by the junior associate and then translation to English by the senior associate. Similar issues arose in translating survey measures from English to Tamil, and in our writing and editing efforts.

I should stress that there is significant give-and-take in these partnerships that moves the academic researcher out of his or her traditional role. Inevitably, one builds relationships that comprise a deep understanding of the life circumstances and constraints faced by one's colleagues. Individually and collectively, working in subsistence contexts, we face personal adversity. We learn to support each other. At the same time, the relationships that we build with individuals in the organizations we work with are also critically important. In the social arena, ultimately, it is individuals who act as champions of specific goals and broader programs. The relationships we build with individuals are, therefore, extraordinarily important.

## Understand Motivations of Partners

I turn now to a related lesson in implementing methods and social initiatives. When one seeks to study complex phenomena through relationships with a diverse set of partners, it may prove necessary to develop a system of incentives well beyond those traditionally associated with academic research, which is especially true for the TCR scholar. Perhaps the most important question in gauging the potential for relationships is that of motivation: What are the prospective partners looking for? The answer is likely to vary widely. The participants in our surveys, interviews, and other research efforts seek a meaningful interaction from which they gain a broader vision, whether it be in educating their communities through marketplace literacy education or in creating a climate in which quality goods and services become available. The community-based organizations, obviously, are looking for our core "product": marketplace literacy education. The local sociopolitical leadership looks to us to help them provide community welfare. Larger social enterprises want the chance to engage in collaborative work that furthers their mission and to derive the benefits of relevant research findings. Local educational institutions also seek new knowledge and see benefit in participation in public events.

The question of incentives and motivations quickly brings us back to the importance of relationships. As in most realms of collaborative human activity, participants in TCR are unlikely to make satisfactory progress when those organizations have significantly different agendas. Alignment is key. When the TCR scholar nurtures strong relationships, well beyond the traditional role of the researcher, he or she is well positioned to make decisions about potential partners.

Drilling down on this issue of incentives, early on we decided not to pay participants to attend our educational program but, instead, to create other appropriate incentives. This approach mitigated issues of fair selection when incentives are offered, as has been highlighted in the literature (Molyneaux et al., 2009). We also decided not to pay recruiters, because we did not want to risk muddying the incentives of a participant who has been recruited (e.g., attendance in exchange for receiving a portion of the recruiting fee). Similarly, paying community-based organizations to run educational programs gave us pause, although we often agreed, after negotiation, to help pay the cost of renting community halls, serving refreshments, and so forth. Our overall aim in setting up incentives was to recruit participants who wanted to be educated, while also asking the communities to make at least a modest investment in the local effort. We believed that signaling our guiding values—in part through our incentives—was important to both the core team and the communities we worked with. At the same time, however, we understood the need for enough flexibility to accommodate the complex realities of subsistence.

## Invest Time to Understand Local Context and Develop Appropriate Methods

Implicit in the methodological issues discussed above is the challenge of immersion in the local context in order to understand that context, develop teams and relationships, and design more tailored methods. We took this challenge seriously, and I can offer myself as a case in point. My own background in no way prepared me for an easy understanding of our target communities. Our open-ended venture into low-literate, low-income consumer behavior as well as subsistence consumer, entrepreneur, and marketplace behavior was intended, in part, to educate myself in an intensive, and thereby efficient, way. As anticipated, this immersion gave me a reasonably powerful bottom-up set of insights into local life circumstances. It also made it possible for me to change our methods more or less in real time, based on what I was learning.

At the same time, my immersion in the field also helped me build my team and establish relationships with partners, not only for research purposes but also for creating targeted social initiatives. Finally, my time in the field enabled me to work closely with my team, setting both direction and tone. Human capital was, and is, our most important asset, and it can only be developed through sustained, in-person interactions. Immersion, for us, was a *sine qua non*.

## Engage in Healthy Disbelief to Refine Methods to Local Needs

I have mentioned several times the importance of refining methodologies in response to on-the-ground learnings to ensure that maximum benefits are delivered to TCR participants. Moving our focus of investigation from the United States to India made this lesson immediately obvious to us, as we sought to serve at-risk individuals in dramatically different contexts.

In the United States, for example, our methods evolved to reflect the particular needs of our participants there: from tutoring and observations in classrooms to open-ended interviews, group shopping observations (based on a class assignment), and one-on-one shopping observations (supplemented with interviews), as well as surveys and experiments. Similarly, in India, we conducted observations, interviews, and experiments in different settings, ranging from community centers to individuals' houses, that emphasized the comfort and needs of the participants. In both contexts, logistical issues needed to be addressed, such as providing participants with transportation to grocery stores.

Beyond that, the specific methods we designed were carefully customized. Interviews in India emphasized learning about larger life circumstances through empathetic conversations. Experiments minimized text-anxiety issues through realistic tasks and stimuli, personal administration, and verbal responses (Viswanathan, Gau, & Chaturvedi, 2008). I believe that this is a generalizable lesson, given the nature of phenomena that are in focus in TCR and also given the constraints of participants. Several cases in point may help illustrate the need for local knowledge combined with iterative design, assessment, and modification. The use of translated statements with seven-point response categories, for example, was a complex task that sometimes led to the same response being given across multiple items. My junior associate devised the approach of asking which side of the scale respondents fell into (i.e., agreement or disagreement), then asking for finer discriminations within those broader categories. Similarly, when administering a questionnaire to female participants, we changed the focus of a scale item from romance to affection.

Our methodological explorations also extended to the design and assessment of the marketplace literacy program. Simply stated, we were attempting to create an education program that drew on (a) my own experience with business education, (b) my associates' extensive local background, acquired both through growing up in similar contexts and through their work in community development, and (c) our ongoing research, including interviews and observations. We sketched out some initial ideas on broader objectives, specific topics, instructional methods, and specific details. Certain conclusions seemed obvious from the outset, such as assuming our audience could not read or write. (This was almost definitional, as we were aiming for the lower levels of literacy and income.) Given the anticipated background of our participants, it seemed likely that even before we attempted to cover specific topics, icebreaking exercises would be very important. We had to make the participants comfortable in an educational setting with which they would not be familiar, and we had to shape and inform their expectations for the program (i.e., the program was not about livelihood skills and would not involve advice on a specific business idea).

Our team members clearly complemented each other as we carried out two key tasks: developing our core topics and identifying the life circumstances, including low literacy, that had to be taken into account. A sharp and exclusive focus on topics to be covered would have been counterproductive at that stage and in that context. Drawing on our different life experiences in these contexts, my associates and I were able to design, assess, and iteratively adapt our educational program. For example, we used picture sortings, simulations of situations, an audio quiz, and small-group assignments and discussions to cover a number of issues. We asked small groups to organize a set of pictures depicting a value chain (e.g., a farmer growing fruit, a retail outlet selling it, consumers buying it) and money (represented by a currency bill) into concentric circles in such a way that the element that is most important to running a successful business wound up in the innermost circle. Many groups initially placed money in the middle. Gradually, however, most amended their "universe" to put the customer at the center. This and other exercises evolved almost continuously. Similarly, the qualitative and quantitative methods we used for assessment purposes also evolved to suit the preferences of participants and reflect our ongoing learning. For example, we learned to take into account the paradoxical outcome that some participants experienced decreased confidence, at least temporarily, in the wake of their educational program, evidently because they realized for the first time how much they did not know.

TCR should assume that there is no particular right way to do things and that a healthy skepticism about precedent is essential throughout the research process. Our methods continue to evolve as we try to scale our program to reach more people. Each setting offers unique challenges, ranging from the logistical to the cultural, and yet we feel duty-bound not to reinvent the wheel in each locale. For example, should different social strata living in different hamlets within a village be combined into one educational program, or should each hamlet be treated separately? There are no easy answers, so I believe that it remains an important question.

The literature makes reference to elements of these methodological lessons in different contexts. For instance, in the context of collaborative research with disadvantaged communities, difficulties due to time-consuming and diverse tasks (e.g., communicating with different stakeholders, offering expertise and advice to help the community) and management of community sensitivities (e.g., conflicts regarding who represents the community) have been noted (MacLean, Warr, & Pyett, 2009). The need to use multiple methods has been emphasized in field research in such areas as health, as has the need to design research based on learning from participants (Israel, Eng, Schulz, Parker, & Satcher, 2005). The importance of social relationships between researchers and field teams, and also between field teams and communities, has been emphasized in the context of conducting research ethically in low-income settings (Molyneaux et al., 2009). A number of issues we discuss have been highlighted in the context of developing partnerships with communities in participatory research (e.g., Wallerstein, Duran, Minkler, & Foley, 2005), reflecting on the research organization's strengths and weaknesses, listening and learning about power dynamics, identifying partners through participation in relevant networks, determining the benefits for the community of working with outside organizations, figuring out the unique needs and imperatives of partners, and understanding the time-intensive nature of building relationships.

## LESSONS ABOUT TRANSFORMATIVE IMPACT

### Education Based on TCR Can Be Transformative

One of the central lessons that we have learned involves the power of education. This may sound like an odd statement, coming as it does from a longtime business educator, but because I started from a vantage point of skepticism and relative unawareness—and, to be sure, a position of relative privilege—coming to understand how nonformal educational programs can have real impact has been an eye-opening experience for me. It has underscored how education can change not only people's skills but also their self-confidence—and, by extension, their awareness and exercising of their rights. It has reminded me of all the things I take for granted as an educated person and how the very act of being treated with dignity in a learning environment, even for a few days, can bring with it enormous benefits. For example, a woman in our program thanked us for educating not just her but also her entire family. Particularly when women are the change agents, that kind of impact tends to spread beyond the family as well, as people share what they learned with others in their community.

The viral nature of information spread became evident to us during qualitative assessments a few months after conducting our pilot educational program. Women in our feedback session talked about sharing their learning throughout their community, particularly in the consumer realm. They told us that they had passed along to friends and acquaintances their learning on such issues as checking prices, buying wholesale, and switching shops. The women in one village talked about the local shopkeeper offering them good deals because they were the "women who had received training." Obviously, in a one-to-one interactional world of intense personal communications, often face-to-face, there exists a powerful potential for the spread of new ideas. When combined with life skills that are immediately relevant and practical for those living in extreme resource constraints, this potential is realized and accentuated.

Combining the powers of research and education places the academic researcher with expertise in each of these areas at the center of research-based educational initiatives. The potential for consumer research that translates into transformative impact through education is tremendous. What TCR scholars can produce—socially relevant knowledge based on rigorous research—in turn can provide the basis for creating powerful educational programs, which are powerful in part due to their viral potential.

Also noteworthy is the power of education that is aimed at know-why, and helping people learn and adapt to changing circumstances. We teach people to proactively shape their marketplaces rather than simply fit in with them. Two strands in the literature are noteworthy in this regard. The path of self-perception from an object reacting to reality to a subject shaping it has been described as "conscientization" (Freire, 1970). This certainly resonates with our work. Similarly, pragmatic learning theory (Dewey, 1910; Elkjaer, 2004; Jayanti & Singh, 2010) emphasizes how experiences lead to awareness of problems (e.g., why something happens), which then leads to inquiry about how problems can be solved, which in turn mobilizes the individual to productive action and ultimately creates a self-reinforcing cycle (Jayanti & Singh, 2010). Central to this approach is that thinking is instrumental to action, which in turn is rooted in situations (Dewey, 1910; Elkjaer, 2004). Our emphasis on know-why, relating to marketplace situations that subsistence consumers and entrepreneurs experience, aims to trigger inquiry and productive action, thereby enabling individuals to gain experience-based knowledge.

### Practical and Theoretical Impact May Not Align

Also noteworthy is the issue of what translates and, perhaps, transforms. Disseminating our findings in a nuanced research article certainly has its value, but it seems evident that the best way to have a substantial impact is through the proactive pursuit of social initiatives based on the broader research program. The research article, by its very nature, tends to involve a funneling of discoveries into a more pointed set of theoretical insights, with the conventional set of implications at the end. In our case, the implications that led to the most important social initiatives flowed out of the dedicated immersion. I am certainly not arguing against rigorous or nuanced thought, but in this particular realm of TCR, what translates from research to practice tends not to overlap with what is central to the typical academic article; instead, it grows out of a more inclusive effort to understand the phenomenon in context.

What really creates transformative impact? (For us, at least, this is the key question.) Our experience is certainly not one of a research project leading to publishable insights, the implications of which were then acted on to create impact. Again, ours is an experience in which a broad understanding through research *preceded*, but then *paralleled*, our educational initiatives. This was perhaps because, in many ways, we were seeking a big picture understanding to educate ourselves. Once the research to social initiative translation efforts are in place, however, the latter lead to nuanced insights that in turn spur research questions. Immersion leads to learning, which aids in the design of an application to improve consumer welfare, which opens the door to deeper and richer insights.

The nature of education in our projects is also noteworthy in this regard. As noted, it is more than skills, in that it extends to self-confidence and awareness of rights. Our focus on know-why helps participants learn how to learn. TCR scholars occupy a unique vantage point in this regard, because their research experiences create nuggets of insights that can be translated into educational efforts. Such efforts may range from public-service announcements to documentaries and from curricular innovations to informal education (see also Mick, Pettigrew, Pechmann, & Ozanne, Chapter 1 of this volume).

Our (understandable) instincts to cover concepts in the education we designed had to be tempered by contextual factors. For example, when working with adults who have not been in a formal educational setting in many years, if ever, their anxieties about what will transpire in the "classroom" have to be taken into consideration. Thus, exercises to make participants feel comfortable and discussions to set expectations are very important. Sociocultural factors, such as social hierarchy, may also need to be taken into account. For instance, in one of our programs, there were three distinct groups that were based on social hierarchy and associated areas of residence within their village. These groups began their experience with us as substantially separate entities that gradually intermingled as time passed, a process that happened at its own pace.

Also paramount in making the translation from TCR to education is design from the vantage point of the end beneficiaries. This is particularly challenging for the academic who focuses primarily, or exclusively, on writing for research journals and teaching university students. Translation, in that case, means turning theory into classroom content for the benefit of a group of students with backgrounds and literacy levels comparable to those of their professors. This is fine, as far as it goes, but we university-based educators tend to be underqualified when it comes to working with low-literate individuals. For one thing, we have to strive to overcome the presumptions that accompany a high level of literacy. In designing programs for low-literate, poor audiences, for example, we have to keep in mind their unfamiliarity and difficulty with abstractions and, instead, emphasize concrete learning experiences. We use local examples from individuals' daily lives, making it easier for them to relate to the concepts at hand. Because our participants possess strong oral language and social skills, we emphasize learning through social interactions. Consistently, we focus on providing benefits in the near term, which underscores the relevance of our "product" to their life circumstances.

Again, I don't mean to suggest that TCR only exerts its influence through practical application or that there are no synergies with core research. In fact, I am convinced that our learning through intuitively designing and administering a program can and does lead to ideas for new, specific research projects. Our engagement in social initiatives provides grounded knowledge that can and should be used to gauge potential research projects for their social relevance. More insights on this feedback loop are discussed later in this chapter.

## TCR Scholars Can Play a Central Role in the Challenge of Scaling

In understanding the challenge of creating large-scale impact, it seems clear that TCR scholars can contribute significantly to that scaling process and also can design new kinds of research as opportunities arise during scaling. First, though, let me say that *scaling* is not the preferred term here, because it connotes "one size fits all." Our purpose is perhaps better expressed as maximizing reach. We have been actively involved in this phase for about 4 years now, and it is very much a work in progress. Based on our experience to date, however, I can point to several key steps along the way, including identifying an important need that is not being served, finding an innovative way to serve it, creating the right technology to deploy to maximize reach, and, eventually, developing an enterprise model. The need for patient human capital—paralleling the need for patient financial capital, which is discussed eloquently by Novogratz (2009)—is critical.

Of all of these, developing an enterprise model is the most elusive and, in some ways, the most important. Identifying a need is insufficient, finding a solution is insufficient, innovating in its delivery is insufficient, and finding the right technology to maximize reach is insufficient. Developing an enterprise model for large-scale application—and, of course, a way to conduct a careful assessment of impact—is essential. Pilot programs are an important learning medium, but unless the learning leads to larger scale application, the real potential for impact is not fully realized. This is particularly true for an educational program.

Given our limited resources, our approach has been to present our program to organizations already capable of wide reach. For example, one of our early scaling efforts involved working with a large foundation that reached some 200 villages. With that foundation, we first attempted to train individuals who would conduct subsequent programs. The costs of this approach proved prohibitive, and we next decided to focus on video-based education. Individuals from such communities created video episodes that we scripted, embedding key aspects of marketplace literacy into the situations that our characters confronted. This process underscores the unique role played by the TCR scholar, who contributes on levels ranging from the conceptual to the operational.

The effort continues. We are currently designing a scaling process whereby facilitators will show videos and run classes with assignments and feedback. The challenge here is that video alone does not create an in-depth educational experience. The actual learning occurs in interactions among participants, such as through small-group exercises in which they apply their learning to their own villages. The involvement of the TCR scholar in such issues of design can be invaluable from the vantage point of gauging the effectiveness of educational approaches and the limitations of technologies, guiding the scaling process while balancing pragmatic constraints.

Unsurprisingly, a host of logistical issues tend to arise. Villages often have a place to meet, but only about 30 of the approximately 200 villages can be reached through computer centers with facilitators that our partner foundation operates. For the remaining villages, we are planning to use a mobile van with a television and DVD player and then use the local community centers to administer modules. The van also has a large-screen capability that we will use to play the video in some central location in an effort to reach others in the village. As noted, many of these villages are divided into different hamlets, reflecting various social strata, which compels us to consider whether to organize classes on a hamlet-by-hamlet basis.

We plan to incorporate immediate and delayed assessments to understand the efficacy of our educational programs, as well as the factors that inhibit or enable entrepreneurship. We will incorporate differences in groups of villages, social strata, and gender of participants to understand the relationships among sociocultural factors and the scaling of in-depth entrepreneurial literacy. Some of the factors we will explore include access to financial resources, membership in social networks, local infrastructure, local livelihood opportunities, governmental support, and family support. Thus, even our scaling process—mainly aimed at increasing our transformative impact— serves as a research endeavor that may lead to new insights.

Concurrently, we are working with one of the largest microfinancing organizations in the world, advising that entity on how to embed marketplace literacy issues in a movie titled *Shakti Rising* (Rajeswari, 2010) that has now been produced. The movie revolves around a woman who joins a self-help group to overcome personal problems and realize her aspirations as an entrepreneur. This movie is intended to serve as a launching platform for a video-based educational program we are designing that addresses marketplace literacy. The program will be self-administered by groups of women and include both in-class assignments based on the movie and out-of-class assignments aimed at applying the learning to their own villages.

To reiterate a lesson discussed earlier about the importance of relationships, scaling is greatly enabled by individuals in organizations who serve as champions and with whom we have developed relationships over time. Challenges in scaling include identifying the appropriate technology and adapting educational content accordingly. Similarly, creating the enterprise model, incentivizing people, and working out logistical issues all impact the educational goals and can benefit from the perspective of the TCR scholar. Finally, scaling in itself offers special opportunities for large-scale field research. Again, TCR scholars have a particularly useful vantage point from which to help design the scaling process. They are in a position to defend the integrity of the planned application—education in the case above—while also making difficult trade-offs. With deep grounding in the underlying research and involvement in the design of the application, the TCR investigator has much to offer larger social-enterprise partners.

A Research Mentality Is Key

In our work, we emphasize a particular kind of inquiry, what might be called our research mentality, that suspends preconceptions (as much as humanly possible). It aims to rigorously analyze the data, strive for new insights, and avoid reinventing the proverbial wheel. For instance, the power of social networks in subsistence contexts is not a new discovery, but our ability to "peel the onion" in a more refined manner has led to novel insights.

Our research mentality is also reflected in how our findings provided the basis for our educational programs. We depended on the listening and immersion phase to design our original educational program. Over time, our research has progressed in parallel with the educational program, in part because a process of continuous assessment of the program also involves a research mentality. Our determination to view our research program as a set of varied insights that can be customized to different situations is another manifestation of the particular research mentality we endorse. This mentality is also crucial in designing the scaling process and its assessment, and in detailing new research projects that stem from such fieldwork, as elaborated in the next section.

Above all, our focus on real impact, rather than the kind of self-perpetuating publicity that all too often predominates in these contexts, captures the research mentality that our program has sought to engender. This is our most important yardstick: Is it hype, or is it real impact? Real impact is also the strongest test of the underlying research and drives our research mentality.

## LESSONS ON THE LOOPS BETWEEN TCR AND ITS POSITIVE IMPACT

Moving from TCR to positive impact has enriched our research, and these lessons—relating to forward and backward loops—are discussed in this section (see Figure 5.2).

### Synergies Between Research and Social Initiatives

Perhaps the most important lesson we have learned to date is the rich synergies that can develop across coordinated research, teaching, and social initiatives. In fact, each of these activities has enriched the others. Research informed the design of the educational program in India. The design and administration of the program has shed light on important research issues and provided nuanced insights. Careful documentation and assessment of the education program also reflects such synergy. As noted, scaling our educational program in turn offers opportunities for new field research.

The relationships and partnerships we developed for social initiatives greatly increase our effectiveness in research, by addressing a number of issues such as shared purposes and incentives among the organizations and individuals we work with. As noted earlier, our ability to demonstrate the larger practical purpose of our research—while also developing activities on the ground that help communities and are aligned with the goals of the organizations with which we work—opens up research opportunities. Explaining and demonstrating the practical implications of our research to our participants increases cooperation.

Looking more broadly, communicating to different audiences also enriches one's research. We communicate to a range of audiences, including participants of a wide range of ages and practitioners in social and commercial enterprises. We view each interaction as an opportunity to strengthen the relevance of the research and develop deeper insights. Similarly, writing for different audiences helps us improve our communication to the academic audience, among others. Working with different groups enriches research by providing a variety of real-world feedback. It also leads to new insights, as managers and social entrepreneurs pose tough questions that force us to be clear about what we are trying to do, which may in turn necessitate more research. These are, in short, virtuous circles.

### Relevant Research Can Emerge From Transformative Interventions

As noted, our efforts to create an application with the potential for social impact led to new research questions. For instance, our efforts to implement the marketplace literacy program led to questions about the need to teach about sustainable consumption and production. In turn, this led to research questions about these topics and the need to understand them. Research on low-literate consumers provided a basis to design educational materials on nutrition. We conducted research, for example, to test the effects of graphical nutrition labels (Viswanathan, Hastak, & Gau, 2009). This led in turn to further thinking on ways to facilitate communication for low-literate consumers in the

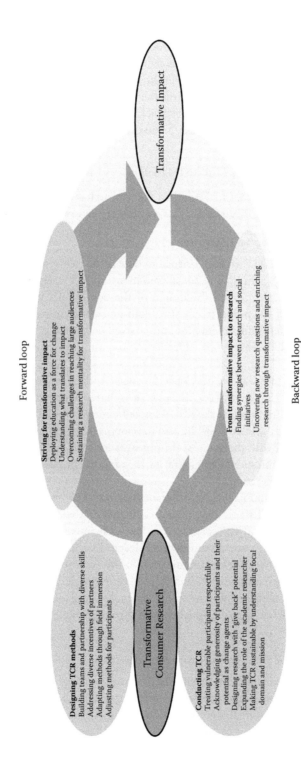

**Figure 5.2**    Forward and backward loops from Transformative Consumer Research to transformative impact.

United States. We are also exploring deeper questions about abstract versus concrete thinking and decision making.

The ongoing scaling process described earlier opens up field research on a larger scale. We plan to study sociocultural differences across villages, the effects of those differences on the development of marketplace literacy, and the extent to which new theoretical issues can be addressed in such settings. It is worth reiterating that such new directions stem from the bottom-up opportunities that arise out of our fieldwork rather than a top-down examination of a predetermined set of variables.

## LESSONS ON THE CONDUCT OF TCR

### Respect At-Risk Participants

We have strived to maintain the highest level of integrity in conducting research and imparting education, especially in the way we treat our participants. Despite the recurrent temptation to sidestep procedures and incentives (e.g., when locals tell us that payment or informed-consent forms are not needed), we have carefully adhered to procedures. Our guiding principle is that we respect the inherent dignity of every human being with whom we interact. By that standard, a subsistence participant cannot be treated any differently than an affluent one. In rural settings, it is not uncommon for a group of people to gather and for several of them to volunteer information about the interviewee, requiring additional effort on the part of the researcher to follow procedures and ensure confidentiality. This is not a trivial issue, as men interviewing women in a closed room is not culturally suitable; yet, issues of privacy and confidentiality cannot be ignored.

In our international immersion experiences, we ensure that *every* individual who shows up to be interviewed by our students is interviewed. In our educational program, we emphasize that what participants have to say is of great value and that they are the experts on their life circumstances. In fact, some arrive on our doorstep, which is actually *their* doorstep, expecting to be scolded for their "incorrect views," and are pleasantly surprised by our nonjudgmental approach. Bridging the perceived status gap is a huge challenge for researchers—indeed, one of the biggest. We take pride when community members decide to trust us, just as we later take pride when they inform us that they benefited from participation in the program.

Our experience underscores the need to follow the spirit of institutional review board procedures and the conduct of ethical research (Wood, 2006). Invariably, field research leads to new situations that require moral judgments on the part of the TCR scholar. We can see the need to go beyond documented informed-consent procedures to ensure that our participants understand their rights. It is safe to predict that this will be an area of increasing concern and study.

### Affirm Participants as Agents of Transformation

Our entire program is based on what might strike some as an unlikely foundation: the generosity of people in opening their homes to us and sharing their lives with us. In the space of an hour or two, they relate their life stories to a stranger. One woman, telling me about the extraordinary adversities she faced, stated that she only normally confided in God on some of these topics. A second woman explained the driving motivation in her life—that no one else should suffer the way she has—as she related overcoming the loss of her husband and her son to support her family. A third woman who had managed a household of abject poverty for 15 years literally became an entrepreneur overnight when her husband became dysfunctional. Some of these interviews go back more than a decade, but I remember them as if they took place yesterday.

Why should people open up their homes and hearts to us? We explicitly and frequently pose this question to ourselves and thereby remind ourselves that our work is built entirely on the generosity of participants in our research, teaching, and social initiatives. At the grassroots level, this is not due to the expectation of concrete rewards. Rather, it is because people respond at the human level to requests from members of my team with whom they are personally acquainted. Secondarily, it is because of an appreciation for our larger objectives and, perhaps, even a sense of shared purpose.

What is that shared purpose? There seem to be several answers. We hear from communities that they benefited from participating in our research. Similarly, we receive positive feedback about the impact of our educational program. As hoped and anticipated, the program enables people to be agents of change by spreading their learning to their communities. In our qualitative assessments, women relate how they have spread the word to many others on issues such as buying wholesale and buying staples like rice at discounts by grouping their purchases. Our participants learn, benefit, and become agents of transformation, and that is our shared purpose.

### TCR Should Be Designed to Give Back

Our foray into low-literate consumer behavior in the United States stemmed from a desire to understand groups who are often left out of policy and business solutions. Equally, it stemmed from a perceived potential to empower individuals and thereby change their status, although there was much uncertainty about how to achieve such outcomes. Our core belief, at the outset, was that understanding marketplace phenomena related to low literacy could lead to the design of solutions that would enable low-literate consumers to participate more effectively in the marketplace.

A similar belief preceded the work on subsistence marketplaces in India. We chose projects not based on anticipated research outcomes but rather on their potential for actual impact through the insights generated, as well as their inherent potential for educating ourselves. Of course, we are far from perfect in our foresight, but we do ask these kinds of tough questions in formulating our research objectives. A case in point is a current project on understanding what *sustainability* means to those living in subsistence. "Planet, profit, and people" is a top-down rendering of this notion, but what are the real elements of sustainability for subsistence consumers and entrepreneurs (or consumer-merchants), and what is the interplay among these elements? What are they actually striving to sustain each day? Livelihood? Culture? Social networks? What began as a throwaway line is stimulating deeper conversations, although the outcome is very uncertain and is likely to range from restating the obvious to deeper insights. Such uncertainty of outcome is, of course, an exciting aspect of this work.

We also deemphasize repetitive studies that show the vulnerabilities of low literacy and poverty. This grows not so much out of wishful thinking but rather out of our determination to avoid studying the obvious and seek more nuanced insights about the circumstances in which low-literate individuals can perform better. For instance, we have identified conditions under which low-literate consumers perform as well as literate counterparts (Viswanathan, Torelli, et al., 2009). In a similar vein, our educational program focuses on overcoming the difficulties posed by abstract thinking by leveraging individuals' inherent social skills to enable learning.

### TCR Transforms the Researcher

A number of lessons learned have related to my own role in bridging different worlds and point to the expanded role of the academic researcher. At the outset, I should state that there is no experience I would substitute for my own journey over more than a decade. This experience has truly been transformative at so many levels, including my own conception of research and how it can and should be conducted. But, the intent here is not so much to prescribe as to describe, in the hope that aspects of this journey can strike a chord in others and perhaps even be useful to them.

Looking again to my own experience, I have been ideally positioned as an academic to shape an educational program, follow through on the administration of that program, and attempt to develop an enterprise model around it. Being responsible both for the dissemination of my own research and its translation into social initiatives gives me a rare opportunity to communicate insights and shape the way the work is used. Moreover, just as effective communication of research is critically important in academic research—with writing being emphasized—so is the dissemination and translation of ideas into social actions. I have told my students that if they do not communicate their work, no one else will. This is no less true for me: If I do not champion the educational program I design by demonstrating it and serving as a resource in its implementation, any inherent transformative potential is unlikely to be realized (see also Wansink, Chapter 3 of this volume). Thus, my experience and inclination have been toward a very proactive approach to social action, especially as it flows from the research.

Results, unsurprisingly, have been mixed. At the very least, we have ensured responsible communication of our work and illustrated socially relevant applications (see Viswanathan, Seth, Gau, & Chaturvedi, 2009, for an example of the centrality of individual and community welfare for businesses). We continue to strive to maximize the reach of our approach. Success in this context would mean not only wide reach but also the demonstration of real impact through bettered lives. This is still a long way from where we are currently.

Again speaking personally, a primary issue relates to my role as an academic versus running a social enterprise. Here, issues have included keeping the mission of the nonprofit clear (i.e., disseminating rather than creating knowledge) and thus not interfering with my academic role at my university. A common issue raised in these circumstances is being an advocate for something versus researching it (see Lehmann & Hill, Chapter 33 of this volume). For me, this has not been a central concern, at least in the conventional sense of pushing for a given outcome (i.e., poverty alleviation) versus conducting research. If anything, having a research orientation has been essential to our cause. Conducting research has enhanced our social initiatives and vice versa. It has also enabled us to constantly focus on assessing the efficacy of our educational program. As we have worked with marketplace literacy over the years, our own proximity to it and its effectiveness need to be constantly questioned through assessment.

Our flexibility is important, especially in thinking more expansively about the nature and effects of marketplace literacy. In this regard, we are wedded to a few special issues: that consumer and entrepreneur are two sides of the same coin (as illustrated by our use of the term *subsistence consumer-merchant*; Viswanathan et al., 2010), that know-why is an important starting point, and that educational experiences need to be concretized, localized, and *socialized*. However, these guidelines are general and provide ample room for customization based on thorough understanding through research.

In short, viewing ourselves as a learning organization with a research mentality is very useful indeed. This does not devalue the importance of complete freedom in making choices; in fact, it underscores the importance of freedom (and the associated integrity) of decision making. Important issues such as funding sources and the requirements of journals have been highlighted in the literature on participatory action research in this regard (David, 2002; Ozanne & Saatcioglu, 2008). Our funding sources have not proven restrictive in any way, although a clear delineation between research and social initiatives based on the intent of grants is very important. Another potential area of separation is between funding from businesses devoted to specific projects in our program versus basic research.

With respect to the requirements of journals, this research has largely been initiated without specific regard to this issue, other than acknowledging the need to conduct research with the highest level of rigor and relevance, both of which having a significant bottom-up flavor. With progress in a series of experiments or qualitative interviews, further understanding has led to the crafting of a potential paper for an academic outlet.

The day-to-day activities and decisions involved in TCR point to an expanded role for the academic researcher well beyond the traditional comfort zones (see also Mick et al., Chapter 1 of this volume). I would caution, however, that an in-depth understanding of what lies ahead is essential for any researcher who chooses to walk down this path.

### Forge Sustainable Transformative Initiatives

A final lesson in the conduct of TCR is simply that it must be sustainable. There are many forms of sustainability, not the least of which is financial, but the financial capital invested in these efforts pales in comparison to the human capital committed. As we traverse new paths, extrinsic rewards are not apparent, and they therefore are unavailable to sustain such human capital. What ultimately can sustain it is a belief in the larger purpose of a specific TCR program and the ability to flow around obstacles, rather than march through or over them.

For this to happen, I submit, TCR scholars have to define their larger purpose and decide up front what success or positive impact will look like. Impact can mean the degree to which we have given a chance to people who have not heretofore had one, especially in improving their well-being. For me, first and foremost, this means giving that chance to impoverished people. Our impact has been minuscule when held up to the millions who live in poverty. Therefore, our tasks remain infinitely large. Second, this means reaching out to diverse audiences. Here I mean not only our participants but also my students, many of whom have not had the benefit (as I have) of opportunities to work toward a sustainable global society. We provide those opportunities. Another related responsibility, closely tied to my own stage of career, is to create opportunities for junior TCR scholars to work in this arena without having to clear the same kinds of hurdles that I did. Third, this means disseminating our learning and implications responsibly to commercial and social enterprises as well as to policy makers. This kind of careful dissemination, in which the TCR scholar is directly involved in both communicating the research and designing applications, increases the likelihood of organizations responsibly serving impoverished communities.

A central focus on mission and domain is important in deciding which paths to go down and which paths to turn away from. For example, our focus could be expanded to adjacent areas, such as health care, that overlap with marketplace activity and consumption. The risk, of course, would be an overall dilution of outcomes, which our central focus on marketplace/consumption perspective might help head off, if not entirely preclude.

## DISCUSSION

At its core, TCR is consumer research that proactively seeks positive social impact. It begins with the choice of important phenomena. In contrast to conventional research, in which theory and method take primacy over the substantive context, in TCR the substantive phenomena take primacy, because infusing research with a grounding in reality is central for transformative potential. The key here is to identify the intersection of theoretical depth and social relevance for the phenomenon at hand, which is accomplished by identifying projects that provide critical understanding that, in turn, can be applied to improve individual and community welfare. Rather than apply existing theories, the goal is to create relevant, actionable knowledge with transformative potential at the intersection of in-depth theory and complex reality. Thus, social relevance is at TCR's core (see also Mick et al., Chapter 1 of this volume; Wansink, Chapter 3 of this volume). The phenomenon in focus is not a methodological context, an afterthought, or an incidental set of implications that flow from basic research; rather, it is central to the work.

TCR, by definition, should offer practical and relevant benefits to the people studied, in other words, the real possibility of transformation. Rigorously assessing the potential for the practical relevance of theories is critical. Also important is the need to develop this promise through articles in diverse academic outlets that welcome contributions about practical implications. Finally, actual involvement in creating applications with transformative potential and assessing their impact is also a logical outcome of TCR. Thus, what is often construed as applied research that is derived from some basic research takes on an important role as bridging research with transformation and, in turn, feeds back into more basic research. Such a bridging blurs the line between basic and applied research and highlights the importance of relevant research in enriching basic research and practice. Also implicit in this lesson, clearly, is the need to assess actual impact.

TCR requires interplay between theory and practice to develop relevant knowledge. Our work points to the challenges of moving from basic research to an education-based application. In a sense, the best test of one's research is whether it translates into actual beneficial impact. Another good test—counterintuitive as it may sometimes sound—is whether the design of applications enriches basic research. Whereas theory and practice inform each other in all research, unique to TCR is the potential to have a genuine and respected transformative impact.

Our approach should be put in perspective as it relates to the literature on relevant topics such as action research. Our approach bears resemblance to action research in some ways, such as the concurrence of research with action (Coghlan, 2004). We began with practical problems that low-literate individuals face, which is another characteristic of action research (Ozanne & Saticioglu, 2008). Our approach blurs the division between theory and practice (Ozanne & Saticioglu, 2008). Aspects of our approach—such as the focus on specific contexts and the emphasis on solving problems therein, the emergent nature of the research based on local conditions, the enrichment of research through experiences of participants, and the notion that the larger test of theory is in its ability to have a positive impact on social problems—also have been discussed in the context of action research (Greenwood & Levin, 1998). However, as the preceding description makes clear, we do not claim anything close to full collaboration with participants, nor have we shaped a collaborative process for authority over and execution of research, as has been discussed with participatory action research (Greenwood, Whyte, & Harkavy, 1993).

I conclude by pointing to the uncertainty that still surrounds our endeavors. Our journey is an *attempt*, and nothing more. While I derive some measure of satisfaction from our research and curricular outcomes, I remain dissatisfied with our inability to reach larger audiences through our educational program. By the metric of changing lives on the ground, we have succeeded qualitatively but not quantitatively. If this writing leads to visions for larger scale impact, then the positive reactions they engender are ones we have not yet fully earned. If those visions are realized, our own investments will in some small way be validated. In the meantime, the journey continues.

## ACKNOWLEDGMENTS

I gratefully acknowledge the support and involvement of various nongovernmental organizations and community-based organizations in India, adult education centers in the United States, and commercial enterprises in several countries. Projects described in this chapter were supported by the National Science Foundation (Grant 0214615; any opinions, findings, and conclusions or recommendations expressed in this material are those of the author and do not necessarily reflect the views of the National Science Foundation); the Center for International Business Education and Research at the University of Illinois, which is funded by the U.S. Department of Education (Grants P220A6000398, P220A020011, and P220A060028); the Social Sciences and Humanities Research Council of Canada (Grant R3414A05); the Association for Consumer Research through a TCR Grant; and the Department of Business Administration, the College of Business, the Campus

Research Board, the Cooperative Extension Program, and the Academy for Entrepreneurial Leadership, all at the University of Illinois.

Many individuals and organizations have been cotravelers on parts of this journey and deserve immense credit. I am indebted to R. Venkatesan and S. Gajendiran, who have been core members of my team for almost a decade. I am grateful for the opportunities to collaborate on research projects and cochair conferences with José Antonio Rosa. I am also grateful for the opportunity to work with Avinish Chaturvedi, Roland Gau, Robin Ritchie, and Srinivas Sridharan, coauthors of a number of research initiatives. I thank John Clarke and Robin Orr, who have encouraged and supported my educational initiatives at the University of Illinois. I also thank Verghese Jacob of Byrraju Foundation and Tara Thyagarajan of Madura Micro Finance Limited for their invaluable support of our endeavors.

## REFERENCES

Arnould, E. J., & Mohr, J. J. (2005). Dynamic transformations for base-of-the-pyramid market clusters. *Journal of the Academy of Marketing Science, 33*(3), 254–274.

Chaturvedi, A., Chiu, C. Y., & Viswanathan, M. (2009). Bounded agency and analytical thinking among low literate Indian women. *Journal of Cross-Cultural Psychology, 40*(5), 880–893.

Coghlan, D. (2004). Action research in the academy: Why and whither? Reflections on the changing nature of research. *Irish Journal of Management, 25*(2), 1–10.

David, M. (2002). Problems of participation: The limits of action research. *International Journal of Social Research Methodology, 5*(1), 11–17.

Dewey, J. (1910). *How we think: A restatement of the relation of reflective thinking to the education process.* Lexington, MA: Heath.

Elkjaer, B. (2004). Organizational learning: The "third way." *Management Learning, 35*(4), 419–434.

Freire, P. (1970). Cultural action for freedom. *Harvard Educational Review Monographs, 1.*

Greenwood, D. J., & Levin, M. (1998). Action research, science, and the co-optation of social research. *Studies in Cultures, Organizations and Societies, 4*(2), 237–261.

Greenwood, D. J., Whyte, W. F., & Harkavy, I. (1993). Participatory action research as a process and as a goal. *Human Relations, 46*(2), 175–192.

Hill, R. P. (1991). Homeless women, special possessions, and the meaning of "home": An ethnographic case study. *Journal of Consumer Research, 18*(3), 298–310.

Israel, B. A., Eng, E., Schulz, A. J., Parker, E. A., & Satcher, D. (2005). *Methods in community-based participatory research for health.* San Francisco: Jossey-Bass.

Jayanti, R. K., & Singh, J. (2010). Pragmatic learning theory: An inquiry-action framework for distributed consumer learning in online communities. *Journal of Consumer Research, 36*(6), 1058–1081.

MacLean, S., Warr, D., & Pyett, P. (2009). Was it good for you too? Impediments to conducting university-based collaborative research with communities experiencing disadvantage. *Australian and New Zealand Journal of Public Health, 33*(5), 407–412.

Molyneux, C., Coudge, J., Russell, S., Chuma, J., Gumede, T., & Gilson, L. (2009). Conducting health-related social science research in low income settings: Ethical dilemmas faced in Kenya and South Africa. *Journal of International Development, 21*(2), 309–326.

Novogratz, J. (2009). *The blue sweater: Bridging the gap between rich and poor in an interconnected world.* New York: Rodale Books.

Ozanne, J. L., & Saatcioglu, B. (2008). Participatory action research. *Journal of Consumer Research, 35*(3), 423–439.

Prahalad, C. K. (2005). *The fortune at the bottom of the pyramid: Eradicating poverty through profits.* Upper Saddle River, NJ: Wharton School Publishing.

Rajeswari, U. (Writer/Director). (2010). *Shakti rising* [Motion picture]. India: Madura Microfinance; Prakrithi JIVA Media.

Viswanathan, M., Gajendiran, S., & Venkatesan, R. (2008a). *Enabling consumer and entrepreneurial literacy in subsistence marketplaces.* Dordrecht, the Netherlands: Springer.

Viswanathan, M., Gajendiran, S., & Venkatesan, R. (2008b). Understanding and enabling marketplace literacy in subsistence contexts: The development of a consumer and entrepreneurial literacy educational program in south India. *International Journal of Educational Development, 28*(3), 300–319.

Viswanathan, M., & Gau, R. (2005). Functional illiteracy and nutritional education in the United States: A research-based approach to the development of nutritional education materials for functionally illiterate consumers. *Journal of Macromarketing, 25*(2), 187–201.

Viswanathan, M., Gau, R., & Chaturvedi, A. (2008). Research methods for subsistence marketplaces. In P. Khandachar & M. Halme (Eds.), *Sustainability challenges and solutions at the base-of-the-pyramid: Business, technology and the poor* (pp. 242–260). Sheffield, England: Greenleaf.

Viswanathan, M., Hastak, M., & Gau, R. (2009). Enabling processing of nutritional labels among low-literate consumers. *Journal of Public Policy & Marketing, 28*(2), 135–145.

Viswanathan, M., & Rosa, J. A. (2007). Product and market development for subsistence marketplaces: Consumption and entrepreneurship beyond literacy and resource barriers. In J. L. C. Cheng, M. A. Hitt (Series Eds.), J. A. Rosa, & M. Viswanathan (Vol. Eds.), *Advances in international management: Vol. 20. Product and market development for subsistence marketplaces* (pp. 1–17). Boston: JAI Press.

Viswanathan, M., & Rosa, J. A. (2010). Understanding subsistence marketplaces: Toward sustainable consumption and commerce for a better world. *Journal of Business Research, 63*(6), 535–537.

Viswanathan, M., Rosa, J. A., & Harris, J. (2005). Decision-making and coping by functionally illiterate consumers and some implications for marketing management. *Journal of Marketing, 69*(1), 15–31.

Viswanathan, M., Rosa, J. A., & Ruth, J. (2010). Exchanges in marketing systems: The case of subsistence consumer merchants in Chennai, India. *Journal of Marketing, 74*(3), 1–18.

Viswanathan, M., Seth, A., Gau, R., & Chaturvedi, A. (2009). Internalizing social good into business processes in subsistence marketplaces: The sustainable market orientation. *Journal of Macromarketing, 29*, 406–425.

Viswanathan, M., & Sridharan, S. (2009, March–April). From subsistence marketplaces to sustainable marketplaces: A bottom-up perspective of the role of business in poverty alleviation. *Ivey Business Journal.* Retrieved December 20, 2010, from http://www.eiu.com/index.asp?layout=EBArticleVW3&article_id=654444850&channel_id=778114477&category_id=&refm=ebCh&page_title=Latest&rf=0

Viswanathan, M., Sridharan, S., Gau, R., & Ritchie, R. (2009). Designing marketplace literacy education in resource-constrained contexts: Implications for public policy and marketing. *Journal of Public Policy & Marketing, 28*(1), 85–94.

Viswanathan, M., Torelli, C., Xia, L., & Gau, R. (2009). Literacy and consumer memory. *Journal of Consumer Psychology, 19*, 389–402.

Wallerstein, N., Duran, B., Minkler, M., & Foley, K. (2005). Developing and maintaining partnerships with communities. In B. A. Israel, E. Eng, A. J. Schulz, & E. A. Parker (Eds.), *Methods in community-based participatory research for health* (pp. 31–51). San Francisco: Jossey-Bass.

Wood, E. (2006). The ethical challenges of field research in conflict zones. *Qualitative Sociology, 29*(3), 373–386.

# 6

# Transformative Consumer Research in Developing Economies
## Perspectives, Trends, and Reflections From the Field

CLIFFORD J. SHULTZ, II AND STANLEY J. SHAPIRO

NOT EVERYTHING THAT CAN BE counted counts, and not everything that counts can be counted.

Albert Einstein

If consumer research is to be truly transformative on a large scale, it must address big challenges that systemically impede or facilitate consumer well-being. Developing economies present such challenges in abundance. In this chapter, we provide an overview of the economic development literature. Encouraged to provide examples from our own empirical studies that might provide fresh and maybe even inspirational insights, we discuss some active research streams in several developing economies. Our review and analysis suggest inherent difficulties and controversies in this field, while also revealing opportunities for consumer researchers to further economic development and, ultimately, enhance consumer well-being. We emphasize that prolonged engagement of research teams, conducting multiple studies of consumers and their consumption environments, and policy change, rather than any single study, are most likely to have a dramatic impact on the development of any given country or region, and consumer transformation therein.

## DEVELOPMENT ECONOMICS

Development economics is a well-established academic discipline focused on enhancing the well-being of nations, communities, and people (e.g., Dapice, 2008). Perspectives, methods, and models to affect these outcomes vary widely, are politically charged, and offer mixed results (e.g., Schumpeter, 1911; Sen, 1999). Further, studies and programs often center more on indicators of economic growth than on actual transformations that enhance the well-being of individual consumers and consumer groups. In this chapter, we introduce current trends and foci in the economic development literature, including various controversies and questions that indicate gaps to suggest potential prospects for Transformative Consumer Research (TCR). We then share synopses of empirical studies in and on Africa, Asia, Europe, and the United States, including some overarching findings. Research from these countries was chosen because of active engagement in them; collectively, they reveal both commonalities and differences, which in turn reveal unique challenges and opportunities. The research presents opportunities for fresh thinking and reinforces the importance of longitudinal, systemic, multimethodological research. Perhaps most importantly, these countries and places—and the consumers from and in them—have provided more than a few eureka moments about the purpose, essence, and value of what increasingly is being described as TCR in the context of developing economies.

We also conclude that TCR can contribute meaningfully to assessing the desirability of both existing systems and proposed alternative courses of action to improve the welfare of the global poor. In this effort, TCR should be viewed as complementary to other disciplines with comparable missions of understanding and providing answers to the complex, interactive, and systemic challenges of economic development and relief for the world's poor consumers. Together, such scholars and practitioners should be able to maximize the contributions by consumers and marketers to social welfare and, thereby, improve the quality of life for the world's less fortunate citizens.

## CONTEXT FOR TCR

Those who conduct TCR in the developing world occupy a specific location within a given country at a particular moment in time. Such researchers must familiarize themselves with the socioeconomic context in which they propose to enhance the lives of consumers. TCR practitioners working in the developing world must also become familiar with the policy literature that explores many different and still controversial dimensions of socioeconomic development. The remainder of this section provides a brief introduction to that rich, diverse, and conflicting literature.

### Development Dimensions

Commentators tend to agree that not only economic indices (e.g., gross national income per capita) but also social measures (e.g., education, literacy, health, the status of women) must be assessed in efforts to gauge developmental progress (Stewart & Deneulin, 2002; World Bank, 2010). In addition, particular attention must be paid to progress in reaching the ambitious millennium development goals set by the United Nations (e.g., Martens, 2005; United Nations Development Programme, 2010).

### Macrofactors

Many macrofactors affect economic development in general and consumers in particular. Topical, timely, and often controversial examples are introduced below.

#### *Geography, Trade, Poverty, and Globalization*

Most development indicators pertain to fairly large geographic boundaries, such as countries, political and economic blocs, and the binary "north versus south" categorization. Although some agreement may have been reached as to how progress in development might be measured, there is no such consensus regarding the most appropriate places, global policies, and international practices for facilitating that development. For example, opinions differ on whether trade and tariffs benefit developing countries and whether they would benefit even more from freer trade (e.g., Akyuz, Milberg, & Wade, 2006; Sutherland, 2007; Tokarick, 2008).

The policy-guided practice of international assistance to developing economies raises a number of questions. Fundamentally, does it help or hinder development? Very different and directly conflicting views exist (e.g., Birdsall, Rodrik, & Subramanian, 2005; Easterly, 2008). The impact of economic development efforts on both poverty reduction and income inequality also remains an area of controversy. How much direct developmental emphasis should be placed on poverty reduction per se, and is such a direct focus the best way to alleviate poverty (Besley & Burgess, 2003; Harrison & McMillan, 2007; Kanbur, 2005; Sumner & Tiwari, 2005)? And, what about the complex issue of globalization? Put more bluntly, the controversy rages over whether the pluses that some have associated with globalization outweigh the minuses that others see (e.g., Grewal, 2006; Trebilcock, 2005; Witkowski, 2005).

## Marketing's Contributions

What about the nature and extent of marketing's contributions? Here, one finds a broad review of the literature on macromarketing and economic development (Klein & Nason, 2001), especially systemic understanding and approaches toward enhanced quality of life (Layton 2007, 2009); a more limited consideration of social marketing and its relation to economic development (Dholakia & Dholakia, 2001); and discussions of the challenge from global poverty and of the many different attempts to alleviate that problem (Kotler, Roberto, & Leisner, 2006). A more direct conflict arises between the proponents of base of the pyramid marketing (Prahalad & Hart, 2002) and an outspoken critic of this same approach (Karnani, 2007).

## Democracy and Markets

Is democracy a precursor to development? What of the cultural, racial, or gender barriers that greatly determine whether certain groups are privileged or disenfranchised? Does development pave the way for democracy, or is there no necessary relationship between the two? Experience suggests that replacing a command economy with a free market—whatever the prevailing political order—does facilitate socioeconomic development with expanded consumption opportunities. China, India, the former Soviet Union and countries in the Eastern bloc, Africa, Latin America, and Southeast Asia all have transitioned from planned to market economies. Who are the winners and losers in this geopolitical economic game? Or does that zero-sum question reflect thinking that is too simplistic, and if so, what forces would facilitate win-win outcomes (Kornai, 2000; Shultz, 2007; Svejnar, 2002)?

## Opportunities for TCR in Developing Economies

Numerous oft-controversial changes capture our attention for their potential to transform consumers' lives on a large scale. Approximately 3 billion people in the aforementioned developing countries or regions are consumers with the relevant needs, wants, expectations, frustrations, behavioral patterns, aspirations, dispositions, feelings, and fantasies typical of consumption experiences (Holbrook, 1995; Holbrook & Hirschman, 1982; see also Viswanathan, Seth, Gau, & Haturvedi, 2009). Individually, and however limited, their consumption defines who they are and what they can become; collectively, their consumer behavior, the systems that enable it, and their connections to consumer communities around the world reveal the extent to which their countries' or locales' economies are developing, have developed, or perhaps have failed to develop. Indeed, a failure to examine economic development from a systemic, dynamic, consumer-centric perspective would represent a missed opportunity. Reframing research objectives and foci accordingly could enhance economic welfare for billions of people, which would provide truly transformative outcomes. Thus, it would be fruitful to explore some of the aforementioned issues and controversies longitudinally and in the context of several countries or regions, with an emphasis on public policy interventions and their implications for enhanced consumer well-being. Such macromarketing explorations may provide useful background and an appropriate context for the ongoing examination of systems, markets, practices, and consumer behaviors (see also Shultz et al., 2010). We next turn to some illustrative studies.

## DEVELOPMENT OPPORTUNITIES: HERE, THERE, EVERYWHERE

As suggested above, developing economies of varying size and scope abound. Here, we share insights from some of our own empirical work, with implications for TCR. In this regard, we framed our thinking and subsequent foci in response to a conceptualization of TCR shared by the lead editor of this compendium, that is, "a movement … that seeks to encourage, support, and publicize research that benefits consumer welfare and quality of life for all beings affected by consumption across the world" (Mick, 2010, para. 1). The spirit and practice of this conceptualization have been captured in research projects introduced or revisited here. The projects are being administered in specific regions, as is typically the case, but also increasingly reflect systemic and global aspects of economic development. We hope that the interconnectedness of consumers and the actual or potential impact of development on consumer well-being will become apparent.

The regions are many and diverse. Countries and places selected for discussion in this chapter are Bangladesh, Burundi-Chicago, Cambodia, the former Yugoslavia and the Balkans, the Republic of Georgia, Myanmar (formerly Burma), South Africa, Thailand, Vietnam, Laos, and Lebanon and the West Bank. A few of these geopolitical entities (e.g., Bangladesh, Cambodia, Myanmar) make just about every list of developing economies based on traditional measures, such as gross national income per capita, Human Development Index, and corruption. Others, such as the countries of the former Yugoslavia, do not; by including some of those countries, especially Croatia and Bosnia-Herzegovina, we make the point that large-scale, acute, and systemic trauma (e.g., war, floods) can have devastating effects to economies that previously were not categorized as developing. Nevertheless, because of the acute trauma, consumers' lives have been profoundly transformed for the worse. Economic development in those contexts, or expeditionary economics (Schramm, 2010), is paramount to recovery and eventually to positive transformations to consumer well-being. Another nontraditional categorization is represented by Burundi-Chicago. Burundi would make the traditional lists, but Chicago would not. But, what of Burundi's poor, illiterate refugees who relocate to suburban Chicago with little command of English, no understanding of that socioeconomic system, and limited skills to thrive in that system? This community also could (and arguably should) be categorized as a developing microeconomy. Moreover, as this microeconomy does develop, the Burundi diaspora has the potential to make contributions to the motherland, its economic development, and the well-being of the consumers still residing there. This model, which we will call *diaspora development*, has been vital worldwide to the economic development and/or recovery of many countries and places. So, economic development can occur at a number of levels: regional, national, communal, and tribal. It can transcend physical boundaries. By thinking of economic development in this more holistic, transcendent way, we are presented with more opportunities to affect consumer transformations toward well-being and improved quality of life.

The development group on which we focus, therefore, is disparate on a few measures, and while our categorization of them as developing economies may be inconsistent with some traditional groupings, they also have commonalities. First, they all evince development challenges of varying sorts, that is, people/consumers live with suboptimal consumption options resulting in, or perhaps caused by, poverty, illiteracy, poor health, disenfranchisement, angst, vulnerability, helplessness, and hopelessness. Again, some of those challenges occur in pockets of affluent nations, and others in massive geographic areas that span national boundaries. Second, each is enmeshed in one or more of the previously introduced controversies. Third, from our perspective as scholars studying development, each is rooted in or connected to a stream of research initiated in Vietnam nearly 20 years ago.

Table 6.1 provides a list of primary research foci vis-à-vis economic development and consumer transformation in each country, region, and place of study. The entries, top to bottom, roughly coincide with the temporal order for the commencement of the projects, most of which are longitudinal studies still being administered today. Each study is intended to have some positive effect on consumer well-being and enhanced quality of life.

Readers will see that the stream of research begins with Vietnam. Vietnam and the methods applied there are discussed in some detail, as the research in this country was the impetus for consumer-centric and macromarketing orientations for all the projects discussed here, which coincide

**Table 6.1**   Examples of Developing Economies and Project Foci

| | |
|---|---|
| Vietnam | • Transition to market, and multisectoral and multiregional development (e.g., coffee in the Dak Lak province)<br>• Women's entrepreneurship<br>• World Trade Organization impact, exports, trade, and foreign direct investment<br>• Global integration<br>• Living standards<br>• Sustainability<br>• Poverty reduction |
| Cambodia | • Genocide recovery, aid and nongovernmental organizations, institution building, foreign direct investment in tourism and agribusiness sectors, and World Trade Organization impact<br>• Women's entrepreneurship, sustainability, and poverty reduction |
| Myanmar | • Authoritarian governance<br>• Boycotts and isolation<br>• Global integration (project stalled) |
| Laos | • Transition to market, globalization, segmentation, and women's entrepreneurship and welfare |
| Balkans | • War recovery<br>• Refugees, possessions, and food marketing and security<br>• European Union integration<br>• Sustainable peace |
| Bangladesh | • Judicial reform<br>• Citizen-consumer participation<br>• Corruption and justice<br>• Poverty reduction |
| Thailand | • Foreign direct investment and tourism development<br>• Minority welfare and global integration |
| West Bank | • Food marketing and trade<br>• Capacity building<br>• Distributive justice (project suspended) |
| Lebanon | • Emergency response and war recovery<br>• Foreign direct investment<br>• Multiculturalism<br>• Sustainable peace |
| Republic of Georgia | • Military invasion<br>• Consumer angst<br>• Geopolitical hegemony and orientation<br>• Market/consumer recovery |
| Burundi-Chicago | • Refugee resettlement<br>• Diaspora development and home country well-being |
| South Africa | • FIFA (International Federation of Association Football) World Cup impact on socioeconomic development and consumer well-being |

*Note:* The entries, top to bottom, roughly coincide with the temporal order for the commencement of the projects, most of which are longitudinal studies still being administered today.

neatly with ideas emerging from the TCR movement. Vietnam also proved to be an early linchpin of a research network of scholars and institutions that continues to collaborate on projects around the world. In addition to developing on some measures, all the countries and places discussed herein have undergone profound trauma, including radical political and/or economic transition, military hostilities, natural disasters, or all the above. Unsurprisingly, the consumers in these countries and places have been profoundly traumatized as well. Quality of life and well-being have deteriorated markedly, and economic development, broadly interpreted, is seen as a catalyst for socioeconomic advancement and recovery or, in other words, for consumer transformation. Below, we provide a synopsis of the development research in and on these regions and their relevance to TCR.

Any developing country or community is a unique amalgam of geographic, historical, cultural, political, economic, institutional, and human forces. The effectiveness with which these interacting forces are managed or mitigated determines the extent to which an economy develops, which, in turn, affects the consumption options and well-being of consumers (e.g., Shultz & Pecotich, 1997; see also Shultz et al., 2010). Regarding commonalities, readers may see some recurrent themes in the research synopses: (a) the interactions of the preceding forces and ultimately the impact on consumer transformation, (b) an eye toward policies and practices vis-à-vis the aforementioned controversies, and (c) text complementary to other themes discussed in the book, such as consumer vulnerability (e.g., Baker & Mason, Chapter 26 of this volume), consumer and merchant/marketing dynamics (Rosa, Geiger-Oneto, & Fajardo, Chapter 7 of this volume), and methodological considerations (Viswanathan, Chapter 5 of this volume).

## VIETNAM

Vietnam has transformed from one of the world's poorest countries to a model of development, with impressive measures for poverty reduction indicating that Vietnam's progress exceeds the millennium goals set for the country (World Bank, 2009) and continues to demonstrate upward trends on basic wellness indicators (United Nations Development Programme, 2009). Its ongoing economic development and transition to a market economy reflect the confluence of evolving policy decisions (both internal and external), expanded domestic production, growth in exports and consumption of Vietnamese products outside the country, foreign direct investment (FDI), and private and public wealth accumulation leading to new consumer options in Vietnam and enhanced consumer well-being for a large number of Vietnamese citizens. In revisiting factors that help explain this turnaround, we shall provide an overview of historical, cultural, political, economic, and systemic forces that once created a desperately inadequate consumption environment in the form of the Socialist Republic of Vietnam but sowed the seeds of the country's rebirth.

### Geography, People, Policy Reforms, Challenges, and Goals

Vietnam is roughly the size of California and is bordered by China to the north, Laos and Cambodia to the west, and the South China Sea to the southeast. The topography is diverse, with rivers, mountains, plains, highlands, islands, and tropical rain forests, all of which affect weather patterns, cause seasonal changes, and shape traditional consumer behaviors. Vietnam has numerous physical assets for economic development and consumption. Its natural wealth plus the industriousness of its people have proven to be both a blessing and a curse, as various civilizations and empires have tried to control the resources of the region for their own consumption-related purposes (Le, 1997).

To command those natural assets and, in turn, ensure its own consumption security, Vietnam's psyche, consumer culture, and present borders were formed from centuries-long resolve and at the cost of nearly 2 millennia of wars (e.g., Karnow, 1997; Shultz, Dapice, Pecotich, & Doan, 2006). The most recent peace accord was brokered in the early 1980s, but war devastation and then an ineffectual Maxist-Leninist political structure rendered Vietnam one of the 10 poorest countries in the world. Poverty was omnipresent. In 1986, amid growing reports of famine and social unrest, the Communist Party implemented a new policy, *doi moi* (change for the new or renovation), that modestly shifted the country toward a market economy. First came agricultural reforms: Farmers were generally permitted to grow what, when, and where they wanted; to set prices; and to keep a portion of their profits. Results were swift and remarkable. Within 3 years, Vietnam transformed from a net importer of rice to the world's third largest exporter. Other cash crops, particularly coffee, were cornerstones of Vietnam's economic rebirth. These successes inspired still further reforms and subsequent consumer transformations (Shultz, 2007).

Today, Vietnamese consumers embody a mixture of local customs and cosmopolitan consumption patterns that have been shaped by other cultures, especially Chinese, French, and American. With the centuries-long southern expansion of Vietnamese civilization through the Cham and Khmer kingdoms, each trade, treaty, invasion, war, and colonial occupation has been transformative in many ways, changing the expectations, outcomes, and traditions of consumers. More recent and relatively benevolent pacts, international agreements, intercultural exchanges, World Trade Organization membership, information technologies, and tourism have brought millions of Vietnamese out of poverty and into the global economy, producing conditions such that a large number of Vietnamese are now aware of the traditions, practices, hopes, dreams, and fears of consumers all around the world (e.g., "Vietnam's Nationalist Bloggers," 2009).

## Development Redux

To facilitate further development, Vietnam has embarked on a strategy to eliminate poverty, enabling Vietnam to become an economically viable, modern, industrialized country by 2020. These goals are especially important for vulnerable groups in the poorer regions of the country. The overarching objectives are to bring Vietnam out of underdevelopment and improve the people's material, cultural, and spiritual lives (World Bank, 2003).

## A Closer Look at a Producer–Consumer Global Dynamic

Given that approximately 75% of Vietnam's 90 million people live in rural areas, agriculture and rural development continue to play vital roles in the country's socioeconomic structure. Improvements in production and marketing have not only resolved the food security problem that has existed for centuries but also have provided increasingly sufficient, diverse, and high-quality food at reasonable prices. As a result, the domestic purchasing/consumption capacity has expanded, thereby supporting the growth of the industrial sector. In short, the agricultural and rural areas are indispensable to securing the stable and sustainable development of an economically sound and equitable society. Consumption of farm products and the aforementioned connectedness have bolstered farmers' purchasing power, ensuring prosperity and giving them consumer options that were literally unimaginable only a decade ago. Although Vietnam remains a poor country with per capita gross national income still below $1,000, one could argue that a nationwide consumer transformation has occurred.

Vietnam's leading crops include coffee, rubber, pepper, cashew nuts, tea, and sugarcane. However, despite obvious successes, one of the biggest inadequacies of Vietnam's agricultural production and consumption system is the limited competitiveness of its goods in the domestic and world markets. The country's agricultural products tend not to enjoy positive country-of-origin effects and little or no brand equity, thus making it difficult to compete in global markets. Additionally, because consumers in overseas markets may not favor Vietnamese agricultural products, the incomes and consumption options of the country's farmers suffer accordingly.

Much of the first author's research has focused on market/consumption/system dynamics, the connectedness (or lack thereof) of consumers with producers, and the effects of policy, investment, trade, brand building, and consumer attitudes on creating value chains that ensure multiwin outcomes. We have been especially interested in positive outcomes for farmers/producers who are lifted from poverty by being part of this consumption/marketing system. Given the preponderance of Vietnamese consumers directly involved in agricultural production as a means to enhance personal, familial, and community consumption, a fundamentally important question therefore concerns whether the evolving production/consumption dynamic of one or more agricultural products could prove to be a test case to affect some of the larger and more nationally systemic desirable outcomes, including those related to farmer and consumer well-being. As a product that connects Vietnamese farmers to consumers around the globe, coffee offers such a test case. For example, Wilkie and Moore (1999) have previously observed that an assessment of coffee from production to consumption can facilitate keen insights into consumer/producer dynamics.

### Vietnam's Coffee Industry

For nearly a decade, Vietnam has been one of the world's largest growers and exporters of coffee ("Coffee Exports Reach $1.3 Billion," 2009; Ministry of Agriculture and Rural Development, 2002). Indeed, coffee production, export, and global consumption have had a profound impact on the levels of income and discretionary spending among millions of rural Vietnamese. The Dak Lak province in Vietnam's central highlands accounts for about half the country's total coffee production and, thereby, became a focal point of our field research.

### World Prices and the Well-Being of Coffee Farmers

Despite obvious successes, current trends hint at a number of challenges confronting coffee growers, suggesting a need for strategic analysis and planning and, beyond that, a better understanding of the dynamics of coffee production and consumption. One challenge is the global price volatility for coffee beans that often forces farmers to sell their crops for less than they cost to produce. In such instances, farmers lack the funds to pay for food, health care, and basic services, keeping them in, or driving them back into, poverty ("Coffee Exports Reach $1.3 Billion," 2009; Nguyet, 2004).

Meanwhile, world consumers have growing expectations for coffee products and companies, including brand meaning, social responsibility, fair trade, and organic growing practices (cf. Arnould, Plastina, & Ball, 2009). These issues offer ways to add value to consumers through coffee consumption while also improving farmer welfare. However, adding value is not an easy solution for coffee growers. Levi and Linton (2003) concluded that the most potent way of regulating the market in favor of coffee growers is through consumers strategically using their purchasing power. A key to helping farmers generate more revenue while giving coffee consumers the "right" price may be how to sell high coffee quality to the "right" consumer, which means that coffee consumers will need to have a better understanding of social responsibility and be assured that part of the profits from coffee retail sales is allocated to coffee growers. More importantly, coffee consumers may attach some value to knowing that farmers receive fair prices for their crops, enabling farmers and their families to have a better quality of life. Tying these associations to brand affinity and profit allocation may be a viable alternative for increasing incomes of small coffee growers and providing more benefits to American and other coffee consumers.

In sum, a number of issues and forces did and still do affect Vietnam's development, particularly vis-à-vis the large number of Vietnamese involved with agriculture in general and the coffee industry in particular. Indeed, it became obvious that a multiskilled research team, well versed in a number of methodologies, would be required to implement a number of studies over time, in the country and elsewhere, if significant and sustainable transformations to large numbers of Vietnamese farmer-consumers are to be achieved. Thus, a longitudinal, multimethodological study was commenced by a research team that included Vietnamese and American scholars, coffee growers, processors, brand owners, and distributors.

### Methods

Conducting fieldwork in developing economies is challenging and can be a delicate process, especially when the research has the potential to affect national policy and citizens' attitudes and entails visits to war zones or areas with other forms of civil unrest (e.g., Shultz, 1997). Many projects require approval from various ministries and local authorities. Moreover, including local scholars and local "experts" can prove valuable and is sometimes legally mandated. Thus, assembling a research team to meet the relevant scholarly and legal requirements is a top priority (see also Viswanathan, Chapter 5 of this volume). Nonetheless, participation in the present research must be fluid in that various members of the team may be involved in some aspects (e.g., field interviews) but not others (e.g., design or administration of quasi-experiments). While the longitudinal study progresses and evolves, findings from all phases of the research are available to all members of the team as well as to interested informants, subjects, and authorities.

Over the years, the methods employed in Vietnam and subsequent sites have been eclectic, that is, qualitative and quantitative, behavioral, psychometric and econometric, ethnographic, and experimental and quasi-experimental. In short, the research questions always determine the methods. Moreover, we regard our timing and methods to research as proceeding in waves from initial examination of macrophenomena to qualitative fieldwork to more focused quantitative study in the form of field and laboratory experiments and quasi-experiments. At each wave, the research team assesses and reassesses findings, returns to the field for qualitative study, conducts new experiments or quasi-experiments, and so on. This prolonged, iterative, multimethod technique has been most helpful in understanding the complex, evolving, and interdependent phenomena that constitute the dynamics of development, market, consumption, and policy inherent in developing markets.

In many respects, the interpretive methods evince an orientation toward participatory action research (Ozanne & Saatcioglu, 2008), with continuous and prolonged engagement by some members of the research team focused on intensive microcycle site immersion (Shultz, Pecotich, & Le, 1994) and prolonged immersion by other indigenous members of the team (Holtzman, 1986). As studies have evolved, particular attention has been paid to the dynamics of consumption and production vis-à-vis particular sectors (e.g., agriculture, tourism, sport), products, and brands. This approach has supported the development of concepts, models, and theory through the identification of emergent themes surfaced via the study of a system in time (e.g., a season or production–delivery–consumption cycle). The research foci for this study are the policies and activities evinced throughout the dynamic coffee production and processing communities, including the subsequent well-being of coffee farmers and farming communities. The specific, multiple techniques for engagement and primary data collection included site observation (cf. Lincoln & Guba, 1985), photographic recording (cf. Holbrook & Kuwahara, 1998), and depth interviews (cf. McCracken, 1988). The findings were verified through "persistent engagement, persistent observation, and triangulation across sources and methods" (Wallendorf & Belk, 1989, p. 71; see also Shultz, Burkink, Grbac, & Renko, 2005).

The research is an ongoing longitudinal study of Vietnam's development, with implications for consumer well-being and social welfare. Data have been collected by members of the research team since 1992. Although we have focused on and collected data throughout Vietnam, some of the most compelling research findings emanated from our site engagement in the central highlands, especially Dak Lak province. In sum, we immersed ourselves in coffee producing and processing communities, as well as in downstream marketing efforts, distribution channels, and consumption venues.

Data sources included various coffee industry experts as well as ordinary people, such as local farmers and their families, whose consumption outcomes are affected by the success of their coffee farms. This empathic approach was especially valuable at sites where ethnic and/or political tensions were most pronounced. Interviews were conducted with representatives from government, businesses (especially throughout the coffee distribution chain), academia, and nongovernmental organizations, as well as with consumers. Thus, informants included coffee producers and consumers, government officials, nongovernmental organization representatives, merchants, distributors, wholesalers, and retailers.

To achieve an accurate understanding of consumer dynamics in developing economies such as Vietnam, one needs to consider a number of personal, familial, local, domestic, institutional, and international forces (Bartels & Jenkins, 1977; Belk, 1988; Shultz, 1997; Shultz et al., 2005; Slater, 1968). Further, a systemic approach is important, because it reveals different and potentially complementary perspectives, which ultimately facilitate comprehensive and appropriate solutions to problems that may hinder consumer well-being (cf. Holbrook 1999).

### Sample Findings From Field Research

A synthesis of the literature and field data led to the conclusion that most Vietnamese coffee growers, as well as many processors and exporters, were production oriented, had little marketing savvy, and possessed virtually no understanding of nuanced consumer preferences for coffee. Moreover, the research team discovered several product dimensions that are relevant to consumers when purchasing coffee (Shultz, Pecotich, & Hoang, 2001). Sharing this information with Vietnamese farmers, processors, distributors, and government officials resulted in a kind of epiphany, namely, that the Vietnamese must be more attuned to the consumers of their coffee in export markets and envision themselves as part of a larger, global production–consumption dynamic. By doing so, the consumer outcomes for the Vietnamese will be enhanced. Encouraging Vietnamese policy makers, farmers, and distributors to view this issue—as well as development more broadly—from such a consumer-centric perspective supports a fresh approach to economic development in important sectors of Vietnam (e.g., An 2004; Shultz, An, Shapiro, & Holbrook, 2010). We hope that this transformation may also be occurring elsewhere, as we now explore some consumer-oriented research project developments in other parts of the world.

## GREATER SOUTHEAST ASIA: CAMBODIA, LAOS, MYANMAR, AND THAILAND

Longitudinal study of Vietnam, its transition to the market, its economic development, and its subsequent improvements to the welfare of its consumers led early on to the study of other countries in the region undergoing similar transitions and/or recovery from war. The fates of Cambodia and Laos, for example, were ineluctably linked to Vietnam via French colonialism, the Mekong River, and the Vietnam War.

Cambodia's destiny has coincided with Vietnam's evolution for centuries; its sovereign territory has diminished, and its current borders have moved farther west and south because of Vietnamese expansion. The two countries fought as recently as 1979, although Vietnam must be credited for liberating the Cambodian people from the genocidal Khmer Rouge. Cambodia subsequently was engaged in a civil war of various levels of intensity into the 1990s and now, some would argue, is under a quasicolonial Vietnamese yoke. Today, Cambodia still struggles to recover from societal evisceration: Some estimates suggest that as many as 3 million people were killed or driven from the country (i.e., about 40–50% of the population at the time) from 1975 to 1978. The intelligentsia, merchant classes, and even the literate were eliminated. By the late 1980s, Cambodia had some of the lowest economic and welfare indicators on the planet (e.g., Shultz & Rahtz, 2006). Aid, while important, was inadequate. Early fieldwork revealed a failed marketing system but unique cultural assets that could link global and local consumers via tourism and FDI. Shultz and Rahtz (2010) are administering a multimethodological longitudinal study, which is well into its 15th year, including ethnographic approaches and survey research on the impact of FDI on consumer well-being. That impact, despite corruption and intractable systemic challenges, tends to be positive, as supported by trends for a number of indicators (e.g., Central Intelligence Agency, 2010b). Nevertheless, Cambodia still reels from the "killing fields," and its people remain mired in a political landscape that hinders more rapid and equitable development.

Laos and Myanmar are especially enigmatic and challenging countries in which to conduct fieldwork. Laos, which is landlocked and encompasses more than 60 ethnic groups and the largest land-to-population ratio in Southeast Asia, has presented opportunities to study the effects of globalization on a comparatively remote country with relatively isolated people. We have largely focused on policy and consumer segments that have emerged and the effects of globalization on well-being. The methods have mostly relied on an analysis of secondary data and interpretive fieldwork (Ardrey, Shultz, & Keane, 2006). Although the government is conservative in its transition, even compared to Vietnam, it is keen to see its economy develop and its consumers' quality of life improve. Myanmar, on the other hand, is home to nearly 50 million consumers held captive in many ways by a government seemingly determined to retard economic development (Central Intelligence Agency, 2010a). Because the country is run by a military junta that deposed the democratically elected Aung San Suu Kyi (who was released from house arrest in November 2010), we do not anticipate the emergence of a marketing system anytime soon to meet the far-reaching needs of consumers in Myanmar. The Myanmarese people suffer accordingly; wide-scale transformation to well-being is not imminent. In sum, Myanmar has proven to be a difficult country in which to conduct research and collect data, even compared to countries actively engaged in intense military hostilities. Accordingly, for the foreseeable future, members of the research team have opted to focus energies elsewhere.

Thailand has recently attracted scholarly interest. This might seem counterintuitive, as it has been on a steady upward trend on most indicators, except for a brief period during the Asian financial crisis, and had been spared acute stress after resolving political unrest in the early 1990s. Indeed, compared to most countries in the region, Thailand is considerably more advanced on most economic indicators. However, a devastating tsunami, corruption, and growing discord within the minority Muslim community have led to a military coup d'état and political paralysis. These events have created opportunities for study. Rahtz and Shultz (2010) have focused on the impact of globalization on the Muslim minority or, more specifically, on what factors might dissuade minority group consumers from becoming radical militants against the majority Thai (Buddhist) population and consumers around the world who embrace tolerance and generally favor globalization.

Finally, longitudinal research across Southeast Asia reveals trends and development phenomena that transcend boundaries. One such trend is the rise of women entrepreneurs in Cambodia, Laos, and Vietnam, who have transformed their own lives by accessing capital and creating wealth to improve their lot. These women also have improved family, community, and national welfare (Ardrey, Pecotich, & Shultz, 2006). Unsurprisingly, women's empowerment and enterprise development are pillars of the United Nations's millennium development goals.

## BANGLADESH

With a population of approximately 160 million people, who are subject to the ravages of typhoons and regular flooding and shackled by ineffectual administration and poor infrastructure, Bangladesh has been mired in a cycle of poor economic performance and poverty since it emerged as an independent country. However, recent policy changes, including market reforms, microloans, and emphases on women's rights, population control, and anticorruption campaigns, have produced an upward spike in some socioeconomic indicators.

The research network's projects in Bangladesh are not so much a logical continuation of research on acute trauma and devastation but a refocusing of interests and a leveraging of expertise and models of core members of the research network. Funded by the World Bank and administered by nongovernmental organizations, the research focus ostensibly was citizens' attitudes on the judiciary in Bangladesh. Pecotich, Rahtz, and Shultz (2010) reconceptualized the project by thinking of citizens as consumers of services provided by the judiciary and the legal system more generally. A survey was designed and administered, before and after which depth interviews were conducted. Findings suggest that access to and efficacy of the judicial system affects consumer confidence in the greater marketing system. In short, consumers believe that their well-being will be enhanced by a more transparent, accessible, and just judicial system.

## FORMER YUGOSLAVIA AND THE BALKANS

As suggested previously, Yugoslavia would not have been categorized as a developing economy, but we argue that acute trauma can be so devastating as to force countries, communities, and consumers to rebuild entire socioeconomic systems; that is, they must (re)develop politically, economically, and socially if the people in this region are to regain the quality of life to which they had grown accustomed. Such is the reality for remnants of Yugoslavia.

Yugoslavia, situated on the Balkans peninsula between East and West, was administered under the softened authoritarianism of Josip Tito and aligned with neither the United States nor the Soviet Union. It was a unique socioeconomic model. Although generally regarded to be socialist or communist, the system permitted and even encouraged some forms of free enterprise and a modest private sector. Citizens enjoyed a fairly high standard of living, freedom to travel, and some property ownership. The country fractured abruptly in the early 1990s, largely because of failures of the political apparatus and the marketing system, although this reality was lost on some observers because the social fabric of the countries most traumatized by the disintegration—namely, Croatia, Bosnia-Herzegovina, Serbia, and Kosovo—quickly reorganized along sectarian lines as Roman Catholic, Eastern Orthodox, or Muslim (Silber & Little, 1995).

The worst fighting seen on European soil in nearly 50 years ensued, with horrific effects on the economy and consumers. Pecotich, Renko, and Shultz (1994) set out to study the disintegration and destruction (i.e., their sources and impact) and possible paths to recovery. Two compelling research foci emerged. The first targeted refugees and displaced persons, particularly attempts to understand their possessions (both actual and lost), changes in consumption experiences, resettlement, reacquisition, and adjustment. This longitudinal study began in 1993 and continues today, as Shultz, Pecotich, and Renko (2010) studied displaced, returning, and resettled victims in Croatia, Bosnia-Herzegovina, Kosovo, Germany, Australia, and the United States. In effect, we have been studying the double transformation of abrupt consumer loss followed by recovery. Early fieldwork has also revealed that a devastated food system must quickly recover if (re)development is to occur; it must connect to consumers in the region and greater Europe (Shultz et al., 2005). Much of the initial work included site observations, videography, and depth interviews. More recently, as the research team has expanded, we have begun to collect and model quantitative data on consumers' attitudes toward food-retailing institutions (Shultz, Renko, & Brčić-Stipčević, 2010).

## LEBANON AND THE WEST BANK

Successes in Southeast Asia and the Balkans have generated interest in the Middle East, which presents complex and seemingly intractable development challenges that may have solutions in TCR. In Lebanon, we have again seen the importance of tethering local marketing activities and consumer preferences to global institutions and processes. These anchors facilitate societal stability, which in turn augments economic development and recovery as well as consumer well-being (e.g., Jallat & Shultz, in press). Israeli and Palestinian academics, various nongovernmental organizations, and the U.S. State Department have approached the first author about replicating in the West Bank some food marketing research projects administered in the Balkans. The logic was to gain rudimentary understanding of the food marketing system and, in turn, create jobs, produce consumer food products, stimulate trade, increase disposable income, and enhance consumer self-esteem and well-being. Unstated, but made clear, was also the goal of connecting people to their humanity, trading hatred and violence for win-win commercial exchanges, and enhancing quality of life for all stakeholders, that is, transforming the social dynamic and the consumers who are part of it. Sadly, funding for this project has been suspended. However, we remain guardedly optimistic about TCR in the West Bank, pending the resources to conduct it.

## REPUBLIC OF GEORGIA

In the summer of 2008, Russian troops entered the sovereign territory of the Republic of Georgia. Official explanations for the invasion (Georgia's perspective) or liberation of South Ossetia (Russia's perspective) conflict. Geopolitical analysis seems to suggest that Russia disfavors Georgia's political and economic orientation toward the European Union and away from Russian influence and vestiges of the dissolved Soviet Empire. Georgia's decision to align and develop in accordance with European Union values and living standards has been interpreted by Moscow as a threat. Regardless, it seemed probable that the effect of the military assault on Georgia and an occupation of Georgian territory by forces backed by a massive military machine would profoundly effect the marketing–consumer dynamics and, of course, consumer perceptions of security and well-being.

Almost immediately after the first shots were fired, scholars and practitioners with shared interests in macromarketing, TCR, and/or political stability assembled a research team to explore the market and consumer transformations that inevitably would result from military hostilities. One member of the research team was a marketing and consumer-behavior professor and Georgian national with an established network on the ground, while another member was an officer serving with United Nations Peacekeeping Forces in Georgia. The individual and collective skills of the team, with their access to people and places, enabled a rough composite of marketing, consumption, and well-being dynamics to emerge. Acute distress, anxiety, and fear were pervasive; marketing and consumption activity varied by location, extent of damage, and whether territories were occupied by Russian troops (Beruchashvili, Shultz, Pearce, & Gentry, 2009).

Although still a work in progress, some conclusions are obvious: Policy change is required to transform consumers' lives for the better in Georgia. Along the legendary Silk Road and with development goals tied to trade and FDI, closer connections to the West remain generally favored by Georgians, as would the security and consumer comforts perceived to be part of those connections. The extent to which Russian policies of intimidation, threats, and military operations permit these outcomes to occur remains to be seen.

## BURUNDI-CHICAGO

The essence of this project was introduced earlier. It emanated from research on refugees and displaced persons in the Balkans. Having recently moved to suburban Chicago, the first author was keen to connect with communities of refugees and displaced persons from the wars that disintegrated Yugoslavia, and he soon discovered that a community of refugees from Burundi and Sudan resided in his own town. This connection conjured thoughts of opportunities to extend a stream of research on refugees. Thus, a new TCR project has begun.

We are examining family dynamics and ways in which they retard or assist development efforts, including the dissemination of best practices for hygiene and wellness, partial repatriation of earnings to family and community members "back home," and other understandings that will emerge from fieldwork in the local community. Again, development occurs in pockets of economically prosperous countries and communities. This microeconomic activity has the potential to facilitate the development of people, communities, and countries from which the refugees were dispossessed and relocated.

## SOUTH AFRICA

While all developing economies are unique in one or more ways, South Africa reveals an especially uncommon history and set of challenges: colonialism, apartheid, natural resources, wealth accumulation by White elites, Black disenfranchisement and poverty, global attention and boycotts, charismatic leadership and peaceful revolution, truth and reconciliation, HIV devastation, and ongoing consumer and societal transformation. It is a compelling study in economic development for any number of reasons, but sometimes the stars align in ways that enable us to leverage our scholarly expertise to coincide with our personal passions. The first author likely would not have taken on a research project in South Africa. However, when the country was awarded the rights to the 2010 FIFA (International Federation of Association Football) World Cup, the game was afoot to design an economic development project that required fieldwork.

A research team of economists, marketing and consumer research scholars, and proprietary marketing researchers from World Cup sponsors is assembling to conduct two studies: (1) on fanatic consumption of this multibillion-dollar, brand-festooned, global, sporting spectacle; and (2) on the event's impact on development and consumer well-being in Africa. The first study requires interpretive fieldwork in South Africa, whereas the second models extant and future economic data. We hasten to add that neither research project likely would have gotten off the ground had the first author not met Steve Burgess, a professor at the University of Cape Town, who presented a study on emerging Africa at the TCR Conference held at Dartmouth in 2007 (Burgess, 2007). When approached about collaborative research vis-à-vis soccer's World Cup, which coincided nicely with his own TCR and economic development efforts in South Africa, he gladly agreed to participate.

Economic development research in South Africa brings us full circle on the matter of controversy. Almost all the controversies mentioned in the early pages of this chapter will surface in this project. For example, is the event itself a modern version of "bread and circus"? Would consumers and policy makers therefore be better served by focusing energy and resources on schools, libraries, and health care? Could South Africans focus on those investments without FDI that will accompany the tournament? FIFA, the world governing body of soccer, and the official sponsors will profit handsomely, but what of local South Africans? Also, what of the intellectual property rights of those sponsors as consumers the world over buy pirated versions of their products? Ultimately, of course, what is the impact on consumer transformation vis-à-vis wellness, quality of life, and happiness? We hope that our research will help answer some of these questions.

## REFLECTIONS AND POSSIBLE INSPIRATIONS

Because of the sheer number of vulnerable and impoverished consumers living in developing markets, they are fruitful environments for researchers interested in TCR. In this connection, under the heading of TCR, we believe that consumer transformation, rather than specific methodological agendas or substantive loyalties, is the primary objective. It therefore stands to reason that consumers would be at the center of considerations for research in developing economies.

As indicated by the preceding research synopses, many methods and foci potentially can affect consumer transformations from a number of vantage points and on a large scale. However, despite any number of positive attributes found in the work of any particular researcher who may want to begin a project in a developing economy, the viability of any research project will be largely determined by key gatekeepers, such as funding sources, as well as by the research network established to conduct the research, efficiently and effectively, over time. Consumers are nestled in a crucible of policies and systems within the developing economy; if the research does not have some catalytic effect on consumers, there is little chance for impact on consumer transformation. Toward the goal of TCR, these and several key points deserve renewed attention.

### Engage for the Long Haul

Although any one study can help transform consumer well-being, prolonged engagement with multimethodological, systemic, and dynamic research streams in developing economies is needed where major goals include policy change and sustainable improvements to consumers' quality of life. Such initiatives will require longitudinal studies administered cooperatively by multimember research teams that include local experts and indigenous scholars. None of these efforts, least of all in countries at war or recovering from disasters, can happen without a well-conceived plan to access the developing economy and conduct research valued by the authorities of the host country. Also, note that, over time, simply being there can add value beyond specific research outcomes. Technology transfer, information dissemination, faculty development, student exchanges, funding, and access to change agents in the system have all resulted simply from "being there for the long haul." Additionally, all have had an impact on consumer transformation beyond any specific outcomes of particular research projects.

### Money Changes Everything

Being there requires money. Indeed, funding is crucial to prolonged fieldwork. Acquiring financial support, setting budgets, and even managing the money can be a daunting process. Institutional seed money is a good initial source, as most research-oriented universities have internal grant programs that provide funds for travel and accommodation, presuming, of course, that one has a well-designed study that likely will lead to more substantial funding from an external source. Incidentally, even if one is only going to model extant data rather than conduct fieldwork in a remote country, data still may need to be purchased, or the scholar will have to allocate time to building a rapport and trust with the data source, which leads to another important consideration.

### Speak Their Language

The institutions that dominate the economic development landscape and control funding and access to places and data are themselves dominated by economists and bankers. One discovers early that they have little or no knowledge of consumer research; experience suggests to us that they know nothing of venerable scholarly associations, such as the Association for Consumer Research, or the journals valued by consumer researchers. A term such as *Transformative Consumer Research* is not likely to impress or even register. Worse, the words *consumer* and *marketing* tend to be derided in these communities. Thus, if one wants to be funded and, in turn, conduct extensive research on economic development, it is important to frame the research in ways that interest these gatekeepers, including the values, lexicon, and measures of economists and bankers. That is, the methods, measures, or other outcomes must be understood and valued by the funding source. Assuring these matters of design, presentation, and proposed outcomes is conducive to viable research.

Since the early 1990s, we have been fortunate to parlay small seed grants and shared interests with colleagues around the world into larger projects funded directly or indirectly by, for example, the World Bank, the United Nations, the Asian Development Bank, various U.S. government departments and agencies, European Union agencies, foundations, governments of host countries in which the research has been conducted, nongovernmental and charitable organizations, and development-oriented consulting firms. We also add that tapping into more familiar institutions (e.g., universities, research institutes) in the country of focus can be enormously helpful in the forms of translators, housing, transportation, databases, and access to economists and bankers working for large multilateral organizations in these countries. Lastly, private companies with interests in markets and consumers in developing economies may also fund projects, but such arrangements may come at some costs. Indeed, a scholar is confronted with many trade-offs when working in developing economies, as suggested by our initial focus on controversies.

### Be Flexible, but Stay True to Your Craft

Conducting research in developing economies requires flexibility. Equipment malfunctions, meetings are canceled, policy changes, laws are selectively enforced, monsoons interrupt, information is withheld, sites become off-limits, soldiers shoot, and shit happens—ad nauseam. Moreover, working in countries that some political scientists and government scholars may categorize as authoritarian raises questions about standards, control, dissemination, and ethics. Frequently, government approval and/or participation may be required, which can raise questions about the purpose of the research, the dissemination of findings, and other aspects of free inquiry. Throughout, and sometimes with difficulty, the research team must guard generally accepted methodological and ethical research practices.

In these efforts, researchers must make strategic choices. We do what we can, often concentrating where our colleagues and governmental authorities share relevant interests. In the case of Vietnam, the government has expressed an interest in agriculture and rural development. It has targeted some crops and value-added products as potential catalysts for poverty reduction. By helping coffee farmers and government authorities understand the global coffee marketing and consumption system and improve production and marketing vis-à-vis the interests of global coffee consumers, researchers can help farmers increase incomes, thereby creating modest wealth and consumption opportunities for their families and communities. Similarly to others, farmers are also consumers, as are their families, members of their communities, and residents of entire coffee growing regions. Their success potentially creates a systemic ripple effect of consumer well-being.

### Persevere

Success can indeed breed success. Perseverance through prolonged engagement, amplified by interesting and valuable findings from our research "waves," has built trust. This trust has, in turn, created new opportunities that include better access to data, places, people, networks, and resources that might otherwise have been unavailable, thus enabling expanded research agendas and potentially greater impacts on economic development.

### Purposeful Serendipity

On further reflection, this morphing and expanding stream of research on economic development has been a kind of purposeful serendipity, which began in a fascination with Vietnam and has resulted in research projects aimed at responsibly integrating several countries into the global economy while enhancing the well-being of consumers. Initial examination of economic data permitted some rudimentary understanding of Vietnam and the Vietnamese. Subsequent interpretive field research, quasi-experiments, and data modeling have enabled meaningful engagement with people around the world—consumers who have suffered, known scarcity, and experienced poverty and injustice, but who also understand that well-being can be improved through policy changes and better access to basic goods and services.

## FINAL REFLECTIONS

Rereading some of the text here, we can fully appreciate why someone might simply ask, why bother? Or perhaps a reader might be inclined to say something such as, "I was trained as an experimentalist, I've been encouraged to focus on extending my dissertation, several influential senior faculty members think this 'Vietnam thing' is a bad idea, and the system won't appreciate my work, let alone reward me." Well, the first author actually uttered the preceding sentence (epithets were deleted), yet there were enough compelling reasons to move forward with work in developing economies, despite several rational arguments not to do so.

Bringing the discussion to some closure, our research and policy recommendations have focused on the humanity of the consumer condition—transformation from suffering to well-being—as well as on development measures. Thus, for nearly 2 decades, consumer transformation has been an important outcome from the systemic study of markets, marketing, policy, and consumers. The process has also been transformative for members of the research teams who have learned an enormous amount about each others' cultures, systems, practices, consumer dynamics, and themselves in ways that have led to still more collaborative projects with the potential to embody and expand the objectives of TCR.

Lastly, TCR in developing economies cannot occur without transformed consumer *researchers*. Choosing to use one's scholarly tool kit to improve the lives of human beings in developing economies; having a substantial impact on the lives of the poor, the frightened, and the vulnerable; looking into the eyes of people who have clearly benefited from (been transformed by) one's research, time, and toil; and seeing a level of gratitude in those eyes that simply cannot be measured or forgotten—all is its own priceless reward.

## ACKNOWLEDGMENTS

The authors thank An Van Khanh—an agricultural economist, former student, and current colleague who embraced consumer-centric economic development—for important contributions to material on Vietnam's coffee industry, and Morris Holbrook for many thoughtful comments on the formative iterations of this chapter. The authors also acknowledge the assistance provided by a global network of governments, multilateral agencies, universities, research institutes, colleagues, interpreters, translators, foundations, and a long list of informants, drivers, and logisticians—too many in number to list here—who were indispensable to this research. We also thank the reviewers and editors who shared helpful comments on earlier drafts. Please contact either author for an unabridged iteration of the chapter.

## REFERENCES

Akyuz, Y., Milberg, W., & Wade, R. (2006). Developing countries and the collapse of the Doha Round. *Challenge, 49*(November/December), 6–19.

An, V. K. (2004). *Consumers' perspectives on Vietnam's coffee value chain, with implications for appropriate management of that chain.* Unpublished doctoral dissertation, Arizona State University, Tempe.

Ardrey, W., Pecotich, A., & Shultz, C. (2006). Entrepreneurial women as catalysts for socioeconomic development in transitioning Cambodia, Laos, and Vietnam. *Consumption, Markets and Culture, 9*(4), 277–300.

Ardrey, W., Shultz, C., & Keane, M. (2006). Laos: Emerging market trends, and the rise of consumers and entrepreneurs. In A. Pecotich & C. Shultz (Eds.), *Handbook of markets and economies: East Asia, Southeast Asia, Australia, New Zealand* (pp. 372–406). Armonk, NY: M.E. Sharpe.

Arnould, E., Plastina, A., & Ball, D. (2009). Does fair trade deliver on its core value proposition? Effects on income, educational attainment, and health in three countries. *Journal of Public Policy & Marketing, 28*(2), 186–201.

Bartels, R., & Jenkins, R. (1977). Macromarketing. *Journal of Marketing, 41*(October), 17–20.

Belk, R. (1988). Third world consumer culture. In E. Kumcu & A. F. Firat (Eds.), *Marketing and development: Towards broader dimensions* (pp. 103–127). Greenwich, CT: JAI Press.

Beruchashvili, M., Shultz, C., Pearce, M., & Gentry, G. (2009). Georgia, Russia, South Ossetia: Preliminary assessment of post-war market and marketing dynamics, with implications for future research. In T. Witkowski (Ed.), *Proceedings of the 34th Macromarketing Conference: Rethinking marketing in a global economy* (p. 207). Kristiansand, Norway: Agder University.

Besley, T., & Burgess, R. (2003). Halving global poverty. *Journal of Economic Perspectives, 17*(Summer), 3–22.

Birdsall, N., Rodrik, D., & Subramanian, A. (2005). How to help poor countries. *Foreign Affairs, 84*(July/August), 136–152.

Burgess, S. (2007, July). Paper presented at the meeting Transformative Consumer Research: Inspiring Scholarship for Collective and Personal Well-Being, Dartmouth College, Hanover, NH.

Central Intelligence Agency. (2010a). Burma. *World factbook.* Washington, DC: Author. Retrieved March 21, 2010, from https://www.cia.gov/library/publications/the-world-factbook/geos/bm.html

Central Intelligence Agency. (2010b). Cambodia, *World factbook.* Washington, DC: Author. Retrieved March 21, 2010, from https://www.cia.gov/library/publications/the-world-factbook/geos/cb.html

Coffee exports reach $1.3 billion. (2009, October 12). *Vietnam News, 19*(6509), 15.

Dapice, D. (2008). What do we know about economic development? *Journal of Macromarketing, 28*(4), 413–417.

Dholakia, R., & Dholakia, N. (2001). Social marketing and development. In P. Bloom & G. Gundlach (Eds.), *Handbook of marketing and society* (pp. 486–505). Thousand Oaks, CA: Sage.

Easterly, W. (2008). Was development assistance a mistake? *American Economic Review, 97*(May), 328–332.

Grewal, D. S. (2006). Is globalization working? *Ethics & International Affairs, 20*(Summer), 247–259.

Harrison, A., & McMillan, M. (2007). On the links between globalization and poverty. *Journal of Economic Inequality, 5,* 123–134.

Holbrook, M. (1995). *Consumer research: Introspective essays on the study of consumption.* Thousand Oaks, CA: Sage.

Holbrook, M. (1999). Higher than the bottom line: Reflections on some recent macromarketing literature. *Journal of Macromarketing, 19*(1), 33–45.

Holbrook, M., & Hirschman, E. (1982). The experiential aspects of consumption: Consumer fantasies, feelings, and fun. *Journal of Consumer Research, 9,* 132–140.

Holbrook, M., & Kuwahara, T. (1998). Collective stereographic photo essays: An integrated approach to probing consumption experiences in depth. *International Journal of Research in Marketing, 15,* 201–221.

Holtzman, J. (1986). *Rapid reconnaissance guidelines for agricultural marketing and food system research in developing countries.* Unpublished manuscript, Michigan State University.

Jallat, F., & Shultz, C. (in press). Lebanon: From cataclysm to opportunity: Crisis management lessons for MNCs in the tourism sector of the Middle East. *Journal of World Business.*

Kanbur, R. (2005). Growth, inequality and poverty: Some hard questions. *Journal of International Affairs, 58*(Spring), 223–232.

Karnani, A. (2007). The mirage of marketing to the bottom of the pyramid: How the private sector can alleviate poverty. *California Management Review, 29*(Summer), 90–111.

Karnow, S. (1997). *Vietnam: A history.* New York: Penguin.

Klein, T., & Nason, R. (2001). Marketing and development: Macromarketing perspectives. In P. Bloom & G. Gundlach (Eds.), *Handbook of marketing and society* (pp. 263–297). Thousand Oaks, CA: Sage.

Kornai, J. (2000). What the change of system from socialism to capitalism does and does not mean. *Journal of Economic Perspectives, 14*(Winter), 27–42.

Kotler, P., Roberto, N., & Leisner, T. (2006). Alleviating poverty: A macro-micro marketing perspective. *Journal of Macromarketing, 26*(December), 233–238.

Layton, R. (2007). Marketing systems: A core macromarketing concept. *Journal of Macromarketing, 27*(3), 227–242.

Layton, R. (2009). On economic growth, marketing systems, and the quality of life. *Journal of Macromarketing, 29*(4), 349–362.

Le, T. (1997). *Viet Nam: The country and its geographical regions.* Hanoi, Vietnam: Gioi.

Levi, M., & Linton, A. (2003). Fair trade: A cup at a time? *Politics & Society, 31*(3), 407–432.

Lincoln, Y., & Guba, E. (1985). *Naturalistic inquiry.* Newbury Park, CA: Sage.

Martens, J. (2005). *Report of the UN Millennium Project "investing in development."* Berlin: Friedrich-Ebert Foundation.

McCracken, B. (1988). *The long interview.* Newbury Park, CA: Sage.

Mick, D. (2010). *Transformative consumer research*. Duluth, MN: Association for Consumer Research. Retrieved January 20, 2010, from http://www.acrwebsite.org/fop/index.asp?itemID=325

Ministry of Agriculture and Rural Development. (2002). *Annual report on agriculture and rural development 2002*. Hanoi, Vietnam: Statistical Publishing House.

Nguyet, H. (2004, June 24). Coffee producers to turn around sector. *VietNamNet*. Retrieved July 15, 2004, from english.vietnamnet.vn/news/2004/06/169318/

Ozanne, J., & Saatcioglu, B. (2008). Participatory action research. *Journal of Consumer Research, 35*(October), 423–438.

Pecotich, A., Rahtz, D. R., & Shultz, C. (2010). Systemic and service dominant socio-economic development: Legal, judicial and market capacity building in Bangladesh. *Australasian Marketing Journal, 18*(4), 248–255.

Pecotich, A., Renko, N., & Shultz, C. (1994). Yugoslav disintegration, war, and consumption in Croatia. *Research in Consumer Behavior, 7*, 1–27.

Prahalad, C. K., & Hart, S. L. (2002). The fortune at the bottom of the pyramid. *Strategy + Business, 26*, 1–14.

Rahtz, D., & Shultz, C. (2010). [Globalization and consumer dynamics in Ko Yao Noi, Thailand]. Unpublished raw data.

Schramm, C. (2010). Expeditionary economics: Spurring growth after conflicts and disasters. *Foreign Affairs, 89*(3), 89–99.

Schumpeter, J. (1911). *Theorie der wirtschaftlichen entwicklung* [The theory of economic development]. Berlin: Duncker & Humblot.

Sen, A. (1999). *Development as freedom*. New York: Knopf.

Shultz, C. (1997). Improving life quality for the destitute: Contributions from multiple-method fieldwork in war-ravaged transition economies. *Journal of Macromarketing, 17*(1), 56–67.

Shultz, C. (2007). Marketing as constructive engagement. *Journal of Public Policy & Marketing, 26*(2), 293–301.

Shultz, C., An, V. K., Shapiro, S., & Holbrook, M. (2010). Vietnam's coffee industry as catalyst to socioeconomic development. Unpublished manuscript, Loyola University Chicago.

Shultz, C., Burkink, T., Grbac, B., & Renko, N. (2005). When policies and marketing systems explode: An assessment of food marketing in the war-ravaged Balkans and implications for recovery, sustainable peace, and prosperity. *Journal of Public Policy & Marketing, 24*(1), 24–37.

Shultz, C., Dapice, D., Pecotich, A., & Doan, H. D. (2006). Vietnam: Expanding market socialism and implications for marketing, consumption and socio-economic development. In A. Pecotich & C. Shultz (Eds.), *Handbook of markets and economies: East Asia, Southeast Asia, Australia, New Zealand* (pp. 656–688). New York: M.E. Sharpe.

Shultz, C., Deshpandé, R., Cornwell, T. B., Ekici, A., Kothandaraman, P., Peterson, M., et al. (2011). *Marketing and public policy: Transformative research in developing markets*. Manuscript submitted for publication.

Shultz, C., & Pecotich, A. (1997). Marketing and development in the transition economies of Southeast Asia: Policy explication, assessment and implications. *Journal of Public Policy & Marketing, 16*(1), 55–68.

Shultz, C., Pecotich, A., & Hoang, T. B. (2001). The coffee purchase consumer behavior model. Unpublished manuscript, Arizona State University, Mesa.

Shultz, C., Pecotich, A., & Le, K. (1994). Changes in marketing activity and consumption in the Socialist Republic of Vietnam. *Research in Consumer Behavior, 7*, 225–257.

Shultz, C., Pecotich, A., & Renko, N. (2010). [Yugoslavia's refugees: Attitudes, possessions and adjustments]. Unpublished raw data.

Shultz, C., & Rahtz, D. (2006). Cambodia: Striving for peace, stability and a sustainable consumer market. In A. Pecotich & C. Shultz (Eds.), *Handbook of markets and economies: East Asia, Southeast Asia, Australia, New Zealand* (pp. 76–106). New York: M.E. Sharpe.

Shultz, C., & Rahtz, D. (2010). [Tourism as a catalyst for socioeconomic development in Cambodia]. Unpublished raw data.

Shultz, C., Renko, S., & Brčić-Stipčević, V. (2010). Grocery store-attributes in recovering economies: An empirical investigation of their importance, using three component contour plotting. *Journal of International Food & Agribusiness Marketing, 22*(1/2), 37–51.

Silber, L., & Little, A. (1995). *Yugoslavia: Death of a nation*. London: Penguin.

Slater, C. (1968). Marketing processes in developing Latin American societies. *Journal of Marketing, 32*(July), 50–53.

Stewart, F., & Deneulin, S. (2002). Amartya Sen's contribution to development thinking. *Studies in Comparative International Development, 37*(Summer), 61–70.

Sumner, A., & Tiwari, M. (2005). Poverty and economic policy: What happens when researchers disagree? *Journal of International Development, 17*(6), 791–801.

Sutherland, P. (2007). Challenges to the multilateral trading system. *World Economics, 8*(January–March), 1–14.

Svejnar, J. (2002). Transition economies: Performance and challenges. *Journal of Economic Perspectives, 16*(Winter), 3–28.

Tokarick, S. (2008). Dispelling some misconceptions about agricultural trade liberalization. *Journal of Economic Perspectives, 22*(Winter), 199–216.

Trebilcock, M. J. (2005). Critiquing the critics of economic globalization. *Journal of International Law and International Relations, 1*(December), 213–236.

United Nations Development Programme. (2009). Viet Nam: The human development index: Going beyond income. *Human Development Report 2009*. New York: Author. Retrieved September 7, 2009, from http://hdrstats.undp.org/en/countries/country_fact_sheets/cty_fs_VNM.html

United Nations Development Programme. (2010). Millennium development goals. New York: Author. Retrieved March 3, 2010, from http://www.undp.org/mdg/

Vietnam's nationalist bloggers: Getting it off your chest. (2009, September 10). *The Economist*, p. 46.

Viswanathan, M., Seth, A., Gau, R., & Haturvedi, A. (2009). Ingraining product-relevant social good into business processes in subsistence marketplaces: The sustainable market orientation. *Journal of Macromarketing, 29*(4), 406–425.

Wallendorf, M., & Belk, R. (1989). Accessing trustworthiness in naturalistic consumer research. In E. C. Hirschman (Ed.), *Interpretive consumer research* (pp. 69–84). Provo, UT: Association for Consumer Research.

Wilkie, W., & Moore, E. (1999). Marketing's contributions to society. *Journal of Marketing, 63*, 198–218.

Witkowski, T. (2005). Antiglobal challenges to marketing in developing countries: Exploring the ideological divide. *Journal of Public Policy & Marketing, 24*(Spring), 7–23.

World Bank. (2003). *Viet Nam development report 2002: Implementing reforms from faster growth and poverty reduction*. Hanoi, Vietnam: Author.

World Bank. (2009). *Vietnam: Country overview*. Washington, DC: Author. Retrieved September 7, 2009, from http://siteresources.worldbank.org/INTVIETNAM/Resources/VietnamCountryOverview.pdf

World Bank. (2010). *WDI 2010*. Washington, DC: Author. Retrieved March 3, 2010, from http://data.worldbank.org/data-catalog/world-development-indicators/wdi-2010

# 7

# Hope and Innovativeness
## Transformative Factors for Subsistence Consumer-Merchants

José Antonio Rosa, Stephanie Geiger-Oneto,
and Andrés Barrios Fajardo

For me, creativity is a state of the soul, a way of surviving. One has made more than just a product. [The person] makes good use of the wood, takes full advantage of the elements to be found in the environment to make things that are unique in order to sell them and meet his needs.... I imagine that when a person creates, it is like a woman giving birth. [Look,] this is my creation. It is something I was not sure I could do, and I did it, and it came out well. It is something that helps the ego, self-esteem, and a whole bunch of other things in the person. One makes good use of tools, of materials ... and that's it.

Nitza
*A 28-year-old single mother of four children, 14 and younger,*
*talking about creativity and innovativeness*

"A state of the soul." "A way of surviving." "Like a woman giving birth." These are far-reaching words and metaphors with which to explain creativity and innovativeness. These are concepts whose full meaning eludes even the highly educated, but they are human enough to be grasped by a woman with 8 years of formal education and living with her mother and children on less than $2 per day. Creativity and innovativeness are popular with business and the academy in light of sustainability concerns, market competitiveness, and rising consumer cocreation of goods and services (Bendapudi & Leone, 2003; Prahalad & Ramaswamy, 2004; von Hippel, 2005). They are also long-standing topics of research interest in the social and administrative sciences (see Burroughs, Moreau, & Mick, 2008, for a historical review) and a matter of concern to the average person, judging from the ease with which even the relatively uneducated can argue their take on creativity and judge artifacts and problem solutions as creative or not creative.

Given the importance of creativity and innovativeness, it is not surprising that research pursuing a more profound understanding of factors that affect these human traits would be included in a tome on Transformative Consumer Research. In addition to giving rise to products and services that can facilitate communications, enhance living conditions, facilitate more efficient and effective use of talents and abilities, and bring healing and comfort where sickness and misery might otherwise prevail, exercising innovativeness is in itself transformative and for the most part beneficial to consumers. More often than not, innovativeness brings about timely solutions to consumption and survival problems, and even in instances when procured solutions are short-lived or ineffective, the sense of well-being that being innovative engenders can have a lasting positive effect on people. For Nitza (quoted above), innovativeness is transformative.

This research focuses on the hope and innovativeness of subsistence consumers, some of whom operate their own microenterprises as subsistence consumer-merchants (SCMs; Viswanathan, Rosa, & Ruth, 2010). SCMs are persons living in poverty who operate one or more small businesses as an integral part of life to provide for their families. The typical consumer-merchant in this study earns less than $4 per day, and some less than $2 per day, in Bogotá, Colombia. To varying degrees, they endure substandard housing, limited property rights, compromised legal protection, and minimal access to necessities such as potable water, sanitation, and health care. None of the informants go hungry, but most do not eat well. Although all have moved from rural areas, they have been established in an urban or semiurban environment for at least 4 years. The study focuses on persons who have been poor a long time and are conscientiously engaging in innovative endeavors. Daily, they suffer needs and yearnings associated with chronic poverty and pursue solutions to such problems. They are vulnerable people whose innovativeness serves as another example of the "resilience of human beings and their capacities to create change" (see Baker & Mason, Chapter 26 of this volume).

We focus on hope and innovativeness among SCMs for several reasons. First, it is valuable for the academy and society to learn more about how hope is associated with innovative behaviors, a relationship sometimes obscured in developed markets by the availability of manufactured goods and services. Hope as an antecedent to consumer attitudes and behaviors (e.g., Lueck, 2007; MacInnis & de Mello, 2005) has been primarily studied in developed retail markets and among persons for whom the most expedient path of action in response to needs and yearnings is to purchase a ready-made solution. This is not to say that affluent consumers are not innovative, as attested to by extant research in this area (Burroughs et al., 2008). Past research, however, has primarily shed light on how hope shapes consumers' beliefs, their responses to environment factors and market information, and their assessment of outcomes from activities such as the use of branded products (e.g., de Mello, MacInnis, & Stewart, 2007; MacInnis & de Mello, 2005). Subsistence consumers, in contrast, can seldom purchase products and services to fulfill their needs and, under most circumstances, must either create solutions to satisfy their yearnings or go without. In contrast to purchasing, which is the typical response to needs and yearnings among the affluent, subsistence consumers more typically must exercise innovativeness to find and implement solutions, and hence they provide a less encumbered view of how hope affects innovative behaviors. Chakravarti (2006) identified possible aspects of consumer thinking and behavior that may be affected by living in subsistence conditions, and the relationship between hope and innovativeness is one such area.

Second, constraints have been shown to stimulate innovativeness (Ridgway & Price, 1994), suggesting that persons living in subsistence conditions may engage in innovative behaviors with greater frequency and intensity on account of the numbers and magnitudes of needs facing them. In addition to facing significant income constraints, subsistence consumers often live in homes that they cannot call their own and that lack basic amenities (i.e., protection against the elements, running water and sewers, security against intruders). These people also lack reliable transportation and are often subject to social and legal inequities because of living beyond the reach of traditional law enforcement. Moreover, many of them endure capricious discrimination, and in some cases extortion, because of not having a legal address. Descriptive research into subsistence consumers (e.g., Hammond, Kramer, Katz, Tran, & Walker, 2007; Prahalad, 2005; Rosa & Viswanathan, 2007; see also Shultz & Shapiro, Chapter 6 of this volume) portrays a daily struggle for survival in which innovativeness and its antecedents are manifest in ways that differ from what can be found in developed markets. Needs and yearnings shower them with countless opportunities to exercise innovativeness and provide consumer researchers who are willing to work in subsistence environments with greater occasion to observe and understand.

Finally, and most germane to Transformative Consumer Research, inquiry into subsistence consumers and their behaviors is valuable by virtue of their sheer numbers and the importance of the segment to global welfare (see Andreasen, Goldberg, & Sirgy, Chapter 2 of this volume). The consumption and innovative potential of over 2.5 billion subsistence consumers, of which roughly half are consumer-merchants (Prahalad, 2005; Roy & Wheeler, 2006), has greatly encouraged research activity among academic and business researchers (e.g., Burgess & Steenkamp, 2006; Chakravarti, 2006; Prahalad & Hammond, 2002; Viswanathan et al., 2010). With aggregate purchasing power in excess of $5 trillion (Hammond et al., 2007), business potential in subsistence markets is high and has triggered efforts by many companies to better understand and serve subsistence populations (e.g., Flores-Letelier, Flores, & Spinosa, 2003; Rajan, 2007; Reck & Wood, 2003). The lives of subsistence consumers in countries like India, Bangladesh, Mexico, and South Africa are already being transformed by better designed products and services and by unprecedented access to information and technologies that can improve their quality of life and preserve their dignity (e.g., Novogratz, 2009; Prahalad, 2005). Particularly important is the role that SCMs play in the distribution and reconfiguration of products and services to better reach subsistence markets (Hawken, 2007; Prahalad, 2005; Simanis, Hart, & Duke, 2008). Through innovative designs, repackaging, pricing, positioning, and usage recommendations that are tailored to their unique environments, SCMs make beneficial products and services more accessible and meaningful to their peers and help unleash the transformative potential of market offerings that are at the same time profitable for the companies that developed them (e.g., Unilever's Project Shakti).

Furthermore, the innovativeness of SCMs may help solve some significant environmental and economic threats. An additional 1 billion new consumers, mostly from developing countries, are expected to enter the global market for discretionary spending before 2020 (Davis & Stephenson, 2006), doubling in a decade the number of consumers who use shampoo, batteries, detergents, cell phones, prepackaged foods, allopathic drugs, fossil fuels, and other life-transforming products. If these new consumers, motivated by common human desires for possessions and enjoyment (Burroughs & Rindfleisch, Chapter 12 of this volume), adopt consumption practices already prevalent in developed markets, the environmental degradation and resource depletion likely to ensue could endanger the quality of life of all consumers (Kilbourne & Mittelstaedt, Chapter 14 of this volume). Rapidly expanding subsistence markets demand product and process designs that promote economic, environmental, and social sustainability. They also demand that the already proven innovativeness of producers and merchants closest to subsistence consumers be channeled and given opportunity to contribute maximally. In the same way that SCMs have closed the gap between companies and subsistence consumers, they are likely to help develop sustainable solutions to consumption problems, solutions that may eventually be retroadapted to developed markets.

For purposes of this research, we adopt a sociocognitive perspective already familiar to consumer research (e.g., Burroughs & Mick, 2004; Hirschman, 1980; Moreau & Dahl, 2005; Ram & Jung, 1989, 1994; Ridgway & Price, 1994), one that purposefully allows the boundaries between thinking and behavior, and between individuals and the social milieu, to be fuzzy. We contribute by specifically investigating how hope and innovativeness inform one another and, to a lesser extent, by qualitatively documenting innovativeness among SCMs. Creativity "involves the retrieval and novel combination of fragments of knowledge from disparate locations in memory, such that it constructively addresses a given issue" (Burroughs et al., 2008, p. 1017); and innovation emerges when the novel arrays prove to be valuable to the developer and others (e.g., Amabile, 1996). Consumer innovativeness exists when recombination and experimentation with known concepts (e.g., products, discarded materials, usage modes and conditions, sensory characteristics) lead to outcomes that creators find valuable, be it for their own immediate benefit or to benefit others.

Value, of course, is subjectively determined, and it is possible that what seems innovative to SCMs may not be so to others. One example of variance in the perception of innovativeness can be drawn from community sanitation in Bangladesh (Kar, 2003), where professional engineers considered bamboo-based latrine designs as not worth pursuing, when in effect they proved highly effective in improving community health because they allowed even the poorest villagers to have access to a family latrine. SCMs in the villages combined locally available building materials with their knowledge of local soil and culture to create innovative and sustainable latrine designs that professional engineers could not envision but recognized as highly effective once implemented. This research focuses on subsistence consumers who are at least temporarily satisfied with the products and services they have developed, and it seeks to learn from them about the process by which their innovations came about and the role that hope plays in their innovativeness.

## HOPING, HAVING HOPE, AND BEING HOPEFUL

Hope is a fundamental motivator of people, necessary for the pursuit of goals (McGeer, 2004) and studied through social science (Lazarus, 1999; McGeer, 2004) and applied science lenses (e.g., MacInnis & de Mello, 2005). Hope is more than warm feelings and wishful thinking (i.e., unfocused yearning); it involves both cognitive and emotional involvement. As with other complex emotions (Peters, Vastfjall, Garling, & Slovic, 2006), hope can have information value, as when people say, "Because hope for victory persists, we are drawing new plans." Hope can also have a focusing effect on thought and action, which we recognize in ideas such as "hope and hard work will save us," and it can be purely energizing, as in the oft-quoted assertion that "hope is passion for what is possible." Through these various mechanisms, hope produces "improvements to the individual's life before any hoped for results are achieved" (Lueck, 2007, p. 251)—improvements that stem from endurance and coping based on having hope, driving toward goals fueled by hoping, and the constructive channeling of cognitive and motivational resources caused by being hopeful (de Mello & MacInnis, 2005). In hope, we "experience ourselves as agents of potential as well as agents in fact" (McGeer, 2004, p. 105) and strive for goals beyond what the objective assessment of resources and capabilities suggest is possible.

Recognizing that hope does more than give people pleasure (Lazarus, 1999), that it can be energizing (Belk, 1996) and in itself be a sought-after outcome (Lueck, 2007), de Mello and MacInnis (2005) argued for three facets of hope in consumer behavior: hoping, having hope, and being hopeful. To hope (or hoping) is an energizing positive emotion that varies in response to the level of yearning for a possible goal-congruent outcome. If an outcome is deemed possible and yearning is strong, hope rises and drives action, and when hope diminishes, people may give up on important desired outcomes (McGeer, 2004), even survival. Hope for desired outcomes, such as recovering from a serious illness or rebuilding one's home after a hurricane, is necessary for persons to work hard and remain alert to opportunities and threats.

To have hope (or having hope) is a pleasurable and nurturing emotional state that arises when goal-congruent outcomes are consciously deemed possible. Having hope promotes a sense of well-being that further motivates the person, because dwelling on a desired outcome being possible is enough to shape the individual's perspective on the future. Having hope generates positive illusions (e.g., Taylor & Brown, 1988) and motivated thinking (Kunda, 1990). Positive illusions exist when people view themselves in what others would consider unrealistically positive terms, believing they have greater control than what is actually the case and holding views of the future that are more rosy than base rate data would justify; positive illusions have also been found to be correlated with higher achievement rates for desired outcomes (Taylor & Brown, 1988). Persons recovering from what were diagnosed as terminal illnesses or surviving accidents and situations that should have been fatal are significantly more likely to hold positive illusions (Taylor, 1989). Having hope leads to positive illusions that reduce fear and anxiety, which in turn attenuates mental load and allows individuals to better recognize opportunities to be exploited and dangers to be averted. Having hope can ultimately lead to better decisions.

Motivated reasoning is thinking about and evaluating information in ways that support a particular directional conclusion (Kunda, 1990). It distorts the validity and meaning of ambiguous information so as to support the expectation of a desired outcome (Averill et al., 1990; Belk, 1996). Motivated reasoning gives rise to situational optimism (Scheier & Carver, 1985) that keeps people in pursuit of desired outcomes and often achieving a portion of those outcomes by appropriating ambiguous and uncommitted resources through enactment (de Mello & MacInnis, 2005).

Being hopeful arises from expectations regarding the likelihood of attaining a desired outcome. If a runner draws energy from entertaining a better than 60% likelihood of running a 5-minute mile, he or she is being hopeful. Being hopeful delivers a positive yet tempering influence on behaviors that stem from hoping and having hope. Highly energized positive illusions and optimistic plans for action are toned down by being hopeful; they are further considered and articulated in ways that often lead to a more cautious pursuit of those outcomes. Being hopeful tempers and directs the energy and activity that come from hoping and having hope.

Hoping, having hope, and being hopeful are interrelated and distinct emotional mechanisms that contribute toward consumers striving for desired outcomes (de Mello & MacInnis, 2005) and as such can result in better decisions and behaviors. Moreover, they are essential to human enterprise (de Mello & MacInnis, 2005; McGeer, 2004), including those of subsistence consumers who yearn for food and clothing to preserve family well-being and shelter for loved ones and their possessions. Subsistence consumers also yearn for generalized outcomes, such as opportunities for self-determination and for their children to be educated, marry well, and achieve a higher standard of living. Moreover, many pursue such immediate and distant outcomes through daily exchange with customers, vendors, and others in their environments (Viswanathan et al., 2010). They pursue reasons to have hope through motivated reasoning and positive illusions, such as when they avoid information that undermines their action plans or when they affirm their positive illusions by speaking frequently and enthusiastically about their desired outcomes (Viswanathan, 2007).

The three facets of hope also have implications for SCM innovativeness. Energy from hoping is likely to result in higher numbers of novel arrays being considered and in an enhanced appreciation of the potential value of any single array, both needed for consumer innovativeness (Burroughs et al., 2008). SCMs who believe in their ability to achieve outcomes will work harder and be more focused. Hope is indispensable for innovativeness to arise in any context, and markedly so among the poor. Having hope is also valuable. The sense of well-being and positive illusions that arise from having hope are attractive and beneficial alternatives to the negative emotions that can easily overtake individuals when resources are nonexistent and environments are hostile and unpredictable. For SCMs, feeling helpless is a frequently occurring emotional state because of surrounding circumstances, and having hope is a likely antidote (Lazarus, 1999). Dwelling on a desired outcome leads SCMs to focus on information that supports their pursuits (motivated reasoning) and to remain mentally engaged as they enact and experiment with novel arrays in the face of difficult odds. It may even lead them to take action when no specific desired outcomes exist but a sense of well-being can be sustained, in the same way that terminally ill patients dwell on positive illusions about beating the disease, going home, and vacationing with loved ones, and in so doing ease their pain and prolong their lives (Taylor & Brown, 1988). Finally, being hopeful can serve a crucial role in making SCM innovativeness safe and productive. Many subsistence consumers live in perpetual states of resource depletion on account of uncertainty in their environments and absolute deprivation, which is a condition that can hinder self-regulation in all manner of consumption-related activities (see Faber & Vohs, Chapter 22 of this volume). Being hopeful, an emotional process that tempers energy and sense of well-being, can result in lower risks being taken by SCMs in their innovative experimentation and ultimately result in long-term well-being even if at the expense of short-term positive emotions. The struggle for survival faced by SCMs demands all three facets of hope to be present and makes the interdependence of hope and innovativeness in subsistence contexts an inescapable phenomenon.

## METHODS

This research was conducted in Bogotá, Colombia, a culture known for energy and hard work despite almost 40% of its 8.5 million citizens living in subsistence conditions (United Nations Development Programme, 2008). Colombia is a country of over 41 million citizens, of which 49.2% live below the poverty line (Central Intelligence Agency, 2009), and Bogotá authorities estimate that as many as 40% of Bogotá residents may live on incomes of less than $2 per day (United Nations Development Programme, 2008). Bogotá receives over 250 new citizens (50+ new family units) daily, and most arrive with not much more than the clothes on their bodies. It is a metropolis where poverty is abundant and makes life difficult, but the culture is not debilitating to individual efforts, and hence is a setting where SCM innovativeness can be found. Complementing the suitability of Bogotá to the research objectives is the fact that two of the authors are fluent in Spanish (Colombia's national language). In contrast to other subsistence settings (e.g., urban India and China), Colombia does not have many dialects among its urban poor, making the quality of communication constant across informants. Participants in the study were identified opportunistically through employees of a local university who were asked for names of subsistence consumers they considered innovative.

Within a 2-week window, 24 informants were identified and contacted, and 18 were interviewed. Twelve of the informants were subsistence consumers who operate small businesses as an integral part of family survival, and their narratives serve as data for this research. Disguised names (i.e., pseudonyms) and demographic information on the informants are presented in Table 7.1. The informants work in different market sectors (e.g., health and beauty aids, construction) and are active in the development of products and services for sale and personal use. Some of the informants work together, but most operate independently. Whenever possible, interviews were conducted and the

**Table 7.1**    Subsistence Consumer-Merchant Informants' Demographic Information

| Pseudonym | Age | Type of Business | Time in Operation | Approximate Annual Income (in U.S. Dollars) |
|---|---|---|---|---|
| José | 42 | Farm manager and inventor | 10 years | $1,200 |
| Antonio | 46 | Farm manager and inventor | 12 years | $1,000 |
| Nestor | 23 | Construction plasterer | 4 years | $1,100 |
| David | 21 | Construction plasterer | 4 years | $1,000 |
| Lorenzo | 48 | Health and beauty aids | 11 years | $1,700 |
| Carolina | 28 | Medicinal and facial soaps | 5 years | $900 |
| Hector | 45 | Detergents and cleaners | 3 years | $800 |
| Arnaldo | 22 | Construction implements | 4 years | $600 |
| Sara | 21 | Construction implements | 5 years | $650 |
| Pablo | 31 | Sugarcane farmer and inventor | 3 years | $500 |
| Iván | 23 | Various | 4 years | $400 |
| Nitza | 28 | Child care | 5 years | $300 |

innovations examined at the informants' homes. In all cases, informants were asked to demonstrate their products and services and explain how they developed (and, in most instances, continue to develop) their innovations. The innovation process and factors that influence the process were probed, including how SCMs test products, how their customers (e.g., neighbors, friends, families) respond to innovations, and their plans to improve the innovations in the future. The interviews were conducted in Spanish, transcribed in the native language, and translated to English.

## OBSERVATIONS ON THE INNOVATION PROCESS

Capabilities and processes associated with innovativeness (Burroughs et al., 2008) are well represented among subsistence consumers. Their innovativeness is deliberate and procedural, adjusting in speed and scope to the demands of uncertain environments but not without discipline. Solution expediency takes precedence over replicability, however, given the low likelihood that identical problem conditions will reoccur. Analogical reasoning (e.g., Burroughs & Mick, 2004) also plays a role in the SCM creative process, which often involves transferring elements from some domains into different ones, such as when José builds alcohol stoves from motorcycle parts, and watering troughs from discarded auto tires and wheels. SCM ideas often emerge from experimentation with scavenged artifacts—touching, feeling, and sensing their way to novel productive applications of someone else's trash.

Other informants combine scavenged items with purchased raw materials (e.g., animal fat from kitchen scraps with purchased chemicals for soap) or take manufactured products from one usage domain (e.g., kitchen foil) into other domains (e.g., wallpaper). Iván, for example, combines what he can grasp from the listed ingredients on hair gel labels with the smell and texture of over-the-counter chemicals to produce hair gel that he sells to friends:

*Iván:* I made gel for the hair.
*Interviewer:* How?
*Iván:* Carbocol, profolamina, profonalicol.
*Interviewer:* You bought the chemicals and made it?
*Iván:* I mixed the chemicals and packed it in bags or whatever I had around.
*Interviewer:* And who taught you to make that gel?
*Iván:* Nobody, because the gel packages [labels] tell you…. To thicken it, I use carbocol, a chemical
       used to make rubber products and all that.
*Interviewer:* To whom did you sell?
*Iván:* My companions at school.

The application of diverse knowledge and innate intelligence is also evident among SCMs, and like Iván, most rely on sensory appraisals (e.g., smell, color, texture, taste) of materials. Such knowledge is integral to how Carolina develops soaps with her mother:

*Interviewer:* And those improvements, how do you make them?
*Carolina:* With my mother—we make some compounds, and then I test them [on myself], and the
       next people who try them are my relatives. And the customers tell me, for example, "I
       liked it a lot for dry skin," or greasy skin, or dry hair. "Look, I really liked that it removed
       the lice from children, but I think it dried their hair," or "It's perfect." Then, we have to
       improve the recipe, so maybe I will add aloe vera for this type of person. A large number
       of trials are needed, and sometimes we lose some batches of product, and it's sort of
       like that.

Similarly, Nitza developed a recipe for nontoxic modeling clay for her day care center:

*Interviewer:* You told me that you made modeling clay.

*Nitza:* I made it because the small children were eating the commercial clay, and that clay is toxic, and they eat it and … It is flour and water, nothing more. Oh, and so it has this consistency, we must add salt.

*Interviewer:* Salt?

*Nitza:* Salt. I do not know why, but it does not let it become hard.

*Interviewer: (later in the interview)* How long did it take to develop the recipe for your modeling clay?

*Nitza:* The consistency was achieved more or less in the course of 1 week.

*Interviewer:* And how did it happen that you added salt?

*Nitza:* I did it for them [the children], so if they eat it, they will find a little flavor. If it was too salty, they did not eat it, however, so I added more salt to it [*laughs*] … and then learned that the salt keeps it humid.

Nestor developed gold-based wall enamel using the same approach:

*Interviewer:* How did you develop the idea? What happened?

*Néstor:* Well, basically it came from looking at paintings and the gold frames…. You may have seen that they put gold frames on them. and so we started experimenting, trying to find the one that worked, until we arrived at this finish [*points at the wall*]…. We started experimenting with the spatula, the paint, trial and error, trial and error…. We used lacquers and varnishes…. Well, we mixed one paint and another paint…. And first we started with some gold dust and some resin they sell to make paints … and we just kept experimenting.

A high reliance on sensory appraisals may uniquely influence SCMs' assessments of whether or not goal-congruent goals are possible and hence affect their innovativeness. Smells and tastes are known to positively or negatively influence consumer assessments of products (Hoch, 2002; Hoegg & Alba, 2007) and influence motivated reasoning across contexts (e.g., Westen, Blagov, Harenski, Kilts, & Hamann, 2006). SCMs who are applying sense-based evaluations to, and experimenting with, different materials are probably shaping their assessments of what is possible, albeit unknowingly, and in so doing, they are elevating or reducing their ability to hope and have hope from new ideas.

Two additional factors common across informants are that many engage in conversation throughout the innovation process, and they perform multiple quick-and-dirty cycles of experimentation and outcome observation until a satisfying solution is found. Some seem to use these tactics to overcome fixation and accelerate the pace of incubation and insight (Ward, Smith, & Finke, 1999). Working and talking, Carolina and her mother develop new recipes for facial soaps in their kitchen, adding ingredients suggested by customers and from newly available materials, and they quickly test the new recipes before making full batches. Similarly, Arnaldo and his friends engaged in conversation as they came up with the idea of an electric wire twister, or *bichiroque*, for the construction trade:

*Interviewer:* How did the idea come up?

*Arnaldo:* One of our group works in construction … in industrial safety. We were sitting at her house one night, and we had like 20 days until the due date for the project, and … we had to make something simple. What do we do? So, let's invent ourselves a tool. So, we began to speak, that we have to invent something that is fast and that people will say "this works," and we began to talk … and then she said, "Why don't we make an electric *bichiroque*, one that belongs to us?"

*Carolina:* Our first reaction was to laugh, because we said, "Not an electric *bichiroque*," … and from there the idea arose.

*Carolina: (later in the interview)* We decided to use a piece of PVC pipe, and we put everything in it.

*Interviewer:* Why PVC pipe? Because somebody had a piece of PVC pipe?

*Carolina:* We obtained our piece of PVC from the rooftop of our friend's house.

*Arnaldo:* We were getting desperate, and we asked her, "Do you have any pipe?" And she went up to her roof and brought down some huge pieces of pipe, and we already had the idea, like the image of the pipe, and so there it is, We got the pipe, and we adapted it. We put an electrical adapter on it, and there it is, ready! And we were very happy.

*Bichiroques* are used to tighten wires that hold steel bars in place during the construction of reinforced cement columns. Extended use of a hand *bichiroque* causes carpal tunnel injuries, and Arnaldo and his team developed a battery-powered tool that reduces wrist strain and the incidence of carpal tunnel injuries. Although admittedly on a small scale, Iván's hair gel, Carolina's soaps, Arnaldo's *bichiroque*, and other SCM-developed products are transformational to themselves and others who use such products.

## IN PURSUIT OF HOPE, HAVING HOPE, AND BEING HOPEFUL

Hoping, having hope, and being hopeful, along with positive illusions and motivated reasoning, were evident among the SCMs. Many of them hoped for something tangible and immediate, such as new shoes, school uniforms for children, or a safer home, but not everything was about material possessions. Sara and her friends, for instance, hope for acceptance from classmates who see themselves as members of a better social class than her:

*Sara:* We launched the [*bichiroque*] idea because of our eagerness to demonstrate to the other people that we, less educated persons, that we also can do [things]. So, we threw ourselves into doing something in the technical area, something that used technology, something that had to do with revolutions and electricity.

Pablo in turn hopes to make a difference in the lives of the poor in his country:

*Interviewer:* And these projects, you say, arose from need.

*Pablo:* From necessity, because we human beings are beautiful projects that go against some types of enterprises, and I am talking about public enterprises. This is a project that if I get it to work, it will go against them [existing business enterprises]. They [the enterprises] are taking away a necessity … or not a necessity, they are taking away a product that is natural [*panela*], that we need, the basis of survival, and they turned it into a business. I want to give it [*panela*] to them [the people], so they can have it without costs, because it is the right of every human being.

Pablo is working on a machine to produce *panela*, edible squares of unrefined sugarcane that are a staple among Colombia's poor. His objective is to reduce the large amounts of manual labor involved in at-home *panela* production and eventually allow for all families in sugarcane growing areas to have their own *panela* machines or no-cost access to one.

Similarly, Nitza hopes to make a difference for children in her day care center:

*Nitza:* I want to have a space where I can have a series of classrooms, but I do not want square classrooms. No, I want circular classrooms. Why circular? I believe that the brain is something compact, but that when we give it information, it expands. Squares have corners, and these corners are like limits. The circle does not have a limit, ... and I can expand it. I can expand the square, but it always has limits, and limits can be good. But in the matter of development, they are not good, because in the matter of development, we need to expand and expand.

Motivated reasoning and positive illusions are discernible in Pablo's belief that his machine will neutralize perceived exploitation of the poor by large *panela* producers, companies that he considers evil. Motivated reasoning and positive illusions are also present in Nitza's belief that classroom shape has a direct influence on children's learning ability. Also noteworthy in Nitza's beliefs is her use of analogical thinking to link sensory information to mental representations of abstract concepts and back to innovative ideas for the day care center. She believes there is a direct connection between the classroom environment and how the mind develops because of their shapes, making round classrooms more compatible with round brains. She was unable to explain how her theories developed, but they seemed grounded in illustrations of the brain she has seen and her experiences with round and square containers.

Lorenzo also holds positive illusions and practices motivated reasoning:

*Interviewer:* Please tell me about your product.
*Lorenzo:* Well, there is a situation that explains it, because it is not only about this product but [also about] a process of life.... The fundamental project that I devised is returning to rural settings, the repopulation of the Colombian countryside, while at the same time preparing retired people for old age so that they can still work productively. What is innovative is that we manage to repopulate [existing rural villages] and make new villages ... with older persons to attract young people toward rural life. Then, there begins a process of chemistry, or more of alchemy than chemistry. It is a work that has to do with adult reeducation and the application of theories like chaos theory, taking it to reality in the making of experiments.

Lorenzo produces a line of skin care products that include snail secretions and with which he is financing his social initiative. He is uneducated but not illiterate; he reads on a sixth- to eighth-grade level. He reads newspapers, books, and magazines and occasionally gets information from the Internet. He does not understand chaos theory, alchemy, or chemistry, but like Nitza has developed intricate theories and positive illusions about harnessing and shaping natural phenomena (e.g., snails), commercial products (e.g., skin creams), and Colombian society. Moreover, using those theories he has developed an elaborate scheme for improving social welfare, and at the same time earns a living for his family.

Motivated reasoning and positive illusions allow informants to hope and have hope and, in so doing, energize their pursuit of innovative ideas and keep them feeling good and optimistic, at least some of the time. Admittedly, most observers who appraise the informants' schemes would consider them nonsensical, although it is important to note that accompanying the motivated reasoning of the informants is notable innovativeness. Most of them have developed products and/or services that other consumers purchase, and they are considered innovative by their peers. (Pablo has yet to deliver a commercial version of his machine.) Moreover, their schemes do not stop at products sold door-to-door or from their homes, but they also involve ways to improve the lives of others and exhibit multiple levels of organization and stages of business growth. Lorenzo envisions multiple villages populated by retired persons creating products and living off the land in happiness. Nitza envisions a school with multiple grades in circular classrooms, and Pablo wants to liberate the masses. Also noteworthy is the energizing and healing effect that SCMs experience from both small achievements and expansive visions. Hoping and working toward envisioned outcomes through innovative activities can be rewarding and restorative:

*Interviewer:* Tell me how you feel when you manage to do something innovative?
*Iván:* Whenever I create a new thing that no one else has thought of, and I see how possible it is to make something, it is happiness.

Pablo is even more expressive, possibly because of the severity of his situation:

*Pablo:* Well, the only thing I want you [the interviewers] to take away is a good memory and to have shared this moment, and sometimes we need to talk to others.... I want to tell you something that only my mother knows. Before I arrived here, I had a problem with my family, my ex-wife, we had problems and we had to separate. I had the project idea and lots of notebooks and diagrams, but I lacked information. A moment arrived when my mind dictated words and I could not articulate them, and my sense of feeling out of place was incredible. Incredible! It was like … I think, not even the most incredible drunken spell can cause this, and the impotence that one feels is hard.... The pain was very hard. Trying to speak and not being able to do it, uttering words that are incomprehensible, it was terrible. It happened to me. And when I came here, I started clearing my mind and clearing, and now I can say that I sleep for 3 hours peacefully.... Being here and communicating has helped me … and being busy, because the ideas come back and gain the same importance as they had before.
*Interviewer:* What set you free?
*Pablo:* Being here … and being able to make the machine work, and when I spoke to them and we coordinated, and I saw it could be made to work, then I felt some relief, and the weight started coming off from me, and that is one of the processes here.

Pablo's hope, and possibly his pursuit of having hope in dark moments, fueled his work on the *panela* machine for 7 years. He described the experimentation as incessant and obsessive, and in his own estimation, the obsession contributed to the marriage failing. Nevertheless, he did not (or maybe could not) give up his hope for the outcome, a yearning so profound that he believes it caused him to not be able to sleep or speak. Such was his state when he came to the vocational center 2 years before we met him, where he was finally able to get some rudimentary guidance on how to build the machine he envisioned. The assistance he receives is minimal, and because he is not a trained engineer, progress toward a prototype has been full of dead ends. Nevertheless, by his own account, Pablo is happier and more fulfilled than he was 2 years ago, even if not all that much closer to achieving his dreams. He seems to have balanced his hope for the machine and relief for the poor, and his quest for simply having hope, with a cooler assessment of the likelihood of success in different facets of the project—with being hopeful. Being hopeful has, in turn, tempered his motivated reasoning and positive illusions and led to better decisions about designs and experiments. Pablo is once again able to speak of his goals and the hurdles that remain. He transitioned away from self-described despair toward a better life and some progress on the machine, even if his marriage could not be saved:

*Pablo:* I am an exaggeratedly emotional person. This feeling inspires not just faith, but the desire to demonstrate to one self that one can do it. That is the only reason, just to say that it makes me very sad to see a person suffering, that someone else is charging them to live. For me, that is hard, because it should not be like that, ... and I want to get [them] out from under those loads, because nobody needs them. [*very emotional*]

*Interviewer:* And to what do you attribute your motivation?

*Pablo:* When I was a child, I had a lot of problems, well not me, but my father and my brothers, and all I did was notice their attitude and behaviors. I noticed they were harming me and were wearing me down and my younger brothers and my mother. And when one sees his mother uncomfortable in front of others, one says, I have to do something. But age gets in the way, because it is impossible to go against someone older. One does not have the strength, and the injustice remains, and it starts to make attitudes change a little ... and one arrives at a moment of maturity. When the veil is removed and one realizes that miracles do not exist, one becomes part of them [the problems]. [*very emotional*]

Pablo's story is illustrative of a potentially dysfunctional by-product of hoping and wanting to have hope without the ability to be hopeful. By his own account, Pablo's yearning was rooted in experiences that went beyond seeing poor people not being able to afford *panela*. He wanted to believe he could make a difference, protect his mother, and make things right, and he was frustrated on all counts. Years later, he connects his work on a *panela* machine to earlier unfulfilled yearnings for hope and desired outcomes, still wanting to address past wrongs in his own life and the lives of those around him. He described years of effort and dozens of attempts at developing the machine using whatever materials were available (e.g., wood and metal scraps, discarded electronics he did not understand) just to keep hope alive, although realistically he lacked the fundamental know-how and materials. He engaged in the work to have hope, and instead of addressing past wrongs, he created new ones. The pursuit of hope in one domain robbed him of hope and well-being in other domains. Nitza expressed similar struggles:

*Nitza:* Traditional education makes us repeat schemas, schemas and more schemas, always the same ... [*increasing agitation in her voice*] and always looking; and because of the anguish, the stress, the fatigue, being locked up in the house, [it] also locks me up.... [*distressed pause*] It is terrible, then I ... [*chokes back tears*] My dream costs too much, ... and I say to him, to God, "I do not know why".... [*distressed and tearful pause*] And every time I see you [referring to one of the interviewers whom she knew beforehand], I see you like an angel. You are an angel, because when I have thoughts of stopping, you appear.... And I say, "Lord, you say to me that I must go on. Well, I am going to go on."

The interviewer's relationship to Nitza was superficial in his own estimation. They had met briefly only a handful of times, and at such encounters, she typically shared with him positive illusions and motivated reasoning about ideas for the day care center, while he listened and offered passive encouragement. The relationship resembles the nondirected nature of Pablo's interactions with others at the vocational center, in that consumer-innovators attribute to others, with whom they share positive illusions and motivated reasoning, a level of power and influence over personal capabilities that surpasses what the listeners see themselves as contributing. Nitza and Pablo seem to benefit from simply conversing with others about their ideas.

As it pertains to pursuing ideas to the point of frustration to keep hope alive, other informants (Iván, Sara, Lorenzo, and Hector) spoke of similar experiences. Iván, for example, did not pursue a single idea but jumped from one idea to another quickly, and sometimes recklessly, and sought solace in the church when things did not go well:

*Iván:* That was my first deal, and I started trying new repairs and learning about systems and computers and things, and put myself to work; and then one day, I was attacked by demons. Ha! And the sister knows how I was attacked by Satan, but now I am calm, thanks to God.

Among the informants, innovative experimentation to gain or restore hope can be harmful, a by-product of hope and innovativeness similar to what arises when consumers overspend on products and services in order to simply have hope (MacInnis & de Mello, 2005). Moreover, some respondents (e.g., Pablo) seem aware of the detrimental effects of their pursuits but continue nevertheless, aware of their vulnerability due to resource depletion but unable to self-regulate (see Faber & Vohs, Chapter 22 of this volume). Such behavior is understandable, however, when one considers that behaviors in pursuit of yearned-for outcomes, even if fruitless, can affirm the possibility of attaining those outcomes. If we take steps toward fulfilling a goal, the steps make it seem more attainable, which in turn gives rise to hope. Having hope becomes a "force that prevents us from disengaging even when faced with obstacles" (Lueck, 2007, p. 251) and sometimes keeps SCMs experimenting and innovating against impossible odds.

Not all of our informants had accounts of frustration and self-damage in their pursuit of having hope. In Carolina's account of how she and her mother develop new soap recipes, there is implicit playfulness and a willingness to abandon ideas if they do not work. Detachment from specific ideas was also evident in Arnaldo's account of his *bichiroque*. Similarly, in what amounts to a classic instance of managing the incubation process (Ward et al., 1999), Antonio frames innovative pursuits as a game, and although he enjoys the positive feeling that comes from having hope, he is not adverse to postponing work on an idea if he reaches an impasse:

*Antonio:* There are many times that … all of a sudden, I am trying to put something together, let's say the lamp, and for some reason, something. [*gestures that it does not work*] So, I put them away [for] 8, 10, 15, 20 days … and suddenly I try it again or tear it apart. Or, at the moment that something did not work out, I start trying to identify [the problem] without having to tear it apart.… The brain has to work permanently, so I can be working on farm chores, milking the cows, weeding the field, and always thinking about how to create new things and getting new small products.

Carolina and Antonio engage in motivated reasoning, discernible from earlier accounts of how they develop product ideas. Their individual pursuits, however, are marked by balance between hoping, having hope, and being hopeful. Although necessarily biased to the positive, they nevertheless hold a tempered assessment of their individual ability to innovate and a level of playfulness to the process. They are consequently able to walk away from ideas that become less likely once experimented on and could prove harmful if pursued further. Pablo and Nitza, in contrast, pursue innovative activities to the detriment of their own well-being and that of others.

Although interviews revealed that some informants did themselves and others harm in the pursuit of innovative ideas, while others were able to walk away from ideas that did not work, it was not possible to query them effectively on what distinguished self-damaging instances from those that were not self-damaging. Retrospectively, it appears that one potential antidote to self-damaging pursuits may be conversation. The most dramatic cases of self-damage (Nitza, Iván, and Pablo) worked alone or with people with whom they could not interact (e.g., children). In contrast,

Antonio and José work and talk together, Carolina works with her mother when developing new soaps, and Arnaldo worked with a team on the electric *bichiroque*.

The importance of conversation to the innovation process is documented (Amabile, 1996; Burroughs et al., 2008), but primarily as it pertains to idea generation. The experiences of informants here suggest that conversation may also help SCMs better sustain hope without becoming reckless in its pursuit, possibly because in sharing with others, they affirm positive illusions and motivated reasoning and, in effect, transform individual hope into collective hope (Braithwaite, 2004). In the pursuit of hope, too much focus on the individual can lead to a lack of regard for potential constraints and an inability to seek assistance from others when needed (McGeer, 2004), which is evident in Pablo's case and implicit in Nitza's. In turning individual hope into collective hope through the sharing of positive illusions and motivated reasoning, the perceived possibility of ultimate success is affirmed (Courville & Piper, 2004), and the activity protects individuals from the despair that momentary setbacks can induce (McGeer, 2004). Having hope is attained through the sharing of the vision, which reduces the need for sustaining hope through (sometimes risky) behaviors and outcomes.

A detrimental aspect of SCMs' innovativeness stems from their continuous experimentation spurred by past success, even when the products being experimented on have proved beneficial to their families and customers. Carolina, for example, responds to customer requests and suggestions as she develops facial and skin soaps, and her strategies endanger both her livelihood and loved ones. As noted, she changes product composition in response to customer requests (e.g., scent, feel, moisture content) and the availability of materials. She does not, however, document the success rates of past formulations, nor does she have documented procedures for producing each one. As a result, changes to recipes often jeopardize customers' satisfaction and have a detrimental effect on her business. In addition, Carolina's product testing practices endanger her family and friends, whom she uses as guinea pigs:

*Interviewer:* And what did you mean by "I have them in trials"?

*Carolina:* That they do not go to market until I know the product will not produce allergic reactions.... We create different mixtures and package samples cooked for different lengths of time and allowed to be exposed to the air and to the sun and to cold and hot temperatures. Four or five persons will try the product, with different types of skin, and if they do not have a reaction, well ... Although my process is homegrown, and it can be improved, this is what we have done until now.

*Interviewer:* And who are the persons who do the trials?

*Carolina:* My family, my sisters, my friends, my mother, and me.

The quick cycles of conceptualization, experimentation, and implementation exhibited by SCMs can yield brilliant solutions and simultaneously cut short the life cycle of any single innovation. Hector's approach is almost identical to Carolina's. He regularly alters products based on consumer requests and the availability of raw materials. Product recipes are thus inconsistent between batches, to the point that people who use his products have more than once asked that he "not change the recipe, because this one works." The inconsistent performance of Hector's products also affects his business. He has to lower prices when batches do not perform well or when they look and smell different from previous ones. He also tests products on his household. In one such episode, he tested one of the homegrown degreasers as an additive in the family laundry and ruined some overalls in the process.

Hector and Carolina illustrate a willingness to experiment that was ubiquitous among the informants. No recipes or designs were sacred, and ideas for new experiments could arise from practically all facets of the environment, even from materials scavenged from discard piles along the road. Moreover, the artisanal nature of the production processes makes variability in the production sequence inevitable and opens the door to unexpected outcomes. None of the informants codify successful designs or recipes to insure consistency between batches.

It appears that the same creative behaviors that engender innovativeness can also undermine the longevity of any one successful innovation, and in that sense, innovativeness may keep SCMs trapped in their impoverished status. The absence of standardized products and processes threatens customer loyalty and makes it difficult to attain economies of scale. Coupling such detrimental outcomes with the damage that can accrue from testing ideas on their possessions, families, and friends, it can be argued that SCMs live with a significant potential for negative outcomes that can neutralize the positives that innovativeness brings them. The transformative potential of SCM innovativeness, therefore, has a dark side. Transformations can lead to a better quality of life or to family members and customers being endangered.

## DISCUSSION AND LIMITATIONS

Different roles for hope, having hope, and being hopeful in SCM innovativeness emerge from the informant narratives and are illustrated in Figure 7.1. Among SCMs, yearnings caused by personal and family needs trigger appraisals of circumstances and possible solutions, and those appraisals

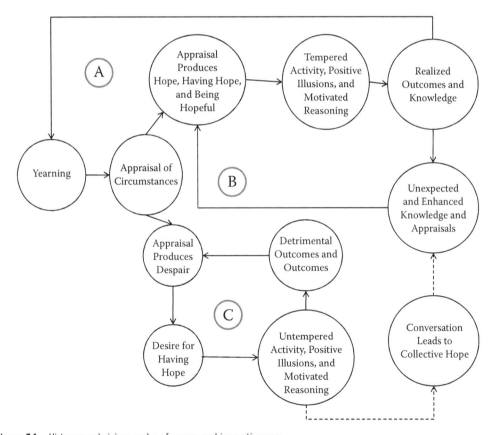

**Figure 7.1**  Virtuous and vicious cycles of agency and innovativeness.
*Note*: A = virtuous cycle of hope to innovativeness; B = vicious cycle from novel outcomes to hope-fueled experimentation; C = vicious cycle of untempered activity in pursuit of hope.

lead to hope (i.e., beliefs that something can be done and the SCM is capable) or despair. In ideal situations, hope, having hope, and being hopeful are present, providing energy and a sense of well-being from regarding outcomes as possible, and assessments of outcome likelihood that are also positive but more guarded. When the three facets of hope are present, they produce motivated reasoning, positive illusions, and tempered activity, which fuels innovativeness. Tempered activity involves multiple cycles of conceptualization, experimentation, and observation; engaging in the creative process (Ward et al., 1999); applying analogical reasoning and preexisting knowledge from diverse domains; and, in some instances, using strategies to move through the creative process more quickly. Moreover, activity fueled by the three facets of hope leads to outcomes and learning. Realized outcomes may not align with envisioned ones but are of sufficient value to satisfy SCMs' needs, encourage market activity for their small businesses, and reinitialize the process through enhanced or new yearnings. This is a virtuous cycle of hope and innovativeness (labeled A in Figure 7.1). Carolina's success with a line of soaps that eliminate lice, for example, triggered yearnings for revenue from serving another market, pet soaps, and led her to innovate in this new arena. Hector was likewise encouraged by success with his household detergents and undertook development of a line of furniture polish. In all instances, the SCMs overcome substantial odds against their development of successful problem solutions by exercising innovative activities guided by positive illusions and motivated thinking and fueled by the complex emotional array that stems from the three facets of hope. Figure 7.1 must not be interpreted as depicting a process that is linear and predictable, since embedded in its circles and arrows are substantial levels of uncertainty and danger, and failed attempts at innovative problem solutions.

A second cycle (labeled B in Figure 7.1) also grows out of the process in which all three facets of hope are present, but this is a vicious cycle triggered by new knowledge (e.g., unexpected outcomes, customer requests, alternative materials). From such knowledge arise new insights, additional factors and possibilities to consider, and possibly new sets of opportunities to pursue or dangers to avert. Unexpected knowledge that results in new and enhanced appraisals further engenders hoping, having hope, and being hopeful and leads to elevated positive illusions and motivated reasoning, new cycles of experimentation, and often the altering of products and services already being offered by SCMs in the market. This is the process illustrated by Carolina's and Hector's adjustments to already successful products and their resulting endangering of the means by which to meet family and personal needs. In such cases, the creative process once again results in innovativeness, but the net effect on subsistence consumer welfare is negative. When the innovation process is segmented, disciplined, and documented, such as one would find in established business enterprises, this second cycle would be a source of market-driven incremental innovation and, as such, be virtuous instead of vicious. In the absence of methods that separate innovation and production processes, however, these cycles of SCM innovation overlay past creations and cut short the value of past innovation.

It seems almost inevitable that SCMs will at some point engage in this vicious cycle because of hope being a force that prevents them from disengaging (Lueck, 2007). The tendency to further experiment with successful products was present among all informants, fueled by the stream of new appraisals that uncertain environments create, ever-present yearnings, and possibly the residual energy (hope) and sense of well-being (having hope) from past successes. Having been able to generate income and meet some family and personal needs through innovativeness, the SCMs' sense of possibilities is likely to increase, which in turn leads to higher levels of positive illusions and motivated reasoning; and because hope is energizing, SCMs are likely to enter new cycles of conceptualization, experimentation, and observation more vigorously. Hope energizes innovativeness toward success and, at the same time, energizes innovativeness toward endangering past success. The informants lack the mental and behavioral discipline required to segregate successful innovations from new experiments, suggesting that the observed pattern may be endemic to SCM innovativeness; whenever hope and innovativeness result in a virtuous cycle that fulfills yearnings, a vicious cycle is also likely to emerge.

A third cycle evident in the narratives (labeled C in Figure 7.1) emerges with appraisals resulting in yearned-for outcomes appearing impossible and leading to despair, such as when Pablo wanted to save his mother, and Nitza measured her capabilities against her dreams and found them lacking. Despair and its accompanying sense of helplessness are negative emotions that are hard to endure and from which most people want to escape. The escape strategy most evident among informants was to engage in activities that help them feel capable of doing something again, which seemed to be Pablo's motivation before connecting with the vocational center and Iván's state of mind when we interviewed him—that is, don't just sit there, do something. It is feasible that activity generates more detailed knowledge of possibilities while channeling energy and motivated reasoning and that the enhanced possibility of yearned-for outcomes that comes from doing, however slim, may give rise to hope and replace the despair. SCMs seem to engage in this type of fervent activity (e.g., new businesses, new approaches) primarily to have hope.

Impulsive activities seldom generate sustainable valuable outcomes, however, and "just do something" cycles often generate detrimental outcomes (e.g., someone gets hurt, resources are wasted). In such cases, despair is affirmed and reinitializes the cycle of activity in pursuit of restoring hope, often causing additional hardship along the way. Such was the case with Pablo as he tried again and again to assemble a working prototype of his machine from materials that were inadequate to the task at hand. Likewise, Nitza tries scheme after scheme to improve the day care center, but she never manages to help the children break out of poverty. In the case of Iván, the dysfunctional cycles seem evident in the list of ill-conceived businesses—from hair gel to soap to picture frames to computer repairs—that never got off the ground. As Iván described his business ventures, he time and again mentioned his primary goals of earning money to make his mother happy and giving up on each venture after a few weeks to start a new business shortly thereafter.

Some SCMs caught in the vicious cycle displayed in part C of Figure 7.1, such as Nitza and Pablo, are able to exit by speaking to others about their positive illusions and motivated reasoning instead of acting further on them, conversation that creates collective hope and sustains them as they slow down their activity, allowing for an eventual tempering of illusions and motivated reasoning. The alternative path is illustrated in Figure 7.1 by a dashed line leading into conversation and collective hope, and from there to unexpected knowledge and appraisals. Hope remains crucial to the process, but the positive illusions, motivated reasoning, and activities that follow are more controlled and focused on achievable outcomes. Nitza and Pablo seem to have exited the vicious cycle of despair, at least temporarily. For Iván, the narratives do not suggest that an exit is imminent.

Conversing with others was important to Nitza and Pablo. Nitza reported regaining hope and focus when speaking with her interviewer friend. For Pablo, talking to others led to changes in his approach and perspective on the project. He started to develop components one at a time instead of making concurrent changes to components. He still moves quickly through cycles of conceptualization, experimentation, and observation, but he allows himself time to assess the likelihood of new ideas and moves away from designs that appear infeasible. Being able to talk to others comes across as an antidote to the despair cycle into which some SCMs fall.

Figure 7.1 emerges from the narratives, so it is admittedly incomplete. The virtuous and vicious cycles identified here are present in the lives of the informants, but their replicability to others is far from certain on account of several limitations of the research. One limitation is that only 12 informants were interviewed, and it is possible that they are unique among SCMs, a possibility enhanced by how they were identified and recruited for the study. These people may have agreed to participate because they recognized their stories as unique compared to those of other SCMs. Another limitation is that all the informants are from a single urban environment that, because of its culture, may induce virtuous and vicious cycles not found elsewhere. With over 2.5 billion SCMs around the globe, the likelihood of finding unique variations in facets of hope, innovativeness, and their interrelationship is high, and more research is needed to fully grasp and appreciate the innovativeness of SCMs and how it is influenced by hope.

Limitations aside, the apparent relationship between hope and innovativeness among SCMs has transformative potential if better understood and eventually harnessed by those same key protagonists. The narratives show that SCMs are capable of developing unique and valuable solutions to subsistence market needs through repeated experimentation and that they can be tireless in their innovative efforts on the strength of the tempered positive illusions and motivated reasoning that the three facets of hope can engender.

## ACKNOWLEDGMENTS

The authors thank Debbie MacInnis, Linda Price, and Julie Ruth for suggestions on prior versions of this chapter, and the Universidad de los Andes (Bogotá, Colombia) and the University of Wyoming for underwriting data collection and analysis.

## REFERENCES

Amabile, T. (1996). *Creativity in context.* Boulder, CO: Westview.

Averill, J. R., Catlin, G., & Chon, K. K. (1990). *Rules of hope.* New York: Springer-Verlag.

Belk, R. W. (1996). On aura, illusion, escape and hope in apocalyptic consumption: The apotheosis of Las Vegas. In S. Brown (Ed.), *Marketing apocalypse: Eschatology, escapology and the illusion of the end* (pp. 87–107). London: Routledge.

Bendapudi, N., & Leone, R. P. (2003). Psychological implications of customer participation in co-production. *Journal of Marketing, 67*(April), 14–28.

Braithwaite, V. (2004). The hope process and social inclusion. *The Annals of the American Academy of Political and Social Science, 592*(1), 128–151.

Burgess, S. M., & Steenkamp, J. E. M. (2006). Marketing renaissance: How research in emerging markets advances marketing science and practice. *International Journal of Research in Marketing, 23*, 337–356.

Burroughs, J. R., & Mick, D. G. (2004). Exploring antecedents and consequences of consumer creativity in a problem solving context. *Journal of Consumer Research, 31*(2), 402–411.

Burroughs, J.R., Moreau, C. P., & Mick, D. G. (2008). Toward a psychology of consumer creativity. In C. P. Haugtvedt, P. M. Herr, & F. R. Kardes (Eds.), *Handbook of consumer psychology* (pp. 1011–1038). New York: Taylor & Francis.

Central Intelligence Agency. (2009). *The world factbook.* Retrieved December 2009 from https://www.cia.gov/library/publications/the-world-factbook/

Chakravarti, D. (2006). Voices unheard: The psychology of consumption in poverty and development. *Journal of Consumer Psychology, 16*(4), 363–376.

Courville, S., & Piper, N. (2004). Harnessing hope through NGO activism. *The Annals of the American Academy of Political and Social Science, 592*(1), 39–61.

Davis, I., & Stephenson, E. (2006). Ten trends to watch in 2006. *McKinsey Quarterly.* Available: http://www.mckinseyquarterly.com/links/22698

de Mello, G., & MacInnis, D. J. (2005). Why and how consumers hope: Motivated reasoning and the marketplace. In S. Ratneshwar & D. G. Mick (Eds.), *Inside consumption: Consumer motives, goals, and desires* (pp. 44–66). New York: Routledge.

de Mello, G., MacInnis, D. J., & Stewart, D. W. (2007). Threats to hope: Effects on reasoning about product information. *Journal of Consumer Research, 34*(2), 153–161.

Flores-Letelier, M., Flores, F., & Spinosa, C. (2003). Developing productive customers in emerging markets. *California Management Review, 45*(Summer), 77–103.

Hammond, A. L., Kramer, W. J., Katz, R. S., Tran, J. T., & Walker, C. (2007). *The next four billion: Market size and business strategy at the base of the pyramid.* Washington, DC: World Resources Institute & International Finance Corporation.

Hawken, P. (2007). *Blessed unrest: How the largest movement in the world came into being and why no one saw it coming*. New York: Viking Penguin.

Hirschman, E. C. (1980). Innovativeness, novelty seeking, and consumer creativity. *Journal of Consumer Research, 7*(3), 283–295.

Hoch, S. (2002). Product experience is seductive. *Journal of Consumer Research, 29*(3), 448–454.

Hoegg, J., & Alba, J. W. (2007). Taste perception: More than meets the tongue. *Journal of Consumer Research, 33*(4), 490–498.

Kar, K. (2003). *Subsidy or self-respect? Participatory total community sanitation in Bangladesh* (IDS Working Paper 184). Brighton, England: Institute of Development Studies.

Kunda, Z. (1990). The case for motivated reasoning. *Psychological Bulletin, 108*(3), 480–498.

Lazarus, R. S. (1999). Hope: An emotion and a vital coping resource against despair. *Social Research, 66*, 653–678.

Lueck, M. A. M. (2007). Hope for a cause as cause for hope: The need for hope in environmental sociology. *The American Sociologist, 38*(3), 250–261.

MacInnis, D. J., & de Mello, G. (2005). The concept of hope and its relevance to product evaluation and choice. *Journal of Marketing, 69*(1), 1–14.

McGeer, V. (2004). The art of good hope. *The Annals of the American Academy of Political and Social Science, 592*(1), 100–127.

Moreau, C. P., & Dahl, D. W. (2005). Designing the solution: The impact of constraints on consumers' creativity. *Journal of Consumer Research, 32*(1), 13–22.

Novogratz, J. (2009). *The blue sweater: Bridging the gap between rich and poor in an interconnected world*. New York: Rodale.

Peters, E., Vastfjall, D., Garling, T., & Slovic, P. (2006). Affect and decision making: A hot topic. *Journal of Behavioral Decision Making, 19*, 79–85.

Prahalad, C. K. (2005). *The fortune at the bottom of the pyramid*. Upper Saddle River, NJ: Wharton School Publishing.

Prahalad, C. K., & Hammond, A. (2002). Serving the world's poor, profitably. *Harvard Business Review, 80*(9), 48–57.

Prahalad, C. K., & Ramaswamy, V. (2004). Co-creation experiences: The next practice in value creation. *Journal of Interactive Marketing, 18*(Summer), 5–14.

Rajan, R. (2007). Unilever's business in India's subsistence economies. In J. Cheng, M. Hitt (Series Eds.), J. A. Rosa, & M. Viswanathan (Vol. Eds.), *Advances in international management: Vol. 20. Product and market development for subsistence marketplaces* (pp. 259–277). Oxford, England: Elsevier.

Ram, S., & Jung, H. (1989). The link between involvement, use innovativeness, and product usage. In T. K. Srull (Ed.), *Advances in consumer research* (Vol. 16, pp. 160–166). Duluth, MN: Association for Consumer Research.

Ram, S., & Jung, H. (1994). Innovativeness in product usage: A comparison of early adopters and early majority. *Psychology and Marketing, 11*(1), 57–67.

Reck, J., & Wood, B. (2003). *What works: Vodacom's community services phone shops: Providing telecommunications to poor communities in South Africa*. Washington, DC: World Resources Institute.

Ridgway, N. M., & Price, L. L. (1994). Exploration in product usage: A model of use innovativeness. *Psychology and Marketing, 11*(1), 69–84.

Rosa, J. A., & Viswanathan, M. (Eds.). (2007). *Product and market development for subsistence marketplaces. Advances in International Management Series* (J. Cheng & M. Hitt, Series Eds.). Oxford, England: Elsevier.

Roy, M., & Wheeler, D. (2006). A survey of micro-enterprise in urban West Africa: Drivers shaping the sector. *Development in Practice, 16*(5), 452–464.

Scheier, M. F., & Carver, C. S. (1985). Optimism, coping, and health: Assessment and implications of generalized outcome expectancies. *Health Psychology, 4*, 219–247.

Simanis, E., Hart, S., & Duke, D. (2008). The base of the pyramid protocol: Beyond "basic needs" business strategies. *Innovations, 3*(1), 57–84.

Taylor, S. E. (1989). *Positive illusions: Creative self-deception and the healthy mind*. New York: Basic Books.

Taylor, S. E., & Brown, J. D. (1988). Illusion and well-being: A social psychological perspective on mental health. *Psychological Bulletin, 103*, 193–210.

United Nations Development Programme. (2008). *Bogotá, una apuesta por Colombia: Informe de desarrollo humano 2008* [Bogotá, a bet on Colombia: Human development report 2008]. Bogotá, Colombia: Author.

Viswanathan, M. (2007). Understanding product and market interactions in subsistence marketplaces: A study in South India. In J. Cheng, M. Hitt (Series Eds.), J. A. Rosa, & M. Viswanathan (Eds.), *Advances in international management: Vol. 20. Product and market development for subsistence marketplaces* (pp. 21–57). Oxford, England: Elsevier.

Viswanathan, M., Rosa, J., & Ruth, J. (2010). Exchanges in marketing systems: The case of subsistence consumer–merchants in Chennai, India. *Journal of Marketing, 74*(May), 1–17.

von Hippel, E. (2005). *Democratizing innovation*. Cambridge, MA: MIT Press.

Ward, T. B., Smith, S. M., & Finke, R. A. (1999). Creative cognition. In R. Sternberg (Ed.), *Handbook of creativity* (pp. 189–212). New York: Cambridge University Press.

Westen, D., Blagov, P. S., Harenski, K., Kilts, C., & Hamann, S. (2006). Neural bases of motivated reasoning: An fMRI study of emotional constraints on partisan political judgment in the 2004 U.S. presidential election. *Journal of Cognitive Neuroscience, 18*(11), 1947–1958.

# 8

# Discrimination and Injustice in the Marketplace

## They Come in All Sizes, Shapes, and Colors

JEROME D. WILLIAMS AND GERALDINE ROSA HENDERSON

LIKE I SAID BEFORE, IT'S 2008. For all we know, we're going to have the first Black president of the United States. We go from slavery to segregation to first Black president all in a span of a century. Now, that is progress! And then this happens.

Priya
*Southeast Asian American, female, 20 years old*

The "this" that Priya describes is marketplace discrimination that she experienced. When examining the extent of general discrimination and injustice in contemporary society, the proverbial question often comes to the fore: Is the glass half empty, or is the glass half full? Another way of putting it is, do we focus on how far we have come, or do we focus on how far we have to go? In this chapter, we focus on the issues of discrimination and injustice in the marketplace. However, the same proverbial question can be asked, as typified by Priya's quote.

From a societal perspective, with the election of the first African American president in the United States, many people feel that the country has reached a point of fulfilling Dr. Martin Luther King's dream despite some vestiges of racial discrimination (Poussaint, 2009). However, others recognize that there is still much work to be done, given continuing disparities in the treatment of various groups in the United States (Hannah, 2009). For example, data from U.S. government agencies highlight the continuing racial inequality in the categories of health, the economy, criminal justice, and education (Cutler, 2009).

Although American society has made significant progress in terms of race relations since the passage of civil rights legislation in the 1960s, the hard reality is that there are still remnants of discrimination in housing, employment, education, and the marketplace (Williams, Qualls, & Grier, 1995).

From a marketplace perspective, we see similar divergent views. For example, the growth and size of the purchasing power of groups that historically have been invisible in the marketplace is frequently touted. The Selig Center data point out that the African American market ($913 billion) and the Hispanic market ($951 billion) are larger than the entire economies of all but 13 countries in the world, as measured by 2007 gross domestic product data in U.S. dollars (Humphreys, 2008). However, there is continuing evidence of economic inequality in the American marketplace. For example, through an examination of 81 federal court decisions made between 1990 and 2002 involving customers' allegations of race and/or ethnic discrimination, Harris, Henderson, and Williams (2005) demonstrated that real and perceived consumer discrimination remains a problem in the U.S. marketplace and concluded that further research is necessary for marketers to address the issue effectively.

Historically, one of the first places researchers turn when examining discrimination and injustice in the marketplace is race and ethnicity. For example, Andreasen, Goldberg, and Sirgy (Chapter 2 of this volume) point out that African Americans have been frustrated and angry for decades about how they have been treated in the marketplace. In this chapter, however, as noted by the title, we want to go beyond race and ethnicity and consider how discrimination and injustice can come in "all sizes, shapes, and colors," and in many types of marketplace venues, both in the United States and abroad. This approach is very much in keeping with the sensitizing principle of intersectionality, which emphasizes that members of marginalized groups are rarely homogeneous and that within any group, there are likely to be distinguishable subgroups whose experiences are contingent on their being at the intersection of more than a single marginalized category (Ozanne & Fischer, Chapter 4 of this volume).

We incorporate the principle of intersectionality by casting a wide net to encompass many different groups that transcend race and ethnicity and also face issues of discrimination and injustice in the marketplace. A number of contributors to this volume consider issues facing these groups from what Ozanne and Fischer (Chapter 4 of this volume) identify as an intracategory perspective. For example, Pettigrew and Moschis (Chapter 27 of this volume) focus on older consumers as a neglected group and suggest that we should actively work against age discrimination in all its guises to promote proper treatment of older consumers in the marketplace. Additionally, Grier and Moore (Chapter 15 of this volume) focus on younger consumers and the epidemic of childhood obesity, Baker and Mason (Chapter 26 of this volume) focus on people with visual impairments and observe that people with disabilities are the single largest minority group in the United States, and Rosa, Geiger-Oneto, and Fajardo (Chapter 7 of this volume) and Viswanathan (Chapter 5 of this volume) focus on issues related to subsistence, low-literate consumers, and low-income consumers. For this chapter, though, we approach the issues from what Ozanne and Fischer identify as an intercategory perspective, by looking at different groups that have experienced marketplace discrimination and offering insight regarding the similarities and differences of those experiences.

Following this introductory section, we first deal with definitions of two important elements in this chapter: (1) what we mean by a subordinate or oppressed group in the marketplace, and (2) what we mean by marketplace discrimination and injustice. We then provide a historical perspective on the treatment of oppressed groups in the marketplace and discuss the theoretical framework of social justice, which we use in providing empirical support in the form of a qualitative study we conducted involving interviews of 124 research participants and their responses to discrimination and injustice in the marketplace. In the analysis and interpretation of these interviews, we begin with an ethnoracial basis for discrimination and, where applicable, extend the discussion to other aspects of the research participants' identity, such as age, religion, appearance, obesity, and gender. We conclude with some recommendations for researchers in supporting the transformation of the lives of consumers in oppressed groups and segments from positions of being discriminated against and experiencing marketplace injustice to a position of fair and equitable treatment in a marketplace reflecting social justice.

## OPPRESSION AND SUBORDINATION

As stated earlier, most researchers naturally turn to race and ethnicity when focusing on marketplace discrimination. However, for this chapter, we will use terminology frequently used in sociology and other social sciences to capture all groups who can face discrimination and injustice in the marketplace. When discussing all such groups and segments, we will refer to them as oppressed, marginalized, or subordinate groups. Although the term *minority* frequently is used in marketing to refer to groups who are subjected to discrimination, this typically is used in reference to racial and ethnic groups. Because the focus of this chapter is beyond race and ethnicity, we prefer to broaden our terminology.

In sociology, *minority* generally means the same as *subordinate*, and *dominant* is used interchangeably with *majority*. For the most part, what does and does not determine minority group status is related to the distribution of power. According to Wagley and Harris (1958), a subordinate group is defined by various dimensions, such as unequal treatment and less power over one's life, distinguishing physical or cultural traits that the dominant group holds in low regard, involuntary membership or ascribed status, and group solidarity awareness of subordinate status and oppression. As noted by Schaefer (2010), subordinate groups can include those beyond race and ethnicity, such as groups set apart on the basis of religion, age, disability, and sexual orientation. Thus, you may have a numerical majority of a particular group (e.g., Latinos in San Antonio, TX) but that does not necessarily equate to a position of dominance and/or power (Grier & Deshpandé, 2001).

Although many of these subordinate groups often are referred to as vulnerable, we agree with the point made by Baker and Mason (Chapter 26 of this volume) that vulnerability should not be regarded as a property of groups or environments. Therefore, when we discuss discrimination against subordinate groups in this chapter and consider vulnerability, our focus will be more on what Baker and Mason refer to as either *environmental vulnerability* (e.g., discriminatory practices by marketers as a cause of the vulnerability) or *situational vulnerability* (e.g., the outcome of personal, social, economic, and ecological conditions such as customer–salesperson interactions).

From a marketplace perspective, these same dimensions of subordinate groups also may apply to groups who have experienced discrimination and injustice in the marketplace. These marketplace groups include those who have received unequal treatment and have had less power over their lives, such as low-income consumers; those who have distinguishing physical or cultural traits that the dominant group holds in low regard, such as consumers with disabilities; and those who have involuntary membership or ascribed status, such as consumers based on gender. For the most part, these segments have not been pursued and given as much attention by advertisers, marketers, or marketing scholars as mainstream segments (Williams, 2003). Therefore, issues of injustice, discrimination, prejudice, and bias among these groups also have not received as much attention (Walsh, 2009).

Also, we should point out that when we speak of various segments receiving unequal treatment, we are referring to *unequal* in the sense of less than as opposed to different from, which is an important distinction due to one of the foundation constructs of effective marketing strategy, namely, market segmentation. Many of the subordinate groups we consider in this chapter also are the targets of segmentation marketing strategies and campaigns, which is where there may be a blurring of the lines. In some instances, treating segments differently is just effective market segmentation (e.g., promoting automobiles to women differently than promoting automobiles to men). However, in other instances, treating the same segments differently reflects marketplace discrimination and injustice. For example, a study at Northwestern University on car dealerships found that salespeople who bargain with customers over the price of a new car make significantly lower final offers to men than to women (Ayres & Siegelman, 1995). Also, housing audits, in which matched pairs of Black and White homeseekers are compared, have indicated that discriminatory behavior may occur as much as 50% of the time (Williams et al., 1995).

## MARKETPLACE DISCRIMINATION AND INJUSTICE

There is various terminology related to marketplace discrimination and injustice that frequently is used in the literature and popular press, such as "shopping while Black" (Gabbidon, 2003, p. 345), consumer racial profiling (Williams, Henderson, & Hakstian, 2010; Williams, Henderson, & Harris, 2001), consumer discrimination (Harris, 2003), and statistical discrimination (Lee, 2000). Almost exclusively, these terms tend to associate marketplace discrimination and injustice with race and ethnicity, most frequently with African Americans. For many researchers, consumer racial profiling is analogized to law enforcement racial profiling, similar to "driving while Black." However, we view consumer racial profiling in a narrow sense as just one type of marketplace discrimination and injustice. Consumer racial profiling typically occurs when law enforcement officers stop, question, investigate, detain, and/or arrest consumers based on their race or ethnicity rather than on probable cause or even a reasonable suspicion that these individuals have engaged in criminal activity, such as shoplifting.

In this chapter, we recognize that, in the marketplace, there may be many types of discrimination and injustice that do not involve suspecting customers of engaging in criminal activity. Therefore, we use *marketplace discrimination* and *injustice* as broader terms to capture not only consumer racial profiling but also other types of discriminatory marketplace situations in which consumers do not receive equal treatment for equal dollars. Essentially, whether there is criminal suspicion or not, we are concerned with any type of differential treatment of consumers in the marketplace based on membership in an oppressed group that constitutes denial of or degradation in the products and/or services offered to the consumer.

In this chapter, we focus on both narrow and broad aspects of marketplace discrimination. Our definition of *marketplace discrimination* also covers consumption experiences beyond shopping in retail stores (Williams, Lwin, Harris, & Gooding, 2007). For example, the Harris et al. (2005) analysis of federal cases demonstrated that marketplace discrimination frequently occurs in places of public accommodation, such as hotels, restaurants, gas stations, and service providers, as well as retail establishments, including grocery/food stores, clothing stores, department stores, home improvement stores, and office equipment stores. Furthermore, marketplace discrimination impacts members of minority groups beyond those classified as Black or African American, such as Hispanic Americans, Asian Americans, Native Americans, and Arab Americans.

We also should note that marketplace discrimination and injustice, by our definition, include what we refer to as both *avoidance* and *annoyance* discrimination (Gabbidon, 2003; Williams et al., 2001). Avoidance discrimination can manifest itself in various forms, including ignoring customers, making them wait an inordinately long time for service, treating them rudely, and waiting on dominant group customers first. Annoyance discrimination occurs when customers are subjected to extra scrutiny by retail security and sales personnel while shopping, like following selected customers closely, observing them in dressing rooms, searching bags, using excessive force (e.g., verbal and/or physical attacks), and requiring additional identification for credit or check purchases. Such scrutiny results from greater suspicion that these types of shoppers will engage in criminal activity, such as shoplifting. Therefore, avoidance discrimination tends to fall into our broader definition, whereas annoyance tends to fall within the narrower view, such as consumer racial profiling.

## HISTORICAL PERSPECTIVE ON DISCRIMINATION
## AND INJUSTICE IN THE MARKETPLACE

Although discrimination and injustice in the marketplace have been understudied by marketing scholars, there is a long history of interest in this topic by researchers, sociologists, historians, civil rights activists, public policy makers, and consumers who have filed lawsuits. However, it has not always been labeled as consumer or marketplace discrimination. For example, at least one study dealing with marketplace discrimination can be traced back to the 1930s. In a cleverly designed study of that era, La Piere (a White male; 1934) traveled widely in the United States with a Chinese couple, stopping at 66 sleeping establishments and 184 eating places. The group of three was refused service only once. However, based on a follow-up mail questionnaire asking whether these same establishments would take "members of the Chinese race as guests in your establishment," 93% of the restaurants and 92% of the hotels said they would not serve Chinese people. The results of this study raised questions concerning discriminatory behaviors manifested in the marketplace and accompanying attitudes.

Also, while the passage of the Civil Rights Act of 1964 is seen as the culmination of the modern Civil Rights movement, we sometimes fail to recognize that this movement is deeply rooted in the marketplace. For example, it was Rosa Parks, a Black seamstress, as a consumer who refused to give up her bus seat to a White man in 1955 and sparked a bus boycott in Montgomery, Alabama, as well as African American college students as consumers who refused to be denied service at F.W. Woolworth lunch counters and instigated sit-ins in Greensboro, North Carolina, in 1960. In fact, we can go back to the post–Civil War era when Congress enacted the Civil Rights Act of 1866; one of its goals was to ensure "that a dollar in the hands of a Negro will purchase the same thing as a dollar in the hands of a white man."

Almost 50 years ago, marketers' attention was turned to marginalized consumers when the question was asked, Do the poor pay more? (Caplovitz, 1963). This triggered what Andreasen (1978) has referred to as the ghetto marketing life cycle, or the cycle of research dealing with problems of marginalized consumers. Generally, the two groups most frequently studied are ethnic minority consumers and those who are financially challenged, or poor (Andreasen, 1982).

Evidence today indicates that the poor are still facing discrimination in the marketplace. There are numerous general press stories about consumers in low-income neighborhoods who pay significantly more for products and services, such as car insurance policies, food, and finance charges (Alwitt & Donley, 1996). Although some of these differences can be attributed to structural factors associated with low-income areas (e.g., higher operating costs in declining neighborhoods), some of the problems faced by marginalized consumers stem from the exploitative behavior of marketers themselves (Williams & Snuggs, 1997). Hill (2008) described dysfunctional business activities that reduce the consumer quality of life of marginalized citizens. Their reactions to this maltreatment then were presented, with an emphasis on the various groups noted. Bell and Burlin (1993) provided further evidence that, in urban areas, the poor still pay more, especially for food, by focusing on redlining, or economic discrimination against certain consumers on the basis of factors such as race, area of residence, gender, and type of employment (see D'Rozario & Williams, 2005, for a discussion of discrimination and the concept of retail redlining).

In the 1960s and 1970s, the poor were reported to perceive themselves as relatively deprived, manipulated externally, powerless, and alienated (Andreasen, 1975). Andreasen (1978) chastised researchers for their relative neglect of public policy issues concerning endemic racism in the marketplace. He proposed a seven-point research agenda (e.g., family decision-making processes, power relationships in channels of distribution, product and brand beliefs) that essentially served as a normative call to action for the field. As noted by Andreasen (1993), in the past, contributions by the academic community have been limited in attempting to understand issues related to the marginalized consumer, and there has been a lack of persistence in researching problems that do not lend themselves to easy solutions (Williams, Qualls, & Ferguson, 2007).

Although the plight of the low-income consumer typically was identified with Black consumers, there also was early evidence that underprivileged Mexican Americans were not well served by retailers and financial institutions (Sturdivant, 1969). Pruden and Longman (1972) examined marketplace alienation and found that Mexican Americans and African Americans believed that they were not receiving equitable treatment as consumers and strongly supported public policy intervention to increase marketplace fairness. This was one of the first studies to acknowledge ethnic discontent with existing marketing practices. The authors used a theoretical perspective of alienation to frame this discussion based on the work of Fromm (1962); alienation referred to a state in which "man does not experience himself as the active bearer of his own powers and richness, but as an impoverished 'thing' dependent on powers outside of himself, unto whom he has projected his living substance" (p. 59). As noted by Pruden and Longman, the lifestyle of the low-income consumer had been identified with alienation as measured by feelings of powerlessness, meaninglessness, anomie, and social isolation. Also, in Fromm's view, the conditions of modem large-scale capitalism alienated consumers from the process of acquisition and consumption of goods.

Research on marketplace discrimination is an emerging field. Jordan, Gabbidon, and Higgins (2009) provided a review of the literature on consumer racial profiling, focusing on interview-based qualitative studies (e.g., Crockett, Grier, & Williams, 2003; Feagin, 1991; Lee, 2000), litigation studies (e.g., Gabbidon, 2003; Harris et al., 2005; Williams, Harris, & Henderson, 2006a, 2006b), experimental and observational studies (e.g., Asquith & Bristow, 2000; Dabney, Dugan, Topalli, & Hollinger, 2006; Dabney, Hollinger, & Dugan, 2004), and victimization surveys (e.g., Gabbidon & Higgins, 2007, 2008; Higgins & Gabbidon, 2009). In addition to these studies, there have been several others focusing on the psychological aspects of discrimination. For example, Carter, Forsyth, Mazzula, and Williams (2005) explored the psychological and emotional effects of racism for people of color through a phenomenologically based qualitative investigation, and Wakefield and Hudley (2005) investigated male African American adolescents' thinking about responses to racial discrimination, including scenarios involving experiences of racial discrimination while making a purchase at a department store and shopping at a mall.

Within the service domain, there have been several studies that address marketplace injustice and discrimination. For example, Baker, Meyer, and Johnson (2008) investigated the role of contextual cues in the evaluation of a service failure. They found that although discrimination is a factor in the evaluation of a service failure for Black versus White customers, contextual cues also play a role in the evaluation of the encounter; for example, when a Black customer experiences a service failure, the failure will be evaluated more severely when no other Black customers are present. The implication is that when serving customers, the race of both the customer and other customers can provide service providers with information relative to the appropriate service recovery effort to implement. Also Ainscough and Motley (2000) examined how customers' visible physical characteristics influence retail service delivery and found that Black and male customers wait significantly longer than White and female customers at retail customer service counters.

As previously indicated, in this chapter, we explore all forms of marketplace discrimination, not just those based on ethnoracial group membership. There have been a few studies conducted that address issues beyond race and ethnicity. For example, Walsh (2009) recognized that discrimination can be attributed also to age, gender, physical ability, and sexual orientation, and drawing on social identification theory, he developed a conceptual model of marketplace discrimination as an outcome of service employees distinguishing between customers in terms of in-group and out-group members, whereby the latter are perceived more negatively.

In terms of discrimination based on sexual orientation, Sen (1996) examined the confluence of marketing and minority civil rights by considering the case of Amendment 2 in Colorado in November 1992. This amendment repealed all existing ordinances and policies in Colorado that protected gays and lesbians from discrimination in housing, employment, and public accommodations on the basis of their sexual orientation and prohibited the passage of similar state or local government antidiscrimination laws in the future. Walters and Moore (2002) reviewed research on homonegative bias and heteronormativity within psychological and sociological domains and illustrated how homonegativity toward perceived lesbians and gays is structurally enacted within the marketplace. Rosenbaum and Montoya (2007) used servicescape frameworks (Bitner, 1992; Tombs & McColl-Kennedy, 2003) as models for illustrating how consumers perceive physical and social elements in consumption settings and demonstrated how physical and place identity elements influence responses among Hispanic and homosexual consumers.

Morton, Zettelmeyer, and Silva-Risso (2003) examined race and gender and found that offline African American and Hispanic consumers pay approximately 2% more than do other offline consumers, while online, they found that minority buyers pay nearly the same prices as do Whites, controlling for consumers' income, education, and neighborhood characteristics. Their results imply that the Internet is particularly beneficial to those whose characteristics disadvantage them in negotiating, such as race and gender. As pointed out by Lwin and Williams (2004), such results suggest that minority consumers may find withholding or even fabrication of certain demographic and other descriptive information online to be a convenient mechanism for shielding themselves from the type of discriminatory behavior they encounter in in-store retail environments (Williams et al., 2007). Thus, we entered our current research endeavor equipped with these previous studies as we sought new understandings of the marketplace discrimination phenomena. Below, we discuss our research questions, followed by our methodology and our interpretation of our empirical findings.

## A QUALITATIVE INQUIRY ON MARKETPLACE DISCRIMINATION AND EXPERIENCES OF DIFFERENT INJUSTICES

Based on the previously mentioned sociodemographic factors that have traditionally formed a basis for marketplace discrimination, we have developed a theoretical perspective on why these injustices are differentially perceived across groups. Thus, our research questions are as follows: Does marketplace discrimination still exist in the Age of Obama? To whom does marketplace discrimination occur and how? Do members of traditionally dominant groups and traditionally marginalized groups differ in the perceptions of marketplace discrimination? How are service provider reactions to allegations of marketplace discrimination perceived by members of marginalized groups? To begin to answer these questions, we employed the methodology described below.

### Methodology

To develop and illustrate our theory of marketplace discrimination, we employed an exploratory research design, collected primary data in the form of depth interviews, and drew heavily from extant literature. We conducted 124 depth interviews of consumers representing various ethnoracial backgrounds, genders, sexual orientations, religions, and so forth (cf. Motley & Henderson, 2008; Motley, Henderson, & Baker, 2003; Spiggle, 1994). The coauthors and 53 student collaborators interviewed 124 people identified in multiple ways: Some were personal contacts (i.e., friends, family members) of the interviewers, others were fellow students and/or coworkers, and a few were identified through the Internet. Informants were from a variety of ethnoracial groups, countries, and ages. Ethnoracial groups included Asian Americans, White Americans, Black Americans, Hispanic Americans, Native Americans, and those of mixed heritage. The informants ranged in age from 18 to 75 years old. Our quoted respondents represent diversity in age (20–72), gender, race (2 Caucasians, 2 Asians, 1 African American, 3 Latinas, and 1 Arab American), and basis for discrimination (language, accent, weight/obesity, religion, ability to pay/income, appearance, skin color, nationality, race, and age).

We did not define marketplace discrimination for them, because we wanted the respondents to tell us how they characterized and perceived such an occurrence. Interviewers were trained to use a standardized interview protocol. They were also trained on probing techniques to determine individual meanings and perceptions, and on the appropriate depth of transcribed discussions. The interviews were conducted either face-to-face or over the telephone via the Internet (e.g., Skype). Each interview was audio- and/or videotaped. The length of the interviews varied, some being as short as 40 minutes and others as long as 90 minutes, depending on the informant's experience with and divulgence of marketplace discrimination. On average, the interviews lasted approximately 60 minutes. Informants provided basic demographic data as well as contact information for subsequent verification of accuracy. We also examined extant literature on discrimination and oppression from numerous disciplines (e.g., sociology, psychology, political science, history) to help understand the issues of social justice. Articles containing either qualitative or quantitative data on the meaning, perception, or responses to marketplace discrimination were analyzed according to Thompson (1997). Thus, our data are rich, as we draw on research collected with multiple methods and from multiple sources, representing views from groups, and numerous disciplines.

### Theoretical Perspective and Findings

We believe that the emergent themes from our data are best captured by the theoretical framework of social justice theory. As previously mentioned, there have been many theoretical perspectives put forth to study and understand discrimination, prejudice, and race relations (e.g., in-group bias theory, social identity theory, intergroup contact theory, liberation psychology, group positioning theory). In this chapter, we highlight the framework of social justice, as we feel that it best captures both our data and an approach that scholars can adapt to further inquiry in this area from a Transformative Consumer Research (TCR) perspective. We present background on the social justice perspective below, along with excerpts from our data for explanatory power.

#### Social Justice

Our respondents almost universally referred to instances of feeling disenfranchised in the marketplace. Their dissatisfying marketplace experiences were based on felt discrimination, and they desired social justice for their marketplace indignities (Ferrell & Ferrell, 2008; Laczniak, 1999; Laczniak & Murphy, 2008; Sirgy, 2008). Throughout this volume, a number of contributors allude to the need for more social justice research in marketing. For example, there is a discussion of the literature in what is called the *new social conscience of marketing*, much of which is in response to what has been labeled "the dark side of the marketplace" (as cited in Andreasen, Goldberg, & Sirgy, Chapter 2 of this volume). Also, Mick, Pettigrew, Pechmann, and Ozanne (Chapter 1 of this volume) note that TCR should seek to improve well-being while maximizing social justice, and Ozanne and Fischer (Chapter 4 of this volume) suggest that research should lead to greater social justice for and empowerment of marginalized groups. Therefore, applying a social justice framework to examine marketplace discrimination seems very apropos.

There are a number of different frameworks used to capture social justice; however, Ross (2009) noted that defining social justice is difficult. Typically, emphasis is placed on protecting the rights of citizens by advocating fair wages, affordable health care, access to education, marketplace access, and proper and safe work and living conditions. However, social justice can mean different things to different people, depending on the audience and the research discipline.

Our data present accounts of social *injustice*, which Levy and Sidel (2006) compared to social *justice*. In fact, they offered one definition of *social injustice* as the denial of economic, sociocultural, political, civil, or human rights of specific populations in the society based on the perception of their inferiority to those with more power or influence. These populations that suffer social injustice may be defined by racial or ethnic status. From a marketing perspective, we consider consumer segments based on these same characteristics as those who might be more susceptible to social injustice due to socioeconomic position, age, gender, sexual orientation, or other perceived group characteristics.

For purposes of our analysis, we will focus on the three-dimensional view of social justice (i.e., distributive justice, procedural justice, interactional justice), which is the approach that seems to be most frequently used in the marketing literature (e.g., Schoefer & Ennew, 2005; Walsh, 2009). Also, this three-dimensional approach is closely linked to fairness theory, equity theory, and research on marketplace discrimination in customer services (Walsh, 2009). Although service failures can occur for any number of reasons, such as poor employee response to customers' special needs, typically when a service failure involves a majority service provider who is a member of the dominant group and a customer who is a member of the subordinate group, the possibility that the failure may be attributed to discrimination is accentuated (Baker et al., 2008). Below, we discuss our data from each of the three social justice perspectives.

*Distributive Justice*

Many of our respondents articulated the need to have their injustice remedied by some type of compensation for their hassle. Distributive justice concerns what is just or right with respect to the allocation of goods in a society and addresses how a community treats its members in terms of the assignments of benefits and burdens according to some standard of fairness (Laczniak & Murphy, 2008). For instance, in the court cases described by Harris et al. (2005), distributive justice was in the form of compensatory damages awarded to plaintiffs. This form of justice is how the marketing system, in terms of its structure, policies, or practices, fairly apportions rewards and penalties among the various parties affected by the market exchange process. One example would be the seeming lack of leverage for subprime borrowers when they try to purchase a home or automobile (Laczniak & Murphy, 2008). We argue that distributive justice is a critical aspect of examining discrimination and injustice in the marketplace and the treatment of oppressed segments of consumers.

Consider the case of Ivonne, a 20-year-old Latina. She was shopping at an upscale national department store chain at a location in a very large metropolitan area in the Southwest. She and her friend were waiting for some assistance in one of the departments, yet the salesclerk refused to give them service. Eventually, the salesclerk told them it was because of her friend's race. This, of course, enraged both the friend and Ivonne, especially since they perceived a relationship with the national department store, at which they had been shopping for years. Thus, Ivonne complained about the salesclerk to the manager and promptly exited the store without making any additional purchases because she was so upset over the ordeal:

> She told us the reason why she wouldn't wait on us, and we demanded to speak to her manager to complain about her customer service. After we spoke with the manager, he forced her to help us, but she still did it in a very disrespectful manner. (Ivonne, personal interview)

In this instance, Ivonne attributed the discrimination to a particular employee and not to the store, especially after the manager became embarrassed and forced the employee to serve them, even though the salesclerk indicated a desire not to do so. The outcome was not compensation per se but a mandate from the manager that Ivonne and her companion be served. Distributive justice has limitations, because quite often compensation and/or service provision are not enough. It is the expectation that frontline service personnel may harbor prejudices and bias, as do all humans. However, it is expected that service personnel will keep their biases in check as they provide service to customers. In this instance, the manager had to compel the service provider to do just that.

Asha, a 22-year-old Hispanic female, had an experience that did lead to compensation. She and a bunch of her friends went out for a happy hour to reunite after a summer of studying abroad. After waiting at the restaurant for half an hour until the rest of her friends got there, the hostess sat them at a table that was too small to accommodate them. Once they were seated, the waitress did not come around for a good 20 minutes; the restaurant was not full, and they were the only people sitting in their section. When the waitress finally came around, she was not very informative about the happy hour specials on the menu, she threw down the drink menu, and she told them to call her whenever they decided what they wanted. Asha and her friends got upset, because they did not know the waitress's name to ask for her, and it took them another 15 minutes to track her down once they knew what they wanted. The waitress was extremely rude when she took their orders and claimed that it was because two of the seven were underage. Four of the seven were so dissatisfied that they left without ordering dinner. The remaining three, including Asha, ordered dinner, but their orders were wrong when the food finally arrived at the table. At this point, Asha and her friends had been there for 2 hours already and were unable to find their server. After receiving the check, they realized that the server had overcharged them by three drinks, then she refused to split the check. As Asha put it,

> We decided to talk to the manager because of the way she was treating us. He offered us complimentary this and that on the next visit, and I assured him that there will be no second or third visit. He also said that if it would have been brought to his attention earlier, we could have gotten something else for free. (Asha, personal interview)

The services literature suggests that a well-executed service recovery can lead to an even more satisfied, loyal customer even more so than if the service failure never happened (Hart, Heskett, & Sasser, 1990; Smith & Bolton, 1998). However, there are some instances that are so egregious that there is no making up for them. Asha's story appears to be one of these. Although she definitely felt as though the manager tried to recover from the mishap, Asha felt as though she had been discriminated against based on her age and that the manager's kindness did not make up for the rudeness of the server.

Saeed, a 21-year-old Arab American male, had a bad experience at Wendy's on a repeated basis. That is, he gave them multiple opportunities to provide him with a satisfying consumer experience, yet he always seemed to have trouble with the staff. They were not very helpful and did not care to be:

> Yeah, I actually have. I remember one time it was bad, because the first two things I ordered, they did not even have it on the menu. And I guess to compensate, they gave me an upgrade size in fries and a free Frosty, which was cool, because I was pretty hungry, but just the hassle was enough to turn me off from Wendy's. (Saeed, personal interview)

The only reason that Saeed went to that particular restaurant is because they were convenient and cheap. He has had a complaint almost inevitably every time and has definitely had concerns about being discriminated against because of his ethnoracial background (Arab American), obesity, religion, language, or accent, but he cannot say that this is the reason for his bad experiences at this restaurant. Most marketing organizations plan on short-term and long-term horizons. In the short term, Wendy's may be able to hold on to Saeed as a customer, since he took the upgrade in fries and the free Frosty. However, in the absence of a true apology and/or an understanding of why the discrimination was an isolated incident not bound to be repeated, he may simply disappear as a customer. That is, when given a choice in fast-food restaurants, why would Saeed deliberately and intentionally choose to return to a place that has blatantly discriminated against him and not apologized for it?

### Procedural Justice

Other respondents focused more on the process than the outcome. For them, it was a matter of procedural (in)justice. Procedural justice is the idea of fairness in the processes that resolve disputes and allocate resources, which includes flexibility to adapt to the customer's recovery needs, the perceived fairness of the policies and procedures by the organization, and efficient service, low waiting times, and helpful service employees. There were many instances of alleged procedural injustice experiences in our data.

Consider the case of Shin, a 26-year-old Asian male. He has had many bad marketplace experiences as an American male with a Korean accent. The worst of his experiences that he shared was with a claims adjuster for Allstate. As a result of these experiences, he has decided to never use Allstate again once his current contract expires. He had a car accident that he claims was not his fault, as he was hit by someone else who was making an illegal U-turn. He had already had difficulty with 911 and the other person's claims adjuster due, in large part, to his accent. However, he did not expect to have such difficulty with his own claims adjuster, a person who works for the insurance company to which he pays a premium every month. Although he was new to the process and had never encountered a claims adjuster before, he did not anticipate the treatment that he received. After numerous failed attempts to reach his claims adjuster or receive return calls, Shin was finally able to speak to him. It became increasingly clear to Shin that because Allstate was the insurance provider for both him and the other driver, the claims adjusters got together and determined Shin was at fault without hearing his side of the story. Shin took up this concern with an Allstate manager, but he still felt as though he did not receive satisfactory treatment. Shin was more concerned about the process than the outcome, since he believed that the unfair process led to the result:

> Yeah. I took some actions to solve this problem. I called the Allstate customer service and sent e-mails to the customer service and the manager of the adjusters. I felt that I was discriminated against, because I'm an Asian man who cannot speak English fluently and the other party is a young White girl. When I tried to complain about my adjuster, staffs of the customer service shuffled off their responsibility on others again. So, it took lots of time to finish the complaint. At the same time, I also tried to contact my adjuster again, but I just had to leave voice messages. Actually, I contacted many people in the Allstate customer service and people who are in the higher position and told about my adjuster and my situation, which I was still trying to solve the insurance problem, and my car was still left without any repair. (Shin, personal interview)

Shin's claims adjuster called later to say that he had made a mistake with the decision. Instead of charging Shin with 100% of the responsibility for the accident, he was only charged with 10% of it, which he accepted reluctantly. Shin felt that he had been ignored by the claims adjuster because he is Asian and speaks English as a second language. As Shin put it, "Some people could think that the reason of the problem would be his laziness, but it was just a small part of this problem. He ignored me. This is unquestionable truth."

Shin's frustration with this incident is palpable, although we were not there to witness it. This is a perfect example of how discrimination-based service failure differs from other types of service failure. Whereas in other types, one may assume that the service provider is simply having a bad day or the service organization is just not very good. However, in discrimination-based service failure, a customer such as Shin cannot help but take the service failure personally. As he poignantly describes above, he believes that the reason for his difficulty are the language and cultural differences between him and the service provider. He also believes that he would have been treated better if he were a woman. This problem is superimposed on top of the lack of accountability within the organization, such that no one wants to assume responsibility for the escalated service failure and opportunity for recovery.

Theresa, a 25-years old Hispanic female, also had an issue of procedural (in)justice, which she attributed, in part, to her younger age. She went to a restaurant named Pappasito's with two of her friends and ordered enchiladas with a different sauce than what is normally served with the dish.

However, when her food arrived 45 minutes later, it contained the sauce listed on the menu rather than the one she ordered:

> This is the same sauce. I don't like it, so … then … I asked her to take it off, and I asked for a manager, and did she take it off? She did take it off the first time. No, she did not take it off, and then she threw the bill on the table. She just threw it like [*reenacts scene with pen*], and that angered me so much … that I got up … grabbed it, and turned around and said, "Where is your manager?" They said, "He's busy." And I said, "I want to talk to him NOW!" So then, finally, the manager comes, and I said, "I don't appreciate her throwing the bill on me. That was disrespectful." And he did not look like he knew what he was doing either. (Theresa, personal interview)

Theresa believes that the manager handled the entire process poorly. Moreover, she believes that the manager's handling of the process is reflective of the overall tolerance for, and perhaps acceptance of, poor employee attitudes such as the ones demonstrated by the server. She believes that the manager did not even seem to care about the situation and how it made her, as his customer, feel:

> I feel angry … I felt like they just, like, pushed me aside, like, oh well. I feel like she got away with it. It's like murder.… It's like unsolved mysteries, like they never caught her. Like she got away with it … I think [the manager] just brushed it aside, 'cause I would have sent her home if I was her manager.

Part of what made Theresa so upset is that she endured this bad service for over 2 hours with long periods of waiting for (in)action in between. Waiting is a recurring theme that we found in our data. The customers either were waiting for what they perceived to be an inordinate amount of time for the initial service, or ended up waiting for a very long time to get the issue escalated, whether or not the initial service failure was resolved.

Divya, a 21-year-old Southeast Asian female, was one of those respondents who had a bad experience with waiting in a retail store. She and her mom went to Rave, a store clothing store similar to Old Navy. Divya tried on many items to determine which, if any, would work for her. The salesperson gave her and her mom a lot of bad attitude, and they felt as if they were being treated differently because they were dark-skinned Southeast Asians. That is, Divya thought that maybe the salesclerk did not think that they could afford everything that Divya was trying on and were just wasting the salesperson's time. Divya's mom was so upset that she threatened to buy everything in the entire store, just so the salesclerk would know that they could afford the items that Divya was trying on. Divya does not recall ever having a discriminatory experience prior to this one and made a point of indicating that she would not normally jump to ethnocentrism and/or elitism as being factors in her treatment. But, given the comparison cases of all of the other people in the store who were not being treated in the same manner, she felt as though the process for her was unjust:

> A part of us wanted to talk to the manager and ask him, "Is there a reason you are treating us this way and not anyone else in the store?" But in the end, we just accepted it and left. I guess she could tell from our body language that we weren't happy with her actions. It was pretty clear that we were upset that we did not appreciate being treated this way because of our skin color. (Divya, personal interview)

Divya's belief is that stereotyping and generalizing are bad in general. She would prefer that everyone live by the golden rule: Treat others as you want to be treated. After all, part of the injustice felt by these respondents is the perception (and to them the knowledge) that the reason they are receiving degraded service is based on some socially identifying characteristic, such as perceptions of skin color, religion, language, or ability to pay, as in Divya's case. This vignette also points out the loss of customers due to this perception and the accompanying customer frustration. Once they exit, the service provider rarely gets a chance to make up for the service failure. Moreover, the spread of negative word of mouth to others in Divya's social network can lead to other problems for the retailer.

### Interactional Justice

Yet, other respondents wanted more than just compensation or a fair process. They wanted to be treated more humanely by a simple acknowledgment by management and/or owners that something foul had happened and they were sorry about it. These respondents wanted interactional justice, which includes an apology, since offering compensation without fair interactional treatment is perceived as hollow justice. Interactional justice includes the manner in which people are treated during the complaint handling process (e.g., courtesy and politeness exhibited by personnel, empathy, effort observed in resolving the situation, the firm's willingness to provide an explanation as to why the failure occurred).

The indignity of marketplace discrimination to these respondents far outweighs any compensation (absent an apology) or emotionless, by-the-book adjudication of a complaint. Shawna, a 31-year-old White female, was shopping in Korea 2 months after having delivered her first child. She had lost all of her baby weight, was 10 pounds under her normal, prepregnancy weight, and was barely an American size 6. She went shopping with some fellow military wives, including a visit to a clothing retailer. Korean women dress very fashionably and thrive on the latest styles, so Shawna was very excited. The prices in Korea were extremely affordable as well, so she thought that it was going to be a fun shopping time. She and her friends noticed the particular shop with attractive clothes hanging in the window and decided to go in. However, as soon as she stepped inside, the Korean shop owner immediately rushed at her and began snapping, "You too big! We have no clothes for you! You too big!" Shawna and her friends were in shock. They were surprised by the owner's behavior, because they had always been treated so nicely in the town. They were so offended that they quickly stepped back out on the street to think about the situation. They eventually decided to go back into the store, much to the shop owner's dismay, and began shopping. Two workers gave them dirty looks and spoke to each other in Korean. Shawna felt as though the employees were talking about Shawna and her friends, given the way that the employees were looking at them. However, Shawna ended up finding some great clothes and happily purchased them.

She and her friends never went back to that particular store. Similar to Divya's mother in the prior case, it was as if they felt compelled to make a successful purchase in that store to prove something to the owner, if not just to themselves:

> The store owner was so rude. I think it is horrible to discriminate against someone for any reason. It was so hurtful to have someone say that you are too big to shop for clothes in their store. The ironic thing is that they sold other items that were not weight related. (Shawna, personal interview)

Shawna points out the irony of the flawed judgment of the store owner. While they were focused on her weight and their perception that she would not be able to purchase any of their clothing, the shop owner and staff almost missed out on the opportunity to sell her accessories and other nonclothing items. Moreover, they missed the opportunity to treat her as a potential goodwill ambassador; although this opportunity may not have resulted in an immediate sale, Shawna could have spread positive word of mouth to other potential customers. The nature of interactional justice, or the lack thereof, is such that the customer is seeking understanding and/or empathy from the service provider. Research on customer lifetime value also suggests that before the incident, Shawna had the potential of being their customer during her lifetime (e.g., for herself, her fellow shoppers, family members, friends; see Blattberg, Getz, & Thomas, 2001; Rust, Zeithaml, & Lemon, 2000).

Jennifer, a 72-year-old Black female, also wanted interactional justice. Her bad experience was at Montgomery Ward department store many years ago before they closed. She attempted to purchase a dress; however, the salesclerk looked right through her, pretended that she was not there, and instead waited on a White customer:

> And I don't like that. I did not like that, because I thought that she was doing that because the other lady was White and I'm Black. So I asked to speak to the manager, and she got the manager over, and I told the manager what had happened, and he apologized. He said, "No, no, no, she did not mean anything like that." And, "No, no, no, I apologize for it," and she apologizes for it. And, "We're not that kind of a store," and he just went on and on and on, but it had really made me angry and upset. And so I told him that it seemed to be clearly that the other lady was White and I was Black that she just assumed that she would wait on her first. And that she was there ahead of me. So, I just threw my item on the counter, and I did not even purchase it. That was a bad experience that I've had. (Jennifer, personal interview)

Even though she did not want the dress any longer, she decided to confront the manager about what had happened to her. Although the manager did apologize to Jennifer about what happened, she still decided to never go to that store again. Like many of our other respondents, she also chose to communicate to others within her social network about her displeasure regarding the way that she was treated. At first glance, one may not understand Jennifer's anger. After all, the manager did apologize for himself and the salesclerk. However, Jennifer has had a lifetime of these experiences, and she feels as though an apology is not enough. That is, in his apology, he suggested that the salesclerk did not mean to do what she did and that she apologized. However, to Jennifer, this interaction was not sufficient, because the manager did not seem to really understand why she was upset or believe that something really occurred to explain her anger. He tried to appease (and perhaps patronize) Jennifer, and in the process, he made the situation worse.

Marty, a 22-year-old White male, remembers vividly his interactional injustice experience. It was so bad that he vowed that he would never go back, and he had not at the time that we interviewed him. The experience occurred at a Home Depot outlet, where he was trying to buy lightbulbs for his house. He lived in a very large house with a lot of lightbulbs in it, and many had gone out, so he went to Home Depot, since they advertise a large inventory and good prices for items like that. He went to the Home Depot by his house and saw a particular deal that he wanted, but there were no such lightbulbs on the shelf. So, Marty rang a nearby bell that calls an employee to come and offer assistance. However, he sat there with his friend and roommate for at least 15 minutes, then rang the bell up to three more times. No one came. Marty got so frustrated at the store for having the bell but not following through on it. Then, when the salesperson finally responded and asked Marty what his problem was, the salesclerk replied that they did not have the item in stock. Marty was shocked, because this was a large mass merchandiser home improvement store, and yet they were out of the advertised lightbulbs. So, Marty asked if there was a rain check or the ability to purchase similar lightbulbs for the same, advertised price. The salesclerk said no. It turned out that it was not just what the salesclerk said but also how it was said. Marty felt as though he was being disrespected by the salesclerk in particular and Home Depot in general. He did not feel valued as a customer and felt as though they did not want his money. He felt as if he had been slapped in the face:

> Honestly, it could be really simple. Just an apology would be great and, you know, maybe like a 50-dollar gift certificate or something. Just an acknowledgment that, hey, that was really wrong on our part, and you should've been charged, you know, the minimum price for what you were trying to buy, what you were doing made sense. And you know, just some responsibility on their part would probably

be enough, not even the gift card. But an apology with a gift card, I would rescind my vow to never shop there again probably. (Marty, personal interview)

The embodiment of interactional justice can be found in Marty's words above. Like Jennifer, he would have been happy to receive at least an apology for what he had endured. Perhaps this tolerance was based on his relatively short-lived exposure to this type of discrimination, being just 22 at the time, or because, in other aspects of his life, he did not feel marginalized.

## DISCUSSION AND CONCLUSION

These experiences of our study's respondents illustrate that marketplace discrimination can come in all sizes, shapes, and colors. This study focuses on discrimination from the perspective of the respondents and felt discrimination that they described to us during the interviews. The responses we received in our interviews concerning discrimination across the various bases are very much in concert with results of surveys concerning attitudes about marketplace discrimination based on race. For example, according to a Gallup poll social audit series on Black–White relations in the United States (Henderson, 2001), 35% of Blacks said they are treated less fairly than Whites in neighborhood shops, 46% said they are treated less fairly in stores downtown or in malls, and 39% said they are treated unfairly in restaurants, bars, and theaters. This poll also indicated that 27% of all Black respondents and 41% of Black males between 18 and 34 years of age felt that they were treated unfairly in the last 30 days in a store where they shop. Similarly, Jordan et al. (2009) conducted a study using data from a national Gallup poll and found support for the belief among Blacks that marketplace discrimination is widespread.

It also is interesting to note that among our respondents, the description of the felt discrimination is often subtle. We expected this, as generally there is a certain degree of ambiguity in service failures attributed to discrimination (Baker et al., 2008). As pointed out by Harris et al. (2005), subtle discrimination is more ambiguous and indirect, and based on their classification scheme, subtle discrimination represents a significant number of cases when marketplace discrimination lawsuits are filed.

### Where Do We Go From Here?

Mick et al. (Chapter 1 of this volume) have advocated for TCR researchers to strive to encourage, support, and publicize research that benefits quality of life for all beings engaged in or affected by consumption trends and practices across the world. Ozanne and Fischer (Chapter 4 of this volume) have also echoed this admonition and have suggested further that researchers should engage with the stakeholders by going beyond merely conducting research to proactively seeking ways to implement change. It is our hope that this chapter will push TCR researchers to move in that direction in terms of bringing more social justice to the marketplace and eradicating discrimination, in whatever size, shape, and color it takes.

Ozanne and Fischer (Chapter 4 of this volume) also have noted that TCR researchers cannot assume that social injustices, also known as trouble, will come looking for them; TCR researchers may have to go looking for trouble by seeking opportunities for improving the well-being of those people who are not benefiting from current social and economic arrangements. As authors of this chapter, we have tried to follow this advice by striving to use the research discussed in this chapter to help transform the lives of individuals who have been subjected to marketplace discrimination. For example, we have given voice to plaintiffs by using our research in expert witness testimony in dozens of lawsuits related to consumer racial profiling. We have used our research in collaborative efforts with the American Civil Liberties Union's national coordinator for the Campaign Against

Racial Profiling. We and other researchers on marketplace discrimination have established the Center for Consumer Equality (http://www.consumerequality.org) to make our research accessible to a wider audience beyond academics. The center's website includes a "Tell Us Your Story" link to capture episodes of marketplace discrimination similar to the ones discussed in this chapter. We also have worked closely with other organizations with similar goals of social justice and eradicating marketplace discrimination, such as the Civil Justice Center (http://www.civiljusticecenter.com). We have not been alone in these efforts. For example, research by other marketplace discrimination scholars (Ainscough & Motley, 2000; Harris, 2003) has been cited in an amicus curiae brief in support of particular petitioners that was filed before the U.S. Supreme Court.

As suggested by these examples of where TCR researchers can go "looking for trouble," linking marketplace discrimination and social justice to public policy is paramount. There are numerous cases in which public policy has made many marketplace practices illegal and unethical outside of marketing, but the laws have not quite caught up with similar practices within marketing. For example, redlining was outlawed in 1968 through the Fair Housing Act of 1968, but *retail* redlining is not illegal (D'Rozario & Williams, 2005). Similarly, discrimination was outlawed in places of public accommodation, such as hotels, restaurants, and movie theaters, by Title II of the Civil Rights Act of 1964, yet most subordinate consumers and their counsel, when filing marketplace discrimination lawsuits, are surprised to discover that retail stores are not considered places of public accommodation under Title II. Hence, discrimination in retail establishments, such as consumer racial profiling, is not covered by the statute (Harris et al., 2005). According to the Supreme Court, "Retail stores, food markets, and the like were excluded from [Title II] for the policy reason [that] there was little, if any, discrimination in the operation of them" (Kennedy, 2001, pp. 335–336). Obviously, such examples indicate that there still are ample opportunities for TCR researchers on marketplace discrimination to have their work impact changes in public policy to benefit consumer welfare and advance social justice.

This chapter has reviewed concepts related to various types of marketplace discrimination and offered empirical evidence through a qualitative study of how social justice can provide a useful framework for assessing the felt discrimination of subordinate consumers. We hope readers of this chapter will take away the message that in today's marketplace, discrimination remains a vexing problem, not only in the domain of race and ethnicity, which has received the majority share of attention, but also in many other domains, including age, gender, religion, physical appearance, nationality, language, skin tone, weight/obesity, and perceived ability to pay. Indeed, discrimination and injustice in the marketplace come in many varieties. Therefore, many opportunities for TCR researchers remain to address social injustices in the marketplace, and we hope this chapter will help TCR scholars continue to identify these areas and spur additional work on marketplace discrimination. Ultimately, it is our hope that this chapter will push other TCR researchers to pursue a path that will bring more social justice and less discrimination to the marketplace. In this way, American consumers—of all sizes, shapes, and colors—can be assured of receiving equitable treatment for equal dollars.

## REFERENCES

Ainscough, T. L., & Motley, C. M. (2000). "Will you help me please?" The effects of race, gender, and manner of dress on retail service. *Marketing Letters, 11*(2), 129–136.

Alwitt, L. F., & Donley, T. D. (1996). *The poor consumer: Adjusting the balance of exchange.* Thousand Oaks, CA: Sage.

Andreasen, A. R. (1975). *The disadvantaged consumer.* New York: Free Press.

Andreasen, A. R. (1978). The ghetto marketing life cycle: A case of underachievement. *Journal of Marketing, 15*(1), 20–28.

Andreasen, A. R. (1982). Judging marketing in the 1980's. *Journal of Macromarketing, 2*(1), 7–13.

Andreasen, A. R. (1993). Revisiting the disadvantaged: Old lessons and new problems. *Journal of Public Policy & Marketing, 12*(2), 270–275.

Asquith, J. L., & Bristow, D. N. (2000). To catch a thief: A pedagogical study of retail shoplifting. *Journal of Education for Business, 75*, 271–276.

Ayres, I., & Siegelman, P. (1995). Race and gender discrimination in bargaining for a new car. *American Economic Review, 85*(3), 304–321.

Baker, T. L., Meyer, T., & Johnson, J. D. (2008). Individual differences in perceptions of service failure and recovery: The role of race and discriminatory bias. *Journal of the Academy of Marketing Science, 36*, 552–564.

Bell, J., & Burlin, B. M. (1993). In urban areas: Many of the poor still pay more for food. *Journal of Public Policy & Marketing, 12*(2), 268–270.

Bitner, M. J. (1992). Servicescapes: The impact of physical surroundings on customers and employees. *Journal of Marketing, 56*(April), 57–72.

Blattberg, R., Getz, G., & Thomas, J. (2001). *Customer equity: Building and managing relationships as valuable assets.* Cambridge, MA: Harvard Business Press.

Caplovitz, D. (1963). *The poor pay more: Consumer practices of low income families.* New York: Free Press of Glencoe.

Carter, R. T., Forsyth, J. M., Mazzula, S. L., & Williams, B. (2005). Racial discrimination and race-based traumatic stress: An exploratory investigation. In R. T. Carter (Ed.), *Handbook of racial-cultural psychology and counseling: Training and practice* (Vol. 2, pp. 447–476). Hoboken, NJ: Wiley.

Crockett, D., Grier, S. A., & Williams, J. A. (2003). Coping with marketplace discrimination: An exploration of the experiences of Black men. *Academy of Marketing Science Review, 4*, 1–21.

Cutler, D. (2009, January 18). Racial inequality in the United States. *Reuters.* Available: http://www.reuters.com/article/companyNewsAndPR/idUSN1342383120090118

Dabney, D. A., Dugan, L., Topalli, V., & Hollinger, R. C. (2006). The impact of implicit stereotyping on offender profiling: Unexpected results from an observational study of shoplifting. *Criminal Justice and Behavior, 33*, 646–674.

Dabney, D. A., Hollinger, R. C., & Dugan, L. (2004). Who actually steals? A study of covertly observed shoplifters. *Justice Quarterly, 21*, 693–728.

D'Rozario, D., & Williams, J. D. (2005). Retail redlining: Definition, theory, typology, and measurement. *Journal of Macromarketing, 25*(2), 175–186.

Feagin, J. R. (1991). The continuing significance of race: Antiblack discrimination in public places. *American Sociological Review, 56*(February), 101–116.

Ferrell, O. C., & Ferrell, L. (2008). A macromarketing ethics framework: Stakeholder orientation and distributive justice. *Journal of Macromarketing, 28*(1), 24–32.

Fromm, E. (1962). Alienation under capitalism. In E. Josephson & M. Josephson (Eds.), *Man alone: Alienation in modern society* (pp. 56–73). New York: Dell.

Gabbidon, S. L. (2003). Racial profiling by store clerks and security personnel in retail establishments. *Journal of Contemporary Criminal Justice, 19*, 345–364.

Gabbidon, S. L., & Higgins, G. E. (2007). Consumer racial profiling and perceived victimization: A phone survey of Philadelphia area residents. *American Journal of Criminal Justice, 32*, 1–11.

Gabbidon, S. L., & Higgins, G. E. (2008). Profiling White Americans: Exploring "shopping while White." In M. J. Lynch, E. B. Patterson, & K. Childs (Eds.), *Racial divide: Race, ethnicity, and criminal justice.* Monsey, NY: Criminal Justice Press.

Grier, S. A., & Deshpandé, R. (2001). Social dimensions of consumer distinctiveness: The influence of social status on group identity and advertising persuasion. *Journal of Marketing Research, 38*(2), 216–224.

Hannah, D. C. (2009, January 19). Obama vs. skyrocketing incarceration rates: Is Dr. King's dream a reality? *DiversityInc.* Available: http://www.diversityinc.com/article/5055/Obama-Vs-Skyrocketing-Incarceration-Rates-Is-Dr-Kings-Dream-a-Reality/

Harris, A. G. (2003). Shopping while Black: Applying 42 U.S.C. § 1981 to cases of consumer racial profiling. *Boston College Third World Law Journal, 23*(1), 1–57.

Harris, A. G., Henderson, G. R., & Williams, J. D. (2005). Courting consumers: Assessing consumer racial profiling and other marketplace discrimination. *Journal of Public Policy & Marketing, 24*(1), 163–171.

Hart, C. W., Heskett, J. L., & Sasser, W. E., Jr. (1990). The profitable art of service recovery. *Harvard Business Review, 68*(4), 148–156.

Henderson, T. P. (2001). Racial profiling general debate. *Stores, 83*(6), 26–32.

Higgins, G. E., & Gabbidon, S. L. (2009). Perceptions of consumer racial profiling and negative emotions: An exploratory study. *Criminal Justice and Behavior, 36*, 77–88.

Hill, R. (2008). Disadvantaged consumers: An ethical approach to consumption by the poor. *Journal of Business Ethics, 80*(1), 77–83.

Humphreys, J. M. (2008). *The multicultural economy 2008*. Athens, GA: Terry College of Business, University of Georgia.

Jordan, K. L., Gabbidon, S. L., & Higgins, G. E. (2009). Exploring the perceived extent of and citizens' support for consumer racial profiling: Results from a national poll. *Journal of Criminal Justice, 37*(4), 353–359.

Kennedy, D. A. (2001). Consumer discrimination: The limitations of federal civil rights protection. *Missouri Law Review, 66*(2), 275–339.

Laczniak, G. R. (1999). Distributive justice, Catholic social teaching, and the moral responsibility of marketers. *Journal of Public Policy & Marketing, 18*(1), 125–129.

Laczniak, G. R., & Murphy, P. E. (2008). Distributive justice: Pressing questions, emerging directions, and the promise of Rawlsian analysis. *Journal of Macromarketing, 28*(1), 5–11.

La Piere, R. T. (1934). Attitudes versus actions. *Social Forces, 13*, 230–237.

Lee, J. (2000). The salience of race in everyday life: Black customers' shopping experiences in Black and White neighborhoods. *Work and Occupations, 27*(3), 353–376.

Levy, B. S., & Sidel, V. W. (2006). The nature of social injustice and its impact on public health. In B. S. Levy & V. W. Sidel (Eds.), *Social injustice and public health* (pp. 5–20). New York: Oxford University Press.

Lwin, M. O., & Williams, J. D. (2004). A model integrating the multidimensional developmental theory of privacy and theory of planned behavior to examine fabrication of information online. *Marketing Letters, 14*(4), 257–272.

Morton, F., Zettelmeyer, F., & Silva-Risso, J. (2003). Consumer information and discrimination: Does the Internet affect the pricing of new cars to women and minorities? *Quantitative Marketing and Economics, 1*(1), 65–92.

Motley, C. M., & Henderson, G. R. (2008). The global hip-hop diaspora: Understanding the culture. *Journal of Business Research, 61*(3), 243–253.

Motley, C. M., Henderson, G. R., & Baker, S. M. (2003). Exploring collective memories associated with African-American advertising memorabilia: The good, the bad, and the ugly. *Journal of Advertising, 32*(1), 47–57.

Poussaint, A. F. (2009, January 19). Commentary: Struggle for MLK's dream isn't over. *CNN Politics.com*. Available: http://www.cnn.com/2009/POLITICS/01/17/poussaint.mlk.obama/index.html#cnnSTCText

Pruden, H. O., & Longman, D. S. (1972). Race, alienation, and consumerism. *Journal of Marketing, 36*(3), 58–63.

Rosenbaum, M. S., & Montoya, D. Y. (2007). "Am I welcome here?" Exploring how ethnic consumers assess their place identity. *Journal of Business Research, 60*(3), 206–214.

Ross, J. I. (2009). Social justice. In H. T. Greene & S. L. Gabbidon (Eds.), *Encyclopedia of race and crime* (pp. 765–766). Newbury Park, CA: Sage.

Rust, R., Zeithaml, V., & Lemon, K. (2000). *Building customer lifetime value*. New York: Free Press.

Schaefer, R. T. (2010). *Race and ethnic groups* (12th ed.). Upper Saddle River, NJ: Pearson/Prentice-Hall.

Schoefer, K., & Ennew, C. (2005). The impact of perceived justice on consumers' emotional responses to service complaint experiences. *Journal of Services Marketing, 19*(5), 261–270.

Sen, S. (1996). Marketing and minority civil rights: The case of Amendment 2 and the Colorado boycott. *Journal of Public Policy & Marketing, 15*(2), 311–318.

Sirgy, M. J. (2008). Ethics and public policy implications of research on consumer well-being. *Journal of Public Policy & Marketing, 27*(2), 207–212.

Smith, A. K., & Bolton, R. N. (1998). An experimental investigation of service failure and recovery: Paradox or peril? *Journal of Service Research, 1*(1), 65–81.

Spiggle, S. (1994). Analysis and interpretation of qualitative data in consumer research. *Journal of Consumer Research, 21*(3), 491–503.

Sturdivant, F. D. (1969). Business and the Mexican-American community. *California Management Review, 11*(Spring), 73–80.

Thompson, C. (1997). Interpreting consumers: A hermeneutical framework for deriving marketing insights from the texts of consumers' consumption stories. *Journal of Marketing Research, 34*(November), 438–455.

Tombs, A., & McColl-Kennedy, J. R. (2003). Social servicescape conceptual model. *Marketing Theory, 3*(4), 447–475.

Wagley, C., & Harris, M. (1958). *Minorities in the new world: Six case studies*. New York: Columbia University Press.

Wakefield, W. D., & Hudley, C. (2005). African-American male adolescents' preferences in responding to racial discrimination: Effects of ethnic identity and situational influences. *Adolescence, 40*(158), 237–256.

Walsh, G. (2009). Disadvantaged consumers' experiences of marketplace discrimination in customer services. *Journal of Marketing Management, 25*(1/2), 143–169.

Walters, A. S., & Moore, L. J. (2002). Attention all shoppers, queer customers in aisle two: Investigating lesbian and gay discrimination in the marketplace. *Consumption, Markets and Culture, 5*(4), 285–303.

Williams, J. D. (2003, May). *Diversity in advertising: Many voices beyond Black and White.* In P. B. Rose & R. L. King (Eds.), *The proceedings of the 2003 Asia-Pacific Conference of the American Academy of Advertising* (pp. 79–82). Richmond, VA: American Academy of Advertising.

Williams, J. D., Harris, A. G., & Henderson, G. R. (2006a). Equal treatment for equal dollars in Illinois: Assessing consumer racial profiling and other marketplace discrimination. *The Law Enforcement Executive Forum, 5*(7), 83–104.

Williams, J. D., Harris, A. G., & Henderson, G. R. (2006b). States of denial and degradation both subtle and overt: Marketplace discrimination across America. In I. M. Martin, D. W. Stewart, & M. Kamins (Eds.), *2006 Marketing & Public Policy Conference proceedings* (Vol. 16, pp. 18–19). Chicago: American Marketing Association.

Williams, J. D., Henderson, G. R., & Hakstian, A. G. (2010). Consumer racial profiling. In H. T. Greene & S. L. Gabbidon (Eds.), *Encyclopedia of race and crime* (pp. 147–151). Newbury Park, CA: Sage.

Williams, J. D., Henderson, G. R., & Harris, A. G. (2001). Consumer racial profiling in retailing: Bigotry goes to market. *Crisis, 108*, 22–24.

Williams, J. D., Lwin, M. O., Harris, A. G., & Gooding, V. A. (2007). Developing a power-responsibility equilibrium model to assess "brick and mortar" retail discrimination: Balancing consumer, corporate, and government interests. In T. M. Lowrey (Ed.), *Brick and mortar shopping in the 21st century* (pp. 171–196). Mahwah, NJ: Erlbaum.

Williams, J. D., Qualls, W. J., & Ferguson, N. (2007). Potential vulnerabilities of U.S. subsistence consumers to persuasive marketing communications. In J. Rosa & M. Viswanathan (Eds.), *Product and market development for subsistence marketplaces: Consumption and entrepreneurship beyond literacy and resource barriers* (pp. 87–110). London: JAI Press.

Williams, J. D., Qualls, W. J., & Grier, S. A. (1995). Racially exclusive real estate advertising: Public policy implications for fair housing practices. *Journal of Public Policy & Marketing, 14*(2), 225–244.

Williams, J. D., & Snuggs, T. (1997). *Survey of attitudes toward customer ethnocentrism and shopping in retail store: The role of race.* In C. Pechmann & S. Ratneshwar (Eds.), *Society for Consumer Psychology 1997 winter conference proceedings* (pp. 161–162). Potsdam, NY: Society for Consumer Psychology.

# III

## *TECHNOLOGICAL EDGES*

# 9

## Internet Indispensability, Online Social Capital, and Consumer Well-Being

Donna L. Hoffman

PEOPLE WOULD NO SOONER GIVE UP THEIR … PCs than they would give up their toilets.

Roger McNamee
*(quoted in Lashinsky, 2003, p. 112)*

The Internet is mainstream. The most recent aggregate statistics show that Internet use continues to penetrate the population (Phillips, 2010). In 2010, 71% of people in the United States used the Internet at least once a month. This figure is expected to rise to 78% of the population by 2014. Now, more than 15 years since the Internet was first commercialized, it is safe to say that Internet use is no longer restricted to highly educated, upper-income, mostly White males. Although Internet use still skews toward those with higher rather than lower incomes, there is no longer a gender divide. The Internet is approximating saturation levels for teenagers and those between the ages of 18 and 44, while the very youngest and oldest are expected to catch up rapidly this decade. The Internet is also becoming more diverse (Phillips, 2009). About three quarters of non-Hispanic Whites and Asians are online, but only 64% of African Americans, 60% of Hispanics, and 53% of Native Americans and related demographic groups (Phillips, 2009). However, these racial disparities are projected to diminish over time.

As the Internet continues its inexorable march toward ubiquity, many are wondering what consequences for consumer well-being lie in its path. The question is becoming more acute as online social networking and "social sharing" behaviors increase and as "always on" Internet use becomes more personal, being accessed as much or more on mobile devices than it is on personal computers. These trends, along with media headlines that carry news of, for example, teens driven to suicide by cyberbullies, online identity theft, and the consequences of compulsive online gaming and cybersex, suggest that the relationships among Internet indispensability, social usage, and individual well-being are complex and may not always be beneficial or benign.

For the purposes of our subsequent discussion, we adopt a broad psychological definition of *well-being* as a person's perceived satisfaction with all or component aspects of their lives (e.g. Diener, Suh, Lucas, & Smith, 1999; Lyubomirsky, King, & Diener, 2005). Novak (Chapter 11 of this volume) introduces the idea of virtual quality of life and proposes a research agenda to examine how the parts of an individual's life that are played out in virtual worlds like Second Life impact their subjective well-being. In the present chapter, we are concerned with the broader implications of how Internet use more generally impacts well-being through the development of social capital.

## CAN THE INTERNET INCREASE WELL-BEING?

In the last several years, researchers interested in the factors influencing longevity have discovered a strong positive connection between being socially active and physical and mental well-being in later life. For example, the more socially active seniors are, the more likely they are to enjoy improved cognitive and motor functioning well into their old age (Yaffe et al., 2009). Another recent study found that the more time seniors spent socializing, the less their motor functions declined (Buchman et al., 2009). Intriguingly, one study has documented a relationship between the size of a person's social network and their perception of pain, such that patients with smaller networks reported more pain and patients with larger networks reported less pain (Mitchinson, Hyungjin, Geisser, Rosenberg, & Hinshaw, 2008). This finding is interesting, because it suggests that larger social networks, regardless of the quality of connections, can have positive influences on consumer welfare. Jetten, Haslam, Haslam, and Branscombe (2009) reviewed a number of studies in this domain and concluded that individuals who are members of many diverse social networks are more resilient and experience more mental and physical well-being compared to individuals who are not as socially connected.

Perhaps not surprisingly, researchers have recently discovered that similar positive benefits may also accrue from online social connections. Collins and Wellman (2010) observed that the more people use the Internet, the more connected they are both online and offline. Bessière, Kiesler, Kraut, and Boneva (2008) found that Internet users motivated by the need to communicate with friends and family had lower depression scores than individuals motivated to use the Internet to meet new people and chat online.

Although research examining the link between Internet use and subjective well-being is still in its early stages, it is reasonable to wonder whether these beneficial effects of Internet use will accrue to all consumers equally. It is therefore worthwhile to examine several key factors that may contribute to whether Internet use will lead to increased consumer well-being. The general hypothesis we explore in this chapter is that consumers who find the Internet indispensable to their daily lives are motivated to build and maintain online social capital and, with that store of online social capital, experience positive outcomes related to mental health and physical well-being. In much the same way that a Harvard undergraduate degree is "immensely valuable, conferring a lifetime of social capital and prestige" (Carey, 2009, para. 6), Internet use offers important opportunities for consumers to build and sustain social capital. We explore this general hypothesis in this chapter and raise what we hope will be interesting questions for an exciting upcoming research area.

In this chapter, we first consider the importance of building online social capital and argue that building and maintaining meaningful social connections in the online sphere can lead to accompanying benefits for some consumers. Next, we review our theory of how Internet indispensability arises, as it grounds our discussion of access and usage issues. We examine both the positive and negative behavioral consequences arising from regular use of the increasingly ubiquitous Internet medium. From there, we evaluate the digital divide and suggest that a behavior-based digital divide may be of greater cause for concern than one based on access. Finally, we conclude with some observations about what can be done to encourage the positive outcomes deriving from Internet use and offer some suggestions for future research directions.

## INTERNET USE CAN BUILD SOCIAL CAPITAL AND IMPROVE CONSUMER WELL-BEING

Most researchers assume that Internet access is a net positive for consumers (e.g. Katz & Rice, 2002; Warschauer, 2003; Youtie, Shapira, & Laudeman, 2004), with the consumer welfare benefits of online access well researched (e.g. Brynjolfsson, Hu, & Smith, 2003; Dutz, Orszag, & Willig,

2009; Keeney, 1999; Zettelmeyer, Morton, & Silva-Risso, 2006). Research that has examined costs of exclusion focus on the monetary (e.g., Cooper, 2000) or broad social costs (e.g., Cooper, 2002; van Dijk, 2004) that may arise from lack of online participation. Hoffman, Novak, and Schlosser (2000) suggested that, looking forward, any gaps in access might be better explained by the social conditions surrounding those who are not online than by any economic considerations. As the digital divide in access now closes (Jones & Fox, 2009), and the Internet becomes increasingly indispensable to consumers in their daily lives, a fuller understanding of the implications of Internet use for consumer well-being can be evaluated by considering how the Internet builds social capital.

Social capital refers to the resources that flow to an individual from the network of his or her relationships (Adler & Kwon 2002). Putnam (1995) observed in the mid-1990s that offline social capital had been in decline in the United States for several decades, owing to more women entering the workforce, more mobility, and the "technological transformation of leisure" (p. 75). This led to the consequence of fewer consumers participating in civic causes, such as political campaigns, town halls, and churchgoing, and more consumers joining larger, impersonal organizations like the AARP. Putnam argued that technology harmed the accumulation of social capital, because larger organizations, although they may satisfy belonging needs, do little to help consumers build a network of relationships from which resources may be acquired.

Running through the many different definitions of *social capital* is the idea of a sense of trust and cooperation fostered between two or more people (e.g. Adler & Kwon, 2002; Putnam, 1995). In addition to fostering trust and cooperation, an important aspect of any definition of *social capital* is that it is relational. Social capital requires some form of interaction to be built, lost, or modified. Early definitions of the construct emphasized community involvement (Alder & Kwon, 2002; Drentea & Moren-Cross, 2005; Putnam, 1995) and the benefits that arose from relationships built from that involvement. More recently, researchers have expanded this definition to include explicit recognition of electronic networks such as the Internet in the formation of social capital (Kavanaugh & Patterson, 2001; Wellman, Haase, Witte, & Hampton, 2001), which expands the idea of weak and strong ties to include connecting with people (across the network) who are not geographically close. Thus, the Internet can be seen as a tool for building and maintaining social capital, both online and offline.

Research shows that accumulating online social capital has positive effects on well-being (Bargh & McKenna, 2004; Ellison, Steinfield, & Lampe, 2007). As the Internet has diffused through modern society, consumers in general are better able to keep in touch with their acquaintances— what Granovetter (1973) calls *weak ties*—and use the Internet to strengthen the bonds underlying their close friends (strong ties). The Internet also offers consumers opportunities to express themselves and build social capital even if they are unable to capitalize on such opportunities offline.

### Early Studies Suggested the Internet Harms Social Capital

In order to study the effect of the Internet on social capital, Kraut et al. (1998) gave a sampling of families a free computer, software, phone line, e-mail account, and Internet access in exchange for allowing their access patterns to be tracked. In addition to tracking online behavior, participants completed periodic surveys regarding their social involvement and psychological well-being. During the 2-year study period, greater Internet usage was associated with less social involvement, greater loneliness, and the incidence of depression. Kraut et al. speculated that the negative social and psychological outcomes were due to online usage displacing offline social activities and strong ties. A similar study by Nie and Erbring (2000) found that more time spent online was associated with participants losing contact with their social environment, which was especially true for those participants spending more than 10 hours per week online.

In addition to research suggesting that Internet connectivity makes users more lonely and depressed, some research has suggested that it can increase conformity (Spears, Postmes, Lea, & Wolbert, 2002). More sensationally, mental health professionals have called to add Internet addiction to the *Diagnostic and Statistical Manual of Mental Disorders*, but much of the research in this area suffers from self-selection bias (see Litt, Pirouz, & Shiv, Chapter 25 of this volume, for a more general discussion of addictive behavior). Although these findings are provocative, it is difficult to know whether Internet use is an antecedent condition to such outcomes or a consequence of existing individual characteristics. Recent research has suggested that the impact of Internet use on a person's well-being is largely a function of the goals people have for interacting (Bargh & McKenna, 2004).

### Long-Run Online Use Positively Contributes to Social Capital

Kavanaugh and Patterson (2001) found limited support for Putnam's (1995) assertion that technology may transform leisure activities and thus reduce the social capital of individuals. In a study of a community computer access program, Kavanaugh and Patterson found that participants who had been online for longer periods of time were more likely to be using the Internet for social capital–building activities than those who had been online for only a relatively short period of time, arguing that this was because those individuals were already building social capital offline and simply using the Internet as a tool to continue those activities.

Contrary to Putnam (1995), Shah, Schimierbach, Hawkins, Espino, and Donavan (2002) found that time spent online was positively related to civic participation and attendance but not to informal socializing. The Shah et al. study departed from the Kraut et al. (1998) and Nie and Erbring (2000) studies by surveying current Web users about their online social capital–building activities. This approach is more representative of the online population as a whole, compared to nonusers who were given free access as part of a social program.

Wellman et al. (2001) analyzed data from one of the first large-scale, Internet-based usage surveys to address the effect of Internet participation on social capital and found that online participation actually supplemented face-to-face and telephone interactions by extending another avenue for communication, although the heaviest users did not reap the benefits to the same degree. Wellman et al. concluded that online participation increases social capital by providing users with yet another method to get in touch with the people with whom they want to communicate. Thus, the Internet is seen as a beneficial tool that complements the tools users already use to maintain their interconnectedness.

Kraut and colleagues (2002) later revisited the findings on the connection between Internet use and loneliness. In a follow-up study, they returned to the same participants as in the Kraut et al. (1998) study and added a sampling of new participants. Among the original participants, the negative effects they initially reported in 1998 had dissipated, although heavier online usage was associated with more stress. In the new sample, the researchers found positive effects of Internet usage for a wide range of social capital variables, including social involvement and community involvement. Additionally, Kraut et al. (2002) found that extroverts took the greatest advantage from online access, whereas introverts experienced worse outcomes from their time online.

### Online Versus Offline Social Capital

Conflicting research results may be due in part to the form of social capital being studied. Early studies emphasized the effects of online usage on offline social capital. More recently, researchers have turned their attention to studying the formation of online social capital (Kobayashi, Ikeda, & Miyata, 2006; Williams, 2006).

Williams (2006) examined both online and offline social capital and found that, despite the fact that using the Internet takes away from the amount of time participants had to work on their offline social capital, the time they spent online helped them build their online social capital. Qualitatively, online social capital was quite different from offline social capital, in that online relationships do not have the same depth and emotional involvement as offline relationships. Although these forms of social capital are quite different, Williams did not believe that the replacement of offline social capital with online social capital was detrimental to the quality of life of the individuals in the study. He concluded that looking at offline social capital as being displaced by online behaviors was not an adequate framework for understanding the complete picture of online and offline social capital. A complete understanding of online social capital should include the study of both psychological variables that moderate relationships and the websites that facilitate those relationships.

Kobayashi et al. (2006) reached a similar conclusion, that online social capital exists and has positive effects on offline social capital. In their study of the effect of participation in virtual communities, such as listservs, bulletin boards, and chat rooms, on social capital, they found that online communities can be powerful tools in building social capital. In particular, Internet users can both experience and participate in reciprocity and reciprocal communications in virtual communities. For those who participate, these interactions help build trust and bolster a sense of reciprocity. These effects also extend to "lurkers," online users who choose not to participate. Due to the public nature of these communications, nonparticipants can witness the ongoing reciprocal communication and trust building happening between others and learn vicariously through their observations. In addition to the reciprocal relationships that are built exclusively online, Kobayashi et al. also showed that virtual communities can be used as a tool to bolster offline social capital when the group goes offline, as with a hobby-focused club or after-hours workers' group.

Pruijt (2002) explored the power of the Internet to increase overall social capital by studying the ability of two different brand communities to positively impact firm behavior. In 1994, a single user discovered a flaw in an Intel processor and posted the findings on a newsgroup. This discussion grew into an intense debate to the point where Intel eventually offered replacements to all users who had purchased computers with the flawed processor. The replacements cost Intel over $400 million, and customers received satisfaction. Pruijt also discussed the evolution of the Linux operating system as a way that people have increased their social capital online. The Linux operating system has been almost entirely user-created by volunteers. In fact, there is still a large community of Internet users who continue to develop the Linux platform. Why do people continue to work on an operating system for free or post messages to newsgroups notifying others of faulty products? Pruijt argued that programmers do this for the social capital they earn in the form of trust and cooperation. He observed that the Internet is a network, and social capital is networking between individuals, and concluded that "the internet *is* social capital" (p. 112, emphasis added).

## Social Capital and Online Social Networking

As social networks proliferate, researchers are turning their attention to the potential for social networking activities to increase social capital. One recent study (Steinfield, Ellison, & Lampe, 2008) found that Facebook increases social capital. Facebook appears to increase the bridging of social capital by building and maintaining weak ties among large groups of distant friends and acquaintances. In addition to increased bridging social capital, Facebook provides the structure to help users maintain their close relationships as well as easily broadcast messages to a large group of friends and acquaintances. One side effect of the use of Facebook was an increased sense of self-esteem in college students who had just left home for school. The website may be useful to maintain bridging social capital by allowing users the possibility to eventually convert these less personal relationships to close relationships, and it allows people with difficulty in maintaining relationships a simple and easy way to maintain contact with a large group of friends and acquaintances.

As social networking sites become ubiquitous, a growing divide may separate those who do and do not use them. Tufekci (2008) found that although 85% of participants used social networking sites, there were significant differences between users and nonusers. There were few differences between the groups with respect to the number of friends and their instrumental use of the Internet, but users also tended to use the Internet for expressive and creative purposes, and nonusers were less interested in the types of social grooming behaviors that users engaged in. Kozinets, Belz, and McDonagh (Chapter 10 of this volume) examine the more general transformative nature of online communities.

Tufekci's (2008) results provide support for the idea we develop below that the digital divide is behavior based, with its roots in the social differences between the networked and nonnetworked. As the social Web becomes increasingly indispensable, lack of access and use has the potential to inhibit full participation in society. We can only wonder, then, if nonusers and light users, missing opportunities to build and maintain important new forms of social capital, will be left on the fringes of an increasingly connected society, peering through the net and wondering what the big deal is. Before we discuss our notion of a behavior-based digital divide, we provide a definition of *Internet indispensability.*

### THE RITUALIZATION OF DAILY ROUTINE GIVES RISE TO INTERNET INDISPENSABILITY

Hoffman, Novak, and Venkatesh (2004) argued that Internet indispensability arises from the microlevel practices of daily routine that become ritualized. For example, checking one's Facebook page each day during breakfast represents a ritualization of the daily routine of reading Facebook. Consumers who have made the Internet a daily ritual are likely to feel varying degrees of disruption if they are disconnected from the Internet. Consider the results from a recent Intel and Harris Interactive survey (Aakre, 2008): 46% of women said they would give up sex for 2 weeks rather than give up the Internet for 2 weeks, and overall, the Internet rated highest among discretionary items that consumers could not live without. In a stark example, several years ago, Yahoo! and OMD conducted an Internet deprivation study ("Yahoo! and OMD Reveal Study," 2004), in which 28 participants were asked to give up Internet access for 14 days. Participants reported intense feelings of withdrawal, frustration, and loss. Nearly 50% were unable to go the entire 14 days without Internet access. Further, the median number of days participants made it without access was only 5 days. The notion of daily ritual that the Internet affords is evident from reading participants' diaries and watching videos of their experiences during the study.

The more consumers use the Internet as a news and information source, for communication and correspondence, to conduct the myriad of life's transactions, for entertainment, and for social interaction (e.g., Turkle, 1998), the more useful they find it. These types of microlevel behaviors are what make the Internet so integral to people's lives (Turow & Kavanaugh, 2003) and lead to its indispensability. It should be clear to the reader that consumers who do not have opportunities to incorporate the Internet into their daily lives will not have the opportunity to experience ritualization that leads to indispensability, and if the Internet is not perceived as indispensable, there will be less opportunity to reap its benefits.

### IS THE DIGITAL DIVIDE A MATTER OF MOTIVATION?

What is the digital divide? At its most basic, the term *digital divide* refers to a gap in Internet access between people who have access and people who do not. The origin of the term has been attributed to Lloyd Morrisett, the former president of the Markle Foundation (Hoffman & Novak, 1998), and appears to have gained popularity in the late 1990s, when the U.S. Department of Commerce first began using the term in official reports (van Dijk, 2006). Although the concept of a digital divide seems straightforward, the reasons behind gaps in access are complex.

Much of the initial research on the digital divide rightly focused on access to the Internet with the rationale that if a consumer simply has no way to gain access to the Internet, it hardly matters how motivated they may or may not be to do so. Many of the early programs that arose from calls to reduce the digital divide therefore focused on attempts to close it by providing computers and Internet service to those who lacked the means to purchase equipment or pay for service (e.g. Jackson et al., 2004; Youtie et al., 2004).

Unfortunately, many of these programs met with limited success. For example, in LaGrange, Georgia, it was discovered that residents who were convinced of the utility of the Internet already had access, while those who remained offline despite the offer of free access did so because they were not convinced that access was either useful or truly free (Youtie et al., 2004). In a similar program (Jackson et al., 2004), HomeNetToo participants in a low-income community were given computers and Internet access in exchange for allowing their behavior to be tracked. Jackson et al. (2004) found that despite having Internet access, use of the Internet by this sample never reached the same levels as those of average Internet users. It turned out that much of the time HomeNetToo users spent online was spent searching for information, with very little time devoted to using the Internet for communication and social purposes, such as e-mail or other forms of online interaction. The authors concluded that the participants' motivation and attitudes toward the Internet were the main influence over usage patterns.

Early attempts to close the digital divide focused on providing equipment and access to those who could not afford it on their own (Jackson et al., 2004; Youtie et al., 2004). In the mid-1990s, the cost of a reasonably simple personal computer capable of accessing the Internet could easily top $2,000 (Warschauer, 2003). Currently, Internet-capable computers can be purchased for as little as a few hundred dollars.

Although the basic equipment has come down in price, the cost of Internet service remains a barrier to access (Chaudhuri, Flamm, & Horrigan, 2005; Savage & Waldman, 2005). Potential Internet users may be put off by the recurring costs and the often confusing array of Internet service options. In a recent study of the barriers to access, Chaudhuri et al. (2005) found that the price of Internet access had a small but significant effect on the decision to purchase Internet access and concluded that providing subsidized basic access is unlikely to have an effect on the digital divide.

## The Demographics of the Digital Divide

In the late 1990s, as researchers and policy makers began to realize that simply providing computers and Internet service was not enough to close the digital divide, research began to focus on the demographic factors influencing the digital divide, including race and ethnicity (e.g., Hoffman & Novak, 1998; Hoffman et al., 2000), psychological makeup (e.g., Chua, Chen, & Wong, 1999), and educational factors (e.g., Robinson, DiMaggio, & Hargittai, 2003). The major thrust of this research emphasizes either getting more people online or describing the differences between those who are online and those who are not without addressing the cost of remaining offline.

Hoffman and Novak (1998) found that the relationship between Internet usage and race and ethnicity was more complex than had been previously believed, as their results showed that household income explained home computer ownership above and beyond race. People with greater household incomes were more likely to own home computers. Additionally, education explained access to a computer in the workplace; people with higher levels of education were more likely to have access to a computer at work regardless of race. However, when looking at students, the picture was not quite so egalitarian. With students, race mattered; overall, White students had greater access to computers and greater rates of Internet usage.

In a follow-up study, Hoffman et al. (2000) found that the digital divide for students was closing but still significant. Additionally, there were still differences in access for African Americans compared to Whites. Hoffman et al. surmised that the digital divide between African Americans and Whites at that time could be explained by apparent cultural differences. The media consumption habits of African Americans tended away from mass media and technology reporting. In addition, schools and churches that African Americans attended were less likely to have websites or use the Internet for communication.

Payton (2003) conducted a small-scale study of 41 African American high school students. Remarkably, only four of the students had ever heard the term *digital divide*. Only one student reported having no access to the Internet, and the majority of the students (83%) had Internet access at home. In addition to the sample of 41 students, Payton conducted a focus group of 10 African American students. In the course of the focus group, all 10 students agreed that "they could not imagine life or school without the computers and the Internet" (p. 91).

The effects of the digital divide go beyond those seen in African American high school students. Robinson et al. (2003) used the results from a nationally representative survey to explore the differences in the advantages afforded by Internet access once people have access. They found that those who had college educations reaped much greater advantages out of their Internet usage than those who had only a high school education. Specifically, those with college educations made better use of the Internet with respect to their work, education, and political engagement.

Clearly, the demographics associated with race and education have played a part in who does and does not have access to the Internet. Do individual difference variables play a role in keeping some people away from the Internet? Studies exploring the psychological aspects of computer use and Internet access are somewhat limited. Chua et al. (1999) conducted a meta-analysis on the correlates of computer anxiety, believing that computer anxiety is in fact one of the psychological barriers to computer use. They found that computer anxiety is a transient emotional state rather than a durable emotional trait and that it can be modified. Based on their study, it can be concluded that the reduction of computer anxiety can lead to greater use of both computers and the Internet.

Research in the late 1990s firmly established that the Internet had not touched all segments of our society equally, and those in the lower socioeconomic levels were among those least likely to enjoy access (Hoffman & Novak, 1998; Hoffman et al., 2000). In the ensuing years, policy makers, educators, and philanthropists have done much to erase this digital divide, resulting in many experts believing that the divide has all but closed (Marriott, 2006). Indeed, recent research supports the conventional wisdom that the falling prices of computers and connectivity, along with the ubiquity of school, library, and other public access wired and wireless hotspots, are rapidly erasing the demographic digital divide (Compaine, 2001). As noted at the beginning of this chapter, over the next few years, African Americans, Hispanics, American Indians, and other underrepresented households are expected to reap connectivity gains, as the American Recovery and Reinvestment Act's Broadband Technology Opportunities Program (U.S. Department of Commerce, 2009) took effect in 2010.

### A Behavior-Based Digital Divide

Although the geodemographic digital divide may be shrinking, another divide is looming. As the Internet mutates from a vast database into a web of social networks, along with a wave of excitement from marketers about social media and Web 2.0, it has gone mostly unnoticed that while the digital divide in *access* may be shrinking, a far more serious *usage* divide is occurring. The Internet is becoming increasingly indispensable to some people in their daily lives but not to everyone.

Although it is hard to argue that whole classes of individuals in our society are shut off from basic access to the Internet, there is increasing evidence that some individuals who have or could have access are choosing not to participate fully in the Internet communications revolution. For example, although African Americans and Hispanics are catching up to Whites and Asians in terms of basic access, according to *eMarketer* ("The Dwindling Digital Divide," 2009), they still lag in significant consumer behavior usage categories. African American and Hispanic Internet users represent the smallest percentage of online buyers (40.6% and 41.8%, respectively), compared to Asian (70%) and all adult (55.8%) Internet users, and make fewer online purchases. Only 10.9% of African American and 12.3% of Hispanic Internet users made five or more online purchases in 2007, compared with 46% of Asians and 35.7% of all adults.

These disparities in usage are important because, as we suggested at the outset, the Internet conveys significant immediate and longer term consumer welfare benefits to its users. In the short run, consumers can easily gather detailed information from multiple sources about products and services, compare products, and search for the lowest prices. Taking the long view, a recent survey found that consumers believe the Internet makes them more productive ("The Dwindling Digital Divide," 2009), and it has been recently argued that the Internet augments cognition and has the potential to make consumers smarter and more creative (Hoffman, 2008).

## CONCLUSIONS

According to a recent PEW Internet & American Life survey (Jones & Fox, 2009), the digital divide in access is closing. As more and more minorities and older Americans gain online access, the monetary, educational, and social costs of online exclusion will become greater and greater for those without access (Tongia & Wilson, 2007). The straightforward case of accessing government documents brings the point home. As the early United States expanded west, it was difficult and expensive to obtain government documents. People had to travel long distances over rough terrain to obtain and file even simple government documents. As more people moved west, the government opened more offices to provide easier access to its citizens. Similarly, as the Internet expands, more government documents are available online for citizens to view, print, and even submit electronically, which means that citizens who do not have or choose not to have online access must physically travel to a government office to retrieve and file documents. As more documents become available online, government offices print fewer hard copies, sometimes making documents and/or certain information available *only* online. Thus, the costs of not being online grow, as more documents and services are available online, and the government closes more local offices.

Researchers assume that Internet access is a net positive for consumers (e.g., Katz & Rice, 2002; Warschauer, 2003; Youtie et al., 2004), with the consumer welfare benefits of online access well researched (e.g., Brynjolfsson et al., 2003; Dutz et al., 2009; Keeney, 1999; Zettelmeyer et al., 2006). Most research that has examined costs of exclusion focus on the monetary (e.g., Cooper & Shah, 2000) or broad social costs (e.g., Cooper, 2002; van Dijk, 2004) that may arise from lack of online participation. Hoffman et al. (2000) suggested that, looking forward, any gaps in access might be better explained by the social conditions surrounding those who are not online than by any economic considerations.

## FUTURE RESEARCH DIRECTIONS

As the digital divide in access now closes (Jones & Fox, 2009), and the Internet becomes increasingly indispensable to many consumers in their daily lives, a fuller understanding of the implications of Internet use for consumer well-being can be evaluated by considering how the Internet builds social capital. More research is needed to evaluate how Internet use, particularly social networks, builds online social capital and to explore the links between online social capital and consumer well-being.

We have argued that, in general, Internet use is likely to enhance social capital and consumer well-being, but more research is needed to understand the conditions under which routinized use of the Internet leads to positive or negative outcomes. Is it a matter of individual differences, usage patterns, or interactions among the two? The more consumers believe they are unable to live without their connection to the Internet, the more the medium is being woven into the larger fabric of global society. Consumers who cannot or do not participate in the online conversation are not only missing out on key benefits that could enrich their lives but also are in danger of becoming socially, commercially, and politically irrelevant in a globally networked consumer society.

## REFERENCES

Aakre, K. (2008, December 14). The Internet: Could you give it up? *Inside Scoop.* Available: http://scoop.intel.com/the_internet_could_you_give_it_up/

Adler, P., & Kwon, S. (2002). Social capital: Prospects for a new concept. *Academy of Management Review, 27,* 17–40.

Bargh, J. A., & McKenna, K. Y. A. (2004). The Internet and social life. *Annual Review of Psychology, 55,* 573–590.

Bessière, K., Kiesler, S., Kraut, R. E., & Boneva, B. (2008). Effects of Internet use and social resources on changes in depression. *Information, Communication & Society, 11,* 47–70.

Brynjolfsson, E., Hu, Y., & Smith, M. D. (2003). Consumer surplus in the digital economy: Estimating the value of increased product variety at online booksellers. *Management Science, 49,* 1580–1596.

Buchman, A. S., Boyle, P. A., Wilson, R. S., Fleischman, D. A., Leurgans, S., & Bennett, D. A. (2009). Association between late-life social activity and motor decline in older adults. *Archives of Internal Medicine, 169*(June), 1139–1146.

Carey, K. (2009, September 28). The "veritas" about Harvard. *Chronicle of Higher Education.* Available: http://chronicle.com/article/Think-Tank-The-Veritas/48590/

Chaudhuri, A., Flamm, K. S., & Horrigan, J. (2005). Analysis of the determinants of Internet access. *Telecommunications Policy, 29,* 731–755.

Chua, S. L., Chen, D., & Wong, A. F. L. (1999). Computer anxiety and its correlates: A meta-analysis. *Computers in Human Behavior, 15,* 609–623.

Collins, J. L., & Wellman, B. (2010). Small town in the Internet society: Chapleau is no longer an island. *American Behavioral Scientist, 53*(9), 1344–1366.

Compaine, B. M. (2001). *The digital divide: Facing a crisis of creating a myth?* Cambridge, MA: MIT Press.

Cooper, M. (2002). Does the digital divide still exist? Bush Administration shrugs, but evidence says "yes." *Consumers Union.* Available: http://www.consumerfed.org/pdfs/DigitalDivideReport20020530.pdf

Cooper, M. N. (2000, October 11). *Disconnected, disadvantaged, and disenfranchised: Explorations in the digital divide.* Washington, DC: Consumer Federation of America & Consumers Union Joint Report.

Diener, E., Suh, E. M., Lucas, R. E., & Smith, H. (1999). Subjective well being: Three decades of progress. *Psychological Bulletin, 125*(2), 276–302.

Drentea, P., & Moren-Cross, J. L. (2005). Social capital and social support on the Web: The case of an Internet mother site. *Sociology of Health & Illness, 27,* 920–943.

Dutz, M., Orszag, J., & Willig, R. (2009). *The substantial consumer benefits of broadband connectivity for U.S. households.* New York: Internet Innovation Alliance.

The dwindling digital divide. (2009, March 12). *eMarketer.*

Ellison, N. B., Steinfield, C., & Lampe, C. (2007). The benefits of Facebook "friends": Social capital and college students' use of online social network sites. *Journal of Computer-Mediated Communication, 12*(4). Available: http://jcmc.indiana.edu/vol12/issue4/ellison.html

Granovetter, M. S. (1973). The strength of weak ties. *American Journal of Sociology, 78,* 1360–1380.

Hoffman, D. L. (2008). *Cognitive augmentation: Can the Internet make you smarter and more creative?* Unpublished manuscript, University of California, Riverside, Sloan Center for Internet Retailing.

Hoffman, D. L., & Novak, T. P. (1998). Bridging the racial divide on the Internet. *Science, 280,* 390–391.

Hoffman, D. L., Novak, T. P., & Schlosser, A. (2000). The evolution of the digital divide: How gaps in Internet access may impact electronic commerce. *Journal of Computer-Mediated Communication, 5.* Available: http://jcmc.indiana.edu/vol5/issue3/hoffman.html

Hoffman, D. L., Novak, T. P., & Venkatesh, A. (2004). Has the Internet become indispensable? *Communications of the ACM, 47*(July), 37–42.

Jackson, L. A., Barbatsis, G., Biocca, F. A., von Eye, A., Zhao, Y., & Fitzgerald, H. E. (2004). Home Internet use in low-income families: Is access enough to eliminate the digital divide? In E. P. Bucy & J. E. Newhagen (Eds.), *Media access: Social and psychological dimensions of new technology use* (pp. 155–183). Mahwah, NJ: Erlbaum.

Jetten, J., Haslam, C., Haslam, S. A., & Branscombe, N. R. (2009, September 9). Groups as therapy? Socializing and mental health. *Scientific American Mind.* Available: http://www.scientificamerican.com/article.cfm?id= the-social-cure

Jones, S., & Fox, S. (2009). *Generations online in 2009.* Washington, DC: Pew Internet & American Life Project. Available: http://www.pewinternet.org/Experts/~/link.aspx?_id=258EE0426A7A487C9BEDAEF9286A D10E&_z=z

Katz, J. E., & Rice, R. E. (2002). *Social consequences of Internet use.* Cambridge, MA: MIT Press.

Kavanaugh, A. L., & Patterson, S. J. (2001). The impact of community computer networks on social capital and community involvement. *American Behavioral Scientist, 45,* 496–509.

Keeney, R. L. (1999). The value of Internet commerce to the customer. *Management Science, 45,* 533–542.

Kobayashi, T., Ikeda, K., & Miyata, K. (2006). Social capital online: Collective use of the Internet and reciprocity as lubricants of democracy. *Information, Communication & Society, 9,* 582–611.

Kraut, R., Kiesler, S., Boneva, B., Cummings, J., Helgelson, V., & Crawford, A. (2002). Internet paradox revisited. *Journal of Social Issues, 58,* 49–74.

Kraut, R., Patterson, M., Lundmark, V., Kiesler, S., Mukopadhyay, T., & Scherlis, W. (1998). Internet paradox: A social technology that reduces social involvement and psychological well-being. *American Psychologist, 53,* 1017–1031.

Lashinsky, A. (2003, May 26). Where the smart money is flowing. *Fortune,* pp. 106–112.

Lyubomirsky, S., King, L., & Diener, E. (2005). The benefits of frequent positive affect: Does happiness lead to success. *Psychological Bulletin, 131*(6), 803–855.

Marriott, M. (2006, March 31). Blacks turn to Internet highway, and digital divide starts to close. *The New York Times Technology Section.* Available: http://query.nytimes.com/gst/fullpage.html?res=950CE3DD1230F9 32A05750C0A9609C8B63

Mitchinson, A. R., Hyungjin, M. K., Geisser, M., Rosenberg, J. M., & Hinshaw, D. B. (2008). Social connectedness and patient recovery after major operations. *Journal of the American College of Surgeons, 206*(February), 292–300.

Nie, N. H., & Erbring, L. (2000). *Internet and society: A preliminary report.* Stanford, CA: Stanford Institute for the Quantitative Study of Society.

Payton, F. C. (2003). Rethinking the digital divide. *Communications of the ACM, 46,* 89–91.

Phillips, L. E. (2009, March 10). African-Americans online. *eMarketer.* Available: http://www.emarketer.com/ Report.aspx?code=emarketer_2000562

Phillips, L. E. (2010, April 7). US Internet users, 2010. *eMarketer.* Available: http://www.emarketer.com/Report. aspx?code=emarketer_2000670

Pruijt, H. (2002). Social capital and the equalizing potential of the Internet. *Social Science Computer Review, 20,* 109–115.

Putnam, R. D. (1995). Bowling alone: America's declining social capital. *Journal of Democracy, 6,* 65–78.

Robinson, J. P., DiMaggio, P., & Hargittai, E. (2003). New social survey perspectives on the digital divide. *IT & Society, 1*(5), 1–22.

Savage, S. J., & Waldman, D. (2005). Broadband Internet access, awareness, and use: Analysis of United States household data. *Telecommunications Policy, 29,* 615–633.

Shah, D., Schimierbach, M., Hawkins, J., Espino, R., & Donavan, J. (2002). Nonrecursive models of Internet use and community engagement: Questioning whether time spent online erodes social capital. *Journalism & Mass Communication Quarterly, 79,* 964–987.

Spears, R., Postmes, T., Lea, M., & Wolbert, A. (2002). When are net effects gross products? The power of influence and the influence of power in computer-mediated communication. *Journal of Social Issues, 58*(1), 91–107.

Steinfield, C., Ellison, N. B., & Lampe, C. (2008). Social capital, self-esteem, and the use of online social network sites: A longitudinal analysis. *Journal of Applied Developmental Psychology, 29*, 434–445.

Tongia, R., & Wilson, E. J. (2007, September). *Turning Metcalfe on his head: The multiple costs of network exclusion.* Paper presented at the 35th annual Telecommunications Policy Research Conference, Arlington, VA.

Tufekci, Z. (2008). Grooming, gossip, Facebook and Myspace. *Information, Communication & Society, 11*, 544–564.

Turkle, S. (1998). Cyborg babies and cy-dough plasm: Ideas about self and life in the culture of simulation. In R. D. Floyd & J. Dumit (Eds.), *Cyborg babies: From techno-sex to techno-tots* (pp. 317–329). New York: Routledge.

Turow, J., & Kavanaugh, A. L. (2003). *The wired homestead: An MIT Press sourcebook on the Internet and the family.* Cambridge, MA: MIT Press.

U.S. Department of Commerce. (2009, February 25). Commerce Department receives $7.9 billion in Recovery Act funding essential to U.S. job creation and economic growth. Available: http://www.commerce.gov/NewsRoom/PressReleases_FactSheets/PROD01_007789

van Dijk, J. A. G. M. (2004). Divides in succession: Possession, skills, and use of new media. In E. P. Bucy & J. E. Newhagen (Eds.), *Media access: Social and psychological dimensions of new technology use* (pp. 233–254). Mahwah, NJ: Erlbaum.

van Dijk, J. A. G. M. (2006). Digital divide research, achievements and shortcomings. *Poetics, 34*, 221–235.

Warschauer, M. (2003). *Technology and social inclusion: Rethinking the digital divide.* Cambridge, MA: MIT Press.

Wellman, B., Haase, A. Q., Witte, J., & Hampton, K. (2001). Does the Internet increase, decrease, or supplement social capital? Social networks, participation, and community commitment. *American Behavioral Scientist, 45*, 436–455.

Williams, D. (2006). The impact of time online: Social capital and cyberbalkanization. *CyberPsychology & Behavior, 10*, 398–406.

Yaffe, K., Fiocco, A. J., Lindquist, K., Vittinghoff, E., Simonsick, E. M., Newman, A. B., et al. (2009). Predictors of maintaining cognitive function in older adults: The health ABC study. *Neurology, 72*(June), 2029–2035.

Yahoo! and OMD reveal study depicting life without the Internet. (2004, September 22). *Yahoo! Media Relations.* Available: docs.yahoo.com/docs/pr/release1183.html

Youtie, J., Shapira, P., & Laudeman, G. (2004). Reducing barriers to access via public information infrastructure: The LaGrange Public Internet Initiative. In E. P. Bucy & J. E. Newhagen (Eds.), *Media access: Social and psychological dimensions of new technology use* (pp. 131–154). Mahwah, NJ: Erlbaum.

Zettelmeyer, F., Morton, F. S., & Silva-Risso, J. (2006). How the Internet lowers prices: Evidence from matched survey and automobile transaction data. *Journal of Marketing Research, 43*, 168–181.

# 10

# Social Media for Social Change
## A Transformative Consumer Research Perspective

Robert V. Kozinets, Frank-Martin Belz, and
Pierre McDonagh

*Groundswell* (Li & Bernoff, 2008). *Here Comes Everybody* (Shirky, 2008). *Join the Conversation* (Jaffe, 2007). *Six Pixels of Separation* (Joel, 2009). *Trust Agents* (Brogan & Smith, 2009). *The New Community Rules* (Weinberg, 2009). *Socialnomics* (Qualman, 2009). The titles of the latest popular business books about marketing leave little doubt that business has recognized the influence of social media. The book titles hint at a tipping point where the social communications of consumers speaking to other consumers online lead to important social and economic outcomes, which marketers and managers are already partaking in and from which many of them are profiting. Just as with Transformative Consumer Research (TCR), the same underlying principles that enable marketers to influence consumers to bond with and buy brands can also be used to further consumer empowerment and well-being. In fact, from the time of some of the earlier theorization about the links between social media and marketing (e.g., Kozinets, 1999; Levine et al., 2000), consumer empowerment—and, explicitly, a moral empowerment—has been hailed as a hallmark of the medium:

> Empowered by information exchange and emboldened by relational interactions, consumers will use their online activities to actively judge consumption offerings, and increasingly resist what they see as misdirected.... The existence of united groups of online consumers implies that power is shifting away from marketers and flowing to consumers. For while consumers are increasingly saying yes to the Internet, to electronic commerce and to online marketing efforts of many kinds, they are also using the medium to say "no" to forms of marketing they find invasive or unethical. Virtual communities are becoming important arenas for organizing consumer resistance [and] have been used for "transformational" interaction aimed at increasing the betterment of the group of consumers as a community, very often by undermining the efforts of those who would profit at their expense. (Kozinets, 1999, p. 258)

In this chapter, we seek to consolidate, broaden, and develop these views. Not only can social media and online community be a site of consumer education and empowerment when dealing with individual companies and brands, but it also can be a place where consumers educate one another about their own attitudes and ideological stances toward consumption itself, as the Kozinets and Handelman (1998) study of the spiritual aspects of online boycotting discussions demonstrated. Not only can these communities and their media be locations where resistance to individual companies and marketing campaigns can be organized (see Kozinets & Handelman, 2004), but they also can be loci where wider visions of communal and social alternatives can be handcrafted, haggled over, hiked up, and handed off and where new paths for consumer well-being can be plowed, stepped on, and perhaps even followed.

The possible application of social media to consumer well-being, and to the TCR that seeks to enhance them, are multifarious. Our notions of the online arena's sphere of influence extend across the gamut of consumption and social activities, from boycotts to body image concerns, from smoking cessation to societal spectacularization. The context we have chosen to focus on in this chapter is environmental, or sustainable, consumption, a topic that is near and dear to all three authors' hearts. However, we intend you to take our implications about social media as general principles about utility and processes, understood as such and then deployed by consumer researchers, social marketers, nonprofits, nongovernmental organizations, regulators, and other agents of social change in ways that can help benefit communities and society in a variety of different ways.

Overridingly, our concern is a practical one. Can social media be used to foster individual and social change resulting in improvements in long-term increases in people's well-being around the world? A part of the answer to this question, and we believe one of the most urgent and important ones, is to get our ecological house in order. How can consumer researchers help foster a more sustainable consumption lifestyle, more sustainable consumption communities, and, ultimately, a more sustainable consumer culture? This is a large question whose three parts are vexingly interconnected. Although it certainly cannot be handled in its entirety in a short format such as this one, this chapter seeks to begin addressing that question by focusing on the role that social media might play in envisioning and empowering these changes.

First, we offer a conceptual overview that sets out our core terminology of online communities, social media, and consumer well-being. Providing additional conceptual backbone, we then take a detour into the real world to examine the theorized role and interrelation of community and sustainability. We look at research that examines the relation between social media and the alleviation of various social problems, then define three types of online social change communities (OSCCs). From there, we broaden our perspective to consider how social media connect to lifestyle-related issues of environmental orientation or sustainability. We offer a brief description and discussion of some different social media sites that illustrate our three variants of OSCCs. The final section offers some important implications of our findings for the understanding of both online communities and sustainable consumption, for the future conduct of consumer research, as well as for the related pragmatic concerns of consumer activists and organizers, corporations, legislators, and others concerned with social and regulatory policies. We develop our notions of social media and social change through the intermediary element of consumer empowerment. As do many of the contributors to this book (see, e.g., Mick, Pettigrew, Pechmann, & Ozanne, Chapter 1 of this volume), we also interrogate the largely neglected role of business academia, and academia in general, in the process of initiating and sustaining social change. The chapter closes with some suggestions for scholars of TCR that include not only the distanced study of social media but also their application and daily use in academic life.

## CONCEPTUAL FOUNDATIONS

### Online Community and Social Media

For the purposes of this chapter and this book, we define *online communities* as persistent computer-mediated forums where groups of people communicate. These communal forums persist and have continuity, participants tend to identify and often recognize other members, and communications can take various forms, such as text, photographs, hyperlinks, and video. *Social media* is the term given to these same communal phenomena as they have spread from newsgroups and website forums to multiple formats and become associated with blogs, wikis, virtual worlds, videogames, social networking sites (e.g., Facebook), microblogs (e.g., Twitter), and their various mobile formats.

The term *social media* tends to have a more pragmatic, tool kit orientation to the phenomenon, viewing them more from the perspective that they are resources that can and should be managed. Because of the action orientation of this chapter and this book, we will preferentially use the term *social media*, unless speaking directly about the core phenomenon of community manifested through computer mediation itself. However, despite connotative differences, the two terms notionally refer to the same phenomenon: The media could not be social without the virtual messengers, and the online community could not communicate without the technological medium.

From a consumer research perspective, the defining characteristic of the social media phenomenon is that it allows collective participation by consumers in a grassroots format that is relatively open and relatively controlled by consumers themselves. Social media are communal locations where consumers

> communicate social information and create and codify group-specific meanings, socially negotiate group-specific identities, form relationships which span from the playfully antagonistic to the deeply romantic and which move between the network and face-to-face interaction, and create norms which serve to organize interaction and to maintain desirable social climates. (Clerc, 1996, pp. 45–46)

Consumer researchers have studied social media phenomena mainly in regard to fan and consumption-related pursuits (e.g., Kozinets, 1999), identity expression and formation (e.g., Schau & Gilly, 2003), user innovation (e.g., Hemetsberger & Reinhardt, 2006), and online word of mouth (e.g., Kozinets, de Valck, Wojnicki, & Wilner. 2010). As noted above, business and marketing research continue to develop and test social media for a variety of marketing purposes, including the influence of word of mouth (see, e.g., Kozinets et al., 2010).

Consumer research is still at a nascent stage in connecting the reality and potential of social media with transformative concerns. In initiating this step, we relate social media to consumer well-being and offer a set of conceptions that we will deepen in the concluding section of this chapter. We draw our notions partially from the psychologically centered subjective well-being conceptions of Ed Diener (e.g., Diener, Suh, Lucas, & Smith, 1999). Diener et al. (1999) noted that reaching goals is an important aspect of the sense of subjective well-being. We suggest that, if an increasingly urgent goal of many people is to live a lifestyle attuned to the limitations of our planet, then furthering that more sustainable lifestyle contributes to consumer well-being on an individual level. Furthermore, if one takes serious the dire nature of climate change and its impact on the planet (see, e.g., Meadows, Randers, & Meadows, 2004; Rees, 2004), then our own immediate perceptions of our own well-being and that of future generations are enhanced by knowledge that we are moving toward a more ecologically sustainable society.

In our conceptions of consumer well-being, we are thus concerned mainly with physical and environmental well-being in the shorter run. However, ecological issues will, as many climate change scientists and environmental thinkers assert, eventually have severe economic, emotional, spiritual, and political ramifications. A conception of sustainability-oriented consumer well-being thus addresses all seven of McGregor and Goldsmith's (1998) dimensions of well-being.

Community and Sustainability

Before proceeding to elaborate on the role of social media in sustainability movements, it may be helpful to relate sustainability to broader themes of communal involvement and the revitalization of community. Ehrenfeld (2009) conceptualized community as a conservative value and as a form of human living and lifestyle that should be valued by political conservatives and liberals alike.

He adopted a conservative definition of the term *community*, considering it "groups of people who share a place and are vested in it, and who can maintain frequent, personal contact with each other" (p. 248). Similarly, Assadourian (2008) defined a community as "a group of geographically rooted people engaged in relationships with each other" (p. 152). Physical proximity and interpersonal engagement are key elements. Like sociologist Robert Putnam, Ehrenfeld (2009) does not believe that "electronic pseudo-communities count as communities, because there is no circumscribed place that their members share, and because the contacts are not personal in the fullest human sense" (p. 248). Ehrenfeld's core definition comes very close to the utopian ideal of the caring and sharing community described in Kozinets's (2002) study of the temporary, experimental community Burning Man: "This communal ideal can be characterized as a group of people living in close proximity with mutual social relations characterized by caring and sharing" (p. 21). Kozinets found that the incursions of markets were widely held to have undermined and weakened this ideal.

Yet, similar to the revitalizing role that caring, sharing hypercommunities played at Burning Man, a number of sustainability scholars have found that functioning, locally rooted, cooperative, grassroots, in-person communities "will be absolutely essential for a manageable transition to a stable, low-energy, low-consumption, and low-waste society" (Ehrenfeld, 2009, p. 248; e.g., Assadourian, 2008; McKibben , 2007). These social thinkers have linked the revival of communities to the fostering of a new relationship between the environment and human lifestyle. Communities draw together in the face of challenge and adversity, such as those we now face on environmental fronts. Communal arrangements facilitate productivity, binding people together into social groups and sponsoring aid for those in need.

Perhaps even more salient to the sustainability topics at hand, in a compartmentalized and tightly knit community, people can observe and directly experience the consequences of their own and their neighbors' actions in a way that they cannot in a globalized, centralized social structure, in which critical decisions are often made in isolation from their social and ecological consequences. Because communities can live in close proximity to each another and the earth, they benefit from a feedback loop that can keep society and nature in healthy balance. As outlined in archaeologist Joseph Tainter's (1988) *The Collapse of Complex Societies*, communities existing in a postabundance, postpetroleum society may regain significant amounts of autonomy as socially structuring forces of amalgamation and centralization weaken or collapse.

The role of communities has been increasingly acknowledged as key to the transition to a more ecologically sustainable society. Ecovillages and other communities in which members intentionally plan their communities around the principles of sustainable consumption are enjoying incredible growth rates. Filled with active, engaged consumers, these community members are collectively enacting practices and making decisions about land use, transportation, and other consumption practices that can be used as a role model of sustainable living to inspire and inform more mainstream consumers. Many of these communities contain some of the world's leaders in sustainable practices and are a hotbed of political innovation and organized political influence (Assadourian, 2010; McKibben, 2007). Many are on the vanguard of localized agricultural practices and the development of local production of other essential goods. They are also developing innovative organizational, marketing, and financial models that provide important alternatives to national and global-level efforts. Summarizing their impact and important, Eric Assadourian (2008) stated that these communities are making "powerful contributions" toward helping facilitate "the transition to a sustainable society" (p. 152).

To summarize, the in-person caring and sharing community has been increasingly invoked as one of the keys to building new social structures that are ecologically sustainable. This perspective holds as critically important the local level of decision making and the presence of feedback loops between individual or household consumption choices and their environmental effects. Through initiatives such as ecovillages and cohousing projects, a collective community spirit has, in this perspective, been revitalized, with positive ecological, social, and even psychological consequences. Social capital has been rebuilt.

However, some of these theorists have adamantly resisted the idea that social media and online communities are real, or authentic, and see no role for them in the social movement to a sustainable human lifestyle. Online communities are viewed negatively as pseudocommunities. In the next section, we seek to explore some of these assertions and evaluations. Through the remainder of this chapter, we take a broad look at social media dedicated to sustainability and speculate on some of their guiding principles, some of the impacts they can make, and the implications they have for the conduct of TCR.

## Extant Research on Social Media and Consumer Empowerment

In much extant empirical research, there is a close relationship between social media participation and in-person commitments to communities, civic engagement, and the construction of social capital, which contradicts the assertions that online communities are somehow lesser communities. A rigorous academic survey of Internet usage in America provided a broad overview of this influence in the American context, suggesting that online communities are linked to (a) the awareness of social causes, (b) participation in them, and (c) participation in new causes. A digital future report of the University of Southern California's Annenberg School (Lebo, 2008) reported that 94% of online community members said that the Internet helps them become more informed about social causes. The same research reported that 75% of online community members said they use the Internet to participate in online communities that were related to social causes, and 87% of online community members who participate in social causes said they got involved in causes that were new to them since the time they began participating in an online community.

A number of broad-based studies (e.g., Kavanaugh & Patterson, 2001; Wellman et al., 1996) suggested that social media facilitate the preexisting expression of wider social involvement. In other words, people who are predisposed to and previously have been involved in social causes will find, through their online participation in the social Web, ways to enhance and deepen this involvement. Jensen, Danziger, and Venkatesh (2007) found that social media are used for political behavior. In their study of the local community civic engagement of 1,203 U.S. residents, they discovered that political engagements are associated with online political information seeking and online political communication. They also found that there is a greater democratization of the political process online. Wellman et al. (1996) concluded, "Internet use increases participatory capital. The more people are on the Internet and the more they are involved in online organizational and political activity, the more they are involved in offline organizational and political activity" (p. 450).

There is also considerable evidence that people use social media for social capital–building activities.

> Whether the community computer network is a new kind of voluntary association or an efficient way of extending traditional associations to new audiences, network users are engaging in communication with their community members. It is this talk or social capital building among community members that builds the social networks and social trust on which community involvement and eventually quality of life thrive. (Kavanaugh & Patterson, 2001, p. 507)

Summarizing this stream of research, McKenna and Seidman (2005) suggested that "if anything, Internet use appears to be bolstering real-world community involvement" (p. 212). In itself, social media appear to bolster quality of life and consumer well-being by increasing individual participation, emotional engagement, and social ties—key elements of the important measures of happiness (Andreasen, Goldberg, & Sirgy, Chapter 2 of this volume; Diener et al., 1999; McGregor, 2010).

Writing in relation to the positive social pressures of "electronic tribes," Olaniran (2008) found that social media "group interests [can] inspire devotees to demand and seek positive change inside and outside the group" (p. 47). Yet, social media are certainly not utopia, and participation is not without its own set of risks. Two important concerns draw from the perpetuation of traditional stereotypes and the continuous coopting of corporations and their interests. Participation in social media seems to provide a sense of social support and empowerment. However, traditional stereotypes persist in online communications and might even be reinforced in them and acculturated through them. Madge and O'Connor (2006) located a paradox in which social media use was simultaneously liberating and constraining in the lives of women partaking in particular communities of practice. Exploitative business and marketing practices are also culpable. Internet forums and portals are often presented as community resources serving the needs of particular groups. Although these communities promise inclusion, support, and authenticity, they position people as consumers whose eyeballs and attention can be sold and directed, whose interests are directed to particular purchases and lifestyle choices, and whose conversations are placed under corporate monitoring and surveillance (see, e.g., Campbell, 2005).

Broader directions for the role of social media in social and political change reveal "new ways of thinking about citizenship and collaboration" in a world in which media audiences are not passive but active (Jenkins, 2006, p. 246), counterinstitutional websites enable workers to have new forms of voices and modalities of resistance (Gossett & Kilker, 2006), and "helplessly inactive" health care recipients are transformed into permanently empowered decision makers through the communal social learning of social media (Jayanti & Singh, 2010, p. 1079). Indeed, Jayanti and Singh asserted that these "consumer communities are incubators of participatory inquiry, akin to communities of practice, that act as learning catalysts for individuals who lack personal inquiry ability" (p. 1080). We thus find that, contrary to past conceptions of online communities as places of escape distanced from real-world interaction, empirical researchers of many stripes find them to be places of engagement where a variety of types of consumer empowerment are occurring.

### Three Types of Online Social Change Communities

There has thus far been little attention paid to the type of online community used to enact consumer empowerment, its defining characteristics, and its differential effects on social capital building and social change efforts. We can distinguish three major types of OSCCs, that is, online groups that use social media in order to attempt to intentionally effect social change. First is the online community related to the local community, which we might term a *locally based OSCC*. This type of community uses social media to coordinate social projects for constituents who are present at a particular local level. Kavanaugh and Patterson (2001) studied Virginia's Blacksburg Electronic Village, a city-based Internet forum that encourages civic involvement and identification, as an example of this type of local online community.

The next type of OSCC can be termed the *support-based OSCC*, which uses social media to allow those with specific informational and emotional needs—usually deriving from particular conditions or group memberships—to easily find one another, communicate, and offer social support. Although a locally based online community would draw from people within a certain geographic area, a support-based online community would not be similarly constrained and could draw from a wide or even global domain. Social media devoted to those with particular illnesses (e.g., Davison et al., 2000; McKay, Glasgow, Feil, Boles, & Barrera, 2002) or to members of stigmatized groups (e.g., McKenna & Bargh, 1998; Williams & Copes, 2005) would fall into this category. In the world of sustainability, those who are concerned about climate change—both pro and con—would also fall into this category.

Finally, there are the issue-based OSCCs, which are online communities that focus on and inform particular social issues, related ideas, and related projects pertaining to them. These communities tend to have a particular agenda that they wish to advance through the use of social media. Possible issues might be social media dedicated to discussions and actions regarding child labor, the sex slave trade, corporate greed, ecotourism, terrorism and its link to the corporate industrial complex, and the real estate industry and the preservation of natural spaces. In this camp, we must include the many organized and freelance "social marketers" who are "creating ads, videos for the Internet, and campaigns to drive awareness about issues as diverse as the dangers of smoking, the importance of family planning, and the problems associated with factory farming" (Assadourian, 2010, p. 20).

Free Range Studios and GRACE's Sustainable Table program created a wildly successful social marketing campaign in 2002. Together, the two organizations created an animated film called the *The Meatrix* (Fox & Sachs, 2003) that spoofs the popular *Matrix* movies. The film uses satire and gentle humor to follow a group of farm animals as they stage a revolution against factory farming and its ecological and social ills. The message spread virally across the Internet, has been translated into 20 languages, and has been viewed by an estimated 20 million viewers to date (interested readers can view it on YouTube or at http://www.themeatrix.com). Our next section provides numerous other examples, as we proceed to discuss sustainability-focused social media and apply our three central community type distinctions in relation to our analysis.

## SOCIAL MEDIA AND SUSTAINABILITY: NETNOGRAPHIC FINDINGS

What impact do social media have on efforts toward a sustainable society? Do social media undermine the sustainability efforts of the real world, or are they, in at least some cases, assisting or even an inextricable part of them? What role might they play in future consumer research investigations and initiatives? As we begin our investigation, it seems as if online communities have far more potential to engage people on local and other levels than many of the sustainability writers may have assumed. For additional discussion on conceptualizing and addressing sustainability issues in TCR, see McDonagh, Dobscha, and Prothero (Chapter 13 of this volume).

Sandlin (2007) has already noted and demonstrated the value of netnography for understanding and studying consumer empowerment through social media. Although the current research is still in its initial and formative stages, we have identified several social media sites for netnographic investigation. Across all of our examples, and throughout our initial investigation, we have identified some intriguing patterns that will require further research to elaborate and develop. We therefore have numerous examples of social media dedicated to issues of sustainability and green consumption. These communities seek to engender better quality of life through sustainable lifestyles and even effect social transformation. We will use the three forms of socially beneficial online communities suggested above—locally based, support based, and issue based—to discuss several types of these sustainability-oriented communities. Following are some initial findings from ongoing netnographic research regarding sustainability-oriented online communities and what they tell us about the possible role of social media in relation to sustainable consumption lifestyle initiatives.

### Locally Based Online Social Change Communities

We first consider social media that use locally based communities to foster and organize sustainability initiatives that seek political change, facilitate communal relations, and inform local members about important environmental issues. Consider, as an initial site, the Baltimore Environment Meetup Group, which uses the Meetup online community site to arrange its meetings. The group is located in the Baltimore area and focused on people who care about sustainability. The group has two different sorts of meetings, or, to emphasize their informality and less structured nature, meet-ups. First are discussion meetings that feature a 30-minute presentation on an environmental or sustainability-related topic, followed by questions, discussions, and networking activities for the affiliated Baltimore Climate Action Network (BCAN), an action-oriented advocacy group. The other type of meet-up is a small group get-together, where people meet to sign up new supporters for BCAN at a farmer's market or a festival. As well, there are associated BCAN meetings and executive meetings.

The goals of this online community are to facilitate the creation of a community, mutual support, networking within the community, education about green lifestyles, and advocacy activities in which they seek to engage politicians locally and on a wider scale. BCAN is local to the Baltimore City and Baltimore County areas, seeks to organize people online for in-person meetings, and is concerned with local engagement, socialization, education, and political activity. There are many such groups spread over the Internet—on forums, using group sites such as Google and Yahoo! Groups, using mailing lists, or using social networking sites. These online communities are very similar to the locally based online communities discussed above, in that they attempt to achieve social betterment through organizing local actions (see, e.g., Kavanaugh & Patterson, 2001).

We find that a particularly salient effect of these locally based OSCCs is the fostering of other, more traditional, more conservative sorts of communities. In particular, the key seems to be in terms of increasing connections (what social network analysts would term an enhancement of both strong and weak ties), which is conceptually important and links into the extensive midsection of this chapter, where we examined the many theoretical interconnections of community and sustainability.

Although a number of authors (e.g., Ehrenfeld, 2009; Putnam, 2000) have decried the corrosive effects of online community on in-person community, our research suggests, instead, that the two can be quite closely linked. Not all social media are transformative, but at least some social media can be. The evidence is that it is used as a useful organizing and recruitment tool for local groups such as the Baltimore Environment Meetup Group and BCAN. Social media enable community members to stay in touch with one another, plan, and exchange information when they are not in physical contact. Relatedly, groups such as the Yarrow EcoVillage, an ecovillage located in Yarrow, British Columbia, use local webpages to inform the world about their local project; gain interest and support; solicit donations; and exchange ideas with, organize with, and inspire other similar projects worldwide (see http://www.yarrowecovillage.ca/ecovillage/).

These sites seem to be directly related to the type of local community organizing that Assadourian (2008) and Ehrenfeld (2009) have valorized. The sites indicate a tighter coupling of online and physically embodied behaviors than many prior theorists envisioned. We are apparently reaching the point "at which we need to reference, study, and understand the data in online communities and cultures" (Kozinets, 2010, pp. 66–67)—as well as its interrelationship with embodied phenomena—in order to effectively and meaningfully study a vast range of social phenomena (see also Garcia, Standless, Bechkoff, & Cui, 2009).

## Support-Based Online Social Change Communities

Next, we consider social media that use support-based communities to educate, motivate, entertain, and offer other resources to those interested in ecologically sustainable lifestyles, such as ecovillages, city farming, and community-supported agriculture and permaculture. Whereas the abovementioned support-based online communities tended to offer support to those with illnesses and stigmatic social situations, we find a range of online communities dedicated to supporting particular ideological types or flavors of sustainable lifestyles or communities. For example, consider the relationship between the permaculture lifestyle and the many online resources dedicated to permaculture. Permaculture is a portmanteau combining *permanent* and *agriculture* and also signifying permanent culture. It is an approach to human lifestyles, settlements, and agricultural systems that seeks to emulate natural ecological relationships (Mollison & Holmgren, 1978). At least partly due to its popularity and accessibility on Internet forums, webpages, blogs, and discussion groups, permaculture has become an influential international movement within the wider sustainability movement.

There are a range of different webpages and blogs that bring to life the permaculture lifestyle. On the Trailer Park Girl: Permaculture and Simple Living in Style blog, we learn, in many ways and through various examples, about what permaculture might mean for our daily lives as a consumer. Here is a quote from Austin, Texas–based "dragonfly jenny" (2009), titled "Pssst! You Don't Need to Buy Shampoo Anymore! Pass It On!":

> I haven't used any shampoo for TWO YEARS. That's right, two years. Two woman-years' worth of plastic shampoo and conditioner bottles kept from the waste-stream. Two woman-years' worth of smelly mysterious chemicals (that ads and marketing departments convince us are a necessary and sufficient condition for "clean") kept from my hair, from the water-treatment system, and from the land. The secret lies in plain ol' baking soda and vinegar. Wash with baking soda, and follow with a cider-vinegar rinse as needed. This article at http://www.instructables.com tells you how. (paras. 1–2)

The Punk Rock Permaculture e-zine blog is managed by "Evan" (n.d.), a 24-year-old resident of Olympia, Washington, who has "a passionate love for permaculture, street art, guerrilla gardening, cooking veggie food, folk punk, harmonica wailin', and riding bikes with friends" (para. 5). His intention for the blog

> is that it will act as [a] link between the personal and communal showcasing examples of all the beneficial work being done for the earth around the world. This is a[n] e-zine about a regenerative culture full of resistance and inspiring creativity. (para. 7)

Finally, the vast PRI's Permaculture Forum website (forums.permaculture.org.au) offers an impressive wealth of discussion, teaching, and information about the permaculture philosophy, lifestyle, and practices. Available to anyone, the forums offer voluminous support for those who are interested in sustainable agriculture on a moderate or small scale. There are over 25,000 posts informing the interested permaculture prosumer (i.e., progressive consumer) about which plants, vegetables, trees, livestock, and aquaculture to cultivate, as well as the elements of composting, food preparation, and storage. Want to design or build your own permaculturally sensitive home, chicken coop, fence, dam, electricity system, watering system, toilet, or gray water filtration system? The answers are on the permaculture forum, as they are for those interested in the lifestyle, permaculture businesses or consultancy, permaculture group in-person meetings and advocacy, or debating politics, energy, conservation, oil, natural resources, genetically modified crops, or spirituality. This community supports, encourages, and—perhaps most importantly—links to an edgy urban lifestyle and identity project, consumption practices associated with permaculture.

These notions of identity, segments, and appropriate conversations are important. In these support-based OSCCs, we found an interesting communal customization phenomenon occurring in the diverse space of the Internet. There were many different types of consumers populating these online communities, coming from many different places geographically, politically, and ideologically. We saw many students, businesspeople and entrepreneurs, and busy parents coexisting with environmental activists. We saw consumers who self-identified as greens or green-spirited members of LOHAS (lifestyles of health and sustainability) and voluntary simplicity followers. The membership thus extended far beyond the alternative milieu of the econiche.

Through the listening and learning orientation of the support-based community, we observed how the community formations took large-scale social issues like sustainability and environmental consumption and chunked them down into bite-sized pieces that are then subject to processes of communal reflection, individuation, and individualization. The process seems related to Williams and Copes's (2005) suggestion that fragmented, postmodern identity weakens commitment, but that social media could mediate between mass media and face-to-face subcultural interaction, facilitating "subcultural diffusion via nomadic Internet users who share subcultural values and feel a part of a virtual community" (p. 86). Social media, in this case, are reformulated by people into a response to the alienation and distance of traditional mass media.

As an alternative to mass media, we find social media fashioned into a lifestyle-related type of ideological commitment. The commitments are often polarized and polarizing and can be superficial and short-lived. Often, they are simplified and oversimplified, and within those commitments exist a range of choices—an ideological supermarket of sustainability options. Yet, as Kozinets et al. (2010) demonstrated in relation to word-of-mouth marketing and its communal-commercial tensions, the communal form is part of a differentiation process that allows consumers to choose how they will address these social issues and how they will alter them for their own needs.

Issue-Based Online Social Change Communities

In this last subsection on netnographic findings, we consider social media that use issue-based communities to inform and focus discussion on particular approaches to sustainability or other environmentally related issues. Finally, there is a range of different online communities dedicated to various aspects of sustainability. Large nonprofits, such as the World Wildlife Fund (WWF) and Greenpeace, offer their own informational websites and give people opportunities for largely one-way communications, such as subscribing to newsletters that are focused on each organization's particular range of issues. There are numerous online resources available for consumers interested in sustainable, environmental, and green consumption issues (Shrode, 2009), and many, if not most, now have a social media component. Kutner (2000) found the Internet to be important to the furtherance of grassroots environmental activism. Likewise, Kim (2006) found the facilitation of consumers' participatory online deliberation about significant public matters to be important to the democratic political process.

For example, as part of their ongoing experiment with social media, the WWF uses Facebook to offer a webpage where people can become fans of the organization. Upon joining as a fan, members see regular postings from the WWF, including such matters as buying WWF gift cards, donating to the WWF through eBay purchases, subscribing to the WWF's Twitter feed, illegal wildlife trafficking, a campaign to call state senators about global climate change, and voting on your favorite great ape. Comments on the stories are usually pithy, but they contain considerable emotion. For example, the 54 comments on the story about illegal trafficking in wildlife-related products contained many expressions of disgust and anger, including ones that did not consider people who did such things to be human and that called out to stop the killing, and ones that compared smugglers to murderers and drug dealers, shared related links, and discussed demand-side solutions to the problem.

A dedicated community that focuses on sustainable consumption within the contemporary capitalist economy is the German online Utopia community (http://utopia.de), which was founded in 2006. Utopia—a term apparently used in the community without the irony that it carries in English-speaking countries—claims to be a change agent and a motor of transformation toward sustainability. It seeks positive change by means of fostering and describing a strategic consumption lifestyle that is characterized by reflective and responsible consumption. This community explores questions of consuming less (reflection) as well as questions of consuming differently (responsibility) by considering ecological and social criteria in the consumption process.

Unlike permaculture or ecovillages, Utopia seeks a more incremental change, working within the current capitalist system, but holding that consuming the correct brands and types of products and services can lead to an improved world. This consumption-centric philosophy toward social improvement is apparent in Utopia's slogan: "Shop and treat yourself, but do it in the right way!" (translation by the authors). In its friendly consumption, business, and marketing online environment, Utopia seeks to sensitize consumers and citizens about consumption-related sustainability issues, inform consumers about sustainable products and services, connect consumers with other consumers, bring change makers together, and provide space for companies and partners.

Utopia follows a cooperative, instead of a confrontational, approach toward corporations:

> Utopia sees itself as bridge-builder between industry and the sustainable needs and wants of consumers. Companies have to learn that it is right and important to take an active approach towards sustainability. That is why we need the support of companies, which are credible and which have already started implementing sustainability into their core business. (Utopia, 2010, translation by the authors)

With more than 45,000 registered users (93% from Germany), Utopia is one of the world's largest online communities of sustainable consumption and the most influential in German-speaking countries.

The overriding finding we discovered in these locations is that social media are important conceptual locations where consumers focus their awareness and attention together on particular options. The area of green and sustainable consumption is complex and linked to a modern carnivalesque panoply of hucksters and (organic!) snake oil salespeople. In instance after instance, we saw online community communications telling members where to focus their attention to have the most meaningful effect. For some, the emphasis was on growing one's own food. For others, it was eating organic, eating family farm–produced food, avoiding automobile ownership, cohousing, or installing wind power in your backyard. Some communities debated scientific evidence that housing and living, eating and drinking, and mobility and energy consumption were key areas that should be attended to, rather than other areas, such as recycling, that were considered extraneous. The online community therefore provided a place where a complex social issue could be boiled down to its most important constituent elements and then "baked in" to the elements of a reasonable, and reasonably viable, lifestyle. Much of the advice seems targeted to answer this sort of modern plea for consumption advice: "Tell me the three things I need to know about what I am buying and two relatively easy things I can do or buy to help." In the next and final section of this chapter, we discuss some of the general understandings we can gain from social media dedicated to sustainability and explore some of their implications for the conduct of TCR.

## SOCIAL MEDIA, SUSTAINABILITY, AND TRANSFORMATIVE CONSUMER RESEARCH

### The Social Roles of Social Media

Can social media be used to foster individual and social change resulting in improvements in long-term increases in people's well-being around the world? Is there sufficient social capital present in social media to constitute a sustainable community movement? Can the combined glare of these illuminated monitors shed sufficient light, if not heat, to effect genuine social change? Can consumer research play a role? We return to these questions with a heightened realization of the role that social media play in engaging and empowering choice, dialogue, and civic engagement. In consumer research on online peer-to-peer problem-solving, Mathwick, Wiertz, and de Ruyter (2008) stated that they "find evidence of an idealized community, led by a noble cadre of wikis who are governed by a culture of voluntarism, trust, and reciprocity as they come to the aid of floundering newbies" (p. 847). In this study, we find many different uses of social media, from ecovillages asking for significant commitment, lifestyle change, and considerable local presence, to widespread, commercially involved offerings that favor consumers shopping their way to a more sustainable lifestyle.

On a macrosocial scale, social media provide a dramatic new source of grassroots information, communal awareness, and personal motivation. We found social media playing a range of important roles related to consumer well-being and quality of life. First, social media narrow consumers' options and thus can make choice simpler. Social issues are complex and multifaceted. Social media, with their wide dispersion and permanent records of conversations, can (in some circumstances) help narrow options and focus choices (e.g., "Forget about recycling and focus on your carbon emissions," "Forget about your auto use and focus on your air travel"). These sorts of consumption heuristics attempted to distill complex scientific information into simple buyer behavior guidelines. By allowing busy, stretched consumers to focus on a limited set of issues, and offering narrowed choices within those sets, social media can leverage consumption decisions for lifestyle change (see also Mick & Schwartz, Chapter 32 of this volume).

Second, social media empower connective options and thus can promote relationship formation. Where social organizers once had to rely on door knocking, placard-carrying protests, and pamphleteering, today's agents of social change can tweet their rallying cries and link up with their cadre of fellow visionaries and resisters. They find each other through Google searches, and the level of commitment to sign a petition has moved to a keystroke or mouse click. Consumers also have the option to turn online connection into in-person action, and face-to-face gathering into ongoing, online connection. The German Utopia website organizes an annual "utopia conference" that brings together key change makers from economics, politics, society, culture, media, and science and features awards given to personalities, corporations, organizations, ideas, products, and services that make a difference in the pursuit of sustainability.

Third, the vast variety of related but different social media fosters communal customization and thus can provide information and skills that are more relevant to particular social mediums' audiences. Where once we focused on individual variegation, we now can increasingly turn our attention to the multitudinous variety of communal forms. There are common patterns in the overall participation in a sustainability movement. However, there are many different movements within this larger movement, and many alternative approaches. Online, consumers are offered an almost dizzying array of ways to address sustainability. Children, teens, businesswomen, male models, lawyers, rappers, Americans, Japanese, combinations of these categories, and other groups all have their own spins on sustainability. Apparently, and perhaps arguably, this level of choice and customization is positive for consumers as well as for social movements themselves—which, it must be added, have to be engaging and multifaceted enough to sponsor this sort of variegation and communal mutation (see also Mick et al., Chapter 1 of this volume).

Finally, and perhaps most importantly, social media's democratization of participation enables more uniform engagement in social change. Jensen et al. (2007) found that civic engagement widened online and allowed people from outside the traditional socioeconomic categories to participate more fully in their local governments and political processes. So too does the social Web allow a more even participation in discussions and debates about sustainability. However, democratization of these ideas and options is also a double-edged sword, as there are major communities of climate change debate active on the Internet, with highly intelligent and influential individuals seeking to influence people's beliefs and decisions about the reality or unreality of climate change. On the social Web, we have 14-year-olds denying and rewriting Wikipedia entries about species devastation, and right-wing ideologues propounding links between fabricated ozone hole photos and government conspiracies. Opening the discussions about sustainability does not mean that people will necessarily "color within the lines" and simply discuss how best they can change their lives to accommodate a lower carbon emissions guideline. On the contrary, through social media, we see enormous and sophisticated push-back from a large and impressively organized variety of dissenters and resisters.

## Social Media and the Empowered Consumer

After our investigation into the socially mediated world of sustainability, we find our initial notions of consumer and societal well-being even more intertwined. Because consumption is a part of society and a part of culture, when the society is nonsustainable, the consumption culture it encourages is nonsustainable. However, sustainable consumption values, beliefs, and practices by consumers and communities begin to manifest a more sustainable society. These values and beliefs, such as "biking is better" or "factory farming is wrong"—or even "climate change is a big, fat lie"—can be spread quite easily through social media. In the consumer education framework in which we work, consumer empowerment is therefore one of the key elements that enables a bridging from unsustainable to sustainable consumer culture (see also Mick et al., Chapter 1 of this volume).

We equate consumer empowerment with the following six characteristics: (1) presence of choices, (2) ability to participate, (3) provision of adequate information, (4) inculcation of positive attitudes, (5) possession of relevant skills, and (6) development of knowledge. Inspired by Wells (1997) and Wells and Atherton (1998), this framework extends the conventional approach to consumer empowerment by adding a focus on responsible consumer citizenship. We can then proceed to outline the role that social media and online community play in consumer empowerment.

In important conceptual groundwork, Jennifer Sandlin (2007) followed adult educators and curriculum theorists by theoretically treating online community resources and gatherings as "sites of informal consumer education" (p. 288). That is, along with other forms of popular culture, and perhaps even more intensely because of its interactive communal qualities, social media act as "a form of informal consumer education that defines what it means to be a citizen and a consumer" (Sandlin, 2007, p. 288). Social media also, we would argue, educate about appropriate and inappropriate consumption beliefs, practices, and alternatives (see, e.g., Bers & Chau, 2006).

Social media thus offer a powerful way for consumers to educate each other about sustainable options, assert their power to choose those options as democratic citizens in a capitalist global economy, and organize as concerned citizens and consumers. Social media enable consumers to share information with other consumers about consumption options that they may not previously have realized were available. Social media can enable an authentic civic exchange and levels of democratic deliberation about how the urgent individual and collective trade-offs required for a sustainable consumption lifestyle can and will occur (see, e.g., McGregor, 2010). Through Facebook, blogs, and Twitter, consumers can and already do encourage positive attitudes and values about sustainability and sustainable consumption. They can teach skills and build a base of knowledge. They can empower each other to make sustainability choices they previously were hesitant or unable to make. Finally, social media offer a unique new forum for participation in discussion and action that can affect the global economy and society worldwide.

### Social Media Research and the Empowered Transformative Consumer Researcher

To close this chapter, let us return to the vital question of the role of the researcher. All along, we have been asking about the role of social media to foster individual and social change. We have been asking about the consumer researcher's role. At this point, aware of the social media's possibilities for empowerment, we can return to those questions.

Rutgers University biology professor David Ehrenfeld (2009) is sweeping and damning in his critique of the role of academics in the university system in our current ecological situation. During his years as a board member of a grant-giving institution, he was "struck by the extreme scarcity of exciting, innovative, useful proposals coming out of the major research universities" (p. 223). Among the major problems he listed that universities are doing little or nothing to address either in research or in teaching are "the deterioration of human communities," materialism, the commercialization of former communal functions, and "the turning away from environmental and human realities in favor of thin, life-sucking electronic substitutes" (p. 223). He stated that universities are "increasingly allying themselves with the commercial forces that are causing them [ecological problems]. The institutions that are supposed to be generating the ideas that nurture and sustain society have abandoned this function in their quest for cash" (p. 223).

Where, in Ehrenfeld's comments, do we locate ourselves? Transformative consumer researchers are positioned unmistakably at the crux of these issues, between the rock of hard science and the hard(-nosed) place of business, often contained in the marketing departments of business schools, concerned with the sociocultural context of issues where corporations meet communities and traditions bump up against technological change. Social media, too, meet in the middle of these issues; they are commercial but also communal (Kozinets et al., 2010), technological but also social, human but also machine.

There is some sense in Ehrenfeld's comments. The majority of marketing and consumer academics are, indeed, situated within business schools, but the blame is not with some abstract set of commercial forces that the universities and, presumably, especially the business schools are allied with (as if we now need to choose sides, and already have done so, for the cash). No, the problem lies much deeper than this. In a system, as our culture and our society are, all the parts are interconnected. There is no outside from which to act, and there are no simply dichotomized sides to choose. There is only change from within the system. There are only parts that change a part of their operation and thereby affect other parts of the system.

For our part, universities seem to be reacting to the need for grounded, local change in the sustainable direction by remaining abstract, disconnected, and identified with a certain kind of rationality. William Rees (2003) suggested that, to promote global sustainability on a finite planet, education "should be oriented toward the life-sustaining values needed to create a society founded on mutual respect, spiritual fulfillment, a cultivated compassion for all others and a sense of participating consciousness with nature," but instead, we have a "cold, hard, alienating enlightenment rationality" (p. 95). Our research and its institutions seem disconnected and disconnecting from the natural world and the ecological crises inflicted on it by our species as well as our economy and its growth imperatives.

Business faculties are increasingly becoming less silo based in their perspectives, though, as interdisciplinary projects focus on sustainability. Consumer researchers straddle both perspectives and, as reflexive educators, are in a surprisingly unique position to bring understanding to many of these issues by questioning widespread assumptions and overturning the occasional sacred academic cow. Going through our references, our colleagues' work, our current research and teaching, the chapters of this wonderful volume, and the courses at our schools (one of which placed first in Aspen Institute's 2009–2010 Beyond Grey Pinstripes ranking of MBA programs that integrate social and environmental stewardship into the curriculum), Ehrenfeld's comments cannot help but strike us as a bit outdated and out of touch.

Are social media truly a "turning away" from human reality? Are they "thin, life-sucking electronic substitutes"? The empirical research in this chapter provides a clear answer. On the contrary, engagement with social media is empowerment, and we believe that Ehrenfeld's underlying message is actually one that urges academics to be more engaged with society, with pressing social issues, and with the empowerment of consumers—citizens—with real solutions. That message should include any effective tools at our disposal, including social media.

The online and physical environment of the university itself offers massive potential for building various forms of local community focused on the values and practices of sustainability as well as illustrating and leading best practices for sustainable consumption. This potential is all too rarely realized. Consider first what we can do in our classrooms. At the business school, a marketing professor might deliver a lecture on the need for more innovative cars that have lower carbon dioxide emissions, then take a big limousine to the airport for a flight to a conference about green marketing. Students see this. Perhaps they even tweet it. Downstairs, the business school's cafeteria serves deep-fried shrimp and French fries (both from a thousand miles away), along with plastic forks and paper plates. In the marketing department, a researcher presents a talk about consumers' menu choices, health, and obesity, and a colleague across the university develops new biodegradable materials. David Orr (1992) suggested that contemporary university students learn a lesson about hypocrisy: "They hear that the vital signs of the planet are in decline without learning to question the de facto energy, food, materials and waste policies of the very institution that presumes to induct them into responsible adulthood" (p. 104). Perhaps social media will encourage them to raise those questions, share them, and demand some answers.

Social media help us pull back the curtain on what we say and what we do. Websites like RateMyProfessors (http://ratemyprofessors.com) already allow students to criticize their professors' teaching styles, manners, and grading (and of course, also rate them as hot or not). As professors, we can provide our students with new social media tools (almost every university provides access to bulletin board systems for its students) as well as encourage them to use existing social media (e.g., Facebook, Twitter, Wikipedia, LinkedIn, YouTube).

We can build these elements into our pedagogy. In a course on consumer behavior, we can have students inquire about what it means to be a green consumer and ask them to create a videography of their findings, as Professor Gary Bamossy does at Georgetown University. We can have new product development students envision sustainable new products (e.g., price a new ecohome; socially market tap water rather than bottled water; debate an ecological book while role-playing hard-nosed, profit-oriented brand managers). We can then have students share their insights—via videos, papers, PowerPoint presentations, class podcasts, book reviews, and so on—with the world through blogs, YouTube postings, and SlideShare. Using social media in the classroom in this way does two important things. First, it encourages students to actually think about and participate in discussions of sustainability, integrating and accessing those ideas in a serious, rather than perfunctory, way in the context of a business education. Second, it opens the discussion to the wider public, shares the insights of students, and in so doing makes them more relevant, ambitious, and alive.

Next, consider our schools themselves. Students and faculty can and should, separately and together, critique and debate the school's social and environmental policies. Is the school ecologically built? Is there green space? Is the school offering adequate non–factory-farmed menu choices? Can one practice an earth-friendly or vegan diet relatively easily? Are organic options available? Is the food locally sourced? Are genetically modified foods on the menu? Is information provided about the food? Are fairly traded foods on the menu? Are there courses that emphasize social and environmental awareness? Are foods from enterprising new firms that feature new environmental innovations available? Are practical partnerships with sustainability-oriented businesses available and pursued? Is the business of business really changing, and are business schools ready to lead, or at least closely follow, that charge? Are business schools a part of the sustainability problem or a part of the solution?

Academics can publicly ask these questions and share the answers that they get. Bloggers often raise customer service issues with companies in their social media posts, which often contain entertainingly and annoyingly familiar bureaucratic responses. The same can be done as we raise questions about the sustainability policies of our own school. Social media are a key tool in prompting, recording, spreading, and organizing this information. If it is done in aggregate and in public, with all of us asking similar questions and comparing our answers in the public sphere, then it may have considerably more impact and power. It may even attract some attention from the press and business school deans (and, yes, we hope you read Mick et al.'s introduction to this volume, in which they equated TCR with "tremendously courageous research").

To paraphrase Mahatma Gandhi, if we want social change, we need to be the change we want to see. Yet again, social media can play a vital part in this process. We firmly believe that what we research, what we write, what we teach, and what we say to our interested public constituents are crucial at this point in our development as a civilization. Social media have a part to play in all of these elements of our own academic practices. Not everyone is going to want to investigate social media and the online communities that thrive and swarm in them. Not every transformative consumer researcher needs or should even be interested in pursuing netnography as a vehicle to understanding consumer empowerment (e.g., Sandlin, 2007).

However, using social media to understand our research topics and gain research insights about important areas of need in the world and about the potential public response to our research can be an extremely important use of the media. If we are researching obesity through behavioral decision theory experiments, our insights into the problem might be enhanced by reading blogs by fat acceptance groups or by looking at social media forums where diet ideas and opinions are shared. If we are modeling online coupon redemption, we might dedicate 30 minutes once a month to looking at the online communities where couponing advice and electronic coupons are being shared. If we are pursuing an ethnography of Chinese nouveau-riche luxury consumption, we might consider posting some initial findings on a webpage related to your topic, hyperlinking that page to some social media posts, and inviting member feedback to let you know what they think about your research, its accuracy, and its importance. If we are conducting participatory action research (Ozanne & Saatcioglu, 2008), then we should use social media to find the community sites we will be working with, stay in touch with them, and communicate our work and our results to other sites where it can be of assistance.

Social media do not just empower the consumers of gasoline, electric lawn mowers, sugary breakfast cereals, and coal-fired energy. They empower academics and all of their constituents. The great critical theorist Antonio Gramsci termed a participative, communicative form of academic as the *organic intellectual*. Perhaps social media encourage not just our bread and cheese purchases to be organic but also our intellectual aspirations.

Social media encourage us not only to get the word up, to journals, conferences, and other academics, but also to get our words out. If we seek to be a positive force for change in the world, we can use social media in ways that we begin to elaborate in this book chapter: to inform, consolidate choices, build relationships, help customize to individual needs, and democratize. We can use social media to learn more about the consumer, corporate, and governmental constituents we seek to assist, transform, and influence positively. Social media enable us to be both better listeners and more effective broadcasters. Through their influence, we can connect our research communities and our academic lives more effectively with each other and the world in a truly transformative way.

So, TCR community, blog, tweet, link, and post. Bloggers are denying climate change, twisting science, and building vast unfounded theories of their own. Online communities are debating the value of green marketing, the necessity of sustainable practices, and the usefulness of university professors. The conversations are out there, in social media space, influencing hundreds of millions of minds. The discussions are happening. The bigger question is, Are we involved in them?

## REFERENCES

Assadourian, E. (2008). Engaging communities for a sustainable world. In G. T. Gardner, T. Prugh, & L. Starke (Eds.), *State of the world 2008: Innovations for a sustainable economy* (25th anniversary ed., pp. 151–165). Washington, DC: W.W. Norton.

Assadourian, E. (2010). The rise and fall of consumer cultures. In E. Assadourian, L. Starke, & L. Mastny (Eds.), *State of the world 2010: Transforming cultures from consumerism to sustainability* (pp. 3–20). Washington, DC: W.W. Norton.

Bers, M. U., & Chau, C. (2006). Fostering civic engagement by building a virtual city. *Journal of Computer-Mediated Communication, 11*(3), 748–770.

Brogan, C., & Smith, J. (2009). *Trust agents: Using the web to build influence, improve reputation, and earn trust.* Hoboken, NJ: Wiley.

Campbell, J. E. (2005). Outing PlanetOut: Surveillance, the marketing and Internet affinity portals. *New Media & Society, 7*(5), 663–683.

Clerc, S. J. (1996). DDEB, GATB, MPPB, and Ratboy: *The X-Files'* media fandom, online and off. In D. Lavery, A. Hague, & M. Cartwright (Eds.), *Deny all knowledge: Reading* The X-Files (pp. 36–51). Syracuse, NY: Syracuse University Press.

Davison, K. P., Pennebaker, J. W., & Dickerson, S. S. (2000). Who talks? The social psychology of illness support groups. *American Psychologist, 55*, 205–217.

Diener, E., Suh, E. M., Lucas, R. E., & Smith, H. L. (1999). Subjective well-being: Three decades of progress. *Psychological Bulletin, 125*(2), 276–302.

dragonfly jenny. (2009, September 2). Pssst! You don't need to buy shampoo anymore! Pass it on! [Weblog]. *Trailer Park Girl: Permaculture and Simple Living in Style.* Retrieved October 18, 2010, from http://www.jennynazak.com/?p=194

Ehrenfeld, D. (2009). *Becoming good ancestors: How we balance nature, community, and technology.* New York: Oxford University Press.

Evan. (n.d.). About Punk Rock Permaculture e-zine. *Punk Rock Permaculture e-zine* [Weblog]. Retrieved October 18, 2010, from http://punkrockpermaculture.com/about

Fox, L. (Writer/Director), & Sachs, J. (Writer). (2003). *The meatrix* [Short flash animation]. United States: Free Range Graphics.

Garcia, A. C., Standless, A. I., Bechkoff, J., & Cui, Y. (2009). Ethnographic approaches to the Internet and computer-mediated communication. *Journal of Contemporary Ethnography, 38*(1), 52–84.

Gossett, L. M., & Kilker, J. (2006). My job sucks: Examining counterinstitutional websites as locations for organizational member voice, dissent, and resistance. *Management Communication Quarterly, 20*(1), 63–90.

Hemetsberger, A., & Reinhardt, C. (2006). Learning and knowledge-building in open-source communities: A social-experiential approach. *Management Learning, 37*(2), 187–214.

Jaffe, J. (2007). *Join the conversation: How to engage marketing-weary consumers with the power of community.* Hoboken, NJ: Wiley.

Jayanti, R. K., & Singh, J. (2010). Pragmatic learning theory: An inquiry-action framework for distributed consumer learning in online communities. *Journal of Consumer Research, 36*(April), 1058–1081.

Jenkins, H. (2006). *Convergence culture.* New York: New York University Press.

Jensen, M. J., Danziger, J. N., & Venkatesh, A. (2007). Civil society and cyber society: The role of the Internet in community associations and democratic politics. *The Information Society, 23*(December), 39–50.

Joel, M. (2009). *Six pixels of separation: Everyone is connected. Connect your business to everyone.* New York: Business Plus.

Kavanaugh A., & Patterson, S. (2001). The impact of community computer networks on social capital and community involvement. *American Behavioral Scientist, 45*, 496–509.

Kim, J. (2006). The impact of Internet use patterns on political engagement: A focus on online deliberation and virtual social capital. *Information Polity, 11*, 35–49.

Kozinets, R. V. (1999). E-tribalized marketing? The strategic implications of virtual communities of consumption. *European Management Journal, 17*(3), 252–264.

Kozinets, R. V. (2002). Can consumers escape the market? Emancipatory illuminations from Burning Man. *Journal of Consumer Research, 29*(June), 20–38.

Kozinets, R. V. (2010). *Netnography*. London: Sage.

Kozinets, R. V., de Valck, K., Wojnicki, A., & Wilner. S. (2010). Networked narratives: Understanding word-of-mouth marketing in online communities. *Journal of Marketing, 74*(March), 71–89.

Kozinets, R. V., & Handelman, J. M. (1998). Ensouling consumption: A netnographic exploration of the meaning of boycotting behavior. In J. Alba & W. Hutchinson (Eds.), *Advances in consumer research* (Vol. 25, pp. 475–480). Provo, UT: Association for Consumer Research.

Kozinets, R. V., & Handelman, J. M. (2004). Adversaries of consumption: Consumer movements, activism, and ideology. *Journal of Consumer Research, 31*(December), 691–704.

Kutner, L. A. (2000). Environmental activism and the Internet. *Electronic Green Journal, 1*(12). Retrieved October 18, 2010, from escholarship.org/uc/item/5vg787tz

Lebo, H. (Ed.). (2008). *The 2008 digital future report: Surveying the digital future, year seven*. Los Angeles: Figueroa Press.

Levine, R., Locke, C., Searls, D., & Weinberger, D. (2000). *The cluetrain manifesto: The end of business as usual*. New York: Perseus.

Li, C., & Bernoff, J. (2008). *Groundswell: Winning in a world transformed by social technologies*. Boston: Harvard Business School Press.

Madge, C., & O'Connor, H. (2006). Parenting gone wired: Empowerment of new mothers on the Internet? *Social & Cultural Geography, 7*(2), 199–220.

Mathwick, C., Wiertz, C., & de Ruyter, K. (2008). Social capital production in a virtual P3 community. *Journal of Consumer Research, 34*(6), 832–849.

McGregor, S. (2010). *Consumer education as a site of political resistance: 50 years of conceptual evolutions* (McGregor Monograph No. 201001). Seabright, NS, Canada: McGregor Consulting Group. Retrieved October 18, 2010, from http://www.consultmcgregor.com/publications.php?cid=6#16

McGregor, S. L. T., & Goldsmith, E. B. (1998). Expanding our understanding of quality of life, standard of living, and well-being. *Journal of Family & Consumer Sciences, 90*(2), 2–6.

McKay, H. G., Glasgow, R. E., Feil, E. G., Boles, S. M., & Barrera, M. (2002). Internet-based diabetes self-management and support initial outcomes from the diabetes network project. *Rehabilitation Psychology, 47*, 31–48.

McKenna, K. Y. A., & J. Bargh, J. A. (1998). Coming out in the age of the Internet: Identity demarginalization through virtual group participation. *Journal of Personality and Social Psychology, 75*, 681–694.

McKenna, K., & Seidman, G. (2005). You, me, and we: Interpersonal processes in electronic groups. In Y. Amichai-Hamburger (Ed.), *The social map: Human behavior in cyberspace* (pp. 191–218). New York: Oxford University Press.

McKibben, B. (2007). *Deep economy*. New York: Henry Holt.

Meadows, D. H., Randers, J., & Meadows, D. L. (2004). *Limits to growth: The 30-year update*. White River Junctions, VT: Chelsea Green.

Mollison, B., & Holmgren, D. (1978). *Permaculture one*. Sydney, Australia: Transworld.

Olaniran, B. (2008). Electronic tribes (e-tribes): Some theoretical perspectives and implications. In T. L. Adams & S. A. Smith (Eds.), *Electronic tribes* (pp. 36–57). Austin: University of Texas Press.

Orr, D. (1992). *Ecological literacy*. Albany: State University of New York Press.

Ozanne, J. L., & Saatcioglu, B. (2008). Participatory action research. *Journal of Consumer Research, 35*(October), 423–439.

Putnam, R. D. (2000). *Bowling alone: The collapse and revival of American community*. New York: Simon & Schuster.

Qualman, E. (2009). *Socialnomics: How social media transforms the way we live and do business*. Hoboken, NJ: Wiley.

Rees, M. J. (2004). *Our final hour*. New York: Basic Books.

Rees, W. (2003). Impeding sustainability? The ecological footprint of higher education. *Planning for Higher Education, 31*(March–May), 95.

Sandlin, J. (2007). Netnography as a consumer education research tool. *International Journal of Consumer Studies, 31*(3), 288–294.

Schau, H. J., & Gilly, M. C. (2003). We are what we post? The presentation of self in personal webspace. *Journal of Consumer Research, 30*(December), 385–404.

Shirky, C. (2008). *Here comes everybody: The power of organizing without organizations.* New York: Penguin.

Shrode, F. (2009). Environmental information sources: Web sites and books. *Electronic Green Journal, 1*(28). Retrieved October 18, 2010, from http://escholarship.org/uc/item/5sm0v2ns

Tainter, J. (1988). *The collapse of complex societies.* New York: Cambridge University Press.

Utopia. (2010). Retreived October 15, 2010, from http://www.utopia.de

Weinberg, T. (2009). *The new community rules: Marketing on the social web.* Sebastopol, CA: O'Reilly.

Wellman, B. Haase, A., Witte, J., & Hampton, K. (2001). Does the Internet increase, decrease, or supplement social capital? Social networks, participation, and community commitment. *American Behavioral Scientist, 45*(3), 436–455.

Wells, J. (1997). *Towards 2000: Consumer education in the classroom.* London: Forbes.

Wells, J., & Atherton, M. (1998, Autumn). Consumer education: Learning for life. *Consumer 21*, pp. 15–20.

Williams, J. P. & Copes, H. (2005). How edge are you? Constructing authentic identities and subcultural boundaries in a straightedge Internet forum. *Symbolic Interaction, 28*(1), 67–89.

# 11

## Quality of Virtual Life

Thomas P. Novak

Current virtual worlds, such as Second Life, The Sims Online, HiPiHi, and There, are visually rich, three-dimensional platforms for social and economic interaction that offer their users the ability to literally live virtual lives. In 2010, at any given point in time, upwards of 70,000 users can be found in avatar form (i.e., as a digital alter ego that provides a virtual representation of the user) inhabiting Second Life, while its counterpart, HiPiHi, has been touted as the vanguard of a vast Chinese project to construct a network of virtual worlds capable of supporting billions of avatars (Keegan, 2007). Driven in part by "a whole generation of children ... growing up on Club Penguin and Webkinz" (Anderson & Rainie, 2008, p. 88), over half of Internet industry experts interviewed by the Pew Internet & American Life Project agreed that by the year 2020, "most well-equipped Internet users will spend some part of their waking hours—at work and at play—at least partially linked to augmentations of the real world or alternate worlds" (Anderson & Rainie, 2008, p. 5). Within these complex immersive environments, the idea of virtual lives that are either complements or substitutes for one's real-world life is already a day-to-day reality for many virtual-world users.

Given that increasing numbers of people are living at least parts of their lives in virtual environments, an important question is how such virtual life impacts one's happiness, well-being, and overall quality of life (QOL). QOL and subjective well-being (SWB) both have vast literatures, and exhaustive reviews are available elsewhere (Diener, Suh, Lucas, & Smith, 1999; Hagerty, et al., 2001; Lyubomirsky, King, & Diener, 2005; Ryan & Deci, 2001; Sirgy et al., 2006). QOL is largely the domain of the social indicators literature, with an economic and public policy focus, whereas SWB is largely the domain of the psychology literature, with an emphasis on the processes underlying SWB. The fundamental motivating questions of this chapter are whether virtual worlds are sufficiently distinct from real-life environments that it makes sense to introduce a new multidimensional quality of virtual life (QOVL) construct, how QOVL would be expected to relate to QOL, and how consideration of QOVL becomes an important consumer welfare issue as people spend increasing amounts of time in virtual environments.

### INTRODUCTION TO QUALITY OF VIRTUAL LIFE

As an example of how QOVL is relevant in virtual worlds, consider the Amsterdam Digital City (*De Digitale Stad*; DDS), an early experimentation in virtual community and social networking that provides an example of how QOVL may be a critical factor in the user acceptance and success of a virtual world. The DDS was established in 1994 as a text-based, digital, public democratic forum for the citizens of Amsterdam (van den Besselaar & Beckers, 2005). DDS rapidly evolved from its political roots into a comprehensive website launched in 1995 and based on a city map metaphor, with cultural, recreational, technological, civic, and political virtual offices rented by both commercial and nonprofit organizations. The offices were organized into 35 city squares, each with a main office building and nine smaller offices. Neighborhoods were located adjacent to these offices, in which digital residents maintained a total of 1,500 virtual houses at no charge. The houses allowed residents to e-mail each other and share information. Emerging three-dimensional virtual reality technology was an obvious next step, given the DDS's metaphor of a real-world city, but while DDS experimented with a three-dimensional interface in 1997, its users' computers and Internet connections were not adequate to support these enhancements, so the interface remained a flat, two-dimensional Web-based map. The DDS population grew from an initial 10,000 virtual citizens to a community of 150,000 by the time of its decline and ultimate abandonment by its users in 2001, as DDS citizens defected to other websites. Van den Besselaar and Beckers offered one intriguing explanation for this decline: DDS citizens "went elsewhere to find a better quality of virtual life" (p. 93).

Although some might dismiss this explanation and offer alternative ones of better usability or improved user experience, those who have experienced the immersive nature of virtual worlds might find themselves nodding in agreement with van den Besselaar and Beckers (2005). The depth of user experience in virtual worlds is orders of magnitudes beyond that found on traditional websites. Hoffman and Novak (2009) argued that the social context, heightened interactivity, sense of place, manipulable environment, and dynamic learning process distinguish virtual worlds from conventional Web-based environments (Hoffman & Novak, 1996; Novak, Hoffman, & Yung, 2000).

The concept of QOVL immediately raises a series of questions regarding its definition. What are the underlying dimensions of QOVL? How do the underlying dimensions of QOVL differ from those in the extensive literature on real-world QOL (Coons, Rao, Keininger, & Hays, 2000; Dolan, Peasgood, & White, 2008; Hagerty et al., 2001; Kahneman, Krueger, Schkade, Schwarz, & Stone, 2004; Noll, 2004; Sirgy et al., 2006) or the literature on SWB and happiness (Diener, 2000; Diener et al., 1999; Diener, Oishi, & Lucas, 2002; Lyubomirsky et al., 2005; Ryan & Deci, 2001)? How would one go about conceptualizing and measuring QOL in a virtual world?

There are also many questions regarding the relationship of QOVL and QOL, with at least three possibilities. First, QOVL and QOL may be independent constructs, although recent empirical evidence has suggested that this is not the case (Bell, Castronova, & Wagner, 2009b). Second, a pessimistic scenario is that although QOVL may compensate for poor real-world QOL, it may not enhance QOL in any meaningful way. For example, the experience of QOVL may provide an escape for some from the problems of the real world, leading at the extreme to addictive online behavior. Third, an optimistic scenario is that QOVL augments real-world QOL and, in the process, enhances QOL. Some have speculated that virtual worlds might in some manner impact QOL, for example, that "virtual environments will be used to help lift people out of mental poverty, even when their real world is immersed in physical poverty" (Anderson & Rainie, 2008, p. 95). There is recognition that participation in virtual worlds can impact QOL for those with physical disabilities. Virtual Ability Island in Second Life was recently awarded a $10,000 annual prize by Linden Lab, given to the virtual-world project that most improves real-world lives. The project, designed by Virtual Ability, offers resources to help people with real-world disabilities learn to use Second Life, where they can "skydive, fish, mountain climb, hike, and even fly" ("Virtual Mobility for Disabled," 2009, para. 3). As the project group's president stated, "[F]or many of us Second Life is not a game—it is a second chance at life" (para. 7).

Given that virtual worlds can impact individuals in positive ways by allowing them to achieve their potential in ways the the real world cannot, or in negative ways by contributing to social isolation or addictive behavior, virtual worlds raise potentially critical consumer welfare issues. To provide a context for understanding these issues, this chapter begins with an overview of virtual worlds and people's motivations for using them. As Second Life is currently the dominant example of a fully realized virtual world, most examples are based on Second Life, but the discussion is relevant to all virtual worlds. The social indicators literature and the well-being literature are examined to identify key definitional, theoretical, and measurement issues relevant to building a conceptual model of QOVL. The final section examines the role of QOVL in the domain of Transformative Consumer Research and sets forth a research agenda for the study of QOVL.

## VIRTUAL WORLDS

### Background

Most generally speaking, virtual worlds are computer-based simulations inhabited by human-controlled avatars. *Virtual world* has been defined as "a synchronous, persistent network of people, represented as avatars, facilitated by networked computers" (Bell, 2008, para. 3) and as "a computer-generated display that allows or compels the user (or users) to have a sense of being present in an environment other than the one they are actually in, and to interact with that environment" (Schroeder, 1996, p. 25). Virtual worlds share six characteristics: (1) persistent, (2) shared spaces with a (3) graphical, two- or three-dimensional user interface involving (4) interactivity in a (5) social context that (6) is experienced by the user. Each of these characteristics is best viewed as a continuum. For example, social context is a continuum ranging from solitary worlds where the only interaction is between the creator of the world and the visitor, to complex social environments where tens of thousands of individuals may be simultaneously engaged with the virtual world. Similarly, immersiveness of experience, or the degree of presence or telepresence (Steuer, 1992), is a continuum defined by the extent of interactivity and vividness of the virtual environment.

Virtual worlds bear some similarities to massive, multiplayer, online role-playing games (MMORPGs), such as World of Warcraft and EverQuest, and to some degree, MMORPGs share the six characteristics of virtual worlds. However, as noted by Schroeder (2008), although MMORPGs can be used for social purposes, online games are designed with specific rules and objectives centered around activities such as accumulating points, reaching new levels, and completing specified missions, whereas virtual worlds have been explicitly designed for the purpose of social activity where users are "asked to make it all up for themselves" (Damer, 2008, para. 4). In reality, the dividing line between MMORPGs and virtual worlds as defined by Schroeder is not so clear-cut. The Sims Online straddles the border between game and social world, in that users are constrained by gaming rules and must follow a prescribed process to acquire skills and virtual game money, yet at the same time, social interaction through live chat is a parallel but unconstrained activity that, for many, dominates the game. Despite the explicit rules of the game that users follow in The Sims Online or MMORPGs, there are always those whose main objective in virtual life is "to find new and exciting ways to disrupt the normal course of gameplay" (Ludlow & Wallace, 2007, p. 93). Such "griefers" bend the rules wherever possible to create consequences unanticipated and largely unenforceable by the game designers, such as harassment of new users. Whenever social interaction is possible in an MMORPG, gameplay will evolve in both positive and negative ways beyond the boundaries prescribed by the formal rules of the game.

The number of virtual-world platforms is steadily increasing. Spence (2008) surveyed 112 distinct virtual worlds, and it is estimated that 900 virtual worlds will be in existence by 2012 ("Growth Forecasts," 2009). These numbers are deceptively low, in that an individual virtual world can be viewed as a platform supporting multiple distinct environments targeted to different user segments. For example, Second Life alone has more than 27,000 distinct regions (M. J. Linden, 2009), with widely different environments, including commercial, entertainment, social, educational, fantasy, and adult themes, and Blue Mars is built on a business model whereby "city developers" lease large, self-contained, autonomous virtual spaces, creating multiple integrated virtual worlds supported by a common platform.

Some virtual worlds have a niche orientation. Club Penguin targets children ages 6–10 with the parental promise that children's interactions will be in a completely safe online environment. Other worlds, for example, Multiverse Places and Kaneva, target adults, but with a singular focus on social interaction. Still other mirror worlds, such as Twinity and Amazing Worlds, specialize in recreating real-life locations (e.g., Berlin, Germany) in virtual form. Next-generation virtual worlds, such as Blue Mars and PlayStation Home, require computers with the latest high-end graphics hardware or powerful home-gaming systems, but provide extremely realistic avatars, three-dimensional immersive environments, and very large numbers of concurrent users. The most broadly based virtual worlds, of which Second Life is the most fully realized current example, allow users to create, explore, entertain, learn, and socialize against the background of a virtual-world economy that is integrated with the real-world economy. In such worlds, virtual currency can be exchanged for real-world currencies using Web-based currency exchanges. Such a virtual economy in Second Life, based on the "Linden dollar," enabled 61,000 users in October 2008 to maintain a positive cash flow, actually earning income in Second Life. Of these users, 211 earned virtual currency equivalent to at least US$5,000 per month, primarily through selling virtual goods or virtual real estate. Since at the time there were 16 million Second Life accounts, of which 1 million used Second Life in October 2008, the odds of striking it rich may sound no better than a Ponzi scheme. Most Second Life users, however, do not enter Second Life with the expectation of earning real-world wages. Basic but functional virtual clothing, homes, furniture, and pets can be obtained for free, and one can outfit his or her avatar in the latest designer fashions and hairstyles for considerably less than the price of a night out at the movies in the real world. The extremely low cost of virtual life, in fact, is one characteristic not well understood by real-world companies that entered Second Life with the explicit objective of striking it rich.

Considerable attention was paid in the business and popular press to the activities of real-world companies in Second Life during the period of 2006–2007. *BusinessWeek* noted that over 200 companies were experimenting in Second Life in 2006 (Hof, 2006b), and it was difficult to open a newspaper or magazine at that time without reading about something some company was doing in Second Life. It is not surprising that companies were so interested. When one broadly defines *virtual goods* as "digital creations of some object that can be used to enhance one's online presence through style, function or self-expression," global virtual goods revenues are expected to increase from $2.2 billion in 2009 to $6 billion by 2013 (Piper Jaffray & Co., 2009). However, success within Second Life has largely eluded mainstream marketers, and by 2008, the list of companies that exited Second Life vastly exceeded those that still remained, a reversal of fortunes also noted by the popular press (Rose, 2007). In retrospect, the presence of real-world companies in Second Life, while capturing the attention of the popular media, was relatively unnoticed among Second Life users who found the virtual storefronts set up by firms like Armani, BMW, Toyota, and Coca-Cola to be significantly less interesting than competing user-generated content, which dominated the corporate content in both quality and quantity. One could say that the corporate content created by design firms, such as Electric Sheep, Millions of Us, and Rivers Run Red, at substantial expense to their corporate clients did little to contribute to QOVL.

### Virtual-World User Behaviors and Motivations

#### *Behaviors*

Human behavior defines the intersection of the real world with virtual worlds. At this intersection, numerous researchers have written about the paradox of parallels and contradictions between real- and virtual-world behavior. Are the real person and his or her avatar equivalent, one and the same? In marketing, there is increasing recognition of the avatar as an independent character, distinct from but related to the consumer's real-life persona (Whang & Chang, 2004). Hemp (2006) argued that marketers need to consider the two-way dynamics internal to the dyad of a real-world consumer and his or her virtual avatar; for example, the real-world consumer can purchase virtual goods for the avatar, while the avatar can purchase real-world goods for its physical creator. But, how closely are the real-world person and his or her avatar linked together?

Empirical research addresses this question from a variety of perspectives (for a collection of recent articles, see Wood & Solomon, 2009). Virtual-world behavior of avatars has been found to mirror real-world behavior, influence real-world behavior, and be influenced by real-world behavior. Further, within virtual worlds, characteristics of one's avatar have been found to influence behavior in the virtual world.

First, consider research from a social perception perspective that shows avatar behavior mirrors real-world behavior. Similar in spirit to the media equation stream of research (Reeves & Nass, 2002), which is grounded in the proposition that people interact with computers and other new media in similar ways that they interact with real people, a growing stream of research has uncovered parallels between virtual-world and real-world social behaviors. In a replication of the classic Milgram (1963) obedience study, Slater et al. (2006) constructed an immersive virtual environment in which participants were required to administer virtual electric shocks to virtual humans and found that "humans tend to respond realistically at subjective, physiological, and behavioral levels in interaction with virtual characters notwithstanding their cognitive certainty that they are not real" (para. 23).

A study of interpersonal distance conducted in the virtual-world Second Life (Yee, Bailenson, Urbanek, Chang, & Merget, 2007) found that norms for interpersonal distance from the physical world were carried forward to the virtual world, specifically that (a) male–male avatar dyads exhibit larger interpersonal distance than female–female avatar dyads, (b) male–male avatar dyads maintain less virtual eye contact, and (c) decreases in interpersonal distance in virtual worlds are met with increased gaze avoidance. Additional evidence that social cues operate similarly in both virtual and real worlds was reported by Eastwick and Gardner (2008), who used the virtual-world There to replicate real-world findings for the door-in-the-face technique, in which an unreasonably large request that is expected to be rejected is followed by a moderate request, and the foot-in-the-door technique, in which a small request is followed by a moderate request. Both techniques increased compliance of the moderate requests using avatar experimenters and avatar subjects in the virtual world. However, despite the above examples demonstrating congruence of real- and virtual-world behavior, it has been recently noted that such congruence is highly dependent on specific behaviors, virtual worlds, and contexts within virtual worlds, and consequently, congruence should not be assumed as a given without validation (Williams, 2010).

In other social contexts, the avatar as virtual representation of the self has been found to affect both virtual-world as well as subsequent real-life behavior. In addition to finding that participants who were given taller avatars were more aggressive negotiators in a virtual environment than participants who were given shorter avatars, Yee and Bailenson (2007) found that those participants who had been given taller avatars were also more aggressive negotiators in subsequent real-world face-to-face interactions than participants who had been given shorter avatars. Fox and Bailenson (2009) found that real-world behavior can be influenced by observation of one's own avatar's behavior. They reported that participants who watched their own avatars run on a virtual treadmill voluntarily exercised more themselves the next day, as compared to participants who watched their avatars standing still or watched a stranger's avatar on a treadmill. Interactions occurring in a virtual environment itself may impact real-world behavior in positive ways. McKenna, Green, and

Gleason (2002) found that participants who met each other for the first time through online chat liked each other more based on that interaction than did participants who met face-to-face for the first time. Even in a subsequent face-to-face meeting when those who met online finally met face-to-face, they continued to like each other more than did participants who first met face-to-face and continued to meet face-to-face.

Yet, real-word personal characteristics and behaviors can, in turn, influence the choice of virtual-world characteristics and behaviors. Dean, Cook, Keating, and Murphy (2009) found that individuals who engage in physical activities in real life also engage in virtual physical activities in Second Life, and individuals who are thinner in real life have thinner avatars. Similarly, Messinger et al. (2008) found that Second Life users tend to customize their avatars to resemble their real selves, but with moderate enhancements, and Second Life users behave in similar ways to real life, although their virtual-world behavior is somewhat less restrained by inhibitions.

Last, there is evidence that the avatar representation of the self affects behavior in virtual environments. As noted, participants with taller avatars are more aggressive negotiators within a virtual world (Yee & Bailenson, 2007). Individuals whose avatars are more attractive than their real selves have been found to behave in a more extroverted manner in virtual worlds, especially when the person is low on extroversion in real life (Messinger et al., 2008). Recent research has found that consumers embodied in an avatar that resembles the typical user of a product have more favorable brand attitudes and greater purchase intention (Yang & Chattopadhyay, 2009). The virtual environment itself also impacts how people view themselves in the virtual setting. Due to anonymity and reduced cost for self-disclosure, individuals interacting through online chat are better able to express their true selves (Rogers, 1951) than individuals in face-to-face interactions (Bargh, McKenna, & Fitzsimons, 2002).

*Motivations*

Why do people use virtual worlds in the first place? Why do they continue using them? Based on a 40-item inventory administered to over 3,000 MMORPG players, Yee (2007) identified three higher order components specifying user motivations to play in massive, multiplayer, online games: achievement, social, and immersion. Each of the three higher order components is, in turn, specified by a number of subcomponents. Achievement consists of advancement (e.g., progress, power, status), mechanics (e.g., game-related numbers, optimization, templating), and competition (e.g., challenging others, provocation, domination). Social includes socializing (e.g., chat, helping other, making friends), relationship (e.g., personal, self-disclosure, providing support), and teamwork (e.g., collaboration, groups). Immersion includes discovery (e.g., exploration, lore, finding hidden things), role-playing (e.g., story line, roles, fantasy), customization (e.g., appearances, accessories, style), and escapism (e.g., relaxing, avoiding real-life problems). These motivational components should also largely apply to virtual worlds, although motivations related to game-specific aspects would be reduced in importance, for example, advancement through progression of prespecified game or character levels. Note, however, that Yee's typology has not yet been validated in the context of virtual worlds and may not capture the full range of motivations for using virtual worlds. Research in progress seeks to determine the fundamental goals people have for using Second Life and how they may differ from goals for using social media in general (Hoffman & Novak, 2010). Still, Yee's typology provides a useful starting point, and I next briefly review other research that has investigated these three broad motivational constructs in the context of social media.

The immersion dimension is particularly important for virtual worlds and other forms of social media, such as online communities, blogs, microblogs, wikis, online chat, and video-sharing sites. Virtual worlds, like social media in general and the Web as a whole, incorporate both goal-directed and experiential user activities. Flow, aesthetic enjoyment, immersion, and escape have been identified as motivating factors for the use of a wide range of social media (Barnes, 2007; Hoffman & Novak, 1996) for both goal-directed activities, such as education, research, and information search (Barnes, 2007; Java, Finin, Song, & Tseng, 2007; Lenhart & Fox, 2006; Ridings & Gefen, 2004; Trammell, Tarkowsi, Hofmokl, & Sapp, 2006; Weiss, Lurie, & Macinnis, 2008), and experiential activities involving fun, relaxation, and enjoyment (Barnes, 2007; Cho, 2007; Jung, Youn, & McClung, 2007; Nov, 2007; Ridings & Gefen, 2004; Stoeckl, Rohnmier, & Hess, 2007; Trammell et al., 2006).

Social motivations identified in social media include altruism, social interaction, communication, development of social capital, and relationships (Barnes, 2007; Butler, Sproull, Kiesler, & Kraut, 2008; Cho, 2007; Daugherty, Eastin, & Bright, 2008; Java et al., 2007; Jung et al., 2007; Lenhart & Fox, 2006; Ridings & Gefen, 2004; Trammell et al., 2006; Weiss et al., 2008). Achievement motivations for social media have been found to involve esteem needs, self-validation, reputation development, external economic incentives, and professional advancement (Barnes, 2007; Cook, 2008; Jung et al., 2007; Kuznetsov, 2006; Li & Bernoff, 2008; Stoeckl et al., 2007; Trammell et al., 2006).

Judged by the wide range of corroborating evidence, Yee's framework provides a useful starting point for understanding the reasons people choose to use virtual worlds. However, there are a few constructs not included in this framework that are relevant for understanding why people use virtual worlds. Social media use has been related to the construct of eudemonic well-being (Ryan & Deci, 2001), which views well-being as realizing one's true nature. For example, Miura and Yamashita (2007) found that blog writing, for example, allows some writers to deepen their understanding of themselves. Barnes (2007) similarly noted that virtual worlds enable the extension of self in a manner that facilitates fulfillment of Maslow's highest order self-actualization need. Self-expression and the creative impulse have been found to motivate social media use. In social media as diverse as Twitter, virtual worlds, online chat, blogs, and Facebook, self-expression is an important motivation (Barnes, 2007; Daugherty et al., 2008; Java et al., 2007; Jung et al., 2007; Lenhart & Fox, 2006; Li & Bernoff, 2008; Miura & Yamashita, 2007; Zhao, Grasmuck, & Martin, 2008).

Last, the desire for control motivates much social media use and takes a range of forms. Those who are motivated to use social media for the control it affords include those attracted to the ability to outsource their memory and achieve lasting access to information (Schotz, 2008), those who use social media for utilitarian purposes and practical solutions (Cook, 2008; Daugherty et al., 2008), and those who seek safety through anonymity (Barnes, 2007). Virtual worlds, by providing an alternative reality offering a new beginning with its own social structure, aesthetic landscape, and economy, also provide a sense of control to those individuals who may not be satisfied with their day-to-day realities.

## QUALITY OF VIRTUAL LIFE

People spend significant amounts of time in virtual worlds. Various research studies have found that users spend on average from 20 hours per week (Castronova, 2001) to 22 hours per week (Repères, 2007), with the heaviest concentration of time occurring on weekends (Fetscherin & Lattemann, 2008). The Repères study of Second Life found that the expert users, 7% of the sample, spent on average over 37 hours per week in Second Life. For many people, time spent in virtual worlds is equivalent to a half-time job. For some, it is equivalent to a full-time job. For some with a full-time real-world job, time spent in Second Life is a significant portion of their workweek. Employees of Linden Lab, the company that operates Second Life, spend on average eight hours of work time per week in Second Life (G. Linden, 2009). Many people are living a virtual life. How do they like it?

A recent large-scale study of 2,094 Second Life users by Bell et al. (2009b) included items measuring both satisfaction with real life and Second Life. Satisfaction was measured on a 10-point scale (0 = *completely dissatisfied*, 10 = *completely satisfied*). Second Life satisfaction (mean 7.57) was slightly higher than real-life satisfaction (mean 7.25), and both Second Life and real-life satisfaction were positively correlated with hours spent in Second Life (Bell, Castronova, & Wagner, 2009a). We may conclude that for at least some people, virtual worlds play a significant enough role in their lives to warrant consideration of the QOVL. Within Second Life, users seem to be at least as satisfied with their virtual lives as they are with their real lives, and the level of satisfaction increases with time spent in the virtual world.

As for whether it really makes sense to consider QOL for virtual worlds, consider that QOL has been studied from a wide range of perspectives, such as sociological, economic, psychological, marketing, health, and occupational (Sirgy et al., 2006). Perhaps the strongest parallel is with quality of work life (QWL). Many of the questions that have been investigated about QWL (Sirgy et al., 2006) can be directly translated to QOVL (simply substitute *QOVL* for *QWL*): "Does QWL contribute significantly to QOL? How does quality of work life contribute to overall QOL? What are other consequences of QWL? What are some factors affecting QWL? How to deploy/QWL programs?" (p. 425).

Also relevant to the discussion of QOVL is the central role of the avatar in virtual worlds. As noted earlier, behavior in virtual worlds can mirror the real world, but in addition, the virtual and real selves can influence each other. To the degree that the avatar is separable from the self, one can visit a virtual world as a person with very different physical and behavioral characteristics than one's real-world self. However, even if the avatar is a reasonably true representation of the real-world self, the virtual environment is likely to significantly differ from the real-world environment. Thus, QOVL can diverge from real-world QOL for two distinct reasons: differences between self and avatar and differences between the real world and the virtual world.

An additional consideration is the type of virtual world for which QOVL is most relevant. In my brief discussion of virtual worlds, I considered broadly based worlds like Second Life, which provide an immersive social context, a functioning economy (in this case, with a currency more stable than the U.S. dollar), and a compelling visual environment that allows the user to suspend disbelief and allows each user to create content and maintain the intellectual property rights of that content within the virtual world. Such broadly based worlds provide the largest base of domains in which QOVL can be assessed, although QOVL can apply in a restricted manner to more limited worlds, for example, those lacking an economic dimension and those that do not provide ways for users to generate content.

In the next sections, I briefly consider some key insights from the QOL and SWB literatures and apply these to build a conceptual model of QOVL. Rather than create a definitive framework for understanding QOVL, my objective is to lay out a range of reasonable components of such a model, and then set forth an agenda for future research.

### Lessons From Quality of Life and Subjective Well-Being

Social indicators consist of both subjective and objective indicators. As noted by Michalos in his discussion of conceptual foundations of QOL (Sirgy et al., 2006), social indicators are sometimes equated with objective indicators, and QOL indicators are sometimes equated with subjective indicators (for additional discussion, see Andreasen, Goldberg, & Sirgy, Chapter 2 of this volume). Subjective indicators overlap to some degree with measures of SWB and are individuals' evaluations of their satisfaction, attitudes, and beliefs. Objective indicators are readily measured by observation and may be obtainable at the aggregate rather than individual level.

As noted by Noll (2004), "social indicators are regarded as instruments for the regular observation and analysis of social change" (p. 154). Given the dynamic evolution of virtual worlds, detection of such social change is particularly important to observe in a timely manner. Traditionally, objective social indicators at the national level have included constructs such as income, employment, divorce rate, productivity, and crime rates. For virtual worlds, although analogies of these physical-world indicators can certainly be obtained, other measures are relevant as well and readily available on essentially a real-time basis for some virtual-world platforms in the form of publicly available economic statistics. For example, Second Life provides raw data files on a daily basis for a set of statistics on its virtual economy, including acres auctioned, land for sale, logged-in users, respondent transactions, Linden dollar money supply, virtual business profits, and consumer spending (e.g., visit secondlife.com/statistics/economy-data.php).

In addition, objective data of user interest in virtual worlds is obtainable through tools such as Google Insights for Search (http:// www.google.com/insights/search/#), which provides downloadable weekly data for up to the past 5 years on search volume for any keyword phrase one enters, for example, "virtual worlds," "Second Life," or "Linden dollar." These search volume trends can be filtered by geographic region or category context (e.g., business, computers, entertainment) and have been successfully used to predict retail sales in the automobile, housing, and travel categories (Choi & Varian, 2009). Search trends for keywords related to virtual worlds would similarly be expected to be predictive of interest and trial of virtual-world platforms, word-of-mouth activity, and other social indicators related to QOVL. Although search volume trends represent the interest of a broader population than the user base of a virtual world, this expression of broader interest is in itself an important objective indicator.

The discussion by Pavot of QOL research from a psychological perspective (Sirgy et al., 2006) provides a concise overview of a number of key issues in SWB. SWB research generally follows the hedonic view, in which maximization of pleasure leads to happiness, as opposed to the eudemonic view, in which well-being is distinct from happiness and derived from the striving to realize one's true potential (Ryan & Deci, 2001). In the hedonic view, SWB consists of three relatively independent constructs: positive affect, negative affect, and a cognitive component operationalized as satisfaction judgments. Thus, the measure of virtual-world satisfaction mentioned earlier that was used by Bell et al. (2009a) represents only one of three distinct components of SWB. SWB, in fact, has been defined even more broadly, with Diener et al. (1999) considering it a broad research area rather than a distinct construct. Although it represents a simplification that some may be uncomfortable with, for purposes of simplicity, I consider SWB a component of a broader QOL domain, consisting of subjective measures of QOL.

*Measurement*

Hagerty et al. (2001, pp. 2–11) presented and applied a list of 14 criteria for evaluating QOL indexes, several of which relate to measurement issues. The criteria specify that a QOL index should be not only reportable as a single number but also decomposable into components, in which the components are reliable, valid, and sensitive to change in public policy or market input. The components of the index should be based on time series data. Seven distinct QOL domains are recommended, with the recognition that these can be supplemented for particular populations or applications: relationships with family and friends, emotional well-being, material well-being, health, work and productive activity, feeling part of one's local community, and personal safety. Within each domain, multi-item rather than single-item measures should be used (Diener et al., 2002; Sirgy et al., 2006;).

*Choice of Domains*

As the domains used for QOVL will differ from QOL, the criteria for selecting domains are important (Hagerty et al., 2001). Again, from the list of criteria provided by Hagerty et al., the components should represent domains which together represent the total of life experience (or virtual life experience), with each domain representing a substantial but separate part of the QOVL construct. The domains should not be idiosyncratic, but each domain must be relevant for most virtual-world users. There should be both objective and subjective indicators for each domain. If an additional domain is included beyond a certain base set of default domains, it must be empirically shown to contribute incremental variance to the QOVL construct above and beyond the base set. Last, the domains should have both cognitive (satisfaction) and affective (positive and negative) components.

*Methodology*

As specified by the requirement that QOVL indexes be based on time series data, longitudinal designs for subjective measures will be required. Self-reports of subjective indicators are problematic, in that they may be influenced by momentary fluctuations in mood (Diener et al., 2002). Experience sampling methodology, which involves the random sampling of subjective measures over a period of time, can be used to address such problems with self-report measures (Kahneman et al., 2004). When aggregating across domains to obtain an overall index of QOVL, the domains should be weighted by importance to the individual (Diener et al., 2002).

*Framework Development*

A QOVL index should be grounded in established theory, which is operationalized as a set of concepts and structural connections between QOL and its domains, antecedents, and consequences. For example, Hagerty et al. (2001) specified a systems theory structure, identifying input, throughput, and output components. In their framework, input components consist of exogenous environmental variables and chronic individual characteristics that impact QOL. Throughput components describe how the individual responds to the environmental variables. These responses are viewed as reflecting choices people make within specific domains. Measures of SWB reside in this framework as an output component.

Toward a Model of Quality of Virtual Life

Figure 11.1 presents a conceptual framework for QOVL that extends the systems theory structure of QOL developed by Hagerty et al. (2001). The right side of the framework is directly drawn from Hagerty et al. (2001) and was first suggested by Veenhoven (1998) and Cummins et al. (1998). Note that the boxes in Figure 11.1 represent broad model components leading to SWB and are identical for both QOVL and QOL. However, within the model components, the specific characteristics leading to SWB will necessarily differ. For example, the individual choices one makes in the real world (e.g., personal health, job choice) will not be exactly the same "life choices" as available in virtual worlds (e.g., avatar appearance, number of identities). As the right side of Figure 11.1 has been explained in detail elsewhere (Hagerty et al., 2001, pp. 79–80), please focus on the left side.

QOVL consists of a range of constructs organized in a structural framework. At the far left, the first column contains input variables consisting of either structural or performance criteria of a virtual-world platform. The structural criteria are the assessment of a specific virtual world on the six characteristics that define virtual worlds: persistence, shared space, interface, interactivity, social environment, and immersive experience. Assessment of the structural criteria requires both objective and subjective indicators. For example, while specific features of the interface can be objectively described, perceptions of interface usability would be determined via survey research or expert judgment. The structural criteria identify strengths and weaknesses of a specific virtual world. As virtual worlds are constantly under development by both the creators and users of the virtual world, structural criteria must be reassessed at regular intervals.

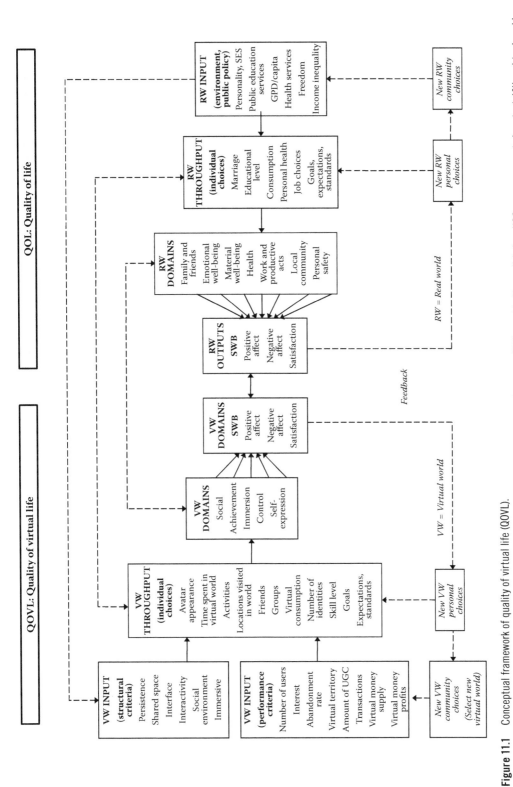

**Figure 11.1**   Conceptual framework of quality of virtual life (QOVL).
*Note.* GPD/capita = gross domestic product per capita; RW = real world; SES = socioeconomic status; SWB = subjective well-being; UGC = user-generated content; VW = virtual world.

Also in the first column are performance criteria. These are aggregate objective indicators of the performance of the virtual world on a range of criteria. As noted earlier, Second Life publishes a set of performance criteria on a daily basis, accessible to the general public. Number of users is a key objective criteria, which can be measured at a variety of levels, for example, total registered accounts, the number of users who have visited the virtual world at least once in a specific time period (e.g., past month, past week), and the number who regularly visited the virtual world in a specific time period. The number of concurrent users is also an important metric, as the number of users simultaneously visiting the virtual world at a given point in time is an indicator of the depth of social interaction possible. In addition, concurrent users can be measured at both global and local levels. In Second Life, while globally over 70,000 users may be logged on simultaneously, in any given local simulator region, the number of concurrent users is much smaller, with a maximum of 100 avatars per region. The region is the basic unit of land in Second Life, with virtual dimensions scaled to represent a square plot of land that is 256 × 256 meters. Actual numbers of concurrent local users in a region do not come close to the maximum, as 45% of regions are completely empty, and only 2% of regions have more than 20 avatars (Varvello, Picconi, Diot, & Biersack, 2008).

As mentioned previously, interest in virtual worlds can be objectively measured using time series data of the number of specific search queries. The abandonment rate for a virtual world can be calculated as the percentage of new sign-ups who enter the world for the first time at time 1 but never return to the virtual world after time 2. There are multiple potential explanations for a high abandonment rate. Ease of use could be poor, people may be trying and discarding alternate avatars, or users may be dissatisfied with the experience.

Additional objective performance criteria include the total amount of available virtual territory, which can increase as server space is added, virtual territory changes ownership, transactions occur, virtual money supply changes, and virtual profits change. Somewhat more difficult to assess is the total amount of user-generated content in a virtual world. Unlike a blog or social networking site, where it is possible to obtain objective counts of the number of discussion posts and comments, counting virtual objects is a bit more challenging, although various approaches are possible. In Second Life, each region is limited to a maximum of 15,000 prims, the basic building unit out of which all other objects are created. One can determine, for each region, the number of prims currently in use, which can serve as an index of the amount of user-generated content in that region. Another example of an index of user-generated content in Second Life would be the number of virtual items offered for sale at central venues such as the Second Life Marketplace (http://marketplace. secondlife.com), a Web-based shop for selling virtual goods that is integrated with Second Life.

The second column of Figure 11.1 contains throughput variables that "describe the individual's response to the environment" (Hagerty et al., 2001, p. 79). These are individual-level variables reflecting choices people make as they use a virtual world. The throughput variables listed in Figure 11.1 are both objective and subjective. It is at least theoretically possible to obtain objective data (counts) on an individual's number of friends, the number of groups the individual has joined, the number and value of transactions, and time spent in a virtual world. However, self-report, and thus necessarily subjective data, must generally be obtained on the type of activities engaged in, locations visited, number of alternative identities, and people's goals or objectives for using a virtual world. Avatar appearance can be assessed by expert judges or by the user and has both objective and subjective components.

In the third column are five domains in which virtual world SWB can be assessed. These represent five primary motivations for using virtual worlds from my previous discussion: social, achievement, immersion, control, and self-expression. Note that these domains diverge significantly from the domains used to assess SWB in the real world, where there are clear norms and institutions for unambiguously defining family, friends, work, and community. The meaning of these terms in virtual worlds is considerably less clear-cut, but the social domain parallels family, friends, and community in the physical world, and the achievement domain parallels work. Health, material well-being, and personal safety are less relevant (but not completely irrelevant) in virtual worlds and are incorporated in domains for control and achievement. As noted earlier, self-expression is a major motivation for using virtual worlds, and while it parallels emotional well-being to some extent, it goes beyond emotional well-being in explaining why people create user-generated content.

Within each domain, SWB can be assessed with subjective indicators. At this stage, this closely parallels the assessment of SWB in the real world. For each of the five virtual-world domains, we can assess both positive and negative affect, as well as satisfaction, and derive an overall index. The arrows at the bottom represent feedback effects of virtual-world SWB. Corresponding to Haggerty et al.'s (2001) discussion of the right side of Figure 11.1 for the feedback effects of SWB in QOL, in virtual worlds, SWB can affect people's personal choices (i.e., virtual-world throughput) as well as their community choices. Community choice represents a fundamental difference between real and virtual worlds. Unlike the real world, in a virtual world, if you are dissatisfied, you always have the option of abandoning the virtual world and finding another one that you believe will have a better QOVL. This is a choice generally unavailable in the real world and presents an outcome that has considerable business, as well as personal, significance.

Also note that there a number of connections between QOVL and QOL specified in Figure 11.1. At the broadest level, virtual-world SWB and real-life SWB can influence each other. While this remains an empirical question, it is not only possible that people who are happier in real life are also happier in virtual worlds, but also that those who experience happiness in virtual worlds can become happier in real life. There are also reciprocal causal links between virtual-world and real-world domains. For example, individuals who have a strong focus on family and friends in the real world may tend toward social activities in virtual worlds. Conversely, people who have difficulty interacting with other people in the real world may be able to establish relationships with others in the virtual world, and those relationships may then extend into the real world. Last, for similar reasons, reciprocal links are indicated between individual choices people make in virtual worlds and choices they make in the real world. One nonreciprocal link in Figure 11.1 is that between the real-world input (exogenous) variables and the virtual-world input variables. People with certain personality characteristics, from certain social strata, or from specific countries may prefer different types of virtual worlds. However, the reverse is generally logically impossible. The choice to qualify this as "generally" impossible is due to exceptions to the rule, such as Ansche Chung, the avatar of real-life Ailin Graef, who accumulated a portfolio of virtual property in Second Life with a market value of US$1 million (Hof, 2006a), thus impacting her real-world socioeconomic status.

## TRANSFORMATIVE ASPECTS OF VIRTUAL WORLDS: A RESEARCH AGENDA FOR QUALITY OF VIRTUAL LIFE

This final section proposes a research agenda, summarized in Table 11.1, which follows from the conceptual framework in Figure 11.1. Rather than expanding on the already stated connections established in Figure 11.1, my discussion here is organized according to a range of ways that virtual worlds may affect well-being. Corresponding to the distinction between QOL/social indicators and SWB/happiness research, the topics I select represent more of a QOL/social indicators focus on policy and societal issues, rather than a SWB/happiness focus on the underlying processes. This decision is due to the conceptual framework, which orients the research agenda more to a broader QOL focus. The objective is not to specificy fairly narrow testable research propositions, but rather to stimulate thinking about virtual worlds and QOL in new directions.

**Table 11.1**    Research Agenda for Quality of Virtual Life

| | |
|---|---|
| Virtual Worlds as an Intervention to Increase SWB | • Does QOVL augment and enhance real-world QOL? |
| | • Can the virtual-world environment compensate for deficiencies in the real-world environment? |
| | • What types of virtual-world interactions most enhance real-world QOL? |
| | • What level of involvement with virtual worlds is required to impact QOL? |
| | • How long do any effects of interventions last? |
| | • How should intervention programs be evaluated? |
| Virtual Consumption as a Substitute for Physical Consumption | • Can real-world consumption activities that contribute to QOL be replaced by virtual consumption activities? |
| | • What are the interrelationships among real-world consumption, virtual consumption, and SWB? |
| | • In terms of satisfying underlying needs, can virtual consumption reduce the desire for material consumption? |
| Virtual Presence as a Substitute for Physical Presence | • Are there aspects of the real world that cannot be captured in the virtual world? |
| | • What contributes to presence in virtual worlds? |
| | • How do individual choices versus characteristics of the virtual world itself contribute to presence? |
| | • Does virtual presence contribute to SWB in virtual worlds, and if so, then how? |
| Perils of Virtual Worlds | • How does the generational digital divide between those growing up with virtual worlds and those who did not affect how virtual-world usage enhances QOL? |
| | • What types of digital divides occur entirely within virtual worlds, and how do these divides impact QOVL? |
| | • What are the situations in which virtual-world use may contribute to addictive behavior? |
| | • Can a focus on QOVL prevent addictive behavior in virtual worlds? |
| Adoption of Virtual Worlds | • What factors contribute to virtual-world use and adoption? |
| | • How does QOVL influence the pace of adoption of virtual worlds? |
| | • What factors impact the adoption of multiple identities within a virtual world or the adoption of multiple virtual worlds? |
| The Advent of Mixed Reality | • How do virtual enhancements or augmentations of the real world impact real-world QOL? |

*Note:* SWB = subjective well-being; QOL = quality of life; QOVL = quality of virtual life.

### Virtual Worlds as an Intervention to Increase Subjective Well-Being

Diener et al. (2002) discussed a number of intervention programs designed to impact SWB. Interventions that have increased SWB include teaching people how to imitate traits of happy people (Fordyce, 1983), kindness interventions (Otake, Shimai, Tanaka-Matsumi, Otsui, & Kredrickson, 2006), gratitude interventions (Emmons & McCullough, 2003), and interventions based on writing tasks (Lyubomirsky, Sousa, & Dickerhoof, 2006). In his summary of prior research on how QWL can contribute to overall QOL, Sirgy (Sirgy et al., 2006, p. 426) noted that affect experienced in the work domain can influence affect experienced in other life domains. Recently, functional magnetic resonance imaging scans of older individuals with limited Internet experience has shown that Internet use can "affect the efficiency of cognitive processing and alter the way the brain encodes new information" ("First-Time Internet Users," 2009, para. 4). Interaction with virtual worlds might similarly influence brain activity and possibly change how people view the real world, providing a biological basis for intervention programs.

There is evidence that virtual worlds can serve as an effective intervention to increase SWB. In a study of gay and lesbian individuals who experienced negative effects in the real world due to their sexual orientations, Cabiria (2008) concluded that virtual worlds can "provide the means to lead a more authentic life" (para. 37) and that positive experience in Second Life spills over into the real world. A recent survey of health-related activities in Second Life uncovered 68 projects that were related to health care, including Second Life projects dealing with autism, Asperger's syndrome, and substance abuse treatment, and the researchers concluded that "simulations that teach users about a specific topic can leave a lasting impact that transfers to the real world" (Beard, Wilson, Morra, & Keelan, 2009, Discussion section, para. 6). The instructional and research activities of 170 educational institutions in Second Life have been recently reviewed (Jennings & Collins, 2007).

Virtual worlds as intervention for improving real-world QOL is a research topic with significant policy implications. To what extent can virtual worlds improve real-life SWB, what degree of immersion in virtual worlds is required, how long do the effects last, and for which types of individuals is such intervention most likely to be successful? What is the critical level of involvement within a virtual world required to have a real impact on QOL both within the virtual world and in the real world? When the real-world environment is less than optimal, can the virtual-world environment compensate in specific real-world domains? How should virtual-world intervention programs for impacting real-world QOL and SWB be designed and evaluated?

## Virtual Consumption as a Substitute for Physical Consumption

The age-old question is, does money make us happy? In reviewing relationships between income and SWB, Diener et al. (1999) summarized the literature as (a) wealthier people are happier than poorer people, but the effect is small; (b) SWB increases or decreases with change in income, but because of adaptation, the effects are temporary; (c) at the national level, SWB does not relate to changes in economic growth; and (d) the largest effects of income and SWB are between national differences in gross national product and purchasing power, but these differences may be confounded by indirect benefits of wealth rather than wealth itself. Although there is some relatively modest relationship between income and happiness, Lyubomirsky et al. (2005) asserted that a portion of the association is due to the reverse causal sequence whereby "happy people are likely to acquire favorable life circumstances" (p. 803). Thus, happiness leads to success.

Csikszentmihalyi (2000) noted that the level of material consumption, in addition to not correlating with people's happiness and SWB, is neither sustainable nor scalable to the world's population and raises the question, "Is it impossible to develop an economy … where consumption involves the processing of ideas, symbols, and emotional experiences rather than the breakdown of matter?" (p. 271). Virtual worlds provide exactly such an economy, where virtual currency changes hands as payment for virtual goods or services to be enjoyed in the world, as payment for activities undertaken or services performed in the world, as compensation for creation of virtual content, as losses or winnings in games of chance, or as rental or payment for ownership rights to virtual property (Castronova, 2005). In fact, the immateriality of virtual goods may alter the very essence of materialism (for a related discussion, see Burroughs & Rindfleisch, Chapter 12 of this volume).

Lin (2008) provided an extensive discussion and documentation of the positive environmental consequences of virtual consumption and argued that virtual worlds can satisfy consumption desires and offer a viable alternative to physical-world consumption. This would appear to have positive environmental implications. However, despite the appealing and almost self-evident argument that virtual consumption is inherently more environmentally friendly than physical consumption, some have questioned the environmental sustainability of virtual consumption. By calculating the power consumption required to support Second Life users' personal computers, Linden Lab servers, and data center cooling requirements, per capita power consumption to annually support a single Second Life avatar is 1,752 kilowatt-hours per year, which is only slightly less than the electricity consumed by the average citizen of Brazil (1,884 kWh/year) and substantially more than the per capita consumption in developing countries (1,015 kWh/year), so while avatars "don't have bodies ... they do leave footprints" (Carr, 2006, para. 10).

A number of research questions follow from this discussion. To what extent can real-world consumption activities that contribute to QOL be replaced by virtual consumption activities? Does virtual consumption have a stronger correlation with SWB than material consumption? Does experience with virtual consumption reduce the desire for material consumption?

### Virtual Presence as a Substitute for Physical Presence

There are clear cost efficiencies to holding events virtually rather than physically. Jim O'Neill, author of Infotoday Blog, commented that a shift from real to virtual meetings

> will happen on the basis of economics and any forthcoming fuel shortages. It is easier (and far less costly in terms of time and money) to have people interact in a virtual world rather than have them traipse around the world. (Anderson & Rainie, 2008, p. 86)

The lack of regulation and greatly simplified logistics in virtual environments also increase the attraction of the virtual option. Technology author Fred Hapgood commented that when "you want to throw a rock concert online you don't have to post bonds, buy insurance, rent portable toilets, and so on" (Anderson & Rainie, 2008, p. 86).

One could argue that interactions in virtual worlds will never be sufficiently real and will suffer due to evolutionary advantages to face-to-face interactions. Similarly, to the degree that attendance at a rock concert is driven by the desire to experience the event in amid a pulsing crowd of humanity, virtual worlds are unlikely for some time to substitute for that experience. Yet, any evolutionary advantage to face-to-face communication did not prevent the widespread adoption of other mediating communication technologies, such as the telephone, online chat, and e-mail. Additionally, while a sweaty, close-pressed crowd appeals to some concert goers, others may actually prefer a less physically immersive alternative at a fraction of the price.

Beyond these considerations, presence as defined as the sense of being immersed in a virtual environment has been studied for many decades in the context of virtual reality (Schuemie, van der Straaten, Krijn, & van der Mast, 2001; Steuer, 1992). Although some attention has to be paid to specific consequences of presence in virtual environments, for example, aggression in video games (Nowak, Kremar, & Farrar, 2008), the causal direction of the relationship of presence to emotional responses is unclear (Schuemie et al., 2001). Considerably greater attention has been paid to the measurement of the experience of presence itself, in that presence is a key outcome measure in the design of virtual environments and has been found to relate to the broader construct of flow in online environments (Csikszentmihalyi, 1997; Hoffman & Novak, 1996, 2009). Flow is an outcome measure that does have significant impact on learning, exploratory behavior, purchase intentions and behavior, and usage (Hoffman & Novak, 2009).

In terms of QOL, a number of important research topics center around presence. As first noted, are there aspects of the real world that simply cannot be adequately represented in the virtual world? One would expect that presence in virtual worlds correlates with measures of virtual SWB, but this needs to be verified and causal relationships determined, including the role of individual differences in the ability to experience presence in virtual worlds with SWB measures. One of the virtual-world domains listed in Figure 11.1, immersion, specifically relates to the construct of presence, but to what extent does presence correlate with SWB measures with all five domains? What leads to presence in virtual worlds? To what extent is presence due to individual choices within a virtual world (e.g., time spent, avatar customization, consumption activities, friends) versus structural characteristics of the virtual-world environment?

## Perils of Virtual Worlds

One broad policy and societal concern is the potential for a new digital divide (Hoffman & Novak, 1998) between those with and without access to virtual worlds (see also Hoffman, Chapter 9 of this volume). As noted in the Pew Internet & American Life Project's *The Future of the Internet III* report, "virtual worlds currently have a generational divide, with younger people readily moving into the world of the scenario, while older people generally do not participate" (Anderson & Rainie, 2008, p. 95). If virtual worlds can enhance real-life QOL, then those without access lack this opportunity. Comparing those who have been familiar with virtual-world environments since their childhood with those who have recently been introduced to virtual worlds, are there differences in how virtual-world usage enhances (or does not enhance) QOL?

While extent of use is perhaps the most obvious divide between virtual haves and have-nots, there is also the concern of a digital divide within virtual worlds themselves, for example, between insiders who belong to a subgroup within the virtual world and outsiders who do not (Axelsson, 2002). In Second Life, there is a definite stigma associated with being a new, unsocialized user, or newbie (Boostrom, 2008), as goes the expression "When a place is filled with newbies, it is about as bad as if it was empty." Thus, even if one has access to a virtual world, one does not immediately have access to the social environment within it. What types of digital divides occur entirely within virtual worlds, and how do these divides impact QOVL?

Joe McCarthy, formerly a principal scientist at Nokia Research Center, commented, "I fear that the time and attention consumed in such worlds will come at the expense of actions that might make the offline world a better place" (Anderson & Rainie, 2008, p. 97). Ignoring the real world for the virtual can have extremely serious consequences, including addictive consumption (see Litt, Pirouz, & Shiv, Chapter 25 of this volume). As noted in a recent editorial calling for inclusion of Internet addiction in the fifth edition of the *Diagnostic and Statistical Manual of Mental Disorders*, because it satisfies the diagnostic criteria of excessive use, withdrawal, tolerance, and negative repercussions, addictive Internet use in South Korea has led to "a series of 10 cardiopulmonary-related deaths in Internet cafes … and a game-related murder" (Block, 2008, p. 306). What are the circumstances under which virtual-world use will contribute to addictive behavior? Can a focus on QOVL prevent addictive behavior?

## Adoption of Virtual Worlds

Not everyone believes that virtual worlds will become a mass phenomenon. *The Future of the Internet III* (Anderson & Rainie, 2008) includes comments from many experts on the evolution of virtual worlds over the next decade. One writer and consultant, Scott Smith, stated that "participation in general metaverses may decline in duration and variety after a short-term peak in usage as users seek to rebalance toward the 'real' and authentic and see fewer benefits in being active in metaverses" (Anderson & Rainie, 2008, p. 94). In fact, according to Google Insights for Search (http://www.google.com/insights/search/#), searches for "Second Life" have been on the decline since early 2007, and searches for "World of Warcraft" have been declining since early 2005. At the same time, Google Insights for Search shows a steady increase in search activity for the generic search term "virtual worlds" over the past 5 years, roughly tripling over that time period.

As the extent to which virtual worlds will be widely adopted as an alternative to physical-world activities is not yet clear, QOL together with broader policy considerations are likely to play a key role in adoption and diffusion. It has been argued that diffusion of innovation goes beyond its usual portrayal as a communication process involving consumer segments who adopt a new product at different points in time, and should also include public policy and technological infrastructure initiatives that may either increase or slow the pace of innovation

(Owen, Ntoko, Zhang, & Dong, 2002). An example of such an initiative is the Beijing Cyber Recreation District project (Keegan, 2007), a 100-square-kilometer real-world site devoted to creating the computing, communications, electrical, financial, and logistics infrastructure that will support a series of "virtual Chinas" (Keating, 2008), each with hundreds of millions of users. Such massive investment has the potential to accelerate the pace of the adoption curve for virtual worlds, but does not by itself guarantee success. An important research question is the role of objective and subjective social indicators in the adoption process for virtual worlds. Which indicators are most predictive of adoption of virtual worlds? What is the role of QOVL in accelerating or dampening the pace of adoption?

One factor that hinders both adoption and QOVL is that different avatar identities are required to experience separate virtual-world platforms. Currently, each virtual world is essentially a closed kingdom. One must redefine oneself for each world—Second Life, There, Amazing Worlds, Blue Mars, and so forth—creating new avatars for each world that have no connection with each other. This is similar to how pre-Web users needed separate accounts to visit AOL, CompuServe, and other such closed networks. A joint project between IBM and Linden Lab seeks to create "universal avatars that can travel between worlds" ("Universal Avatars Bestride Worlds," 2007), but any widespread implementation is unlikely in the near to midterm future. Although this creates barriers to adoption, it also raises important research questions about how one should construct a multiworld model of QOVL. Figure 11.1 suggests that world switching can occur through the feedback link leading away from virtual-world SWB. However, many people do concurrently explore multiple virtual worlds, and one important research direction is a QOVL model that takes into account both multiple identities and multiple worlds. What factors impact the adoption of multiple identities with a virtual world or the adoption of multiple virtual worlds?

The Advent of Mixed Reality

Virtual worlds represent a clear dichotomy between the real world and a computer-generated world. At one extreme is a vision of the future where large numbers of people are sequestered in virtual environments for a significant portion of their waking hours. This is not the only scenario, and the real threat to the widespread adoption of virtual worlds may not lie in reality but in virtuality. Mixed reality merges the real world and a virtual world along a virtuality continuum ranging from the real world at one extreme to a completely virtual environment at the other (Milgran & Kishino, 1994). At points along this continuum, the real and virtual are mixed together in varying proportions. On one hand, augmented reality denotes systems in which the real world is dominant but enhanced by means of computer-generated, primarily visual displays that overlay information or representations of virtual objects on the real world. On the other hand, in augmented virtuality, the virtual world is dominant, but aspects of the real environment are present in the virtual world, for example, a live camera connection to a live real-world speaker from a virtual-world conference attended by avatars. Mixed reality offers prospects for enhancing SWB in conventional QOL domains. For example, virtual interactions with distant loved ones may impact the family and friends domain, and eventual holographic projections of virtual objects into the real world that enhance one's physical surroundings may impact the material well-being domain. Research questions include the degree to which virtual enhancements or augmentations of the real world impact QOL in different domains.

In conclusion, virtual worlds are with us today and are expected to become much more prominent in the coming decade either as alternatives to living in the real world or as a means of enhancing real-world conditions, becoming indispensable (Hoffman, Chapter 9 of this volume) to increasing numbers of users. As outlined in this chapter, QOVL is a critical topic for consumer welfare, given the potential for experience and interaction in virtual spaces to impact real-world QOL and SWB.

In the quest for happiness and life satisfaction, virtual worlds can open doors to experiences that are simply not available in the real world. The evolution of online environments began with static websites with limited interpersonal interaction whose quality was assessed with usability metrics. More recent interactive social media Web 2.0 applications require deeper user experience metrics that go beyond the mere usability of the applications. Immersive virtual worlds and spaces, in which people literally live portions of their lives, require even more complex and multidimensional QOVL metrics. Just as successful early websites were designed to maximize usability, and successful social media applications maximize user experience, virtual worlds can and should be designed to maximize QOVL. In the search for the killer application that will propel virtual worlds to the next level of user adoption, developers would be wise to think in terms of how the application would maximize QOVL.

## REFERENCES

Anderson, J. Q., & Rainie, L. (2008). *The future of the Internet III*. Washington, DC: Pew Internet & American Life Project.

Axelsson, A. (2002). The digital divide: Status differences in virtual environments. In R. Schroeder (Ed.), *The social life of avatars: Presence and interaction in shared virtual environments* (pp. 188–204). London: Springer-Verlag.

Bargh, J. A., McKenna, K. Y., & Fitzsimons, G. M. (2002). Can you see the real me? Activation and expression of the "true self" on the Internet. *Journal of Social Issues, 58*(1), 33–48.

Barnes, S. (2007). Virtual worlds as a medium for advertising. *The Data Base for Advances in Information Systems, 38*(4), 45–55.

Beard, L., Wilson, K., Morra, D., & Keelan, J. (2009). A survey of health-related activities on Second Life. *Journal of Medical Internet Reseach, 11*(2). Available: http://www.jmir.org/2009/2/e17#ref30

Bell, M. W. (2008). Toward a definition of "virtual worlds." *Journal of Virtual Worlds Research, 1*(1). Available: http://journals.tdl.org/jvwr/article/view/283/237

Bell, M. W., Castronova, E., & Wagner, G. G. (2009a, June 10). *Comparing real and virtual quality of life data using a self-interview method: Presentation transcript*. Retrieved September 17, 2009, from http://www.slideshare.net/storygeek/comparing-real-and-virtual-quality-of-life-data-using-a-virtual-assisted-selfinterview-method

Bell, M. W., Castronova, E., & Wagner, G. G. (2009b, June 12). *Surveying the virtual world: A large scale survey in Second Life using the Virtual Data Collection Interface (VDCI)*. Available: http://ssrn.com/abstract=1418562

Block, J. J. (2008). Issue for DSM-V: Internet addiction. *American Journal of Psychiatry, 165*, 306–307.

Boostrom, R. (2008). The social construction of virtual reality and the stigmatized identity of the newbie. *Journal of Virtual Worlds Reserach, 1*(2). Available: http://journals.tdl.org/jvwr/article/view/302/269

Butler, B., Sproull, S., Kiesler, S., & Kraut, R. (2008). Community effort in online groups: Who does the work and why? In S. P. Weisband (Ed.), *Leadership at a distance: Research in technologically supported work* (pp. 171–193). New York: Erlbaum.

Cabiria, J. (2008). Virtual world and real world permeability: Transference of positive benefits for marginalized gay and lesbian populations. *Journal of Virtual Worlds Research, 1*(1). Available: http://journals.tdl.org/jvwr/article/view/284/238

Carr, N. (2006, December 5). Avatars consume as much electricity as Brazilians [Web log]. *Rough Type*. Retrieved September 18, 2009, from http://www.roughtype.com/archives/2006/12/avatars_consume.php

Castronova, E. (2001, December). *Virtual worlds: A first-hand account of market and society on the cyberian frontier* (CESifo Working Paper No. 618). Unpublished manuscript.

Castronova, E. (2005). *Synthetic worlds: The business and culture of online games*. Chicago: University of Chicago Press.

Cho, S. H. (2007). Effects of motivations and gender on adolescents' self-disclosure in online chatting. *CyberPsychology & Behavior, 10*(3), 339–345.

Choi, H., & Varian, H. (2009). *Predicting the present with Google trends*. Unpublished manuscript, Google, Inc.

Cook, S. (2008). The contribution revolution: Letting volunteers build your business. *Harvard Business Review, 86*(10), 60–69.

Coons, S. J., Rao, S., Keininger, D. L., & Hays, R. D. (2000). A comparative review of generic quality-of-life instruments. *Pharmacoeconomica, 17*(1), 13–35.

Csikszentmihalyi, M. (1997). *Finding flow: The psychology of engagement with everyday life.* New York: Basic Books.

Csikszentmihalyi, M. (2000). The costs and benefits of consuming. *Journal of Consumer Research, 27*(2), 267–272.

Cummins, R. A., Andelman, R., Board, R., Carman, L. L., Feriss, A., Friedman, P., et al. (1998). *Quality of life definition and terminology: A discussion document.* Blacksburg, VA: International Society for Quality-of-Life Studies.

Damer, B. (2008). Meeting in the ether: A brief history of virtual worlds as a medium for user-created events. *Journal of Virtual Worlds Research, 1*(1). Available: http://journals.tdl.org/jvwr/article/view/285/239

Daugherty, T., Eastin, M. S., & Bright, L. (2008). Exploring consumer motivations for creating user-generated content. *Journal of Interactive Advertising, 8*(2). Available: http://jiad.org/article101

Dean, E., Cook, S., Keating, M., & Murphy, J. (2009). Does this avatar make me look fat? Obesity and interviewing in Second Life. *Journal of Virtual Worlds Research, 2*(2). Available: https://journals.tdl.org/jvwr/article/view/621/495

Diener, E. (2000). Subjective well-being: The science of happiness. *American Psychologist, 55*(1), 34–43.

Diener, E., Oishi, S., & Lucas, R. E. (2002). Subjective well-being: The science of happiness and life. In C. R. Snyder & S. J. Lopez (Eds.), *The handbook of positive psychology* (pp. 63–73). Oxford, England: Oxford University Press.

Diener, E., Suh, E. M., Lucas, R. E., & Smith, H. (1999). Subjective well being: Three decades of progress. *Psychological Bulletin, 125*(2), 276–302.

Dolan, P., Peasgood, T., & White, M. (2008). Do we really know what makes us happy? A review of the economic literature on the factors associated with subjective well-being. *Journal of Economic Psychology, 29*(1), 94–122.

Eastwick, P. W., & Gardner, W. L. (2008). Is it a game? Evidence for social influence in the virtual world. *Social Influence, 4*(1), 18–32.

Emmons, R. A., & McCullough, M. E. (2003). Counting blessing versus burdens: An experimental investigation of gratitude and subjective well being in daily life. *Journal of Personality and Social Psychology, 84,* 377–389.

Fetscherin, M., & Lattemann, C. (2008). User acceptance of virtual worlds. *Journal of Electronic Commerce Research, 9*(3), 231–242.

First-time Internet users find boost in brain function after just one week. (2009, October 19). *ScienceDaily.* Retrieved April 25, 2010, from http://www.sciencedaily.com/releases/2009/10/091019134707.htm

Fordyce, M. W. (1983). A program to increase happiness. *Journal of Counceling Psychology, 30,* 483–498.

Fox, J., & Bailenson, J. (2009). Virtual self-modeling: The effects of vicarious reinforcement and identification on exercise behaviors. *Media Psychology, 12*(1), 1–25.

Growth forecasts for the virtual worlds sector. (2009). *Kzero Worldswide.* Retrieved September 17, 2009, from http://www.kzero.co.uk/blog/?p=2845

Hagerty, M. R., Cummins, R. A., Ferriss, A. L., Land, K., Michalos, A. C., Peterson, M., et al. (2001). Quality of life indexes for national policy: Review and agenda for research. *Social Indicators Research, 55*(1), 1–96.

Hemp, P. (2006). Avatar-based marketing. *Harvard Business Review 84*(6), 48–57.

Hof, R. (2006a, November 26). Second Life's first millionaire. *BusinessWeek.* Retrieved September 17, 2009, from http://www.businessweek.com/the_thread/techbeat/archives/2006/11/second_lifes_fi.html

Hof, R. D. (2006b, May 1). My virtual life. *BusinessWeek.* Available: http://www.businessweek.com/magazine/content/06_18/b3982001.htm

Hoffman, D. L., & Novak, T. P. (1996). Marketing in hypermedia computer-mediated environments: Conceptual foundations. *Journal of Marketing, 60*(July), 50–68.

Hoffman, D. L., & Novak, T. P. (1998). Bridging the racial divide on the Internet. *Science, 280*(April), 390–391.

Hoffman, D. L., & Novak, T. P. (2009). Flow online: Lessons learned and future prospects. *Journal of Interactive Marketing, 23*(1), 23–34.

Hoffman, D. L., & Novak, T. P. (2010, June). *Roles and goals: Consumer motivations to use social media.* Paper presented at the 32nd annual INFORMS Marketing Science Conference, Cologne, Germany.

Java, A., Finin, T., Song, X., & Tseng, B. (2007). Why we Twitter: Understanding microblogging usage and communities. In H. Zhang et al. (Eds.), *Proceedings of the joint ninth WEBKDD and first SNA-KDD 2007 workshop on Web mining and social network analysis* (pp. 56–65). New York: Association for Computing Machinery.

Jennings, N., & Collins, C. (2007). Virtual or virtually U: Educational institutions in Second Life. *International Journal of Social Sciences, 2*, 180–186.

Jung, T., Youn, H., & McClung, S. (2007). Motivations and self-presentation strategies on Korean-based "cyworld" Weblog format personal homepages. *CyberPsychology & Behavior, 10*(1), 24–31.

Kahneman, D., Krueger, A. B., Schkade, D., Schwarz, N., & Stone, A. (2004). Toward national well-being accounts. *American Economic Review, 94*(2), 429–434.

Keating, J. E. (2008, May/June). Fake China. *Foreign Policy*, p. 92.

Keegan, V. (2007, November 1). Virtual China looks for real benefits. *The Guardian*, p. 4.

Kuznetsov, S. (2006). Motivations of contributors to Wikipedia. *Computers & Society, 36*(2), article 1.

Lenhart, A., & Fox, S. (2006). *Bloggers: A portrait of the Internet's new storytellers.* Washington, DC: Pew Internet & American Life Project.

Li, C., & Bernoff, J. (2008). *Groundswell: Winning in a world transformed by social technologies.* Boston: Harvard Business Press.

Lin, A. C. (2008). Virtual consumption: A *Second Life* for earth. *Brigham Young Uniersity Law Review, 1*, article 2.

Linden, G. (2009, April 21). Linden Lab use of Second Life [Web log]. *Second Life Blogs.* Retrieved September 17, 2009, from https://blogs.secondlife.com/community/workinginworld/blog/2009/04/21/linden-lab-use-of-second-life

Linden, M. J. (2009, May 15). Land Expo 2009 [Web log]. *Second Life Blogs.* Retrieved September 17, 2009, from https://blogs.secondlife.com/community/land/blog/2009/05/15/land-expo-2009

Ludlow, P., & Wallace, M. (2007). *The* Second Life Herald: *The virtual tabloid that witnessed the dawn of the metaverse.* Cambridge, MA: MIT Press.

Lyubomirsky, S., King, L., & Diener, E. (2005). The benefits of frequent positive affect: Does happiness lead to success? *Psychological Bulletin, 131*(6), 803–855.

Lyubomirsky, S., Sousa, L., & Dickerhoof, R. (2006). The costs and benefits of writing, talking, and thinking about life's triumphs and defeats. *Journal of Personality and Social Psychology, 90*, 692–708.

McKenna, K. Y., Green, A. S., & Gleason, M. E. (2002). Relationship formation on the Internet: What's the big attraction? *Journal of Social Issues, 58*(1), 9–31.

Messinger, P. R., Ge, X., Stroulia, E., Lyons, K., Smirnov, K., & Bone, M. (2008). On the relationship between my avatar and myself. *Journal of Virtual Worlds Reseach, 1*(2). Available: https://journals.tdl.org/jvwr/article/view/352/263

Milgram, S. (1963). Behavioral study of obedience. *Journal of Abnormal and Social Psychology, 67*, 371–378.

Milgran, P., & Kishino, F. (1994). A taxonomy of mixed reality visual displays. *IEICE Transactions on Information Systems, 77*, 1321–1329.

Miura, A., & Yamashita, K. (2007). Psychological and social influences on blog writing: An online survey of blog authors in Japan. *Journal of Computer-Mediated Communication, 12*, 1452–1472.

Noll, H. (2004). Social indicators and quality of life research: Background, achievements and current trends. In N. Genov (Ed.), *Advances in sociological knowledge over a half century* (pp. 151–181). Wiesbaden, Germany: Verlag für Sozialwissenschaften.

Nov, O. (2007). What motivates Wikipedians? *Communications of the ACM, 50*(11), 60–64.

Novak, T. P., Hoffman, D. L., & Yung, Y. (2000). Measuring the consumer experience in online environments: A structural modeling approach. *Marketing Science, 19*(Winter), 22–42.

Nowak, K. L., Kremar, M., & Farrar, K. M. (2008). The causes and consequences of presence: Considering the influence of violent video games on presence and aggression. *Presence, 17*(3), 256–268.

Otake, K., Shimai, S., Tanaka-Matsumi, J., Otsui, K., & Kredrickson, B. L. (2006). Happy people become happier through kindness: A counting kindness intervention. *Journal of Happiness Studies, 7*(3), 361–375.

Owen, R., Ntoko, A., Zhang, D., & Dong, J. (2002). Public policy and diffusion of innovation. *Social Indiators Research, 60*(December), 179–190.

Piper Jaffray & Co. (2009). Virtual goods revenues worldwide, 2008–2013 [Chart]. *eMarketer.* Available: http://www.emarketer.com/Results.aspx?dsNav=Rpp:25,N:4294966212-1143&xsrc=TopicsPanel

Reeves, B., & Nass, C. (2002). *The media equation: How people treat computers, television, and new media like real people and places.* Chicago: University of Chicago Press.

Repères. (2007). *Main research findings: Purchase habits in Second Life.* Paris: Author.

Ridings, C., & Gefen, D. (2004). Virtual community attraction: Why people hang out online. *Journal of Computer-Mediated Communication, 10*(1), article 4.

Rogers, C. (1951). *Client-centered therapy.* Boston: Houghton Mifflin.

Rose, F. (2007, July 24). How Madison Avenue is wasting millions on a deserted Second LIfe. *Wired, 15*(8). Available: http://www.wired.com/techbiz/media/magazine/15-08/ff_sheep

Ryan, R. M., & Deci, E. L. (2001). On happiness and human potentials: A review of reserach on hedonic and eudaimonic well-being. *Annual Review of Psychology, 52*(1), 141–166.

Schotz, T. (2008). *Motivations for participation* [Slideshow]. Retrieved September 17, 2009, from https://www.slide share.net/trebor/motivating-people-to-participate

Schroeder, R. (1996). *Possible worlds: The social dynamic of virtual reality technologies.* Boulder, CO: Westview Press.

Schroeder, R. (2008). Defining virtual worlds and virtual environments. *Journal of Virtual Worlds Research, 1*(1). Available: http://journals.tdl.org/jvwr/article/view/294/248

Schuemie, M. J., van der Straaten, P., Krijn, M., & van der Mast, C. A. (2001). Research on presence in virtual reality: A survey. *CyberPsychology & Behavior, 4*(2), 183–201.

Sirgy, M. J., Michalos, A. C., Ferriss, A. L., Easterlin, R. A., Patrick, D., & Pavot, W. (2006). The quality-of-life (QOL) research movement: Past, present and future. *Social Indicators Research, 76*(3), 343–466.

Slater, M., Antley, A., Davison, A., Swapp, D., Guger, C., Barker, C., et al. (2006). A virtual reprise of the Stanley Milgram obedience experiments. *PLoS One, 1*(1), e39.

Spence, J. (2008). Demographics of virtual worlds. *Journal of Virtual Worlds Research, 1*(2). Available: http://journals.tdl.org/jvwr/article/view/360/272

Steuer, J. (1992). Defining virtual realities: Dimensions determining telepresence. *Journal of Communication, 42*, 73–79.

Stoeckl, R., Rohnmier, P., & Hess, T. (2007, June). *Motivations to produce user generated content: Differences between webloggers and videobloggers.* Paper presented at the 20th annual Bled eConference on eMergence: Merging and emerging technologies, processes, and institutions, Bled, Slovenia.

Trammell, K. D., Tarkowsi, A., Hofmokl, J., & Sapp, A. M. (2006). Rzeczpospolita blogów [Republic of blog]: Examining Polish bloggers through content analysis. *Journal of Computer-Mediated Communication, 11*(3), 702–722.

Universal avatars bestride worlds. (2007, October 11). *BBC News.* Retrieved September 17, 2009, from http://news.bbc.co.uk/2/hi/technology/7038039.stm

van den Besselaar, P., & Beckers, D. (2005). The life and death of the great Amsterdam Digital City. In D. Hutchison et al. (Series Eds.), P. van den Besselaar, & S. Koizumi (Vol. Eds.), *Lecture notes in computer science: Vol. 3081. Digital cities 2003* (pp. 66–96). Berlin: Springer-Verlag.

Varvello, M., Picconi, F., Diot, C., & Biersack, E. (2008, December). *Is there life in Second Life?* Paper presented at the annual conference of CoNEXT, Madrid, Spain.

Veenhoven, R. (1998). Quality-of-life and happiness: Not quite the same. In G. DeGirolamo et al. (Eds.), *Health and quality-of-life* (pp. 67–95). Rome: Il Pensierro Scientifico.

Virtual mobility for disabled wins Second Life prize. (2009, May 2). *Physorg.com.* Retrieved September 17, 2009, from http://www.physorg.com/news160459222.html

Weiss, A. M., Lurie, N. H., & Macinnis, D. J. (2008). Listening to strangers: Whose responses are valuable, how valuable are they, and why? *Journal of Marketing Reserch, 45*(August), 425–436.

Whang, L. S., & Chang, G. (2004). Lifestyles of virtual world residents: Living in the on-line game lineage. *CyberPsychology & Behavior, 7*(5), 592–600.

Williams, D. (2010). The mapping principle, and a research framework for virtual worlds. *Communication Theory, 20*, 451–470.

Wood, N. T., & Solomon, M. R. (Eds.). (2009). *Virtual social identity and consumer behavior.* Armonk, NY: M.E. Sharpe.

Yang, H., & Chattopadhyay, A. (2009). *Marketing to avatars: The impact of metaverse embodiment on consumer self-concept and behavior.* Unpublished manuscript, INSEAD.

Yee, N. (2007). Motivations of play in online games. *CyberPsychology & Behavior, 9*, 772–775.

Yee, N., & Bailenson, J. N. (2007). The Proteus effect: The effect of transformed self-representation on behavior. *Human Communication Research, 33*(3), 271–290.

Yee, N., Bailenson, J. N., Urbanek, M., Chang, G., & Merget, D. (2007). The unbearable likeness of being digital: The persistence of nonverbal social norms in online virtual environments. *CyberPsychology & Behavior, 10*(1), 115–121.

Zhao, S., Grasmuck, S., & Martin, J. (2008). Identity construction in Facebook: Digital empowerment in anchored relationships. *Computers in Human Behavior, 24*(5), 1816–1836.

# IV

## *MATERIALISM AND THE ENVIRONMENT*

# 12

## *What Welfare?*
## On the Definition and Domain of Transformative Consumer Research and the Foundational Role of Materialism

JAMES E. BURROUGHS AND ARIC RINDFLEISCH

In his widely lauded 2005 presidential address to the Association for Consumer Research (ACR), David Glen Mick (2006) offered the stark observation that the consumer research field had done very little to enhance the welfare of consumers. Mick's pronouncement contained a certain degree of irony, as one of ACR's founding principles in 1973 was to promote consumer well-being (Kernan, 1979). Over the past 4 decades, ACR members have produced an impressive body of research on consumer behavior. Unfortunately, little of this research has benefited consumers themselves. In short, the hopes and aspirations of the ACR as an agent of change have not been realized.

Mick's address strongly resonated throughout the ACR community, as many of its members share a collective sense of disappointment that we have not done better. Prompted by this call to action, the past 5 years have witnessed a resurgent interest in consumer welfare and the birth of the Transformative Consumer Research (TCR) movement. While TCR offers renewed hope and a sense of urgency, there is also fear and trepidation. The task is daunting, and the consumer research community has engaged in these self-recriminations before (Andreasen, Goldberg, & Sirgy, Chapter 2 of this volume; Mick, 2006). The ultimate success of the TCR movement hinges on developing and directing research that produces demonstrable positive change for consumers in all corners of the world, and there is a firm belief that the collective talents of ACR can be marshaled to this end (Mick, Pettigrew, Pechmann, & Ozanne, Chapter 1 of this volume). However, our ability to make an important and lasting difference in consumers' lives will require a realistic assessment of TCR's domain and focus.

Our objective is to provide such an assessment by taking inventory of recent developments in the TCR movement and establishing the value of materialism for advancing this cause. Based on careful reflection and our many years researching this topic, we believe materialism has the potential to serve as a foundational construct in TCR, both in terms of defining the scope of consumer welfare and as a lens through which many other TCR concerns may be viewed (e.g., Burroughs & Rindfleisch, 2002; Rindfleisch, Burroughs, & Denton, 1997; Rindfleisch, Burroughs, & Wong, 2009). Our assessment begins by framing the domain of TCR and situating materialism research within it. We then examine prior conceptions of consumer welfare and introduce a new concept that we term the *material trap*. We conclude with a discussion of three endowments for escaping the material trap and suggest ways that future research can be directed to leverage and augment these endowments. Our hope is that this assessment, along with the other chapters in this volume, will help establish the parameters of an emerging discipline, one with the explicit aim of enhancing consumer welfare.

## DOMAIN OF TRANSFORMATIVE CONSUMER RESEARCH

A survey of the TCR landscape reveals that the bulk of extant research falls into one of four over-lapping categories: (1) suboptimal decision making, (2) consumption-related disorders, (3) macro-social concerns, and (4) materialism (see Figure 12.1). The first category of research, suboptimal decision making, refers to the myriad (often cognitive) deficiencies that lead consumers to make poor consumption choices, either because they forego a better choice or would have been better off by not engaging in the act of consumption in the first place. There is abundant research that sug-gests that consumers are subject to deception in the marketplace (Boush, Friestad, & Wright, 2009), prone to immediate gratification at the expense of a larger, deferred benefit (Malkoc & Zauberman, 2006), and systematically irrational in their decision making (Ariely, 2008). These shortcomings are not aberrations among a select few consumers, but instead are widely present among what are considered to be "normal" consumers.

The second area of TCR inquiry concentrates on consumption-related disorders, which are psychological afflictions that manifest in various consumption settings. The most prominent example is compulsive consumption, which is believed to be part of an impulse spectrum disorder (see Faber & Vohs, Chapter 22 of this volume; O'Guinn & Faber, 1989; Ridgeway, Kukar-Kinney, & Monroe, 2008). Other forms of consumption-related disorders include uncontrolled gambling,

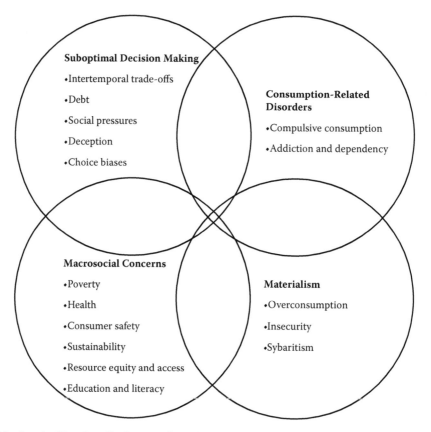

**Figure 12.1**  Domain of Transformative Consumer Research.

addiction to pornography, substance dependency, and eating disorders (see Albright, Chapter 24 of this volume; Cotte & LaTour, 2009, Chapter 23 of this volume; Faber, Christenson, de Zwaan, & Mitchell, 1995).

The third area of TCR relates to the macrosocial concerns that transcend society, including the institutional structures that dictate access to material resources and services (see Kilbourne & Mittelstaedt, Chapter 14 of this volume). This area covers a wide array of issues, including poverty, environmental degradation, economic development, and health care access (Hill, 2001; Kilbourne, McDonagh, & Prothero, 1997; Shultz & Shapiro, Chapter 6 of this volume; Viswanathan, Chapter 5 of this volume; Viswanathan, Rosa, & Ruth, 2010). Although these issues are primarily macro in scope, this does not preclude researchers from focusing on specific problems and affected consumer groups. For example, while poverty is a global concern, Viswanathan's research (see Viswanathan, Chapter 5 of this volume; Viswanathan et al., 2010) concentrates on impoverished and low-literate consumers in Chennai, India, and seeks ways to empower these individuals to make better consumption decisions and decrease their vulnerability to unscrupulous marketing practices. Other macroissues, such as health care or sustainability, might similarly be approached at either a societal or more localized level.

The fourth area of TCR focuses on materialism. *Materialism* can be defined as the importance or value placed on the acquisition and ownership of material objects, as opposed to other important sources of meaning, such as family, spirituality, or community. Materialism is multidimensional in nature and entails the centrality of material possessions to one's sense of self, their role as a sign of success, and the importance of acquiring possessions as a means of happiness (Richins & Dawson, 1992). Since its inception, research on materialism has been centrally concerned with how these values influence consumer welfare. Most of this research has examined materialism's negative relation to individual well-being, particularly personal happiness and life satisfaction (see Burroughs & Rindfleisch, 2002). Although materialistic individuals believe objects will make them happier and more fulfilled, the opposite often turns out to be the case (Kasser, 2002).

In contrast to the other three areas of TCR, materialism is the one topic that is homegrown within the field of consumer research (e.g., Belk, 1985; Richins & Dawson, 1992). Thus, as consumer researchers, we possess a high level of expertise in this area and stand to advance research on other social concerns through our unique understanding of materialism. Indeed, many of the issues that have attracted the interest of TCR scholars (e.g., addictive behaviors, deceptive marketing practices, sustainability concerns) appear to be closely linked to materialism. For example, gambling taps into materialistic desires to get rich quick and live a lavish lifestyle. Similarly, unscrupulous marketers are often able to deceive consumers by exploiting their materialistic vulnerabilities. Moreover, materialism can be directly implicated in the excess consumption that threatens our environment. As each of these examples shows, materialism research has considerable value for TCR scholars, even those primarily interested in other areas.

Figure 12.1 also illustrates other areas of overlap across the four subdomains of TCR, and each intersection represents an opportunity to combine one or more TCR topics. For example, prior research has linked materialism to consumer disorders such as compulsive consumption (Rindfleisch et al., 1997), to suboptimal decision making such as weakened capacity for delayed gratification (Kasser, 2002), and to macrosocial issues such as concern for the environment (Kasser & Sheldon, 2000). Although it is not possible to consider all the potential ways materialism research could be extended into these other areas, these examples further reinforce the value of materialism for widening TCR scholarship (for additional research opportunities, see Burroughs et al., 2011). Of course, transformative consumer researchers can also utilize this framework to examine the intersection of other consumer welfare issues, such as debt and compulsive consumption, poverty and intertemporal trade-offs, or health and social pressures. However, while Figure 12.1 highlights opportunities for spanning research boundaries, it also shows that this overlap is only partial. Consumer researchers must therefore be mindful not to overreach. For example, materialism may be only peripherally related to issues such as consumer safety or choice biases. In sum, TCR scholarship encompasses a wide variety of issues, united in their focus on consumer welfare.

## DEFINING CONSUMER WELFARE

Interestingly, Mick (2006) never explicitly defined *consumer welfare* in his presidential address, although he referenced any number of consumer welfare–related issues (e.g., smoking, gambling, product safety). Considering that the goal of his speech was to inspire an audience, becoming mired in definitions may have been counterproductive, but surely someone would have since taken up this mantle?

We searched broadly for a definition of *consumer welfare* beginning with the *Journal of Consumer Research*'s "Special Issue on Consumer Welfare" in 2008. Although the organization of the articles in this issue help frame what consumer welfare might entail, and it is clear that the authors have given the issue some thought (see Mick, 2008; Ozanne & Saatcioglu, 2008), none of these articles explicitly define what consumer welfare is or delineate its scope of inquiry, nor could we find a definition in any of the other foundational writings on TCR (e.g., Bazerman, 2001; Hill, 2001; Mari, 2008). Furthermore, we could find no suitable definition in allied areas such as sustainable consumption (Kilbourne et al., 1997; Varey, 2010), macromarketing (Mittelstaedt, Kilbourne, & Mittelstaedt, 2006; Wilkie & Moore, 2006), social marketing (Andreasen, 2002; Sprott & Miyazaki, 2002), or quality-of-life marketing (Lee & Sirgy, 2004).

Only with this volume has the definition of *consumer welfare* finally been taken up in TCR. Mick et al. (Chapter 1 of this issue) define it as "a state of flourishing that involves health, happiness, and prosperity" and note how consumer welfare is comprised of seven dimensions or contributing factors: "emotional, social, economic, physical, spiritual, environmental, and political" (see also McGregor & Goldsmith, 1998). Mick and colleagues acknowledge that this is a wide array of factors and will likely involve trade-offs across them. Andreasen et al. (Chapter 2 of this volume), by comparison, suggest that consumer welfare is fundamentally about human development and reflects both personal (e.g., happiness, life satisfaction) and societal aspects (e.g., economic health, environmental health). These authors provide a remarkable historical overview of prior research in this domain and suggest that consumer well-being must be redressed through considerations of sovereignty, nonmalfeasance, social justice, and stakeholder claims.

The lack of a clear and consistent definition to mobilize the TCR movement suggests that consumer welfare may mean different things to different researchers. As a result, the topics that garner the attention and resources of TCR scholars are likely to encompass a considerable amount of variance, and our efforts may become diluted as a consequence. ACR Fellow Don Lehmann aptly summarized the situation at a TCR roundtable when he opined, "If the TCR movement is to have any chance of succeeding, we better make darn sure that the first fight we pick is one we are going to win" (comment made during a panel discussion following Mick's ACR presidential address, Mick, 2006). In other words, if TCR is to succeed, it must show immediate, if limited, progress, which necessarily requires a certain amount of prioritization by the field. Conversely, if transformative consumer researchers rush headlong into social problems of such variety and magnitude that there is little chance of making any measurable difference, the movement will founder. We believe that positive results will be best achieved by limiting our efforts to a tractable set of research issues built around a shared set of concepts and points of focus.

Consider the tracks at the second TCR conference recently held in Philadelphia, Pennsylvania (Ozanne, in press). They included poverty, environmental sustainability, materialism, health, nutrition and obesity, developing markets, at-risk populations, social justice, and immigration. Clearly, these are important issues, and consumer researchers are doing important work on all of them. However, this is a remarkable array of topics, and the meaning of consumer welfare may vary from one area to another. For example, some of these topics center on economic and social welfare (e.g., poverty, social justice, at-risk populations), whereas others focus on psychological and physical welfare (e.g., health, nutrition and obesity). In short, there remains a need to define the parameters of consumer welfare. In addition to establishing TCR's conceptual boundaries, we must also consider what unique value we can bring to these varied topics, nearly all of which have been the subject of decades of research and public policy efforts. The issue of obesity alone claims dozens of dedicated academic journals (e.g., *Journal of Obesity, International Journal of Obesity, Obesity and Weight Management, International Journal of Pediatric Obesity, Current Opinion in Endocrinology, Diabetes and Obesity, Diabetes, Obesity & Metabolism*). To be sure, consumer researchers need to step out of their silos, and solving these problems will require cross-disciplinary collaboration, but we must also carefully consider the unique expertise that we can offer to these efforts.

We believe that research on materialism can help establish a common understanding of what is meant by consumer welfare as well as provide a valuable lens for TCR scholars interested in these other areas of inquiry. In the remainder of this section, we provide a review of consumer welfare viewed from both the individual (psychological) and societal (economic) perspectives and relate these views to materialism. In the end, we do not define consumer welfare strictly in terms of increased individual well-being, such as enhanced happiness, social connection, or physical health, although these will certainly be a product of our efforts. Nor do we believe that consumer welfare is achieved strictly through some systemic or economic means like optimal resource distribution, although it is difficult to envision any sustained form of consumer welfare without addressing these broader social ramifications. Rather, it is our contention that consumer welfare must encompass both of these elements. Therefore, we define *consumer welfare* as the alignment of individual and societal needs (i.e., physical, psychological, economic, social) as they relate through consumption. Consumer welfare is optimized when an individual recognizes and balances these varied interests in their decision making. Making the case for our approach to consumer welfare requires a review of past research on consumer well-being.

### Individual and Psychological Perspectives on Consumer Welfare

Consumer researchers have historically viewed individual well-being through the lens of rational choice theory (Bettman, 1974; Howard & Sheth, 1969). Because this theory is well known to consumer researchers, we will keep our comments brief. According to rational choice theory, individuals carefully select and consume products because they expect to benefit from these purchases. An exemplar of this perspective is the large literature that now exists on consumer satisfaction, which posits that satisfaction is a direct function of the degree to which a product delivers anticipated utility (e.g., Fournier & Mick, 1999; Oliver, 1997). Unfortunately, due to bounded rationality, consumers often make suboptimal choices. They often have difficulty comprehending intertemporal trade-offs (Malkoc & Zauberman, 2006), exhibit a variety of biases in their decision making (Ariely, 2008; Tversky & Kahneman, 1974), and are vulnerable to deceptive marketing practices (Boush et al., 2009). Consumers may even use products that are detrimental to aspects of their well-being, such as cigarettes (Pechmann, Biglan, Grube, & Cody, Chapter 17 of this volume; Pechmann & Knight, 2002; Pechmann & Riebling, 2006).

As a result of these and other limitations, consumer researchers have dedicated substantial effort to understanding the psychological aspects of consumer welfare (Baumeister, 2002; Csikszentmihalyi, 2000; Moiso & Beruchashvili, 2010). As might be expected, these discussions are decidedly individualistic in their approach to well-being, with a heavy emphasis on subjective indicants, such as happiness and life satisfaction, or adverse consequences like anxiety and depression (Baumeister, 2002; Hirschman, 1991; Labroo & Patrick, 2009; Raghunathan & Irwin, 2008). Interest in the physical manifestations of well-being has also grown dramatically in consumer research, with recent topics of obesity, oral care, and breast cancer, to name but a few (Block et al., in press; Du, Sen, & Bhattacharya, 2008; Grier & Moore, Chapter 15 of this volume; Scammon et al., in press; Sharpe, Staelin, & Huber, 2008; Wong & Kim, 2010; Wong & King, 2008). Finally, consumer researchers have started to consider the social aspects of well-being, with an emphasis being at the dyadic or small-group level, such as social support or family connection (Epp & Price, Chapter 29 of this volume; Hoffman, Chapter 9 of this volume; Kozinets, Belz, & McDonagh, Chapter 10 of this volume).

Over the past 2 decades, materialism researchers have been at the forefront of consumer research on individual well-being. This body of research has consistently demonstrated that consumers who highly value material acquisition (e.g., designer clothes, luxury automobiles) exhibit lower levels of psychological adjustment (see Burroughs & Rindfleisch, 2002), and there is emerging evidence that materialistic tendencies can even be detrimental to physical health (Kasser, 2002; Kasser & Ahuvia, 2002). In sum, the data indicate that materialism is harmful to both mind and body.

### Economic and Societal Perspectives on Consumer Welfare

Although consumer researchers have concentrated on the psychological and physical aspects of well-being, many of the issues that transformative consumer researchers are interested in (e.g., poverty, overconsumption, sustainability) are societal in scope. To date, these more collective aspects of consumer welfare have received decidedly less attention from consumer scholars. Thus, to help address this gap, we provide a review of some foundational concepts and works in this area.

In contrast to the more individualistic view of well-being described previously, economic and social welfare focuses on the health of an entire society or economic system, in terms of both total welfare and welfare distribution. Termed the *social welfare function*, economists define *welfare* as the sum total of the well-being of all the citizens that comprise a society (Pattanaik, 2008; Sen, 1970). From an economic perspective, monetary and material resources are the primary metric of well-being, although welfare economists now often consider nonmonetary indicants of societal health as well (e.g., education, sanitation, crime). Nonetheless, there remains a trenchant belief that material resources are fungible and can therefore be translated into other forms of well-being.

The goal of welfare economics is to maximize total social welfare, which is captured in the concept of the Pareto optimum (i.e., a state where no further redistribution of resources can produce an increase in benefit to one individual without a larger offsetting loss to someone else). Since, presumably, individuals will pursue those objects and outcomes that maximize their personal utility, a foundational axiom in welfare economics is that resource distribution is optimized through a decentralized system in which individual actors egoistically pursue their own self-interests, or at least there is a presumption that such a system is superior to "a large class of possible alternative dispositions" (Arrow & Hahn, 1971, p. xi).

Although the idea that individual interest will maximize the collective good is long-standing in economic thought, the problem with the Pareto optimality is that it can be satisfied in conditions when "some people are rolling in luxury and others are near starvation, as long as the starvers cannot be made better off without cutting into the pleasures of the rich" (Sen, 1970, p. 22). This inequity stems from two rather well-known flaws of free-market economics. The first is the presumption of free choice (i.e., unconstrained access to market offerings from which an individual gets to choose). Unfortunately, institutional barriers, such as access to education and health care, often falsify this assumption. In other words, not everyone begins the resource race at the same starting line. The second limitation is the presumption that individuals are fully capable of making informed choices. The limits to human rationality are increasingly highlighted in the emerging subfield of behavioral economics (see Mazar, Amir, & Ariely, 2008). Due to these two limitations, disparities in personal welfare typically arise, even within wealthy societies (Sen, 1973).

Because some individuals are able to capture and consume a disproportionate share of a society's wealth (Sen, 1979), economists have historically been left with two rather unattractive choices when it comes to maximizing social welfare. One is to accept the status quo that egoistic pursuit produces the maximum total output, and then hope for an acceptable level of trickle-down. The other is to intervene in the distribution of resources through alternative forms of social governance, accepting attendant inefficiencies in the process. Because, at its heart, the TCR movement is focused on challenging accepted paradigms and upsetting the status quo, we shall consider these two options more deeply.

The interventionist approach is nicely captured in Barry's (1973) notion of altruistic collaboration and Rawls's (1971) maximin principle. Barry (1973) argues that a society should strive to benefit all its members even at the expense of efficiency and personal enhancement, whereas Rawls (1971) asserts that society should be structured to maximize the position of those who are least well off. Rawls's maximin argument is based on what is known as the veil of ignorance. According to this logic, it is in any individual's best interest to ascribe to a system that protects the lowest echelons of society, because one can never know the fate of one's own future economic fortunes. Moreover, according to Rawls (as cited in Arrow, 1973), because

> superiorities of intelligence or strength do not themselves create any claims to greater rewards the principles of justice are "an agreement to regard the distribution of natural talents as a common asset and to share in the benefits of this distribution." (p. 247)

Finally, Rawls (1971) holds a more sanguine view of human nature than most economists when he speaks of humans' "natural sociability" (p. 584) and one for which he "anticipates a more spontaneous public spiritedness to cement a commitment to both the right and the good" (Chapman, 1975, p. 589).

Both Barry's and Rawls's writings emote a certain liberal idealism that, although appealing in principle, have proven exceedingly difficult to implement. Unfortunately, the free rider problem endemic to these systems creates a large disincentive to individual initiative and industriousness. To the extent that aspiration and opportunity are important elements of human welfare in their own right, such egalitarianism appears to create as many problems as it solves. Arrow (1973) recognized this disincentive and provided a stiff rebuttal to Rawls by asking the simple question, "[I]s not an individual entitled to what he creates?" (p. 248). Finally, interventionists such as Rawls offer little guidance on how much sacrifice at the top should be necessary for elevating the welfare of the bottom (Sen, 1979), other than when the top becomes the bottom, which is self-defeating.

Nonetheless, the persistent inequality of the free market has led a faction of economists to mount a powerful challenge to the long-standing assumption of individual self-interest as the guiding principle of resource distribution. As Sen (1979) aptly points out, there are many intermediate alternatives between a purely egoistic system and a purely altruistic one. According to Sen (1973, 1977), there is a third possibility that individuals might also be guided by moral or sympathetic motives (what he terms *commitments*) even in a system predicated on individual self-interest. Individuals can, and do, make decisions that enhance the welfare of others, even at personal expense. Sen's ideas hold out the possibility of maximizing, or at least greatly enhancing, social good while preserving individual initiative. However, the natural question that arises in Sen's writings is how to foster this more enlightened decision making without institutionally mandating it. Even Sen (1977) acknowledges that altruistic decisions are a distinct minority compared to self-interested decisions in any capitalist arrangement. A challenge for the TCR movement, then, is to find ways to enhance both personal and collective welfare without severely jeopardizing one for the other.

Although the tension between personal and collective welfare is an enduring dilemma in the social sciences (see Mills, 1959), these two forms of well-being are inextricably tied together and may be more naturally aligned than they first appear. While individuals may derive certain short-run benefits by overconsuming at the expense of others, they cannot maximize long-term welfare by depleting the system that sustains them. A lavish fur coat, a gas-guzzling sport-utility vehicle, and a shiny wood floor harvested from old-growth forest may all feel good to consume in the short run. However, such materialism harbors long-term negative consequences for both the individual and the broader society. Thus, the tension between personal and collective welfare represents a critical challenge for the TCR movement. We believe that viewing this tension through the vantage of the material trap can open a host of valuable insights.

## MATERIAL TRAP

Thus far, we have argued that materialism is a foundational concept in TCR and a key element of consumer welfare. In the remainder of this chapter, we employ materialism as a lens for looking ahead. Specifically, we explore the etiology of materialism and how a materialistic orientation unwittingly traps consumers into a set of behaviors that are detrimental to both themselves and society. We finish with a consideration of potential ways to escape the material trap, and the consequences if we do not.

Materialism scholars have devoted substantial attention to understanding the antecedents and origins of material values. This body of research has found that material values are formed at an early age and are often an adaptive response to developmental, economic, social, or existential insecurity (Rindfleisch et al., 1997, 2009). This adaptation is facilitated by exposure to materialistic messages and imagery via television and other socialization agents (Shrum, Burroughs, & Rindfleisch, 2005). In sum, the extant literature has suggested that materialism is overwhelmingly a product of nurture rather than nature. We wonder, however, whether it could be the other way around.

We realize this assertion is likely to be somewhat controversial, but consider the argument, if humans evolved with an instinct for self-preservation, why wouldn't we also evolve an instinct for self-enhancement? As documented by Galbraith (1958), for most of human history, affluence and luxury have been the exception rather than the rule. Given that human existence has been characterized by deprivation and shortage, the development of an acquisitive orientation would confer many advantages.

The premise that materialism may be at least partially innate is supported by recent research in neurology, which found that the brain is hardwired to develop a sense of autonomous possession (Rochat, 2010). At age 2, some of the first words out of a child's mouth are "me" and "mine" (Rochat, in press). Conceptions of possession are essential to navigating the natural environment. Such possessiveness quite literally signals developmental changes in the prefrontal cortex regions of the brain as the body struggles to control its immediate surroundings (Rochat, 2010). From there, the brain quickly and progressively develops the ability to recognize a socialized, and potentially coveting, other, but egoistic possession remains inalienable and nonnegotiable (Rochat, 2010). Only later, from age 3 to 5, does the brain become capable of more complex social concepts such as sharing, at which time possession becomes an important foundation for a moral space and notions of distributive justice (Rochat et al., 2009). It is also at this point that potential differences in possessiveness due to cultural influence become possible (Rochat et al., 2009). These findings reinforce the notion that even if materialism is heavily socialized, it has an important innate component.

Because a materialistic disposition appears to be part of our DNA as well as our social development, materialism can be an exceedingly difficult trap to avoid. The problem is that humans are not well adapted to conditions of abundance and cannot easily turn this material drive off. While material objects are necessary for survival, they are of very limited value in satisfying higher order needs, yet humans often persist in trying to use objects for this purpose (Diener & Biswas-Diener, 2008; Kasser & Ahuvia, 2002; Myers, 2008; Wong, Rindfleisch, & Burroughs, 2003). To illustrate, one survey conducted by the National Opinion Research Center showed a positive relationship between household income and happiness up to a level of about $65,000 (Myers, 2008). However, once household income passes this level (i.e., where all essential needs are met), the association between income and happiness basically disappears. Nonetheless, when asked the one thing that would make them happier, Americans' overwhelming response is "more money" (Myers, 2008). Indeed, while most of us would agree with the adage that money cannot buy happiness, our expressed preferences (e.g., lobbying for pay raises, buying lottery cards) reveal that we often think and act differently. Like Samuel Gompers, we tend to assume that we would be satisfied if we had just a little more. Unfortunately, this belief is illusory, as a considerable body of research has shown that materialism decreases rather than increases life satisfaction (see Burroughs & Rindfleisch, 2002, for a review).

In addition to being personally detrimental, materialism may also be harmful to collective well-being (Kasser, 2002). Our entire economic system is predicated on continually expanding cycles of growth and consumption, which is now straining our planet's resources and creating substantial social inequities (Speth, 2008). The result is what we refer to as the material trap, a situation in which the short-term payoffs of consumption undermine the longer term personal and societal benefits of moderation and restraint. The more ravenous our consumption becomes, the more difficult it becomes to extricate ourselves from this cycle. In many respects, the material trap is a modern incarnation of the tragedy of the commons, in which the pursuit of immediate self-interests undermines broader social welfare and ultimately circles back to harm the individual (Hardin, 1968; Platt, 1973; Schelling, 1971). Unfortunately, these adverse consequences are usually lagged and hidden. For example, Americans' desire for less expensive goods often requires the relocation of production to less expensive labor markets, which increases the distance these goods must travel, which necessitates the building of massive cargo ships that pollute the environment, which eventually requires these ships to be dismantled, which occurs in squalid working conditions in places of extreme poverty (Buerk, 2006; Dauvergne, 2008). This chain of consequences rarely enters the lexicon of individual decision making and is just as rarely considered by consumer researchers.

To recap, we propose that consumer welfare, or at least an important component of it, involves the alignment of individual and societal interests. While we acknowledge that there may be other valid views of consumer welfare,* we nonetheless hope that our view is a provocative one that prompts consumer researchers to think more broadly about the problems they study. Such a view suggests a matrix of trade-offs that transformative consumer scholars should consider in their research: What are the individual benefits and costs? What are the societal benefits and costs? What is the distance between individual and societal outcomes? What do consumers expect in return if asked to give something up? Ultimately, these questions are concerned with altering the ratio of the equation in the material trap or getting people to understand it differently. The question is, how?

---

* Moving forward, it would be useful to consider how other views of consumer welfare might contribute to our understanding of the material trap. For example, feminist theory, which has advanced the welfare of women, has also been criticized for failing to sufficiently distinguish between freedom of choice and the notion having it all (i.e., family, career, personal life) when these choices necessarily involve trade-offs. Women who fail to recognize this difference often end up feeling overwhelmed (Hewlett, 2003).

## ESCAPING THE MATERIAL TRAP

We have described how our penchant for materialism is deeply seated and presents a pernicious trap. Although consumer researchers have made substantial progress in identifying materialism's causes and consequences, they have made relatively little progress in offering viable solutions for reducing materialism or ameliorating its negative effects. Because materialism is widely presumed to be socially constructed, most attempts to combat it try to either block exposure to materialistic messages or counter these messages with antimaterialistic media campaigns. For example, a popular proposal for lessening materialism is to reduce exposure to materialistic messages by controlling or limiting contact with mass media (Hammerslough, 2002; Kasser, 2002). Although getting Americans, and most of the rest of the world, to watch less television is certainly a laudable goal, trying to prevent materialism in this way is exceedingly difficult, if not unrealistic. Trying to convince people that they should not be materialistic is akin to trying to convince them that they should not like sex or fatty foods. We may learn to control our impulses, but we cannot remove the underlying desire.

Throughout this chapter, we have tried to propose a different way of thinking about materialism, which naturally implies a different set of solutions. Fortunately, humans have three powerful endowments for escaping the material trap in the forms of our mental capacities for social organization, future thinking, and analogical reasoning.* These capacities, in turn, lead to three solutions for escaping the material trap: (1) aligning individual and collective interests, (2) narrowing the conceptual distance between micromotives and macroconsequences, and (3) framing behaviors to raise the saliency of their impact.

### Aligning Individual and Collective Interests

Humans have a propensity to make decisions that weigh individual benefits but discount societal costs. Fortunately, our ability to organize socially has the potential to overcome this problem by aligning these interests. In fact, "a good part of social organization—of what we call society— consists of institutional arrangements to overcome these divergences" (Schelling, 1971, p. 68). These institutional arrangements include conventions, rules, and laws, all of which are designed to elicit conformance to a set of behaviors that are mutually beneficial, even when individual interests might suggest otherwise.

A good example of an institutional attempt to align individual and social interests is the introduction of high-occupancy vehicle (HOV) lanes in major U.S. urban areas. Although most of us prefer to drive our own vehicles, this preference exacts a severe environmental cost, as well as a heavy personal toll due to increased traffic congestion. The introduction of specially designated lanes for vehicles with multiple passengers was intended to help alleviate both of these problems.

Unfortunately, most HOV lanes stand nearly empty at rush hour because individuals are largely unwilling to devote the time and energy needed to form a carpool. Thus, when developing their HOV initiatives, urban planners apparently failed to account for this aspect of the decision matrix. However, a recent remedy to this shortcoming has been the emergence of slug lines in the greater Washington, DC, area, which are predetermined routes between the suburban ring and the city center that facilitate carpooling among complete strangers (i.e., sluggers). To achieve such

---

\* To this initial set of three endowments, a fourth endowment might be added, namely, the capacity for moral reasoning. Humans appear to possess a unique capacity for moral judgment (Bloom, 2010; Haidt, 2007), and this capacity can lead to prosocial behaviors. However, the failures of moral appeals to effect lasting social change are well documented and may be because moral appeals often rely on prohibition which does not automatically help an individual see how behavioral change is in their own self-interest, or at least not to the degree the other endowments do. For this reason, moral appeals would probably be best used in conjunction with one or more of the other three endowments.

cooperation among strangers, slugging has a defined set of rules. Sluggers do not talk to the driver or each another, do not talk on their cell phones, do not change the radio station set by the driver, and do not ask to be picked up or dropped off anywhere other than one of the predetermined locations, which are strategically selected to be maximally convenient to the driver. These and other rules make carpooling as maximally similar to solo driving as possible. The success of this social initiative demonstrates how individuals can escape the material trap by creating a path of least resistance between individual benefits and collective costs.[*]

Narrowing the Conceptual Distance Between Micromotives and Macroconsequences

In his recent treatise on human nature and happiness, Gilbert (2005) boldly proclaims that the most important human endowment is our ability to conceive the future. Gilbert goes on to detail how the emergence of the frontal lobe (i.e., the portion of the brain that renders us capable of future thought) is a recent evolutionary development and a unique human capability. This endowment also provides a second possible escape route from the material trap by helping concretize the macrosocial consequences of micromotivated decisions before these consequences become irreversible. We use the simple example of grass to illustrate this principle in action.

If one were asked to list the most important consumer products, one could be forgiven if grass did not immediately come to mind. In a certain sense, this thinking should be right. Grass is plentiful and relatively cheap. Its ubiquity belies the fact that grass only grows naturally in substantive quantities in a handful of places in the world, including the pampas of South America, the prairies of North America, and the steppes of central Asia (Ridley, 1996). It also grows abundantly on the savannahs of Africa, which happen to be where humans transitioned to the upright-walking, future-thinking, socially organizing beings we are today (Ridley, 1996). Thus, we seem to have a natural affinity for grassy environs, and we plant grass nearly everywhere we live and play, including not only our homes and parks but also golf courses in the desert, green spaces on rooftops, and even cruise ships in the open ocean. Moreover, all of our most important agricultural crops are grass derivatives (i.e., corn, wheat, rice), and virtually all of our livestock has been historically grass-fed (Ridley, 1996).[†]

More importantly, the epitome of the American dream is to own a large home with an expansive manicured lawn. Thus, homeowners spend countless hours cultivating *Poa pratensis* (Kentucky bluegrass) and ridding their lawns of *Stellara media* (chickweed). To an alien observer, the way we privilege one small green plant over another must appear quite absurd, and in a way, it is. We dump massive quantities of costly and dangerous fertilizers and herbicides on the ground in the pursuit of the picture-perfect lawn. Unfortunately, these chemicals ultimately end up in the groundwater and disrupt delicate marine ecosystems. For example, fertilizer is responsible for massive and harmful algae blooms that threaten to suffocate the Chesapeake Bay (McCartney, 2010).

---

[*] Another interesting suggestion for aligning individual and societal interests in consumption is collective forms of ownership. Fractional and cooperative forms of ownership have recently become popular for a number of products, including cars and bicycles. Using museums and libraries has long been a way for people to enjoy the benefits of ownership without the costs (e.g., expense, storage, maintenance, insurance), and there are ways this model can be extended. For example, a recent initiative is the formation of toy libraries, which operate on the same principle as their literary counterparts: Children check out toys, play with them until they tire of or outgrow them, and then return them for the next child to use (Ozanne & Ozanne, in press). Toy libraries reduce the reinforcement of materialism in children, while allowing parents to get many of the benefits of possession without the costs.

[†] In recent years, many farmers have shifted their livestock, especially cows, from natural grass diets to grains, such as certain varieties of corn. The effects on the livestock, the environment, and human diets and health have been increasingly documented and criticized (see Mick & Schwartz, Chapter 32 of this volume, and their discussion of Michael Pollan's related writings).

Fortunately, a new trend has started to take hold in places like Northern Virginia and other suburban areas within the Chesapeake watershed (McCartney, 2010). Rather than cultivating large open expanses of grass that are costly and laborious to maintain, this movement promotes much smaller grass spaces, while allowing the balance of these areas to grow as they would naturally. This natural landscaping movement has even taken hold in tony neighborhoods where unsightly weeds would have been unthinkable a few short years ago. The ability to envision the future—in this case specifically, the loss of the Chesapeake Bay—provides a sense of personal urgency (i.e., the loss of a recreation area, the loss of fresh local seafood, the loss of a place of great beauty) compared to some abstract and distal notion of harming the planet. As a result, many people living within the watershed have taken much greater ownership of their consumer behaviors in this regard. To recap, this example illustrates that one means of escaping the material trap is by narrowing the distance between micromotives (i.e., a well-manicured superficial lawn) and macroconsequences (i.e., destroying an important natural resource).

### Framing Behaviors to Raise the Saliency of Their Impact

A third path for escaping the material trap is to employ our unique capacity for analogical thinking, which is not only highly developed but also fundamental to human cognition (Lakoff & Johnson, 1980; Ortony, 1993). To illustrate the power of analogical thinking, consider the following statistics, all drawn from a variety of areas but likely to be of interest to TCR scholars. According to the United Nations's report *The State of Food Insecurity in the World 2005* (Food and Agriculture Organization of the United Nations, 2005), about 6 million children die each year of malnutrition. During the period from August 2008 to July 2009, the Brazilian National Institute for Space Research (2010) estimated that 7,464 square kilometers of Amazon rainforest disappeared. According to the U.S. State Department (2005), an estimated 600,000 to 800,000 women and children are involuntarily forced across borders and into the sex trade each year. To be sure, malnutrition, deforestation, and human trafficking are serious issues, but these numbers are all so large as to defy easy comprehension. Humans are not well equipped to think at these magnitudes, because life is not experienced on these scales. As a result, these problems risk being discounted or even dismissed.

Consider what happens when these statistics are recast as the following analogies: Every single day, the equivalent of six Boeing 747 jumbo jets of women and children are loaded onto one-way flights bound for the sex trade. Every single hour, the equivalent of two U.S. elementary schools of children are wiped off the face of the earth by starvation. Every single minute, the equivalent of two football fields of rain forest disappear from the Amazon rain forest forever because of clear-cutting. In effect, by leveraging our capacity for analogical reasoning, statistical reframing can raise the saliency of the material trap.

In addition to raising attention of materialism's consequences, TCR scholars should also seek to provide consumers with alternative sources of meaning and security. As noted earlier, materialism may be innate, but it is often manifest in response to insecurity. Material objects provide tangible sources of meaning in an uncertain world, and current events are unlikely to promote increased feelings of security (Rindfleisch et al., 2009). Thus, any effort geared toward attenuating materialism should offer consumers useful alternatives, such as reconnecting with traditional sources of meaning like family and spirituality (Burroughs & Rindfleisch, 2002; Rindfleisch, Wong, & Burroughs, 2010), as well as other virtues like hope (MacInnis & Chun, 2007) and gratitude (Polak & McCullough, 2006). Although we believe our proposed solutions can help consumers and society escape the material trap, they are challenging to implement and will require sustained effort on the part of TCR scholars. As we collectively work on these research initiatives, it may be helpful to keep in mind the consequences of remaining mired in this trap.

## FAILURE TO ESCAPE THE MATERIAL TRAP

When President Franklin Roosevelt delivered his famous "Four Freedoms" speech in 1941, one of these essential freedoms was a freedom from want. In the 70 years since, few Americans have experienced this freedom. It appears Roosevelt underestimated the human appetite for consumption. Although Americans' appetite for material goods is intense, it is hardly unique. Much like ancient Rome, the United States and other Western societies risk imploding under the weight of their own lavish excesses (Tainter, 1990). This tendency toward self-implosion is a recurrent theme throughout civilization. For example, in his analysis of the reasons societies fail, Diamond (2005) identified seven contributing factors: deforestation, erosion, water shortages, overhunting and overfishing, the introduction of invasive species, overpopulation, and unsustainable per capita consumption. In essence, societies fail when their resources are squandered. According to Diamond, as societies grow in size and scope, it becomes increasingly difficult to effectively manage the core resources that form the foundation of that civilization, and it is this mismanagement that ultimately proves to be a society's undoing. Note how all seven of the factors Diamond identified directly implicate materialism. Even invasive species, which at first glance might appear to fall outside the purview of materialism, are often deliberately smuggled into new locales as exotic species in black-market exchanges or introduced as stowaways on cargo ships plying the global trade for cheap goods.

In a related analysis of the reasons societies collapse, Tainter (1990) also concluded that the core reasons come down to ones of overconsumption. However, his reasoning diverges somewhat from Diamond's. Tainter argues that complex societies collapse as a result of diminishing marginal returns from the resources on which they depend. Historically, these have primarily been agricultural resources, but in modern societies, they could be extended to include energy, health care, and intellectual capital. While Tainter (1990) acknowledges that resource mismanagement can be a contributing factor to a society's demise, in his view, inefficiency is built into the system. Social expansion comes with a self-defeating mechanism of social complacency, such that innovation fails to keep pace with rising consumption, insuring a civilization's eventual decline. In essence, Tainter suggests that growing consumption (i.e., materialism) ultimately proves to be a society's undoing. This viewpoint is out of step with conventional wisdom, which largely views economic expansion as not only desirable but also beneficial. However, a growing number of scholars and social activists have begun to question the extent to which economic expansion is a requirement for a flourishing society (Hamilton, 2003; Jackson, 2009; Kassiola, 1990; Speth, 2008).

Although the historical perspectives offered by both Diamond and Tainter provide a valuable backdrop for understanding the impact of materialism on collective well-being, there is an important difference between their analyses and the situation we face today. At the height of the Roman Empire (circa the first century), the earth's total population was about 200 million, most of whom resided in small, insular communities. In contrast, the earth's present population has exploded to nearly 7 billion people, the majority of whom now reside in densely packed urban centers connected through revolutions in transportation and communication. Thus, any consideration of material strivings now has global repercussions (Burroughs, 2010; Speth, 2008).

To give some perspective to the problem, the United States represents merely 5% of the global population but consumes 26% of the world's oil, 25% of its coal, and 27% of its natural gas (Worldwatch Institute, 2004). Similarly, while the United States and Western Europe account for only about 12% of the world's population, they control 60% of its consumer spending (Worldwatch Institute, 2004). These statistics take on new meaning when one considers the rapid transition of places like India and China to consumer-driven economies. Within the next 20 years, China and India will contribute almost 400 million new consumers to the world, many with a high degree of discretionary income (Jackson, 2009). China is already the world's largest consumer of automobiles, adding more than 11,000 cars to the roads every day (Worldwatch Institute, 2004). If the material aspirations of these new consumers eventually rise to the levels of their Western counterparts, the strain on the earth's carrying capacity will be staggering. According to one estimate, if China and India were to match the consumption levels of the United States and Japan, these two countries alone would consume all the world's resources (Worldwatch Institute, 2006).

This situation is unfolding in a world already strained. For example, our current thirst for water is so great that four of the world's most important rivers—the Nile, Ganges, Yellow, and Colorado—no longer reach the ocean in the dry season, having been entirely diverted to human uses. Runoff from fertilizers and other industrial pollutants has created more than 200 dead zones in the world's oceans. The earth's population of pelagic fish has shrunk by 90%, and the tropics are being deforested at a rate of one acre per second (Speth, 2008).

The threat of the material trap is no longer the province of fringe alarmists. Even *The Wall Street Journal* recognizes these dangers and has made the issue front-page news:

> Now and then across the centuries, powerful voices have warned that human activity would overwhelm the earth's resources. The Cassandras always proved wrong. Each time, there were new resources to discover, new technologies to propel growth. [However,] as the world grows more populous it is also growing more prosperous. The average person is consuming more food, water, metal and power. Growing numbers of China's 1.3 billion people and India's 1.1 billion are stepping up to the middle class, adopting the high-protein diets, gasoline-fueled transport, and electric gadgets that developed nations enjoy. The result is that demand for resources has soared. If supplies don't keep pace, prices are likely to climb further, economic growth in rich and poor nations alike could suffer, and some fear violent conflicts could ensue. Some of the resources now in great demand have no substitutes. In the 18th century, England responded to dwindling timber supplies by shifting to abundant coal. But there can be no such replacement for arable land and fresh water. (Lahart, Barta, & Batson, 2008, p. A1)

To this list of problems, consider that much of the strife in the Middle East can be traced to America's voracious demand for oil, that the near implosion of the global banking system was driven by unbridled greed on the part of both lenders and borrowers, and that the recent collapse of the Greek economy is a direct result of government profligacy done to placate the consuming masses. Each of these trenchant social problems represents a type of material trap. As Taleb (2007) pointed out in his influential book *The Black Swan: The Impact of the Highly Improbable*, it is a human tendency to believe that because something has never happened, it cannot happen, and then get blindsided as a result. One must wonder whether the material trap is modern society's "black swan."

## CONCLUDING THOUGHTS

Materialism is not only a foundational concept to the domain of TCR but also a useful lens for examining a variety of related topics that affect both personal and collective consumer welfare. Indeed, many of the other topics discussed in this volume, including sustainability (McDonagh, Dobscha, & Prothero, Chapter 13 of this volume), credit card abuse (Soman, Cheema, & Chan, Chapter 20 of this volume), compulsive consumption (Faber & Vohs, Chapter 22 of this volume), gambling (Cotte & LaTour, Chapter 23 of this volume), and even sharing (Belk & Llamas, Chapter 30 of this volume), are at least partially rooted in materialism or its aftermath. Moreover, in contrast to the other domains that scholars of TCR may be interested in, materialism is the only one that has been primarily developed by consumer researchers. Thus, by studying material-ism, TCR scholars have access to a wealth of prior literature, a solid theoretical foundation, and an opportunity to meaningfully impact a broad range of consumer welfare issues. Given recent world events and trends, the need for this expertise has never been greater. For these reasons, we believe that materialism commands special attention within the TCR community, and we strongly encourage other TCR scholars to join us in working to identify and remedy its harmful effects on consumer welfare. To paraphrase Don Lehmann, this is a fight we better win.

# REFERENCES

Andreasen, A. R. (2002). Marketing social marketing in the social change marketplace. *Journal of Public Policy & Marketing, 21*(Spring), 3–13.

Ariely, D. (2008). *Predictably irrational: The hidden forces that shape our decisions.* New York: HarperCollins.

Arrow, K. J. (1973). Some ordinalist-utilitarian notes on Rawls's theory of justice. *Journal of Philosophy, 70*(9), 245–263.

Arrow, K. J., & Hahn, F. H. (1971). *General competitive analysis.* Amsterdam: North-Holland.

Barry, B. (1973). *The liberal theory of justice.* Oxford, England: Clarendon Press.

Baumeister, R. F. (2002). Yielding to temptation: Self-control failure, impulsive purchasing, and consumer behavior. *Journal of Consumer Research, 28*(March), 670–676.

Bazerman, M. (2001). Consumer research for consumers. *Journal of Consumer Research, 27*(March), 499–504.

Belk, R. W. (1985). Trait aspects of living in the material world. *Journal of Consumer Research, 12*(December), 265–280.

Bettman, J. R. (1974). *An information processing theory of consumer choice.* Reading, MA: Addison-Wesley.

Block, L. G., Grier, S. A., Childers, T. L., Davis, B., Ebert, J. E. J., Kumanyika, S., et al. (in press). *From nutrients to nurturance: A conceptual introduction to food well-being. Journal of Public Policy & Marketing, 30*(1).

Bloom, P. (2010). How do morals change? *Nature, 464*(March), 490.

Boush, D. M., Friestad, M., & Wright, P. (2009). *Deception in the marketplace: The psychology of deceptive persuasion and consumer self-protection.* New York: Routledge.

Buerk, R. (2006). *Breaking ships: How supertankers and cargo ships are dismantled on the beaches of Bangladesh.* New York: Penguin.

Burroughs, J. E. (2010). Can consumer culture be contained? Comment on "marketing means and ends for a sustainable society." *Journal of Macromarketing, 30*(June), *30*(2), 127–132.

Burroughs, J. E., Chaplin, L. N., Pandelaere, M., Norton, M., Ordabayeva, N., Gunz, A., et al. (2011). *Gaps and opportunities for research on reducing materialism: Overview, agenda, and policy implications.* Unpublished manuscript, McIntire School of Commerce, University of Virginia, Charlottesville.

Burroughs, J. E., & Rindfleisch, A. (2002). Materialism and well-being: A conflicting values perspective. *Journal of Consumer Research, 29*(December), 348–370.

Chapman, J. W. (1975). Rawls's theory of justice. *American Political Science Review, 69*(June), 588–593.

Cotte, J., & LaTour, K. A. (2009). Blackjack in the kitchen: Understanding online versus casino gambling. *Journal of Consumer Research, 35*(5), 742–758.

Csikszentmihalyi, M. (2000). The costs and benefits of consuming. *Journal of Consumer Research, 27*(September), 267–272.

Dauvergne, P. (2008). *The shadows of consumption: Consequences for the global environment.* Cambridge, MA: MIT Press.

Diamond, J. (2005). *Collapse: How societies choose to fail or succeed.* New York: Penguin.

Diener, E., & Biswas-Diener, R. (2008). *Happiness: Unlocking the mysteries of psychological wealth.* Malden, MA: Blackwell.

Du, S., Sen, S., & Bhattacharya, C. B. (2008). Exploring the social and business returns of a corporate oral health initiative aimed at disadvantaged Hispanic families. *Journal of Consumer Research, 35*(October), 483–494.

Faber, R. J., Christenson, G. A., de Zwaan, M., & Mitchell, J. (1995). Two forms of compulsive consumption: Comorbidity of compulsive buying and binge eating. *Journal of Consumer Research, 22*(December), 296–304.

Food and Agriculture Organization of the United Nations. (2005). *The state of food insecurity in the world 2005.* Rome: Author. Available: ftp://ftp.fao.org/docrep/fao/008/a0200e/a0200e.pdf

Fournier, S., & Mick, D. G. (1999). Rediscovering satisfaction. *Journal of Marketing, 63*(October), 5–23.

Galbraith, J. K. (1958). *The affluent society.* New York: Houghton Mifflin.

Gilbert, D. (2005). *Stumbling on happiness*. New York: Vintage.

Haidt, J. (2007). The new synthesis in moral psychology. *Science, 316*, 998–1002.

Hamilton, C. (2003). *Growth fetish*. Sydney, Australia: Allen & Unwin.

Hammerslough, J. (2002). *Dematerializing: Taming the power of possessions*. Cambridge, MA: Perseus.

Hardin, G. (1968). The tragedy of the commons. *Science, 162*, 1243–1248.

Hewlett, S. A. (2003). *Creating a life: What every woman needs to know about having a baby and a career*. New York: Hyperion.

Hill, R. P. (2001). *Surviving in a material world: The lived experience of people in poverty*. Notre Dame, IN: University of Notre Dame Press.

Hirschman, E. C. (1991). Presidential address: Secular mortality and the dark side of consumer behavior. In M. R. Solomon & R. Holman (Eds.), *Advances in consumer research* (Vol. 17, pp. 1–4). Provo, UT: Association for Consumer Research.

Howard, J. A., & Sheth, J. N. (1969). *Theory of buyer behavior*. New York: John Wiley.

Jackson, T. (2009). *Prosperity without growth? The transition to a sustainable economy*. London: Sustainable Development Commission.

Kasser, T. (2002). *The high price of materialism*. Cambridge, MA: MIT Press.

Kasser, T., & Ahuvia, A. (2002). Materialistic values and well being in business students. *European Journal of Social Psychology, 32*(January/February), 137–146.

Kasser, T., & Sheldon, K. (2000). On wealth and death: Materialism, mortality salience, and consumption behavior. *Psychological Science, 11*(July), 348–351.

Kassiola, J. J. (1990). *The death of industrial civilization: The limits to economic growth and the repoliticization of advanced industrial society*. Albany: State University of New York Press.

Kernan, J. B. (1979). Presidential address: Consumer research and the public purpose. In W. L. Wilkie (Ed.), *Advances in consumer research* (Vol. 6, pp. 1–2). Ann Arbor, MI: Association for Consumer Research.

Kilbourne, W. E., McDonagh, P., & Prothero, A. (1997). Sustainable consumption and the quality of life: A macromarketing challenge to the dominant social paradigm. *Journal of Macromarketing, 17*(Spring), 4–24.

Labroo, A. A., & Patrick, V. M. (2009). Psychological distancing: Why happiness helps you see the big picture. *Journal of Consumer Research, 35*(February), 800–809.

Lahart, J., Barta, P., & Batson, A. (2008, March 24). New limits to growth spread Malthusian fears. *The Wall Street Journal*, p. A1.

Lakoff, G., & Johnson, M. (1980). *Metaphors we live by*. Chicago: University of Chicago Press.

Lee, D., & Sirgy, M. J. (2004). Quality-of-life (QOL) marketing: Proposed antecedents and consequences. *Journal of Macromarketing, 24*(June), 44–58.

MacInnis, D., & Chun, H. E. (2007). Understanding hope and its implications for consumer behavior: I hope, therefore I consume. *Foundations and Trends in Marketing, 1*(2), 97–188.

Malkoc, S., & Zauberman, G. (2006). Deferring versus expediting consumption: The effect of outcome concreteness on sensitivity to time horizon. *Journal of Marketing Research, 43*(4), 618–627.

Mari, C. (2008). Doctoral education and transformative consumer research. *Journal of Marketing Education, 30*(5), 5–11.

Mazar, N., Amir, O., & Ariely, D. (2008). The dishonesty of honest people: A theory of self-concept maintenance. *Journal of Marketing Research, 45*(December), 633–644.

McCartney, R. (2010, April 25). Redefining the beautiful lawn when it comes to Chesapeake Bay's health. *The Washington Post*, p. C1.

McGregor, S. L. T., & Goldsmith, E. B. (1998). Expanding our understanding of quality of life, standard of living, and well-being. *Journal of Family & Consumer Sciences, 90*(2), 2–6.

Mick, D. G. (2006). Meaning and mattering through transformative consumer research. In C. Pechmann & L. L. Price (Eds.), *Advances in consumer research* (Vol. 33, pp. 1–4). Duluth, MN: Association for Consumer Research.

Mick, D. G. (2008). Introduction: The moment and place for a special issue. *Journal of Consumer Research, 35*(October), 377–379.

Mills, C. W. (1959). *The sociological imagination*. New York: Oxford University Press.

Mittelstaedt, J. D., Kilbourne, W. E., & Mittelstaedt, R. A. (2006). Macromarketing as agorology: Macromarketing theory and the study of the agora. *Journal of Macromarketing, 26*(December), 131–142.

Moiso, R., & Beruchashvili, M. (2010). Questing for well-being at Weight Watchers: The role of the spiritual-therapeutic model in a support group. *Journal of Consumer Research, 36*(February), 857–875.

Myers, D. G. (2008). Will money buy happiness? In S. Lopez (Ed.), *Positive psychology: Exploring the best in people* (pp. 37–56). Westport, CT: Praeger.

National Institute for Space Research. (2010). *Specific data of PRODES/INPE confirms the range of the Amazon deforestation.* Available: http://www.inpe.br/ingles/news/news_dest117.php

O'Guinn, T. C., & Faber, R. J. (1989). Compulsive buying: A phenomenological exploration. *Journal of Consumer Research, 16*(September), 147–157.

Oliver, R. L. (1997). *Satisfaction: A behavioral perspective on the consumer.* New York: Irwin.

Ortony, A. (Ed.). (1993). *Metaphor and thought.* New York: Cambridge University Press.

Ozanne, J. L. (in press). Introduction to the special issue on transformative consumer research: Creating dialogical spaces for policy and action research. *Journal of Public Policy & Marketing.*

Ozanne, J. L., & Saatcioglu, B. (2008). Participatory action research. *Journal of Consumer Research, 35*(October), 423–439.

Ozanne, L. K., & Ozanne, J. L. (in press). *A child's right to play: The social construction of civic virtues in toy libraries. Journal of Public Policy & Marketing.*

Pattanaik, P. K. (2008). Social welfare function. In S. N. Durlauf & L. E. Blume (Eds.), *The new Palgrave dictionary of economics* (pp. 955–958). New York: Palgrave Macmillan. Available: http://www.dictionaryofeconomics.com/dictionary

Pechmann, C., & Knight, S. J. (2002). An experimental investigation of the joint effects of advertising and peers on adolescents' beliefs and intentions about cigarette consumption. *Journal of Consumer Research, 29,* 5–19.

Pechmann, C., & Reibling, E. T. (2006). Antismoking advertisements for youth: An independent evaluation of health, counter-industry, and industry approaches. *American Journal of Public Health, 96*(May), 906–913.

Platt, J. (1973). Social traps. *American Psychologist, 28*(August), 641–651.

Polak, E. L., & McCullough, M. E. (2006). Is gratitude an alternative to materialism? *Journal of Happiness Studies, 7,* 343–360.

Raghunathan, R., & Irwin, J. R. (2008). Walking the hedonic product treadmill: Default contrast and mood-based assimilation in judgments of predicted happiness with a target product. *Journal of Consumer Research, 28*(December), 355–368.

Rawls, J. (1971). *A theory of justice.* Cambridge, MA: Belknap Press.

Richins, M. L., & Dawson, S. (1992). A consumer values orientation for materialism and its measurement: Scale development and validation. *Journal of Consumer Research, 19*(December), 303–316.

Ridgeway, N. M., Kukar-Kinney, M., & Monroe, K. B. (2008). An expanded conceptualization and a new measure of compulsive buying. *Journal of Consumer Research, 35*(December), 622–639.

Ridley, M. (1996). *The origins of virtue: Human instincts and the evolution of cooperation.* New York: Penguin.

Rindfleisch, A., Burroughs, J. E., & Denton, F. (1997). Family structure, materialism, and compulsive consumption. *Journal of Consumer Research, 23*(March), 312–325.

Rindfleisch, A., Burroughs, J. E., & Wong, N. (2009). The safety of objects: Materialism, existential insecurity and brand connection. *Journal of Consumer Research, 36*(June), 1–16.

Rindfleisch, A., Wong, N., & Burroughs, J. E. (2010). God and Mammon: The influence of religiosity on brand connections. In S. Wuyts, M. G. Dekimpe, E. Gijsbrechts, & R. Pieters (Eds.), *The connected customer* (pp. 163–201). New York: Routledge.

Rochat, P. (2010). The innate sense of the body develops to become a public affair by 2–3 years. *Neuropsycholgia, 48*(February), 738–745.

Rochat, P. (in press). Possession and morality in early development. *New Directions for Child and Adolescent Development.*

Rochat, P., Dias, M. D. G, Guo, L., Broesch, T., Passos-Ferreira, C., & Winning, A. (2009). Fairness in distributive justice by 3- and 5-year-olds across seven cultures. *Journal of Cross-Cultural Psychology, 40*(May), 327–348.

Scammon, D. L., Keller, A. P., Albinsson, P. A., Bahl, S., Catlin, J. R., Haws, K. L., et al. (in press). Transforming consumer health. *Journal of Public Policy & Marketing, 30*(1).

Schelling, T. C. (1971). On the ecology of micromotives. *Public Interest, 25,* 61–98.

Sen, A. K. (1970). *Collective choice and social welfare.* London: Holden-Day.

Sen, A. K. (1973). *On economic inequality.* New York: Oxford University Press.

Sen, A. K. (1977). Rational fools: A critique of the behavioral foundations of economic theory. *Philosophy & Public Affairs, 6*(Summer), 317–344.

Sen, A. K. (1979, May 22). *Equality of what? The Tanner lecture on human values.* Stanford, CA: Stanford University.

Sharpe, K. M., Staelin, R., & Huber, J. (2008). Using extremeness aversion to fight obesity: Policy implications of context dependent demand. *Journal of Consumer Research, 35*(October), 406–422.

Shrum, L. J., Burroughs, J. E., & Rindfleisch, A. (2005). Television's cultivation of material values. *Journal of Consumer Research, 32*(December), 473–479.

Speth, J. G. (2008). *The bridge at the end of the world: Capitalism, the environment, and crossing from crisis to sustainability*. New Haven, CT: Yale University Press.

Sprott, D. E., & Miyazaki, A. D. (2002). Two decades of contributions to marketing and public policy: An analysis of research published in the *Journal of Public Policy & Marketing*. *Journal of Public Policy & Marketing, 21*(Spring), 105–125.

Tainter, J. (1990). *The collapse of complex societies*. New York: Cambridge University Press.

Taleb, N. N. (2007). *The black swan: The impact of the highly improbable*. New York: Random House.

Tversky, A., & Kahneman, D. (1974). Judgment under uncertainty: Heuristics and biases. *Science, 185*, 1124–1131.

U.S. Department of State. (2005). *Trafficking in persons report*. Washington, DC: U.S. Department of State, Office to Monitor and Combat Trafficking in Persons. Available: http://www.state.gov/g/tip/rls/tiprpt/2005/46606.htm

Varey, R. J. (2010). Marketing means and ends for a sustainable society: A welfare agenda for transformative change. *Journal of Macromarketing, 30*(2), 112–126.

Viswanathan, M., Rosa, J. A., & Ruth, J. A. (2010). Exchanges in marketing systems: The case of subsistence consumer-merchants in Chennai, India. *Journal of Marketing, 74*(3), 1–17.

Wilkie, W. L., & Moore, E. S. (2006). Macromarketing as a pillar of marketing thought. *Journal of Macromarketing, 26*(December), 224–232.

Wong, N. Y., & Kim, M. (2010). Ecological factors and childhood obesity: A structural look. In R. Batra, P. A. Keller, & V. Streecher (Eds.), *Leveraging consumer psychology for effective health communications: The obesity challenge* (pp. 272–291). Armonk, NY: M.E. Sharpe.

Wong, N. Y., & King, T. (2008). The cultural construction of risk: Understandings through illness narratives. *Journal of Consumer Research, 34*(February), 579–594.

Wong, N. Y., Rindfleisch, A., & Burroughs, J. E. (2003). Do reverse-worded items confound measures in cross-cultural consumer research? The case of the material values scale. *Journal of Consumer Research, 30*(June), 72–91.

Worldwatch Institute, (2004). *The state of consumption today*. Washington, DC: Author. Available: http://www.world watch.org/node/810

Worldwatch Institute. (2006). *State of the world 2006: Special focus China and India*. Washington, DC: Author. Available: http://www.worldwatch.org/node/3866

Zhao, X., & Belk, R. W. (2008). Politicizing consumer culture: Advertising's appropriation of political ideology in China's social transition. *Journal of Consumer Research, 35*(August), 231–244.

# 13

# *Sustainable Consumption and Production*
## Challenges for Transformative Consumer Research

Pierre McDonagh, Susan Dobscha, and Andrea Prothero

The purpose of this chapter is to juxtapose contemporary perspectives on Transformative Consumer Research (TCR) with views on sustainability as represented by the recent call for sustainable consumption and production (SC&P) in society. In this chapter, we first provide a brief overview of the extant research on sustainability (environmental/green consumption) in consumer research (see Kilbourne & Beckmann, 1998, for a thorough review of the marketing field's contributions through the mid-1990s), then introduce the concept of SC&P. We conclude by connecting SC&P with TCR by highlighting how the combined efforts of these two perspectives can propel TCR forward in the domains of research and teaching.

Almost 20 years ago, Beck (1992) drew our attention to the question of how researchers understand the environment and its consequences:

> Environmental problems are *not* problems of our surroundings, but—in their origins and through their consequences—are thoroughly *social* problems, *problems of people*, their history, their living conditions, their relation to the world and reality, their social, cultural and political situations. The industrially transformed "domestic nature" of the cultural world must frankly be understood as an exemplary *non*-environment, as an *inner* environment, in the face of which all of our highly bred possibilities of distancing and excluding ourselves *fail*. At the end of the twentieth century nature *is* society and society is also "*nature*". Anyone who continues to speak of nature as non-society is speaking in terms from a different century, which no longer captures our reality. (p. 81)

Since Beck issued this warning, researchers in a diversity of traditions have, without doubt, given more consideration to the environment and the consequences of unsustainable consumption and production (e.g., Assadourian, 2010; Jackson, 2005; Jackson & Michaelis, 2003). Kilbourne (2004) argued that unless the basic assumptions that underpin research on ecological sustainability are questioned, and new environmental paradigms are encouraged and supported, substantive changes in society will never occur (see also Kilbourne & Mittelstaedt, Chapter 14 of this volume). In order to achieve the goal of ecological sustainability, all facets of the system of production and consumption must be critically examined, and perhaps dismantled and reformed, using new assumptions, rules, and methods. We suggest that TCR provides a unique prism for considering the important changes that need to occur to achieve this daunting goal within consumer research.

## A DOMINANT PRACTICE OF CONSUMER RESEARCH

Issues such as resource depletion, global warming, overpopulation, and pollution are facing all nations the world over. The negative consequences of this global environmental crisis are both immediate (e.g., towns washing away into the oceans as a result of rising water levels) and long term (e.g., ozone depletion creating a warmer planet with long-term deleterious effects on wildlife and plant life). Consumer research needs to take a harder look at the role it has (or has not) played and the degree of responsibility for the current ecological crisis by promoting the ideology of consumption. Kilbourne, McDonagh, & Prothero (1997) define the ideology of consumption as the "prevailing belief within industrial societies that the sure and only road to happiness is through consumption" (p. 4). This ideology is built on the assumptions that consumption solves problems, creates confidence, and will, in its presence or absence, serve the purpose of mediating unethical or immoral marketplace activity. The challenge is to alter both the theoretical framing and practical lens through which we look at consumers, consumer research, human needs, well-being, humanity, and community within the marketplace. This new framework should be reflected in the core values of the TCR movement.

To what extent has consumer research contributed to this ideology of consumption? The dominant social paradigm (DSP; Milbrath, 1989) reinforces the overarching consumption ideology of most developed nations by promoting the benefits of capitalism and ignoring the negative consequences of overconsumption and materialism. Green consumerism and green marketing have been conceived within the system of the DSP, in which political, economic, and technological institutions have contributed to global environmental decline (Kilbourne, 2004; Kilbourne et al., 1997; McDonagh, 1998). Thus, in order for SC&P to take center stage in both organizational and individual decision making, significant structural and institutional changes must occur. Sanne (2002) argues that "limited advances can be made by changing consumer habits but further progress demands that the political system overcomes the dogma of economic growth or redefines it in terms of individual welfare of a less material dominated kind" (p. 279). This echoes what Bauman (1998, 2007) refers to as the prevailing (social) order. SC&P directly challenges TCR to play a leading role in moving society toward a better prevailing order—a state of less environmental damage. In this chapter, we evoke SC&P to provoke and challenge the reader's view of what consumer research is and question the very nature of the TCR agenda—transformative from what to what? If TCR is the answer, what is the question, ecologically speaking? The editors of this book (Mick, Pettigrew, Pechmann, & Ozanne, Chapter 1 of this volume) describe TCR as rigorous and applied consumer research for improving human and earthly welfare. They go on to say that "TCR seeks to improve well-being while maximizing social justice and the fair allocation of opportunities and resources. Meeting such a challenge will require open-mindedness, compassion, and the best scientific research."

SC&P, we argue, can reinform ecological TCR and vice versa, which would mark out ways of constructing ecological solutions for humankind. It is essential for consumer research to note that "transmogrification of consumption values from *consuming to live* into *living to consume* is the mainstay of the marketing academy" (Kilbourne et al., 1997, pp. 5–6). We submit that for consumer research, such transmogrification needs to be substantiated through transformative practices and research in which SC&P is prioritized within TCR, that is, to question and shift the prevailing ideology of consumption. This point mirrors the call to arms within consumer culture theory to include in our analyses those "historical and institutional forces that have shaped the marketplace and the consumer as a social category" (Arnould & Thompson, 2005, p. 876).

Environmental Research in the Consumer Field

As one reviews the literature exploring environmental consumption practices, one sees the cyclical nature of these studies, from the initial focus during the 1970s, to its brief reemergence in the late 1980s, to its third incarnation at the start of the millennium. During these three significant time periods, various terms were used to describe sustainable consumers, significant research developments emerged, and the discourse itself has varied. The terminology to describe sustainable consumers has evolved from "responsible" (Fisk, 1973), "environmentally/ecologically concerned" (Kinnear & Taylor, 1973; Murphy, Kangun, & Locander, 1978), and "socially conscious" (Anderson & Cunningham, 1972; Antil, 1984) to "green consumers" (Prothero, 1990; Straughan & Roberts, 1999) and "semi-ethicals" or "ethical consumers" (Berry & McEachern, 2005; Strong, 1996). More recently, "sustainable consumers" has begun to replace "green consumers" (Connolly & Prothero, 2003). (For clarity and consistency in this chapter, we use the terms *sustainable consumer* and *sustainable consumption* to refer to previous work in the field that have dealt with environmental issues, even though some of those works may have used different terminology.)

In addition to the different labels placed on these consumers, studies have also attempted to profile the sustainable consumer. Studies in the 1980s and 1990s focused on the reasons behind consumers making green choices and considered the various determinants of green behavior, with an emphasis on both internal (e.g., individual reasoning on health considerations) and external factors (e.g., concern for the state of the planet). More recent studies provided rich narratives of sustainable consumers' worldviews and practices (Autio, Heiskanen, & Heinonen, 2009; Connolly & Prothero, 2008; Dobscha & Ozanne, 2001). Earlier studies tended to focus on consumers having to give something up in order to lead a greener lifestyle; for instance, the quality of environmental products were often identified as being poorer quality or more expensive than more mainstream brands. Recent research considers the hedonism and enjoyment of leading a greener lifestyle (Autio et al., 2009).

It was not until the latter part of the 1990s that a shift occurred in the types of questions asked and studies conducted. Consumers were no longer the sole focus of research, as it was recognized that companies, policy makers, and national and international legislation also impact sustainable consumption (Menon & Menon, 1997). This shift in focus coincided with the movement within the field to question the predominant views of the role of consumption in everyday life and society. Thus, there was a focus not only on environmentally friendlier products but also on alternative forms of consumption and even nonconsumption (Dobscha & Ozanne, 2001).

Consequently, it would seem that the literature on green consumption most certainly has a peak/trough pattern, which has been echoed in our daily lives. A plethora of environmentally friendly products flooded the marketplace in the late 1980s and early 1990s, and then again at the start of the new millennium. Market research agencies have shown interest, too. Mintel, for example, conducted special reports on ethical and green consumers in both 1999 and 2007. In 2007, a GfK NOP (Grande, 2007b) survey declared ethical consumption as one of the most important issues in branding, and the *Financial Times* (Grande, 2007a) reported on the expected increased use of environmental advertising messages by companies. The managing director of the Center for Research on Environmental Decisions, an environmental consultancy in the United Kingdom, stated that environmental actions have become a lifestyle choice for some consumers (Harvey & Wiggins, 2006). Although much of these discussions have been eclipsed by the global recession and an industry and consumer emphasis on price-consciousness, during this third wave, environmental brands have remained, and environmental issues have not disappeared from either consumer or industry agendas.

The combined literature on sustainable consumption highlights a number of key factors. First, environmental actions are obviously influenced by the values and belief systems of individual consumers; these values are, however, context specific. For instance, consumers with concerns about global warming may not be so concerned with more locally based environmental pollution issues and vice versa, and industry sectors will be affected by issues in different ways. Second, as well as being context specific, we know that individuals' values and belief systems, at least from an environmental perspective, are complex, confusing, and even contradictory. This is highlighted by the very different results from consumer classification studies and, more recently, studies highlighting how an environmentally conscious consumer, who is anti–big business, regularly purchases cigarettes produced by a large multinational corporation or takes long-haul journeys (Connolly & Prothero, 2008). The third tranche of research has also begun to highlight how complicated environmental decision making can be. For instance, should one buy a locally produced product or an organic, fairly traded one that has been shipped thousands of miles (McDonagh, 2002; Shaw & Newholm, 2002)?

As a result, we can now see that consumption as practice (Ropke, 2009) is far more complicated than simple consumer choice. As such, research is focusing on not simply which green products consumers buy but also how green consumers behave in their actual consumption practices, by focusing, for instance, not just on the product itself but also on its entire life cycle: from production to consumption, reuse, and disposal. At the same time, there is also an emphasis on consumer responsibilities and the reasons behind these practices. Thus, research has begun to explore both the individual and collective reasons behind consumers' actions (Connolly & Prothero, 2008).

Although there has been a focus on individual actions, it has been recognized that this is for both individual and global reasons; actions are curtailed by the dominant social, political, and corporate institutions and by the DSP that transcends consumer actions. As a result, consumers need better decision-making tools for SC&P (see Kilbourne & Mittelstaedt, Chapter 14 of this volume) or may have choices that are not actually available to them, since some institutions do not allow certain products to be available in certain regions. These situations echo Sanne's (2002) comments about consumers being locked in. Within the DSP, there are many types of individuals attempting to live greener lifestyles within systemic confines. For instance, there are those voluntary simplifiers and downshifters who attempt, as best as possible, to live off grid and outside the DSP, with various degrees of success. Below we offer a summary of the issues of categorization of green consumption that acknowledges the influence of the prevailing order of the DSP and any desire to move toward SC&P.

## SUSTAINABLE CONSUMPTION AND PRODUCTION (SC&P)

Consumer actions have been set against a backdrop of national and international legislation and regulations, on an international scale never seen before. The second wave of green consumerism coincided with the 1983 World Commission on Environment and Development (the Brundtland Report), which was the first time sustainability became a truly global issue, as discussions focused more on the destruction of the entire planet and less on specific single issues such as the dangers of pesticide use. Sustainable development was part of a global agenda, and the Brundtland Report was followed by the Kyoto Protocol in 1997, the 2002 World Summit on Sustainable Development, and a summit planned for 2012 that coincides with the 20th anniversary of the 1982 Rio Earth Summit.

From an industry perspective, organizations have been complying with government-based policies, at global, supranational, national, and local levels, and also adhering to voluntary standards, the most widely used of which is ISO 14001 (Prakash & Potoski, 2006), the environmental management standard of the International Organization for Standardization based in Geneva, Switzerland. ISO 14001 was launched in 1995, and nearly 37,000 firms had adopted the standard by 2004 (Neumayer & Perkins, 2004). There are also specific firm-based environmental standards, which large organizations apply to all of their international operations, oftentimes to protect the reputational capital of the company (Angel & Rock, 2005). Many companies engaging in environmental activities also remain relatively quiet about their actions. Over the years, environmental laws and policies and various voluntary standards have been subject to praise and criticism by environmental groups, and as such, two clear issues seem apparent. First, greater legislation and compliance are expected to occur at global and national levels in the future; and, second, existing difficulties with both compliance-based and voluntary-based measures will need to be addressed. Various commentators have stressed how environmental industries, such as alternative energies, can play a significant role in helping job creation and economic growth in the aftermath of the global recession. For example, in the United States, President Barack Obama released a white paper in September 2009 entitled "A Strategy for American Innovation: Driving Towards Sustainable Growth and Quality Jobs" (National Economic Council, 2009) with a considerable focus on green innovations to lead the United States out of recession. The strategy emphasized an increased use of renewable energies, support for energy-efficient industries, the construction of green buildings, and the development of a national high-speed rail network.

In more recent times, governments in both developing and developed nations are becoming ever more serious about dealing with global environmental challenges. Supranational blocs, such as the European Union, have extensive environmental policies; similarly, individual countries have their own policies at both national and local levels, and a mix of incentive- and disincentive-based policies have been adopted. Legislation and regulations affecting governments, industry, and society will continue into the future. One result of existing norms has been the recognition of the importance of SC&P in tackling many of the environmental problems already highlighted.

The previous section gave an overview of some of the research conducted within the consumer research field generally. Within consumer research, the topic of sustainable consumption has been studied to varying degrees for over four decades, but it is not a mainstream concern. Outside the field of consumer research, in particular on the production side of SC&P, there is considerable research in domains such as industrial ecology and ecological economics. We believe that TCR can engage some of these issues to make its own contributions to the SC&P field.

Recently, the United Nations Environment Programme (2009) defined *sustainable consumption and production* as

> the use of services and related products, which respond to basic needs and bring a better quality of life while minimizing the use of natural resources and toxic materials as well as the emissions of waste and pollutants over the life cycle of the service or product so as not to jeopardize the needs of further generations. (p. 8)

Many researchers, however, have focused on only the consumption aspect of this definition. Over a decade ago, Kilbourne et al. (1997) pointed to the direct connection between changes in consumption and changes in society and posited that the required change in society is predicated on the improvement of consumers' knowledge of ecological sustainability, in order to facilitate movement from traditional consumption practices, namely hyperconsumption, to a more meritorious state of sustainable consumption. Sanne (2002) echoed this analysis by depicting consumers as being locked in via life circumstances, such as the length of the workweek that makes such change difficult to enact; McDonagh (1998) also noted that "people have their own life interests which they place before ecological concerns" (p. 607). For all intents and purposes, the majority of consumers—*consensus consumers*, as we call them—are happy with their lot and not necessarily worried by heightened ecological concerns, which they may prioritize under paying bills, vacationing, budget shopping, or investing in family education. As consumers have a number of social conflicts (McDonagh, 1998) that they need to address in their everyday lives, they cannot easily separate ecological concerns from their personal concerns (e.g., long work hours, health concerns, job security, pay negotiations). Anthony Giddens (1991) referred to this as people's life politics. As a consequence, many researchers have shifted their sustainability focus to incorporate the production side of the process of consumption, following life cycle analysis.

### Adding Production

While consumer research has understandably placed a heavy emphasis on understanding the consumption dimensions of ecological sustainability, scholars in other fields, as indicated above, have tackled the equally important role of production. Scholars in industrial ecology (e.g., Jackson, 2005) have studied the policies that may stimulate or inhibit sustainable lifestyles. Early evidence has suggested that initiatives like plastic bag taxes force shoppers to at least contemplate the effects of their everyday habits, while simultaneously asking polluters to actively engage in creating SC&P by making product developments more sustainable. While consumer researchers in SC&P have emphasized the need to change consumers' consumption patterns, those in other disciplines (Jackson & Michaelis, 2003; Tukker, Cohen, Hubacek, & Mont, 2010) have emphasized consuming differently and efficiently, which incorporates, in an important way, the role of production and design in accomplishing sustainability goals.

Researchers in ecological economics (e.g., Ropke, 2009) have adopted a practice theory approach, arguing that certain practices that are resource intensive need to be identified and killed off in peoples' everyday lives in favor of more collective efforts toward sustainability. These researchers have claimed that consumers engage in social practices that include consumption, yet often the connection between the two is insidious or hidden. As a result, they have submitted that all practices of social life, or what Hoffman (Chapter 9 this volume) calls the "ritualization of daily routine," should fall under scrutiny.

In an attempt to unify the consumption and production elements of sustainability, the United Nations Environment Programme (2009) developed a 10-year plan using a multistakeholder approach. This approach, *Frequently Asked Questions: The Marrakech Process*, has identified the key stakeholders in the SC&P process and assisted in the development of regional programs worldwide and the implementation of concrete sustainability projects led by governments and volunteer organizations. As an opportunity to reach out, our TCR community can opt in favor of inclusivity so the outreach is to business leaders, business philanthropists, policy makers, consumer associations, nongovernmental organizations, watchdog bodies, environmental consultancies, professional bodies, grant-awarding trusts, our own university institutions, and consumer activists (see also Wansink, Chapter 3 of this volume). Such pluralistic actions can play a role in considering how society should adopt or best foster a practical wisdom for SC&P (see Mick & Schwartz, Chapter 32 of this volume), and thus combine both United Nations Environment Programme and TCR initiatives to improve life quality and minimize unneeded depletion of resources.

### FOSTERING SC&P

Our review of existing literature suggests that although we know much more about SC&P activities than we did 20 years ago, there is still a lot to learn. What then is required for the role of TCR in this future learning process? Without a doubt, the planet is suffering from a sustainability crisis. However, some choose to not believe this, others agree with the issues but choose to ignore them (an oft-cited reason being "I'll be dead before it becomes a real issue"), and many others do small things, through both consumption and nonconsumption acts, but it is generally accepted that these acts are not enough. Consumers, as discussed earlier, may be curtailed by their own individual desires and/or limited in their actions by the existing prevailing order. There are a small number of consumers—referred to as either downshifters, voluntary simplifiers, or those who live off-grid—whose sustainable lifestyles are praised, but their small numbers mean that their overall sustainable impact is minimal.

This conundrum is similar to other TCR topics. For instance, some obese people know they are obese and know there are health risks as a consequence of their condition, but they choose to continue eating at an individually unsustainable level. Similarly, most smokers are all too aware of the risks of smoking, but for whatever reason, many choose to continue with their smoking habits. Thus, if TCR is concerned with transforming lives and the planet for the better, we must first stand back and recognize that on an individual level, there are individuals who do not want their lives and consumption activities transformed. From a sustainability perspective, how do we address this key problem?

From a TCR perspective, how do we inculcate SC&P into core TCR values and envisionments (see Mick, Pettigrew, Pechmann, & Ozanne, Chapter 1 of this volume) or into what is perceived as wise consumer behavior (see Mick & Schwartz, Chapter 32 of this volume)? Can we really convince people that a sustainable lifestyle is much better than one of hyperconsumption, and if so, how? Shankar and Fitchett (2002); Shankar, Whittaker, and Fitchett (2006); and others have talked of how materialism and consumers' constant need for more goods lead to dissatisfaction facilitated through the free market, which makes consumers aware of goods they could have. While these authors and others (Prothero & Fitchett, 2000; Prothero, McDonagh, & Dobscha, 2010) have discussed possible routes to tackle this issue (e.g., via a green commodity form), consumer research now needs to actively engage innovatively in this field.

We do not need any more research that highlights the complex, contradictory, and confusing nature of sustainability! What we require are tangible examples as to how SC&P becomes *the* way of life and not simply *a* way of life. With that in mind, is there a role for TCR to foster research that explores how transforming society toward SC&P mutually benefits the planet and human life quality? For instance, following the work of Autio et al. (2009), what are the hedonistic, pleasurable, or fulfilling benefits of being sustainable? How can being sustainable save money for individuals? How can being sustainable free up extra time for family activities or leisure? In other words, how can the social practices of SC&P impact life quality in a positive way? Research on sharing (Belk & Llamas, Chapter 30 of this volume) echoes this sentiment. Some specific paths that can be explored include examining the individual, the academy, and the institutions of human society, where it is imperative that future research examine both the production and consumption aspects of SC&P. Looking at both in isolation or in individual disciplines will not be as fruitful, we contend, as interdisciplinary research, which does not mean that interdisciplinary research is going to be easier or that it is some sort of SC&P panacea. It is possible that the reverse may transpire if the work is poorly orchestrated or the micropolitics of faculties mismanaging research grants rule the day. With this in mind, we suggest the task at hand is all the more challenging, but certainly one not beyond the scope or capabilities of SC&P and TCR researchers.

### The Individual Within the Community

#### Connecting With Core Values: The Downshifter/Voluntary Simplifier

Earlier, we discussed the lives of those who chose to opt out of the market in various guises. We know that these lifestyles are unlikely to become the norm for the masses, but are there activities that these citizens engage in that could be applied to the masses? Allotments and growing your own food, for instance, are suddenly de rigueur among consumers, so how can we build on these developments? How can we learn from these consumers' core value sets, and how might we use that knowledge to motivate others? Connecting with nature has been examined by exemplary scholars, such as Carolyn Merchant, for a number of years, requiring researchers to espouse a more holistic framing of the human–planet connection. This in itself challenges the human condition to its very limits.

In addition to learning about core values and consumption practices, how can our knowledge of these consumers contribute to the production issue, besides the obvious examples of their nonconsumption actions? Are there any consumption practices that these consumers engage in that could have implications for how products are produced (or not produced) in the future? Do they have innovative uses for products and packaging from which both producers and consumers can learn (see also Rosa, Geiger-Oneto, & Fajardo, Chapter 7 of this volume)? Could future product designers, manufacturers, and engineers learn from their consumption practices? Future research that includes interdisciplinary research teams examining the lifestyles and consumption practices of those who choose to live off-grid could prove most rewarding in addressing both the production and consumption sides of SC&P.

### Constraints on Greening

We also discussed earlier the many constraints individuals face in attempting to lead more sustainable lifestyles. What are these constraints, and how can we learn from them? How can we categorize these constraints, which are a result of individual factors (e.g., contradictory beliefs) and also macroinstitutional forces (e.g., the banking sector privileging money as the dominant exchange form as opposed to sharing; see Belk & Llamas, Chapter 30 of this volume)? Once we have a clearer understanding of the constraints, how can we overcome them? How can we tackle problems of practical wisdom as discussed in the Richard and Carol case described by Mick and Schwartz (Chapter 32 of this volume) in terms of improving better SC&P consumer knowledge, product availability, financial costs, and so forth? One area of existing research shows that there is much consumer confusion over environmental labels, so how can TCR help address this confusion (cf. Grunert, Bolton, & Raats, Chapter 16 of this volume, on nutritional labeling)? Can TCR play a role in ensuring better and more widely accepted information provision in the future?

From a TCR perspective, we must consider research that begins to universally tackle these constraints and also offer solutions of a greener path to follow in the future, which again requires interdisciplinary research. Thus, consumer researchers may explore individual and macroconstraints in more detail, but if this is done in conjunction with other disciplines, solutions to some problems may be addressed more quickly. For example, if consumer researchers are able to identify specific product reasons for why some consumers do not engage in sustainable behavior sharing, these findings might lead scientific researchers to solutions to the identified issues. Of course, this research, in isolation, will not solve the wider sustainability problem of too much consumption, but it can play a leading role in making the consumption that does take place more sustainable.

### Consensus Consumers

How can TCR contribute to the difficult problem of bringing consensus consumers into the picture? These consumers are happy with their status quo and do not want to transform their consumer behaviors. Unlike other TCR strands, the sustainability one emphasizes the need to transform consumers for the good of the earth, not necessarily for themselves individually. Thus, two things in altering the frame of reference adopted by consensus consumers become paramount here: How can they be convinced to become sustainable for the good of the planet on the one hand, but on the other, are there any ways in which they can be convinced that sustainability, despite their initial doubts, might support their life quality and the common good? Can what we learn from the core values of the voluntary simplifiers be useful here? Can we use marketing techniques to convince people of the benefits of less consumption (Prothero & Fitchett, 2000; see also Andreasen, Goldberg, & Sirgy, Chapter 2 of this volume)? These are all questions that TCR should encourage. Such research directly focuses on the consumption end of SC&P research, but if this is conducted in conjunction with production research, then we can begin to tackle all of the elements of SC&P research. As we make ourselves more aware of the reasons why so many people are not willing to change their lifestyles, we can consider how marketing techniques might be utilized to address this issue.

## Celebratory Sustainability

There is a need to conduct and report research on successful stories of sustainability, which range from small acts, such as the introduction of the plastic bag tax in Ireland, to larger ones, such as the efforts on the Danish island of Samsø, which, via the use of wind power, has no carbon footprint and is selling its excess supply of power back to the Danish mainland. Success stories are at individual, societal, and institutional levels. What are these success stories, and how can we learn from them? What impacts can the constructs of quality of life (Andreasen, Goldberg, & Sirgy, Chapter 2 of this volume) and quality of virtual life (see Novak, Chapter 11 of this volume) play in this regard? We noted earlier in this chapter how all too often acts of sustainability are portrayed in some type of negative manner; in other words, to go green means you have to give something up, whether in the form of poorer product quality or sacrificing consumption needs or desires for the good of the planet.

Not all sustainability acts are perceived as negative in some way. We have mentioned recent research that talks about the hedonism or pleasures of sustainable consumption acts, and TCR can play a significant role in building on the positive aspects. Indeed, some consumption practices can be sustainable, but the sustainability issue itself is not at the forefront of those engaging in the acts. During the current economic recession, as with previous recessions or times of hardship, we learn all the time of new and innovative ways to make products last longer, share products with our friends or family, or swap clothes with our friends rather than buy new ones. Further TCR investigations that celebrate and publish these practices are warranted. At the same time, sharing the findings with other disciplines to address production issues arising from these celebratory practices may yield useful results in making the acts more widespread among consumers and in changing production acts for the future.

Related to these points is the very real prospect of SC&P and TCR building on Arvidsson's (2008) concepts of the ethical economy of coproduction. He claimed that as people continuously develop spimes (i.e., objects that can be tracked through space and time) in communities of coproduction, there is an enhanced ability to contribute more ethical production once they get materialized or produced. The example Arvidsson foresaw as eminently feasible, and connects both TCR and SC&P, is the incorporation of radio frequency identification technology into our shopping experiences or everyday lives. Being able to scan your iPhone or Blackberry over a piece of clothing in the mall to automatically receive its ecocredentials is no longer the realm of science fiction. This also opens a rich vein or confluence of interdisciplinary research potential between TCR, SC&P, and the traditional sciences.

## Credibility of SC&P

Illustrations of SC&P practices as transformative at the individual level (e.g., freedom from materialism, better saving strategies, spending time instead of money), the institutional level (e.g., undertaking a green agenda from top to bottom can improve the bottom line), and a global level (e.g., efforts can add up to help the overall health of the planet) will help legitimate a credibility for consumption to be seen not as a devastating force but as a life-affirming choice. Extension of the social practices model explored in sociology by Spaargaren (2003) seems apposite here. Future TCR research that highlights these transformative practices, as discussed above, will help in ensuring all aspects of SC&P are addressed, which means that the responses of the consumer research academy to issues of sustainability can be seen as holistic and not piecemeal, as it has been so often criticized in the past.

## Academic Perspectives

We need improvements in writing and teaching about consumption as well. How can we encourage changes in our students, so life is not always about consumption (and money) at the individual level? Let us consider the curriculum and teaching about SC&P and TCR. TCR initiatives may serve to facilitate change in the mainstream consumer behavior curriculum to include important consumption issues, such as poverty, literacy, obesity, and, hopefully, SC&P. The first place where SC&P could be better integrated into the educational domain is in doctoral education. Mari (2008) argued effectively for wide-scale change in doctoral education by incorporating TCR into the three primary domains of concepts and theories, methodology, and substantive issues. We argue that incorporating TCR into doctoral education would serve to fuel the SC&P research domain by introducing students to the key historical contexts that impact consumption practices (Arnould, & Thompson, 2005) It would also expose them to broader societal issues such as consumerism; teach them new methodological tools that would enable deeper, context-dependent inquiries into consumers' everyday lives; and generally socialize them to the possibilities of building a career around important social topics, such as vulnerable consumer groups, negative and positive consumption behaviors, and the complexities of a heterogeneous society (Mari, 2008).

While Mari's recommendations state that curricula should be programmatic, we extend this idea to recommend the creation of specific doctoral programs related to TCR topics, in this case, SC&P. Fortunately, we see evidence that this movement is already afoot, with 2010 being the inaugural year of the sustainable marketing doctoral program at the University of Wyoming (2010). As well as programmatic doctoral themes, there is also potential for greater interdisciplinary research. SC&P is a prime example of scrutinizing the success of markets and their ecological consequences; it is a global research approach that can develop solutions from all academic disciplines. We will not enact SC&P if, as consumer researchers, we remain in our individual academic silos. As a newly established movement emanating from an already internationally recognized body (i.e., the Association for Consumer Research), TCR should seek to foster and develop links with other disciplines (e.g., Grier & Yumanyika, 2008; Pechmann & Reibling, 2006). As TCR embraces SC&P, it should also lobby funding bodies to think outside the box and develop research funding for likeminded interdisciplinary projects. If this happens, there is then much more likelihood that the community research we discuss above becomes a reality and not a pipe dream.

Initiatives such as these promote more programmatic study of a topic, as opposed to the snapshot techniques of most doctoral programs (Wells, 1993). The creation of new doctoral programs allows for researchers to branch out of their academic comfort zones and give students and teachers alike more freedom to pursue topics of interest rather than topics that are deemed managerially relevant or academically iterative.

In addition, when updating doctoral curricula to reflect new perspectives, there must be a sea change in how we convey consumer behavior to both our undergraduate and postgraduate students, particularly our MBA students. Since MBA students are our future business leaders, any exposure to SC&P principles will benefit both these students and the companies they will be leading. For example, if MBA students majoring in finance and accounting were exposed to the idea of cradle-to-cradle design and manufacturing principles (McDonough & Braungart, 2002), perhaps they would increasingly assert alternative solutions and positively valuate sustainable investments. Better understanding of SC&P may lead future business leaders to make different decisions regarding issues such as outsourcing of production and services, information technology investment, packaging, distribution methods, farming practices, and advertising and promotional efforts.

Business school graduates are consistently criticized for lacking historical perspective (Schumpeter, 2009). While the financial institutions around the world crumbled in 2009, business schools walked away unscathed, when in fact they were primary contributors to the employment pool of those failing institutions. If business education does not shift to incorporate more sustainable and ethical principles, we are doomed to repeat our mistakes. This shift requires a significant reformulation of the business curriculum to reflect what it purports to deliver; in the case of Harvard Business School (2010), this is to "educate leaders who make a difference in the world." The

March 2010 issue of *Harvard Business Review* has a focus on ethical leadership, and *Businessweek* asked in February 2009 if business schools were failing to give graduates the tools to act ethically once they reach the marketplace. To show the transformative effects of SC&P would go a long way in delivering students to the business world who would have the requisite perspectives and skills to make a positive difference to all of our futures.

Organizations such as the Aspen Institute (2010) foster environmental education in both high schools and universities. Its successful Beyond Grey Pinstripes biennial awards, for example, focus on business education that fosters business and society teaching, including environmental issues. Similarly, its 2010 MBA awards for energy and environmental sustainability are another example. Although many may consider such rankings as these to be nonmainstream, there is evidence they are having an impact on where students choose to study. At the same time, we are also at last witnessing the importance of business and society, including sustainability, within more mainstream bodies. The EFMD (European Foundation for Management Development; 2010), a European accreditation body, has highlighted the importance of corporate social responsibility being taught in various curricula. The Association to Advance Collegiate Schools of Business (AACSB) International (n.d.), the largest business school accreditation body, maintains that ethics and sustainability are crucial components of business education because of the complex ethical issues that business entities encounter today (see http://www.AACSB.edu). Bentley University was recently highlighted on the AACSB website for its continued emphasis on ethics, social responsibility, and sustainability, having created its Center for Business Ethics in 1976, through its current teaching, research, and community outreach programs. Notre Dame's Mendoza College of Business, ranked number one in undergraduate business education in 2010 by *Businessweek*, has cited its strong commitment to business ethics as a key contributor to securing the coveted top spot (Elliott, 2010). TCR, as an organization, needs to play a significant role in ensuring such issues remain on the consumer research and teaching agendas for the future; collaborating with groups such as the Aspen Institute is but one possibility.

From a purely environmental perspective, SC&P would be better delivered in various curricula if, as teachers of consumer behavior (in its many guises), we focused less on individual consumption, which is an unfortunate throwback to our economics roots, and delivered insights about consumers as they exist in communities, often with shared consumption behaviors, with collective goals in mind. As Schiffman and Kanuk (2010) defined it,

> [C]onsumer behavior focuses on how individual consumers and families or households make decisions to spend their available resources … on consumption-related items. That includes what they buy, why they buy it, how often they buy it, how often they use it, how they evaluate it after the purchase, the impact of such evaluations on future purchases, and how they dispose of it. (p. 5)

Yet, in order to transform communities into more sustainable entities, many constituencies must manage and work together for mutual benefit (Baker, 2009). Referring to Shankar and Fitchett (2002) above, consumption behavior is about *being* as well as *having*, and our curricula and textbooks should reflect this. In so doing, they will play a dual role in educating managers and consumers of the future to consider consumption practices from a sustainability and a being perspective.

The Institution

The Association for Consumer Research and the *Journal of Consumer Research* have made great strides over the years toward broadening the scope of consumer research (see, e.g., Deighton, Macinnis, McGill, & Shiv, 2010). TCR is now an important part of that history. As well as programmatic doctoral education in TCR, there is a need for greater interdisciplinary work. SC&P is a prime example of a global challenge that requires solutions from all academic disciplines, and as we have highlighted above, we will not solve these problems in our individual academic silos. As a newly established, but already internationally recognized, movement, TCR should seek to foster and develop links with other disciplines and also lobby governments and funding bodies to think creatively and develop research funding for SC&P interdisciplinary projects for both research and teaching purposes. Allied to this, this book on TCR bears testimony to a wave of new thinking that permeates the Association in the exciting form of TCR. Our primary concern is for TCR to calibrate itself closely with the goals of SC&P. In this way, it can play a centrifugal role in bringing SC&P to fruition and helping shape a research agenda toward that end. If, as an institution, TCR plays a significant role in fostering interdisciplinary research and teaching partnerships, then it will become much easier to address the future research and teaching agendas we discuss above. We will then be in a position to truly tackle all issues of importance in moving toward a society in which SC&P is the norm and not the exception.

Parallels with other disciplines are worth remarking on at this juncture. Compare the purposive nature of TCR to what happened with the more organic, less systematic development of environmental literary studies (ELS). Glotfelty and Fromm (1996) note that ELS developed in the 1980s from the works of individual literary and cultural scholars who had been developing ecologically informed criticism and theory since the 1970s. Glotfelty and Fromm observed that, unlike their disciplinary cousins, ELS researchers did not organize themselves into an identifiable group, and as a consequence, their efforts were not recognized as belonging to a distinct critical school or movement. Individual studies appeared, and disunity prospered. As a result, ecocriticism did not become a presence in the major institutions of power in the profession, such as the Modern Language Association. It was only in the mid-1980s, as scholars undertook collaborative projects in the field of environmental projects, that the research strand was allowed to prosper and grow in the early 1990s. By comparison to the development of ELS, we have the benefit of a clearly identifiable group, TCR. We recognize this is not by mere chance, fluke, or favorable circumstance but rather foresight and dogged determination, allied to a dedication to the professional body of the Association of Consumer Research. Therefore, we suggest that all the contributors to this text owe a debt of gratitude to the TCR organization. This gratitude also extends to the editors of this book for constructing professional space to transform and change the very essence of consumer research and, in so doing, allowing us to press the SC&P case for readers' consideration.

## CONCLUSION

At present, one can accuse TCR of being overly anthropocentric and lacking in what McDonagh and Prothero (1997) and Dobscha and Ozanne (2001) termed a robust rumination of the consequences of ecocentric thought. This would not be surprising, given TCR's focus on the consumer, but we submit that in terms of SC&P, we need to calibrate TCR research so that its contribution does not remain peripheral to the sustainability megatrend (Lubin & Esty, 2010) in the 21st century. This chapter has outlined some opportunities to promote the SC&P imperative and provide a challenge to TCR to play a more central and proactive role in researching and shaping the SC&P agenda.

In a recent article in *Newsweek*, Begley (2010) notes that changes in consumer behavior alone will not solve global environmental problems, which is indeed why SC&P is so critical for our future. She emphasizes that focusing solely on consumption behaviors is an act of collective laziness on society's part, because to do so is much easier than tackling the bigger systemic picture. As consumer researchers, it is absolutely imperative that as we move forward, TCR should debate and contribute to research that fosters solutions to the bigger systemic picture, which requires interdisciplinary collaborations to tackle consumption and production issues as well as legislative issues.

We hope that in our discussions above, we have provided some possible avenues for future action that focuses on the systemic aspects of SC&P and not the lazy issues identified in the *Newsweek* article. It is apparent that academics, oftentimes outside the consumer research discipline, and the popular press now widely recognize that changing our consumption behaviors alone is not going to solve the environmental crisis the planet currently faces. It is one of the responsibilities of TCR to ensure that, as academic researchers, we do our utmost to contribute to solutions that effect change to benefit not just humankind but also the planet, because, as we know, the two can never really be separated.

## REFERENCES

Anderson, T. W., & Cunningham, W. H. (1972). The socially conscious consumer. *Journal of Marketing, 36*, 23–31.

Angel, D. P., & Rock, M. T. (2005). Global standards and the environmental performance of industry. *Environment and Planning, 37*, 1903–1918.

Antil, J. H. (1984). Socially responsible consumers: Profile and implications for public policy. *Journal of Macromarketing, 4*(2), 18–39.

Arnould, E. J., & Thompson, C. J. (2005). Consumer culture theory (CCT): Twenty years of research. *Journal of Consumer Research, 31*(March), 868–882.

Arvidsson, A. (2008). The ethical economy of customer coproduction. *Journal of Macromarketing, 28*(4), 326–338.

The Aspen Institute. (2010). *The Aspen Institute mission statement.* Retrieved October 20, 2010, from http://www.aspeninstitute.org/about

Assadourian, E. (2010). The rise and fall of consumer cultures. In E. Assadourian, L. Starke, & L. Mastny (Eds.), *State of the world 2010: Transforming cultures from consumerism to sustainability* (pp. 3–20). New York: W.W. Norton.

Association to Advance Collegiate Schools of Business. (n.d.). *Ethics/Sustainability Resource Center.* Retrieved April 29th, 2010, from http://www.aacsb.edu/resources/ethics-sustainability/about.asp

Autio, M., Heiskanen, E., & Heinonen, V. (2009). Narratives of "green" consumers: The antihero, the environmental hero and the anarchist. *Journal of Consumer Behaviour, 8*, 40–53.

Baker, S. M. (2009). Vulnerability and resilience in natural disasters: A Marketing and public policy perspective. *Journal of Public Policy & Marketing, 28*(Spring), 114–123.

Bauman, Z. (1998). *Work, consumerism and the new poor.* Philadelphia: Open University Press.

Bauman, Z. (2007). *Consuming life.* Malden, MA: Polity Press.

Beck, U. (1992). *Risk society: Towards a new modernity.* Newbury Park, CA: Sage.

Begley, S. (2010). On the 40th anniversary of Earth Day, let's … go shopping! *Newsweek.* Retrieved April 28, 2010, from http://www.newsweek.com/id/236722/page/1

Berry, H., & McEachern, M. (2005). Informing ethical consumers. In R. Harrison, T. Newholm, & D. Shaw (Eds.), *The ethical consumer* (pp. 69–87). Thousand Oaks, CA: Sage.

Connolly, J., & Prothero, A. (2003). Sustainable consumption: Consumption, consumers and the commodity discourse. *Consumption, Markets and Culture, 6*(4), 275–291.

Connolly, J., & Prothero, A. (2008). Green consumption: Life-politics, risk and contradictions. *Journal of Consumer Culture, 8*(1), 117–145.

Deighton, J., Macinnis, D., McGill, A., & Shiv, B. (2010). Editorial: Broadening the scope of consumer research. *Journal of Consumer Research, 36*(6), 1–3.

Dobscha, S. (1993). Women and the environment: Applying ecofeminism to environmentally-related consumption. In L. McAlister & M. L. Rothschild (Eds.), *Advances in consumer research* (Vol. 20, pp. 36–40). Provo, UT: Association for Consumer Research.

Dobscha, S., & Ozanne, J. (2001). An ecofeminist analysis of environmentally sensitive women: Qualitative findings on the emancipatory potential of an ecological life. *Journal of Public Policy & Marketing, 20*(2), 201–214.

EFMD. (2010). *What is EQUIS?* Retrieved October 20, 2010, from http://www.efmd.org/index.php/accreditation-/equis/what-is-equis

Elliott, C. (2010, May 7). *Notre Dame business school gets high marks in Bloomberg Businessweek specialty rankings.* Retrieved October 21, 2010, from http://business.nd.edu/news_and_events/news_articles_article.aspx?id=6639

Fisk, G. (1973). Criteria for a theory of responsible consumption. *Journal of Marketing, 37*, 24–31.

Giddens, A. (1991). *Modernity and self-identity: Self and society in the late modern age.* Stanford, CA: Stanford University Press.

Glotfelty, C. & Fromm, H. (1996). Introduction. In C. Glotfelty & H. Fromm (Eds.), *The ecocriticism reader: Landmarks in literary ecology* (pp. xv–xxxvii). Athens: University of Georgia Press.

Grande, C. (2007a, February 12). Wave of eco-marketing predicted. *Financial Times.* Retrieved October 20, 2010, from http://www.ft.com/cms/s/0/ec520b18-ba3d-11db-89c8-0000779e2340.html#axzz17Y5vchst

Grande, C. (2007b, February 20). Ethical consumption makes mark on branding. *Financial Times.* Retrieved October 20, 2010, from http://www.ft.com/cms/s/2/d54c45ec-c086-11db-995a-000b5df10621.html

Grier, S. A., & Kumanyika, S. K. (2008). The context for choice: Health implications of targeted food and beverage marketing to African Americans. *American Journal of Public Health, 98*(9), 1616–1629.

Harvard Business School. (2010). *Our mission.* Retrieved October 21, 2010, from http://www.hbs.edu/about/

Harvey, F., & Wiggins, J. (2006, September 13). Companies cash in on environment awareness. *Financial Times.* Retrieved October 20, 2010, from http://www.ft.com/cms/s/0/13121c36-434a-11db-9574-0000779e2340.html#axzz17YCdanZD

Jackson, T. (2005). Live better by consuming less? Is there a "double dividend" in sustainable consumption? *Journal of Industrial Ecology, 9*(1/2), 19–36.

Jackson, T., & Michaelis, L. (2003). *Policies for sustainable consumption.* London: Sustainable Development Commission.

Kilbourne, W. E. (2004). Sustainable communication and the dominant social paradigm: Can they be integrated? *Marketing Theory, 4*(3), 187–208.

Kilbourne, W. E., & Beckmann, S. C. (1998). Review and critical assessment of research on marketing and the environment. *Journal of Marketing Management, 14*, 513–532.

Kilbourne, W. E., McDonagh, P., & Prothero., A. (1997). Sustainable consumption and the quality of life: A macromarketing challenge to the dominant social paradigm. *Journal of Macromarketing, 17*(1), 4–24.

Kinnear, T. C., & Taylor, J. A. (1973). The effect of ecological concern on brand perceptions. *Journal of Marketing Research, 10*(2), 191–197.

Lubin, D. A., & Esty, D. C. (2010). The sustainability imperative. *Harvard Business Review, 88*(5), 42–50.

Mari, C. (2008). Doctoral education and transformative consumer research. *Journal of Marketing Education, 30*(1), 5–11.

McDonagh, P. (1998). Towards a theory of sustainable communication in risk society: An empirical analysis relating issues of sustainability to marketing communications. *Journal of Marketing Management, 14*, 591–622.

McDonagh, P. (2002). Communicative campaigns to effect anti-slavery and fair trade. *European Journal of Marketing, 36*(5/6), 642–666.

McDonagh, P., & Prothero, A. (1997). Leap frog marketing: The contribution of ecofeminist thought to the world of patriarchal marketing. *Marketing Intelligence & Planning, 15*(7), 361–368.

McDonough, W., & Braungart, M. (2002). *Cradle to cradle: Remaking the way we make things.* New York: North Point Press.

Menon, A., & Menon, A. (1997). Enviropreneurial marketing strategy: The emergence of corporate environmentalism as marketing strategy. *Journal of Marketing, 61*(1), 51–67.

Milbrath, L. (1989). *Environmentalists: Vanguards for a new society.* Albany: State University of New York Press.

Murphy, P. E., Kangun, N., & Locander, W. B. (1978). Environmentally concerned consumers: Racial variations. *Journal of Marketing, 42*(4), 61–66.

National Economic Council. (2009). *A strategy for American innovation: Driving towards sustainable growth and quality jobs.* Retrieved March 28, 2010, from http://www.whitehouse.gov/administration/eop/nec/StrategyforAmericanInnovation/

Neumayer, E., & Perkins, R. (2004). What explains the uneven take-up of ISO 14001 at the global level? A panel-data analysis. *Environment and Planning, 36*, 823–839.

Pechmann, C., & Reibling, E. T. (2006). Antismoking advertisements for youths: An independent evaluation of health, counter-industry, and industry approaches. *American Journal of Public Health, 96*, 906–913.

Prakash, A., & Potoski, M. (2006). Racing to the bottom? Trade, environmental governance, and ISO 14001. *American Journal of Political Science, 50*(2), 350–364.

Prothero, A. (1990). Green consumerism and the societal marketing concept: Marketing strategies for the 1990s. *Journal of Marketing Management, 6*(2), 87–103.

Prothero, A., & Fitchett, J. A. (2000). Greening capitalism: Opportunities for a green commodity. *Journal of Macromarketing, 20*(1), 46–55.

Prothero, A., McDonagh, P., & Dobscha, S. (2010). Is green the new black? Reflections on a green commodity discourse. *Journal of Macromarketing, 30*(2), 147–159.

Ropke, I. (2009). Theories of practice: New inspiration for ecological economics studies on consumption. *Ecological Economics, 68*(10), 2490–2497.

Sanne, C. (2002). Willing consumers—or locked-in? Policies for a sustainable consumption. *Ecological Economics, 42*, 273–287.

Schegelmilch, B. B. (1994). Green, ethical and charitable: Another marketing ploy or a new marketing era? In M. J. Baker (Ed.), *Perspectives on marketing management* (Vol. 4, pp. 55–72). New York: Wiley.

Scheppard, N. (2002). Anarcho-environmentalists, ascetics of late modernity. *Journal of Contemporary Ethnography, 31*(2), 135–137.

Schiffman, L. G., & Kanuk, L. L. (2010). *Consumer behavior.* Upper Saddle River, NJ: Prentice Hall.

Schumpeter, J. (2009, September 24). The pedagogy of the privileged: Business schools have done too little to reform themselves in light of the credit crunch. *The Economist.* Retrieved October 20, 2010, from http://www.economist.com/node/14493183

Shankar, A., & Fitchett, J. A. (2002). Having, being and consumption. *Journal of Marketing Management, 18*, 501–516.

Shankar, A., Whittaker, J., & Fitchett, J. A. (2006). Heaven knows I'm miserable now. *Marketing Theory, 6*(4), 485–505.

Shaw, D., & Newholm, T. (2002). Voluntary simplicity and the ethics of consumption. *Psychology & Marketing, 19*(2), 167–185.

Spaargaren, G. (2003). Sustainable consumption: A theoretical and environmental policy perspective. *Society & Natural Resources, 16*, 687–701.

Straughan, R. D., & Roberts, J. A. (1999). Environmental segmentation alternatives: A look at green consumer behavior in the new millennium. *Journal of Consumer Marketing, 16*(6), 558–575.

Strong, C. (1996). Features contributing to the growth of ethical consumerism. *Marketing Intelligence & Planning, 14*(5), 5–13.

Tukker, A., Cohen, M. J., Hubacek, K., & Mont, O. (2010). Sustainable consumption and production. *Journal of Industrial Ecology, 14*(1), 1–3.

United Nations Environment Programme. (2009). *Frequently asked questions: The Marrakech process: Towards a 10-year framework of programmes on sustainable consumption and production.* Paris: Author. Retrieved October 20, 2010, from http://www.unep.fr/scp/publications/details.asp?id=DTI/1177/PA%20

University of Wyoming. (2010). *College of Business PhD in marketing: Sustainable business practices.* Retrieved April 14, 2010, from http://business.uwyo.edu/phdmarketing

Wells, W. D. (1993). Discovery-oriented consumer research. *Journal of Consumer Research, 19*, 489–504.

# 14

# *From Profligacy to Sustainability: Can We Get There From Here?*

## Transforming the Ideology of Consumption

WILLIAM KILBOURNE AND JOHN MITTELSTAEDT

The purposes of this chapter are to consider the effects of the ideology of consumption on our environment and offer a research agenda for Transformative Consumer Research (TCR) to address the impact of consumption on the environment. While we generally accept that consumer behaviors reflect attitudes, preferences, and experiences, there is a deeper, more fundamental driver of behavior as well: consumption as a cultural imperative, or what we will call the ideology of consumption (see also Mick, 2003). In many ways, consumption ideology—our beliefs about the necessity of consumption in our lives and our culture—affects when, where, how consciously and mindfully, and (most importantly) how much we consume, just as attitudes and preferences affect our choices among alternatives. What distinguishes attitudes from these deeper convictions is that while the attitudes vary among individuals, consumption ideology is held collectively. These deeper convictions constitute the dominant social paradigm (DSP; Kilbourne, McDonagh, & Prothero, 1997; McDonagh, Dobscha, & Prothero, Chapter 13 of this volume) that sets the tone and context for consumption. If TCR is to make a difference in the long-term sustainability of the environment, it must address the antecedents and consequences of consumption as a cultural orientation, just as it addresses other important issues of consumer welfare. As such, it must, at this level at least, adopt a critical stance in exposing the ideology as ideology, which is one of the critical foci of TCR.

The concept of ideology is used here as usually considered in the sociology of knowledge, in which it refers to (a) beliefs that were justified in an earlier historical context but can no longer be justified and (b) beliefs that present a specific interest as the general interest. From the perspective of consumption, this reflects, in the first instance, that increasing levels of consumption in historical contexts, in which needs are not being satisfied and resources are plentiful, are easily justified. However, when this context is surpassed, and needs are being created to absorb excess production (i.e., profligate consumption) and resources are becoming scarce, continuous growth cannot be justified from a consumer well-being perspective. In the second case, the question of interests must be considered. The *specific interest* refers to the interests of a small segment of society that reaps the greatest benefits of economic growth and increased consumption. The *general interest* refers to the well-being of the remainder of society, that is, the consumers whose well-being is not being enhanced by further growth and, by recent accounts of materialism, whose well-being may be diminishing with further growth. This is the case of the one pulling the plow being convinced that he is riding in a golden chariot. As a result of these ideological forces, consumers come to believe that more consumption leads to greater happiness.

Stern (2000) raised the challenge of consumption ideology for us when he noted that all environmental problems are, at their core, problems of consumption. Our economic and social structures are built around ever-increasing aggregate consumption, in which more is assumed to be better. Between 1970 and 2000, global economic output increased 338% (DeLong, 1998), with concurrent increases in health, welfare, and standards of living. Today, all but a handful of countries (i.e., Myanmar, North Korea, and Cuba) accept all or most of the central tenets of the Industrial Revolution as the basis of economic growth and welfare. In many ways, the story of consumption, and the economic systems that support it, is the story of human success.

Although excessive consumption works for us in economic terms, it pushes us to the limits environmentally. The Intergovernmental Panel on Climate Change calculated that carbon dioxide emissions grew 80% between 1970 and 2004 (Metz, Davidson, Bosch, Dave, & Meyer, 2007). Atmospheric concentrations of carbon dioxide now hover around 390 parts per million (ppm), an increase of 100 ppm since the beginning of the Industrial Revolution and 40 ppm above levels estimated to sustain human life in the long run (Hansen, et al., 2007). Because environmental consequences are separated from the choices made by consumers in daily market exchanges, this trend cannot be reduced or reversed unless we change the role of consumption in society. In short, our capacity to consume is outstripping our ideology.

Consumption, as an ideology, in its manifestations of acquisition, use, and disposal, is as much a product of the Enlightenment as the goods and services we consume. Until the Industrial Revolution, and the ability to produce, acquire, and accumulate on a mass scale, *consumption* referred to the subsistence behavior of survival. Modern capitalism, as such, reflects our beliefs about the role and value of consumption, just as choice models of behavior are the fruits of industrial production. When Adam Smith (1776/1937) said, "Consumption is the sole end and purpose of all production" (p. 376), he was advocating consumption as profligacy, or extravagance, not consumption as subsistence. Frugality became the enemy of capitalism, at least as we practice it today.

The purpose of this chapter is to understand the origins and consequences of profligate consumption as an ideological imperative, its role in the structure of marketing systems, and its environmental consequences. Today, 80% of developed economies are consumption driven, meaning that we are all dependent on the level of consumption of others regardless of the individual choices they make. In this sense, consumption is not merely the aggregation of choices but also an orientation, a paradigm, an ideology. This chapter intends to explore and understand the origins and consequences of the ideology of consumption, so TCR can better affect the daily behavior of consumers. If we hope to influence the choices consumers make, we must first understand the role consumption plays in their worldview.

## TRANSFORMATIVE CONSUMER RESEARCH AND SUSTAINABLE CONSUMPTION

Although TCR is in its infancy and has not been specifically defined yet, the working definition we adopt in this chapter is that it entails research that intends to result in the enhancement of consumer well-being in its largest sense. In underdeveloped countries, this might include how to increase levels of consumption for those who have too little. In more developed countries and at the individual consumer level, it would entail research that would empower consumers to enact the lives that they desire, which is the approach taken by McDonagh, Dobscha, and Prothero (Chapter 13 of this volume) as well as Burroughs and Rindfleisch (Chapter 12 of this volume). From a systems level, TCR would examine the institutional structures in which consumers are embedded and help them understand the nature of their existence within a particular historic, cultural context. This would lead to a better understanding of how and why choices are made and what the larger consequences of those choices aggregated across society are. To this end, a series of 13 questions (labeled TCRQ) is posed at appropriate points in this chapter.

TCR is concerned with two levels of consumption, the individual and the collective (Mick, 2006). TCR at the level of the individual focuses on issues of access, opportunity, and choice. Recent work on choice restriction (Botti et al., 2008) and vulnerability (Baker, Gentry, & Rittenburg, 2005) are excellent examples of this form of research. Additionally, Baker and Mason (Chapter 26 of this volume) consider the role of TCR in navigating the role for the visually impaired, from vulnerability to resiliency. At the collective level, though, TCR should focus on issues of aggregate consumption, or consumption at the systems or institutional level of society. These two perspectives can be at odds. If a household spends less and saves more, it may improve its future opportunities. If all households spend less and save more, though, the results can be economic catastrophe. This Keynesian paradox is at the heart of our consumption-driven economy and raises issues of the individual and the aggregate in consumption research, both of which are important to the intersection of consumption and sustainability. The approach taken in this chapter is the systems perspective, examining the institutional framework within which consumption takes place.

Sustainable consumption is consumption that meets the needs of the present generation without compromising the ability of future generations to meet their own needs (World Commission on Economic and Development, 1987). The role of consumption in environmental sustainability is twofold. For consumption to be sustainable, we must (1) improve the environmental impact of what we consume, and (2) reduce the total amount of consumption. TCR at the individual level is focused on the first question: How do we help people make better choices, given the realities of environmental limits? This is fundamentally a problem of consumer selection, and answers to it necessarily deal with the choice processes of consumers, information gaps, cognitive-processing capabilities, and the assortment of offerings. Sustainable consumption requires that consumers incorporate better decision-making tools into their decision processes, and to do this, TCR needs to move consumer-behavior research beyond the merely descriptive into the realm of prescriptive rules that limit our environmental impact.

TCR at the aggregate level focuses on to the second question: How much do we consume, and how we can reduce the overall volume of consumption to sustainable levels? Even if we make better choices, the total amount of resources consumed by humanity will, sooner or later, outstrip the resource capabilities, regarding both sources and sinks, of the planet. Issues of climate change, carbon dioxide emissions, and global warming are affected mostly by aggregate consumption, not the individual choices we make, and avoiding an environmental disaster is not a problem we can fix by consuming better but only by consuming less. So, why do we consume as much as we do? Why do we see consumption as the solution to the problems of our daily lives? Answers to these questions lie in our society's ideology of consumption.

TCRQ1. Do consumers believe that consumption leads to happiness and enhanced well-being, and, if so, to what extent do they understand why they believe this? What do we know about the motivations that lead to excessive consumption? Is compulsive shopping abnormal behavior or just excessive behavior?

TCRQ2. How do consumers understand the full consequences, both personal and environmental, of their consumption choices? Neither buyers nor sellers are incentivized to examine the full costs of their behaviors. Why is this the case?

TCRQ3. What are the institutional forces at work that lead to profligate (excessive) consumption on a national scale, and how do they relate to each other in an integrated paradigm influencing consumption behavior? Put another way, when the going gets tough, why do the tough go shopping?

## CONSUMPTION AS A DRIVER OF MARKETING SYSTEMS

The systems, or institutional, approach taken in this chapter expands on the view of marketing as agorology (Mittelstaedt, Kilbourne, & Mittelstaedt, 2006) to become thesmology (the study of institutions), which entails incorporating what the agorology approach considers to be philosophical antecedents so that the sustainability problem is framed as a problem of institutions. This approach will include the institutions that Kilbourne, McDonagh, and Prothero (1997) argued are part of the DSP of Western industrial societies. Hodgson (2001) defined *institutions* as "durable systems of established and embedded social rules and conventions that structure social interactions" (p. 295). The focus is on institutions because it is at this level of social structures that the predefined control of human conduct within society is developed (Berger & Luckmann, 1966). It is through institutions that individuals' patterns of thought and behavior manifest themselves as rational behavior, or that which is expected of certain actors in certain situations. These patterns become the taken-for-granted routines of society that exist outside the individual and are experienced as objective reality. This broad definition would include political, economic, and technological institutions making up the DSP. This is also consistent with the consumer culture theorists' call for research that examines the "institutional and social structures that systematically influence consumption" (Arnould & Thompson, 2005, p. 874).

## PHILOSOPHICAL ORIGINS OF PROFLIGACY AS THE IDEOLOGY OF CONSUMPTION

Although profligacy with its typical connotation of extravagant expenditure and extreme self-indulgence has been a concern for ancient Greek philosophers including Pythagoras and Plato, as well as for prominent Romans such as Cicero and Marcus Aurelius, concern among these philosophers and statesmen related to the pernicious effects on the individual and society. For them, profligacy had social and ethical dimensions but not an ecological dimension. During the Middle Ages, profligacy had more religious significance with its basis in biblical scripture. Wealth possessed badly had pernicious effects on one's faith. This conflict persisted for centuries within the church. This theme resonates in Eco's (1983) *The Name of the Rose*, in which medieval Scholastics are convening a meeting to determine if Jesus owned his own clothes. If he did, then private property would be considered a legitimate institution. Although private property had been given legal status in the Magna Carta in 1215, it was almost 600 years before the religious proscriptions on excess accumulation of property began to subside (see, e.g., Tawney, 1962).

### Man and the Natural State of Consumption

With the publication of Locke's *The Second Treatise of Civil Government* in 1690, the legitimacy of accumulation was sealed, and the proscriptions on excess consumption were not only relaxed but also transformed into a virtue. Yet, once the ethical concerns for profligacy were removed, the ecological ramifications began to take hold. Locke cautioned on the institutionalization of excess, arguing that accumulation was desirable so long as there was "enough, and as good" (ch. 5, sec. 27) for others to behave similarly. To him, this seemed a minimal constraint, because America, at the time, seemed to be a vast, though not limitless, storehouse of resources. In effect, Locke opened the door to what Rifkin (1980) referred to as the environmentalist's nightmare: infinite growth in a finite system. Little note was taken of this problem until Mill's (1848/1872) treatment of it in what he referred to as the inevitable stationary state that occurs when the salutary consequence of increasing wealth diminishes and technical growth sufficient to continue accumulation cannot be maintained. In this early account of the social and physical limits to growth, Mill considered both the ethical and ecological limits, arguing that the individual and the environment are diminished. Both dimensions of the sustainability problem were picked up by the Romantic poets as well.

TCRQ4. In a contemporary economy, what are the consumer-behavior implications of a steady-state economy? How would consumption be different if we assigned a moral value to a steady-state economy?

From this brief assessment, it can be seen that consumption profligacy has had a long and varied history, having gone from a vice to a virtue and back again. Although its relationship to sustainability has only been recent from a historical perspective, overconsumption is now problematic, having been linked almost unequivocally to environmental degradation. The question posed in the chapter title is derived from and concurs with this view. If both the quantity (too much) and the quality (the wrong kind) of global consumption are clearly linked to environmental degradation, then why do the problems appear intractable? Western industrial societies are certainly the most educated, self-aware, and socially integrated populations in history (although, as educators, we may sometimes doubt this). Yet, if this is true, then we are faced with a conundrum. Why do so many smart people do so many seemingly stupid things, such as overconsume or consume without regard to long-term consequences to themselves (e.g., using tobacco products) or for society (e.g., ignoring externalities like air and water pollution)?

The persistence of the consumption problem can be attributed to both its complexity and its ubiquity. The operative word in the question posed above is *seemingly*, because it may be that these smart people are doing the wrong thing in the sincere belief that they are doing the right thing. If this is the case, then we may be caught in the vortex of a positive feedback loop moving us further from sustainability as we redouble our efforts to achieve it. The implication of this is that there are forces within cultures that are opaque, but these forces direct behavior in ways that consumers neither understand nor would condone if they did understand. To pursue such an analytical course, we must take Thomas Paine's (1776/1997) admonition to heart: "A long habit of not thinking a thing wrong, gives it a superficial appearance of being right, and raises at first a formidable outcry in defense of custom" (p. 1).

It is the "defense of custom" that becomes important, because it is the custom of overconsumption that, as a type of commons problem (Shultz & Holbrook, 1999), must be overcome if Western societies are to move from profligacy to sustainability regarding consumption behavior. That is, if we each sacrificed a little now and consumed less, the long-term sustainability gain could be highly significant. Yet, we, particularly in the United States, do not seem willing to do that and instead take full measure of our pleasures with little regard for the future of ourselves, our progeny, or abstract future generations because of our sense of our role in the natural order and the institutions that support and reinforce the DSP.

TCRQ5. How do consumers see themselves in the natural order, and does it affect their consumption behavior? If their position were different, would they consume differently? Put another way, why is consumption considered natural behavior?

## Consumption and the Natural State of Man

Before such an analysis is possible, certain assumptions about custom must be clarified. At the risk of being labeled heretical, we begin with the proposition that Adam Smith's view of humanity was wrong. Both Rousseau (1983) and Nietzche (1878/1986) argued that philosophers had for centuries before them tried to put humans in their natural state, but they had only succeeded in putting them in their social state, and for them, nature and state were to be differentiated (MacIntyre, 1996). In this case, Smith (1776/1937) assumed that the "propensity to truck, barter, and exchange" (p. 21) was a natural human propensity that enabled capitalist market relations to develop. Thus, it was an intrinsic part of the human character that was waiting for the opportunity to emerge (see also Burroughs & Rindfleisch, Chapter 12 of this volume). More contemporary assessments have argued that it was expanding market relations of incipient capitalism that precipitated the exchange relationship as the model of behavior between individuals (MacPherson, 1962), which had been developing for three centuries before Smith (see, e.g., Wood, 2002). This social transformation of institutions from feudal society to capitalist society is well documented by Polanyi (1944). However, even if one rejected the analyses of Wood and Polanyi and assumed that "trucking and bartering" were natural, the form of social relations that issue from that propensity could be different under different social relations. Dewey (1989) states:

> For example, if our American culture is largely a pecuniary culture, it is not because the original or innate structure of human nature tends of itself to obtaining pecuniary profit. It is rather that a certain complex culture stimulates, promotes and consolidates native tendencies so as to produce a certain pattern of desires and purposes. (p. 22)

Polanyi (1944) concurs with this, arguing that the necessary market institutions had to be constructed to make capitalism work in 18th- and 19th-century England. Wood (2002) goes even further, stating that "coercion by the state, in other words, was required to impose the coercion of the market" (p. 69). Finally, Dryzek (1996) concludes "that there is nothing natural, still less universal, about rational egoism in human social, economic, and political life" (p. 94). If we were to assume that the propensity to consume more and more were a natural propensity, then the prospects for a successful TCR initiative would be severely limited. If such behavior is shaped by existing institutions, however, then change, while difficult, becomes possible through institutional transformation using the same processes that created the institutions initially. Thus, we derive two major premises for this chapter. First, as it is found, behavior is seldom the sole product of human nature regardless of how common it is. Second, institutions can be transformed in periods of extraordinary necessity.

Regarding the nature of consumption activities, the standard neoclassical assumptions are called into question here. Among these are rational egoism (i.e., self-interest) (Dryzek, 1996), exogenous consumer preference functions (Sagoff, 1988), atomistic individualism (Taylor, 1991), procedural neutrality in politics (Sandel, 1996), and innate human material greed (Thurow, 1980). Taken together, these assumptions indicate that unrestrained consumption within impersonal market mechanisms is the means through which individuals satisfy their needs in the most efficient manner, and they should not or could not, if a product of human nature, be inhibited from behaving according to these conditions. If these assumptions are true, then the solution to the sustainability problem would be to free markets even more so that they will work the magic of the invisible hand through which sustainability will inevitably evolve. If the market argument is not true, however, then mutually coercive institutions that persuade people to consume properly would be necessary.

Ophuls (1977) refers to this as mutual coercion, mutually agreed upon. If the market argument fails, assuming that it is the neoliberal conception of markets that is the cause of environmental degradation rather than the solution to sustainability, then one must conclude that existing institutions serve to transmogrify social relations to meet the exigencies of mass production and capital accumulation, and these exigencies are, at present, incompatible with sustainability (Speth, 2008). Then, we find ourselves with Einstein's problem framework suggesting that you cannot solve the problems you have created with the same framework of thought used to create them. Thus, the starting point and underlying assumption for this assessment is that consumers behave the way they do because of institutional forces (i.e., the DSP) that they do not attend to, do not control, and generally do not understand. While these institutions are ubiquitous and most often opaque precisely because of their ubiquity, they can be understood and transformed because no institution is so well integrated as to be immune to change, as Berger and Luckmann (1966) point out. Wapner and Willoughby (2005) concur, suggesting that, although the structures of society that can pervert ecologically sound living are rigid, they are not eternal. Thus, the problem becomes exposing ideology masquerading as fact. Marcuse (1964) and the critical theorists have argued that the task is to expose false consciousness that is inured to its falseness. Finally, it is through critical macromarketing (Kilbourne et al., 1997) and TCR that the nature and logic of these institutions, and their underlying ideologies, can be understood and changed.

TCRQ6. Why will consumers readily accept the coercion of the market but are reluctant to accept political coercion even for an acceptable cause?

Institutions That Shape the DSP

Although there are many institutions that may be complicit in the profligate consumer behavior that is driving Western societies toward a sustainability crisis, three play a dominant role and are considered to be integral in the DSP of Western societies: political, economic, and technological institutions that have a direct relationship to consumer behavior. Each of these institutions will be examined for its role in the development of that particular orientation toward consumption commonly referred to as *materialism*. It has been argued that the global spread of materialism (Stiglitz, 2002) is unsustainable (Daly, 1996), and despite its many negative consequences, it is spreading (Ger & Belk, 1996) and threatening the well-being of citizens individually, socially, and ecologically around the world (Ger, 1997; Kilbourne, 2004).

The questions to be addressed here are What is happening? and Why is it happening? Although this may seem trite, it will be argued that it is much more complex than the marketing discipline has understood. The attitude–behavior gap seems well established (Alwitt & Pitts, 1996) and suggests that, although citizens in most countries are becoming ecologically aware and cognizant of the role of human behavior in environmental degradation, their consumption behavior changes very little. We must conclude from this that making consumers aware of the problem is a necessary but insufficient approach to sustainability, because the institutional structure of Western societies (i.e., political, economic, technological) is incompatible with sustainability.

As a result, while serious efforts are being made to inform consumers and appeal to their ethical sensibilities for behavioral change, the institutions that surround them in their everyday lives communicate a ubiquitous, antisustainability message. For example, through numerous cultural apparatuses, the consistent message is that more stuff will make you happier. This message is the product of and compatible with the DSP of Western industrial societies, promotes profligacy on a global scale, and contrary to many observers, is not a strategy for increasing profitability per se. It is an imperative of the competitive market system through which needs are met in Western industrial societies, and the global spread of materialism is a product of this imperative. Sustainability initiatives incorporating TCR are likely to be effective only at the margin if consideration is not given to this imperative.

TCRQ7. Is the global spread of profligate consumption an imperative of capitalism? If so, then why? What are the consequences of the global spread of profligate consumption?

What will be demonstrated in the remainder of the chapter is the nature and evolution of the DSP within which the market imperative resides. It will be argued that the political, economic, and technological dimensions of the DSP work in harmony and are mutually supportive in engendering profligate consumption behavior that is the inevitable outcome of materialism. To do this, we will first examine the nature of paradigms in general and show that environmentalists' desire to initiate a new environmental paradigm to replace the current DSP, although well intentioned, is substantively vacuous. Thus, the possibility of effecting such a change is severely limited because paradigm change is seldom brought about by the power of the better argument (Kuhn, 1962). We will then develop a characterization of the DSP of Western industrial societies to demonstrate its consistency with and necessity for materialistic behavior. The intent here is to show that the competitive market system cannot exist without materialism and profligate consumption and also that deriding materialistic consumers for their behavior is what Ryan (1976) referred to as "blaming the victim."

Thus, the basic premise here is that it is not errant consumers who craft institutions consistent with their misguided or natural desires, but the institutions of Western industrial society that mold consumer behavior to be consistent with its own unique requirements. This creates a circular relationship through which overconsumption and marketing reinforce each other. Within the DSP of Western industrial societies, materialism is both necessary and desirable, as it is consistent with and fully supports the exigencies of mass production (Ewen, 1976) in which economic efficiency is the tribunal of last resort. Material simplicity has no purchase in this court, nor does justice or nature. Sustainability requires simplicity, social justice, intrinsic value in nature, and efficiency, so the transition from profligacy to sustainability is problematic from within the DSP of Western industrial societies because these social qualities are anathema to progress, defined for more than a century as material progress (Bury, 1932). When TCR is predicated on this proposition, then it becomes possible to address sustainability in a more comprehensive way. What this suggests is that marketing scholarship should be cautious of technological quick fixes, green mythology, and the triple bottom line (i.e., people, planet, profit) in the popular press and begin to take note of the institutional foundations of the marketing process noted by Mittelstaedt et al. (2006).

TCRQ8. Why have consumer orientations such as voluntary simplicity failed to spread, and do voluntary simplifiers answer the TCR questions differently? Why do they see it differently?

This framing of the sustainability problem does not suggest that TCR can only be at the institutional level, as consumer well-being is a complex phenomenon and exists at many levels. However, it does suggest that Ozanne and Saatcioglu's (2008) caveat about action research should be heeded. The quality of individual-level research should be assessed partly, at least, through its ability in helping consumers understand their social reality, thus creating catalytic validity that transcends the immediacy of action research. One objective should be to effect social change up to the global level by expanding consumers' knowledge about the institutions under which they function on a daily basis. This renders transparent the ideology behind opaque institutions and provides the function of democratizing knowledge. That is, once individuals understand the institutions that influence them, they are in a better position to deal with them. This, in turn, enables one to enact the life one chooses to live by expanding positive freedom, or capabilities, as they are referred to by Sen (1993, 1999), within the framework of negative freedom that simply adds rights by removing constraints to one's social existence. It takes many levels of knowledge and freedom to create a life worthy of living that is also sustainable.

TCRQ9. Can an action research approach that works within the existing system lead to catalytic validity, or do we need more dramatic new approaches that seek to challenge the DSP?

### Evolutions of the Dominant Social Paradigm

The idea of a paradigm was first popularized by Kuhn (1962) in the context of scientific development, then adapted by Pirages and Ehrlich (1974) to apply to the social context. They described a paradigm as the institutions, values, and beliefs that provide the lens through which members of society view and interpret their world. Kuhn also states that one's paradigm determines which objects are of interest in society and the relationship between them. Kilbourne and Beckmann (2002) add an evaluative dimension to social paradigms, suggesting that they provide the criteria by which one judges good and bad outcomes. As for the dominance of a paradigm within a society, Cotgrove (1982) argues that it is not the majority adhering to a paradigm that makes it dominant, but rather the worldview held by the dominant class who use it to legitimize their position in society. All these factors taken together indicate that a DSP functions as ideology. As presented here, the DSP of Western industrial societies was engendered during the Enlightenment and has functioned as ideology since that time.

The authority of the DSP rests, to a large extent, on a variation of the naturalistic fallacy referred to as the is—ought problem through which the conventional categories within the paradigm are presented, not as the outcome of unique social conditions (i.e., prevailing institutions) but as the natural condition of society. Because it exists, it ought to exist, and no other outcome makes sense within the paradigm. Berger and Luckmann (1966) concur with this, suggesting that institutions appear as self-evident and that institutions themselves cannot be understood without understanding the historical process that engendered them. Using the conventional institutions of capitalism provides a useful demonstration of the application of paradigmatic thought. A conventional priority within capitalism, as indicated earlier, is the imperative of economic growth, which has achieved, through institution building during the 20th century (see, e.g., Ewen, 1976), the status of *summum bonum* within Western industrial societies. Because economic growth is what capitalism produces best, and is necessary for the reproduction of capital, there was no discussion about whether economic growth was, in fact, good or even desirable under all circumstances at the inception of capitalism (Mirowski, 1988; Polanyi, 1944). It was simply necessary to make the system work. Within this context, it was necessary to create the ultimate end, or the good, as that which reinforced and legitimized the institutions of capitalism, primarily economic growth and its concomitant, expanding consumption opportunities sufficient to sustain growth.

Contrary to popular opinion within capitalist societies, however, exponentially increasing consumption was not a priority of any society in the past, particularly Protestant-based societies such as the United States. Thus, material consumption had to be engendered and valorized as the ultimate end because it was the only such goal that would serve the interest of the dominant class, and that interest was the endless increase of production, that is, economic growth (Ewen, 1976; Polanyi, 1944). This entailed equating individual consumption with individual well-being and progress.

The model of the well-functioning society became one in which material affluence was perpetually increasing. Societies with the greatest affluence were those associated with capitalism because only capitalism was capable of producing enough economic growth for perpetually increasing affluence (i.e., the *sine qua non* of well-being), which then legitimates the institutions of capitalism. As can be seen, the reasoning is quite circular. Capitalism produces growth, growth produces affluence, affluence is good, and, therefore, capitalism is good. In Western industrial societies, this has entered the realm of self-evident truths that, as suggested by Bauman (1998), are used to explain the world but do not need to be explained themselves. The qualities that the institutions of capitalism do not produce are not a part of the equation, and no explanation is needed as to why they are not. Such qualities as justice, equality, and security do not enter into the assessment because by these criteria, capitalism would not legitimate itself, and the dominant classes would have to find alternative criteria for legitimation.

Wachtel (1989), Polanyi (1944), and Speth (2008) provide accounts of the development and consequences of this process of institution building and argue that, because they have become part of the habits of thought and are self-evidently true, we are unable to see the larger collection of institutions that support and engender these beliefs. As a result, we remain "chained to the wheel of economic growth" (Wachtel, 1989, p. 116) and are transformed by the procrustean competitive market system of allocation. The fact that the institutions are arbitrary, capricious, and anything but natural escapes notice because they are already built into the paradigm and remain unexamined.

We now turn to a brief account of the institutions that have, thus far, only been mentioned in the abstract. If TCR is to be effective in engendering long-term change in consumption behavior, we must understand how these institutions influence the behavior that needs to be changed. If consumer researchers fail to consider the institutional structure in which the consumer resides, then change, even if it is created, will be short-lived. If the institutions that created and reinforce the original profligate behavior are left in intact, then they will be continuously affecting consumer behavior, recreating it in its original form.

## DIMENSIONS OF THE IDEOLOGY OF CONSUMPTION

Although there are a large number of institutions that might be considered complicit in the development and reinforcement of profligate consumption as an end in itself, a small number, such as science, liberalism, and markets, have contributed greatly. Whereas none of the institutions is sufficient to direct a society, their confluence in a single society has a significant impact in enabling and rewarding profligate consumption. It is argued here that one goal of TCR should be to transform these institutions so that they lead societies away from profligacy and toward sustainability. It should be recalled that we are using the term *institutions* in the largest sense, as suggested by Berger and Luckmann (1966), Searle (1995), and Hodgson (2001), and it is the confluence of these taken-for-granted habits of thought and action that constitutes the DSP of a society.

The DSP of Western industrial societies had its origins in the Enlightenment, during which the break with feudal society became complete. This means that a new set of institutions was created out of the old, and these institutions have been in development since that time. They now form the basis, or the background, within which subsequent habits of thought and action have evolved, and they have shaped consumption behavior that is now at issue. Although no individual can reasonably be assigned the lead role in this process, three are particularly important in the DSP of Western societies. The works of Francis Bacon, John Locke, and Adam Smith have become classics in Western science (technology), politics, and economics, respectively. While a full analysis of how their ideas developed in harmony is beyond the scope of this chapter, their confluence is immediately evident in the sense that each prepared the way for the next. Bacon, in 1620, opened the door for the systematic study of both nature and society through the experimental method and argued that the purpose of science was liberation from the inconveniences of man's estate, which included both man's relation to nature and the relations between men. The advance of learning served the dual purpose of satisfying material wants and repressing the instinctual desires that threatened peace (Leiss, 1972). It was within this social context that Locke was to work in the late 17th century after political revolution, in the form of the English civil war, opened the door for democracy and political analysis in general. Smith, in 1776, followed Locke and was able to capitalize on both his work and the Industrial Revolution, which made possible the full-scale development of capitalism and formed the basis of his economics. Each then had "stood on the shoulders of giants" whose visions and historical circumstances shaped the Enlightenment.

### The Technology of Profligate Consumption

The specific institutions of interest here should be considered as enabling conditions in the development of profligate consumption, but not causal conditions. Enabling conditions do not necessarily lead to specific modes of consumption, but profligate consumption can scarcely be considered without them. Because of this relationship, they are of paramount importance to TCR. The institution of interest is the Baconian principle that science is for the purpose of bettering (increasing) the material conditions of existence through the judicious development of technology that forces nature to yield its assets to mankind (see also Mick, Pettigrew, Pechmann, & Ozanne, Chapter 1 of this volume, regarding conventional science and practical wisdom), which results in the reductionist transformation of nature from intrinsic to instrumental value in service to humanity and separates humans from nature placing them above it. This is the move that Merchant (1980) refers to as "the death of nature." Once nature is transformed from an organic unity within which human development takes place to a mechanical device that is controlled by humans in developing the material conditions of existence, the human relation to nature is transformed. This creates new habits of thought and behavior toward nature that become an integral part of the new institutional structure of Western industrial societies.

TCRQ10. How do consumers see nature and their place in it? Is nature fragile or resilient? How can we reenchant nature? Do we consume differently depending on our view? Do other cultures see it differently?

In the new technological institutions, nature is reduced to instrumental value in service to humanity. Reverence for its grandeur and mystery recedes as it becomes the object of manipulation for purely human purposes. Because of the vastness of nature at that time, it appeared to be an inexhaustible supply of resources that were valueless unless enlisted in the service of humanity. This was a reasonable assumption at that historical moment, but even the earlier theorists like Locke and Mill indicated that the supply would not last forever. What is more important here, however, is the transformation in thought regarding technology and how that impacted the role of consumption in society. The one-eyed prophets of technology, who see only the good and not the bad, saw only the advances in material progress that technological development was bringing, but they failed to see the institutional transformations taking place at the same time (Postman, 1993). The confluence of technology and industry was creating a new rationality with new ideological biases that were changing language, thought, and reality to bring them into conformity with the new material conception of the world. Truth was no longer found in religion or tradition but in the language of technology: efficiency, objectivity, and progress. This reductionist move finds ultimate meaning not in a proper relationship with the eternal but only in technique and its product, material consumption, which are inherently short term in their temporal focus.

TCRQ11. What is the relationship between technological optimism and profligate consumption? Does technological change revise the social contract? Do consumers see that their lives and consumption are technologically mediated?

Bacon anticipated that, with the mastery of nature, the mastery of human nature would follow close behind. It is here, however, that the Enlightenment project has failed. While the definition of *freedom* has been limited within technological rationality to mean freedom from external constraint imposed by nature, which is manifested in the freedom to consume whatever and as much as one chooses—that is, the freedom to enact the life one chooses, or what Sen (1999) refers to as substantive freedom—the essence of freedom remains unsatisfied. Leiss (1972) concurs with this assessment arguing that individuals work toward progress through technological rationality, but there is no reward for their efforts in the end. Yet, this limitation is consistent with the role of paradigms outlined earlier. Technology can provide negative freedom, that is, the freedom from pernicious nature (within ecological limits), and it has done this for a small percentage of the world's population during the last century, so mastery over nature becomes the criterion by which technological progress is judged. In this way, material progress and exponentially increasing consumption legitimate technological rationality. However, emancipation writ large has not become part of the equation because technology cannot provide it. Leiss (1972) further argued that a persistent illusion in Western society is that the mastery of nature has actually been achieved. Rather, technological rationality is characterized as an inferior mode of thought by Thoreau (1854/1962), who stated, "Our inventions are wont to be pretty toys, which distract our attention from serious things. They are but improved means to an unimproved end, an end which it was already but too easy to arrive at" (p. 151).

The imperative of technology in the modern era has been reduced to a limited set of objectives. Foremost among these, according to Leiss (1972), is getting the goods. He stated, "In short: to get what we want (or think we need in order to be happy) by transforming the planet into nothing but a supplier of our wants—an abundant, unlimited, never-ending variety of goods" (p. xxv). He then concluded, "The attempt to achieve this goal by means of humanity's technological mastery over nature will fail" (p. xxvi). This is a brief accounting of how we have chosen to get the goods through scientific and technological development and why the goods produced through the process have been defined as desirable, but it does not address the question of why we feel an entitlement to the goods so obtained. This is, at its core, a political question to which we now turn.

## The Politics of Profligate Consumption

Because the means for producing goods through scientific progress had been developing for half a century before Locke arrived on the political scene, a number of sociopolitical problems inhibited the full development of incipient capitalism. This was essentially a legitimation problem, because there were still both religious (see, e.g., Tawney, 1962; Weber, 1904–1905/1992) and social restraints (see, e.g., Ashton, 1964; Polanyi, 1944) on consumption. As suggested earlier, increased capacity for production is impotent without increased capacity for consumption. The legitimation project was left to Locke, who met the challenge through the development of political liberalism. This new philosophy was predicated on three institutions that, although not new at the time, were not integrated into a single coherent form: possessive individualism, private property, and limited democratic government.

These three factors form the basis for the political dimension of the DSP in Western industrial societies today. Free and independent individuals who are in possession of themselves are entitled to acquire property through the exercise of their labor, which can be directly, as in agriculture, or indirectly through the sale of their labor. In the latter case, the laborer receives a wage through which property can be acquired, but the fruits of one's labors rightfully belong to the supplier of wages, which is predicated on the assumption that labor is alienable. Through their efforts, individuals can accumulate private property (i.e., material goods) that becomes theirs by the application of their labor (MacPherson, 1962). Unlike earlier ages, this property is protected by law and is exclusively theirs. To insure that both the individual and property are protected, a limited democratic government is empowered to protect the property in one's self and one's goods and enforce contracts that were legitimately formed, which was, for Locke, a necessary arrangement that ensured that the system would function smoothly.

There were three outcomes of the institutionalization of individualism, private property, and limited government that are particularly relevant for our purposes. First, Locke described and legitimated nature as a storehouse for human development. He argued that nature, undeveloped for human purposes, was a waste and was to be condemned as such. Second, he developed the cornucopian view of nature that implied that, in the foreseeable future, nature's bounty was unlimited. His justification for this was the American frontier that appeared to him and his contemporaries to be virtually unlimited (MacPherson, 1962). Most important, he transformed the ideas of increasing consumption and unlimited accumulation of property from vices to virtues. Locke's institutional legacy cannot be overestimated in Western industrial society, as profligate consumption practices are virtually inconceivable without them. Without atomistic individuals pursuing their own interests unconstrained by external forces, then integrated, competitive markets cannot function. Without assurance that one's property is protected, there is little motivation to exchange and accumulate. Although markets had not yet become fully integrated, Locke opened the door for their full development under capitalism a century later. Yet, from this perspective, it is clear that without Locke, Adam Smith's philosophies would not have been possible.

TCRQ12. To what extent do consumers define freedom as the freedom to consume? Do myriad options in the market create an illusion of choice and freedom? How do we get consumers to understand the consequences of their individual choices in the aggregate (i.e., social traps)?

### The Economics of Profligate Consumption

The full development of capitalism was enabled by Locke but legitimized by Adam Smith, whose underlying assumptions have become institutionalized in modern capitalism. Primary among these are that free markets are the most efficient way to allocate resources, self-interest is the sole motivator of individual behavior, and that if markets are left to the devices of atomistic individuals, then their natural propensity to truck and barter will result in the most beneficial outcome for society. Casual examination of any account of the current economic crisis in the United States confirms that these assumptions are still prevalent. It is becoming increasingly clear, however, that they are questionable, and for Rousseau (1762/1968), they would be highly questionable. The two issues raised are (1) is exchange a natural or a social propensity, and (2) does the will of all necessarily equal the general will? About these assumptions, Polanyi (1944) argues, "In retrospect it can be said that no misreading of the past ever proved more prophetic for the future" (p. 43). With regard to the first assumption, he argues that it was not the propensity to truck and barter that created markets but the opposite. Exchange behavior derives from the existence of markets, and because they are of relatively recent origin, this is where economists focused their attention. As a result, the capitalistic psychology has become the mainstay of economic analysis and leads to the conclusion driving most analyses that market behavior is natural. However, as suggested earlier, Rousseau (1762/1968) and Nietzsche (1878/1986), and more contemporaneously Searle (1995) and Polanyi (1944), argue that philosophers have for centuries tried to put man in his natural state, but they have only succeeded in putting him in his social state and calling it natural.

The error in economic analysis, and in Adam Smith's theories, was in assuming that which was to be proved. That is, he assumed a capitalistic psychology that was only waiting for competitive market relations to evolve. Because the capitalistic psychology has now been institutionalized, it is the basic premise on which profligate consumption thrives. Atomistic individuals functioning in unconstrained markets exercise preferences that they believe will lead to their well-being, but the growing volume of research at both the individual and social levels suggests that this is not true. Consumers seldom know what contributes to their long-run well-being either as an individual or a member of a collective. It is this lack of knowledge that leads to the "poverty of affluence" described by Wachtel (1989) on the individual level and social traps and commons dilemmas described by Dawes (1980), Hardin (1968), Shultz and Holbrook (1999), and many others on the collective level.

Rousseau (1762/1968) also addressed the second assumption above. Here, he argued that the will of all (i.e., what they would will, considering their own personal interests) is seldom equal to the general will (i.e., what each would will, if their own personal interests were set aside). The equality of the will of all and the general will is the very basis for market society, which assumes a single, all-encompassing preference function that does not distinguish between consumer preferences and citizen preferences. Here, the market logic suggests that the sum total of whatever consumers choose in competitive markets results in the best outcome for society, because all of their individual actions are guided by an invisible hand that guarantees the outcome, which is true even when the global disparity in wealth is as large as it is today (Boyle & Simms, 2009). We now know from decades of research that this is not necessarily true except in a very limited sense (see, e.g., Daly, 1972; Shultz & Holbrook, 1999). If the objective of market allocations is to maximize economic growth, which is the imperative of capitalism, then markets can be said to function efficiently. But, if virtually any other objective is imposed, then the outcome is not so clear.

TCRQ13. How do consumers understand markets and their function? Are they economically rational and think that everyone else is, too? Is all behavior motivated by self-interest?

## TRANSFORMATIVE CONSUMER RESEARCH: A SYSTEMS PERSPECTIVE

What has been suggested thus far is that nature cannot withstand the levels of consumption currently found in developed economies if these levels are extrapolated to the rest of the world. It is doubtful that the profligate consumption styles of the West can be maintained into the indefinite future even if globalization does not result in their spread, which leaves us a number of problems with which to deal. Foremost among these is a transformation from profligacy to sustainability that entails a transformation of consumer lifestyles in Western industrial societies. Although green marketing, conservation initiatives, and lean production have all been initiated, they will result in too little too late if consumption levels continue to expand. What is required is that consumers shift both the quality and quantity of consumption. We must consume better and less if sustainability is to become a reality.

It is also suggested that the change from profligacy to sustainability requires transformation at the individual and social levels, although the focus of this chapter is on the social. This becomes the role of TCR. It is clear that some initial changes are in evidence, as reflected by such initiatives as toy libraries, slow food, and the New Zealand anticonsumption group. Clearly, scholars are taking the problem seriously, but there remains a problem with this approach in that it is incomplete because it focuses on the individual level of consumption and fails to consider the institutional, or paradigm, level of analysis. It is argued here that a number of institutions making up the DSP of Western industrial societies remain in place while the individual initiatives are being developed.

Throughout the chapter, we have provided TCR questions that need to be addressed. It must be acknowledged, however, that answering these questions is the beginning of the TCR process. The answer to every question must ultimately be framed in a consumer policy agenda. Whereas at the individual level of analysis, TCR questions can be used to transform individual consumers' behavior, at the social level, the transformation must be made at the policy level. This requires that the answers to the questions posed lead us to leverage points that can result in large changes in institutional structures. These changes can be directed at both the individual consumer level and the level of business practices. In the first instance, this would complement the development of the consumer/citizen, and in the second instance, build constraints into the promotion of profligate consumption through a combination of incentives and disincentives for business. If the evolution of the consumer/citizen is successful, business practices would be subject to both market and political forces in a joint effort to achieve sustainable practices.

Among the premises comprising the ideology of consumption that reinforce profligacy are (a) technological progress means material consumption that is defined as progress, (b) possessive individualism allows individuals to pursue their own version of the good that is defined again as material accumulation, (c) the proper mode of possession is private property that is protected by the state, and (d) the state's only true function is to protect negative freedoms and not establish its own version of the good. Each individual must remain free to pursue his or her version of the good (Sandel, 1996).

The ideology of consumption perpetuates itself through unconstrained, competitive markets within which individuals engage in exchange to enhance their own self-interest as they see it. The difficulty here is that the primary function of these institutions is the maintenance of the paradigm through which they were initiated over the past 300 years. Each of these institutions plays a role in maintaining the legitimacy of the system of modern capitalism. But, as argued earlier by many proponents of sustainability (see, e.g., Capra, 1982; Daly, 1991; Kassiola, 1990; Ophuls, 1977; Speth, 2008), while the ideology of consumption served to develop material conditions of the Western world to unimaginable levels, that same development and growth now threatens the viability of the system itself. As a result, TCR needs to address the problem of profligacy at its core to get at the root causes of environmental decline, which means an expansion in the domain of TCR to include not just individual behaviors but also the institutional structures that precipitate and maintain those behaviors. Although TCR at the individual level is imperative, if the initiatives lack the catalytic validity to transcend the immediacy of the consumption situation, then the institutions proffering profligate consumption will remain intact and militate against substantive, long-term change. In this case, the transformative nature of individual consumer change will be lost.

## TRANSFORMATIVE CONSUMER RESEARCH AND A NEW IDEOLOGY OF CONSUMPTION: A RESEARCH AGENDA

The science of climate change is no longer in dispute. As we read of it in the papers, the discussion is now political rather than scientific. If anything, revisions to climate models now indicate that our time line of opportunity is shorter than we previously imagined (Hansen et al., 2007). Given the relationship between environmental decay and consumption, TCR bears a particular responsibility to create a new relationship between consumption and the environment. To do this, we propose that TCR should address the root assumptions of the current ideology of consumption and imagine a new agora—a new ideology of consumption. In this final section, we offer four general questions that consumer and marketing scholars are uniquely equipped to address. Each deals with fundamental issues at the heart of the DSP.

First, what would the agora look like if consumption were not separated from its environmental consequences? Put another way, how would consumer behavior change if we bore responsibility for the environmental impact of the choices we make? This is the intent of public policy options such as a carbon tax or a carbon cap-and-trade system. TCR should give voice to the consumer in this debate. For example, what can we learn from voluntary participation in carbon offset programs about consumers' understanding of the relationship between consumption and the environment? Or, what effects does participation by companies in cap-and-trade systems, like the Chicago Climate Exchange, have on consumer welfare?

Second, what would the agora—the public space where market activities and social discourse take place—look like if consumption were not an implicit political right or an implicit political responsibility? Asked either way, this question goes to the heart of whether and how markets empower consumers to express their better virtues. What can we learn from water use reduction programs (Grinstein & Nisan, 2009) about transformation of consumer behavior from entitlement to responsibility?

Third, what would the agora look like if we broke the link between consumption and carbon emissions? Mullen, Doney, Mrad, and Sheng (2009) examine the macromarketing implications for carbon emissions of rising standards of living and indicate that as incomes rise, per capita carbon dioxide emissions fall. They offer insights into the kinds of political structures necessary to make this happen.

Finally, all of these lead us back to the question of the nature of humanity. What would the agora look like if the propensity to consume, and with it to truck and barter, were not the natural state of humans? This is the kind of questions we should address if we are to offer consumers and marketers an ideology of consumption that improves the lives of current market participants without sacrificing the options of future generations.

Answers to these four questions form the foundation of a new ideology of consumption. TCR is our best hope for transforming the effects of markets and marketing systems on the environment. Let's hope it isn't our last.

## REFERENCES

Alwitt, L. F., & Pitts, R. E. (1996). Predicting purchase intentions for an environmentally sensitive product. *Journal of Consumer Psychology, 5*(1), 49–64.

Arnould, E. J., & Thompson, C. J. (2005). Consumer culture theory (CCT): Twenty years of research. *Journal of Consumer Research, 31*(March), 868–882.

Ashton, T. S. (1964). *The Industrial Revolution: 1760–1830.* New York: Oxford University Press.

Baker, S. M., Gentry, J. W., & Rittenburg, T. L. (2005). Building understanding of the domain of consumer vulnerability. *Journal of Macromarketing, 25*(2), 128–139.

Bauman, Z. (1998). *Globalization: The human consequences.* New York: Columbia University Press.

Berger, P. L., & Luckmann, T. (1966). *The social construction of reality.* Garden City, NY: Doubleday.

Botti, S., Broniar, S., Haubl, G., Hill, R., Huang, Y., Kahn, B., et al. (2008). Choices under restriction. *Marketing Letters, 19*, 183–199.

Boyle, D., & Simms, A. (2009). *A new economics: The bigger picture.* London: Earthscan.

Bury, J. B. (1932). *The idea of progress.* New York: Macmillan.

Capra, F. (1982). *The turning point: Science, society, and the rising culture.* London: Flamingo.

Cotgrove, S. (1982). *Catastrophe or cornucopia: The environment, politics, and the future.* New York: Wiley.

Daly, H. E. (1972). *Toward a steady-state economy.* San Francisco: W.H. Freeman.

Daly, H. E. (1991). *Steady-state economics.* Washington, DC: Island Press.

Daly, H. E. (1996). *Beyond growth: The economics of sustainable development.* Boston: Beacon Press.

Dawes, R. M. (1980). Social dilemmas. *Annual Review of Psychology, 46*, 190–203.

DeLong, J. B. (1998). Estimating world GDP, one million B.C.–present. Retrieved October 21, 2010, from http://www.j-bradford-delong.net/TCEH/1998_Draft/World_GDP/Estimating_World_GDP.html

Dewey, J. (1989). *Freedom and culture.* Amherst, NY: Prometheus Books.

Dryzek, J. S. (1996). *Democracy in capitalist times: Ideals, limits, and struggles.* New York: Oxford University Press.

Eco, U. (1983). *The name of the rose.* New York: Warner Books.

Ewen, S. (1976). *Captains of consciousness.* New York: McGraw-Hill.

Ger, G. (1997). Human development and humane consumption: Well-being beyond the "good life." *Journal of Public Policy & Marketing, 16*(1), 110–126.

Ger, G., & Belk, R. W. (1996). Cross-cultural differences in materialism. *Journal of Economic Psychology, 17*(1), 55–77.

Grinstein, A., & Nisan, U. (2009). Demarketing, minorities and national attachment. *Journal of Marketing, 73*(March), 105–122.

Hansen, J., Sato, M., Ruedy, R., Kharecha, P., Lasic, A., Miller, R., et al. (2007). Dangerous human-made interference with climate: A GISS modelE study. *Atmospheric Chemistry and Physics, 7*(9), 2287–2312.

Hardin, G. (1968). The tragedy of the commons. *Science, 162*, 1243–1248.

Hodgson, G. M. (2001). *How economics forgot history: The problem of historical specificity in social science.* New York: Routledge.

Kassiola, J. (1990). *The death of industrial civilization.* Albany: State University of New York Press.

Kilbourne, W. E. (2004). Globalization and development: An expanded macromarketing view. *Journal of Macromarketing, 24*(2), 122–135.

Kilbourne, W. E., & Beckmann, S. C. (2002). Rationality and the reconciliation of the DSP with the NEP. In S. C. Beckmann & E. K. Madsen (Eds.), *Environmental regulation and rationality: Multidisciplinary perspectives* (pp. 51–70). Aarhus, Denmark: Aarhus University Press.

Kilbourne, W., McDonagh, P., & Prothero, A. (1997). Sustainable consumption and the quality of life: A macromarketing challenge to the dominant social paradigm. *Journal of Macromarketing, 17*(1), 4–24.

Kuhn, T. S. (1962). *The structure of scientific revolutions*. Chicago: University of Chicago Press.

Leiss, W. (1972). *The domination of nature*. New York: George Braziller.

Locke, J. (1690). *The second treatise of civil government*. Retrieved October 21, 2010, from http://www.constitution .org/jl/2ndtr05.htm

MacIntyre, A. (1996). *A short history of ethics*. Notre Dame, IN: University of Notre Dame Press.

MacPherson, C. B. (1962). *The political theory of possessive individualism: Hobbes to Locke*. Oxford, England: Clarendon.

Marcuse, H. (1964). *One-dimensional man: Studies in the ideology of advanced inndustrial society*. Boston: Beacon Press.

Merchant, C. (1980). *The death of nature: Women, ecology, and the scientific revolution*. London: Wildwood House.

Metz, B., Davidson, O. R., Bosch, P. R., Dave, R., & Meyer, L. A. (Eds.). (2007). *Climate change 2007: Mitigation of climate change*. New York: Cambridge University Press.

Mick, D. G. (2003). Editorial: Appreciaton, advice, and some aspirations for consumer research. *Journal of Consumer Research, 29*(4), 455–462.

Mick, D. G. (2006). Meaning and mattering through transformative consumer research. In C. Pechmann & L. L. Price (Eds.), *Advances in consumer research* (Vol. 33, pp. 1–4). Duluth, MN: Association for Consumer Research.

Mill, J. S. (1872). *Principles of political economy: With some of their applications to social philosophy* (5th London ed.). New York: D. Appleton. (Original work published 1848)

Mirowski, P. (1988). *Against mechanism: Protecting economics from science*. Lanham, MD: Rowman & Littlefield.

Mittelstaedt, J. D., Kilbourne, W. E., & Mittelstaedt, R. A. (2006). Macromarketing as agorology: Macromarketing theory and the study of the agora. *Journal of Macromarketing, 26*(2), 131–142.

Mullen, M. R., Doney, P. M., Mrad, S. B., & Sheng, S. Y. (2009). Effects of international trade and economic development on quality of life. *Journal of Macromarketing, 29*(3), 244–258.

Nietzsche, F. (1986). *Human, all too human: A book for free spirits* (R. J. Hollingdale, Trans., 2nd ed.). New York: Cambridge University Press. (Original work published 1878)

Ophuls, W. (1977). *Ecology and the politics of scarcity: A prologue to a political theory of the steady state*. San Francisco: Freeman.

Ozanne, J. L., & Saatcioglu, B. (2008). Participatory action research. *Journal of Consumer Research, 35*(October), 423–439.

Paine, T. (1997). *Common sense* (R. Herder, Ed.). Mineola, NY: Dover. (Original work published 1776)

Pirages, D. C., & Ehrlich, P. R. (1974). *Ark II: Social response to environmental imperatives*. San Francisco: Freeman.

Polanyi, K. (1944). *The great transformation: The political and economic origins of our time*. Boston: Beacon Press.

Postman, N. (1993). *Technopoly: The surrender of culture to technology*. New York: Vintage Books.

Rifkin, J. (1980). *Entropy: A new world view*. New York: Vintage Press.

Rousseau, J. (1968). *The social contract* (M. Cranston, Trans.). New York: Penguin Books. (Original work published 1762)

Rousseau, J. (1983). *The essential Rousseau* (L. Bair, Trans.). New York: Meridian.

Ryan, W. (1976). *Blaming the victim*. New York: Vintage Books.

Sagoff, M. (1988). *The economy of the earth: Philosophy, law, and the environment*. New York: Cambridge University Press.

Sandel, M. J. (1996). *Democracy's discontent: America in search of a public philosophy*. Cambridge, MA: Belknap Press.

Searle, J. R. (1995). *The construction of social reality*. London: Allen Lane.

Sen, A. (1993). Capability and well-being. In M. C. Nussbaum & A. Sen (Eds.), *The quality of life* (pp. 30–53). Oxford, England: Clarendon.

Sen, A. (1999). *Development as freedom*. New York: Knopf.

Shultz, C. J., & Holbrook, M. B. (1999). Marketing and the tragedy of the commons: A synthesis, commentary, and analysis for action. *Journal of Public Policy & Marketing, 18*(2), 218–229.

Smith, A. (1937). *An inquiry into the nature and causes of the wealth of nations* (E. Cannan, Ed.). New York: Random House. (Original work published 1776)

Speth, J. G. (2008). *The bridge at the edge of the world*. New Haven, CT: Yale University Press.

Stern, P. C. (2000). Toward a coherent theory of environmentally significant behavior. *Journal of Social Issues, 56*(3), 407–424.

Stiglitz, J. E. (2002). *Globalization and its discontents*. New York: W.W. Norton.

Tawney, R. H. (1962). *Religion and the rise of capitalism*. Gloucester, MA: Peter Smith.

Taylor, C. R. (1991). *The ethics of authenticity*. Cambridge, MA: Harvard University Press.

Thoreau, H. D. (1962). *Walden and other writings* (J. W. Krutch, Ed.). New York: Bantam Dell. (*Walden* originally published 1854)

Thurow, L. C. (1980). *The zero-sum society: Distribution and the possibilities for economic change*. New York: Basic Books.

Wachtel, P. L. (1989). *The poverty of affluence: A psychological portrait of the American way of life*. New York: Free Press.

Wapner, P., & Willoughby, J. (2005). The irony of environmentalism: The ecological futility but political necessity of lifestyle change. *Ethics & International Affairs, 19*(3), 77–89.

Weber, M. (1992). *The Protestant ethic and the spirit of capitalism* (A. Giddens, Trans.). New York: Routledge. (Original work published 1904–1905)

Wood, E. M. (2002). *The origin of capitalism: A longer view*. London: Verso.

World Commission on Economic and Development. (1987). *Our common future*. New York: Oxford University Press.

# V

## ENHANCING HEALTH

# 15

# *Tackling the Childhood Obesity Epidemic*
## An Opportunity for Transformative Consumer Research

SONYA A. GRIER AND ELIZABETH S. MOORE

Obesity among children and adolescents has become a major societal concern around the world. Estimates have indicated that 110 million children are overweight worldwide (Caprio et al., 2008; World Health Organization, 2009). In the United States, the prevalence of obesity among all age groups has increased (Wang & Beydoun, 2007), tripling among children (ages 6–11) and adolescents (ages 12–17) since 1980 (Ogden et al., 2006). The most recent national data from the National Health and Nutrition Examination Survey show that in 2006, 31.9% of youth ages 2–19 were overweight or obese. As shown in Table 15.1, obesity rates also differ significantly by gender and ethnicity (Ogden, Carroll, & Flegal, 2008).

In some countries in Central Europe, Latin America, the Caribbean, the Middle East, and North Africa, levels among some age groups are as high as in the United States (Martorell, Khan, Hughes, & Grummer-Strawn, 2000; Musaiger & Gregory, 2000). Obesity rates among youth have also increased in countries where malnutrition has historically been a critical issue and still persists (Wang, Monteiro, & Popkin, 2002). It is not only the scale of the problem but also the rapid increase that make childhood obesity such a challenging issue (Kipping, Jago, & Lawlor, 2008).

Obesity has significant adverse health and psychosocial consequences for the child and creates social and economic costs for society. Excess weight in children has been associated with asthma, fatty liver problems, kidney disease, and orthopedic problems, as well as increased risk for diabetes and cardiovascular disease (Caprio et al., 2008). Psychosocial consequences include low self-esteem, social isolation, and poor school performance (Caprio et al., 2008; Kipping et al., 2008). Further, obese children are more likely to become overweight adults, with all the attendant health risks (Daniels, 2006).

Although consumer researchers have long studied children, the primary focus has been on topics such as children's processing of advertising (D. R. John, 1999), the impacts of parenting styles and intergenerational influences (Carlson & Grossbart, 1988; Moore, Wilkie, & Lutz, 2002), and children's influence on family purchase decisions (Palan & Wilkes, 1997). There is very little consumer research that investigates the many factors that contribute to childhood obesity and how it might be alleviated or prevented (for an exception, see Goldberg & Gunasti, 2007, for an analysis of marketing impacts).

There is significant research in other fields, however (e.g., nutrition, pediatrics, public health, anthropology, psychology), that can be useful in gaining insights into the obesity problem. The Institute of Medicine emphasizes the need for preventative approaches that can help children who are at a healthy weight avoid becoming obese, as well as the need for targeted

**Table 15.1**  Prevalence of Obesity and Overweight Among U.S. Children by Gender, Age, and Ethnicity, 2007–2008

|  | Gender | Ages | White American | African American | Hispanic American |
|---|---|---|---|---|---|
| Prevalence of obesity (BMI > 95th percentile of the CDC growth charts) | Boys | 2–5 | 6.6 | 11.1 | 17.8 |
|  |  | 6–11 | 20.5 | 17.7 | 28.3 |
|  |  | 12–19 | 16.7 | 19.8 | 25.5 |
|  | Girls | 2–5 | 12.0 | 11.7 | 10.4 |
|  |  | 6–11 | 17.4 | 21.2 | 21.9 |
|  |  | 12–19 | 14.5 | 29.2 | 17.5 |
| Prevalence of overweight (BMI > 85th percentile of the CDC growth charts) | Boys | 2–5 | 15.6 | 28.1 | 30.7 |
|  |  | 6–11 | 34.6 | 36.4 | 43.7 |
|  |  | 12–19 | 32.6 | 33.0 | 42.7 |
|  | Girls | 2–5 | 19.5 | 23.9 | 24.3 |
|  |  | 6–11 | 34.3 | 38.9 | 41.5 |
|  |  | 12–19 | 29.9 | 46.3 | 39.7 |

*Note:* BMI = Body Mass Index; CDC = Centers for Disease Control and Prevention.

*Source:* Adapted from "Prevalence of High Body Mass Index in US Children and Adolescents, 2007–2008," by C. L. Ogden, M. D. Carroll, L. R. Curtin, M. M. Lamb, and K. M. Flegal, *Journal of the American Medical Association, 303*(3), 242–249, 2010.

approaches aimed at high-risk groups. Review articles have assessed different types of interventions at the school, family, community, or societal level and identified current best practices (e.g., Barlow & the Expert Committee, 2007; Horgen & Brownell, 2002; Story, Kaphingst, Robinson-O'Brien, & Glanz, 2008; Whitt-Glover & Kumanyika, 2009). However, the effect sizes observed in many obesity interventions are small[*] (e.g., Stice, Shaw, & Marti, 2006), and much still needs to be learned. For example, in a recent review, Cook-Cottone, Casey, Feeley, and Baran (2009) concluded that the psychological and emotional dimensions of overeating have not been much studied, and they argued that this may account, in part, for the limited success of some interventions.

New, transformative approaches to research and intervention are needed. Consumer researchers are well positioned to do this work, given the collective expertise in areas such as learning and decision making, processes of persuasion, the emotional aspects of consumption, social and situational influences, consumer culture, and the consumer socialization of children. Scholars in our field also have the capacity to bring a range of research methods to bear in addition to the survey and experimental methods that typify this area. In this chapter, we review relevant research with an emphasis on priorities for consumer researchers wishing to advance theory and practice. We draw on a broad ecological framework, adapted from the literature, that encompasses both internal factors (e.g., individual predispositions, heritability) and external factors (e.g., social and environmental forces) to understand key contributors to childhood obesity and identify possible leverage points for intervention (see Figure 15.1; also Booth et al., 2001; Koplan, Liverman, & Kraak, 2005; Kumanyika, 2007). We hope that this chapter will allow consumer researchers to gain new insights and facilitate the development of Transformative Consumer Research that helps children live happier, healthier lives.

---

[*] When thinking about effect size of interventions with individuals, consider that if the goal is prevention, the desired effect is no effect (i.e., no weight gain). There is an additional problem with the effect size for environmental and policy interventions, in that the changes may be too distal to the weight outcome to show an effect. Finally, specific interventions may not work alone and will not have an effect if there are no other enabling interventions.

## THE CONTEXT IN WHICH CONSUMPTION OCCURS

Before we turn to a discussion of the primary contributors to obesity, it is useful to first consider the changing circumstances in which children and families are making consumption decisions today. A focus on eating and activity as solely determined by individual choices has been replaced by one which also considers context as integral to the development of effective interventions (Kumanyika, 2002). Consumer researchers have long understood that behavior may be influenced by the setting within which it occurs (e.g., Belk, 1975; Stayman & Deshpande, 1989). The primary environments where children and adolescents eat, shop, or participate in physical activity include their home, neighborhood (including friends' homes), schools and day care centers, recreation areas, and retail outlets. Situational factors operating within these environments, such as time, cost, convenience, and accessibility, can also support or inhibit healthy eating and physical activity choices among children and families.

Environmental and lifestyle changes that have made energy-dense foods more accessible and reduced opportunities for energy expenditure are relevant to obesity via their influence on energy balance (e.g., French, Story, & Jeffery, 2001). A decline in family meals, increases in restaurant meals, larger portion sizes, and more snacking all encourage overeating (French, Story, Neumark-Sztainer, Fulkerson, & Hannan, 2001; Sturm, 2005a). People underestimate portion sizes and calorie content, especially when outside the home (Harnack, Jeffery, & Boutelle, 2000; Young & Nestle, 2002). Adolescents in particular consume more calories when they eat out, and almost a third of youths eat at fast-food restaurants on any given day (Bowman, Gortmaker, Ebbeling, Pereira, & Ludwig, 2004; Nielsen, Siega-Riz, & Popkin, 2002). Consumption of sugar-sweetened beverages (SSBs) has also increased among U.S. children, who consume about 172 calories from SSBs daily, and among other groups, including, for example, adolescents from Mexico (Barquera et al. 2008; Brownell et al., 2009). Such increases are of concern, because consumption of SSBs has been directly linked to obesity risk (Malik, Schulze, & Hu, 2006; Vartanian, Schwartz, & Brownell, 2007).

At the same time, sedentary behaviors have increased (French et al., 2001). For example, in a nationally representative study of U.S. children ages 9–13 and their parents, it was reported that 61.5% do not participate in organized physical activity outside of school, and almost a quarter (22.6%) do not engage in physical activity in their free time (Centers for Disease Control and Prevention, 2002). Playing outdoors and walking to school are no longer typical. Among children ages 5–15, walking declined from 20.2% of trips to school in 1977 to 12.5% in 2001 (Sturm, 2005a, 2005b).

While physical activity has decreased, computer use and television viewing have increased over time (Kimm et al., 2000; Nelson, Neumark-Stzainer, Hannan, Sirard, & Story, 2006; Rideout, Foehr, & Roberts, 2010). Children's "screen time" is a key concern among health providers, given the well-established (positive) correlation with obesity (Dietz & Gortmaker, 2001). The time that American children and teens (ages 8–18) spend watching television or movies, whether during an original broadcast or via new media platforms such as the Internet, cell phones, or iPods, averages 4 hours and 29 minutes per day (Rideout et al., 2010). When computer, video games, and music are added to the mix, exposure swells to over 7.5 hours per day.* Concerns center on not only the time spent in sedentary activities but also the tendency to eat while viewing and likely increased exposure to food advertising. Decreased television viewing can result in lowered body mass index (BMI) among children (Robinson, 1999). However, 71% of U.S. children have a television in their bedroom, and about half also have a DVD player or VCR and video game console (Rideout et al., 2010). Children with a television in their bedroom spend about 1 hour more per day watching

---

* Because this age group also spends a significant amount of time (29%) using two or more media concurrently, they are actually exposed to more than 10.5 hours of media content per day, which still does not include time spent texting or talking on cell phones (Rideout et al., 2010).

television than those without. More than 50% of children report that their parents do not impose limits on how much television they watch, which is the backdrop for understanding weight issues among children.

## KEY CONTRIBUTORS TO CHILDHOOD OBESITY

In essence, obesity is caused by an imbalance between the amount of energy consumed and the amount of energy expended. Although seemingly simple, this imbalance is the result of a complex interplay of many factors that occur across time. Some of these factors are unique to the child, and others are a product of the social and situational contexts in which learning and influence occur. Our discussion focuses first on individual-level factors, then we turn to the people and settings (i.e., family, friends, communities) that shape children's everyday lives while also considering broader societal-level influences, both cultural and institutional.

## INTERNAL CONTRIBUTORS

As shown in Figure 15.1, there are a number of individual factors that play a role in the development of obesity. A child is shaped in fundamental ways by his or her genetic inheritance, physiological profile, and psychological characteristics such as temperament. Although these factors may not be readily amenable to outside intervention, it is crucial to understand them, because they lay the foundation for consumption attitudes and behaviors. Individuals differ in their metabolic susceptibility to weight gain, and some may be at particular risk in the current obesogenic environment,

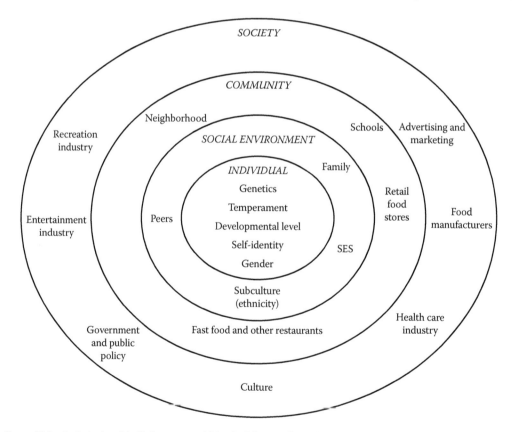

**Figure 15.1**   Ecological model of influences on child and adolescent diet and activity.

with its ready availability of palatable foods and vast opportunities for sedentary pursuits. Children of obese parents have a much greater chance of becoming overweight, a relationship that reflects a child's biological predispositions and the environment in which preferences develop (Whitaker, Wright, Pepe, Seidel, & Dietz, 1997).

## Biological Predispositions

It is difficult to disentangle the interactive effects of genetic contributors, an individual's metabolic characteristics, and the environment (Birch, 1999), despite advances highlighting the role of molecular genetics in determining an individual's susceptibility to weight gain (J. O. Hill & Trowbridge, 1998). Endocrinologists have discovered specific hormones, such as leptin, that regulate appetite (Gale, Castracane, & Mantzoros, 2004), and geneticists have studied familial impacts on weight (Maes, Neale, & Eaves, 1997). One way that genetic influences may be evident is in innate preferences for specific tastes and nutrients. Humans have predispositions to prefer some tastes (sweet and salty) over others (sour and bitter; Savage, Fisher, & Birch, 2007). Although these are universal tendencies, they can be affected by genetics via varying sensitivity to taste dimensions. For example, there is a heritability component in preferences for, and intake of, macronutrients, primarily dietary fat (Reed, Bachmanov, Beauchamp, Tordoff, & Price, 1997). Sensitivity to bitter tastes also has a genetic basis, which accounts for some differences in children's preferences for sweet beverages (Mennella, Pepino, & Reed, 2005).

Recent research has also questioned whether there may be a heritable component to behaviors such as reduced sensitivity to satiety cues, eating in the absence of hunger, and hyperresponsiveness to food cues. For example, in a large study of twins ($n = 5390$ families), it was shown that a child's responsiveness to internal satiety cues and general interest in eating are more strongly related in genetically identical (i.e., monozygotic) twins than those who share only a portion of their genes (i.e., dizygotic; Carnell, Haworth, Plomin, & Wardle, 2008). Studies of adult twins have also shown that dietary restraint (e.g., restricting intake to control weight) has a genetic component, but dietary disinhibition (e.g., overeating in response to availability of palatable foods or emotional distress) does not (de Castro & Lilenfeld, 2005). Further discoveries as to which appetite-related behaviors have a genetic basis are surely forthcoming. Calls for interdisciplinary studies that integrate the natural and behavioral sciences in public health research have been made (Glass & McAtee, 2006), which is an area that seems well suited to such collaboration. Behavioral researchers can contribute by building an understanding of environmental factors that facilitate the phenotypic expression of appetite-related genetic predispositions.

## Behavioral Predispositions

Temperament also needs to be included as part of any system describing influences on, and variation in, childhood obesity. *Temperament* refers to individual differences in a child's behavioral style and is characterized in terms such as activity, adaptability, mood, attention span, distractibility, and intensity (Carey, Hegvik, & McDevitt, 1988). Differences along these dimensions appear in infancy and are relatively stable across time and context. Specific aspects of temperament are related to weight gain in children. For example, irritability in infancy is a predictor of carbohydrate intake in young children (ages 2–3) and some indicators of body fat (Wells et al., 1997), which may suggest that some caregivers rely too heavily on sugary foods to soothe their children when distressed. More difficult aspects of temperament (e.g., lower persistence, withdrawal, low adaptability, anger or frustration, negative mood, high intensity) have also been related to weight gain in older children (Carey et al., 1988; Zeller, Boles, & Reiter-Purtill, 2008). These may also mediate the relationship between parent BMI and child BMI, although precisely how is not yet clear (Agras, Hammer, McNicholas, & Kraemer, 2004).

This brief review does not do justice to the complexity of temperament's role in obesity. It is instructive, however, in showing that behavioral style interacts with aspects of the external environment in ways that are not yet well understood. In particular, parents may face greater challenges with children of particular temperaments in controlling intake, avoiding overfeeding, and introducing change into family meals. Research is needed to understand how these challenges are manifested in the home and how parents might best address them.

### Developmental Readiness

Food preferences, eating behaviors, and habits as well as receptivity to marketing stimuli are just a few of the outcomes affected by a child's developmental trajectory. Throughout childhood and into young adulthood, significant changes occur that are pertinent to obesity risk.

In early childhood (ages 0–5), behaviors that serve as the basis for future eating patterns emerge (Savage et al., 2007). During this period, children learn what, when, and how much to eat. Although innate preferences may be a factor that promotes intake, children's acceptance of specific foods is also affected by their early experiences with them. Food neophobia (i.e., refusal to try new foods) can be a problem, but repeated, noncoercive exposure to fruits and vegetables enhances children's liking and preferences for them (Savage et al., 2007). Yet, parents may need to be persuaded to offer healthy options repeatedly, as surveys have shown that many young children are consuming a high-calorie, nutritionally poor diet (Fox, Pac, Devaney, & Jankowski, 2004).

In addition to the choice of which foods to eat, young children also learn what quantities to consume. Very young children eat in response to hunger and satiety cues and attend to physiological signals that tell them when to eat and when to stop. However, as children mature, they are socialized to adopt the eating conventions of others. Even as toddlers, children become sensitive to external cues, such as portion size and number of meals offered, and begin to adjust intake accordingly (Fox, Devaney, Reidy, Razafindrakoto, & Ziegler, 2006; Rolls, Engell, & Birch, 2000). So, although children are biologically equipped to control their food intake, the environment can quickly teach them to override these signals. The strategies parents use to monitor children's diets are a critical feature of that milieu, a topic we turn to in a later section.

Forces outside the home are also relevant. Children's capacity to understand and defend themselves against marketing messages undergoes significant change from early childhood to adolescence (Andreasen, Goldberg, & Sirgy, Chapter 2 of this volume; D. R. John, 1999). Young children (ages 3–7) are the most vulnerable to persuasive attempts and have not yet acquired efficient information-processing strategies. Children ages 7–11 have a better understanding of advertising (D. R. John, 1999); however, even 10–11-year-olds may not draw from this knowledge unless reminded (Brucks, Armstrong, & Goldberg, 1988; Moore & Lutz, 2000). Teens generally have the cognitive skills to understand advertising but are more impulsive and self-conscious than adults. Impulsivity may impact decision making, with teens less likely to consider the consequences of excessive consumption (e.g., Pechmann, Levine, Loughlin, & Leslie, 2005), a key issue given the many opportunities they have for independent food and activity choices. Relatively little is known about adolescents' responsiveness to marketing messages, particularly in new media, despite evidence of their potential vulnerability. Almost all research in this domain has focused on children ages 12 and younger and their understanding of ads in traditional media, which is clearly an area in need of further study and one which consumer researchers are particularly well positioned to pursue.

### Self-Identity and Self-Esteem

Identity formation is a universal developmental task, fraught with challenges. In particular, adolescence has long been characterized as a period when individuals explore and examine the self as a means to discover who they are and how they fit into their social world (Steinberg & Morris,

2001). For obese children and teens, there are additional concerns about how weight may impact self-perceptions, body satisfaction, and ultimately self-esteem. Reviews of research have indicated that there is a relationship between BMI and body dissatisfaction in children, particularly among girls (Wardle & Cooke, 2005). There is also an inverse association between obesity and self-esteem, but effects are small and by no means universal (Puhl & Latner, 2007; for related discussion, see also Faber & Vohs, Chapter 22 of this volume).

## EXTERNAL CONTRIBUTORS: PROXIMAL AND DISTAL

As we have seen, some factors that put children at risk for obesity are specific to the individual (e.g., genetics, temperament), but others are a product of the environments in which children are socialized. Socialization is the process by which individuals develop the beliefs, values, and behaviors needed to function in society (Maccoby, 2007). Theory suggests that childhood learning is sufficiently powerful that the beliefs and attitudes formed during this period persist into adulthood, a premise supported by research in psychology, political science, sociology, and consumer behavior (Maccoby, 2007; Prinz, Chapter 28 of this volume). Socialization theory is a useful perspective from which to consider environmental factors that put children at risk for obesity. Children are embedded in families, peer groups, ethnic groups, social classes, and cultures from which they are learning every day (see Figure 15.1). To understand the child, we need insight into the settings in which learning and influence occur.

Family Influences

Whether or not childhood obesity develops depends to a large extent on family-related influences, including genetic predispositions passed on to a child and consumption practices in the household. Parental obesity increases the risk of adult obesity among both overweight and normal-weight children. For children under age 10, the level of risk more than doubles when at least one parent is obese (Whitaker et al., 1997). The family is the first and typically the most powerful agent of socialization, with parents, siblings, and other family members serving as sources of information, support, and social pressure.

*Parent Recognition*

A surprising yet well-documented research finding is that parents often fail to recognize when their child is overweight. Estimates vary, but somewhere between just under one third and well over two thirds of parents of overweight children do not realize their child has a weight problem (Carnell, Edwards, Croker, Boniface, & Wardle, 2005; V. B. Gray et al., 2007; Maynard, Galuska, Blanck, & Serdula, 2003). This phenomenon has been replicated in the Netherlands and the United Kingdom (Jansen & Brug, 2006), demonstrating that these misperceptions are not purely a by-product of American culture. Some child characteristics may moderate this pattern. Younger children are more likely to be classified incorrectly than older children (Eckstein et al., 2006), for example, suggesting that parents may find it difficult to distinguish between a real weight issue and baby fat that a child will outgrow. Parents of the most obese children are more accurate than those whose children are just overweight (e.g., Jeffery, Voss, Metcalf, Alba, & Wilkin, 2005; Maynard et al., 2003), and mothers are better able to recognize their daughters' at-risk status than their sons' (Anderson, Bandini, & Must, 2005; Baughcum, Chamberlin, Deeks, Powers, & Whitaker, 2000; May et al., 2007; Maynard et al., 2003). There is also some initial evidence that parents' conceptions of weight and what it means for their child's health vary. For example, low-income mothers of preschoolers may perceive their heavier children as healthier as long as they are happy and active (Jain et al., 2001). Despite the frequency of parental misperception, little is known about the specific cues parents use to judge their children's weight or those that signal a need for concern, which is a key topic for future research. If parents do not discern their child's weight problem, or if they discount it, any efforts to resolve it are unlikely.

### Parents' Nutrition Knowledge

Parents' nutrition knowledge is a precursor to ensuring that children eat a well-balanced diet. Children of knowledgeable mothers consume more fruits and vegetables, eat less fat, and are less likely to be overweight (Contento et al., 1993; Cooke et al., 2004). Knowledge is multidimensional, however, and varies across the population. Although a majority of U.S. parents know basic nutrition facts, such as the number of recommended daily servings of fruits and vegetables, and are aware of basic health problems related to diet (Variyam, 2001), this does not necessarily extend to knowledge of appropriate portion sizes or the nutritional quality of individual foods. Why some parents are more knowledgeable than others is not yet well understood. In the United States, low levels of education have been linked to limited nutrition knowledge, particularly among some Latino groups (Boulanger, Pérez-Escamilla, Himmelgreen, Segura-Millán, & Haldeman, 2002). A study of Australian parents suggests that knowledge may also vary by social class, with those from advantaged backgrounds better able to discuss nutrition in terms informed by prevailing health and medical priorities (C. John, 2005).

Greater insight into the predictors of parental knowledge as well as its role in shaping the family diet is needed. One of the challenges is that consumers may not act on what they know, a reality that accounts in part for the limited impact of many communication campaigns. Despite understanding the components of a healthy diet, parents may not draw on their knowledge unless motivated and empowered to do so, which is tantamount to everyday practical wisdom (see Mick & Schwartz, Chapter 32 of this volume). Research is needed to better understand not only what parents know but also how to help them enact dietary recommendations. What parents and children believe to be healthy behaviors and the social norms that inform them also need to be better understood, which will require studies that look across layers within the ecological model and at the interactions between parent understanding and the contextual factors that constrain them.

### Intergenerational Influences

The knowledge, dietary, and exercise patterns children learn at home shape their preferences and habits. If children learn to prefer energy-dense foods, for example, this puts them at risk of becoming overweight. Similarly, if they develop preferences for fruits and vegetables, this can be a protective factor (Davison & Birch, 2001).

Intergenerational influence refers to the transmission of information, resources, and preferences between family generations. In consumer research, there is evidence of intergenerational influences on aspects of consumer buying style as well as brand choice for packaged goods, including foods and beverages (Moore et al., 2002). Nutrition and public health researchers, however, have focused at the product category rather than brand level (Borah-Giddens & Falciglia, 1993). Some of these studies have revealed significant intergenerational effects, as well as sibling similarities, for product preferences (Pliner & Pelchat, 1986), while others have suggested more modest relationships (Rozin, 1991), which may, in part, be accounted for by different research methods and the set of product categories examined. Research is needed to clarify the range of intergenerational effects on food preferences and the factors that explain variation across families (Moore et al., 2002).

Actual dietary intake has also been examined. Intergenerational studies in the United States and the United Kingdom have pointed to significant similarities in the intake of fat (Cullen, Lara, & de Moor, 2002; Oliveria et al., 1992), soft drinks and milk (Fisher, Mitchell, Smiciklas-Wright, Mannino, & Birch, 2004; Grimm, Harnack, & Story, 2004), as well as fruits and/or vegetables (Cooke et al., 2004; Fisher, Mitchell, Smiciklas-Wright, & Birch, 2002; Hansson, Karnehed, Tynelius, & Rasmussen, 2009; Matheson, Robinson, Varady, & Killen, 2006). Results are robust, as a variety of age groups, ethnicities, and genders are represented in these studies. Yet, research provides little insight into the mechanisms by which intergenerational relationships are established. Although commonalities might be attributed in part to genetically driven taste preferences, similarities have also been found among individuals living in the same household who are not genetically related, thus suggesting that environmental forces are also at work (Davison & Birch, 2001), such as the family meal. Longitudinal data have shown that regular family meals in early adolescence contribute to healthy diets 5 years later (Burgess-Champoux, Larson, Neumark-Sztainer, Hannan, & Story, 2009; for a related discussion on family time, see Epp & Price, Chapter 29 of this volume).

On the activity side of the energy balance equation, a Finnish study revealed significant yet modest intergenerational consistency in vigorous physical activity levels between parents and children ages 7–12. However, a much stronger relationship was observed between parents' and children's inactivity levels (Fogelholm, Nuutinen, Pasanen, Myöhänen, & Säätelä, 1999), which suggests that parental support of children's participation in a physical activity or sport (e.g., attendance at child's sporting events), although necessary (Davison & Lawson, 2006), is insufficient. Parental modeling via their own regular physical exercise may also be needed.

More broadly, greater insight is needed into parental modeling of dietary and activity-related behaviors. Within consumer research, there is much discussion of parental modeling as a primary process by which children learn, yet very little is known about what specifically is being modeled and what cues children use to either accept or reject what they observe.

*Parenting Practices*

A key question in thinking about the role of the family centers on parenting practices. These are localized, behavioral strategies and tactics that a parent might use to monitor and control what, how much, and when children eat (Ventura & Birch, 2008). Most research on this topic has focused on young children.

Parents' feeding decisions affect their children's weight trajectory as early as infancy (Savage et al., 2007). Breast-feeding, for example, may provide protection against obesity over the life course, beyond its immunological benefits (Owen, Martin, Whincup, Smith, & Cook, 2005). The American Academy of Pediatrics recommends exclusive breast-feeding for the first 6 months of life with continued support during the first year (American Academy of Pediatrics, 2005). Most studies of this issue have centered on young, low-income women of African American, Native American, or Mexican American descent (Bentley, Gavin, Black, & Teti, 1999; Houghton & Graybeal, 2001; Zive et al., 1992). Many of these women find it difficult to adhere to the American Academy of Pediatrics recommendations. Bentley et al. (1999) used ethnography to understand the nature of young mothers' decisions relating to this practice. They discovered a social norm among these women to bottle-feed cereal and introduce other semisolid foods in the first month of life and that this norm was reinforced by grandmothers who play a dominant role in feeding decisions. Additional studies, grounded in cultural insights, are needed to understand the tensions women face in making these choices and how they negotiate pressures applied from family members and others.

As a child moves beyond infancy, there is an array of feeding approaches that may be used by parents to control children's diets, such as restricting access to certain foods; pressuring a child to eat; involving them in meal preparation; using food as a bribe, pacifier, or reward; or withholding it as a punishment. Many studies using a variety of research methods have been conducted to understand the consequences of parents' actions (Faith, Scanlon, Birch, Francis, & Sherry, 2004; Ventura & Birch, 2008). Two parenting practices, restriction (e.g., limiting access to junk food) and pressure to eat (e.g., encouraging children to eat healthful foods), have been a common focus of study. Researchers have speculated that strong parental controls may teach children to focus attention on external cues such as portion size or rewards, thus undermining their capacity to respond to internal cues signaling hunger and satiety (Savage et al., 2007).

Experimental studies have indicated that by restricting access to appealing foods that are high in sugar or fat, parents may increase their children's preference for these foods, resulting in overeating when they are available (Fisher & Birch, 1999; Savage et al., 2007). Longitudinal data have shown that high levels of parental restriction at age 5 predicts young White girls eating in the absence of hunger at ages 7 and 9, with the magnitude of effects greatest for girls who were already overweight at age 5 (Birch, Fisher, & Davison, 2003). Studies drawing on more ethnically diverse samples have not observed such impacts (Robinson, Kiernan, Matheson, & Haydel, 2001; SpruijtMetz, Lindquist, Birch, Fisher, & Goran, 2002). Why outcomes differ across studies is unclear. It may be that real yet not well-understood ethnic differences exist or that metrics used in some studies have tapped into beneficial aspects of parental control while others have accessed problematic dimensions. Parents likely need to exert some controls, but the key questions are Under what circumstances? and How much is too much?

Researchers have also studied the impact of parents' pressuring their children to eat. Cross-sectional surveys have revealed negative correlations between parental pressure and children's fruit and vegetable consumption (Wardle, Carnell, & Cooke, 2005). Parental modeling seems to be more effective in increasing children's intake than applying overt pressure (Galloway, Fiorito, Lee, & Birch, 2005; Wardle, Volz, & Golding, 1995). Experimental studies have provided further insight into causality. For example, when preschoolers were pressured to eat (e.g., "Finish your soup") in a lab setting, they made more negative comments about the soups, consumed less, and had reduced preferences for them after the experimental trials (Galloway, Fiorito, Francis, & Birch, 2006). Further, when food is used as a reward (e.g., "If you finish your vegetables, you may have a dessert"), children eat more of the vegetables on that occasion, but preference for them declines (Birch, Marlin, & Rotter, 1984). So, applying pressure to eat healthy options may not have the results parents intend.

To this point, researchers have focused on a relatively constrained set of parenting practices that impact young children's food consumption. Other than the importance of regular family meals, relatively little is known about the strategies parents use to try to influence the dietary choices of older children and teens, who likely have greater freedoms and opportunities to make independent decisions. A broader perspective on parenting practices is needed (see, e.g., Prinz, Chapter 28 of this volume), not only with regard to child age but also in terms of the settings in which such practices are enacted. For example, we need a better understanding of how parents attempt to mediate the marketing environment for their children (e.g., exert control over children's ad exposure, food choices in the store, availability of foods in the home) as well as the types of strategies that are most effective in leading to the dietary behaviors parents prefer.

Also missing from this literature are studies of the child's influence on the family, yet there is significant evidence in the consumer socialization literature that even young children exert considerable influence on foods purchased and consumed in the household (Isler, Popper, & Ward, 1987). To fully understand diet-related parenting practices, and what makes them successful (or not), requires an understanding of the ways in which children respond and how this response shapes subsequent parental attempts. This is an important area for research, because it is in these day-to-day interactions that preferences and habits are established.

### Socioeconomic Status

To this point, we have implicitly framed the discussion as though children have equal life chances. However, it is obvious that children and families are situated within a set of socioeconomic circumstances that impact the resources and thus the choices that can be made. Poverty rates for children worldwide are substantial, with almost one in five children living without adequate family income, nutritious food, or health care (R. P. Hill, 2001). Rates differ by country, with one in two children living in poverty in developing countries. Socioeconomic status (SES) is typically defined in terms of income, education, occupation, or wealth, and among children, by parents' attributes. The relationship between SES and weight status varies both across and within countries (Gordon-Larsen, Adair, & Popkin, 2003; O'Dea, 2008; Wang, 2001). For example, higher SES youth are more likely to be obese in China, Egypt, and Russia, but in the United States, lower SES groups are at greater risk (Wang, 2001). A recent review has demonstrated an increase in positive associations between SES and obesity, and a decrease in negative associations, as one moves from countries with high levels of socioeconomic development to those with lower levels (McLaren, 2007). Further, results vary depending on the SES indicator used (e.g., income, education). At the macrolevel, the mechanisms, structures, and specific processes underlying the relationship between socioeconomic development and obesity remain to be identified.

At an individual level, SES may influence parenting beliefs, practices, and knowledge, independent of other demographic factors (N. E. Hill, 2006). Poor consumers face economic, physical, and marketplace limitations, which may affect their ability to eat healthfully or easily pursue physical activity (Andreasen, 1975; Andreasen, Goldberg, & Sirgy, Chapter 2 of this volume; Baker & Mason, Chapter 26 of this volume; Grier & Kumanyika, 2008; R. P. Hill, 2001). Economic constraints increase the importance of food and beverage costs, and the lowest priced items are typically relatively high in fat and sugar (Drewnowski, 2007). In Canada, low-income consumers are considered nutritionally vulnerable, because income constraints do not allow them to buy adequate amounts of nutritionally adequate food (Power, 2005). Research has suggested that the poor pay more, that is, higher prices for lower quality goods (Bell & Burlin, 1993). Price is also closely coupled with distribution, whereby the limited access to supermarkets among low-income consumers may result in them paying higher prices (Grier & Kumanyika, 2008). Economic disadvantage may mean living in neighborhoods with less access to recreation facilities and infrastructure that support physical activity (Addy et al., 2004; Molnar, Gortmaker, Bull, & Buka, 2004). A lack of health insurance may also be related to SES and is positively associated with overweight among adolescents (Haas et al., 2003). The effects of childhood poverty are long term. For example, poor socioeconomic conditions experienced as a child relate to adult women's BMI and weight status (Parsons, Power, Logan, & Summerbell, 1999), although attitudes toward obesity may moderate or mediate this relationship (Sobal & Stunkard, 1989). SES may also interact with factors such as ethnicity, which we discuss in a later section.

Peer Influences

Although family members are typically regarded as the first and most important socialization agents, peers become increasingly significant as a child matures. Through peer interactions, children learn how to build and maintain relationships as well as develop problem-solving skills. Beginning in early adolescence, peers also aid in the development of personal identity and in the search for autonomy that characterizes this life stage (Steinberg & Morris, 2001). Peers impact the diet, physical activity, and psychosocial functioning of overweight children in a number of ways and can be a positive force. For example, adolescent girls with higher levels of body satisfaction reported having friends who encourage healthy eating and exercising to stay fit (Kelly, Wall, Eisenberg, Story, & Neumark-Sztainer, 2005). However, it is the negative aspects of peer interactions, particularly weight-based stigmatization and victimization, that have been a major research focus (V. B. Gray et al., 2007).

Weight-based stereotyping behaviors are common among children, and these biases are already apparent in preschoolers (Musher-Eizenman, Holub, Miller, Goldstein, & Edwards-Leeper, 2004; Neumark-Sztainer, Story, & Faibisch, 1998; Penny & Haddock, 2007), which is an international phenomenon, having been observed in the United States, the United Kingdom, Sweden, and Australia (Hansson et al., 2009; Penny & Haddock, 2007; Tiggemann & Anesbury, 2000; Turnbull, Heaslip, & McLeod, 2000). Overweight children are more likely to be ascribed with negative attributes, such as ugly, sloppy, lazy, selfish, or stupid, with some variation by age group (Wardle, 1995). Several studies have indicated that overweight children are just as likely as normal-weight children to hold these negative views (Cramer & Steinwert, 1998). Despite the recent rise in childhood obesity, there is no indication that these prejudices are on the wane, and in fact, they appear to have increased over time (Latner & Stunkard, 2003).

Overweight children and adolescents are more likely to be found at the periphery of their social networks than their normal-weight peers and are less likely to be nominated as a friend, have fewer reciprocated friendships, and are described as less popular (Strauss & Pollack, 2003; Zeller, Reiter-Purtill, & Ramey, 2008). However, friendship nominations increase when adolescents join in school sports or clubs, irrespective of weight. Children and teens also tend to be more accepting when they believe that an overweight child is not to blame for his or her weight problem (Iobst et al., 2009; Tiggemann & Anesbury, 2000). Although there is substantial evidence that weight-related biases exist, relatively little is known about the genesis of them, which is an important area for future research if interventions are to be developed to reduce the stigmatizing effects of these prejudices.

Obese children are also at increased risk for overt victimization (e.g., gossip, weight-based teasing, exclusion, bullying) by their peers (W. N. Gray et al., 2009). Clearly, such aggression is a much broader social problem and affects large numbers of children, irrespective of their weight status, at some point in their lives. In a large sample of Midwestern teens, Neumark-Sztainer, Story, Hannan, and Croll (2002) found that over 40% of overweight teens have reported being teased by their peers, which rose to close to 60% among the most obese. Teasing about body weight is associated with lower body satisfaction, low self-esteem, and depressive symptoms among teens, particularly girls (Adams & Bukowski, 2008; Neumark-Sztainer et al., 1998). Younger, prepubescent children who are overweight may also be involved in bullying, for girls primarily as a victim and for boys as either victim or perpetrator (Griffiths, Wolke, Page, & Horwood, 2006). Although many studies have examined the link between obesity and reduced self-concept, little evidence of a direct relationship exists (Puhl & Latner, 2007). Rather, it is weight-based teasing that mediates the relationship between obesity and lower self-concept (Davison & Birch, 2001).

Peers can also affect the exercise habits and eating behavior of overweight youth. Victimization by peers reduces physical activity in overweight children and teens (W. N. Gray et al., 2008; Storch et al., 2007). This is particularly problematic, because obese children and adolescents engage in less physical activity than their normal-weight peers anyway (Ekelund et al., 2002; Trost et al., 2002), and these differences are already apparent in early childhood (Trost, Sirard, Dowda, Pfeiffer, & Pate, 2003). Peers can also act as a positive force in this domain. In a small event-sampling study, overweight teens (mean age 13) were more likely to report intense physical activity when in the presence of peers or friends than when alone (Salvy et al., 2008). Social context also affects the eating behavior of overweight children (Salvy, Coelho, Kieffer, & Epstein, 2007; Salvy, Romero, Paluch, & Epstein, 2007). Overweight children ages 6–10 tend to eat less with peers than when alone, but this pattern is reversed for normal-weight children. So, the presence of peers may suppress the consumption of obese children, but research is needed to explore the social motives (e.g., impression management, informational modeling) and situational dimensions that might account for these effects. It would also be helpful to learn more about the positive influence of peers in weight control. Much of the research focus has been on negative impacts, yet with greater understanding of the nature and processes of positive peer influence, it may be possible to develop interventions that promote healthy behaviors through peer-based models.

## Cultural Influences

The influence of family and peers takes shape within a broader cultural context or meaning system that is learned and transmitted across generations. Aspects of culture may be visible or invisible, physical or subjective (Bétancourt & López, 1993; de Mooij, 2004; Triandis, 1989). A result is that certain behaviors just seem natural to us (Kumanyika, 2008). The psychological aspects of culture, reflected in attitudes, beliefs, and values, as well as the relationships between consumption and cultural meanings, have received considerable attention from consumer researchers (e.g., Arnould & Thompson, 2005; de Mooij, 2004).

Cultural influence may stem from global, national, or subcultural levels. In consumer research, some authors have posited a global youth culture, while others have illustrated how youth culture is glocalized (Kjeldgaard & Askegaard, 2006). Country-level influences may include broad characterizations of national culture, such as the trends characterized at the start of this chapter. Societies worldwide are also made up of subcultures that differ by nationality, ethnicity, religion, and geography. Cultural influence is context dependent, because we may be members of multiple cultures or subcultures that each exert varying influences simultaneously (Triandis, 1989). Cultural influences may be reflected in the beliefs, attitudes, values, and norms among members of a particular group with regard to eating and physical activity and constitute a context for consumer response to obesity interventions. Three particularly important areas for understanding weight issues among youth are level of acculturation, body image, and food habits.

### Level of Acculturation

Consumer acculturation is the acquisition of consumer-related knowledge, skills, and the adoption of habits and behaviors upon moving into a new culture (Penaloza, 1989, 1995). The results of this process may be positive or negative. For example, African American girls whose mothers are less acculturated show less body image discrepancy and weight concern than other girls (Beech et al., 2004). Acculturation to the United States among Hispanics has been related to a shift from a traditional diet of vegetables, meats, and whole grains to more heavily processed, sugar-laden, and high-fat foods (Unger et al., 2004). It has also been linked to decreased physical activity, increased fast-food consumption, and obesity among Hispanic and Asian American adolescents (Gordon-Larsen, Harris, Ward, & Popkin, 2003; Popkin & Udry, 1998; Unger et al., 2004). Scholars have posited that the adoption of the eating-related behaviors of a new society may be viewed as a way to integrate and gain acceptance. It may manifest as a preference among immigrant consumers for foods viewed as "American" (e.g., fast food, pizza) in an attempt to fit in or as parental pride in taking their family to a fast-food restaurant (Kipke, Iverson, & Booker, 2005; Renzaho, 2004; Unger et al., 2004). Worldwide increases in immigration highlight the importance of understanding the influence of acculturation on obesity-related behaviors and how the positive aspects of culture can be maintained in new environments. Investigations of how food consumption may contribute to social acceptance through qualitative or experimental study of social norms may provide important insights.

### Body Image

Although obesity is generally stigmatized in the United States, attitudes and norms regarding ideal body shape and size vary across cultures (Brown, 1991; Flynn & Fitzgibbon, 1995; Kumanyika, 1995; Rguibi & Belahsen, 2004). In some parts of the world, excess weight has been considered a sign of wealth, success, and good health (Brown, 1991; Crawford, 2001; Renzaho,

2004; Sobal & Stunkard, 1989). For example, a study of weight perceptions among teenage girls and women in Morocco found that the majority of the women viewed their size as appropriate and had no desire to lose weight despite a high prevalence of overweight among them (Rguibi & Belahsen, 2006). Broad cultural perspectives related to body image overlap with subcultural factors such as ethnicity. For example, in an Australian study, obese Aboriginal, Middle Eastern/Arabic, and Pacific Islander female adolescents were less likely than their Caucasian or Asian peers to perceive themselves as too fat (O'Dea, 2008).

In the United States, significant differences in ideal body shape, size, and weight preoccupation are evident between ethnic-majority and ethnic-minority adolescents and adults, which are often attributed to differences in cultural norms (Flynn & Fitzgibbon, 1995). However, other research has suggested the need for additional within-group segmentation to understand body image percep-tions. While some studies have shown that Black females consider overweight bodies more attrac-tive, others have found that Black females prefer normal weight (Flynn & Fitzgibbon, 1998). Cultural perceptions of body shapes and sizes may also interact with observed realities. Communities where excess weight is normative may influence what is perceived to be attractive (Kumanyika, 2002). Although researchers have addressed body image and cultural differences, less emphasis has been placed on understanding how these physical perceptions may manifest in consumption-related attitudes, norms, and behaviors, which is an area ripe for consumer research attention.

*Food Habits*

Food habits are influenced by culture and encompass the ways people use, obtain, prepare, serve, and consume foods (Kittler & Sucher, 2001). Although the same foods may be served across differ-ent cultures, the meanings of those foods may vary (Airhihenbuwa et al., 1996; Andreasen, 2006). Significant cross-cultural differences exist in the extent to which food serves as pleasure versus a stressor (Rozin, 1999). Cultural beliefs and influences on eating behavior apply not only to the eat-ing patterns of adults but also, as noted earlier in our discussion of intergenerational influences, to how parents feed and socialize their children (Kumanyika, 2008, Moore et al., 2002). Culture influ-ences the foods that a child is exposed to and develops a preference for, as well as norms regarding the appropriateness of certain foods in certain situations, such as when and where certain foods are eaten (Airhihenbuwa et al., 1996; Wardle & Cooke, 2008). Children internalize their own culture's ideas about what foods are appropriate at certain mealtimes as early as preschool, and these are reinforced within families (Birch et al., 1984). Given the overlap of lower income with certain sub-cultural groups, economic deprivation may also lead to the acceptability of overeating when food is available (Kumanyika, 2008). Research on the specific cultural meanings of food among children and youth is very limited, and more is needed.

Subcultural Influences: Ethnicity

One specific dimension of culture that is of significance to understanding obesity is ethnicity. Countries worldwide are experiencing increasing ethnic diversity. In the United Kingdom, the minority ethnic population grew by 53% from 1991 to 2001 and tends to be younger and have larger families (D. Burton, 2002; Oldroyd, Banerjee, Heald, & Cruickshank, 2005). In the United States, first- and second-generation immigrants comprise one of the fastest growing segments of the child population (Zhou, 1997). Ethnic-minority families in the United States are also younger and more likely to have more children than ethnic-majority populations (D. Burton, 2002; Frey, 2003, Humphreys, 2006). Further, although multigenerational families are increasing generally in the United States, the trend is disproportionately occurring among minority populations (Taylor et al., 2010). The relationship between ethnic-group membership and obesity is an increasing focus, given observed higher rates among some groups. Ethnic-minority youth are significantly more likely to be overweight or at risk of overweight in the United States, England, Australia, and other countries (O'Dea, 2008; Ogden et al., 2008; Saxena, Ambler, Cole, & Majeed, 2004; Will, Zeeb, & Baune, 2005). Although the association between ethnicity and obesity is often assumed to be a product of income differences, research has suggested that the effects of ethnicity may be independent. A study of overweight children in England found differences by ethnicity and gender but not social class (Saxena et al., 2004). In the United States, while obesity generally declines with parental increases in education or income among White children, rates may increase with income or show no consistent pattern among Black and Hispanic children (see Kumanyika & Grier, 2006, for more detailed discussion).

Ethnic influences relevant to eating and activity behaviors include social roles, attitudes toward exercise, social norms, and ethnic food habits, beliefs, and practices related to food and feeding (Airhihenbuwa et al., 1996; Kumanyika, 2004; Kumanyika & Grier, 2006). Some researchers have characterized the cultural milieu of ethnic minorities in the United States as obesity tolerant and suggested that sociocontextual conditions may influence attitudes and behaviors (Kumanyika, 2002). Research among ethnically diverse parents of 2–12-year-old children found that greater exposure to fast-food promotion was associated with beliefs that eating fast food is normative in their community, and these norms mediated the association of exposure to fast-food promotion with greater consumption of fast food by their children (Grier, Mensinger, Huang, Kumanyika, & Stettler, 2007). Researchers have posited that differences in repeated exposure to food and beverage marketing, as well as differences in obesity rates among ethnic-minority adults, may mean that minority youth are more likely to regard less healthful eating patterns and related behaviors as normative (Grier et al., 2007; Kumanyika & Grier, 2006).

Sociocultural group memberships, such as ethnicity, are complementary cultural influences. For example, minority youth are confronted with ethnic identity concerns as a contributor to their self-esteem as well (Castro, 2004). Further, ethnic influences may reflect many other factors on which minority populations differ, such as household type and composition, health care access, and neighborhood characteristics, including safety, available services, and the degree of racial and ethnic segregation (Kumanyika, 2004, 2008; Kumanyika & Grier, 2006). For example, lower SES is more prevalent in ethnic-minority populations, and weight disparities may be mediated by conditions associated with lower income (Koplan et al., 2005). Thus, it is challenging to distinguish ethnic-group differences based on subcultural influences from those related to SES or other sociodemographic factors that may disproportionately affect ethnic-minority populations (Kumanyika, 2004).

The changing demographics of societies combined with the higher obesity rates among certain ethnic-minority populations make this an area for proactive, forward-thinking transformational research. Despite considerable attention to culture in consumer research, only limited effort has been focused on the role of subculture and, relatedly, SES in obesity, overconsumption or relevant attitudes, values, and practices. More research is needed to understand independent and interactive effects of ethnicity and SES on child and adolescent weight, especially for groups that are at higher risk. It is necessary to understand which causes of obesity are especially influential, how aspects of the social, cultural, and economic environment support or reinforce the effects of such factors, and what changes can contribute to obesity reduction (Kumanyika & Grier, 2006). Studies across multiple subcultures may highlight novel intervention points. Research investigations of consumption in context, via ethnographic or other qualitative approaches, may help identify important overlooked yet modifiable factors (e.g., Crockett & Wallendorf, 2004). Such research not only is relevant to understanding ethnic minorities but also may contribute to a more general understanding of behavior change.

## The Marketing Environment

As our ecological framework reflects, it is also necessary to look to the community and societal institutions that shape a child's consumption opportunities and constraints if we are to understand the obesity problem. In the sections that follow, we turn to issues relevant to marketing, the local community, and the health care industry.

### Retail Food Outlets

Children and families purchase foods and beverages in many settings, including supermarkets, convenience stores, malls, restaurants, vendor carts, cafeterias, and vending machines. Retail food outlets represent the food industry at a local level and are the direct interface with consumers. The presence or absence of these outlets, the products they offer, the information they provide, and the prices they charge can have considerable influence on the eating behavior of patrons. For example, information provided in restaurants and fast-food outlets can support families' ability to make informed choices and assist them in limiting calorie intake. Most adults are unaware of the nutritional content of restaurant offerings, yet providing this information may increase healthy choices (S. Burton et al., 2006), including choices regarding what parents buy for their children. Whether nutritional data will support healthier choices by youth is unclear, and more research is needed.

In one experiment, adolescents (ages 11–18) made food selections first from a menu without nutritional information and then again from the same menu with nutritional information. Of the 29% that changed their selections, 80% shifted to healthier options (Yamamoto, Yamamoto, & Yamamoto, 2005). However, other studies have indicated that providing calorie information has little effect on food choice, especially among those who regularly patronize fast-food restaurants (Harnack & French, 2008; Harnack et al., 2008). Understanding the conditions in which the provision of nutrition information leads to better choices, and among what types of consumers, seems to be an important policy-relevant avenue for future research (for further discussion, see Grunert, Bolton, & Raats, Chapter 16 of this volume). In addition, sales of fast-food chains are fueled by promotions, frequently price promotions, focused on local markets (Feltenstein, 1983). Analyses of in-store and outdoor advertising have indicated more promotion of less healthful foods in African American and Hispanic communities relative to White communities (Lewis et al., 2005; Yancey et al., 2009). Thus, food outlet operators may have the opportunity to promote healthier products to specific groups, and consumer research could inform specific approaches.

Local outlets also impact consumer access to food. The term *food desert* describes communities with limited access to healthy foods (Whitacre, Tsai, & Mulligan, 2009; Wrigley, Warm, & Margetts, 2003). In the United States, food deserts are especially prevalent in low-income, inner-city, and rural areas that have fewer supermarkets and less access to healthy items such as fruits and vegetables (Whitacre et al., 2009). Systematic reviews have provided clear evidence of disparities in food access in the United States as a function of both income and race (Beaulac, Kristjansson, & Cummins, 2009; Grier & Kumanyika, 2008). A national U.S. study of supermarket availability found that in 2000, access to supermarkets for African Americans was 52% of the access of Caucasians, Hispanics had 33% of the access of non-Hispanics, and lower-income neighborhoods had lower access than middle- and upper-income neighborhoods (Powell, Slater, Mirtcheva, Bao, & Chaloupka, 2006). Availability of supermarkets has been linked to better dietary quality among African American consumers but not White consumers in the United States (Morland, Wing, & Roux, 2002). Changes in food pricing and increased access to supermarkets can have measurable effects on weight outcomes of children ages 6–17, especially those from low-income families (Powell & Ba, 2009).

Fast-food outlet operators are especially important, because as noted, children and youth frequently consume fast food, a pattern that contributes to higher calories and lower nutritional quality (Bowman et al., 2004; French, Story, Neumark-Sztainer, et al., 2001). Youth exposed to fast food around their schools or who have fewer supermarkets in their neighborhoods consume more unhealthy food and are more likely to be overweight (Davis & Carpenter, 2009; Powell, Auld, Chaloupka, O'Malley, & Johnston, 2007). African American and Hispanic students in urban schools that are near fast-food restaurants are three times more likely to have a higher BMI than the general population of students (Davis & Grier, 2009). Parental attitudes toward fast-food outlets have suggested that they value the child-friendly aspects, yet feel marketing challenges their ability to control their children's diets (Ayala, Mueller, Lopez-Madurga, Campbell, & Elder, 2005; Jones, 2002). Research has highlighted the need for a more nuanced understanding of the influence of local food marketing environments on eating behaviors (Grier & Kumanyika, 2008).

*Food Manufacturers*

At a broader level, questions are being asked about the contribution of food marketing to the obesity epidemic. Three comprehensive research reviews of marketing's impacts on children have been published, one by the Food Standards Agency in the United Kingdom (Hastings et al., 2003), another in response to a congressional directive by the Institute of Medicine (McGinnis, Gootman, & Kraak, 2006), and a third commissioned by the World Health Organization (Cairns, Augus, & Hastings, 2009). Each of these reviews focused primarily on the effects of television advertising. In its analysis, the Institute of Medicine reported that television advertising influences key dietary precursors, including children's (ages 2–11) food and beverage preferences, purchase requests, and short-term consumption. Correlational evidence has also linked advertising exposure to children's weight. One of the Institute of Medicine's key conclusions was that "food and beverage marketing practices geared to children and youth are out of balance with healthful diets and contribute to an environment that puts their health at risk" (p. 10). The impact of television advertising on children is an area of study that consumer researchers have made many contributions to over the years. However, the world of marketing to children has changed of late. Much less is known about the impacts of integrated marketing communications programs that may include product placements; special packaging; promotions; events; in-school, online, and other digital marketing; as well as television and print media (Moore, 2004; Moore & Rideout, 2007). This is an area clearly in need of research and one to which consumer researchers are very well positioned to contribute.

*Recreation and Entertainment Industries*

Impacts on childhood obesity extend beyond the food industry to the recreation and entertainment industries. Firms catering to both active (e.g., bicycles, health clubs, sporting goods) and sedentary (e.g., spectator sports, television) pursuits have benefited from significant growth, although the growth has been steeper for sedentary activities (Koplan et al., 2005). Unsurprisingly, sports, both organized and unorganized, and other types of physical activity are negatively associated with obesity, whereas television watching and video game use are positive risk factors (Tremblay & Williams, 2003). Public health researchers argue that the motivation to be physically active is challenged by the heavy marketing of seductive sedentary entertainment. American children spend only about 12 minutes per day in vigorous physical activity, yet 75% of their waking hours are spent being inactive (Strauss, Rodzilsky, Burack, & Colin, 2001). Increased time spent on sedentary activities relative to active pursuits has been associated with higher rates of obesity (French et al., 2001). Opportunities exist for these industries to support increased physical activity through product innovation, market development, and shifts in the allocation of promotional resources. Consumer research can provide needed insights on the types of changes most likely to be successful.

### The Local Community

Communities also influence the incidence of obesity. Local government officials (e.g., mayors, city planners, health departments) make decisions that influence the settings where children and adolescents make food choices, including convenience stores, restaurants and fast-food outlets, shopping malls, schools, and vending machines (Story, Neumark-Sztainer, & French, 2002). Lack of access to recreation facilities and supportive infrastructure, such as sidewalks, bike paths, safe playgrounds, controlled intersections, and public transportation, as well as crime rates negatively impact children's participation in physical activity (Davison & Lawson, 2006; Ebbeling, Pawlak, & Ludwig, 2002). Ease of access to and increased appeal of recreation facilities can facilitate physical activity, suggesting that youth sport and recreation leaders can play an important role through local organizations, summer day camps, and active transportation (Koplan et al., 2005; Yancey et al., 2004). The lack of a public health practice infrastructure for the promotion of physical activity at the local level may also influence weight-related behaviors among children and adolescents (Yancey et al., 2007). Since many communities do not adequately invest in environments that encourage physical activity, often favoring real estate development over open space (Ebbeling et al., 2004; Sallis & Glanz, 2006), opportunities may exist for local governments to encourage healthy development.

### Health Care Industry

Health care workers have the opportunity to not only diagnose obesity but also encourage healthy lifestyles. Clinicians are challenged to convey the seriousness of weight issues to youth and families who may be sensitive or ashamed (Barlow & Dietz, 1998). Pediatric practitioners, nurses, dieticians, psychologists, and other specialists have perceived that intervention in child and adolescent obesity is important, yet they face barriers with regard to obesity prevention and treatment, including discomfort and a lack of preparation and competence, as well as unmotivated patients, lack of family involvement, and inadequate support services (Story, Neumark-Stzainer, Sherwood, et al., 2002). Resource needs of the patient and/or health practitioner may also hinder health care workers. Management and health care institutions may need to incorporate added training, education, and advocacy efforts into medical curricula and continuing education programs for physicians as a means to integrate weight issues into the primary care setting (Jelalian, Boergers, Alday, & Frank, 2003; Story, Neumark-Stzainer, Sherwood, et al., 2002).

In the U.S. health insurance industry, reimbursement for medical treatment of childhood obesity is poor to nonexistent, which affects treatment resources available to patients (Tershakovec, Watson, Wenner, & Marx, 1999). In addition to a primary care provider, obesity treatment for pediatric patients may necessitate a dietician, psychologist, and/or physical activity specialist, resources which may not be available, leaving the physician faced with requests that they cannot fulfill alone (Stettler, 2004). Research that examines best practices for integrating childhood obesity concerns, given the realities and constraints of the clinical context, can assist in identifying solutions.

## TOWARD INTEGRATIVE CONSUMER RESEARCH ON CHILDHOOD OBESITY

The goals of childhood obesity prevention are to maintain healthy diets and regular physical activity in the context of healthy development (Koplan et al., 2005). As is the case in other areas of public health behavior management (Rothschild, 1999), obesity prevention approaches have relied heavily on education and rational decision making. Although education can play an important role by making target groups aware of opportunities, it is limited in its capacity to remove actual or perceived barriers to behavior change.

One of the criticisms of intervention studies in public health is that they have tended to ignore the social context that affects behavior, which is due in part to evidence demonstrating that socio-economic differences across a wide variety of health outcomes persist even after adjusting for individual-level risk factors (Glass & McAtee, 2006). Diet and activity behaviors are often conceptualized primarily as if they are voluntary decisions without regard to the social constraints, inducements, or pressures that children and families face. Yet, children and their families may alternatively be eager, reluctant, capable, or unable to meet program goals.

An ecological perspective highlights how prevention efforts must be informed by an understanding of the multiple contexts in which people live and make choices. Although many childhood obesity researchers have recognized that such a perspective is appropriate, research in this domain has remained largely anchored within individual layers of the model. However, the more we have learned about this topic, the more we have become convinced that a real shift in perspective is needed, one that attempts to frame research questions and designs in a way that takes the ecological model more seriously with respect to the reciprocal determinism and interactions across layers. This is no easy task. Yet, Transformative Consumer Research is an applied movement that draws on an array of theories, concepts, and research approaches to understand its substantive domain. It is this breadth of perspective and methodological eclecticism that makes it particularly well suited to undertake this work. It became clear to us from the analysis of the individual, social, and environmental contributors to childhood obesity that a deeper understanding of consumer experience is needed. Social marketers, who focus not on education but on behavior change, have recommended that consumer research should be conducted to better understand target audiences before interventions are initiated (Andreasen, 2002). This may prove to be good advice in this case, because although the behaviors that lead to childhood obesity are well recognized, much less is known about how they come about, are maintained, and can be changed.

Our discussion to this point has identified a number of research needs, yet many of these are nested within individual layers of the ecological model. There are a number of issues that might benefit from a more integrative perspective. Here, we mention just a few. For example, what are the independent and interactive effects of ethnicity, family structure, and SES on child and adolescent weight? Which causes of obesity are especially influential in particular subpopulations? It is very clear that a richer knowledge base is needed to address the disparities in risk status evident among children. To this point, most obesity studies have focused on White, middle-class children. Investigations are needed that work to identify the contextual factors that both enable and constrain a healthy way of life within a diverse population.

Other issues might also benefit from a more integrative perspective. For example, in a relatively short period of time, family structure in the United States has diversified considerably. Large numbers of children are living with single parents or in multigenerational families, and more parents are working outside the home, thus creating additional challenges in daily life. Links between working parents and childhood obesity have been suggested due to fewer family meals, increased emphasis on convenience foods, and latchkey children engaged in sedentary after-school activities (e.g., Koplan et al., 2005). Although more needs to be learned about consumers' experiences with regard to these challenges, integrative approaches that are well grounded in sociological and economic analysis are also needed to understand what kinds of community and industry support structures would aid parents in promoting healthy lifestyles.

Questions about how upstream changes might affect end consumers are also pertinent. For example, how do contextual changes at a national level (e.g., in the types and nature of products promoted, information, or services provided) influence community-level perceptions and the individual choices of parents and youth? Consumer researchers can draw from a vast array of behavior change theories, such as the theory of planned behavior, marketing theories such as the persuasion knowledge model, or segmentation strategies such as the stages of change model, to undergird such investigations.

Community-based prevention marketing, participatory action research, and community-based participatory research can involve consumers through the development of research partnerships with community members and stakeholders (Ammerman et al., 2007; Bryant et al., 2007; Ozanne & Saatcioglu, 2008). The obesity research paradigm developed by the African American Collaborative Obesity Research Network presents an ecological model that includes contextual variables specifically focused on studying African American communities and may be adapted to examine other subcultural groups (Kumanyika et al., 2007). Approaches such as these that examine key factors across several layers of influence can create an environment that supports healthier behaviors.

Our burgeoning understanding of social marketing suggests that it can also be an effective tool. Social marketing is increasingly being used to try to address factors that impact obesity, such as the demand for healthy snacks, increased availability of healthy choices (via targeted efforts aimed at the food industry), and increased physical activity (Grier & Bryant, 2005). For example, VERB™ was a national, multicultural program created by the Centers for Disease Control and Prevention and aimed at increasing physical activity among tweens (ages 9–13; Wong et al., 2003). First-year results revealed increased weekly free-time physical activity sessions, suggesting that social marketing campaigns can impact children's weight-related behaviors (Huhman et al., 2005).

Social marketing shares commercial marketing's consumer orientation as well as its recognition of the value of the entire marketing mix, not just education or advertising (Grier & Bryant, 2005). Interventions can be targeted at the "right people," those who affect social change, whether they be consumers, policy makers, public health practitioners, medical professionals, or industry leaders. Social marketing's disciplinary roots may also enable its use in creating interventions to counteract any potential negative impacts of commercial marketing on children's choices. Although there have been some self-regulatory policy developments, questions remain as to how effective they will be in shifting demand and altering children's food preferences and, ultimately, weight status. A more nuanced understanding of parents' and children's responses to industry initiatives such as new labeling programs, packaging innovations, creation of more nutritious offerings, and increased marketing of healthier items would be helpful in this regard.

Consumer researchers need not struggle alone. Cross-disciplinary and cross-sector collaborations with other academics, government agencies, state health departments, and private-sector marketers can support the development of investigations that cut across layers of the ecological model. Multiple initiatives that bring together resources to address childhood obesity exist, including local and national coalitions such as the Consortium to Lower Obesity in Chicago Children and the California Convergence, private foundation programs such as the Healthy Eating Research and Active Living Research programs of the Robert Wood Johnson Foundation, and national government efforts such as the Let's Move campaign launched by Michelle Obama. Such collaborations may also assist in providing complementary expertise, community partners, and funds necessary to pursue multilayered studies.

It is also important to keep in mind that weight-related issues are a sensitive domain, especially among children, and research into relevant topics can involve a variety of ethical issues. For example, representations may stigmatize obese children or groups who have historically been disadvantaged, or parents may be made to feel inadequate. Although a full discussion of the types and nature of ethical issues are beyond the scope of this chapter, it is an important area worthy of mention, and researchers should consider and anticipate any potential issues and unintended effects of research or interventions.

As is surely evident by now, the problem of childhood obesity is serious, complex, and not easily remedied. Despite extensive study in other fields, there remain real opportunities to advance understanding and develop novel strategies for intervention and transformation. Scholars in the arena of Transformative Consumer Research can bring new perspectives, theories, substantive insights, and methodological strengths to this issue. It is our hope that this chapter will provide a basis for pursuing this important work and, ultimately, in helping children live happier, healthier lives.

## REFERENCES

Adams, R. E., & Bukowski, W. M. (2008). Peer victimization as a predictor of depression and body mass index in obese and non-obese adolescents. *Journal of Child Psychology and Psychiatry, 49*(8), 858–866.

Addy, C. L., Wilson, D. K., Kirtland, K. A., Ainsworth, B. E., Sharpe, P., & Kimsey, D. (2004). Associations of perceived social and physical environmental supports with physical activity and walking behavior. *American Journal of Public Health, 94*(3), 440–443.

Agras, W. S., Hammer, L. D., McNicholas, F., & Kraemer, H. C. (2004). Risk factors for childhood overweight: A prospective study from birth to 9.5 years. *Journal of Pediatrics, 145*(1), 20–25.

Airhihenbuwa, C. O., Kumanyika, S., Agurs, T. D., Lowe, A., Saunders, D., & Morssink, C. B. (1996). Cultural aspects of African American eating patterns. *Ethnicity & Health, 1*(3), 245–260.

American Academy of Pediatrics. (2005). Breastfeeding and the use of human milk [Policy statement]. *Pediatrics, 115*(2), 496–506.

Ammerman, A. S., Samuel-Hodge, C. D., Sommers, J. K., Leung, M. M., Paxton, A. E., & Vu, M. B. (2007). Community-based approaches to obesity prevention: The role of environmental and policy change. In S. Kumanyika & R. C. Brownson (Eds.), *Handbook of obesity prevention: A resource for health professionals* (pp. 263–284). New York: Springer.

Anderson, S. E., Bandini, L. G., & Must, A. (2005). Child temperament does not predict adolescent body composition in girls. *International Journal of Obesity, 29*(1), 47–53.

Andreasen, A. R. (1975). *The disadvantaged consumer*. New York: Free Press.

Andreasen, A. (2002). Marketing social marketing in the social change marketplace. *Journal of Public Policy & Marketing, 21*(1), 3–13.

Andreasen, A. R. (2006). *Social marketing in the 21st century*. Thousand Oaks, CA: Sage.

Arnould, E. J., & Thompson, C. J. (2005). Consumer culture theory (CCT): Twenty years of research. *Journal of Consumer Research, 31*(4), 868–882.

Ayala, G. X., Mueller, K., Lopez-Madurga, E., Campbell, N., & Elder, J. (2005). Restaurant and food shopping selections among Latino women in Southern California. *Journal of the American Dietetic Association, 105*(1), 38–45.

Barlow, S. E., & Dietz, W. H. (1998). Obesity evaluation and treatment: Expert committee recommendations. *Pediatrics, 102*(3), 1–11.

Barlow, S. E., & and the Expert Committee. (2007). Expert committee recommendations regarding the prevention, assessment, and treatment of child and adolescent overweight and obesity: Summary report. *Pediatrics, 120*(Suppl. 4), S164–S192.

Barquera, S., Hernandez-Barrera, L., Tolentino, M. L., Espinosa, J., Ng, S. W., Rivera, J. A., et al. (2008). Energy intake from beverages is increasing among Mexican adolescents and adults. *Journal of Nutrition, 138*(12), 2454–2461.

Baughcum, A. E., Chamberlin, L. A., Deeks, C. M., Powers, S. W., & Whitaker, R. C. (2000). Maternal perceptions of overweight preschool children. *Pediatrics, 106*(6), 1380–1386.

Beaulac, J., Kristjansson, E., & Cummins, S. (2009). A systematic review of food deserts: 1966–2007. *Preventing Chronic Disease, 6*(3). Available: http://www.cdc.gov/pcd/issues/2009/jul/08_0163.htm

Beech, B. M., Kumanyika, S. K., Baranowski, T., Davis, M., Robinson, T. N., Sherwood, N. E., et al. (2004). Parental cultural perspectives in relation to weight-related behaviors and concerns of African-American girls. *Obesity, 12*(Suppl. 9), 7S–19S.

Belk, R. W. (1975). Situational variables and consumer behavior. *Journal of Consumer Research, 2*(3), 157–164.

Bell, J., & Burlin, B. M. (1993). In urban areas: Many of the poor still pay more for food. *Journal of Public Policy & Marketing, 12*(2), 268–270.

Bentley, M. E., Gavin, L., Black, M. M., & Teti, L. (1999). Infant feeding practices of low-income, African-American, adolescent mothers: An ecological multigenerational perspective. *Social Science & Medicine, 49*(8), 1085–1110.

Bétancourt, H., & López, S. R. (1993). The study of culture, ethnicity, and race in American psychology. *American Psychologist, 48*(6), 629–637.

Birch, L. L. (1999). Development of food preferences. *Annual Review of Nutrition, 19*(1), 41–62.

Birch, L. L., Fisher, J. O., & Davison, K. K. (2003). Learning to overeat: Maternal use of restrictive feeding practices promotes girls' eating in the absence of hunger. *American Journal of Clinical Nutrition, 78*(2), 215–220.

Birch, L. L., Marlin, D. W., & Rotter, J. (1984). Eating as the "means" activity in a contingency: Effects on young children's food preference. *Child Development, 55*(2), 431–439.

Booth, S. L., Sallis, J. F., Ritenbaugh, C., Hill, J. O., Birch, L. L., Frank, L. D., et al. (2001). Environmental and societal factors affect food choice and physical activity: Rationale, influences, and leverage points. *Nutrition Reviews, 59*(3), S21–S39.

Borah-Giddens, J., & Falciglia, G. A. (1993). A meta-analysis of the relationship in food preferences between parents and children. *Journal of Nutrition Education & Behavior, 25*(3), 102–107.

Boulanger, P. M., Pérez-Escamilla, R., Himmelgreen, D., Segura-Millán, S., & Haldeman, L. (2002). Determinants of nutrition knowledge among low-income, Latino caretakers in Hartford, Conn. *Journal of the American Dietetic Association, 102*(7), 978–981.

Bowman, S., Gortmaker, S., Ebbeling, C., Pereira, M., & Ludwig, D. (2004). Effects of fast-food consumption on energy intake and diet quality among children in a national household survey. *Pediatrics, 113*, 112–118.

Brown, P. J. (1991). Culture and the evolution of obesity. *Human Nature, 2*(1), 31–57.

Brownell, K. D., Farley, T., Willett, W. C., Popkin, B. M., Chaloupka, F. J., Thompson, J. W., et al. (2009). The public health and economic benefits of taxing sugar-sweetened beverages. *New England Journal of Medicine, 361*(16), 1599–1605.

Brucks, M., Armstrong, G. M., & Goldberg, M. E. (1988). Children's use of cognitive defenses against television advertising: A cognitive response approach. *Journal of Consumer Research, 14*(4), 471–482.

Bryant, C. A., McCormack, K., McCormack, K., Forthofer, M. S., Bumpus, E. C., Calkins, S. A., et al. (2007). Community-based prevention marketing: Organizing a community for health behavior intervention. *Journal of Health Promotion Practice, 8*(2), 154–163.

Burgess-Champoux, T., Larson, N., Neumark-Sztainer, D., Hannan, P. J., & Story, M. (2009). Are family meal patterns associated with overall diet quality during the transition from early to middle adolescence? *Journal of Nutrition Education & Behavior, 41*(2), 79–86.

Burton, D. (2002). Incorporating ethnicity into marketing intelligence and planning. *Marketing Intelligence & Planning, 20*(7), 442–451.

Burton, S., Creyer, E. H., Kees, J., & Huggins, K. (2006). Attacking the obesity epidemic: The potential health benefits of providing nutrition information in restaurants. *American Journal of Public Health, 96*(9), 1669–1675.

Cairns, G., Angus, K., & Hastings, G. (2009). *The extent, nature and effects of food promotion to children: A review of the evidence to December 2008.* Geneva, Switzerland: World Health Organization Press.

Caprio, S., Daniels, S. R., Drewnowski, A., Kaufman, F. R., Palinkas, L. A., Rosenbloom, A. L., et al. (2008). Influence of race, ethnicity, and culture on childhood obesity: Implications for prevention and treatment. *Diabetes Care, 31*(11), 2211–2221.

Carey, W. B., Hegvik, R. L., & McDevitt, S. C. (1988). Temperamental factors associated with rapid weight gain and obesity in middle childhood. *Journal of Developmental & Behavioral Pediatrics, 9*(4), 194–198.

Carlson, L., & Grossbart, S. (1988). Parental style and consumer socialization of children. *Journal of Consumer Research, 15*(June), 77–94.

Carnell, S., Edwards, C., Croker, H., Boniface, D., & Wardle, J. (2005). Parental perceptions of overweight in 3–5 y olds. *International Journal of Obesity, 29*(4), 353–355.

Carnell, S., Haworth, C. M. A., Plomin, R., & Wardle, J. (2008). Genetic influence on appetite in children. *International Journal of Obesity, 32*(10), 1468–1473.

Castro, F. G. (2004). Physiological, psychological, social, and cultural influences on the use of menthol cigarettes among Blacks and Hispanics. *Nicotine Tobacco Research, 6*(Suppl. 1), S29–S41.

Centers for Disease Control and Prevention. (2002). Physical activity levels among children aged 9–13 years: United States, 2002. *Morbidity and Mortality Weekly Report, 52*(33), 785–788. Available: http://www.cdc.gov/mmwr/preview/mmwrhtml/mm5233a1.htm

Contento, I. R., Basch, C., Shea, S., Gutin, B., Zybert, P., Michela, J. L., et al. (1993). Relationship of mothers' food choice criteria to food intake of preschool children: Identification of family subgroups. *Health Education Quarterly, 20*(2), 243–259.

Cook-Cottone, C., Casey, C. M., Feeley, T. H., & Baran, J. (2009). A meta-analytic review of obesity prevention in the schools: 1997–2008. *Psychology in the Schools, 46*(8), 695–719.

Cooke, L. J., Wardle, J., Gibson, E. L., Sapochnik, M., Sheiham, A., & Lawson, M. (2004). Demographic, familial and trait predictors of fruit and vegetable consumption by preschool children. *Public Health Nutrition, 7*(2), 295–302.

Cramer, P., & Steinwert, T. (1998). Thin is good, fat is bad: How early does it begin? *Journal of Applied Developmental Psychology, 19*(3), 429–451.

Crawford, P. B. (2001, October). *Perceptions of child weight and health in Hispanic parents: Implications for the California FitWIC Childhood Obesity Prevention Project.* Paper presented at the 129th annual meeting of the American Public Health Association, Atlanta, GA.

Crockett, D., & Wallendorf, M. (2004). The role of normative political ideology in consumer behavior. *Journal of Consumer Research, 31*(3), 511–528.

Cullen, K. W., Lara, K. M., & de Moor, C. (2002). Familial concordance of dietary fat practices and intake. *Family & Community Health, 25*(2), 65–75.

Daniels, S. R. (2006). The consequences of childhood overweight and obesity. *The Future of Children, 16*(1), 47–67.

Davis, B., & Carpenter, C. (2009). Proximity of fast-food restaurants to schools and adolescent obesity. *American Journal of Public Health, 99*(3), 505–510.

Davis, B., & Grier, S. (2009, February). *Access to healthy versus unhealthy food in developing countries: What can be learned from low-income areas of the United States?* Paper presented at the American Marketing Association Winter Educators' Conference, Tampa, FL.

Davison, K. K., & Birch, L. L. (2001). Childhood overweight: A contextual model and recommendations for future research. *Obesity Reviews, 2*(3), 159–171.

Davison, K. K., & Lawson, C. (2006). Do attributes in the physical environment influence children's physical activity? A review of the literature. *International Journal of Behavioral Nutrition and Physical Activity, 3*(1), 1–19.

de Castro, J. M., & Lilenfeld, L. R. R. (2005). Influence of heredity on dietary restraint, disinhibition, and perceived hunger in humans. *Nutrition, 21*(4), 446–455.

de Mooij, M. K. (2004). *Consumer behavior and culture: Consequences for global marketing and advertising.* Thousand Oaks, CA: Sage.

Dietz, W. H., & Gortmaker, S. L. (2001). Preventing obesity in children and adolescents. *Annual Review of Public Health, 22*, 309–335.

Drewnowski, A. (2007). The real contribution of added sugars and fats to obesity. *Epidemiological Review, 29*(1), 160–171.

Ebbeling, C. B., Pawlak, D. B., & Ludwig, D. S. (2002). Childhood obesity: Public-health crisis, common sense cure. *Lancet, 360*(9331), 473–482.

Ebbeling, C. B., Sinclair, K., Pereira, M., Garcia-Lago, E., Feldman, H., & Ludwig, D. (2004). Compensation for energy intake from fast food among overweight and lean adolescents. *Journal of the American Medical Association, 291*, 2828–2833.

Eckstein, K. C., Mikhail, L. M., Ariza, A. J., Thomson, J. S., Millard, S. C., & Binns, H. J. (2006). Parents' perceptions of their child's weight and health. *Pediatrics, 117*(3), 681–690.

Ekelund, U., Aman, J., Yngve, A., Renman, C., Westerterp, K., & Sjöström, M. (2002). Physical activity but not energy expenditure is reduced in obese adolescents: A case-control study. *American Journal of Clinical Nutrition, 76*(5), 935–941.

Faith, M. S., Scanlon, K. S., Birch, L. L., Francis, L. A., & Sherry, B. (2004). Parent-child feeding strategies and their relationships to child eating and weight status. *Obesity Research, 12*(11), 1711–1722.

Feltenstein, T. (1983). *Restaurant profits through advertising and promotion: The indispensable plan.* New York: CBI.

Fisher, J. O., & Birch, L. L. (1999). Restricting access to palatable foods affects children's behavioral response, food selection, and intake. *American Journal of Clinical Nutrition, 69*(6), 1264–1272.

Fisher, J. O., Mitchell, D. C., Smiciklas-Wright, H., & Birch, L. L. (2002). Parental influences on young girls' fruit and vegetable, micronutrient, and fat intakes. *Journal of the American Dietetic Association, 102*(1), 58–64.

Fisher, J. O., Mitchell, D. C., Smiciklas-Wright, H., Mannino, M. L., & Birch, L. L. (2004). Meeting calcium recommendations during middle childhood reflects mother–daughter beverage choices and predicts bone mineral status. *American Journal of Clinical Nutrition, 79*(4), 698–706.

Flynn, K., & Fitzgibbon, M. (1995). Body image ideals of low-income African American mothers and their preadolescent daughters. *Journal of Youth and Adolescence, 25*(5), 615–630.

Flynn, K., & Fitzgibbon, M. (1998). Body images and obesity risk among Black females: A review of the literature. *Annals of Behavioral Medicine, 20*(1), 13–24.

Fogelholm, M., Nuutinen, O., Pasanen, M., Myöhänen, E., & Säätelä, T. (1999). Parent–child relationship of physical activity patterns and obesity. *International Journal of Obesity and Related Metabolic Disorders, 23*(12), 1262–1268.

Fox, M. K., Pac, S., Devaney, B., & Jankowski, L. (2004). Feeding infants and toddlers study: What foods are infants and toddlers eating? *Journal of the American Dietetic Association, 104*, 22–30.

Fox, M. K., Devaney, B., Reidy, K., Razafindrakoto, C., & Ziegler, P. (2006). Relationship between portion size and energy intake among infants and toddlers: Evidence of self-regulation. *Journal of the American Dietetic Association, 106*(January), S77–S83.

French, S. A., Story, M., & Jeffery, R. W. (2001). Environmental influences on eating and physical activity. *Annual Review of Public Health, 22*, 309–335.

French, S. A., Story, M., Neumark-Sztainer, D., Fulkerson, J., & Hannan, P. (2001). Fast food restaurant use among adolescents: Association with nutrient intake, food choices and behavioral and psychosocial variables. *International Journal of Obesity and Related Metabolic Disorders, 25*, 1823–1833.

Frey, W. (2003). Married with children. *American Demographics, 25*, 17–19.

Gale, S. M., Castracane, V. D., & Mantzoros, C. S. (2004). Energy homeostasis, obesity and eating disorders: Recent advances in endocrinology. *Journal of Nutrition, 134*(2), 295–298.

Galloway, A. T., Fiorito, L. M., Francis, L. A., & Birch, L. L. (2006). "Finish your soup": Counterproductive effects of pressuring children to eat on intake and affect. *Appetite, 46*(3), 318–323.

Galloway, A. T., Fiorito, L. M., Lee, Y., & Birch, L. L. (2005). Parental pressure, dietary patterns, and weight status among girls who are "picky eaters." *Journal of the American Dietetic Association, 105*(4), 541–548.

Glass, T. A., & McAtee, M. J. (2006). Behavioral science at the crossroads in public health: Extending horizons envisioning the future. *Social Science & Medicine, 62*, 1650–1671.

Goldberg, M. E., & Gunasti, K. (2007). Creating an environment in which youths are encouraged to eat a healthier diet. *Journal of Public Policy & Marketing, 26*(2), 162–181.

Gordon-Larsen, P., Adair, L. S., & Popkin, B. M. (2003). The relationship of ethnicity, socioeconomic factors, and overweight in US adolescents. *Obesity Research, 11*(1), 121–129. (Erratum, *Obesity Research*, 2003, *11*(4), 597)

Gordon-Larsen, P., Harris, K. M., Ward, D. S., & Popkin, B. M. (2003). Acculturation and overweight-related behaviors among Hispanic immigrants to the US: The National Longitudinal Study of Adolescent Health. *Social Science & Medicine, 57*(11), 2023–2034.

Gray, V. B., Byrd, S. H., Cossman, J. S., Chromiak, J. A., Cheek, W., & Jackson, G. (2007). Parental attitudes toward child nutrition and weight have a limited relationship with child's weight status. *Nutrition Research, 27*(9), 548–558.

Gray, W. N., Janicke, D. M., Ingerski, L. M., & Silverstein, J. H. (2008). The impact of peer victimization, parent distress and child depression on barrier formation and physical activity in overweight youth. *Journal of Developmental & Behavioral Pediatrics, 29*(1), 26–33.

Gray, W. N., Kahhan, N. A., & Janicke, D. M. (2009). Peer victimization and pediatric obesity: A review of the literature. *Psychology in the Schools, 46*(8), 720–727.

Grier, S., & Bryant, C. A. (2005). Social marketing in public health. *Annual Review of Public Health, 26*, 319–339.

Grier, S. A., & Kumanyika, S. K. (2008). The context for choice: Health implications of targeted food and beverage marketing to African Americans. *American Journal of Public Health, 98*(9), 1616–1629.

Grier, S. A., Mensinger, J., Huang, S. H., Kumanyika, S. K., & Stettler, N. (2007). Fast food marketing and children's fast food consumption: Exploring parental influences in an ethnically diverse sample. *Journal of Public Policy & Marketing, 26*(2), 221–235.

Griffiths, I. J., Wolke, D., Page, A. S., & Horwood, J. P. (2006). Obesity and bullying: Different effects for boys and girls. *Archives of Disease in Childhood, 91*(2), 121–125.

Grimm, G. C., Harnack, L., & Story, M. (2004). Factors associated with soft drink consumption in school-aged children. *Journal of the American Dietetic Association, 104*(8), 1244–1249.

Haas, J., Lee, L., Kaplan, C., Sonneborn, D., Phillips, K., & Liang, S. (2003). The association of race, socioeconomic status, and health insurance status with the prevalence of overweight among children and adolescents. *American Journal of Public Health, 93*, 2105–2110.

Hansson, L. M., Karnehed, N., Tynelius, P., & Rasmussen, F. (2009). Prejudice against obesity among 10-year-olds: A nationwide population-based study. *Acta Paediatrica, 98*(7), 1176–1182.

Harnack, L. J., & French, S. A. (2008). Effect of point-of-purchase calorie labeling on restaurant and cafeteria food choices: A review of the literature. *International Journal of Behavioral Nutrition and Physical Activity*, 5(1), 51.

Harnack, L. J., French, S. A., Oakes, J. M., Story, M. T., Jeffery, R. W., & Rydell, S. A. (2008). Effects of calorie labeling and value size pricing on fast food meal choices: Results from an experimental trial. *International Journal of Behavioral Nutrition and Physical Activity*, 5(1), 63.

Harnack, L. J., Jeffery, R. W., & Boutelle, K. N. (2000). Temporal trends in energy intake in the United States: An ecologic perspective. *American Journal of Clinical Nutrition*, 71(6), 1478–1484.

Hastings, G., Stead, M., McDermott, L., Forsyth, A., MacKintosh, A. M., & Rayner, M. (2003). *Review of research on the effects of food promotion to children: Final report*. Glasgow, Scotland: Centre for Social Marketing, University of Strathclyde.

Hill, J. O., & Trowbridge, F. L. (1998). Childhood obesity: Future directions and research priorities. *Pediatrics*, 101(3, Pt. 2), 570–574.

Hill, N. E. (2006). Disentangling ethnicity, socioeconomic status and parenting: Interactions, influences and meaning. *Vulnerable Children and Youth Studies*, 1(1), 114–124.

Hill, R. P. (2001). Surviving in a material world: Evidence from ethnographic consumer research on people in poverty. *Journal of Contemporary Ethnography*, 30, 364–391.

Horgen, K. B., & Brownell, K. D. (2002). Comparison of price change and health message interventions in promoting healthy food choices. *Journal of Health Psychology*, 21(5), 505–512.

Houghton, M. D., & Graybeal, T. E. (2001). Breast-feeding practices of Native American mothers participating in WIC. *Journal of the American Dietetic Association*, 101(2), 245–247.

Huhman, M., Potter, L. D., Wong, F. L., Banspach, S. W., Duke, J. C., & Heitzler, C. D. (2005). Effects of a mass media campaign to increase physical activity among children: Year-1 results of the VERB campaign. *Pediatrics*, 116(2), e277–e284.

Humphreys, J. M. (2006). The multicultural economy 2006. *Georgia, Business and Economic Conditions*, 66(3), 1–14.

Iobst, E. A., Ritchey, P. N., Nabors, L. A., Stutz, R., Ghee, K., & Smith, D. T. (2009). Children's acceptance of a peer who is overweight: Relations among gender, age and blame for weight status. *International Journal of Obesity*, 33(7), 736–742.

Isler, L., Popper, E., & Ward, S. (1987). Children's purchase requests and parental responses: Results from a diary study. *Journal of Advertising Research*, 27, 28–39.

Jain, A., Sherman, S. N., Chamberlin, L. A., Carter, Y., Powers, S. W., & Whitaker, R. C. (2001). Why don't low-income mothers worry about their preschoolers being overweight? *Pediatrics*, 107(5), 1138–1146.

Jansen, W., & Brug, J. (2006). Parents often do not recognize overweight in their child, regardless of their socio-demographic background. *European Journal of Public Health*, 16(6), 645–647.

Jeffery, A. N., Voss, L. D., Metcalf, B. S., Alba, S., & Wilkin, T. J. (2005). Parents' awareness of overweight in themselves and their children: Cross sectional study within a cohort (EarlyBird 21). *British Medical Journal*, 330(1), 23–24.

Jelalian, E., Boergers, J., Alday, C. S., & Frank, R. (2003). Survey of physician attitudes and practices related to pediatric obesity. *Clinical Pediatrics*, 42(3), 235–245.

John, C. (2005). A qualitative study exploring socio-economic differences in parental lay knowledge of food and health: Implications for public health nutrition. *Public Health Nutrition*, 8(3), 290–297.

John, D. R. (1999). Consumer socialization of children: A retrospective look at twenty-five years of research. *Journal of Consumer Research*, 26(December), 183–213.

Jones, S. J. (2002). *The measurement of food security at the community level: Geographic information systems and participatory ethnographic methods*. Unpublished doctoral dissertation, University of North Carolina at Chapel Hill.

Kelly, A. M., Wall, M., Eisenberg, M. E., Story, M., & Neumark-Sztainer, D. (2005). Adolescent girls with high body satisfaction: Who are they and what can they teach us? *Journal of Adolescent Health*, 37(5), 391–396.

Kimm, S. Y. S., Glynn, N. W., Kriska, A. M., Fitzgerald, S. L., Aaron, D. J., Similo, S. L., et al. (2000). Longitudinal changes in physical activity in a biracial cohort during adolescence. *Medicine & Science in Sports & Exercise*, 32(8), 1445–1454.

Kipke, M., Iverson, E., & Booker, C. (2005). Community level risks for obesity. *Obesity Research*, 13, A7.

Kipping, R. R., Jago, R., & Lawlor, D. A. (2008). Obesity in children. Part 1: Epidemiology, measurement, risk factors, and screening. *British Medical Journal*, 337, 6.

Kittler, P., & Sucher, K. (2001). *Food and culture*. Belmont, CA: Wadsworth Thomson Learning.

Kjeldgaard, D., & Askegaard, S. (2006). The glocalization of youth culture: The global youth segment as structures of common difference. *Journal of Consumer Research, 33*(2), 231–247.

Koplan, J., Liverman, C., & Kraak, V. (Eds.). (2005). *Preventing childhood obesity: Health in the balance.* Washington, DC: National Academies Press.

Kraig, K. A., & Keel, P. K. (2001). Weight-based stigmatization in children. *International Journal of Obesity and Related Metabolic Disorders, 25*(11), 1661–1667.

Kumanyika, S. (1995). Cultural factors in desirable body shapes and their impact on weight loss and maintenance. *Obesity Treatment, 278,* 79–82.

Kumanyika, S. (2002). The minority factor in the obesity epidemic. *Ethnicity & Disease, 12*(3), 316–319.

Kumanyika, S. (2004). Cultural differences as influences on approaches to obesity treatment. In G. A. Bray & C. Bouchard (Eds.), *Handbook of obesity: Clinical applications* (2nd ed., pp. 45–67). New York: Marcel Dekker.

Kumanyika, S. (2007). Obesity prevention concepts and frameworks. In S. Kumanyika & R. C. Brownson (Eds.), *Handbook of obesity prevention: A resource for health professionals* (pp. 85–114). New York: Springer.

Kumanyika, S. K. (2008). Environmental influences on childhood obesity: Ethnic and cultural influences in context. *Physiology & Behavior, 94*(1), 61–70.

Kumanyika, S. K., & Grier, S. (2006). Targeting interventions for ethnic minority and low-income populations. *The Future of Children, 16*(1), 187–207.

Kumanyika, S. K., Whitt-Glover, M. C., Gary, T. L., Prewitt, T. E., Odoms-Young, A. M., Banks-Wallace, J., et al. (2007). Expanding the obesity research paradigm to reach African American communities. *Preventing Chronic Disease, 4*(4), 1–22.

Latner, J. D., & Stunkard, A. J. (2003). Getting worse: The stigmatization of obese children. *Obesity Research, 11*(3), 452–456.

Lewis, L. B., Sloane, D. C., Nascimento, L. M., Diamant, A. L., Guinyard, J. J., Yancey, A. K., et al. (2005). African Americans' access to healthy food options in South Los Angeles restaurants. *American Journal of Public Health, 95*(4), 668–673.

Maccoby, E. E. (2007). Historical overview of socialization research and theory. In J. E. Grusec & P. D. Hastings (Eds.), *Handbook of socialization* (pp. 13–41). New York: Guilford Press.

Maes, H. M., Neale, M. C., & Eaves, L. J. (1997). Genetic and environmental factors in relative body weight and human adiposity. *Behavior Genetics, 27*(4), 325–351.

Malik, V. S., Schulze, M. B., & Hu, F. B. (2006). Intake of sugar-sweetened beverages and weight gain: A systematic review. *American Journal of Clinical Nutrition, 84*(2), 274–288.

Martorell, R., Khan, L., Hughes, M., & Grummer-Strawn, L. (2000). Overweight and obesity in preschool children from developing countries. *International Journal of Obesity, 24*(8), 959–967.

Matheson, D. M., Robinson, T. N., Varady, A., & Killen, J. D. (2006). Do Mexican-American mothers' food-related parenting practices influence their children's weight and dietary intake? *Journal of the American Dietetic Association, 106*(11), 1861–1865.

May, A. L., Donohue, M., Scanlon, K. S., Sherry, B., Dalenius, K., Faulkner, P., et al. (2007). Child-feeding strategies are associated with maternal concern about children becoming overweight, but not children's weight status. *Journal of the American Dietetic Association, 107*(7), 1167–1174.

Maynard, L. M., Galuska, D. A., Blanck, H. M., & Serdula, M. K. (2003). Maternal perceptions of weight status of children. *Pediatrics, 111*(5), 1226–1231.

McGinnis, J. M., Gootman, J. A., & Kraak, V. I. (Eds.). (2006). *Food marketing to children and youth: Threat or opportunity?* Washington, DC: National Academies Press.

McLaren, L. (2007). Socioeconomic status and obesity. *Epidemiological Review, 29*(1), 29–48.

Mennella, J. A., Pepino, M. Y., & Reed, D. R. (2005). Genetic and environmental determinants of bitter perception and sweet preferences. *Pediatrics, 115*(2), e216–e222.

Molnar, B., Gortmaker, S., Bull, F., & Buka, S. (2004). Unsafe to play? Neighborhood disorder and lack of safety predict reduced physical activity among urban children and adolescents. *American Journal of Health Promotion, 18*(5), 378–386.

Moore, E. S. (2004). Children and the changing world of advertising. *Journal of Business Ethics, 52*(2), 161–167.

Moore, E. S., & Lutz, R. J. (2000). Children, advertising, and product experiences: A multimethod inquiry. *Journal of Consumer Research, 27*(1), 31–48.

Moore, E. S., & Rideout, V. J. (2007). The online marketing of food to children: Is it just fun and games? *Journal of Public Policy & Marketing, 26*(2), 202–220.

Moore, E. S., Wilkie, W. L., & Lutz, R. J. (2002). Passing the torch: Intergenerational influences as a source of brand equity. *Journal of Marketing, 66*(2), 17–37.

Morland, K., Wing, S., & Roux, A. D. (2002). The contextual effect of the local food environment on residents' diets: The atherosclerosis risk in communities study. *American Journal of Public Health.*, *92*(11), 1761–1767.

Musaiger, A., & Gregory, W. (2000). Profile of body composition of school children (6–18y) in Bahrain. *International Journal of Obesity*, *24*(9), 1093–1096.

Musher-Eizenman, D., Holub, S. C., Miller, A. B., Goldstein, S. E., & Edwards-Leeper, L. (2004). Body size stigmatization in preschool children: The role of control attributions. *Journal of Pediatric Psychology*, *29*(8), 613–620.

Nelson, M. C., Neumark-Stzainer, D., Hannan, P. J., Sirard, J. R., & Story, M. (2006). Longitudinal and secular trends in physical activity and sedentary behavior during adolescence. *Pediatrics*, *118*(6), e1627–e1634.

Neumark-Sztainer, D., Story, M., & Faibisch, L. (1998). Perceived stigmatization among overweight African-American and Caucasian adolescent girls. *Journal of Adolescent Health*, *23*(5), 264–270.

Neumark-Sztainer, D., Story, M., Hannan, P. J., & Croll, J. (2002). Overweight status and eating patterns among adolescents: Where do youths stand in comparison with the *Healthy People 2010* objectives? *American Journal of Public Health*, *92*, 844–851.

Nielsen, S. J., Siega-Riz, A. M., & Popkin, B. M. (2002). Trends in food locations and sources among adolescents and young adults. *Preventive Medicine*, *35*(2), 107–113.

O'Dea, J. A. (2008). Gender, ethnicity, culture and social class influences on childhood obesity among Australian schoolchildren: Implications for treatment, prevention and community education. *Health & Social Care in the Community*, *16*(3), 282–290.

Ogden, C. L., Carroll, M. D., Curtin, L. R., McDowell, M. A., Tabak, C. J., & Flegal, K. M. (2006). Prevalence of overweight and obesity in the United States, 1999-2004. *Journal of the American Medical Association*, *295*(13), 1549–1555.

Ogden, C. L., Carroll, M. D., & Flegal, K. M. (2008). High body mass index for age among U.S. children and adolescents, 2003-2006. *Journal of the American Medical Association*, *299*(20), 2401–2405.

Oldroyd, J., Banerjee, M., Heald, A., & Cruickshank, K. (2005). Diabetes and ethnic minorities. *Postgraduate Medical Journal*, *81*(958), 486–490.

Oliveria, S. A., Ellison, R. C., Moore, L. L., Gillman, M. W., Garrahie, E. J., & Singer, M. (1992). Parent–child relationships in nutrient intake: The Framingham Children's Study. *American Journal of Clinical Nutrition*, *56*(3), 593–598.

Owen, C. G., Martin, R. M., Whincup, P. H., Smith, G. D., & Cook, D. G. (2005). Effect of infant feeding on the risk of obesity across the life course: A quantitative review of published evidence. *Pediatrics*, *115*(5), 1367–1377.

Ozanne, J. L., & Saatcioglu, B. (2008). Participatory action research. *Journal of Consumer Research*, *35*(3), 423–439.

Palan, K. M., & Wilkes, R. E. (1997). Adolescent–parent interaction in family decision making. *Journal of Consumer Research*, *24*(2), 159–169.

Parsons, T. J., Power, C., Logan, S., & Summerbell, C. D. (1999). Childhood predictors of adult obesity: A systematic review. *International Journal of Obesity and Related Metabolic Disorders*, *23*(Suppl. 8), S1–S107.

Pechmann, C., Levine, L., Loughlin, S., & Leslie, F. (2005). Impulsive and self-conscious: Adolescents' vulnerability to advertising and promotion. *Journal of Public Policy & Marketing*, *24*(2), 202–221.

Penaloza, L. N. (1989). Immigrant consumer acculturation. In T. K. Srull (Ed.), *Advances in consumer research* (Vol. 16, pp. 110–118). Provo, UT: Association for Consumer Research.

Penaloza, L. (1995). *Atravesando fronteras*/border crossings: A critical ethnographic exploration of the consumer acculturation of Mexican immigrants. *Journal of Consumer Research*, *21*(1), 32–54.

Penny, H., & Haddock, G. (2007). Anti-fat prejudice among children: The "mere proximity" effect in 5–10 year olds. *Journal of Experimental Social Psychology*, *43*(4), 678–683.

Pliner, P., & Pelchat, M. L. (1986). Similarities in food preferences between children and their siblings and parents. *Appetite*, *7*(4), 333–342.

Popkin, B. M., & Udry, J. R. (1998). Adolescent obesity increases significantly in second and third generation U.S. immigrants: The National Longitudinal Study of Adolescent Health. *Journal of Nutrition*, *128*(4), 701–706.

Powell, L. M., Auld, M. C., Chaloupka, F. J., O'Malley, P. M., & Johnston, L. D. (2007). Associations between access to food stores and adolescent body mass index. *American Journal of Preventive Medicine*, *33*(4, Suppl. 1), S301–S307.

Powell, L. M., & Ba, Y. (2009). Food prices, access to food outlets and child weight. *Economics & Human Biology*, *7*(1), 64–72.

Powell, L. M., Slater, S., Mirtcheva, D., Bao, Y., & Chaloupka, F. J. (2006). Food store availability and neighborhood characteristics in the United States. *Preventive Medicine, 44*(3), 189–195.

Power, E. M. (2005). Determinants of healthy eating among low-income Canadians. *Canadian Journal of Public Health, 96*(Suppl. 3), S37–42.

Puhl, R. M., & Latner, J. D. (2007). Stigma, obesity, and the health of the nation's children. *Psychological Bulletin, 133*(4), 557–580.

Reed, D. R., Bachmanov, A. A., Beauchamp, G. K., Tordoff, M. G., & Price, R. A. (1997). Heritable variation in food preferences and their contribution to obesity. *Behavior Genetics, 27*(4), 373–387.

Renzaho, A. M. N. (2004). Fat, rich and beautiful: Changing socio-cultural paradigms associated with obesity risk, nutritional status and refugee children from sub-Saharan Africa. *Health & Place, 10,* 105–113.

Rguibi, M., & Belahsen, R. (2004). Overweight and obesity among urban Sahraoui women of South Morocco. *Ethnicity & Disease, 14,* 542–547.

Rguibi, M., & Belahsen, R. (2006). Body size preferences and sociocultural influences on attitudes towards obesity among Moroccan Sahraoui women. *Journal of Body Image, 3,* 359–400.

Rideout, V. J., Foehr, U. G., & Roberts, D. F. (2010). *Generation M²: Media in the lives of 8- to 18-year-olds.* Menlo Park, CA: Henry J. Kaiser Family Foundation.

Robinson, T. N. (1999). Reducing children's television viewing to prevent obesity: A randomized controlled trial. *Journal of the American Medical Association, 282*(16), 1561–1567.

Robinson, T. N., Kiernan, M., Matheson, D. M., & Haydel, K. F. (2001). Is parental control over children's eating associated with childhood obesity? Results from a population-based sample of third graders. *Obesity Research, 9*(5), 306–312.

Rolls, B. J., Engell, D., & Birch, L. L. (2000). Serving portion size influences 5-year-old but not 3-year-old children's food intakes. *Journal of the American Dietetic Association, 100*(2), 232–234.

Rothschild, M. L. (1999). Carrots, sticks, and promises. *Journal of Marketing, 63,* 24–27.

Rozin, P. (1991). Family resemblance in food and other domains: The family paradox and the role of parental congruence. *Appetite, 16*(2), 93–102.

Rozin, P. (1999). Attitudes to food and the role of food in life in the U.S.A., Japan, Flemish Belgium and France: Possible implications for the diet–health debate. *Appetite, 33*(2), 163–180.

Sallis, J. F., & Glanz, K. (2006). The role of built environments in physical activity, eating, and obesity in childhood. *The Future of Children, 16*(1), 89–108.

Salvy, S. J., Bowker, J. W., Roemmich, J. N., Romero, N., Kieffer, E., Paluch, R., et al. (2008). Peer influence on children's physical activity: An experience sampling study. *Journal of Pediatric Psychology, 33*(1), 39–49.

Salvy, S. J., Coelho, J. S., Kieffer, E., & Epstein, L. H. (2007). Effects of social contexts on overweight and normal-weight children's food intake. *Physiology & Behavior, 92*(5), 840–846.

Salvy, S. J., Romero, N., Paluch, R., & Epstein, L. H. (2007). Peer influence on pre-adolescent girls' snack intake: Effects of weight status. *Appetite, 49*(1), 177–182.

Savage, J. S., Fisher, J. O., & Birch, L. L. (2007). Parental influence on eating behavior: Conception to adolescence. *Journal of Law, Medicine & Ethics, 35*(1), 22–34.

Saxena, S., Ambler, G., Cole, T., & Majeed, A. (2004). Ethnic group differences in overweight and obese children and young people in England: Cross sectional survey. *Archives of Disease in Childhood, 89,* 30–36.

Sobal, J., & Stunkard, A. J. (1989). Socioeconomic status and obesity: A review of the literature. *Psychological Bulletin, 105*(2), 260–275.

Spruijt-Metz, D., Lindquist, C. H., Birch, L. L., Fisher, J. O., & Goran, M. I. (2002). Relation between mothers' child-feeding practices and children's adiposity. *American Journal of Clinical Nutrition, 75*(3), 581–586.

Stayman, D., & Deshpande, R. (1989). Situational ethnicity and consumer behavior. *Journal of Consumer Research, 16*(3), 361–371.

Steinberg, L., & Morris, A. S. (2001). Adolescent development. *Annual Review of Psychology, 52*(1), 83–110.

Stettler, N. (2004). The global epidemic of childhood obesity: Is there a role for the paediatrician? *Obesity Reviews, 5*(Suppl. 1), 1–3.

Stice, E., Shaw, H., & Marti, N. (2006). A meta-analytic review of obesity prevention programs for children and adolescents: The skinny on interventions that work. *Psychological Bulletin, 132*(5), 667–691.

Storch, E. A., Milsom, V. A., Debraganza, N., Lewin, A. B., Geffken, G. R., & Silverstein, J. H. (2007). Peer victimization, psychosocial adjustment, and physical activity in overweight and at-risk-for-overweight youth. *Journal of Pediatric Psychology, 32*(1), 80–89.

Story, M., Kaphingst, K. M., Robinson-O'Brien, R., & Glanz, K. (2008). Creating healthy food and eating environments: Policy and environmental approaches. *Annual Review of Public Health, 29*(1), 253–272.

Story, M., Neumark-Sztainer, D., & French, S. (2002). Individual and environmental influences on adolescent eating behaviors. *Journal of the American Dietetic Association, 102*(3), S40–S51.

Story, M. T., Neumark-Stzainer, D. R., Sherwood, N., Holt, K., Sofka, D. L.,Trowbridge, F., & Barlow, S. E. (2002). Management of child and adolescent obesity: Attitudes, barriers, skills, and training needs among health care professionals. *Pediatrics, 110*(1), 210–214.

Strauss, R. S., & Pollack, H. A. (2003). Social marginalization of overweight children. *Archives of Pediatrics & Adolescent Medicine, 157*(8), 746–752.

Strauss, R. S., Rodzilsky, D., Burack, G., & Colin, M. (2001). Psychosocial correlates of physical activity in healthy children. *Archives of Pediatrics & Adolescent Medicine, 155*(8), 897–902.

Sturm, R. (2005a). Childhood obesity—what we can learn from existing data on societal trends, part 1. *Preventing Chronic Disease, 2*(1). Available: http://www.cdc.gov/pcd/issues/2005/jan/pdf/04_0038.pdf

Sturm, R. (2005b). Childhood obesity—what we can learn from existing data on societal trends, part 2. *Preventing Chronic Disease, 2*(2). Available: http://www.cdc.gov/pcd/issues/2005/apr/04_0039.htm

Taylor, P., Passel, J., Fry, R., Morin, R., Wang, W., Velasco, G., et al. (2010). *The return of the multi-generational family household.* Washington, DC: Pew Research Center.

Tershakovec, A. M., Watson, M. H., Wenner, W. J., & Marx, A. L. (1999). Insurance reimbursement for the treatment of obesity in children. *Journal of Pediatrics, 134*(5), 573–578.

Tiggemann, M., & Anesbury, T. (2000). Negative stereotyping of obesity in children: The role of controllability beliefs. *Journal of Applied Social Psychology, 30*(9), 1977–1993.

Tremblay, M. S., & Williams, J. D. (2003). Is the Canadian childhood obesity epidemic related to physical inactivity? *International Journal of Obesity and Related Metabolic Disorders, 27*(9), 1100–1105.

Triandis, H. C. (1989). The self and social behavior in differing cultural contexts. *Psychological Review, 96*(3), 506–520.

Trost, S. G., Pate, R. R., Sallis, J. F., Freedson, P. S., Taylor, W. C., Dowda, M., et al. (2002). Age and gender differences in objectively measured physical activity in youth. *Medicine & Science in Sports & Exercise, 34*(2), 350–355.

Trost, S. G., Sirard, J. R., Dowda, M., Pfeiffer, K. A., & Pate, R. R. (2003). Physical activity in overweight and non-overweight preschool children. *International Journal of Obesity and Related Metabolic Disorders, 27*(7), 834–839.

Turnbull, J. D., Heaslip, S., & McLeod, H. A. (2000). Pre-school children's attitudes to fat and normal male and female stimulus figures. *International Journal of Obesity and Related Metabolic Disorders, 24*(12), 1705–1706.

Unger, J. B., Reynolds, K., Shakib, S., Spruijt-Metz, D., Sun, P., & Johnson, C. A. (2004). Acculturation, physical activity, and fast-food consumption among Asian-American and Hispanic adolescents. *Journal of Community Health, 29*(6), 467–481.

Variyam, J. N. (2001). Overweight children: Is parental nutrition knowledge a factor? *Food Review, 24*(2), 18–22.

Vartanian, L. R., Schwartz, M. B., & Brownell, K. D. (2007). Effects of soft drink consumption on nutrition and health: A systematic review and meta-analysis. *American Journal of Public Health, 97*(4), 667–675.

Ventura, A. K., & Birch, L. L. (2008). Does parenting affect children's eating and weight status? *International Journal of Behavioral Nutrition and Physical Activity, 5*, 15.

Wang, Y. (2001). Cross-national comparison of childhood obesity: The epidemic and the relationship between obesity and socioeconomic status. *International Journal of Epidemiology, 30*, 1129–1136.

Wang, Y., & Beydoun, M. A. (2007). The obesity epidemic in the United States—gender, age, socioeconomic, racial/ethnic, and geographic characteristics: A systematic review and meta-regression analysis. *Epidemiological Review, 29*(1), 6–28.

Wang, Y., Monteiro, C., & Popkin, B. M. (2002). Trends of obesity and underweight in older children and adolescents in the United States, Brazil, China, and Russia. *American Journal of Clinical Nutrition, 75*(6), 971–977.

Wardle, J. (1995). Parental influences on children's diets. *Proceedings of the Nutrition Society, 544*(3), 747–758.

Wardle, J., Carnell, S., & Cooke, L. (2005). Parental control over feeding and children's fruit and vegetable intake: How are they related? *Journal of the American Dietetic Association, 105*(2), 227–232.

Wardle, J., & Cooke, L. (2005). The impact of obesity on psychological well-being. *Best Practice Research in Clinical Endocrinology & Metabolism, 19*(3), 421–440.

Wardle, J., & Cooke, L. J. (2008). Genetic and environmental determinants of children's food preferences. *British Journal of Nutrition, 99*(Suppl.), S15–S21.

Wardle, J., Volz, C., & Golding, C. (1995). Social variation in attitudes to obesity in children. *International Journal of Obesity and Related Metabolic Disorders, 19*(8), 562–569.

Wells, J. C. K., Stanley, M., Laidlaw, A. S., Day, J. M. E., Stafford, M., & Davies, P. S. W. (1997). Investigation of the relationship between infant temperament and later body composition. *International Journal of Obesity and Related Metabolic Disorders, 21*(5), 400–406.

Whitacre, P. T., Tsai, P., & Mulligan, J. (Eds.). (2009). *The public health effects of food deserts: Workshop summary.* Washington, DC: National Academies Press.

Whitaker, R. C., Wright, J. A., Pepe, M. S., Seidel, K. D., & Dietz, W. H. (1997). Predicting obesity in young adulthood from childhood and parental obesity. *New England Journal of Medicine, 337*(13), 869–873.

Whitt-Glover, M., & Kumanyika, S. K. (2009). Systematic review of interventions to increase physical activity and physical fitness in African-Americans. *American Journal of Health Promotion, 23*(6), S33–S56.

Will, B., Zeeb, H., & Baune, B. (2005). Overweight and obesity at school entry among migrant and German children: A cross-sectional study. *BMC Public Health, 5*(1), 45.

Wong, F., Huhman, M., Heitzler, C., Asbury, L., Bretthauer-Mueller, R., McCarthy, S., et al. (2003). VERB™—a social marketing campaign to increase physical activity among youth. *Preventing. Chronic Disease, 1*(3). Available: http://www.cdc.gov/pcd/issues/2004/jul/04_0043.htm

World Health Organization. (2009). *Childhood overweight and obesity.* Retrieved February 23, 2009, from http://www.who.int/dietphysicalactivity/childhood/en/index.html

Wrigley, N., Warm, D., & Margetts, B. (2003). Deprivation, diet, and food-retail access: Findings from the Leeds "food deserts" study. *Environment and Planning, 35*(1), 151–188.

Yamamoto, J., Yamamoto, B., & Yamamoto, L. (2005). Adolescent fast food and restaurant ordering behavior with and without calorie and fat content menu information. *Journal of Adolescent Health, 37*, 397–402.

Yancey, A. K., Cole, B. L., Brown, R., Williams, J. D., Hillier, A., Kline, R. S., et al. (2009). A cross-sectional prevalence study of ethnically targeted and general audience outdoor obesity-related advertising. *Milbank Quarterly, 87*(1), 155–184.

Yancey, A. K., Fielding, J. E., Flores, G. R., Sallis, J. F., William, J. M., & Breslow, L. (2007). Creating a robust public health infrastructure for physical activity promotion. *American Journal of Preventive Medicine, 32*(1), 68–78.

Yancey, A. K., Kumanyka, S. K., Ponce, N. A., McCarthy, W. J., Fielding, J. E., Leslie, J. P., et al. (2004). Population-based interventions engaging communitites of color in healthy eating and active learning: A review. *Preventing Chronic Disease, 1*(1), 1–18.

Young, L. R., & Nestle, M. (2002). The contribution of expanding portion sizes to the US obesity epidemic. *American Journal of Public Health, 92*(2), 246–249.

Zeller, M. H., Boles, R. E., & Reiter-Purtill, J. (2008). The additive and interactive effects of parenting style and temperament in obese youth seeking treatment. *International Journal of Obesity, 32*(10), 1474–1480.

Zeller, M. H., Reiter-Purtill, J., & Ramey, C. (2008). Negative peer perceptions of obese children in the classroom environment. *Obesity, 16*(4), 755–762.

Zhou, M. (1997). Growing up American: The challenge confronting immigrant children and children of immigrants. *Annual Review of Sociology, 23*, 63–95.

Zive, M. M., McKay, H., Frank-Spohrer, G., Broyles, S. L., Nelson, J. A., & Nader, P. R. (1992). Infant-feeding practices and adiposity in 4-y-old Anglo- and Mexican-Americans. *American Journal of Clinical Nutrition, 55*(6), 1104–1108.

# 16

# *Processing and Acting on Nutrition Labeling on Food*
## The State of Knowledge and New Directions for Transformative Consumer Research

Klaus G. Grunert, Lisa E. Bolton, and Monique M. Raats

Noncommunicable diseases (e.g., cardiovascular diseases, diabetes, cancers, chronic respiratory diseases) were globally estimated to cause 60% of all deaths in 2005 (World Health Organization, 2005). Five of the 10 leading causes of death were related to noncommunicable diseases, an estimate expected to rise to 8 of 10 by 2030 (World Health Organization, 2008). Diet is a major modifiable risk factor underlying chronic diseases (World Cancer Research Fund & American Institute for Cancer Research, 2007; World Health Organization, 2005).

Nutrition labeling is widely regarded as one of the most promising instruments for fighting unhealthy eating habits and rising obesity rates (Baltas, 2001). Nutrition labeling refers to a list of nutrients on a food label along with some means of quantification (Hawkes, 2004). From a policy perspective, it holds the promise of furthering healthy eating while preserving freedom of choice. From a consumer perspective, it provides a means of reducing the information asymmetry that exists between producers and consumers by providing product-specific information. From a producer or retailer perspective, it provides a means of exhibiting positive nutritional characteristics of products in a credible way.

In this chapter, we will give a brief introduction to the current practice of nutrition labeling in the United States and the European Union. We will then address the question of how nutrition labeling affects consumer behavior, reviewing extant research and proposing an agenda for future research. Our discussion will focus on the effects of nutrition labeling that occur via their impact on consumer behavior. Labeling may also have effects on the supply side; for example, as labeling makes certain nutritional properties of a product more visible, new product development and product reformulation may take place to create positive nutritional profiles. Such effects, although potentially very important from a public health perspective, will not be addressed in this chapter (for investigation of such effects, see Moorman, 1998; Moorman, Du, & Mela, 2005).

## NUTRITION LABELING IN THE UNITED STATES AND EUROPEAN UNION: AN OVERVIEW

When examining the history of nutrition labeling in the United States, Golan, Kuchler, Mitchell, Greene, and Amber (2001) reported the first explicit reports linking labels with the social goal of health of the nation to the White House Conference on Food, Nutrition, and Health in 1969. One of the major recommendations from this conference was that the federal government should consider developing a system for identifying the nutritional qualities of food to help address deficiencies in the U.S. diet (U.S. Food and Drug Administration [FDA], 1998). Around the world, regulation by transparency has become an important regulatory tool, of which nutritional labeling is one form (Weil, Fung, Graham, & Fagotto, 2006). The U.S. Nutrition Labeling and Education Act (NLEA), enacted in 1990, explicitly seeks to reduce heart disease, cancer, and other chronic diseases through changing consumers' habits and encouraging companies to market healthier products. In their review of transparency policies, Weil et al. (2006) concluded that these policies are only effective when the information they produce becomes embedded in the everyday decision-making routines of information users and information disclosers.

Prior to the NLEA, nutrition labeling in the United States was voluntary. The NLEA mandated that packaged foods display a nutrition facts panel, listing selected nutrients per food serving as well as nutrients as a percentage of recommended daily values. An additional labeling requirement for trans fat content went into effect in 2006. The U.S. Department of Agriculture's Food Safety and Inspection Service adopted similar labeling rules for meat, poultry, and eggs. In contrast, labeling is not mandated for raw produce. A sample U.S. nutrition panel is shown in Figure 16.1. Usually, this panel appears on the side or back of packaging (BOP). Although the FDA estimated the monetary value of the health benefits of the NLEA at $4.4 to $26.5 billion in 1991, compared against estimated costs of $1.4 to $2.3 billion to implement, research is scant on whether these health benefits were achieved (Variyam & Cawley, 2006).

More recently, various voluntary labeling schemes, many of them appearing on the front of packaging (FOP), have been adopted by industry to augment the nutrition facts panel in the United States. Many of these are health logos, that is, logos awarded to products regarded as nutritionally superior based on selected criteria (see Figure 16.1 for some examples). Some of these labels

**Figure 16.1**   Examples of nutrition labels in the United States.
*Note:* Heart Check Mark is a registered trademark of the American Heart Association, Inc.

are awarded by independent bodies, like the American Heart Association's heart-check mark for foods that meet certain fat, sodium, and other criteria. Others are run by firms, like Kraft's Sensible Solution program, which identifies products that are "better for you" among Kraft offerings with a green flag. Finally, a health logo effort of multiple firms (e.g., Kraft, Kellogg, Unilever) was voluntarily halted after a short period in 2009. The Smart Choices program featured a green checkmark label and labeling decisions were guided by a panel of food executives, academics, and health academics. However, the program was widely criticized when the Smart Choice label appeared on products like Fruit Loops and Fudgsicle. According to FDA Commissioner Margaret Hamburg, "There's a growing proliferation of forms and symbols, check marks, numerical ratings, stars, icons and the like.... There's truly a cacophony of approaches, not unlike the tower of Babel" (CBS News, 2009, para. 12). The FDA has announced intentions to review voluntary FOP labels for misleading health claims and to research labeling that would help consumers make healthier choices, including the challenging question of realistic serving sizes. There have also been recent initiatives to institute nutrition labeling of restaurant menus, such as the Menu Education and Labeling Act, which was introduced but never passed at the federal level, and various state and city initiatives in the United States.

Mandatory nutrition-labeling legislation can also be found in other countries, including Argentina, Australia, Canada, Israel, Malaysia, and New Zealand (Hawkes, 2004). In the European Union, giving nutrition information on food labels is voluntary, unless the product carries a nutrition or health claim, that is, promotes certain nutritional or health-related properties (for overviews of the E.U. situation, see Cheftel, 2005; Przyrembel, 2004). The European Commission, which is the executive body of the European Union, has presented a proposal for making such information compulsory, including easily legible FOP information. In addition, numerous voluntary schemes are in place in the European Union, some promoted by major food producers or retail chains. BOP information is usually a table or list giving information on content of various nutrients in grams per 100 grams, per serving, and/or per package, supplemented with information on calories. In addition, the per serving information may also be stated as a percentage of guideline daily allowances (GDA), which are a guide to the amount of energy (calories) and maximum amount of some nutrients (e.g., fat, saturated fat/saturates, salt, sugars) a person should eat in a day; it is usually computed for an adult female with a moderate level of physical activity.

FOP information is more simplified, and three types of FOP labeling are prevalent: GDA labels, traffic light labels, and health logos. GDA labels usually give information on calories, fat, saturated fat, sugar, and salt both in grams per serving and in percentage of the GDA. GDA labels are promoted by parts of the food industry and have been adopted by several multinational food producers as well as some major retail chains. Traffic light labels also give information on calories and the four key nutrients (i.e., fat, saturated fat, sugar, salt); instead of GDA percentages for nutrients and calories, these labels are color-coded as red, yellow, or green to reflect whether the nutrient and energy content is high, medium, or low, based on some preestablished standards. Traffic light labels are used by some producers and retail chains in the United Kingdom, where the Food Standards Agency (2007) has set nutrition criteria for the red, amber, and green colorcoding that provides information on the high, medium, or low levels of individual nutrients in the product. Traffic light labels are the type of label preferred by most European consumer associations, many of which look with some suspicion at GDA labels, which they believe are too complicated for consumers to use and may be misleading (BEUC, 2006). Finally, health logos are used in Europe as well. The best known and oldest example in Europe is the Swedish keyhole logo, which signals that a product contains less fat, less sugar, less salt, and more fiber than similar products in the same category; a newer example is the Healthy Choice logo promoted by the Choices International Foundation. Sometimes these three types of labels are designated as nondirective, semidirective, and directive, based on the extent to which they direct consumers to what to buy if they want to make a healthier choice (Hodgkins et al., 2009). Figure 16.2 shows examples of the major formats used in Europe.

A recent audit of almost 40,000 products in all 27 E.U. member states and Turkey (Storcksdieck genannt Bonsmann et al., 2010) showed that 85% of the products had BOP nutrition information, and 48% also had FOP nutrition information. GDA labels were the most common form of FOP nutrition information (25% of the products audited). In the United States, a 1995 survey indicated that 96% of processed foods had nutrition facts labels (as cited in French, Story, & Jeffery, 2001). Thus, use of nutrition labeling is widespread, which begs the questions as to whether and how it works.

## APPROACHES TO ANALYZING THE EFFECTS OF NUTRITION LABELING

The effects of nutrition labeling on consumer behavior can be analyzed from producer and public health perspectives. Although a food producer may have a genuine interest in contributing to public health, nutrition labeling is also a positioning and branding tool for the producer. For example, the mere presence of a FOP nutrition label on a range of products might be perceived by consumers as an indicator of overall healthiness of the product line. The major difference between a producer perspective and a public health perspective, though, is that a producer perspective is primarily concerned with the effect of nutrition labeling on brand choice, whereas a public health perspective is primarily concerned with a healthier overall dietary intake—goals that are not necessarily aligned and may frequently compete. When analyzing the effects of nutrition labeling on consumer behavior, it therefore makes sense to distinguish between effects on brand choice and effects on dietary intake. In this chapter, and in line with the philosophy of Transformative Consumer Research, we will look at the effects of nutrition labeling on consumer behavior both in terms of brand choice and in terms of effects on dietary intake.

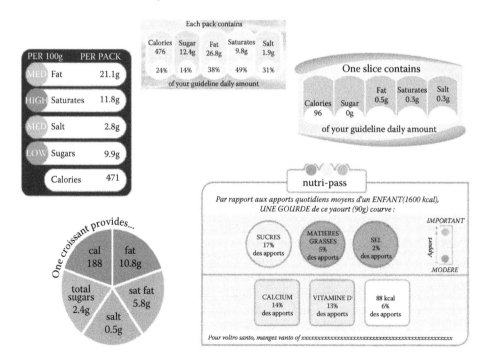

**Figure 16.2**   Examples of nutrition labels in Europe.

Brand Choice

To understand the impact of nutrition labeling on brand choice, a broad range of theoretical concepts may be invoked. One simple way of structuring the problem area is to use a dual-processing hierarchy of effects framework, as illustrated in Figure 16.3 (see also Balasubramanian & Cole, 2002; Grunert & Wills, 2007; Moorman, 1990). Consumers need to be exposed to the nutrition information. BOP nutrition information will mostly require intentional exposure inasmuch as consumers have to turn the package around and look at the back in order to see the information, whereas FOP nutrition information is more likely to result in incidental exposure. Perception of the BOP information is therefore most likely dependent on the consumer's motivation and ability to process nutrition information and use nutritional content as a criterion in decision making, whereas perception of FOP information also will be affected by the attention-getting properties of the label. If (part of) the nutrition label is indeed perceived, further processing can follow two paths.

Path 1 (see Figure 16.3) is cognitively dominated and involves conscious efforts to assign meaning to the labeling information. The process of assigning meaning can be subdivided into understanding and inferences. Understanding includes, for example, whether the consumer understands the concepts on which the information is based (e.g., whether the information is per serving or per 100 grams), understands the definition of GDA, and understands what a health logo stands for. Inferences are the conclusions about the healthiness of the product that the consumer draws from his or her understanding of the label; in addition, nutrition labels can serve as the basis for inferring other product attributes, like the taste. Both understanding and inferences depend on the nutritional competence of the consumer, that is, their declarative (e.g., too much saturated fat is unhealthy) and procedural (e.g., how to choose a low-sugar product) knowledge with regard to nutrition and healthy eating. This includes knowledge about expert recommendations (e.g., "Do not eat too much fat"), about nutritional properties of certain products (e.g., alcohol is high in calories, fish is high in unsaturated fat), principles of healthy eating (e.g., "Eat a varied diet"), and making trade-offs in choices (e.g., "Salt content is more important than calories" or vice versa, depending on your health status). Health inferences may not be based on the nutrition label alone, as perceptions of the healthiness of product categories differ considerably, and consumers may infer healthiness also from a range of other indicators, like degree of processing, use of additives, organic production, or the brand. Nutrition and health will, in most cases, not be the only criterion in food choice, and hence the effect of the nutrition information on brand choice will depend on how the inferences made about healthiness will be integrated with or traded off against other criteria, like taste, family liking, convenience, and price.

Path 1, sketched above, traces the cognitive effects of nutrition labeling, and processing via this path will depend on the levels of both motivation and ability to process nutrition information when buying food. However, food is frequently bought, some product categories may be low-involvement purchases for the consumer, and many brand choices may be habit based. In addition, nutrition and health may not even be prominent motives in some people's food choices. In such cases, the nutrition-labeling information may just be ignored, or it may have affective effects as described by path 2 in Figure 16.3. We have already noted that the mere presence of a FOP nutrition label can be taken as a signal of healthiness, and our framework proposes that such labels may also elicit affective responses. For example, the presence of green or red traffic lights on the FOP may elicit positive or negative emotions that impact brand choice without further cognitive processing. The literature has typically not distinguished between these paths and tended to focus on cognitive responses; research on affective response to nutritional labeling is scant.

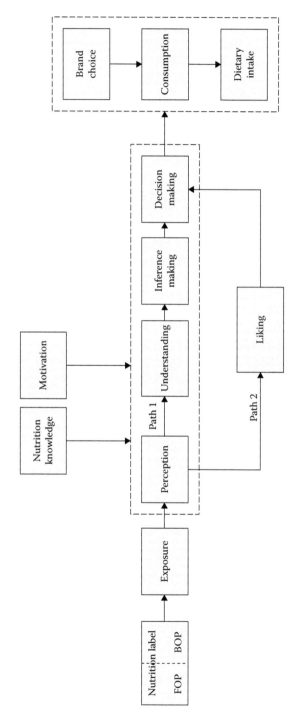

**Figure 16.3** Hierarchy of effects model of nutrition labeling.
*Note:* BOP = back of packaging; FOP = front of packaging.

Dietary Intake

From a dietary intake perspective, nutritional labeling should result in healthier choices in a product category, which should, in turn, have a positive, albeit small, effect on the healthiness of overall dietary intake (Roodenburg, Temme, Howell, & Seidell, 2009). However, several important qualifiers affect whether this conclusion can be drawn. First, the nutrition label must have driven the healthier choice; hence, determining whether consumers are able to use labels correctly and whether such labels impact choice is an important precursor of effects on dietary intake. Second, the positive effect of healthier choices assumes that all other aspects of buying, preparing, and eating food remain the same, which is an assumption that may be questionable. The label may affect the quantity eaten within the category (e.g., consumers may eat more of a product if they perceive it as low-fat) or across categories (e.g., eating healthier during regular meals may lead consumers to think they can indulge in more snacking), and even changes in meal patterns and eating habits (e.g., substituting dining out for ready-made meals after realizing the latter are high in fat and salt). The single-brand choice represents one of a large number of decisions that have an impact on dietary intake. In addition to the totality of brand choices in the food area, dietary impact will be influenced by decisions on menus, meal preparation methods, choice of recipes, eating in versus eating out, meal patterns, and snacking habits. Although many of these may not be directly affected by nutrition labels, indirect effects may occur that either reinforce or counteract healthier brand choices. Given this complexity, the net effects of nutrition labeling on dietary intake at the aggregate level are probably not huge.

Compared to explaining brand choices, the body of consumer-behavior theory we can draw from is considerably sparser when it comes to explaining meal preparation, meal patterns, and other aspects of dietary intake at the aggregate level. Economic models of demand have possible substitutions between various product categories built in, and although relative prices are viewed as the primary determinant of demand in economics, effects of information, including health information, are being analyzed as part of demand models (see, e.g., Mazocchi, Traill, & Shogren, 2009). Sociological approaches have also been employed to analyze changes in meal patterns in response to changes in society, and the introduction of nutrition labeling can be viewed as an aspect of changing societal discourse on health that impacts also on meal patterns (e.g., Mennel, Murcott, & van Otterloo, 1992). The question of how nutrition labeling affects dietary intake remains, therefore, largely unanswered.

## PREVIOUS RESEARCH ON NUTRITION LABELING

Consumer research on the effects of nutrition labeling has been conducted for decades (for previous reviews, see Cowburn & Stockley, 2005; Drichoutis, Lazaridis, & Nayga, 2006; Grunert & Wills, 2007). Such research has tended to drill deep on certain effects of nutrition labeling, for example, focusing only on one or few dependent variables, like self-reported use of the label or liking different label formats. The following section highlights some of the results that have been obtained in existing research.

### Motivation to Process Nutrition Labels

In their review of European research on the topic, Grunert and Wills (2007) concluded that there is "a surprising degree of consistency in the conclusions about consumer interest in nutrition information and in their interest in getting this information from nutrition labels on food products" (p. 389). Their review suggested that consumers were generally aware of the link between food and health, indicated an interest in nutrition, and also expressed an interest in getting information about the nutritional properties of the food they eat. It was also clear, however, that nutrition information was not the top interest with regard to food, even in those countries where nutrition issues are of higher interest. In a Dutch study, for example, informants would rather talk about tasty food, food safety, or issues like genetically modified foods than nutrition (van Dillen, Hiddink, Koelen, de Graaf, & van Woerkum, 2003). In a Swedish study, respondents ranked health and nutrition sixth in importance after food safety, freshness, taste, lack of pesticides, and animal welfare (Svederberg, 2002). In a study on what kind of information consumers would like to see on meat labels in Europe, nutrition information was rated as of medium importance, lower than information on origin and the best before date (Bernues, Olaizola, & Corcoran, 2003). Demographic differences exist: Women have a higher interest in nutrition than men, interest in health and nutrition increases with age, and there is more interest in Northern compared to Southern Europe. Interest in getting nutritional information was also higher for products with a higher degree of processing, and less for products that are regarded as a treat; it was also higher when products were bought for the first time. Across a range of studies, the nutrition information that respondents were most interested in were calories and fat, followed by sugar, salt, carbohydrates, vitamins, and calcium. As expected, motivation to process nutrition information is related to actually processing label information, both in a lab setting (Moorman, 1990) and in the real world (Grunert, Fernández-Celemin, Wills, Storcksdieck genannt Bonsmann, & Nureeva, 2010). That is, motivation drives consumers to process nutrition labels along path 1 in Figure 16.3.

### Nutrition Knowledge

Knowledge or ability is an important driver of behavior, although the influence of nutrition knowledge on food-related behaviors has not received consistent support from the scientific literature (Worseley, 2002). In his review, Worseley drew on the distinction between (a) declarative knowledge, that is, knowledge of "what is" and awareness of things and processes (e.g., good sources of particular nutrients or diet–disease relationships), and (b) procedural knowledge, that is, knowledge about how to do things (e.g., how to choose a low-salt product). There is some evidence of a relationship between higher nutrition knowledge and healthier food intakes (e.g., Wardle, Parmenter, & Waller, 2000). Overall, however, Worseley suggested that the lack of significant evidence for nutrition knowledge improving dietary behaviors is a result of (a) poor conceptualization of nutrition knowledge, (b) lack of relevance (e.g., saturated fat knowledge may be more relevant to middle-aged consumers than teenagers), (c) poor measurement (i.e., lack of well-validated questionnaires), (d) poor matching of knowledge and outcome variables, and (e) small studies (i.e., no statistical power to detect any influence; see also Obayashi, Bianchi, & Song, 2003). Turning to the processing of nutrition labels, Elbon, Johnson, Fischer, and Searcy (2000) found that high nutrition knowledge and positive nutrition-related health-seeking behaviors (i.e., interest) were strongly associated with the reading of nutrition information panels on food products. However, such effects may not be forthcoming if consumers with higher levels of nutrition knowledge feel that processing of nutrition labels is unnecessary. Hence, nutrition knowledge may be a second factor, beyond motivation, that affects path 1 processing in Figure 16.3, but support for this relationship is weaker, compared to motivation, in the literature.

### Self-Reported Perception and Use in Decision Making

By far, most research carried out on perception and use of nutrition information on food labels is based on self-reported measures; that is, respondents are asked, "How often do you read...?" or "How often do you use...when buying...?" Reading and use are often treated as synonymous in this type of research, and it may indeed be difficult to ask consumers whether they read but did not use nutrition information. However, these processes are conceptually distinct, and reading may not imply use. In their review of nutrition-labeling research conducted until 2002, Cowburn and Stockley (2005) concluded that "most consumers claimed to look at nutrition labels often or at least sometimes" (p. 24). The review of research after 2002 by Grunert and Wills (2007) comes to a similar conclusion, finding that usually about 50% of the sample claimed that they read or used nutrition information always or often. Women reported more use than men, and people with higher levels of education and higher incomes reported more frequent use, as do people with higher levels of interest in health and nutrition and/or with a health status that implies special dietary needs. Higher levels of nutritional knowledge also correlated with higher self-reported use. When asked for reasons for not using nutrition labels, factors mentioned include lack of time, small print, lack of understanding, and concerns about accuracy of the information. Other information available on the food package, like the presence of a health claim, may also impact the likelihood of reported label use (Roe, Levy, & Derby, 1999).

Measures of self-reported retrospective behavior can lead to considerable overreporting with regard to behaviors that are regarded as socially desirable (Podsakoff, MacKenzie, Lee, & Podsakoff, 2003), and as we will note below, more direct evidence on reading and use of nutrition information in the shops has suggested that actual reading and usage rates may be considerably lower. A recent study conducted in six European countries (Grunert et al., 2010) that employed both observation of purchases and measures of self-reported use when buying the same product category found levels of overreporting varying between 0% and 100% and suggested that some of these differences may be attributable to differences in how much health and nutrition have been prominent in the public discourse in those countries. Also, self-reported use does not distinguish whether processing followed the cognitive path 1 or the affective path 2 (Figure 16.3).

### Liking Different Labeling Formats

A range of studies has looked at consumer liking or preferences for different label types and formats. However, most of these studies, although sometimes highly cited in the public debate on nutrition labeling, are not specific about the theoretical status of liking. In our framework, liking is an affective reaction (path 2 in Figure 16.3), whereby nutrition labels can affect choice with minimal cognitive processing. Grunert and Wills (2007), in reviewing the evidence on consumers liking different labeling formats, suggested three underlying dimensions (see also Levy, Fein, & Schucker, 1996). First, consumers like simplification. They know that in a real shopping situation, they have limited time and opportunity to look at comprehensive, especially BOP, nutrition information. They also find it difficult to interpret various nutrients and compare numbers and are generally wary about the cognitive load that comes with trying to make use of nutrient tables. Second, consumers may be wary of simplification and respond negatively. When presented with simplified information like traffic lights or health logos, consumers want to know what the simplified information stands for (e.g., how the red light or the health logo was determined) and are wary of letting even credible others make these judgments for them. Third, nutrition information can create resistance in consumers when they feel coerced or pushed to make choices that they do not want. Obviously, these three responses may conflict, and consumers may differ in the weight with which these responses determine their liking for various labeling formats.

Such heterogeneity may explain why results on liking different formats are not always clear, especially when comparisons are made across the three major formats of FOP labeling (i.e., GDA labels, traffic light labels, health logos). Health logos are simple, but consumers may be suspicious about the underlying criteria. GDA labels are much more complete in the information provided but are more complex. Traffic light labels are somewhere in between, with the color-coding reducing the complexity but, at the same time, possibly adding an element of perceived coerciveness that could lead to reactance. Results on liking are considerably more clear-cut when the basic type of label is held constant and only presentational elements are changed, with a higher liking for bigger fonts, use of colors, and use of whole numbers instead of decimals.

### Understanding and Health Inferences

Understanding has two distinct dimensions: subjective understanding (i.e., whether consumers believe they understand the label information) and objective understanding (i.e., whether the consumer interprets the information correctly based on some external standard). Subjective understanding is usually high, especially for the simplified FOP formats. Objective understanding, unsurprisingly, depends on the design of the task. Usually, a majority of respondents can correctly recall information given on one nutrient, although the percentage of correct answers may depend on the format in which the information is given. For example, a study commissioned by the Food Standards Agency (2005) in the United Kingdom asked respondents to evaluate whether a product was high, medium, or low on two key nutrients. Of four formats tested, the multiple traffic lights format led to most correct answers, ahead of the color-coded GDA information, presumably because the multiple traffic lights provided exactly this information. However, when respondents were asked which of two products was higher on these two key nutrients, the color-coded GDA outperformed the traffic light system. In another study (Conquest Research, 2006), the multiple traffic lights system clearly outperformed various versions of a GDA-based system when the task was to find out whether the level of four nutrients in the product was low, medium, or high. A U.S. study (Levy, Fein & Schucker, 1996) showed that the format in which respondents performed best in comparing nutrient content across products was different from the format that best facilitated computing overall daily intakes of a particular nutrient, which again was different from the format best for finding out how to balance a diet across nutrients. Most of these results can be interpreted on the background of the simple hypothesis that share of correct answers increases in line with a decrease in the requirements for processing the information provided in order to give a correct answer. That is, objective understanding improves when the measure matches the label. Such measurement artifact makes it difficult to determine whether label formats actually affect true comprehension.

Research on inference making from nutrition labeling is more limited, and again, results depend on characteristics of the study design. When respondents were asked to compare or rank two or three products from the same product category in terms of overall healthiness, based on some kind of FOP-labeling format, most respondents are able to do so correctly, and the percentages of correct answers did not differ considerably between the various formats of FOP labels (see Conquest Research, 2006; Grunert et al., 2010; Malam, Clegg, Kirwan, & McGinigal, 2009). That is, any structured and legible presentation of key nutrient and energy information, regardless of FOP format, is sufficient to enable consumers to detect the healthier alternative. For more difficult tasks (i.e., monadic and product comparisons), however, objective understanding declines, and label format appears to matter (e.g., Barone, Rose, Manning, & Miniard, 1996; Malam et al., 2009).

Health inferences may, of course, be based on other information than the nutrition label. A recent European study (Grunert et al., 2010) indicated that level of processing is the most commonly used information when making inferences about healthiness; information on ingredients and additives are also commonly used. Although the presence of health and nutrition claims affects the likelihood of reading the BOP information (Roe et al., 1999), their presence does not appear to interact with nutrition information when judging overall healthiness of a product (Keller et al., 1997; Kozup, Creyer, & Burton, 2003; Mitra, Hastak, Ford, & Ringold, 1999). Given the recent interest in adding FOP nutrition and health claims to food products, the issue of how such claims combined with standard nutrition labeling affect consumer response is important to investigate.

## Actual Use in Decision Making

The high levels of self-reported use, coupled with the evidence for accurate health inferences, could suggest that the impact of nutrition labels on food choice and dietary intake is considerable. However, as already noted, self-reported use probably reflects an overreporting bias. The limited evidence that is available based on observational methods or verbal protocol analyses suggests that actual levels of usage may be a good deal lower, and/or that consumers may merely look at the label but not process the information further (Cowburn & Stockley, 2005). A recent study conducted in six European countries (Grunert et al., 2010) provided the most accurate picture of actual label use to date. Shoppers were observed at six different aisles in supermarkets (i.e., breakfast cereal, soft drinks, yogurts, savory snacks, confectionary, ready-made meals), and time spent, products handled, and selections made were recorded. Upon leaving the aisle, shoppers were intercepted and interviewed about the selections just made. When respondents answered the question "Did you look for any nutrition information when selecting this product?" affirmatively, they were asked to name the nutrient(s) on which they sought information, characterize the product as high or low on that nutrient, and show the interviewer where on the package they had found this information. Respondents who answered these questions were classified as having processed nutrition information. From 9% (in France) to 27% (in the United Kingdom) of shoppers appeared to process nutrition information, with considerable variation across product categories (i.e., from 11% for confectionary to 25% for breakfast cereals).

It should be noted that this methodology only taps explicit knowledge of nutrition information on the package. Research on price knowledge (Dickson & Sawyer, 1990; Vanhuele & Dreze, 2002) has suggested that shoppers may also have implicit knowledge of the products they buy, which could be measured by a recognition task but not by a recall task, as explored above. Explicit knowledge is more likely to result from cognitive processing of the label information (path 1 of Figure 16.3) than from affective processing (path 2), and it is thus conceivable that this type of methodology underestimates cognitive and affective processing of nutrition labels.

## Dietary Intake

Processing nutrition information does not necessarily imply that the information will have an impact on the choice made or that the impact results in an objectively healthier choice. Moreover, even if individual choices improved, an impact on overall dietary intake may not emerge at the aggregate level. Indeed, the empirical evidence is rather weak. Three types of studies have been conducted to address the effects of nutritional labeling on dietary intake. The first type was based on survey data and related people's self-reported food intake to the same people's self-reported use of nutrition labels (e.g., Coulson, 2000; Kim, Nayga, & Capps, 2001; Kristal, Hedderson, Patterson, & Neuhauser, 2001; Lin, Lee, & Yen, 2004: Neuhouser, Kristal, & Patterson, 1999; Weaver & Finke, 2003), finding that there was indeed a positive relationship. Apart from potential biases resulting from social desirability and consistency, correlational evidence cannot provide evidence of causality. (The interpretation that people with a healthier lifestyle consult nutrition labels more often is at least as plausible as the hypothesis that use of nutrition labels results in a healthier lifestyle.) The causality problem is less severe in longitudinal studies, and a recent analysis using National Health Interview Survey data pre- and post-NLEA found that self-reported use of nutrition labeling reduced BMI for only one demographic group, non-Hispanic white women (Variyam & Cawley, 2006). The second type of study consisted of econometric studies using household budget data, in which researchers attempted to incorporate health information as a potential predictor of demand for product categories that involve a health issue (e.g., eggs, animal fat). Usually, an index of health information is constructed based, for example, by counting media appearances of a certain issue (e.g., cholesterol) or counting appearances of the issue in the scientific press, based on the argument that this information eventually will trickle down to consumers. Indeed, such an association can be found in a number of U.S. studies (e.g., Brown & Schrader, 1990; Chern, Loehman, & Yen, 1995).

Although such studies have shown that the presence of a food and health issue in the public discourse has an effect on consumer demand, they have not shed much light on the effect of nutrition labeling. The closest we have come to real evidence on how nutrition labeling affects consumer choices were some studies comparing purchase patterns before and after changes in the U.S. legislation on nutrition labeling, with mixed evidence (e.g., Mathios, 1998; Mojduszka, Caswell, & Harris, 2001). Finally, the third type of study referred to experimental work in which the focus is not on brand choice but on consumption decisions. For example, Wansink and Chandon (2006) demonstrated that providing information on low-fat content led to increased calorie intake by adjusting the perception of the appropriate serving size upward and decreasing consumption guilt. Although this approach provides stronger evidence of causality, it remains focused on a single consumption episode rather than the totality of consumption that, in the aggregate, determines dietary intake.

## THEORETICAL AND METHODOLOGICAL CHALLENGES

A review of the existing research on nutrition labeling is not easily summarized. A large proportion of consumers are aware of the link between food and health and have a basic interest in obtaining and using information that could help them eat healthily. When making food choices, using nutrition-labeling information is regarded as good and desirable behavior. Still, evidence has been limited for actual use of such information in the shop. To explain this gap, the discussion has, for a long time, focused mainly on problems with availability of labels, understandability of labels, and comparability of information. Yet, much progress has been made on these fronts: Availability is now improved due to legislation and retailer and producer initiatives. Understandability has also improved inasmuch as FOP labels help consumers, when prompted, to identify healthier options. Nonetheless, actual usage of nutrition labels remains low, which raises two major questions for future research: (1) Why is the current level of usage of nutrition-labeling information not higher than it is? (2) When nutrition-labeling information indeed is used, does it have a positive effect on healthy product choice and dietary intake? Answering the first question may require a shift from the information-processing approach of prior research on nutrition labels to an approach that emphasizes motivational issues, goal setting, and self-regulation. Answering the second may require a shift from the study of individual brand choice to an approach that emphasizes actual consumption and, in the aggregate, dietary intake. Providing answers to these questions would provide help in designing nutrition-labeling schemes that indeed will be used and inform the regulatory debate on nutrition labeling. To encourage real progress in addressing these questions, we focus on three theoretical and methodological challenges: the need to do in-store and in-home research, the challenge of analyzing consumer choices that are not discrete but form a continuous pattern, and the difficulty of analyzing the link from food choice to dietary intake.

### In-Store and In-Home Research

Given the large amount of research that has been done on brand choice, it is astonishing how little has been conducted where most such choices are made: in the shop or restaurant. Of course, there are good reasons for moving studies into the lab, where the information-overloaded supermarket environment can be replaced with a controlled environment, and for relying on retrospective accounts of one's own behavior instead of observations of the actual behavior, given the cost and time needed to conduct observational studies in the field, along with the challenge of finding retailers with which to partner. Nonetheless, it seems imperative to consider the effects that nutrition labeling has at the place where it occurs. Observations at the aisle, combined with interviews conducted with close temporal proximity to the observed behavior, can help researchers determine whether consumers looked at the label, for how long, what they looked for, whether they found what they looked for, and how consumers believe that the information has entered their decisions. Mobile eye trackers may be another way of measuring processing at the microlevel in a real-world setting, despite concerns about reactivity. Conducting in-store experiments with different forms of labeling may ultimately be the gold standard for investigating how different forms of labeling can affect perception, understanding, health inferences, and use in decision making, especially when combined with the scanner data automatically generated in retail outlets.

Another location that may merit greater research is the home. Exposure to nutrition labels continues at home, with both the shopper and other family members potentially being exposed, and nutrition may become an element in the family discourse that shapes the next shopping trip. Unfortunately, the home is at least as difficult to access as the shop. Unobtrusive observation is not easy, and input from different family members may be needed to get a more complete picture of family interactions.

## Ongoing Choice and Consumption

For decades, the bulk of brand choice research has explicitly or implicitly followed a paradigm focusing on individual brand choices rather than a continuing process of interrelated choices. In fast-moving consumer goods, it has of course been recognized that category purchases are made frequently, and specific instances of brand choice, therefore, are part of an ongoing process in which choices are interrelated. Food choice is probably the most extreme form of such interrelated choices. Most people eat several times each day, and the process of planning meals, buying food, preparing meals, and eating is therefore an ongoing process that pervades much of daily life. What people eat is the result of many small decisions triggered by events like experiences with current meals, remarks by family members, remembering the need to pack school lunches, looking into the fridge to find out what is there and what is missing, and so forth (Khare & Inman, 2006). To illustrate this issue, Figure 16.4 depicts the results of a network analysis of all food-related thoughts that 10 respondents recorded during a 1-week period (Scholderer, 2005).

Ideally, the role of nutrition labeling needs to be related to this ongoing decision-making process, not just to the brand choice of the product on which the label appears. The challenge, of course, is that very little is currently known about this ongoing decision-making process or about which decisions are made when, triggered by which environmental events, and with what outcome: When was the decision made to have steak for dinner tonight? When was the subsequent decision made to combine it with creamy potato gratin instead of baked potato, and what triggered that decision? Was the decision to buy reduced-fat crème fraîche made in the shop, with the potato gratin in mind, or was reduced-fat crème fraîche only used because it had been bought earlier as part of stocking up on foods? Did the label on the bottle of olive oil standing in the kitchen trigger the decision to fry the steaks in oil instead of butter? It seems difficult to make claims about a possible role of nutrition labeling when so little groundwork has been done on ongoing choice and consumption in the food domain. More generally, we expect that cultural and social norms will play an important role in food-related decisions and so may shape the role that nutrition labeling could play.

## Food Choice Versus Dietary Intake

Personal health is affected by overall dietary intake not by individual brand choices, which represents a final challenge for nutrition-labeling research. First, effects of nutrition labeling have to be held up against some objective standard of what constitutes a healthy diet.

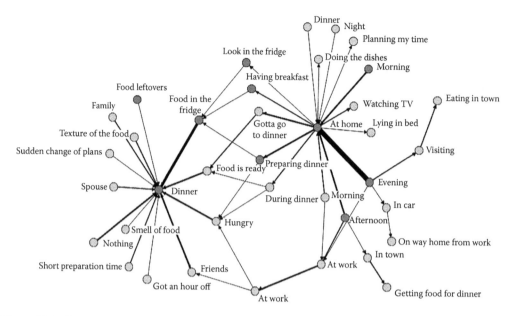

**Figure 16.4** Network of food-related thoughts of 10 informants over a 1-week period. (From Scholderer, J., *Traps and Pitfalls in Research on Healthy Food Choices: On Selective Accessibility, Assimilation and Contrast, and the Look-in-the-Fridge Heuristic*, paper presented at the 5th annual International Conference on Food Choice and Healthy Eating, Kauhajoki, Finland, 2005.)

Second, since nutrition labeling is developed to aid consumer decision making at the product level, we need to analyze and understand the link between product decisions and the overall dietary intake. This link may be straightforward; for example, if nutrition labeling encourages consumers to substitute fat-rich ready-made meals with less fat-rich ready-made meals, and the rest of the diet remains mostly unchanged, then overall dietary intake should improve in healthiness. However, the link may also be more complex and less direct; for example, nutrition labeling that encourages consumers to substitute butter with margarine or olive oil may lead to changes in recipes and substitutions between categories that eventually lead to shifts in eating styles. In such cases, the relationships between product choice and overall dietary intake are much more intricate and require a more holistic understanding of ongoing consumption patterns.

Importantly, researchers should also consider whether nutrition labeling may have unintended consequences on dietary intake. Prior research has suggested that exposure to weight-management drug marketing increases consumption of high-fat foods (Bhattacharjee, Bolton, & Reed, 2009) and undermines healthy lifestyle intentions (Bolton, Reed, Volpp, & Armstrong, 2008), consistent with the notion that remedies may serve as "get out of jail free cards" that encourage risky behavior (Bolton, Cohen, & Bloom, 2006). In the food domain, research by Wansink and Chandon (2006) found that low-fat labels increase consumption of such food; consumers appear to compensate for the improved healthfulness of the item by consuming greater quantities. Preliminary research has also suggested that functional foods can boomerang on subsequent eating intentions (Garvey & Bolton, 2010), perhaps because consumers infer progress on a health goal and then switch to other goals like indulgence (cf. Fishbach & Dhar, 2005). These findings point to the importance of investigating not just brand choice but also the impact of nutritional labeling on consumption and dietary intake.

## AGENDA FOR RESEARCH

Based on our discussion of the challenges in this domain, we would like to propose five problem areas that are in need of research in order to provide a better basis for the design of nutrition labeling that can improve public health. First, we are in urgent need of studies of peripheral processing of labels, both in the shop and at home, that is, studies that take into account principles of low-involvement learning and subconscious processing and, therefore, do not put respondents into a forced exposure situation (Grunert, 1996). In-store label processing, if it occurs at all, will be mostly in situations of time pressure and as part of decisions in which habitual behavior and the use of heuristics play a large role. In-store label perception can be studied by observational methods and by at-the-shelf interviewing methods analogous to those that have been used in price perception research (e.g., Dickson & Sawyer, 1990). Such studies can be complemented by eye-tracking experiments in the laboratory (Pieters & Warlop, 1999) and choice experiments that do not involve forced exposure to labels. Developing insight into low-involvement and real-world label processing would allow the formulation of realistic expectations about the impact of nutrition labels on brand choice and dietary intake. Moreover, such insights could also give important guidance to improve label exposure, design and identify label formats that encourage processing, and perhaps even develop accompanying in-store measures that encourage label usage.

A second area that needs more attention is the inferences that consumers make from label information, including how the label information interacts with other information and consumers' prior beliefs about what makes a food product healthy. Consumers may draw inferences from nutrient information, ways of presenting the information, and patterns of information across the key nutrients. In addition, consumers may infer healthiness from the product category, the brand, the list of ingredients and additives, the degree and type of processing (e.g., freezing vs. canning vs. high-pressure treatment), organic and natural attributes, and a range of other factors that together constitute their personal set of metabeliefs for what constitutes healthy food. Such research, which should also incorporate differences in consumer motivation and ability to process nutritional information, would yield insight into how consumers' personal health theories affect the way in which they interpret nutrition labels and how label information interacts with other cues used for health inferences. This insight, in turn, could be used to improve the design of labels and perhaps, more importantly, calibrate the way in which labels are integrated into comprehensive systems for conveying nutrition information.

Third, we need more insight into whether and how labels actually are used in guiding buying decisions and with what effect, which is a difficult problem and requires a combination of approaches. An obvious starting point is analysis of scanner data from retailers. For product categories that are labeled or partly labeled, a hedonic pricing approach (Rosen, 1974) would allow researchers to detect whether certain patterns of labeling information carry a positive hedonic price, and evidence that consumers appreciate this information. Another analytic approach, using sales as the dependent variable, would attempt to examine whether label information, controlling for other important determinants like price, promotions, and shelf space, influences sales. This approach would be complemented by research that looks more closely at the way consumers use labeling in their decision making, distinguishing different forms of processing corresponding to the two paths in Figure 16.3. Research methods might include think-aloud studies and choice experiments to understand the ways in which nutritional labeling information is, or is not, used in decision making.

Fourth, recent research on goal setting and balancing seems relevant to understanding how consumers make food and consumption choices and also raises the questions of whether and how goals interact with labeling. Research has suggested that making some progress toward a goal frees consumers to pursue other goals, implying that ordering a healthy main course in a restaurant may be viewed as a license to indulge with the dessert, akin to the boomerang effect discussed earlier. Nutrition labeling could not only facilitate choices when a health goal is dominant but could also affect goal balancing. Indeed, labeling, and packaging, may make salient healthful goals that improve consumer choice, consumption, and ultimately dietary intake.

A final research issue has to do with the personalization and customization of nutrition information. Nutrigenomics has established that people's different genomic makeups lead to different nutritional needs, and there hence is a need for personalized diets, personalized nutrition information, or even personalized food products. Although these ideas are still in their infancy, and neither producers nor consumers may be ready for them (Ronteltap, van Trijp, & Renes, 2007, 2009), it is clear that nutrition labeling, in its current form, is still very standardized. How do consumers interpret nutritional information and adapt it to their personal needs, both to their personal physiological profile (e.g., body weight, age, level of physical activity) and their more specific health needs (e.g., diabetes, obesity, bone loss)? How do consumers with competing health goals (e.g., reduce sugar for losing weight, increase polyunsaturated fat for preventing heart disease) balance these personal goals, as well as goals of family members, when shopping and using labeling information? Current nutrition labels are standardized and do not address such individualized needs, which may represent one potential future direction for nutritional labeling in society.

## CONCLUSION

As noted at the beginning of this chapter, nutrition labeling is widely regarded as one of the most promising instruments for fighting unhealthy eating habits and rising obesity rates. Yet, as this chapter has shown, numerous questions regarding the effects of nutrition labeling remain unanswered. From the evidence already at hand, it seems fair to warn against exaggerated hopes with regard to the effects of nutrition labeling. Dietary intake is a complex matter affected by a multitude of factors (see also Grier & Moore, Chapter 15 of this volume), and nutrition labeling is only one of many factors that have an influence. More importantly, although nutrition labeling can be viewed as one of many instruments aimed at increasing consumer resilience (Maddi, Chapter 31 of this volume), we should also note that most arguments advanced for nutrition labeling have assumed that consumers are both motivated and able to cognitively process the information. Peripheral processing, including affective responses, is largely uninvestigated in the area of nutrition labeling, and it is unclear whether such processing would move dietary intake in a healthy direction. Just as partial, biased beliefs about what constitutes a healthy diet may cause more harm than good (Rozin, Fischler, Imada, Sarubin, & Wrzesniewski, 1999), so may a partial, biased understanding of nutrition labeling.

## REFERENCES

Balasubramanian, S. K., & Cole, C. (2002). Consumers' search and use of nutrition information: The challenge and promise of the Nutrition Labeling and Education Act. *Journal of Marketing, 66*(3), 112–127.

Baltas, G. (2001). Nutrition labeling: Issues and policies. *European Journal of Marketing, 35,* 708–721.

Barone, M. J., Rose, R. R., Manning, K. C., & Miniard, P. W. (1996). Another look at the impact of reference information on consumer impressions of nutrition information. *Journal of Public Policy & Marketing, 15,* 55–62.

Bernues, A., Olaizola, A., & Corcoran, K. (2003). Labeling information demanded by European consumers and relationships with purchasing motives, quality and safety of meat. *Meat Science, 65,* 1095–1106.

BEUC (The European Consumers' Organisation). (2006). *Discussion Group on Simplified Labelling: Simpler labelling for healthier choices* (BEUC/X/044/2006). Brussels, Belgium: Author.

Bhattarcharjee, A., Bolton, L. E., & Reed, A. (2009). *License to lapse: The effects of weight management product marketing on a healthy lifestyle.* Unpublished manuscript, University of Pennsylvania, Philadelphia, & Pennsylvania State University, State College.

Bolton, L. E., Cohen, J. B., & Bloom, P. N. (2006). Does marketing products as remedies create "get out of jail free cards"? *Journal of Consumer Research, 33,* 71–81.

Bolton, L. E., Reed, A., II, Volpp, K. G., & Armstrong, K. (2008). How does drug and supplement marketing affect a healthy lifestyle? *Journal of Consumer Research, 34,* 713–726.

Brown, D. J., & Schrader, L. F. (1990). Cholesterol information and shell egg consumption. *American Journal of Agricultural Economics, 72,* 548–555.

CBS News. (2009, October 20). *FDA cracks down on deceptive food labels.* Retrieved December 21, 2010, from http://www.cbsnews.com/stories/2009/10/20/health/main5402704.shtml

Cheftel, J. C. (2005). Food and nutrition labeling in the European Union. *Food Chemistry, 93,* 531–550.

Chern, W. S., Loehman, E. T., & Yen, S. T. (1995). Information, health risk beliefs and the demand for fats and oils. *Review of Economics and Statistics, 77,* 555–564.

Conquest Research. (2006). *Food labelling study prepared for Which?* London: Author.

Coulson, N. S. (2000). An application of the stages of change model to consumer use of food labels. *British Food Journal, 10,* 661–668.

Cowburn, G., & Stockley, L. (2005). Consumer understanding and use of nutrition labeling: A systematic review. *Public Health Nutrition, 8,* 21–28.

Dickson, P. R., & Sawyer, A. G. (1990). The price knowledge and search of supermarket shoppers. *Journal of Marketing, 54*(3), 42–53.

Drichoutis, A., Lazaridis, P., & Nayga, R. M. (2006). Consumers' use of nutritional labels: A review of research studies and issues. *Academy of Marketing Science Review, 9.* Available: http://www.amsreview.org/articles/drichoutis09-2006.pdf

Elbon, S. M., Johnson, M. A., Fischer, J. G., & Searcy, C.A. (2000). Demographic factors, nutrition knowledge, and health seeking behaviors influence nutrition label reading behaviors among older American adults. *Journal of Nutrition for the Elderly, 19,* 31–48.

Fishbach, A., & Dhar, R. (2005). Goals as excuses or guides: The liberating effect of perceived goal progress on choice. *Journal of Consumer Research, 34,* 370–377.

Food Standards Agency. (2005). *Quantitative evaluation of alternative food signposting concepts.* London: Synovate.

Food Standards Agency. (2007). *Front-of-pack traffic light signpost labelling: Technical guidance, 2.* London: Author.

French, S. A., Story, M., & Jeffery, M. (2001). Environmental influences on eating and physical activity. *Annual Review of Public Health, 22,* 309–335.

Garvey, A., & Bolton, L. E. (2010, February). *Hedonic-utilitarian goal balancing as the result of functional food consumption.* Paper presented at the annual conference of the Society for Consumer Psychology, St. Petersburg, FL.

Golan, E., Kuchler, F., Mitchell, L., Greene, C., & Amber, J. (2001). Economics of food labeling. *Journal of Consumer Policy, 24,* 117–184.

Grunert, K. G. (1996). Automatic and strategic processes in advertising effects. *Journal of Marketing, 60*(4), 88–101.

Grunert, K. G., Fernández-Celemin, L., Wills, J. C., Storcksdieck genannt Bonsmann, S., & Nureeva, L. (2010). Use and understanding of nutrition information on food labels in six European countries. *Journal of Public Health, 18,* 261–277.

Grunert, K. G., & Wills, J. M. (2007). A review of European research on consumer response to nutrition information on food labels. *Journal of Public Health, 15,* 385–399.

Hawkes, C. (2004). *Nutrition labels and health claims: The global regulatory environment.* Geneva, Switzerland: World Health Organization.

Hodgkins, C., Raats, M., Barnett, J., Wasowicz-Kirylo, G., Stysko-Kunkowska, M., Gulcan Y., et al. (2009). *Derivation of a typology for nutritional labelling.* Brussels, Belgium: European Food Information Council.

Keller, S. B., Landry, M., Olson, J., Velliquette, A. M., Burton, S., & Andrews, J. C. (1997). The effects of nutrition package claims, nutrition facts panels, and motivation to process nutrition information on consumer product evaluations. *Journal of Public Policy & Marketing, 16,* 256–269.

Khare, A., & Inman, J. J. (2006). Habitual behavior in American eating patterns: The role of meal occasions. *Journal of Consumer Research, 32,* 567–575.

Kim, S., Nayga, R. M., Jr., & Capps, O., Jr. (2001). Food label use, self-selectivity, and diet quality. *Journal of Consumer Affairs, 35,* 346–363.

Kozup, J. C., Creyer, E. H., & Burton, S. (2003). Making healthful food choices: The influence of health claims and nutrition information on consumers' evaluations of packaged food products and restaurant menu items. *Journal of Marketing, 67*(2), 19–34.

Kristal, A. R., Hedderson, M. M., Patterson, R. E., & Neuhauser, M. L. (2001). Predictors of self-initiated, healthful dietary change. *Journal of the American Dietetic Association, 101*, 762–766.

Levy, A. S., Fein, S. B., & Schucker, R. E. (1996). Performance characteristics of seven nutrition label formats. *Journal of Public Policy & Marketing, 15*, 1–15.

Lin, C. T. J., Lee, J. Y., & Yen, S. T. (2004). Do dietary intakes affect search for nutrient information on food labels? *Social Science & Medicine, 59*, 1955–1967.

Malam, S., Clegg, S., Kirwan, S., & McGinigal, S. (with Raats, M., Barnett, J., et al.). (2009). *Comprehension and use of UK nutrition signpost labelling schemes.* London: British Market Research Bureau.

Mathios, A. D. (1998). The importance of nutrition labeling and health claim regulation on product choice: An analysis of the cooking oils market. *Agricultural and Resource Economics Review, 27*, 159–168.

Mazzocchi, M., Traill, W. B., & Shogren, J. (2009). *Fat economics: Nutrition, health and economic policy.* Oxford, England: Oxford University Press.

Mennel, S., Murcott, A., & van Otterloo, A. H. (1992). *The sociology of food: Eating, diet and culture.* London: Sage.

Mitra, A., Hastak, M., Ford, G. T., & Ringold, D. J. (1999). Can the educationally disadvantaged interpret the FDA-mandated nutrition facts panel in the presence of an implied health claim? *Journal of Public Policy & Marketing, 18*, 106–117.

Mojduszka, E. M., Caswell, J. A., & Harris, J. M. (2001). Consumer choice of food products and the implications for price competition and government policy. *Agribusiness, 17*, 81–104.

Moorman, C. (1990). The effects of stimulus and consumer characteristics on the utilization of nutrition information. *Journal of Consumer Research, 17*, 362–374.

Moorman, C. (1998). Market-level effects of information: Competitive responses and consumer dynamics. *Journal of Marketing Research, 35*, 82–98.

Moorman, C., Du, R., & Mela, C. F. (2005). The effect of standardized information on firm survival and marketing strategies. *Marketing Science, 24*, 263–274.

Neuhouser, M. L., Kristal, A. R., & Patterson, R. E. (1999). Use of food nutrition labels is associated with lower fat intake. *Journal of the American Dietetic Association, 99*, 45–53.

Obayashi, S., Bianchi, L. J., & Song, W. O. (2003). Reliability and validity of nutrition knowledge, social-psychological factors, and food label use scales from the 1995 diet and health knowledge survey. *Journal of Nutrition Education and Behavior, 35*, 83–92.

Pieters, R., & Warlop, L. (1999). Visual attention during brand choice: The impact of time pressure and task motivation. *International Journal of Research in Marketing, 16*, 1–16.

Podsakoff, P. M., MacKenzie, S. B., Lee, J., & Podsakoff, N. P. (2003). Common method biases in behavioral research: A critical review of the literature and recommended remedies. *Journal of Applied Psychology, 88*, 879–903.

Przyrembel, H. (2004). Food labeling legislation in the EU and consumer information. *Trends in Food Science & Technology, 15*, 360–365.

Roe, B., Levy, A. S., & Derby, B. M. (1999). The impact of health claims on consumer search and product evaluation outcomes: Results from FDA experimental data. *Journal of Public Policy & Marketing, 18*, 89–105.

Ronteltap, A., van Trijp, J. C. M., & Renes, R. J. (2007). Expert views on critical success and failure factors for nutrigenomics. *Trends in Food Science & Technology, 18*, 189–200.

Ronteltap, A., van Trijp, J. C. M., & Renes, R. J. (2009). Consumer acceptance of nutrigenomics-based personalised nutrition. *British Journal of Nutrition, 101*, 132–144.

Roodenburg, A. J. C., Temme, E. H. M., Howell, D. O., & Seidell, J. C. (2009). Potential impact of the Choices Programme on nutrient intakes in the Dutch population. *Nutrition Bulletin, 34*, 318–323.

Rosen, S. (1974). Hedonic prices and implicit markets: Product differentiation in pure competition. *Journal of Political Economy, 82*, 34–55.

Rozin, P., Fischler, C., Imada, S., Sarubin, A., & Wrzesniewski, A. (1999). Attitudes to food and the role of food in life in the U.S.A., Japan, Flemish Belgium and France: Possible implications for the diet–health debate. *Appetite, 33*, 163–180.

Scholderer, J. (2005, September). *Traps and pitfalls in research on healthy food choices: On selective accessibility, assimilation and contrast, and the look-in-the-fridge heuristic.* Paper presented at the 5th annual International Conference on Food Choice and Healthy Eating, Kauhajoki, Finland.

Storcksdieck genannt Bonsmann, S., Celemín, L. F., Larrañaga, A., Egger, S., Wills, J. M., Hodgkins, C., et al. (2010). Penetration of nutrition information on food labels across the EU-27 plus Turkey. *European Journal of Clinical Nutrition*. Available: http://www.nature.com/ejcn/journal/vaop/ncurrent/abs/ejcn2010179a.html

Svederberg, E. (2002). *Consumers' views regarding health claims on two food packages*. Lund, Sweden: Lund University.

U.S. Food and Drug Administration. (1998). *Good reading for good eating*. Washington, DC: Author.

van Dillen, S. M. E., Hiddink, G. J., Koelen, M. A., de Graaf, C., & van Woerkum, C. M. J. (2003). Understanding nutrition communication between health professionals and consumers: Development of a model for nutrition awareness based on qualitative consumer research. *American Journal of Clinical Nutrition, 77*, 1065S–1072S.

Vanhuele, M., & Dreze, X. (2002). Measuring the price knowledge shoppers bring to the store. *Journal of Marketing, 66*, 72–85.

Variyam, J. N., & Cawley, J. (2006). *Nutrition labels and obesity* (NBER. Working Paper No. 11956). Cambridge, MA: National Bureau of Economic Research.

Wansink, B., & Chandon, P. (2006). Can "low-fat" nutrition labels lead to obesity? *Journal of Marketing Research, 43*, 605–618.

Wansink, B., Sonka, S. T., & Hasler, C. M. (2004). Front-label health claims: When less is more. *Food Policy, 29*, 659–667.

Wardle, J., Parmenter, K., & Waller, J. (2000). Nutrition knowledge and food intake. *Appetite, 34*, 269–275.

Weaver, D., & Finke, M. (2003). The relationship between the use of sugar content information on nutrition labels and the consumption of added sugars. *Food Policy, 28*, 213–219.

Weil, D., Fung, A., Graham, M., & Fagotto, E. (2006). The effectiveness of regulatory disclosure policies. *Journal of Policy Analysis and Management, 25*, 155–181.

World Cancer Research Fund & American Institute for Cancer Research. (2007). *Food, nutrition, physical activity, and the prevention of cancer: A global perspective*. Washington, DC: Author. Available: http://www.dietandcancerreport.org

World Health Organization. (2005). *Preventing chronic diseases: A vital investment*. Geneva, Switzerland: Author.

World Health Organization. (2008). *World health statistics 2008*. Geneva, Switzerland: Author.

Worseley, A. (2002). Nutrition knowledge and food consumption: Can nutrition knowledge change food behaviour? *Asia Pacific Journal of Clinical Nutrition, 11*(Suppl.), S579–S585.

# 17

# Transformative Consumer Research for Addressing Tobacco and Alcohol Consumption

CORNELIA PECHMANN, ANTHONY BIGLAN,
JOEL W. GRUBE, AND CHRISTINE CODY

A MAN HATH NO BETTER THING UNDER THE SUN, than to eat, and to drink, and to be merry.

Ecclesiastes 8:15

AND A WOMAN IS ONLY A WOMAN, but a good cigar is a smoke.

Joseph Rudyard Kipling (1865–1936)

For eons, millions of people have consumed and enjoyed alcohol and tobacco, and there are pharmacological and psychosocial benefits to consuming alcohol (Varlinskaya & Spear, 2002) and tobacco (Geier, Mucha, & Pauli, 2000). However, the preponderance of scientific evidence has indicated that alcohol abuse and most tobacco use lead to significant health problems, and marketing encourages use of both products (Davis, Gilpin, Loken, Viswanath, & Wakefield, 2008; Martin & Mail, 1995). This chapter will summarize research about the effects of alcohol and tobacco marketing, particularly on youth but also on adults. In addition, we will summarize research on the regulation of marketing and the use of social marketing (demarketing) to help consumers, especially youth, make better decisions regarding alcohol and tobacco consumption.

The main aim of this chapter is to inform researchers globally who, as transformative consumer researchers or social marketing researchers, have made a commitment to conduct and disseminate research that will result in positive consumption changes to benefit individuals and societies, including consumption changes related to alcohol or tobacco. We hope this chapter will serve as a key resource by providing a comprehensive overview of major research areas and findings related to the marketing and demarketing of tobacco and alcohol and the effects on consumers. To our knowledge, this is the first major attempt to compare consumer research related to tobacco and alcohol. Although most of the literature that we review comes from U.S. researchers and primarily examines U.S. marketing and demarketing practices, we provide a global perspective in the initial (background) and final (policy) sections, and we cite international researchers whenever they have provided crucial research in an area (e.g., advertising bans).

There is voluminous research on both alcohol and tobacco, in part because of the substantial use and health effects of both substances worldwide. We cannot realistically review all the research here, but we have sought to address every major research topic related to alcohol and tobacco marketing and demarketing and consumers. Although there has been an impressive amount of research, we identified several research gaps that we will discuss throughout the chapter and at the end. For additional information about tobacco and alcohol research, readers should refer to these useful resources: National Institute on Alcohol Abuse and Alcoholism (2002) monographs; National Cancer Institute (2010) tobacco monographs (see also Davis et al., 2008); Institute of Medicine books on youth and alcohol (Bonnie & O'Connell, 2004) and youth and tobacco (Lynch & Bonnie, 1994); the United Kingdom's National Institute for Health and Clinical Excellence (2007, 2008) monographs on youth and alcohol and tobacco; books on alcohol politics (Babor et al., 2010), tobacco politics (Chapman, 2007; Jha & Chaloupka, 1999) and tobacco risk perceptions (Slovic, 2001; Viscusi, 1992); and policy websites on alcohol (e.g., College Drinking—Changing the Culture, http://www.collegedrinkingprevention.gov/policies/default.aspx; World Health Organization [WHO]: Management of Substance Abuse, http://www.who.int/substance_abuse/publications/alcohol/en/index.html) and tobacco (e.g., Campaign for Tobacco-Free Kids, http://www.tobaccofreekids.org/index.php; WHO: Tobacco Free Initiative, http://www.who.int/tobacco/en/).

## ALCOHOL AND TOBACCO PREVALENCES

Vast numbers of consumers use alcohol and tobacco in the United States and worldwide. Among U.S. youth, use of both substances has actually been declining for about a decade but remains high: In 2008, the percentages of youth reporting alcohol use in the past 30 days were 43% of 12th graders, 29% of 10th graders, and 16% of 8th graders (Johnston, O'Malley, Bachman, & Schulenberg, 2008a). Thirty-day cigarette prevalence was about half that of alcohol: 20% of 12th graders, 12% of 10th graders, and 7% of 8th graders (Johnston, O'Malley, Bachman, & Schulenberg, 2008b).

Among the general U.S. population ages 12 or older in 2007, 51% used alcohol in the past 30 days, and 7% were repeat binge drinkers; also, 24% used cigarettes (Substance Abuse & Mental Health Services Administration, 2007). Globally, drinking rates have varied widely, with 41% of adults classified as repeat binge drinkers in the United Kingdom, 15% in Mexico, 2% in Russia, 1% in India, and 0% in Egypt (WHO, 2004). Worldwide smoking rates have varied by gender: 47% of men and 12% of women reported smoking. Among men, 35% reported smoking in developed countries, 50% in developing countries, and 67% in China (Shafey, Dolwick, & Guindon, 2003). About 30% of youth have reported smoking worldwide (Shafey et al., 2003). The reliability of these estimates is unclear, however.

## ALCOHOL AND TOBACCO HEALTH RISKS

The health risks of alcohol and tobacco use are substantial. Overall in the United States, alcohol is associated with about 75,000 deaths annually (Centers for Disease Control and Prevention [CDC], 2004) and also risky sexual behavior (Carpenter, 2005), suicide (Carpenter, 2004), and nonviolent crime (Carpenter, 2007). In the United States in 2004, about 17,000 (39%) of traffic deaths were related to alcohol (National Highway Traffic Safety Administration, 2004). In comparison in the United States, on an annual basis, an estimated 443,000 people die from smoking or secondhand smoke and another 8.6 million suffer from smoking-related diseases (CDC, 2008). Tobacco use is the single most preventable cause of disease and death in the United States. Smokers die primarily of lung cancer, heart disease, lung disease, other cancers, or stroke (CDC, 2008).

Globally, alcohol is the second leading cause of disability-adjusted life years (i.e., healthy years lost) among males, although some countries escape this prognosis because of very low alcohol use (WHO, 2004). Alcohol caused 1.8 million deaths, or 3.2% of all deaths, worldwide in 2004; and about half were due to injuries (WHO, 2004, 2007). By contrast, smoking caused 5.4 million deaths, or 9.6% of all deaths, worldwide in 2004, which were split nearly evenly between developed and developing countries (Shafey et al., 2003; WHO, 2008). Projections indicate that smoking will cause 9 million deaths by 2020, 7 million of those in developing countries (Shafey et al., 2003).

Worldwide, the most common government regulation involving alcohol and tobacco is a minimum purchase and/or sell-to age, which is typically age 18 but ranges from ages 14 through 25, with the tobacco purchase ages trending slightly younger (International Center for Alcohol Policies, 2009; Shafey et al., 2003). In all U.S. states, people must be at least 21 years old to purchase alcohol and at least 18 years old to purchase tobacco. Countries and states vary on whether they regulate actual product consumption by age, but laws to prevent driving under the influence of alcohol are prevalent. In the United States, drivers ages 21 and over cannot exceed a blood alcohol content ranging from 0.08% to 0.10%, and drivers under age 21 cannot exceed 0.02% due to so-called zero-tolerance laws (Carpenter, 2007).

Research has indicated that age-related restrictions on alcohol and tobacco purchase and/or use are beneficial, because until about age 21, the brain undergoes massive change and reorganization; thus, the adolescent brain is especially vulnerable to damage from and addiction to alcohol and nicotine (Pechmann, Levine, Loughlin, & Leslie, 2005; see also Litt, Pirouz, & Shiv, Chapter 25 of this volume). Research has also indicated that early initiation of alcohol and/or tobacco elevates the health risks, and delaying initiation helps prevent consumers from taking up these habits (Bonnie & O'Connell, 2004; U.S. Department of Health and Human Services, 1989). However, more research is needed on age-of-purchase and age-of-use restrictions for both alcohol and tobacco to ascertain the advantages and disadvantages of different age-of-use policies and how these may vary by country and culture.

Substantial research exists about how tobacco and alcohol marketing affect youth and other consumers; there is also much consideration of government regulations to minimize the individual and societal health risks. We will review these literatures thoroughly, starting with the tobacco literature, because it is more comprehensive. For information on other addictive products, see Faber and Vons (Chapter 22 of this volume) on eating and spending, Cotte and LaTour (Chapter 23 of this volume) on gambling, and Litt et al. (Chapter 25 of this volume) on addictive substances including illicit drugs.

## RESEARCH ON TOBACCO MARKETING

### Cigarette Advertising Prevalence

Cigarette advertising and promotions are prevalent in the United States and many other countries (e.g., China). In 2006 in the United States, the five largest cigarette firms spent $12.5 billion on advertising and promotion (Federal Trade Commission, 2009). The largest spending category was promotional assistance to retailers to provide price discounts, which amounted to $9.21 billion, or 74% of the total. An additional $50 million was spent on magazine advertising; that spending peaked in 1984, when firms spent $426 million, or 20% percent of the total. Tobacco firms spent $243 million on point-of-sale promotions, or 2% of the total, which later peaked in 1993 at $401 million. Although there are no reliable estimates of worldwide tobacco marketing expenditures, they are estimated to be in the tens of billions of U.S. dollars annually (Mackay & Eriksen, 2010).

### Causal Effects of Cigarette Advertising

#### Historical Analyses of Cigarette Campaigns

There is considerable evidence that tobacco marketing affects consumption, based on studies using diverse methodologies (Biglan, 2004a; Davis et al., 2008). Some of the evidence comes from historical analyses of advertising campaigns and is descriptive. Other evidence comes from surveys and is correlational; it shows associations but cannot prove causal effects. Additional evidence comes from experiments or randomized controlled trials that test for the causal effects. Finally, econometric studies provide additional evidence, by relating advertising expenditures or exposures to consumption across markets and/or times, after controlling for confounds or covariates.

Pierce and Gilpin (1995) analyzed historical periods in the 20th century when there were major increases in smoking, and their research indicates that tobacco marketing innovations prompted many major sales increases. For example, in the 1920s, the American Tobacco Company began marketing Lucky Strike cigarettes to women; the slogan was "Reach for a Lucky Instead of a Sweet" (see Figure 17.1). This campaign doubled the proportion of young women who smoked, from about 15% to 30%. When the modern women's liberation movement began in the early 1970s, Philip Morris introduced Virginia Slims cigarettes for liberated women. Pierce and Gilpin (1995) found that the Virginia Slims campaign and similar campaigns during the period were associated with increases in smoking initiation among adolescent women but not among men.

One of the most successful cigarette marketing campaigns was for Marlboro, which began in the 1950s (Hemdev, 2005). By associating Marlboro with rugged, masculine autonomy and good looks, Marlboro gradually attained a dominant market share as the newly recruited youth smokers aged into the adult population. As Myron Johnston, a Philip Morris economist, wrote in a 1981 memo, "Today's teenager is tomorrow's potential regular customer, and the overwhelming majority of smokers first begin to smoke while still in their teens.... The smoking patterns of teenagers are particularly important to Philip Morris" (Legacy Tobacco Documents Library, n.d.b, p. 7).

Tobacco industry documents discovered in lawsuits reveal that the R.J. Reynolds Tobacco Company had long tried to wrest more of the youth market from Philip Morris's Marlboro cigarettes. R.J. Reynolds tried several Camel campaigns emphasizing rugged masculinity, but these were unsuccessful (Biglan, 2004a; Cohen, 2000). Then, they created the cartoon character Joe Camel and commissioned a brilliant advertising campaign to establish Joe Camel as the coolest guy on earth, the one who had everything and could do everything (see Figure 17.1). For example, R.J. Reynolds research findings showed the following:

> Joe Camel's car and style of clothing quickly portrayed him as cool, sophisticated, debonair, and attractive. The fact that he was with an attractive female helped him to appear as leading a lifestyle of ladies' man.... Many respondents mentioned that they would like to live this lifestyle. (Legacy Tobacco Documents Library, n.d.a, p. 5)

### Surveys

Surveys have indicated that the Joe Camel ad campaign was successful at recruiting young smokers. Figure 17.2 shows the rates of growth and decline for Camel and Marlboro among 18–24-year-olds from 1982 to 1992 (this is a company document, and due to legal concerns, it did not look at market share among those under 18 in this study). As the figure shows, the large increases in young adults smoking Camels occurred after the campaign had aired for 2 years, presumably when the younger teens affected by the campaign had reached age 18. Public health data have also indicated that the Joe Camel ad campaign appealed to youth (CDC, 1992, 1994): By 1993, 13% of 12- to 18-year-old smokers smoked Camels, while Camel's market share across all ages remained at 4%. Pierce et al.'s (1991) findings indicate that by 1990, 25% of boys and 22% of girls (ages 12–17) in California smoked Camel, and Camel advertising was about twice as effective among youth as young adults. Evans, Farkas, Gilpin, Berry, and Pierce (1995) found that 36% of 12- and 13-year-olds named Camel ads as their favorite cigarette ads.

Surveys have also shown an association between cigarette advertising for other brands and youth smoking. Pierce, Choi, Gilpin, Farkas, and Berry (1998) surveyed thousands of nonsmoking youth twice, 3 years apart. Having a favorite cigarette ad or a cigarette promotion item significantly

**Figure 17.1**    A Lucky Strike cigarettes ad from the 1920s and a Camel cigarettes ad from the 1990s.

predicted later smoking among these youth. Unger, Johnson, and Rohrbach (1995) found that youth who reported greater liking of cigarette ads were more likely to smoke or intend to smoke.

*Experiments*

Controlled experiments have provided additional evidence that cigarette advertising encourages youth to smoke. For example, Turco (1997) found that nonsmokers who were randomly exposed

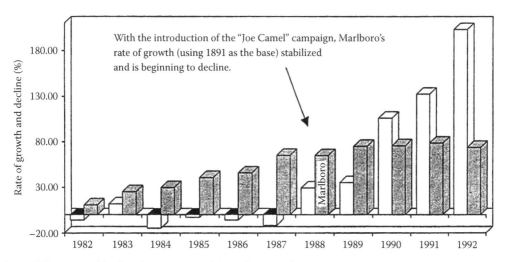

**Figure 17.2**    Impact of Joe Camel ads on young adult smoking rates: Camel's and Marlboro's rate of growth among 18–24-year-olds from 1982 to 1992.
*Note*: Dark bars = Marlboro cigarettes' rates of growth and decline; white bars = Camel cigarettes' rates of growth.

(vs. not exposed) to cigarette ads expressed more positive attitudes toward smoking and smokers. Donovan, Jancey, and Jones (2002) found that point-of-sale ads had a stronger impact on youth than simply viewing a pack of cigarettes. Youth who saw a Benson & Hedges cigarettes ad (vs. pack) rated the smokers of this brand as more relaxed, interesting, cool, rich, adventurous, and classy, whereas those who saw a Marlboro ad (vs. pack) rated this brand's smokers as more adventurous. Henriksen, Flora, Feighery, and Fortmann (2002) showed youth pictures of a convenience store with (vs. without) cigarette advertising, and youth who saw the advertising perceived cigarettes to be more available and youth smoking to be more prevalent, and expressed less support for tobacco control policies. Other research has shown that youth who have positive attitudes or beliefs about smoking or think it is prevalent are more likely to smoke currently and in the future (Chassin, Presson, Sherman, Corty, & Olshavsky, 1984; Dinh, Sarason, Peterson, & Onstad, 1995; Leventhal, Glynn, & Fleming, 1987).

Experiments have indicated that cigarette advertising makes youth who smoke look more attractive to their peers or, in effect, that cigarette advertising works synergistically with peer influences. Pechmann and Ratneshwar (1994) randomly assigned seventh-grade students to see either cigarette ads or control ads in a magazine, and then the students rated a peer who was described either as a smoker or nonsmoker. Students who saw cigarette (vs. control) ads had a greater proportion of positive thoughts about smokers. Later, Pechmann and Knight (2002) randomly assigned ninth graders to view one of eight videos about teens that contained one of the following: four cigarette ads, four antismoking ads, four cigarette ads and one antismoking ad, or four control ads. The tapes also showed either smoking or nonsmoking teens. Students who saw both cigarette ads and smoking teens had significantly more positive beliefs about smokers and a higher smoking intent, even those reporting no recall of the cigarette ads, and their beliefs mediated intent. Other research has indicated that smoking intent is significantly predictive of actual smoking behavior (Pierce, Choi, Gilpin, Farkas, & Merritt, 1996).

*Econometric Studies*

Numerous econometric studies of longitudinal (i.e., time series) data have shown that cigarette advertising has a positive effect on consumption (Chetwynd, Coope, Brodie, & Wells, 1988; McGuinness & Cowling, 1975; Radfar, 1985; Telser, 1962), so the evidence is quite conclusive, although skeptics remain (Harrison, Chetwynd, & Brodie, 1989). For example, one study examined 28 years of data on 12 brands in the U.S. market and found that both current and lagged advertising expenditures generally predicted brand sales, although sometimes sales predicted advertising (Holak & Tang, 1990).

Another study examined U.S. cigarette advertising expenditures and brand shares among adolescents and adults from 1979 to 1983 (Pollay et al., 1996). Adolescents were found to be about three times as responsive to cigarette brand advertising as adults were. For instance, a brand with a 10% market share and a 10% advertising share that doubled its advertising share could expect to increase its youth and adult market shares by 9% and 3%, respectively. Overall, a meta-analysis of 48 studies in different countries from 1933 to 1990 (Andrews & Franke, 1991) concluded that higher cigarette advertising generally led to higher cigarette consumption.

Tobacco in Entertainment Media

Substantial research has indicated that movies have depicted extensive smoking, and depicted it positively, which has encouraged youth to smoke (Pechmann & Shih, 1999). Tobacco firms paid for cigarettes to be placed in movies for promotional purposes until 1990, when the firms agreed to stop paid placements after a scandal over a hit youth movie that included a paid placement (Charlesworth & Glantz, 2005). Unpaid placements continue, however, and content analyses of

U.S. movies have documented extensive smoking content. For example, a study of 600 hit U.S. movies from 1988 to 1999 (Sargent et al., 2001) found a median of one smoking incident for movies rated G (general audience), four for movies rated PG and PG-13 (parental guidance), and nine for movies rated R (restricted to viewers ages 17 and over). A later study of hit U.S. movies (Sargent, Tanski, & Gibson, 2007) found that 74% portrayed smoking; as a result, the average U.S. youth (ages 10–14) witnessed about 120 instances of smoking in movies per year. A different study (Worth, Cin, & Sargent, 2006) found that 21% of the adult characters in movies smoked, which was roughly the same smoking prevalence as in the U.S. adult population. Most smoking portrayals in movies have been positive, demonstrating that attractive people smoke and suffer no ill health effects (Charlesworth & Glantz, 2005).

Additional longitudinal findings have indicated a relationship between youth's exposure to smoking in movies and youth's later smoking initiation. For example, a longitudinal, global study (Hanewinkel & Sargent, 2008) analyzed 400 mainly U.S. movies that were hits in Germany, 74% of which depicted smoking. The study indicated that the average German youth witnessed 36 instances of smoking per year in these movies, and youth in the highest (vs. lowest) movie smoking quartile were at least two times more likely to have tried smoking 1 year later, after controlling for confounds. Similarly, Dalton et al. (2003) found that U.S. youth (ages 10–14) in the highest (vs. lowest) movie smoking quartile were 2.7 times more likely to initiate smoking one to 2 years later. Then, 6 years later (Dalton et al., 2009), the youth in the highest (vs. lowest) quartile were two times more likely to become established smokers (i.e., 100 or more cigarettes smoked in total). A cross-sectional U.S. study (Sargent et al., 2005) concluded that exposure to movie smoking was more strongly associated with youth initiation than parental smoking was (2.6 vs. 1.8 adjusted odds ratio). Another cross-sectional U.S. study (Song, Ling, Neilands, & Glantz, 2007) concluded that movie smoking also affected young adults ages 18–25: those in the highest (vs. lowest) quartile were 1.8 times more likely to smoke in the past 30 days and 1.9 times more likely to become established smokers.

There is also experimental evidence that movie smoking has causally affected youth smoking. Pechmann and Shih (1999) randomly exposed nonsmoking youth (ages 14–15) to a full-length PG-13–rated (youth) movie either with smoking or with the smoking professionally edited out. Youth who saw the smoking reported feeling positive arousal, consistent with smoking being viewed as "forbidden fruit." In addition, their perception of a smoker's social stature became more positive, and they reported a higher intent to smoke. However, showing a strong 30-second antismoking ad before the movie, which portrayed social disapproval of smokers, prevented the smoking scenes from eliciting positive arousal or positively affecting smoking-related beliefs or intent. These results do not seem to be explained by a demand effect from the antismoking ad, because virtually none of the youths suspected the study was about smoking (see Edwards, Harris, Cook, Bedford, & Zuo, 2004, for similar results).

## Marketing of Light Cigarettes

In a landmark federal tobacco case, *United States of America et al. v. Philip Morris et al.* (*USA v. PM*; 2006), the judge ruled that the tobacco industry had marketed light cigarettes to smokers with the intent of keeping them from quitting and that light cigarettes do not deliver substantially less tar and nicotine to smokers. Therefore, tobacco firms were ordered to stop advertising cigarettes as light or low tar, and this ruling was subsequently upheld on appeal ("Tobacco Companies Lose Appeal," 2009). Before this ruling, the Federal Trade Commission (FTC) had allowed tobacco firms to market cigarettes as light or low tar, because the FTC had inaccurately estimated the cigarettes' tar and nicotine delivery. Tobacco firms had ventilated the sides of light cigarette filters with microscopic holes or channels, which increased air delivery and could potentially dilute the amount of tar and nicotine delivered, and the FTC had tested the cigarettes with a machine that "smoked" by taking consistent puffs. However, studies with actual smokers indicated that smokers often blocked the ventilation holes and also often compensated for the lower levels of nicotine by puffing more intensely and/or more frequently, negating the possible health benefits of light cigarettes (Kozlowski, Pillitteri, & Sweeney, 1994; Kozlowski, Sweeney, & Pillitteri, 1996; Robinson, Pritchard, & Davis, 1992; Sweeney, Kozlowski, & Parsa, 1999; Weinhold & Stitzer, 1989).

Although tobacco firms knew that people were smoking light cigarettes in ways that precluded them from getting health benefits, the firms intentionally and successfully marketed light cigarettes to smokers as safer to keep smokers from quitting (*USA v. PM*, 2006). Cataldo and Malone (2008) reviewed industry documents and found that light cigarettes were marketed to older smokers who were contemplating quitting, because such smokers would be less likely to quit if they believed light cigarettes were safer (Cummings, 2004; Cummings, Hyland, Bansal, & Giovino, 2004; Etter, Kozlowski, & Perneger, 2003; Gilpin, Emery, White, & Pierce, 2002; Kozlowski et al., 1998). Lee and Kahende (2007) compared people who had quit with those who had not, and quitters were less likely to have smoked light cigarettes.

## Marketing of Other Nicotine Products

For decades, tobacco firms have marketed smokeless tobacco products that users apply to their gums to deliver nicotine, including (a) coarsely shredded chewing tobacco; (b) dipping tobacco or moist snuff, which is ground and pasty; and (c) snus, primarily from Sweden, like moist snuff but processed under much higher temperatures, and often placed in small sachets. Research has indicated that most smokeless tobacco products cause oral cancer (Stratton, Shetty, Wallace, & Bondurant, 2001) and noncancerous lesions (Foulds, Ramstrom, Burke, & Fagerström, 2003). Snus poses a lower oral cancer risk, although it might possibly increase cardiovascular risk due to its sodium content (Foulds et al., 2003). In effect, because snus differs from snuff and related products in production and nicotine delivery, it poses less of a health risk.

Snus has been marketed in Sweden principally for historical reasons rather than for public health reasons, and over the past 25 years, large numbers of Swedish males have switched to snus instead of smoking cigarettes (Goldberg, 2008); the nicotine delivery is quite comparable (Foulds et al., 2003). Apparently as a result, Swedish males have experienced positive health outcomes (e.g., fewer lung cancers and heart attacks), as compared to males elsewhere in Europe who continued to smoke cigarettes (Foulds et al., 2003). There is little evidence that snus is a gateway to cigarettes, and thus Sweden allows manufacturers to market snus as a safer alternative to smoking. However, the global public health community is divided over whether to endorse snus as a harm-reduction product. Snus recently became available in the United States, and the rest of Europe has loosened restrictions on it (Goldberg, 2008). However, there is very little research on consumer perceptions of snus, so research is needed in this area.

In the late 1980s, U.S. tobacco firms began marketing a completely different type of tobacco products that are smoked but produce minimal secondhand smoke (Pederson & Nelson, 2007). We will refer to them as reduced-exposure products, short for potential reduced-exposure products (Pederson & Nelson, 2007), but tobacco firms often refer to them as modified-risk products (Family Smoking Prevention and Tobacco Control Act [FSPTCA], 2009). The most common of these reduced-exposure products are electronic cigarettes that heat tobacco rather than burn it, reducing smoke substantially (e.g., Eclipse cigarettes) or even eliminating it (e.g., Accord cigarettes). Some of these products also reduce carbon monoxide in smokers' expired air (Hughes & Keely, 2004), but other products actually increase it, and the long term effects are unknown (Breland, Buchhalter, Evans, & Eissenberg, 2002). These products also substitute imperfectly for cigarettes, because they do not eliminate nicotine cravings. One study found that, although cigarette consumption by users of reduced-exposure products dropped by 33%, total consumption across cigarettes and reduced-exposure products rose (Hughes & Keely, 2004).

Research has also indicated that after smokers viewed ads for reduced-exposure products, many incorrectly inferred that these products are safer than light cigarettes or are quitting aids, or that the government has approved the ad claims (Hamilton et al., 2004; O'Connor et al., 2007; Pederson & Nelson, 2007). Also, most smokers have found reduced-exposure products to be less satisfying in terms of nicotine delivery and taste (O'Connor et al., 2007), so these products have had very low sales and advertising budgets (Pederson & Nelson, 2007). Research is needed to track consumers' evolving perceptions and acceptance of reduced-exposure tobacco products.

Since the 1970s, pharmaceutical firms have marketed nicotine replacement therapies that deliver nicotine without smoke, smoking, or even tobacco (Shiffman, Ferguson, Rohay, & Gitchell, 2008), including over-the-counter nicotine patches, gums, and lozenges as well as prescription nicotine nasal sprays and inhalers. Nicotine replacement therapies are effective cessation aids that have approval from the U.S. Food and Drug Administration (FDA) and related government entities worldwide (Pederson & Nelson, 2007). Research has indicated that these therapies nearly double long-term (e.g., 6-month) smoking cessation rates (Shiffman et al., 2008; Silagy, Lancaster, Stead, Mant, & Fowler, 2004). Therefore, nicotine replacement therapies are rapidly becoming part of the standard of care for smokers who are trying to quit and stay quit, but these therapies alone are often insufficient. Substantial research has indicated that cessation outcomes significantly improve when nicotine replacement therapies are combined with counseling (Strecher, Shiffman, & West, 2005), cessation websites (Muñoz et al., 2009), or other social support (Brendryen & Kraft, 2008) and when the purchase costs are subsidized (Kaper, Wagena, Willemsen, & van Schayck, 2005).

Research has also indicated that consumers need to learn more about nicotine replacement therapies. Virtually all cessation websites discuss these therapies (Cheh, Ribisl, & Wildemuth, 2003), but only about one third of smokers use such therapies in their quit attempts (Shiffman et al., 2008). Also, whereas 34% of smokers reported believing that nicotine replacement therapies are safe, 26% did not, and 40% were unsure. In fact, research has not identified any significant cardiovascular risks or other risks associated with using these therapies (Benowitz, 1999). Therefore, consumers have misperceptions about nicotine replacement therapies. Although many public health officials support consumer education or even aggressive marketing to encourage smokers to use these therapies (Shiffman et al., 2008), some remain skeptical, in part because these therapies alone are often insufficient, as most smokers require additional services. One study (Bolton, Cohen, & Bloom, 2006) suggested that ads for nicotine replacement therapies may actually discourage smokers from quitting by giving them false security about the ease of quitting, that is, by offering a quick and easy remedy for smoking risks.

## RESEARCH ON TOBACCO DEMARKETING

### Advertising Bans

Many countries, particularly in Europe, have banned tobacco advertising and sponsorships (Saffer & Chaloupka, 2000). It has been concluded that tobacco advertising is so harmful to the public health that a ban is warranted. In effect, tobacco advertising is treated as a public health risk and disallowed, similar to how other risky corporate behavior is disallowed, such as dumping pollutants in water bodies or operating hazardous mines (e.g., Rosner & Markowitz, 1987). Several econometric studies examined the effects of cigarette advertising bans, especially in Europe, and generally found that these bans significantly lowered cigarette consumption (Laugesen & Meads, 1991; Smee, 1992). Weaker advertising restrictions typically had weaker effects on consumption (Rimpela, Aaro, & Rimpela, 1993). In contrast, some studies that concluded that cigarette advertising bans and restrictions had no impact (Aero, Wold, Kannas, & Rampela, 1986; Boddewyn, 1986, 1989; van Reek, Andriaanse, & Aaro, 1991), but these studies generally used a problematic method, comparing smoking rates across countries in a single year. Hence, a country with a very high smoking rate and a ban was deemed a failure relative to one with a perpetually low smoking rate and no ban, even if the country with a high smoking rate had substantially reduced smoking through its ban. Overall, the evidence has suggested that comprehensive cigarette advertising and sponsorship bans seem to be effective.

Counteradvertising

Some U.S. states, such as California, have utilized counteradvertising (i.e., antismoking ads) for over 20 years (Pechmann, 2002). Notwithstanding, only a few states have funded tobacco control at recommended levels, despite substantial money from the U.S. states' comprehensive tobacco settlement in 1998 (National Association of Attorneys General [NAAG], 1998) and tobacco surtaxes (American Lung Association, 2010). The CDC (2008) has recommended that states should spend $12.30 per capita on tobacco control annually, including $2.30 per capita on counteradvertising. Most states have never allocated the recommended amounts, whereas a few states, such as Massachusetts, allocated the recommended amount for counteradvertising for a while but then cut funding due to a budget crisis (American Lung Association, 2010).

The American Legacy Foundation (2007) began a national antismoking ad campaign for youth called Truth that was well funded for several years, paid for by the U.S. states' comprehensive tobacco settlement in 1998 (NAAG, 1998). Initially, the foundation spent about $0.90 per capita, or $275 million, annually. Due to a legal loophole, though, tobacco firms cut their annual payments to the foundation from $300 million in the years 1999–2003 to $40 million or less now, nearly decimating the Truth campaign.

Studies have suggested that well-funded and well-crafted antismoking media campaigns can significantly reduce both adult and youth smoking rates. California had the leading antismoking media campaign in the United States in terms of funding. Pierce, Gilpin, et al. (1998) compared adult per capita cigarette consumption in California with the rest of the United States during 1982–1988 (prior to the counteradvertising campaign), 1989–1993 (higher expenditure period on the campaign, about $3 per capita), and 1994–1996 (lower expenditure period, about $1.80 per capita). During the preprogram period, 1982–1988, California roughly mirrored the United States in per capita cigarette consumption decline (−0.42 vs. −0.36, respectively). During the higher expenditure period, California's rate of decline accelerated (−0.64 vs. −0.42, respectively). During the lower expenditure period, California's rate of decline weakened but was still faster than the average U.S. rate (−0.17 vs. 0.04, respectively). Overall, California's counteradvertising campaign amounted to about 15% of tobacco marketing expenditures in the state.

Studies have indicated that antismoking ads can deter youth smoking, too. Flynn and colleagues (1992, 1994) from the University of Vermont tested a youth antismoking television ad campaign in two communities and tracked youth's smoking behavior there and in two matched control communities. Ads initially ran for several months and then periodically thereafter. Youth who were exposed to the antismoking ads were much less likely to smoke; for instance, at age 15, 13% of the ad group versus 20% of the control group smoked.

Farrelly, Davis, Haviland, Messeri, and Healton (2005) evaluated the American Legacy Foundation's youth antismoking Truth campaign in its first 2 years, 2000–2002. The study assessed pre–post and dose–response effects, because different media markets happened to vary in ad dose (i.e., gross rating points). Monitoring the Future school surveys (Johnston, O'Malley, & Bachman, 2001) were used to assess youth smoking outcomes. The annual decline in past 30-day youth smoking was 3.2% at baseline (1998–1999), which improved significantly to 6.8% after the campaign commenced (2000–2002). A higher ad dose in a media market, measured in targeted gross rating points, increased the rate of decline. In fact, youth smoking has been declining in the United States from 1996 to 2009 (Johnston, O'Malley, Bachman, & Schulenberg, 2009), perhaps in part to the Truth campaign's well-funded effort from 2000 to 2004.

The youth-targeted antismoking ad campaigns often used different messages, leading to questions about relative message efficacy. The Vermont researchers' ad messages were primarily normative about smoking and secondhand smoke leading to social disapproval (Worden et al., 1988). The Truth ad messages were primarily anti-industry, about tobacco firms duping people into smoking and youth refusing to be duped. The Massachusetts ads stressed health effects. Pechmann and colleagues (Pechmann & Reibling, 2006; Pechmann, Zhao, Goldberg, & Reibling, 2003) randomly assigned youth to view either ads with a certain antismoking message or control messages; then the youths completed a survey about their smoking beliefs and intent. Two messages appeared to reduce youth's smoking intent significantly: social disapproval messages, often about secondhand smoke, and health messages about youth who were victims and that evoked disgust directed at the industry. Later research indicated that valence mattered, too; negative messages about social disapproval of smoking were effective for safety- or prevention-focused youth, whereas positive messages about social approval of nonsmoking were effective for aspiration- or promotion-focused youth (Zhao & Pechmann, 2007).

It is unclear why the anti-industry ads did not fare better in the above controlled lab studies (Pechmann & Reibling, 2006; Pechmann et al., 2003), but the lab studies took place in California, where anti-industry ads had already aired for many years, so the ads might have worn out. The American Legacy Foundation's evaluation of its Truth campaign indicated that its ads were worn out in California; that is, the ads were shown to have no discernible effect at any exposure level (Thrasher et al., 2004). More research is needed on the Truth counteradvertising approach and possible wear-out, and on related approaches that stress media literacy (see Andreasen, Goldberg, & Sirgy, Chapter 2 of this volume). Further, since it is difficult to predict a specific ad's effectiveness, it is advisable to copy test or pretest ads before airing (Foley & Pechmann, 2004; Pechmann & Andrews, in press) and monitor the ads for wear-out.

Warning Labels

Research has suggested that health warnings on cigarette packs and in ads can have beneficial effects, particularly if the warnings are graphic and changed frequently enough to ensure novelty. However, tobacco warnings could have null effects or even boomerang if not properly constructed, for example, if worn out or dogmatic (Stewart & Martin, 1994). On the positive side, numerous studies have suggested that those who are exposed to on-pack cigarette warnings are more likely to think about the harms of smoking and intend to quit (e.g., Borland et al., 2009; Krugman, Fox, Fletcher, & Fischer, 1994; Nimbarte, Aghazadeh, & Harvey, 2005; White, Webster, & Wakefield, 2008). Additionally, Golmier, Chebat, and Gélinas-Chebat (2007) found that when teens viewed warnings prior to seeing smoking depicted in movies, the warnings immunized them from the smoking depictions.

There has also been evidence that higher impact warnings (e.g., graphic pictures rather than just verbal descriptions of the health risks) are more effective at attracting attention and motivating quitting (Hammond et al., 2007; Nimbarte et al., 2005). For example, Willemsen (2005) surveyed Dutch smokers about the new graphic European Union warnings and found that, although smokers preferred packs without warnings, 10% said they smoked less due to the warnings and 18% said they were more motivated to quit. In the findings by Hammond et al. (2007), smokers who saw the new U.K. graphic warnings reported higher levels of awareness and impact. Kees, Burton, Andrews, and Kozup (2006) found that smokers who saw the new Canadian graphic warnings reported less package liking, more negative affect (e.g., fear), and less intent to smoke. White et al. (2008) found that Australian youth's processing of warning labels rose when new graphic warnings accompanied a media campaign.

In contrast, Krugman et al. (1994) found that U.S. youth simply did not attend to the old cigarette ad warnings, instead only attending to novel warnings, which indicated that warnings do wear out. An older U.K. study found that cigarette ads with (vs. without) the government health warning actually increased smokers' desire to smoke and had no effect on nonsmokers (Hyland & Birrell, 1979). To our knowledge, no randomized controlled trials have looked at the impact of warning labels on actual smoking, which indicates that more research is needed.

### Smoking Restrictions in Buildings

A number of researchers have examined whether restrictions on smoking in workplaces, restaurants, and other public buildings and places reduce smoking exposure and smoking behavior, and the bulk of the evidence indicates that they do. Albers and colleagues (Albers, Siegel, Cheng, Rigotti, & Biener, 2004; Siegel, Albers, Cheng, Biener, & Rigotti, 2004) studied the relationships among smoking bans in restaurants, smoke exposure, and smoking behavior among adults and youth in 301 Massachusetts communities. Communities with the strongest regulations had fewer adults and youth exposed to smoking (Albers et al., 2004; Siegel et al., 2004). Also, adult smokers who had made at least one previous quit attempt were more likely to try again if they lived in communities with strong regulations (Siegel et al., 2004). Finally, youth in communities with strong regulations were significantly less likely to start smoking, especially if the regulations had been in place for at least 2 years (Siegel, Albers, Cheng, Biener, & Rigotti, 2005; Siegel, Albers, Cheng, Hamilton, & Biener, 2008). However, Deverell, Randolph, Albers, Hamilton, and Siegel (2006) found that smoking bans were correlated with residents' education levels, suggesting some possible confounding.

There is also evidence that smoking bans in the workplace influence people to quit. Evans, Family, and Montgomery (2006) used a nationally representative sample of Americans to evaluate the impact of workplace smoking bans and found that bans increased the percentage of workers who quit smoking and decreased average daily consumption. These researchers argued that workplace bans might have a bigger effect than bans in other locations, because they prohibit smoking over a larger part of the day. Jha, Chaloupka, Corrao, and Jacob (2006) reviewed trends in the regulation of tobacco use around the world and concluded that restrictions on smoking in public places and workplaces substantially reduced smoking prevalence.

### Restricting Retail Sales to Youth

Because most smokers start when they are minors (i.e., younger than age 18), when legally they should not be able to purchase tobacco, a variety of methods have attempted to strengthen the impact of youth access laws. In the United States, the most common method has been merchant education, or informing and motivating retail clerks, managers, and store owners to stop selling to minors, but studies have indicated that merchant education has little lasting impact on sales to minors (Altman, Rasenick-Douss, Foster, & Tye, 1991). A second method is to reward clerks for not selling to minors. Biglan and colleagues (1995, 1996) found that this significantly reduced the proportion of stores that were willing to sell to minors, and Embry, Biglan, Hankins, Dahl, and Galloway (2009) recently replicated this effect in two states. Finally, it is possible to prosecute clerks for selling tobacco to minors, which has been shown to reduce such sales (Forster et al., 1998; Forster & Wolfson, 1998).

However, it is unclear whether reducing tobacco sales to minors reduces their smoking prevalence. Therefore, more research is needed to determine when and why youth smoking behavior is affected or not. Some survey evidence has suggested that restricting youth's access to tobacco does deter their smoking (DiFranza, Carlson, & Caisse, 1992; Forster et al., 1998; Hinds, 1992; Jason, Ji, Anes, & Birkhead, 1991). However, several studies have failed to find this to be a deterrent (Altman, Wheelis, McFarlane, Lee, & Fortmann, 1999; Cummings, Hyland, Perla, & Giovino, 2003; DiFranza et al., 1992; Rigotti et al., 1997). The null effect on youth smoking for restricting youth access to tobacco was confirmed in a meta-analysis across multiple studies (Fichtenberg & Glantz, 2002).

There are at least two reasons why reducing youth's access to cigarettes may not prevent youth smoking. Even a small number of retailers selling to youth could provide a sufficient supply (DiFranza, 2000; Forster & Wolfson, 1998). Also, as it becomes more difficult for youth to buy cigarettes, they may still get cigarettes from social sources, such as friends and family (Forster et al., 1998; Jones, Sharp, Husten, & Crossett, 2002). In sum, although tobacco firms have widely publicized their merchant education programs to discourage sales to minors, it appears the effects have been minimal. In fact, there is considerable evidence from tobacco firm documents that the prime purpose of these efforts has been to deter policy makers from restricting youth tobacco marketing (Biglan, 2004a, 2004b).

### Prices and Taxes

Evidence from econometric studies of the effects of increased prices on cigarette smoking indicates that increasing the price of cigarettes reduces overall cigarette consumption (Chung et al., 2002) and the number of youth who initiate smoking (Liang & Chaloupka, 2002; Slater, Chaloupka, Wakefield, Johnston, & O'Malley, 2007). In fact, raising taxes on cigarettes may be the single most cost-effective intervention to reduce smoking. Slater et al. (2007) studied the impact of price increases on youth smoking and concluded that increasing prices had a stronger effect than restricting retail sales. In addition to its direct impact on smoking, raising cigarette prices through taxes generates revenue that can fund further antitobacco activities, such as evidence-based counteradvertising campaigns, subsidized nicotine replacement therapies, and other smoking cessation and prevention programs. In sum, there are strong reasons to increase the cost of cigarettes through increased taxation.

## RESEARCH ON ALCOHOL MARKETING

### Alcohol Advertising Prevalence

Alcohol advertising and promotions are prevalent in most of the world, except in Muslim countries where alcohol consumption is highly restricted or banned. In 2005 in the United States, the alcoholic beverage industries spent over $3 billion on advertising (FTC, 2008). About 42% was spent on television, radio, print, and outdoor advertising; 40% on promotional assistance to retailers and wholesalers to provide price discounts; 16% on sponsorships of sporting events and athletes; and 2% on other promotional activities, including Internet ads and product placements.

Since alcohol does not cause significant harm to adults if used as recommended (e.g., in moderation, not while driving), many researchers have focused on alcohol use by underage youth and alcohol marketing that reaches youth (American Academy of Pediatrics, 2006). Using alcohol industry data, the FTC (2008) concluded that 92% of alcohol media advertising in 2005 met industry standards in terms of having a minimum of 70% adult audience. Yet, there remains concern that youth exposure to alcohol advertising is high and that a substantial number of alcohol ads appear in youth-popular media (Jernigan, Ostroff, & Ross, 2005). Estimates have shown, for example, that the average underage television viewer has encountered as many as 245 televised alcohol ads annually, and the heaviest viewers, or 30%, have seen as many as 780 alcohol ads each year. Further, even though most cable television alcohol ads appear in programming with 30% or less youth audience, advertising for beer, spirits, and alcohol refreshers, or alcopops actually increased as the size of the youth audience grew from 0% to 30% (Chung et al., 2010).

Alcohol ads have also been common in magazines popular with youth readers (Austin & Hust, 2005). Based on a content analysis of the top 103 national magazines, Jernigan, Ostroff, Ross, and O'Hara (2004) concluded that underage youth, compared with youth ages 21 and over, were exposed to 45% more beer ads, 12% more spirits ads, and 65% more alcopop ads, but 69% fewer wine ads. Other studies have similarly found that the number of magazine ads for beer and spirits increased directly with the size of the youth readership until the 30% maximum standard was reached (Garfield, Chung, & Rathouz, 2003). Other analyses controlling for readership demographics and overall readership, however, provided no evidence that youth were the targets of magazine alcohol ads (Nelson & Young, 2008). Regardless of marketers' intent, youth regularly encounter alcohol advertising in magazines.

Research has also indicated that between 20% and 37% of outdoor alcohol advertising (e.g., billboards, transit ads) in Los Angeles and Louisiana were within 500 feet of schools, playgrounds, or churches (Scott, Cohen, Schonlau, Farley, & Blumenthal, 2008). Also, outdoor and point-of-sale alcohol advertising was concentrated in low-income and minority areas and often used cultural icons or depicted persons of color to appeal to specific ethnic groups (Howard, Flora, Scheicher, & Gonzalez, 2004; Pasch, Komro, Perry, Hearst, & Farbakhsh, 2009; Scott et al., 2008).

The recent expansion of alcohol advertising into new media and nontraditional forms of promotion (e.g., Internet, e-mail, cell phones, product placements) have raised further concerns about youth exposure (Babor et al., 2010; see also Hoffman, Chapter 9 of this volume). Internet advertising is of particular concern because of youths' already high and ever-increasing exposure to the Internet, often without parental oversight or controls. Alcohol industry websites have voluntary controls to prevent underage access, requiring users to state their birth dates and then disallowing access to minors based on that information (Beer Institute, 2006). However, youth are quite adept at circumventing these alcohol website controls. For example, a tracking study found that, in the last 6 months of 2003, over 700,000 underage youth visited 55 alcohol industry Internet websites (Jernigan et al., 2005). Research is needed to determine how to protect minors more effectively from proalcohol, and protobacco, messages online.

### Causal Effects of Alcohol Advertising

*Surveys*

Research has indicated that alcohol advertising has been associated with prodrinking knowledge, beliefs, attitudes, and behaviors (Martin & Mail, 1995). However, much of the evidence was survey based and correlational, and did not establish with certainty that alcohol advertising causally affected drinking (Grube, 2004; Grube & Waiters, 2005). A few experimental studies and several econometric studies have also suggested that alcohol advertising causally affected beliefs and behavior, but some of these studies have found null effects.

Many surveys have found that youth find alcohol advertising appealing (Chen & Grube, 2002; Chen, Grube, Bersamin, Waiters, & Keefe, 2005; Waiters, Treno, & Grube, 2001). Also, youth who encountered more alcohol advertising were more knowledgeable about alcohol brands and slogans (Collins, Schell, Ellickson, & McCaffrey, 2003; Grube & Wallack, 1994). In addition, youth who reported more favorable responses to alcohol ads also reported more proalcohol beliefs (Collins et al., 2003; Fleming, Thorson, & Atkin, 2004; Unger, Schuster, Zogg, Dent, & Stacy, 2003). Similar findings have been reported for youth subgroups; for example, Mastro and Atkin (2002) found that exposure to alcohol billboards was related to prodrinking attitudes and beliefs among Mexican American youth.

Further, numerous surveys have provided evidence that exposure to alcohol advertising has been associated with self-reported drinking and drinking problems (Anderson, de Bruijn, Angus, Gordon, & Hastings, 2009; Connolly, Casswell, Zhang, & Silva, 1994; Smith & Foxcroft, 2009; Wyllie, Zhang, & Casswell, 1998a, 1998b). For example, in two longitudinal surveys, it was found that exposure to and liking of alcohol advertising at age 18 was related to higher levels of beer consumption and to alcohol-related aggression at age 21 (Casswell & Zhang, 1998) and to heavier drinking among males in adulthood (Casswell, Pledger, & Pratap, 2002). Another longitudinal study indicated that market-level alcohol advertising expenditures were related to self-reported exposure to alcohol advertising and alcohol consumption among both youth and young adults (Martin et al., 2002; Snyder, Milici, Slater, Sun, & Strizhakova, 2006).

Even preadolescents seem to be affected by alcohol advertising. In a study of fifth- and sixth-grade children, Grube and Wallack (1994) found positive relationships between awareness of alcohol advertising, increased knowledge of beer brands and slogans, more positive beliefs about drinking, and intent to drink as an adult. Another study found that seventh graders' exposure to alcohol advertising predicted alcohol use in eighth grade (Stacy, Zogg, Unger, & Dent, 2004). Similarly, sixth graders' self-reported exposure to alcohol ads and ownership of beer-related promotional items in sixth grade were associated with drinking and intent to drink in seventh grade (Collins, Ellickson, McCaffrey, & Hambarsoomians, 2007). Youth in the 75th percentile of exposure in this study were 50% more likely to drink than were those in the 25th percentile (see also Ellickson, Collins, Hambarsoomians, & McCaffrey, 2005). Exposure to alcohol advertising on billboards, when measured as density around schools attended in sixth grade, has had a relationship with self-reported intent to drink in eighth grade (Pasch et al., 2009).

*Experiments*

Relatively few experiments have been conducted on alcohol advertising effects. A few experiments involving youth have found that exposure to alcohol advertising promoted beliefs that were more favorable to drinking (Kohn & Smart, 1984). For instance, an experiment involving fourth- and fifth-grade students (Dunn & Yniguez, 1999) found that viewing alcohol ads activated positive and arousing expectancies in memory, suggesting that these ads may predispose youth to drinking. However, some experiments have found no alcohol advertising effects on youth (Kohn, Smart, & Ogborne, 1984; Sobell et al., 1986). No studies examined whether alcohol advertising might work synergistically with peer influences to drink (Pechmann & Knight, 2002), so studies should examine this.

*Econometric Studies*

Many econometric studies have indicated that alcohol advertising has been related to aggregate-level alcohol consumption and/or alcohol problems, although some studies have found null effects. For example, researchers found that youth from media markets with greater (vs. lesser) alcohol advertising expenditures were more likely to drink (Snyder et al., 2006). It was estimated that each dollar per capita spent on alcohol advertising increased the number of drinks consumed by 1–3%. Another study found that higher levels of alcohol advertising in the top 75 U.S. media markets were related to increased total and nighttime motor vehicle fatalities (Saffer, 1997). However, several studies have not found significant effects of alcohol advertising on consumption (Duffy, 1995, 2001; Fisher & Cook, 1995; Gius, 1996; Goel & Morey, 1995; Nelson, 1999; Nelson, Coulson, & Moran, 2001). For instance, using annual U.S. data from 1964 to 1990, Nelson and Moran (1995) found that alcohol advertising effects were nonsignificant after controlling for income, price, age, and other product advertising.

One concern about these economic studies is that they lacked data on advertising exposure (e.g., gross rating points) and relied on advertising expenditures as a proxy. Further, researchers often treated advertising costs across media types as equivalent, whereas the one study that accounted for differential media costs found significant advertising effects (Saffer, 1997). Also, differences in advertising expenditures across years or markets may be very small relative to total dollars spent; thus, it may be possible to document only small effects (Saffer, 1997). In other words, assuming firms are rational and allocate close to an optimal amount on advertising, one would not expect much variation in allocations; hence, one would not expect much of an effect on consumption from those small variations. Finally, most econometric studies have not examined youth alcohol consumption, which could be the most sensitive outcome (Pollay et al., 1996), and studies of this kind are needed.

### Alcohol in Entertainment Media

Paid alcohol placements have been common in television, movies, music, and music videos, and unpaid or uncompensated portrayals of alcohol use have been even more common (Dal Cin, Worth, Dalton, & Sargent, 2008; Gruber, Thau, Hill, Fisher, & Grube, 2005; Gunasekera, Chapman, & Campbell, 2005). A recent content analysis found that 83% of the top-rated movies released between 1998 and 2003 contained alcohol use, and 52% contained brand or product placements (Dal Cin et al., 2008). Intoxication appeared in roughly 32% of the top-rated films (Gunasekera et al., 2005). Depictions of underage drinking and intoxication have also been common in some television series that are popular with youth (Russell, Russell, & Grube, 2009; Van Den Bulck, Simons, & Van Gorp, 2008). These alcohol portrayals have been largely positive or, at best, neutral, often associating drinking with positive consequences and desirable attributes. The shows rarely portrayed serious negative consequences of drinking, such as car accidents.

An analysis of music popular with youth found that, across genres, 17% of the lyrics contained references to alcohol (Roberts, Henriksen, & Christensen, 1999). Rap music mentioned alcohol substantially more frequently (47%) than other genres. A common theme was getting intoxicated, although drinking was also associated with wealth and luxury, sexual activity, and crime and violence. Very few songs mentioned negative consequences of drinking, and antiuse messages occurred very rarely. Product or brand placements occurred in about 30% of the songs that discussed drinking, and were especially common in rap music (48%). In music videos, alcohol was present in about 56% of rap/hip-hop videos, 27% of rock videos, 26% of rhythm and blues videos, and 27% of pop videos (Gruber et al., 2005).

Longitudinal studies have investigated the effects of exposure to entertainment media portrayals of drinking among youth and young adults. Robinson, Chen, and Killen (1998) found that each one-hour increase in music video viewing was associated with a 31% increased risk of drinking during the next 18 months. Wingood et al. (2003) studied young African American females and found that those with greatest exposure to rap music videos were 1.5 times more likely to have used alcohol at the 12-month follow-up. In studies of German and Belgian youth (Hanewinkel & Sargent, 2009; Van Den Bulck & Beullens, 2005), exposure to movies, television, and music videos with alcohol use was associated with drinking intent and heavy episodic drinking (i.e., five or more consecutive drinks) in later time periods.

Recent longitudinal analyses of data from a national sample of U.S. youth indicated that level of exposure to movie alcohol use was related to increased use of alcohol and more alcohol problems up to 2 years later (Dal Cin et al., 2009; Stoolmiller, Gerrard, Sargent, Worth, & Gibbons, 2010; Wils, Sargent, Gibbons, Gerrard, & Stoolmiller, 2009). Perceived alcohol use by friends (norms), alcohol expectancies, and willingness to use alcohol mediated the effects of movie exposure, indicating pathways through which such portrayals may influence behavior. The effects of exposure to drinking in popular media may be more severe for youth who are more highly connected to the characters in the portrayal (Russell et al., 2009).

Parental monitoring of and restrictions on youth media use have been found to decrease the likelihood of youth drinking and may moderate the effects of media exposure (Dalton et al., 2002, 2006; Hanewinkel, Morgenstern, Tanski, & Sargent, 2008; see also Prinz, Chapter 28 of this volume.) For example, Dalton et al. (2002) found that the prevalence of having tried alcohol was 46% for youth with no parental movie viewing restrictions, 16% for youth with partial restrictions, and 4% for youth with complete restrictions. These prevalence rates held constant after controlling for other variables such as student and parenting characteristics (see also Hanewinkel et al., 2008).

In sum, alcohol portrayals have been common in youth-popular media, even in materials with ratings indicating the intended audiences are children and youth. The portrayals have been typically positive or neutral, and drinking is often associated with desirable outcomes and attributes. There is some evidence that these portrayals can affect youth's attitudes, intentions, and behaviors. Parental monitoring and restrictions on youth media use may counter such effects.

## RESEARCH ON ALCOHOL DEMARKETING

### Advertising Bans

A seminal study of 17 European and North American countries (Saffer, 1991) indicated that restrictions on broadcast alcohol advertising reduced alcohol consumption and related health problems (i.e., liver cirrhosis mortality, motor vehicle fatalities). Countries with partial restrictions (e.g., no spirits advertised on television) had alcohol consumption rates about 16% lower than countries with no restrictions, and countries with complete bans had consumption rates 11% lower than countries with partial restrictions. The corresponding reductions in motor vehicle fatalities were 10% and 23%, respectively. However, some researchers have challenged these findings, arguing that there was reverse causality: Countries with low rates of alcohol consumption and problems were more likely to restrict or ban alcohol advertising (Young, 1993). The original author (Saffer, 1991, 1993) asserted his models were correctly specified, while Young's models were misspecified. Saffer and Dave's (2002) comprehensive updated analysis of data from 20 countries again indicated that both partial and compete bans on alcohol advertising reduced alcohol consumption, with each added restriction reducing consumption by 5–8%. A recent review estimated that a complete ban on alcohol advertising in the United States would reduce alcohol deaths by 7,609 lives and cut life years lost by 16.4% (Hollingworth et al., 2006).

Nevertheless, controversy persists regarding the relationships between alcohol advertising restrictions and alcohol consumption and related health outcomes (Nelson, 2001, 2008; Nelson & Young, 2001). For example, a recent study using data from 17 countries from 1975 to 2000 investigated restrictions on alcohol advertising on per capita consumption while controlling for other alcohol control policies, price, tourism, unemployment, population structure, and wine consumption (Nelson, 2008). Effects of advertising bans and restrictions in reducing drinking were significant in some model specifications, but overall, the author concluded that there were no consistent effects. Studies generally have not considered the effects of alcohol advertising bans on youth drinking, so more research is needed in this area.

### Counteradvertising

Social marketing campaigns have tried to discourage underage drinking by targeting youth directly or both youth and their parents. The campaigns have used a number of approaches, including providing information about the risks of alcohol use and abuse, attempting to correct erroneous drinking norms, encouraging parent–child communication, and supporting advocacy and policy changes (DeJong, 2002). A recent review concluded that social marketing campaigns related to alcohol and other substance use often have the desired effects on youth's beliefs and behaviors across a range of target audiences (Gordon, McDermott, Stead, & Angus, 2006).

A novel and ambitious campaign to discourage drunk driving in the United States was the Harvard Alcohol Project's Designated Driver campaign, which was launched nationally in 1988 (Winsten, 1994). Television writers were persuaded to put designated driver messages in top television shows to educate viewers and establish this as a norm. A designated driver is someone who agrees not to drink alcohol, or to drink very little, so they can safely drive everyone else. Surveys to evaluate the campaign indicated that within a few years, 97% of the target populations were familiar with and accepting of designated drivers. Eventually, beer companies began promoting designated drivers in their own public service television announcements. A follow-up survey 10 years later, using a nationally representative sample of college students, found that college students still used designated drivers to avoid impaired driving (DeJong & Winsten, 1999). Among students who drank alcohol, 36% said they had served as a designated driver in the past month, and of these, 40% said they avoiding binge drinking when serving as the driver, with the vast majority having 0–1 drinks. However, 22% said they had extra drinks when someone else was the designated driver, indicating that the strategy had some unexpected consequences.

Because binge drinking remains a serious problem on U.S. college campuses, with associated health risks and even deaths, some campuses have begun using social marketing campaigns to change students' drinking norms. Some studies have found that these campaigns are effective at reducing drinking (DeJong et al., 2006; Haines & Spear, 1996; Mattern & Neighbors, 2004; Slater et al., 2006), but other studies have found no effects (DeJong et al., 2009; Flynn et al., 2006) or even boomerang or adverse effects (Campo & Cameron, 2006). For example, Werch and colleagues (2000) randomly assigned college students to receive or not receive antidrinking normative messages, such as "64% [of your follow students] reported that they have *not* engaged in heavy drinking recently" (p. 86). These messages lowered drinking rates and perceived norms among most students but boomeranged among some heavy drinkers.

Wechsler et al. (2003) compared trends in self-reported alcohol use at 37 colleges that adopted social norm antidrinking campaigns and 61 colleges that did not. A typical antidrinking message was "most students have five or fewer drinks when they party" (p. 485). Heavy episodic drinking increased from 46% to 49% in colleges that ran antidrinking campaigns and stayed at about 41% in colleges without these campaigns. However, colleges that ran (vs. did not run) the antidrinking campaigns were more likely to be large and public and have high drinking rates to begin with. Covariates were used to adjust for respondents' age, gender, and race, but this may not have adequately corrected for inherent differences among campuses. Research is needed to ascertain what types of antidrinking messages and/or exposure levels are efficacious and which result in null effects or boomerangs. In the meantime, since antidrinking ads might sometimes boomerang or have adverse effects, it may be especially beneficial to copy test or pretest these ads before use.

Warning Labels

There has been little indication that warning labels on alcohol containers and/or alcohol advertising have been effective as currently implemented in the United States. In 1988, the U.S. government mandated that alcoholic beverage containers include one of the following warning labels: Drinking alcohol causes birth defects, causes health problems, impairs your ability to drive, or impairs your ability to operate machinery (MacKinnon, Pentz, & Stacy, 1993). An early evaluation of these warning labels found that about one fifth of a nationally representative sample remembered seeing them (Kaskutas & Greenfield, 1992). Although somewhat greater proportions of key groups (e.g., heavy drinkers, young men at risk for drunk driving) remembered seeing the warnings, there were no improvements in knowledge about these risks. A similar study of U.S. youth found high awareness and memory of the warning labels; however, most youth already knew the risks, so their knowledge was unaffected (MacKinnon et al., 1993).

Snyder and Blood (1992) found that the warnings against drinking alcohol when pregnant or driving actually caused boomerang effects. For example, the warnings caused male college student drinkers to increase their intent to drink, while having no effect on nondrinkers. Other researchers (MacKinnon & Lapin, 1998) were unable to replicate the Snyder and Blood results, however. Few, if any, studies have addressed alcohol warnings in other media (e.g., music videos) or settings (e.g., bars). Overall, there is little evidence that the alcohol warnings used in the United States reduce drinking or drinking problems among adults or youth (Wilkinson & Room, 2009). Research is needed to identify more effective alcohol warning messages and strategies.

### Restricting Retail Sales to Youth

A key intervention involving alcohol and youth focused on the retail market and its compliance with minimum-age purchase or sell-to laws. In 1984, the U.S. National Minimum Drinking Age Act required states to enact a minimum age of 21 years for purchase or public possession of alcohol or risk losing federal highway funds. Since 1987, the minimum legal drinking age in the United States has been 21 years in all 50 states and the District of Columbia. Reviews of the available studies have indicated that increasing the minimum legal drinking age significantly decreased drinking and drinking problems among youth (Wagenaar & Toomey, 2002).

Despite the uniform minimum legal drinking age of 21, underage youth are able to obtain alcohol from both commercial and social sources. Purchase surveys, for example, have found that about 30–40% of alcohol outlets will sell to underage buyers (e.g., Freisthler, Gruenewald, Treno, & Lee, 2003; Grube, 1997; Paschall, Grube, Black, Flewelling, et al., 2007; Paschall, Grube, Black, & Ringwalt, 2007). In part, these high sales rates resulted from low and inconsistent enforcement (Wagenaar & Wolfson, 1995). Thus, even moderate increases in enforcement of sell-to laws have been shown to substantially reduce alcohol sales to minors (Grube, 1997; Scribner & Cohen, 2001; Wagenaar, Salois, & Komro, 2009). Decreases in underage sales following increased enforcement may be of limited duration, however, unless routine compliance checks are done (Wagenaar, Toomey, & Erickson, 2005).

Enforcement of sell-to alcohol laws might also reduce youth alcohol consumption (Barry et al., 2004). One study found that youth's perceptions of retail access to alcohol showed a direct relation to their 30-day frequency of alcohol use, heavy drinking, alcohol use at school, and drinking and driving (Dent, Grube, & Biglan, 2005). Also, communities with higher perceived enforcement of alcohol sell-to laws had lower rates of alcohol use and heavy drinking, and the use of social and retail sources of alcohol expanded and contracted depending on perceived enforcement. However, more research is needed on enforcement of sell-to laws for alcohol, and comparisons with tobacco should be done. Based on lessons learned from tobacco research, youth may be particularly adept at identifying retailers that continue to sell to minors despite enforcement efforts, or may shift to social sources when retail access becomes difficult.

### Prices and Taxes

Research has indicated that alcohol is price-sensitive; that is, alcohol consumption and its associated problems decrease as price increases (Cook, 2007). A recent meta-analysis of 112 studies confirms that consumption of beer, wine, and spirits is price-sensitive (Wagenaar et al., 2009). In part because of infrequent increases in state and federal alcohol taxes, the inflation-adjusted price of alcohol has actually declined substantially over the past half century in the United States

(Chaloupka, 2004). Research using data from the U.S. National Longitudinal Survey of Youth suggests that doubling the tax on beer would reduce beer consumption among youth by 3–6% (Pacula, 1998).

Other estimates indicate that increasing alcohol taxes in the United States to keep pace with inflation would lead to a 19% reduction in heavy drinking and a 6% reduction in very high-risk drinking by youth (Laixuthai & Chaloupka, 1993). Although taxation and price increases may be effective prevention strategies, social, environmental, and/or economic factors may moderate price elasticity. As a result, the price sensitivity of alcohol could vary considerably across time, states, and communities (Meier, Purshouse, & Brennan, 2010). For example, drink specials (i.e., reduced-price promotions) in bars have been associated with increased drinking and intoxication by college students (O'Mara et al., 2009) and could offset the effects of higher taxes.

A recent study indicated that increasing beer taxes and the minimum legal drinking age led to fewer youth traffic fatalities (Ponicki, Gruenewald, & LaScala, 2007). A given change in price, however, caused a larger proportional change in fatalities when the minimum legal drinking age was low than when it was high. Specifically, a 10% increase in price could reduce traffic fatalities among youth an estimated 3.1% if the legal drinking age were 18, versus 1.9% if the legal drinking age were 21. The conclusion was that communities with relatively strong policies might expect alcohol tax increases to have smaller impacts on alcohol-related problems, whereas communities with weak policies might expect larger benefits. Further, price increases could lead to consumption changes, such as switching to less expensive alcoholic beverages, without reducing overall consumption (Gruenewald, Millar, Ponicki, & Brinkley, 2000).

## REGULATION OF TOBACCO AND ALCOHOL MARKETING

### Industry Self-Regulation

Industry self-regulation of tobacco and alcohol varies by country, and so, for pragmatic reasons, we will again focus primarily on the United States. In the United States, government regulation has largely superseded tobacco industry self-regulation, as we will discuss below, but self-regulation still governs in the area of tobacco product placement. Health groups, such as Smoke Free Movies, the American Medical Association, the World Health Organization, and the U.S. states' attorneys general have demanded industry self-regulation of product placement, specifically that (a) the Motion Picture Association of America rate new movies with smoking as R, (b) studios certify no payments for cigarette placements in movies, (c) studios stop identifying tobacco brands within movies, and (d) theaters run strong antismoking ads before movies (Smoke Free Movies, n.d.). These groups have had some success at influencing tobacco industry self-regulation of product placement. In 2007, the Motion Picture Association of America (2007) agreed to consider smoking in its movie ratings. In 2008, the major U.S. movie studios agreed to put antismoking ads on the DVDs of youth-targeted movies that depict smoking (Schuker, 2008), consistent with research suggesting that this has been effective at deterring youth smoking (Pechmann & Shih, 1999). Nevertheless, most youth-targeted movies with smoking still have PG or PG-13 ratings, antismoking ads virtually never play in movie theaters, and it is unclear how long antismoking ads will continue to be placed on movie DVDs for youths. Therefore, although industry self-regulation has increased in this area because of intense public pressure, even more is needed if the industry truly wants to protect youth from smoking scenes in movies.

In the United States, the main forms of industry self-regulations for alcohol are the beer, distilled spirits, and wine industries' voluntary marketing codes. The Beer Institute's (2006) voluntary advertising and marketing code contains the following provisions: (a) Beer ads, materials, and product placements should not depict drunk driving; should not contain excessive drinking, illegal acts, lewd or indecent language or images, graphic nudity, sexually explicit activity, or acceptance of drunken behavior; and should not claim or represent that beer consumption is required for success or status; (b) beer ads and placements should be restricted to media where 70% or more of the audience is likely to be of legal drinking age (i.e., 21 or older), and beer premiums, samples, and event marketing should be restricted to venues where people are, or should be, of legal drinking age; and (c) beer ad models should be at least 25 years old and look at least 21, beer placement models should be at least 21, and beer billboards should be 500 feet or more from schools and playgrounds.

The voluntary marketing code of the Distilled Spirits Council of the United States (2009) restricts distilled spirit (i.e., hard liquor) ads to media with at least 70% of the audience of legal drinking age and bans billboards within 500 feet of schools. The voluntary Wine Institute (2005) advertising code restricts wine ads to media with a 70% or more adult audience and prohibits advertising on college campuses or in college newspapers; it also precludes underage or youthful-looking models touting the alcohol content of wine, and depicting heavy drinking or drinking in risky situations (e.g., drinking and driving). Finally, the voluntary Outdoor Advertising Association of America (2009) code of conduct prohibits outdoor advertising within 500 feet of schools, playgrounds, and churches for any age-restricted product, including alcohol.

Based on the research viewed earlier, these self-regulatory marketing codes could have some beneficial effects in terms of deterring youth targeting and youth alcohol use. However, U.S. alcohol marketers can still advertise in general audience media and reach people under age 21 who cannot legally purchase alcohol, if less than 30% of the audience is under 21; as a basis of comparison, 30% of the general population is under 21 (Day, 1996). In addition, no government or nonprofit entity is responsible for the monitoring and enforcement of the alcohol codes, and cooperation is voluntary. Finally, many public health advocates argue that self-regulatory marketing codes are aimed more at placating policy makers than protecting public health (Barbeau, DeJong, Brugge, & Rand, 1998).

## U.S. Government Regulation of Tobacco Marketing

In 1971, the U.S. Congress banned tobacco ads on television and radio (Lewit, Coate, & Grossman, 1981). It was not until 1998 that further restrictions on tobacco marketing were imposed by the U.S. Master Settlement Agreement, which was negotiated by individual states' attorneys general (NAAG, 1998), although a few states' attorneys general did not sign it. The Master Settlement Agreement prohibits direct or indirect targeting of youth below the legal smoking age of 18. It bans cartoon advertising models (e.g., Joe Camel), paid brand placements, brand premiums (e.g., free nontobacco items with the brand logos), packs with fewer than 20 cigarettes, outdoor advertising except in tobacco retail and adult-only (i.e., ages 18 and over) venues, brand name sponsorships of sport and music events and events with significant percentages of youth in attendance, and free samples except in adult-only venues.

However, the Master Settlement Agreement lacks an oversight body that can identify and punish violators. Therefore, after the agreement was signed, researchers found that virtually all of the major tobacco firms, especially R.J. Reynolds, continued to place ads in magazines that reached substantial numbers of youth (Hamilton, Turner-Bowker, Celebucki, & Connolly, 2002; *People of the State of California v. R.J. Reynolds Tobacco Company*, 2002). For example, King, Siegel, Celebucki, and Connolly (1998) studied tobacco ads in leading U.S. magazines after the Master Settlement Agreement and found that if one third of a magazine's readership consisted of youth, the magazine contained an average of nine ads for youth brands and just two ads for adult brands.

In June 2009 in the United States, the landmark FSPTCA (Tobacco Act; 2009) became law. The Tobacco Act gives the FDA authority to oversee tobacco marketing, which tobacco firms will pay for with user fees. The Tobacco Act formalizes most of the Master Settlement Agreement regulations and, in addition, contains virtually all of the regulations to prevent tobacco marketing to youth that the FDA tried to implement in 1996 but could not, because the Supreme Court ruled that the FDA lacked regulatory authority over tobacco. Tobacco firms are challenging the Tobacco Act for allegedly violating their right to free speech under the First Amendment (Wilson, 2009). These legal challenges have been unsuccessful to date, but nonetheless, the various lawsuits and appeals that may ensue may hold up implementation of the Tobacco Act provisions for years to come, with the final outcomes uncertain. In addition, much detailed work and time are needed to write the specific regulations to make the Tobacco Act operative. Therefore, although we will describe the act's major provisions below, there is no guarantee that they will make it into the specific regulations (see Andreasen, Goldberg, & Sirgy, Chapter 2 of this volume).

The 2009 Tobacco Act goes beyond the Master Settlement Agreement in protecting youth, because it adopts the extensive provisions set out by the FDA that the Supreme Count initially disallowed (FDA, 1996). Specifically, the Tobacco Act limits print advertising to black text on a white background except in adult publications, defined as having less than 15% of readers under age 18 and also less than 2 million readers under age 18. These criteria are quite stringent but reasonable, because 25% of the U.S. population, or 74 million people, are under 18 (Day, 1996). The Tobacco Act bans outdoor advertising within 1,000 feet of schools and playgrounds except for the type of ad that the First Amendment protects (e.g., tobacco retailer signage). It also bans gifts with purchase or proof of purchase, vending machine sales except in adult-only venues, and free cigarette samples, but it allows smoke-free tobacco samples in qualified adult-only venues. The act bans sales to those under age 18 and requires retailers to verify the purchaser's age under federal law; previously, this was only state law. However, the Tobacco Act does not address product placements in movies or on television.

The Tobacco Act addresses adult smokers as well (FSPTCA, 2009). It mandates that cigarette packs include specified health warnings on the top 50% of both the front and back of the packaging and that print cigarette ads include the same health warnings on the top 20% of their pages. In a few years, the warnings must include graphic pictures that depict the health risks of smoking. The act specifies the text of the warnings to be used, such as "WARNING: Cigarettes are addictive" and "WARNING: Cigarettes cause cancer," although different statements can be imposed through rule-making. Further, tobacco firms must divulge ingredient lists and nicotine contents by brand, disclose their research on health effects, and forgo flavorings except menthol.

Further, the Tobacco Act defines *modified-risk products* as those that claim to reduce risk, have less or none of an ingredient, or be light or mild, but it excludes smokeless claims. The act specifies that a firm cannot market a new or existing modified-risk product unless it can prove that the product will "(A) significantly reduce harm and the risk of tobacco-related disease to individual tobacco users; and (B) benefit the health of the population as a whole" (sec. 911.g.1). The Tobacco Act bans terms like *light, mild,* and *low tar* outright. The FDA must set up a committee to advise it on modified-risk products. However, the FDA cannot ban tobacco products or nicotine outright, require prescriptions for such products, or mandate ad preapproval.

The Tobacco Act should deter youth targeting, as its authors based the youth provisions on extensive research compiled by the American Psychological Association (FDA, 1995). Also, the act prevents advertising in most general audience media. Further, the FDA is responsible for monitoring and enforcement and will receive funding to perform both functions. The Tobacco Act should also deter adult smoking, because it bans misleading marketing terms (e.g., *light cigarettes*) and requires manufacturers to substantiate all claims about modified-risk products. The act will eventually mandate graphic, pictorial warnings on cigarette packs, which should be beneficial.

The Tobacco Act lists nine specific warnings to be used in rotation, although research has indicated that it is more effective to ensure the warnings are novel, rather than repeating the same warnings in rotation (Krugman et al., 1994). Also, all nine warnings address health risks rather than social risks or the health benefits of quitting. The FDA is authorized to change the warning text through rule making, though, so researchers should examine if this is truly the optimal type of warning. Research has indicated that warning messages about social risks (e.g., disapproval of secondhand smoke) have worked particularly well with youth (Pechmann et al., 2003), so perhaps these types of warnings are needed. Research has also suggested that it may be beneficial to intersperse messages about the benefits of quitting with ones about the costs of not quitting, to reach people who are promotion or benefit focused as well as those who are prevention or cost focused (Zhao & Pechmann, 2007), so perhaps these types of warning are needed, too. More research is needed on these issues, as they relate to both tobacco and alcohol warnings.

## Global Efforts to Regulate Alcohol and Tobacco

The global community has done little to regulate alcohol on a comprehensive and unified scale, so we will offer no discussion of this. However, the global community has made substantial progress in regulating tobacco marketing. Most countries have signed a global treaty called the WHO Framework Convention on Tobacco Control, which was adopted at the World Health Assembly in 2003 and implemented in 2005 (WHO, 2003). This comprehensive, global tobacco control framework has the following major provisions: Countries must establish and finance a national tobacco control body, implement tobacco taxes to discourage consumption, and prohibit tobacco smuggling. They must restrict tobacco sales to minors, protect people from secondhand smoke, regulate tobacco product ingredients, and require tobacco firms to disclose their ingredients.

In addition, the treaty requires that countries use rotating graphic health warnings, which does not preclude novel warnings, that cover at least 30% and ideally 50% of the cigarette package, and they must ban misleading marketing claims, such as "light" or "mild" cigarettes. Further, countries must ban all tobacco advertising, promotion, and sponsorship. If a country's constitution prohibits a comprehensive ban, it must use all available means to restrict tobacco advertising and marketing. Countries must restrict purchase incentives, such as price promotions, and require tobacco firms to disclose promotional, advertising, and sponsorship expenditures. Countries must adopt effective measures to promote cessation, provide treatment for tobacco dependence, and provide access to educational and awareness programs about the health risks of tobacco use. This treaty should dramatically reduce the lives lost worldwide from tobacco use.

## CONCLUDING THOUGHTS AND FUTURE RESEARCH DIRECTIONS

Tobacco use and alcohol abuse are of significant concern to transformative consumer researchers, social marketing researchers, and other researchers worldwide who are concerned about individual and societal health and well-being. Past research has documented that numerous tobacco and alcohol marketing activities encourage product use among youth and adults, including not only advertising but also more covert marketing activities such as product placements. Governments have successfully used social marketing to discourage consumption, such as advertising bans, counteradvertising, health warnings, restrictions in product use (e.g., no smoking in public buildings), and higher prices through taxations, which seem to be effective in many cases, but sometimes these efforts (e.g., counteradvertising) are not sustained or are overshadowed by tobacco and alcohol marketing efforts. Industry self-regulation has been limited and weak for both alcohol and tobacco, although intense public pressure has yielded some new self-regulation related to tobacco placements in movies.

Recent actions have substantially strengthened government regulation of tobacco marketing in the United States and worldwide. The 2009 U.S. FSPTCA is a comprehensive attempt to regulate tobacco marketing, especially to protect youth, although it is silent about counteradvertising and product placement. The 2003 WHO Framework Convention on Tobacco Control is a landmark treaty that should be highly effective at reducing tobacco marketing and tobacco use globally. In comparison to tobacco, alcohol marketing restrictions in the United States and most of the world are much more limited and dependent on industry self-regulation. Perhaps the significant advances in tobacco policies in the United States and globally will serve as an impetus for more comprehensive alcohol policies.

Throughout this chapter, we have identified numerous research gaps and future research directions that may interest Transformative Consumer Research scholars and others. To highlight a few of the gaps, research is still needed to examine the behavioral effects of cigarette and alcohol warning labels on products for both youth and adults. We could not find a single study that examined how alcohol warnings or cigarette warnings affected actual behavior, either in the short- or long-term, although a few studies have examined the new graphic cigarette warnings and self-reported behavior or intent. Studies are also needed on whether tobacco or alcohol warning labels should include social messages (e.g., about the harm to others of secondhand smoke or drunk driving) and whether some warnings should be worded positively (e.g., stressing the benefits of quitting), rather than negatively (e.g., stressing the costs of not quitting), to appeal to different consumers.

Also, future studies should explore consumers' perceptions of snus and the new reduced-exposure tobacco products, and their misperceptions of nicotine replacement therapies. There is a need for more cross-country and cross-cultural research on the impact of different legal ages for purchasing alcohol and tobacco to determine both the short- and longer term impacts of lower age limits. More ethnographic studies should focus on youth and their drinking and smoking habits around the world, and the role of marketing in potentially influencing these habits. Since the recent U.S. and global tobacco control efforts do not include counteradvertising, key research questions are Why did this happen? and Is this exclusion warranted?

Overall, more carefully controlled research is needed in the alcohol area, because many of these studies are correlational and cannot ascertain causality, especially in comparison with the tobacco area. In particular, more research is needed on the effects of enforcing laws that disallow alcohol sales to minors to see if youth alcohol consumption actually declines. Also, more research is needed to determine to what extent alcohol advertising influences alcohol consumption and to what extent alcohol counteradvertising causes boomerangs. In the tobacco area, numerous studies have established that cigarette advertising influences cigarette consumption, and virtually no studies have found that cigarette counteradvertising causes boomerangs. In the alcohol area, the advertising–consumption link is less well established, and counteradvertising has boomeranged. These findings imply that advertising and counteradvertising are more powerful and predictable for tobacco than alcohol, but can we really conclude this? Or, has the tobacco research community been more focused on conducting studies that support tobacco control, while the alcohol research community has sought to identify both the pros and cons of alcohol control?

Research is needed that has no specific agenda, so we know when the right decision for consumers and society is more government intervention or less. This chapter clearly demonstrates that considerable research has already been conducted on tobacco and alcohol marketing and consumers, yet major research gaps remain for transformative consumer researchers and others to address. Hopefully, this chapter also demonstrates that this type of research can truly transform researchers, consumers, and societies.

# REFERENCES

Aero, L. F., Wold, B., Kannas, L., & Rampela, M. (1986). Health behavior in school children: A WHO cross national study. *Health Promotion, 1*, 17–32.

Albers, A. B., Siegel, M., Cheng, D. M., Rigotti, N. A., & Biener, L. (2004). Effects of restaurant and bar smoking regulations on exposure to environmental tobacco smoke among Massachusetts adults. *American Journal of Public Health, 94*(11), 1959–1964.

Altman, D. G., Rasenick-Douss, L., Foster, V., & Tye, J. B. (1991). Sustained effects of an educational program to reduce sales of cigarettes to minors. *American Journal of Public Health, 81*(7), 891–893.

Altman, D. G., Wheelis, A. Y., McFarlane, M., Lee, H., & Fortmann, S. P. (1999). The relationship between tobacco access and use among adolescents: A four-community study. *Social Science & Medicine, 48*(6), 759–775.

American Academy of Pediatrics, Committee on Communications. (2006). Policy statement: Children, adolescents, and advertising. *Pediatrics, 118*(6), 2563–2569. Available: http://pediatrics.aappublications.org/cgi/content/full/118/6/2563

American Legacy Foundation. (2007). *Saving lives, saving money II: Tobacco-free states spend less on Medicaid* (Policy Report No. 4). Washington, DC: Author. Available: http://www.americanlegacy.org/PDFPublications/saving_lives_saving_money.pdf

American Lung Association. (2010). *State Legislated Actions on Tobacco Issues (SLATI) overview*. Available: http://slati.lungusa.org/StateLegislateAction.asp

Anderson, P., de Bruijn, A., Angus, K., Gordon, R., & Hastings, G. (2009). Impact of alcohol advertising and media exposure on adolescent alcohol use: A systematic review of longitudinal studies. *Alcohol and Alcoholism, 44*(3), 229–243.

Andrews, R. L., & Franke, G. R. (1991). The determinants of cigarette consumption: A meta-analysis. *Journal of Public Policy & Marketing, 10*(Spring), 81–100.

Austin, E. W., Chen, M., & Grube, J. W. (2006). How does alcohol advertising influence underage drinking? The role of desirability, identification and skepticism. *Journal of Adolescent Health, 38*(4), 376–384.

Austin, E. W., & Hust, S. J. (2005). Targeting adolescents? The content and frequency of alcoholic and nonalcoholic beverage ads in magazine and video formats November 1999–April 2000. *Journal of Health Communication, 10*(8), 769–785.

Babor, T., Caetano, R., Casswell, C., Edwards, G., Giesbrecht, N., Graham, K., et al. (2010). *Alcohol: No ordinary commodity: Research and public policy* (2nd ed.). New York: Oxford University Press.

Barbeau, E. M., DeJong, W., Brugge, D. M., & Rand, W. M. (1998). Does cigarette print advertising adhere to the Tobacco Institute's voluntary advertising and promotion code? An assessment. *Journal of Public Health Policy, 19*(4), 473–488.

Barry, R., Edwards, E., Pelletier, A., Brewer, R., Miller, J., Naimi, T., et al. (2004). Enhanced enforcement of laws to prevent alcohol sales to underage persons—New Hampshire, 1999–2004. *Journal of the American Medical Association, 292*(5), 561–562.

Beer Institute. (2006). *Advertising and marketing code*. Washington, DC: Author. Available: http://www.beerinstitute.org/beerInstitute/files/ccLibraryFiles/Filename/000000000384/2006ADCODE.pdf

Benowitz, N. (1999). Nicotine addiction. *Primary Care, 26*(3), 611–631.

Biglan, A. (2004a). Written testimony in U.S. vs. Philip Morris et al, 99-cv-02496. Available: http://www.ori.org/oht/Testimony/3_Biglan_PhilipMorris_December_2004.pdf

Biglan, A. (2004b). Written direct testimony in U.S. v. PM et al, 99-cv-02496. Demonstrative 19, citing Legacy Tobacco Documents online. Bates Number 506866008. Available: http://www.ori.org/oht/Testimony/Demonstrative19_RJR_Joe_Camel_December_2004.pdf

Biglan, A., Ary, D. V., Koehn, V., Levings, D., Smith, S., Wright, Z., et al. (1996). Mobilizing positive reinforcement in communities to reduce youth access to tobacco. *American Journal of Community Psychology, 24*(5), 625–638.

Biglan, A., Henderson, J., Humphreys, D., Yasui, M., Whisman, R., Black, C., et al. (1995). Mobilising positive reinforcement to reduce youth access to tobacco. *Tobacco Control, 4*(1), 42–48.

Boddewyn, J. J. (1986). *Tobacco advertising bans and consumption in 16 countries*. New York: International Advertising Association.

Boddewyn, J. J. (1989). *Juvenile smoking initiation and advertising*. New York: International Advertising Association.

Bolton, L. E., Cohen, J. B., & Bloom, P. N. (2006). Does marketing products as remedies create "get out of jail free cards?" *Journal of Consumer Research, 33*(1), 71–81.

Bonnie, R. J., & O'Connell, M. E. (2004). *Reducing underage drinking*. Washington, DC: National Academies Press.

Borland, R., Yong, H. H., Wilson, N., Fong, G. T., Hammond, D., Cummings, K. M., et al. (2009). How reactions to cigarette-packet health warnings influence quitting: Findings from the ITC Four-Country survey. *Addiction, 104*(4), 669–675.

Breland, A. B., Buchhalter, A. R., Evans, S. E., & Eissenberg, T. (2002). Evaluating acute effects of potential reduced-exposure products for smokers: Clinical laboratory methodology. *Nicotine & Tobacco Research, 4*(Suppl. 2), S131–140.

Brendryen, H., & Kraft, P. (2008). Happy ending: A randomized controlled trial of a digital multi-media smoking cessation intervention. *Addiction, 103*(3), 478–484.

Campo, S., & Cameron, K. A. (2006). Differential effects of exposure to social norms campaigns: A cause for concern. *Health Communication, 19*(3), 209–219.

Carpenter, C. (2004). Heavy alcohol use and youth suicide: Evidence from tougher drunk driving laws. *Journal of Policy Analysis & Management, 23*(4), 831–842.

Carpenter, C. (2005). Youth alcohol use and risky sexual behavior: Evidence from underage drunk driving laws. *Journal of Health Economics, 24*(3), 613–628.

Carpenter, C. (2007). Heavy alcohol use and crime: Evidence from underage drunk-driving laws. *Journal of Law and Economics, 50*(August), 539–557.

Casswell, S., Pledger, M., & Pratap, S. (2002). Trajectories of drinking from 18 to 26 years: Identification and prediction. *Addiction, 97*(11), 1427–1437.

Casswell, S., & Zhang, J. F. (1998). Impact of liking for advertising and brand allegiance on drinking and alcohol-related aggression: A longitudinal study. *Addiction, 93*(8), 1209–1217.

Cataldo, J. K., & Malone, R. E. (2008). False promises: The tobacco industry, "low tar" cigarettes, and older smokers. *Journal of the American Geriatrics Society, 56*(9), 1716–1723.

Centers for Disease Control and Prevention. (1992). Comparison of the cigarette brand preferences of adult and teenaged smokers: United States, 1989 and 10 U.S. communities, 1988 and 1990. *Morbidity and Mortality Weekly Report, 41*(10), 169–173, 179–181.

Centers for Disease Control and Prevention. (1994). Changes in the cigarette brand preferences of adolescent smokers: United States, 1989–1993. *Morbidity and Mortality Weekly Report, 43*(32), 577–581.

Centers for Disease Control and Prevention. (2004). Alcohol-attributable deaths and years of potential life lost—United States 2001. *Morbidity and Mortality Weekly Report, 53*(37), 866–870.

Centers for Disease Control and Prevention. (2008). Smoking-attributable mortality, years of potential life lost, and productivity losses—United States, 2000–2004. *Morbidity and Mortality Weekly Report, 57*(45), 1226–1228.

Chaloupka, F. J. (2004). The effects of price on alcohol use, abuse, and their consequences. In R. Bonnie & M. E. O'Connell (Eds.), *Reducing underage drinking: A collective responsibility* (pp. 541–564). Washington, DC: National Academies Press.

Chapman, S. (2007). *Public health advocacy and tobacco control: Making smoking history*. Oxford, England: Blackwell.

Charlesworth, A., & Glantz, S. A. (2005). Smoking in the movies increases adolescent smoking: A review. *Pediatrics, 116*, 1516–1528.

Chassin, L., Presson, C. C., Sherman, S. J., Corty, E., & Olshavsky, R. W. (1984). Predicting the onset of cigarette smoking in adolescents: A longitudinal study. *Journal of Applied Social Psychology, 14*(3), 224–243.

Cheh, J. A., Ribisl, K. M., & Wildemuth, B. M. (2003). An assessment of the quality and usability of smoking cessation information on the Internet. *Health Promotion Practice, 4*(3), 278–287.

Chen, M., & Grube, J. W. (2002). TV beer and soft drink advertising: What young people like and what effects? In S. E. Martin, L. B. Snyder, M. Hamilton, F. Fleming-Milici, M. D. Slater, A. Stacy, et al. (Eds.), Alcohol advertising and youth [Special section]. *Alcoholism: Clinical and Experimental Research, 26*(6), 900–906.

Chen, M., Grube, J. W., Bersamin, M., Waiters, E., & Keefe, D. B. (2005). Alcohol advertising: What makes it attractive to youth? *Journal of Health Communication, 10*(6), 553–565.

Chetwynd, J., Coope, P., Brodie, R. J., & Wells, E. (1988). Impact of cigarette advertising on aggregate demand for cigarettes in New Zealand. *British Journal of Addiction, 83*, 409–414.

Chung, P. J., Garfield, C. F., Elliott, M. N., Ostroff, J., Ross, C., Jernigan, D. H., et al. (2010). Association between adolescent viewership and alcohol advertising on cable television. *American Journal of Public Health, 100*(3), 555–562.

Chung, P. J., Garfield, C. F., Rathouz, P. J., Lauderdale, D. S., Best, D., & Lantos, J. (2002). Youth targeting by tobacco manufacturers since the Master Settlement Agreement. *Health Affairs, 21*(2), 254–263.

Cohen, J. B. (2000). Playing to win: Marketing and public policy at odds over Joe Camel. *Journal of Public Policy & Marketing, 19*(2), 155–167.

Collins, R. L., Ellickson, P. L., McCaffrey, D., & Hambarsoomians, K. (2007). Early adolescent exposure to alcohol advertising and its relationship to underage drinking. *Journal of Adolescent Health, 40*(6), 527–534.

Collins, R. L., Schell, T., Ellickson, P. L., & McCaffrey, D. (2003). Predictors of beer advertising awareness among eighth graders. *Addiction, 98*(9), 1297–1306.

Connolly, G. M., Casswell, S., Zhang, J., & Silva, P. A. (1994). Alcohol in the mass media and drinking by adolescents: A longitudinal study. *Addiction, 89*(10), 1255–1263.

Cook, P. J. (2007). *Paying the tab: The costs and benefits of alcohol control.* Princeton, NJ: Princeton University Press.

Cummings, K. M. (2004). Tobacco risk perceptions and behavior: Implications for tobacco control. *Nicotine & Tobacco Research, 6*(Suppl. 3), 285–288.

Cummings, K. M., Hyland, A., Bansal, M. A., & Giovino, G. A. (2004). What do Marlboro Lights smokers know about low-tar cigarettes? *Nicotine & Tobacco Research, 6*(Suppl. 3), 323–332.

Cummings, K. M., Hyland, A., Perla, J., & Giovino, G. A. (2003). Is the prevalence of youth smoking affected by efforts to increase retailer compliance with a minors' access law? *Nicotine & Tobacco Research, 5*(4), 465–471.

Dal Cin, S., Worth, K. A., Dalton, M. A., & Sargent, J. D. (2008). Youth exposure to alcohol use and brand appearances in popular contemporary movies. *Addiction, 103*(12), 1925–1932.

Dal Cin, S., Worth, K. A., Gerrard, M., Gibbons, F. X., Stoolmiller, M., Wills, T. A., et al. (2009). Watching and drinking: Expectancies, prototypes, and peer affiliations mediate the effect of exposure to alcohol use in movies on adolescent drinking. *Health Psychology, 28*(4), 473–483.

Dalton, M. A., Adachi-Mejia, A. M., Longacre, M. R., Titus-Ernstoff, L. T., Gibson, J. J., Martin, S. K., et al. (2006). Parental rules and monitoring of children's movie viewing associated with children's risk for smoking and drinking. *Pediatrics, 118*(5), 1932–1942.

Dalton, M. A., Ahrens, M. B., Sargent, J. D., Mott, L. A., Beach, M. L., Tickle, J. J., et al. (2002). Relation between parental restrictions on movies and adolescent use of tobacco and alcohol. *Effective Clinical Practice, 5*(1), 1–10.

Dalton, M. A., Beach, M. L., Adachi-Mejia A. M., Longacre, M. R., Matzkin, A. L., Sargent, J. D., et al. (2009). Early exposure to movie smoking predicts established smoking by older teens and young adults. *Pediatrics, 123*(4), e551–e558.

Dalton, M. A., Sargent, J. D., Beach, M. L., Titus-Ernstoff, L., Gibson, J. J., Ahrens, M. B., et al. (2003). Effect of viewing smoking in movies on adolescent smoking initiation: A cohort study. *Lancet, 362*(9380), 281–285.

Davis, R. M., Gilpin, E. A., Loken, B., Viswanath, K., & Wakefield, M. A. (Eds.). (2008). *The role of the media in promoting and reducing tobacco use* (NCI Tobacco Control Monograph No. 19). Bethesda, MD: U.S. Department of Health and Human Services, National Institutes of Health, National Cancer Institute.

Day, J. C. (1996). *Population projections of the United States by age, sex, race, and Hispanic origin: 1995 to 2050.* U.S. Bureau of the Census, Current Population Reports, P25-1130. Washington, DC: U.S. Government Printing Office. Available: http://www.census.gov/prod/1/pop/p25-1130.pdf

DeJong, W. (2002). The role of mass media campaigns in reducing high-risk drinking among college students. *Journal of Studies on Alcohol, 63*(Suppl. 14), 182–192.

DeJong, W., Schneider, S. K., Towvim, L. G., Murphy, M. J., Doerr, E. E., Simonsen, N. R., et al. (2006). A multisite randomized trial of social norms marketing campaigns to reduce college student drinking. *Journal of Studies on Alcohol, 67*(6), 868–879.

DeJong, W., Schneider, S. K., Towvim, L. G., Murphy, M. J., Doerr, E. E., Simonsen, N. R., et al. (2009). A multisite randomized trial of social norms marketing campaigns to reduce college student drinking: A replication failure. *Substance Abuse, 30*(2), 127–140.

DeJong, W., & Winsten, J. A. (1999). The use of designated drivers by U.S. college students: A national study. *Journal of American College Health, 47*(4), 151–156.

Dent, C., Grube, J. W., & Biglan, A. (2005). Community level alcohol availability and enforcement of possession laws as predictors of youth drinking. *Preventive Medicine, 40*(3), 355–362.

Deverell, M., Randolph, C., Albers, A., Hamilton, W., & Siegel, M. (2006). Diffusion of local restaurant smoking regulations in Massachusetts: Identifying disparities in health or protection for population subgroups. *Journal of Public Health Management and Practice, 12*(3), 262–269.

DiFranza, J. R. (2000). World's best practice in tobacco control: Reducing youth access to tobacco. *Tobacco Control, 9*(2), 235–236.

DiFranza, J. R., Carlson, R. P., & Caisse, R. E., Jr. (1992). Reducing youth access to tobacco [Letter to the editor]. *Tobacco Control, 1*(1), 58.

Dinh, K. T., Sarason, I. G., Peterson, A. V., & Onstad, L. E. (1995). Children's perceptions of smokers and nonsmokers: A longitudinal study. *Health Psychology, 14*(1), 32–40.

Distilled Spirits Council of the United States. (2009). *Code of responsible practices for beverage alcohol advertising and marketing.* Washington, DC: Author. Available: http://www.discus.org/industry/code/code.htm

Donovan, R. J., Jancey, J., & Jones, S. (2002). Tobacco point of sale advertising increases positive brand user imagery. *Tobacco Control, 11*(3), 191–194.

Duffy, M. (1995). Advertising in demand systems for alcoholic drinks and tobacco: A comparative study. *Journal of Policy Modeling, 17*(6), 557–577.

Duffy, M. (2001). Advertising in consumer allocation models: Choice of functional form. *Applied Economics, 33*(4), 437–456.

Dunn, M. E., & Yniguez, R. M. (1999). Experimental demonstration of the influence of alcohol advertising on the activation of alcohol expectancies in memory among fourth- and fifth-grade children. *Experimental & Clinical Pharmacology, 7*(4), 473–483.

Edwards, C. A., Harris, W. C., Cook, D. R., Bedford, K. F., & Zuo, Y. (2004). Out of the smokescreen: Does an antismoking advertisement affect young women's perception of smoking in movies and their intention to smoke? *Tobacco Control, 13*(3), 277–282.

Ellickson, P. L., Collins, R. L., Hambarsoomians, K., & McCaffrey, D. F. (2005). Does alcohol advertising promote adolescent drinking? Results from a longitudinal study. *Addiction, 100*(8), 235–246.

Embry, D. D., Biglan, A., Hankins, M., Dahl, M. J., & Galloway, D. (2009). *Effectiveness trial using Reward & Reminder‴ visits to reduce tobacco sales to, and tobacco use by, young people: A multiple-baseline across two states.* Manuscript submitted for publication.

Etter, J. F., Kozlowski, L. T., & Perneger, T. V. (2003). What smokers believe about light and ultralight cigarettes. *Preventive Medicine, 36*(1), 92–98.

Evans, N., Farkas, A., Gilpin, E., Berry, C. C., & Pierce, J. P. (1995). Influence of tobacco marketing and exposure to smokers on adolescent susceptibility to smoking. *Journal of the National Cancer Institute, 87*(20), 1538–1545.

Evans, W. N., Family, M. C., & Montgomery, E. (2006). Do workplace smoking bans reduce smoking? In K. E. Warner (Ed.), *Tobacco control policy* (pp. 233–261). San Francisco: Jossey-Bass.

Family Smoking Prevention and Tobacco Control Act, H.R. 1256, Pub. L. No. 111-31 (2009). Available: http://www.govtrack.us/congress/billtext.xpd?bill=h111-1256

Farrelly, M. C., Davis, K. C., Haviland, M. L., Messeri, P., & Healton, C. G. (2005). Evidence of a dose–response relationship between "truth" antismoking ads and youth smoking prevalence. *American Journal of Public Health, 95*(3), 425–431.

Federal Trade Commission. (2008). *Self-regulation in the alcohol industry: Report of the Federal Trade Commission.* Washington, DC: Author. Available: http://www.ftc.gov/os/2008/06/080626alcoholreport.pdf

Federal Trade Commission. (2009, August 12). *FTC releases reports on cigarette and smokeless tobacco sales and marketing expenditures.* Available: http://www.ftc.gov/opa/2009/08/tobacco.shtm

Fichtenberg, C. M., & Glantz, S. A. (2002). Youth access interventions do not affect youth smoking. *Pediatrics, 109*(6), 1088–1092.

Fisher, J. C., & Cook, P. A. (1995). *Advertising, alcohol consumption, and mortality: An empirical investigation.* Westport, CT: Greenwood.

Fleming, K., Thorson, E., & Atkin, C. K. (2004). Alcohol advertising exposure and perceptions: Links with alcohol expectancies and intentions to drink or drinking in underaged youth and young adults. *Journal of Health Communication, 9*(1), 3–29.

Flynn, B. S., Worden, J. K., Bunn, J. Y., Dorwaldt, A. L., Dana, G. S., & Callas, P. W. (2006). Mass media and community interventions to reduce alcohol use by early adolescents. *Journal of Studies on Alcohol, 67*(1), 66–74.

Flynn, B. S., Worden, J. K., Secker-Walker, R. H., Badger, G. J., Geller, B. M., & Costanza, M. C. (1992). Prevention of cigarette smoking through mass media intervention and school programs. *American Journal of Public Health, 82*(6), 827–834.

Flynn, B. S., Worden, J. K., Secker-Walker, R. H., Pirie, P. L., Badger, G. J., Carpenter, J. A., et al. (1994). Mass media and school interventions for cigarette smoking prevention: Effects 2 years after completion. *American Journal of Public Health, 84*(7), 1148–1150.

Foley, D., & Pechmann, C. (2004). The National Youth Anti-Drug Media Campaign Copy Test System. *Social Marketing Quarterly, 10*(2), 34–42.

Forster, J. L., Murray, D. M., Wolfson, M., Blaine, T. M., Wagenaar, A. C., & Hennrikus, D. J. (1998). The effects of community policies to reduce youth access to tobacco. *American Journal of Public Health, 88*(8), 1193–1198.

Forster, J. L., & Wolfson, M. (1998). Youth access to tobacco: Policies and politics. *Annual Review of Public Health, 19*(1), 203–235.

Foulds, J., Ramstrom, L., Burke, M., & Fagerström, K. (2003). Effect of smokeless tobacco (snus) on smoking and public health in Sweden. *Tobacco Control, 12*(4), 349–359.

Freisthler, B., Gruenewald, P. J., Treno, A. J., & Lee, J. (2003). Evaluating alcohol access and the alcohol environment in neighborhood areas. *Alcoholism: Clinical and Experimental Research, 27*(3), 477–484.

Garfield, C. F., Chung, P. J., & Rathouz, P. J. (2003). Alcohol advertising in magazines and adolescent readership. *Journal of the American Medical Association. 289*(18), 1028–1029.

Geier, A., Mucha, R. F., & Pauli, P. (2000). Appetitive nature of drug cues confirmed with physiological measures in a model using pictures of smoking. *Psychopharmacology, 150*(3), 283–291.

Gilpin, E. A., Emery, S., White, M. M., & Pierce, J. P. (2002). Does tobacco industry marketing of "light" cigarettes give smokers a rationale for postponing quitting? *Nicotine & Tobacco Research, 4*(Suppl. 2), S147–S155.

Gius, M. P. (1996). Using panel data to determine the effect of advertising on brand-level distilled spirits sales. *Journal of Studies on Alcohol, 57*(1), 73–76.

Goel, R. K. & Morey, M. J. (1995). The interdependence of cigarette and liquor demand. *Southern Economic Journal, 62*(2), 451–459.

Goldberg, M. E. (2008). Why new tobacco harm-reduction products should be regulated. *Journal of Public Policy & Marketing, 27*(2), 182–186.

Golmier, I., Chebat, J. C., & Gélinas-Chebat, C. (2007). Can cigarette warnings counterbalance effects of smoking scenes in movies? *Psychological Reports, 100*(1), 3–18.

Gordon, R., McDermott, L., Stead, M., & Angus, K. (2006). The effectiveness of social marketing interventions for health improvement: What's the evidence? *Public Health, 120*(12), 1133–1139.

Grube, J. W. (1997). Preventing sales of alcohol to minors: Results from a community trial. *Addiction, 92*(Suppl. 2), S251–S260.

Grube, J. W. (2004). Alcohol in the media: Drinking portrayals, alcohol advertising, and alcohol consumption among youth. In R. J. Bonnie & M. E. O'Connell (Eds.), *Reducing underage drinking: A collective responsibility* (pp. 597–624). Washington, DC: National Academies Press.

Grube, J. W., & Waiters, E. D. (2005). Alcohol in the media: Content and effects on drinking beliefs and behaviors among youth. *Adolescent Medicine Clinics, 16*(2), 327–343.

Grube, J. W., & Wallack, L. (1994). Television beer advertising and drinking knowledge, beliefs, and intentions among schoolchildren. *American Journal of Public Health, 84*(2), 254–259.

Gruber, E. L., Thau, H. M., Hill, D. L., Fisher, D. A., & Grube, J. W. (2005). Alcohol, tobacco, and illicit substances in music videos: A content analysis of prevalence and genre. *Journal of Adolescent Health, 37*(1), 81–83.

Gruenewald, P. J., Millar, A., Ponicki, W. R., & Brinkley, G. (2000). Physical and economic access to alcohol: The application of geostatistical methods to small area analysis in community settings. In R. A. Wilson & M. C. Dufour (Eds.), *The epidemiology of alcohol problems in small geographic areas* (pp. 163–212). Bethesda, MD: National Institute on Alcohol Abuse and Alcoholism.

Gunasekera, H., Chapman, S., & Campbell, S. (2005). Sex and drugs in popular movies: An analysis of the top 200 films. *Journal of the Royal Society of Medicine, 98*(10), 464–570.

Haines, M., & Spear, S. F. (1996). Changing the perception of the norm: A strategy to decrease binge drinking among college students. *Journal of American College Health, 45*(3), 134–140.

Hamilton, W. L., Norton, G. D., Ouellette, T. K., Rhodes, W. M., Kling, R., & Connolly, G. N. (2004). Smokers' responses to advertisements for regular and light cigarettes and potential reduced-exposure tobacco products. *Nicotine & Tobacco Research, 6*(Suppl. 3), 353–362.

Hamilton, W. L., Turner-Bowker, D. M., Celebucki, C. C., & Connolly, G. N. (2002). Cigarette advertising in magazines: The tobacco industry response to the Master Settlement Agreement and to public pressure. *Tobacco Control, 11*(Suppl. 2), ii54–ii58.

Hammond, D., Fong, G. T., Borland, R., Cummings, K. M., McNeill, A., & Driezen, P. (2007). Text and graphic warnings on cigarette packages: Findings from the International Tobacco Control Four Country Study. *American Journal of Preventive Medicine, 32*(3), 202–209.

Hanewinkel, R., Morgenstern, M., Tanski, S. E., & Sargent, J. D. (2008). Longitudinal study of parental movie restriction on teen smoking and drinking in Germany. *Addiction, 103*(10), 1722–1730.

Hanewinkel, R., & Sargent, J. D. (2008). Exposure to smoking in internationally distributed American movies and youth smoking in Germany: A cross-cultural cohort study. *Pediatrics, 121*(1), 108–117.

Hanewinkel, R., & Sargent, J. D. (2009). Longitudinal study of exposure to entertainment media and alcohol use among German adolescents. *Pediatrics, 123*(3), 989–995.

Harrison, R., Chetwynd, J., & Brodie, R. J. (1989). The influence of advertising on tobacco consumption: A reply to Jackson and Ekelund. *British Journal of Addiction, 84,* 1251–1254.

Hemdev, P. A. (2005). Marlboro: A mini case study. *Marketing Review, 5*(1), 73–96.

Henriksen, L., Flora, J. A., Feighery, E., & Fortmann, S. P. (2002). Effects on youth exposure to retail tobacco advertising. *Journal of Applied Social Psychology, 32*(9), 1771–1789.

Hinds, M. W. (1992). Impact of a local ordinance banning tobacco sales to minors. *Public Health Reports, 107*(3), 355–358.

Holak, S. L., & Tang, Y. E. (1990). Advertising's effect on the product evolutionary cycle. *Journal of Marketing, 54,* 16–29.

Hollingworth, W., Ebel, B. E., McCarty, C. A., Garrison, M. M., Christakis, D. A., & Rivara, F. P. (2006). Prevention of deaths from harmful drinking in the United States: The potential effects of tax increases and advertising bans on young drinkers. *Journal of Studies on Alcohol, 67*(2), 300–308.

Hornik, R., Jacobsohn, L., Orwin, R., Piesse, A., & Kalton, G. (2008). Effects of the National Youth Anti-Drug Media Campaign on youths. *American Journal of Public Health, 98*(12), 2229–2236.

Howard, K. A., Flora, J. A., Scheicher, N. C., & Gonzalez, E. M. (2004). Alcohol point-of-purchase advertising and promotions: Prevalence, content, and targeting. *Contemporary Drug Problems, 31*(3), 561–583.

Hughes, J. R., & Keely, J. P. (2004). The effect of a novel smoking system—Accord—on ongoing smoking and toxin exposure. *Nicotine & Tobacco Research, 6*(6), 1021–1027.

Hyland, M., & Birrell, J. (1979). Government health warnings and the "boomerang" effect. *Psychological Reports, 44*(2), 643–647.

International Center for Alcohol Policies. (2009). *Minimum age limits worldwide* [Table]. Available: http://www.icap.org/Table/MinimumAgeLimitsWorldwide

Jason, L. A., Ji, P. Y., Anes, M. D., & Birkhead, S. H. (1991). Active enforcement of cigarette control laws in the prevention of cigarette sales to minors. *Journal of the American Medical Association, 266*(22), 3159–3161.

Jernigan, D. H., Ostroff, J., & Ross, C. (2005). Alcohol advertising and youth: A measured approach. *Journal of Public Health Policy, 26*(3), 312–325.

Jernigan, D. H, Ostroff, J., Ross, C., & O'Hara, J. A. (2004). Sex differences in adolescent exposure to alcohol advertising in magazines. *Archives of Pediatric & Adolescent Medicine, 158*(7), 629–634.

Jha, P., & Chaloupka, F. J. (1999). *Curbing the epidemic: Governments and the economics of tobacco control.* Washington, DC: World Bank.

Jha, P., Chaloupka, F. J., Corrao, M., & Jacob, B. (2006). Reducing the burden of smoking world-wide: Effectiveness of interventions and their coverage. *Drug and Alcohol Review, 25*(6), 597–609.

Johnston, L. D., O'Malley, P. M., & Bachman, J. G. (2001). *The Monitoring the Future national survey results on adolescent drug use: Overview of key findings, 2000* (NIH Publication No. 01-4923). Bethesda, MD: National Institute on Drug Abuse.

Johnston, L. D., O'Malley, P. M., Bachman, J. G., & Schulenberg, J. E. (2008a, December 11). *More good news on teen smoking: Rates at or near record lows.* Ann Arbor: University of Michigan News Service. Available: http://www.monitoringthefuture.org/data/08data.html

Johnston, L. D., O'Malley, P. M., Bachman, J. G., & Schulenberg, J. E. (2008b, December 11). *Various stimulant drugs show continuing gradual declines among teens in 2008, most illicit drugs hold steady.* Ann Arbor: University of Michigan News Service. Available: http://www.monitoringthefuture.org/data/08data.html

Johnston, L. D., O'Malley, P. M., Bachman, J. G., & Schulenberg, J. E. (2009, December 14). Smoking continues gradual decline among U.S. teens, smokeless tobacco threatens a comeback. Ann Arbor: University of Michigan News Service. Available: http://monitoringthefuture.org/data/09data.html#2009data-cigs

Jones, S. E., Sharp, D. J., Husten, C. G., & Crossett, L. S. (2002). Cigarette acquisition and proof of age among US high school students who smoke. *Tobacco Control, 11*(1), 20–25.

Kaper, J., Wagena, E. J., Willemsen, M. C., & van Schayck, C. P. (2005). Reimbursement for smoking cessation treatment may double the abstinence rate: Results of a randomized trial. *Addiction, 100*(7), 1012–1020.

Kaskutas, L., & Greenfield, T. K. (1992). First effects of warning labels on alcoholic beverage containers. *Drug and Alcohol Dependence, 31*(1), 1–14.

Kees, J., Burton, S., Andrews, J. C., & Kozup, J. (2006). Tests of graphic visuals and cigarette package warning combinations: Implications for the framework convention on tobacco control. *Journal of Public Policy & Marketing, 25*(2), 212–223.

King, C., Siegel, M., Celebucki, C., & Connolly, G. N. (1998). Adolescent exposure to cigarette advertising in magazines: An evaluation of brand-specific advertising in relation to youth readership. *Journal of the American Medical Association, 279*(7), 516–520.

Kohn, P., & Smart, R. (1984). The impact of television advertising on alcohol consumption: An experiment. *Journal of Studies on Alcohol, 45*(4), 295–301.

Kohn, P., Smart, R., & Ogborne, A. (1984). Effects of two kinds of alcohol advertising on subsequent consumption. *Journal of Advertising, 13*(1), 34–48.

Kozlowski, L. T., Goldberg, M. E., Yost, B. A., White, E. L., Sweeney, C. T., & Pillitteri, J. L. (1998). Smokers' misperceptions of light and ultra-light cigarettes may keep them smoking. *American Journal of Preventive Medicine, 15*(1), 9–16.

Kozlowski, L. T., Pillitteri, J. L., & Sweeney, C. T. (1994). Misuse of "light" cigarettes by means of vent blocking. *Journal of Substance Abuse, 6*(3), 333–336.

Kozlowski, L. T., Sweeney, C. T., & Pillitteri, J. L. (1996). Blocking cigarette filter vents with lips more than doubles carbon monoxide intake from ultra-low tar cigarettes. *Experimental and Clinical Psychopharmacology, 4*(4), 404–408.

Krugman, D. M., Fox, R. J., Fletcher, J. E., & Fischer, P. M. (1994). Do adolescents attend to warnings in cigarette advertising? An eye-tracking approach. *Journal of Advertising Research, 34*(6), 39–52.

Laixuthai, A., & Chaloupka, F. J. (1993). Youth alcohol use and public policy. *Contemporary Economic Policy, 11*(4), 70–81.

Laugesen, M., & Meads, C. (1991). Tobacco advertising restrictions, price, income and tobacco consumption in OECD countries, 1960–1986. *British Journal of Addiction, 86*(10), 1343–1354.

Lee, C. W., & Kahende, J. (2007). Factors associated with successful smoking cessation in the United States, 2000. *American Journal of Public Health, 97*(3), 1503–1509.

Legacy Tobacco Documents Library. (n.d.a). *Camel qualitative research in Dallas.* Memorandum from M. R. Bolger. Available: http://legacy.library.ucsf.edu/tid/wxf44d00/pdf

Legacy Tobacco Documents Library. (n.d.b). *Young smokers: Prevalence, trends, implications, and related demographic trends.* Memorandum from Myron Johnston. Available: http://legacy.library.ucsf.edu/tid/qfl70g00/pdf

Leventhal, H., Glynn, K., & Fleming, R. (1987). Is the smoking decision an "informed choice?" Effect of smoking risk factors on smoking beliefs. *Journal of the American Medical Association, 257,* 3373–3376.

Lewit, E. M., Coate, D., & Grossman, M. (1981). The effects of government regulation on teenage smoking. *Journal of Law and Economics, 24*(3), 545–569.

Liang, L., & Chaloupka, F. J. (2002). Differential effects of cigarette price on youth smoking intensity. *Nicotine & Tobacco Research, 4*(1), 109–114.

Lynch, B. S., & Bonnie, R. J. (1994). *Growing up tobacco free: Preventing nicotine addiction in children and youths.* Washington DC: National Academies Press.

Mackay, J., & Eriksen, M. (Eds.). (2010). Tobacco industry promotion [Chart]. In *The tobacco atlas* (pp. 58–59). Geneva, Switzerland: World Health Organization. Available: http://www.who.int/tobacco/en/atlas22.pdf

MacKinnon, D. P., & Lapin, A. (1998). Effects of alcohol warnings and advertisements: A test of the boomerang hypothesis. *Psychology & Marketing, 15*(7), 707–726.

MacKinnon, D. P., Pentz, M. A., & Stacy, A. W. (1993). Alcohol warning labels and adolescents: The first year. *American Journal of Public Health, 83*(4), 585–587.

Martin, S. E., & Mail, P. (1995). *Effects of the mass media on the use and abuse of alcohol.* Bethesda, MD: National Institute on Alcohol Abuse and Alcoholism.

Martin, S. E., Snyder, L. B., Hamilton, M., Fleming-Milici, F., Slater, M. D., Stacy, A., et al. (2002). Alcohol advertising and youth. *Alcoholism: Clinical and Experimental Research, 26*(6), 900–906.

Mastro, D. E., & Atkin, C. (2002). Exposure to alcohol billboards and beliefs and attitudes to drinking among Mexican American high school students. *Howard Journal of Communication, 13*(2), 129–151.

Mattern, J. L., & Neighbors, C. (2004). Social norms campaigns: Examining the relationship between changes in perceived norms and changes in drinking levels. *Journal of Studies on Alcohol, 65*(4), 489–493.

McGinness, T., & Cowling, K. (1975). Advertising and the aggregate demand for cigarettes. *European Economic Review, 6*(3), 311–328.

Meier, P. S., Purshouse, R., & Brennan, A. (2010). Policy options for alcohol price regulation: The importance of modeling population heterogeneity. *Addiction, 105*(3), 383–393.

Motion Picture Association of America. (2007, May 10). *Film rating board to consider smoking as a factor.* Available: http://www.mpaa.org/resources/9d558a6b-9e9a-41d2-9ac8-d7b2361ef965.pdf

Muñoz, R. F., Barrera, A. Z., Delucchi, K., Penilla, C., Torres, L. D., & Perez-Stable, E. J. (2009). International Spanish/English Internet smoking cessation trial yields 20% abstinence rates at 1 year. *Nicotine & Tobacco Research, 11*(9), 1025–1034.

National Association of Attorneys General. (1998). *Master settlement agreement.* Available: http://www.naag.org/backpages/naag/tobacco/msa/msa-pdf

National Cancer Institute. (2010). Tobacco monographs [List]. Available: https://cissecure.nci.nih.gov/ncipubs/home.aspx?js=1

National Highway Traffic Safety Administration. (2004). *Alcohol impairment.* Available: www.nhtsa.gov/Research/Human+Factors/Alcohol+Impairment

National Institute for Health and Clinical Excellence. (2007). *Interventions in schools to prevent and reduce alcohol use among children and young people* (NICE Public Health Guidance Report No. 7). London: Author. Available: http://guidance.nice.org.uk/PH7/Guidance/pdf/English

National Institute for Health and Clinical Excellence. (2008). *Mass-media and point-of-sales measures to prevent the uptake of smoking by children and young people* (NICE Public Health Guidance Report No. 14). London: Author. Available: http://guidance.nice.org.uk/PH14/Guidance/pdf/English

National Institute on Alcohol Abuse and Alcoholism. (2002). *Research monographs* [List]. Available: pubs.niaaa.nih.gov/publications/monograp.htm

Nelson, J. P. (1999). Broadcast advertising in the U.S. and demand for alcoholic beverages. *Southern Economic Journal, 65*(4), 774–790.

Nelson, J. P. (2001). Alcohol advertising and advertising bans: A survey of research methods, results, and policy implications. In M. R. Baye & J. P. Nelson (Eds.), *Advances in applied microeconomics: Advertising and differentiated products* (Vol. 10, pp. 239–295). Amsterdam: JAI Press.

Nelson, J. P. (2008). Alcohol advertising bans, consumption, and control policies in seventeen OECD countries, 1975–2000. *Applied Economics, 42*(7), 803–823. Abstract available: http://www.informaworld.com/smpp/content~db=all?content=10.1080/00036840701720952

Nelson, J. P., Coulson, N. E., & Moran, J. R. (2001). The long-run demand for alcoholic beverages and the advertising debate: A cointegration approach. In M. R. Baye & J. P. Nelson (Eds.), *Advances in applied microeconomics: Advertising and differentiated products* (Vol. 10, pp. 31–54). Amsterdam: JAI Press.

Nelson, J. P., & Moran, J. R. (1995). Advertising and US alcoholic beverage demand: System-wide estimates. *Applied Economics, 27*(12), 1225–1236.

Nelson, J. P., & Young, D. J. (2001). Do advertising bans work? An international comparison. *International Journal of Advertising, 20*(3), 273–296.

Nelson, J. P., & Young, D. J. (2008). Effects of youth, price, and audience size on alcohol advertising in magazines. *Health Economics, 17*(4), 551–556.

Nimbarte, A., Aghazadeh, F., & Harvey, C. (2005). Comparison of current U.S. and Canadian cigarette pack warnings. *International Quarterly of Community Health Education, 24*(1), 3–27.

O'Connor, R. J., Ashare, R. L., Fix, B. V., Hawk, L. W., Cummings, K. M., & Schmidt, W. C. (2007). College students' expectancies for light cigarettes and potential reduced exposure products. *American Journal of Health Behavior, 31*(4), 402–410.

O'Mara, R. J., Thombs, D. L., Wagenaar, A. C., Rossheim, M. E., Merves, M. L., Hou, W., et al. (2009). Alcohol price and intoxication in college bars. *Alcoholism: Clinical and Experimental Research, 33*(11), 1973–1980.

Outdoor Advertising Association of America. (2009). *Industry code: The OAAA code of industry principles.* Available: http://www.oaaa.org/about/IndustryCode.aspx

Pacula, R. L. (1998). Does increasing the beer tax reduce marijuana consumption? *Journal of Health Economics, 17*(5), 557–585.

Pasch, K. E., Komro, K. A., Perry, C. P., Hearst, M. O., & Farbakhsh, K. (2009). Does outdoor alcohol advertising around elementary schools vary by the ethnicity of students in the school? *Ethnicity & Health, 14*(2), 225–236.

Paschall, M. J., Grube, J. W., Black, C., Flewelling, R. L., Ringwalt, C. L., & Biglan, A. (2007). Alcohol outlet characteristics and alcohol sales to youth: Results of alcohol purchase surveys in 45 Oregon communities. *Prevention Science, 8*(2), 153–159.

Paschall, M. J., Grube, J. W., Black, C. A., & Ringwalt, C. L. (2007). Is commercial alcohol availability related to adolescent alcohol sources and alcohol use? Findings from a multi-level study. *Journal of Adolescent Health, 41*(2), 168–174.

Pechmann, C. (2002). Changing adolescent smoking prevalence: Impact of advertising interventions. In D. Burns (Ed.), *Changing adolescent smoking prevalence: Where it is and why* (pp. 171–181). Silver Spring, MD: National Cancer Institute.

Pechmann, C., & Andrews, J. C. (in press). Copy test methods to pretest advertisements. In J. Sheth, N. Malhotra (Series Eds.), M. Belch, & G. Belch (Vol. Eds.), *Wiley international encyclopedia of marketing. Vol. 4: Advertising and integrated communication.* Oxford, England: Wiley-Blackwell.

Pechmann, C., & Knight, S. J. (2002). An experimental investigation of the joint effects of advertising and peers on adolescents' beliefs and intentions about cigarette consumption. *Journal of Consumer Research, 29*(1), 5–19.

Pechmann, C., Levine, L., Loughlin, S., & Leslie, F. (2005). Impulsive and self-conscious: Adolescents' vulnerability to advertising and promotion. *Journal of Public Policy & Marketing, 24*(2), 202–221.

Pechmann, C., & Ratneshwar, S. (1994). The effects of antismoking and cigarette advertising on young adolescents' perceptions of peers who smoke. *Journal of Consumer Research, 21*(2), 236–251.

Pechmann, C., & Reibling, E. T. (2006). Antismoking advertisements for youth: An independent evaluation of health, counter-industry, and industry approaches. *American Journal of Public Health, 96*(May), 906–913.

Pechmann, C., & Shih, C. (1999). Smoking scenes in movies and antismoking advertisements before movies: Effects on youth. *Journal of Marketing, 63*(3), 1–13.

Pechmann, C., Zhao, G., Goldberg, M. E., & Reibling, E. T. (2003). What to convey in antismoking advertisements for adolescents? The use of protection motivation theory to identify effective message themes. *Journal of Marketing, 67*(2), 1–18.

Pederson, L. L., & Nelson, D. E. (2007). Literature review and summary of perceptions, attitudes, beliefs, and marketing of potentially reduced exposure products: Communication implications. *Nicotine & Tobacco Research, 9*(5), 525–534.

People of the State of California v. R.J. Reynolds Tobacco Company (Case No. GIC 764118). (2002, June 6). *Statement of decision.*

Pierce, J. P., Choi, W. S., Gilpin, E. A., Farkas, A. J., & Berry, C. C. (1998). Tobacco industry promotion of cigarettes and adolescent smoking. *Journal of the American Medical Association, 279*(7), 511–515.

Pierce, J. P., Choi, W. S., Gilpin, E. A., Farkas, A. J., & Merritt, R. K. (1996). Validation of susceptibility as a predictor of which adolescents take up smoking in the United States. *Health Psychology, 15*(5), 355–361.

Pierce, J. P., & Gilpin, E. A. (1995). A historical analysis of tobacco marketing and the uptake of smoking by youth in the United States: 1890–1977. *Health Psychology, 14*(6), 500–508.

Pierce, J. P., Gilpin, E. A., Bums, D. M., Whalen, E., Rosbrook, B., Shopland, D. R., et al. (1991). Does tobacco advertising target young people to start smoking? Evidence from California. *Journal of the American Medical Association, 266*(22), 3154–3158.

Pierce, J. P., Gilpin, E. A., Emery, S. L., White, M. M., Rosbrook, B., & Berry, C. C. (1998). Has the California Tobacco Control Program reduced smoking? *Journal of the American Medical Association, 280*(10), 893–899.

Pollay, R. W., Siddarth, S., Siegel, M., Haddix, A., Merritt, R. K., Giovino, G. A., et al. (1996). The last straw? Cigarette advertising and realized market shares among youths and adults, 1979–1993. *Journal of Marketing, 60*(2), 1–16.

Ponicki, W. R., Gruenewald, P. J., & LaScala, E. A. (2007). Joint impacts of minimum legal drinking age and beer taxes on US youth traffic fatalities, 1975 to 2001. *Alcoholism: Clinical and Experimental Research, 31*(5), 804–813.

Radfar, M. (1985). The effect of advertising on total consumption of cigarettes in the U.K.: A comment. *European Economic Review, 29*(2), 225–231.

Rigotti, N. A., DiFranza, J. R., Chang, Y. C., Tisdale, T., Kemp, B., & Singer, E. (1997). The effect of enforcing tobacco-sales laws on adolescents' access to tobacco and smoking behavior. *New England Journal of Medicine, 337*(15), 1044–1051.

Rimpela, M. K., Aaro, L. E., & Rimpela, A. H. (1993). The effects of tobacco sales promotion on initiation of smoking: Experiences from Finland and Norway. *Scandinavian Journal of Social Medicine, 49*(Suppl.), 5–23.

Roberts, D. F., Henriksen, L., & Christensen, P. G. (with Kelly, M., Carbone, S., & Wilson, A. B.). (1999). *Substance use in popular movies and music.* Washington, DC: Office of National Drug Control Policy & U.S. Department of Health and Human Services, Substance Abuse & Mental Health Services Administration.

Robinson, J. H., Pritchard, W. S., & Davis, R. A. (1992). Psychopharmacological effects of smoking a cigarette with typical "tar" and carbon monoxide yields but minimal nicotine. *Psychopharmacology, 108*(4), 466–472.

Robinson, T.N., Chen, H. L., & Killen, J. D. (1998). Television and music video exposure and risk of adolescent alcohol use [Abstract]. *Pediatrics, 102*(5), e54. Available: http://pediatrics.aappublications.org/cgi/content/abstract/102/5/e54

Rosner, D., & Markowitz, G. E. (1987). *Dying for work: Workers' safety and health in twentieth-century America.* Bloomington: Indiana University Press.

Russell, C. A., Russell, D. W. & Grube, J. W. (2009). Nature and impact of alcohol messages in a youth-oriented television series. *Journal of Advertising, 38*(3), 92–112.

Saffer, H. (1991). Alcohol advertising bans and alcohol abuse: An international perspective. *Journal of Health Economics, 10*(1), 65–79.

Saffer, H. (1993). Alcohol advertising bans and alcohol abuse: Reply. *Journal of Health Economics, 12*(2), 229–234.

Saffer, H. (1997). Alcohol advertising and motor vehicle fatalities. *Review of Economics and Statistics, 79*(3), 431–442.

Saffer, H. (2002). Alcohol advertising and youth. *Journal of Studies on Alcohol and Drugs, 63*(Suppl. 14), 173–181.

Saffer, H., & Chaloupka, F. (2000). The effect of tobacco advertising bans on tobacco consumption. *Journal of Health Economics, 19*(6), 1117–1137.

Saffer, H., & Dave, D. (2002). Alcohol consumption and alcohol advertising bans. *Applied Economics, 34*(11), 1325–1334.

Sargent, J. D., Beach, M. L., Adachi-Mejia, A. M., Gibson, J. J., Titus-Ernstoff, L. T., Carusi, C. P., et al. (2005). Exposure to movie smoking: Its relation to smoking initiation among US adolescents. *Journal of Pediatrics, 116*(5), 1183–1191.

Sargent, J. D., Beach, M. L., Dalton, M. A., Mott, L. A., Tickle, J. J., Ahrens, M. B., et al. (2001). Effect of seeing tobacco use in films on trying smoking among adolescents: Cross-sectional study. *British Medical Journal, 323*(7326), 1394–1397.

Sargent, J. D., Tanski, S. E., & Gibson, J. (2007). Exposure to movie smoking among US adolescents aged 10–14 years: A population estimate. *Pediatrics, 119*(5), e1167–e1176.

Schuker, L. A. (2008, July 12). DVDs will include antismoking announcements. *The Wall Street Journal*, p. A3.

Scott, M. M., Cohen, D. A., Schonlau, M., Farley, T. A., & Blumenthal, R. N. (2008). Alcohol and tobacco marketing: Evaluating compliance with outdoor advertising guidelines. *American Journal of Preventive Medicine, 35*(3), 203–209.

Scribner, R., & Cohen, D. (2001). The effect of enforcement on merchant compliance with the minimum legal drinking age law. *Journal of Drug Issues, 31*(4), 857–866.

Shafey, O., Dolwick, S., & Guindon, G. E. (Eds.). (2003). *Tobacco control country profiles* (2nd ed.). Atlanta, GA: American Cancer Society, World Health Organization, & International Union Against Cancer. Available: http://www.wpro.who.int/internet/resources.ashx/TFI/TCCP2.pdf

Shiffman, S., Ferguson, S. G., Rohay, J., & Gitchell, J. G. (2008). Perceived safety and efficacy of nicotine replacement therapies among US smokers and ex-smokers: Relationship with use and compliance. *Addiction, 103*(8), 1371–1378.

Siegel, M., Albers, A. B., Cheng, D. M., Biener, L., & Rigotti, N. A. (2004). Effect of local restaurant smoking regulations on environmental tobacco smoke exposure among youths. *American Journal of Public Health, 94*(2), 321–325.

Siegel, M., Albers, A. B., Cheng, D. M., Biener, L., & Rigotti, N. A. (2005). Effect of local restaurant smoking regulations on progression to established smoking among youths. *Tobacco Control, 14*(5), 300–306.

Siegel, M., Albers, A. B., Cheng, D. M., Hamilton, W. L., & Biener, L. (2008). Local restaurant smoking regulations and the adolescent smoking initiation process: Results of a multilevel contextual analysis among Massachusetts youth. *Archives of Pediatrics & Adolescent Medicine, 162*(5), 477–483.

Silagy, C., Lancaster, T., Stead, L., Mant, D., & Fowler, G. (2004). Nicotine replacement therapy for smoking cessation. *Cochrane Database of Systematic Reviews, 3*, 1–106.

Slater, M., Kelly, K., Edwards, R., Thurman, P., Plested, B., Keefe, T., et al. (2006). Combining in-school and community-based media efforts: Reducing marijuana and alcohol uptake among younger adolescents. *Health Education Research, 21*(1), 157–167.

Slater, S. J., Chaloupka, F. J., Wakefield, M., Johnston, L., & O'Malley, P. M. (2007). The impact of retail cigarette marketing practices on youth smoking uptake. *Archives of Pediatrics & Adolescent Medicine, 161*(5), 440–445.

Slovic, P. (2001). *Smoking: Risk, perception and policy.* Thousand Oaks, CA: Sage.

Smee, C. (1992). *Effect of tobacco advertising on tobacco consumption: A discussion document reviewing the evidence.* London: Department of Health, Economics & Operational Research Division.

Smith, L., & Foxcroft, D. (2009). The effect of alcohol advertising, marketing and portrayal on drinking behaviour in young people: Systematic review of prospective cohort studies. *BMC Public Health, 9*, 51. Available: http://www.biomedcentral.com/1471-2458/9/51

Smoke Free Movies. (n.d.). *The solution.* Available: smokefreemovies.ucsf.edu/solution/index.html

Snyder, L. B., & Blood, D. J. (1992). Caution: The Surgeon General's alcohol warnings and alcohol advertising may have adverse effects on young adults. *Journal of Applied Communication Research, 20*(1), 37–53.

Snyder, L. B., Milici, F. F., Slater, M., Sun, H., & Strizhakova, Y. (2006). Effects of alcohol advertising exposure on drinking among youth. *Archives of Pediatric & Adolescent Medicine, 160*(1), 18–24.

Sobell, L., Sobell, M., Riley, D., Klanjer, F., Leo, G., Pavan, D., et al. (1986). Effect of television programming and advertising on alcohol consumption in normal drinkers. *Journal of Studies on Alcohol, 47*(4), 333–340.

Song, A. V., Ling, P. M., Neilands, T. B., & Glantz, S. A. (2007). Smoking in movies and increased smoking among young adults. *American Journal of Preventive Medicine, 33*(5), 396–403.

Stacy, A. W., Zogg, J. B., Unger, J. B., & Dent, C. W. (2004). Exposure to televised alcohol ads and subsequent adolescent alcohol use. *American Journal of Health Behavior, 28*(6), 498–509.

Stewart, D. W., & Martin, I. M. (1994). Intended and unintended consequences of warning messages: A review and synthesis of empirical research. *Journal of Public Policy & Marketing, 13*(1), 1–19.

Stoolmiller, M., Gerrard, M., Sargent, J. D., Worth, K. A., & Gibbons, F. X. (2010). R-rated movie viewing, growth in sensation seeking and alcohol initiation: Reciprocal and moderation effects. *Prevention Science, 11*(1), 1–13.

Stratton, K., Shetty, P., Wallace, R., & Bondurant, S. (2001). Clearing the smoke: The science base for tobacco harm reduction—executive summary. *Tobacco Control, 10*(2), 189–195.

Strecher, V. J., Shiffman, S., & West, R. (2005). Randomized controlled trial of a Web-based computer-tailored smoking cessation program as a supplement to nicotine patch therapy. *Addiction, 100*(5), 682–688.

Substance Abuse & Mental Health Services Administration. (2007). Table 2.1B—Tobacco product and alcohol use in lifetime, past year, and past month among persons aged 12 or older: Percentages 2006 and 2007 [Table]. In *2007 National Survey on Drug Use & Health: Detailed tables.* Rockville, MD: U.S. Department of Health and Human Services, Substance Abuse & Mental Health Services Administration. Available: http://oas.samhsa.gov/NSDUH/2k7NSDUH/tabs/Sect2peTabs1to42.htm#Tab2.1B

Sweeney, C. T., Kozlowski, L. T., & Parsa, P. (1999). Effect of filter vent blocking on carbon monoxide exposure from selected lower tar cigarette brands. *Pharmacology Biochemistry & Behavior, 63*(1), 167–173.

Telser, L. G. (1962). Advertising and cigarettes. *Journal of Political Economy, 70,* 471–499.

Thrasher, J. F., Niederdeppe, J., Farrelly, M. C., Davis, K. C., Ribisl, K. M., & Haviland, M. L. (2004). The impact of anti-tobacco industry prevention messages in tobacco producing regions: Evidence from the US truth campaign. *Tobacco Control, 13*(3), 283–288.

Tobacco companies lose appeal. (2009, May 23). *The New York Times,* p. A11. Available: http://www.nytimes.com/2009/05/23/us/23tobacco.html

Turco, R. M. (1997). Effects of exposure to cigarette advertisements on adolescents' attitudes toward smoking. *Journal of Applied Social Psychology, 27*(13), 1115–1130.

Unger, J. B., Johnson, C. A., & Rohrbach, L. A. (1995). Recognition and liking of tobacco and alcohol advertisements among adolescents: Relationships with susceptibility to substance use. *Preventive Medicine, 24*(5), 461–466.

Unger, J. B., Schuster, D., Zogg, J., Dent, C. W., & Stacy, A. W. (2003). Alcohol advertising exposure and adolescent alcohol use: A comparison of exposure measures. *Addiction Research & Theory, 11*(3), 177–193.

United States of America et al. v. Philip Morris USA et al. (2006, August 17). *Civil Action No. 99-2496 (GK): Final opinion.* Available: http://www.tobaccofreekids.org/reports/doj/FinalOpinion.pdf

U.S. Department of Health and Human Services. (1989). *Reducing the health consequences of smoking: 25 years of progress: A report of the Surgeon General* (DHHS Publication No. CDC 89-8411). Rockville, MD: U.S. Department of Health and Human Services, Centers for Disease Control, Center for Chronic Disease Prevention and Health Promotion.

U.S. Food and Drug Administration. (1995). Regulations restricting the sale and distribution of cigarettes and smokeless tobacco products to protect children and adolescents: Proposed rule. *Federal Register, 60*(155), 41314–41375.

U.S. Food and Drug Administration. (1996). Regulations restricting the sale and distribution of cigarettes and smokeless tobacco products to protect children and adolescents; final rule. *Federal Register, 61*(168), 44615–44618.

Van Den Bulck, H., & Beullens, K. (2005). Television and music video exposure and adolescent alcohol use while going out. *Alcohol and Alcoholism, 40*(3), 249–253.

Van Den Bulck, H., Simons, N., & Van Gorp, B. (2008). Let's drink and be merry: The framing of alcohol in the prime-time American youth series *The OC. Journal of Studies on Alcohol and Drugs, 69*(6), 933–940.

van Reek, J., Andriaanse, H., & Aaro, L. (1991). Smoking by school children in eleven European countries. In B. Durston & K. Jamrozik (Eds.), *Proceedings of the seventh World Conference on Tobacco and Health* (pp. 301–302). East Perth, WA, Australia: Organising Committee of the Seventh World Conference on Tobacco and Health.

Varlinskaya, E. I., & Spear, L. P. (2002). Acute effects of ethanol on social behavior of adolescent and adult rats: Role of familiarity of the test situation. *Alcoholism: Clinical & Experimental Research, 26*(10), 1502–1511.

Viscusi, W. K. (1992). *Smoking: Making the risky decision.* New York: Oxford University Press.

Wagenaar, A. C., Salois, M. J., & Komro, K. A. (2009). Effects of beverage alcohol price and tax levels on drinking: A meta-analysis of 1003 estimates from 112 studies. *Addiction, 104*(2), 179–190.

Wagenaar, A. C., & Toomey, T. L. (2002). Effects of minimum drinking age laws: Review and analyses of the literature from 1960 to 2000. *Journal of Studies on Alcohol, 63*(Suppl. 14), 206–225.

Wagenaar, A. C., Toomey, T. L., & Erickson, D. J. (2005). Preventing youth access to alcohol: Outcomes from a multi-community time-series trial. *Addiction, 100*(3), 335–345.

Wagenaar, A. C., & Wolfson, M. (1995). Deterring sales and provision of alcohol to minors: A study of enforcement in 295 counties in four states. *Public Health Reports, 110*(4), 419–427.

Waiters, E. D., Treno, A. J., & Grube, J. W. (2001). Alcohol advertising and youth: A focus group analysis of what young people find appealing in alcohol advertising. *Contemporary Drug Problems, 28*(4), 695–718.

Wechsler, H., Nelson, T. E., Lee, J. E., Seibring, M., Lewis, C., & Keeling, R. P. (2003). Perception and reality: A national evaluation of social norms marketing interventions to reduce college students' heavy alcohol use. *Journal of Studies on Alcohol, 64*(4), 484–494.

Weinhold, L. L., & Stitzer, M. L. (1989). Effects of puff number and puff spacing on carbon monoxide exposure from commercial brand cigarettes. *Pharmacology Biochemistry & Behavior, 33*(4), 853–858.

Werch, C. E., Pappas, D. M., Carlson, J. M., DiClemente, C. C., Chally, P. S., & Sinder, J. A. (2000). Results of a social norm intervention to prevent binge drinking among first-year residential college students. *Journal of American College Health, 49*(2), 85–92.

White, V., Webster, B., & Wakefield, M. (2008). Do graphic health warning labels have an impact on adolescents' smoking-related beliefs and behaviours? *Addiction, 103*(9), 1562–1571.

Wilkinson, C., & Room, R. (2009). Warnings on alcohol containers and advertisements: International experience and evidence on effects. *Drug and Alcohol Review, 28*(4), 426–435.

Willemsen, M. C. (2005). The new EU cigarette health warnings benefit smokers who want to quit the habit: Results from the Dutch Continuous Survey of Smoking Habits. *European Journal of Public Health, 15*(4), 389–392.

Wils, T. A., Sargent, J. D., Gibbons, F. X., Gerrard, M., & Stoolmiller, M. (2009). Movie exposure to alcohol cues and adolescent alcohol problems: A longitudinal analysis in a national sample. *Psychology of Addictive Behaviors, 23*(1), 23–35.

Wilson, D. (2009, August 31). Tobacco companies sue to block marketing law. *The New York Times,* p. B1.

Wine Institute. (2005). *Code of advertising standards* (Amended). Available: http://www.wineinstitute.org/initiatives/issuesandpolicy/adcode/details

Wingood, G. M., DiClemente, R. J., Bernhardt, J. M., Harrington, K., Davies, S. L., Robillard, A., et al. (2003). A prospective study of exposure to rap music videos and African American female adolescents' health. *American Journal of Public Health, 93*(3), 437–439.

Winsten, J. A. (1994). Promoting designated drivers: The Harvard Alcohol Project. *American Journal of Preventive Medicine, 10*(3), 11–14.

Worden, J. K., Flynn, B. S., Geller, B. M., Chen, M., Shelton, L. G., Secker-Walker, R. H., et al. (1988). Development of a smoking prevention mass media program using diagnostic and formative research. *Preventive Medicine, 17*(5), 531–558.

World Health Organization. (2003). *WHO Framework Convention on Tobacco Control.* Geneva, Switzerland: Author. Available: http://www.who.int/fctc/text_download/en/index.html

World Health Organization. (2004). *Global status report on alcohol 2004.* Geneva, Switzerland: Author. Available: http://www.who.int/substance_abuse/publications/global_status_report_2004_overview.pdf

World Health Organization. (2007). *Alcohol and injury in emergency departments: Summary of the report from the WHO Collaborative Study on Alcohol and Injuries.* Geneva, Switzerland: Author. Available: http://www.who.int/substance_abuse/publications/alcohol_injury_summary.pdf

World Health Organization. (2008). *The global burden of disease: 2004 update.* Geneva, Switzerland: Author. Available: http://www.who.int/healthinfo/global_burden_disease/GBD_report_2004update_full.pdf

Worth, K. A., Cin, S. D., & Sargent, J. D. (2006). Prevalence of smoking among major movie characters: 1996–2004. *Tobacco Control, 15*(6), 442–446.

Wyllie, A., Zhang, J. F., & Casswell, S. (1998a). Positive responses to televised beer advertisements associated with drinking and problems reported by 18 to 29-year-olds. *Addiction*, *93*(5), 749–760.

Wyllie, A., Zhang, J. F., & Casswell, S. (1998b). Responses to televised alcohol advertisements associated with drinking behavior of 10–17-year-olds. *Addiction*, *93*(3), 361–371.

Young, D. J. (1993). Alcohol advertising bans and alcohol abuse: Comment. *Journal of Health Economics*, *12*(2), 213–228.

Zhao, G., & Pechmann, C. (2007). The impact of regulatory focus on adolescents' response to antismoking advertising campaigns. *Journal of Marketing Research*, *44*(4), 671–687.

# 18

## Using Behavioral Theory to Transform Consumers and Their Environments to Prevent the Spread of Sexually Transmitted Infections

Martin Fishbein and Susan E. Middlestadt

Health and well-being result from individuals acting in their environments. Our central proposition is that, through a behavioral analysis, we can transform consumers and the environments that influence their behaviors and, through this transformation, we can improve health and well-being. We begin by making the case that reducing sexually transmitted infections (STIs) can improve well-being for a substantial proportion of the world, and describing the role behavior plays in sexual transmission. We present the Integrative Model (IM), the most recent formulation of a Reasoned Action Approach, and show how research guided by this model can help develop interventions to transform consumers. We describe two interventions that have successfully transformed behavior, both of which take the typical, straightforward approach of identifying and modifying beliefs associated with condom use and thereby increasing condom use, an end health behavior. Then, we argue for an expanded use of a theory-based behavioral analysis, one that takes a public health perspective. Stated another way, we argue that a behavioral analysis can be used to develop the more complex, multilevel, or multicomponent interventions recognized as essential in public health. More specifically, we explain how a behavioral analysis can be used to understand the upstream behaviors that lead to the end health behavior, identify aspects of the environment that might be addressed by structural interventions, and determine how to change the behavior of agents who control the environments that influence our behavior. We conclude with recommendations for research based on this expanded use of a behavioral analysis.

### SEXUALLY TRANSMITTED INFECTIONS

STIs present a major challenge to well-being in both developing and industrialized countries. While precise information about infection rates is often unavailable, the World Health Organization (2010) estimates that 457 million cases of curable STIs occur each year among men and women worldwide. Infection rates vary enormously by region, country, and population within country. The largest number of new infections occurred in South and Southeast Asia, followed by sub-Saharan Africa, Latin America, and the Caribbean. Globally, the prevalence is higher among those residing in urban areas, unmarried individuals, and the young. In fact, worldwide, about two thirds of new cases occur among people younger than 25 years of age.

In the United States, according to the Centers for Disease Control and Prevention (CDC), about 19 million new infections occur each year, and almost half of these infections occur among young people 15–24 years of age (Weinstock, Berman, & Cates, 2004). In the United States, STIs disproportionately affect minority populations. For example, a recent surveillance report (CDC, 2009) indicated that Blacks, who represented 12% of the population, accounted for 70% of reported cases of gonorrhea and about half of all cases of chlamydia and syphilis. Poverty and socioeconomic status have been demonstrated to be factors underlying these sexual health disparities.

STIs are a major cause of illness and death and result in a range of serious psychological and medical consequences for infected individuals, their partners, and their children. If not treated, syphilis can damage the heart and the nervous system. Chlamydia and gonorrhea pose a particular risk to the health of women, as both can result in infertility if left untreated. A number of STIs can influence the course of a pregnancy: Pregnant women with trichomoniasis are more likely to experience preterm and low-birth-weight deliveries, and gonorrhea is associated with septic abortions, prematurity, and other complications that adversely affect the infant. Syphilis and chlamydia can be transmitted to infants born of infected women. Chlamydia and gonorrhea, along with syphilis and herpes, have been associated with increased HIV transmission. The CDC estimates that STIs cost the U.S. health system as much as $15.3 billion annually (Chesson et al., 2004). Additionally, beyond health, medical, and financial costs, the threat of sexual transmission is likely to have social and psychological impacts on well-being through effects on intimate partner relationships.

There can be little doubt that reducing the prevalence and incidence of STIs is a critical and global public health challenge, one that requires an interdisciplinary approach (Wasserheit, Aral, & Holmes, 1991). It is important to recognize, however, that whether one does or does not transmit or acquire an STI is not a behavior but an outcome of performing one or more behaviors. Thus, the success of any behavioral intervention will depend on the relationship between the behavior(s) addressed and biological outcomes. Unfortunately, this relationship is not a simple one.

To understand, at least in part, the complex relationship between behavioral and biological outcomes, one can use the May and Anderson (1987) model: $R_0 = \beta cD$. In this model, $R_0$ is the reproductive rate of infection, which is the number of secondary infections expected to arise from a single infected case early in the epidemic when there is no immunity and almost all individuals are susceptible (Pinkerton & Abramson, 1994). When $R_0$ is greater than 1, the epidemic is on the rise; when it is less than 1, the epidemic is dying out. According to this model, three factors influence the reproductive rate: $\beta$ is transmission efficiency, or the ease with which an infected person transmits the disease to an uninfected partner; $c$ is the rate of partner exchange, or the average number of sexual partners per unit time; and $D$ is the length of time a person is infectious. The reproductive rate is lower when transmission efficiency is decreased, the rate of partner exchange is decreased, and the length of time a person is infectious is decreased. Behavior can influence each of these three factors ($\beta$, $c$, and $D$), which will, in turn, influence the reproductive rate and course of the epidemic. Transmission efficiency ($\beta$) can be reduced by increasing condom use or delaying sexual activity, the rate of partner exchange ($c$) can be decreased by reducing the number of sexual partners, and the length of time a person is infectious ($D$) can be reduced by increasing the likelihood that the person will seek care in a timely fashion through participation in screening programs or regular health checkups.

For a number of reasons, one should not expect a simple linear relationship between changes in behavior and the incidence of an STI. The effect on the reproductive rate of a change in one factor will depend on the values of the other two factors. For example, the impact of an increase in condom use will depend on both the prevalence of the disease and the sexual mixing patterns in the segment of the population. If there is little disease in a segment, increases in condom use to reduce transmission efficiency will have little effect on the spread of the disease. In contrast, an increase in condom use in a segment of the population likely to transmit the STI can, depending on prevalence of the disease in that segment, have a big impact on the epidemic (see Reiss & Leik, 1989). To complicate matters further, it must also be recognized that changes in one factor may have effects on the other factors. To continue with the condom use example, a program that successfully increases condom use might have the unintended consequence of increasing the number of sexual partners people choose to have, because they feel protected when they use condoms. If this happens, the condom use program would not necessarily lead to a decrease in the reproductive rate of the STI.

As another example of the complexity of the relationship between behavior change and STI incidence, it must be recognized that people may behave quite differently with partners they perceive as safe compared to partners they perceive as risky. People are more likely to use condoms with occasional partners than with a spouse or main partner (e.g., Peterman et al., 2000). Similarly, people may be more likely to get tested after having unprotected sex with a casual partner than with a regular partner or after having unprotected anal sex than unprotected oral sex. Moreover, many factors other than condom use may influence transmission efficiency. Since the degree of infectivity of the donor, characteristics of the host, and type and frequency of sexual practices all influence transmission efficiency, variations in these factors will also influence the nature of the relation between behavior change and STI incidence.

Finally, STIs have different transmissibility rates, and condoms are not equally effective in reducing transmission efficiency. Although condom use with all partners can prevent HIV, gonorrhea, syphilis, and probably chlamydia, condoms are less effective at preventing transmission of herpes and genital warts (Cates & Holmes, 1996). Although it is always better to use a condom, the impact of condom use will vary by STI. Additionally, it is possible to acquire an infection even when condoms are used. As Warner and his colleagues (Warner, Clay-Warner, Boles, & Williamson, 1998; Warner et al., 2008) have noted, there are many ways a condom can be used incorrectly, and condom use errors occur with surprisingly high frequency.

## A BEHAVIORAL ANALYSIS BASED ON THE INTEGRATIVE MODEL

So, what can we do to prevent the spread of STIs? Clearly, based on the description of STIs presented above, one route to preventing and controlling STIs is by changing the behavior of consumers. There are a number of behaviors that could be addressed. Interventions could be developed to encourage condom use, promote abstinence, reduce the number of partners (particularly concurrent partners), encourage getting tested and treated, or promote regular health care seeking. Once a behavior has been identified, it is necessary to understand why the relevant consumers do or do not engage in the selected behavior. Consistent with the principles of Transformative Consumer Research articulated elsewhere in this book (e.g., Mick, Pettigrew, Pechmann, & Ozanne, Chapter 1 of this volume), the argument we make here is that a theory-based behavioral analysis is useful for research to design programs. Simply put, the more one knows about the factors influencing a given behavior in a particular segment of consumers, the better one's chances of developing a successful intervention to transform these consumers. Although every individual and every behavior are unique, and although there are literally hundreds of variables that might be considered in attempts to predict and explain behavior, the Reasoned Action Approach suggests that only a limited number of variables needs to be considered to predict and understand a specific behavior (see, e.g., Fishbein & Ajzen, 2010). This limited set of variables makes up the central core of the Integrative Model, which is the most recent formulation of the Reasoned Action Approach to understanding and predicting human behavior (Fishbein, 2000; Institute of Medicine, 2002; Sackett & Mavor, 2002).

### The Integrative Model

The IM is presented in Figure 18.1 and was developed largely as a result of a 1991 National Institute of Mental Health workshop held to identify similarities and differences among some of the major theories of behavior (Fishbein, Triandis, et al., 2001). The model attempts to integrate the variables common to these several theories within a single framework. According to the IM, if a person has made a strong commitment, or formed a strong intention, to perform a given behavior, if he or she has the abilities and skills necessary to perform that behavior, and if there are no environmental barriers to prevent the performance of that behavior, it is likely that he or she will perform the behavior. Generally speaking, the model assumes that intention is the best predictor of behavior. It recognizes, however, that one may not always be able to act on one's intention. In particular, one might not have the skills and abilities needed to perform the behavior, and one might encounter barriers or other types of environmental constraints that can prevent behavioral performance. Thus, when the behavior is not being performed, it is important to know whether the problem is due to the lack of intention, the lack of skills or abilities, and/or the presence or absence of environmental factors that make behavioral performance difficult, if not impossible.

The intention to perform a given behavior is viewed as a function of three variables: the attitude toward performing the behavior, the perception of the social pressure to perform the behavior, and the perception of control or self-efficacy with respect to performing the behavior. The more positive one's attitude toward performing the behavior (i.e., the more favorably one feels about performing the behavior), the more one feels social pressure to perform the behavior (i.e., the more one believes that important others think one should (or should not) perform the behavior and/or that important others or "others like me" are themselves performing the behavior), and the stronger one's sense of personal agency or self-efficacy with respect to performance of the behavior (i.e., the more one believes that he or she has the necessary skills and abilities to perform the behavior even under a number of difficult circumstances), the stronger one's intention to perform

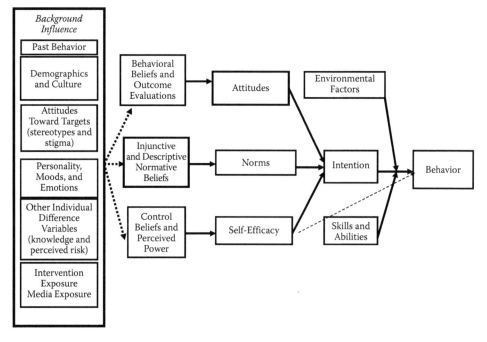

**Figure 18.1**   An Integrative Model.

the behavior. The model also states that the relative importance of these three variables as determinants of behavior is a function of both the behavior and the segment of the population being considered. Although some behaviors are primarily determined by attitudinal considerations, others may be more influenced by normative considerations and still others by issues of efficacy. Similarly, a behavior that is largely driven by attitudinal considerations in one population may be primarily driven by normative or efficacy considerations in a different one. A given intention may be influenced by all three, two, or only one of these primary determinants. When a behavior is not being performed, and it has been determined that nonperformance is primarily due to a lack of intention, one needs to know the extent to which that lack of intention is a function of attitude, perceived normative pressure, and/or self-efficacy when determining how to transform the consumer.

Attitudes, perceived social pressure, and self-efficacy are themselves assumed to be based on underlying beliefs. Attitudes are seen as a function of beliefs that performing the behavior will lead to various outcomes. Referred to as behavioral beliefs in the Theories of Reasoned Action and Planned Behavior, as outcome expectancies in Social Cognitive Theory, and as perceived costs and benefits in the Health Belief Model, it is assumed that the more one believes that performing the behavior will lead to positive outcomes and prevent negative ones, the more favorable will be one's attitude. Perceived normative pressure is viewed as a function of beliefs that specific individuals or groups think one should or should not perform the behavior (i.e., injunctive normative beliefs) as well as beliefs that specific relevant others are themselves performing or not performing the behavior (i.e., descriptive normative beliefs). The more one believes that referent others think one should perform the behavior and/or are themselves performing the behavior, the stronger will be the perceived social pressure to perform that behavior. Similarly, self-efficacy is seen as a function of beliefs that one can perform the behavior, even in the face of specific barriers.

Thus, according to the IM, one's behavior is ultimately determined by one's beliefs concerning the behavior. To fully understand why some people do and others do not perform a given behavior, it is necessary to identify the beliefs that underlie that behavior. A salient belief elicitation (Middlestadt, Bhattacharyya, Rosenbaum, Fishbein, & Shepherd, 1996) to identify the specific consequences, referents, and circumstances relevant to that behavior in the specific group of consumers is a necessary step in a full behavioral analysis.

Finally, the theory recognizes that there are a large number of variables that may influence these underlying behavioral, normative, and efficacy beliefs. For example, rich and poor, high and low sensation seekers, those who are scared or not scared, those who are anxious or relaxed, those who perceive they are or are not at risk for a serious illness, as well as those differing in ethnicity, age, and gender may have similar beliefs with respect to some behaviors but very different beliefs with respect to others. According to the IM, these upstream or background variables influence intention and behavior through their effect on the underlying belief structure.

## Using the Integrative Model to Develop Interventions

Let us now consider how a behavioral analysis based on the IM can help develop effective interventions to transform a consumer. A behavioral analysis is a series of evidence and theory-based decisions, beginning with the health outcome to be addressed, identifying the behavior to be changed, and then tracing the factors that influence this behavior upstream to the underlying beliefs (Fishbein, Middlestadt, & Hitchcock, 1991). The first step in a behavioral analysis of STI rates is the selection of the behavior most likely to have an impact in the population under consideration. The success of any behavioral intervention in reducing STI incidence in a given population will depend on the relationship between the behavior(s) addressed and the biological outcome in that population. Although it is beyond the scope of this chapter to detail all of the biological and behavioral issues involved in transmission dynamics, it should be clear from the brief description above that input from epidemiologists and clinicians familiar with the particular disease and with the evidence on the sexual and health care–seeking behaviors of the proposed segment of consumers is important in selecting the behavior. In addition, since the ultimate goal of this analysis is an intervention to transform consumers, we argue that input from an applied behavioral scientist, the planner designing the program, and members and stakeholders from the community is also important (Middlestadt, 2007).

The behavioral scientist will help the intervention team clearly define the behavior to be addressed. In selecting the behavior, one must recognize that there is a difference between specific behaviors (e.g., walking for 20 minutes almost every day), behavioral categories that include several specific behaviors (e.g., exercising, dieting), and behavioral goals or outcomes (e.g., losing weight). Although the IM can be applied to any intention (i.e., perform specific behaviors, engage in a category of behaviors, reach a specific goal), the prediction of a specific behavior from a behavioral intention is likely to be much more successful than is the prediction of engaging in a behavioral category from the intention to engage in that category or of attaining a given outcome or goal from the intention to reach that goal (see Fishbein & Ajzen, 2010). In sum, we have been more successful when we have directed interventions at changing specific behaviors.

One must also recognize that defining a behavior means considering four elements. More specifically, a behavior can be viewed as performing an action, directed at a target, performed in a given context, and at a certain point in time. Although the definitions of the four elements of action, target, context, and time are somewhat arbitrary, it is useful to explicitly consider each element. The factors underlying condom use behaviors will differ depending on target, context, and time factors, such as the type of intercourse (e.g., vaginal, anal), the type of condoms (e.g., the various styles of male and female condoms), the type of sexual partner (e.g., main, new, occasional), and the time frame (e.g., first time, every time for the next 12 months). Similarly, the factors underlying the behaviors of seeking screening or treatment will depend on factors such as the type of screening or treatment (e.g., urine test, pelvic exam), the type of health care facility (e.g., STD clinic, women's clinic, primary health care provider), the context of the visit (e.g., with symptoms, part of a primary health care visit), and the time frame of the visit. It is important to note that behaviors can be defined with a high level of specificity (e.g., buying [action] Trojan condoms [target] at your local drugstore [context] at 9 p.m. on March 3 [time]) or can be left quite general (e.g., buying [action] condoms [target and context left unspecified] in the past 12 months [time]). From the perspective of the Reasoned Action Approach, the level of specificity of any given behavior should depend on the nature of the problem and the setting. Under some circumstances, one might be interested in understanding why women select a specific type of store to purchase condoms; at other times, one may simply be trying to understand why some women did, whereas others did not, purchase condoms.

Irrespective of the level of specificity one chooses to define a behavior, once that behavior has been defined, the Reasoned Action Approach suggests that a change in any one of these elements changes the behavior under consideration and thus changes the factors that explain the behavior. Thus, for example, obtaining condoms from a clinic is a different behavior than is obtaining them from a pharmacy. Similarly, using a condom with one's spouse is a very different behavior than using a condom with an occasional or new sexual partner, and using a condom during vaginal sex is a very different behavior than using a condom during anal sex.

According to the Reasoned Action Approach, for intention to accurately predict behavior, the measure of intention must correspond to the measure of behavior. The principle of compatibility or correspondence states that the intention being studied must involve exactly the same four elements as the behavior of interest (Ajzen, 1988; Ajzen & Fishbein, 1977). If the intention is defined specifically with respect to target, context, and time, the behavior must be defined at the same level of specificity for those elements. Research has demonstrated that the greater the correspondence between the measure of intention and the measure of behavior, the higher the correlation. To achieve the best prediction, the principle of correspondence suggests that intention and behavior, as well as all other IM components, should be measured at equivalent levels of specificity.

Despite the fact that intention is the best single predictor of whether or not a behavior will be performed, intentions do not always predict corresponding behaviors. According to the IM, very different interventions are necessary if one has formed an intention but is unable to act on it than if one has little or no intention to perform the behavior. If the problem is a lack of intention, then the intervention should be directed at forming an intention. If the issue is not intention but skills or environmental constraints, then the intervention should be directed at improving skills, changing environmental factors, or helping people deal with environmental barriers.

Unfortunately, when people are not performing behaviors that we think they should perform, often our first reaction is to assume that they have the "wrong" attitude, because they do not have the knowledge to make the "correct" decision. Many interventions are designed to influence attitudes by providing knowledge. Unsurprisingly, however, many times these interventions do not work. Clearly, if people already intend to perform the behavior in question but are not acting on these intentions, it is likely that they have enough knowledge and the "right" attitude. The reason these people are not performing the behavior is because they either do not have the necessary skills and abilities, or internal or external barriers are preventing them from acting on their intentions. In these cases, it is unlikely that a knowledge-based intervention designed to change attitudes will be effective. Instead, the appropriate intervention is one directed at building skills, improving the environment, or helping people overcome or avoid barriers.

However, the problem is different if people are not performing a behavior because they have not formed an intention to do so. According to the IM, the three primary determinants of intention are the attitude toward performing the behavior in question, normative influence or the amount of social pressure one feels about performing the behavior, and one's sense of self-efficacy or personal agency with respect to performing the behavior. The relative weight or importance of these three primary psychosocial variables as determinants of intention will vary as a function of both the segment of the population and the specific behavior under study. Thus, when developing interventions to change intentions, one must first identify the degree to which that intention is under attitudinal, normative, or self-efficacy control. Different interventions are needed for behaviors under attitudinal control than those under the influence of normative factors or those that are most influenced by self-efficacy.

Given that a behavior is primarily influenced by attitudinal, normative, or control factors, how does one change these variables? As can be seen in Figure 18.1, attitudes, perceived norms, and self-efficacy themselves can be seen as determined by underlying beliefs, the perceived consequences of performing the behavior in question in the case of attitude, the normative proscriptions and/or behaviors of specific referents in the case of perceived norms, and the perception of the specific circumstances that make the behavior easier or more difficult to perform in the case of self-efficacy. It is at the level of underlying beliefs that the differences among behaviors defined at different levels of specificity are most evident. To put this somewhat differently, a change in any one of the four elements defining the behavior is likely to have a large impact on the beliefs underlying that behavior. For example, the perceived consequences of going to a women's clinic to get condoms may be different from the consequences of going to a local pharmacy to get them. Or, the normative beliefs of using a condom for vaginal sex with one's spouse or main sexual partner may be very different from the normative beliefs of using a condom for vaginal sex with a new or occasional partner. Similarly, the self-efficacy beliefs about using a male condom may be very different from the self-efficacy beliefs about using a female condom.

Yet, it is these behavioral, normative, and self-efficacy beliefs that must be addressed by an intervention if one wishes to change intentions and behavior. Although one can develop measures of attitudes, perceived norms, and self-efficacy based solely on the definition of the behavior, one must go to members of that population to identify the salient outcomes, referents, and barriers and facilitators that are underlying these three primary determinants. Stated another way, one must understand the behavior from the perspective of the segment of consumers under consideration by conducting open-ended research to identify the salient beliefs relevant to the specific behavior and the specific priority group of interest (Middlestadt, Bhattacharyya, Rosenbaum, Fishbein, et al., 1996).

### Two Illustrations

The Reasoned Action Approach has been used successfully in a number of domains to understand the psychosocial factors underlying people's decisions to engage in health behaviors with the goal of improving health. Typically, this approach is applied to a single behavior as practiced by a segment of the population relevant to the health outcome. Also, again typically, the behavior selected is one that has been demonstrated to be the immediate or most proximal determinant of the health condition through epidemiological or other evidence. To illustrate how the IM can be used in the typical setting, we will briefly review two multisite studies designed, among other things, to increase condom use.

#### The AIDS Community Demonstration Project

The CDC initiated the AIDS Community Demonstration Project to increase consistent condom use and consistent needle sterilization to reduce HIV infections in high-risk communities (Corby & Wolitski, 1997; Fishbein et al., 1997; Yzer, Fishbein, & Hennessy, 2008). The project involved five U.S. cities and several at-risk populations: men who have sex with men but do not identify themselves as being gay, injecting drug users, female sex partners of male injecting drug users, female sex workers, and youth in high-risk situations (O'Reilly & Higgins, 1991). Altogether, interventions were implemented in 10 different high-risk communities, and reports of risk behavior in these communities were compared to similar data obtained in 10 matched control communities that were not exposed to the intervention. The central element of the intervention consisted of role model stories that were distributed to members of the intervention communities through community newsletters and other small media materials. The role model stories were based on formative research and directed at either attitudes, perceived norms, or perceived control for the specific risk behaviors in the specific at-risk population.

The intervention had a significant impact on the condom use behavior of participants in the intervention communities. According to the IM, in order to produce these changes in condom use behaviors, the intervention should have led to changes in underlying beliefs, which in turn, should have led to changes in condom use attitudes, perceived normative pressure, and/or perceived control. Moreover, changes in one or more of these central components of the theory should have led to changes in intention and behavior. Somewhat surprisingly, with respect to using condoms consistently with either main partners or occasional partners, there was little differential change between intervention and control communities in either attitudes or perceived norms. Perceived self-efficacy, however, increased significantly in the intervention communities, as did intentions to use condoms consistently with respect to both types of partner (Yzer,

2007; Yzer et al., 2008), and each of these changes was significantly greater than the changes that occurred in the control communities. It seems reasonable to conclude that the intervention increased people's confidence that they could use condoms consistently with their main and occasional partners, and these changes in self-efficacy produced corresponding increases in intentions and behavior.

*Project RESPECT*

Through Project RESPECT, the CDC tested an intervention designed to prevent the spread of STIs by encouraging people to use condoms consistently (Kamb, Dillon, Fishbein, & Willis, 1996; Kamb et al., 1998). A multisite randomized control trial was conducted in sexually transmitted diseases clinics located in five U.S. cities. Participants were assigned at random to one of three individual face-to-face prevention strategies, two experimental interventions, and a control condition. The brief counseling intervention consisted of two 20-minute sessions administered 10 days apart. In the first session, risk behaviors were discussed, possible barriers to consistent condom use were identified, and participants were encouraged to take steps to begin using condoms with their main and occasional partners. In the second session, reasons for the failure were discussed. The second intervention, an enhanced counseling component developed in accordance with the IM, consisted of four sessions over a 2-week period. The initial 20-minute session of enhanced counseling was identical to the first session in the brief counseling condition. Each of the subsequent 60-minute sessions was directed at one of the IM's main components: One session tried to make attitudes toward consistent condom use more favorable by discussing the consequences of this behavior, reinforcing supportive beliefs, and countering negative beliefs brought up in the discussion; another session dealt with normative beliefs by pointing to changes in the community in support of condom use (e.g., condom store openings) and trying to convince participants that important referents approve of consistent condom use; and the third session addressed factors that could prevent or facilitate consistent condom use and tried to provide participants with needed resources and skills. Participants in the control, or educational, condition received general information about HIV/AIDS and its prevention in two didactic 5-minute sessions that were 10 days apart.

The questionnaire, administered prior to the intervention, immediately after the intervention, and at each follow-up visit, contained measures of the basic IM constructs with respect to consistent condom use for vaginal sex with main or occasional partners. In addition to direct measures of attitude, perceived norm, perceived control, and intention, the questionnaire assessed salient behavioral and normative beliefs as well as perceived barriers with respect to consistent condom use. The beliefs and perceived barriers had earlier been elicited as part of the formative research conducted in preparation for the intervention. Both path analyses (Rhodes, Stein, Fishbein, Goldstein, & Rotheram-Borus, 2007) and growth curve analyses (Fishbein, Hennessy, et al., 2001) provided strong evidence that the interventions produced significant changes in condom use behavior. For example, both enhanced and brief counseling significantly increased women's use of condoms with their main partners, but only enhanced counseling increased the frequency with which men used a condom with their main partners. Why were both interventions successful for women but only the enhanced intervention for men? The answer is relatively straightforward. Although both enhanced and brief counseling changed women's behavioral and efficacy beliefs, and thus attitudes, self-efficacy, and intentions, only enhanced counseling changed men's behavioral and efficacy beliefs. Brief counseling had virtually no effect on the men's beliefs. Perhaps most important, in comparison to the control condition, these significant increases in condom use that resulted from both enhanced and brief counseling significantly reduced the overall incidence of STIs (Kamb et al., 1998).

## AN EXPANDED BEHAVIORAL ANALYSIS FOR MULTICOMPONENT AND MULTILEVEL INTERVENTIONS

In the first part of this chapter, we showed how a Reasoned Action Approach and the IM can be used to inform a behavioral analysis in the typical setting of understanding and changing a single behavior. In this section, we are arguing for an expanded application of a behavioral analysis to help us develop more complex interventions. In public health and perhaps in Transformative Consumer Research, we increasingly find ourselves in need of approaches that can help us develop interventions that address more than the one end behavior that is the immediate determinant of a health outcome. In many settings, the ultimate health behavior is just one in a long sequence of behaviors. Furthermore, public health professionals have been challenged to recognize the major role that environments play and to take a systems approach to improving health (Leischow & Milstein, 2006). The argument being made here is that a behavioral analysis informed by a Reasoned Action Approach can be one of the tools we use to develop the more complex, multicomponent, or multilevel interventions we now look for in public health. To illustrate this expanded approach, we present three examples in the domain of preventing and controlling STIs: applying the approach to understand the several behaviors that lead up to the performance of the end consumer or health behavior, using the results of the analysis of the underlying belief structure to identify environmental changes, and applying the approach to the behavior of agents in order to modify the systems that influence behavior and health outcomes.

### Illustration 1: Apply the Reasoned Action Approach to Understand Several Behaviors Implicated in the Performance of the End Consumer or Health Behavior

In many situations, there are a number of behaviors that may need to be performed to correctly and consistently perform the end health behavior that is associated with or most proximal to the biological or health outcome. In these situations, the intervention designer may need to develop intervention components that target these supportive behaviors in addition to or before addressing the end or most proximal health behavior. For example, screening and timely treatment is an effective approach to control some STIs. When it comes to encouraging members of an at-risk priority group to get tested for an STI, the practitioner may need to understand several supportive behaviors, such as going to a primary care provider for a test or a regular health care visit, asking the provider to test for the STI, contacting the provider for results of the test and treatment recommendations, following treatment recommendations, or taking steps to notify sex partners.

When it comes to condom use, there is considerable evidence confirming the role of a number of supportive or precursor behaviors. In a meta-analysis of 121 empirical studies of condom use, Sheeran, Abraham, and Orbell (1999) found that three preparatory behaviors (i.e., carrying condoms, ensuring condom availability, communication with sexual partners about condoms) were among the strongest associates of condom use. Meekers and Klein (2002) found gender differences in purchasing condoms that seemed to explain the lower levels of condom use among young women in Cameroon and that exposure to condom advertising seemed to reduce women's shyness at buying condoms and lead to greater use. To address the lower level of condom use among young women in Brazil, the national AIDS commission developed, implemented, and evaluated a mass media campaign encouraging women to purchase condoms (Porto, 2007). In Malawi, condom use is increasing outside of marriage, but condom use within married couples is negligible. Qualitative data suggest that even discussing the use of condoms in a marriage is disruptive, because condoms are believed to interfere with sex and procreation (Chimbiri, 2007). In this case, the behavior of discussing condoms must be understood and addressed before the issue of condom use can be tackled. Finally, one team of researchers developed a research method to identify which supportive behaviors are important to different priority groups. They applied this method to condom use and identified one sequence relevant to adolescents (Schaalma, Kok, Poelman, & Reinders, 1994) and another sequence for men who have sex with men (Van Kesteren, Hospers, Kok, & Van Empelen, 2005).

Although it is unlikely that it will be necessary or possible to conduct a behavioral analysis to understand all of these precursor behaviors and all of their underlying factors, it is possible that interventions to encourage condom use would be improved if the IM was applied to understand the factors underlying people's performance of some of these supportive behaviors. Although there is considerable research using the Reasoned Action Approach to understand the end health behavior of condom use (e.g., Albarracin, Johnson, Fishbein, & Muellerleile, 2001), less research has attempted to understand the behaviors that support condom use. We did, however, identify three studies that used a Reasoned Action Approach to understand a supportive behavior. First, in a study of condom carrying among adolescents from the United Kingdom, Arden and Armitage (2008) found that self-efficacy and attitude toward carrying condoms, but not subjective norm with respect to carrying condoms, were predictive of condom carrying intention and behavior. Second, Van Empelen and Kok (2008) applied the Theory of Planned Behavior to understand two condom use behaviors (i.e., with a steady partner, with a casual partner) and two preparatory behaviors (i.e., buying and carrying condoms). In their study of Dutch adolescents, they found that intention to use condoms did not automatically lead to buying or carrying them and that perceived social norms were associated with intention both to buy and carry condoms. Based on this evidence, the authors urged for programs that address preparatory behaviors like buying and carrying as well as the end health behavior of using condoms.

Third, in an elicitation study based on the Reasoned Action Approach with White and African American heterosexual young adults in casual or steady relationships from three cities in the United States, Middlestadt and colleagues (Middlestadt, Bhattacharyya, Rosenbaum, Baume, & Weiss, 1996; Middlestadt, Bhattacharyya, Rosenbaum, Fishbein, & Shepherd, 1996) examined the belief structure underlying four behaviors: using a condom every time, discussing condom use with one's partner, the female putting the condom on the male, and refusing to have sex without a condom. Some of the underlying beliefs (e.g., prevent pregnancy, prevent STIs, would lead to a negative partner reaction) were elicited for all four of the behaviors. However, some of the underlying beliefs were different for the different behaviors. For example, the consequence "would arouse me" was the most frequently elicited advantage of the woman putting the condom on the man. As another example, "would learn about each other's views, beliefs, and expectations" was elicited as an advantage of discussing condoms with one's partner. This comparative behavioral analysis of four behaviors (i.e., one condom use behavior and three supportive behaviors) found that there are common as well as unique beliefs across the four behaviors in the condom sequence. The finding of several common and some unique beliefs suggests that it might be possible to develop a multicomponent intervention to deal with all four behaviors efficiently by developing some components to change the common beliefs and some to change the unique ones.

Illustration 2: Use the Results From the Analysis of the Underlying Behavioral, Normative, and Control Belief Structure to Identify Environmental Changes

It is often assumed that the Reasoned Action Approach limits its focus to the individual, relies on cognitive changes (often through persuasive communication or education programs), and neglects environmental change. In fact, most applications of the Reasoned Action Approach result in an individual persuasion approach. However, although the Reasoned Action Approach clearly states that it is what people believe about a behavior that influences whether they do or do not perform the behavior, it does not necessarily follow that the only route to changing behavior is through persuasive communication or education designed to change these beliefs. A person's beliefs are formed based on a variety of direct and indirect factors, including performing the behavior and experiencing the consequences, the approval or disapproval of significant others, and/or the circumstances that facilitate or hinder the behavior. Thus, while it may be that a communication will be a successful tactic to help someone view a behavior differently, the intervention planner may need to change the environment to bring about the necessary belief change and resultant behavior change. Alternatively, the practitioner may choose to create a multicomponent intervention that includes communication components as well as components that support changes in the environment.

Going beyond communication and education is consistent with several models of social change. Social marketing, defined as the use of marketing principles and techniques for social and health issues, recommends addressing price, product, and place in addition to promotion (see Andreasen, Goldberg, & Sirgy, Chapter 2 of this volume). Smith (1991) applies social marketing principles to the development of large-scale STI prevention interventions and points out that addressing price and place often means structural change. In his articulation of a marketing approach, Rothschild (1999) recommends that planners should consider marketing tools as well as education and policy tools for social change. Here, marketing involves exchange and is defined as making the environment more favorable by offering benefits and reinforcing desired behavior. Within public health, the PRECEDE-PROCEED planning model (Green & Kreuter, 1999) requires the intervention designer to conduct social, environmental, administrative, and policy assessments as well as educational and behavioral assessments to identify factors to modify. Finally, the various statements of the Social Ecological Model (e.g., McLeroy, Bibeau, Steckler, & Glanz, 1988) maintain that it is necessary to consider factors beyond intrapersonal factors, including interpersonal, primary group, institutional, community, and public policy factors. The purpose of this section is to show how the results of the analysis of the behavioral, normative, and control belief structures underlying a behavior can help the designer identify the aspects of the environment that, if changed, will support behavior change. Stated another way, the beliefs of the participants identified during research using the IM or the Reasoned Action Approach can be used as one lens through which to view the environment at its multiple levels and thus can suggest aspects of the environment to change.

### Behavioral Beliefs

As a first example, let us consider the behavioral beliefs underlying attitude toward condom use. A number of studies have identified the belief that using a condom reduces pleasure as a significant determinant of intention. Jemmott et al. (2007) found that belief about the effect of condom use on pleasure was associated with intention to use condoms among adolescents from Xhosa, South Africa. Similarly, in a study of university students in Ghana, Bosompra (2001) found that beliefs about the consequence of ruining the moment and reducing pleasure differentiated intenders from nonintenders. Given this behavioral belief, what kind of intervention might transform the consumer and support condom use? One clear recommendation is to change the environment, that is, change the actual consequences experienced. To accomplish this, one might improve the product by developing a condom that does not have the expected negative impact on sexual pleasure and instead enhances it. In fact, condom manufacturers are working to develop condoms that are sized to fit (Reece et al., 2008) and include vibrators. Recently, Trojan released the Ecstasy condom line with several features designed to increase pleasure for both partners.

### Normative Beliefs

As a second example, a number of studies have identified a variety of normative beliefs as factors underlying the social pressure to use condoms. In a study of Norwegian adolescents, Myklestad and Rise (2008) found that beliefs about what friends believed was associated with condom use intentions for boys, whereas beliefs about what parents believed was associated with condom use intentions for girls. Salabarria-Pena, Lee, Montgomery, Hopp, and Muralles (2003) found that the normative belief about the expectations of female friends was the strongest predictor of subjective norm among immigrant women from Central America living in Los Angeles. How these findings are best used to develop interventions to transform behaviors might depend on what the significant others actually believed. For example, suppose the normative belief from the sexual partner was a key factor in condom use. In this case, a persuasive communication pointing out that most sexual partners wanted to use condoms would be effective if most partners actually want condoms to be used but had not communicated this to their partners. If partners actually were opposed to condom use, a communication strategy aimed at letting the participants know what their partners expected would likely be ineffective. Here, it would be necessary to change the social environment.

### Self-Efficacy Beliefs

As a third example, consider the beliefs underlying the person's self-efficacy or sense of personal agency with respect to performing some behavior, which is likely to be the part of the belief structure with the clearest environmental implications. Myklestad and Rise (2008) found that two efficacy beliefs predicted intention to use condoms among boys: (1) Condoms are more difficult to use if there is no condom vending machine at the boy's school or youth club, and (2) buying condoms is too expensive. These results clearly support two environmental interventions that might be effective: a structural intervention that ensures that condom vending machines are placed in the environment, and policies or structural supports to keep the price of condoms low.

### Illustration 3: Apply the Reasoned Action Approach to Understand the Behavior of Agents Who Influence the Environment

Given that one wants to change the environment that a consumer experiences, how might we go about transforming this environment? One approach is to change the behavior of the agents who control or influence that environment. One of the advantages of the Reasoned Action Approach is that it can be used on behaviors of all types, not just health behaviors. In particular, this approach can be used to understand the social behaviors of the agents who shape the environment and influence the systems that affect the behavior of consumers. Thus, an intervention planner can use the theory to understand and craft interventions to change the behavior of agents at several levels in the environment. Although many planners recognize the need to get input from stakeholders, theories of behavior are rarely used to obtain this input. In this section, we describe how a Reasoned Action Approach might be used to understand and influence agents in two organizations important in the environment of sexual health behaviors: the school system and the health care system.

### Providing Effective Sex Health Education in Schools by Changing the Behavior of Parents, Administrators, Classroom Teachers, and Other School Stakeholders

Given the statistics outlined at the beginning of this chapter, adolescents and young adults are one of the priority groups at higher risk for getting STIs. The classroom has long been identified as a setting for delivering interventions that help our nation's youth learn to practice healthy behaviors, including sexual health behaviors. Furthermore, research reviewing school-based sexual health programs demonstrates that a number of effective interventions exist (James-Traore, Finger, Ruland, & Savariaud, 2004; Kirby, 2002a; Kirby et al., 1994; Shuey, Babishangire, & Omiat, 1999). However, the school continues to be a controversial setting for sexual health education, and there is considerable evidence that effective programs are not always being offered in schools (Guttmacher

Institute, 2010; Kirby, 2002b; Lindberg, Santelli, & Singh, 2006). We propose that a behavioral analysis of the behaviors of agents in the school setting can help us change the school environment.

We could find no studies that used the Reasoned Action Approach to understand and modify the behavior of parents, administrators, teachers, or other school stakeholders. The literature on school stakeholders that we did find supports the need for theory-based research. That is, although research attempting to diagnose the problem has suggested that the beliefs and attitudes of administrators, school boards, parents, and teachers are critical when it comes to adopting and fully implementing sex education programs in schools (Blinn-Pike, 2008; Buston, Wight, Hart, & Scott, 2002; Giacquinta, 1975; Milton, 2003; Mufune, 2008), this research was, by and large, not guided by any behavioral theories. Furthermore, some health planners have explicitly called for theory-based programs addressing parents, teachers, administrators, and other stakeholders to encourage them to adopt and fully implement effective sex education in schools (e.g., Schaalma, Abraham, Gillmore, & Kok, 2004).

Thus, we would argue that a behavioral analysis following a Reasoned Action Approach is one approach to formative research to understand and modify the behaviors of agents who shape the school environment in order to offer and fully implement sexual health education. The behaviors would be different for the different stakeholders. In the case of parents, since research has demonstrated the role of parental approval on administrator and teacher behavior with respect to implementing school-based sexual health education, we might want to examine the behavior of parents speaking out in support of sex education in schools. In the case of administrators, the behavior to select, as a target of intervention research, will depend on the level of the administrator and the place in the school system where curricular decisions are made. In some settings, administrator support of a particular type of sex education program in a school system is critical. In other settings, school boards are involved in the decision about which, if any, program to offer in a school district. Thus, a Reasoned Action Approach can be used to understand the behavior of voting for a particular sex education program by either administrators or school board members.

Finally, for the classroom teachers expected to deliver the program, the issue is often one of increasing the likelihood that they will fully implement the activities and all components of the program. Effective sex education programs go beyond providing information and almost always consist of activities that are experiential, aimed at improving skills and self-efficacy through role-playing, and require a sensitive discussion of difficult issues of relationships and sexuality. Often, teachers do not fully implement these programs and leave out interactive or sensitive components. Research following the Reasoned Action Approach would be useful to understand the factors that determine whether a teacher fully implements the curriculum. Such information could be used to develop teacher training and other supportive interventions to ensure complete delivery.

### Ensuring Testing for STIs by Modifying the Behavior of Primary Care Providers

The health care systems we experience can have a profound effect on our health behavior and outcomes. Physicians and other medical providers are agents who play a major role in how the care system works and even whether and when individuals seek health care. A number of provider factors have been identified as important associates of intention to seek STI care (e.g., Amaro & Gornermann, 1991; Pavlin, Gunn, Parker, Fairley, & Hocking, 2006). Thus, it is reasonable to use a behavioral analysis to understand the behaviors of health care providers as the agents who influence health care organizations and the health care environment.

In contrast to the literature on agents in the school system, we found a number of studies that used a Reasoned Action Approach to understand provider behavior. For example, one study analyzed physician beliefs about prescribing emergency contraception (Sable, Schwartz, Kelly,

Lisbon, & Hall, 2006), and another tried to understand physician beliefs with respect to talking with adolescents about STI prevention (Millstein, 1996). A third example, the Gonorrhea Community Action Project, was a multilevel intervention that took a Reasoned Action Approach directed at reducing the incidence of gonorrhea and chlamydia among adolescents and young adults by addressing both consumers and providers (Middlestadt, VanDevanter, et al., 2002). Timely treatment can control the spread of an STI by reducing the length of time individuals are infectious. Reproductive health guidelines indicate that sexually active adolescents and young adults should be screened for gonorrhea and chlamydia and treated if they test positive. However, the literature revealed that many primary care providers were reluctant to discuss sexual activity with their adolescent and young adult clients, did not determine that these clients were sexually active, and did not test and treat them for STIs.

One approach to facilitating early and effective treatment is multilevel: Consumers who are at risk are encouraged to seek health care, and at the same time, providers are encouraged to test and treat. In the case of the Gonorrhea Community Action Project, adolescents and young adults were encouraged to go for a primary care visit, primary care providers were encouraged to ask adolescents and young adults if they were sexually active at every visit and test for an STI if the youth were sexually active, and steps were taken to ensure the accessibility of urine-based screening tests. Formative research based on the Reasoned Action Approach found that normative, control, and attitudinal factors predicted providers' intentions to ask adolescents about sexual behavior at every visit (Middlestadt et al., 2001). This research was used to develop an intervention to encourage primary care providers to ask their adolescent and young adult patients about sexual behavior at every visit and screen for gonorrhea and chlamydia if they were sexually active (Middlestadt, Malotte, et al., 2002). This provider intervention was accompanied by educational and communication interventions with adolescents and young adults to encourage them to go for a primary health care visit (VanDevanter et al., 2005), and both components were found to be effective.

## CONCLUSION

STIs represent a major public health problem around the world, a problem that is responsible for substantial morbidity, mortality, health care and other costs, and reduced quality of life. Reducing STIs requires transforming consumers and the environments in which they live. In this chapter, we have argued that interventions to transform consumers need to be guided by theory-based research. More specifically, with a step-by-step approach, we have tried to show how a behavioral analysis based on a particular behavioral theory, the IM, can be used to understand and change behavior and identify ways to improve sexual health. First, we outlined the role behavior plays within the dynamics of infection. Second, we presented the IM as the most recent formulation of the Reasoned Action Approach and showed how a behavioral analysis based on this model can be used to conduct research to plan effective interventions. Then, we described two multisite interventions based on the IM that have successfully changed condom use. Like most applications of the Reasoned Action Approach, these two interventions took a straightforward approach of understanding the psychosocial factors underlying a health behavior that was the most proximal determinant of a health behavior in a priority group.

In the second half of the chapter, we made the case for an expanded use of a theory-based behavioral analysis, one that can help the field develop more complex, multicomponent, or multilevel interventions. We provided three illustrations of an expanded behavioral analysis: one that outlines how a Reasoned Action Approach can be used to understand the upstream behaviors that support the end health behavior, one that shows how the underlying beliefs identified from research based on the IM can be used to identify features of the environment that, if transformed, would change behavior, and one that articulates a behavioral approach to organizational change, in which we try to understand and modify the social behaviors of the agents and stakeholders who control the environment and the systems that surround us.

Hopefully, these examples illustrate how the IM can be used beyond the typical application of understanding the psychosocial factors underlying a single behavior that is the immediate determinant of a health outcome with the goal of developing a communication or educational intervention directed at the individual. Three things became clear in developing these illustrations. First, it is likely that other illustrations of an expanded behavior analysis are possible. One reviewer suggested using the IM to systematically develop a series of interventions tailored to helping transform sexual behavior over the stages of the life cycle. It is clear that one size does not fit all when it comes to sexual health decision making. The factors that influence a young adolescent new to sexual activity will differ from those of the older adolescent who has had a number of partners (Guilamo-Ramos, Jaccard, Dittus, Gonzalez, & Bouris, 2008). Similarly, factors will differ for divorced adults or older adults thinking about sexual activity in their maturity. Research on these factors guided by a common theory-based framework could lead to a series of progressive interventions. Another reviewer suggested helping consumers change which referent group to attend to in making behavioral decisions as a way to transform behavior. We hope researchers and practitioners in the field of behavior change will explore other expanded illustrations.

Second, although the Reasoned Action Approach has received much attention in the research literature, we found few studies that used it or the IM in an expanded way. In fact, most applications in the sexual health arena focused on the three primary determinants of intention and did not even assess the underlying cognitive structure. Thus, we recommend that researchers should take the time to use the full model and assess the underlying cognitive structure, identify and try to understand a range of behaviors that lead to end health behaviors, and conduct theory-based research to understand the social behaviors of agents in the environment. Finally, although our focus has been on the IM as the most recent formulation of the Reasoned Action Approach, we recognize that this chapter could have been written from the perspective of other behavioral theories. What we hope we have made clear, however, is the role that a sound, empirically supported behavioral analysis can play in Transformative Consumer Research.

## ACKNOWLEDGMENTS

Martin Fishbein, my coauthor, colleague, and close friend, died in November 2009 after we submitted the first draft of this chapter. I have revised the chapter based on the comments from the editor and three reviewers, James Jaccard, Gerald Gorn, and Kevin Malotte. First, I wish to thank these reviewers for their support and help. Second, I would like to let readers know that Marty and I did not finish arguing about a number of the points in the second part of this chapter. Finally, I would like to take the opportunity to thank Marty for his enormous contribution to the field and to my own personal and professional development.

## REFERENCES

Ajzen, I. (1988). *Attitudes, personality, and behavior*. Chicago: Dorsey Press.

Ajzen, I. (1991). The theory of planned behavior. *Organizational Behavior and Human Decision Processes, 50*, 179–211.

Ajzen, I., & Fishbein, M. (1977). Attitude–behavior relations: A theoretical analysis and review of empirical research. *Psychological Bulletin, 84*, 888–918.

Albarracin, D., Johnson, B. T., Fishbein, M., & Muellerleile, P. A. (2001). Theories of reasoned action and planned behavior as models of condom use: A meta-analysis. *Psychological Bulletin, 127*, 142–161.

Amaro, H., & Gornermann, I. (1991). Health care utilization for sexually transmitted diseases: Influence of patient and provider characteristics. In J. N. Wasserheit, S. O. Aral, & K. K. Holmes (Eds.), *Research issues in human behavior and sexually transmitted diseases in the AIDS era* (pp. 140–160). Washington, DC: American Society for Microbiology.

Arden, M. A., & Armitage, C. J. (2008). Predicting and explaining transtheoretical model stage transitions in relation to condom-carrying behaviors. *British Journal of Health Psychology, 13,* 719–735.

Blinn-Pike, L. (2008). Sex education in rural schools in the United States: Impact of rural educators' identities. *Sex Education, 8,* 77–92.

Bosompra, K. (2001). Determinants of condom use intentions of university students in Ghana: An application of the theory of reasoned action. *Social Science & Medicine, 52,* 1057–1069.

Buston, K., Wight, D., Hart, G., & Scott, S. (2002). Implementation of a teacher delivered sex education programme: Obstacles and facilitating factors. *Health Education Research, 17,* 59–72.

Cates, W., Jr., & Holmes, K. K. (1996). Re: Condom efficacy against gonorrhea and nongonococcol urethritis. *American Journal of Epidemiology, 143,* 843–844.

Centers for Disease Control and Prevention. (2009). *Trends in reportable sexually transmitted diseases in the United States, 2007: National surveillance date for Chlamydia, gonorrhea, and syphilis.* Available: http://www.cdc.gov/std/stats07/trends.pdf

Chesson H. W., Blandford, J. M., Gift, T. L., Tao, G., & Irwin, K. L. (2004). The estimated direct medical cost of sexually transmitted diseases among American youth, 2000. *Perspectives on Sexual and Reproductive Health, 36*(1), 11–19.

Chimbiri, A. M. (2007). The condom is an "intruder" in marriage: Evidence from rural Malawi. *Social Science & Medicine, 64,* 1102–1115.

Corby, N. H., & Wolitski, R. J. (Eds.). (1997). *Community HIV prevention: The Long Beach AIDS Community Demonstration Project.* Long Beach: California State University Press.

Fishbein, M. (2000). The role of theory in HIV prevention. *AIDS Care, 12*(3), 273–278.

Fishbein, M. (2008). A reasoned action approach to health promotion. *Medical Decision Making, 28*(6), 834–844.

Fishbein, M., & Ajzen, I. (2010). *Predicting and changing behavior: A reasoned action approach.* New York: Psychology Press.

Fishbein, M., Guenther-Grey, C., Johnson, W., Wolitski, R. J., McAlister, A., Rietmeijer, C. A., et al. (1997). Using a theory-based community intervention to reduce AIDS risk behaviors: The CDC's AIDS community demonstration projects. In M. E. Goldberg, M. Fishbein, & S. Middlestadt (Eds.), *Social marketing: Theoretical and practical perspectives* (pp. 123–146). Mahwah, NJ: Erlbaum.

Fishbein, M., Hennessy, M., Kamb, M., Bolan, G. A., Hoxworth, T., Iatesta, M., et al. (2001). Using intervention theory to model factors influencing behavior change: Project RESPECT. *Evaluation & the Health Professions, 24,* 363–384.

Fishbein, M., Middlestadt, S. E., & Hitchcock, P. J. (1991). Using information to change STD-related behaviors: An analysis based on the theory of reasoned action. In J. N. Wasserheit, S. O. Aral, & K. K. Holmes (Eds.), *Research issues in human behavior and sexually transmitted diseases in the AIDS era* (pp. 243–257). Washington, DC: American Society for Microbiology.

Fishbein, M., Triandis, H. C., Kanfer, F. H., Becker, M., Middlestadt, S. E., & Eichler, A. (2001). Factors influencing behavior and behavior change. In A. Baum, T. A. Revenson, & J. E. Singer (Eds), *Handbook of health psychology* (pp. 1–7). Mahwah, NJ: Erlbaum.

Giacquinta, J. B. (1975). Status, risk and receptivity to innovations in complex organizations: A study of the responses of four groups of educators to the proposed introduction of sex education in elementary school. *Sociology of Education, 48,* 38–58.

Green, L. W., & Kreuter, M. W. (1999). *Health promotion planning: An educational and ecological approach* (3rd ed.). Mountain View, CA: Mayfield.

Guilamo-Ramos, V., Jaccard, J., Dittus, P., Gonzalez, B., & Bouris, A. (2008). A conceptual framework for the analysis of risk and problem behaviors: The case of adolescent sexual behavior. *Social Work Research, 32,* 29–45.

Guttmacher Institute. (2010). State policies in brief as of October 1, 2010: Sex and STI/HIV education. Retrieved December 15, 2010, from http://www.guttmacherinstitute.org/statecenter/spibs/spib_SE.pdf

Institute of Medicine, Committee on Communication for Behavior Change in the 21st Century: Improving the Health of Diverse Populations. (2002). *Speaking of health: Assessing health communication strategies for diverse populations.* Washington, DC: National Academies Press.

James-Traore, T., Finger, W., Ruland, C., & Savariaud, S. (2004). *Teacher training: Essential for school-based reproductive health and HIV/AIDS education: Focus on sub-Saharan Africa* (Youth Issues Paper No. 3). Arlington, VA: Family Health International, Youth Net Program.

Jemmott, J. B., Heeren, G., Ngwane, Z., Hewitt, N., Jemmott, L. S., Shell, R., et al. (2007). Theory of planned behavior predictors of intention to use condoms among Xhosa adolescents in South Africa. *AIDS Care*, *19*, 677–684.

Kamb, M. L., Dillon, B. A., Fishbein, M., & Willis, K. L. (1996). Quality assurance of HIV prevention counseling in a multi-center randomized controlled trial. *Public Health Reports*, *111*, 99–107.

Kamb, M. L., Fishbein, M., Douglas, J. M., Rhodes, F., Rogers, J., Bolan, G., et al. (1998). Efficacy of risk-reduction counseling to prevent human immunodeficiency virus and sexually transmitted diseases. *Journal of the American Medical Association*, *280*, 1161–1167.

Kirby, D. (2002a). Effective approaches to reducing adolescent unprotected sex, pregnancy, and childbearing, *Journal of Sex Research*, *39*, 51–57.

Kirby, D. (2002b). The impact of schools and school programs upon adolescent sexual behavior. *Journal of Sex Research*, *39*, 27–33.

Kirby, D., Short, L., Collins, J., Rugg, D., Kolbe, L., Howard, M., et al. (1994). School-based programs to reduce sexual risk behaviors: A review of effectiveness. *Public Health Reports*, *10*, 339–360.

Leischow, S. J., & Milstein, B. (2006). Systems thinking and modeling for public health practice. *American Journal of Public Health*, *96*(3), 403–405.

Lindberg L. D., Santelli, J. S., & Singh, S. (2006). Changes in formal sex education: 1994–2002. *Perspectives on Sexual and Reproductive Health*, *38*(4), 182–189.

May, R. M., & Anderson, R. M. (1987). Transmission dynamics of HIV infection. *Nature*, *326*, 137–142.

McLeroy, K. R., Bibeau, D., Steckler, A., & Glanz, K. (1988). An ecological perspective on health promotion programs. *Health Education Quarterly*, *15*, 351–377.

Meekers, D., & Klein, M. (2002). Understanding gender differences in condom use self-efficacy among youth in urban Cameroon. *AIDS Education and Prevention*, *14*, 62–72.

Middlestadt, S. E. (2007). What is the behavior? Strategies for selecting the behavior to be addressed by health promotion interventions. In I. Ajzen, D. Albarracin, & R. Hornik (Eds.), *Prediction and change of health behavior: Applying the reasoned action approach* (pp. 129–147). Mahwah, NJ: Erlbaum.

Middlestadt, S. E., Bhattacharyya, K., Rosenbaum, J., Baume, C., & Weiss, L. (1996). *Exploring condom use behaviors of young adults: An elicitation study*. Washington, DC: Academy for Educational Development.

Middlestadt, S. E., Bhattacharyya, K., Rosenbaum, J. E., Fishbein, M., & Shepherd, M. (1996). The use of theory-based semi-structured elicitation questionnaires: Formative research for CDC's Prevention Marketing Initiative. *Public Health Reports*, *3*(Suppl. 1), 18–27.

Middlestadt, S. E., Malotte, C. K., VanDevanter, N., Hogben, M., St. Lawrence, J. S., Ledsky, R., et al. (2002, November). *STD care beliefs and behaviors: Effects of a workshop for primary care providers from three communities*. Paper presented at the 130th annual meeting of the American Public Health Association, Philadelphia.

Middlestadt, S. E., Malotte, C. K., VanDevanter, N., Hogben, M., Ledsky, R., Cohall, A., et al. (2001, October). *Asking adolescents about sexual behavior at every visit: Correlates among primary care providers*. Paper presented at the 129th annual meeting of the American Public Health Association, Atlanta, GA.

Middlestadt, S. E., VanDevanter, N., Malotte, C. K., Gift, T., Messeri, P., Ledsky, R., et al. (2002, February–March). *The Gonorrhea Community Action Project*. Paper presented at the National STD Prevention Conference, San Diego, CA.

Millstein, S. G. (1996). Utility of the theories of reasoned action and planned behavior for predicting provider behavior: A prospective analysis. *Health Psychology*, *15*, 398–402.

Milton, J. (2003). Primary school sex education programs: View and experiences of teachers in four primary schools in Sydney, Australia. *Sex Education*, *3*, 241–256.

Mufune, P. (2008). Stakeholder perceptions and attitudes towards sexual and reproductive health education in Namibia. *Sex Education*, *8*, 145–157.

Myklestad, I., & Rise, J. (2008). Predicting intentions to perform protective sexual behaviors among Norwegian adolescents. *Sex Education*, *8*, 107–124.

O'Reilly, K., & Higgins, D. L. (1991). AIDS community demonstration projects for HIV prevention among hard-to-reach groups. *Public Health Reports*, *106*, 714–720.

Pavlin, N. L., Gunn, J. M., Parker, R., Fairley, C. K., & Hocking, J. (2006). Implementing chlamydia screening: What do women think? A systematic review of the literature. *BMC Public Health*, *6*, 221.

Peterman, T. A., Lin, L. S., Newman, D. R., Kamb, M.L., Bolan, G., Zenilman, J., et al. (2000). Does measured behavior reflect STD risk? An analysis of data from a controlled behavioral intervention study. *Sexually Transmitted Diseases*, *27*(8), 446–451.

Pinkerton, S. D., & Abramson, P. R. (1994). An alternative model of the reproductive rate of HIV infection: Formulation, evaluation, and implications for risk reduction interventions. *Evaluation Review, 18*(4), 371–388.

Porto, M. P. (2007). Fighting AIDS among adolescent women: Effects of a public communication campaign in Brazil. *Health Communication, 12,* 121–132.

Reece, M., Herbenick, D., Sanders, S. A., Monahan, P., Temkit, M., & Yarber, W. L. (2008). Breakage, slippage and acceptability outcomes of a condom fitted to penile dimensions. *Sexually Transmitted Diseases, 84,* 143–149.

Reiss, I. L., & Leik, R. K. (1989). Evaluating strategies to avoid AIDS: Number of partners vs. use of condoms. *Journal of Sex Research, 26,* 411–433.

Rhodes, F., Stein, J. A., Fishbein, M., Goldstein, R. B., & Rotheram-Borus, M. J. (2007). Using theory to understand how interventions work: Project RESPECT, condom use, and the integrative model. *AIDS and Behavior, 11,* 393–407.

Rothschild, M. L. (1999). Carrots, sticks, and promises: A conceptual framework for the management of public health and social issue behaviors. *Journal of Marketing, 63,* 24–37.

Sable, M. R., Schwartz, L. R., Kelly, P. J., Lisbon, E., & Hall, M. A. (2006). Using the theory of reasoned action to explain physician intention to prescribe emergency contraception. *Perspectives on Sexual and Reproductive Health, 38,* 20–27.

Sackett, P., & Mavor, A. (Eds.). (2002). *Attitudes, aptitudes, and aspirations of American youth: Implications for military recruitment.* Washington, DC: National Academies Press.

Salabarria-Pena, Y., Lee, J. W., Montgomery, S., Hopp, H. W., & Muralles, A. A. (2003). Determinants of female and male condom use among immigrant women of Central American descent. *AIDS and Behavior, 7,* 163–174.

Schaalma, H. P., Abraham, C., Gillmore, M. R., & Kok, G. (2004). Sex education as health promotion. *Archives of Sexual Behavior, 33,* 259–269.

Schaalma, H. P., Kok, G., Poelman, J., & Reinders, J. (1994). The development of AIDS education for Dutch secondary schools: A systematic approach based on research, theories, and co-operation. In D. R. Rutter & L. Quine (Eds.), *Social psychology and health: European perspectives* (pp. 175–194). Aldershot, England: Avebury.

Sheeran, P., Abraham, C., & Orbell, S. (1999). Psychosocial correlates of heterosexual condom use: A meta-analysis. *Psychological Bulletin, 125,* 90–132.

Shuey, D. A., Babishangire, B., & Omiat, S. (1999). Increased sexual abstinence among in-school adolescents as a result of school health education in Soroti district, Uganda. *Health Education Research, 14,* 411–419.

Smith, W. A. (1991). Organizing large-scale interventions for sexually transmitted disease prevention. In J. N. Wasserheit, S. O. Aral, & K. K. Holmes (Eds.), *Research issues in human behavior and sexually transmitted diseases in the AIDS era* (pp. 219–242). Washington, DC: American Society for Microbiology.

VanDevanter, N., Middlestadt, S. E., Messeri, P., Bleakley, A., Ledsky, R., Merzel, C., et al. (2005). Community-based intervention to increase preventive health care seeking in adolescents: The Gonorrhea Community Action Project. *American Journal of Public Health, 95*(2), 331–338.

Van Empelen, P., & Kok, G. (2008). Action-specific cognitions of planned and preparatory behaviors of condom use among Dutch adolescents. *Archives of Sexual Behavior, 37,* 626–640.

Van Kesteren, N. M. C., Hospers, J. J., Kok, G., & van Empelen, P. (2005). Sex and sexual risk behavior in HIV positive men who have sex with men. *Qualitative Health Research, 15,* 145–168.

Warner, L., Clay-Warner, J., Boles, J., & Williamson, J. (1998). Assessing condom use practices: Implications for evaluating method and user effectiveness. *Sexually Transmitted Diseases, 25,* 273–277.

Warner, L., Newman, D. R., Kamb, M. L., Fishbein, M., Douglas, J. M., Jr., Zenilman, J., et al. (2008). Problems with condom use among patients attending sexually transmitted disease clinics: Prevalence, predictors, and relation to incident gonorrhea and chlamydia. *American Journal of Epidemiology. 167,* 341–349.

Wasserheit, J., Aral, S., & Holmes, K. (Eds.). (1991). *Research issues in human behavior and sexually transmitted diseases in the AIDS era.* Washington, DC: American Society for Microbiology.

Weinstock, H., Berman, S., & Cates, W., Jr. (2004). Sexually transmitted diseases among American youth: Incidence and prevalence estimates, 2000. *Perspectives on Sexual and Reproductive Health, 36*(1), 6–10.

World Health Organization. (2010). *WHO sexual and reproductive health medium-term strategic plan for 2010–2015 and programme budget for 2010–2011.* Geneva, Switzerland: Author.

Yzer, M. (2007). Perceived control moderates attitudinal and normative effects on intention: I'd like to, but I can't, so I won't. In I. Ajzen, R. Hornik, & D. Albarracin (Eds.), *Prediction and change of behavior: Applying the reasoned action approach* (pp. 111–127). Mahwah, NJ: Erlbaum.

Yzer, M. C., Fishbein, M., & Hennessy, M. (2008). HIV prevention interventions affect behavior indirectly: Results from the AIDS Community Demonstration Projects. *AIDS Care, 20*, 456–461.

# VI

## CONSUMER FINANCES

# 19

# *Addition by Division*

## Partitioning Real Accounts for Financial Well-Being

GEORGE LOEWENSTEIN, CYNTHIA E. CRYDER,
SHLOMO BENARTZI, AND ALESSANDRO PREVITERO

If consumers had infinite computing capacity and perfect self-control, they would estimate their total lifetime accumulation of wealth and decide whether to make each purchase by comparing the utility of that purchase to the utility of the next best use of the money, or in some cases, to the best use of money, in which case the purchase would not occur. However, for a variety of reasons, consumers find it useful to set up mental accounts (Thaler, 1985, 1999), which help classify different sources of income (Henderson & Peterson, 1992), different pools of savings (e.g., Shefrin & Thaler, 1992; Thaler & Shefrin, 1981), and different categories of spending (e.g., Heath & Soll, 1996), in some cases linking one set of categories (e.g., income sources) to another (e.g., spending categories; see, e.g., O'Curry, 1997). Although mental accounting strategies can yield patterns of behavior that deviate from rational standards (e.g., Arkes & Blumer, 1985; Tversky & Kahneman, 1981), people employ mental accounting for a reason. Mental accounts help consumers rationalize expenditures and enhance self-control (see Thaler, 1985, 1999) and can, in certain situations, also help consumers derive greater enjoyment from their spending (Loewenstein & O'Donoghue, 2006).

The concept of mental accounting, as well as many specific features of mental accounts, derives inspiration from real financial accounts. As Thaler (1999) writes, "Perhaps the easiest way to define [mental accounting] is to compare it with financial and managerial accounting as practiced by organizations" (p. 184). Much of the literature on mental accounting has assumed that mental accounts are determined, in part, by the real financial accounts that are available to consumers, such as the common division of bank holdings into checking and savings accounts (Shefrin & Thaler, 1981, 1992).

In this chapter, we suggest that inspiration can work the other way around. Financial institutions can seek inspiration from consumers' natural mental accounting strategies and then create financial accounts that encourage the establishment of specific mental accounts. We argue that investment and bank accounts should be subdivided in ways that could, despite being only paper changes, have profound effects on individual behavior and satisfaction. Such accounts can address a variety of specific problems that bedevil spenders and savers and can produce benefits such as improved investment decisions, increased savings, and even increased enjoyment of spending. Below we describe four common problems that challenge consumers' ability to save adequately or enjoy saving and spending. For each problem, we propose a division of real financial accounts to address it.

## PROBLEM 1: THE DESIRE TO MEDDLE
## SOLUTION: NEST EGG AND FUN ACCOUNTS

Investing can be fun, an observation that, however obvious, has been ignored in the academic literature on individual investor behavior. Testing one's theories about which stocks will take off is exhilarating and has the potential to be financially rewarding. It turns out, however, that increased stock trading is associated with decreased returns; on average, the more a person meddles or plays with their portfolio, beyond perhaps periodic rebalancing, the worse off they seem to be. A 2001 study (Barber & Odean, 2001), for example, found that women and men trade stocks at different rates and consequently experience different portfolio performance levels. Women holding common stock portfolios turned over their holdings at a rate of 53% annually, whereas men holding common stock portfolios turned their holdings at a rate of 77% annually—a significant difference. Portfolio performance was negatively related to the amount of trading, not only due to transaction costs but also because there was a tendency to buy stocks that performed worse than those that were sold. The consequence was worse overall portfolio performance for men, whose returns were 2.65% below average market returns, compared to women, whose returns were 1.72% below average market returns.

The simple solution seems obvious: Encourage consumers to buy reliable index funds that provide less temptation for interference. Yet, buying index funds is a bore. Between the pleasure of gambling, the irresistible lure of stock tips and hunches, and the conceit that one is smarter than the market, the urge to actively trade individual stocks can be overwhelming, particularly for some individuals. Protecting such individuals, without totally squashing their pleasure, calls for a financial account solution that gives investors an outlet for their urge to play the market, but does not put (much of) their savings at risk. We propose separate nest egg and fun accounts to meet these requirements.

The nest egg account would be designed to house the bulk of one's savings, and the funds would be managed primarily by investment professionals in "safe" mutual funds. This account would be kept largely out of the investor's sight, so it could grow unhindered. In contrast, the smaller fun account would be designed to include individual stocks that are actively managed by the investor, as well as limited liability derivatives (e.g., purchases but not sales of options). The investor can use this small account to test their hunches about stock performance and potentially even make some money. However, at the same time that consumers are enjoying playing the stock market with this fun account, they are not putting their life savings at risk. By protecting the majority of one's savings in the nest egg account and playing with a smaller piece in the fun account, the investor both gets to enjoy investing and protects his or her savings and future spending ability.

## PROBLEM 2: LACK OF PLEASURE OR REASSURANCE FROM SAVING
## SOLUTION: EARMARKED ACCOUNTS

Of the many reasons that saving money is difficult, perhaps the most fundamental is that immediate uses of money tend to be far more concrete, and hence compelling, than delayed uses of the same money (see Rick & Loewenstein, 2008). John Rae, who wrote the first book-length treatment of saving in 1834, focused on the first part of the problem—the concreteness of immediate consumption—when he famously wrote,

> The actual presence of the immediate object of desire in the mind by exciting the attention, seems to rouse all the faculties, as it were to fix their view on it, and leads them to a very lively conception of the enjoyments which it offers to their instant possession. (as cited in James, 1965, p. 120)

Böhm-Bawerk (1889/2006), author of the second significant treatise on the topic, focused on the second part of the problem—the intangibility of delayed consumption—when he wrote that "we limn a more or less incomplete picture of our future wants and especially of the remotely distant ones" (pp. 268–269). The concreteness of immediate expenditures, as contrasted with the relative intangibility of the delayed consequences of spending, can tip the balance toward spending now as opposed to saving for the future.

One way to prompt increased savings, then, is to make saving for the future more vivid, and one tactic for accomplishing this goal is to attach specific goals to selected buckets of savings. For example, a consumer could earmark a savings account specifically for his or her children's college savings. Once earmarked, it is then more satisfying to save $10,000, because it is easier to imagine how $10,000 will make a meaningful difference to a college savings fund than to a general savings fund. The college savings fund is tied to the specific and imaginable outcomes of a child's education.

Financial institutions can help consumers establish such earmarked accounts for savings. From the vantage point of the bank, this involves a purely paper change, dividing a pool of money into smaller components. From the vantage point of the saver, earmarked accounts can help increase the commensurability, and hence quality of trade-offs, between immediate and delayed expenditures. The multiple savings account system can be customized to fit individuals' savings and spending goals and can even be expanded to include accounts for esoteric savings goals, such as saving for wine collections or electronics.

Earmarked savings accounts also can provide greater peace of mind about one's future. For example, when a consumer worries about paying for future health care, he or she can find comfort in the savings account set aside specifically for health care expenses. Similarly, earmarked retirement accounts can provide peace of mind about general spending needs after retirement and, like the "spend it" accounts that we will discuss later, can also be more easily spent and enjoyed during retirement (see also Keller & Lusardi, Chapter 21 of this volume). In sum, the point of these multiple earmarked savings accounts is that moving saving from an abstract process to a concrete one makes saving more gratifying and, hence, more likely.

## PROBLEM 3: DIMINISHING MOTIVATION TO SAVE
## SOLUTION: "OLD MONEY" AND "NEW MONEY" ACCOUNTS

When people invest their savings, they often mass them into a single investment account and, especially if this account consists largely of mutual funds, are likely to pay attention to a single number: the total value of the account. This common practice turns out to be relatively unconducive to saving beyond a particular point, because contributing to this single pot of money becomes less satisfying with each contribution. As consumers get further away from the starting point or reference point in their savings account, usually $0 of savings, they experience diminishing marginal utility for each contribution (Kahneman & Tversky, 1979). Each additional dollar added feels less satisfying, because it has less of a proportional impact on the increasingly larger account. For example, adding a $10,000 contribution to a $50,000 savings account is more gratifying than adding the same contribution to a larger $1,000,000 savings account. An initial zeal for building a savings account can turn to indifference, as additional contributions feel like only a drop in the bucket.

Moreover, if savings are invested in risky assets, as the value of the portfolio grows, it becomes increasingly likely that fluctuations in the principal amount resulting from market changes will overwhelm the impact of incremental contributions. Depending on the vicissitudes of the stock market, with a large portfolio, even if one adds a substantial amount in any year, it is quite likely that the value of the portfolio will shrink in any given year. Needless to say, this is a demoralizing outcome given the sacrifice entailed by putting the money aside.

To combat this problem of diminishing motivation to save, we suggest the periodic establishment of "new money" accounts that separate new contributions from accumulated past contributions held in "old money" accounts. New money accounts could be established either based on timing (e.g., a new account created every 5 years and old accounts denoted by time intervals, such as "savings between 2005 and 2010") or based on amount accumulated (e.g., old money could be partitioned into buckets of $500,000).

Beyond combating the decline in motivation to save that might otherwise occur, the creation of old and new money accounts could also yield benefits when it comes to wise investment decisions. Similar to the nest egg and fun accounts that we proposed earlier, consumers could be encouraged to actively manage new money accounts, which are small enough to minimize damage, while old money accounts could be put into long-term, out-of-sight, out-of-mind, age-based funds that shift toward more conservative investments as the consumer ages.

## PROBLEM 4: THE PAIN OF PAYING
## SOLUTION: "SAVE IT" AND "SPEND IT" ACCOUNTS

Standard economic theory assumes that the cost of a particular purchase is the (typically future) consumption that must be forgone as a result of indulging oneself in the present. However, in reality, consumers rarely consider what they are giving up when they make a purchase (Frederick, Novemsky, Wang, Dhar, & Nowlis, 2009). Instead, they experience an immediate, psychological pain of paying (Knutson, Rick, Wimmer, Prelec, & Loewenstein, 2007; Prelec & Loewenstein, 1998). This pain of paying helps rationalize spending by providing an immediate, tangible cost to making a purchase that can be compared to the immediate benefit. The downside of the pain of paying, however, is that it decreases enjoyment that consumers obtain from their purchases. This damper on pleasure leads to the following paradoxical situation: Consumers spend too much, according to the dismally low rates of consumer savings, but at the same time, the pain of paying limits their enjoyment of the purchases that they make. Neurological studies have confirmed the existence of the pain of paying; studies in which shoppers' brains are scanned while they decide whether to purchase goods have found that showing the price of a good activates neural systems associated with pain processing, an effect which is accentuated when the price of the good is perceived to be excessively high (Knutson et al., 2007).

A recently developed spendthrift–tightwad scale measures individual differences in the tendency to experience the pain of paying (Rick, Cryder, & Loewenstein, 2008). Individuals on the spendthrift end of the scale typically experience minimal pain of paying and, therefore, tend to spend more than they would ideally like to. Individuals on the tightwad end typically experience intense pain of paying and, therefore, tend to spend less than they would ideally like to. Individuals in the middle of the scale, termed *unconflicted consumers*, experience a moderate amount of the pain of paying and experience minimal divergence between their desired and actual spending levels. One's status as a spendthrift or tightwad predicts a wide range of important spending outcomes; for example, spendthrifts who use credit cards are three times more likely to carry debt than are tightwads who use credit cards, even after controlling for income (Rick et al., 2008).

Average savings rates in the United States and the general attention to undersaving suggest that tightwads represent a sparse segment of the American population; however, tightwaddism is actually quite prevalent. In some large samples (e.g., a sample of more than 10,000 *New York Times* readers), tightwads outnumber spendthrifts three to two (Rick et al., 2008). Although underspending does not make headlines, it seems to affect a substantial portion of the population (see also Kivetz & Simonson, 2002).

Tightwads are not the only ones that experience this pain of paying. All consumers experience this pain to some degree, and some situations exist that make spending painful for nearly everyone, such as paying credit card bills for past purchases after the pleasure of those purchases has long past

(Prelec & Loewenstein, 1998). Moreover, in the current tense economic situation, consumers may experience the pain of paying more intensely than usual. Many consumers are walking a financial tightrope, making almost every purchase stressful and psychologically painful.

To help alleviate this pain, we propose that consumers should go beyond common implicit saving and spending budgets and actually create real accounts designed to formally partition saving and spending; we call these accounts "save it" and "spend it" accounts. Checking and savings accounts already often provide structures ready to partition money for saving and spending; however, consumers tend to use fuzzy rules to allocate the money into these checking (spending) and saving buckets. For example, people often use checking accounts to receive and house their monthly paycheck, and savings accounts to hold any leftovers at the end of the month. This unsystematic division inevitably results in little to no money saved by the end of the month and an uncomfortable sliding budget for spending. With the slightly reframed save it and spend it accounts, a preset fraction of each paycheck would automatically go into each account, with the predetermined amount dictated by the individual's saving goals. A main benefit of establishing these accounts is that clearly partitioning money into saving and spending accounts provides a bright-line spending limit for consumers. The bright line can not only help constrain spending, but also simply knowing that the bright line is there can reduce the anxiety that one might be overspending.

The second benefit is that these accounts allow more relaxed spending from the "spend it" account. By having some money specifically designated to be spent, consumers can more easily use that money without fear of going into debt or restricting future spending ability. In the same way that some consumers help themselves save by establishing savings accounts that are designed to be psychologically costly to draw from, they can establish a spend it account that is intended to be psychologically easy to spend from, thus reducing the psychological costs of paying.

These partitioned accounts for spending allow consumers to essentially prepay for consumption. A model of prospective accounting proposed by Prelec and Loewenstein (1998) suggests that future payments can hang over our heads to cloud the pleasure of current consumption, whereas past payments are written off, so consumption that has already been paid for can be enjoyed almost as if it were free. People often prefer to pay ahead of time for experiences such as vacations, so they can enjoy the experience unburdened from thoughts of payment (Prelec & Loewenstein, 1998). Similarly, prepaid spending accounts can reduce the anxiety of thinking about where the money to fund a particular expenditure is going to come from. Mental accounts for spending also help relieve the pain of paying by reducing thoughts about opportunity costs. Once the money is in the spending account, the choice about how to use it is a pleasurable one of deciding between different forms of short-term gratification, rather than a potentially more painful one about consuming now versus later, such as choosing between a nice restaurant dinner tonight and a fraction of one's child's college education in the future. These partitioned spend it accounts may be especially attractive not only to individuals who are tightwads but also to other groups who experience high levels of the pain of paying, such as people who are worried about overspending due to tough economic times and retired individuals who need to finance their spending out of capital rather than a steady income.

## HOW FINANCIAL INSTITUTIONS CAN HELP

We have proposed that the creation of multiple formal financial accounts can help consumers with different types of spending and saving challenges. Financial institutions, for their part, can help customers establish these financial accounts by asking their customers to describe their financial issues, advising them on what types of accounts to create, and making it easy for consumers to open and manage multiple accounts. The primary benefits of the multiple accounting system accrue to consumers; however, benefits exist for financial institutions as well. First, encouraging accounts that help consumers enjoy saving and spending can only make customers more satisfied with their banking institutions. In addition, most of the multiple accounting systems that we propose encourage saving, thus increasing the account balances that consumers house at their financial institutions.

Some currently available budgeting services take an intermediate step of helping consumers formalize their mental budgeting strategies. For example, www.mint.com provides free online budgeting tools to consumers that allow them to establish budgeting and saving goals, allocate spending to different categories, and then receive feedback every week about how they are performing toward their goals, all based on information that Mint pulls directly from consumers' credit card purchases and checking account withdrawal data. However, establishing real, institutionalized, financial accounts has several benefits beyond using mental accounts or even budgeting tools like Quicken and Mint. Establishing real accounts relieves some of the mental tracking and budget management burden from the consumer, making maintenance of budgets easier and the overall budgeting effort more likely to succeed. In addition, real financial accounts encourage consumers to stick to their original plans. It is more difficult to spend or save outside of one's budget when the accounts are real rather than mental (i.e., in one's head), due to not only the time costs of transferring funds but also the impossibility of engaging in the kind of slippery math that is possible with purely mental accounts. In fact, formalizing implicit mental accounts has been shown to help consumers meet their financial goals. When a set amount of money is formally partitioned for savings, even if that partition is as simple as a separate envelope of cash, people save more than if money is not set aside (Cheema & Soman, 2009).

Another reason that formally establishing a multiple accounts system ahead of time can be successful is that once people set up financial accounting systems, they are unlikely to change them. Samuelson and Zeckhauser (1988) investigated the decision patterns of 1987 TIAA-CREF investors and found that the median number of changes in asset allocation over participants' lifetimes was zero. A more recent study found a similar result; in a 10-year study of TIAA-CREF investors, almost half made zero changes to their allocation structure over the 10 years (Ameriks & Zeldes, 2000). If people set up the portfolios of multiple financial accounts that are proposed in this chapter, they are likely to stick with them if for no other reason than a resilient tendency to stick with the status quo.

An important feature of all of these proposed accounts is that they rely on immediate withdrawal or debit systems. People spend more carefully when transactions are immediate (i.e., in debit systems) as opposed to delayed (i.e., in credit systems; Soman, 2001). In addition, debit systems provide access to resources that an individual actually has available, in contrast to credit systems, especially credit cards, which provide easy access to resources that the individual does not have and that will put them in debt if they are used (see Soman, Cheema, & Chan, Chapter 20 of this volume).

Another potential design feature of these financial accounts is of note. The multiple accounts system can be designed so that people place deposits into their spending accounts at a regular interval. When the money is depleted for an account, it is gone, and no more can be spent until the next period without trading off resources from another account, a deliberate process that promotes judicious use of resources. When money is left unspent for a week, the consumer can be reminded of the excess in the next week when it is time for the next deposit, promoting use and enjoyment of resources that are available. With this system, consumers have extra checks in place that help them stick to their original goals of saving and spending certain amounts.

## HOW RESEARCHERS CAN HELP

Although past research and theories from social science have suggested that partitioned financial accounts will help consumers reach their spending and savings goals, the only real way to know the effectiveness of each type of account is to experimentally test each one and measure consumers' savings and satisfaction outcomes. Ideally, these tests could be done in the field in partnerships with financial institutions. Although financial institutions may desire to know whether partitioned accounts work, they may not have the expertise to run their own experiments to find out how useful, and profitable, each type of account can be. This is where experienced researchers come in. Partnerships between financial institutions and academic researchers allow gains for both groups. The financial institutions gain the expertise from the researcher to run the experiments, while the researchers gain access to field data from the financial institutions that they otherwise would not have access to.

As an example, a simple test of the solution to problem 4 above could measure the benefit of automatically allocating predetermined percentages of consumers' paychecks to checking and savings accounts (i.e., spend it and save it accounts) in contrast to the standard procedure of sending one's entire paycheck to the checking account and then depositing leftovers into the savings account later. To conduct the test, a group of consumers at a financial institution who do not already partition their paychecks ahead of time could be selected for the experiment. Then, half could be randomly selected to be encouraged to divide their paycheck deposit ahead of time between spend it and save it accounts. Even though not all of the consumers in the experimental group would choose to divide their paycheck ahead of time, some would, and the group as a whole could be compared to the control group (i.e., an intention to treat analysis). Using surveys to measure satisfaction, researchers could then determine if there is benefit to encouraging the partitioning of savings and spending ahead of time in terms of accumulated savings and spending enjoyment. Then, they also could look specifically at those individuals who adopted the new accounts to measure the magnitude of the gain for individuals who chose to adopt the new allocation procedure.

Similar tests could be done with all the different types of accounts that we propose, such as encouraging the old and new money accounts or earmarked accounts. For all of these tests, a big question is whether consumers will in fact be interested in adopting the accounts. Although many of them seem likely to be beneficial once adopted, the accounts may not be automatically appealing to the consumer. This concern seems especially applicable to the nest egg and fun accounts, which require a consumer to recognize that his or her own stock picks will likely perform worse than standard mutual funds. Thus, with all of these tests, it is important not only to measure the difference in outcomes for groups given and not given access to the new accounts but also to track real adoption rates and measure outcomes for those who actually did and did not adopt the new account strategies and test different approaches to marketing. For example, with the nest egg and fun accounts, if few people adopted the accounts, but those who did experienced success, that success information can be used to develop marketing messages that encourage more consumers to adopt such accounts.

In summary, past research has suggested that partitioned financial accounts yield many benefits to consumers in terms of increased savings and satisfaction. However, experimental tests in the field are necessary to determine both the adoption rate of these accounts and their success once adopted. Partnerships between academic researchers and financial institutions can provide financial institutions with the research expertise to test the impact of different configurations of accounts and give academic researchers the opportunity to test their ideas in the ultimate proving ground of the real world.

## CONCLUSIONS

Consumers rely on mental accounting strategies to help them code, categorize, and efficiently manage financial decisions (Thaler, 1980, 1985). Although these strategies can yield behavior that deviates from rational standards (e.g., Arkes & Blumer, 1985; Tversky & Kahneman, 1981), they can help consumers by allowing them to make sense of their financial situation and exert self-control. In this chapter, we propose that financial institutions can enhance the positive effects of consumers' mental accounting strategies by offering real financial accounts that match, and in some cases guide, consumers' mental accounts. Restructured financial accounts could provide diverse benefits to consumers, including increased enjoyment from saving, increased savings, and increased enjoyment of spending. Because of the many benefits that multiple financial accounts can provide to consumers, and because of the almost nonexistent risks and costs of using multiple accounts, we consider multiple financial accounts for consumers to be a case of hedonic arbitrage (Benartzi, Loewenstein, & Previtero, 2008). That is, multiple accounts can allow consumers to enhance their hedonic experience without necessarily increasing their resources or incurring meaningful costs or risks.

Thaler and Shefrin (Shefrin & Thaler, 1992; Thaler & Shefrin, 1981) have discussed how consumers' mental accounts are often modeled after real financial accounts, for example in the way that consumers implicitly treat money in savings and checking accounts differently. In this chapter, we propose going much further in exploiting and taking control of the effects that real accounts can have on consumer thinking, feeling, and behavior. New types of formal accounts that use ideas from psychology and behavioral economics to help consumers achieve their goals have the potential to benefit both consumers and their financial institutions.

## ACKNOWLEDGMENTS

We thank Shane Frederick for helpful comments, and Scott Rick for helpful comments and for suggesting this chapter's title.

## REFERENCES

Ainslie, G. (1975). Specious reward: A behavioral theory of impulsiveness and impulse control. *Psychological Bulletin, 82*(4), 463–496.

Ameriks, J., & Zeldes, S. (2000). *How do household portfolio shares vary with age?* Unpublished manuscript, Columbia University, New York.

Arkes, H., & Blumer, C. (1985). The psychology of sunk cost. *Organizational Behavior and Human Decision Processes, 35*(1), 124–140.

Barber, B., & Odean, T. (2001). Boys will be boys: Gender, overconfidence, and common stock investment. *Quarterly Journal of Economics, 116*(1), 261–292.

Benartzi, S., Loewenstein, G., & Previtero, A. (2008, March). *Hedonic arbitrage.* Paper presented at the annual meeting of the Behavioral Finance Forum, Miami, FL. Available: http://www.rand.org/labor/centers/befi/resources/pdf/conference/befi_2008_topic6.pdf/

Böhm-Bawerk, E. v. (2006). *The positive theory of capital* (W. Smart, Trans.). New York: Cosimo. (Original work published 1889)

Bureau of Economic Analysis. (2007). *Gross domestic product: Fourth quarter 2006 (advance).* Washington, DC: U.S. Department of Commerce. Retrieved September 24, 2009, from http://www.bea.gov/newsreleases/national/gdp/2007/pdf/gdp406a.pdf

Bureau of Economic Analysis. (2009). *Personal saving rate* [Table]. Washington, DC: U.S. Department of Commerce. Retrieved September 22, 2009, from http://www.bea.gov/briefrm/saving.htm

Cheema, A., & Soman, D. (2008). The effect of partitions on controlling consumption. *Journal of Marketing Research, 45*(6), 665–675.

Cheema, A., & Soman, D. (2009). *Earmarking and partitioning: Increasing saving by low-income households*. Unpublished manuscript, University of Virginia, Charlottesville.

Choi, J. J., Laibson, D., Madrian, B. C., & Metrick, A. (2004). For better or for worse: Default effects and 401(k) savings behavior. In D. A. Wise (Ed.), *Perspectives on the economics of aging* (pp. 81–125). Chicago: University of Chicago Press.

Farkus, S., & Johnson, J. (1997). *Miles to go: A status report on Americans' plans for retirement*. New York: Public Agenda.

Feinberg, R. A. (1986). Credit cards as spending facilitating stimuli: A conditioning interpretation. *Journal of Consumer Research, 13*(3), 348–356.

Fetherstonhaugh, D., Slovic, P., Johnson, S. M., & Friedrich, J. (1997). Insensitivity to the value of human life: A study of psychophysical numbing. *Journal of Risk and Uncertainty, 14*(3), 283–300.

Frederick, S., Loewenstein, G., & O'Donoghue, T. (2002). Time discounting and time preference: A critical review. *Journal of Economic Literature, 40*(2), 351–401.

Frederick, S., Novemsky, N., Wang, J., Dhar, R., & Nowlis, S. (2009). Opportunity cost neglect. *Journal of Consumer Research, 36*(4), 553–561.

Gourville, J., & Soman D. (1998). Payment depreciation: The behavioral effects of temporally separating payments from consumption. *Journal of Consumer Research, 25*(2), 160–174.

Heath, C., & Soll, J. (1996). Mental budgeting and consumer decisions. *Journal of Consumer Research, 23*(1), 40–52.

Henderson, P. W., & Peterson, R. A. (1992). Mental accounting and categorization. *Organizational Behavior and Human Decision Processes, 51*(1), 92–117.

James, R. W. (Ed.). (1965). *John Rae, political economist: An account of his life and a compilation of his main writings. Vol. 2: Statement of some new principles on the subject of political economy*. Toronto, ON, Canada: University of Toronto Press.

Kahneman, D., Knetsch, J. L., & Thaler, R. H. (1990). Experimental tests of the endowment effect and the Coase theorem. *Journal of Political Economy, 98*(6), 1325–1348.

Kahneman, D., & Tversky, A. (1979). Prospect theory: An analysis of decision under risk. *Econometrica, 47*(2), 263–292.

Kivetz, R., & Simonson, I. (2002). Self-control for the righteous: Toward a theory of precommitment to indulgence. *Journal of Consumer Research, 29*(2), 199–217.

Knetsch, J. L., & Sinden, J. A. (1984). Willingness to pay and compensation demanded: Experimental evidence of an unexpected disparity in measures of value. *Quarterly Journal of Economics, 99*(3), 507–521.

Knutson, B., Rick, S., Wimmer, G. E., Prelec, D., & Loewenstein, G. (2007). Neural predictors of purchases. *Neuron, 53*(1), 147–156.

Laibson, D. (1997). Golden eggs and hyperbolic discounting. *Quarterly Journal of Economics, 112*(2), 443–477.

Loewenstein, G., & Lerner, J. (2003). The role of affect in decision making. In R. J. Davidson, H. H. Goldsmith, & K. R. Scherer (Eds.), *Handbook of affective science* (pp. 619–642). New York: Oxford University Press.

Loewenstein, G., & O'Donoghue, T. (2006). "We can do this the easy way or the hard way": Negative emotions, self-regulation and the law. *University of Chicago Law Review, 73*(1), 183–206.

O'Curry, S. (1997). *Income source effects*. Unpublished manuscript, DePaul University, Chicago.

Odean, T. (1998). Are investors reluctant to realize their losses? *Journal of Finance, 53*(6), 1775–1798.

O'Donoghue, T., & Rabin, M. (2002). The economics of immediate gratification. *Journal of Behavioral Decision Making, 13*(2), 233–250.

The Pew Research Center for the Public & the Press. (2008). *Economic discontent deepens as inflation concerns rise: Growing rich–poor divide in affording necessities*. Washington, DC: Pew Research Center. Retrieved September 22, 2009, from people-press.org/report/395/economic-discontent-deepens-as-inflation-concerns-rise

Prelec, D., & Loewenstein, G. (1998). The red and the black: Mental accounting of savings and debt. *Marketing Science, 17*(1), 4–28.

Prelec, D., & Simester, D. (2001). Always leave home without it: A further investigation of the credit-card effect on willingness to pay. *Marketing Letters, 12*(1), 5–12.

Rick, S. (2007). *The influence of anticipatory affect on consumer choice*. Unpublished doctoral dissertation, Carnegie Mellon University, Pittsburgh, PA.

Rick, S., Cryder, C. E., & Loewenstein, G. (2008). Tightwads and spendthrifts. *Journal of Consumer Research, 34*(6), 767–782.

Rick, S., & Loewenstein, G. (2008). Intangibility in intertemporal choice. *Philosophical Transactions B, 363*(1511), 3813–3824.

Samuelson, W., & Zeckhauser, R. (1988). Status quo bias in decision making. *Journal of Risk and Uncertainty, 1*(1), 7–59.

Shefrin, H. M., & Thaler, R. H. (1992). Mental accounting, saving, and self-control. In G. Loewenstein & J. Elster (Eds.), *Choice over time* (pp. 287–330). New York: Russell Sage Foundation.

Soman, D. (2001). Effects of payment mechanism on spending behavior: The role of rehearsal and immediacy of payments. *Journal of Consumer Research, 27*(4), 460–474.

Soman, D., & Cheema, A. (2002). The effect of credit on spending decisions: The role of credit limit and credibility. *Marketing Science, 21*(1), 32–53.

Thaler, R. H. (1980). Toward a positive theory of consumer choice. *Journal of Economic Behavior and Organization, 1*(1), 39–60.

Thaler, R. H. (1985). Mental accounting and consumer choice. *Marketing Science, 4*(3), 199–214.

Thaler, R. H. (1999). Mental accounting matters. *Journal of Behavioral Decision Making, 12*(3), 183–206.

Thaler, R. H., & Bernartzi, S. (2004). Save more tomorrow: Using behavioral economics to increase employee savings. *Journal of Political Economy, 112*(1), 164–187.

Thaler, R. H., & Shefrin, H. M. (1981). An economic theory of self-control. *Journal of Political Economy, 89*(2), 392–406.

Tversky, A., & Kahneman, D. (1974). Judgment under uncertainty: Heuristics and biases. *Science, 185*(4157), 1124–1131.

Tversky, A., & Kahneman, D. (1981). The framing of decisions and the psychology of choice. *Science, 211*(4481), 453–458.

# 20

# *Understanding Consumer Psychology to Avoid Abuse of Credit Cards*

## Dilip Soman, Amar Cheema, and Eugene Y. Chan

On February 8, 1949, Frank McNamara dined with his wife and colleagues at Major's Cabin Grill in New York City. When it was time to pay the bill, he realized that he had forgotten his wallet. His wife was able to rescue him from his predicament, but on that fateful winter's day, McNamara had come up with an inspiration to avoid further embarrassment. One year later, McNamara went back to Major's Cabin Grill and presented Diners Club, the world's first credit card (Diners Club, 2008). The idea for Diners Club was simple: Cardholders would be able to present the card to merchants as an alternative to cash, merchants would charge the card company for the expenses, and cardholders would then pay back the card company shortly afterward. This paved the way for further credit cards to come, namely, American Express in 1958, MasterCard in 1966, and Visa in 1970. As of 2006, there were more than 173 million credit cardholders in the United States alone, with more than half of the U.S. population owning at least two credit cards (*The Nilson Report*, 2009). Worldwide, credit card usage was at $1.24 trillion in 2000 and grew to $1.95 trillion in 2006.

Little did McNamara know that his solution to avoid a personal pickle would lead to the most popular method of payment in many parts of the world. By the turn of the 21st century, consumer credit was widely accessible. Credit cards come easily in the mail, allowing consumers to maintain a lifestyle that they cannot afford otherwise. In 2000, credit card debt in the United States alone was $680 billion. In 2008, the number grew to $972.73 billion, with the average American household owing approximately $8,329 in credit card debt (*The Nilson Report*, 2009). This is particularly remarkable given that the average American household's mean gross income was $50,233 in 2007 (DeNavas-Walt, Proctor, & Smith, 2008).

The ease of access to consumer credit has spawned a culture of materialism (Kilbourne & Mittelstaedt, Chapter 14 of this volume), which in turn further fueled the demand for consumer credit. Indeed, the growth in credit card debt is so worrying that economists have warned that, following the recent mortgage crisis that began in the United States, "the next meltdown will be in credit cards" (Silver-Greenberg, 2008, para. 2).

Standard economic models of the consumer assume rationality, the idea that consumers make decisions by weighing costs, benefits, and preferences. However, the behavioral sciences have demonstrated that situational and cognitive limitations exist in the utility decision-making process. For instance, preferences are malleable, the framing of decisions can manipulate choices, and the limited capacity of cognitive resources often leads to problem-solving errors (Kahneman & Tversky, 1979). The behavioral perspective would suggest that the management of credit card debt by households is most effective if viewed through the lens of consumer psychology, perhaps with the aid of behavioral interventions dictated by policy (cf. Thaler & Sunstein, 2008).

Recognizing that individuals might fall prey to biases in their adoption and usage of credit cards, the U.S. Congress passed the Credit Card Accountability, Responsibility, and Disclosure (CARD) Act of 2009 (see also Credit Card Reform Act of 2009). The aim of the act was "to protect consumers—and especially young consumers—from skyrocketing credit card debt, unfair credit card practices, and deceptive credit card offers" (Credit Card Reform Act of 2009, p. 1). In Canada, the government also released new proposed regulations aimed at limiting business practices that are not beneficial to consumers and providing clear and timely information to Canadians about credit cards (Department of Finance Canada, 2009). Later in this chapter, we review the provisions of these acts and offer our thoughts on what past behavioral research would suggest about the efficacy of the provisions.

In the sections to follow, we build on a behavioral model of the consumer and describe its implications in understanding credit card debt. We first give an overview of the economics of consumer credit, with a particular focus on the behavioral life cycle hypothesis (Shefrin & Thaler, 1988). We then provide an overview of prior and current research on credit card use among consumers and the implications for understanding credit card debt. We also report results from two empirical studies, discuss the CARD Act, and conclude with a set of prescriptive recommendations to avoid abuse of credit cards.

## THE ECONOMICS OF CONSUMER CREDIT

Over the course of an individual's lifetime, there is a mismatch between the income he or she earns and the lifestyle he or she consumes in any given time period. Incomes typically vary over time, but individuals like to maintain or improve their lifestyles from year to year. The life cycle hypothesis postulates that, in the face of a mismatch between their income stream and their desired consumption stream, consumers should allocate their lifetime income over time to smooth their consumption (Ando & Modigliani, 1963; Modigliani & Brumberg, 1954; cf. Friedman, 1957). More formally, the hypothesis specifies that the cumulative discounted consumption stream over an individual's lifetime is exactly equal to the sum of the cumulative discounted income stream and all assets. Empirical testing of the theory has found that the propensity to spend (a) increases as a function of initial assets, (b) decreases as a function of expected lifetime, and (c) increases as a function of human wealth (Courant, Gramlich, & Laitner, 1986; Johnson, Kotlikoff, & Samuelson, 1987; Kotlikoff, Samuelson, & Johnson, 1988).

Consumers can use their past income in the future, because they can store it in the form of savings and investments. However, it is practically impossible for consumers to use future income in the present, because the future income does not yet physically exist. In order to use future income, a consumer needs to have access to an account that can act as an intertemporal intermediary between the future lender and the present borrower. Consumer credit plays exactly this role. Hence, it can be said that credit cards are an agent that enables spending in accordance with the life cycle hypothesis.

That said, the use of credit in a rational manner calls for a cognitively complex processing of information. In particular, consumers need to correctly value their present and future resources and interest rates, perform complicated net present value calculations to compute their lifetime income, and apportion its appropriately interest-adjusted value throughout their lifetime. In an experiment in which subjects were asked to make preferred consumption choices under hypothetical life cycle economic conditions, Johnson et al. (1987) found that individuals repeatedly made substantial computational errors (cf. Kotlikoff et al., 1988). Their experiment led them to conclude that their results "raise serious questions about the life-cycle model's ability to describe consumption choice" (Johnson et al., 1987, p. 42). In a summary paper, Courant et al. (1986) similarly concluded that despite its elegance and rationality, "the life-cycle model has not tested very well" (p. 279). An additional complication in the real world is the fact that the future is never certain for most individuals. Although it appears that consumers may have the right intuitions about intertemporal allocations (Shefrin & Thaler, 1988), the life cycle hypothesis is not an accurate descriptor of their behavior. Accordingly, Shefrin and Thaler proposed a psychologically enriched version of the life cycle model. The behavioral life cycle hypothesis highlights the role of consumers' self-control in their economic lives.

## CONSUMER SELF-CONTROL

Fisher (1930) first described the notion of self-control in *The Theory of Interest*. Because the future is uncertain, and consumers do not have the cognitive apparatus to perform the complex optimization problem, it is important for consumers to ensure that they do not excessively borrow from the future. Prior research has shown that individuals pervasively discount the future, as a result of which immediate consumption always seems to be an attractive alternative to future consumption (Ainslie & Haslam, 1992; Benzion, Rapoport, & Yagil, 1989; Faber & Vohs, Chapter 22 of this volume; Kirby, 1997; Shiv & Fedorikhin, 1999).

How do consumers exert self-control? Thaler and Shefrin (1981) considered the consumer as both a "farsighted planner and a myopic doer" (p. 392). The planner looks at the long run, but the doer wants immediate gratification. The model suggests that when consumers are asked about their preferences, their planner comes forth, and they respond with a "should" option. However, when they face a tempting opportunity, the doer comes forth and pushes them toward the "want" option. The literature on self-control has often focused on curbing impulses with restraints (Hoch & Loewenstein, 1991). For instance, a dieter's desire for a rich piece of chocolate cake requires an inhibiting goal to maintain his or her diet; similarly, a consumer desiring to splurge on a big-screen plasma television screen must find a way to limit his or her other spending. The increase in access to debt only highlights the importance of understanding and controlling consumer overspending. Impulsive purchases, after all, are failures in self-control. Crucially, impulses to buy are strong when self-control capacity is low (Vohs & Faber, 2005). Self-control often fails because of conflicting goals or difficulties in self-monitoring or diminishing "muscle" power (Baumeister, 2002; Faber & Vohs, Chapter 22 of this volume; Muraven & Baumeister, 2000). In view of this, consumers have to self-impose rules in order to curb their spending (Baumeister, Heatherton, & Tice, 1994; Hoch & Loewenstein, 1991).

A second theoretical account that researchers often use to explain how individuals make should/want choices is the theory of hyperbolic discounting (Ainslie & Haslam, 1992). At the heart of the theory is the idea that consumers pervasively tend to devalue the future and thus prefer a smaller sooner (SS) reward over a larger later (LL) reward. Economists model this devaluation by using discount rates designed to capture the rate of the trade-off between the present and the future (Benzion et al., 1989). However, the mere discounting of the future is not enough.

Consider the following simple choice task:

- Option A: Receive $10 today, versus Option B: Receive $12 at the end of one week.
- Option A*: Receive $10 at the end of 52 weeks, versus Option B*: Receive $12 at the end of 53 weeks.

At first blush, it might appear that the choice between A and B is functionally identical to the choice between A\* and B\*, hence the pattern on choices should be similar. However, numerous researchers have found, using stimuli like the ones shown above, that when consumers view the options from a distance, they choose the LL option. However, when SS draws closer, the pattern of choices reverses. This can be best explained by the theory of hyperbolic discounting, which says that consumers discount the value of future outcomes steeply and close in time to the outcome but more gently further away. As a result, when consumers see a choice between SS and LL options in the future, they discount both options greatly, hence the present value of LL appears greater than the present value of SS. This is why people who view the two options from the present choose the LL option over the SS option.

However, things get interesting when consumers get very close in time to SS. Because of the steep discounting of LL, but not of SS, the perceived value of SS is now larger than the perceived value of LL. The region close to SS is called the *lapse zone*, which represents points in time when the individual could make a mistake and prefer the SS reward over the LL reward (Ainslie & Haslam, 1992), which happens because the SS option is so close in time that people can almost imagine having the reward. To wait longer for the LL reward induces a sense of deprivation, hence people succumb to temptation. Note that the SS and LL rewards are a handy metaphor for should versus want options. In the domain of spending, for instance, SS might stand for impulsive spending and LL for future savings.

There is much consensus that exerting self-control is an effortful process, and several researchers have advised that consumers need to construct and adhere to a set of well-defined rules or precommitment devices (Elster, 1979; Schelling, 1984). For instance, a consumer could use a matching rule in which the consumption in any period *t* is constrained by the income available in *t*. Similarly, consumers may adopt a rule whereby they allow themselves to have credit balances up to a specified limit (Weber, 1996). For instance, financial advice websites typically tell consumers that it is important to budget wisely but also remind them that credit cards allow the flexibility of paying credit card bills over time. Some further recommend that outstanding credit balances should not exceed anywhere from one fifth to one third of total annual income.

What needs to be done to snap a consumer out of a lapse zone and get him or her to think prudently about the consumption decision at hand? Soman, Cheema, and Xu (2010) proposed that individuals could be prompted into controlling their consumption behavior by providing what they call decision points. Consumers start off in a deliberative mode, in which they actually think explicitly about the pros and cons of consumption. However, after they start consuming, they move quickly to an automatic mode, and continued consumption becomes mindless and habitual. The provision of a decision point allows the individual to snap back to a deliberative mode; for a consumer who is trying to control consumption, this typically entails a call to vigilance, which often results in the termination of the act of consumption. A decision point occurs as a result of any intervention that is designed to get an individual to pause and think about the consumption that he or she is currently engaged in, and can be created in several ways, including inserting transaction costs, working on the premise that requiring the individual to take a positive action makes him or her deliberate on the consumption decision; providing reminders or information, working on the premise that drawing attention to a neglected activity can provide the impetus to get it done; and creating interruptions to the consumption activity, working on the premise that the interruption allows the individual to pause and think. Research by Keller and Lusardi (Chapter 21 of this volume), which has shown that making savings too easy actually reduces the likelihood of savings, is also consistent with the decision points idea.

In a purchasing context, traditional payment mechanisms like cash and checks create natural decision points. The process of visiting an automatic teller machine to withdraw cash or writing out a check for a purchase allows a consumer enough time to critically think about whether the purchase is justified. However, payment mechanisms like credit cards remove this natural decision point; a consumer can quickly whip out a card and complete the transaction. Online retailers make this process even faster and simpler, with many now encouraging consumers to enter their payment information as part of the site-registration process, which enables the retailers to offer consumers a one-click purchase option that makes future purchasing events nearly instantaneous. That is, a click on this button automatically triggers a purchase. The lack of a decision point was evident in a comment that one of our respondents made to us about one-click purchasing: "Before I knew it, I had purchased it."

A different method of exerting self-control is to use mental accounts (Heath & Soll, 1996; Shefrin & Thaler, 1988; Thaler, 1985, 1999). Budgets assist consumers in not overspending on tempting products that they may otherwise want to buy, but that they should not. The reason that such precommitment devices are effective in exerting self-control is that people do not arbitrarily choose tempting alternatives just because they are attractive (Hsee, 1995). Specifically, precommitment changes the incentives under which people will make their future choice, such that giving in to temptation will be costly (Wertenbroch, 1998). However, recent research has also shown that if there is any degree of ambiguity in the structure of the mental accounts, consumers can exploit this to justify choosing a tempting course of action (Soman & Cheema, 2001; Soman & Gourville, 2001). Soman and Cheema showed that subjects were willing to use an unbudgeted windfall gain to purchase a tempting product by using the windfall money to augment the spending budget.

In the present research, we propose that the availability of credit lines plays a role similar to the windfall gain in Soman and Cheema's experiments. For further discussion on new ways to conceive of mental accounts to benefit consumer spending, see Loewenstein, Cryder, Benartzi, and Previtero (Chapter 19 of this volume). The behavioral research has contributed to a rich understanding of consumer decisions to (a) adopt credit cards, (b) use them, and also (c) study the long-term consequences of their usage. In the next sections, we present a discussion on each of these.

## THE ADOPTION AND USE OF CREDIT CARDS

One implication of the research on intertemporal choice and myopia (Ainslie & Haslam, 1992) discussed earlier has to do with the effect of immediate incentives on consumer choice. Consider an individual looking to adopt a credit card from two options, one of which has a low interest or annual percentage rate (APR), whereas the other has a marginally higher interest but offers a giveaway incentive at sign-up. Past research would suggest that a consumer might be unduly influenced by the incentive and choose the second card even if the net present value of the bundle is relatively lower. This happens because (a) the value of the benefit is certain, whereas the additional interest costs will only occur with some probability (for a discussion on related risk aversion, see Kahneman & Tversky, 1979); (b) consumers optimistically expect that their own likelihood of winding up in debt is low (for a discussion on optimism bias, see Kahneman & Lovallo, 1993); and (c) the value of the benefit is undiscounted, whereas the additional cost of the interest charges is fuzzy and discounted (Ainslie & Haslam, 1992).

The effect of the APR on consumer decisions and welfare is a particularly interesting area for research. Ausubel (1991) showed empirically that credit card interest rates did not respond to the decline in market interest rates between 1983 and 1988 in the United States (i.e., they were sticky), and at the same time, banks earned three to five times more than the ordinary rate of return of the banking industry from their credit card branches. In his research, Ausubel has classified consumers of credit cards into three main groups, and there is almost a consensus on this classification in the literature. The first group comprises convenience users who pay their bill in full each month and hence do not borrow on their credit cards. The second group comprises revolvers, also known as *high-risk* or *illiquid consumers*, who intend to use the credit option of their cards and borrow on their credit cards heavily. The last group represents consumers who are behaviorally most interesting, because they do not intend to borrow on their credit cards but frequently find themselves doing so. The fact that consumers have a prediction bias that reflects as overconfidence in their own future actions has been documented extensively in the literature in psychology (Buehler & Griffin, 2003; Buehler, Griffin, & MacDonald, 1997) and marketing (Gourville & Soman, in press). This last group of consumers is the most profitable consumer segment for banks, because they borrow at high interest rates and generally pay their debts—and the greater the size of this group, the stickier the interest rates become.

In addition to simply being optimistic about not carrying credit card balances in the future, prior research has also shown that consumers are unable to comprehend the impact of small changes in compound interest rates and APR rates on the net present value of the borrowing cost (Eisenstein & Hoch, 2007; McKenzie & Liersch, 2009). As a result, consumers tend to not weight the APR as heavily as they should in their credit card choice and usage decisions.

A final set of biases that speak to credit card pricing arise from the practice of partitioned pricing (Morwitz, Greenleaf, & Johnson, 1998). Morwitz and colleagues showed that marketers are better off by presenting prices in a divided manner (e.g., $50 + $5 shipping + $7 taxes) rather than as an integrated number (e.g., $62). This happens for two types of reasons, most notably because either consumers often forget or overlook the smaller amounts, or even when they do remember all the information, the act of dividing the price softens the psychological impact. Credit card marketers have tended to adopt a divide and prosper policy, much like the title of Morwitz et al.'s 1998 paper. As the popular press has noted, credit card issuers in the United States often do not "clearly disclose penalties, variable interest rates and other fees, leaving consumers confused about the true cost of using plastic to pay for everyday transactions" (Day, 2006, para. 1). Reporting the results of a U.S.'s Government Accountability Office study, Day further concluded that pricing in the industry was complex and inadequately communicated to consumers. As prior research has suggested (cf. Schwartz, 2004), increasing complexity reduces the likelihood of the information being used in decision making, therefore resulting in suboptimal choices. Once the decision to use a credit card has been made, a separate set of behavioral phenomena come into play that affect consumption behavior.

## THE EFFECT OF CREDIT CARDS AND MENTAL ACCOUNTING ON SPENDING

A large body of literature in the area of mental accounting has documented the processes that consumers use to track—and often control—their expenses over time. Contrary to the belief that money is fungible (i.e., money from different sources is used interchangeably), funds in the various mental accounts are nonfungible (Thaler, 1990). The manner in which consumers allocate funds to different mental accounts has implications for their consumption and savings decisions (Thaler, 1980, 1981, 1985; see also Loewenstein et al., Chapter 19 of this volume). For instance, consumers may divide funds into those that pay bills and those that are for fun (Zelizer, 1989, 1997). Similarly, consumers may consider money won in a football betting pool as free money for entertainment expenses but use a tax refund for home renovations (O'Curry, 2000). One implication of funds being nonfungible in mental accounting is that there exists a cost–benefit analysis of the transaction that uses those funds (Prelec & Loewenstein, 1998; Thaler, 1980, 1999). For instance, a mother may pay $150 for a baby stroller, but she does not recover this cost until she receives the benefit of the stroller, for instance, by taking a leisure walk in the park with her baby in that stroller. As we shall discuss, this transaction coupling between the cost and benefit of the transaction is useful in understanding credit card usage and credit card debt.

There is considerable evidence in support of the nonfungibility hypothesis of the behavioral life cycle hypothesis. In the original introduction of the behavioral model, participants who imagined that they were the beneficiaries of some financial bonus spent the money if they coded the bonus as current income rather than future income or current assets; also, they indicated that they would spend the least portion of the bonus if they coded it as future income versus the others (Shefrin & Thaler, 1988). In recent years, research has also shown that the Save More Tomorrow program in the workplace increases employees' savings by diverting a part of their future income increases toward retirement savings accounts (Thaler & Benartzi, 2004). Similarly, full-time professors at American University in Washington, DC, can choose to receive their pay for the standard 9-month teaching appointment spread over either 9 months or 1 year. Subsequently, salary for summer teaching creates an unbalanced salary distribution for those who elect the 12-month salary plan, because they get more pay in the summer months than the rest of the year. As predicted by the behavioral model, more professors under the 1-year plan than under the 9-month one earmark their savings toward ongoing expenses (e.g., club memberships) that they normally would not pay for from their 9-month salaries (Graham & Isaac, 2002).

To understand precisely how credit cards result in excessive spending, we first articulate how a consumer might arrive at the decision to make a specific discretionary purchase. An economic approach would suggest simply that the consumer would compute the utility gained from consuming the product and compare it to the disutility of spending the money. In the case of a cash-and-carry transaction, such as buying a sandwich for lunch, the consumer would purchase if the utility of the sandwich exceeded the disutility of its price. In a mental-accounting sense, the consumer would set up a transaction-specific mental account and ascertain whether the account would need to be closed in the black (i.e., with a net positive value) or in the red (Prelec & Loewenstein, 1998; Soman, 2001).

However, research has also shown that consumers perform poorly when evaluating the utility of products (Ariely, Loewenstein, & Prelec, 2003). In addition, products are never purchased in isolation but in the context of a consumption stream. In particular, the spending likelihood is a function of spending on similar items in the recent past (Heath & Soll, 1996). The exact relationship is captured in the budgeting model proposed by Heath and Soll, in which consumers proactively divide their monthly planned spending into different categories or accounts (e.g., rent, utility bills, food, entertainment) and prospectively set budgets for each category. Spending decisions in a given category are then made as a function of how much unused budgets remain in the respective categories.

In contrast to this prospective-budgeting story, Soman (2001) proposed an alternate, retrospective-budgeting accounting. Soman (2001) proposed that consumers might not proactively set budgets, monitor spending, and update available budgets on an ongoing basis. Instead, when faced with a consumption opportunity, they might make a general judgment about how much they had spent on similar items in the recent past; if they believed they had spent a lot, they would be less likely to purchase than if they believed they had spent only a little. This account produces results that are similar to the prospective-budgeting model but provides a different process account for why those effects arise.

In parallel, a stream of research has started documenting the fact that consumers who use credit cards tend to spend more than comparable consumers who use cash or checks. In perhaps the first notable demonstration of facilitated spending by credit cards, Feinberg (1986) found that participants were willing to pay up to 50% more for dresses, tents, sweaters, and lamps when the MasterCard logo was present on the table and were likely to tip more at a restaurant when using credit cards versus other forms of payment. Since then, a wealth of research has shown similar findings. For instance, consumers have self-reported that they tend to spend more on everyday goods with credit cards than with cash (Burman, 1974; Mathews & Slocum, 1968), there is a correlation between merely owning a credit card and feelings of antic-ipation and actualization of future use (Hirschman, 1979; Wise, Brown, & Cox, 1977), and credit card images increase mere willingness to pay (Prelec & Simester, 2001). Although some of the earlier studies documented greater spending for credit card users, they suffered from the problem of self-selection. Prelec and Simester were the first to use random assignment of participants to credit card versus cash conditions in an auction setting and showed that consumers in the credit card condition bid significantly more. Why and how do credit cards facilitate spending?

Soman's (2001) retrospective accounting model provided two explanations for why peo-ple using credit cards spend more. The first explanation relates to the memorability of past expenses and hence the accuracy of the mental accounting. When paying by check, consumers write down the total amount in words and figures and consequently rehearse the past spending amount. When paying with a card, they simply sign a receipt, and no rehearsal occurs. Soman intercepted patrons of a bookstore right after they had made a purchase, and found that those who had paid by check or cash could indeed recall their past expenses more accurately than those who paid by credit cards. Because of this difference, people who use credit cards tend to underestimate their past expenses in a given month, overestimate their available funds, and hence spend more.

A second factor that drives the effect of credit cards on spending relates to the so-called pain of paying (Prelec & Loewenstein, 1998; Zellermayer, 1996). Zellermayer argued that some pay-ments seem more painful than others because of the nature of the transaction. For instance, cash payments are painful, because the consumer has to physically endure the act of parting with his or her hard-earned money. However, payment by plastic mechanisms (i.e., credit or debit cards) is conceptually—and physically—very different from paying with cash. The transaction via plastic mechanisms is simpler and shorter, as no money actually exchanges hands. Although cash and checks are still prevalent in some parts of the world, plastic payment mechanisms are more com-monplace in most economies (Soman & Lam, 2002). In some countries, even these payment mecha-nisms are getting dated and being replaced by more advanced mechanisms. For instance, in Hong Kong, a contactless and rechargeable smart card allows consumers to pay their bus and train fares, buy snacks at vending machines and cafés, pay parking fees, and also pay for access to sporting facilities. In many countries, it is possible to pay for a vending machine snack by simply dialing a number on one's mobile phone and having the amount charged to one's phone bill. The advent of this so-called electronic money has resulted in payment mechanisms that are increasingly per-ceptually distant as compared to conventional cash-and-carry transactions (Schneider, 2002; cf. Gourville & Soman, 1998).

Soman (2003) captured the notion of pain of payment in a construct called *payment transpar-ency*, which he defined as "the relative salience of the payment, both in terms of physical form and the amount, relative to paying by cash" (p. 175). In a series of field studies comparing the spending behaviors of two groups of consumers who used payment mechanisms that differed on transparency, his research showed that the pain of payment, and hence the likelihood of saving, was lowest when the payment was relatively nontransparent. Raghubir and Srivastava (2008) built on this idea when they made individual payments salient using a piecemeal decomposi-tion strategy as opposed to a holistic estimate resembling credit card bills that lump separate purchases into one (Menon, 1997). By doing so, Raghubir and Srivastava attenuated consumers' willingness to pay using credit cards. Such findings are consistent with the mental accounting view of credit card spending in that it attenuates the salience of the pain from paying at the point of purchase.

A third factor that plays a role in the greater spending by credit cards relates to the research of transaction decoupling and payment depreciation (Gourville & Soman, 1998; Soman & Gourville, 2001; Thaler, 1999). In a standard cash-and-carry world, the linkage between the consumption benefit (i.e., the sandwich) and the cost (i.e., the price) is unambiguous, and the two are said to be tightly coupled. However, in many real-world transactions, the degree of coupling could decrease. Likewise, if there is a temporal separation between the payment and the consumption, as in the case of advance purchases, consumers gradually adapt to the pain of the payment over time, such that when the time to consume finally arrives, the payment is no longer aversive, and the good appears to be a free good. In a series of demonstrations, Gourville and Soman (1998; Soman & Gourville, 2001) showed that when transactions are decoupled or temporally disjointed, the tendency to purchase might go up, because the pain of the payment is diminished. When contemplating a cash purchase for $10, the payment is immediate and segregated. When contemplating a credit card purchase for $10, the payment will be delayed and integrated with other items in the credit card bill. Based on the predictions of prospect theory (Kahneman & Tversky, 1979), the payment will not sting as much in the bundled credit card condition, because it is integrated with other losses.

A fourth factor relates to the role of feedback on behavior. Research has suggested that in domains in which consumers are unable to keep track of behaviors, such as prior spending, the provision of feedback allows them to learn and hence update their behavior (Hogarth, Gibbs, McKenzie, & Marquis, 1991). As a specific example, Soman (2001) was able to attenuate the effects of credit cards on spending by providing consumers with feedback on their cumulative spending to date in the given month. However, in order for feedback to be effective, it should be expressive or vivid, timely or immediate, and consistent or suitable (Hogarth et al. 1991). In the case of credit cards, feedback arrives in the form of credit card statements that are neither timely (e.g., a sample of 54 credit card users reported that the delay between purchase and the receipt of the statement for the first item was anywhere between 24 and 46 days) nor consistent; specifically, whereas most household budgeting cycles and income cycles start on the first day of the month, not a single respondent reported that their credit card cycles started on the first day, and the earliest start date was the eighth day of the month. Consequently, feedback does not help greatly.

A fifth factor that can drive the effects of credit cards has to do with the role of the credit limit. Younger consumers have fewer experiences with credit cards and, therefore, typically treat their credit limit as a signal of their future earnings (Soman & Cheema, 2002). Thus, a younger consumer with a high credit limit may infer that he or she will have a higher income than someone with a low credit limit. In Study 1, Soman and Cheema found that participants with a $5,000 credit limit were more likely to spend than those with a $2,000 credit limit. However, as participants realized that the credit limit was not a credible signal of their future earnings, they discounted its importance as a predictor of future earnings, thereby decreasing their likelihood to spend. Participants who considered their credit limit to be low in credibility did not differ in their likelihood to spend regardless of credit limit. In fact, their likelihood to spend was lower than those with high credibility but a low credit limit of $2,000. The roles of the credit limit and credibility of that limit in spending decisions thus make younger and less educated consumers susceptible to overspending with their credit cards. In Study 3, the authors found that credit limit was more important than current liquidity on the propensity to spend. These results are consistent with the behavioral life cycle hypothesis (Shefrin & Thaler, 1988). The hypothesis posits that while consumers make use of future income in the present to construct the highest and smoothest consumption path, they are also unable to correctly calculate or predict the available future income for use in the present. The credit limit offers a solution to this problem, but at the same time, it makes consumers feel wealthier than they are, increasing their likelihood to incur credit card debt (Gross & Souleles, 2001).

In sum, although credit cards serve as devices that enable the intertemporal allocation of income, their usage is likely to have unintended consequences (i.e., excessive spending) because of the following:

- *Decision points:* A payment mechanism that is effortful and involves some transaction costs can serve as a decision point for consumers to evaluate their expenses. However, credit cards remove those decision points and hence make spending easier.
- *Memorability of past expenses:* The memory for past payments decreases; consequently, consumers believe they have access to more funds than they actually do.
- *Payment transparency:* The pain of payment is lower for credit cards, because the payment is nontransparent, hence consumers do not think as much about incurring an expense.
- *Mismatch of feedback and budgeting cycles:* Feedback on credit card expenses in the form of credit card statements is delayed, and the payment cycles do not coincide with budgeting cycles.
- *Decoupling:* Rather than evaluating an expense as a segregated amount, credit cards allow consumers to integrate their payments with other payments, hence reducing their hedonic impact.
- *Credit limit:* Consumers interpret the credit limit given to them by credit card issuers as a signal of the consumers' spending power. In the absence of expertise in making intertemporal income allocations, this leads to overreliance on credit limits.

We note that some of these effects are not limited to credit cards but could work in the case of other payment mechanisms as well. In Table 20.1, we list several payment mechanisms and propose which of these effects would be particularly strong for each payment mechanism.

As discussed in the preceding paragraphs, a fair bit of past work is relevant to understanding how credit cards influence spending patterns. This literature is relevant, though, in situations in which consumers have made the decision to adopt a credit card and continue to use it. In the next section, we discuss the implication of past research on the adoption decision.

**Table 20.1**  Payment Mechanisms and Consumer Psychology, Leveled to Show Proposed Effect of Mechanism Use

|  | Cash | Checks | Debit Cards | Credit Cards | Electronic Payments | Payroll Deductions |
|---|---|---|---|---|---|---|
| Decision point at purchase | High | High | Low | Low | Very low | None |
| Memorability | High | High | Low | Low | Low | Low |
| Pain of payment | High | High | Low | Low | Low | Low |
| Degree of coupling | High | High | Medium | Low | Medium | Medium |
| Quality of feedback | High | High | Medium | Low | Low | Low |
| Effects of credit limits | Not applicable | Not applicable | Not applicable | High | Not applicable | Not applicable |

## CREDIT CARDS, THE PAIN OF PAYMENT, AND SPENDING: NEW EMPIRICAL EVIDENCE

In this section, we report the results of two new studies in which we manipulate the specific features of the available credit and examine the effects on the decision to purchase. As noted above, one mechanism that prevents consumers from overspending is that paying for a product is usually psychologically painful (Zelizer, 1997). In the context of mental accounting, the analogy drawn is typically one of a moral tax (Prelec & Loewenstein, 1998; Soman & Ahn, 2010; Thaler, 1999). When deciding to spend a dollar, a consumer needs to pay this moral tax to move the dollar from savings to spending. However, once the moral tax has been paid, the money is easier to spend. When consumes go to a store expecting to spend $100 but only end up spending $50 due to a promotion, they are likely to spend the newfound $50 on expenses they would otherwise not have incurred (Soman & Ahn, 2010). Likewise, when an international traveler purchases foreign exchange, the psychological tax associated with the money has been paid, hence the traveler tends to spend the money relatively frivolously.

### Study 1: Moral Tax Payments and Spending

Credit card loans have much the same nature as sums of money in which the moral tax has already been paid. Once a consumer is granted a credit limit of, say, $5,000, there is little by way of a psychological barrier to constrain spending within that amount. In our first study, we make a contrast between two lines of credit: one in which consumers pay the psychological moral tax as a lump sum when setting up the account, similar to a credit card account, and another in which consumers need to pay a moral tax as they go, similar to a line of credit labeled a *piecemeal loan*. We show that when consumers make upfront moral tax payments, they are less willing to set up the account, but subsequent spending from such an account, after it has been set up, is relatively easy. In contrast, an account in which the consumer makes moral tax payments on a pay-per-use basis is easier to set up, but the consumer is less likely to subsequently spend from such an account, because the pain of payment for each transaction is higher relative to the other payment mechanism.

*Participants, Design, and Procedure*

One hundred students at a large U.S. university's student center completed the study. The study scenario asked participants to imagine that after finishing college, they move to a foreign country to start a new job, and their salary is 3,000 boons per month (1 boon = 1 U.S. dollar). Participants read that their monthly expenses on essentials like rent, food, and utilities is about 2,500 boons, with miscellaneous expenses accounting for a further 200 boons. Because they have no prior savings, this does not leave participants with much money for other discretionary expenses like clothes, entertainment, and home appliances. Participants then read that they are thinking about purchasing a television and microwave that they do not really need but are looking forward to getting.

We then manipulated the credit availability between subjects (i.e., not set up [select condition] vs. already set up [use condition]). Half of the participants—those in the select condition—read that because they expect their salary to increase over the next few months, they decide to look for some form of consumer credit to buy the appliances. The agent at the bank where they have their checking accounts informs them that two forms of consumer credit are popular and could be extended with a limit of 3,000 boons. The rest of the subjects, those in the use condition, read that they had already established two forms of loans. Participants read that because they had expected their salary to increase over the next few months, they had looked for some form of consumer credit to buy the appliances. At the time they had opened a checking account with their bank, they had also signed up for two popular consumer credit schemes, each with a 3,000 boons limit.

All participants then saw the description of two consumer credit schemes corresponding to the piecemeal loan and lump-sum loan formats described earlier. The surveys did not use these labels but rather two names (i.e., signature account, gold line) in which assignment to the two formats was counterbalanced. The surveys described the schemes as follows:

- *Lump-sum loan:* The bank would transfer 3,000 boons to your account that you could spend by writing checks as usual from your checking account. Interest would accrue only on the portion of the credit you actually use. The principal and interest would need to be repaid at the end of one year.
- *Piecemeal loan:* The bank would not actually transfer money into your account but would give you access to a separate account from which you could spend up to $3,000 by writing checks, and you would be issued a separate set of checks for this loan. Interest would accrue only on the portion of the credit you actually use. The principal and interest would need to be repaid at the end of one year.

All participants read that the interest rate was 10%, which represented a fairly low rate of interest in the foreign country. Finally, all participants answered two questions after reading the scenario. First, participants in the select condition chose one of the two loans to set up, while participants in the use condition chose one of the two loans to use for the appliance purchases. Second, all participants indicated their relative strength of preference between the two alternatives on a 9-point scale (1 = *definitely prefer lump-sum loan;* 9 = *definitely prefer piecemeal loan*).

*Results and Discussion*

Consistent with our expectation, we found that participants who had to set up a loan (select condition) were less likely to choose the lump-sum loan (34%) versus the piecemeal loan (66%; $\chi^2 = 5.12$, $p < .05$). In contrast, participants who had use of the two previously set up loans (use condition) were more likely to use the lump-sum loan (64%) versus the piecemeal loan (36%; $\chi^2 = 3.92$, $p < .05$). Thus, more people were likely to choose the lump-sum loan in the use versus the select condition ($\chi^2 = 8.72$, $p < .005$). Responses to the second question revealed a similar pattern, with greater preference for the piecemeal loan in the select condition than in the use condition ($M_{select} = 5.92$ vs. $M_{use} = 4.50$; $F[1, 98] = 3.42$, $p < .001$). This is consistent with the expectation that the upfront pain of payment of the former loan format is lower than that of the latter, likely being incurred when the money is spent (i.e., transferred into the participant's bank account and used). Similar to credit cards, this supports the prediction that it may be less painful to spend from the lump-sum loan, in which the psychological cost is incurred up front when the loan is set up.

These results suggest that, left to themselves, consumers may not willingly sign up for credit cards when other credit mechanisms are available. From a public policy perspective, therefore, limiting the aggressive marketing of credit cards—especially to younger consumers—may be a useful mechanism to slow credit adoption, a strategy that is currently being considered by lawmakers (Levisohn, 2009). Our results also suggest that once consumers do have a credit card, they may spend more readily on credit than through other forms of payment. As discussed previously, multiple mechanisms such as conditioning (Feinberg, 1986), decoupling, and reduced pain of payment may drive such spending. Next, we discuss how such automatic spending may be slowed by introducing a need for justification and decreasing perceived ownership of the credit limit as spending money.

## Study 2: Automatic Aspects of Spending With Credit Cards

In a second study, we highlight the automatic aspect of spending with credit cards. If the decision to utilize credit is one that requires justification, consumers' likelihood of spending decreases significantly. Furthermore, if consumers believe that they are spending "someone else's money," then they may be less profligate if they assume the credit is their own money. These manipulations suggest interventions that are likely to increase deliberation and decrease spending with credit cards. Participants in this experiment were presented with a scenario in which they had the opportunity to buy a desired item on credit. The nature of the available loan was manipulated across subjects, such that the consumer either had direct or indirect access to the loan amount (theirs or someone else's money), and the loan was either exclusive or shared, with the need for justification being higher for a shared loan.

*Participants, Design, and Procedure*

We asked 120 students at cafeterias on the campus of a large U.S. university to complete the survey in return for a snack of their choice. All subjects read a scenario in which they have recently graduated, and they and a former classmate (George) have started up their own small businesses. A third friend, Rich, now works for a financing company and has arranged a small low-interest loan to help the participant and George with their start-ups. The amount of the loan is $4,000 for each of them and is meant to finance short-term operational expenses. The loan amount must be spent in six months and be repaid in two years. The interest rate on the loan is 6%. The study employed a 2 (access: direct, indirect) × 2 (exclusivity: unique, shared) full factorial design with random assignment. The format of the loan was next described and created by completely crossing the access (i.e., direct, indirect) and exclusivity (i.e., unique, shared) factors.

To manipulate access, participants in the direct access condition read, "The loan is in the form of a cash advance whereby Rich has transferred (the loan amount to an account in your name). You can pay for expenses by writing checks from this account." In contrast, participants in the indirect access condition read, "The loan is administered through a bank account that is managed by Rich but from which (you) are authorized to utilize (the loan amount). You can pay for expenses by writing checks from this account."

Exclusivity was manipulated by changing the details within parentheses in the above sentences. All subjects were told that they and George both had a credit limit of $4,000. However, participants in the unique condition read either, "Rich has transferred $4,000 each to two separate bank accounts, one in your name and one in George's," or "The loan is administered through a bank account that is managed by Rich but from which you are authorized to utilize up to $4,000. There are two separate bank accounts, one for you and one for George." On the other hand, participants in the shared condition read either, "The loan is in the form of a cash advance whereby Rich has transferred $8,000 to a bank account set up jointly in your name and George's," or "The loan is administered through a bank account that is managed by Rich but from which you and George are authorized to utilize up to $8,000." In both cases, subjects were also told, "While there is a single account, there is an understanding that neither you nor George will utilize more than $4,000 each." All subjects were also told that interest would only accrue on the amount actually utilized.

All participants then saw a purchase opportunity. They read that five months have passed, and they have used a sum of $2,500 of the loan. They do not see any further need to draw from the loan. Just then, their partner suggests that their office could use some new furniture. A local store is offering a complete set of office furniture at a great sale price of $800. Although they do not really need the new furniture, it would be nice to have. Also, they realize that they do not have enough money to buy the furniture, but they will earn enough within the next year to afford it. In this context, they wonder whether they should use the unused part of the low-interest loan to buy the furniture. Finally, all participants then reported their willingness to use the loan to buy furniture (1 = *definitely not use loan*; 9 = *definitely use loan*). Second, they indicated their perceived ownership of the money by responding to the statement "The loan amount belongs to me and has been assigned to me for my spending" (1 = *disagree*; 9 = *agree*).

*Results and Discussion*

We analyzed participants' willingness to use the loan in a 2 (access: direct, indirect) × 2 (exclusivity: unique, shared) ANOVA. A significant main effect of access indicated that participants who had direct, versus indirect, access were more likely to use the loan ($M_{direct}$ = 6.20 vs. $M_{indirect}$ = 4.27; $F[1, 116]$ = 23.52, $p < .001$). In addition, a main effect of exclusivity revealed that participants who had unique, versus shared, ownership were more likely to use the loan money ($M_{unique}$ = 5.72 vs. $M_{shared}$ = 4.75; $F[1, 116]$ = 5.88, $p < .02$). The access × exclusivity interaction did not approach significance ($p > .80$). The two main effects led to the pattern shown in Figure 20.1, in which the willingness to use the loan was highest when the loan was given as a cash advance, rather than through an account managed by the lender, and when the loan amount was uniquely assigned (i.e., $4,000 to each individual instead of $8,000 jointly).

The perceived ownership measure showed a similar pattern of results, with significant main effects of access ($M_{direct}$ = 5.98 vs. $M_{indirect}$ = 4.42; $F[1, 116]$ = 22.90, $p < .001$) and exclusivity ($M_{unique}$ = 5.63 vs. $M_{shared}$ = 4.77; $F[1, 116]$ = 7.01, $p < .01$), while the two-way interaction between these factors did not approach significance ($p > .20$). Furthermore, this perceived ownership measure mediated the effect of the manipulated variables on participants' willingness to use the loan to buy the furniture, as shown in Figure 20.2. These results support the expectation that the propensity to spend credit is greater when the consumer perceived ownership of the loan amount. The perception of ownership is high when the loan amount is within the consumer's direct access and when the consumer does not share the loan with others. As avenues of future research, communications that challenge consumers' beliefs about owning the credit limit are likely to decrease their likelihood of incurring debt.

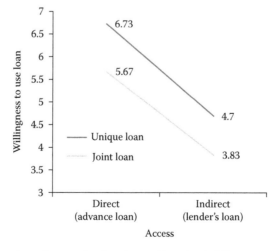

**Figure 20.1**   Mean willingness to use loan as a function of ownership and exclusivity.

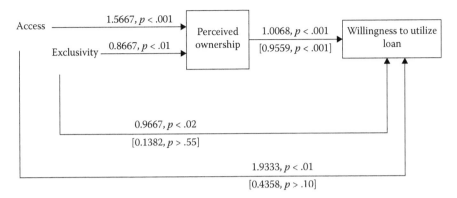

**Figure 20.2**  Mediating effect of perceived ownership.
*Note:* Numbers above the lines indicate regression coefficients and *p* values for those variables directly connected by the arrows. Numbers below the arrows are results when perceived ownership is used as a covariate in a regression of willingness to utilize loan in the presence of the independent variables.

## THE CREDIT CARD REFORM ACT OF 2009

In response to the financial crisis of 2008 and the so-called mortgage meltdown, the U.S. Congress passed the CARD Act of 2009. The act took effect as of February 2010 and encompasses the following key provisions:

- Prevents unfair interest rate increases and term changes
- Prohibits unnecessary fees
- Requires fairness in the timing and amounts of credit card payments
- Protects the rights of financially responsible credit card users
- Provides for enhanced disclosures of credit card terms and conditions
- Calls for adequate safeguards for young people
- Calls for transparent credit card pricing

What effects would this provision have in the context of the research presented in this chapter? We discuss this in the next few paragraphs, with references to section numbers of the act, as is available in the full text provided online by the U.S. Congress (http://www.opencongress.org/bill/111-s392/text).

One family of provisions in the CARD Act directly addresses the biases that are prevalent in consumers' adoption decisions. As discussed earlier, short-term rewards and incentives play a disproportionate role in influencing consumers, especially those who are younger, to adopt credit cards. To this end, Section 304 of the CARD Act puts constraints on the marketing of credit cards to college students. In particular, issuers are prohibited from giving any inducements or incentives for signing up, and as a further deterrent, colleges are encouraged to track all credit card marketing activities and offer debt education and counseling services as part of orientation programs.

A second family of provisions has to do with enhanced consumer protection as it relates to interest rates, fees, and repayment. As discussed earlier, many consumers are aware of their interest rates at the time of adoption, but as rates change, they tend to not remember the new interest rates. In addition, a number of fees are hidden. To address these concerns, Title 1 of the new law mandates credit card providers to provide advance notice of rate increases, puts limits on APR and fee increases, and requires that if specific factors are used to increase APR, the same factors should be used to decrease it.

A related set of provisions in the law deals with the application of credit card payments and the protection of financially responsible consumers. The new law requires credit card statements be mailed 21 days in advance of the payment date, prohibits issuers from setting early morning deadlines for payments, and requires payments in excess of the minimum to be applied first to the credit card balance with the highest rate of interest. The law also prohibits credit card issuers from imposing any late fees arising due to delays in crediting payments and requires payments made at local branches to be credited on the same day.

The provisions of the CARD Act are largely all consistent with a subset of the research reported in this chapter. In particular, we note that the provisions will definitely help address some of the biases in the domain of credit card adoption, and in mitigating the effects of hidden fees and changing interest rates. However, further work is needed on two dimensions. First, we note that while some provisions of the act are designed to help consumers, there may be perverse effects. For instance, the act encourages consumers to pay bills online, because payments made on the due date cannot be penalized with late fees. However, past research (Soman, 2001, 2003) has suggested that making payments online can reduce the pain of payment by masking the salience of the payment. Likewise, as credit card issuers find that the new regulations impact revenues, there remains the possibility that consumers will be faced with increasing annual fees, as well as new forms of charges like inactivity and reinstatement fees.

Second, our position on helping consumers resonates with the stand taken by Thaler and Sunstein (2008). In particular, we believe that the battle against credit card and consumer debt problems needs to be fought on three fronts. The first front is exemplified by the CARD Act and refers to a set of laws and guidelines for credit card issuers and marketers. The second front is aimed at consumers and, in our opinion, is best delivered through a program of financial literacy. However, research has shown that self-control problems arise even for well educated and sophisticated consumers (see Faber & Vohs, Chapter 22 of this volume). The third front, therefore, refers to a series of behavioral interventions designed to inform and influence consumers at the precise times that they make relevant decisions. In our next section, we outline a series of prescriptive recommendations along these lines.

## PRESCRIPTIVE RECOMMENDATIONS

Based on the research summarized in this chapter, what prescriptive recommendations could we offer to consumers who want to control their spending and to policy makers who need to develop guidelines for issuers of credit cards, and indeed other payment mechanisms? For instance, asking consumers to keep track of their credit card spending (Soman, 2001), by providing feedback on the amount spent (Soman & Lam, 2002) and calling into question the credibility of assigned credit limits (Soman & Cheema, 2002), can mitigate the illusion of liquidity. Data presented in this chapter also indicate that the propensity to spend on credit is likely to decline with increased deliberation and the requirement to justify the expense to others.

As discussed at the conclusion of Study 1, the decision to adopt credit seems to be driven as much, if not more, by marketing tactics than by economic parameters of the offer (Bertrand, Karlan, Mullainathan, Shafir, & Zinman, 2005). Consequently, greater scrutiny of such marketing tactics is likely to prove useful for improved consumer education. Also, Study 2 results suggest that manipulating perceived ownership of the credit amount (i.e., as the lender's money) or increasing the need to justify credit expenses to parents or a significant other may be useful mechanisms to reduce spending tendencies. We organize our list of prescriptive suggestions around the basic drivers of the credit card effects as discussed earlier.

## Self-Control Strategies and Decision Points

As a counter to a popular credit card advertisement that implored consumers to "never leave home without it," Prelec and Simester entitled their 2001 paper "Always Leave Home Without It." The point they make is simple: By imposing a transaction cost on the use of a credit card, consumers might be encouraged to elaborate more on the pros or cons of the purchase. This is also consistent with the notion of a cooling-off period (Loewenstein, O'Donoghue, & Rabin, 2003), which suggests that decision makers should be encouraged to impose a period of time between an emotional event and a decision, so decisions are not made in the heat of the moment (Mick & Schwartz, Chapter 32 of this volume). The popular press also talks about tactics like freezing a credit card into a block of ice (Smith, 2008), which ensures that the consumer has access to credit in the case of a real emergency but cannot whip it out and use it quickly in response to a purchase impulse. In the language of our chapter, these interventions create a decision point for consumers.

Additionally, there are other ways to create decision points. Imagine a utopian world in which a consumer who clicks on the purchase button at an online retailer sees a screen with the question "Are you sure you would like to make this purchase?" Alternately, they might be faced with a short delay in a typical store setting and asked this question. The research reviewed here suggests that this would result in greater elaboration, and the purchase likelihood would reduce. A similar intervention could be created at the checkout terminals of retail stores where consumers swipe their own cards.

In an ongoing field experiment with a cooperative bank in Asia, consumers who have access to a certain credit limit on their cards are allowed to select intermediate decision points at which they are warned about their spending to date. For instance, a consumer might have a credit limit of $2,000 but chooses to receive an alert at $500, $1,000, and $1,500. When he or she attempts to make a purchase that tips his or her balance over $500, the consumer receives an alert either via the checkout terminal or through a text message on his or her mobile phone. Early results have suggested that this intervention successfully increases prudence and reduces spending. Another simple tip for using the decision point idea effectively is for consumers to set aside their spending budgets in a separate account. Once the account has been depleted, it provides a decision point and forces the consumer to think about the next purchase, also acting as a simple and unambiguous piece of feedback. Interestingly, current bank fee structures in at least some countries discourage this, so there would be public policy implications to prevent this from occurring.

## Interventions That Influence the Mental Accounting of Consumers

We join other contributors in this volume (Keller & Lusardi, Chapter 21 of this volume; Loewenstein et al., Chapter 19 of this volume) in suggesting that interventions that influence the mental accounting practices of consumers have a significant role to play in influencing savings behavior. The key themes emerging from our review relate to the fact that consumers could make mental accounting errors, because the memorability of past expenses goes down, and feedback is not immediate and consistent. Thankfully, technology today should allow for the development of tools that provide solutions in this regard. In our utopian world, for instance, a law might mandate that every time a consumer swipes a credit card at a store terminal, the screen gives him or her a listing of the last 20 purchases made. With some technological refinement, the screen might also be able to sort the purchases into different categories and alert the consumer if the spending in a particular category has exceeded the predetermined budgets. However, since our utopian world is still some way off, our advice to consumers is simple: Maintain a register of expenses; tally cumulative spending at the end of, say, every week; and compare the total spent to one's available budgets. In this regard, a simple policy intervention might ask consumers to write the amount in words and figures before they sign a credit card docket at a retail establishment, which would help increase the memorability of past expenses and hence decrease the illusion of liquidity (Soman, 2001).

Research reviewed here suggests that the credit limit plays a significant role in spending behavior. Ideally, credit limits should reflect future earning potential and, therefore, be calculated using a set of appropriate indexes that allow banks to estimate future earnings potential. Soman and Cheema (2002) pointed to a need for a common set of guidelines that would result in credit limits that more accurately reflect the future earnings potential of the consumer, as well as a need for policy measures to control the seemingly indiscriminate increases in credit limits. The research also calls for a policy requiring banks and other lending institutions to inform consumers about the procedures used to determine or increase their credit limits. The practice of telling consumers that they deserve increases in their credit limits is not only uninformative but might also mislead consumers into believing that their net worth has actually increased.

Finally, the research reported in this chapter also has implications for the design of financial literacy programs. In the past, these programs tended to focus on providing information about financial products, but we believe that they should additionally teach consumers about human psychology and also about possible interventions that they could use in regulating their own behavior. In addition, the research also suggests that programs need to go beyond simple literacy and also introduce consumers to products and practices that help them execute on their desire to save more (see Soman, Cheema, & Xu, 2010). Recent work has already demonstrated a few examples of the kinds of products and programs that could augment education. For instance, Thaler and Benartzi (2004) and Ashraf, Karlan, and Yin (2010) report success with precommitment-based savings program, while Soman, Cheema , and Xu (2009) show that simple products can help people save more, such as a budgeting board and a buddy system–based safety deposit box. Our position is simply that while it is important to invest in financial literacy programs that inform and educate, it is equally important to invest in programs and products that help consumers actually accomplish their intentions.

## REFERENCES

Ainslie, G., & Haslam, N. (1992). Self-control. In G. Loewenstein & J. Elster (Eds.), *Choice over time* (pp. 177–209). New York: Sage.

Ando, A., & Modigliani, F. (1963). The "life cycle" hypothesis of saving: Aggregate implications and tests. *American Economic Review, 53*, 55–84.

Ariely, D., Loewenstein, G., & Prelec, D. (2003). Coherent arbitrariness: Stable demand curves without stable preferences. *Quarterly Journal of Economics, 118*, 73–105.

Ashraf, N., Karlan, D., & Yin, W. (2010). Female empowerment: Impact of a commitment savings product in the Philippines. *World Development, 38*(3), 333–344.

Ausubel, L. M. (1991). The failure of competition in the credit card market. *American Economic Review, 81*, 50–81.

Baumeister, R. F. (2002). Yielding to temptation: Self-control failure, impulsive purchasing, and consumer behavior. *Journal of Consumer Research, 28*, 670–676.

Baumeister, R. F., Heatherton, T. F., & Tice, D. M. (1994). *Losing control: How and why people fail at self-regulation.* San Diego, CA: Academic Press.

Benzion, U., Rapoport, A., & Yagil, J. (1989). Discount rates inferred from decisions: An experimental study. *Management Science, 35*, 270–284.

Bertrand, M., Karlan, D. S., Mullainathan, S., Shafir, E., & Zinman, J. (2005). *What's psychology worth? A field experiment in the consumer credit market* (Discussion Paper No. 918). New Haven, CT: Economic Growth Center, Yale University.

Buehler, R., & Griffin, D. (2003). Planning, personality, and prediction: The role of future focus in optimistic time predictions. *Organizational Behavior and Human Decision Processes, 92*, 80–90.

Buehler, R., Griffin, D., & MacDonald, H. (1997). The role of motivated reasoning in optimistic time predictions. *Personality and Social Psychology Bulletin, 23*, 238–247.

Burman, D. (1974). Do people overspend with credit cards? *Journal of Consumer Credit Management, 5*, 98–103.

Courant, P., Gramlich, E., & Laitner, J. (1986). A dynamic micro estimate of the life-cycle model. In H. G. Aaron & G. Burtless (Eds.), *Retirement and economic behavior* (pp. 279–314). Washington, DC: Brookings Institute.

Credit Card Accountability, Responsibility, and Disclosure Act of 2009, Pub. L. No. 111-24 (2009).

Credit Card Reform Act of 2009, S. 392, 111th Cong. (2009). Available: http://www.opencongress.org/bill/111-s392/show

Day, K. (2006, October 12). Credit cards' hidden costs. *The Washington Post*. Available: http://www.washingtonpost.com/wp-dyn/content/article/2006/10/11/AR2006101101850.html

DeNavas-Walt, C., Proctor, B. D., & Smith, J. C. (2008). *Income, poverty, and health insurance coverage in the United States: 2007* (Current Population Reports No. P60-235). Washington, DC: U.S. Department of Commerce, Economics and Statistics Administration, U.S. Census Bureau.

Department of Finance Canada. (2009). *Backgrounder: Regulatory measures related to credit.* Available: http://www.fin.gc.ca/n08/data/09-048_1-eng.asp

Diners Club International. (2008). *Company history.* Available: https://www.dinersclubus.com/dce_content/aboutdinersclub/companyhistory

Eisenstein, E. M., & Hoch, S. J. (2007). *Intuitive compounding: Framing, temporal perspective, and expertise.* Unpublished manuscript, Cornell University, Ithaca, NY.

Elster, J. (1979). *Ulysses and the Sirens: Studies in rationality and irrationality.* New York: Cambridge University Press.

Feinberg, R. A. (1986). Credit cards as spending facilitating stimuli: A conditioning interpretation. *Journal of Consumer Research, 12*, 348–356.

Fisher, I. (1930). *The theory of interest.* New York: Macmillan.

Friedman, M. (1957). The permanent income hypothesis: Comment. *American Economic Review, 48*, 990–991.

Gourville, J., & Soman, D. (1998). Payment depreciation: The behavioral effects of temporally separating payments from consumption. *Journal of Consumer Research, 25*, 160–174.

Gourville, J., & Soman, D. (in press). Consumer psychology of mail-in rebates. *Journal of Product & Brand Management.*

Graham, F., & Isaac, A. G. (2002). The behavioral life-cycle theory of consumer behavior: Survey evidence. *Journal of Economic Behavior & Organizations, 48*, 391–401.

Gross, D., & Souleles, N. S. (2001). *Consumer response to changes in credit supply: Evidence from credit card data* (Working Paper No. 01-10). Philadelphia: Financial Institutions Center, Wharton School, University of Pennsylvania.

Heath, C., & Soll, J. B. (1996). Mental budgeting and consumer decisions. *Journal of Consumer Research, 23*, 40–52.

Hirschman, E. C. (1979). Differences in consumer purchase behavior by credit card payment system. *Journal of Consumer Research, 6*, 58–66.

Hoch, S. J., & Loewenstein, G. F. (1991). Time-inconsistent preferences and consumer self-control. *Journal of Consumer Research, 17*, 492–507.

Hogarth, R. M., Gibbs, B. J., McKenzie, C. R. M., & Marquis, M. A. (1991). Learning from feedback: Exacting and incentives. *Journal of Experimental Psychology: Learning, Memory, and Cognition, 17*, 734–752.

Hsee, C. K. (1995). Elastic justification: How tempting but task-irrelevant factors influence decisions. *Organizational Behavior and Human Decision Processes, 62*, 330–337.

Johnson, S., Kotlikoff, L. J., & Samuelson, W. (1987). *Can people compute? An experimental test of the life cycle consumption model* (NBER Working Paper No. 2183). Cambridge, MA: National Bureau of Economic Research.

Kahneman, D., & Lovallo, D. (1993). Timid choices and bold forecasts: A cognitive perspective on risk-taking. *Management Science, 39*, 17–31.

Kahneman, D., & Tversky, A. (1979). Prospect theory: An analysis of decisions under risk. *Econometrica, 47*, 313–327.

Kirby, K. (1997). Bidding on the future: Evidence against normative discounting of delayed rewards. *Journal of Experimental Psychology, 126*, 57–71.

Kotlikoff, L. J., Samuelson, W., & Johnson, S. (1988). Consumption, computation mistakes, and fiscal policy. *American Economic Review, 78*, 408–412.

Levisohn, B. (2009, September 9). Dodging credit-card reform. *BusinessWeek*. Available: http://www.business week.com/magazine/content/09_38/b4147026262530.htm

Loewenstein, G., O'Donoghue, T., & Rabin, M. (2003). Projection bias in predicting future utility. *Quarterly Journal of Economics, 118*, 1209–1248.

Mathews, H. L., & Slocum, J. W., Jr. (1968). *Marketing strategies in the commercial bank credit card field*. Chicago: Bank Public Relations and Marketing Association.

McKenzie, C. R. M., & Liersch, M. J. (2009). *Misunderstanding savings growth: Implications for retirement savings*. Unpublished manuscript, University of California, San Diego.

Menon, G. (1997). Are the parts better than the whole? The effects of decompositional questions on judgments of frequent behaviors. *Journal of Marketing Research, 32*, 335–346.

Modigliani, F., & Brumberg, R. H. (1954). Utility analysis and the consumption function: An interpretation of cross-section data. In K. K. Kurihara (Ed.), *Post-Keynesian economics* (pp. 388–436). New Brunswick, NJ: Rutgers University Press.

Morwitz, V. G., Greenleaf, E. A., & Johnson, E. J. (1998). Divide and prosper: Consumers' reactions to partitioned prices. *Journal of Marketing Research, 35*, 453–463.

Muraven, M., & Baumeister, R. F. (2000). Self-regulation and depletion of limited resources: Does self-control resemble a muscle? *Psychological Bulletin, 126*, 247–259.

*The Nilson Report*. (2009, March). Issue 922. Carpinteria, CA: HSN Consultants.

O'Curry, S. (2000). *Income source effects*. Unpublished manuscript, DePaul University, Chicago.

Prelec, D., & Loewenstein, G. (1998). The red and the black: Mental accounting of savings and debt. *Marketing Science, 17*, 4–28.

Prelec, D., & Simester, D. (2001). Always leave home without it: A further investigation of the credit-card effect on willingness to pay. *Marketing Letters, 12*, 5–12.

Raghubir, P., & Srivastava, J. (2008). Monopoly money: The effect of payment coupling and form on spending behavior. *Journal of Experimental Psychology: Applied, 14*, 213–225.

Schelling, T. C. (1984). Self-command in practice, in policy, and in a theory of rational choice. *American Economic Review, 74*, 1–11.

Schneider, G. P. (2002). *Electronic commerce* (2nd ed.). Cambridge, MA: Thomson Course Technology.

Schwartz, B. (2004). *The paradox of choice: Why more is less*. New York: Ecco.

Shefrin, H. M., & Thaler, R. H. (1988). The behavioral life-cycle hypothesis. *Economic Inquiry, 26*, 609–643.

Shiv, B., & Fedorikhin, A. (1999). Heart and mind in conflict: The interplay of affect and cognition in consumer decision making. *Journal of Consumer Research, 26*(3), 278–292.

Silver-Greenberg, J. (2008, October 9). The next meltdown: Credit-card debt. *BusinessWeek*. Available: http:// www.businessweek.com/magazine/content/08_42/b4104024799703.htm

Smith, M. (2008, January 5). Putting your credit card on ice. *Lending Club Blog*. Available: http://blog.lendingclub .com/2008/01/05/putting-your-credit-card-on-ice/

Soman, D. (2001). Effects of payment mechanism on spending behavior: The role of rehearsal and immediacy of payments. *Journal of Consumer Research, 27*, 460–474.

Soman, D. (2003). The effect of payment transparency on consumption: Quasi experiments from the field. *Marketing Letters, 14*, 173–183.

Soman, D., & Ahn, H. (2010). Mental accounting and individual welfare. In G. Keren (Ed.), *Perspectives on framing* (pp. 65–92). New York: Psychology Press.

Soman, D., & Cheema, A. (2001). The effect of windfall gains on the sunk cost effect. *Marketing Letters, 12*, 49–60.

Soman, D., & Cheema, A. (2002). The effect of credit on spending decisions: The effect of credit limit and credibility. *Marketing Science, 21*, 32–53.

Soman, D., Cheema, A., & Xu, J. (2010, Winter). Decision points: A theory emerges. *Rotman Magazine*, pp. 64–74.

Soman, D., & Gourville, J. T. (2001). Transaction decoupling: How price bundling affects the decision to consume. *Journal of Marketing Research, 38*, 30–44.

Soman, D., & Lam, V. (2002). The effects of prior spending on future spending decisions: The role of acquisition liabilities and payments. *Marketing Letters, 13*, 359–372.

Thaler, R. H. (1980). Toward a positive theory of consumer choice. *Journal of Economic Behavior & Organization, 1*, 39–60.

Thaler, R. H. (1981). Some empirical evidence on dynamic inconsistency. *Economic Letters, 8*, 201–207.

Thaler, R. H. (1985). Mental accounting and consumer choice. *Marketing Science, 4*, 199–214.

Thaler, R. H. (1990). Saving, fungibility and mental accounts. *Journal of Economic Perspectives, 4*, 193–205.

Thaler, R. H. (1999). Mental accounting matters. *Journal of Behavioral Decision Making, 12*, 183–206.

Thaler, R. H., & Benartzi, S. (2004). Save More Tomorrow: Using behavioral economics to increase employee saving. *Journal of Political Economy, 112,* 164–187.

Thaler, R. H., & Shefrin, H. M. (1981). An economic theory of self-control. *Journal of Political Economy, 89,* 392–406.

Thaler, R. H., & Sunstein, C. R. (2008). *Nudge: Improving decisions about health, wealth, and happiness.* New Haven, CT: Yale University Press.

Vohs, K. D., & Faber, R. J. (2005). *Spent resources: Self-regulatory resource availability impulse buying.* Unpublished manuscript, University of Minnesota, Minneapolis.

Weber, J. (with Booraem, C. D.). (1996). *Credit limits.* Santa Ana, CA: Eight Fourteen.

Wertenbroch, K. (1998). Consumption self-control by rationing purchase quantities of virtue and vice. *Marketing Science, 17,* 317–337.

Wise, G., Brown, H., & Cox, M. (1977). Profiling the heavy user of consumer credit. *Journal of Consumer Credit Management, 8,* 116–123.

Zelizer, V. A. (1989). The social meaning of money: "Special moneys." *American Journal of Sociology, 95,* 342–377.

Zelizer, V. A. (1997). The many enhancements of money. In K. Erikson (Ed.), *Sociological visions* (pp. 83–94). Lanham, MD: Rowman & Littlefield.

Zellermayer, O. (1996). *The pain of paying.* Unpublished doctoral dissertation, Carnegie Mellon University, Pittsburgh, PA.

# 21

## Employee Retirement Savings

### What We Know and Are Discovering for Helping People Prepare for Life After Work

PUNAM ANAND KELLER AND ANNAMARIA LUSARDI

Crisis seems like an extreme descriptor, but crisis is how the current state of retirement savings has been characterized by many. Several factors contribute to the fact that nearly 45% of Americans will be at risk of being unable to maintain their standard of living in retirement. Current retirees make it look deceptively simple, because they live in a world of Social Security, defined benefit pensions, employee retirement plans, and savings.

Let us fast-forward to future retirees. Increasingly, the responsibility to secure a comfortable retirement has been shifted from the government and the employer onto individual workers. With the shift from defined-benefit to defined-contribution pensions, workers have to decide how much to save and how to allocate retirement wealth over a longer life span. According to the U.S. Census Bureau, the average retirement age in the United States is 62, and the average life expectancy is 77, meaning that 20% of the average American's life span would need to be financially covered between personal savings and Social Security.

One of the reasons why workers have difficulty looking ahead and making plans for the future is that these plans require a lot of information and complex calculations. At the minimum, to calculate lifetime income, one would have to discount the entire stream of future income. In fact, the majority of workers are not very numerate. Several papers have shown that people have difficulties performing simple calculations (Lusardi & Mitchell, 2006). Moreover, financial markets have become more complex, and people have to navigate a system that requires both financial knowledge and financial skills.

President Barack Obama's administration has outlined four initiatives to make it simpler to save. First, the plan calls for expanding opportunities for automatic enrollment in employee 401(k) and other retirement savings plans. Another approach would be to gradually increase worker contribution over time, automatically stepping up contributions with the worker's approval each year. Second, officials hope to make it easier for people to save a portion or all of their tax refunds in the form of a savings bond by checking a box on their tax returns. Senior administration officials said they hope putting tax return money into a savings bond will help whet the appetite of those without a retirement account to start becoming more active in saving. Third, planners want to enable workers to convert their unused vacation or other similar leave into additional retirement savings. Fourth, officials hope to help workers and their employers better understand the available options for tax-favored retirement saving through clear, easy-to-understand language. The Internal Revenue Service and the U.S. Department of the Treasury are creating a plain English, easy-to-follow guide and a website to help people navigate what are often complicated waters, especially for workers changing jobs and are often unsure how best to continue saving for retirement. Rule simplification should encourage, not discourage, people to save.

## WHAT WE ARE DISCOVERING ABOUT WHY AMERICANS DO NOT SAVE

The four initiatives proposed by the Obama Administration involve immediate steps that will help make it easier and more automatic for families to save. Our research on why individuals do not save supports the need for more user-friendly and simplified materials. We undertook several steps to examine the behavioral reasons for retirement saving decisions. We conducted in-depth interviews, focus groups, and field studies to provide insights on why Americans are not motivated and/or are unable to save for retirement (Lusardi, Keller, & Keller, 2008). This initial work was used as the basis for the new research described later in this chapter.

### Motivation: Looking Ahead and Priorities

Younger employees are less likely to save for retirement than older employees and may put off planning for retirement if they subconsciously believe that someone or some thing (e.g., the government, relatives, good luck) will bail them out (Bolton, Cohen, & Bloom, 2006). Even if they believe they need a retirement plan, many younger workers feel like retirement is far away and put off saving for it to pay for current expenses. It is very difficult to choose saving over spending when the latter bestows immediate benefits. In addition, younger employees believe their incomes are malleable, in that they will have more discretionary income and need less income in the future. In one study, only 26% of individuals 30 years of age or younger participated in their supplementary retirement accounts (SRAs) versus 58% of those 60 years of age and older with at least 10 years on the job (Employee Benefits Research Institute, 2007). Hewitt Associates reported that most people put priority on saving for a house, saving for their children's education, or paying for their children's needs rather than retirement (Smith, 2006). Americans are also more likely to prioritize health care benefits over retirement savings. Although the majority of working Americans participated in their companies' health plans in 2004, only a minority of employees participated in their companies' sponsored savings plans (Employee Benefits Research Institute, 2007).

### Ability

An overwhelming decision process hampers retirement saving implementation goals. In focus groups and interviews, employees repeatedly voice uncertainty about how much to invest and how to allocate their investments (Lusardi et al., 2008). There seems to be growing mistrust in the financial markets, and low savers point to people who lost their entire retirement savings despite following the advice of financial experts. Current retirees believe inability to save is related to the younger generations' need for immediate gratification and lack of mindfulness about the future.

We found that lack of attention and absence of planning trip up even those employees who want to save for retirement. Several employees, especially those making less than $35,000 per year and females, stated that the process of beginning and participating in a retirement plan, such as a typical 401(k), can be very overwhelming. The initial process often is perceived as confusing, long, and tedious. Many individuals do not feel comfortable making financial decisions like how to manage their money within an employee plan or 401(k), and they do not read prospectuses or other investor materials. Consistent with this view, many people do not understand how small their savings for retirement actually are. In fact, according to survey results released by the Consumer Federation of America and the Financial Planning Association (2006), 21% of Americans think that winning the lottery, rather than saving, is the most practical way to accumulate several hundred thousands of dollars.

## TARGET AUDIENCE

Our goal is to encourage new employees to voluntarily save for retirement. We focus on female and low-income employees, since this group faces unique saving challenges (Lusardi et al., 2008). These segments of the population are disproportionately less likely to save or take advantage of tax-favored programs and also display low financial literacy. We refer to this group as the target group henceforth.

Employees typically have relied on benefit fairs, carrier presentations, websites, annual benefits packets, and human resource counseling to get information on the value of saving for retirement. In addition, new employees have access to an orientation session when they join an organization. Although important, these programs fail to sufficiently engage the target group to save more for retirement. Prior to our project, the enrollment rate for SRAs was in single digits (~8%). Our goal is to increase SRA election rates to at least 20% among the target audience.

## CONSUMER RESEARCH RELATED TO ENHANCING MOTIVATION TO SAVE

Our review of consumer research was guided by two main issues: (1) how to motivate people to save for retirement, and (2) how to help motivated people implement their saving goals. We turned to the literature related to lay theories on resource slack and self-control to shed light on the communication programs designed to encourage saving for retirement. We relied on the literature on implemental mind-sets, goals, and planning to design communication programs to increase the employees' ability to save for retirement.

### Lay Theories That Undermine Saving for Retirement

Lay theories are basic assumptions that ordinary people hold about themselves and their world (Wyer, 2004). Once acquired, lay theories form an integral part of an individual's belief system (Wyer, 2004) and, therefore, influence judgments and behavior across many, if not most, domains of human behavior (Mukhopadhyay & Johar, 2005). Consumer research has extensively studied lay theories as manifested in decision-making biases (e.g., Dhar & Nowlis, 1999). Given our interest in retirement savings, we were particularly interested in lay theories about resource (i.e., time, money) slack and self-control.

### Resource Slack

Insufficient resources in the form of time and money are probably the most common excuses for not undertaking a task immediately (Soman, 1998, 2004; Zauberman & Lynch, 2005). When consequences occur at different points in time, people tend to accept small rewards in the short term instead of larger long-term rewards. Money and time are discounted in the future, because the value of both future costs and benefits is smaller than their value in the present (Ainslie & Haslam, 1992; Frederick, Loewenstein, & O'Donoghue, 2002; Soman, 2004).

Rather than giving up any future benefit, most people have a lay theory about how they will make up in the future any cost they have not expended in the present. This belief stems from lay theories on resource slack, such as "I will have more (money/time) resources in the future," coupled with "I will need fewer (money/time) resources in the future." Consistent with this premise, Zauberman and Lynch (2005) proposed higher delay discounting or procrastination when (a) an immediate investment in a retirement account would block individuals from obtaining other, more proximal activated goals (e.g., vacation) that require the same resource (i.e., discretionary dollars); and (b) in the future, they would have more slack (e.g., fewer expenses) and thus less sacrifice of other highly valued goals (e.g., vacation). They find that time has more slack than money. Resources that are more fungible (e.g., money compared to time) are more predictable.

How does one reverse delay discounting? Reverse delay discounting will occur when slack in the future is perceived to be lower than slack in the present. In a retirement saving context, overturning lay theories by arguing that there will be less money in the future (i.e., higher taxes, higher health costs, more money spent on kids' colleges) or less ability to work (i.e., poorer health, less energy and time to earn) should reverse delay discounting and encourage retirement savings.

### Self-Control

Consumers tend to be overconfident in their lay theories about how much self-control they have. In general, they believe they will manage the future despite not investing in the present. Mukhopadhyay and Johar (2005) identify two distinct dimensions of lay theories of self-control. First, consumers may differ on how much self-control they and others have, ranging from very small, that is, limited theorists who believe that reserves of self-control are inherently limited (Muraven & Baumeister, 2000), to very large, that is, unlimited theorists who believe that reserves of self-control are practically unlimited, as per much of Western philosophy (cf. Descartes, 1649/1996). A second dimension relevant to such lay theories is whether consumers believe that reserves of self-control can be changed over time. Those who tend to believe they can increase or decrease their self-control over time are malleable theorists, whereas those leaning toward the inclination that reserves of self-control are fixed for all time are fixed theorists. According to this perspective, the least likely to save would be employees who believe they will have large, malleable reserves of self-control in the future.

Consumer researchers have demonstrated the role of lay theories in a savings context. Kivetz and Simonson (2002) found that some people have a lay theory that people in general have too much self-control and, if gifted cash, would spend the money on practical things. Hence, they would prefer to give hedonic items as gifts. The literature also indicates that failure to exert self-control or follow personal rules results in guilt, regret, and loss of faith in oneself (Herrnstein & Prelec, 1991). Soman (2004) calls these psychological costs of breaking personal rules *transgression costs*.

Consumers rely on several counteractive self-control measures to reduce transgression costs. Decision point theory explains one mechanism to enhance self-control or consumption control. The theory of decision points suggests that external interventions can help individuals curb excessive spending or enhance saving by providing them with an opportunity to pause and think about whether they really need to consume more. Soman, Cheema, and Xu (2010) show that decision points can prompt a more deliberative decision-making mode instead of the default automatic mode among motivated individuals who are seeking to control consumption (see also Soman, Cheema, & Chan, Chapter 20 of this volume). Tactics used for enhancing self-control include partitioning or dividing a pool of resources (e.g., food, money, effort) into subsets by creating somewhat artificial boundaries, such as two packets of popcorn or two envelopes of money (Cheema & Soman, 2008); exercising willpower (Hoch & Loewenstein, 1989); precommitments and price premiums (Wertenbroch, 1998); deadlines (Ariely & Wertenbroch, 2002); and binding behaviors, such as restricting access (e.g., vegan restaurants), buying small packages (e.g., 10-calorie packs), and signing contracts (Wertenbroch, 1998).

### Design of Communication Interventions to Motivate Retirement Saving

The literature on resource slack and self-control provides direct evidence on the temptation to procrastinate saving for retirement. The literature on lay theories provides guidelines on why people may be comfortable delaying the saving decision: They believe they will have more time, money, and self-control in the future. In order to design a communication program that would change these lay theories about resource slack and self-control, we first surveyed a group of employees to verify they indeed had these two types of lay theories. A significant percentage of our sample did not believe they needed resources for the following: (a) retirement (40%), (b) emergencies (26%), (c) unexpected expenses (28%), (d) medical expenses (55%), (e) to support children and/or grandchildren (61%), (f) to pay for large durable goods (49%), and (g) security (39%).

Despite overlap on these lay theories, we found that beliefs about saving barriers, retirement lifestyle, and retirement horizons varied by gender and age. For instance, younger women (i.e., less than 35 years of age) were more likely than younger males to believe they would be able to sustain their lifestyle in the future ($t = 3.42$, $p = .07$). Younger males were more worried than older (i.e., more than 35 years of age) males about maintaining their lifestyles in the future ($t = 3.45$, $p = .07$). Lifestyle beliefs were not significantly different among females in different age groups.

Younger women and older men had similar beliefs about why they did not have resource slack. Compared to younger men, younger women believed they could not save for retirement, because they had many unexpected family expenses ($t = 3.55$, $p = .06$) and high debt ($t = 4.29$, $p = .04$). Similarly, compared to younger males, older males were prevented from saving more for retirement due to unexpected family expenses ($t = 3.55$, $p = .06$) and high debt ($t = 4.29$, $p = .04$).

As expected, compared to older females, younger females were more likely to believe that it was hard to save for retirement, because it seemed so far away ($t = 40.12$, $p = .00$), but these beliefs were not significantly different among males in different age groups. Additional retirement saving difficulties for younger women were due to unexpected family expenses ($t = 3.32$, $p = .07$) and from not knowing how much they would need in the future ($t = 4.28$, $p = .04$). Again, younger males did not believe these factors were related to resource slack. Finally, lay theories were remarkably similar among older male and female employees.

To make these lay theories salient and identify ways in which employees challenged their lay theories, we interviewed several employees and elected to videotape four—a younger male, an older male, a low-income female, and a high-income female—all discussing their lay theories, as well as why and how they save for retirement. The interviewer asked specific questions on lay theories, such as "Do you think you will need less for retirement?" and "Do you think you will be able to keep working when you are older?" These four videos may be viewed on the website of the Office of Human Resources at Dartmouth College (http://www.dartmouth.edu/~hrs/benefits/saving_for_retirement.html).

## CONSUMER RESEARCH RELATED TO ENHANCED ABILITY TO SAVE

Behavior that is goal directed depends on some level of planning. However, not all goals are carried out. Often, goals seem more ambitious than the resources we have to carry them out (Ajzen, 1985). The literature identifies several barriers for goal attainment. Uncertainty associated with choice can become burdensome. For example, increasing the number of choice options can undermine motivation (Iyengar & Lepper, 2000). In difficult choice situations, the literature indicates the almost unavoidable propensity of individuals to avoid the decision altogether (Luce, Payne, & Bettman, 2000) or use simple heuristics to make choices, with serious consequences. Methods to reduce choice avoidance range from structuring the choice task to make it simpler (Thaler & Sunstein, 2008) to extreme measures, such as "no choice" default (e.g., autoenrollment; for a critique of these approaches, see Mick & Schwartz, Chapter 32 of this volume). In addition, consumer researchers are questioning the role of unrestricted choice as empowering by examining the downside of having to exercise self-control, experience regret, and overload (Wathieu et al., 2002). We reviewed the literature on the role of process versus outcome information and implemental mind-sets to guide our design of communication programs that would help motivate people to implement their saving goals.

## Plans Versus Outcomes

In contrast to conventional wisdom that focuses on the outcomes of retirement, both positive (e.g., sailing or playing golf without a care in the world) and negative (e.g., going bankrupt), the literature recommends focusing on the process for meeting goals rather than these outcomes. Instructions to simulate how one would achieve the goal result in more goal attainment than simulations that focus on outcomes (Escalas & Luce, 2003, 2004). Escalas and Luce found that mental simulations that required participants to imagine how they would use the product being advertised resulted in higher intentions to purchase than imagining the benefits they would gain from using the product, especially when the advertisement contained strong arguments. The authors expected process-focused thoughts to involve plans, because process simulations are episodic; people imagine events unfolding over time, linking actions to outcomes in a causal manner. Process-focused simulations encourage plan formation of detailed steps to achieve an outcome. By contrast, outcome simulations emphasize the end of the story without the steps being illustrated, which may remain fantasies (Escalas & Luce, 2003).

This literature recommends providing people with instructions to develop a plan by imagining how they would achieve a goal or giving them a concrete plan that is easy to imagine. Although these findings on process-focused mental simulation are prevalent in the consumer and psychology literatures, they contradict much self-help retirement saving advice delivered online or via benefits packets provided to employees by human resources (HR) staff. These findings suggest we may not automatically plan even if we are motivated, and planning aids that focus on the process can facilitate goal attainment.

## Implemental Mind-Sets

Gollwitzer and his colleagues (Gollwitzer 1990; Gollwitzer & Brandstätter, 1997; Gollwitzer, Heckhausen, & Ratajczak, 1990) have shown that unique tasks associated with the different action phases of goal pursuit lead to the activation of appropriate cognitive procedures or mind-sets. When people are deciding whether they should do something, they are in a deliberative mind-set. People switch to an implemental mind-set when they are in the planning phases of goal pursuit. Implementation intentions were more effective in completing difficult tasks than easy ones (Gollwitzer & Brandstätter, 1997). In fact, the effectiveness of forming implementation intentions increases for less routine tasks (Brandstätter, Lengfelder, & Gollwitzer, 2001).

Implemental mind-sets are also especially effective for achieving goals like savings that are possible but not desirable. Brandstätter and Frank (2002) found that an implemental mind-set only enhanced persistence on a task when there was a behavioral conflict between the perceived feasibility and desirability of the task. When feasibility and desirability are low, persistence is higher in the deliberative mind-set condition, whereas an implemental mind-set is more effective when feasibility is high but desirability is low.

The literature provides several guidelines for prompting an implemental mind-set. One method for successful implementation is delegating control to the environment (Gollwitzer, 1990). Relinquishing control to time, for example, might mean taking your vitamins at 10:00 every morning, depositing savings on the first of the month, or setting a deadline (Ariely & Wertenbroch, 2002). Such delegation also converts the choice from passive to active and from a deliberative mind-set to an implemental one.

In addition to an implemental mind-set, plans are more likely to be implemented if they are memorable. Work by Keller and McGill (1994), McGill and Anand (1989), and Krishnamurthy and Sujan (1999) indicates that contextual details facilitate imagery, and more easily imagined information has a disproportionate weight on memory and decision making. There is considerable evidence that mental simulations enhance the subjective probability of an event's occurrence; they contain an implicit plan and can enhance motivation and arousal of an action sequence (Block & Keller, 1997; Keller & Block, 1997; McGill & Anand, 1989; Petrova & Cialdini, 2005; Taylor & Pham, 1999).

## Design of Communication Interventions to Enhance Ability to Save for Retirement

The literature on process versus outcomes and implemental mind-sets provides solid guidelines on ways to enhance employee ability to undertake the various steps required to successfully save for retirement. We used this literature to develop hypotheses on the role of structure, planning, and deadlines to enhance retirement saving behavior. Three approaches were used to design the plan for enhancing employee ability to save for retirement. Given the literature on self-control, we first undertook a series of field experiments to identify the role of deadlines and commitment to reduce the need for self-control and thereby reduce procrastination (Ariely & Wertenbroch, 2002). Then, based on the literature on imagery, we developed a vivid flyer that identified the barriers that undermine ability to save for retirement and provided concrete recommendations to overcome these barriers. Finally, we used consumer literature on implemental mind-sets and process guidelines to develop a step-by-step plan to open a SRA.

### Field Test of Tactics to Reduce Procrastination to Save

We conducted two studies with a broader sample to provide guidelines for interventions that would enhance saving for retirement. The key dependent measure was the same across experiments: whether the employee was willing to join a hypothetical saving program now or 1 year later. In Experiment 1, we varied commitment (low = no contract; high = contract) and deadline (no deadline = put savings in a designated box in your office on any day of the month; deadline = put savings in a box in the central HR office on the first of the month). In Experiment 2, in addition to the commitment (i.e., contract) manipulation, we varied the deadline while keeping the location constant (i.e., no deadline vs. deadline). Experiment 2 was designed to separate the effect of the location and the deadline. Exhibit 21.1 contains sample employee instructions.

The findings across both experiments indicate that deadlines are an effective means of reducing procrastination (see Figure 21.1). There was a main effect of deadline in both experiments (Experiment 1: $F[1, 86] = 3.27, p < .07$; Experiment 2: $F[1, 65] = 4.86, p < .05$). In Experiment 1, more than twice as many employees were willing to wait to join the program a year later in the absence of a deadline (lockbox in office on any day of the month: 36%) versus when a deadline was present (HR on the first of the month: 16%). In Experiment 2, 45% of the employees preferred to wait when the program did not have a deadline (i.e., HR any day of the month) versus the program with a deadline (20th of the month: 19%). In other words, 84% and 81% of employees were willing to join the saving program right away when they were given a saving deadline.

By contrast, the contract increased procrastination in Experiment 1. Sixteen percent of the employees said they would join the program now if they had to sign a contract versus 36% of employees who would join now in the no-contract condition ($F[1, 86] = 3.75, p < .06$). Procrastination increased when the task did not contain a deadline but required high commitment. Forty-six percent of employees preferred to wait a year when they were required to sign a contract with no deadline as compared to only 27% of employees choosing to procrastinate in the high commitment/deadline condition in which they were required to sign a contract and deposit their savings in HR on the first of the month. In Experiment 2, 28% of the employees said they would join now if there was no contract, whereas 37% said they would join now if they had to sign a contract, although this effect was insignificant ($F[1,66] = 0.56, p < .46$).

**Exhibit 21.1**   Sample employee instructions for Experiments 1 and 2

Experiment 1

- *No deadline/low commitment condition:* We would like you to imagine that you are interested in increasing your personal wealth. Your employer tells you about a *hypothetical* program that recommends you contribute $20 per month. You will need to put your money in a locked box that will be in your office.
- *Deadline/low commitment condition:* We would like you to imagine that you are interested in increasing your personal wealth. Your employer tells you about a *hypothetical* program that recommends you contribute $20 per month. You will need to put your money in an envelope with your name and deposit it in the human resources office on the first of every month.
- *No deadline/high commitment condition:* We would like you to imagine that you are interested in increasing your personal wealth. Your employer tells you about a *hypothetical* program in which you sign an annual contract to contribute $20 per month. You will need to put your money in a locked box that will be in your office.
- *Deadline/high commitment condition:* We would like you to imagine that you are interested in increasing your personal wealth. Your employer tells you about a *hypothetical* program in which you sign an annual contract to contribute $20 per month. You will need to put your money in an envelope with your name and deposit it in the human resources office on the first of every month.

Experiment 2

- *No deadline/low commitment condition:* We would like you to imagine that you are interested in increasing your personal wealth. Your employer tells you about a *hypothetical* program that recommends you contribute $20 per month. You will need to put your money in an envelope with your name and deposit it in the human resources office on any day of the month.
- *Deadline/low commitment condition:* We would like you to imagine that you are interested in increasing your personal wealth. Your employer tells you about a *hypothetical* program that recommends you contribute $20 per month. You will need to put your money in an envelope with your name and deposit it in the human resources office on the first of every month.
- *No deadline/high commitment condition:* We would like you to imagine that you are interested in increasing your personal wealth. Your employer tells you about a *hypothetical* program in which you sign an annual contract to contribute $20 per month. You will need to put your money in an envelope with your name and deposit it in the human resources office on any day of the month.
- *Deadline/high commitment condition:* We would like you to imagine that you are interested in increasing your personal wealth. Your employer tells you about a *hypothetical* program in which you sign an annual contract to contribute $20 per month. You will need to put your money in an envelope with your name and deposit it in the human resources office on the first of every month.

Key Dependent Variable Across Conditions

You have the choice of contributing immediately or after one year. Which would you prefer?

Now _____ One year later _____

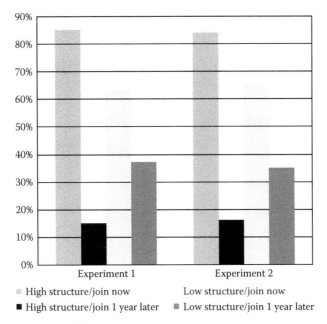

**Figure 21.1**    Field experiment results: High versus low structure.

We also gathered additional information on employee beliefs and attitudes about the hypothetical saving program in Experiment 2. Although employees acknowledged that it would be simpler for them to go to HR any day of the month (i.e., no deadline condition), they were more confident and felt more committed when they were given a deadline (see Table 21.1). The effect of commitment and the interaction effects were insignificant across these dependent measures. The experimental findings suggest the need to convey a sense of urgency and provide employees with the motivation and ability to save for retirement when they are already in the HR office rather than relying on the employees to figure it out for themselves in their workplace.

*Design of Flyer to Overcome Saving Barriers*

We used consumer research on imagery and vividness to design a flyer that addressed the key barriers to saving and ways to overcome these barriers (Keller & McGill, 1994; Krishnamurthy & Sujan, 1999; McGill & Anand, 1989). The barriers were identified in our employee surveys and focus groups (Lusardi et al., 2008) and are contained in Table 21.2. We included several contextual details to facilitate imagery because of the previously mentioned tendency for more easily imagined

**Table 21.1**    Field Experiment Results: Active Versus Passive Choice

|  | Low Structure (any day of month) | High Structure (first day of month) | F Value (significant at $p < .05$) |
|---|---|---|---|
| Decision timing | 1.55 | 1.19 | 4.99 |
| Simple program design | 5.00 | 6.00 | 4.76 |
| Feel confident | 4.73 | 5.52 | 3.42 |
| Feel committed | 4.86 | 5.65 | 3.37 |
| Like program | 4.83 | 5.57 | 3.32 |

**Table 21.2**    Average Ratings of Barriers to Saving for Retirement for Nontarget (>35k Males) and Target (<35k Males and Females, >35k Female) Employees

| Barriers[1] | Mean | $t$ Value (significant at $p < .05$) |
|---|---|---|
| *No time now* | | 2.72 |
| >35k males | 1.39 | |
| <35k males and females + >35k females | 1.72 | |
| *Do not know where to put money* | | 2.25 |
| >35k males | 1.61 | |
| <35k males and females + >35k females | 1.98 | |
| *Few people like me do it* | | 2.82 |
| >35k males | 1.23 | |
| <35k males and females + >35k females | 1.60 | |
| *Do not know how much I will need* | | 1.99 |
| >35k males | 1.60 | |
| <35k males and females + >35k females | 1.90 | |
| *Too many unexpected expenses* | | 2.26 |
| >35k males | 2.10 | |
| <35k males and females + >35k females | 2.57 | |
| *My debt is too expensive* | | 2.06 |
| >35k males | 1.88 | |
| <35k males and females + >35k females | 2.28 | |

[1] Based on orientation survey questions: Please indicate your level of agreement or disagreement with the following statements: 1 (strongly disagree), 3 (neither agree or disagree), 5 (strongly agree).

information to have a disproportionate weight on decision making. To prime imagery, we showed a picture of a woman imagining all the barriers as well as the solutions to help her save more. A sample of this communication intervention is in Figure 21.2.

*Design of Plan to Open a SRA*

We used the findings from the field experiment and the literature on the importance of process versus outcomes, and partitioning, to design a step-by-step plan to help employees open a SRA. The plan used three main findings from the consumer literature: (1) we used the literature on self-control and the results of our field experiments by asking the employees to set a deadline for themselves (Ariely & Wertenbroch, 2002), (2) we broke down the task into small parts to increase self-control (Cheema & Soman, 2008), and (3) we described the saving steps in concrete language, with pictures for each step to enhance imageability (Escalas & Luce, 2003).

Our employee survey indicated that compared to the nontarget group of high-income males, our target group faced six main challenges to save for retirement. Three additional challenges were identified by HR (i.e., do not have income, do not know how to use Flex Online, do not have a computer). These nine barriers were presented in a foldout to subjects with accompanying solutions, as shown in Figure 21.2. Note that the retirement saving information received by employees was provided in the same packet as the health information. Moreover, employees were asked to elect supplementary retirement saving before receiving their first paycheck. It is unclear whether many employees know their net salary (i.e., after taxes and all other contributions) prior to receiving their first check. The process for enrolling in the supplemental pension presents several additional complexities: Employees have to access a provider website to make their investment allocation and have to be able to complete the enrollment process in 20 minutes. For security reasons, the

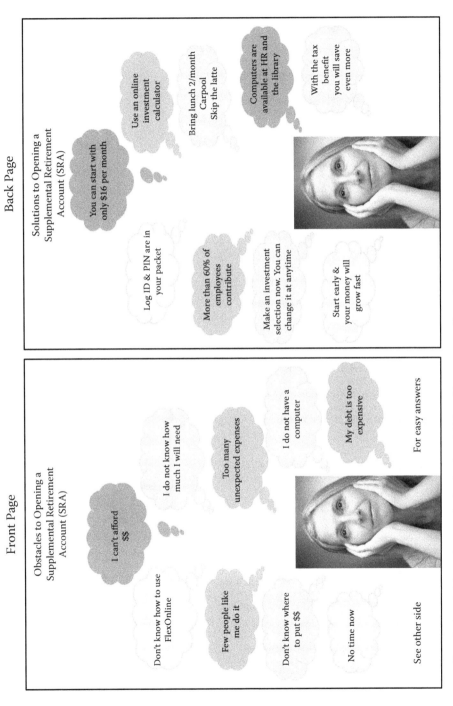

**Figure 21.2** The effect of acknowledging and overturning barriers in a vivid format to encourage retirement savings.

enrollment process automatically restarts if more than 20 minutes elapse. To be able to complete the enrollment in the allocated time, employees need to have prepared in advance. In developing our planning aid, we focused on providing information on how to enroll and ways to simplify enrollment by dividing the task into small, manageable steps. A copy of the planning intervention is in Figure 21.3.

We have outlined seven simple steps to help you
complete the application.

1. Select a 30-minute time slot right now to complete the online contribution to your Supplemental Retirement Account (SRA) during the next week.

2. <u>3 minutes.</u> Check to see if you have the following materials: a) worksheet in your benefits packet _√_, and b) the name and Social Security number of a beneficiary _√_.

3. Select the amount you want to invest for 2007 (minimum: $16/month, maximum: $1,292/month), even if you don't know your take-home pay in your first month. If you want, you can change this amount at a later date. This voluntary contribution is tax deferred, you will not pay taxes on it until you withdraw the funds.

4. <u>5 minutes.</u> Select a carrier. If you do not select a carrier, Dartmouth will invest the nonvoluntary portion of your college funds in a Fidelity Freedom Fund, a fund that automatically changes asset allocation as people age.

5. <u>5 minutes.</u> Now you are ready to complete your worksheet. Complete the worksheet even though you may be unsure of some options. You can change the options in the future.

6. Take your completed worksheet to a computer that is available for 20 minutes. If you like, you can use the one in the Human Resources office at 7 Lebanon Street, Suite 203.

7. <u>15-20 minutes.</u> Log on to Flex Online and complete your online SRA registration within the 20 assigned minutes. Be sure to click on the investment company (TIAA-CREF, Fidelity, or Calvert) to complete the application. You need to set up your account—otherwise your savings will not reach the carrier.

**Figure 21.3** Plan for successfully opening a supplementary retirement account.

## Methodology for New Employee Orientation Intervention

### Dependent Measures

We measured (a) anxiety about future retirement needs; (b) awareness about financial knowledge, including interest in professional advice; and (c) the percentage of female and low-income new college employees who opened a SRA.

### Data Collection Period

We tested the effectiveness of our communication programs by asking employees to compare how they felt before and after exposure to the communication programs. The flyer and plan were included in the benefits packet. One of four videos was shown during orientation.

We selected the first half of the year to test the effectiveness of our communication program, because the second half consisted mainly of male faculty making more than $35,000 who are not in our target group. Of the 24 weeks in the first half of 2008, one of four videos was shown within 12 weeks and not shown during orientation in the remaining weeks. In our target audience, 124 new employees attended orientation from January 2008 through June 2008, 64 of whom watched the video, whereas 60 did not during an otherwise identical orientation session.

## Findings

Our communication interventions attained all three objectives: (1) reduced anxiety levels about future retirement needs; (2) increased awareness about financial knowledge, including interest in professional advice; and (3) increased participation and contribution to SRAs among female and low-income workers compared to a control condition.

### Anxiety

Target employees reported feeling less anxious about future retirement needs after exposure to our communication programs (see Table 21.3). The programs were able to counter the overwhelming impact of the economic crisis on employee anxiety. In an American Psychological Association poll in September 2008, 80% of those surveyed reported that the economy was causing them significant stress, up from 66% of people surveyed the previous April, especially among women. The U.S. Department of the Treasury, the U.S. Department of Labor, and other U.S. federal departments started a website for people experiencing stress. Viewed from this perspective, we could consider the significant reduction in anxiety levels a very positive indicator of the effectiveness of our communication programs.

### Financial Awareness

Our communication programs significantly increased awareness and understanding about future financial needs (see Table 21.3). We added several additional measures to test dimensions of increased salience of financial needs. In particular, our communication programs increased the importance of thinking about the future, the need for personal control over retirement saving, perceived manageability of the future, and the importance of job stability (see Table 21.3).

### Retirement Saving Behavior

We determined the effectiveness of our video programs by comparing the SRA election rates for targeted new employees who watched the videos with those of targeted employees who did not during the same time period of January–June 2008. Table 21.4 contains the election results among employees in our target group who did or did not have a chance to watch the video. Our communication

**Table 21.3** Effects of Communication Programs on Anxiety and Awareness and Understanding of Future Financial Needs

|  | n | Mean | Mean Difference | t Value (significant at p < .01) |
|---|---|---|---|---|
| Anxious about the future[1] | 67 | 3.43 | 0.433 | 4.768 |
| Increased awareness and understanding of future financial needs | 66 | 3.71 | 0.712 | 7.419 |
| Importance of thinking about retirement | 66 | 3.86 | 0.864 | 9.458 |
| Need for personal control over retirement savings | 66 | 3.41 | 0.409 | 4.740 |
| Future seems more manageable | 64 | 3.72 | 0.719 | 7.509 |
| Decision-making process simpler | 66 | 3.42 | 0.424 | 4.281 |
| Importance of job stability | 67 | 3.76 | 0.761 | 7.007 |

[1] Based on orientation survey question: How did the information presented in the video and seven steps make you feel: 1 (less than before), 3 (same as before), 5 (more than before)?

program resulted in a 56.2% increase in election behavior within 30 days of viewing the communications, compared to SRA election rates among targeted employees who were not exposed to our communication program during the same period. The increase was 26.6% after 60 days and 14.1% after 90 days. Thus, we exceeded the goal of a 20% increase in SRA election rates.

To further verify the reliability of our results, we compared SRA election rates for those employees in the target group who watched the video with employees in the target group who did not watch it during the same time period a year earlier, January–June 2007. The election result of the two groups is shown in Table 21.5. Our video program resulted in a 147% increase in election behavior within 30 days of viewing the communication program compared to SRA election rates among targeted employees who were not exposed to it during the same period. The increase was 94% after 60 days and 104% after 90 days. Thus, we obtained dramatic increases in SRA election by showing the video to low-income and female employees.

We examined the effectiveness of the seven-step plan by comparing the group who received it to a control group of new employees who attended employee orientation and received the standard

**Table 21.4** Mean Percentage of Targeted New Employees Electing to Open a Supplementary Retirement Account Among Those Who Watched the Video and Those Who Did Not, January–June 2008

|  | n | Mean |
|---|---|---|
| *Election less than 30 days* | | |
| Did not watch video | 60 | 0.2000 |
| Watched video | 64 | 0.3125 |
| Total | 124 | 0.2581 |
| *Election less than 60 days* | | |
| Did not watch video | 60 | 0.3333 |
| Watched video | 64 | 0.4219 |
| Total | 124 | 0.3790 |
| *Election less than 90 days* | | |
| Did not watch video | 60 | 0.3833 |
| Watched video | 64 | 0.4375 |
| Total | 124 | 0.4113 |

**Table 21.5**  Mean Percent of Targeted New Employees Electing to Open a Supplementary Retirement Account Before (January–June 2007) and After (January–June 2008) the Communication Program

|  | *n* | **Mean** |
|---|---|---|
| *Election less than 30 days* | | |
| Did not watch video | 83 | 0.1325 |
| Watched video | 61 | 0.3279 |
| Total | 144 | 0.2153 |
| *Election less than 60 days* | | |
| Did not watch video | 83 | 0.2169 |
| Watched video | 61 | 0.4262 |
| Total | 144 | 0.3056 |
| *Election less than 90 days* | | |
| Did not watch video | 83 | 0.2169 |
| Watched video | 61 | 0.4426 |
| Total | 144 | 0.3125 |

packet but not the seven-step plan. The control period selected was January 1–July 30, 2006, because online data were not available prior to this period. Those eligible for the control condition were 183 new employees, because they had low incomes or were women. We compared the SRA election within 30 and 60 days between the control and treatment groups. The two groups had comparable demographic characteristics. For example, the average age in the control group was 37.4 (standard deviation [SD] = 10.5), the proportion of low-income employees was 0.428 (SD = 0.49), and the proportion of women was 0.427 (SD = 0.49). The corresponding figures in the treatment groups were 36.42 (SD = 11.0), 0.48 (SD = 0.50), and 0.57 (SD = 0.49).

Table 21.6 contains the effect of the modified planning aid on enrollment at 30 days and 60 days. With respect to the control group, in which 7.3% of targeted employees enrolled in an SRA after 30 days, the percentage of targeted employees who opened an SRA in 30 days tripled (21.7%) after being exposed to our intervention. A much higher fraction, 44.7%, opened an SRA within 60 days, versus an enrollment of 28.9% in the control group after 60 days. Thus, this simple planning aid was extremely effective in inducing targeted employees to enroll in SRAs.

## DISCUSSION

### Meeting the Retirement Saving Challenge

We rarely abandon goals. Instead, we bear the costs of unfulfilled goals. In general, unfulfilled goals can produce a range of feelings from mild regret to extreme despair. In the case of retirement,

**Table 21.6**  Percentage of Targeted Employees Electing Supplementary Retirement Accounts Before and After the Planning Aids

|  | 30 Days After Hire Date | 60 Days After Hire Date | Number of Observations |
|---|---|---|---|
| Control group | 7.3% | 28.9% | 210 |
| Group who received the seven-step intervention | 21.7% | 44.7% | 166 |

unfulfilled retirement goals can also produce serious consequences, such as homelessness and bankruptcy, and can cause unfulfilled health goals.

It is important to understand the barriers that prevent us from attaining goals, especially those that produce extreme economic distress during retirement. Retirement goals often require significant resources in the form of time, ability, money, and in some cases, connections, such as family support. It is no wonder that being motivated to plan and enact goal execution takes on a whole new meaning, such that even serious health consequences or large economic incentives are insufficient for goal attainment.

Our research findings indicate that employees face seemingly insurmountable barriers to attain goals such as saving for retirement. We traced the underlying causes to lack of sufficient motivation and ability. Lay theories have noted that resource slack and self-control lead to low motivation, because employees believe they will have more resource (i.e., money, time) slack in the future, as they will have more and need less. Lack of ability stemmed from small issues (e.g., access to a computer, not knowing the Social Security number of a beneficiary) to large issues (e.g., perceptions of insufficient income, lack of information, not knowing where to start, absence of a plan).

Three cost-effective motivation and planning tools significantly encouraged new female and low-income employees to take immediate action to save in a SRA: (1) we developed a series of employee videos to change lay theories about resource slack, (2) we designed a flyer to encourage employees to imagine their saving barriers and solutions to those barriers, and (3) we created a simple step-by-step plan to open a SRA account. We observed a sharp increase in SRA election for the first intervention compared to a control condition; the election rate more than tripled in the 30-day period and doubled in the 60-day period. The second intervention further improved SRA election, from 21.7% to 27.6%, in the 30-day period and sustained the lift obtained with the first intervention in the 60-day period. Our video program resulted in a 56.2% increase in election behavior within 30 days of viewing the communication program, compared to SRA election rates among targeted employees who were not exposed to it during the same period.

Our research provides valuable insights into designing saving programs. The social marketing approach we employ is atypical for designing saving programs, but it is well suited to deal with the many differences in saving behavior that we observe among individuals. The program relies on motivating and enabling low-income and female employees to overcome barriers to saving. Similar processes can be undertaken to identify barriers and customize programs for different target audiences.

Our approach is a significant departure from other initiatives that have been undertaken to promote saving and contributions to pension plans. Most of these initiatives have relied on automatic enrollment in pension plans. However, contribution rates and asset allocations set by employers hardly match employees' needs. Rather than taking away control, in our approach, we conferred control to employees with the help of an implementation plan. We relied on the consumer research literature for guidelines on substitutes for low self-control. In addition to enhancing self-control in the near future by changing lay theories about the distant future (Mukhopadhyay & Johar, 2005), we made communication more memorable by using concrete, vivid materials (Keller & Block, 1997), encouraged self-imposed deadlines (Ariely & Wertenbroch, 2002), and relied on a step-by-step process rather than encouraging a focus on saving outcomes (Escalas & Luce, 2003, 2004).

The planning aid is not a substitute for automatic enrollment. In fact, with small modification, our aid can complement automatic enrollment programs very well. For example, it can keep employees motivated to stay in pension plans as well as modify their contribution rate and asset allocation to best fit their specific needs. We plan to continue working in this direction and motivate employees to make plans for their retirement.

## Future Research

There are a myriad of consumer research–based interventions that may be used to encourage retirement saving by enhancing self-control and employee empowerment, including emotions based on the emotional appraisal literature; social norms, especially among subcultures; and decision rules that prompt reflection points and increase the feasibility and desirability of retirement saving. The literature on goal progress and abandonment also provides a host of rich guidelines that require testing in a financial planning context. Our findings build on extant research on obstacles to goal fulfillment. In particular, we discuss the role of misplaced beliefs from lay theories, overestimating resource slack, task difficulty, and absence of self-control as key factors that prevent goal achievement. We further rely on the literature to identify tactics to overcome these barriers, including making employees aware of their debilitating lay theories and providing concrete implementation plans with self-imposed deadlines to overcome procrastination. We stay away from specific saving targets, since such targets have been shown to discourage individuals who are already thinking about their actions concretely (Ulkumen & Cheema, 2010). We also recommend that employees should select a date to take action rather than set a deadline. This approach is consistent with lower completion rates for people who fail to meet a deadline versus those who do not set one initially (Soman & Cheema, 2004).

Our interventions do not manage emotion regulation. Although our findings indicate that participants were less anxious after viewing our videos, we do not rely on fear appeals or other emotional appeals in our communication strategy. We chose to use a problem–solution approach rather than a fear-arousal approach to guide our intervention. We chose employees who had saved successfully and opened a SRA rather than employees who were fearful, anxious, and depressed. Our goal was to provide positive role models, a sense of empowerment, and concrete saving methods. Future research should incorporate the role of negative emotions on future planning (i.e., goal abandonment) in general and procrastination, loss of self-control, and intertemporal discounting in particular.

The literature on the best saving methods is equivocal on the role of specific saving goals (e.g., $550) versus ambiguous goals. Specific saving goals have been found to enhance commitment (Hollenbeck & Klein, 1987). However, specific goals can also undermine commitment if they do not provide regular self-reinforcement (Kirschenbaum, Humphrey, & Malett, 1981; Naylor & Ilgen, 1984) or are ambitious (Soman & Cheema, 2004).

We encourage the use of tailored saving interventions. Although our survey suggests the benefits of this, we do not test different implementation plans for different types of employees. Our sample size did not permit an examination of gender/age congruency between the video spokesperson and the employee. In addition to the demographic variables, recent research has promoted the use of construal level (Ulkumen & Cheema, 2010) and regulatory focus (Lee, Keller, & Sternthal, 2010) as possible moderating variables. Ulkumen and Cheema found that specific saving goals are more important and effective for people who think about why they pursue other goals (e.g., physical health) versus people who think about how they pursue other goals. Lee, Keller, and Sternthal found that people who strive for achievement and growth (i.e., a promotion orientation) are more persuaded by information that is construed at high levels, such as why they should save, whereas people who are regulated by safety and security (i.e., a prevention orientation) are more persuaded by information that is construed at lower levels, such as how much to save. Together, these studies have supported the use of psychological segmentation variables, especially those related to goal formation to promote saving behaviors.

## CONCLUSIONS

When examining the reasons why so many households do not save, Lusardi and Mitchell (2006) found that only one third of older respondents have ever tried to calculate how much they need to save for their retirement. Widespread lack of planning is also evident in studies about workers' knowledge of Social Security and pensions, two of the most important components of retirement wealth. As many as half of older workers do not know or are wrong about the type of pensions they have, whether defined benefit, defined contribution, or a combination of the two, and even fewer know how much money they have in their pensions. Only a small fraction of workers know about the rules governing their Social Security benefits. As noted in the Employee Benefit Research Institute report on the 2007 annual Retirement Confidence Survey, even though it has been 24 years since legislation was passed that increased in increments the normal retirement age for Social Security and despite 8 years of annual mailings of individual benefit statements from the Social Security Administration, only 18% of workers know the age at which they will be entitled to full Social Security benefits. The major drawback of extant company approaches to enhance retirement saving is that they either do not involve the customer/employee at all (e.g., autoenrollment), or they only appeal to audiences who already have considerable financial assets.

We have developed a unique approach to counter the retirement saving challenge by devising relatively inexpensive motivation and implementation tools for low-income and female employees. We have two main recommendations. First, we recommend designing communication initiatives to overcome barriers to save for retirement. We have identified barriers and solutions that can be used by other organizations. A simple flyer describing the barriers and providing simple solutions and a step-by-step saving plan went a long way in simplifying an overwhelming financial decision process.

Our second recommendation is based on the premise that there is no one-size-fits-all solution to the retirement savings crisis. Our findings demonstrate the importance of tailoring motivational and implementation materials for low-income and female employees. Based on employee input, we created four videos: two for females varying in income and two for males varying in age. Our data from the focus groups and in-depth interviews may be used by other organizations seeking to create their own employee videos, or they may use ours. We have demonstrated that we can dramatically increase retirement saving by tailoring communications for different employee audiences. Overall, the opportunities are promising for Transformative Consumer Research to make important and useful discoveries for assisting people in saving for retirement.

## ACKNOWLEDGMENTS

We would like to thank the National Endowment for Financial Education for its guidance and financial support. We would also like to thank Vice President of Finance Adam Keller and the staff of the Office of Human Resources at Dartmouth College.

## REFERENCES

Ainslie, G., & Haslam, N. (1992). Self-control. In G. Loewenstein & J. Elster (Eds.), *Choice over time* (pp. 57–92). New York: Russell Sage Foundation.

Ajzen, I. (1985). From intentions to actions: A theory of planned behavior. In J. Kuhl & J. Beckmann (Eds.), *Action control: From cognition to behavior* (pp. 429–438). Berlin: Heidelberg.

Ariely, D., & Wertenbroch, K. (2002). Procrastination, deadlines, and performance: Self-control by precommitment. *Psychological Science, 13*(3), 219–224.

Block, L. G., & Keller, P. A. (1997). Effects of self-efficacy and vividness on the persuasiveness of health communications. *Journal of Consumer Psychology, 6*(1), 31–54.

Bolton, L. E., Cohen, J. B., & Bloom, P. N. (2006). Does marketing products as remedies create "get out of jail free cards"? *Journal of Consumer Research, 33*(June), 71–81.

Brandstätter, V., & Frank, E. (2002). Effects of deliberative and implemental mindsets on persistence in goal-directed behavior. *Personality and Social Psychology Bulletin, 18,* 1366–1378.

Brandstätter, V., Lengfelder, A., & Gollwitzer, P. M. (2001). Implementation intentions and efficient action initiation. *Journal of Personality and Social Psychology, 81*, 946–960.

Cheema, A., & Soman, D. (2008). The effect of partitions on controlling consumption. *Journal of Marketing Research, 45*(December), 665–675.

Consumer Federation of America & Financial Planning Association. (2006, January 9). *How Americans view personal wealth vs. how financial planners view this wealth*. Available: http://www.consumerfed.org/index .php/financial-services/saving-and-spending

Descartes, R. (1996). Les passions de l'âme [The passions of the soul]. In C. Adam & P. Tannery (Eds.), *Oeuvres de Descartes. Vol. 11* (pp. 368–369), Paris: Vrin/CNRS. (Original work published 1649)

Dhar, R., & Nowlis, S. M. (1999). The effect of time pressure on consumer choice deferral. *Journal of Consumer Research, 25*(March), 369–384.

Employee Benefits Research Institute. (2007). *Retirement confidence survey—2007 results*. Washington, DC: Author. Available: http://www.ebri.org/surveys/rcs/2007

Escalas, J., & Luce, M. F. (2003). Process vs. outcome thought-focus and narrative advertising. *Journal of Consumer Psychology, 13*(3), 246–254.

Escalas, J., & Luce, M. F. (2004). Understanding the effects of process-focused versus outcome-focused thought during advertising. *Journal of Consumer Research, 31*(2), 274–286.

Frederick, S., Loewenstein, G., & O'Donoghue, T. (2002). Time discounting and time preference: A critical review. *Journal of Economic Literature, 40*, 351–401.

Gollwitzer, P. M. (1990). Implementation intentions: Strong effects of simple plans. *American Psychologist, 54*, 493–503.

Gollwitzer, P. M. (1996). The volitional benefits of planning. In J. Bargh & P. Gollwitzer (Eds.), *The psychology of action* (pp. 287–312). New York: Guilford.

Gollwitzer, P. M., & Brandstätter, V. (1997). Implementation intentions and effective goal pursuit. *Journal of Personality and Social Psychology, 73*, 186–199.

Gollwitzer, P. M., Heckhausen, H., & Ratajczak, H. (1990). From weighing to willing: Approaching a change decision through pre- or postdecisional mentation. *Organization Behavior and Human Decision Processes, 45*, 41–65.

Herrnstein, R. J., & Prelec, D. (1991). Melioration: A theory of distributed choice. *Journal of Economic Perspectives, 5*(3), 137–156.

Hoch, S. J., & Loewenstein, G. F. (1989). Outcome feedback: Hindsight and information. *Journal of Experimental Psychology: Learning, Memory, and Cognition, 15*(4), 605–619.

Hollenbeck, J. R., & Klein, H. J. (1987). Goal commitment and the goal-setting process: Problems, prospects and proposals for future research. *Journal of Applied Psychology, 72*(2), 212–220.

Iyengar, S., & Lepper, M. R. (2000). When choice is demotivating: Can one desire too much of a good thing? *Journal of Personality and Social Psychology, 79*(6), 995–1006.

Keller, P. A., & Block, L. G. (1997). Vividness effects: A resource-matching perspective. *Journal of Consumer Research, 24*(December), 295–304.

Keller, P. A., & McGill, A. (1994). Differences in the relative influence of product attributes under alternative processing conditions: Attribute importance versus attribute ease of imageability. *Journal of Consumer Psychology, 3*(1), 29–49.

Kirschenbaum, D. S., Humphrey, L., & Malett, S. D. (1981). Specificity of planning in adult self-control: An applied investigation. *Journal of Personality and Social Psychology, 40*, 941–950.

Kivetz, R., & Simonson, I. (2002). Self-control for the righteous: Towards a theory of pre-commitment to indulgence. *Journal of Consumer Research, 29*(September), 199–217.

Krishnamurthy, P., & Sujan, M. (1999), Remembering versus anticipating: The role of the ad under retrospective and anticipatory self-referencing. *Journal of Consumer Research, 26*(June), 55–69.

Lee, A. Y., Keller, P. A., & Sternthal, B. (2010). Value from regulatory construal fit: The persuasive impact of fit between consumer goals and message concreteness. *Journal of Consumer Research, 36*(February), 735–748.

Luce, M. F., Payne, J. W., & Bettman, J. R. (2000). Coping with unfavorable attribute values in choice. *Organizational Behavior and Human Decision Processes, 81*(2), 274–299.

Lusardi, A., & Keller, P. A. (2006). *Message design to change behavior*. Unpublished manuscript, Dartmouth College, Hanover, NH.

Lusardi, A., Keller, P. A., & Keller, A. M. (2008). New ways to make people save: A social marketing approach. In A. Lusardi (Ed.), *Overcoming the saving slump: How to increase the effectiveness of financial education and saving programs* (pp. 209–220). Chicago: University of Chicago Press.

Lusardi, A., & Mitchell, O. S. (2006). *Financial literacy and planning: Implications for retirement wellbeing.* Unpublished manuscript, Pension Research Council, The Wharton School, University of Pennsylvania, Philadelphia.

Lusardi, A., & Mitchell, O. S. (2007). Baby boomer retirement security: The role of planning, financial literacy, and housing wealth. *Journal of Monetary Economics, 54,* 205–224.

McGill, A. L., & Anand, P. (1989). The effect of imagery on information processing strategy in a multiattribute choice task. *Marketing Letters, 1,* 7–16.

Mukhopadhyay, A., &. Johar, G. V. (2005). Where there is a will, is there a way? Effects of lay theories of self-control on setting and keeping resolutions. *Journal of Consumer Research, 31*(March), 779–786.

Muraven, M., & Baumeister, R. (2000). Self-regulation of limited resources: Does self-control resemble a muscle? *Psychological Bulletin, 126*(March), 247–259.

Naylor, J. C., & Ilgen, D. R. (1984). Goal setting: A theoretical analysis of a motivational technology. In L. Commings & B. Staw (Eds.), *Research in organizational behavior* (Vol. 6, pp. 95–140). Greenwich, CT: JAI Press.

Petrova, P. K., & Cialdini. R. B. (2005). Fluency of consumption imagery and the backfire effects of imagery appeals. *Journal of Consumer Research, 32*(December), 442–452.

Smith, L. (2006, July 16). The generation gap. *Investopedia.* Available: http://www.investopedia.com/articles/pf/06/generationgap.asp?viewed=1

Soman, D. (1998). The illusion of delayed incentives: Evaluating future money–effort transactions. *Journal of Marketing Research, 34,* 427–437.

Soman, D. (2000). The mental accounting of sunk time costs: Why time is not like money. *Journal of Behavioral Decision Making, 14*(3), 169–185.

Soman, D. (2004). The effect of time delay on multi-attribute choice. *Journal of Economic Psychology, 25*(2), 153–175.

Soman, D., & Cheema, A. (2002). The effect of credit on spending decisions: The role of the credit limit and credibility. *Marketing Science, 21*(1), 32–53.

Soman, D., & Cheema, A. (2004). When goals are counterproductive: Effects of violation of a behavioral goal on subsequent performance. *Journal of Consumer Research, 31*(June), 52–62.

Soman, D., Cheema, A., & Xu, J. (2010, Winter). Decision points: A theory emerges. *Rotman Magazine,* pp. 64–74.

Taylor, S. E., & Pham, L. B. (1999). From thought to action: Effects of process- versus outcome-based mental simulations on performance. *Personality and Social Psychology Bulletin, 25*(2), 250–260.

Thaler. R. H., & Sunstein, C. R. (2008). *Nudge: Improving decisions about health, wealth, and happiness.* New Haven, CT: Yale University Press.

Ulkumen, G., & Cheema, A. (2010). *Framing goals to influence personal savings: The role of specificity and construal level.* Unpublished manuscript, University of Virginia, Charlottesville.

Wathieu, L., Brenner, L., Carmon, Z., Chattopadhyay, A., Wertenbroch, K., Drolet, A., et al. (2002). Consumer control and empowerment: A primer. *Marketing Letters, 3*(August), 297–305.

Wertenbroch, K. (1998). Consumption self-control by rationing purchase quantities of virtue and vice. *Marketing Science, 17*(4), 317–337.

Wyer, R. S., Jr. (2004). *Social comprehension and judgment: The role of situation models, narratives, and implicit theories.* Mahwah, NJ: Erlbaum.

Zauberman, G., & Lynch, J. G. (2005). Resource slack and propensity to discount delayed investments of time versus money. *Journal of Experimental Psychology, 134*(1), 23–37.

# VII

## *OTHER RISKY BEHAVIORS AND AT-RISK CONSUMERS*

# 22

# A Model of Self-Regulation
## Insights for Impulsive and Compulsive Problems With Eating and Buying

RONALD J. FABER AND KATHLEEN D. VOHS

Self-regulation is both a boon and burden for modern humans. The elongated time perception that enables people to envision the future (Suddendorf & Busby, 2003; Wheeler, Stuss, & Tulving, 1997), and therefore form the basis for self-regulation (Baumeister, 2005), is said to be one of humankind's most unique capacities (Roberts, 2002). As a boon, self-regulation enables people to direct their actions and modulate their innermost thoughts and feelings, which is necessary for the accomplishment of goals that must occur over time. As a burden, self-regulation is psychologically costly (Baumeister, Bratslavsky, Muraven, & Tice, 1998; Vohs & Heatherton, 2000), requires multiple steps for success (Carver & Scheier, 1990), and is vulnerable to subtle cognitive biases (Zhang, Fishbach, & Kruglanski, 2007). Considering all of the spheres that play a role in self-regulation (i.e., attention, performance, emotion, cognition, impulses), it is unsurprising that self-regulatory failures are common. The causes and consequences of these failures are exceptionally important in understanding and modifying human behavior.

A small lapse in self-regulation may not be a big concern. A dieter may give in to eating a fattening desert, a person trying to save money may succumb to purchasing a new pair of shoes, or an individual trying to complete a work project may yield to the temptation to stop working and engage in a pleasurable activity. After the lapse, if the individual can reestablish self-control and maintain it, the indiscretion is unlikely to harm the achievement of the overall goal. However, over time, repeated lapses may thwart the achievement of desired goals.

For some people and in some situations, a lapse in self-regulation can snowball, which is sometimes described as an abstinence violation effect (Marlatt, 1985) and is most common when a person is trying to completely avoid consuming a forbidden substance or activity. There is no room for tolerance of failure when the goal is complete abstinence. If an initial violation occurs in this situation, it is likely to create an emotional response, such as a feeling of hopelessness or guilt. The effort to contain these negative emotions requires attention and self-regulatory effort, which further depletes resources, and the result is often even greater consumption of the forbidden substance (Baumeister, Heatherton, & Tice, 1994). In this situation, people often view their long-term goal as hopeless and give up trying.

Another factor that can cause a temporary self-regulation failure is deindividualism (Le Bon, 1895/2002), which refers to a loss of self-awareness that can occur when a person feels submerged in a group. In this situation, the group norms or standards replace those of the individual. Thus, a person may decide not to imbibe alcohol or eat fattening foods, but when they get together with friends, they momentarily forget about those plans and go along with what everyone else is doing. This lack of self-awareness prevents monitoring one's progress toward a goal and allows for a lapse in self-control.

The examples above represent normal failures of self-regulation and may be overcome with better knowledge and planning. However, in extreme cases, there can be a complete breakdown of self-regulation. In this case, a problem behavior becomes chronic and uncontrollable and leads to severe problems for the individual. Disorders such as bulimia, binge-eating behavior, and compulsive buying represent examples of these types of problems. These self-regulatory failures occur for different reasons than ordinary lapses and typically require professional intervention to overcome. People suffering from these problems may allow self-regulation failures to occur to provide temporary relief from an overwhelming sense of negative self-feelings. Experiencing a temporary relief reinforces these behaviors and fosters chronic and repetitive self-regulatory failure.

The consumption domain is particularly interesting and valuable to the study of these different types of self-regulation failures. As humans evolved to form groups that then developed into cultures, the role of people as consumers (cf. *Homo economicus*; Horan, Bulte, & Shogren, 2005) grew in importance and brought about advances in trade, innovation, and attendant life quality. Studying consumption is still crucial today, not to help advance culture but to understand the challenges to self-regulation that arise from the abundance of consumption opportunities that impinge on consumers. Defining consumption broadly, it is not an overstatement to say that people are consumers almost every moment awake. As a result, the ability to regulate their consumption behaviors has a big impact on their lives. This chapter focuses on two realms of consumption—eating and purchasing—to illustrate how self-regulation works and why failures of self-regulation occur. It is hoped that by understanding when and why we have failures in self-regulation, we can develop better strategies to overcome them and help people achieve the long-terms goals they desire.

## DEFINITIONS AND CONCEPTUAL CONSIDERATIONS

There are several related terms that are often confused for one another. The term *self-control* refers to intentional, conscious processes related to suppressing or maintaining targeted behaviors or responses. A related term, *self-discipline*, indicates people's actions to achieve deliberate goals that are often in the service of self-improvement. Thus, the concept of self-control is superordinate to the narrower construct of self-discipline. The terms *self-control* and *self-regulation* are also frequently used interchangeably but differ in subtlety. *Self-regulation* is a broader term used to indicate the changing or guidance of responses (i.e., automatic, conscious), aimed at achieving goal attainment, whereas the term *self-control* is limited to conscious, volitional efforts (Vohs & Baumeister, 2004). Last, there is the concept of executive functioning. This multidimensional construct is often invoked in cognitive or clinical science and is frequently connected to neurology. The term *executive functioning* is generally interpreted as meaning the ability to set goals or plans, the capacity to inhibit prepotent impulses, a motivational component related to the actual process of goal pursuit, and flexibility in changing plans as needed. Executive functioning is so close to self-control that its definition often includes this phrase: "freeing an organism from innate, hard-wired drives and reflexes, as well as from over-practiced, over-learned, and prepotent responses" (Suchy, 2009, p. 106), which is precisely what self-control is said to do as well. This chapter is aimed at explicating the ability to exert self-control and its impact on eating and spending. In doing so, we include discussion of many self-regulation and executive functioning processes but not as much in the way of self-discipline.

## A MODEL OF SELF-REGULATION

Self-regulation is viewed by some behavioral scientists as among the most important determinants of achieving a healthy, successful, and happy life (Vohs & Baumeister, 2004). There are three primary components to the self-regulation process: (1) setting or establishing self-standards, (2) monitoring the distance between one's current state and the standard, and (3) moving from one's current state to the desired one. Problems in self-regulation and self-control can occur at each stage.

One may fail to recognize the need to engage in self-control. Students, for example, sometimes fail to control their buying behavior, because they believe that their parents will bail them out if they get into financial difficulty, or they fail to appreciate that debt will be a problem at some point. Additionally, problems in setting appropriate goals can occur because of conflicting standards. College students often experience this problem when they initially go off to school. They may have been raised with one set of standards (e.g., do not stay up too late, do not engage in sexual activities, study hard), but when they get to college, they may observe people they admire behaving differently from their own behavior. This can create confusion about which of the conflicting set of standards they want for themselves, and this confusion may ultimately result in poor self-regulation.

Second, failure to monitor can cause self-regulatory lapses. This aspect of self-regulation failure often involves a lack of self-awareness. For example, alcohol consumption may make people less aware of their own behaviors and thus less able to engage in self-control (Hull, 1981). Similarly, preoccupation with one concern, such as a romantic relationship, may make it difficult for people to attend to other areas of their lives, and hence they fail to engage in self-control.

The third step of self-regulation, behaving in a way consistent with moving toward a desired goal, is where many problems in self-control occur. One can think of this aspect as a competition between the desire to engage in a behavior that is in opposition to one's goal (e.g., wanting to eat a piece of chocolate cake while trying to lose weight) and the strength of the self-regulatory system being the ability to stop the desire and keep people on the path toward their goal (e.g., lose weight). Self-regulatory resources can make a huge difference between success and failure. These resources are needed to help the person carry through on their goal.

## Limited-Resource Model of Self-Regulation

People typically have goals in many different areas at any point in time, and these multiple goals can conflict or influence each other. The limited-resource model of self-regulation (Baumeister & Heatherton, 1996) posits that the ability to self-regulate is governed by a common pool of volitional resources. Thus, if one is exerting self-control in one domain, such as focusing on writing a manuscript, then he or she may have fewer resources available in the short term to maintain self-regulation in another area, such as eating healthy foods. The limited-resource model states that self-regulation acts much like a muscle, such that it can be built up with frequent use in the long term, but it can be fatigued by excessive effort in the short term.

Direct tests of the limited-resource model of self-regulation have demonstrated that self-regulatory depletion occurs when immediately preceded by another self-regulatory endeavor. Vohs and Baumeister (2004) identified five major domains of self-control: attention control, impulse override, emotion modification or maintenance, thought suppression, and behavioral guidance. Recent findings show that making choices also taps into this limited well of resources (Vohs et al., 2008). More than 130 published studies support a hang-over effect of prior self-control or decision making on later self-control. Although theorists had implicated self-regulation resources as an important predictive mechanism in consumer behavior (Baumeister, 2002), until recently, there had been little empirical evidence to support this assumption. However, recent work has begun to show the importance of self-regulation and the regulatory resource model for consumer actions and decisions. For instance, one recent study found that persisting on a difficult task leaves people less able to resist a persuasive sales message (Fennis, Janssen, & Vohs, 2009). Similarly, making decisions about consumer products weakens people's ability to drink a healthy but bad-tasting drink in a setting akin to asking people to take their medicine (Vohs et al., 2008). These studies illustrate that the self-regulatory demands that occur in consumption situations can temporarily deplete global self-regulatory strength. A better understanding of these can help us develop more successful strategies for achieving desired goals. The following sections try to demonstrate this in the domains of eating and purchasing.

Dieting Failure Due to a Loss of Self-Control

The importance of self-regulation and temptation in eating has long been recognized by theoreticians and empiricists. Delay of gratification experiments by Mischel and colleagues (e.g., Mischel, Shoda, & Peake, 1988) illustrated the difficulty in self-stopping under tempting conditions. Festinger (1962) argued in dissonance theory that people who resist temptation under conditions of mild threat will come to devalue the object and desire it less. Conversely, people who resist temptation under conditions of strong threat will increase their desire for the object. For instance, a child whose older brother casts a disapproving look at a beloved toy might react to this mild threat by wanting to play with the toy less than before. Yet, if the same child's mother says that he or she absolutely cannot under any circumstances play with the toy, this might result in a stronger wanting for it. New research (Litt, Khan, & Shiv, 2010) indicates that although this situation might bring about an increase in wanting for the toy, the perceived attractiveness of the toy is diminished in a clear separation of wanting and liking (Litt, Pirouz, & Shiv, Chapter 25 of this volume; Robinson & Berridge, 1993).

Experiments conducted by researchers examining dissonance and delay of gratification have typically used external demands to manipulate the need to resist temptation. However, in daily life, people most often decide for themselves whether an object is off-limits or should be denied. Thus, people frequently create their own regulatory guides (Higgins, 1996).

Dieting provides an excellent example of a common experience that requires resisting temptation. First, dieting is one of the most commonly self-regulated behaviors in contemporary Western society. Americans spend tens of billions of dollars on dieting programs each year. One survey of college women showed that at least half of them are actively trying to lose weight, and 70% consider their current body weight to be at least 10 pounds too heavy (Heatherton, Nichols, Mahamedi, & Keel, 1995). Second, there is substantial evidence that long-term weight loss is extremely difficult to achieve. Extensive reviews of the literature indicate that fewer than 5% of people who lose weight maintain their weight loss over 5 years. Moreover, many people who lose weight not only regain the pounds they lost but also add additional pounds to their prediet weight (Mann et al., 2007). Therefore, the goal of weight loss, which is frequently accompanied by regulation of caloric intake, appears to be an especially elusive one. In short, dietary inhibition is an important and practical domain in which to study consumption problems (see also Grier & Moore, Chapter 15 of this volume).

Dieters engage in classic self-regulatory behavior when they try to override normal eating motives (i.e., hunger) by focusing on long-term weight loss goals. As mentioned, most of these self-regulatory efforts end in failure. There have been many factors cited as contributing to difficulty restricting calories, such as biological theories (e.g., Meyer & Stunkard, 1993), eating to overcome negative feelings (Vohs, Bardone, Joiner, Abramson, & Heatherton, 1999), intrusion of processes that produce boomerang or counterproductive results due to suppressing thoughts about food (Herman & Polivy, 1993), and the necessity of food for individual survival and evolution of the species (Heatherton & Vohs, 1998). In the end, however, the main reason that diets fail is that dieters occasionally or frequently give in to temptation, and the ensuing disinhibited eating sabotages weight loss goals.

The work on dieting represented an excellent example of how self-regulation theory can apply to real-life consumption situations, insofar as it uses situational manipulations that mirror everyday experiences. One area of study in self-regulation is the impact of proximity to temptation (Vohs & Heatherton, 2000; Wansink, Painter, & Lee, 2006). People seated next to desirable candies devote more cognitive energies to thinking about them, feel more tempted to eat them, and consume more than those sitting more physically distant from the candies.

Vohs and Heatherton (2000) were interested in determining whether being highly tempted through close proximity would lead dieters to use up some of their self-regulatory resources to resist eating candies. After first sitting either near or farther away from M&M's, participants were asked to taste and rate three flavors of ice cream to assess taste attributes (e.g., creaminess, saltiness). In actuality, the researchers were interested in the quantity of ice cream consumed, since one only needs to sample a small amount to perform the ratings task. As predicted, sitting next to tempting snacks, rather than sitting farther way, depleted the self-regulatory capacity of dieters more, as evidenced by their eating larger amounts of ice cream in the subsequent ratings task. This finding is intriguing, because eating a great amount of ice cream is a behavior counter to the goal of controlling caloric intake. Dieters who were seated farther away from the M&M's were not depleted, however, as evidenced by their eating an equivalent amount of ice cream as dieters who were not exposed to the tempting candies at all.

Although these experiments only focused on one domain (i.e., food), additional experiments in this study showed that the limited-resource model of self-regulation operates across domains. One experiment demonstrated that dieters, after being tempted by snacks considered to be off-limits because of their high-fat and high-calorie content, were less able to persist at a challenging, unsolvable task relative to dieters who performed the same task but had not been previously tempted by snack foods. In another experiment, the eating versus noneating self-regulation domains were transposed. Dieters watched an extremely sad movie clip either naturally (i.e., "as if you were in your own home") or while being asked to suppress all emotional reactions (i.e., "as if someone watching you could not tell that you were feeling anything whatsoever"). Later, they were given the ice cream taste and rate task described before. As expected, having to suppress their emotions burdened their self-control system and led them to be less successful in keeping their diet. The dieters who were told to control their emotions ate more ice cream than did those who watched the same movie while letting their emotions flow. As these experiments have shown, depleting self-regulatory resources is not domain specific.

In sum, the failure to maintain control over eating is a pernicious problem for today's society. For the first time in known history, children have a lower life expectancy than their parents due to rising obesity rates (Grier & Moore, Chapter 15 of this volume; Olshansky et al., 2005). This shocking prediction tells scholars two things: (1) It is clearly quite difficult to manage one's weight; and (2) if societies do not start addressing this epidemic soon, money and lives will be wasted. While a great many factors contribute to the problem of obesity, we believe that the limited-resource model of self-regulation can help explain why some failures occur and can be useful in helping people better maintain control of their eating.

## Impulse Buying Due to a Loss of Self-Control

Another domain in which people regularly develop self-restraint goals is in their spending. People are frequently trying to accumulate money for specific purchases (e.g., car, vacation, new clothes). One needs to practice self-control to refrain from buying some products in order to afford others. As a result, exerting some degree of self-regulation regarding spending is often necessary (see also Loewenstein, Cryder, Benartzi, & Previtero, Chapter 19 of this volume). Many people experience self-control failure here, too. Although Americans' savings rate has been going up slightly the past few years, due in part to negative economic conditions and the fear of unemployment, it is still low. According to the U.S. Bureau of Economic Analysis (2010), Americans are currently saving about 5% of disposal income, although for most of this decade, the savings rate has been below 3%.

One difficulty people have in regulating their spending behavior is with resisting impulse purchases. Impulse buying is generally considered to be an unplanned purchase when there is a compelling urge to buy, a desire for immediate gratification, and the decision process is made rapidly and without thoughtful deliberation (Kacen & Lee, 2002; Piron, 1991). It has been characterized as resulting from a conflict between desire and self-control (Hoch & Loewenstein, 1991). Sometimes, desire can be greatly heightened, such as when one encounters a great sale or price discount or finds an item that meets a long-held need. Often, however, impulse buying results from a temporary drop in willpower. Despite the fact that consumers have often reported that impulse buying occurs in response to strong urges (Rook, 1987; Rook & Hoch, 1985), one study found that the urge to buy only accounted for 20% of the variance in impulse buying (Beatty & Ferrell, 1998). Thus, it would seem that factors influencing the ability to exert self-control may be particularly important in achieving spending goals.

Proximity influences a person's ability to resist a buying urge. As was the case with eating behavior, being physically near a product makes it harder to resist (Hoch & Loewenstein, 1991). Temporal proximity may also make it difficult to resist buying. Consumers have described impulse buying as an unexpected, immediate, and intense urge to buy (Rook, 1987; Rook & Hoch, 1985). Some consumers stated that they try to control this initial rush of desire by practicing delay strategies to prevent themselves from buying (Rook & Hoch, 1985). For example, they may decide to think about the item for a while before buying, and if they still want it later, then they can come back and buy it. This temporal delay provides an opportunity for consumers to escape the initial surge of desire and control the urge to buy.

Another factor that influences impulse buying is mood state (Rook & Gardner, 1993; Weinberg & Gottwald, 1982). Consumers are more likely to buy impulsively when they are in a good mood (Beatty & Ferrell, 1998; Rook & Gardner, 1993). This may be because they are trying to extend this pleasant feeling (Rook & Gardner, 1993), or being in a positive mood may bias judgments in a positive direction (Gardner, 1985).

A recent series of experiments has also shown that depleted self-regulatory resources can affect impulse buying (Vohs & Faber, 2003, 2007). In one study (Vohs & Faber, 2003), participants in the resource depletion condition were instructed to watch a boring, silent video but avoid looking at random words appearing on the bottom of the screen. The control (i.e., no depletion) participants viewed the same tape but with no instructions to avoid attention to any content. Following exposure to the video, participants completed a supposedly unrelated task that included filling out a modified version of the buying impulsiveness scale (Rook & Fisher, 1995). This scale was designed to assess trait impulse buying, but in the current experiment, it was reworded to assess the desire to buy impulsively at that point in time (i.e., state scale). The results of this study indicated that participants in the resource depletion condition scored significantly higher on the modified (i.e., state) buying impulsiveness scale than did the no depletion participants. Thus, reducing self-regulatory resources seemed to increase the propensity for impulse buying.

In another experiment (Vohs & Faber, 2007), self-regulatory resources were similarly manipulated with an attention control task, after which participants were shown pictures of 18 high-priced items (e.g., expensive watches, luxury cars). Participants were asked to indicate how much they would be willing to pay for each item. The results showed that participants with depleted resources reported that they would pay significantly more for the items than did the no depletion participants. A more recent study (Ackerman, Goldstein, Shapiro, & Bargh, 2009) found that just imagining having to engage in self-regulation (e.g., not eating tempting food) was enough to lead people to say they would pay more for products.

A third experiment used a different manipulation of self-regulatory resources to assess actual impulse buying. Here, people were told that the researchers were interested in thoughts as they naturally occur in people's minds. Accordingly, they were asked to write down all of their thoughts as they occurred during the next few minutes. Those in the depletion condition were told to think about anything except a white bear. These participants were told that they should not think about a white bear, but if they did, they needed to stop and refocus on another thought. Suppressing thoughts requires effort and self-control (Wegner, 1994) and should, therefore, deplete the resource pool. The people in the no thought suppression condition were told that they could think about anything, including a white bear. After the manipulation, participants were given the opportunity to buy items at a discounted price that commonly would be found in a college bookstore or convenience store. Participants who experienced resource depletion bought more items and spent more money than those whose regulatory resources were not depleted. This finding was especially strong among participants who were high in trait impulsive buying, as measured by the original buying impulsiveness scale (Rook & Fisher, 1995), suggesting that among people for whom impulsive purchasing is a problem, having few regulatory resources available considerably increases the prospect of spending impulsively.

A final experiment showed that depleted resources reduce control over all types of purchase decisions not only affectively desirable choices (cf. Shiv & Fedorikhin, 1999). Depletion participants were asked to read aloud a series of boring historical biographies while exaggerating their hand gestures, facial expressions, and emotionality. This task required self-control, because it involved amplifying and creating an emotional reaction while reading dull biographies that lacked emotional content. Participants in the no depletion condition read aloud the same biographies but were not asked to change their reading styles. Participants were then allowed to purchase as many or as few snack food items as they wanted from among eight choices. Half of the items were relatively healthy alternatives, and the others were less healthy. The results of this study replicated previous findings by showing that people impulsively spent after being depleted. Furthermore, this effect occurred equally for healthy and less healthy alternatives. Thus, it appears that depleting self-regulatory resources makes one more likely to give in to impulse buying regardless of the type of purchase being considered.

## Strategies for Avoiding Self-Regulation Lapses

Perhaps the most important element in maintaining effective self-regulation is managing attention (Rueda, Posner, & Rothbart, 2004). Attention is important in two ways. First, to be successful in practicing self-control, one must be able to ignore desirable stimuli. The best way to do this is through avoidance (Hoch & Loewenstein, 1991). In some situations, people can try to avoid coming into proximity with tempting objects. A person who wants to cut down on or give up drinking might be well advised to stay away from bars and places where alcohol will be served. For some types of self-regulation goals, though, complete avoidance is not possible. People need to eat, and it is generally true that they must engage in some shopping. However, if there are specific items that are particularly tempting, we can try to avoid these. If a person has a favorite clothing store or tends to impulsively buy at bookstores, he or she could stay away from these particular places.

Avoidance may be seen as a form of removing the negative effect of proximity on self-regulation. By distancing oneself from the tempting object, the consumer can interrupt thoughts of it more easily and thus improve the likelihood of successfully practicing self-control (Hoch & Loewenstein, 1991). Another way to remove the impact of proximity is by postponement or delaying strategies. Many consumers develop rules for themselves to avoid focusing too much on a desired good (Hoch & Loewenstein, 1991). As noted earlier, this can involve removing temporal proximity as well as physical proximity. As one respondent in an impulsive behavior study reported,

> I have a rule about eating—once I finish what is on my plate, I make myself wait half an hour before thinking about dessert. By that time, I'm usually doing something else or I'm not hungry anymore. I do the same thing when shopping. (Rook & Hoch, 1985, p. 26)

Distraction is another form of creating distance from an object and avoiding thinking about it. Work by Mischel and Ebbesen (1970) showed that children were able to wait longer for a reward if they distracted themselves while waiting. Consumers can do the same when confronted with tempting situations (Rook & Hoch, 1985).

Another possible strategy in self-control is to focus attention on long-term goals instead of the immediate temptation. For example, a dieter may find a picture of himself/herself at his or her target weight and place it in a prominent place in the house (e.g., on the refrigerator) to keep this goal salient at crucial times. Similarly, the dieter may circle a date on the calendar or place an outfit he or she is trying to fit into in a prominent place as a reminder of the weight goal. Consumers indicated that this strategy was the most common way they tried to practice self-control over impulse purchasing urges (Rook & Hoch, 1985). However, such distal goals tend to be abstract and require one to transcend the immediate environment to focus beyond it. Such transcendence is particularly difficult when one is preoccupied with other issues or depleted of self-regulation resources. Hence, breaking goals into concrete situation–response plans, such as implementation intentions (Gollwitzer & Brandstätter, 1997), can be an effective strategy to close the gap between consumers' (good) intentions and their behavior.

Instead of turning attention forward to the potential benefits of self-control, one may try to focus backward on past failures and the feelings they engendered. Research has found that people will avoid actions they anticipate regretting (Bell, 1982). Recalling the guilt or shame one felt the last time he or she gave in to an impulse may help in avoiding the current desire. Similarly, recalling a prior experience in which acting on an impulse did not provide as much pleasure as anticipated (e.g., "I bought that jacket that looked so good in the store, but I ended up never wearing it") may also help people maintain their self-control.

Attentional factors are not the only way that people can maintain self-regulation. Another strategy is substitution (Hoch & Lowenstein, 1991; Rook & Hoch, 1985). Substitution involves allowing oneself a small lapse in exchange for resisting a much larger impulse. For example, a dieter might give himself or herself permission to eat a serving of low-fat chocolate pudding instead of consuming the higher calorie ice cream sundae that he or she really wants. Such a trade-off may provide enough immediate gratification to distance oneself from the more intense desire or minimize the feeling of deprivation. However, there is a risk that this alternative might not reduce desire and instead lead to wholesale failure of self-control in dieting (Hoch & Loewenstein, 1991).

Still another strategy to avoid self-regulation failure is precommitment, which requires recognizing that a self-regulation failure may occur and doing something proactively to prevent it from being able to happen. A solution for people who know they may spend more than they should might be not carrying credit cards or excess cash. Some recreational gamblers only bring as much money to a casino as they are prepared to lose. A precommitment approach that helps some people save involves having their paychecks directly deposited into a savings account. Not seeing the money makes it less likely that they will spend it. Another precommitment strategy might be making a list of items to purchase before going shopping and sticking to it to avoid being tempted by unnecessary items in the store. People may also choose to bring someone who will disapprove of their overspending when shopping. Shopping with a spouse, for example, may help control impulse urges by seeing spending through the spouse's eyes or the comments he or she makes.

## SEVERE LOSSES OF CONSUMPTION CONTROL

Lapses in self-regulation are typically seen as situations in which desire has exceeded willpower, which often occurs because desire to purchase or consume a specific item is extremely high or willpower is reduced at that given point in time. Desire can occur because a particular food item smells good, or we can recall how good it tasted in previous trials. Willpower might be reduced when we have had a hard day or recently made many efforts to control prior behaviors. Environmental factors can play a large role in these lapses. Failures occur episodically, but afterward, control can be reestablished. The objective here is to reduce the number or frequency of the failures in order to achieve the desired goal.

For some individuals, however, self-regulatory failures in a particular domain can be far more severe. This may involve a far more serious psychological condition (an impulse control disorder), and may have genetic and neurochemical antecedents. The desire for the specific item consumed is often minimal. Instead, the behavior is motivated and reinforced by an ability to temporarily reduce negative self-feelings (Baumeister, 1991; Faber & Vohs, 2004; Heatherton & Baumeister, 1991), which ultimately leads to highly repetitive, uncontrollable, and extreme regulatory failures. Examples of these are discussed below.

Bulimia: Compulsive Eating

*Bulimia nervosa* is a pernicious condition, consisting of three primary components: bingeing, in which large quantities of food are consumed uncontrollably during a confined time period; purging, in which vomiting, excessive exercise, laxatives, or other means are used to expel calories consumed during the binge; and excessive concern about weight or body shape (American Psychiatric Association, 1994). Vohs et al. (1999) developed a model of bulimia that focuses on personality traits in combination with proximal feelings abut the self that together serve to affect self-regulation. In this model, the personality traits are perfectionism and self-esteem, whereas the proximal component is self-perceptions or feelings that one is overweight. Perfectionism makes people set unrealistic goals for themselves. For many people, feeling overweight serves as feedback that one has failed in achieving a weight- or appearance-related goal. Finally, low self-esteem is an outcome of the perception that one has frequently failed to meet one's goals. One of the key aspects of this model is that it is the combination of all three factors (i.e., perfectionism, low self-esteem, seeing oneself as overweight) that results in bulimic symptoms. On their own, each factor presents a risk but does not produce bulimic symptoms.

*Perfectionism* is defined as the presence of high, and perhaps even unattainable, standards for oneself that represent a vulnerability to bulimic symptoms. Perfectionism is problematic for bulimia only insofar as the woman[*] comes to believe that she is not meeting self-standards. From this perspective, failure to achieve one's high self-standards becomes a stressor that, when combined with perfectionism, creates an undesirable self-image.

At this juncture enters the notion of escaping self-awareness (e.g., Heatherton & Baumeister, 1991). The essence of this idea is that many harmful self-directed behaviors come from a desire to escape from aversive self-awareness and attendant negative affect. Heatherton and Baumeister (1991) linked this process to binge eating, although escaping self-awareness also has been cited as a precursor to alcohol use, sadomasochism, and suicide (Baumeister, 1991; Vohs & Baumeister, 2000). Heatherton and Baumeister's central hypothesis was that a desire to escape from aversive self-awareness and negative affect motivates a cognitive shift to immediate, concrete thinking, resulting in the removal of inhibitions and, in turn, binge eating. They concluded that aversive self-awareness and negative affect motivate escape through cognitive deconstruction, which results in irrational thought and a loosening of inhibitions, including disinhibited, or binge, eating.

---

[*] The model has only been tested on women thus far, but there is no theoretical reason that it would not apply to men. Indeed, some work related to this model has been tested on both men and women (Joiner, Vohs, & Heatherton, 2000). Future research is needed to address whether or with what modifications the model can predict the incidence of bulimic symptoms among men.

According to this notion, then, the immediate precursors of binge eating are the aversive cognitive and affective states that motivate escape.

Vohs et al. (1999, 2001) outlined the pathway to binge eating and subsequent purging as starting from perfectionistic standards that can* lead to a perception of failure to meet weight or shape expectations. This, in turn, leads to a flood of unflattering self-appraisals and negative emotions, a state from which women seek to escape via binge eating and subsequent purging. Empirical support for this hypothesis has been found in data showing that the two-way combination of perfectionism and feeling overweight predicts bulimic symptoms (Joiner, Heatherton, Rudd, & Schmidt, 1997; Vohs et al., 1999).

It was hypothesized that the detrimental aspects of perfectionism become activated only in the presence of a stressor, such as seeing oneself as overweight (Vohs et al., 1999). To test this assertion, the researchers asked women to self-classify their weight as not overweight versus overweight. The interaction of general (i.e., not weight-specific) perfectionism scores and perceptions of weight status was then computed to predict reports of bulimic symptoms. The results indicated that when highly perfectionistic women felt overweight, they reported elevated bulimic symptoms. Conversely, highly perfectionistic women who did not feel overweight were not prone to bulimic symptoms. The interaction between perfectionism and feeling overweight remained significant even when statistically controlling for actual body weight, and its predictability held across two measures of bulimic symptomatology. Thus, it was a woman's self-perception of weight, rather than her actual weight, that predicted severity of bulimic symptoms.

These findings raised the question of why perfectionistic women who think they are overweight respond by bingeing, which is counterproductive to the goal of losing weight. It would seem to be more productive to enact goal-directed behaviors (e.g., dieting, exercise). In our view, a person's self-esteem will determine whether she responds to failures and setbacks by viewing them as short-term and changeable or global and permanent. A person who catastrophizes an adverse event (e.g., a person with low self-esteem) will likely experience accompanying states of aversive self-awareness and negative affect that may set the stage for self-escape through binge eating (Heatherton & Baumeister, 1991). Thus, self-esteem moderates the perfectionism-perceived overweight relationship in predicting bulimic symptoms.

This hypothesis was tested in a prospective study of 342 women who were tracked for an average of 9 months (Vohs et al., 1999). After statistically controlling for baseline bulimic symptoms and actual weight, the triple interaction of perfectionism, perceptions of overweight versus not overweight, and self-esteem predicted later bulimic symptoms. As expected, only among low self-esteem women was the interaction of perfectionism and feeling overweight predictive of increased bulimic symptoms. In contrast, women high in self-esteem did not develop bulimic symptoms even if they were perfectionists and regarded themselves as overweight. A subsequent study of 70 college women across a 5-week time span replicated these results using a different measure of self-esteem and conceptualizing the stressor as body dissatisfaction (Vohs et al., 2001). Again, high body dissatisfaction and high perfectionism predicted increased bulimic symptoms for low, but not high, self-esteem women. These findings point to the protective function of positive self-views in the development of bulimic symptoms.

This model of high perfectionism, feeling overweight, and low self-esteem or low self-efficacy has been shown to predict depressive as well as bulimic symptoms (Vohs et al., 2001). Given that the model emphasizes a specific combination of three variables in creating a complete self-regulation

---

* Readers may think that high standards will inevitably engender a self-perception that one is not achieving them. The two constructs (i.e., perfectionism scores, self-perceptions), in this case of weight or body shape, are in fact only moderately correlated around 0.40. Hence, they are not isomorphic.

failure in eating behavior, we are optimistic that changes in any one of them would reduce bulimic, and perhaps depressive, symptoms. It is hoped that this model can help uncover underlying pathways for overcoming extreme self-regulatory failure.

Compulsive Buying

*Compulsive buying* is defined as chronic, repetitive purchasing driven by negative feelings and experienced as an uncontrollable urge to buy, which ultimately causes harm to the individual and/or others (Faber & O'Guinn, 2008; O'Guinn & Faber, 1989). It was originally identified as a psychiatric disorder in the early 1900s under the term *oniomania* (Bleuler, 1924; Kraepelin, 1915). However, there was little discussion of this problem in the academic literature until the late 1980s, when research teams in the United States, Canada, and Germany began to report on the disorder (d'Astous, 1990; Faber & O'Guinn, 1988; Faber, O'Guinn, & Krych, 1987; O'Guinn & Faber, 1989; Scherhorn, Reisch, & Raab, 1990). Recent studies using population-based samples to determine prevalence estimates have reported that 5.8% of the U.S. adult population and over 7% of the adult German population suffer from compulsive buying (Koran, Faber, Aboujaoude, Large, & Serpe, 2006; Neuner, Raab, & Reisch, 2005).

Compulsive buying is internally generated rather than externally, and it is triggered by negative affect or an uncontrollable urge to buy (O'Guinn & Faber, 1989). Compulsive buyers score no higher on measures such as possessiveness or object attachment than do ordinary consumers (Edwards, 1992; O'Guinn & Faber, 1989; Scherhorn et al., 1990). The need or desire to compulsively buy often begins well before the person is in a location where buying can take place and is said to feel like a mounting tension that can only be relieved by making a purchase (Christenson et al., 1994). Several researchers have noted that compulsive buyers frequently do not use the items they purchase, and often these items are not removed from the bags or boxes in which they came (Boundy, 2000; O'Guinn & Faber, 1989; Ridgway, Kukar-Kinney, & Monroe, 2008). Such neglect of purchases differs markedly from the behavior of impulsive and excessive buyers, who sometimes gain considerable pleasure from using the items they purchase (Ditmar, Beattie, & Friese, 1996; Yurchisin & Johnson, 2004).

Instead, compulsive buying seems to be motivated by a desire to escape from aversive self-awareness. Compulsive buyers have been found to hold lofty self-standards and score high on measures of perfectionism (DeSarbo & Edwards, 1996; Faber, 2000; O'Guinn & Faber, 1989). Data from in-depth interviews with compulsive buyers suggest that both high standards and a feeling of failure from not attaining them date back to failed efforts to please their parents during childhood (Faber & O'Guinn, 1988; O'Guinn & Faber, 1989). As one informant reported,

> Because you are the oldest you're suppose to be the good little person. I was always trying to win their (parents) approval but couldn't. You know you could have stood on your head and turned blue and it wouldn't matter. I got straight A's and all kinds of honors and it never mattered. (as cited in Faber, 2004, p. 178)

The desire to be perfect and the inability to meet these impossible standards is often accompanied by low self-esteem in compulsive buyers. A low level of self-esteem among compulsive buyers has been reported in numerous studies (Elliott, 1994; Friese & Koenig, 1993; O'Guinn & Faber, 1989; Ridgway et al., 2008; Scherhorn et al., 1990). Depth interviews with compulsive buyers have suggested that low self-esteem coupled with idealized visions of siblings can create aversive feelings of self-awareness (Faber, 2004; O'Guinn & Faber, 1989).

Chronic depression and anxiety can result from aversive self-awareness (Higgins, 1987), which appears to be the case for compulsive buyers. Several studies have reported that compulsive buyers have higher than average levels of depression (McElroy, Keck, Pope, Smith, & Strakowski, 1994; Schlosser, Black, Repertinger, & Freet, 1994) and anxiety (Christenson et al., 1994; Ridgway et al.,

2008; Scherhorn et al., 1990). Between 25% and 50% of compulsive buyers have a clinical history of major depressive disorder (Christenson et al., 1994; McElroy et al., 1994; Schlosser et al., 1994). Compulsive buyers also score significantly higher than matched control subjects on a measure of stress reaction that assesses the frequency and intensity of negative emotional states experienced under everyday life conditions (Faber, Peterson, & Christenson, 1994).

Just as Vohs et al. (1999) found that a stressor was present to activate the impact of perfectionism for bulimia, so too does a negative factor appear to trigger compulsive buying episodes. Research with compulsive buyers has consistently found that negative mood states precede buying episodes (Elliott, 1994; Faber & Christenson, 1996; Faber et al., 1987). One study asked compulsive buyers to complete the following sentence fragment, "I am most likely to buy myself something when …" (Faber et al., 1987). Almost 75% of these respondents included some mention of a negative mood, such as "I'm depressed" or "I feel bad about myself." In comparison, this same sentence fragment was used by Belk (1985) with normal consumers, and only about 20% mentioned any type of emotion, either negative or positive, in response.

A different approach to examining triggers for compulsive buying episodes was used by Faber, Ristvedt, Mackenzie, and Christenson (1996), who asked compulsive buyers to indicate from a list of over 400 items which factors were associated with a worsening of their compulsive buying problems. The specific items on the list had either been identified in prior research with compulsive buyers or in studies examining other types of impulse control disorders. Twenty-three items were selected by at least a third of the sample, and these formed two primary factors. The first represented shopping-related stimuli (e.g., malls, stores, having money, credit cards). The second factor represented negative emotions, including boredom, stress, depression, anger, hurt, and irritability, as well as feeling fat or overweight. As with bulimia, negative affect can trigger extreme self-regulatory failure regarding buying among low self-esteem perfectionists.

### Explaining Complete Self-Regulatory Failure

In both bulimia and compulsive buying, aversive self-awareness triggers a desire to escape from these negative thoughts. One way to accomplish this is by focusing on immediate, concrete low-level tasks or activities (Baumeister, 1991; Heatherton & Baumeister, 1991). Shopping and buying serve this purpose for compulsive buyers, who find that when they are engaged in a compulsive-buying episode, physical sensations such as textures, smells, colors, and sounds become heightened, and these sensations are able to block out all other thoughts (O'Guinn & Faber, 1989; Schlosser et al., 1994). The tendency to become immersed in self-involving experiences triggered by external sources is sometimes referred to as absorption. Compulsive buyers have been found to score higher on absorption than a matched control group (Faber et al., 1994). This tendency may be what makes some people particularly prone to developing disorders such as bulimia and compulsive buying.

The ability to become immersed in this concrete, low-level thinking may explain why some compulsive buyers claim that shopping is the only thing that provides relief from negative feelings (Elliott, 1994; Friese & Koenig, 1993). It may also explain why compulsive buyers prefer to shop by themselves (Elliott, 1994; Schlosser et al., 1994). The presence of others is likely to interfere with the cognitive narrowing that can take place and prevent the escape that compulsive buyers seek.

Cognitive narrowing not only blocks thoughts of negative self-awareness but also prevents consideration of the longer term consequences of the action, which creates disinhibition (Heatherton & Baumeister, 1991; Heatherton & Vohs, 1998). Another consequence of cognitive narrowing is the failure to recognize the implausibility of beliefs, allowing noncritical, irrational thoughts to emerge that produce magical or fanciful thinking (Heatherton & Baumeister, 1991). This can be seen in the way many compulsive buyers describe a compulsive buying episode as feeling intoxicated, powerful, high, or elated (Elliott, 1994; Faber & Christenson, 1996; Faber et al.,

1987; Scherhorn et al., 1990). Similarly, during buying episodes, they view themselves as being more powerful or admired (Krueger, 2000; Scherhorn et al., 1990). These feelings of grandiosity may also allow them to think that they will be able to handle the debt or expenses they are incurring.

Compulsive buying and bulimia can be seen as chronic and large-scale breakdowns of the self-regulatory process, which occur because the goal of maintaining emotional stability or avoiding mental pain overwhelms efforts to maintain food consumption or purchasing goals. This is consistent with work that has found that when there is a conflict between regulating affect or behavior, priority will be given to feeling good (Tice, Bratslavsky, & Baumeister, 2001). Giving in to the behavior can result in cognitive narrowing that prohibits one from monitoring one's goals. This can be seen in the quasidissociative states some compulsive buyers and binge eaters report experiencing, in which they feel they are outside their bodies watching someone else act.

### Recovering From Extreme Self-Regulation Failure

For compulsive buyers, bulimics, and those with other impulse control disorders, recovery is often a long and difficult road, frequently requiring the help of a doctor or therapist. The good news is that there are routes to break these destructive failures. As was found with bulimia, being a perfectionist, having feelings of low self-esteem, and experiencing a negative affective trigger may all be necessary to cause a complete loss of self-control. Changing even one of these factors might help avoid this extreme failure.

One approach to treating bulimia and compulsive buying is via traditional psychotherapy or group therapy sessions. The purpose here is to get at the underlying causes of low self-esteem, depression, and anxiety (Krueger, 2000). The impact of a common root problem separate from the specific area of a loss of self-control can be seen in the high degree of comorbidity between different disorders. Several studies, for example, have shown that compulsive buyers have lifetime histories of other psychopathology, including eating disorders, alcoholism, drug abuse, various impulse control disorders, anxiety, and depression (Christenson et al., 1994; Goldsmith & McElroy, 2000; Schlosser et al., 1994). Similar findings have also been found among people with bulimia and binge-eating disorder (Mitchell, 1990). In all of these cases, consumption-related disorders have been found to be related to depression, anxiety, and low self-esteem. Psychodynamic therapy may help some people uncover the cause of their negative self-feelings and remove this component of their chronic regulatory failure.

Research has also shown some potential impact of drug therapy, although results are mixed (Benson & Gengler, 2004). Several authors have treated these patients with various antidepressants, typically those that target serotonin reuptake (Black, Monahan, & Gabel, 1997; McElroy et al., 1994; Ninan et al., 2000). Results have often shown a complete or partial reduction in buying urges and behavior. However, it is important to point out that when double-blind studies have been used, there is often not just an improvement in the treatment group but also a similar improvement in the control group (Black, Gabel, Hansen, & Schlosser, 2000; Ninan et al., 2000). Thus, it is uncertain if the success of drug treatments are because they block or modify depression and negative self-feelings, or because of the support and attention people receive, which helps them control the urges (Benson & Gengler, 2004).

The third major approach to treatment is the use of cognitive behavioral therapy, which is usually done in a group but can also be on an individual level. This type of therapy tries to approach the problem on several levels (Burgard & Mitchell, 2000). It helps people recognize the triggers for their problem behaviors; helps them restructure the associations they have between thoughts, feelings, and behaviors; and tries to replace responses to problematic cues or triggers with less problematic behaviors. An additional strategy in cognitive behavioral therapy is to teach people improved coping mechanisms for stress and anxiety, including such simple things as eating well, getting an adequate amount of sleep, establishing and maintaining friendships, arranging for some relaxation time each day, and improving problem-solving skills (see also Maddi, Chapter 31 of this volume). Successful outcomes from cognitive behavioral therapy programs have been reported for both eating disorders and compulsive buying (Mitchell, Burgard, Faber, Crosby, & de Zwaan, 2006).

## FUTURE RESEARCH

It appears that an understanding of self-regulation can offer a great deal of insight into the causes of consumption-related self-regulation failures as well as provide insights for how to avoid such failures and treat extreme self-control problems. We have tried to clearly differentiate between lapses in self-control and extreme regulatory disorders in specific realms. Much of the work in consumer behavior has tended to treat these as part of a continuous dimension of behavior. However, we see them as qualitatively different. Lapses in self-control involve underregulation, often occurring because of a depletion of regulatory resources, which makes exerting willpower difficult and allows desire to overwhelm control. Extreme failures, however, involve misregulation when people experience behavioral failure in the service of meeting affective needs. It represents a situation of wanting without liking. More research is needed to more fully distinguish these two different types of regulatory failure and how each might best be resolved.

In this chapter, we discussed self-regulatory failure with regard to eating and buying. However, many other important consumption areas may also be affected by self-regulation. For example, studies have frequently found that less than 50% of patients are fully compliant with taking their medications (Osterberg & Blaschke, 2005). Poor adherence in taking medication is responsible for between one third and two thirds of all medication-related hospital admissions and accounts for $100 billion in medical costs in the United States each year (O'Connor, 2006; Osterberg & Blaschke, 2005). Although many factors contribute to poor compliance, one contributing factor can be poor self-regulation. Patients may need to overcome resistance to taking their medications due to tiredness, dislike of side effects, or difficulty swallowing pills (Wu et al., 2008). Some have reported greater difficulty in taking pills later in the day when self-regulatory resources are most likely to be depleted (Wu et al., 2008). At least one study has shown that swallowing a bad tasting liquid, analogous to taking some medications, is lower when resources have been depleted (Vohs et al., 2008). Thus, self-control findings may help identify ways of improving compliance.

Future developments in self-regulation may provide important contributions to consumer welfare and suggest additional ways of helping people achieve their desired goals. One potentially important area of research would be examining what factors can serve to improve regulatory resources. Do certain activities such as meditation, relaxation techniques, or exercise help people restore depleted resources more quickly? A muscle analogy has been used to describe resource depletion. If this analogy holds, can exercises or activities be designed to help strengthen resources over the long run? Finally, factors such as proximity have been found to reduce one's ability to practice self-control. Are there also situational factors that can enhance it? The end result of these efforts may help promote happier and healthier consumers.

## REFERENCES

Ackerman, J. M., Goldstein, N. J., Shapiro, J. R., & Bargh, J. A. (2009). You wear me out: The vicarious depletion of self-control. *Psychological Science, 20*(3), 326–332.

American Psychiatric Association. (1994). *Diagnostic and statistical manual of mental disorders* (4th ed.). Washington, DC: Author.

Baumeister, R. F. (1991). *Escaping the self: Alcoholism, spirituality, masochism, and other flights from the burden of selfhood.* New York: Basic Books.

Baumeister, R. F. (2002). Yielding to temptation: Self-control failure, impulsive purchasing, and consumer behavior. *Journal of Consumer Research, 28,* 670–676.

Baumeister, R. F. (2005). *The cultural animal: Human nature, meaning, and social life.* New York: Oxford University Press.

Baumeister, R. F., Bratslavsky, E., Muraven, M., & Tice., D. M. (1998). Ego depletion: Is the active self a limited resource? *Journal of Personality and Social Psychology, 74,* 1252–1265.

Baumeister, R. F., & Heatherton, T. F. (1996). Self-regulation failure: An overview. *Psychological Inquiry, 7,* 1–15.

Baumeister, R. F., Heatherton, T. F., & Tice, D. M. (1994). *Losing control: How and why people fail at self-regulation.* San Diego, CA: Academic Press.

Beatty, S. E., & Ferrell, M. E. (1998). Impulse buying: Modeling its precursors. *Journal of Retailing, 74,* 169–191.

Belk, R. W. (1985). Materialism: Trait aspects of living in the material world. *Journal of Consumer Research, 12,* 265–280.

Bell, D. E. (1982). Regret in decision making under uncertainty. *Operations Research, 30,* 961–981.

Benson, A. L., & Gengler, M. (2004). Treating compulsive buying. In R. H. Coombs (Ed.), *Handbook of addictive disorders: A practical guide to diagnosis and treatment* (pp. 451–491). New York: John Wiley.

Black, D. W., Gabel, J., Hansen, J., & Schlosser, S. (2000). A double-blind comparison of Fluvoxamine versus placebo in the treatment of compulsive buying disorder. *Annals of Clinical Psychiatry, 12,* 205–211.

Black, D. W., Monahan, P., & Gabel, J. (1997). Fluvoxamine in the treatment of compulsive buying. *Journal of Clinical Psychiatry, 58*(4), 159–163.

Bleuler, E. (1924). *Textbook of psychiatry.* New York: Macmillan.

Boundy, D. (2000). When money is the drug. In A. L. Benson (Ed.), *I shop, therefore I am: Compulsive buying and the search for self* (pp. 3–26). Northvale, NJ: Aronson Press.

Burgard, M., & Mitchell, J. E. (2000). Group cognitive behavioral therapy for buying disorder. In A. L. Benson (Ed.), *I shop, therefore I am: Compulsive buying and the search for self* (pp. 367–397). Northvale, NJ: Aronson Press.

Carver, C. S., & Scheier, M. F. (1990). Origins and functions of positive and negative affect: A control-process view. *Psychological Review, 97,* 19–35.

Christenson, G. A., Faber, R. J., de Zwaan, M., Raymond, N., Specker, S., Eckert, M. D., et al. (1994). Compulsive buying: Descriptive characteristics and psychiatric comorbidity. *Journal of Clinical Psychiatry, 55,* 5–11.

d'Astous, A. (1990). An inquiry into the compulsive side of "normal" consumers. *Journal of Consumer Policy, 13,* 15–31.

DeSarbo, W. S., & Edwards, E. A. (1996). Typologies of compulsive buying behavior: A constrained clusterwise regression approach. *Journal of Consumer Psychology, 5,* 231–262.

Ditmar, H., Beattie, J., & Friese, S. (1996). Objects, decision considerations and self-image in men's and women's impulse purchases. *Acta Psychologica, 93,* 187–206.

Edwards, E. A. (1992). The measurement and modeling of compulsive buying behavior (Doctoral dissertation, University of Michigan, 1992). *Dissertation Abstracts International, 53,* 11A. (UMI No. 9308304)

Elliott, R. (1994). Addictive consumption: Function and fragmentation in postmodernity. *Journal of Consumer Policy, 17,* 159–179.

Faber, R. J. (2000). A systematic investigation into compulsive buying. In A. L. Benson (Ed.), *I shop, therefore I am: Compulsive buying and the search for self* (pp. 27–54). Northvale, NJ: Aronson Press.

Faber, R. J. (2004). Self-control and compulsive buying. In T. Kasser & A. Kanner (Eds.), *Psychology and the culture of consumption* (pp. 169–188). Washington, DC: American Psychological Association.

Faber, R. J., & Christenson, G. A. (1996). In the mood to buy: Differences in the mood states experienced by compulsive buyers and other consumers. *Psychology & Marketing, 13,* 803–820.

Faber, R. J., & O'Guinn, T. C. (1988). Dysfunctional consumer socialization: A search for the roots of compulsive buying. In P. Vanden Abeele (Ed.), *Psychology in micro and macro economics* (Vol. 1, pp. 1–15). Leuven, Belgium: International Association for Research in Economic Psychology.

Faber, R. J., & O'Guinn, T. C. (2008). Compulsive buying: Review and reflection. In C. P. Haugtvedt, P. M. Herr, & F. R. Kardes (Eds.), *Handbook of consumer psychology* (pp. 1039–1056). New York: Taylor & Francis.

Faber, R. J., O'Guinn, T. C., & Krych, R. (1987). Compulsive consumption. In M. Wallendorf & P. Anderson (Eds.), *Advances in consumer research* (Vol. 14, pp. 132–135). Provo, UT: Association for Consumer Research.

Faber, R. J., Peterson, C., & Christenson, G. A. (1994, August). *Characteristics of compulsive buyers: An examination of stress reaction and absorption.* Paper presented at the annual meeting of the American Psychological Association Conference, Los Angeles.

Faber, R. J., Ristvedt, S. L., Mackenzie, T. B., & Christenson, G. A. (1996, October). *Cues that trigger compulsive buying*. Paper presented at the annual meeting of the Association for Consumer Research, Tucson, AZ.

Faber, R. J., & Vohs, K. D. (2004). To buy or not to buy? Self-control and self-regulatory failure in purchase behavior. In R. Baumeister & K. Vohs (Eds.), *The handbook of self-regulation* (pp. 509–524). New York: Guilford.

Fennis, B. M., Janssen, L., & Vohs, K. D. (2009). Acts of benevolence: A limited-resource account of compliance with charitable requests. *Journal of Consumer Research, 35*, 906–924.

Festinger, L. (1962). Cognitive dissonance. *Scientific American, 207*, 93–107.

Friese, S., & Koenig, H. (1993). Shopping for trouble. *Advancing the Consumer Interest, 5*(1), 24–29.

Gardner, M. P. (1985). Mood states and consumer behavior: A critical review. *Journal of Consumer Research, 12*, 281–300.

Goldsmith, T., & McElroy, S. (2000). Compulsive buying: Associated disorders and drug treatment. In A.L. Benson (Ed.), *I shop, therefore I am: Compulsive buying and the search for self* (pp. 217–242). Northvale, NJ: Aronson Press.

Gollwitzer, P. M., & Brandstätter, V. (1997). Implementation intentions and effective goal pursuit. *Journal of Personality and Social Psychology, 73*, 186–199.

Heatherton, T. F., & Baumeister, R. F. (1991). Binge eating as an escape from self-awareness. *Psychological Bulletin, 110*, 86–108.

Heatherton, T. F., Nichols, P., Mahamedi, F., & Keel, P. K. (1995). Body weight, dieting, and eating disorder symptoms among college students: 1982 to 1992. *American Journal of Psychiatry, 152*, 1623–1629.

Heatherton, T. F., & Vohs, K. D. (1998). Why is it so difficult to inhibit behavior? *Psychological Inquiry, 9*, 212–215.

Herman, C. P., & Polivy, J. (1993). Mental control of eating: Excitatory and inhibitory food thoughts. In D. M. Wegner & J. W. Pennebaker (Eds.), *Handbook of mental control* (pp. 491–505). Englewood Cliffs, NJ: Prentice-Hall.

Higgins, E. T. (1987). Self-discrepancy: A theory relating self to affect. *Psychological Review, 94*, 319–340.

Higgins, E. T. (1996). The "self digest": Self-knowledge serving self-regulatory functions. *Journal of Personality and Social Psychology, 71*, 1062–1083.

Hoch, S. J., & Loewenstein, G. F. (1991). Time inconsistent preferences and consumer self-control. *Journal of Consumer Research, 18*, 492–507.

Horan, R. N., Bulte, E., & Shogren, J. (2005). How trade saved humanity from biological exclusion: An economic theory of Neanderthal extinction. *Journal of Economic Behavior & Organization, 58*, 1–29.

Hull, J. G. (1981). A self-awareness model of the causes and effects of alcohol consumption. *Journal of Abnormal Psychology, 90*, 586–600.

Joiner, T. E., Jr., Heatherton, T. F., Rudd, M. D., & Schmidt, N. (1997). Perfectionism, perceived weight status, and bulimic symptoms: Two studies testing a diathesis-stress model. *Journal of Abnormal Psychology, 106*, 145–153.

Joiner, T. E., Vohs, K. D., & Heatherton, T. F. (2000). Three studies on the factorial distinctiveness of binge eating and bulimic symptoms among non-clinical men and women. *International Journal of Eating Disorders, 27*, 198–205.

Kacen, J. J., & Lee, J. A. (2002). The influence of culture on consumer impulsive buying behavior. *Journal of Consumer Psychology, 12*, 163–176.

Koran, L. M., Faber, R. J., Aboujaoude, E., Large, M. D., & Serpe, R. T. (2006). Estimated prevalence of compulsive buying in the United States. *American Journal of Psychiatry, 163*, 1806–1812.

Kraepelin, E. (1915). *Psychiatrie* (8th ed.). Leipzig, Germany: Johann Ambrosius Barth.

Krueger, D. (2000). The use of money as an action symptom. In A. L. Benson (Ed.), *I shop, therefore I am: Compulsive buying and the search for self* (pp. 288–310). Northvale, NJ: Aronson Press.

Le Bon, G. (2002). *The crowd: A study of the popular mind*. Mineola, NY: Dover. (Original work published 1895)

Litt, A., Khan, U., & Shiv, B. (2010). Lusting while loathing: Parallel counterdriving of wanting and liking. *Psychological Science, 21*, 118–125.

Mann, T., Tomiyama, A. J., Westling, E., Lew, A., Samuels, B., & Chatman., J. (2007). Medicare's search for effective obesity treatments: Diets are not the answer. *American Psychologist, 62*, 220–233.

Marlatt, G. A. (1985). Relapse prevention: Theoretical rationale and overview of the model. In G. A. Marlatt & J. R. Gordon (Eds.), *Relapse prevention: Maintenance strategies in the treatment of addictive behaviors* (pp. 3–70). New York: Guilford.

McElroy, S. L., Keck, P. E., Jr., Pope, H. J., Jr., Smith, J. M., & Strakowski, S. M. (1994). Compulsive buying: A report of 20 cases. *Journal of Clinical Psychiatry, 55*, 242–248.

Meyer, J. M., & Stunkard, A. J. (1993). Genetics and human obesity. In A. J. Stunkard & T. Wadden (Eds.), *Obesity therapy and treatment* (pp. 137–149). New York: Raven.

Mischel, W., & Ebbesen, E. B. (1970). Attention in delay of gratification. *Journal of Personality and Social Psychology, 16*, 329–337.

Mischel, W., Shoda, Y., & Peake, P. K. (1988). The nature of adolescent competencies predicted by preschool delay of gratification. *Journal of Personality and Social Psychology, 54*, 687–696.

Mitchell, J. E. (1990). *Bulimia nervosa.* Minneapolis: University of Minnesota Press.

Mitchell, J. E., Burgard, M., Faber, R. J., Crosby, R. D., & de Zwaan, M. (2006). Cognitive behavioral therapy for compulsive buying disorder. *Behaviour Research and Therapy, 44*, 1859–1865.

Neuner, M., Raab, G., & Reisch, L. (2005). Compulsive buying in maturing consumer societies: An empirical re-inquiry. *Journal of Economic Psychology, 26*, 509–522.

Ninan, P. T., McElroy, S. L., Kane, C. P., Knight, B. T., Casuto, L. S., Rose, S. E., et al. (2000). Placebo-controlled study of Fluvoxamine in the treatment of patients with compulsive buying. *Journal of Clinical Psychopharmacology, 20*(3), 362–366.

O'Connor, P. J. (2006). Improving medication adherence: Challenges for physicians, payers and policy makers. *Archives of Internal Medicine, 166*, 1802–1804.

O'Guinn, T. C., & Faber, R. J. (1989). Compulsive buying: A phenomenological exploration. *Journal of Consumer Research, 16*, 147–157.

Olshansky, S. J., Passaro, D. J., Hershow, R. C., Layden, J., Carnes, B. A., Brody, J., et al. (2005). A potential decline in life expectancy in the United States in the 21st century. *New England Journal of Medicine, 352*, 1138–1145.

Osterberg, L., & Blaschke, T. (2005). Drug therapy: Adherence to medication. *New England Journal of Medicine, 353*, 487–497.

Piron, F. (1991). Defining impulse purchasing. In R. Holman & M. Solomon (Eds.), *Advances in consumer research* (Vol. 18, pp. 509–514). Provo, UT: Association of Consumer Research.

Ridgway, N. M., Kukar-Kinney, M., & Monroe, K. (2008). An expanded conceptualization and a new measure of compulsive buying. *Journal of Consumer Research, 35*, 350–406.

Roberts, W. A. (2002). Are animals stuck in time? *Psychological Bulletin, 128*, 473–489.

Robinson, T. E., & Berridge, K. C. (1993). The neural basis of drug craving: An incentive-sensitization theory of addiction. *Brain Research Reviews, 18*, 247–291.

Rook, D. W. (1987). The buying impulse. *Journal of Consumer Research, 14*, 189–199.

Rook, D. W., & Fisher, R. J. (1995). Normative influences on impulsive buying behavior. *Journal of Consumer Research, 22*, 305–313.

Rook, D. W., & Gardner, M. P. (1993). In the mood: Impulse buying's affective antecedents. *Research in Consumer Behavior, 6*, 1–28.

Rook, D. W., & Hoch, S. J. (1985). Consuming impulses. In M. Holbrook & E. Hirschman (Eds.), *Advances in consumer research* (Vol. 12, pp. 23–27). Provo, UT: Association of Consumer Research.

Rueda, M. R., Posner, M. I., & Rothbart, M. K. (2004). Attentional control and self-regulation. In R. F. Baumeister & K. D. Vohs (Eds.), *Handbook of self-regulation: Research, theory, and applications* (pp. 33–42). New York: Guilford.

Scherhorn, G., Reisch, L. A., & Raab, G. (1990). Addictive buying in West Germany: An empirical study. *Journal of Consumer Policy, 13*, 355–387.

Schlosser, S., Black, D. W., Repertinger, S., & Freet, D. (1994). Compulsive buying: Demography, phenomenology, and comorbidity in 46 subjects. *General Hospital Psychiatry, 16*, 205–212.

Shiv, B., & Fedorikhin, A. (1999). Heart and mind in conflict: Interplay of affect and cognition in consumer decision making. *Journal of Consumer Research, 26*, 278–282.

Suchy, Y. (2009). Executive functioning: Overview, assessment, and research issues for non-neuropsychologists. *Annals of Behavioral Medicine, 37*, 106–116.

Suddendorf, T., & Busby, J. (2003). Mental time travel in animals? *Trends in Cognitive Sciences, 7*, 391–396.

Tice, D. M., Bratslavsky, E., & Baumeister, R. F. (2001). Emotional distress regulation takes precedence over impulse control: If you feel bad, do it! *Journal of Personality and Social Psychology, 80*, 53–67.

U.S. Bureau of Economic Analysis. (2010). *National economic accounts.* Retrieved December 9, 2010, from http://www.bea.gov/national/nipaweb/TableView.asp?SelectedTable=58&ViewSeries=NO&Java=no&Request3Place=N&3Place=N&FromView=YES&Freq=Year&FirstYear=2000&LastYear=2009&3Place=N&Update=Update&JavaBox=no#Mid

Vohs, K. D., Bardone, A. M., Joiner, T. E., Jr., Abramson, L. Y., & Heatherton, T. F. (1999). Perfectionism, perceived weight status, and self-esteem interact to predict bulimic symptoms: A model of bulimic symptom development. *Journal of Abnormal Psychology, 108*, 695–700.

Vohs, K. D., & Baumeister, R. F. (2000). Escaping the self consumes regulatory resources: A self-regulatory model of suicide. In T. E. Joiner, Jr. & M. D. Rudd (Eds.), *Suicide science: Expanding boundaries* (pp. 33–42). Boston: Kluwer Academic.

Vohs, K. D., & Baumeister, R. F. (2004). Understanding self-regulation: An introduction. In R. F. Baumeister & K. D. Vohs (Eds.), *Handbook of self-regulation: Research, theory, and applications* (pp. 1–9). New York: Guilford.

Vohs, K. D., Baumeister, R. F., Schmeichel, B. J., Twenge, J. M., Nelson, N. M., & Tice, D. M. (2008). Making choices impairs subsequent self-control: A limited resource account of decision making, self-regulation, and active initiative. *Journal of Personality and Social Psychology, 94,* 883–898.

Vohs, K. D., & Faber, R. J. (2003, October). *Self-regulatory abilities and impulsive spending.* Paper presented at the annual meeting of the Association for Consumer Research, Toronto, ON, Canada.

Vohs, K. D., & Faber, R. J. (2007). Spent resources: Self-regulatory resource availability affects impulse buying. *Journal of Consumer Research, 33,* 537–547.

Vohs, K. D., & Heatherton, T. F. (2000). Self-regulatory failure: A resource-depletion approach. *Psychological Science, 11,* 249–254.

Vohs, K. D., Voelz, Z. R., Pettit, J. W., Bardone, A. M., Katz, J., Abramson, L. Y., et al. (2001). Perfectionism, body dissatisfaction, and self-esteem: An interactive model of bulimic symptom development. *Journal of Social and Clinical Psychology, 20,* 476–497.

Wansink, B., Painter, J. E., & Lee, Y. K. (2006). The office candy dish: Proximity's influence on estimated and actual candy consumption. *International Journal of Obesity, 30,* 871–875.

Wegner, D. M. (1994). Ironic processes of mental control. *Psychological Review, 101,* 34–52.

Weinberg, P., & Gottwald, W. (1982). Impulsive consumer buying as a result of emotions. *Journal of Business Research, 10,* 43–57.

Wheeler, M. A., Stuss, D. T., & Tulving, E. (1997). Toward a theory of episodic memory: The frontal lobes and autonoetic consciousness. *Psychological Bulletin, 121,* 331–354.

Wu, J. R., Moser, D. K., Lennie, T. A., Peden, A. R., Chen, Y. C., & Heo, S. (2008). Factors influencing medication adherence in patients with heart failure. *Heart & Lung: The Journal of Acute and Critical Care, 37,* 8–16.

Yurchisin, J., & Johnson, K. K. P. (2004). Compulsive buying behavior and its relationship to perceived social status associated with buying, materialism, self-esteem, and apparel-product involvement. *Family & Consumer Sciences Research Journal, 32,* 291–314.

Zhang, Y., Fishbach, A., & Kruglanski, A. W. (2007). The dilution model: How additional goals undermine the perceived instrumentality of a shared path. *Journal of Personality and Social Psychology, 92,* 389–401.

# 23

# *Gambling Beliefs Versus Reality*
## Implications for Transformative Public Policy

JUNE COTTE AND KATHRYN A. LaTOUR

THERE ARE NOW MORE THAN 500 CASINOS IN THE U.S., most of them set up over the last two decades. They account for more than half of the almost $100 billion that Americans wager every year.

Christopher Caldwell
*The New York Times,* April 13, 2008

IN JANUARY 2008 THERE WERE 2,132 Internet gambling web sites owned by 477 companies from 49 different jurisdictions.

Sally M. Monaghan
*Computers in Human Behavior, 25,* 2009

Gambling, both casino- and Internet-based, is big business. In 2007, U.S. casino revenues, not including Native American casinos, totaled $32.2 billion, and American consumers lost, on average, $138 million per day at U.S. casinos (Basham & Kwon, 2008). Unfortunately, about a quarter of that revenue was supplied by problem gamblers (Williams & Wood, 2004). Given the growth trends of virtually all forms of gambling, it appears as though consumer attitudes toward gambling are changing as well, with gambling increasingly perceived to be simply another form of leisure entertainment (Currie, Hodgins, Wang, & Chen, 2009). It has been estimated that online gambling revenues range from $10 billion to $12 billion yearly (Schwartz, 2006). Although online gambling is illegal in the United States, consumer attitudes generally do not reflect this, with a 2007 poll reporting that almost half of Americans agreed that "Internet gambling should be permitted as long as it's regulated by the government" (Ipsos, 2008, para. 9).

Researchers have created quite a lot of knowledge around casino gambling, and our own recent research increases knowledge about online gambling (Cotte & LaTour, 2009). However, we believe there are some common misunderstandings, conventional wisdoms, and unfounded beliefs about gambling as consumption that, when examined closely, can productively lead to better public policy–oriented research and actions. This chapter will identify some of the main misconceptions regarding gambling and compare them to gambling realities. Although some of the misconceptions are commonly held societal perceptions, others are actually based on research that has been inappropriately generalized. We will explore the misconceptions by bringing in new literatures from diverse sources and also point out several unanswered questions relevant to public policy. We end with a discussion of possible future research.

## RESEARCH-BASED BELIEF: CONSUMERS ARE LOSS AVERSE

The judgment and decision-making literature is an appropriate starting point for our discussion regarding views of gambling, as it addresses how consumers approach risky decision making.

Prospect theory (Kahneman & Tversky, 1979) concludes that consumers are loss averse, and another related theory on the endowment effect (Thaler, 1980) states that it is more painful for consumers to give up a current asset than it is pleasurable to buy that same asset. If either of these theories held in reality, casinos would not be successful, as they rely on consumers giving up current assets (i.e., money) to engage in an activity that involves risk. A closer look at the experimental paradigms used to study risk in the judgment and decision-making areas offers insight into why consumers' theorized loss aversion does not always hold up in practice in gambling, as well as how public policy makers can make gambling losses a more salient part of the consumer's decision process.

Prospect theory is used to describe how a person addresses risk and uncertainty and posits that when outcomes are framed as positive gains, people are more risk averse; however, in the same situation, when outcomes are framed negatively as losses, people become risk seeking. The Asian disease problem is one traditional paradigm used to study risk taking (Tversky & Kahneman, 1981). In this paradigm, in the gain frame condition, participants were asked to imagine the United States is preparing for the outbreak of an Asian disease expected to kill 600 people. However, if program A is adopted, 200 people will be saved, and if program B is adopted, there is a one-third probability that 600 people will be saved and a two-thirds probability that no people will be saved. Although the expected utility or outcomes of both programs is the same, about 70% of people in the gain frame (i.e., lives saved) condition preferred program A, which is the risk-averse solution, in which there will be a certain gain. In other words, people in a gain frame prefer certain positive outcomes over gambling for a potential larger positive outcome, which suggests that when people have money they have gained (i.e., a certainty), they should not risk it by gambling but often do. This finding also suggests that when gamblers win once, they should stop gambling but often do not.

However, when the outcomes are presented differently and framed in terms of losses, people's choices change. People in the loss condition were told that if program C is adopted, 400 people will die; however, if program D is adopted, there is a one-third probability that nobody will die and a two-thirds probability that 600 people will die. The expected utility or outcome is again the same for both programs, yet more people (roughly 70%) in the loss (i.e., lives lost) frame preferred program D, which is the risk-seeking solution, because the exact negative outcome is unknown or probabilistic. Here, people chose uncertainty to avoid a certain loss, as certainty exaggerated the aversiveness of the loss. This finding suggests that gamblers should be deterred by the certainty of long-term losses, but the problem is that gamblers never know they will lose with certainty on the next gamble, and the certain long-term losses fail to deter them. Finally, an important underlying tenet of prospect theory is that "the displeasure associated with losing a sum of money is generally greater than pleasure associated with winning the same amount" (Tversky & Kahneman 1981, p. 454), which would suggest that people would not gamble at all. Yet, many do.

There are several problems relating the results of the prospect theory (Tversky & Kahneman, 1981) paradigm to casino gambling. First, in the paradigm, the risks are known for the decision maker. For the gambler in a casino, the outcome is usually random, in the case of slot machines, or changing based on context, in the case of table games like blackjack. Second, in the prospect theory paradigm, the consumer typically chooses between two choices. In the casino, however, the choices are limitless: People can choose to continue to play; end their play; move their play to another machine, table, or game; get a drink and then decide whether to continue to play; and so on. Of course, most relevant is that in this paradigm, the consumer is not making a choice about gambling their own money. Whereas the focus of prospect theory is a choice the consumer makes and whether that choice reflects risk taking or aversion, the reality is that in casinos, we are not only concerned about the risk of consumers placing one bet (i.e., one choice), but also that they initially make the choice to become part of a gambling environment and then continue to put money toward betting on options in which the odds of winning are against them.

The research on heuristics and biases, coming from the judgment and decision-making literature, also helps explain the discrepancy between consumers' documented loss aversion and the
reality of casino play. For example, one could argue that the casinos distort risk by highlighting
winnings, with the loud noises and lights of winning machines, and featuring images of past winners, such as on a "wall of fame," that make the consumer feel winning is more likely via the repre-
sentativeness bias. Additionally, the casinos may create a context in which gambling is seen as more
acceptable and within social norms; that is, everyone else is gambling, so I should, too (Cialdini,
Reno, & Kallgren, 1990).

We will use similar decision-making explanations as we address reasons why people may gamble.
In terms of the potential takeaway for public policy, the judgment and decision-making literature
suggests that making the consumers' current money and monetary gains more salient and highlighting the gains of the casino as a whole, such as the lavish decor, will make consumers become
more risk averse. In terms of understanding the actual gambling behavior itself, the judgment and
decision-making literature does not offer much insight, so we need to turn to research conducted
on gamblers in more real-world settings. As we do so, we need to take into account the environment
in which gambling occurs and how it influences the way gamblers approach their decision making. The rational mind advocated by most economists, wherein the consumer maximizes utility,
does not hold in the casino setting. Simmons and Novemsky (2008) pointed out that "while many
experiments aim to understand risky choice, only a small fraction explicitly links their results to
real-world risk taking behavior" (p. 15).

## RESEARCH-BASED BELIEF: THE CASINO ENVIRONMENT MAKES THE GAMBLER MORE EMOTIONAL, WHICH LEADS TO IRRATIONAL BEHAVIOR

Gamblers' heart rates increase in the casino, but not the lab, when playing blackjack, poker, and slot
machines and when betting on horses (Anderson & Brown, 1984; Carroll & Huxley, 1994; Dickerson,
Hinchy, England, Fabre, & Cunnigham, 1992; Griffiths, 1993; Leary & Dickerson, 1985). Heart rates
increase in proportion to the monetary stakes, so slot machines cause less of an increase than high-
stakes blackjack. This is also one reason why lab-based studies of gambling (e.g., for points, contests)
do not typically represent casino gambling adequately, as heart rate increases only happen appreciably when gamblers risk their own money. In addition, the correlation between the size of the bet
made and heart rate increases is only significant in real casinos with real money (Anderson & Brown,
1984). Further, researchers have found that there is a significant negative correlation between the
telic dominance scale (i.e., arousal avoidance, a planful orientation, serious-mindedness) and the
size of blackjack bets, but only in the casino and not when the same issues are measured in a laboratory (Anderson & Brown, 1987). Also, sensation seeking, combined with the size of a bet, affect
arousal for real casino gamblers but not subjects in the lab (Anderson & Brown, 1984).

In another study, regular gamblers playing blackjack in a real casino with their own money
were compared to the same gamblers playing cards in a casino for nonmonetary stakes. Results
showed that when playing for money, gamblers showed increased cardiovascular activity as well
as increased neuroendocrine activity, as measured by salivary cortisol levels (Meyer et al., 2000).
Together, these physical reactions are evidence that money-based, real casino gambling produces
alterations in stress hormones as well as heart rate increases, and both persisted for a number of
hours. Meyer et al. argued that the increase in cortisol helps gamblers feel less tired, and this gam-
bling-induced physiological arousal may reinforce gambling behaviors, contributing to problem
gambling. Litt, Pirouz, and Shiv (Chapter 25 of this volume) also discuss some of these neurological
aspects of addictive behavior. In a study with problem gamblers, Meyer and colleagues found that
while heart rate, norepinephrine levels, and dopamine levels increased during blackjack play for all

gamblers, problem gamblers showed higher levels of all of these than regular, nonproblem gamblers (Meyer et al., 2004). This suggests that problem gamblers have higher physiological arousal and activation while gambling than do regular, nonpathological gamblers.

The physiological arousal and emotional engagement of gamblers suggest that gamblers might not be making rational decisions. Several researchers have documented the presence of irrational beliefs as people gamble, and there is a positive relationship between increasing irrational beliefs and increasing level of gambling intensity and risk-taking (Delfabbro & Winefield, 2000; Gaboury & Ladouceur, 1988; May, Whelan, Meyers, & Steenbergh, 2005; Toneatto, Blitz-Miller, Calderwood, Dragonetti, & Tsanos, 1997). As May et al. summarized, there are several forms of irrationality in gambling, including the gambler believing he or she has control over a purely chance game, believing there are patterns in chance games like roulette where none exist, making rationalizations about near misses, engaging in rituals shrouded in superstitions, and developing personifications of the betting machines. Burroughs and Rindfleisch (Chapter 12 of this volume) discuss more generally some of the irrational psychological aspects of compulsive consumptive disorders.

Our next section focuses on the irrational behaviors thought to be associated with gambling. Because many of these behaviors are a result of the highly intense and emotional casino environment, public policy efforts to reduce gambling losses need to focus on getting the gambler to disengage from the environment, such as the cooling-off period seen on some Internet gambling sites in which gamblers have to wait a certain amount of time before more money can be added to their account and play can resume. The presence of automatic teller (banking) machines and easy access to credit lines for the high rollers in casinos reduce the potential opportunity for them to disengage from their highly involved play.

## RESEARCH-BASED BELIEF: RESEARCH ON PROBLEM GAMBLERS PROVIDES INSIGHTS FOR UNDERSTANDING ALL GAMBLERS

Much of the funded research on gambling has been on the problem gambler, as government research funding has focused on understanding and preventing problem gambling. However, although this research has helped in our understanding of the 1–3% of the gambling population who are problem gamblers, we know less about others that do not fit that definition and little about the process of moving from recreational usage to problem usage. As Clarke et al. (2007) point out, most gambling theories have been developed to explain pathological gambling and are often based on clinical samples or students; very few are attempting to explain real recreational gambling.

Cotte (1997) used three behavioral heuristics for identifying recreational casino gamblers: those who (a) gambled with small stakes on each bet, (b) moved between different types of games, and (c) took breaks to dine or shop within the broader casino complex. However, gamblers who were not studied included those betting very large sums of money on each hand of poker or blackjack, those who had been at the table for a long period of time, and those who came in, went straight to one game, and stayed intently at that game until they left the casino. Other observational field researchers may want to consider using these criteria.

Researchers more typically use survey items developed to diagnose pathological gamblers, such as the *Diagnostic and Statistical Manual of Mental Disorders* (American Psychiatric Association, 2000) or the South Oaks Gambling Screen (Lesieur & Blume, 1987). *Recreational gambler* is thus defined by default as a nonproblem or nonpathological gambler. Recently, Currie et al. (2009) identified cutoffs or limits above which gamblers would be subject to harm from gambling, including spending more than 1% of income on gambling and gambling more than two or three times per month. This can also help researchers identify recreational gamblers as those who gamble smaller amounts or less frequently.

Clarke at al.'s (2007) work demonstrated that the motives for gambling among pathological gamblers are much stronger than those held by recreational gamblers, and there are some striking differences in motives that should concern those who may consider using the literature generated on pathological gamblers to inform the study of recreational gambling. Cotte (1997) identified some of the motives driving U.S.-based recreational casino gambling: learning and evaluating, seeking a rush, self-definition, risk-taking, cognitive self-classification, emotional self-classification, competing, and communing. Some of these were affirmed by Clarke et al.'s study of New Zealand gamblers, but because these researchers investigated both recreational and pathological gamblers, they were able to outline some stark differences. Pathological gamblers were far more likely to chase losses than recreational gamblers and were also more likely to turn to gambling as an escape from stress. Although the desire for excitement or a rush (Cotte, 1997) exists for both groups, Clarke at al. (2007) showed that it wears off for recreational gamblers but not pathological gamblers. Unsurprisingly, documented behavioral differences between pathological and recreational gamblers include spending more time and more money on gambling activities (Ferris & Wynne, 2001). Although we know that recreational and problem gamblers are different, we do not yet know how that difference develops, which is important for public policy researchers. Understanding what triggers one to move from being a recreational player to becoming more compulsive is an area of research that needs much more attention.

## SOCIETAL-BASED BELIEF: GAMBLERS CHASE LOSSES

One common gambling assumption is the idea that gamblers chase losses. That is, gamblers become more risk seeking as they lose; that is, they continue to gamble, thereby increasing their losses as they attempt to recover previous losses. This is consistent with prospect theory, which posits that people in a loss frame tend to be more risk seeking (Kahneman & Tversky, 1979). Lab-based neuroscience researchers, using functional magnetic resonance imaging (fMRI; i.e., brain imaging) techniques, have recently argued that loss chasing reflects conflicting motivations, and the decision to stop chasing losses takes longer and takes place in a different part of the brain, as compared to the decision to continue to chase losses (Campbell-Meiklejohn, Woolrich, Passingham, & Rogers, 2008). These authors conclude that loss chasing shows the expectancy of later positive outcomes, and the decision to chase losses looks similar, at a neural level, to hunger or a craving for a drug among addicts.

However, the perception that gamblers chase losses is in part a misconception, because gamblers do not often do this. In one of the earliest studies to rigorously compare results from the lab and fMRI techniques to results in a real casino, researchers discovered that 75% of gamblers in the real casino bet more when they were ahead, whereas 61% of gamblers in a lab bet more when they were behind, and only 33% of gamblers used the same gambling strategy in both the casino and the lab (Anderson & Brown, 1984). This seems to suggest that the anecdotal phenomenon of chasing losses might be more prevalent in a lab.

Whereas a simulated gambling task showed evidence of chasing losses, or risk-seeking (Gehring & Willoughby, 2002), a longitudinal study of real Internet gamblers showed that those who self-identified as having a gambling problem, and ultimately quit, first placed higher probability or safer bets, then closed their Internet gambling accounts altogether; that is, they gradually became more risk averse (Xuan & Shaffer, 2009). These researchers suggest a productive avenue is to look for and examine the break points where gamblers shift from a risk-seeking to a risk-averse motivation. For public policy researchers, understanding when and why chasing losses occurs is important, because it may be a signal that what was recreational gambling is becoming something more serious. In addition, anecdotal evidence suggests that it is during the loss chasing when consumers typically lose the most money.

## SOCIETAL-BASED BELIEF: NEAR MISSES MOTIVATE GAMBLERS TO CONTINUE GAMBLING

A near miss is when the slot machine displays the reel as if one of the columns was just one notch away from a win; imagine two cherries lined up, with the third reel one notch away from a third cherry, which would have caused a win. With near misses, "the player is not constantly losing but constantly nearly winning" (Parke & Griffiths, 2004, p. 407). Today's slot machines are now virtually controlled, and the probabilities of winning are not what they appear to be, because they are based on random number generation not the physical reels presented to the gambler. In the United States and Canada, but not Australia and New Zealand, casino operators are allowed to use a clustering algorithm to create the perception of more near misses than is statistically likely to occur (Harrigan, 2009). From a consumer welfare perspective, this is a bad thing; the occurrences of near misses correspond with increasing time spent gambling on the machine (Cote, Caron, Aubert, & Ladouceur, 2003; Kassinove & Schare, 2001). In addition, near misses are experienced as closer to a win than another random collection of symbols, which increases gambling (Dixon & Schreiber, 2004). A lab-based study in 2006 did not support this finding (Ghezzi, Wilson, & Porter, 2006), but there were significant differences between the simulated gambles and real gambling, including playing for points instead of money. Harrigan quite convincingly argues that near misses caused by virtual reels and clustering are a form of player entrapment.

Using lab-based and fMRI studies, but allowing real money wins on a slot machine task, Clark, Lawrence, Astley-Jones, and Gray (2009) examined the near miss effect. Participants reported that subjectively, near misses felt worse but increased their intention to continue playing. This result was much stronger for those who had higher perceived control (i.e., they thought they had some skill); for them, near misses were less pleasant but far more motivating. The neural responses also showed that near misses recruit the win (i.e., expected positive outcome) areas of the brain, which is why they promote more gambling play, especially when gamblers feel they are in control of the game (Clark et al., 2009).

## SOCIETAL-BASED BELIEF: GAMBLERS DO NOT UNDERSTAND LAWS OF PROBABILITY, SO TEACHING THEM WILL REDUCE GAMBLING PROBLEMS

The gambler's fallacy is a belief in a negative autocorrelation for a noncorrelated or random sequence. It is one case of the representative heuristic, or the law of small numbers (Rabin, 2002; Tversky & Kahneman, 1971), in which people think a short random sequence should be representative of the underlying probability (e.g., after three reds [Rs], black [B] will come up next, because RRRB is more representative of the actual probability than RRRR). Croson and Sundali (2005; Sundali & Croson, 2006) examined the gambler's fallacy and the hot hand biases, as discussed below, in actual casinos, using data from 18 hours of 139 roulette players making 24,131 bets. The data were collected using a Nevada casino's security tapes. Croson and Sundali found gambler's fallacy behavior in the casino, as gamblers bet consistently with the fallacy in mind after streaks of five or more outcomes of one color; that is, they bet against that color coming up again. After streaks of six or more, 85% of bets were consistent with the fallacy. With this behavior at least, there seems to be some correspondence between lab- and casino-based research.

The hot hand is not exactly the opposite of the gambler's fallacy, as it is a belief in positive autocorrelation for a noncorrelated series. People believe that they or other people have control over the random event, which is an illusion of control bias (Langer, 1975). Gamblers who believe in a hot hand do not think an outcome is hot (e.g., red vs. black) but rather that a particular gambler is hot; for example, whatever they choose to bet on will win (Croson & Sundali, 2005; Gilovich, Vallone, & Tversky, 1985; Sundali & Croson, 2006). That is, "in the gambler's fallacy the coin is due; in the hot hand the person is hot" (Sundali & Croson, 2006, p. 1). Lab studies have shown that gamblers bet more after they win (Ayton & Fischer, 2004), but field evidence has shown that sports betting (Camerer, 1989) and lottery ticket sales are weaker after wins (Clotfelter & Cook, 1989). For roulette and some other casino games, field evidence for hot hands has been stronger. Croson and Sundali (2005) show that 80% of roulette players quit after losing a spin, whereas only 20% quit after winning, and roulette players place more bets when they have just won than when they have previously lost; both observed behaviors are consistent with the hot hand belief. Sundali and Croson (2006) report that some gamblers cannot be reliably classified, but of those that can, they are about equally split between gambler's fallacy bettors and hot hand bettors. The researchers speculate, but did not test, that those with an internal locus of control are more likely to fall prey to either the hot hand or the gambler's fallacy.

One might conclude that teaching gamblers about the laws of probability would reduce these irrational behaviors, but apparently that is not the case. In Williams and Connolly's (2006) study, 470 university students either took a semester of probability and statistic lectures, with labs concentrating on gambling, or attended nonmathematics control lectures. The researchers found that the students in the statistical course had improved ability to calculate gambling odds and greater awareness of common irrational thoughts, as compared with the control students. However, they also found no significant difference between the groups in terms of likelihood of gambling, being a problem gambler, amount of time or money spent gambling, or overall attitudes toward gambling. Similarly, Hertwig, Barron, Weber, and Erev (2004) found that even students who were educated on the probabilities of winning were more likely to gamble on unlikely outcomes more often than statistically optimal outcomes. Hence, in terms of public policy, education about gambling odds may improve consumers' overall knowledge, but that knowledge may not necessarily be activated or used in a casino setting. Other interventions are therefore called for.

## SOCIETAL-BASED BELIEF: RESPONSIBLE GAMBLING CAN BE SUCCESSFULLY PROMOTED

There is the overriding belief that measures can be taken to help promote responsible gambling. For example, the American Gaming Association (2003) offers a resource guide for gaming operators to promote responsible gaming and solicits funding from these operators. In an effort to appear socially conscious, most casinos mandate that their employees go through training to recognize problem gambling and post signs in their casinos to alert gamblers to potential problems. Indeed, one of the main intents of the government-sponsored research on problem gambling has been to develop interventions to mitigate this problem. Increasingly, the term *responsible gambling* has appeared, with little effort to clearly define what it means (Blaszczynski, Ladouceur, & Shaffer, 2004). Exhortations to "please gamble responsibly" make little sense without a definition of what responsible gambling would look like. In reality, we know that for some people, any gambling is dangerous financially, socially, and psychologically.

The truth is that most interventions for promoting responsible gambling come too late or are relatively ineffective. Risk factors found to be associated with problem gambling include starting at a young age (Johansson, Grant, Kim, Odlaug, & Gotestam, 2009). A recent survey of teenagers ages 15–17 in the Canadian province of Ontario found that of those teens who gambled, the average age at which both problem and nonproblem gamblers reported first gambling was 13, with money used from either jobs or parental allowances (White, Mun, Kauffman, Whelan, & Regan, 2007). Some other known risk factors for problem gambling include being male, lower income, and non-Caucasian, and having only a high school education or less; thus, it appears that these individuals can be explicitly targeted. However, even after controlling for all these factors, more frequent gambling behavior, regardless of how "responsible," is still more likely to lead to gambling problems.

For example, Currie at al. (2009) demonstrated that people who gamble weekly or more, regardless of spending, are about 13 times more likely to experience gambling-related harm, independent of their age, gender, and socioeconomic status.

Recent survey work in the United States indicates that the rates of problem gambling are not appreciably higher for adolescents than adults (Welte, Barnes, Tidwell, & Hoffman, 2008). However, the more types of gambling for which youths were old enough to participate in legally, the more gambling involvement and problem gambling occurred (Welte, Barnes, Tidwell, & Hoffman, 2009). Although not all gamblers who begin gambling as teenagers become problem gamblers, most adult problem gamblers began their gambling as teenagers (Burge, Pietrzak, Molina, & Petry, 2004). In addition, there is a definite gender difference in adolescent gambling. Most studies of teenagers have shown that the prevalence of males gambling is much higher than that of females (e.g., Stinchfield, Cassuto, Winters, & Latimer, 1997; Volberg, 1998; Welte et al., 2008; Westphal, Rush, Stevens, & Johnson, 2000).

From a public policy standpoint, this means that education about the potential problems of gambling needs to come early, such as through schools or parents. Cotte and LaTour (2009) demonstrated the effect of family socialization on gambling, whereby the adoption of gambling was more acceptable if the youth came from a family that gambled. Clarke at al. (2007) demonstrated that a risk factor for pathological gambling is being introduced to gambling by friends and family. With increasing access to gambling, it is easy to imagine more progambling socialization influences and thereby more risk for gambling problems. However, public policy might possibly be able to use socialization agents to deter gambling rather than encourage it.

## SOCIETAL-BASED BELIEF: BAD PEOPLE CAUSE PROBLEM GAMBLING

A general belief among many people is that casinos and other entities that benefit from gambling are guilty of causing problem gambling. However, because problem gamblers are such a small percentage of the general population, and these gamblers tend to gamble more money than they have, they are not the ideal target market for casinos, which thrive on long-term relationships with paying customers. However, greater availability to gambling opportunities is a key risk factor for problematic gambling; those countries with the highest availability of gambling have the highest rates of problem gambling (Campbell & Lester, 1999; Johansson et al., 2009). The number of gambling options available to a person is positively related to whether he or she gambles, how frequently, and whether he or she develops gambling problems (Welte et al., 2009). Indeed, for American survey participants ages 18–21, the chance of being a problem gambler, as opposed to never having tried gambling, increased 39% for each additional type of legal gambling available in one's home state (Welte et al., 2009).

A growing public policy issue regarding availability concerns Internet gambling, because it has exploded, resulting in gambling being available virtually 100% to those with access to a computer with an Internet connection. Recently, researchers have demonstrated that the prevalence of problem gambling is higher for those gamblers who participate, versus those who do not, in Internet gambling, and the problem gambling percentages are much higher for Internet gamblers (over 20%) as compared to casino-based problem gamblers, for which estimates are typically in the range of 1–3% (Ladd & Petry, 2002; Wood, Williams, & Lawton, 2007). This is a very underresearched area, with just a few preliminary attempts at understanding possible public policy interventions (Currie, Hodgins, Wang, el-Guebaly, Wynne, & Miller, 2008; Delfabbro, 2008; Shandley & Moore, 2008). In particular,

> [T]here is currently little empirical support for the efficacy of online responsible gambling programs. Therefore, the majority of responsible gambling measures used online are not based on empirical data

demonstrating their effectiveness, but created on the face value of the presumed effect or extrapolated from strategies used for other forms of gambling, which also may lack empirical validity. (Monaghan, 2009, p. 203)

Many websites do not seriously attempt to protect players, for example, by verifying age or clearly indicating time and money spent while gambling. In fact, most responsible gambling initiatives are implemented by the Internet gambling sites themselves, which are unlikely to want to damage the site revenues (Monaghan, 2009; Smeaton & Griffiths, 2004). Most gamblers have reported some degree of losing track of time and a narrow focus on the game, rather than on other aspects of life, which is a phenomenon known as dissociation (Diskin & Hodgins, 1999; Jacobs, 1986, 1988; Noseworthy & Finlay, 2009). Dissociation is stronger for gamblers with a problem and appears to be stronger for Internet gamblers as well (Monaghan, 2009). Thus, it is particularly important to draw the attention of gamblers away from the game to help them take stock of their spending, in both time and money terms.

Cotte and LaTour (2009) recently argued for the regulation of online gambling, citing the possible use of pop-up messages to remind gamblers of their standings. There is some empirical research that suggests this could be helpful, including research on the use of pop-up messages on electronic gambling machines (Monaghan, 2008) and electronic roulette games (Floyd, Whelan, & Meyers, 2006). Also, in a lab study, researchers have found that participants placed in a warning message group demonstrated less risky gambling behavior and reported fewer irrational beliefs than those in the control, or no warning message, condition (Floyd et al., 2006). Using simple warning messages, such as, "Winning is completely due to chance. No luck is involved," and "If you continue gambling, you will eventually lose your money," the people in the aforementioned study were more risk averse. This research indicates that warning messages could be an effective solution to addictive and excessive gambling. Monaghan (2009) suggests also that the use of pop-up messages could promote more responsible gambling without affecting nonproblem gamblers. In further research, Monaghan and Blaszczynski (2010) suggest that the most effective warnings might be ones that get gamblers to self-reflect on their behavior. This would be an important policy consideration, as legislators would likely be pressured by legitimate casino businesses not to do this for fear it might interfere with the revenue generated by nonproblem gambling.

## SOCIETAL-BASED BELIEF: THERE ARE NO UPSIDES TO GAMBLING

Although this chapter has focused on the problems associated with gambling, there are some benefits as well. For instance, taxes on gambling help fund education, the casinos provide employment, and even for the problem gamblers, casinos provide a venue for social connections. In our own research, we found that going to casinos gave many Las Vegas retirees a "reason to get out of the house" and connect with their friends. Other researchers also found some psychological benefits from gambling for older consumers (e.g., Hope & Havir, 2002; Loroz, 2004). However, because the retiree population is often targeted and a focus of public policy (see, e.g., the discussion of Andreasen, Goldberg, & Sirgy, Chapter 2 of this volume), researchers need to provide oversight, so this population is not targeted with deceptive materials.

## WHERE TO FROM HERE?

Our review of the gambling literature identifies some potential areas for future research, ranging from ideal research methodologies (e.g., lab vs. casino settings) to different types of gamblers (e.g., how recreational gamblers become pathological gamblers) to new technologies that can be used in gambler education as well as the regulation of these new technologies in Internet spaces. These issues are discussed in more detail below.

### Research Methodologies

Lab studies of gambling are most commonplace and obviously easier for academic researchers to control. However, as we have discussed, these laboratory findings have not always translated into actual gambling behavior. For example, studies without real financial upside potential for gamblers will not activate goals for winning money, whereas many casino gamblers have definite goals and plans for their winnings. Many gamblers in a lab are limited to winning a token prize amount, if anything; few social science researchers are funded to the extent that they could cover true gambling wins. In addition, players in real casinos are usually playing to beat the house, not to win points or prizes in a gambling study. Finally, and perhaps most importantly, there is no real risk in a lab study without a monetary investment; the presence of risk is typically necessary to create the high levels of arousal found in real gamblers while gambling (Anderson & Brown, 1984; Conlisk, 1993; Cotte, 1997). University ethics boards may not allow research studies to expose gamblers to true risks, particularly studies focusing on the most serious risks.

Lab studies will therefore continue to be an important part of future research on gambling. However, if researchers can identify reasons for the differences in findings between a lab environment and a real casino environment (e.g., arousal, emotional engagement), then researchers can try to simulate real experiences in the lab to better approach real gambling. The lack of sensory stimulation and physiological arousal may account for some of the differences. However, some researchers have suggested that as long as gamblers are allowed to win and lose real money, field and lab results will be roughly the same (Ladouceur, Gaboury, Bujold, Lachance, & Tremblay, 1991).

### Gambling Populations

As discussed earlier, the majority of research thus far has been on pathological or problem gamblers. There is little understanding on how a recreational gambler moves from exhibiting normal gambling to problem gambling. There is quite a bit of research on the susceptibility of the young to later gambling problems, which is, of course, a population of interest to public policy makers. The research on the elderly, however, has been limited, and because of this group's frequent gambling, future research ought to address how to help them maintain a healthy gambling lifestyle. In doing so, researchers would help provide insight into what "responsible gambling" might look like.

### The Internet

LaBrie, Kaplan, LaPlante, Nelson, and Shaffer (2008) found that rates of Internet gambling are low compared to other types of gambling. However, they identified the potential of online gambling to grow and attract players because of some uniquely appealing aspects, such as anonymity, proximity, and a greater sense of control. Moreover, the loose regulations implemented by many gambling websites, combined with younger generations' familiarity with, interest in, and access to computer technology, signal that underage gambling may become a more serious public health concern in the future. Internet gambling presents an entirely different set of challenges for governments, regulators, and antigambling advocates. There are few reliable methods to verify Internet gamblers' true ages, and little is known about how to truly educate and warn them about the negative effects of excessive gambling. Research also suggests that online gamblers are more likely to be problem gamblers (Griffiths & Barnes, 2008).

Further research and the gathering of recent empirical evidence about Internet gambling will lead to a deeper understanding of this new phenomenon. However, it seems to be difficult to gather accurate Internet gambling data, as many of these websites are unregistered or located in countries that do not track or regulate gambling activity; yet, Canada may prove to be a new research site, as several provinces are moving to regulate online gambling. Specific research is limited, but general studies have concluded that technological advances in Internet-based gambling will increase the potential for problem gambling globally (Griffiths & Parke, 2002). Griffiths, Parke, Wood, and Parke (2006) identified multiple factors that may make Internet gambling potentially more seductive and/or addictive, including anonymity of the gambler, convenience to gamble anywhere, escape from everyday reality without having to leave home, easy accessibility to gambling and the means to gamble (i.e., credit cards), higher frequency of gambling, and interactivity between gamblers in a virtual casino (for a discussion of quality of virtual life, see Novak, Chapter 11 of this volume).

One potential solution for regulating Internet gambling is a self-limit feature that users can select. However, the literature shows that self-limiting features are not always effective. Nelson et al. (2008) found that self-limiting gamblers played a wider variety of games, placed more bets than they did before imposing limits on themselves, and did not reduce the amount they wagered per bet. Screening questions to help identify problem gamblers on the Internet or in casinos tend to be qualitative in nature, for example, often asking gamblers whether they spend more than they planned to or whether gambling creates a problem for those around them. Recently, there have been calls to use more research-based, quantitative questions to help identify problem gamblers. Questions about actual quantities (e.g., "Do you gamble more than three times per month?") have been shown to be very good predictors of problem gambling and could be used to generate harm-reduction strategies (Currie, Hodgins, Wang, el-Guebaly, & Wynne, 2008; Currie, Hodgins, Wang, el-Guebaly, Wynne, & Miller, 2008; Grun & McKeigue, 2000). There are many potential avenues for further public policy work in this area, and we encourage more Transformative Consumer Research on the topic of gambling. The odds of making an impact with your research will likely be in your favor!

## REFERENCES

American Gaming Association. (2003). *Code of conduct for responsible gaming.* Washington, DC: Author. Retrieved January 7, 2011, from http://www.americangaming.org/assets/files/Code_with_bookmarks.pdf

American Psychiatric Association. (2000). *Diagnostic and statistical manual of mental disorders* (4th ed., text rev.). Washington, DC: Author.

Anderson, G., & Brown, R. I. F. (1984). Real and laboratory gambling, sensation seeking and arousal. *British Journal of Psychology, 85,* 401–410.

Anderson, G., & Brown, R. I. F. (1987). Some applications of reversal theory to the explanation of gambling and gambling addictions. *Journal of Gambling Behavior, 3*(Fall), 179–189.

Ayton, P., & Fischer, I. (2004). The gambler's fallacy and the hot hand fallacy: Two faces of subjective randomness? *Memory & Cognition, 32,* 1369–1378.

Basham, M., & Kwon, E. Y. (2009). *Industry surveys: Lodging & gaming.* New York: Standard & Poor's.

Blaszczynski, A., Ladouceur, R., & Shaffer, H. J. (2004). A science-based framework for responsible gambling: The Reno model. *Journal of Gambling Studies, 20,* 301–317.

Burge, A. N., Pietrzak, R. H., Molina, C. A., & Petry, N. M. (2004). Age of gambling initiation and severity of gambling and health problems among the older adult problem gamblers. *Psychiatric Services, 55,* 1437–1439.

Caldwell, C. (2008, April 13). Bad bet. *The New York Times,* p. 13.

Camerer, C. (1989). Does the basketball market believe in the "hot hand"? *American Economic Review, 79,* 1257–1261.

Campbell, F., & Lester, D. (1999). The impact of gambling opportunities on compulsive gambling. *Journal of Social Psychology, 139,* 126–127.

Campbell-Meiklejohn, D. K., Woolrich, M. W., Passingham, R. E., & Rogers, R. D. (2008). Knowing when to stop: The brain mechanisms of chasing losses. *Biological Psychiatry, 63,* 293–300.

Carroll, D., & Huxley, J. A. A. (1994). Cognitive, dispositional, and psychophysical correlates of dependent slot machine gambling in young people. *Journal of Applied Social Psychology, 24,* 1070–1083.

Chau, A., & Phillips, J. (1995). Effects of perceived control upon wagering and attributions in computer blackjack. *Journal of General Psychology, 122,* 252–269.

Cialdini, R. B., Reno, R. R., & Kallgren, C. A. (1990). A focus theory of normative conduct: Recycling the concept of norms to reduce littering in public places. *Journal of Personality and Social Psychology, 58*(June), 1015–1026.

Clark, L., Lawrence, A. J., Astley-Jones, F., & Gray, N. (2009). Gambling near-misses enhance motivation to gamble and recruit win-related brain circuitry. *Neuron, 61*(3), 481–490.

Clarke, D., Tse, S., Abbott, M. W., Townsend, S., Kingi, P., & Manaia, W. (2007). Reasons for starting and continuing gambling in a mixed ethnic community sample of pathological and non-problem gamblers. *International Gambling Studies, 7*(3), 299–313.

Clotfelter, C., & Cook, P. (1989). *Selling hope: State lotteries in America.* Cambridge, MA: Harvard University Press.

Conlisk, J. (1993). The utility of gambling. *Journal of Risk and Uncertainty, 6*(June), 255–275.

Cote, D., Caron, A., Aubert, J., & Ladouceur, R. (2003). Near wins prolong gambling on a video lottery terminal. *Journal of Gambling Studies, 19*(4), 380–407.

Cotte, J. (1997). Chances, trances, and lots of slots: Gambling motives and consumption experiences. *Journal of Leisure Research, 29*(4), 380–406.

Cotte, J., & LaTour, K. (2009). Blackjack in the kitchen: Understanding online versus casino gambling. *Journal of Consumer Research, 35*(February), 742–758.

Croson, R. L., & Sundali, J. (2005). The gambler's fallacy and the hot hand: Empirical data from casinos. *Journal of Risk and Uncertainty, 30*(93), 195–209.

Currie, S. R., Hodgins, D. C., Wang, J., & Chen, S. (2009). *Risk of harm among gamblers in the general population as a function of level of participation in gambling activities.* Unpublished manuscript, Alberta Gaming Research Institute.

Currie, S. R., Hodgins, D. C., Wang, J., el-Guebaly, N., & Wynne, H. (2008). In pursuit of empirically based responsible gambling limits. *International Gambling Studies, 8*(2), 207–227.

Currie, S. R., Hodgins, D. C., Wang, J., el-Guebaly, N., Wynne, H., & Miller, N. (2008). Replication of low-risk gambling limits using Canadian provincial gambling prevalence data. *Journal of Gambling Studies, 24,* 321–335.

Delfabbro, P. (2008). Evaluating the effectiveness of a limited reduction in electronic gaming machine availability on perceived gambling behavior and objective expenditure. *International Gambling Studies, 8*(2), 151–165.

Delfabbro, P. H., & Winefield, A. H. (2000). Predictors of irrational thinking in regular slot machine gamblers. *Journal of Psychology, 134*(7), 117–128.

Dickerson, M., Hinchy, J., England, S. L., Fabre, J., & Cunnigham, R. (1992). On the determinants of persistent gambling behavior: High frequency poker machine players. *British Journal of Psychology, 83,* 237–248.

Diskin, K., & Hodgins, D. (1999). Narrowing of attention and dissociation in pathological video lottery gamblers. *Journal of Gambling Studies, 15,* 17–28.

Dixon, M. R., & Schreiber, J. E. (2004). Near-miss effects on response latencies and win estimation of slot machine players. *Psychological Record, 54*(3), 335–348.

Ferris, J., & Wynne, H. J. (2001). *The Canadian problem gambling index final report.* Ottawa, ON: Canadian Centre on Substance Abuse.

Floyd, K., Whelan, J. P., & Meyers, A. W. (2006). Use of warning messages to modify gambling beliefs and behavior in a laboratory investigation. *Psychology of Addictive Behaviors, 20,* 69–74.

Gaboury, A., & Ladouceur, R. (1988). Irrational thinking and gambling. In W. R. Eadington (Ed.), *Gambling research: Proceedings of the seventh International Conference on Gambling and Risk Taking* (Vol. 3, pp. 142–163). Reno: University of Nevada.

Gehring, W. J., & Willoughby, A. R. (2002). The medial frontal cortex and the rapid processing of monetary gains and losses. *Science, 295,* 2279–2281.

Ghezzi, P. M., Wilson, G. R., & Porter, J. (2006). The near-miss effect in simulated slot machine play. In P. M. Ghezzi, C. A. Lyons, M. R. Dixon, & G. R. Wilson (Eds.), *Gambling: Behavior theory, research, and application* (pp. 155–170). Reno, NV: Context Press.

Gilovich, T., Vallone, R., & Tversky, A. (1985). The hot hand in basketball: On the misperception of random sequences. *Cognitive Psychology, 17,* 295–314.

Griffiths, M. (1993). Tolerance in gambling: An objective measure using the psychophysiological analysis of male fruit machine gamblers. *Addictive Behavior, 18,* 365–372.

Griffiths, M. D., & Barnes, A. (2008). Internet gambling: An online empirical study among gamblers. *International Journal of Mental Health Addiction, 6*(2), 194–204.

Griffiths, M., & Delfabbro, P. (2001). The biopsychosocial approach to gambling: Contextual factors in research and clinical interventions. *Electronic Journal of Gambling Issues*, issue 5. Available: http://jgi.camh.net/toc/jgi//5

Griffiths, M. D., & Parke, A. (2002). The social impact of internet gambling. *Social Science Computer Review*, *20*(3), 312–320.

Griffiths, M. D., Parke, A., Wood, R. T. A., & Parke, J. (2006). Internet gambling: An overview of psychosocial impacts. *Gaming Research & Review Journal*, *27*(1), 27–39.

Grun, L., & McKeigue, P. (2000). Prevalence of excessive gambling before and after introduction of a national lottery in the United Kingdom: Another example of the single distribution theory. *Addiction*, *95*, 959–966.

Harrigan, K. A. (2009). Slot machines: Pursuing responsible gaming practices for virtual reels and near misses. *International Journal of Mental Health Addiction*, *7*, 68–83.

Hertwig, R., Barron, G., Weber, E., & Erev, I. (2004). Decisions from experience and the effect of rare events in risky choice. *Psychological Science*, *15*, 534–539.

Hope, J., & Havir, L. (2002). You bet they're having fun! Older Americans and casino gambling. *Journal of Aging Studies*, *16*, 177–197.

Ipsos. (2008). *Canada and US public perceptions of Internet gambling*. Retrieved October 29, 2010, from http://www.ipsos-na.com/news-polls/pressrelease.aspx?id=3792

Jacobs, D. (1986). A general theory of addictions: A new theoretical model. *Journal of Gambling Behavior*, *2*, 15–31.

Jacobs, D. (1988). Evidence for a common dissociative-like reaction among addicts. *Journal of Gambling Behavior*, *4*, 27–37.

Johansson, A., Grant, J. E., Kim, S. W., Odlaug, B. L., & Gotestam, K. G. (2009). Risk factors for problematic gambling: A critical literature review. *Journal of Gambling Studies*, *25*, 67–92.

Kahneman, D., & Tversky, A. (1979). Prospect theory: An analysis of decision under risk. *Econometrica*, *47*, 253–292.

Kassinove, J., & Schare, M. (2001). Effects of the "near miss" and the "big win" at persistence in slot machine gambling. *Psychology of Addictive Behaviors*, *15*(2), 155–158.

LaBrie, R. A., Kaplan, S., LaPlante, D. A., Nelson, S. E., & Shaffer, H. J. (2008). Inside the virtual casino: A prospective longitudinal study of Internet casino gambling. *European Journal of Public Health*, *18*(4), 410–416.

Ladd, G. T., & Petry, N. M. (2002). Disordered gambling among university-based medical and dental patients: A focus on Internet gambling. *Psychology of Addictive Behaviors*, *16*, 76–79.

Ladouceur, R., Gaboury, A., Bujold, A., Lachance, N., & Tremblay, S. (1991). Ecological validity of laboratory studies of videopoker gaming. *Journal of Gambling Studies*, *7*(2), 109–116.

Langer, E. (1975). The illusion of control. *Journal of Personality and Social Psychology*, *32*, 311–328.

Leary, K., & Dickerson, M. (1985). Levels of arousal in high- and low-frequency gamblers. *Behavioral Research Therapy*, *23*, 635–640.

Lesieur, H., & Blume, S. (1987). The South Oaks Gambling Screen (SOGS): A new instrument for the identification of pathological gamblers. *American Journal of Psychiatry*, *144*, 1185–1188.

Loroz, P. S. (2004). Golden age gambling: Psychological benefits and self-concept dynamics in aging consumers' consumption experiences. *Psychology & Marketing*, *21*(5), 323–349.

May, R. K., Whelan, J. P., Meyers, A. W., & Steenbergh, T. A. (2005). Gambling-related irrational beliefs in the maintenance and modification of gambling behaviour. *International Gambling Studies*, *5*(2), 155–167.

Meyer, G., Hauffa, B. P., Schedlowski, M., Pawlak, C., Stadler, M. A., & Exton, M. S. (2000). Casino gambling increases heart rate and salivary cortisol in regular gamblers. *Biological Psychiatry*, *48*, 948–953.

Meyer, G., Schwertfeger, J., Exton, M. S., Janssen, O. E., Knapp, W., Stadler, M. A., et al. (2004). Neuroendocrine responses to casino gambling in problem gamblers. *Psychoneuroendocrinology*, *29*, 1272–1280.

Monaghan, S. (2008). Review of pop-up messages on electronic gaming machines as a proposed responsible gambling strategy. *International Journal of Mental Health & Addiction*, *6*, 214–222.

Monaghan, S. M. (2009). Responsible gambling strategies for Internet gambling: The theoretical and empirical base of using pop-up messages to encourage self-awareness. *Computers in Human Behavior*, *25*, 202–207.

Monaghan, S., & Blaszczynski, A. (2010). Electronic gaming machine warning messages: Information versus self-evaluation. *Journal of Psychology*, *144*(1), 83–96.

Nelson, S. E., LaPlante, D. A., Peller, A .J., Schumann, A., LaBrie, R. A., & Shaffer, H. J. (2008). Real limits in the virtual world: Self-limiting behavior of Internet gamblers. *Journal of Gambling Studies*, *24*, 463–477.

Noseworthy, T. J., & Finlay, K. (2009). A comparison of ambient casino sound and music: Effects on dissociation and on perceptions of elapsed time while playing slot machines. *Journal of Gambling Studies*, *25*(September), 331–342.

Parke, J., & Griffiths, M. D. (2004). Gambling addiction and the evolution of the near miss. *Addiction Theory and Research, 12,* 407–411.

Petry, N. M. (2005). *Pathological gambling: Etiology, comorbidity, and treatment.* Washington, DC: American Psychological Association.

Rabin, M. (2002). Inference by believers in the law of small numbers. *Quarterly Journal of Economics, 157,* 775–816.

Schwartz, M. (2006, June 11). The hold-'em holdup. *The New York Times.* Available: http://www.nytimes .com/2006/06/11/magazine/11poker.html?_r=1

Shandley, K., & Moore, S. (2008). Evaluation of gambler's helpline: A consumer perspective. *International Gambling Studies, 8*(3), 315–330.

Simmons, J. P., & Novemsky, N. (2008). *From loss aversion to loss acceptance: How casino contexts can undermine loss aversion.* Unpublished manuscript, Yale University, New Haven, CT.

Smeaton, M., & Griffiths, M. (2004). Internet gambling and social responsibility: An exploratory study. *CyberPsychology and Behavior, 7,* 49–57.

Stinchfield, R., Cassuto, N., Winters, K., & Latimer, W. (1997). Prevalence of gambling among Minnesota public school students in 1992 and 1995. *Journal of Gambling Studies, 13*(1), 25–48.

Sundali, J., & Croson, R. (2006). Biases in casino betting: The hot hand and the gambler's fallacy. *Judgment and Decision Making, 1*(1), 1–12.

Thaler, R. (1980). Toward a positive theory of consumer choice. *Journal of Economic Behavior & Organization, 1*(1), 39–60.

Toneatto, T., Blitz-Miller, T., Calderwood, K., Dragonetti, R., & Tsanos, A. (1997). Cognitive distortions in heavy gambling. *Journal of Gambling Studies, 13,* 253–266.

Tversky, A., & Kahneman, D. (1971). Belief in the law of small numbers. *Psychological Bulletin, 76,* 105–110.

Tversky, A., & Kahneman, D. (1981). The framing of decisions and the psychology of choice. *Science, 211*(4481), 453–458.

Volberg, R. A. (1998). *Gambling and problem gambling among adolescents in New York.* Albany: New York Council on Problem Gambling.

Welte, J. W., Barnes, G. M., Tidwell, M. O., & Hoffman, J. H. (2008). The prevalence of problem gambling among U.S. adolescents and young adults: Results from a national survey. *Journal of Gambling Studies, 24,* 119–133.

Welte, J. W., Barnes, G. M., Tidwell, M. O., & Hoffman, J. H. (2009). Legal gambling availability and problem gambling among adolescents and young adults. *International Gambling Studies, 9*(2), 89–99.

Westphal, J. R., Rush, J. A., Stevens, L., & Johnson, L. J. (2000). Gambling behavior of Louisiana students in grades 6 through 12. *Psychiatric Services, 51*(1), 96–99.

White, M. A., Mun, P., Kauffman, N., Whelan, C., & Regan, M. (2007). *Teen gambling in Ontario: Behaviors and perceptions among 15 to 17 year-olds.* Toronto: Responsible Gaming Council.

Williams, R. J., & Connolly, R. (2006). Does learning about mathematics of gambling change gambling behavior? *Psychology of Addictive Behaviors, 20,* 62–68.

Williams, R. J., & Wood, R. T. (2004). The proportion of gaming revenue derived from problem gamblers: Examining the issues in a Canadian context. *Analyses of Social Issues and Public Policy, 4,* 33–45.

Wood, R. T., Williams, R. J., & Lawton, P. K. (2007). Why do Internet gamblers prefer online versus land-based venues: Some preliminary findings and implications. *Journal of Gambling Issues, 20,* 235–252.

Xuan, Z., & Shaffer, H. (2009). How do gamblers end gambling: Longitudinal analysis of Internet gambling behaviors prior to account closure due to gambling related problems. *Journal of Gambling Studies, 25,* 239–252.

# 24

# *Porn 2.0*

## The Libidinal Economy and the Consumption of Desire in the Digital Age

JULIE M. ALBRIGHT

As a point of entry into the consumption of porn in the digital era, I offer the following case example: With a slight tilt of her head, eyes sparkling, and a bright smile, blonde and vivacious Jesse Logan was the image of the all-American high school cheerleader, the kind of girl many aspire to be. In an increasingly common act among teens today, Jesse took and sent sexy, nude photos of herself to her teenaged boyfriend, seemingly without much thought to the consequences. Fueled by passion and hormones but not enough maturity to weather the inevitable storms, the relationship flamed out. When it did, Jesse's boyfriend, perhaps feeling jilted and as an act of revenge, digitally distributed the photos to classmates at school. Soon, Jesse's grades plummeted, and she began skipping school to avoid bullying by the girls, who in *Mean Girls* fashion, threw objects at her and called her a slut, whore, and porn queen. Humiliated, depressed, and ashamed, Jesse went on television to warn other teens of the dangers of taking and distributing nude photos. In the taped interview, disguised in a cloak of anonymity, she can be heard saying, "I just want to make sure no one else will have to go through this again." Two months later, her mother discovered Jesse hanging in her bedroom. She was 18 years old (Celizic, 2009, para. 2).

Jesse Logan wasn't a "bad girl," a porn queen, or even that unusual. Lest we think her case an isolated example of teens and porn, consider the following recent newspaper reports. A 17-year-old Wisconsin student was charged with possessing child pornography after posting naked pictures that his teenaged ex-girlfriend sent him on his MySpace page. In Pennsylvania, three teenage girls and three male classmates were charged with child pornography after the girls sent naked or partially naked photos of themselves to the boys. In Rochester, New York, a 16-year-old boy faces 7 years in jail after he forwarded a naked picture that his 15-year-old girlfriend sent to his friends.

Such examples of producing and distributing pornographic images have been termed *sexting*, which is becoming increasingly common among schoolchildren in the United States today. One poll put the number at one in five American teenagers, while another put it as high as one in three (National Campaign, 2009). It seems pornography has become a part of the youth cultural zeitgeist: Soft-core porn arises from mass media advertising and television shows (Rossi, 2007), hip-hop videos sell sexual desire with strippers gyrating and looking sexy (Railton & Watson, 2007), and hard-core sexual photos appear alongside pictures of high school friends on MySpace. Pornographic references in popular culture have become so commonplace that one author has referred to them as "porno chic" (McNair, 2002). Kids are not just being passively victimized by inadvertent exposure to pornography (e.g., accidently stumbling on it via a Google search while doing homework), but they are also active consumers themselves. A 2009 report by Symantec of the top 10 most frequent terms searched for online by kids from February to July 2009 identified number four as "sex" and number six as "porn," while "boobs" came in at number 28 (Whitney, 2009). Interactive social media sites like Chatroullette and even MySpace foster a Wild West–like atmosphere where kids can readily see hard-core and live streaming pornographic images with the click of a mouse. Growing up in this "pornosphere" (McNair, 2002), it perhaps comes as no surprise that kids now are more sexually precocious than those of earlier generations. By age 15, already a quarter of both boys and girls have had intercourse (Mosher, Chandra, & Jones, 2005), as opposed to only 4% of those turning 15 in 1954–1963, 6% in 1964–1973, 10% in 1974–1983, and 13% in 1984–1993 (Finer, 2007).

Adults are also consuming porn in record numbers. A U.S. national poll conducted on MSNBC. com, a mainstream online news website, found that 75% of men and 41% of women admitted they had intentionally downloaded or viewed porn (Albright, 2008), while an international study of 9,000 adults in 12 countries found that 4 out of 10 adults in all countries had visited porn sites ("Sex, Porn, Team Jacob," 2009). Despite Apple's attempt to keep porn off its iPhones, worldwide revenue from mobile phone pornography alone is expected to rise to $1 billion and could grow to three times that number within a few years (Bryan-Low & Pringle, 2005). What is new is that both kids and adults are now not only porn consumers but are active cocreators of it as well. Marketing research has addressed the notion of cocreation (Vargo & Lusch, 2004), in which consumers become producers; research in this area has focused on cocreation and branding (C. T. Allen, Fournier, & Miller, 2008), product development (Sawhney, Verona, & Prandelli, 2005), advertising (Berthon, Pitt, & Campbell, 2008), and brand communities (Schau, Muñiz, & Arnould, 2009). New technologies such as multimedia message service (MMS) cell phone texting, digital recorders in both cameras and phones, e-mail, social networking sites like MySpace, dating sites like AdultFriendFinder, and amateur porn sites like RedTube and YouPorn are facilitating the cocreation and distribution of pornography, creating an atmosphere of what could be called participatory porn or Porn 2.0 (Mowlabocus, 2010), with some "amateurs" doing it for pay.

The lines between public and private, sex work and sexuality, and porn and pop culture are being blurred by these new technologies, creating new issues and inspiring the need for new research. As such, this chapter aims to explore the social, legal, and policy issues raised by Porn 2.0, and its broader implications, including the "pornification" of mainstream marketing and consumer culture, through the tropes of porn's visual culture, including the sexualized girl-child Lolita, bondage, strippers, ménage à trois, and interracial sex. These sexed-up images in turn provide new ways for teens and children to act sexy, posing new challenges for parents, policy makers, and school administrators. My goals for this chapter are to outline the historical development of porn to contextualize Porn 2.0, consider its impacts, and outline emerging areas in need of future research.

## WHAT AND WHERE IS PORN?

Porn itself is not a new historical development; rather, erotic depictions can be traced back to the roots of humankind. It has historically threaded through visual culture alongside the technological capabilities of its time and, in some cases, has helped drive the development of those technologies. The mutable nature of porn has vexed researchers and lawmakers alike who try to define it, as its shape shifts into new forms and distribution channels faster than lawmakers can keep up with it. Pornography pushes the bounds of decency based on current community values, often themselves contested. What is permissible to produce and consume has changed drastically since the advent of film, television, and digital media, making pinning down a single definition of *porn* difficult, as evidenced by U.S. Chief Justice Potter Stewart's famous utterance,

"I'll know it when I see it" (Silver, 2003, p. 1). In the late 1990s, Robert Jensen and Gail Dines (1998), an antiporn feminist, defined *pornography* as "the material sold in pornography shops for the purposes of producing sexual arousal for mostly male consumers" (p. 65). Since the explosion of pornography on the Internet since the late 1990s, this definition seems almost quaint, in that the containment of porn within the "erogenous zone" of the "adult" store is part of what defines it. Yet, the pornographic cat is out of that bag, and the privatization of porn via pay-per-view television and the Internet has had vast and, as yet, largely underexplored ramifications for its consumption, production, and distribution.

Pre-Internet, if we were to imagine the portrait of a porn consumer, would probably bring to mind a "certain kind" of male, perhaps of questionable character, skulking in and out of a forlorn strip mall porn shop with a bright pink XXX neon sign beckoning from its window. Few women and no teens would have been found there, and certainly no children. We have come a long way in just the last 10 years in changing this profile as a result of digital technologies. In the following section, I offer a brief sketch of the stages of technological development linked to porn, and the changing porn consumer, and highlight some of the social and legal issues that arose at each stage of development to the present day.

### The Secret Life of Porn

The nude was a central figure in classical art tracing back to Roman and Greek antiquities, as an erotic signifier of sexuality for the male gaze (Mulvey, 1975). Overt sexuality, erect phalluses, and even homosexual sex acts were commonly depicted in art and on decorative objects, like pottery and cups of the ancient Greek and Roman eras. In the 1600s, artists like Peter Paul Rubens painted dozens of images of classical Greek mythological figures, shown nude and clearly eroticized. Later, in the 1800s, when trade between the African continent and Europe became more common, images of odalisques became a recurring trope in the Orientalist tradition; shown white, nude, and reclining, these portraits of chambermaids to the concubines of sultans from the Middle East captured the erotic imaginations of Europeans about the raw and exotic sexuality of "the Orient" and harem life at the time. Nochlin (1994) describes the typical depiction as "disempowered, pacified, prettified, exaggeratedly sexualized or purified" (p. 59), a description that could be readily lifted and applied to modern porn stars.

Although erotic imagery can be traced back to premodern man in sculpture, painting, and mosaics, the term *pornography* did not come into the public lexicon until the mid-1800s, from the Greek word *pornographos*, meaning to write about prostitutes (Kendrick, 1987). The invention of the printing press was a key technological driver during this time. The widespread availability of books, pamphlets, and other printed materials expanded the scope of people who could read, ushering in the erotic novel and with it, the first widespread public concern about porn. Most of the original authors of erotic novels were male, the most famous of these being the Marquis de Sade and his now classic *120 Days of Sodom*. At the time, clear class distinctions were made in terms of access to erotic or pornographic materials. Erotic novels and art were housed away from public view in secretoriums, or secret museums, where only elite educated or upper-class men had access (Kendrick, 1987). By the early 1900s, warnings were issued about such material getting into the hands of the masses, because they were thought to lack the education, class, and cultural capital to properly interpret the art; without proper interpretation by people with the right background, erotic art was thought to be merely obscene (Fonsegrive, 1912). Yet, the cheap cost of producing books, pamphlets, and similar materials meant erotic writing inevitably found its way into the hands of the masses. Bénedict Morel, an early practitioner of psychophysiology, called such material "alcohol for the brain," which was likely to result in deleterious effects similar to alcohol consumed in excess (Stora-Lamarre, 2005, p. 56).

In France, many erotic novels were seized; the books, some 900 in all, were collected in a reposi-tory called the L'Enfer de la Bibliothèque National, or the Hell Collection of the National Library, with the reference to hell indicating the plans to burn them (Stora-Lamarre, 2005). By the late 1800s, concern about the spread of pornography rose to the point that an international congress on pornography, founded by Protestants, was convened in Bern, Switzerland. Subsequently, an International Bureau Against Immoral Literature was created by the Swiss to act as a dike against what was seen as a flood of pornography (Stora-Lamarre, 2005). During this same period, porno-graphic cartoons became popular. In addition to coding the erotic, they served a second purpose as a political tool to satirize and criticize political and religious authorities by eroticizing and portray-ing them as impotent, amoral, and, in the case of Marie Antoinette, castrating (Hunt, 1993). Such political usage has survived into modern times, when, for example, sexualized cartoons of strong female political figures like Margaret Thatcher of Britain and America's Hillary Clinton have been shown in sadistic and masochistic attire in venues like *Playboy* magazine, perhaps as a way to blow off steam or sublimate men's resentment of such powerful women by portraying them in an overtly sexual and, thus, humiliating manner.

In England, the Obscene Publications Act of 1857 was one of the first attempts to make illegal the sale of written pornography: This law gave the courts the right to seize and destroy porno-graphic material (Hunt, 1993). English case law later responded with the Hicklin test, through *Regina v. Hicklin* (1868), which states that a legislature can outlaw anything that "depraves and corrupts those whose minds are open to such immoral influences and into whose hands a publica-tion of this sort might fall" (sec. 00). In the United States, the courts looked to *Regina v. Hincklin* to develop the Comstock Act of 1873, which criminalized the transmission and receipt of "obscene, lewd, and/or lascivious" materials through the U.S. mail (Lamay, 1997, p. 16). These legal responses were designed with the overt intention of protecting the masses, particularly youth, from the cor-rupting and immoral influence of pornography.

## Photography, *Playboy*, and the "Girls Next Door"

The invention of photography at the end of the 1800s and later advances in printing halftone black-and-white photographic images ushered in an entirely new era of pornography. Depictions of real women, rather than stylized artist renderings, brought a new erotic charge to pornogra-phy, as well as new social and legal challenges. Beginning in France and later crossing the Atlantic to the United States, magazines appeared that purported to focus on "nature" scenes featuring nude actresses, models, or burlesque entertainers. These magazines were quite controversial at the time (Rodley, Bailey, Williams, & Varma, 2006). Prior to 1930, early stag films were pro-duced, containing themes of nudity, prostitution, and drug use. Covertly made and consumed by small, male audiences, these films were later made illegal by the Production Code of 1934, also known as the Hays Code, which became a stern film industry code to restrict the production of films and regulate "morally offensive" content. The code insisted that the "sanctity of home and marriage should be upheld," and "pictures should not infer that low forms of sex relation-ships are the accepted or common thing" (Association of Motion Picture Producers, Inc., 1930). Responding to the racial and eugenics concerns of the time, the code explicitly denounced sexual depictions of white slavery and miscegenation, defined as sex relationships between Whites and Blacks. The Hays Code remained in place for the film industry until the 1960s, when American mores in regard to sexuality began to change, and the code was replaced by the modern film rating system.

During World War II, many soldiers serving overseas were exposed to porn as an act of enemy propaganda. Both the Germans and the Japanese printed and dropped leaflets featuring pinups in an attempt to demoralize the troops, yet they had quite the opposite effect. Joseph Balkoski

(1989), in his memoir *Beyond the Beachhead: The 29th Infantry Division in Normandy*, describes the impact of the porn dropped on them:

> The enemy's leaflets were nothing more than appeals to the American soldier's sexual instincts. A typical leaflet featured a sketch of an attractive and scantily clad woman in the arms of a happy male civilian. The caption asked what the G.I.'s thought they would be doing if they were home instead of in the army. The 29ers chuckled and hoped the Germans would send more over the lines. (p. 237)

The Japanese also dropped sexually explicit pictures of beautiful women on the troops, private parts and all, including some with the headline, "You can have this if you surrender." The propaganda bombers came every day, and the troops began trading the leaflets like baseball cards (Daws, 1994, p. 66).

The exposure to porn during the war set the stage for it to come out of the closet after the troops returned home. In 1953, Hugh Hefner debuted a sex-themed magazine for discerning gentlemen titled *Playboy* (n.d.). With the creation of *Playboy*, porn went mainstream. Soon after, a number of Playboy Clubs opened across the country, fostering an elite atmosphere catering to the sophisticated businessman. While there, men would be attended to by "bunnies," costumed to emphasize their figures and bustlines and fueling the sexual fantasy of the submissive, sexually available woman. The clubs reached their zenith in the 1980s, then lost ground and closed, but the Playboy bunny has lived on to become one of the most recognizable corporate logos in the world. Recently, the brand has enjoyed a renaissance of sorts, with a television series, *The Girls Next Door* (Burns & Hefner, 2005–2011), focused on the Playboy lifestyle, featuring a bevy of blonde girlfriends living with "Hef" at the Playboy mansion. Following the show's success, the Playboy Club recently reopened in Las Vegas, with other locations planned.

*Playboy* relied on a "girl next door" type of sexuality for its appeal. The photo spreads were considered soft-core and did not feature genitalia or other hard-core depictions. Some *Playboy* models, like Marilyn Monroe, Anna Nicole Smith, and Pamela Anderson, later went on to lucrative mainstream modeling, television, and film careers after their features in *Playboy*. Young women who were not porn actresses or porn models were willing, and still are, to pose nude for *Playboy* because of its branding as mainstream sexuality. Yet, controversy over decency still swirled around the relatively tame *Playboy*, by today's standards. Hefner was arrested for obscenity for a pictorial titled "The Nudist Jayne Mansfield," but was later acquitted (Breitbart & Ebner, 2004). Other, more hard-core magazines followed, such as *Hustler* and *Penthouse*, both of which featured full nudity and genitalia. *Playboy* reached a circulation high in 1978, with a total of 7,161,561 subscribers (Playboy, 2009). Since then, its circulation has fallen by half, as competition from both the hard-core imagery of the Internet and the soft-core porn featured in popular lad mags, like *Maxim*, *FHM*, and *Stuff*, have negatively impacted sales.

Limp Dicks and Art House Porn: The Video Era

The 1960s' sexual revolution marked another cultural flash point in terms of legally defining what is or is not pornographic or obscene, as adult videos intensified the public debate about porn. During the 1960s and 1970s, a good number of porn actors, porn directors, and art house theater owners were arrested, resulting in obscenity cases that went all the way to the U.S. Supreme Court. One case of note was *Jacobellis v. Ohio* (1964), when an Ohio man was arrested for showing French director Louis Malle's *The Lovers* at his art house theater. Such a film would barely raise an eyebrow in the current cultural milieu. Yet, the Supreme Court heard the landmark case, described by Bob Woodward, the reporter from Watergate, and Scott Armstrong in their book *The Brethren: Inside the Supreme Court*, who outlined Supreme Court "movie nights," when the chief justices would sit down with popcorn and screen pornographic films to define what was obscene. Their law clerks devised shorthand definitions for the various justices' definitions of *obscenity*. Looking back now, in light of our current culture, the struggle to define the term seems somewhat amusing. According to Justice Byron White, "No erect penises, no intercourse, no oral or anal sodomy ... equaled no obscenity." Justice William Brennan, Jr.'s take was deemed the "limp dick test." It was, simply put, no erections. Oral sex or penetration was tolerable, as long as there were no erections involved. Finally, Justice Stewart's version, himself a former Navy lieutenant in World War II who had seen men bring back pornography from Europe, was called the "Casablanca test." Stewart was the justice who uttered the now infamous line, "I'll know it when I see it" (Woodward & Armstrong, 1979, p. 193).

Despite the arrests in the 1960s and early 1970s, pornographic films continued to be shown on theater screens across the nation. The 1970s became the crossover decade of porn into the public zeitgeist, with films like *Deep Throat*, *The Devil in Miss Jones*, and *Behind the Green Door* being seen by large audiences (Paasonen & Saarenmaa, 2007). It was said that even Jackie Kennedy went to see *Deep Throat* in an art house cinema. Something about these films excited the social imagination, and lines formed around the block at theaters around the country to see them. In the late and post-1960s "free love" era, people in the United States were apparently ready to consume sexual displays in a public arena. Yet, despite their urban popularity, controversy continued to swirl around these films. Arrests were made, and obscenity trials waged in Tennessee and other places, leading to the conviction of the director and one of the stars of *Deep Throat* (Allyn, 2001).

The invention and proliferation of VCRs in the late 1970s changed the game for porn, privatizing consumption within people's homes and bringing it into the bedroom communities of America's suburbs, which led some social analysts to call the 1970s the heyday of porn (Grahame-Smith, 2005). The increased private consumption of porn seemed to change Americans' values toward pornography, as much more blatant forms of sexual imagery became prevalent across American society. According to survey data from the General Social Survey in the years 1973–1992, one fourth of Americans had consumed porn in the previous year (Buzzell, 2005). Pay-per-view continued the privatization of porn consumption in both homes and hotel rooms across the nation, eschewing the need to venture out in public to buy or rent a videotape. Estimates of pay-per-view rentals of adult films in 2005 were $282 million for adult video on demand and $199 million in pay-per-view sales (Braiker, 2007). Overall, one conservative estimate of the U.S. porn industry put its 2007 revenues at $6 billion ("Hard Times," 2009).

### Porn Consumption in the Digital Age

The Internet has no doubt been the biggest factor in the mass production and distribution of porn in the United States. Although early 1990s bulletin boards provided pornographic images via dial-up on telephone line modems, with slow connections that could take 30 minutes to download one picture, millions of Americans had no computer access as yet or lacked the skills to download porn. The creation of the World Wide Web and the expansion of broadband capabilities have meant that images and films can now be uploaded or downloaded with ease, changing the industry of porn production, distribution, and consumption tremendously. The digital porn era exploded in the late 1990s to early 2000s, expanding the consumer market for porn within the privacy of homes. Despite this expansion, few studies exist on its consumption and impacts, probably due to its taboo nature. Many of the extant studies were conducted in the late 1990s or before, at the very beginning of the Internet boom. Since this time, with the advent of digital technologies, porn has become so ubiquitous that one analyst has charged that American society has now become "pornified" (Paul, 2005).

Males remain the predominant consumers of porn, regardless of technological format (Buzzell, 2005), yet an increasing number of females are also consuming it, most likely because of the triple

A engine of affordability, accessibility, and anonymity afforded by the Internet (Cooper, Scherer, Boies, & Gordon, 1999). A 2004 online poll conducted on MSNBC.com of more than 15,000 adults found that 75% of men and 41% of women have intentionally downloaded or viewed porn (Albright, 2008). Further, a 2008 study of young adults ages 18–26 revealed that nearly 9 of 10 young men (87%) and almost a third of young women (31%) in the study reported viewing pornography (Carroll et al., 2008). In addition, the majority of young men in the study (67%) and half the young women (49%) agreed that viewing pornography is acceptable (Carroll et al., 2008). A surprising number of teens and children under 18 have also accessed porn online. One study of 1,500 Internet users between 10 and 17 years old found that 42% of them reported being exposed to pornography on the Internet (Wolak, Mitchell, & Finkelhor, 2007). A 2009 study by Norton Online Family found that "sex" was the number four most frequently searched term by boys on Google; for girls, "sex" came in at number five ("Sex, Porn, Team Jacob," 2009). Youth at particular risk for exposure to porn include those most vulnerable, namely, youth who have reported being harassed or sexually solicited online or interpersonally victimized offline and individuals who have clinically diagnosed depression (Mitchell, Finkelhor, & Wolak, 2007). A 2005 survey by the same authors found that 13% of Internet users 10–17 years old had visited X-rated websites on purpose in the past year (Wolak et al., 2007). Unscrupulous website operators sometimes steer unwitting children to porn websites when they undertake keyword searches on search engines like Google by embedding invisible HTML keywords on their webpages, like "Barbie," "Barney," "candy," and other similar words popular with children.

Porn is also increasingly reaching children through the popular social-networking site MySpace, where children as young as 11—or perhaps even younger, although the official age is 14—have pages to keep in touch with their friends. I went on MySpace last year to prepare for a television interview, knowing that many in the adult entertainment industry have webpages there; I was more than surprised by the extent of hard-core and readily available pornographic images. I encountered images of a girl with a ball gag in her mouth, a man with his head between the legs of a woman in full cunnilingus, images of a stripper recreating the erotic chair dance from the movie *Flashdance*, and a variety of other actual sexual depictions. I sent a few of the images to the reporter doing the story. Concerned, she asked her manager about these images, and he told her they were too hardcore to be shown on television. What is perhaps most troubling is not just the unwanted exposure to porn but also the fact that child sexual predators can prepare or groom their victims prior to sexually assaulting them through games, candy, and, oftentimes, exposure to porn (Ost, 2009). On MySpace, kids are already pregroomed by interacting in a space peppered with pornographic imagery, a potentially dangerous and volatile atmosphere.

The juxtaposition of porn and children is troublesome for other reasons. One study reported higher rates of exposure and use of hard-core pornography among adult rapists and both heterosexual and homosexual child molesters when these individuals were juveniles, as compared to a group of adults without such offenses (Marshall, 1988). These rapists and molesters were also more likely to seek out such materials as children and consume more porn as adults (Marshall, 1988). A second study of juvenile sexual offenders versus violent crime offenders whose offenses were nonsexual found that 42% of the sex offenders, compared with 29% of the violent crime offenders, had consumed hard-core, sexually explicit magazines as kids (Ford & Linney, 1995).

The increased availability of porn, and changing social mores around it, poses perplexing theoretical and practical problems in defining it. As one researcher put it, "Pornography is an elusive term with a range of meanings, dependent not only on cultural, social, and historical contexts, but also on individuals' own experiences and beliefs" (Kendrick, 1996, pp. x–xii). Porn is now sometimes differentiated from erotica, which contains less hard-core or overt sexual depictions, yet for some, this distinction in terms of outcomes is mute (Russell, 1998). The Miller test, also known as the three prong obscenity test, adopted by the U.S. Supreme Court in *Miller v. California* (1973), is the standing definition for *obscenity*, which entails three criteria: (1) whether the average person, applying contemporary community standards, would find that the work, taken as a whole, appeals to the prurient interest; (2) whether the work depicts or describes, in a patently offensive way, sexual conduct or excretory functions specifically defined by applicable state law; and (3) whether the work, taken as a whole, lacks serious literary, artistic, political, and scientific value. The work is considered obscene only if all three conditions are satisfied. Some have argued from a communications perspective that halting a message at its source, thereby eliminating its consumption, as the Miller test was designed to do, will mediate porn's potentially negative effects (Wackwitz, 2002).

The new challenge of porn consumption by children online is probably the most stubborn and troubling aspect of its increased availability, and lawmakers and policy makers have been scrambling to keep up. Although all the top social-networking sites, like Facebook, Friendster, and MySpace, have antiporn policies, MySpace is the only one that does not edit for content, including porn, and the result is striking. On one hand, Facebook shows the occasional bikini or sexy club attire, but porn is markedly absent. MySpace, on the other hand, is filled with images from sexy strippers revealing their buttocks or breasts to hard-core sexual depictions. Concerned about the juxtaposition of children and porn, a number of states' attorneys general complained to the owners of MySpace. To identify issues and inform policy related to this issue, the Multi-State Working Group on Social Networking was formed in 2008, led by attorneys general Roy Cooper of North Carolina and Richard Blumenthal of Connecticut and now including the attorneys general of 47 other U.S. states and the District of Columbia. MySpace issued a statement that they would be working to address issues related to pornography and child predation on their site. MySpace then began cross-referencing lists of known sexual offenders with their user lists. As of March 2009, it identified 90,000 registered sex offenders who are registered on the site and, consequently, MySpace ejected them (Olivarez-Giles, 2009). Although MySpace most likely refrained from culling members' pornographic content in order not to decrease their hit count (i.e., the number of visitors, which is used to attract advertiser dollars), doing so may have worked against them. At present, MySpace is losing ground in terms of the number of people accessing and using their site, whereas Facebook is experiencing exponential growth, recently hitting the 400 million user mark (Facebook, 2010).

Educators have also been challenged by the easy availability of porn on the Internet to under-aged students. Some public libraries have installed Net Nanny screening software, in an attempt to weed out pornographic websites and images. The move has resulted in some unintended consequences, however, such as blocking health-related searches for both kids and low-income people who type in search terms like "breast cancer" (Richardson, Resnick, Hansen, Derry, & Rideout, 2002). Educational settings like universities may find themselves in difficult positions trying to regulate porn within their bounds, since the framing of porn as free speech has made banning it in such settings unconstitutional. Antiporn feminists like Andrea Dworkin and Catherine MacKinnon have argued virulently against this, saying that porn not only is words but also has real-world implications, as it depicts acts of rape and the subjugation of women (MacKinnon, 1993). Dworkin and MacKinnon proposed a law to ban pornography on the grounds that it exists as defamation or hate speech against women. Robert Jensen (2007), in his book *Getting Off: Pornography and the End of Masculinity*, took up a similar battle in the digital era, raising the question, "Why do so many pornographic movies include scenes where the woman seems to be in pain?" (p. 74). He problematizes porn in a similar way to the antiporn feminists:

> Sex is a sphere in which men are trained to see themselves as naturally dominant and women as naturally passive. Rape is both nominally illegal and completely normal at the same time, which is why men can engage in self-described behavior that meets the legal definition of rape and be certain they have never raped anyone. (p. 75)

Although porn in general has been protected as free speech, with restrictions for obscenity, the U.S. Supreme Court has narrowed the scope of consumption of pornography as a protected act when it involves child pornography. This tactic has removed it from the protection of the free speech umbrella, coming to terms that, as MacKinnon (1993) puts it, "child pornography conveys very effectively that children like to have sex with adults … child pornography is prohibited as child abuse, based on the use of children to make it" (p. 25). The Child Pornography Prevention Act of 1996 was enacted to restrict the production and consumption of virtual child porn, or child porn created through computer graphics. However, it was later struck down in *Ashcroft v. Free Speech Coalition* as being overly broad and not containing the elements of obscenity as outlined by *Miller v. California* (Cisneros, 2002).

## THE PORNIFICATION OF POPULAR CULTURE

The easy availability of digital porn seems to have led to a crossover effect in sexualized imagery in popular culture, resulting in an increase in depictions of women and children in an overtly sexualized manner. This crossover is no doubt an attempt by marketers to find an edge that arouses and differentiate their products in an increasingly noisy visual marketplace. As such, many have turned to porn, evoking the now familiar tropes of the sexualized girl-child Lolita, bondage, sadism and masochism (S&M), strippers, ménage à trois, and interracial sex. Porn in mainstream advertising and popular culture is becoming both more common and more hard-core. Examples range from Calvin Klein's ode to child porn (Agins, 1995), campaigns for Abercrombie & Fitch that feature threesomes (Kilbourne & Jhally, 2000), and H&M outdoor billboards hinting at bisexual flirting between women models (Rossi, 2007) to the unabashedly pornographic campaign for American Apparel. In the latter case, one ad of four panels featured four photographs of the same model in a yellow one-piece bodysuit, with the title "Unzip." In the last two shots, she does unzip, revealing her breasts. Another series from American Apparel featured porn actress Sasha Grey, fully nude except for a pair of thigh-high striped socks and a strategically placed hand covering her pubic area, with pubic hair still peeking out from underneath, and her face twisted into orgasmic pleasure. The campaign was so racy that one news fashion site declared, "American Apparel is officially in the porn business" (Saynt, 2008).

Since the 1960s, such sex appeals have been on the rise in Western countries and are becoming more overt (LaTour & Henthorne, 1994). Advertisers have had to up the ante to more hard-core and blatant sexual themes to take advantage of the attention-grabbing value of porn (Taflinger, 1996) and compete with other hard-core imagery available online. Studies have found that younger consumers in China, Australia, and the United States are more responsive to these kinds of appeals (Liu, Cheng, & Li, 2009), a fact that may suggest a greater porn exposure effect as compared to older consumers with less Internet experience.

Porn is increasingly crossing over into pop culture as well. Madonna began the trend, shocking audiences in the 1980s with her racy imagery onstage and in her music videos, which evoked bondage, leather, and S&M depictions, all culminating in her book with the unambiguous title *Sex*. With Madonna having aged out of the pop princess market, Britney Spears became the heir apparent in 2000 to Madonna's pop culture crown and quickly followed in her sexual footsteps. Spears's carefully packaged image as a budding 16-year-old pop star was based on the sexualized girl-child Lolita, attired in a modified schoolgirl uniform, tied at the waist to expose her midriff for maximum sexual appeal (Albright, 2002). More recently, Spears has included tropes from S&M for her 2009 "Circus" tour. Her designers admitted that their costuming of the former teen idol was drawn from bondage porn. In one scene, she appeared onstage in an outfit bearing nipple tassels and is blindfolded in another.

The newest entry into the pop-porn culture market has been Lady Gaga. Seeking a new edge, she appears in her videos in lingerie or nude, save for a G-string and sky-high heels. The video for her song "Telephone" is peopled with porn stars and sexual themes. In the opening scene, she is led into a prison for "bitches," while heavily made-up, scantily clad women make suggestive faces as she passes by their cells. Upon reaching her cell, the two butch female guards strip her down to a G-string and two pieces of tape forming an X over each nipple. Afterward, one female guard says, "I told you she doesn't have a dick." Another video in which Lady Gaga appears is a clear homage to sexting, with the lyrics "Do you like what you see? You wanna video me?" (Knowles, 2009).

Lady Gaga clearly has the edge right now in popular culture, and other female artists, including Shakira and Christina Aguilera, are pushing the porn envelope to keep up. Aguilera's most recent video for "Not Myself Tonight" evokes hard-core and S&M imagery, including showing her in a full fetishistic latex bodysuit and 7″ stiletto heels. She appears nude, tied to a chair with diamond-encrusted ropes, and a rhinestone-encrusted ball gag in her mouth; she also wears a full latex hood with "XXX" stitched across where the face would be, as she is pulled down amid a crowd of men and women involved in a group sex scene. This video draws liberally from the visual references of hard-core sadomasochistic porn. McQuarrie and Mick (1999) pointed out in their analysis of the visual rhetoric of advertising that the visual elements carry crucial meanings to those with the ability to process them; that is, one must have a level of cultural competency to interpret the subtextual meanings. It is interesting to note then that music videos like Lady Gaga's or Christina Aguilerra's (e.g., "Not Myself Tonight") are a form of advertising aimed at selling records and target a young teen or young adult demographic. As such, one may assume the audience for these videos has enough pornographic literacy that they understand the visual references of S&M in these videos and the excitement that such images encode and invite.

Suburban adolescents are also being exposed to familiar tropes drawn from porn on an increasing basis, as strippers and porn stars more and more often inhabit their world of hip-hop videos and video games. Kanye West, a popular rap artist among teen boys, has used the sexually edgy Lady Gaga to appeal to his teen boy demographic. He posted an "artistic" trailer clip online to promote his "Fame Kills" tour, featuring Gaga styled after a 1970s porn film. In it, she appears naked, with the bright red O of her lips accentuated by her alabaster skin, as she lies on her back with the side of her breast visible. The camera pans slowly to reveal one hand clasped against her breast, and then she is seen lying in the arms of an unseen black man, whom viewers are left to imagine is West. To garner attention, this video uses the trope of interracial sex, which is a familiar theme in porn that codes the exotic. Realizing that West's main audience is adolescent males, this video reveals again how pornography has become normative and mainstream enough that a rap artist would use it to sell an upcoming concert tour to kids.

Popular cultural forms targeting boys and young men often evoke the kind of atmosphere found in all-male spaces such as locker rooms where, in the words of a famous Snoop Doggy Dogg (1993) song, "it ain't no fun if the homies can't have none." Hip-hop videos have become hypermasculine, hypersexualized soft-core porn, filled with "video vixens" acting out "male sexual dream worlds or fantasies" (Cullity & Younger, 2004, p. 99). Women are routinely disparaged and devalued as bitches and "hos" and talked about or shown what they are good for (Jensen, 2007). The voyeuristic pleasures these videos engender are intended for a male consumer, from his point of view, and for his consumption. Nelly put an exclamation on this point in his controversial "Tip Drill" video, when he looked into the camera and slid a credit card down the crack of a woman's backside. In the fantasy world created in these videos, the men are in control, and the women are just another object of conspicuous consumption alongside the rapper's jewelry, "cribs," and luxury cars (Perry, 2003). These videos have become so overtly sexual that some rappers are actually making two versions of their videos: one for mainstream television and an X-rated version available online, again blurring the lines between porn and popular culture.

Themes of "pimpin'" and pimp culture have historically threaded through rap and hip-hop, providing a natural jumping-off point into the sexual commodification of porn. Snoop Dogg was the first to film a full-length pornographic video, titled *Snoop Dogg's Doggystyle*, for Hustler Videos in 2001. It subsequently became the best-selling porn video of 2001 (Internet Movie Database, 2010). Other mainstream hip-hop stars, including Ice-T, Lil Jon, and 50 Cent, have entered the pornography market as well. 50 Cent produced an interactive porn video with his rap group G-Unit for the Digital Sin pornographic film studio, in which the viewer interacts with 17 beautiful women, identified as groupies, by controlling the sexual positions and camera angles.

Bracher (1993) has said that the consumption of these kinds of sexualized images "make natural" these specific subjectivities and sexual relations (p. 97). He says that pornography resolves the impossibility of sexual rapport between men and women by allowing men "to experience their own desire and the Other Sex's desire as complementary, natural forces that exist in a pre-established harmony" (p. 97). The outcome of this "making natural" of sexual relations is that men are drawn to conclude that all women "ultimately desire to have done to them exactly what men desire to do" (p. 97). The themes of control, dominance, and sexuality shown in both mainstream and adult hip-hop and rap videos are repeated and intensified in video games popular with males. Jenna Jameson, a well-known brand by herself in the porn industry, became the voice-over for the video game *Grand Theft Auto: Vice City*. As of July 2006, it became the best-selling game for PlayStation of all time. As of 2008, the entire *Grand Theft Auto* series (2010) had sold more than 70 million units worldwide. In *Grand Theft Auto IV*, the sexual themes are heightened. A player can visit a strip club, pick up a prostitute in the player's car, and pay to have sex with them. Afterward, the player can kill the woman in a variety of brutal ways to get the money back, including beating her with a baseball bat, running her over with the car, and bombing her with a petrol bomb, by which she burns to death. Players in online interactive forums, such as WeGame.com, compare notes and videos on how to kill prostitutes (e.g., http://www.wegame.com/watch/GTA_IV_prostitutes_how_do_you_kill_yours/). The narrative themes that run through many hip-hop and rap videos and video games like Grand Theft Auto "make natural" the particular subjectivity of women as gold diggers who deserve exactly what the male wants to do to them, including using and discarding them like objects or inflicting cruelty, sexual violence, or even murder.

Another example of the pornification of pop culture is the increasing sexualization of children in the media in recent years. Advertisements featuring pouting nymphets in full make-up and suggestive poses have turned up in child beauty pageants (Giroux, 2000), music videos, and mainstream advertising (Walkerdine, 1997), successfully attracting the consumer's attention. After Calvin Klein used soft-porn (Reisman, 1991) images reminiscent of child pornography in a jeans campaign, sales rose from $113 million to over $462 million in one year (Ozzard, 1996). The sexualized Lolita image allows advertisers to inject a new kind of sexual fantasy into their advertising that is "doubly prohibited and therefore doubly exciting" (Walkerdine, 1997, p. 183). Although a few popular books and articles have expressed concern regarding the seeming increase of the sexualized child in advertising and pop culture (Giroux, 2000; "Pure Intentions," 1997), little research exists on this issue, perhaps because of its inherently taboo nature (Walkerdine, 1997; Walkerdine, Lucey, & Melody, 2001).

Levin and Kilbourne (2008) have cautioned that these kinds of pornographic depictions, including the soft-core pornography increasingly seen in advertising like the Calvin Klein ad campaigns, provide models or guidelines to girls for sexualizing themselves and encourage sexual violence. A recent example of a viral video on the Internet is a good illustration. The YouTube video titled "Girls Goin' Hard on Single Ladies" shows a dance troupe of 6- and 7-year-old girls—all with matching pageboy haircuts and clad in black and red bras, panties, and gartered high stockings—dancing to Beyoncé's "Single Ladies." For 5 minutes, the girls dance, gyrate their pelvises, and booty shake their way through the song in an overtly sexualized manner. The video caused an uproar and received wide play on a number of national media outlets, including CNN, in part because such Lolita-esque images garner attention. As a result, the video received millions of online hits and was eventually recategorized as adult content on YouTube, begging the question, Is this child porn?

The American Psychological Association's (2010) report on the sexualization of girls in popular culture included examples culled from (a) advertisements, such as the Skechers "naughty and nice" ad that featured Christina Aguilera dressed as a schoolgirl in pigtails, with her shirt unbuttoned and licking a lollipop; (b) dolls, such as the Bratz line dressed in sexualized clothing like miniskirts, fishnet stockings, and feather boas; (c) clothing, such as thongs sized for 7–10-year-olds, some printed with slogans like "wink wink"; and (d) television programs, such as a fashion show in which adult models in lingerie were presented as young girls. Other depictions include the soft-core reality video series *Girls Gone Wild*, which earned its owner Joe Francis over $100 million in direct-mail sales and made *going wild* a common phrase in the popular lexicon (Eldredge, 2004). Sold on late night television for $9.95 each, the tapes depict girls next door willingly going wild, with some appearing in Lolita-esque pigtails and schoolgirl uniforms while proclaiming they are barely 18 (Pitcher, 2006). Apparently, not all of the girls in the videos are in fact 18. In 2003, Francis was arrested in connection with filming underaged girls, paying them $100 to shower and masturbate together and another $50 to touch his penis ("Girls Gone Wild," 2003). After following Francis's cameras around for a few days, Ariel Levy became a vocal critic of the franchise for its promotion of raunch culture, which she says many young women view as a triumph of feminism and sexual liberation rather than a sign of its failure (Levy, 2005). Joe Francis was sentenced to pay $1.6 million in criminal fines for failing to maintain age and identity records for the films he produced under Mantra Films, operating as Girls Gone Wild (Department of Justice, 2006). He subsequently spent 35 days in jail for contempt of court, after shouting obscenities during settlement negotiations for a civil suit filed by seven girls who were minors when they were filmed by his company ("Joe Francis Sentenced to Jail for Contempt," 2007).

Following the text-interpretive tradition, Giroux has discussed the semiotics of these kinds of images, stating that the proliferation of sexualized images of young girls in the media in recent years has resulted in "innocence [becoming a] fractured sign … used unapologetically to present children as objects of desire for adults as voyeurs" (Giroux, 2000, p. 60). Giroux argues that we must examine such social practices in order to resist ways in which young women's bodies and identities are being appropriated to satisfy adult needs and desires (Giroux, 2000). Indeed, the American Psychological Association (2010) concluded its report on the topic by saying that "documenting the pervasiveness and influence of such products and portrayals is sorely needed" (para. 9). One pressing reason is that these images may fuel a desire for sexual relations; a troubling indicator is an increase in global sex trafficking, as adult males travel to foreign countries seeking sex with girls (Farr, 2004). A number of websites have cropped up promoting sex tourism, providing "potential child sex tourists with pornographic accounts written by other child sex tourists" (Nair, 2009, para. 7). One such website offers "nights of sex 'with two young Thai girls for the price of a tank of gas'" (Nair, 2009, para. 7), illustrating further how sexualized images of children may have very troubling real-world implications.

There has been a move in recent years toward increasingly draconian laws in relation to images considered child pornography. In the United States, federal statutes place heavy penalties on the production, consumption, and reproduction of child pornography, from a 15–30-year sentence for production and up to 20 years for receipt or distribution (U.S. Department of Justice, 2009). Additionally, section 2257 of the U.S. Code states that anyone producing sexually explicit videos "shall create and maintain individually identifiable records pertaining to every performer portrayed in such a visual depiction," including name and birth date information. Although intended to harass porn producers, the unintended consequence has been a stabilization and expansion of the industry itself. To address the concerns about children accessing and being involved in porn, the industry has employed more self-regulation measures, including age checks and credit card filters on their websites, as a way to limit access by children. Globally, too, other countries are beefing up laws regarding child pornography, yet such moves are not purely to protect children. Rather, by separating off and regulating child pornography, the adult sphere is left as a protected market (Milter & Slade, 2005). Such self-regulation often comes in advance of regulations sought by politicians in these markets.

## IMPACTS OF PORN CONSUMPTION

What is the impact of all this porn consumption? The research in this area has been sparse and often contradictory. In this next section, I attempt to summarize some of the key findings from both laboratory and more naturalistic studies in terms of addiction, aggression, rape, relationships, bodies, and body image.

### Porn Addiction

Many media reports have focused on porn's addictive potential. One researcher team claims that fully 40–50% of individuals who consume porn will eventually develop signs of addiction, resulting in the need for interventions by family and counselors (Landau, Garrett, & Webb, 2008). Others have called porn consumption a "hidden health hazard exploding because very few are recognizing it as such" (Cooper, Delmonico, & Burg, 2000, p. 25). Such alarmist accounts seem to be overblown by the media. Using Cooper, Griffin-Shelley, Delmonico, and Mathy's (2001) definition of *porn addiction*, or compulsive use of porn online, as 11 or more hours per week, a large national survey found that only 2% of adults fell into the compulsive zone (Albright, 2008), while another study put the estimate at only 1% (Cooper et al., 2000). Cooper et al. (2000) also point out that far from problematic for most users, the Internet actually has given couples new ways to connect with their romantic partners.

Many psychiatric professionals are at odds about labeling a set level of porn consumption as an addiction. Debate has similarly raged around these issues in the creation of the next edition of the *Diagnostic and Statistical Manual of Mental Disorders*, as to whether to include fetishism as a kinky preference or a full-blown mental disorder. As Foucault (1978) discussed in his work on the history of sexuality, the discipline of bodies and the categorization of sexuality are tied to particular historical and cultural moments. Labeling sexual activities as normal or deviant, according to Foucault (1976), is a way to bring them into the scope of discourse in order to regulate and control them. As such, doing so makes academics as complicit in the production of postmodern rubrics of sexuality as pornographers and consumers. The increased consumption of pornography in general in the digital era and hard-core pornography in particular, including depictions of bondage, discipline, S&M , bestiality, and various fetishes, combined with the secularization of society and the loosening overall sexual mores, makes labeling such variations of sexuality as deviant or as mental disorders much more difficult to justify.

### Porn Consumption and Aggression

Much of the discussion about porn in the news media and the blogosphere has centered around its negative impacts, often without much solid research backing up the claims. Many political factions, including sex-negative feminists and religious fundamentalists in the United States, have argued for restrictions on pornography. These sex-negative feminists have spoken out aggressively against it, claiming that men find in pornography models of violent behavior against women that encourage rape and sexual coercion (Brownmiller, 1975; Dworkin, 1981; MacKinnon, 1993).

In terms of actual research findings, it is noteworthy that many of the studies related to porn consumption and aggression were conducted in experimental settings and, thus, may not reflect the experiences of average adults' real-world settings (Einsiedel, 1992). The findings can be summarized as follows: Some studies of college students have found a connection between viewing violent pornography and an increased propensity to agree with rape myths (e.g., "She was dressed seductively, so she must have asked for it") (M. Allen, Emmers, Gebhardt, & Giery, 1995). In addition, a meta-analysis of laboratory findings has linked violent sexual depictions to attitudes supporting sexual aggression and an increase in actual aggression in these settings (M. Allen, D'Alessio, & Brezgel, 2006). Malamuth, Addison, and Koss (2000), in a meta-analytic study of 16 experiments, found that increases in aggression were significantly related only to violent pornography, not nonviolent pornography. Donnerstein, Linz, and Penrod (1987) found similar effects in another laboratory study, showing that aggression increased more after exposure to violent sexual material as compared to nonviolent sexual material or nonsexual nudity alone.

A meta-analysis of consumers of porn in more naturalistic settings among college students found a meager average positive correlation between consumption of porn and attitudes toward sexual aggression ($r = 0.06$), which the researchers reasonably concluded does not show a significant, reliable relationship (M. Allen et al., 1995). Malamuth's et al.'s (2000) key finding after their meta-analysis was that pornography use cannot be viewed as a cause or an outcome of sexual aggressive tendencies, leading them to suggest that it may be that aggressive men interpret and react to the same pornography differently than nonaggressive men, as opposed to pornography itself triggering such aggression. Yet, Boeringer (1994) has found a connection between higher exposure to violent pornography and engaging in sexual aggression and believing oneself capable of sexual violence. Overall, much of the research has shown mixed results in terms of the effects of porn consumption. Some research even points to some positive effects of porn consumption for couples, which will be described later.

Porn Consumption and Rape

Some researchers have gone so far as to suggest that porn may actually be a substitute for rape, as a way to sublimate violent impulses. Supporting this hypothesis is Wilson's (1978) study, which found that males who developed deviant patterns of sexual behavior in adulthood suffered relative deprivation of porn in adolescence, suggesting that exposure to porn may actually inhibit these patterns. Although other studies suffered from numerous methodological difficulties in terms of finding this causal connection (Tovar, Elias, & Chang, 1999), studies of international sexual violence rates actually point to an inverse relationship between an increase in pornography and a decrease in violent sexual crime (Diamond & Uchiyama, 1999). Diamond and Uchiyama looked to the U.S. Department of Justice's crime statistics for 1975–1995 and found a drop in rates of rape. This decline was most marked in the years 1993–1996, when dial-up sites were available for downloading porn via modem, corresponding during the same period to a 60% nationwide decrease in forcible rape. Although an intriguing finding, prior to 1999, the Internet had not reached the point of saturation in the United States that it has today, and with it, the increased ease of accessing porn online. Now, just over 10 years later, and with the huge increase of pornography available online, the relationship still holds. According to the FBI (Federal Bureau of Investigation; 2007), forcible rape dropped 13% nationwide between 1998 and 2006, and an additional 2.5% drop was seen between 2006 and 2008. Likewise, Kimmel and Linders's (1996) studies of six U.S cities found no increase in rates of rape linked to the circulation of adult-themed magazines. The research seems to indicate that it is the sexualization of violence, rather than pornographic or sexual depictions themselves, that leads to negative effects related to the consumption of pornography.

## Porn Consumption and Relationships

In terms of porn's impact on relationships, some negative impacts have been found. Married women are more likely to experience distress over a partner's pornography use than are women in dating relationships (Bridges, Bergner, & Hesson-McInnis, 2003), most likely because they view porn consumption as a kind of infidelity (Whitty, 2003). A poll of over 15,000 adults on MSNBC.com found a number of gender-specific positive and negative impacts of watching porn. In terms of negative outcomes, women were significantly and notably more likely than men to report that watching pornography decreased the amount of actual sex that they had, and they felt their partner was more critical of their bodies (Albright, 2008). Women also were more likely to express feeling pressured to perform the sexual acts seen in porn films. Men were more likely to agree that pornography lowered their interest in actually having sex and, confirming the women's fears, that viewing porn made them more critical of their partner's body (Albright, 2008). In fact, the more hours people consumed porn per week, the more likely they were to express a decreased interest in actual sex (Albright, 2008), suggesting that for more frequent users, viewing pornography and the self-stimulation that often goes along with it seem to be substituting for actual sexual relations.

Research has pointed to some potentially positive impacts of porn consumption, including more positive lovemaking experiences with their partners due to its instructive and pleasurable features as a matter of sex education (Barak & Fisher, 2001; Brecher et al., 1984). The gender-specific positive impacts of watching porn were that women reported more relational benefits, including being more open to new things, making it easier to say what they want, and increasing arousal when watching with their partner. Men were more likely to report an individualistic benefit, such as enhancing arousal when alone (Albright, 2008).

## Porn, Bodies, and Body Image

Porn seems also to have spurred some unforeseen dysfunctional behaviors among consumers, including behavior linked to the body, body image, and bodily performance, and these effects are clearly delineated along gendered lines. For women, there has been a 162% increase in cosmetic surgical procedures since 1997 (Plastic Surgery Research.info, 2009). Women are expressing new forms of body dysmorphism and new desires to change their bodies to match the images they see on the screen (Albright, 2007) to look and perform more like men's fantasies of the porn stars they see online. Surgical procedures range from breast enlargements, which is the number one most frequently performed procedure, sometimes to unreal proportions (Plastic Surgery Research.info, 2009), to vaginal "rejuvenation" and plastic surgery, so their vulvas more closely resemble those of popular porn stars. As such, more research on the relationship between pornography consumption among women and their sexual partners, on body image disturbances, and on motivations and effects of related plastic surgery seems an important area of inquiry.

For men, plastic surgery is up less than 10% in recent years; instead of body changes, men seem to be focused on trying to enhance sexual performance. Sales of performance-enhancing drugs like Cialis and Viagra may be linked not only to an aging population but also to the seemingly nonstop performance of porn stars, who may themselves be taking such drugs. Use of such drugs by young men for recreational purposes has also been reported, with one study citing that it has tripled in recreational use among men under 45 in 1998–2002 (Delate, Simmons, & Motheral, 2004), corresponding to increases in porn consumption during that period. Use of drugs like Viagra is also prevalent among users of other supposed sex-enhancing drugs like ecstasy, crystal meth, and opiates, particularly among men who have sex with men (Fisher, Reynolds, & Napper, 2010). More research into the consumption of porn, notions of performance and the body, and recreational use of Viagra and other sex-enhancing drugs is warranted.

## EMERGING ISSUES

### Fandom and Public Consumption of Porn

Prior to the Internet boom, men who bought or subscribed to adult magazines may have hidden them in brown paper bags or received them by mail in unmarked envelopes to conceal the contents. Driving along recently in Los Angeles, it became apparent how out of the closet porn has become when I spotted billboards advertising Adultcon 2009, a pornography convention in business since 2001. Adultcon (2009) describes itself on its website as a place where fans go "to get personalized autographed Magazines, Photos and DVD's *directly* from over 69 Porn Stars and to take photos with your favorite stars while watching their performance *with* them on the big screen" (para. 4). Adult and swinger conventions like these are cropping up around the country with increasing frequency in places like Los Angeles, Miami, and Las Vegas (Adultcon, 2009). The AVN Adult Entertainment Expo has also drawn more than 30,000 attendees a year (Esch & Mayer, 2007). The increasing popularity of these meet-and-greet conventions, coupled with their blatant advertising via billboards on the sides of freeways in suburban areas, with no apparent public outcry, shows just how far the mainstreaming of porn has evolved. Far from being hidden on back roads or in strip mall shops with adult neon signs flirtatiously announcing their whereabouts, the open display of pornographic wares and porn stars in convention halls across the country and their coverage on local news stations may garner no more than snickers from the reporters. Research is needed into the public consumption of sex-related materials and the construction of consumer groups and communities of interest around particular porn stars.

### Erogenous Zoning

With its potential to distribute child porn and other potentially harmful or illegal fetishes through communities of interest online, the Internet still evokes fear and distrust among many, which in some aspects may be well founded. To deal with the juxtaposition of children and porn on MySpace, for example, several U.S. states' attorneys general have put pressure on MySpace to cull the porn from its site. More research on the frequency of porn exposure to children on such sites, the unwanted or unsolicited sexual advances by strangers, and the tactic of sexual grooming through porn is in order. Policy makers may want to consider regulations and laws demanding the creation of erogenous zones on virtual sites. Erogenous zoning, or restricting the location of sexually themed businesses, was first conceived of by city leaders who did not want sex-themed businesses like porn shops or strip bars in close proximity to schools. Policy makers may need to call for virtual erogenous zoning in places like MySpace, where children and porn may interact, to protect children from potentially harmful early exposure to porn as well as sexual predators who take advantage of this dangerous milieu (Furlow, 2000). Legal challenges have made such zoning difficult. An attempt was made to enforce the erogenous zoning case *Voyeur Dorm, L.C. v. City of Tampa* (2002) in Florida. The founders of Voyeur Dorm set up webcams to film young women in their homes for the adult website that alleged to show "girls who are fresh, naturally erotic, and as young as 18. Catch them in the most intimate acts of youthful indiscretion" (*Voyeur Dorm*, 2001, sec. 1). The appeals court overturned an earlier ruling, stating that "[the Tampa court] erroneously found that Voyeur Dorm offered adult entertainment to the public at the residence in question" (sec. 1). The laws have had difficulty keeping up with activities in a virtual world, even though some activities have very real-world implications, such as those outlined above.

This latter case points to the vexing issues raised by Porn 2.0 and the production and consumption of porn by amateurs. Websites for showcasing amateur porn are cropping up to ever-increasing audiences, including YouPorn and RedTube. These sites offer free access, potentially to children, to hard-core pornographic depictions from both professional and amateur actors in short clip form, increasingly favored by consumers who may now view them even on their smartphones. Policy makers may want to consider erogenous zoning on the Internet to keep children and porn separated in a sphere where there is increasing crossover between the two.

## Celebrity Sex Tapes

The availability of porn in popular culture, and the ready access to it online, sets up social models for both adults and kids to follow. Kids may want to be considered hot, equating to popularity, even if they do not yet have a full grasp of what that means. Impetuous acts like filming and posting or sending sexual photos and films have led to embarrassing results in the later careers of a number of actors, actresses, and models, including a recent Miss USA who had eight sex tapes and 30 naked photos surface, leading to public embarrassment and the removal of her crown (Duke, 2009). Yet, sex tapes have led to career boosts for Kim Kardashian, Paris Hilton, and Pamela Anderson; as a result, more seem to be coming out all the time, with the most recent featuring "Housewives of New Jersey," including Danielle Staub, and Kendra Wilkinson, a former "Girl Next Door" and Hugh Hefner girlfriend. Celebrity sex tapes represent a growing segment of the porn market, as the lens of fame fueled by the paparazzi opens ever wider to include the once private aspects of performers' personal lives for public consumption. In this milieu, the bedroom becomes a stage, the last bastion of celebrity and performance for those trying to stay in the spotlight and those trying to get in.

For the average person, however, sex tapes and photos can lead to embarrassing personal, career, or even legal repercussions. The education of parents, teachers, and others in positions of influence to guide children is important, especially in terms of understanding the technological possibilities for producing and distributing pornographic imagery, including via cell phones, video cameras, and webcams. Children need to be advised on the repercussions of public sex activities and supervised to avoid future embarrassment and career derailment.

## Amateur Porn and Hooking Up

Websites are increasingly cropping up for people to post amateur porn photos and videos in the hopes of "hooking up" for casual sex or meeting a romantic partner, such as AdultFriendFinder and AdultMatchdoctor. Although the wisdom of posting such videos may be questioned, researchers may be interested in looking at what role, if any, such early sexual exposure may have in the formation of sexual and romantic relationships. The development of instant intimacy and a new set of sexual expectations during relationship initiation may yield unexpected consequences. Also, research is needed into what role these sites may be playing in terms of marital disruption as new, ready sexual partners are easily found, facilitating risky sexual behavior and potentially increasing sexually transmitted diseases like HIV.

## Reaction Videos

The ability to e-mail or post videos on sites like YouTube has generated an unexpected phenomenon that could be called an *aggregate of interest* and *reaction video*. Here, the production and distribution capabilities related to digital video have resulted in some unusual and unexpected social behaviors. Reaction videos are made of a person or people watching particularly extreme and rare forms of fetishism, including bestiality and scatology (i.e., sex involving feces and/or urination). The videos are shot alone or in groups, with a webcam aimed at the person watching the sex video to capture his or her reaction, which is then posted online for others to see. The first of these videos was shot in reaction to a viral video called "Mr. Hands," which despite its extreme content, was circulated widely among coworkers and friends of all ages and both genders. Mr. Hands was a nickname for Kenneth Pinyan, an engineer at Boeing, who enjoyed the fetish of bestiality, particularly receptive anal sex with horses at a farm in the state of Washington. A documentary titled *Zoo* of his life and eventual death from a perforated bowel was released in 2007 to critical acclaim at film festivals ("Enumclaw Horse Sex Case," 2009). Although bestiality is thought to be an exceedingly rare paraphilia, teenagers and others across the country, alone and in groups, have watched the uncensored, hard-core video of Pinyan being gored by an impossibly large horse phallus. Reaction videos have been posted on YouTube. A search for "Mr. Hands reaction" or "two guys one horse" yields thousands of results. The "Mr. Hands" video made the rounds of offices via e-mail and became a viral phenomenon.

As a takeoff on these reaction videos, "Two Girls One Cup" was produced, featuring scatology. Two young girls are shown eliminating into a cup, followed by licking and eating the contents in a completely disgusting manner. This video also prompted a series of reaction videos on YouTube by a cast of unlikely reactors, ranging from teenagers to grandmothers. A search of "two girls one cup reaction" on YouTube leads to over 15,000 results. These reaction videos have become spectacles in themselves. No research has been conducted to date on reaction videos as recorded documentation of the emotional reaction linked to the consumption of porn. In addition, more research is needed into the etiology and social behaviors surrounding fetishes online and the voyeuristic fascination with them, since the Internet may be fueling and encouraging previously unexplored behaviors such as these, which can lead to serious legal implications, high-risk sexual behaviors, relationship or marital discord, or even mental illness.

## Communities of Porn

Consumer behavior research has had a growing interest in recent years in communities, including brand communities and special-interest and lifestyle communities as well as place-centric gathering places both online and offline (McAlexander, Schouten, & Koenig, 2002; Muñiz & O'Guinn, 2001; Muñiz, O'Guinn, & Fine, 2006; Schouten & McAlexander, 1995). In need of further study is the Internet's ability to create consumer communities around porn. Communities of interest have cropped up surrounding every possible sexual proclivity, from smoking fetishes (Albright, 2002) to bestiality (Earls & Lalumière, 2009). Fetishes like bestiality and zoophilia (i.e., love of animals) were once thought to be rare and mainly confined to rural individuals and the mentally retarded. Special-interest groups have formed on Yahoo! and other sites to meet, discuss, and trade pictures related to these and other fetishes. Based on new data emerging from the Internet, researchers are now saying that they are not as rare as once thought and, in fact, may be the purview of highly intelligent, educated individuals (Earls & Lalumière, 2009). Communities of porn linked to sex tourism, beauty pageants and the sexualization of children, fetishes, porn conventions, and porn star fandom are areas understudied and in need of further research.

## New Technologies, New Challenges

As technologies continue to advance, porn will continue to morph and adapt to them. It has already been suggested that the first "porn in space" video may be produced soon. Virgin Galactic, the company planning to take tourists to the edge of space, has apparently already turned down a $1 million offer to shoot a sex in space movie (de Selding, 2008). New venues like Second Life offer participants the chance to experiment with sex in three-dimensional (3D) virtual reality, which counselors say has led to an increase in cases of marital discord, including at least one divorce (Hartley, 2008).

Smartphones like the iPhone and the Droid are expected to dominate the cell phone market in another year. Apple, the maker of the popular iPhone, has resisted granting approval to applications that play porn; Apple executives have pointed users instead to Google's Android phone to download porn. Yet, some pirated applications are apparently aiming to facilitate iPorn's videos on iPhones. The iPorn company circumvented Apple's censorship policy on iTunes by offering its application free on its website. Thus, cell phones continue to be a growing venue for people to send one another erotic photographs or videos, as well as view more hard-core, professional renditions of porn. This will be an emerging issue for teens, as cell phone technology becomes less expensive, and greater capabilities allow longer videos and more photographs to be stored and transferred. Policy makers and lawmakers need to give careful thought to the arrest and prosecution of children for child porn when the children involved in the filming are themselves or when they receive videos from those with whom they are romantically involved. The lessons learned from the suicide of Jesse Logan over sexting should be neither forgotten nor overlooked; the fallout of "adult" pictures taken by children can be deleterious to their health and well-being. Adults need to be involved to help guide conversations and set proper limits for children who are too emotionally immature to handle the consequences of their actions. At the same time, lawmakers and policy makers need to grapple with the legal implications of this complex issue, as new challenges are posed by production and distribution technologies not dreamed of when the laws regulating child porn were first written and enacted.

Last, pornographers continue to chase and create new means for exciting their customer base in an increasingly noisy sexual field, as mainstream media catches up with porn's sexual arousal. No doubt, they will turn to 3D technology as their next frontier. Although 3D movies have been available for some time now, both high-definition and 3D television will make porn in the home more engaging than ever. As such, one wonders what the impact will be when porn becomes more and more lifelike, appearing in 3D and eventually in full holographic images in the privacy of one's home.

## CONCLUSION

In this chapter, I have attempted to contextualize Porn 2.0 as pertaining to the production, distribution, and consumption of porn in the digital age by outlining some of the technological, social, and behavioral changes that have impacted this arena. Surely, the developments in this milieu will be more challenging than ever to marriages, families, and the development of children due to increased access to porn as well as its significant dilemmas for legal and policy analysts, educators, marketers, and others. The developments in the porn market in terms of new distribution channels, brand communities, and the crossover of porn to mainstream popular culture, and vice versa, are certain to open up areas ripe for Transformative Consumer Research, with far-reaching implications for well-being among individuals and societies. Porn has historically helped encourage and push technological development and will continue to do so in the future. Porn is sure to be a continually evolving subject for consumer research, as new interactive technologies, games, and other vehicles for consumption practices come into the marketplace and provide new ways for the production and consumption of desire in the libidinal economy.

## REFERENCES

Adultcon. (2009). *About Adultcon.* Retrieved October 29, 2010, from adultcon.com/indexa.html

Agins, T. (1995, September 8). FBI has designs on Calvin Klein in child porn probe. *The Wall Street Journal,* p. A1.

Albright, J. (2002, June). Lolita online: Sex and under-aged smoking on the Internet. *International Journal of Critical Psychology*, pp. 25–51.

Albright, J. (2007). Impossible bodies: TV viewing habits, body image, and plastic surgery attitudes among college students in Los Angeles and Buffalo, New York. *Configurations*, *15*(2), 103–123.

Albright, J. (2008). Sex in America online: An exploration of sex, marital status and sexual indentity in Internet sex-seeking. *Journal of Sex Research*, *45*(2), 175–186.

Allen, C. T., Fournier, S., & Miller, F. (2008). Brands and their meaning makers. In C. P. Haugtvedt, P. M. Herr, & F. R. Kardes (Eds.), *Handbook of consumer psychology* (pp. 781–822). New York: Taylor & Francis.

Allen, M., D'Alessio, D., & Brezgel, K. (2006). A meta-analysis summarizing the effects of pornography II aggression after exposure. *Human Communication Research*, *22*(2), 258–283.

Allen, M., Emmers, T., Gebhardt, L., & Giery, M. A. (1995). Exposure to pornography and acceptance of rape myths. *Journal of Communication*, *45*(1), 5–26.

Allyn, D. (2001). *Make love, not war: The sexual revolution, an unfettered history*. New York: Routledge.

American Psychological Association. (2010). *Sexualization of girls: Executive summary*. Retrieved June 12, 2010, from http://www.apa.org/pi/women/programs/girls/report.aspx?item=2

Balkoski, J. (1989). *Beyond the beachhead: The 29th Infantry Division in Normandy*. Harrisburg, PA: Stackpole Books.

Barak, A., & Fisher, W. A. (2001). Toward an Internet-driven, theoretically-based, innovative approach to sex education. *Journal of Sex Research*, *38*(4), 324–332.

Berthon, P., Pitt, L., & Campbell, C. (2008). Ad lib: When customers create the ad. *California Management Review*, *50*(4), 6–30.

Boeringer, S. B. (1994). Pornography and sexual aggression: Associations of violent and nonviolent depictions with rape and rape proclivity. *Deviant Behavior*, *15*(3), 289–304.

Bracher, M. (1993). *Lacan, discourse, and social change: A psychoanalytic cultural criticism*. Ithaca, NY: Cornell University Press.

Braiker, B. (2007, February 8). Hard times for the porn industry? *Newsweek*. Retrieved December 14, 2010, from http://tinyurl.com/272xnl4

Brecher, E. M., & the editors of *Consumer Reports* books. (1984). *Love, sex, and aging: A Consumers Union report*. Boston: Little, Brown.

Breitbart, A., & Ebner, M. C. (2004). *Hollywood, interrupted: Insanity chic in Babylon—the case against celebrity*. New York: Wiley.

Bridges, A. J., Bergner, R. M., & Hesson-McInnis, M. (2003). Romantic partners' use of pornography: Its significance for women. *Journal of Sex & Marital Therapy*, *29*(1), 1–14.

Brownmiller, S. (1975). *Against our will: Men, women, and rape*. New York: Simon & Schuster.

Burns, K., & Hefner, H. (Creators). (2005–2011). *The girls next door* [Television series]. Los Angeles: E! Entertainment Television.

Buzzell, T. (2005). The effects of sophistication, access and monitoring on use of pornography in three technological contexts. *Deviant Behavior*, *26*(2), 109–132.

Carroll, J. S., Padilla-Walker, L. M., Nelson, L. J., Olson, C. D., Barry, C. M., & Madsen, S. D. (2008). Generation XXX: Pornography acceptance and use among emerging adults. *Journal of Adolescent Research*, *23*(1), 6–30.

Cassell, B., & Pringle, D. (2005, May 12). Sex cells: Wireless operators find that racy cellphone video drives surge in broadband use. *The Wall Street Journal*, p. B1.

Celizic, M. (2009, March 6). Her teen committed suicide over "sexting." *MSNBC.com*. Retrieved June 7, 2010, from http://www.msnbc.msn.com/id/29546030

Cisneros, D. (2002 ). "Virtual child" pornography on the Internet: A "virtual" victim? *Duke Law & Technology Review*. Retrieved June 10, 2010, from http://www.law.duke.edu/journals/dltr/articles/2002dltr0019.html

Cooper, A., Delmonico, D., & Burg, R. (2000). Cybersex users, abusers, and compulsives: New findings and implications. *Sexual Addiction & Compulsivity: Journal of Treatment & Prevention*, *7*, 5–30.

Cooper, A., Griffin-Shelley, E., Delmonico, D., & Mathy, R. (2001). Online sexual problems: Assessment and predictive variables. *Sexual Addiction & Compulsivity: Journal of Treatment & Prevention*, *8*(3), 267–285.

Cooper, A., Scherer, C. R., Boies, S. C., & Gordon, B. L. (1999). Sexuality on the Internet: From sexual exploration to pathological expression. *Professional Psychology: Research and Practice*, *30*(2), 154–164.

Cullity, J., & Younger, P. (2004). Sex appeal and cultural liberty: A feminist inquiry into MTV India. *Frontiers: Journal of Women Studies*, *25*(2), 96–122.

Daws, G. (1994). *Prisoners of the Japanese: POWs of World War II in the Pacific*. New York: William Morrow.

Delate, T., Simmons, V. A., & Motheral, B. R. (2004). Patterns of use of sildenafil among commercially insured adults in the United States: 1998–2002. *International Journal of Impotence Research*, *16*(4), 313–318.

Department of Justice. (2006). *"Girls Gone Wild" company sentenced to pay $1.6 million in fines in sexual exploitation case*. Retrieved January 10, 2011, from http://tinyurl.com/2eghvhu

de Selding, P. B. (2008, October 2). Virgin Galactic rejects $1 million space porn. *MSNBC.com*. Retrieved November 5, 2009, from http://www.msnbc.msn.com/id/26991760/

Diamond, M., & Uchiyama, A. (1999). Pornography, rape, and sex crimes in Japan. *International Journal of Law and Psychiatry, 22*(1), 1–22.

Dines, G., Jensen, R., & Russo, A. (1998). *Pornography: The production and consumption of inequality*. New York: Routledge.

Donnerstein, E., Linz, D., & Penrod, S. (1987). *The question of pornography: Scientific findings and policy implications*. New York: Free Press.

Duke, A. (2009, November 4). Source: Carrie Prejean "sex tape" spurred pageant settlement. *CNN*. Retrieved December 14, 2010, from http://bit.ly/tu3j

Dworkin, A. (1981). *Pornography: Men possessing women*. New York: Putnam.

Earls, C. M., & Lalumière, M. L. (2009). A case study of preferential bestiality. *Archives of Sexual Behavior, 38*(4), 605–609.

Einsiedel, E. (1992). The experimental research evidence: Effects of pornography on the "average" individual. In C. Itzin (Ed.), *Pornography: Women, violence and civil liberties* (pp. 248–283). New York: Oxford University Press.

Eldredge, R. L. (2004). Now it's the guys "gone wild" on video. *The Atlanta Journal-Constitution*, p. B1.

Enumclaw horse sex case. (2010, October 28). *Wikipedia*. Retrieved October 29, 2010, from http://en.wikipedia.org/wiki/Kenneth_Pinyan

Esch, K., & Mayer, V. (2007). How unprofessional: The profitable partnership of amateur porn and celebrity culture. In S. Paasonen, K. Nikunen, & L. Saarenmaa (Eds.), *Pornification* (pp. 99–114). New York: Berg.

Facebook. (2010). *Statistics*. Retrieved June 11, 2010, from http://www.facebook.com/press/info.php?statistics

Farr, K. (2004). *Sex trafficking: The global market in women and children*. New York: Worth.

Federal Bureau of Investigation. (2007). *Crime in the United States, 2007: Table 1A* [Table]. Retrieved October 29, 2010, from http://www2.fbi.gov/ucr/cius2007/data/table_01a.html

Finer, L. B. (2007). Trends in premarital sex in the United States, 1954–2003. *Public Health Reports, 122*(1), 73–78.

Fisher, D. G., Reynolds, G. L., & Napper, L. E. (2010). Use of crystal methamphetamine, Viagra, and sexual behavior. *Current Opinion in Infectious Diseases, 23*(1), 53–56.

Fonsegrive, G. (1912). *Art et pornographie* [Art and pornography]. Paris: Bloud.

Ford, M. E., & Linney, J. A. (1995). Comparative analysis of juvenile sexual offenders, violent nonsexual offenders, and status offenders. *Journal of Interpersonal Violence, 10*(1), 56–70.

Foucault, M. (1976). *The history of sexuality vol. 1: The will to knowledge*. London: Penguin.

Foucault, M. (1978). *The history of sexuality: An introduction* (Vol. 1). New York: Pantheon.

Furlow, C. T. (2000). Erogenous zoning on the cyber-frontier. *Virginia Journal of Law and Technology, 7*(Spring), 1522–1687.

"Girls Gone Wild" boss busted. (2003, April 4). *The Smoking Gun*. Retrieved June 11, 2010, from http://www.thesmokinggun.com/archive/ggwild1.html

Giroux, H. A. (2000). *Stealing innocence: Youth, corporate power, and the politics of culture*. New York: St. Martin's.

Grahame-Smith, S. (2005). *The big book of porn: A penetrating look at the world of dirty movies*. Philadelphia: Quirk Books.

Grand Theft Auto (series). (2010, October 30). On *Wikipedia*. Retrieved October 30, 2010, from http://en.wikipedia.org/wiki/Grand_Theft_Auto_(series)

Hard times: The trouble with pornography. (2009, September 10). *The Economist*. Retrieved November 11, 2009, from http://www.economist.com/node/14416740?story_id=14416740

Hartley, A. (2008, November 13). Discovery of Second Life sex leads to divorce. *TechRadar*. Retrieved November 7, 2009, from http://www.techradar.com/news/internet/discovery-of-second-life-sex-leads-to-divorce-484673#ixzz0qnp1bz6u

Hunt, L. (1993). *The invention of pornography: Obscenity and the origins of modernity, 1500–1800*. Cambridge, MA: MIT Press.

Internet Movie Database. (2010). *Doggystyle*. Retrieved June 9, 2010, from http://www.imdb.com/title/tt0282988/

Jacobellis v. Ohio, 378 U.S. 184 (1964).

Jensen, R. (2007). *Getting off: Pornography and the end of masculinity*. Cambridge, MA: South End Press.

Jensen, R., & Dines, G. (1998). The content of mass-marketed pornography. In G. Dines, R. Jensen, & A. Russo (Eds.), *Pornography: The production and consumption of inequality* (pp. 65–100). New York: Routledge.

Joe Francis sentenced to jail for contempt. (2007, April 23). *People*. Retrieved January 10, 2011, from http://tinyurl.com/2afjhxw

Kendrick, W. M. (1987). *The secret museum: Pornography in modern culture*. New York: Viking.

Kendrick, W. M. (1996). *The secret museum: Pornography in modern culture*. Berkeley: University of California Press.

Kilbourne, J. (Creator), & Jhally, S. (Producer/Director/Editor). (2000). *Killing us softly 3: Advertising's image of women* [Motion picture]. Northampton, MA: Media Education Foundation.

Kimmel, M., & Linders, A. (1996). Does censorship make a difference? An aggregate empirical analysis of pornography and rape. *Journal of Psychology and Human Sexuality, 8*(3), 1–20.

Knowles, B. (2009). Video phone. [Recorded by Beyonce & Lady Gaga]. On *I am...Sasha Fierce* (Deluxe ed.) [Record]. Atlanta, GA: Bangladesh, Patchwerk, and Silent Sound Studios.

Lamay, C. L. (1997). America's censor: Anthony Comstock and free speech. *Communications and the Law, 19*(3), 1–59.

Landau, J., Garrett, J., & Webb, R. (2008). Assisting a concerned person to motivate someone experiencing cybersex into treatment application of invitational intervention: The arise model to cybersex. *Journal of Marital & Family Therapy, 34*(4), 498–511.

LaTour, M., & Henthorne, T. L. (1994). Ethical judgements of sexual appeals in print advertising. *Journal of Advertising, 23*(3), 81–90.

Levin, D. E., & Kilbourne, J. (2008). *So sexy so soon: The new sexualized childhood, and what parents can do to protect their kids*. New York: Ballantine.

Levy, A. (2005). *Female chauvinist pigs: Women and the rise of raunch culture*. New York: Free Press.

Liu, F., Cheng, H., & Li, J. (2009). Consumer responses to sex appeal advertising: A cross-cultural study. *International Marketing Review, 26*(4/5), 501–520.

MacKinnon, C. A. (1993). *Only words*. Cambridge, MA: Harvard University Press.

Malamuth, N., Addison, T., & Koss, M. (2000). Pornography and sexual aggression: Are there reliable effects and can we understand them? *Annual Review of Sex Research, 11*, 26–91.

Marshall, W. L. (1988). The use of sexually explicit stimuli by rapists, child molesters, and nonoffenders. *Journal of Sex Research, 25*(2), 267–288.

McAlexander, J. H., Schouten, J. W., & Koenig, H. F. (2002). Building brand community. *Journal of Marketing, 66*(1), 38–54.

McNair, B. (2002). *Striptease culture: Sex, media and the democratisation of desire*. New York: Routledge.

McQuarrie, E. F., & Mick, D. G. (1999). Visual rhetoric in advertising: Text-interpretive, experimental, and reader-response analyses. *Journal of Consumer Research, 26*(1), 37–54.

Miller v. California, 413 U.S. 15 (1973).

Milter, K. S., & Slade, J. W. (2005). Global traffic in pornography: The Hungarian example. In L. Z. Sigel (Ed.), *International exposure: Perspectives on modern European pornography, 1800–2000* (pp. 173–204). New Brunswick, NJ: Rutgers University Press.

Mitchell, K. J., Finkelhor, D., & Wolak, J. (2007). Youth Internet users at risk for the most serious online sexual solicitations. *American Journal of Preventive Medicine, 32*(6), 532–537.

Mosher, W. D., Chandra, A., & Jones, J. (2005). Sexual behavior and selected health measures: Men and women 15–44 years of age, United States, 2002. *Advance Data From Vital and Health Statistics*, issue 362, 1–55.

Mowlabocus, S. (2010). Porn 2.0? Technology, social practice and the new online porn industry. In F. Attwood (Ed.), *Porn.com* (pp. 69–87). New York: Peter Lang.

Mulvey, L. (1975). Visual pleasure and narrative cinema. *Screen, 16*(3), 6–18.

Muñiz, A. M., Jr., & O'Guinn, T. C. (2001). Brand community. *Journal of Consumer Research, 27*(4), 412–432.

Muñiz, A. M., Jr., O'Guinn, T. C., & Fine, G. A. (2006). Rumor in brand community. In D. A. Hantula (Ed.), *Advances in social and organizational psychology: A tribute to Ralph Rosnow* (pp. 227–247). Mahwah, NJ: Erlbaum.

Nair, S. (2009). *Child sex tourism*. Washington, DC: U.S. Department of Justice, Child Exploitation and Obscenity Section. Retrieved June 7, 2010, from http://www.justice.gov/criminal/ceos/sextour.html

The National Campaign to Prevent Teen and Unplanned Pregnancy & CosmoGirl.com. (2009). *Sex and tech: Results from a survey of teens and young adults*. Washington, DC: Author. Retrieved June 7, 2010, from http://www.thenationalcampaign.org/sextech/pdf/sextech_summary.pdf

Newcomer, R. (2006). *Moments in film: An essential understanding*. Dubuque, IA: Kendall/Hunt.

Nochlin, L. (1994). Géricault, or the absence of women. *October, 68*(Spring), 45–59.

Olivarez-Giles, N. (2009, February 4). More sex offenders joined Myspace than previously acknowledged. *Los Angeles Times*. Retrieved December 14, 2010, from http://tiny.cc/ek9wm

Ost, S. (2009). *Child pornography and sexual grooming: Legal and societal responses*. New York: Cambridge University Press.

Ozzard, J. (1996). CK Jeans rides again: Global push planned to cap the comeback. *Women's World, 30*, 6–7.

Paasonen, S., & Saarenmaa, L. (2007). The golden age of porn: Nostalgia and history in cinema. In S. Paasonen, K. Nikunen, & L. Saarenmaa (Eds.), *Pornification* (pp. 23–31). New York: Berg.

Paul, P. (2005). *Pornified: How pornography is transforming our lives, our relationships, and our families*. New York: Times Books.

Perry, I. (2003). Who(se) am I? The identity and image of women in hip-hop. In G. Dines & J. M. Humez (Eds.), *Gender, race and class in media: A text-reader* (2nd ed., pp. 136–148). Thousand Oaks, CA: Sage.

Pitcher, K. C. (2006). The staging of agency in *Girls Gone Wild. Critical Studies in Media Communication, 23*(3), 200–218.

Plastic Surgery Research.info. (2009). *Cosmetic plastic surgery research: Statistics and trends for 2001–2008*. Retrieved June 5, 2010, from http://www.cosmeticplasticsurgerystatistics.com/statistics.html

Playboy. (n.d.). *The Playboy FAQ*. Retrieved November 7, 2009, from http://www.playboy.com/articles/the-playboy-faq/index.html

Pure intentions. (1997). *Advertising Age, 68*(2), 42.

Railton, D., & Watson, P. (2007). Sexed authorship and pronographic address in music videos. In S. Paasonen, K. Nikunen, & L. Saarenmaa (Eds.), *Pornification* (pp. 115–126). New York: Berg.

Regina v. Hicklin (1868), L.R. 3 Q.B. 360, United Kingdom.

Reisman, J. A. (1991). *"Soft porn" plays hardball: Its tragic effects on women, children, and the family*. Lafayette, LA: Huntington House.

Richardson, C. R., Resnick, P. J., Hansen, D. L., Derry, H. A., & Rideout, V. J. (2002). Does pornography-blocking software block access to health information on the Internet? *Journal of the American Medical Association, 288*(22), 2887–2894.

Rodley, C. (Writer/Director), Bailey, F., Williams, K., & Varma, D. (Directors). (2006). *Pornography: The secret history of civilisation* [Television series]. Port Washington, NY: Koch Vision.

Rossi, L. (2007). Outdoor pornification: Advertising heterosexuality in the streets. In S. Paasonen, K. Nikunen, & L. Saarenmaa (Eds.), *Pornification* (pp. 127–138). New York: Berg.

Russell, D. E. H. (1998). *Dangerous relationships: Pornography, misogyny, and rape*. Thousand Oaks, CA: Sage.

Sawhney, M., Verona, G., & Prandelli, E. (2005). Collaborating to create: The Internet as a platform for customer engagement in product innovation. *Journal of Interactive Marketing, 19*(4), 4–17.

Saynt. (2008, December 27). Fashion porn: American Apparel is officially in the porn business. *Fashion Indie*. Retrieved October 30, 2010, from http://fashionindie.com/american-apparel-is-officially-in-the-porn-business

Schau, H. J., Muñiz, A. M., Jr., & Arnould, E. J. (2009). How brand community practices create value. *Journal of Marketing, 73*(5), 30–51.

Schouten, J. W., & McAlexander, J. H. (1995). Subcultures of consumption: An ethnography of the new bikers. *Journal of Consumer Research, 22*(1), 43–61.

Sex, porn, Team Jacob, and Michael Jackson make Norton's 100 top kids' online searches of 2009. (2009, December 17). *Symantec*. Retrieved June 7, 2010, from http://www.symantec.com/about/news/release/article.jsp?prid=20091217_01

Silver, J. A. (2003). Movie day at the Supreme Court or "I know it when I see it": A history of the definition of obscenity. *FindLaw*. Retrieved June 7, 2010, from http://library.findlaw.com/2003/May/15/132747.html

Snoop Doggy Dogg. (1993). Ain't no fun (if the homies can't have none). On *Doggystyle* [Record]. Los Angeles: Death Row, Interscope, & Atlantic.

Stora-Lamarre, A. (2005). Censorship in republican times: Censorship and pornographic novels located in L'Enfer de la Bibliothèque National, 1800–1900. In L. Z. Sigel (Ed.), *International exposure: Perspectives on modern European pornography, 1800–2000* (pp. 48–66). New Brunswick, NJ: Rutgers University Press.

Taflinger, R. (1996, May 28). *You and me, babe: Sex and advertising*. Retrieved March 16, 2004, from http://www.wsu.ede:80801-taflinger/sex.html

Tovar, E., Elias, J. E., & Chang, J. (1999). An overview of the effects of pornography on sex offending. In J. E. Elias, V. D. Elias, V. L. Bullough, G. Brewer, J. J. Douglas, & W. Jarvis (Eds.), *Porn 101: Eroticism, pornography, and the First Amendment* (pp. 261–278). Amherst, NY: Prometheus Books.

U.S. Department of Justice, Child Exploitation and Obscenity Section. (2009). *Child pornography*. Washington, DC: Author. Retrieved November 11, 2009, from http://www.justice.gov/criminal/ceos/childporn.html

Vargo, S. L., & Lusch, R. F. (2004). Evolving to a new dominant logic for marketing. *Journal of Marketing, 68*(1), 1–17.

Voyeur Dorm, L.C. v. City of Tampa, 265 F.3d 1232 (11th Cir. 2001), *cert. denied*, 534 U.S. 1161 (2002).

Wackwitz, L. A. (2002). Burger on Miller: Obscene effects and the filth of a nation. *Journal of Communication*, *52*(1), 196–210.

Walkerdine, V. (1997). *Daddy's girl: Young girls and popular culture*. Cambridge, MA: Harvard University Press.

Walkerdine, V., Lucey, H., & Melody, J. (2001). *Growing up girl: Psychosocial explorations of gender and class*. New York: New York University Press.

Whitney, L. (2009, August 11). Kids' search terms: Sex, games, rock 'n' roll. *Gaming and Culture*. Retrieved September 20, 2009, from http://news.cnet.com/8301-10797_3-10306357-235.html

Whitty, M. T. (2003). Pushing the wrong buttons: Men's and women's attitudes toward online and offline infidelity. *Cyberpsychology & Behavior*, *6*(6), 569–579.

Wilson, W. C. (1978). Can pornography contribute to the prevention of sexual problems? In C. B. Qualls, J. P. Wincze, & D. H. Barlow (Ed.), *The prevention of sexual disorders: Issues and approaches* (pp. 159–179). New York: Plenum Press.

Wolak, J., Mitchell, K., & Finkelhor, D. (2007). Unwanted and wanted exposure to online pornography in a national sample of youth Internet users. *Pediatrics*, *119*(2), 247–257.

Woodward, B., & Armstrong, S. (1979). *The brethren: Inside the Supreme Court*. New York: Simon & Schuster.

# 25

## Neuroscience and Addictive Consumption

### Ab Litt, Dante M. Pirouz, and Baba Shiv

The tragic irony of addiction—the root of the ensuing emotional suffering, crippling loss of control, and irrepressibly self-destructive behavior—is that it arises from precisely the same interacting brain mechanisms that enable us to choose, think, and act in ways that keep us safe and make us happy. We have evolved an array of interacting neural systems for processing joy and displeasure, expectations and evaluations, immediate and long-term goals, and desire versus hedonic experience. When acting in harmony, these systems underpin our ability to successfully interact with constantly changing environments, and to flexibly learn (and learn to like) adaptive behaviors. Yet, when they are corrupted, decoupled, or adversely affected, the result can be the pathological desire, pursuit, and consumption patterns characteristic of addiction.

Understanding these basic neurophysiological mechanisms not only gives us insight into the roots of addictive consumption but also, in so doing, can enrich conceptions of and predictions regarding key behavioral phenomena in choice, control, and compulsion (e.g., those discussed by Faber & Vohs, Chapter 22 of this volume). It also illuminates causal and exacerbating forces driving addictive consumption, and opportunities for and impediments to avoidance, coping, and overcoming by individuals. Examining the bases of addictive consumption can highlight key issues and inform practical recommendations for policy makers and others working to improve consumer well-being, and illuminate important and promising new questions warranting deeper exploration by researchers. In this chapter, we address these and related dimensions relevant to protecting and enhancing consumer well-being and quality of life across both immediate and long-term perspectives. To do so, we present an integrative review of key results from consumer psychology, psychopharmacology, and neuroscientific research.

We first provide a basic inventory of key domains of addictive consumption. We outline properties and threats to consumer well-being shared by and characteristic of each, and evaluate the rationales and consequences of differences in scope and treatment of addiction to licit versus illicit substances. How society can and should make such disjunctions for the maximal collective benefit is a central issue benefited by understanding the neural mechanisms of addiction.

We turn next to describing these mechanisms in detail through the lenses of affective and decision neuroscience, consumer behavior, and integrative approaches. As we illustrate, consumer research is enlightened not only by neural and pharmacological research into mechanisms of addiction, but also by results, theories, and scenarios developed by consumer psychologists who have offered fruitful insights into core addiction processes and phenomena. We review converging evidence for various and often counterposed systems by which the brain encodes value and pleasure and engages in motivational processing that determines desire and pursuit actions. Such a fundamental deconstruction of value lies at the heart of the problem of addiction: When dissociable valuation subsystems are adversely driven apart by substances or situations, behaviors characteristic of addiction, such as wanting without liking, anhedonic consumption, and compulsive yet remorseful actions, can be the inexorable result.

From a detailed understanding of these basic neural, psychological, and pharmacological mechanisms, it becomes possible to construct a more enlightened and biologically informed array of policy viewpoints and recommendations regarding the prevention, treatment, and punishment of addictive behavior, as well as the regulation of addictive substances and their marketing. We outline a series of such public policy implications and salient issues informed by and derived from results from the neuroscience of addictive consumption. Policy administrators, nonprofit groups, health professionals, and individual consumers have much to gain from a perspective on these matters, informed directly by modern insights into addiction based on integrative neuroscientific, pharmacological, and behavioral investigations.

## ADDICTIVE SUBSTANCES AND BEHAVIORAL PATTERNS

We focus here on a basic enumeration and classification of some key specific domains of addictive-pattern behavior and outline their impact on consumer well-being. Underlying mechanisms of action are described in depth in a subsequent section.

### Illicit Substances

Discussions of addiction typically center on several classes of globally controlled and interdicted substances of abuse, which we describe briefly here (for additional details, see Koob, 1992; Nestler, 2005). Psychostimulants such as cocaine and amphetamine-class drugs, including methamphetamine, enhance activity in the central and peripheral nervous systems, typically inducing hyperactivity, increases in blood pressure and heart rate, decreases in perceptions of food and sleep requirements, hypersexuality and increased sexual pleasure, and euphoria. Chronic abuse greatly increases risks of seizures, paranoid delusions, and hallucinations, as well as heart attack, stroke, and cerebral hemorrhage, which may lead to death directly or via respiratory or renal failure caused by hyperthermia-induced muscle destruction. Tolerance can develop rapidly and acutely, with withdrawal leading to bounce-back effects such as depression, excessive eating and sleeping, and heightened drug craving with related anxiety.

Natural and synthetic opioids, such as heroin, morphine, and related derivatives, also cause intense euphoria but act through depressant rather than stimulant effects on neural and physiological function. Effects besides euphoria making users prone to abuse include pain relief, amnesia, anxiety reduction, and profound feelings of physical and psychological relaxation. The combined effects of nausea, sedation, and shallow breathing make aspiration of vomit while unconscious a significant mortality risk. Respiratory depression alone may be extreme enough to lead to fatal cessation of breathing. Risks of opioid tolerance and dependence are notably acute, with highly unpleasant withdrawal symptoms and extraordinarily intense drug craving in the immediate discontinuation phase, and continued cravings over longer periods leading to high risk of relapse. Barbiturates such as Quaaludes and benzodiazepines (e.g., Valium) are also widely addictive depressants and have similar tolerance and risk profiles, given sufficient dosages and chronic abuse patterns. These substances occupy a gray area between generally illicit for nonindicated and recreational uses and available with prescription for specific purposes. Although the euphoric effects of these substances tend to be somewhat less pronounced in intensity than those of opioids, their powerful anxiolytic, sedative, relaxing, and inhibition-reducing effects make them highly attractive for recreational, and often addictive-pattern, usage.

This is, of course, not a full compendium of addictive illicit substances. For example, cannabis, a psychoactive drug causing a mix of stimulant and depressive effects, has a comparably much lower addictive profile, but one with an increasingly well-characterized biological mechanism (Fattore, Fadda, Spano, Pistis, & Fratta, 2008), although significant controversies regarding its dependence profile remain to be resolved (e.g., Grinspoon, Bakalar, & Zimmer, 1997). Yet, these cases encompass the large majority of controlled and interdicted drugs prone to addictive-pattern abuse.

## Licit Behaviors and Consumables

The aforementioned addictive drugs are certainly highly destructive to the lives and well-being of many people. In the United States alone, the 2006 National Survey on Drug Use and Health (Office of Applied Studies, 2007) reported within-year use of cocaine by 6 million individuals, methamphetamine by 1.9 million, and heroin by 560,000. Similar relative levels of abuse exist in Western Europe. However, in both usage prevalence and mortality rates, these and other illicit drugs pale in comparison to two substances with comparably minimal control and interdiction in much of the world: tobacco, which is a stimulant, and alcohol, which is a depressant. For 2002, the World Health Organization estimated 185 million users of all types of illicit drugs, versus 2 billion alcohol users and 1.3 billion smokers (Shafey, Dolwick, & Guindon, 2003). Any purported tameness of effects of these substances relative to harder illicit drugs is swamped at the level of aggregate destructive effects on health and well-being (see Pechmann, Biglan, Grube, & Cody, Chapter 17 of this volume). Alcohol is responsible for more than eight times the number of worldwide deaths as illicit drugs, and tobacco more than 20 times. Globally, tobacco smoking has killed more than 100 million people in the past 100 years, and it has been estimated that it could kill 1 billion over the next 100 years (World Health Organization, 2008). Perhaps contrary to expectations based on their generally legal and less controlled status, alcohol has a dependence risk comparable to barbiturates and benzodiazepines, and tobacco has an addictive profile nearly as acute as that of cocaine (Nutt, King, Saulsbury, & Blakemore, 2007).

Caffeine is another dependence-inducing psychoactive stimulant that is generally uncontrolled worldwide. Whereas specific negative effects on health are comparably minor (e.g., nervousness, irritability, disturbed sleep, diarrhea), with dangerous effects on heart and liver function occurring only with extreme and difficult-to-achieve overdose levels, tolerance is quick to develop, and withdrawal can be accompanied by unpleasant symptoms (e.g., severe headache, joint and stomach pain, concentration disruption). More pertinent to the current discussion is the economic impact of caffeine dependence in consumers in terms of product manufacture, marketing, and sales. Sixteen billion pounds of coffee beans are produced and brought to market each year, and tea is the second most consumed liquid on earth, after water. In the United States alone, the market for high-caffeine energy drinks grew from $3 billion in 2005 to $5.4 billion in 2007 and was predicted to reach $10 billion by 2010. Overall, 9 in 10 Americans consume caffeine in one form or another every day (Lovett, 2005). This wide and deep-rooted reach into the brain chemistry and pocketbooks of consumers has undoubtedly been abetted by the addictive-dependence profile of caffeine.

Besides usage of licit and illicit psychoactive substances, addictive-pattern behavior is also prevalent in other domains of consumption. Compulsive buying or shopping behavior has been estimated to be exhibited by as high as 9% of the U.S. population (Ridgway, Kukar-Kinney, & Monroe, 2008; see also Faber & Vohs, Chapter 22 of this volume) and is associated and commonly comorbid with compulsive hoarding behavior (Mueller, Mitchell, Crosby, Glaesmer, & de Zwaan, 2009). Problem gambling has an estimated prevalence of 1.3% of the North American population at a clinical, pathological level and at a subclinical but serious problem and potentially pathological level of 4.9% (Cotte & LaTour, Chapter 23 of this volume; Shaffer, Hall, & Vander Bilt, 1999). Also receiving study and characterization as addictive-type disorders have been compulsive overeating (Davis & Carter, 2009; Faber & Vohs, Chapter 22 of this volume; Kessler, 2009), sex and Internet pornography addiction (Albright, Chapter 24 of this volume; Bostwick & Bucci, 2008), excessive tanning bed usage (Kaur et al., 2006; Warthan, Uchida, & Wagner, 2005), and even dependence and withdrawal issues with regard to video gaming and television viewing (Kubey & Csikszentmihalyi, 2002). In each of these cases, rather than addictive responses to specific and well-defined neuroactive chemicals, behavioral patterns consistent with addiction, such as craving, dependence, inability to restrain consumption in line with higher level goals, risk of relapse into abusive consumption after periods of abstention, and often even tolerance and withdrawal effects, occur in response to more varied, higher order, and physiologically and psychologically complex rewarding stimuli.

### Licit, Illicit, and Related Disjunctions Versus an Expansive View of Addictive-Pattern Consumption

Strong disjunctions are often drawn in discussions of addictive behavioral patterns. Common besides licit versus illicit, although intrinsically related, are drug versus nondrug, physical versus psychological addiction, and demarcations based on perceived outcome severity (e.g., heroin abuse vs. excessive video gaming). As we describe further in a later section on public policy issues, these disjunctions have important implications and real-world consequences regarding which consumers are stigmatized and which are not, with consequent implications for homelessness and family strife, who risks conflict with the criminal justice system, how extensive and well funded are available treatment options, and other issues.

But is making such strong disjunctions the best way to approach problems of addictive consumption, from the standpoints of either science or practical well-being enhancement? Addictive behaviors across such boundaries often exhibit significant co-occurrence patterns (Greenberg, Lewis, & Dodd, 1999), and consumer research has shown wide-ranging generality effects in reward-seeking across disparate domains (Wadhwa, Shiv, & Nowlis, 2008). Looking to the basic neural mechanisms of addictive consumption, we argue that a more useful and biologically accurate approach to understanding addiction, and designing appropriate policies to improve consumer well-being, is more unified, expansive, and nondisjunctive. Although, of course, specific differences between addictive consumption domains are important and often crucial for understanding and treating any specific addiction, addictive behaviors across domains share a high degree of commonality in basic underlying mechanisms (Nestler, 2005), as we review in the next section. Thus, a neuroscientific view not only deepens our understanding of how addictive behaviors arise but also motivates an integrative approach to conceptualizing the fundamental problems and their solutions, rather than relying on disjunctive categorizations that have often been favored by policy makers and researchers.

## CENTRAL PHENOMENA AND MECHANISMS

Here, we describe the basic neural underpinnings of addiction, tying them to the consumption domains described previously. (The key neural regions we highlight are illustrated in Figure 25.1.) We then review essential findings and consequences regarding these basic mechanisms from both neurophysiological and behavioral research. In particular, we focus this discussion on results specifically relevant to consumer choice, valuation, and issues central to overall happiness and well-being.

### Key Neural Pathways, Regions, and Activity Patterns

An ever-increasing body of neural and pharmacological evidence points to an essentially bipartite view of the processes underlying the array of addictive-pattern behaviors: the craving to obtain a stimulus, and the compulsion to produce and perseverate in stimulus-seeking and consumption actions, even when they no longer give pleasure or stand explicitly against higher level goals to desist (Naqvi & Bechara, 2009; O'Brien, Childress, Ehrman, & Robbins, 1998; Volkow & Fowler, 2000). These processes are implemented in the brain by dissociable but interacting networks of activity, whose adverse or decoupled activation leads to the maladaptive outcomes of addiction that

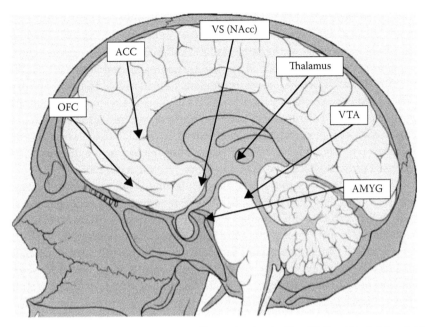

**Figure 25.1**   Medial view of the brain with localizations of key regions involved in addiction. (Adapted from Patrick J. Lynch, medical illustrator; C. Carl Jaffe, MD, cardiologist. Creative Commons Attribution 2.5 License 2006. With permission.)
*Note:* ACC = anterior cingulate cortex; AMYG = amygdala; NAcc = nucleus accumbens, a subregion of the ventral striatum; OFC = orbitofrontal cortex; VS = ventral striatum; VTA = ventral tegmental area. Insula is not pictured, as it is located more laterally in the brain.

are so detrimental to consumer well-being. This underlying process distinctness also raises interesting new possibilities for exploration by consumer researchers, which we describe later.

Central to the first component of addiction, craving, is the stimulus-induced, or stimulus-indicative cue-induced, release of dopamine from the ventral tegmental area of the midbrain (i.e., mesencephalon) projected to receptor regions in the limbic areas of the brain, most crucially the nucleus accumbens region of the ventral striatum (see Figure 25.1). As reviewed by Naqvi and Bechara (2009), this mesolimbic dopaminergic pathway was first identified as central to reward and addiction in the 1980s by Wise (Wise, 1988; Wise & Bozarth, 1982, 1987), and much work since has continued to refine and enrich these early efforts. Interestingly, and lamentably converse to its treatment by the popular media and less neuroscientifically expert researchers, this dopaminergic reward pathway has little to do directly with mediating the pleasure obtained from reinforcing stimuli. Rather, it is crucial for determining the attractiveness, or incentive value, of these stimuli, that is, the motivational impetus to obtain these stimuli. Despite the popular prevalence to this day of the "pleasure chemical" view of dopamine, in his early efforts Wise accurately characterized this dopaminergic pathway as central instead to the approach response to rewards such as addictive drugs, rather than the experienced pleasure they might bring (Wise & Bozarth, 1987). Additional limbic regions are also important for representing and amplifying the incentive value of rewarding stimuli and associated emotional responses, including the amygdala and extended regions (Baxter & Murray, 2002), which has been shown to be crucial to linking reward values to action selection through connections with prefrontal regions of the brain (Baxter, Parker, Lindner, Izquierdo, & Murray, 2000; Bechara, Damasio, & Damasio, 2003).

Supporting a unified model of addiction, there is evidence for essentially all stimuli prone to addictive abuse activating this mesolimbic dopamine pathway to induce reward responses. While some stimuli (e.g., cocaine, nicotine) act to directly stimulate dopamine release to accumbens, others (e.g., opioids, alcohol) act through second-order (i.e., indirect) pathways and on different types of dopamine receptors but lead to the same result (Nestler, 2005). Whereas mesolimbic engagement mechanisms are being characterized for directly neuroactive addictive substances (e.g., caffeine, barbiturates, benzodiazepines, psychostimulants), the incentive and craving characteristics of more complex addictive consumption domains are also being tied to this system. Pathological gambling has been linked to disruption of the mesolimbic dopamine pathway (Reuter et al., 2005). In a now famous case, Mirapex, a dopamine-active drug designed to treat Parkinson's disease, also induced pathological gambling behavior in previous nongamblers, as the drug acted on a type of dopamine receptor primarily localized in limbic regions (Dodd et al., 2005).

Naltrexone, an opioid blocker that thus disrupts a second-order pathway to dopamine release in limbic reward regions, has been used as an effective treatment of Internet pornography addiction (Bostwick & Bucci, 2008). This drug has also been seen to reduce ultraviolet light preference in frequent, but not infrequent, users of tanning beds, even inducing withdrawal-like symptoms in some (Kaur et al., 2006). Similar mesolimbic activity association has been described for overeating-related behaviors (Davis & Carter, 2009; Kessler, 2009; Volkow & Wise, 2005). These results show how a neural view of addiction can unify our understanding of diverse domains of addiction, and provide telling evidence for a broader conceptualization of the key phenomena, rather than such disjunctions as between licit and illicit, drug and nondrug, or physical and psychological.

Additionally, recent evidence points to a key role for the insula region of the brain in inducing conscious, felt urges to consume rewarding substances. In a striking study, damage to the insula immediately and completely ablated felt urges to smoke in long-time smokers, thus disrupting addiction (Naqvi, Rudrauf, Damasio, & Bechara, 2007). Because of its extensive inputs from both limbic areas and regions representing bodily states, such as the thalamus, a recently proposed mechanism for the insula's role in conscious, motivated craving is in computing and translating felt, internal states (i.e., interoception) into feelings of desire, and biasing behavioral responses toward desired stimuli accordingly (Contreras, Ceric, & Torrealba, 2007; Naqvi & Bechara, 2009). Such internal states crucially include those experienced during preconsumption rituals and the consumption act, such as the bitter taste of cocaine, or the act of striking a match to light a cigarette. The existence of highly characteristic consumption and preconsumption rituals and experiences extends across addictive domains, so the insula's role in craving also seems one which crosses the disjunctions typically drawn between these domains.

The second fundamental component system of addiction, compulsion to produce seeking and consumption behaviors with respect to the addictive target, seems served at a basic level by a primarily dopaminergic pathway from the striatum through the thalamus to frontal cortical regions, most notably the orbitofrontal and anterior cingulate cortices. Like the insula, to which they are both directly connected, these frontal regions are ideally situated and networked to monitor and integrate bodily states central to valuation and choice behavior, such as satiety levels and potential conflicting goals (Baxter et al., 2000; Botvinick, Cohen, & Carter, 2004). Along with a wide-ranging and richly conceptualized role in value computation (Padoa-Schioppa & Assad, 2006; Plassmann, O'Doherty, & Rangel, 2007), the orbitofrontal cortex plays a critical role in regulating compulsive, impulsive, repetitive, and disinhibited behavior (Bechara, Damasio, Damasio, & Anderson, 1994; Damasio, Grabowski, Frank, Galburda, & Damasio, 1994). It is abnormally activated in drug-addicted subjects: underactive during protracted withdrawal in proportion to dopaminergic links from the striatum, and hyperactive during and immediately after addictive target consumption in proportion to the intensity of craving (Volkow & Fowler, 2000). Cocaine-dependent individuals have shown decreased concentrations of neurons in the orbitofrontal and anterior cingulate cortices (Franklin et al., 2002); depressed or otherwise abnormal activation in these regions underlies compulsive behavior in Tourette's syndrome and obsessive-compulsive disorders such as compulsive hoarding (Saxena et al., 2004; Volkow & Fowler, 2000), which, as described before, seems closely associated with compulsive shopping behavior.

With additional connectivity to the insula, evidence supports the anterior cingulate playing a major role in integrating the inside (i.e., interoception of bodily states) with the outside (i.e., environmental cues and objects, valuations of external stimuli computed in the orbitofrontal cortex) to evaluate competing and often conflicting goals and responses and link them to behavioral choices (Botvinick et al., 2004; Shima & Tanji, 1998; Williams, Bush, Rauch, Cosgrove, & Eskandar, 2004). This role has been characterized as the core of behavioral will (Peoples, 2002). The anterior cingulate cortex is where conflicts between goals and associated behaviors are waged, with damage or abnormal activity leading to the winning out of impulsive and compulsive choices, ranging from perseveration in drug consumption (Nestler, 2005) to overselection of first-impulse, but incorrect, responses in Stroop tasks (Whalen et al., 1998). It is the distinctness of this circuit regulating compulsive and impulsive behavioral selection that, in the case of addiction, leads to the persistence of seeking and consumption behaviors even when the associated stimulus is no longer pleasurable, there are adverse reactions to the stimulus, and there are active countergoals to refrain from consumption.

Intense craving and irrepressible seeking and consumption behaviors are further exacerbated by the development of tolerance to addictive targets and the experience of unpleasant withdrawal symptoms during cessation attempts. Both of these outcomes are due to homeostatic responses of the dopaminergic system (Nestler, 2005). Chronic ramping up via abuse of addictive targets reduces baseline levels of dopamine function, which leads both to increasing tolerance as abuse continues, and thus the requirement of greater and greater levels of stimulation to ameliorate cravings and produce pleasurable responses; and to negative emotional symptoms during subsequent withdrawal periods, with the associated persistence of intense cravings increasing the risk of relapse.

Individuals differ greatly in their risk of developing addictions, and as described previously, diverse addictive-pattern behaviors are often co-occurring. Those high in general reward sensitivity are likely to overeat and prefer foods high in fat and sugar (Davis et al., 2007), and high novelty seeking has been shown to lead to impulse control disorders (Kim & Grant, 2001). In a similar vein, Kuhnen and Chiao (2009) found that individuals with a 7-repeat allele (variant) of the dopamine receptor D4, a gene known to regulate dopamine and serotonin neurotransmission, are significantly more risk-seeking compared to those without the 7-repeat allele, with direct implications for risk of developing addictions. Understanding addiction as the interaction of specific neural systems offers a natural means for characterizing such between-individual differences and within-individual generalities of behavior. Individual brains differ in the strength of mesolimbic dopaminergic pathways, sensitivities of output reward regions such as the orbitofrontal cortex and ventral striatum, and interconnectivity with integrative regions such as the anterior cingulate and insula. This provides a natural and mechanistic framework for explaining and predicting when and why individuals differ in addictive behaviors and risk factors. Moreover, the commonality of the underlying neural architecture explains why such individual differences may extend quite generally across diverse forms of addictive behavior.

### Desire–Satisfaction Dissociation: Anhedonic and Counterhedonic Consumption

Incentive salience mediated by mesolimbic dopamine has been conceptualized by Berridge and colleagues as "wanting" rewarding targets, which captures desire and pursuit motivation, as contrasted with "liking" the same targets, which relates instead to the pleasure and satisfaction they bring (Berridge & Robinson, 1995). Although less definitively characterized, the latter seems underpinned by opioid output activity in primary sensory and valuation regions, such as the orbitofrontal cortex (Berridge, 1996). The dissociable nature of these constructs has been demonstrated across a range of physiological and pharmacological investigations, identifying broad neurological disjunctions between wanting- and liking-related activities (Berridge, 2007; Berridge & Zajonc, 1991; Kelley & Berridge, 2002; Robinson & Berridge, 1993; Wyvell & Berridge, 2000). This is a key dissociation for understanding addiction and related behaviors.

When wanting and liking are driven apart, as is frequent in addiction, individuals may desire and pursue targets that not only are counter to high-level goals and destructive to well-being but bring little happiness as well. Joyless and anhedonic consumption, even in the presence of knowledge of dangerous and destructive consequences, is a tragic hallmark of chronic addiction (O'Brien et al., 1998; Rogers et al., 1999). Of the same form, consumption that is insensitive to pleasure signals seems key to the phenomenon of mindless eating (Wansink, 2007). This desire–satisfaction deconstruction of value that is at the heart of addiction can be further enlightened by consumer research and, in turn, may inspire interesting new questions in consumer research warranting investigation. We turn to a discussion of these issues next.

### Manifestations in Consumer Behavior, Choice, and Valuation

In a related dichotomy to wanting versus liking, Higgins (2006), in reviewing 8 decades of research in animal and human psychology, proposes value as being determined by the individual and interactive effects of the hedonic experience of a stimulus, and the engagement strength with which the organism desires or pursues the stimulus. The nature of the interaction of these effects can vary widely. In some cases, engagement, pursuit, and wanting can shape subsequent liking. Actions requiring higher effort can increase the relative attractiveness of both unobtained (Aronson, 1961) and obtained rewards (Norton & Ariely, 2009). In a notable case of the latter from consumer behavior research, identical potato chips packaged in difficult- rather than easy-to-open polyvinyl bags, which were opened by the participants, were rated as crisper and tastier and were preferred overall (McDaniel & Baker, 1977).

From a neural perspective, by directly interfering with dopamine transmission to nucleus accumbens in rats, Salamone and colleagues (Salamone & Correa, 2002; Salamone, Correa, Farrar, & Mingote, 2007; Salamone, Correa, Mingote, & Weber, 2005) have implicated the mesolimbic pathway as centrally involved in the degree to which organisms engage in effortful responding to obtain rewarding stimuli. This point is echoed by neuroimaging results that have shown increased ventral striatum activity with the expenditure of effort to obtain rewards (Zink, Pagnoni, Martin-Skurski, Chappelow, & Berns, 2004). How this fits with the incentive salience view of this same pathway is a question of great current interest to neuroscientists and should be so as well for those interested in both addiction and the wider issues of consumer desire and satisfaction.

More broadly construed, these phenomena are examples of motivational influences on experienced utility, that is, liking derived from wanting to like a stimulus. Other such examples are marketing placebo effects, in which heightened expectations and quality signals, such as through higher reported product prices, can lead to a motivated enhancement of the actual efficacy of drugs and performance-enhancing stimuli (Shiv, Carmon, & Ariely, 2005; Waber, Shiv, Carmon, & Ariely, 2008) and, of particular relevance for the current discussion, experienced beverage flavor pleasantness as tracked by orbitofrontal cortex activity (Plassmann, O'Doherty, Shiv, & Rangel, 2008). This work is of interest to neuroscientists studying fundamental addiction circuits, as they have widely documented a role of expectations of a seemingly opposite nature, namely, attenuation (Seymour & McClure, 2008). Understanding when and how expectations potentiate heightened pleasure responses, as in marketing placebo and price placebo work versus attenuated responses with expectations matching, are key questions whose resolutions will likely require the efforts of both behavioral and neurobiological researchers.

In addition to absolute effects of engagement and desire on liking of stimuli, consumer researchers have shown that relative or subjective values can also be influenced by such consumption antecedents. Actions requiring high levels of effort can shift the qualitative nature of relative reward preferences, for example, toward luxuries and away from necessities (Kivetz & Simonson, 2002), or toward specific types of rewards that are more superficially congruent with the nature of the specific actions selected and engaged in (Kivetz, 2005). Energy levels and mental states can also shift relative reward preferences in favor or against consumption requiring additional cognitive effort expenditure (Gibbs & Drolet, 2003).

Conversely, generalized wanting or desire states have been shown in both behavioral and neuroscientific paradigms to be created by viewing or being primed with images of other, wholly unrelated desire-inducing stimuli (Gibbs, 1997; Knutson, Wimmer, Kuhnen, & Winkielman, 2008) and also through cueing via nonsatiating consumption experiences, such as samples of a pleasant-tasting, flavored beverage (Wadhwa et al., 2008). The underlying mechanism typically proposed for these results is one of prepotentiation of the mesolimbic dopamine pathway and seems related to the previously described role of the insula in translating preconsumption rituals and reward cues into felt cravings. It may also help explain certain cases of cross-tolerance and cross-sensitization that have been observed for different drugs, with respect to their effects on craving and compulsive consumption behavior (Nestler, 2005).

Another striking example from consumer research that is both inspired by and further enriching the wanting–liking dichotomy of neural pathways central to addiction is that these systems are not simply dissociable, but can actually be counterdriven in opposing directions by single experiences as well. In particular, affect-laden "jilting," involving the frustrating denial of a desired and pursued outcome, can simultaneously increase desire and engagement in pursuit of that outcome, or even a superficially similar proxy target, but decrease the attractiveness and appraisal of the target itself due to its tainting by the negativity of the preceding jilting experience (Litt, Khan, & Shiv, 2010). This persists even if and after desire has been satisfied. In such cases, the outcome is wanted more but liked less.

Supportive results have been reported in neuroscientific investigations of the bases of rejection feelings in romantic love: rejected lovers viewing pictures of the partners who had jilted them showed increased activity, relative to happy, unrejected lovers, in both the nucleus accumbens and surrounding regions as well as areas of the anterior insula, operculum, and lateral orbitofrontal cortex, associated with pain and evaluating punishers (Fisher, Aron, & Brown, 2006; Fisher et al., 2005). This result may have broad and important implications for understanding and predicting differences across consumer behavior metrics more associated with wanting (e.g., product demand, persistence in pursuit of scarce products) versus liking (e.g., return rates, reported satisfaction, repeat purchase tendencies), and even more basic issues such as the non-one-to-one ratio between willingness to pay and willingness to accept. For understanding addiction, the notion of wanting–liking counterdriving underscores the dissociability of these constructs and may inspire new ideas and experimental paradigms to explore how they come to be adversely and distinctly influenced during addictive consumption.

## NEUROSCIENCE AND THE PUBLIC DEBATE REGARDING ADDICTION

As we have described thus far, neuroscientific advances are rapidly providing a more complete characterization of the fundamental bases of addiction. By building on this knowledge, Transformative Consumer Research may benefit from a greatly enriched understanding of the effects of advertising and marketing actions on the consumption of addictive products. In addition, with a detailed understanding of the neural, psychological, and pharmacological mechanisms of addiction, it becomes possible to construct a more fair, effective, and actionable array of policy recommendations for preventing, treating, and punishing addictive behavior, as well as regulating addictive substances and their marketing.

Regrettably, despite progress in understanding the neural bases of addiction, the formulation and implementation of specific public policy measures based on these findings lag behind. For the most part, consumer behavior research has not played a prominent role in the development of regulations governing the marketing of addictive products either. A complete understanding of addictive consumption stands at the nexus of these, until recently far removed, research approaches. Consumer behavior and decision neuroscience researchers thus have an opportunity to meaningfully influence public policy discourse by developing integrative research streams, predictions, and ideas that address key theoretical and practical issues regarding interactions between marketing actions and addictive consumption. Here, we briefly review the state of public policy positions and initiatives intended to curtail and control addictive consumption and the marketing of addictive products (for a more thorough treatment, see Pechmann et al., Chapter 17 of this volume). We then outline a series of public policy implications and possibilities informed by results from the neuroscience of addictive consumption.

## Current Policy Efforts Regarding Addictive-Product Marketing

Much policy effort in the United States has focused on addiction prevention through educational campaigns targeting children, adolescents, and parents (Dackis & O'Brien, 2005). An example of such an initiative is the National Youth Anti-Drug Media Campaign. Over $1 billion has been spent by Congress through this campaign, with the goals of educating young people to reject illegal drugs and encouraging drug users to quit (Hornik, Jacobsohn, Orwin, Piesse, & Kalton, 2008). The antidrug campaign targets adolescents ages 9–18, their parents, and other influential adults via television, radio, websites, magazines, and movie theaters. However, the effectiveness of these types of campaigns has been debated. Some research has shown that they are effective, especially when combined with a school- or community-based education program (Farrelly, Davis, Haviland, Healton, & Messeri, 2005; Farrelly, Niederdeppe, & Yarsevich, 2003). However, a recent study on the effectiveness of the National Youth Anti-Drug campaign found no effect on intent to avoid marijuana use and may have had some delayed unfavorable effects (Hornik et al., 2008).

A wide array of policies regulating the marketing and sale of addictive products have been implemented globally (Bernheim & Rangel, 2005). A central stream is the restriction of advertising and promotion efforts, including full bans, bans on outdoor advertising close to schools and playgrounds or in publications with significant youth readerships, bans of free samples or giveaways with the purchase of products, and bans of tobacco and alcohol brand sponsorships of sports and entertainment events. A related push is the regulation of the nature and content of marketing efforts, such as restricting cigarette advertising to black-and-white visuals accompanied by only spoken word audio; another example is the voluntary industry code by alcohol producers, with advertising showing consumption only in a responsible manner, avoiding the depiction or encouragement of drunk driving, risky behavior, excessive intoxication, or illegal activities (Federal Trade Commission, 2003). Another policy initiative involves strengthening health warnings and labeling on products. In the case of cigarettes, this can entail requiring warnings to cover a certain percentage of packages; using graphic, viscerally arousing warning labels (e.g., diseased lungs); and prohibiting the use of terms such as *light*, *mild*, and *low tar* (Family Smoking Prevention and Tobacco Control Act, 2009).

As to potentially addictive products beyond tobacco and alcohol, regulation stipulating limitations on marketing and advertising tactics has been sporadic at best. Although the U.S. Food and Drug Administration has regulated the advertising of prescription drugs since 1962 (Kessler &

Pines, 1990), consideration of other potentially addictive products and their dependency risks, the regulation of the marketing of gambling outlets, the regulation of credit cards and similar enablers of compulsive shopping, and so forth have been scant.

Public Policy Implications of Neuroscience for Addictive Consumption

There are a number of public policy implications that can be informed by findings in neuroscience and psychopharmacological research (see, e.g., Bernheim & Rangel, 2005). Aforementioned youth-targeted education programs might be enhanced in efficacy by leveraging neuroscientific findings regarding learning and memory differences in the developing brains of adolescents and children (Dackis & O'Brien, 2005). For instance, beyond even more basic neurodevelopmental hurdles of reduced inhibitory control and long-term perspective taking, the ability to simply maintain in memory one's prospective intentions for future actions is reduced and still developing throughout adolescence (Blakemore & Choudhury, 2006). Thus, even if education campaigns are effective in inducing youth intentions to avoid addictive consumption traps and behaviors, their impact may be much attenuated at later points in time when the intention to avoid must still be active to guide behavior. Knowledge of this and similar developmental issues, derived from the neuroscientific study of changes across the life span, should guide both the high-level design of educational campaigns and key basic-level implementation steps. One such recommendation is the reduction of spatial, contextual, and temporal distances between anticonsumption messages and consumption temptations, such as putting the messages directly at the point of purchase. Relatedly, regulatory efforts banning the display of tobacco and alcohol products and paraphernalia in retail outlets open to youths may be particularly warranted and efficacious.

This example is embedded in a larger body of neuroscientific literature indicating unique neural vulnerabilities across age and population groups. Developmental changes in the brain across the life span may indicate specific age-related vulnerabilities to the effects of addictive-product marketing. One such case is the nonlinear neural development of adolescents, which may make them especially susceptible to risk and addictive behaviors (Chambers, Taylor, & Potenza, 2003; Crews, He, & Hodge, 2007). An adolescent undergoes significant changes to the reward circuitry underlying addictive behavior, such as increases in connectivity from prefrontal cortex to the nucleus accumbens (Doremus-Fitzwater, Varlinskaya, & Spear, 2009), which have been implicated in regulating drug-seeking behavior (Kalivas, Volkow, & Seamans, 2005). Adolescents seem to be more sensitive than adults to the positive, rewarding properties of drug stimuli and less sensitive to their negative, aversive effects. However, specific links between extensive findings in behavioral and consumer research on adolescents and their susceptibility to persuasive messages (e.g., regarding drugs, smoking, or drinking; see Pechmann & Knight, 2002; Pechmann & Ratneshwar, 1994; Shadel, Niaura, & Abrams, 2002; Shadel, Tharp-Taylor, & Fryer, 2008) and the neurological development trajectory of the adolescent brain are still relatively new in the literature. Neuroscience research might offer more well-informed and integrated approaches to designing programs and messages that effectively deter experimentation and initiation during this vulnerable developmental period. Overall, a richer understanding of neurological differences across the life span and between population groups could greatly inform the design of regulations, prevention messages, and treatment approaches (Pfefferbaum, Rosenbloom, Crusan, & Jernigan, 1988; Volkow & Wise, 2005).

As previously described, neuroscience provides a natural means of characterizing a vast array of individual differences, such as age, in terms of their implications for addictive consumption, which, in turn, can meaningfully influence the development of policy interventions. For instance, consider one relevant individual difference mentioned earlier, sensation seeking. Palmgreen, Donohew, Lorch, Hoyle, and Stephenson (2001) have developed a sensation-seeking targeted prevention approach, which has been shown to significantly reduce marijuana use among adolescents who are high in sensation seeking (Byrne, Dickson, Derevensky, Gupta, & Lussier, 2005). The framing and development of counteradvertising messages, as well as predictions regarding their relative efficacy between individuals, can thus benefit from an understanding of how individuals and populations differ along neurological and developmental dimensions. Neuroscience provides rich insight into the mechanistic bases of such differences and their interrelationships and is, thus, critical for informing public policy recommendations.

Another public policy issue that could be usefully informed by neuroscience research is the nature of content regulation in advertising and marketing materials for addictive products. Since environmental cues have been shown to influence addictive behaviors, it has been suggested that the restriction or elimination of these cues through regulation may help reduce the elicited craving and desire for addictive products (Bernheim & Rangel, 2005). However, it is unclear what elements in advertising and marketing materials should specifically be targeted in such regulations. Some lawmakers, for example, have attempted to restrict tobacco advertising to black-and-white representations. Is such a restriction effective in lowering cue reactivity in vulnerable consumers? What are the precise effects on underlying memory, attention, and emotional neural circuits of the use of human models, cartoon characters, and lifestyle imagery in addictive product advertising (Kelly, Slater, & Karan, 2002; Kelly, Slater, Karan, & Hunn, 2000), and how in turn do any such effects influence the craving and compulsion neural networks? Neuroscience and psychopharmacology may provide critical insights into the mechanisms driving reactive responses to addictive cues and, therefore, address these critical open questions for policy makers.

Given that addiction often leads to cravings and compulsive behavior at odds with higher level goals, such as persistent wanting of what is no longer liked, it is critical for public health policy to understand the efficacy of treatment interventions that aim to strengthen the exertion of cognitive control over cravings and compulsive behaviors. Recent research on such cognitive interventions is encouraging. For instance, Volkow and colleagues (2010) demonstrate that, when cocaine abusers purposefully inhibited craving when exposed to conditioned drug cues, metabolic activity decreased in the nucleus accumbens and medial orbitofrontal cortex. Thus, cognitive interventions that strengthen a weakened circuit between the accumbens and frontal cortical regions may improve cocaine abusers' abilities to reduce drug craving responses. At a higher level, showing that even strongly addicted individuals retain the ability to exercise some effortful control over craving (see also Ahmed & Koob, 2009), and that these efforts directly influence the critical neural circuitry underlying addiction, suggests that such cognitive interventions may play a useful role in treating addictive behavior.

Neuroscience research could be similarly helpful in identifying factors that might make addiction countercampaigns more effective. Much work in decision neuroscience has revealed how marketing elements can have profound effects on emotional processing in the brain (McClure et al., 2004; Plassmann et al., 2008; Shiv, 2007; Shiv, Bechara, et al., 2005), with implications for advertisers that are still being formalized and debated (Plassmann, Ambler, Braeutigam, & Kenning, 2007). For example, what should be predicted regarding the effectiveness of emotionally vivid antismoking imagery? Do graphic antismoking labels enhance message effectiveness, or because they are typically encountered at a moment of high craving (e.g., point of purchase, upon opening a package to take out a cigarette), might the "just say no" message possibly enhance the emotional intensity of the craving? The development of regulation regarding specific design elements of addictive product advertising should strive to minimize potential boomerang countereffects, and neuroscience offers valuable techniques and extant results for identifying such risk factors.

Although fundamental and imperative for survival, even food consumption can become problematic and detrimental when driven by addictive-pattern urges and compulsions (Davis & Carter,

2009; Kessler, 2009; Volkow & Wise, 2005). As in drug abuse, food consumption can become craved, habitual, and no longer functional or even pleasurable for the individual. To break the addictive cycle of overeating, people must break conditioned responses to cues, such as advertising or plate size, that drive them to eat more than they should (Wansink, 2007). Treatment for compulsive eating might benefit from cognitive and behavioral techniques used for treating drug abuse, which strive to coax the brain to unlearn detrimental addictive habits.

The fundamental challenge in unlearning existing habits is the two semidistinct neural pathways underpinning addiction: one responsible for felt urges and cravings and the approach motivation, and the other for regulating compulsive, repetitive behavior. Even clever ways of mitigating reactivity and responses to food-related cues often only affect one of these pathways, so addictive consumption behavior tends to persist or bounce back after a brief period of abstaining. Substitution strategies, in which an existing habit is substituted with a similar but healthier one, may work especially well precisely because they leverage existing learned compulsive behaviors. This may be why replacement habits are more likely to work when they are as similar to the target behavior as possible, for example, replacing chocolates with carrot sticks as a solution to a mindless-eating habit.

Neurocompromised groups, such as the previously described patients who were prescribed Mirapex for Parkinson's disease, are clearly a population who will be better identified, served, and protected as policy makers and public health professionals pay more attention to the neural bases of addiction. The Mirapex affair illustrates the need for regulatory institutions, such as the U.S. Food and Drug Administration, to more completely examine the potential for effects on complex high-level psychological behaviors, such as problem gambling, sexual compulsion, and patterns of decision making when evaluating drugs. Doing so in a well-informed fashion requires attention to specific neural pathways of action, and developing theories regarding how their interplay produces complex behaviors. These issues have a similar bearing on product liability laws and the parameters of such liabilities.

The specific constructs and systems emerging from a neural understanding of addictive consumption can also directly inspire predictions and recommendations regarding policy actions and treatment efforts. As we have outlined, the neural circuitry of addiction can be disentangled into processes driving felt cravings for rewarding stimuli, versus those underpinning their compulsive consumption and related persistence of dependence. The connected but dissociable manner in which these responses are computed by the brain suggests potentially divergent implications of interventions on the suppression of craving versus the attenuation or reversal of dependent behavior. This may serve as an important caution, because it means that policy and treatment interventions may have multiple potential failure points. Efforts that simply tamp down craving may do little to attenuate already developed compulsive behavioral patterns, and those that simply go after compulsive behaviors may similarly be doomed to failure, as pent-up craving impulses lead to an eventual bounce-back relapse into dependent behavior.

Effective therapies and policy interventions should counteract both the urge to consume and the existing developed compulsions to perform the behavior. For instance, habit substitution approaches, in which a learned compulsive behavior is replaced with a similar but less harmful one (e.g., sucking on a lollipop rather than putting a cigarette in one's mouth), seem primarily active on the compulsion side of addictive behavior. Such approaches should ideally be yoked with efforts to also suppress and counteract craving (e.g., chewing nicotine replacement gum). From a policy perspective, it is important to recognize that actions disrupting dependent behavioral patterns (e.g., making addictive products more difficult to obtain, putting them out of sight and thus out of mind at the point of purchase, regulations disrupting developed habits of consumption in the workplace or elsewhere) may operate in a fundamentally different manner than those meant to counteract desire and the urge to consume addictive products (e.g., graphic warning labels, counteradvertising appeals, banning appealing tobacco and alcohol flavorings). Policy actions disproportionately addressing only one of these are likely to be less effective at lastingly reducing addictive consumption than those that tackle both. Thus, the neuroscience of addiction can inform high-level strategic decisions regarding the optimal character of public policy actions.

On this front, an overarching recommendation of potential promise is a more holistic public policy approach for regulating the marketing and sale of addictive products. Currently, most policy regulations focus on addressing specific and singular addictive domains. In contrast, neuroscientific and neurobiological evidence indicates a common basic neural architecture underlying addictive behaviors (Goldstein & Volkow, 2002; Nestler, 2005; Volkow & Fowler, 2000). Exposure to the marketing of an addictive product might possibly lead to a generalized motivational drive to increase consumption of different reward-satiating products and promote craving-satiating behaviors unrelated to the originally cued domain, but perhaps equally or even more deleterious (Wadhwa et al., 2008). Is it enough to regulate cigarette advertising tightly while ignoring the effects of, for example, casino and lottery marketing? Can policies regulating the marketing of addictive products be maximally effective if they are created and implemented in a domain-specific, piecewise fashion, often by disparate policy makers?

As we have outlined, neuroscience characterizes a shared neural underpinning for diverse addictions, a range of domain-general risk factors for addiction (e.g., sensation seeking, novelty seeking, reward sensitivity, cue reactivity), and specific neural circuits, attention to which is likely to yield generalizable prevention and treatment approaches. Neuroscience can thus provide the means for holistic public policy approaches that (a) take a broad view of potential addictive-pattern behaviors; (b) recognize the shared risk factors across such addictive domains and the potential for cross-domain stimulation of reward circuitry; (c) formulate and implement principled, coherent approaches to counteracting both craving and behavioral compulsion; and (d) develop and provide treatments and interventions that by acting on basic reward and valuation circuitry, show promise for combating addiction across domains. Such approaches may share some kinship with prevention efforts based on the notion of gateway or entry-level drugs, whereby preventing smoking is seen as a critical first step in preventing marijuana use, which in turn mitigates risk of usage of harder drugs, and so on. To the extent that addictive behaviors are deeply interrelated via their shared circuitry, neuroscience provides some justification for this viewpoint. We would, however, argue for a broader ranging, less hierarchical, and more weblike view of the multiplicity of related and cross-reinforcing addictive domains, particularly because perceptions of addictive substance dangers do not always match their addictive profiles per se (Nutt et al., 2007), and addictive-pattern behavior may extend beyond drug abuse.

Finally, addiction has often been viewed by the public and lawmakers as a character flaw of the abuser (Dackis & O'Brien, 2005). Thus, addicts are blamed for their addictions and discriminated against, and their behavior is criminalized. This is a view of addiction through a moral lens, namely, addictive behavior is due to weakness in character. As a result, addicts are often stigmatized, have difficulty gaining access to psychological and biological treatments, and, in many cases, end up in the legal system or, ultimately, in jail. In contrast, most addiction researchers have argued for the replacement of this weakness of character view of addiction with a brain disease model. In this model, addiction can be viewed as a chronic, relapsing brain disease affecting the reward centers of the brain, leading to uncontrollable cravings and irrepressible substance-seeking behaviors (Dackis & O'Brien, 2005; Hall, 2006).

By providing clear and specific evidence of the true underlying mechanisms, the neuroscientific study of addiction can play a large role in changing stereotypes regarding drug addiction and, thus, facilitating more humane public policy actions for treating it. These actions can include ensuring access to effective treatments, the reduced social stigmatization and legal system entanglement of addicts, and the protection of vulnerable populations from environmental cues, such as advertising and marketing, that may induce unwanted and deleterious consumption behaviors. A major challenge for researchers in this area will be the development of a biological, neurological, and genetic understanding of addiction that integrates the myriad of individual and social influences that impact the addictive behavior (Hall, 2006).

## Potential Caveats of Using Neuroscience Methods

Possible risks and downsides of taking a neuroscientific approach to addiction policies should also be acknowledged. There are concerns that such research might be misconstrued or otherwise yield misguided social policy. For example, findings from genetic or neurobiological studies may be used by policy makers to create more coercive policies (Hall, 2006). There is debate over whether addicts have the capacity to give free and informed consent to participate in many studies and clinical trials, especially those involving administration of addictive substances (Charland, 2002; Hall, Carter, & Morley, 2003, 2004). There is also a need to ensure that the often complex and nuanced findings from neuroscientific research on the effects of marketing actions on addictive behaviors are disseminated accurately, both in the popular media and among those researchers who are less engaged and less expert in neuroscience. With increased public interest in such work, there are significant risks of it being misunderstood and/or misinterpreted by journalists, policy makers, and consumers (Hall et al., 2004). Researchers need to ensure that accurate information is communicated to the media, while also taking an active role in helping educate nonacademics in how to understand and interpret results.

## CONCLUSION

In his 1839 *Prize Essay on the Freedom of the Will*, Schopenhauer (1839/1999) remarked that "man can do what he wants, but he cannot want what he wants." In the case of addiction, as we have reviewed in this chapter, this seems at most a half-truth. Not only is what one desires beyond the power of the will, but so often, too, are one's actions. It does not require a detailed neuroscientific view of addiction to reach this partial invalidation of Schopenhauer's claim, as numerous behavioral studies of goal-conflicting habitual and compulsive behaviors provide a wide array of relevant evidence. Yet where neuroscience proves its worth is in revealing precisely why and how such dual failures of the will occur in addiction, and how they lead to characteristic and destructive behavioral and psychological phenomena. Interestingly, in delineating the mechanisms of addiction, neuroscience confirms the deeper veracity of Schopenhauer's process disjunction between desire and action. Craving (i.e., desire beyond will) and compulsion (i.e., action beyond will) reveal themselves as crucial and clearly dissociable component neural pathways underlying the initiation and persistence of addictive consumption. The interactions of these processes have been verified and enriched by behavioral consumer research on motivation, satisfaction, impulsivity, and effort—scholarship that either has been inspired by or is deeply relevant to ongoing neuroscientific investigations.

It is the unraveling of the operations of these dissociable neural systems that leads to the dreadful destructive aspects of addiction: wanting what one no longer likes and wanting also what one knows to be harmful, including continued consumption against higher level goals to refrain and also the ever looming risk of relapse when the addiction seems to have been escaped. It may appear that by elucidating clear and deep-seated biological underpinnings for the motivational and behavioral processes underlying addiction, the problems seem even more daunting and intractable. But knowing about and fully understanding such fundamental bases is also our greatest hope for designing more effective treatments, regulations, policies, and campaigns to prevent and combat addiction and predict and evaluate the efficacy of current efforts. Perhaps most crucially, a wider understanding of the real and well-defined neurobiological substrates of addictive behavior may change the still common attitudes toward sufferers and induce a shift away from the social and legal stigmatization that so often serves only to compound the serious health problems of the addictive disease state. Scholars in Transformative Consumer Research may thus find that leveraging an understanding of the brain is the best way to change minds.

## REFERENCES

Ahmed, S. E., & Koob, G. F. (2009). Rapid extinction of cocaine craving: Toward a novel cue exposure therapy. *Nature Precedings*. Available: precedings.nature.com/documents/2980/version/1/html

Aronson, E. (1961). The effect of effort on the attractiveness of rewarded and unrewarded stimuli. *Journal of Abnormal and Social Psychology, 63*, 375–380.

Baxter, M. G., & Murray, E. A. (2002). The amygdala and reward. *Nature Reviews Neuroscience, 3*(7), 563–573.

Baxter, M. G., Parker, A., Lindner, C. C., Izquierdo, A. D., & Murray, E. A. (2000). Control of response selection by reinforcer value requires interaction of amygdala and orbital prefrontal cortex. *Journal of Neuroscience, 20*(11), 4311–4319.

Bechara, A., Damasio, A. R., Damasio, H., & Anderson, S. (1994). Insensitivity to future consequences following damage to human prefrontal cortex. *Cognition, 50*, 7–15.

Bechara, A., Damasio, H., & Damasio, A. R. (2003). Role of the amygdala in decision-making. *Annals of the New York Academy of Sciences, 985*, 356–369.

Bernheim, B. D., & Rangel, A. (2005). From neuroscience to public policy: A new economic view of addiction. *Swedish Economic Policy Review, 12*(2), 99–144.

Berridge, K. C. (1996). Food reward: Brain substrates of wanting and liking. *Neuroscience & Biobehavioral Reviews, 20*(1), 1–25.

Berridge, K. C. (2007). The debate over dopamine's role in reward: The case for incentive salience. *Psychopharmacology, 191*(3), 391–431.

Berridge, K. C., & Robinson, T. E. (1995). The mind of an addicted brain: Neural sensitization of wanting versus liking. *Current Directions in Psychological Science, 4*(3), 71–76.

Berridge, K. C., & Zajonc, R. B. (1991). Hypothalamic cooling elicits eating: Differential effects on motivation and pleasure. *Psychological Science, 2*(3), 184–188.

Blakemore, S., & Choudhury, S. (2006). Development of the adolescent brain: Implications for executive function and social cognition. *Journal of Child Psychology and Psychiatry, 47*(3/4), 296–312.

Bostwick, J. M., & Bucci, J. A. (2008). Internet sex addiction treated with naltrexone. *Mayo Clinic Proceedings, 83*(2), 226–230.

Botvinick, M. M., Cohen, J. D., & Carter, C. S. (2004). Conflict monitoring and anterior cingulate cortex: An update. *Trends in Cognitive Sciences, 8*(12), 539–546.

Byrne, A. M., Dickson, L., Derevensky, J. L., Gupta, R., & Lussier, I. (2005). The application of youth substance use media campaigns to problem gambling: A critical evaluation. *Journal of Health Communication, 10*(8), 681–700.

Chambers, R. A., Taylor, J. R., & Potenza, M. N. (2003). Developmental neurocircuitry of motivation in adolescence: A critical period of addiction vulnerability. *American Journal of Psychiatry, 160*(6), 1041–1052.

Charland, L. C. (2002). Cynthia's dilemma: Consenting to heroin prescription. *American Journal of Bioethics, 2*, 37–47.

Contreras, M., Ceric, F., & Torrealba, F. (2007). Inactivation of the interoceptive insula disrupts drug craving and malaise induced by lithium. *Science, 318*(5850), 655–658.

Crews, F., He, J., & Hodge, C. (2007). Adolescent cortical development: A critical period of vulnerability for addiction. *Pharmacology Biochemistry & Behavior, 86*(2), 189–199.

Dackis, C., & O'Brien, C. (2005). Neurobiology of addiction: Treatment and public policy ramifications. *Nature Neuroscience, 8*(11), 1431–1436.

Damasio, H., Grabowski, T., Frank, R., Galburda, A. M., & Damasio, A. R. (1994). The return of Phineas Gage: Clues about the brain from the skull of a famous patient. *Science, 264*, 1102–1104.

Davis, C., & Carter, J. C. (2009). Compulsive overeating as an addiction disorder: A review of theory and evidence. *Appetite, 53*(1), 1–8.

Davis, C., Patte, K., Levitan, R., Reid, C., Tweed, S., & Curtis, C. (2007). From motivation to behaviour: A model of reward sensitivity, overeating, and food preferences in the risk profile for obesity. *Appetite, 48*, 12–19.

Dodd, M. L., Klos, K. J., Bower, J. H., Geda, Y. E., Josephs, K. A., & Ahlskog, J. E. (2005). Pathological gambling caused by drugs used to treat Parkinson disease. *Archives of Neurology, 62*(9), 1377–1381.

Doremus-Fitzwater, T. L., Varlinskaya, E. I., & Spear, L. P. (2009). Motivational systems in adolescence: Possible implications for age differences in substance abuse and other risk-taking behaviors. *Brain and Cognition, 72*, 114–123.

Family Smoking Prevention and Tobacco Control Act of 2009, Pub. L. No. 111-31 (2009).

Farrelly, M. C., Davis, K. C., Haviland, M. L., Healton, C. G., & Messeri, P. (2005). Evidence of a dose–response relationship between "truth" antismoking ads and youth smoking prevalence. *American Journal of Public Health, 95*(3), 425–431.

Farrelly, M. C., Niederdeppe, J., & Yarsevich, J. (2003). Youth tobacco prevention mass media campaigns: Past, present, and future directions. *Tobacco Control, 12*(90001), i35–i47.

Fattore, L., Fadda, P., Spano, M. S., Pistis, M., & Fratta, W. (2008). Neurobiological mechanisms of cannabinoid addiction. *Molecular and Cellular Endocrinology, 286*(1/2, Suppl. 1), S97–S107.

Federal Trade Commission. (2003). *Alcohol marketing and advertising: A report to Congress.* Retrieved August 30, 2009, from http://www.ftc.gov/os/2003/09/alcohol08report.pdf

Fisher, H. E., Aron, A., & Brown, L. L. (2006). Romantic love: A mammalian brain system for mate choice. *Philosophical Transactions B, 361*(1476), 2173–2186.

Fisher, H. E., Aron, A., Mashek, D. J., Strong, G., Li, H. F., & Brown, L. L. (2005, November). *Motivation and emotion systems associated with romantic love following rejection: An fMRI study.* Poster presented at the annual meeting of the Society for Neuroscience, Washington, DC.

Franklin, T. R., Acton, P. D., Maldjian, J. A., Gray, J. D., Croft, J. R., Dackis, C. A., et al. (2002). Decreased gray matter concentration in the insular, orbitofrontal, cingulate, and temporal cortices of cocaine patients. *Biological Psychiatry, 51*(2), 134–142.

Gibbs, B. J. (1997). Predisposing the decision maker versus framing the decision: A consumer-manipulation approach to dynamic preference. *Marketing Letters, 8*(1), 71–83.

Gibbs, B. J., & Drolet, A. (2003). Consumption effort: The mental cost of generating utility and the role of consumer energy level in ambitious consumption. *Journal of Consumer Psychology, 13*(3), 268–277.

Goldstein, R., & Volkow, N. (2002). Drug addiction and its underlying neurobiological basis: Neuroimaging evidence for the involvement of the frontal cortex. *American Journal of Psychiatry, 159*(10), 1642–1652.

Greenberg, J. L., Lewis, S. E., & Dodd, D. K. (1999). Overlapping addictions and self-esteem among college men and women. *Addictive Behaviors, 24*(4), 565–571.

Grinspoon, L., Bakalar, J. B., & Zimmer, L. (1997). Marijuana addiction. *Science, 277*(5327), 749–753.

Hall, W. (2006). Avoiding potential misuses of addiction brain science. *Addiction, 101*(11), 1529–1532.

Hall, W., Carter, L., & Morley, K. I. (2003). Addiction, neuroscience and ethics. *Addiction, 98*(7), 867–870.

Hall, W., Carter, L., & Morley, K. I. (2004). Neuroscience research on the addictions: A prospectus for future ethical and policy analysis. *Addictive Behaviors, 29*(7), 1481–1495.

Higgins, E. T. (2006). Value from hedonic experience and engagement. *Psychological Review, 113*(3), 439–460.

Hornik, R., Jacobsohn, L., Orwin, R., Piesse, A., & Kalton, G. (2008). Effects of the National Youth Anti-Drug Media Campaign on Youths. *American Journal of Public Health, 98*(12), 2229–2236.

Kalivas, P. W., Volkow, N., & Seamans, J. (2005). Unmanageable motivation in addiction: A pathology in prefrontal-accumbens glutamate transmission. *Neuron, 45*(5), 647–650.

Kaur, M., Liguori, A., Lang, W., Rapp, S. R., Fleischer, A. B., & Feldman, S. R. (2006). Induction of withdrawal-like symptoms in a small randomized, controlled trial of opioid blockade in frequent tanners. *Journal of the American Academy of Dermatology, 54*(4), 709–711.

Kelley, A. E., & Berridge, K. C. (2002). The neuroscience of natural rewards: Relevance to addictive drugs. *Journal of Neuroscience, 22*(9), 3306–3311.

Kelly, K. J., Slater, M. D., & Karan, D. (2002). Image advertisements' influence on adolescents' perceptions of the desirability of beer and cigarettes. *Journal of Public Policy & Marketing, 21*(2), 295–304.

Kelly, K. J., Slater, M. D., Karan, D., & Hunn, L. (2000). The use of human models and cartoon characters in magazine advertisements for cigarettes, beer, and nonalcoholic beverages. *Journal of Public Policy & Marketing, 19*(2), 189–200.

Kessler, D. A. (2009). *The end of overeating: Taking control of the insatiable American appetite.* New York: Rodale Press.

Kessler, D. A., & Pines, W. L. (1990). The federal regulation of prescription drug advertising and promotion. *Journal of the American Medical Association, 264*(18), 2409–2415.

Kim, S. W., & Grant, J. E. (2001). Personality dimensions among pathological gambling disorder and obsessive-compulsive disorder patients. *Psychiatry Research, 104*, 205–212.

Kivetz, R. (2005). Promotion reactance: The role of effort–reward congruity. *Journal of Consumer Research, 31*, 725–736.

Kivetz, R., & Simonson, I. (2002). Earning the right to indulge: Effort as a determinant of customer preferences toward frequency program rewards. *Journal of Marketing Research, 39*(2), 155–170.

Knutson, B., Wimmer, G., Kuhnen, C. M., & Winkielman, P. (2008). Nucleus accumbens activation mediates the influence of reward cues on financial risk taking. *Neuroreport, 19*(5), 509–513.

Koob, G. F. (1992). Drugs of abuse: Anatomy, pharmacology and function of reward pathways. *Trends in Pharmacological Sciences, 13,* 177–184.

Kubey, R., & Csikszentmihalyi, M. (2002). Television addiction is no mere metaphor. *Scientific American, 286*(2), 62–68.

Kuhnen, C. M., & Chiao, J. Y. (2009). Genetic determinants of financial risk taking. *PLoS ONE, 4*(2), e4362.

Litt, A., Khan, U., & Shiv, B. (2010). Lusting while loathing: Parallel counter-driving of wanting and liking. *Psychological Science, 21*(1), 118–125.

Lovett, R. (2005). Coffee: The demon drink? *New Scientist, 24,* 2518–2522.

McClure, S. M., Li, J., Tomlin, D., Cypert, K. S., Montague, L. M., & Montague, P. R. (2004). Neural correlates of behavioral preference for culturally familiar drinks. *Neuron, 44*(2), 379–387.

McDaniel, C., & Baker, R. C. (1977). Convenience food packaging and the perception of product quality. *Journal of Marketing, 41*(4), 57–58.

Mueller, A., Mitchell, J. E., Crosby, R. D., Glaesmer, H., & de Zwaan, M. (2009). The prevalence of compulsive hoarding and its association with compulsive buying in a German population-based sample. *Behaviour Research and Therapy, 47*(8), 705–709.

Naqvi, N. H., & Bechara, A. (2009). The hidden island of addiction: The insula. *Trends in Neurosciences, 32*(1), 56–67.

Naqvi, N. H., Rudrauf, D., Damasio, H., & Bechara, A. (2007). Damage to the insula disrupts addiction to cigarette smoking. *Science, 315*(5811), 531–534.

National Association of Attorneys General. (1998). *Master settlement agreement.* Retrieved August 30, 2009, from http://www.naag.org/backpages/naag/tobacco/msa/msa-pdf/

Nestler, E. J. (2005). Is there a common molecular pathway for addiction? *Nature Neuroscience, 8*(11), 1445–1449.

Norton, M. I., & Ariely, D. (2009, January). *The IKEA effect: When labor leads to love.* Poster presented at the annual meeting of the Society for Personality and Social Psychology, Tampa, FL.

Nutt, D., King, L. A., Saulsbury, W., & Blakemore, C. (2007). Development of a rational scale to assess the harm of drugs of potential misuse. *Lancet, 369*(9566), 1047–1053.

O'Brien, C. P., Childress, A. R., Ehrman, R., & Robbins, S. J. (1998). Conditioning factors in drug abuse: Can they explain compulsion? *Journal of Psychopharmacology, 12*(1), 15–22.

Office of Applied Studies. (2007). *2006 national survey on drug use and health: National results.* Washington, DC: Department of Health and Human Services. Retrieved January 6, 2011, from http://www.oas.samhsa.gov/nsduh/2k6nsduh/2k6results.cfm

Padoa-Schioppa, C., & Assad, J. A. (2006). Neurons in the orbitofrontal cortex encode economic value. *Nature, 441*(7090), 223–226.

Palmgreen, P., Donohew, L., Lorch, E. P., Hoyle, R. H., & Stephenson, M. T. (2001). Television campaigns and adolescent marijuana use: Tests of sensation seeking targeting. *American Journal of Public Health, 91*(2), 292–296.

Pechmann, C., & Knight, S. J. (2002). An experimental investigation of the joint effects of advertising and peers on adolescents' beliefs and intentions about cigarette consumption. *Journal of Consumer Research, 29*(1), 5–19.

Pechmann, C., Levine, L. J., Loughlin, S., & Leslie, F. (2005). Self-conscious and impulsive: Adolescents' vulnerability to advertising and promotions. *Journal of Public Policy & Marketing, 24*(2), 202–221.

Pechmann, C., & Ratneshwar, S. (1994). The effects of antismoking and cigarette advertising on young adolescents' perceptions of peers who smoke. *Journal of Consumer Research, 21*(2), 236–251.

Peoples, L. L. (2002). Will, anterior cingulate cortex, and addiction. *Science, 296,* 1623–1624.

Pfefferbaum, A., Rosenbloom, M., Crusan, K., & Jernigan, T. L. (1988). Brain CT changes in alcoholics: Effects of age and alcohol consumption. *Alcoholism: Clinical & Experimental Research, 12*(1), 81–87.

Plassmann, H., Ambler, T., Braeutigam, S., & Kenning, P. (2007). What can advertisers learn from neuroscience? *International Journal of Advertising, 26*(2), 151–175.

Plassmann, H., O'Doherty, J., & Rangel, A. (2007). Orbitofrontal cortex encodes willingness to pay in everyday economic transactions. *Journal of Neuroscience, 27*(37), 9984–9988.

Plassmann, H., O'Doherty, J., Shiv, B., & Rangel, A. (2008). Marketing actions can modulate neural representations of experienced pleasantness. *Proceedings of the National Academy of Sciences, 105*(3), 1050–1054.

Reuter, J., Raedler, T., Rose, M., Hand, I., Gläscher, J., & Büchel, C. (2005). Pathological gambling is linked to reduced activation of the mesolimbic reward system. *Nature Neuroscience, 8*(2), 147–148.

Ridgway, N. M., Kukar-Kinney, M., & Monroe, K. B. (2008). An expanded conceptualization and a new measure of compulsive buying. *Journal of Consumer Research, 35*(4), 622–639.

Robinson, T. E., & Berridge, K. C. (1993). The neural basis of drug craving: An incentive-sensitization theory of addiction. *Brain Research Reviews, 18*(3), 247–291.

Rogers, R. D., Everitt, B. J., Baldacchino, A., Swainson, R., Wynne, K., Baker, N. B., et al. (1999). Dissociable deficits in the decision-making cognition of chronic amphetamine abusers, opiate abusers, patients with focal damage to prefrontal cortex, and tryptophan-depleted normal volunteers: Evidence for monoaminergic mechanisms. *Neuropsychopharmacology, 20*(4), 322–339.

Salamone, J. D., & Correa, M. (2002). Motivational views of reinforcement: Implications for understanding the behavioral functions of nucleus accumbens dopamine. *Behavioural Brain Research, 137*, 3–25.

Salamone, J. D., Correa, M., Farrar, A., & Mingote, S. M. (2007). Effort-related functions of nucleus accumbens dopamine and associated forebrain circuits. *Psychopharmacology, 191*(3), 461–482.

Salamone, J. D., Correa, M., Mingote, S. M., & Weber, S. M. (2005). Beyond the reward hypothesis: Alternative functions of nucleus accumbens dopamine. *Current Opinion in Pharmacology, 5*(1), 34–41.

Saxena, S., Brody, A. L., Maidment, K. M., Smith, E. C., Zohrabi, N., Katz, E., et al. (2004). Cerebral glucose metabolism in obsessive-compulsive hoarding. *American Journal of Psychiatry, 161*(6), 1038–1048.

Schopenhauer, A. (1999). *Prize essay on the freedom of the will* (G. Zoller, Ed., & E. J. Payne, Trans.). Cambridge, England: Cambridge University Press. (Original work published 1839)

Seymour, B., & McClure, S. M. (2008). Anchors, scales and the relative coding of value in the brain. *Current Opinion in Neurobiology, 18*(2), 173–178.

Shadel, W. G., Niaura, R., & Abrams, D. B. (2002). Adolescents' reactions to the imagery displayed in smoking and antismoking advertisements. *Psychology of Addictive Behaviors, 16*(2), 173–176.

Shadel, W. G., Tharp-Taylor, S., & Fryer, C. S. (2008). Exposure to cigarette advertising and adolescents' intentions to smoke: The moderating role of the developing self-concept. *Journal of Pediatric Psychology, 33*(7), 751–760.

Shafey, O., Dolwick, S., & Guindon, G. E. (Eds.). (2003). *Tobacco control country profiles* (2nd ed.). Atlanta, GA: American Cancer Society. Available: http://www.who.int/tobacco/global_data/country_profiles/en/

Shaffer, H. J., Hall, M. N., & Vander Bilt, J. (1999). Estimating the prevalence of disordered gambling behavior in the United States and Canada: A research synthesis. *American Journal of Public Health, 89*(9), 1369–1376.

Shima, K., & Tanji, J. (1998). Role for cingulate motor area cells in voluntary movement selection based on reward. *Science, 282*(5392), 1335–1338.

Shiv, B. (2007). Emotions, decisions, and the brain. *Journal of Consumer Psychology, 17*(3), 174–178.

Shiv, B., Bechara, A., Levin, I., Alba, J. W., Bettman, J. R., Dube, L., et al. (2005). Decision neuroscience. *Marketing Letters, 16*(3/4), 375–386.

Shiv, B., Carmon, Z., & Ariely, D. (2005). Placebo effects of marketing actions: Consumers may get what they pay for. *Journal of Marketing Research, 42*(4), 383–393.

Tobacco Control Legal Consortium. (2009). *Tobacco product marketing restrictions: Federal regulation of tobacco: Impact on state and local authority*. Saint Paul, MN: Author. Available: tobaccolawcenter.org/documents/fda-5.pdf

Volkow, N. D., & Fowler, J. S. (2000). Addiction, a disease of compulsion and drive: Involvement of the orbitofrontal cortex. *Cerebral Cortex, 10*(3), 318–325.

Volkow, N. D., Fowler, J. S., Wang, G. J., & Swanson, J. M. (2004). Dopamine in drug abuse and addiction: Results from imaging studies and treatment implications. *Molecular Psychiatry, 9*(6), 557–569.

Volkow, N. D., Fowler, J. S., Wang, G. J., Telang, F., Logan, J., Jayne, M., et al. (2010). Cognitive control of drug craving inhibits brain reward regions in cocaine abusers. *Neuroimage, 49*, 2536–2543.

Volkow, N. D., & Wise, R. A. (2005). How can drug addiction help us understand obesity? *Nature Neuroscience, 8*, 555–560.

Waber, R. L., Shiv, B., Carmon, Z., & Ariely, D. (2008). Commercial features of placebo and therapeutic efficacy. *Journal of the American Medical Association, 299*(9), 1016–1017.

Wadhwa, M., Shiv, B., & Nowlis, S. M. (2008). A bite to whet the reward appetite: The influence of sampling on reward-seeking behaviors. *Journal of Marketing Research, 45*(4), 403–413.

Wansink, B. (2007). *Mindless eating: Why we eat more than we think*. New York: Bantam Dell.

Warthan, M. M., Uchida, T., & Wagner, R. F. (2005). UV light tanning as a type of substance-related disorder. *Archives of Dermatology, 141*(8), 963–966.

Whalen, P. J., Bush, G., McNally, R. J., Wilhelm, S., McInerney, S. C., Jenike, M. A., et al. (1998). The emotional counting Stroop paradigm: A functional magnetic resonance imaging probe of the anterior cingulate affective division. *Biological Psychiatry, 44*(12), 1219–1228.

Williams, Z. M., Bush, G., Rauch, S. L., Cosgrove, G. R., & Eskandar, E. N. (2004). Human anterior cingulate neurons and the integration of monetary reward with motor responses. *Nature Neuroscience, 7,* 1370–1375.

Wise, R. A. (1988). The neurobiology of craving: Implications for the understanding and treatment of addiction. *Journal of Abnormal Psychology, 97*(2), 118–132.

Wise, R. A., & Bozarth, M. A. (1982). Action of drugs of abuse on brain reward systems: An update with specific attention to opiates. *Pharmacology Biochemistry and Behavior, 17*(2), 239–243.

Wise, R. A., & Bozarth, M. A. (1987). A psychomotor stimulant theory of addiction. *Psychological Review, 94*(4), 469–492.

World Health Organization. (2008). *WHO report on the global tobacco epidemic, 2008: The MPOWER package.* Geneva: Author.

Wyvell, C. L., & Berridge, K. C. (2000). Intra-accumbens amphetamine increases the conditioned incentive salience of sucrose reward: Enhancement of reward "wanting" without enhanced "liking" or response reinforcement. *Journal of Neuroscience, 20*(21), 8122–8130.

Zink, C. F., Pagnoni, G., Martin-Skurski M. E., Chappelow, J. C., & Berns, G. S. (2004). Human striatal responses to monetary reward depend on saliency. *Neuron, 42*(3), 509–517.

Zink, C. F., Pagnoni, G., Martin, M. E., Dhamala, M., & Berns, G. S. (2003). Human striatal response to salient nonrewarding stimuli. *Journal of Neuroscience, 23,* 8092–8097.

# 26

## Toward a Process Theory of Consumer Vulnerability and Resilience
### Illuminating Its Transformative Potential

Stacey Menzel Baker and Marlys Mason

Although the world is full of suffering, it is full also of the overcoming of it.

Helen Keller (1880–1968)

Consumer research widely acknowledges the role that the consumption of goods, services, and brands, as well as interactions with markets, plays in the construction, maintenance, and reconstitution of consumer identities (Arnould & Thompson, 2005; Baker, 2006; Belk, 1988). What is not as commonly recognized in the literature is the personal and social instability, or vulnerability, related to the lack of access to consumption and markets (Baker, Gentry, & Rittenburg, 2005; Hill, 2001; Hoffman, Chapter 9 of this volume; Sachs, 2005). In other words, markets and consumption are sources of meaning, relational connections, and freedom on the one hand, and sources of risk, vulnerability, and social conflict on the other. As it turns out, both seemingly dichotomous perspectives are essential in highlighting the situational and sociocultural contexts within which consumer behavior transpires.

This chapter is about what makes people vulnerable and also the resilience of human beings and their capacities to create individual and social change (see also Maddi, Chapter 31 of this volume). How people construct an understanding of vulnerability is important, because the conceptualization of vulnerability affects how and to whom social and economic resources are distributed. Conceptualizations of vulnerability also impact how society and individuals perceive consumer identities and respective positions or participation in the marketplace. The intent of this review piece is to illuminate how vulnerability, when understood as a multidimensional process, has transformative potential for consumers. Our review illustrates the process by which persons may experience vulnerability and the pathways to building resilience. The theoretical framework offered here suggests that through the cooperation of multiple stakeholder groups, including consumers, more can be done to enhance consumer well-being (Mick, 2006) and achieve constructive or authentic engagement (Santos & Laczniak, 2009; Shultz, 2007) for consumers experiencing vulnerability. If we (i.e., researchers, marketers, policy makers, nonprofit organizations) do our jobs well, we will never have another Helen Keller who has to fight a system of injustices. Instead, human beings may experience freedom in action, choice, and opportunity within the bounds of their capabilities (Sen, 1999).

This chapter begins with a discussion of alternative conceptualizations of vulnerability, showing the assumptions behind each, the benefits, and the solutions derived from the analysis. Next, drawing from previous literature on vulnerability, we present a theoretical model believed to be useful as transformative consumer researchers seek to address the access constraints faced by consumers in the marketplace, marketspace, and everyday living. Then, we illustrate applications of the theoretical model in the contexts of marketplace experiences for people with disabilities and recovery experiences for people in communities impacted by natural disasters. We conclude with a discussion on multiple issues ripe for research and by suggesting that a process theory of consumer vulnerability and resilience is a powerful theoretical tool in the Transformative Consumer Research (TCR) agenda.

## VULNERABILITY ANALYSIS

Vulnerability analysis has a rich and varied tradition within the social sciences, arising primarily as a theoretical lens through which to view at-risk groups, social injustices, or hazardous situations. Wisner (2004) presents a typology of four different approaches to vulnerability analysis consisting of demographics, taxonomic (i.e., environmental), situational, and contextual, proactive approaches. In this chapter, we adopt a similar initial classification scheme but offer our interpretation of each approach. Each approach to vulnerability analysis differs in terms of its underlying assumptions for why vulnerability is or will be experienced, benefits, and implications for solutions (see Table 26.1).

### Vulnerability Defined by Demographics

Demographic approaches define *vulnerability* as a status, with the implication that people within particular social categories (e.g., income, ethnicity, gender, age) possess characteristics that make them vulnerable. That is, the problem creating the vulnerability resides within the individual (Baker et al., 2005). Based on objective, and perhaps subjective, perceptions, susceptibility to harm is calculated, and individuals within groups are assumed to be homogeneous. The temporal orientation of vulnerability defined by demographics is both past- and future-oriented. Typically, definitions are based on objective historical data that have demonstrated inequities in access; then, historical data are used to predict the likelihood of future injustices (Commuri & Ekici, 2008).

The benefit of the demographic approach is that it allows for succinct descriptions of who is vulnerable and who should receive assistance. However, people who may not be vulnerable but fall within these demographic boundaries may be labeled as vulnerable, and people who are vulnerable but outside the demographic description may not be recognized in the analysis. For example,

**Table 26.1**    Alternative Approaches to Vulnerability Analysis

|  | Demographic | Environmental | Situational | Community and Context |
|---|---|---|---|---|
| Perspective on vulnerability | A status based on particular social categories in which people are presumed to be vulnerable (e.g., racial and gender profiling) | A status based on perceived causal agents of social, economic, environmental, and information factors | A dynamic state that considers a person embedded in a particular situation | A community-defined dynamic state with emphasis on local knowledge; considers complex social and material relations and processes |
| Assumptions | Homogeneity within group | Expert knowledge of external constraints on causal agents | Heterogeneity in daily life and actual situations | Produced and resolved by co-constitution |
| Benefits of approach | Description | Explanation | Understanding | Social change |
| Solution | Fixing the person | Altering the environment | Accommodation for variances in lived experiences | Community participation and activism |

a person with a physical impairment may be empowered, regularly participate in market activities, be embedded in an extensive social and professional network, and have a rewarding, high-paying career. Yet, a demographic approach would not distinguish this individual from an underemployed, disconnected person with a physical impairment who regularly struggles with marketplace interactions and access in meeting his or her basic consumption needs. Similarly, in disaster management, teens often are not considered a vulnerable group. The failure of relief workers to recognize at least some teens as vulnerable in the aftermath of the 2004 tsunami in Southeast Asia provides at least one explanation for why many teens' consumer needs were unmet (Klein & Huang, 2007).

Ultimately, demographic approaches reduce real people to a "homogenized, culturally undifferentiated mass of humanity variously associated with powerlessness, passivity, ignorance, hunger, illiteracy, neediness, oppression and inertia" (Bankoff, 2001, p. 23). This approach, which aggregates vulnerability data and treats vulnerability as one-dimensional, has been criticized as paternalistic, failing to recognize the resource assets of individuals, framing people as flawed or disempowered victims, and too narrow a definition of individuals' identities (Baker, et al., 2005; Bankoff, 2001; Cardona, 2004; Sen, 1999; Wisner, 2004). Thus, in recent times. many social scientists, legal analysts, and public policy makers use alternative approaches in vulnerability analysis.

## Vulnerability Defined by Environments in Which People Live

The focal point of analysis when vulnerability is defined by environments is the perceived causal agents for barriers to full participation in society (Wisner, 2004). Often, taxonomies are constructed to differentiate between different types of vulnerability and explain how environmental forces expose some social groups to greater hazards than other groups (Wisner, 2004). Lack of access to material and financial resources, living conditions, ecological characteristics, cultural values, and exploitive practices by marketers are examples of environmental variables that might explain the causes for the vulnerability of people (Andreasen, 1975).

From a moral perspective, this approach is better than the first, because it does not place the blame for vulnerability on particular characteristics of individuals; instead, blame is placed on characteristics of the environment. In this approach, vulnerability continues to be treated as a one-dimensional, static state and a property of the environment, with the assumption that the society and people exposed to these causal agents will always be vulnerable (Wisner, 2004). The downfall of this approach is its limited perspective and the narrow solutions it produces. Just as demographics provide an incomplete description of consumer experiences, so too do disabling conditions and homogenic attempts to fix the environment (Stephens & Bergman, 1995). For example, Kaufman-Scarborough (1999), in her analysis of access for consumers with mobility impairments, noted that "legislation is likely to fail if it provides mandates for the design of 'any store' without examining the behaviors that take place within it" (p. 503). Such approaches to vulnerability analysis have provided researchers, marketers, and policy makers much insight into the constraints imposed on consumers by the environment, and although changes in the environment are necessary, they are insufficient to reduce vulnerability.

## Vulnerability Defined by the Situation

Situational approaches view vulnerability as a dynamic multidimensional state characterized by powerlessness and dependence and followed by resilience. Blame is not fixed on any one point, such as on a demographic personal characteristic or environmental factor, but instead is focused on alternative directions and treated as a complex, multidimensional process rather than a unidimensional state (Gergen, McNamee, & Barrett, 2001). In other words, a number of factors (e.g., personal, social, contextual) simultaneously work to disempower consumers and create vulnerability. Vulnerability is regarded not as a property of groups or environments but as an outcome of personal, social, economic, and ecological conditions (Baker et al., 2005; Hill & Stamey, 1990; Wisner, 2004). Research from this perspective conceptualizes vulnerability as fluid and socially constructed rather than fixed and objective (Cardona, 2004; Gentry, Kennedy, Paul, & Hill, 1995; Wisner, 2004).

The situational approach, which considers a person embedded in a particular situation, allows for the heterogeneity of needs and responses in market and consumption experiences. The benefit to this approach is that it allows for understanding the multitude of factors that may contribute to vulnerability and takes temporal factors into account by recognizing that people can and often do work through their vulnerabilities (Baker et al., 2005; Shultz & Holbrook, 2009). Solutions derived from this approach focus on accommodating variances in lived experiences and allow for diversity in how individuals define their relationship to their environments. This perspective is developed by acknowledging the developmental capacity of individuals and allows for alternative conceptualizations of power and control.

The situational approach provides a more sensitive theoretical analysis of the powerlessness and dependence of people than the first two approaches, but it has been criticized for a lack of generalizability. Certainly, empirical findings from the analysis of one consumption experience cannot be equated to another situation, but frameworks for analysis (e.g., constructs, nomological networks) can be generalized and provide useful guides for creating solutions (Baker, 2009). Indeed, Garrett and Toumanoff (2010) analyzed 24,000 complaints to the Better Business Bureau over a 13-year period and found no support for the demographic approach to conceptualizing vulnerability; instead, their study shows powerful support for the situational approach to vulnerability analysis and how practical solutions can be derived from such an approach. However, still troublesome in the situational approach is that the unit of the analysis tends to be the individual, which may constrain derived solutions from being used to proactively create social change. Creative solutions may require a more systemic approach that includes stakeholders in impacted communities as well as other citizens and business, government, and nongovernmental organizations (NGOs).

### Vulnerability Defined by Community and Context

The fourth perspective in vulnerability analysis has emerged in recent years as a response to calls for a proactive approach to creating social change, particularly based on unmet needs for social groups, such as people living in poverty, people with disabilities, and people reconstituting their lives in disasters. This approach, which Wisner (2004) labels as "contextual and proactive" (p. 187) and criticizes for its inability to inspire practical solutions, is identified as community and context. We argue that it is the only current approach to vulnerability analysis possible for driving social change. In contrast, the situational approach is useful for understanding individual experiences and driving individual change. Researchers utilizing the community and context approach work with community members who define their perceived strengths and weaknesses and decide which risks they can manage and which need to be reduced. The power of this approach is that multiple stakeholder voices are heard, and vulnerability is considered within the context of the complex relationship between people, the economic and material realities of their lives, social forces, and the natural and built environments (Baker, 2009).

Contextual and proactive approaches tend to be community based and recognize that transformation occurs by "facilitating the collaborative construction of new realities" (Gergen et al., 2001, p. 697). For example, in attempting to reduce vulnerability in a natural hazard context, Mileti (1999) argued the importance that a "participatory process be engaged in, for the information it generates and distributes, for the sense of community it can foster, for the ideas that grow out of it, and for the sense of ownership it creates" (p. 34). Through co-constitution and the validation and affirmation of the realities of the constraints faced by different stakeholder groups, community members work to reconstruct a system that maximizes access and potential for underrepresented groups (Ozanne & Fischer, Chapter 4 of this volume; Ozanne & Saatcioglu, 2008; Viswanathan, Sridharan, Gau, & Ritchie, 2009).

The inherent weakness of such approaches is that they are laden with conflict. Community is not univocal. Members of different groups within a community possess different views, even ideological stances, about individuals, contributing problems, resource allocation, and how each should be prioritized and addressed. Within cultures, ideological views, particularly those with an emphasis on individualism and an assumption of competition with resultant winners and losers, may present obstacles for engagement in a participatory, cooperative community approach (Mileti, 1999). However, recent consumer research highlighting the pervasiveness of sharing in our daily lives may refute such cautionary naysaying. Consumers commonly share possessions, spaces, and resources with family, friends, and even strangers and, by doing so, help foster both individual and collective well-being (Belk & Llamas, Chapter 30 of this volume). Such sharing tendencies and behaviors might be directed toward community engagement and participatory, cooperative solutions. Finally, another concern with this approach is that the boundaries between researcher and community activist may become blurred, although we argue that perhaps these boundaries must be fluid if the intent of TCR is to enhance consumers' lives.

## Summary

At present, many social scientists are moving away from viewing vulnerability as a static state and toward viewing it as dynamic and processual (Baker et al., 2005; Cardona, 2004; Wisner, 2004). This chapter adopts the latter perspective in building the theoretical framework presented in the next section. Vulnerability occurs when losses exceed the capacity of an individual or collective to act in their own best interests in the short run (Baker et al., 2005; Cardona, 2004; Gentry et al., 1995; Hill, 2001). Vulnerability necessitates that individuals and/or collectives are dependent on external sources to assist in relieving the threat. Thus, vulnerability is powerlessness and dependence embedded in complex social, ecological, and material relations and processes (Baker, 2009). Vulnerability is not an acceptable state of being, and people (i.e., those impacted, those wishing to have positive social impact, or both) may actively work to overcome threats to identity and well-being.

## A PROCESS THEORY OF CONSUMER VULNERABILITY AND RESILIENCE

Figure 26.1 presents a conceptual model illustrating a process theory of consumer vulnerability and resilience, which builds on previous vulnerability research and is consistent with the progression of vulnerability analysis to a situational and contextual, proactive approach as outlined in the previous section. The model is also inductively constructed from observations and patterns detected in studies of the consumption experiences of consumers with disabilities (e.g., Baker, 2006; Kaufman-Scarborough & Baker, 2005; Mason & Pavia, 2006) and studies of community recovery during disaster (e.g., Baker, 2009; Baker, Hunt, & Rittenburg, 2007). Finally, the model builds on vulnerability work by Baker and colleagues (Baker et al., 2005; Baker, Hunt, & Rittenburg, 2007; Baker, Stephens, & Hill, 2001), but differs from this work by (a) articulating additional pressures that increase the likelihood of vulnerability, (b) more clearly articulating potential cumulative effects of repeated exposure to trigger events, (c) showing the potential for aftershocks that exacerbate vulnerability, and (d) moving toward a deeper understanding of vulnerability as a shared experience.

The model presents a macroperspective believed to be useful in future studies and actions designed to facilitate the reduction of vulnerability and the enhancement of power and access. The transformative model embraces a dynamic, systemic perspective by recognizing the complex

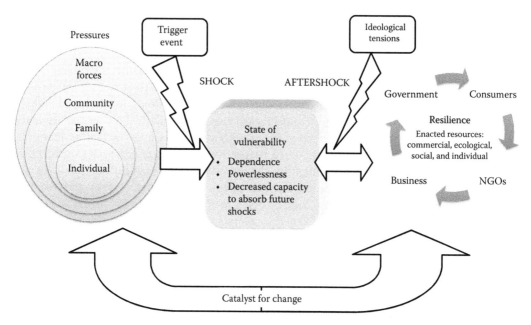

**Figure 26.1**   Conceptual model of a process theory of consumer vulnerability and resilience.
*Note:* NGOs = nongovernmental organizations.

pressures leading to vulnerability, the trigger events in the marketplace and marketspace that can shock one into a state of vulnerability, the actual state of vulnerability, the socially situated aftershocks that can exacerbate vulnerability, and the resulting responses by numerous stakeholders that can lead to greater resiliency and ultimately create the catalyst for social change. Furthermore, six major tenets underlie the development of our theoretical model, which we discuss next in conjunction with each stage of the model (i.e., pressures, trigger events, state of vulnerability, resilience, aftershocks).

### A Transformative Model of Consumer Vulnerability and Resilience

*Pressures and Tenet 1*

Individual, family, community, and macroforces put pressure on the everyday lives of consumers. These pressures, represented by the concentric circles on the left side of the model, increase the effects of exposure to a trigger event and increase the likelihood of experiencing vulnerability. In other words, we see pressures as risk factors, in which risk is understood as potential for future harm. Pressure factors are separate and distinct from the actual experience of vulnerability (Baker, 2009; Cardona, 2004).

The everyday lives of people are characterized by a variety of pressures related to self, family, community, and the macroenvironment. These pressures increase the effects of exposure to a trigger event and the likelihood of experiencing vulnerability. An example scenario is as follows: A single father living from month to month works the assembly line in an automobile manufacturing plant, which is in an industry plagued by effects from recessions; 2 months later, he is laid off and cannot find employment. The father's limited income, family structure, and current economic conditions put pressures on his life. These pressures represent risk factors that increase his exposure to disruptive events, but he copes with his present circumstances by living month to month. Then, a trigger event occurs (e.g., he is laid off), and he becomes powerless and dependent on a range of factors (e.g., his skills, his initiative, opportunities available to him) so that he can be resilient. What would happen to our interpretation of the experience if we just described the scenario as, "a single father has been laid off from his job"? The point of these contrasting scenarios is threefold: (1) One-dimensional representations of vulnerability experiences do not accurately portray their content; (2) risk and vulnerability are not synonymous, that is, vulnerability is the materialization of risk (Baker, 2009; Cardona, 2004); and (3) in states of vulnerability, people are dependent on internal and external resources to recover.

## Individual

Consumer research has a rich tradition of examining the individual influences on daily lives. Moschis (1992) groups individual influences into biophysical (e.g., impairment, sex, cognitive ability) and psychosocial (e.g., perceived skills, self-concept, socioeconomic status) categories. Variables within these categories can be used to illuminate the pressures on the individual (for a review, see Baker et al., 2005). To date, most studies in consumer research related to vulnerability have used the individual as the unit of analysis (see Mason & Pavia, 2006, for an exception).

## Family

Families are argued as being the closest network that helps fulfill basic consumption and support needs (Commuri & Gentry, 2005; Epp & Price, Chapter 29 of this volume). The family serves as an ongoing connection and buffer to the outside world, perhaps even more so for individuals with substantial physical and/or cognitive constraints (Mason & Pavia, 2006). The literature on family structure, communication styles, adaptation skills, roles, and rituals could be analyzed for pressures experienced within the family unit and may provide important bases for developing an understanding of the adaptive role of these constructs and facilitating solutions to enhance family well-being.

## Community

Community constitutes a set of relational, rather than simply geographic, connections. People who share the same set of pressures (e.g., limited access to goods and services) and are impacted by the same or similar trigger events may share the experience of vulnerability (Baker, Hunt, & Rittenburg, 2007); however, each individual, family unit, and community may interpret and respond to its vulnerability in unique ways. Consumers with visual impairments may participate in multiple communities, such as those at work or church, and in special-interest groups that can include those united by the common experience of disability. No studies in consumer research have used community as the unit of analysis to explore how social groups that are formed from a basis of impairment (e.g., National Federation of the Blind, American Foundation for the Blind) unite around common consumption goals, or how conflicts emerge and play out with respect to strategies for achieving consumption aspirations.

## Macroforces

Macroenvironmental factors such as natural and built environments, social structures, regulations, technology availability and access, and the distribution of social resources are pressures that could contribute to vulnerability. For example, lack of access to public transportation and retail stores designed with able-bodied assumptions may constrain options for consumers with sensory, cognitive, or mobility impairments (Kaufman-Scarborough & Baker, 2005; Mason & Pavia, 2006). To summarize, the concentric circles in Figure 26.1 represent risk factors, or factors that increase the chance and effects of exposure to a trigger event, perhaps leading to the experience of vulnerability. Although the concentric circles in the figure are discussed as an inward to outward movement of effects, there is a dynamic interplay between the effects of self, family, community, and the environment. Further, it is important to note that consumers do not experience a state of actual vulnerability simply because of these pressures. That is, consumers typically do not experience an active powerlessness and dependency associated with vulnerability until a trigger event creates a shock that overwhelms their capacity to absorb the incident in light of the individual, family, community, and macroenvironmental forces putting pressure on their everyday lives (see also Hill, 2001).

### Trigger Events and Tenet 2

A trigger event (i.e., shock) affects the direction and/or strength of the relationship between pressures and a state of vulnerability. Most relevant to marketing and consumer research are trigger events related to marketplace and marketspace access and consumption experiences, including being taken advantage of by unscrupulous business practices, but also relevant could be disruptive triggers that impact day-to-day markets and consumption behavior. A trigger event often illuminates an imbalance in marketplace interaction or consumption experiences and is usually a discrete event that signals a crisis or rock bottom for the individual, family, or community (Baker et al., 2005; Baker, Hunt, & Rittenburg, 2007; Hill, 2001; Pavia & Mason, 2004). Such disruptive events have been described as emerging from external crises such as natural disasters, personal crises such as job loss or divorce, or life crises such as a serious health threat or the death of a loved one (Gentry et al., 1995; Mason & Pavia, 1998). Although people may not be blameless due to their life choices, as such crisis categorizations suggest, their movement into vulnerability is often beyond their control (Hill, 2001; Hill & Stamey, 1990; Mason & Pavia, 1998).

### State of Vulnerability and Tenet 3

Vulnerability is a state of human existence characterized by powerlessness and lack of control. External resources are required to enhance the capacity of the impacted person or persons to respond. All humans have the potential to experience consumer vulnerability. Anyone at any time under the right conditions with a trigger event has the potential to experience a state of vulnerability (Baker et al., 2005; Gentry et al., 1995). When individuals, families, or communities experience vulnerability, they have a decreased capacity to absorb future shocks, and their needs always exceed available resources. Vulnerability is the outcome of one or more of the pressure factors (i.e., self, family community, macroenvironment) interacting with a trigger event or hazard. Dependence intensifies during periods of increased stress, and if the stressful situation cannot be resolved, self-concept is eroded (Baker et al., 2005; Hill, 1991, 2001; Moschis, 1992).

### Resilience and Tenet 4

Consumer vulnerability induces resiliency behaviors. Individuals and communities are resilient when they transform their material, social, or ecological environments to reduce the negative impact and/or improve their quality of life (Baker & Hill, 2010). The capacity for individuals and communities to be resilient can be built through the actions of multiple stakeholder groups, including business, consumers, government, and NGOs. Previous studies have shown that in many situations, individuals do not passively accept their powerlessness but, instead, actively and constructively resist their constraints (Baker, 2006; Hill, 1991; Pavia & Mason, 2004).

Because the present is uncertain, vulnerability also relates to a lack of future orientation (Hill, 2001; Pavia & Mason, 2004; Viswanathan et al., 2009), which may impact choices and actions taken in response to vulnerability (see also Rosa, Geiger-Oneto, & Fajardo, Chapter 7 of this volume; Shultz & Shapiro, Chapter 6 of this volume). Resiliency behaviors reflect the capacity of individuals and/or collectives to adjust to threats or change (Baker & Hill, 2010; Maddi, Chapter 31 of this volume). As the model in Figure 26.1 shows, the capacity for resilience is built through the efforts of the impacted consumers, other consumers, businesses, governments, and NGOs, who engage the resources (e.g., human, technological, material) they have available to them. When all stakeholders are not working toward the same goal with the same set of understandings, capacity may not be at optimal functioning. The ability of the individual or collective to recover is reduced, perhaps exacerbating vulnerability and lengthening time to recovery, as denoted by the bidirectional arrow between state of vulnerability and resiliency in Figure 26.1.

*Aftershocks and Tenet 5*

Aftershocks affect the direction and strength of the relationship between resilience responses and a state of vulnerability. Ideological tensions between stakeholder groups and individuals are one type of aftershock. Aftershocks and actions taken by members of different stakeholder groups may exacerbate and continue vulnerability, as denoted by the bidirectional arrow between state of vulnerability and resiliency in Figure 26.1.

Vulnerability experiences may be exacerbated or continued over time if in attempts to respond to threats, new forces (i.e., aftershocks) impinge on resiliency behaviors. Aftershocks may include ideological tensions, such as between personal and social responsibility and between equality and individuation (Baker & Hill, 2010). These ideological tensions not only affect the direction and/or strength of the relationship between resilience and a state of vulnerability but also may be important catalysts for social change (Baker & Hill, 2010).

*The Process Model and Tenet 6*

Vulnerability as a process is a catalyst for change. Responses to threats (i.e., shocks) may transform the pressures (i.e., individual, family, community, and macroforces). The pressures also affect the nature of the resiliency response, as denoted by the bidirectional arrow labeled "catalyst for change" in Figure 26.1.

Summary

The model presented here expands on previous views of vulnerability by moving beyond adaptive behaviors of individuals and communities to try to envision participatory approaches in which multiple stakeholders are involved in stimulating a cycle of resilience and ultimately being the catalyst for social change to reduce the pressures contributing to vulnerability. Cultures and consumers are in continuous motion. It is through this dynamic state that consumers, businesses, governments, and NGOs can actively work to create a resilient environment. Opportunities for resilience are influenced by self, family, community, and macroenvironmental factors. In other words, pressures can, and often do, have positive social consequences in the process of social change.

## CONTEXTUALIZING A PROCESS THEORY OF VULNERABILITY AND RESILIENCE

A process theory of consumer vulnerability and resilience is a sensitive theoretical tool useful for informing analysis, developing deep understanding of situational and sociohistorical consumption contexts, and creating solutions to inspire individual and social change. To address how TCR can enhance consumers' lives in regard to vulnerabilities, we now illuminate how our theoretical framework has broad applicability across contexts in which restrictions in choice, access, and resources for consumers pose threats to consumer well-being. Next, we highlight two contextual areas in marketing and consumer research—disability and disaster—where this theoretical framework would provide recommendations for guiding transformations. Then, we briefly discuss how the framework applies to other TCR contexts.

Disability

Access, whether to the marketplace or resource pathways, for people with disabilities is a problem that cuts across all socioeconomic layers and cultures. In the United States, people with disabilities are the single largest minority group, with nearly 50 million individuals reported to have a disability (Brault, 2008). This means that nearly one in five consumers has some type of disability that can present unique needs and challenges in the marketplace, yet these consumers are often unacknowledged by marketers and policy makers.

Studies in rich market and consumption contexts in the developed world have provided insights and understanding into the nature of disability. Disability is not solely a human characteristic, as environments and social interactions also may be disabled. In other words, consumption constraints may flow from individual abilities, competencies, or confidence in some situations, but barriers also come from the environments in which people operate (Baker et al., 2001, 2005; Kaufman-Scarborough & Baker, 2005; Kaufman-Scarborough & Childers, 2009). Thus, solutions to choice, access, and resource restrictions must address both individual competencies and environmental barriers.

Shopping and consumption studies illuminate the uniqueness of each person's experience of vulnerability and the value of different types of adaptation strategies (Baker et al., 2001). The studies show how individuals adapt shopping patterns to cope with access barriers (Baker, 2006) and how families adapt roles, norms, and rituals to meet marketplace challenges (Mason & Pavia, 2006). Finally, they demonstrate how online environments can increase access to opportunities and manage consumption needs (Childers & Kaufman-Scarborough, 2009; Kaufman-Scarborough & Childers, 2009). These studies highlight the heterogeneity of adaptive responses in consumption venues. For example, some consumers with visual impairment prefer to be independent shoppers despite others' willingness to assist, whereas others seek out shopping assistance from friends, family, or service providers. Some consumers have reported disliking overt attempts at accommodation by service providers, but others have reported concerns about being ignored or not readily acknowledged. Given these different expectations or concerns about the consumption environment, what defines an enabling environment for one consumer with an impairment may be an unwelcoming and disabling environment for another. In addition, what is an enabling environment for a consumer with a visual impairment one time may not be enabling for that same consumer the next time. Such heterogeneity in service needs and preferences emphasizes the need to understand disability and its intersectionality within sociocultural and situational contexts. Thus, consumption experiences must be designed around an understanding of the needs and movements of consumers with a wide range of capabilities rather than around the flaw of averages.

If we assume that marketers empower consumers, alter physical structures, and educate service providers, then the marketplace should be more accessible, and all is resolved. However, although such improvements are important starting points, unwelcoming servicescapes and access barriers reveal larger systemic concerns about vulnerability, such as stigmatization and repression in the marketplace. When understood on a deeper theoretical basis, these concerns can be challenged and changed across a broad array of marketing contexts and groups, while contributing more broadly to the study of the power relations in consumption practices and consumer identity projects. The consistent need for adaptation by or exclusion of consumers with visual impairments provides a window into issues of power and control in the marketplace. For all consumers, environments send important signals of social valuation and devaluation (Baker, 2006; Baker, Holland, & Kaufman-Scarborough, 2007). Welcoming signals convey to consumers with impairments that they are recognized and valued members of this marketplace and society. In contrast, unwelcoming environments communicate a message of devaluation and exclusion. Such signals can shape all consumers' attitudes and attitudinal barriers about who should or should not be in the market venue and who is valued or not valued as part of the consumption landscape. Future research should address systemic issues of power and social valuation, for example, through the lens of social justice (Scott et al., in press), while providing creative solutions to the marginalization of consumers' identities.

Most, if not all, of the research conducted at the intersection of disability, markets, and consumption has been conducted in the developed world. Yet, the nature of the problem will manifest and be contextualized differently in the developing world. For example, most people with vision loss (about 83%) live in the developing world, where blindness rates are higher and the size of the population is larger compared to industrialized nations (World Health Organization, 2009). In the developing world, visual disability reveals additional concerns of access. According to the World Health Organization, an estimated 85% of visual impairment and 75% of blindness is preventable or treatable globally if individuals have access to resources such as improved nutrition, treatment and prevention of infectious eye disease, and access to eye services and surgery. In addition, the issue of visual disability and access constraints is not diminishing. Current predictions suggest that the number of cases of visual impairments will grow due to global population growth and aging demographics (World Health Organization, 2009). Future research that involves consumers with disabilities in the developing world and addresses choice, access, and resource pathway constraints is sorely needed (see Viswanathan, Chapter 5 of this volume, for lessons learned from his research in subsistence markets).

*Summary*

In the context of disability, a process theory of consumer vulnerability and resilience:

- Treats the presence of a disability and negative environmental factors (e.g., structural barriers) as pressure (i.e., risk) factors that increase the chance of exposure to an event triggering vulnerability
- Recognizes that a trigger event (e.g., job loss, discontinued bus route) exposes latent pressures
- Shows that vulnerability is a high point where pressures have materialized to create powerlessness and dependence in a situation in which people with disabilities have decreased ability to absorb future shocks
- Appreciates the resiliency of people with disabilities, particularly when businesses, consumers, government, and NGOs enact resources to build the capacity of impacted people to respond to threats
- Acknowledges that different stakeholder groups will have different interests, values, and adaptive strategies that may reduce or exacerbate vulnerability
- Recognizes the transformative potential of exposing pressures and experiencing vulnerability

This theoretical framework is powerful in this context, because it acknowledges that understandings of disability, access, and public accommodations must be fluid in nature to account for cultural changes (e.g., growth of electronic commerce) as well as situational and contextual interactions.

Disaster, Markets, and Consumption

In the decade between 1997 and 2006, 2.7 billion global citizens experienced substantial damage to their well-being in the form of 1.2 million human fatalities and $800 billion in economic losses, directly attributable to natural hazard events (e.g., earthquakes, droughts, tornadoes). From the previous decade, the number of disasters grew by 60%, the number of people impacted increased by 17%, the death toll doubled, and the cost of material damage increased by 12% in 2006 prices (International Federation of Red Cross and Red Crescent Societies, 2007). The impacts of disaster on commercial, social, and ecological factors were substantial, and the probability of future harm to consumer well-being is considerable.

For TCR to have an impact in the disaster context, we must first understand what disaster is. Scholars from geography, engineering, anthropology, sociology, psychology, and business employ different definitions of *disaster*, including (1) caused by a hazard, or fleeting event, such as an earthquake, tornado, or hurricane; (2) equivalent to hazard (i.e., the earthquake is the disaster); and (3) created at the intersection of natural and social phenomenon (Perry, 2007). A fourth and more recent, emerging definition suggests that disaster occurs at the intersection of ecological, social, and material phenomena (Baker, 2009). These definitions are not mutually exclusive, but the definition is important, because it impacts how and to whom resources are allocated and, therefore, how resources are engaged to fuel resilience processes.

The fourth perspective of disaster appears most appropriate to TCR, because transformative consumer researchers are concerned with the relationship between well-being and sociocultural and situational contexts of consumption (Mick, Pettigrew, Pechmann, & Ozanne, Chapter 1 of this volume). Clearly, disasters affect every facet of life (e.g., biological, commercial, social, ecological), create vulnerability, and necessitate resilience. What role do markets and consumption play in resilience processes in disasters? Importantly, a process theory of consumer vulnerability and resilience provides the conceptual link between disaster, well-being, and consumption.

Studies linking these three often focus on loss of material possession attachments as well as disparities in resource distribution efforts. Losses of material possessions force consumers to transform values toward possessions and render many other possessions meaningless due to loss of context (Sayre, 1994). The absence of meaningful possessions may become a catalyst for change in consumers' lives (Sayre, 1994), at least temporarily. Additionally, there is transformative power in shared losses and shared recovery related to material and interpersonal relationships (Baker, Hunt, & Rittenburg, 2007). Resource distribution efforts reproduce power relationships (Marshall, 1979) and expose latent disparities with respect to race and income (Austin, 2006; Guion, Scammon, & Borders, 2007). In addition, victims' and survivors' needs often are not considered in response efforts, which focus on the needs of responders (Guion et al., 2007).

*Summary*

In the context of disaster, the process theory of consumer vulnerability and resilience:

- Treats the presence of demographic factors and possession attachments as pressure, or risk, factors that increase the chance of exposure to an event triggering vulnerability (e.g., people choosing to live in low-lying areas more at risk of flooding), while ensuring these factors on their own are neither necessary nor sufficient for classifying people impacted by a disaster
- Recognizes that a trigger event (e.g., hurricane) exposes pressures, such as latent disparities with respect to race
- Shows that vulnerability is a high point where pressures have materialized to create powerlessness and dependence in a situation in which people impacted by disasters have decreased ability to absorb future shocks
- Appreciates the resiliency of people impacted by disasters, particularly when businesses, consumers, governments, and NGOs enact resources to build the capacity of impacted people to respond to threats

- Acknowledges that different stakeholder groups will have different interests, values, and adaptive strategies that may reduce or exacerbate vulnerability
- Recognizes the transformative potential of exposing pressures and experiencing vulnerability

This theoretical framework is powerful in this context, because it acknowledges that understandings of disaster, well-being, and consumption must be fluid in nature to account for differences in perceptions between stakeholder groups (e.g., valuing needs, assigning responsibility) as well as situational and contextual interactions.

### Extending the Theoretical Framework Beyond Disability and Disaster

Table 26.2 highlights the five components of this theoretical model and places it within various contexts of consumers experiencing vulnerability. Table 26.2 briefly demonstrates how this framework may be used as a theoretical tool to understand the process of vulnerability and resilience for consumers in poverty, those with health problems, and those who have recently immigrated. It is important to note that within each of these groups, substantial pressures may lead to susceptibility to a trigger event, which pushes the consumer to experience a state of vulnerability. Given the overwhelming nature of their situations, resilience is co-constructed through engagement of the individual and other stakeholders and often in light of ideological tensions.

## A CALL TO ARMS

TCR strives to make a difference in people's lives and enhances consumer welfare (Mick, 2006). To achieve this, "TCR must be a devoted engagement with consumers and the world we all inhabit to address problems and opportunities of well-being in a manner that speaks of shared values, empathy, immediacy, and usefulness" (Mick et al., Chapter 1 of this volume). In other words, TCR looks at real problems from the point of view of impacted publics and works together to enhance everyday lives and solve social problems (see also Ozanne & Fischer, Chapter 4 of this volume).

Given such admirable goals, how can TCR facilitate access to consumption and markets? How can TCR help level the playing field with consumers living with visual impairments or health limitations, having few financial resources, confronted with the aftermath of disasters, or experiencing stigmatized identities due to discriminating legal constraints? In this chapter, we have argued that a process theory of consumer vulnerability and resilience is a robust theoretical tool for the TCR agenda. We advocate that working together in a participatory manner to conduct research and solve problems with, rather than for, disadvantaged consumers is an approach that recognizes and unleashes the empowerment in such actions (Mick et al., Chapter 1 of this volume). This perspective is the foundational premise of our process model for transforming vulnerability toward resiliency through individual and social change. In this section, we outline the implications of this framework for theory and practice, then call transformative consumer researchers to action, for example, by employing the six tenets of our theory.

### Transformative Theory

Prior consumer research has highlighted substantial differences in consumption experiences and access opportunities for groups who may be marginalized and has shown larger systemic and ideological issues within the global consumer society paradigm (Crockett & Wallendorf, 2004; Hill, 2005). What is revealed in this research is that consumption experiences and access barriers are much more than misunderstood service encounters or physical structural constraints. Lack

**Table 26.2**   A Process Model of Vulnerability and Resilience in Context

| | Pressures | Trigger Events | Vulnerability | Ideological Tensions | Resilience |
|---|---|---|---|---|---|
| What this is | Phenomena related to self, interpersonal networks, community, and macroforces that increase the likelihood that a trigger event can overwhelm and lead to vulnerability | An event or series of related effects from a trigger event that overwhelm the individual beyond the pressures they already absorb, which leads to vulnerability | Ongoing, overwhelming feeling and experience of dependency, powerlessness, and inability to absorb current shocks | Ideological tensions that enable or prohibit resilience | Positive adjustments in the face of adversity; a state in which consumers living under conditions of restriction are empowered in terms of increased choices, access, or resources resulting in greater absorption of future pressures |
| What this might consist of | • *Individual*—Biophysical characteristics, psychosocial characteristics, emotional states, life events<br>• *Interpersonal*—Family network (structure, conflict), peer network, normative models, support systems<br>• *Community*—Infrastructure and resources, support agencies, opportunities for resource attainment, normative anomie and illegitimate opportunities, collective identity and involvement<br>• *Macroforces*—Poverty, distribution of resources, economic forces, inequality and stigmatization, physical and logistical elements, public policies and legal forces, cultural and institutional views | • *Individual*—Job loss, illness<br>• *Interpersonal*—Divorce, death of loved one<br>• *Community*—Natural disaster, plant closing<br>• *Macroforces*—Access discrimination | • Powerlessness<br>• Dependency<br>• Inability to absorb future shocks | • *Individual*—Low self-esteem<br>• *Interpersonal*—Family conflicts<br>• *Community*—Stigmatization in distributing resources<br>• *Macroforces*—Views of personal responsibility vs. assistance | Responses from<br>• Consumers<br>• Nongovernmental organizations<br>• Businesses<br>• Government |

**How this process may occur with different consumers**

| | | | | |
|---|---|---|---|---|
| Impoverished consumer | • *Individual*—High school dropout with limited skills maintains a minimum-wage job in retail <br> • *Interpersonal*—Single mother raising a small child, limited ties to a chemically dependent parent, problematic relationship with abusive partner but relies on his financial support, limited peer network with similar normative models of conflict <br> • *Community*—Dependent on affordable day care while working, receives nutrition assistance for her child <br> • *Macroforces*—Limited education and employment opportunities in small community | • Partner abuse episode forces individual and child out of home. | • Dependence on others for housing, basic needs, and protection <br> • Powerless to find well-paying job with current skills <br> • Difficulty attaining skills with limited resources <br> • Dependence for resources and fear for safety reduce ability to absorb further shocks <br><br> • Conflicts between work, family, and education <br> • Ideological tensions about funding assistance and welfare reform | • Local government helps fund safe houses for women and children experiencing abuse. <br> • Community agencies connect to counseling and educational opportunities. <br> • Peer networks form to share child care and offer support when engaging in marketplace. <br> • The consumers and local agencies work together to advocate for enforcement of legal and privacy protections. |
| Consumer with health crisis | • *Individual*—Middle-class male in late 40s with highly involved sales position requiring frequent travel and customer interaction on 100% commission-based salary <br> • *Interpersonal*—Married, wife stays home to raise three children, other family members scattered across country | Diagnosis of a debilitating chronic illness requires medical intervention and change in lifestyle (e.g., time demands for medical needs, draining side effects of treatment). | • Dependence on medical treatments and reduced health impacting job performance, family life, and community involvement <br> • Powerless to maintain level of performance, resulting in lost wages, and job and insurance fears <br><br> • Conflict between job performance and personal medical needs <br> • Affordable health insurance tied to continued employment | • Employer and individual revisit job responsibilities, compensation plan, and time demands. <br> • Family members alter their schedules to facilitate medical needs. <br> • Spouse finds employment. |

*continued*

**Table 26.2**    A Process Model of Vulnerability and Resilience in Context (Continued)

| | Pressures | Trigger Events | Vulnerability | Ideological Tensions | Resilience |
|---|---|---|---|---|---|
| | • *Community*—Involved in community through schools, church, and community organizations<br>• *Macroforces*—Economic cycle putting increased pressure on sales and job performance, layoffs occurring | | • Resource loss, family conflicts, and weakened networks reducing ability to absorb shocks | | • Renegotiate roles within the family system.<br>• Consumer groups work to pass state and federal health policy. |
| Immigrant facing marginalization | • *Individual*—Hispanic, male, undocumented blue-collar worker living in the United States for 11 years in an apartment but saving to buy a home<br>• *Interpersonal*—Extended family living in Mexico whom he helps support, one child born in the United States, close friends are documented and undocumented immigrants<br>• *Community*—Attends local Hispanic church but not involved in community, tries to remain outside of system to avoid detection<br>• *Macroforces*— Strong impact on his life by immigration policy and employment opportunities | • Immigration policy passed that restricts access to employment, housing, transportation, health care, and education.<br>• Racial profiling and random documentation checks occur in marketplace. | • Dependence on others or illegal means to attain basic resources (e.g., housing, employment, transportation)<br>• Powerless to prevent racial profiling and random stops<br>• Fear and dependency on others reducing ability to absorb further shocks | • Tension between providing services for those in need and not breaking the law<br>• Ideological conflicts in views of citizens and immigrants | • Documented friends help rent apartments, find employment, and shop.<br>• Empathetic employers and community members take risks to help.<br>• Hispanic community members, families, and undocumented individuals unite to fight the new policy, lobby, and create positive image in larger community. |

of access to resource pathways, exclusion, and the consistent need for adaptation by members in some social groups provide a window into the larger themes of power, control, and social valuation. These themes require marketers to do more than undertake education efforts and modify environments to provide improved or fixed accommodations. They require a reassessment of marketplace ideologies concerning individual rights to participate in the market, while not always bearing the burden of adaptation or exclusion, and deeper reflection on the role that consumption plays in affording dignity and verifying participation in the human race (Baker, 2006; Hill, 2005; Klein & Hill, 2008; Scott et al., in press).

Recall for a moment our opening quote by Helen Keller, an internationally known writer, speaker, and human rights activist who was deaf and blind because of a childhood illness. Her story reveals a young woman overcoming a physical impairment despite categorization in a group that was seen as uniformly possessing little capability and societal value. She overcame a system that institutionalized lack of access and inequality. While confronting a legal system that not only ignored her needs but also failed to recognize that her needs even existed, Keller transformed the hearts and minds of others and changed how society saw, understood, and responded to individuals with disabilities. Through a process theory of consumer vulnerability and resilience, we come to understand the transformative power of Keller and the potential of TCR.

To conceptualize this transformation, our theoretical model has as its basis an assumption of the resiliency of human beings. We believe in the ability of individuals, with support from a collective network and social system, to adapt and emerge stronger from overwhelming adversity. It is important to note that this theoretical framework is not context specific. Its flexibility can guide scholarly thought about the creation of resilience and social change across consumer contexts and with a variety of social groups. In contrast to earlier models that view vulnerability as a static state, this model recognizes the dynamic and systemic nature of the creation and resolution of vulnerability. The model conveys vulnerability not as a problem of the individual to be fixed (i.e., demographic perspective) or of the environment to be corrected (i.e., environmental perspective) but as a systemic development that requires systemic engagement for changing lives and enhancing consumer well-being. For example, previous consumer research illuminates the transformative power of low-income or subsistence consumers becoming empowered through collective action and resource-sensitive providers and channels (Viswanathan, Chapter 5 of this volume; Viswanathan et al., 2009). These studies highlight the possibility of transformative change in particular service programs and contexts, but considerable knowledge gaps into the process of broad and sustainable social change that foster resilience and well-being still exist. A process theory of vulnerability and resilience is offered here as a systemic approach to help fill that gap.

This framework can push our understanding of how vulnerability emerges. By recognizing that vulnerability is an outcome of multiple, embedded pressures that underlie the reactions to trigger events, consumer researchers can begin to more fully explore the relationships between upstream pressures and the experience of vulnerability. Specifically, our model acknowledges the powerful pressures that social systems (e.g., institutions, norms, social stratification) exert on consumers and advocate that if such systems are consciously evolved in a participatory manner, they can play a transformative role toward building consumer resiliency. Our framework also can be used to explore how to build capacity and foster strengths that exist downstream to empower people and communities to move beyond vulnerability toward resilience—not just a temporary resolution but also an ongoing, more sustainable resilience.

This framework also recognizes the interdependencies between human life and market access (Mittelstaedt, Kilbourne, & Mittelstaedt, 2006), as well as the emancipatory potential of participatory approaches that draw on the strengths of all actors within the system (Ozanne,

Corus, & Saatcioglu, 2009; Ozanne & Saatcioglu, 2008). At the same time, this framework recognizes the simple truth that when individuals, families, or communities experience a trigger event, or shock to the system, they will seek to reconstitute their lives, regardless of whether they were previously in a survival or prosperity mode or in a transition between the two. To be sure, actions by any one or more of the downstream players may exacerbate and continue the cycle of vulnerability. Yet, also possible is that downstream players, most especially the impacted consumers themselves, may find adaptive solutions to their consumptive needs, even if the solutions are temporary or based on a survivalist mode.

Transformative Practice

Social movements occur when there is dissatisfaction with current conditions. How social issues and conditions are framed guides the actions designed to address them. When individuals within groups (e.g., women, elderly, disabled) are assumed to be homogeneous, or when environments are seen to be a static property of society, then issues are framed in such a way that change cannot be envisioned. Consider the transformative potential of changing our understanding of the term *disability* from a characteristic of an individual to an impairment that resides in the interaction between a person and his or her environment. Consider the transformative potential of changing our understanding of disasters as an extreme environmental event necessitating recovery response to conceiving them as an embedded convergence of major systems (e.g., ecological, commercial, material, social), which allows shifts such as mitigation efforts, participatory approaches, and sustainability efforts to emerge (Baker, 2009; Mileti, 1999). How pressures, trigger events, and vulnerability are conceptualized will alter what actions, if any, are undertaken to address resolution. A process theory of consumer vulnerability and resilience recognizes that vulnerability is a dynamic process produced and resolved by co-constitution. The interdependencies that exist within the social system require participation and voice from all stakeholders in social and material relations and practices.

How is participation and voice achieved? How can research facilitate transformation? We believe stakeholders (e.g., consumers, policy makers, researchers, NGOs) can achieve deeper understanding and foster social change through (1) recognition, (2) respect, and (3) responsibility. First, those in power and public positions must recognize the diverse and disenfranchised voices within communities. In particular, those consumers whose voices have been silenced or devalued must be identified and heard. This can be achieved through community assessments; interactions with grassroots organizations and agencies serving disadvantaged people; the democratic processes of elections, town hall, or community meetings; and so on.

Second, individuals who are marginalized or seen through a second-class lens must be given respect and an authentic voice. If participation in democratic processes is allowed in voicing how collective resources and spaces are shared, then individuals are likely to feel and be valued. Ideally, this participation will result in a deeper engagement and cocreation of systemic processes that help empower and balance inequalities. For example, allowing the working poor to have a stronger voice in processes for attaining food assistance, rather than imposing an institutionalized model focused on scrutiny and screening, could help create a more empowering delivery and service system that values all persons. Furthermore, once these voices are heard, they should be respected and valued through societal debate and actions that transform overburdening institutionalized pressures that contribute to vulnerability.

Third, beyond recognizing and respecting consumers' experiences and viewpoints, responsibility must be incorporated into the resolutions for vulnerability. Consumers and stakeholders must assume responsibility and participation in helping others understand the pressures contributing to vulnerability, creating systems to aid vulnerable consumers, and negotiating ideological tensions surrounding perceived societal value and access to collective resources and services for quality of life (e.g., education, health care). For example, anti-immigration laws passed in some southwestern U.S. states have led numerous immigrants and other stakeholders to organize, form rallies and protests, publicly speaking out against such discrimination, call for changes in federal policy, and work with state systems to roll back the policies. By accepting a need to responsibly engage, these consumer collectives may achieve the change that silence, complacency, and individual effort cannot.

Our model identifies four stakeholder groups who actively participate in co-constructing resolutions to foster resilience for those experiencing vulnerability, but what can these stakeholders do? Although no one individual or entity can solve market access issues, as a collective, strides can be made to enhance access and draw on strengths of each actor within the system. First, consumers facing adversity and pressures must engage in the marketplace and express their consumption needs and desires. In doing so, they foster resilience by achieving self-completion in the marketplace and paving a path for themselves and others to follow (Baker, 2006). Marketers and businesses that recognize the heterogeneity of consumers with impairments can help strip away the barriers that deter access and inclusion. To ignore diverse persons' needs is to devalue them as consumers and members of society.

Government has the power to mandate and enforce social change. By passing laws, such as the Americans With Disabilities Act or requiring unique markings on currency, the government has required accommodation for disability and attempted to remove structural barriers associated with pressures that may increase the likelihood of experiencing vulnerability. Also, through these mandated acts, the government is helping change the tone that is the foundation of attitudinal barriers. An implicit message is sent that if this behavior is illegal, then it also must be ethically wrong. In addition, the government can encourage social change through upstream remedies, such as funding targeted toward lessening the root pressures within the model. In effect, root pressures on individuals' lives could be alleviated if, for example, access to medical services and appropriate assortments of them could be assured (Mittelstaedt, Duke, & Mittelstaedt, 2009), because in the majority of cases, blindness may be treatable and preventable (World Health Organization, 2009).

Finally, NGOs are involved in upstream remedies by identifying participants and helping deliver programs and services designed to alleviate root pressures. For example, some NGOs train consumers with visual impairments how to shop independently, while others may help create greater educational and job opportunities for their clients. Globally, NGOs work to connect the visually impaired with preventive measures, such as good nutrition and eye services, and assist communities to remove environmental hazards that contribute to infectious eye diseases. NGOs can also play an important role in educating communities about the nature of visual impairment and reduce the stigmatization of these consumers.

Scholars of TCR are uniquely poised to understand, engage, empower, and give voice to the story of transformation, as well as explain the relationship between consumers and social spaces, and marketplace access and identity. Uncovering unmet needs, identifying resource strengths, and working with consumers to create solutions to diminish or eliminate consumption constraints of access, choice, and resources are tasks consistent with our strengths as consumer researchers. We encourage future research on each of the six tenets of the process theory of consumer vulnerability and resilience. We welcome and encourage debate, extensions, and empirical testing of this theoretical model, but first and foremost, we encourage TCR that makes a difference in consumers' lives and enhances consumer well-being.

## ACKNOWLEDGMENTS

We thank Jim Gentry, Ron Hill, John Mittelstaedt, and Cliff Shultz for insightful comments on an earlier version of this chapter.

## REFERENCES

Andreasen, A. R. (1975). *The disadvantaged consumer*. New York: Free Press.

Arnould, E. J., & Thompson, C. J. (2005). Consumer culture theory (CCT): Twenty years of research. *Journal of Consumer Research, 31*(March), 868–882.

Austin, D. E. (2006). Coastal exploitation, land loss, and hurricanes: A recipe for disaster. *American Anthropologist, 108*(4), 671–691.

Baker, S. M. (2006). Consumer normalcy: Understanding the value of shopping through narratives of consumers with visual impairments. *Journal of Retailing, 82*(1), 37–50.

Baker, S. M. (2009). Vulnerability and resilience in natural disasters: A marketing and public policy perspective. *Journal of Public Policy & Marketing, 28*(Spring), 114–123.

Baker, S. M., Gentry, J. W., & Rittenburg, T. L. (2005). Building understanding of the domain of consumer vulnerability. *Journal of Macromarketing, 25*(2), 128–139.

Baker, S. M., & Hill, R. P. (2010). *Negotiated fate and community reconstitution: The role of marketing in disaster recovery*. Manuscript submitted for publication.

Baker, S. M., Holland, J., & Kaufman-Scarborough, C. (2007). How consumers with disabilities perceive "welcome" in retail servicescapes: A critical incident study. *Journal of Services Marketing, 21*(3), 160–173.

Baker, S. M., Hunt, D. M., & Rittenburg, T. L. (2007). Consumer vulnerability as a shared experience: Tornado recovery process in Wright, Wyoming. *Journal of Public Policy & Marketing, 26*(Spring), 6–19.

Baker, S. M., Stephens, D. L., & Hill, R. P. (2001). Marketplace experiences of consumers with visual impairments: Beyond the Americans with Disabilities Act. *Journal of Public Policy & Marketing, 20*(Fall), 215–224.

Bankoff, G. (2001). Rendering the world unsafe: "Vulnerability" as Western discourse. *Disasters, 25*(1), 19–35.

Belk, R. W. (1988). Possessions and the extended self. *Journal of Consumer Research, 15*(September), 139–168.

Brault, M. W. (2008). *Americans with disabilities: 2005* (Current Population Reports No. P70-117). Washington, DC: U.S. Census Bureau. Retrieved September 2009 from http://www.census.gov/prod/2008pubs/p70-117.pdf

Cardona, O. D. (2004). The need for rethinking the concepts of vulnerability and risk from a holistic perspective: A necessary review and criticism for effective risk management. In G. Bankoff, G. Frerks, & D. Hilhorst (Eds.), *Mapping vulnerability: Disasters, development and people* (pp. 37–51). London: Earthscan.

Childers, T. L., & Kaufman-Scarborough, C. (2009). Expanding opportunities for online shoppers with disabilities. *Journal of Business Research, 62*(May), 572–578.

Commuri, S., & Ekici, A. (2008). An enlargement of the notion of consumer vulnerability. *Journal of Macromarketing, 28*(June), 182–186.

Commuri, S., & Gentry, J. W. (2005). Resource allocation in households with women as chief wage earners. *Journal of Consumer Research, 32*(September), 185–195.

Crockett, D. K., & Wallendorf, M. (2005). The role of normative political ideology in consumer behavior. *Journal of Consumer Research, 31*(December), 511–528.

Garrett, D. E., & Toumanoff, P. G. (2010). Are consumers disadvantaged or vulnerable? An examination of consumer complaints to the Better Business Bureau. *Journal of Consumer Affairs, 44*(1), 3–34.

Gentry, J. W., Kennedy, P. F., Paul, K., & Hill, R. P. (1995). The vulnerability of those grieving the death of a loved one: Implications for public policy. *Journal of Public Policy & Marketing, 14*(Spring), 128–142.

Gergen, K. J., McNamee, S., & Barrett, F. J. (2001). Toward transformative dialogue. *International Journal of Public Administration, 24*(7/8), 679–707.

Guion, D., Scammon, D. L., & Borders, A. L. (2007). Weathering the storm: A social marketing perspective on disaster preparedness and response with lessons from hurricane Katrina. *Journal of Public Policy & Marketing, 26*(1), 20–32.

Hill, R. P. (1991). Homeless women, special possessions, and the meaning of "home": An ethnographic case study. *Journal of Consumer Research, 18*(December), 298–310.

Hill, R. P. (2001). Surviving in a material world: Evidence from ethnographic consumer research on people in poverty. *Journal of Contemporary Ethnography, 30*(August), 364–391.

Hill, R. P. (2005). Do the poor deserve less than surfers? An essay for the special issue on vulnerable consumers. *Journal of Macromarketing, 25*(December), 215–218.

Hill, R. P., & Stamey, M. (1990). The homeless in America: An examination of possessions and consumption behaviors. *Journal of Consumer Research, 17*(December), 303–321.

International Federation of Red Cross and Red Crescent Societies. (2007). *World disasters report: Focus on discrimination*. Bloomfield, CT: Kumarian Press.

Kaufman-Scarborough, C. (1999). Reasonable access for mobility-disabled persons is more than widening the door. *Journal of Retailing, 75*(4), 479–508.

Kaufman-Scarborough, C., & Baker, S. M. (2005). Do people with disabilities believe the ADA has served their consumer interests? *Journal of Consumer Affairs, 39*(Summer), 1–26.

Kaufman-Scarborough, C., & Childers, T. L. (2009). Understanding markets as online public places: Insights from consumers with visual impairments. *Journal of Public Policy & Marketing, 28*(Spring), 16–28.

Klein, J. G., & Hill, R. P. (2008). Rethinking macro-level theories of consumption: Research findings from Nazi concentration camps. *Journal of Macromarketing, 28*(September), 228–242.

Klein, J. G., & Huang, L. (2007). After all is lost: Meeting the material needs of adolescent disaster survivors. *Journal of Public Policy & Marketing, 26*(1), 54–59.

Marshall, M. (1979). Natural and unnatural disaster in the Mortlock Islands of Micronesia. *Human Organization, 38*(3), 265–272.

Mason, M., & Pavia, T. (1998). The disruption of the consumer life cycle by serious illness: The case of breast cancer. In J. W. Alba & J. W. Hutchinson (Eds.), *Advances in consumer research* (Vol. 25, pp. 416–20). Provo, UT: Association for Consumer Research.

Mason, M., & Pavia, T. (2006). When the family system includes disability: Adaptation in the marketplace, roles, and identity. *Journal of Marketing Management, 22*, 1009–1030.

Mick, D. G. (2006). Meaning and mattering through transformative consumer research. In C. Pechmann & L. L. Price (Eds.), *Advances in consumer research* (Vol. 33, pp. 1–4). Duluth, MN: Association for Consumer Research.

Mileti, D. S. (1999). *Disasters by design: A reassessment of natural hazards in the United States.* Washington, DC: John Henry Press.

Mittelstaedt, J. D., Duke, C. R., & Mittelstaedt, R. A. (2009). Health care choices in the United States and the constrained consumers: A marketing systems perspective on access and assortment in health care. *Journal of Public Policy & Marketing, 28*(Spring), 95–101.

Mittelstaedt, J. D., Kilbourne, W. E., & Mittelstaedt, R. A. (2006). Macromarketing as agorology: Macromarketing theory and the study of the agora. *Journal of Macromarketing, 26*(Fall), 131–142.

Moschis, G. C. (1992). *Marketing to older consumers: A handbook of information for strategy development.* Westport, CT: Quorum.

Ozanne, J. L., Corus, C., & Saatcioglu, B. (2009). The philosophy and methods of deliberative democracy: Implications for public policy and marketing. *Journal of Public Policy & Marketing, 28*(Spring), 29–40.

Ozanne, J. L., & Saatcioglu, B. (2008). Participatory action research. *Journal of Consumer Research, 35*(October), 423–439.

Pavia, T. M., & Mason, M. J. (2004). The reflexive relationship between consumer behavior and adaptive coping. *Journal of Consumer Research, 31*(December), 441–454.

Perry, R. W. (2007). What is a disaster? In H. Rodríguez, E. L. Quarantelli, & R. R. Dynes (Eds.), *Handbook of disaster research* (pp. 1–15). New York: Springer.

Sachs, J. (2005). *The end of poverty: Economic possibilities for our time.* New York: Penguin Books.

Santos, N., & Laczniak, E. (2009). Marketing to the poor: An integrative justice model for engaging impoverished market segments. *Journal of Public Policy & Marketing, 28*(Spring), 3–15.

Sayre, S. (1994). Possessions and identity in crisis: Meaning and change for victims of the Oakland firestorm. In C. T. Allen & D. R. John (Eds.), *Advances in consumer research* (Vol. 21, pp. 109–114). Provo, UT: Association for Consumer Research.

Scott, L., Williams, J. D., Baker, S. M., Brace-Govan, J., Downey, H., Hakstian, A., et al. (in press). Beyond poverty: Social justice in a global marketplace. *Journal of Public Policy & Marketing.*

Sen, A. (1999). *Development as freedom.* New York: Alfred A. Knopf.

Shultz, C. J., II. (2007). Marketing as constructive engagement. *Journal of Public Policy & Marketing, 26*(Fall), 293–301.

Shultz, C. J., II, & Holbrook, M. B. (2009). The paradoxical relationships between marketing and vulnerability. *Journal of Public Policy & Marketing, 28*(Spring), 124–127.

Stephens, D. L., & Bergman, K. (1995). The Americans with Disabilities Act: A mandate for marketers. *Journal of Public Policy & Marketing, 14*(1), 164–168.

Viswanathan, M., Sridharan, S., Gau, R., & Ritchie, R. (2009). Designing marketplace literacy education in resource-constrained contexts: Implications for public policy and marketing. *Journal of Public Policy & Marketing, 28*(Spring), 85–94.

Wisner, B. (2004). Assessment of capability and vulnerability. In G. Bankoff, G. Frerks, & D. Hilhorst (Eds.), *Mapping vulnerability: Disasters, development and people* (pp. 183–193). London: Earthscan.

World Health Organization. (2009). *Visual impairment and blindness* (Fact Sheet No. 282). Retrieved September 2009 from http://www.who.int/mediacentre/factsheets/fs282/en/index.html

# 27

# Consumer Well-Being in Later Life

Simone Pettigrew and George Moschis

Over the last 2 decades, there has been a marked increase in the number of consumer studies investigating purchase and consumption processes from the perspective of the older consumer. This increase has been triggered, at least in part, by the demographic reality of rapid population aging across the globe. Past studies have been useful in improving our limited understanding of the older consumer from a marketing perspective, but there remains enormous potential to explore the aging process in terms of opportunities for transforming people's lives in positive and enduring ways. Such an approach is timely and appropriate, given the numerous individual and societal implications of population aging that need to be addressed in the coming years.

The aging of the earth's population will result in increased personal and societal expenditure on retirement funding and health service delivery. These pressures will necessitate a focus on preparing consumers for better health, active lifestyles, and financial independence in their later years. This chapter outlines possible means of assisting consumers to achieve these ends and proposes methods that have the potential to provide further insight into our understanding of aging and the many and varied implications for consumer welfare. The chapter is structured into the following sections: (a) a demographic description of current and future older consumers, (b) an explanation of why older consumers are worthy of greater research attention, (c) an account of the major areas of relevant current knowledge, (d) a discussion of the gaps in this knowledge and where future efforts could be directed to positively transform older consumers' lives, and (e) suggestions for methods to generate this new knowledge.

## OLDER CONSUMERS: NOW AND IN THE FUTURE

Around 10% of the global population is already over 60 years of age (World Health Organization [WHO], 2008), which represents 650 million people, a number that is forecast to increase to 2 billion by 2050 (WHO, 2007). Growth rates among those in the oldest age brackets are especially high; the segment of those aged 80 and over is projected to increase from 105 million globally in 2010 to around 438 million in 2050 (U.S. Census Bureau, 2009). The majority of the world's older people live in developing countries (WHO, 1999), and by 2050 their numbers will have quadrupled, such that 80% of the 2 billion people aged 60 and over will reside in these nations (WHO, 2002).

Three age demarcations are typically used in both academic and practitioner research to define someone as old: 50, 60, and 65. The latter two are the most common and generally reflect the age at which men retire from the workforce. For example, average retirement rates in China and the United States are 58 and 63 years, respectively (Munnell, Buessing, Soto, & Sass, 2006; Wang, Wang, & Su, 2009). Retirement age and the time at which people could access Social Security payments used to reflect life expectancy (Moschis, 1992), but this is no longer the case. Although the global average life expectancy today is 68 years, in many developed countries, such as Australia,

France, Japan, and the United Kingdom, it now exceeds 80 years (WHO, 2009). In these countries, many people will live for around another 20 years after ceasing paid employment. The substantial increase in longevity and the implications for ensuring older members of society are financially secure are resulting in a trend toward encouraging, and in some cases requiring, individuals to work until more advanced ages (Bonoli & Palier, 2007). This strategy aims to (a) reduce the amount of time for which individuals are reliant on age pensions, (b) maintain the workforce in the face of smaller post–baby boomer cohorts, and (c) maximize the tax base from which increases in health care costs and age pensions will need to be funded (Blake & Mayhew, 2006; WHO, 2002). However, increasing the number of older workers reduces the number of seniors available to engage in volunteer work, which will have significant consequences, given the substantial proportion of volunteers who are retirees (Matsuba, Hart, & Atkins, 2007) and the large contributions to the economy that result from their volunteer efforts (Erlinghagen & Hank, 2006). In particular, older people are often the primary caregivers for other older people (Stone, Cafferata, & Sangl, 1987), thereby providing much needed caring services that reduce costs to national health systems. It is unclear how an increased retirement age will impact the demand and supply of caregiver services over time.

The aging of the world's population has been the result of two main forces: a sharp increase in life expectancy and high birth rates in the post–World War II years. The WHO (2000) noted that as life expectancy is a critical indicator of the health of a population, global aging is "first and foremost a success story for humanity" (p. 5). The increase in life expectancy during the 20th century, which was only 31 years in 1900, roughly equates to the improvements achieved over the preceding 5,000 years (Acemoglu & Johnson, 2007; Butler, 1989), largely the result of advances in medicine and hygiene (Easterlin, 1999). In some countries, such as Japan, Switzerland, and France, life expectancy is continuing to increase each year by around 3 months (Robine, 2005), illustrating that we have not yet reached the limits of human longevity.

In light of progressive improvements in the health of older people (Schroll, 2005), longer life expectancy, and the likelihood of extended working years, it is time to revise our definitions of old age and focus on preparing individuals to live longer. In an era of longevity, in which those defined as grandchildren can be as young as newborns or as old as retirees, conceptions of what it means to be old need to be more flexible and less dependent on chronological age as a determining factor. Such an approach is consistent with the notion that older consumers can be best differentiated based on their physical health and psychosocial states, rather than just their chronological age (Moschis, 1996). While acknowledging this, given the review status of this chapter, we continue to use the term *older consumers* to refer to those of current average retirement age or older, as this reflects the orientation of the referenced work.

## WHY STUDY OLDER CONSUMERS?

Although the number of consumer studies involving seniors is growing, this increase is commencing from a low base, and it is recognized that older people continue to be underrepresented in consumer research (Yoon, Cole, & Lee, 2009). There are numerous reasons why older consumers should receive greater research attention. First, as noted above, the senior segment is now substantial in size and growing rapidly. The sheer size of the segment justifies calls to closely examine the current and future needs of older consumers and how these may be better accommodated in the marketplace. Growing segment size combined with increasing affluence make seniors a more attractive target market than previously recognized. Although many older people are reliant on modest pensions, a growing number are financially comfortable because of lower levels of housing debt, fewer child-related costs, and effective retirement planning (Hansen, Slagsvold, & Moum, 2008). In Australia, for example, those aged 55 and older represent one fifth of the population, yet they possess 39% of the country's household wealth and 25% of its disposable income (Access Economics Pty Ltd, 2001). In the public sphere, the swelling ranks of seniors may see them acquire considerable political clout because of their voting power, with important implications for the way public resources will be allocated (Binstock, 2000). These attributes highlight the importance of understanding older consumers' beliefs, attitudes, and preferences across a wide range of consumption-related areas.

Second, the characteristics of older consumers also constitute a methodological advantage. Recruitment can be easier, because those who are fully or partly retired experience fewer time constraints and, as a result, have greater discretionary time (Krantz-Kent & Stewart, 2007). In addition, people often experience a growing desire to give back to society as they age (Cohen, 2001), which can act as an inducement to participate in research projects. Further, there is a tendency for older people to live in close proximity to each other (Hagestad & Uhlenberg, 2006), which can simplify data collection. Importantly, their extensive life experiences make them interesting and informative research subjects.

Third, governments and other funding bodies are becoming increasingly concerned about the economic and social implications of aging populations. As a result, aging is often designated as a priority area for research funding allocations. Given academics' growing reliance on external research funding sources, choosing to study older consumers, especially in health-related contexts, can reap benefits in terms of access to funding.

Last but not least, the underresearched nature of older consumers represents an opportunity for those researchers wishing to make a meaningful contribution to social welfare. Seniors can experience particular life challenges that make them vulnerable on numerous fronts, including their marketplace interactions (Lee & Geistfeld, 1999; Lee & Soberon-Ferrer, 1997; see also Andreasen, Goldberg, & Sirgy, Chapter 2 of this volume; Baker & Mason, Chapter 26 of this volume). Consumer research can play an important role in generating the information required to protect older consumers' interests and improve their well-being. Those willing to take up the challenge can receive exposure to many related fields that can broaden our knowledge base within the discipline. For example, a foray into the world of the older consumer can involve insights into the fields of gerontology, neurobiology, epidemiology, preventive medicine, and health promotion. There is the potential for these insights to be imported into mainstream consumer research to facilitate new perspectives on other consumer issues.

## WHAT DO WE ALREADY KNOW ABOUT OLDER CONSUMERS?

In this section, we present a summary of current knowledge relating to the aging process and its physical, psychological, and social impacts on the individual. These impacts have positive and negative outcomes that can contribute either to older people's strengths or their vulnerabilities. The concept of successful aging is discussed, and possible means of impeding the negative effects of the aging process are outlined. The findings of consumption studies focusing on older people are then summarized, and the literature relating to seniors' decision-making processes and the implications for their marketplace behaviors is reviewed. For additional discussion on elderly consumers, see Andreasen et al. (Chapter 2 of this volume).

### The Aging Process

#### Physical Aging

Physiological models of aging focus on biological changes in the organism and its subsystems. Changes in cells and tissues cause development and deterioration (i.e., aging) of the biological system, increasing susceptibility to disease and death (Rockstein & Susman, 1979). Consequently, the incidence of illnesses such as cancer, heart disease, and dementia increases with age (Mathurs & Vos,

2000). Some of the most common age-related physical conditions include loss in bone density, incontinence, reduced mobility and dexterity, and deterioration in sight, hearing, and taste discernment (Freidrich, 2001; Leventhal, 2007; Mathurs & Vos, 2000). These alterations in physical health have implications for an individual's ability to function in the marketplace. For example, as people age, they have increasing difficulty reading fine print and distinguishing stimuli presented in certain colors, especially those along the blue–green spectrum (Braus, 1995). They also become more sensitive to glare and take more time to adjust to certain light conditions (Stuen & Faye, 2003). Reductions in manual dexterity can cause difficulty in holding and manipulating objects, such as when attempting to open cans, bottles, and other packages (Carmeli, Patish, & Coleman, 2003).

Although there are typical onset ages for physiological decline (e.g., many adults begin to require reading glasses between the ages of 40 and 50; Stuen & Faye, 2003), people age differently and, as a result, can experience physical changes at different ages and at different rates. These variations occur because of genetic inheritance as well as environmental factors (WHO, 2002). Inability to deal with physical changes in later life can undermine a person's self-esteem and well-being (Horowitz, 2003). Access and willingness to use assistive devices can be instrumental in determining the quality of life of the older individual who has experienced substantial physical decline (Day, Jutai, & Campbell, 2002; McCreadie & Tinker, 2005). Not all reductions in physical functioning are inevitable, however, and behaviors earlier in life can affect the likelihood and rate of decline. For example, smoking accelerates normal age-related deterioration in respiratory and cardiac functions, and loss of hearing can be experienced earlier than usual among those who have been exposed to loud music or equipment noise (Agrawal, Platz, & Niparko, 2008). Many older people worry about suffering some form of serious physical impairment (Moschis & Mathur, 2007) and thus may be willing to take steps to reduce their level of risk. However, these concerns need to be made salient among younger people to ensure preventive actions are taken in time to be effective in later life (WHO, 2002).

*Psychological Aging*

Models of psychological aging focus on the development of and change in personality and cognition. Personality models attempt to explain the development of behavioral patterns and self-concept. Cognition (i.e., the processes of perception, memory, judgment, reasoning, and decision making) accounts for a person's mental responses. Resource deficit models conceptualize age-related differences in memory, intelligence, problem-solving, and reasoning in terms of deficits in processing resources (Salthouse, 1991). These models have been used by consumer researchers to account for age-related variations in consumer behavior (e.g., Cole & Gaeth, 1990; Cole & Houston, 1987; Yoon, 1997). For example, children's and seniors' greater susceptibility to advertising has been attributed, respectively, to their inadequately developed and declining cognitive abilities (Moschis, 1992).

Age-related cognitive decline involves the deterioration of neural pathways to the brain, resulting in the older person having less attentional capacity (Wahl & Heyl, 2003). When processing information, it has been postulated that the older brain needs to recruit both hemispheres to a greater extent than younger brains, which can result in longer processing times (Li, 2002). This makes cognitive processing more challenging, especially in the case of unfamiliar stimuli (e.g., new product information). Two outcomes of cognitive deterioration are that older people are less likely than younger people to change their beliefs in the face of new, contradictory information (Rice & Okun, 1994), and they can experience greater difficulty recalling the source of new information (Yoon et al., 2005). In addition, older people have been found to allocate more attention to the affective aspects of a message than the factual elements, whereas younger people are more likely to attend to both equally (Carstensen & Turk-Charles, 1994). This can be problematic, as a bias toward affect reduces the accuracy of information recall (Hashtroudi, Johnson, Vnek, & Ferguson, 1994). These cognition-related outcomes have the potential to make older consumers more vulnerable in the marketplace. For example, older people are more likely than younger people to recall negative product information (e.g., defect warnings) as positive, most likely because the increased familiarity resulting from repeated exposure overrides the actual content of the message (Skurnik, Yoon, Park, & Schwarz, 2005).

However, as is the case with physical deterioration, debilitating cognitive decline is neither inevitable nor uniform across individuals. There is even intraindividual variation, with factors such as time of day contributing to cognitive processing ability; Yoon, Lee, and Danziger (2007) found that seniors typically perform better on cognitive tasks in the morning. Aging is not the only trigger for cognitive decline; other factors such as education level, social isolation, lack of motivation or confidence, and alcohol and medication usage are also significant contributors (Schroll, 2005; WHO, 2002).

The components of the cognitive system relating to knowledge and crystallized abilities are derived from environmental experience and, as such, are believed to be immune to deterioration associated with programmed biological aging (Perlmutter, 1988). Instead, they can adapt to the environment, such as when a person experiences some deterioration in a component skill but learns new skills to maintain the same level of performance (Perlmutter, 1988; Salthouse, 1991). Recent consumer research suggests that the declining ability to process information from television commercials may result in older consumers engaging in more frequent stimulus generalization processes when assessing new products, such as by using brand name, price, or type of outlet to judge expected performance (Walsh & Mitchell, 2005).

It seems that certain components of the cognitive system can improve or emerge with age as a result of internal experience with the system's own activity. The idea that cognition becomes the object of itself reflects the view of some developmental psychologists and sociologists, such as Piaget's (1983) reflective abstraction and Flavell's (1977) metacognition. In the context of the older person, skills underlying an activity that is especially well mastered are expected to show continuous improvement with age and be quantitatively larger than a novice's, regardless of age (Baltes, Dittman-Kohl, & Dixon, 1986). Some consumer studies have provided support for the notion that cognitive processes can be improved over time. For example, Gaeth and Heath (1987) found that training in later life can decrease older adults' susceptibility to misleading advertising, while Cole and Gaeth (1990) showed that older people can improve their ability to use complex decision rules.

Variations in the rate of psychological aging may account for the discrepancies that have been identified between cognitive age and chronological age. Cognitive, or psychological, age is the term given to how old one feels, as compared to how old one is in years, which is their chronological age (see Stephens, 1991). Consumers' cognitive age influences how they react to the depiction of seniors in the media. For example, some older people have been found to be concerned about a lack of representation of seniors in advertisements, and some self-identify with younger models and sources and are alienated by images of people their own chronological age, while others do not have a strong preference either way (Greco & Swayne, 1992; Johnson, 1996; Long, 1998). In general, however, it seems that the stigma attached to aging in Western societies exerts a downward pressure on cognitive age, which can prevent seniors from adopting goods and services designed specifically for them (Russell & Kendig, 1999).

*Social Aging*

Social aging relates to the quantity and quality of individuals' relationships and the various life roles they enact. Social capital accumulated over the life span is very important to the older person, as it acts as a reserve that can provide a buffer against the negative consequences of physical and psychological aging (Grundy, 2006). Some of the social roles adopted in later life relate to an individual's situation and preferences (e.g., volunteering at a local museum), whereas others are directly associated with older age (e.g., the roles of retiree and grandparent). As they assume new roles and responsibilities, individuals develop new knowledge, consumer skills, and needs for products suitable for those roles (Mathur, Moschis, & Lee 2008).

Productive roles, such as being a paid or volunteer worker or caregiver, are particularly important to a person's well-being (Hinterlong, Morrow-Howell, & Rozario, 2007). Greater engagement in the activities associated with productive roles has been associated with higher levels of life satisfaction and happiness (Baker, Cahalin, Gerst, & Burr, 2005). Older people who frequently volunteer tend to have higher levels of perceived health (Van Willigen, 2000), less functional impairment (Hinterlong et al., 2007), and lower mortality (Harris & Thoresen, 2005). Although reverse causality cannot be ruled out, there appears to be a dose–response relationship, whereby higher levels of volunteering yield more positive outcomes (Morrow-Howell, Hinterlong, Rozario, & Tang, 2003). There are two primary mechanisms for the positive association between the assumption and enactment of nonobligatory roles and various health indicators. First, people with a larger number of roles are more likely to be exposed to social contacts that can serve as sources of information for better health (Frytak, Hartley, & Finch, 2003). Second, people with multiple roles may have more social support groups that can assist them in overcoming physical and emotional challenges (Moschis & Mathur, 2007).

While taking on new roles can be invigorating, involuntary role changes in later life, such as those relating to the loss of a spouse, can be detrimental to an older person's well-being. Shrinking social networks increase the likelihood of experiencing loneliness (Bondevik & Skogstad, 1998; Kim, 1999), which is one of the main mental health problems suffered by older people (Riddick & Keller, 1992). Reflecting their greater longevity, older women tend to suffer more from loneliness than do older men (Savikko, Routasalo, Tilvis, Strandberg, & Pitkala, 2005). On a positive note, technological advances such as the Internet are allowing older people with physical limitations to remain socially connected (Williamson & Shaffer, 2007). Although take-up rates have been slower among older people, seniors constitute a rapidly growing segment of Internet users who primarily use it to keep in contact with others, stay informed of current events, and obtain health-related information (Reisenwitz, Iyer, Kuhlmeier, & Eastman, 2007).

## Successful Aging

As noted above, aging occurs across the entire life span, and decisions made earlier in life can be critical in determining aging outcomes in later life (WHO, 2002). The concept of successful aging, also known as active, positive, or optimal aging, has been developed to bring into focus the factors that contribute to positive physical, mental, and social outcomes (Jorm et al., 1997; Vaillant & Mukamal, 2001; von Faber et al., 2001). Some aspects of aging are not within the individual's control due to the role of genetics, but many can be modified by decisions made and behaviors enacted. Examples of specific behaviors within the individual's control that have been associated with successful aging include being a nonsmoker and engaging in regular physical activity (Colombe & Kramer, 2003; Jorm et al., 1997; Vaillant & Mukamal, 2001).

In their review of the literature on this topic, Brown, Allen, Dwozan, Mercer, and Warren (2004) listed the following as primary contributors to successful aging: cognitive efficiency and self-mastery, adaptable values, ability to use compensatory strategies, ability to establish and maintain harmonious relationships, being productive, feeling engaged with life, and enjoying good physical health. Older people who do not demonstrate at least some of these attributes are unlikely to possess the reserves necessary to cope with life's challenges and are therefore less likely to age successfully (Grundy, 2006). This outcome tends to be most common among those who suffer financial disadvantage and have low levels of education (Schroll, 2005). Unfortunately, we lack adequate knowledge about how to ensure individuals acquire these attributes across the life span and retain them in their later years. We also lack an understanding of how successful aging is currently defined in different cultures, especially in the developing world.

## Aging and Consumption

The aging process has implications for consumption behaviors in later life. The physical, psychological, and social aspects of aging can influence the types of products favored, product utilization behaviors, customer service preferences, and how product information is sought and processed. However, before outlining how seniors are different, it is worth noting that their product-related attitudes and behaviors have often been found to be very similar to those of younger cohorts (Fisher, Johnson, Marchand, Smeeding, & Torrey, 2007; Simcock, Sudbury, & Wright, 2006; Uncles & Ehrenberg, 1990). For example, consumers of all ages tend to prioritize functionality, value for money, convenience, and customer service, and leading brands within product categories tend to be popular among all age groups, not just those of a certain age cohort (Uncles & Lee, 2006). In addition, the many variations in manifestation of the physical, psychological, and social aspects of aging mean that older consumers constitute a highly heterogeneous group (Moschis, Lee, & Mathur, 1997). Past research has identified numerous age and lifestyle subsegments within the senior segment (Goodwin & McElwee, 1999; Oates, Shufeldt, & Vaught, 1996), suggesting that variation within the group may be as substantial as variation between older and younger consumers.

However, in general, older consumers have been found to exhibit somewhat higher levels of customer loyalty (Lambert-Pandraud, Laurent, & Lapersonne, 2005; Patterson, 2007) and more limited brand repertoires (Uncles & Ehrenberg, 1990) than younger consumers. Older consumers can also be more concerned about store reputation than the specific brands stocked by a store (Lumpkin, 1985). Possibly as a result of their greater experience as consumers, seniors have been found to have higher quality expectations (Moschis & Mathur, 1993) and lower price sensitivity (Moschis & Mathur, 2007; Tongren, 1988), and they can be more concerned than younger consumers about the risks associated with a purchase (Simcock et al., 2006). Reflecting their greater reliance on affective processing, older consumers can have a heightened appreciation for emotional appeals in advertising (Williams & Drolet, 2005; Yoon et al., 2005), especially those featuring nostalgia (Gruca & Schewe, 1992).

Customer service is particularly important to older consumers, possibly as a consequence of their shrinking social networks and increasing dependence on shopping for social interaction (Kim, Kang, & Kim, 2005). Some researchers have expressed concern that a dependence on shopping for social interaction can make the elderly more vulnerable to suboptimal or unethical marketing practices (Lee & Geistfeld, 1999; Lee & Soberon-Ferrer, 1997). However, seniors are also considered to be generally more skeptical of marketing efforts and have a better appreciation of the persuasion tactics often used by salespeople (Kirmani & Campbell, 2004).

There has been a tendency in consumer studies to focus on seniors' vulnerability, primarily in terms of the psychological resource deficit and social dependency models noted earlier. However, there is a growing appreciation of the positive aspects of aging and the role of consumption in producing life satisfaction (e.g., Price, Arnould, & Curasi, 2000). Consumers in their postretirement phase continue to transform their identities and lifestyles, and their consumption decisions are an important part of this process. Schau, Gilly, and Wolfinbarger's (2009) exploration of consumption behaviors after retirement identified two primary forms of identity work: the revival or continuation of identities held earlier in life, such as when a retiree volunteers in a role similar to that held as a paid employee, and the launching of new identities, such as taking up a new sport. Through their revitalized or emergent life projects, Schau et al.'s retirees demonstrated a desire to remain active and take advantage of new opportunities to use consumption as a means of fulfillment and personal evolution. This finding is in line with Gilleard, Higgs, Hyde, Wiggins, and Blane's (2005) proposition that while the working years have a strong production orientation, retirement presents the opportunity to focus on consumption. Their research found that levels of postretirement consumption are associated with the occupational category of the individual immediately prior to retirement as well as the particular birth cohort to which the individual belonged. They argue that age per se is relatively insignificant in determining consumption patterns, because economic considerations, as reflected in preretirement occupation, and extent of consumer socialization, as reflected in birth cohort, are much more important predictors of consumption behavior. For example, the tendency for baby boomers to be more materialistic than their parents has been attributed to their consumer socialization during more prosperous times and greater exposure to the mass media (Moschis & Mathur, 2007).

## RESEARCH GAPS

Corresponding with the view of aging as a negative force that has costly implications for individuals and society, much previous research has focused on ways to enhance older people's productive capacity to reduce the burden they place on society. Although this focus may be beneficial to older individuals, because maintaining physical, psychological, and social engagement can impede age-related decline, greater attention also needs to be given to seniors' consumption behaviors to better understand how they can enhance quality of life. A critical mass of knowledge is being developed on older consumers within the disciplines of marketing and consumer behavior, but much remains to be done to bring our understanding of the consumption motivations and behaviors of this group closer to the knowledge levels that have been achieved for younger age groups. In particular, relatively little research has examined seniors' consumption behaviors other than those pertaining to health-related goods and services. There is a need for work across a wider range of consumption contexts. Possible future areas of research focus that have the potential to be transformational for seniors are described below under the categories of marketing strategy, consumer education, and public policy.

### Marketing Strategy

Almost all aspects of seniors' consumer behavior would benefit from increased research attention to compensate for past neglect of this group. As it would not be possible to outline all areas of relevance to marketing strategy, this section focuses on a few issues that have the potential to improve our understanding in ways that are both meaningful to marketers and beneficial to consumers. In the first instance, the burgeoning size of the senior market brings a need to predict future demand patterns across and within industries. Extrapolation of existing demand levels according to segment growth forecasts is unlikely to be sufficient due to the different characteristics of past, present, and future senior cohorts that are likely to result in varying consumption behaviors. We do not yet know, for instance, how higher levels of education and income and greater expectations relating to quality of life among future seniors will play out in terms of their demand for specific goods and services (Brown et al., 2004). Will complaint rates among seniors increase in future cohorts as a result of their different consumer socialization experiences? How will delayed retirement and moves toward more gradual departures from the workplace influence seniors' consumption levels at the individual and aggregate levels? How will seniors of the future cope with their caregiving responsibilities, and will their coping strategies translate into stronger or weaker demand for specific goods and services (e.g., meal delivery services, high-care residential facilities, online health information services)? How will they feel about using assistive devices, and what are the implications for the design and promotion of such devices?

The trend toward increasing age segregation in developed nations has important implications for consumption patterns and, as such, needs to be monitored and analyzed for strategic potential. Other macroenvironmental factors may either strengthen or weaken this trend over time. A shrinking workforce may increase pressures on mothers to return to work and result in more grandparents acting as child caregivers, a situation that may encourage multigenerational living arrangements. Alternatively, the provision of health services to a growing number of seniors may be better facilitated through further age segregation in living quarters. The outcome of these competing forces is important to marketers, because households of different sizes exhibit varying consumption patterns across a wide range of product categories (Wilkes, 1995). In developing nations, there is a closer integration of elders within the extended family due to the utility of this family structure where Social Security is nonexistent and caregiving services, whether they be for children or the elderly, are not readily available outside of the family unit (Neysmith & Edwardh, 1984). However, the global aging phenomenon is placing strain on traditional family structures in these countries, and there are concerns that they will become unsustainable in the future (Cameron & Cobb-Clark, 2008; Lunenfeld, 2008).

Relatedly, future research could examine how seniors' consumption varies according to their level of integration, both physical and emotional, with the extended family. Explorations of family relationships and associated consumption behaviors have illustrated the complex nature of the roles older people can play within the extended family (Curasi, Price, & Arnould, 2004; Price et al., 2000). Changing demographic structures are likely to impact these relationships, altering current patterns of interaction and consumption enactments. For example, declining birth rates are resulting in a substantial reduction in the number of grandchildren a person is likely to have, possibly manifesting in more intense relationships between grandparents and their fewer grandchildren. Gifting rituals between grandparents and their grandchildren and caregiving practices between elderly parents and their adult children, who have fewer of their own children to care for, may alter accordingly. Such trends will be of particular interest to those in the toy and eldercare industries, respectively.

Research should also investigate the most effective means of informing consumers of the consumption options available to them that can assist in attenuating the negative effects of aging and enhance any transformative benefits. Ambivalent consumer responses to assistive devices and the below-average usage rates of information technology among older people have suggested that there are knowledge barriers relating to the possible benefits of these items and/or psychosocial barriers relating to their adoption. A deeper understanding of these barriers is needed to develop appropriate strategies to increase take-up rates where this would improve seniors' quality of life. For example, marketers of hearing aids may find they can improve sales by designing their products so that they more closely resemble the earphones that are now commonly worn by consumers of all ages. It may also be possible to emphasize product attributes that are desirable to a wider cross section of consumers, such as if the device has the ability to not only restore lost hearing but also provide the wearer with access to a broader sound spectrum than can be registered by the normal ear. Positioning the product as beneficial to all consumers because of its technological advancement may encourage adoption by reducing age-related stigma. In light of Schau et al.'s (2009) findings related to postretirement identity work, further research could be directed at explicating the role of consumption activities in facilitating seniors' efforts to create or revive meaningful identities that provide them with an enhanced sense of purpose and well-being. A detailed understanding of the roles played by specific products in identity formation and maintenance would assist marketers in positioning these products appropriately and facilitating their adoption in ways that can benefit older consumers.

Lastly, recent work on cognitive processing provides promising avenues for future research. With the increasing use of neuroimaging methods of data collection in marketing (e.g., Hedgcock

& Rao, 2009; Litt, Perouz, & Shiv, Chapter 25 of this volume; Yoon, Gutchess, Feinberg, & Polk, 2006), there is the potential to better understand the differences in decision-making processes between age groups and the outcomes of these differences. This information can inform marketing strategies designed to, for instance, enhance seniors' decision making at the point of sale, where they are more susceptible to processing limitations resulting from time pressure (Yoon et al., 2009). In addition, the varying time horizon perspectives that were found by Williams and Drolet (2005) to influence older consumers' reactions to advertising appeals could be applied to other aspects of consumption to explore their wider relevance to seniors. The relationships between attitudes, intentions, and behaviors, for instance, may vary according to the time horizon adopted.

### Consumer Education

Most of the factors listed earlier as contributing to successful aging are amenable to change, especially if efforts to do so commence early in life. As such, there is a growing appreciation of the need to encourage individuals to take appropriate actions across the life span to increase the likelihood of aging well (Rowe & Kahn, 1998; Schroll, 2005; WHO, 2002). From a Transformative Consumer Research perspective, the challenge is thus to encourage people at every stage of life to modify their consumption habits to those aligned with successful aging. A basic premise for such a lifelong prevention strategy is that people are willing to make behavioral changes in the present for a future payoff. Unfortunately, trade-offs between the present and the future are difficult, and consumers have been found to frequently discount future benefits relative to outcomes in the present (Hoch & Loewenstein, 1991). Social marketers and those working in the health sciences have long struggled to identify effective means of convincing individuals to take preventive actions to optimize their future well-being. As indicated by the health belief model (Rosenstock, 1966), motivating preventive action requires individuals to be knowledgeable about (a) the likelihood of experiencing age-related decline if recommended behaviors are not adopted, and (b) the resulting consequences for their future quality of life. Much work is required to identify effective ways to sensitize consumers to their ability to influence the aging process, educate them about how to achieve this goal, and motivate them to take appropriate preventive actions. This will involve convincing them of both the short- and long-term benefits of such actions to provide adequate impetus for behavioral change in the present (Hastings, 2003).

A related area of research focus is the relative effectiveness of various communication methods in triggering consumers' transformation from being passive and accepting of the traditional aging process to being more active planners of their future welfare. For example, how effective is consumer education in the form of public-service announcements versus inclusion of information in school curricula or information seminars delivered in workplaces and retirement villages? At what age should consumer education on the subject of aging commence, and which aspects of successful aging should be prioritized over others? Who should take responsibility for managing this education process? Further research to add to our growing understanding of the effects of emotional versus factual approaches in information provision could assist in ensuring that information delivered at different life stages is assimilated effectively. Similarly, more attention could be given to the differing health-related motivations of older and younger consumers and how these translate into different propensities to attend to health-related messages (Moorman & Matulich, 1993).

The stress associated with transition into new roles can interfere with optimal decision making and increase the older person's dependency on external sources for guidance and information (Moschis, 1992). Research could address whether, how, and why stress interferes with sound judgment in later life and the possible resources or skills that could help combat vulnerability. In addition, future research could examine the extent to which less socially integrated older persons are susceptible to potentially misleading marketing communications and how this vulnerability can be reduced. In a similar vein, the prevention and alleviation of unwanted social isolation is an important future research focus (Kendig, Andrews, Browning, Quine, & Parsons, 2000). Little work relating to loneliness appears in the consumer behavior literature, but this is a promising area due to the potential of various consumption behaviors to alleviate this condition (Pettigrew, 2007). Finally, other possible areas of research relating to consumer education could involve identifying the most effective means of (a) encouraging the development of hobbies and interests that are mentally challenging and immune to physical aging; (b) discouraging negative consumption activities, such as smoking and excessive alcohol consumption; and (c) instilling knowledge and skills relating to fraudulent business practices and complaint processes.

## Public Policy

In line with models of resiliency that highlight the importance of both individual and macrolevel factors (see Baker & Mason, Chapter 26 of this volume; Maddi, Chapter 31 of this volume), the WHO (2002) has emphasized the importance of engendering supportive environments that orient individuals throughout their lives toward making choices that will enhance their later years. Governments have an important role to play in creating such environments through the enactment of appropriate policies. To facilitate successful aging at the population level, policy needs to address macrofactors such as economic security, equitable and efficient health systems, and civic participation (Brown et al., 2004; Venne, 2005). There is also the need to facilitate age-friendly societies that feature universal design in all aspects of life, including health care systems, transport systems, and neighborhood environments (e.g., pavement, street lighting; WHO, 2002). Age-friendly societies make good use of new technologies to enhance individuals' lives (Heinisch, 2004; Schroll, 2005) and actively work against age discrimination in all its guises (WHO, 2002). Examples of the latter include setting marketplace standards and establishing expectations for the proper treatment of older consumers.

Achieving these goals will require focused research to explicate the barriers and facilitators to creating "a society for all ages" (United Nations, 2002, p. 1). With its emphasis on understanding individuals' thoughts, feelings, and behaviors, consumer behavior as a discipline has much to offer public policy makers in this regard. With its explicit focus on consumer welfare, Transformative Consumer Research is especially relevant because of its objective of empowering individuals and societies to optimize well-being (Mick, 2006; Mick, Pettigrew, Pechmann, & Ozanne, Chapter 1 of this volume). Formative research that explores older consumers' needs and preferences can ensure new systems and services are truly senior friendly and identify appropriate means of communicating with target audiences about changes in policies and programs as they occur. For example, at the program level, it is important for administrators to understand any differences in the aging experience between urban and rural dwellers and those of varying ethnic backgrounds to ensure that government-funded services offered in different locations are appropriate (Walker, Cook, & Traynor, 2004). In addition, policy makers need to appreciate seniors' important roles as caregivers for both other older people and younger generations (Brown et al., 2004; WHO, 1999), as these responsibilities influence seniors' mental states and physical health.

## RESEARCH METHODS

Consumer research over the life course has been predominantly cross sectional, focusing on the behavior of different age groups and describing the observed differences that exist across age categories, rather than explaining how and why changes in consumer behavior occur throughout life. Many of the research tasks discussed above will require methods that take a long-term perspective by examining behaviors in relation to earlier life stages within historical and cultural contexts.

Some traditional data collection methods, such as interviews and surveys, could partially address this need with some modification to overcome age-related limitations, such as using mail rather than phone surveys to allow respondents to self-pace their responses and applying generous font sizes to all written materials (Gruca & Schewe, 1992). These methods may also need to be modified to take into account societal perceptions of aging and how these may constrain interviewees' readiness to discuss the subject frankly. Matching interviewer and interviewee characteristics, personal disclosure on behalf of the interviewer, multiple interviews with the same interviewees, careful consideration of interview locations, and demonstration of a genuine interest in interviewees' welfare may assist in generating the level of rapport required for the extensive sharing of feelings and experiences (Reinharz, 1992; Smith 1999).

Other approaches that have been used less frequently in marketing and consumer behavior also have the potential to offer additional insights into the many and varied factors associated with successful aging. In particular, methods conducive to the collection of rich, detailed data relating to the complex interrelationships between individuals and their sociocultural and situational contexts are needed (Ozanne & Fischer, Chapter 4 of this volume; Settersten & Mayer, 1997; Wansink, Chapter 3 of this volume; Yoon et al., 2009). Methods such as memory work (Onyx & Small, 2001) and life history (Dhunpath, 2000) have the capacity to provide detailed life course data to allow identification of experiences in earlier life stages that affect patterns of consumer behavior and well-being in later life. In addition, participatory action research (Ozanne & Saatcioglu, 2008) may assist in generating possible solutions to common problems experienced by older consumers. For example, peer discussions on issues such as financial restriction, loneliness, and health information may lead to recommendations relating to new forms of cohousing or the establishment of neighborhood health circles. These kinds of methods take advantage of many older people's desire to contribute to the world's stock of wisdom and their enjoyment of storytelling (Cohen, 2001).

Within life course research, there has been the development of statistical models for analyzing discrete state, continuous time stochastic processes using probability theory, which are collectively known as event history analysis. Most event history analysis models are defined by expressing the hazard rate of an event, or transition rate when a shift to one of several states is possible, as a specific function of a relevant time dimension (e.g., duration, age), measured covariates, and unmeasured random disturbances (Mayer & Tuma, 1990). Event history analysis enables researchers to incorporate variables into their models that are derived from different levels of aggregation, such as historical eras, market conditions, social structures, and group and individual characteristics (Helsen & Schmittlein, 1993; Mortimer & Shanahan, 2003).

When researching older consumers, other key methodological considerations include researcher characteristics and internationalizing the research process. The heightened social interaction needs of many older people, and particularly their desire for meaningful interaction with others their own age, points to the benefits of employing seniors to perform data collection tasks. This can reduce any social barriers while ensuring inclusion of end users in the research process (European Research Area in Ageing, 2008). Collaborating with researchers in other countries can facilitate comparison of data to provide insights into alternative ways of achieving successful aging at both individual and population levels. It is especially important to work with researchers in developing nations whenever possible to facilitate the transfer of knowledge to assist these countries in coping with the challenges of population aging in the context of limited resources.

## CONCLUSION

Population aging constitutes an opportunity for consumer researchers to inform marketing strategy, consumer education initiatives, and public policy to assist consumers age successfully.

Using a transformative lens, we can make an important contribution by focusing on the delay or prevention of the negative aspects of aging and the optimization of the positive aspects. Novice and experienced researchers alike have much to gain from studying the aging process and its consumption implications—if not for the challenge of understanding such complex phenomena, then for our own future quality of life.

## ACKNOWLEDGMENTS

We thank our insightful reviewers: Carolyn Yoon, Anil Mathur, and Helen Christensen.

## REFERENCES

Access Economics Pty Ltd. (2001). *Population ageing and the economy*. Canberra, Australia: Commonwealth Department of Health and Aged Care.

Acemoglu, D., & Johnson, S. (2007). Disease and development: The effect of life expectancy on economic growth. *Journal of Political Economy, 115*(6), 925–985.

Agrawal, Y., Platz, E. A., & Niparko, J. K. (2008). Prevalence of hearing loss and differences by demographic characteristic among US adults: Data from the national health and nutrition examination survey, 1999–2004. *Archives of Internal Medicine, 168*(14), 1522–1530.

Baker, L. A., Cahalin, L. P., Gerst, K., & Burr, J. A. (2005). Productive activities and subjective well-being among older adults: The influence of number of activities and time commitment. *Social Indicators Research, 73*, 431–458.

Baltes, P. B., Dittman-Kohl, F., & Dixon, R. A. (1986). Multidisciplinary propositions on the development of intelligence during adulthood and old age. In A. B. Sorensen, G. E. Weinert, & L. R. Sherrod (Eds.), *Human development and the life course* (pp. 467–507). Hillsdale, NJ: Erlbaum.

Binstock, R. H. (2000). Older people and voting participation: Past and future. *Gerontologist, 40*(1), 18–31.

Blake, D., & Mayhew, L. (2006). On the sustainability of the UK state pension system in the light of population ageing and declining fertility. *Economic Journal, 116*, F286–F305.

Bondevik, M., & Skogstad, A. (1998). The oldest old, ADL, social network, and loneliness. *Western Journal of Nursing Research, 20*(3), 325–343.

Bonoli, G., & Palier, B. (2007). When past reforms open new opportunities: Comparing old-age insurance reforms in Bismarckian welfare systems. *Social Policy & Administration, 41*(6), 555–573.

Braus, P. (1995). Vision in an ageing America. *American Demographics, 17*(6), 34–38.

Brown, V. M., Allen, A. C., Dwozan, M., Mercer, I., & Warren, K. (2004). Indoor gardening and older adults: Effects on socialization, activities of daily living, and loneliness. *Gerontological Nursing, 30*(10), 34–42.

Butler, R. N. (1989). Dispelling ageism: The cross-cutting intervention. *Annals of the American Academy of Political and Social Science, 503*, 138–147.

Cameron, L. A., & Cobb-Clark, D. (2008). Do coresidency and financial transfers from the children reduce the need for elderly parents to work in developing countries? *Journal of Population Economics, 21*, 1007–1033.

Carmeli, E., Patish, H., & Coleman, R. (2003). The aging hand. *Journal of Gerontology, 58A*(2), 146–152.

Carstensen, L. L., & Turk-Charles, S. (1994). The salience of emotion across the adult life span. *Psychology and Aging, 9*(2), 259–264.

Cohen, G. D. (2001). Creativity with ageing: Four phases of potential in the second half of life. *Geriatrics, 56*(4), 51–57.

Cole, C. A., & Gaeth, G. J. (1990). Cognitive and age-related differences in the ability to use nutritional information in a complex environment. *Journal of Marketing Research, 27*(2), 175–184.

Cole, C. A., & Houston, M. J. (1987). Encoding and media effects on consumer learning deficiencies in the elderly. *Journal of Marketing Research, 24*, 55–63.

Colombe, S., & Kramer, A. F. (2003). Fitness effects on the cognitive function of older adults: A meta-analytic study. *Psychological Science 14*, 125–130.

Curasi, C. F., Price, L. L., & Arnould, E. J. (2004). How individuals' cherished possessions become families' inalienable wealth. *Journal of Consumer Research, 31*, 609–622.

Day, H., Jutai, J., & Campbell, K. A. (2002). Development of a scale to measure the psychosocial impact of assistive devices: Lessons learned and the road ahead. *Disability & Rehabilitation, 24*, 31–37.

Dhunpath, R. (2000). Life history methodology: "Narradigm" regained. *Qualitative Studies in Education, 13*(5), 543–551.

Easterlin, R. A. (1999). How beneficial is the market? A look at the modern history of mortality. *European Review of Economic History, 3,* 257–294.

Erlinghagen, M., & Hank, K. (2006). The participation of older Europeans in volunteer work. *Ageing & Society, 26,* 567–584.

European Research Area in Ageing. (2008). *Executive summaries of recommendations taken from ERA-AGE forum meeting and ERA-AGE scientific workshop reports.* Sheffield, England: Author.

Fisher, J. D., Johnson, D. S., Marchand, J. T., Smeeding, T. M., & Torrey, B. B. (2007). No place like home: Older adults and their housing. *Journals of Gerontology, 62B*(2), S120–S128.

Flavell, J. H. (1977). Cognitive changes in adulthood. In L. Goulet & P. Baltes (Eds.), *Life-span developmental psychology: Research and theory* (pp. 248–253). New York: Academic Press.

Freidrich, M. J. (2001). Women, exercise, and aging: Strong message for the "weaker" sex. *Journal of the American Medical Association, 285*(11), 1429–1431.

Frytak, J. R., Hartley, C. R., & Finch, M. D. (2003). Socioeconomic states and health over life course. In J. T. Mortimer & M. J. Shanahan (Eds.), *Handbook of the life course* (pp. 623–643). New York: Kluwer Academic/Plenum.

Gaeth, G. J., & Heath, T. B. (1987). The cognitive processing of misleading advertising in young and old adults: Assessment and training. *Journal of Consumer Research, 14,* 43–54.

Gilleard, C., Higgs, P., Hyde, M., Wiggins, R., & Blane, D. (2005). Class, cohort, and consumption: The British experience of the third age. *Journals of Gerontology, 60B*(6), S305–S310.

Goodwin, D. R., & McElwee, R. E. (1999). Grocery shopping and an ageing population: Research note. *International Review of Retail, Distribution and Consumer Research, 9*(4), 403–409.

Greco, A. J., & Swayne, L. E. (1992). Sales response of elderly consumers to point-of-purchase advertising. *Journal of Advertising Research, 32*(5), 43–53.

Gruca, T. S., & Schewe, C. D. (1992). Researching older consumers. *Marketing Research, 4*(3), 18–26.

Grundy, E. (2006). Ageing and vulnerable elderly people: European perspectives. *Ageing & Society, 26,* 105–134.

Hagestad, G. O., & Uhlenberg, P. (2006). Should we be concerned about age segregation? Some theoretical and empirical explorations. *Research on Aging, 28,* 638–653.

Hansen, T., Slagsvold, B., & Moum, T. (2008). Financial satisfaction in old age: A satisfaction paradox or a result of accumulated wealth? *Social Indicators Research, 89*(2), 323–347.

Harris, A. H. S., & Thoresen, C. E. (2005). Volunteering is associated with delayed mortality in older people: Analysis of the longitudinal study of aging. *Journal of Health Psychology, 10,* 739–752.

Hashtroudi, S., Johnson, M. K., Vnek, N., & Ferguson, S. A. (1994). Aging and the effects of affective and factual focus on source monitoring and recall. *Psychology and Aging, 9*(1), 160–170.

Hastings, G. (2003). Competition in social marketing. *Social Marketing Quarterly, 9*(3), 6–10.

Hedgcock, W., & Rao, A. R. (2009). Trade-off aversion as an explanation for the attraction effect: A functional magnetic resonance imaging study. *Journal of Marketing Research, 46*(1), 1–13.

Heinisch, M. (2004). *Towards the seventh framework programme for research: Research needs in the area of demographic change: Quality of life of elderly persons and technological requirements.* Brussels, Belgium: European Economic and Social Committee.

Helsen, K., & Schmittlein, D. (1993). Analyzing duration times in marketing: Evidence of effectiveness of hazard models. *Marketing Science, 1*(4), 395–414.

Hinterlong, J. E., Morrow-Howell, N., & Rozario, P. A. (2007). Productive engagement and late life physical and mental health: Findings from a nationally representative panel study. *Research on Aging, 29,* 348–370.

Hoch, S. J., & Loewenstein, G. F. (1991). Time-inconsistent preferences and consumer self-control. *Journal of Consumer Research, 17*(4), 492–507.

Horowitz, A. (2003). Depression and vision and hearing impairments in later life. *Generations, 27*(1), 32–38.

Johnson, E. B. (1996). Cognitive age: Understanding consumer alienation in the mature market. *Review of Business, 1*(3), 35–40.

Jorm, A. F., Christensen, H., Henderson, A. S., Jacomb, P. A., Korten, A. E., & Mackinnon, A. (1997). Factors associated with successful ageing. *Australasian Journal on Ageing, 17*(1), 33–37.

Kendig, H. L., Andrews, G., Browning, C., Quine, S., & Parsons, A. (2000). *A review of healthy ageing research in Australia.* Canberra, Australia: Department of Health and Aged Care.

Kim, O. (1999). Predictors of loneliness in elderly Korean immigrant women living in the United States of America. *Journal of Advanced Nursing, 29*(5), 1082–1088.

Kim, Y., Kang, J., & Kim, M. (2005). The relationships among family and social interaction, loneliness, mall shopping motivation, and mall spending of older consumers. *Psychology & Marketing, 22*(12), 995–1015.

Kirmani, A., & Campbell, M. C. (2004). Goal seeker and persuasion sentry: How consumer targets respond to interpersonal marketing persuasion. *Journal of Consumer Research, 31*, 573–582.

Krantz-Kent, R., & Stewart, J. (2007). How do older Americans spend their time? *Monthly Labor Review, 130*(5), 8–26.

Lambert-Pandraud, R., Laurent, G., & Lapersonne, E. (2005). Repeat purchasing of new automobiles by older consumers: Empirical evidence and interpretations. *Journal of Marketing, 69*, 97–113.

Lee, J., & Geistfeld, L. V. (1999). Elderly consumers' receptiveness to telemarketing fraud. *Journal of Public Policy & Marketing, 18*(2), 208–217.

Lee, J., & Soberon-Ferrer, H. (1997). Consumer vulnerability to fraud: Influencing factors. *Journal of Consumer Affairs, 31*, 70–90.

Leventhal, E. (2007). Ageing and health. In S. Ayers, A. Baum, C. McManus, S. Newman, K. Wallston, J. Weinman, et al. (Eds.), *Cambridge handbook of psychology, health and medicine* (2nd ed., pp. 20–22). New York: Cambridge University Press.

Li, S. (2002). Connecting the many levels and facets of cognitive aging. *Current Directions in Psychological Science, 11*(1), 38–43.

Long, N. (1998). Broken down by age and sex: Exploring the ways we approach the elderly consumer. *Journal of the Market Research Society, 40*(2), 73–91.

Lumpkin, J. R. (1985). Shopping orientation segmentation of the elderly consumer. *Journal of the Academy of Marketing Science, 13*(2), 271–289.

Lunenfeld, B. (2008). An aging world: Demographics and challenges. *Gynecological Endocrinology, 24*(1), 1–3.

Mathur, A., Moschis, G. P., & Lee, E. (2008). A longitudinal study of the effects of life status changes on changes in consumer preferences. *Journal of the Academy of Marketing Science, 36*(2), 234–246.

Mathurs, C., & Vos, T. (2000). The burden of disease and injury among older Australians. *Australasian Journal on Ageing, 19*(2), 54–56.

Matsuba, M. K., Hart, D., & Atkins, R. (2007). Psychological and social-structural influences on commitment to volunteering. *Journal of Research in Personality, 41*, 889–907.

Mayer, K. U., & Tuma, N. B. (1990). Life course research and event history analysis: An overview. In K. U. Mayer & N. B. Tuma (Eds.), *Event history analysis in life course research* (pp. 3–20). Madison: University of Wisconsin Press.

McCreadie, C., & Tinker, A. (2005). The acceptability of assistive technology to older people. *Ageing & Society, 25*(1), 91–110.

Mick, D. G. (2006). Meaning and mattering through transformative consumer research. In C. Pechmann & L. L. Price (Eds.), *Advances in consumer research* (Vol. 33, pp. 1–4). Duluth, MN: Association for Consumer Research.

Moorman, C., & Matulich, E. (1993). A model of consumers' preventive health behaviors: The role of health motivation and health ability. *Journal of Consumer Research, 20*, 208–228.

Morrow-Howell, N., Hinterlong, J., Rozario, P. A., & Tang, F. (2003). Effects of volunteering on the well-being of older adults. *Journals of Gerontology, 58B*(3), S137–S145.

Mortimer, J. T., & Shanahan, M. J. (Eds.). (2003). *Handbook of the life course.* New York: Plenum.

Moschis, G. P. (1992). *Marketing to older consumers.* Westport, CT: Quorum Books.

Moschis, G. P. (1996). *Gerontographics.* Westport, CT: Quorum Books.

Moschis, G. P., Lee, E., & Mathur, A. (1997). Targeting the mature market: Opportunities and challenges. *Journal of Consumer Marketing, 14*(4), 282–293.

Moschis, G. P., & Mathur, A. (1993). How they're acting their age. *Marketing Management, 2*(2), 40–50.

Moschis, G. P., & Mathur, A. (2007). *Baby boomers and their parents: Surprising findings about their lifestyles, mindsets, and well-being.* Ithaca, NY: Paramount Books.

Munnell, A. H., Buessing, M., Soto, M., & Sass, S. (2006). *Will we have to work forever?* Chestnut Hill, MA: Boston College, Center for Retirement Research.

Neysmith, S. M., & Edwardh, J. (1984). Economic dependency in the 1980s: Its impact on third world elderly. *Ageing & Society, 4*(1), 21–44.

Oates, B., Shufeldt, L., & Vaught, B. (1996). A psychographic study of the elderly and retail store attributes. *Journal of Consumer Marketing, 13*(6), 14–27.

Onyx, J., & Small, J. (2001). Memory-work: The method. *Qualitative Inquiry, 7*, 773–786.

Ozanne, J. L., & Saatcioglu, B. (2008). Participatory action research. *Journal of Consumer Research, 35*(3), 423–439.

Patterson, P. G. (2007). Demographic correlates of loyalty in a service context. *Journal of Services Marketing, 21*(2), 112–121.

Perlmutter, M. (1988). Cognitive potential throughout life. In J. E. Birren & V. L. Bengtson (Eds.), *Emergent theories of aging* (pp. 247–268). New York: Springer.

Pettigrew, S. (2007). Reducing the experience of loneliness among older consumers. *Journal of Research for Consumers*, issue 12. Available: http://www.jrconsumers.com/academic_articles/issue_12_2007

Piaget, J. (1983). Piaget's theory. In P. H. Mussen (Series Ed.) & W. Kesson (Vol. Ed.), *Handbook of child psychology. Vol. 1: History, theory, and methods* (4th ed., pp. 103–128). New York: Wiley.

Price, L. L., Arnould, E. J., & Curasi, C. F. (2000). Older consumers' disposition of special possessions. *Journal of Consumer Research, 27*(2), 179–201.

Reinharz, S. (with Davidman, L.). (1992). *Feminist methods in social research.* New York: Oxford University Press.

Reisenwitz, T., Iyer, R., Kuhlmeier, D. B., & Eastman, J. K. (2007). The elderly's Internet usage: An updated look. *Journal of Consumer Marketing, 24*(7), 406–418.

Rice, G. E., & Okun, M. A. (1994). Older readers' processing of medical information that contradicts their beliefs. *Journal of Gerontology, 49*(3), 119–128.

Riddick, C. C., & Keller, M. J. (1992). Efficacy of recreation on influencing the social psychological health of elders. *Parks & Recreation, 27*(3), 20–21, 23–24, 61.

Robine, J. (2005). *Human longevity research issues.* Sheffield, England: European Forum on Population Ageing Research, European Group on Quality of Life.

Rockstein, M., & Susman, M. (1979). *Biology of aging.* Belmont, CA: Wadsworth.

Rosenstock, I. M. (1966). Why people use health services. *Milbank Quarterly, 83*(4), 1–32.

Rowe, J. W., & Kahn, R. L. (1998). *Successful aging.* New York: Pantheon Books.

Russell, C., & Kendig, H. L. (1999). Social policy and research for older citizens. *Australasian Journal on Ageing, 18*(3), 44–49.

Salthouse, T. A. (1991). *Theoretical perspectives on cognitive aging.* Hillsdale, NJ: Erlbaum.

Savikko, N., Routasalo, P., Tilvis, R. S., Strandberg, T. E., & Pitkala, K. H. (2005). Predictors and subjective causes of loneliness in an aged population. *Aging & Mental Health, 41*, 223–233.

Schau, H. J., Gilly, M. C., & Wolfinbarger, M. (2009). Consumer identity renaissance: The resurgence of identity-inspired consumption in retirement. *Journal of Consumer Research, 36*, 255–276.

Schroll, M. (2005). *Health and social care management for older people.* Sheffield, England: European Forum on Population Ageing Research, European Group on Quality of Life.

Settersten, R. A., Jr., & Mayer, K. U. (1997). The measurement of age, age structuring, and the life course. *Annual Review of Sociology, 23*, 233–261.

Simcock, P., Sudbury, L., & Wright, G. (2006). Age, perceived risk and satisfaction in consumer decision making: A review and extension. *Journal of Marketing Management, 22*, 355–377.

Skurnik, I., Yoon, C., Park, D. C., & Schwarz, N. (2005). How warnings about false claims become recommendations. *Journal of Consumer Research, 31*, 713–724.

Smith, L. T. (1999). *Decolonizing methodologies: Research and indigenous peoples.* Dunedin, New Zealand: University of Otago Press.

Stephens, N. (1991). Cognitive age: A useful concept for advertising. *Journal of Advertising, 20*(4), 37–48.

Stone, R., Cafferata, G. L., & Sangl, J. (1987). Caregivers of the frail elderly: A national profile. *Gerontologist, 27*(5), 616–626.

Stuen, C., & Faye, E. E. (2003). Vision loss: Normal and not normal changes among older adults. *Generations, 27*(1), 8–14.

Tongren, H. N. (1988). Determinant behavior characteristics of older consumers. *Journal of Consumer Affairs, 22*(1), 136–157.

Uncles, M. D., & Ehrenberg, A. S. C. (1990). Brand choice among older consumers. *Journal of Advertising Research, 30*(4), 19–22.

Uncles, M. D., & Lee, D. (2006). Brand purchasing by older consumers: An investigation using the Juster scale and the Dirichlet model. *Marketing Letters, 17*, 17–29.

United Nations. (2002). *Population ageing: Facts and figures.* New York: Author. Available: http://www.un.org/swaa2002/

U.S. Census Bureau. (2009). *International data base* [Data file]. Washington, DC: Author. Available: http://www.census.gov/ipc/www/idb/region.php

Vaillant, G. E., & Mukamal, K. (2001). Successful aging. *American Journal of Psychiatry, 158*(6), 839–847.

Van Willigen, M. (2000). Differential benefits of volunteering across the life course. *Journals of Gerontology, 55B*(5), S308–S318.

Venne, R. (2005). *Mainstreaming the concerns of older persons into the social development agenda.* New York: United Nations. Available: http://www.un.org/esa/socdev/ageing/documents/mainstreaming/position paper.pdf

von Faber, M., Bootsma-van der Wiel, A., van Exel, E., Gussekloo, J., Lagaay, A. M., van Dongen, E., et al. (2001). Successful aging in the oldest old: Who can be characterized as successfully aged? *Archives of Internal Medicine, 161,* 2694–2700.

Wahl, H., & Heyl, V. (2003). Connections between vision, hearing, and cognitive function in old age. *Generations, 27*(1), 39–45.

Walker, A., Cook, J., & Traynor, P. (2004). *European research priorities in the field of ageing.* Sheffield, England: European Forum on Population Ageing Research, European Commission.

Walsh, G., & Mitchell, V. (2005). Consumer vulnerability to perceived product similarity problems: Scale development and identification. *Journal of Macromarketing, 25*(2), 140–152.

Wang, M., Wang, Y., & Su, Y. (2009). The actuarial model for implicit pension debt of China. *Modern Applied Science, 3*(7), 99–102.

Wilkes, R. E. (1995). Household life-cycle stages, transitions, and product expenditures. *Journal of Consumer Research, 22*(1), 27–42.

Williams, P., & Drolet, A. (2005). Age-related differences in responses to emotional advertisements. *Journal of Consumer Research, 32,* 343–354.

Williamson, G. M., & Shaffer, D. R. (2007). Age and physical functioning. In S. Ayers, A. Baum, C. McManus, S. Newman, K. Wallston, J. Weinman, et al. (Eds.), *Cambridge handbook of psychology, health and medicine* (2nd ed., pp. 10–14). New York: Cambridge University Press.

World Health Organization. (1999). *Ageing: Exploding the myths.* Geneva, Switzerland: Author. Available: http://www.who.int/docstore/world-health-day/en/pages1999/whd99_1.html

World Health Organization. (2000). *Social development and ageing: Crisis or opportunity?* Geneva, Switzerland: Author. Available: http://www.who.int/ageing/publications/development/alc_social_development.pdf

World Health Organization. (2002). *Active ageing: A policy framework.* Geneva, Switzerland: Author. Available: http://whqlibdoc.who.int/hq/2002/WHO_NMH_NPH_02.8.pdf

World Health Organization. (2007). *10 facts on ageing and the life course.* Geneva, Switzerland: Author. Available: http://www.who.int/features/factfiles/ageing/en/

World Health Organization. (2008). *World health statistics 2008.* Geneva, Switzerland: Author. Available: http://www.who.int/whosis/whostat/2008/en/index.html

World Health Organization. (2009). *World health statistics 2009.* World Geneva, Switzerland: Author. Available: http://www.who.int/whosis/whostat/2009/en/index.html

Yoon, C. (1997). Age differences in consumers' processing strategies: An investigation of moderating influences. *Journal of Consumer Research, 24*(3), 329–342.

Yoon, C., Cole, C. A., & Lee, M. P. (2009). Consumer decision making and aging: Current knowledge and future directions. *Journal of Consumer Psychology, 19,* 2–16.

Yoon, C., Gutchess, A., Feinberg, F., & Polk, T. A. (2006). A functional magnetic resonance imaging study of neural dissociations between brand and person judgments. *Journal of Consumer Research, 33,* 31–40.

Yoon, C., Laurent, G., Fung, H. H., Gonzales, R., Gutchess, A. H., Hedden, T., et al. (2005). Cognition, persuasion and decision making in older consumers. *Marketing Letters, 16*(3/4), 429–441.

Yoon, C., Lee, M. P., & Danziger, S. (2007). The effects of optimal time of day on persuasion processes in older adults. *Psychology & Marketing, 24*(5), 475–495.

# VIII

## FAMILY MATTERS

# 28

## Effective Parenting to Prevent Adverse Outcomes and Promote Child Well-Being at a Population Level

RONALD J. PRINZ

Parenting variables are implicated either directly or as exacerbating factors in a large variety of child and adolescent outcomes and societal problems, including but not limited to attention deficit hyperactivity disorder, childhood aggression and oppositional defiant disorder, conduct disorder and delinquency, low school readiness, school dropout, substance abuse, teen pregnancy, youth depression, and child maltreatment (Biglan, Brennan, Foster, & Holder, 2004; Collins, Maccoby, Steinberg, Hetherington, & Bornstein, 2000; Hawkins, Catalano, & Miller, 1992; Jones & Prinz, 2005; Patterson, 1982; Patterson, Reid, & Dishion, 1992). Several decades of research have produced an impressive collection of parenting and family-based interventions that can be readily applied to the promotion of positive child development and the prevention of adverse outcomes, such as mental health problems, substance abuse, academic failure, and delinquency. Much of the effort in evidence-supported parenting and family interventions has been grounded in a comprehensive array of parenting strategies and practices associated with beneficial child outcomes.

Efficacious parenting and family interventions have emerged for the prevention of a variety of target outcomes. Many of these interventions have several elements in common, although specific implementation varies with age group, application, and contextual factors. Despite the documented advantages and benefits of parenting and family interventions, however, the field is struggling with insufficient impact. In answer to this challenge, a newer paradigm is emerging in the parenting intervention field that emphasizes wide-scale dissemination and population impact.

The purpose of this chapter is to articulate a conceptual foundation for a population-based approach to parenting intervention aimed at preventing adverse outcomes in children and adolescents and broadly promoting children's health and well-being. In doing so, the hope is to provide new insights and guidance to scholars in Transformative Consumer Research who are interested in joining in and contributing to this vitally important area of social life. As a backdrop, the first part of the chapter describes basic assumptions about what constitutes many of the beneficial parenting strategies and practices that are central to most of the evidence-based parenting and family interventions in the field. This section is meant to be a distillation of key principles and not a substantive and methodological review of the many studies that have contributed to the body of knowledge. For the latter, the reader is referred to Benjet and Kazdin (2003); Bornstein (2008); Cowan and Hetherington (1991); Holden and Edwards (1989); Polster, Dangel, and Rasp (1987); and Taylor and Biglan (1998) as starting points.

The second part of the chapter identifies some of the more prominent parenting and family interventions in prevention. This discussion is meant to provide examples rather than be exhaustive. The last section of the chapter discusses several critical issues related to population-based prevention and parenting and family interventions, including common elements shared by most interventions, questions about whether long-term studies are always necessary, movement toward wide-scale prevention, whether interventions are designed for broad dissemination, goals to reduce population-level prevalence rates, and improvement in parent accessibility to evidence-based parenting information and support.

## BENEFICIAL PARENTING STRATEGIES AND PRACTICES

Undoubtedly, there are many ways to parent successfully, and the identification of effective parenting methods is not meant to imply otherwise. That said, elements of parenting strategies and practices associated with positive child adjustment and healthy parent–child relationships are known and form the basis for viable preventive interventions (Hart & Risley, 1995; Taylor & Biglan, 1998). A number of tenets underlie beneficial parenting. One such tenet is grounded in how the parental role is characterized and is useful to construe parenting as more like that of a teacher than an enforcer. Learning to speak, tie one's shoes, cross the street safely, use the bathroom, share with other children, and show good manners all require patient and continual teaching (cf. Becker, 1971). Beneficial parenting is also developmentally appropriate. Expectations, rules, requests, and interactions should match a child's developmental level, not too high or too low. For example, the frequent holding of infants, coddling them, and goggling over them are not only developmentally appropriate but also highly desirable. Doing the same thing with 10- or 12-year-olds, however, would be quite inappropriate and would infantilize and embarrass children at this age. Parents can and should find ways to express affection to older children, but the mode of affection should be developmentally matched.

Related to developmental appropriateness is the notion of starting with what a child can already do and building on that, something that effective classroom teachers routinely do (Alberto & Troutman, 1999). Before young children can form words, they need to make sounds that imitate what they hear. Before a child can use the toilet on his or her own, the child needs to acquire requisite skills (e.g., recognition of the urge, pulling down his or her pants). Before a teenager can learn to drive, he or she needs to be aware of traffic patterns, how drivers navigate, and rules of the road. When parents are trying to help a child learn a new skill or way of behaving, it is important to break down that goal into its parts and make sure the prerequisite elements are mastered first.

Harsh and coercive parenting tactics, particularly in the absence of frequent positive interactions, are counterproductive (Hutchinson, 1977). Frequent reliance on threats, slapping and hitting, angry criticism, and other coercive parental tactics can sometimes produce the illusion of immediate gains (e.g., momentary obedience) but runs the pronounced risk of long-term side effects. Chronic use of harsh and coercive parenting is associated with several problematic outcomes, such as resentment and retaliatory behavior, anxiety and lack of confidence, running away from home, delinquency, and aggressive or violent behavior with others (Patterson, 1982; Patterson et al., 1992; Prinz & Connell, 1997).

Beneficial parenting encompasses many strategies and practices. Some of the more prominent ones found in evidence-supported parenting interventions include:

- Give rules and instructions before situations begin. Children do better when they know what the rules and expectations are ahead of time. Clear and simple instructions about what to do and not do in a pending situation (e.g., before taking a child into a store), and what the consequences will be for cooperation or problematic behavior, increase the likelihood of success (Webster-Stratton, 2006).

- Give frequent attention to positive behaviors. Most interchanges by parents with children should be about things the children are doing well or correctly. Every positive child behavior does not have to produce parental praise, but parental attention for positive child behavior should greatly overshadow parental attention for negative child behavior for optimal impact (Dangel & Polster, 1984; Hutchinson, 1977).

- Give prompts, coaching, and correction. Frequent and/or acerbic criticism is not optimal parenting. However, children do need corrective feedback for healthy and prosocial growth. Parents can use minimal prompts, positive coaching, and nonnegative corrections in modest proportion in child socialization (Sanders, 2004).

- Set clear limits and boundaries. Children benefit from knowing what is and is not acceptable in terms of conduct. Humane and effective parenting does not mean discarding limits for child behavior. However, there are ways to communicate and back up such limits that do not demean or overcontrol children. If parents teach a self-regulatory approach, children can learn to be partners in acquiring self-control and adhering to limits and boundaries (Sanders, 2004).

- Ignore harmless but annoying behavior. When a parent frequently engages a child about minor behaviors that the parent finds annoying, the result is often the opposite of what the parent intended; that is, the annoying behaviors occur more often over time. This is particularly true if the child behavior is an attempt to gain an audience among those watching (Dangel & Polster, 1984; Sanders, 2004).

- Recognize and reward the opposite of the problem. Successful parents and teachers will tell you that they cannot simply punish their way to good child outcomes. A more promising and useful general strategy is to strengthen positive behaviors that can replace the problematic behaviors through recognition and reward. The key is to pick a positive behavior that is truly incompatible with the problematic behavior, such as chewing food with mouth closed rather than open, putting clothes and toys in the hamper rather than leaving a mess, playing gently and talking in a nice way with other children rather than hitting and yelling, and staying in school the whole day rather than being truant. Technically, this process is called direct reinforcement of other behavior (Dangel & Polster, 1984; Sanders, 2004; Webster-Stratton, 2006).

- Use naturally occurring rewards. When the lay public hears the word *reward*, the impression is that this entails payment or prize, but there is a more palatable way of thinking about rewards, which are called reinforcers in the technical literature. Positive attention, fun activities, access to special places (e.g., playroom), public recognition, and other naturally occurring events in the environment are actually better and more durable rewards than money or prizes. Parents can arrange the environment to take advantage of such opportunities. For example, a parent can say to a child, "Finish your homework, and then I will play catch with you," or "When you are ready for bed, we will read a story."

These are just examples of some of the many parenting practices that contribute to positive child adjustment and good long-term outcomes.

## PARENTING AND FAMILY-BASED INTERVENTIONS FOR PREVENTION

Parenting and family-based interventions represent a critical domain in the prevention of child and adolescent mental health problems, substance abuse, and other adverse outcomes, as well as for the promotion of child well-being. Family-related risk factors such as coercive discipline practices, an inconsistent or disorganized parenting style, strained parent–child relations, incomplete or ineffective socialization by parents, and marked family conflict have been implicated as proximal and distal influences for child and adolescent mental health problems and substance abuse. Parenting and family interventions have been deployed to pursue a number of prevention goals, including (a) risk reduction for a specific outcome, such as oppositional defiant disorder or conduct disorder in children or substance abuse in adolescence; (b) risk reduction for multiproblem outcomes in adolescence (Biglan et al., 2004); and (c) reduction of parenting and family risk factors as a general strategy without linking the intervention to specific adverse outcomes. Some of the parenting and family interventions serve more than one of these prevention goals, which is particularly true for interventions applied to parents of younger children (i.e., toddler, preschool, early elementary school).

There are universal preventive interventions that focus on all families, selected interventions that address families at collective risk (e.g., families living in poverty, premature infants, divorcing families), and indicated interventions that assist families in which children have begun to show early signs of emerging problems. Extensive reviews of parenting and family interventions can be found in Barrett and Turner (2004); Biglan et al. (2004); Dadds and Fraser (2003); Donovan and Spence (2000); Lochman and van den Steenhoven (2002); Petrie, Bunn, and Byrne (2007); Prinz and Dumas (2004); Prinz and Jones (2003); and Sutton (2007). Additionally, there are other prevention initiatives that have a parenting and family intervention embedded with several other intervention components (e.g., Fast Track). Other components besides a parenting and family intervention might include classroom and school programs, social skills training, child intervention, and academic tutoring. Multicomponent prevention programs are not considered here, primarily because it is generally not possible to determine what contribution the parenting and family intervention component made to any observed outcomes. Multicomponent approaches are useful to the field and should be considered in their own right. However, a big advantage of stand-alone parenting and family interventions is that the cooperation of multiple settings is not a necessary condition for successful dissemination; also, stand-alone programs can be evaluated more effectively.

Developmental considerations play out explicitly and implicitly in the body of literature on evidence-based parenting and family interventions. The greatest distinction is between parenting and family interventions for preadolescents versus adolescents. For parenting and family interventions aimed at families with preadolescents, especially toddlers and young children, the emphasis is on the parent or caregiver role as a socialization agent. Parenting and family interventions for this age group concentrate on positive and effective strategies for handling misbehavior, teaching new behaviors, promoting positive behaviors, enhancing the affective quality of parent–child interactions and family relations in general, and anticipating future challenges. The specific parenting strategies vary across developmental periods (e.g., toddler, preschool, elementary school), but the principles of effective parenting across those ages are generally robust.

Parenting and family interventions for families with adolescents concentrate more on family communication issues, risky behavior and its prevention, parental monitoring and supervision of adolescents when they are out of the home, and parenting strategies aimed at strengthening adolescent self-regulation and responsible independence. Programs for the adolescent age group are also more likely to involve the youth directly in the intervention, in either family sessions or concurrent youth sessions. Parenting and family interventions draw from a number of theoretical and conceptual frameworks, including but not limited to social learning and social-interactional theories, cognitive-behavioral principles, developmental psychopathology, attribution theory, attachment theory, public health, and an array of child and family development models.

## Prevention of Preadolescent Problems

Family-based prevention of oppositional defiant disorder and related behavior problems in children is one of the more successful parenting and family intervention application areas. There are numerous interventions that have demonstrated varying degrees of impact in reducing or preventing child aggressive behavior, defiant uncooperative behavior, and associated difficulties. The interventions described below, although not exhaustive, are intended to represent the strength of the evidence-based parenting and family interventions and illustrate some unique and innovative features.

The Incredible Years program developed by Webster-Stratton and colleagues focuses primarily on parents of 3–8-year-old children with oppositional defiant disorder or conduct problems (Webster-Stratton & Reid, 2003). This program, which is typically administered to groups of parents over the course of 12–14 weekly sessions, mainly functions as either an indicated preventive intervention or a clinical treatment. However, the Incredible Years has also been implemented as a selected preventive intervention with parents of children in Head Start programs. In an impressive series of controlled outcome studies spanning over 20 years, the core parenting program produced reductions in child aggressive and destructive behavior and improved parent–child interactions and parenting competence. The Incredible Years is flexible in that it can be implemented in a variety of settings, including preschools, elementary schools, and clinics. There are also companion programs in the form of child group training and teacher classroom management. The program has produced favorable cost–benefit data.

The Incredible Years has been successfully disseminated in the United States and elsewhere. With respect to the parenting and family intervention prevention goals mentioned at the beginning, the Incredible Years mainly serves the first goal: risk reductions for a specific outcome, which in this case is oppositional defiant disorder and associated conduct problems. However, the program also addresses concomitant internalizing problems, such as anxiety and fears, that are seen in the indicated populations. Additionally, the selected intervention application of the Incredible Years (e.g., with Head Start parents) fits the third goal to some degree, namely, the general reduction of parenting and family risk factors (The Incredible Years, 2009).

Another well-supported parenting and family intervention, but one that takes a somewhat different structural approach than The Incredible Years and other similar programs, is the Triple P—Positive Parenting Program (Sanders, 2008; Sanders, Turner, & Markie-Dadds, 2002). Triple P, which is actually a system of parenting interventions rather than a single one, is intended in its fullest implementation to be a population-wide strategy for prevention of childhood social, emotional, and behavioral problems. Although the system runs from infancy through age 16, this discussion focuses only on the 1–12-year-old age range for comparison purposes. Triple P incorporates five levels of intervention on a tiered continuum of increasing strength but with narrowing utilization by parents. The five levels are summarized in Table 28.1.

Triple P was designed from the outset for population dissemination in terms of the materials, portability of the interventions, utilization of multiple disciplines and settings in the existing workforce, and a standardized professional training process. The ultimate goals of the system are to strengthen parenting across the population and reduce the prevalence of common child social, behavioral, and emotional problems. To this end, the multilevel interventions of increasing intensity subscribe to the public principle of taking the minimally sufficient action to solve the problem at hand. The assumption is that much can be accomplished across the population with a universal media-based program, which is relatively cost-efficient compared to professionally delivered programming, plus the other lower levels of intervention, and if a family needs or wants more assistance, the higher intensity interventions are still available. Over 25 years of empirical work went into the development and refinement of Triple P.

**Table 28.1**   Five Intervention Levels for the Triple P—Positive Parenting Program System

| Level | Focus | Variants |
|---|---|---|
| *Level 1*—Universal | • Coordinated media and communication strategies<br>• Access by all interested parents to useful information about parenting | Not applicable |
| *Level 2*—Selected | • Brief intervention<br>• Early anticipatory developmental guidance<br>• Addressing normative concerns and mild behavior problems | • *Individual*—Brief and flexible consultation<br>• *Parenting seminars*—Large group |
| *Level 3*—Primary care | • Narrowly focused parent training in a brief (up to four contacts) and flexible consultation mode | Brief and flexible consultation |
| *Level 4*—Standard | • Intensive parenting intervention to address moderate to severe social, behavioral, and emotional difficulties<br>• Indicated prevention | • *Standard format*—Individual families<br>• *Group format*—Multiple families<br>• *Stepping Stones*—Families of children with developmental disabilities<br>• *Self-directed format*<br>• *Lifestyles*—Parents of obese children |
| *Level 5*—Enhanced | • Add-on to level 4<br>• For families also experiencing family difficulties (e.g., parental depression or stress, conflict between partners) | • *Enhanced*—For family difficulties<br>• *Pathways*—For child abuse risk |

A sizable number of effectiveness trials and a few dissemination studies have been conducted with various components of the Triple P system, including over 40 randomized trials and several field evaluation studies. These have yielded consistently positive results in terms of reduced child externalizing problems, and internalizing problems where appropriate, reduced use of coercive parenting methods, improved parent–child interactions and relations, and benefits for other aspects of parent and family functioning. Favorable cost–benefit data have been reported for Triple P, and it is currently being disseminated in 16 countries including the United States. The system is sufficiently flexible that organizations and communities can adopt some or one of the interventions and still accrue benefits. However, the elegance of this approach is in the synergy of the various levels and program formats (see Table 28.1). The universal media piece is intended to not only convey positive parenting information but also normalize and destigmatize the accessing of parenting and family support (http://www.pfsc.uq.edu.au/research/publications).

Prevention of Adolescent Problems

In the area of adolescent substance abuse, there is some evidence that parenting and family interventions can delay onset and reduce the extent of substance abuse. One of the best examples is found in the Strengthening Families Program (Molgaard & Spoth, 2001; Spoth, Randall, Shin, & Redmond, 2005). This universal preventive intervention, typically but not exclusively conducted in school settings, consists of seven group sessions with parents while concurrent group sessions are conducted with the youth. It has shown impressive preventive effects in randomized trials in terms of lower levels of drug, tobacco, and alcohol use; lower rates of aggressive and destructive behaviors; and better parent–youth interactions. Strengthening Families has yielded positive cost–benefit data, too. The intervention model is relatively efficient but can be expanded with booster sessions. It is primarily a school-based parenting and family intervention but presumably can be implemented in a community center or house of faith. The intervention lends itself well for dissemination in terms of materials, family recruitment, and technical support.

An approach that is built on a blended prevention model is the Adolescent Transitions Program developed by Dishion and Kavanagh (2003), which is consistent with the aforementioned goal number 2, risk reduction for multiple outcomes. This program targets reduction of risk for adolescent substance abuse, behavior problems, and school failure and combines universal, selected, and indicated interventions into a blended prevention strategy. Delivered in middle or high schools, the Adolescent Transitions Program includes the following:

- A universal access family resource center that includes brief consultation with parents either face-to-face or by telephone, feedback when solicited to parents about their teenager's behavior at school, and resource videos and books
- A selected intervention called the Family Check Up, which is offered to families of youth who are identified as high risk for behavior problems based on teacher ratings, consisting of three family sessions emphasizing motivational interviewing and culminating in feedback about family strengths, needs, and possible intervention linkages
- An indicated intervention that relevant families choose from a menu of family-centered interventions that provide support for family management practices conducive to positive adolescent development

In a randomized study, the Adolescent Transitions Program resulted in slower growth of externalizing behavior problems and alcohol, tobacco, and marijuana use from age 11 through 17 and decreased risk for substance abuse and police arrests by age 18. More work needs to be done on the portability and dissemination of the program; nonetheless, it is a unique and promising multilevel preventive intervention.

Evidence-supported parenting and family interventions that specifically target the prevention of anxiety disorders in adolescence have not emerged. Most of the work on family-based intervention related to adolescent anxiety disorders has been in the context of treatment for youth already experiencing diagnosable problems. A potentially fruitful area in need of research and development is family-based prevention of anxiety problems in the offspring of adults who have an anxiety disorder. The testing of selected prevention of anxiety disorder would be well justified, given the likely genetic, modeling, and socialization contributions parents might make to their children.

With respect to the prevention of conduct disorder, parenting and family interventions geared toward parents of adolescents (e.g., Adolescent Transitions Program, Strengthening Families Program) have shown reduction of risk for externalizing problems. However, it is not clear yet how well parenting and family interventions that are initiated during adolescence can prevent the emergence of actual cases of conduct disorder. Part of the problem is that by adolescence, youth who are going to qualify for a conduct disorder diagnosis may already have done so when an intervention is being offered. In this regard, there might be some blurring of definitions regarding treatment versus prevention, compounded by timing issues.

Family-based prevention of depression in adolescence, like the anxiety area, is not well developed. Most of the family-based intervention work in this area centers around treatment of depressed youth, with one notable exception. A selected preventive intervention, the Clinician-Based Cognitive Psychoeducational Intervention (Beardslee, Gladstone, Wright, & Cooper, 2003) is a family-based approach for the offspring of parents who have significant mood disorders. This intervention shows promise in terms of improving youth and family functioning, increasing knowledge about affective disorders and the resilience of children, and reducing risk for internalizing disorders. The extent to which it can reduce the prevalence of adolescent depression is not yet known; however, the strategy seems well justified. Also, the intervention has the potential to link youth to treatment earlier than usual and thereby possibly prevent the long-term debilitating sequelae associated with untreated depression. Offspring of depressed parents have at least a fourfold greater likelihood of developing depression during adolescence and early adulthood. In terms of potential dissemination impact, what is not as well known is the extent to which depressed parents are able to be involved in the treatment with their offspring. Nonetheless, this intervention deserves more research, given the dearth of family-based strategies for prevention of depression.

Additionally, a few of the universal interventions (e.g., those based on the work of Hawkins and colleagues), geared primarily for parents of adolescent youth and the prevention of substance abuse, have begun to show promise in terms of reducing depressive symptoms. There is some lack of clarity in the field as to whether changes in depressive-type symptoms correspond to prevention of clinical depression. Added research including independent replication should help bolster this promising work.

Another parenting and family intervention focuses on children of divorce and fits the third prevention goal noted at the outset in terms of reducing parenting and family risk factors as a general strategy not tied to a specific disorder or outcome. The New Beginnings Program helps divorced mothers promote resilience in their children (Wolchik, Sandler, Weiss, & Winslow, 2007). It is sort of a hybrid of the standard kinds of parenting and family interventions for all families plus normative and useful information about divorce-specific issues, such as parental guilt reactions and multiple household issues. Although not yet ready for broad dissemination, the New Beginnings Program in controlled research has shown promise in reducing risk for internalizing and externalizing problems.

## SAMPLING OF CRITICAL ISSUES

### Distillation of Common Elements

Across the various preventive interventions and domains, the evidence-supported parenting and family interventions have a number of common elements or features:

- *Action focused*—Parents actually do things during the intervention rather than simply engage in conversation with the interventionist.
- *Problem-solving oriented*—Parenting and family interventions generally work toward addressing specific challenges and solving problems. A problem-solving orientation does not preclude building on child, parent, and family strengths. What it means, though, is that parental goals are pursued. Parents want to solve the challenges they are facing in child rearing. For example, if a child is frequently exhibiting violent tantrums in public places, such as restaurants and shopping malls, and seems to have difficulty with emotional regulation, then the parent is looking for effective ways of solving this stressful problem. Parenting and family interventions offer strategies that have a reasonable probability of solving the problems at hand rather than just talking about the child's problems without generating action plans.
- *Specific, concrete, and practical parenting strategies*—Although it is important for parents to induce general principles that they can apply in future situations, parenting and family interventions still try to focus on practical parenting strategies that parents can readily implement. Parents need and want suggestions for action. Parenting and family interventions typically offer a menu of specific parenting strategies, so parents can find the best fit for their personal style and still address the issue at hand. Instead of vague generalities, such as "Show your child a lot of love," the interventions focus, for example, on specific

ways to build closer, more affectionate parent–child relationships. For more complex situations, interventionists walk parents through specific but straightforward steps to implement a strategy.

- *Collaborative goal setting*—Parenting and family interventions seem to work better if parents set the specific goals for themselves and their children, in consultation with the interventionist. The professional asks facilitative questions and helps parents articulate useful and specific goals. The parents' role in this process is paramount. They are not passive participants but rather a consumers who have a major stake in what happens with their children and families. The interventions typically involve identification and sharpening of parents' goals for their children. Parents often begin with distress and concern as they discuss their children's adjustment. It is the interventionist's job to join with the parents and help them figure out what the needs are in terms of the specific challenges relevant to their children's development and functioning.
- *Consultative rather than prescriptive*—Although not all parenting and family interventions subscribe to this principle equally, there is a general trend toward making the intervention consultative, in line with collaborative goal setting noted above, rather than prescribing to the parent what they must do. Providing menu options and answering parents' questions are important facets of the consultative approach.
- *Adopting a positive frame*—Parents do not need to feel blamed or inept for an intervention to be successful. Successful parenting and family interventions adopt a positive frame about the child, the parent, the program tasks, and the intervention itself.

## Engagement of Parents

One of the biggest challenges in the successful implementation of parenting and family interventions is the engagement of parents initially (i.e., recruitment) and then throughout the program. Compared with 15 years ago, program implementers have become savvier in addressing potential barriers to participation by being more sensitive to program time and location, availability of transportation and child care, and other logistical considerations. From a dissemination perspective, however, delivery systems and staff may or may not share the same flexibility. We know more about parental engagement now than we used to, but it is still a major challenge. Who delivers a parenting and family intervention, how they deliver it, in what context it is offered, and how the community perceives it are just some of the critical variables that can impact engagement.

## Are Long-Term Studies of Every Intervention Needed?

There is no doubt that long-term longitudinal and preventive intervention studies have contributed to progress in parenting and family-based prevention. Nonetheless, it is a debatable issue whether every parenting and family intervention needs to be subjected to a long-term study that is both costly and potentially delaying. For example, suppose that a parenting and family intervention shows strong positive impact on parenting competence and child behavior when a child is 5, and the effects sustain over a 2-year period. If in other research those constructs (i.e., same facets of parenting competence and child behavior) have been shown to be pertinent to prevention of substance abuse, is it necessary or advisable to test the parenting and family intervention over a 10-year follow-up period? Or, is it sufficient to draw inferences across studies to arrive at a conclusion about the parenting and family intervention's impact on precursor risk factors in childhood? Individual studies or sources of evidence should not be considered in isolation or out of context. Parenting and family interventions that can reduce the prevalence of known parenting and family-related risk factors at the time of implementation are useful whether 10-year forecast data are available or not.

## MOVING TOWARD WIDE-SCALE PREVENTION

The field has produced efficacious interventions for improving parenting and parent–child relations and preventing or ameliorating children's social, emotional, behavioral, and health problems
(Miller & Prinz, 2003; Olds, Sadler, & Kitzman, 2007; Prinz & Dumas, 2004; Zubrick et al., 2005).
Also emerging is evidence that parenting interventions can reduce child maltreatment and children's injuries (Prinz, 2007; Prinz, Sanders, Shapiro, Whitaker, & Lutzker, 2009). Despite strong
evidence for positive impact, most of the parenting and family interventions have not met with
wide adoption. The limitations of these interventions collectively are apparent with respect to not
achieving, or even attempting to achieve, broad or population-level effects. In part as a response to
this state of affairs, a paradigm shift is beginning to take place that emphasizes a public health and
population approach over one that is strictly clinical and focused on high-risk children (Biglan &
Metzler, 1998; Prinz & Sanders, 2007).

### Interventions Designed for Broad Dissemination

Many of the existing parenting and family interventions were designed for potentially cumber-
some, or at least not very practical, efficacy trials. This issue cuts two ways. First, a parenting and
family intervention that shows efficacy but cannot be readily disseminated is not a good candidate
for widespread adoption. Second, if the efficacious intervention has to be modified before dissemination, the disseminated version may not retain the same level of efficacy as the original version.
As new interventions are readied for efficacy testing, it makes sense that the end state goal of dissemination be taken into account up front when the intervention is being designed. This recommendation pertains to intervention materials, length and efficiency, provider training methods,
promotion and verification of intervention fidelity, and ease of administration.

### Targeting Reduction of Population Prevalence

As attempts are being made to more widely disseminate parenting and family interventions, greater
attention is being paid to the challenges and requirements of going to full scale. Generally speaking, however, the field does not appear to be making the reduction of population prevalence (e.g.,
child mental health problems, child maltreatment) the overarching goal. From a public health perspective, if society spends billions of dollars on prevention, but the problem remains at the same
prevalence level, the approach has not succeeded. Reframing the prevention challenge in terms
of prevalence reduction at a population level is a major undertaking that will require a concerted
paradigm shift. Additionally, our community surveillance systems need to be overhauled and
improved, so population effects can be more readily detected.

### Improving Accessibility to Parenting Interventions and Information

One of the keys to moving toward a population-wide approach to family-based prevention is
improving the accessibility of parenting interventions and information. This means utilizing many
settings including nontraditional ones, so parents can "bump into" programming wherever it is
convenient and most advantageous to them, and also requires a shift in the paradigm. Typically,
mental health–type interventions have been guarded by mental health providers, at least in certain
disciplines. Although parenting is obviously a major influence on children's mental health and
well-being, it is also something that belongs to a broader domain. Parenting interventions for the
most part need to be demedicalized and destigmatized. Drawing on many settings and types of
providers is one way to start that process.

Research on media-based approaches to improving parenting has begun to emerge but is still in
its infancy. The greatest advances in this work in relation to evidence-based parenting and family

interventions and media utilization have been made by Sanders and colleagues (Calam, Sanders, Miller, Sadhnani, & Carmont, 2008; Sanders, Calam, Durand, Liversidge, & Carmont, 2008; Sanders & Prinz, 2008). Three studies have demonstrated the potential benefits of using media delivery for an evidence-based parenting and family intervention such as Triple P, as described earlier. In the first media study, Sanders, Montgomery, and Brechman-Toussaint (2000) established the feasibility of using an infotainment-style television series with embedded segments on parenting to promote positive family outcomes. Using a controlled design, the investigators found that 12 half-hour episodes led to fewer child behavior problems and better child adjustment, as well as greater parental confidence, in comparison to the wait list control. The second study examined the effects of Triple P as a reality series on British television (Sanders et al., 2008). The six-episode documentary television series *Driving Mum and Dad Mad* (Campbell, 2005–2006) depicted the experiences and emotional journey of five families with young children who had severe conduct problems, as the parents participated in Group Triple P (an eight-session intensive group program).

A randomized trial involving approximately 500 families examined the impact of viewing the television series. The intricacies of the study are beyond the scope of the discussion here, but a primary finding is that substantial benefits could be accrued from parental viewing of the series with respect to child behavior, dysfunctional parenting, parental anger about child behavior, and parental disagreements about the use of discipline. The third study (Calam et al., 2008) also investigated the effectiveness of *Driving Mum and Dad Mad* and involved 723 families who were randomly assigned to either a standard viewing condition or a technology-enhanced one, which provided additional online support. Parents in both conditions reported significant improvements from preintervention to postintervention in child behavior, dysfunctional parenting, parental anger, depression, and self-efficacy, and these improvements were maintained at the 6-month follow-up. Of particular importance is that Calam et al. demonstrated that the television series approach had positive benefits for a diverse range of families with respect to socioeconomic level. In contrast to the aforementioned work supporting media strategies grounded in evidence-based parenting and family interventions, there are non-evidence-based television programs related to parenting, such as *Nanny 911* and *Supernanny*, that have not been scientifically tested. Society does not know not only the potential benefits of such programs but also whether there are potentially iatrogenic or harmful effects from these particular television approaches.

Pertinent to the media discussion and furthering the paradigm of taking a population approach to parenting and family support, a few recent studies have integrated media strategies with parenting and family interventions delivered face-to-face. One of the larger of such studies is the U.S. Triple P System Population Trial funded by the Centers for Disease Control and Prevention (Prinz et al., 2009). Aimed at the prevention of child maltreatment among parents of children ages 0–8, 18 counties were randomized to either the Triple P system, including a media component, or community services as usual. Hundreds of service workers in many settings (e.g., clinics, schools, daycare centers, health centers, community nongovernmental centers, churches) were trained in the delivery of Triple P.

All levels of the Triple P system were implemented (see Table 28.1). There were also concurrent media and communication strategies involving local newspaper stories and articles with parenting tips, newsletter mass mailing, radio public service announcements, website information, and information distributed at community events. After controlling for baseline levels, counties in the Triple P system condition yielded significantly lower rates of substantiated maltreatment, child out-of-home placements (i.e., foster care), and child injuries resulting in hospital treatment, compared with the counties randomized to services as usual. Although it was not possible to tease out the separate effects of the media strategies from those of direct services, prior media-only studies coupled with studies on individual-level Triple P suggested that there was possibly a synergistic effect. Media strategies for improving parenting and child adjustment are promising, but there is much to study before the field knows their full potential as well as their limitations.

## CONCLUSION

Children and families can benefit from well-tested parenting and family support interventions that are practical, action oriented, problem solving, and efficient and delivered collaboratively in partnership with parents regarding goals and parenting options. Although not yet fully adopted, the field has begun to move toward a newer paradigm that emphasizes broad dissemination, impact on prevalence rates at a population level, and integration of media strategies with more traditional modes of service delivery. Consumer researchers who specialize in social marketing, vulnerable populations, and quality of life have much to contribute to this area (see Andreasen, Goldberg, & Sirgy, Chapter 2 of this volume; Grier & Moore, Chapter 15 of this volume; Pechmann, Biglan, Grube, & Cody, Chapter 17 of this volume), in addition to those whose expertise includes families (Epp & Price, Chapter 29 of this volume), online communities (Hoffman, Chapter 9 of this volume; Kozinets, Belz, & McDonagh, Chapter 10 of this volume), materialism (Burroughs & Rindfleisch, Chapter 12 of this volume), and practical wisdom (Mick & Schwartz, Chapter 32 of this volume). Overall, there are many opportunities for Transformative Consumer Research to contribute to understanding and positively influencing effective parenting of young and maturing consumers.

## REFERENCES

Alberto, P., & Troutman, A. C. (1999). *Applied behavior analysis for teachers*. New York: Prentice Hall.

Barrett, P. M., & Turner, C. M. (2004). Prevention of childhood anxiety and depression. In P. M. Barrett & T. H. Ollendick (Eds.), *Handbook of interventions that work with children and adolescents: Prevention and treatment* (pp. 475–488). Hoboken, NJ: Wiley.

Beardslee, W. R., Gladstone, T. R., Wright, J., & Cooper, A. B. (2003). A family-based approach to the prevention of depressive symptoms in children at risk: Evidence of parental and child change. *Pediatrics, 11*, 119–131.

Becker, W. C. (1971). *Parents as teachers: A child management program*. Champaign, IL: Research Press.

Benjet, C., & Kazdin A. E. (2003). Spanking children: The controversies, findings, and new directions. *Clinical Psychology Review, 23*, 197–224.

Biglan, A., Brennan, P. A., Foster, S. L., & Holder, H. D. (2004). *Helping adolescents at risk: Prevention of multiple behaviors*. New York: Guilford.

Biglan, A., & Metzler, C. (1998). A public health perspective for research on family-focused interventions. In R. S. Ashery, E. B. Robertson, & K. L. Kumpfer (Eds.), *Drug abuse prevention through family interventions* (NIDA Research Monograph 177, NIH Publication No. 994135, pp. 430–458). Washington, DC: National Institute on Drug Abuse.

Bornstein, M. (Ed.). (2008). *Handbook of parenting. Vol. 5: Practical issues in parenting* (2nd ed.). New York: Erlbaum.

Calam, R., Sanders, M. R., Miller, C., Sadhnani, V., & Carmont, S. A. (2008). Can technology and the media help reduce dysfunctional parenting and increase engagement with preventative parenting interventions? *Child Maltreatment, 13*, 347–361.

Campbell, S. (Director). (2005–2006). *Driving mum and dad mad* [Television series]. London: London Weekend Television.

Collins, W. A., Maccoby, E. E., Steinberg, L., Hetherington, E. M., & Bornstein, M. H. (2000). Contemporary research on parenting: The case for nature and nurture. *American Psychologist, 55*, 218–232.

Cowan, P. A., & Hetherington, E. M. (1991). *Family transitions*. New York: Family Research Council.

Dadds, M. R., & Fraser, J. A. (2003). Prevention programs. In C. A. Essau (Ed.), *Conduct and oppositional defiant disorders: Epidemiology, risk factors, and treatment* (pp. 193–222). Mahwah, NJ: Erlbaum.

Dangel, R. F., & Polster, R. A. (Eds.). (1984). *Parent training: Foundations for research and practice*. New York: Guilford.

Dishion, T. J., & Kavanagh, K. (2003). *Intervening in adolescent problem behavior: A family-centered approach*. New York: Guilford.

Donovan, C. L., & Spence, S. H. (2000). Prevention of childhood anxiety disorders. *Clinical Psychology Review, 20*, 509–531.

Foster, E. M., Prinz, R. J., Sanders, M. R., & Shapiro, C. J. (2008). The costs of a public health infrastructure for delivering parenting and family support. *Children and Youth Services Review, 30*, 493–501.

Hart, B., & Risley, T. R. (1995). *Meaningful differences in the everyday experience of young American children.* Baltimore: Paul H. Brookes.

Hawkins, J. D., Catalano, R. F., & Miller, J. Y. (1992). Risk and protective factors for alcohol and other drug problems in adolescence and early adulthood: Implications for substance abuse prevention. *Psychological Bulletin, 112*, 64–105.

Holden, G. W., & Edwards, L. A. (1989). Parental attitudes toward child rearing: Instruments, issues, and implications. *Psychological Bulletin, 106*, 29–58.

Hutchinson, R. R. (1977). By-products of aversive control. In W. K. Honig & J. E. R. Staddon (Eds.), *Handbook of behavior* (pp. 415–431). Englewood Cliffs, NJ: Prentice Hall.

The Incredible Years. (2009). *Evidence of effectiveness.* Seattle, WA: Author. Available: http://www.incredibleyears .com/ResearchEval/effective.asp

Jones, T. L., & Prinz, R. J. (2005). Potential roles of parental self-efficacy in parent and child adjustment: A review. *Clinical Psychology Review, 25*, 341–363.

Lochman, J. E., & van den Steenhoven, A. (2002). Family-based approaches to substance abuse prevention. *Journal of Primary Prevention, 23*, 49–114.

Miller, G. E., & Prinz, R. J. (2003). Engagement of families in treatment for childhood conduct problems. *Behavior Therapy, 34*, 517–534.

Molgaard, V., & Spoth, R. (2001). Strengthening Families Program for young adolescents: Overview and outcomes. In S. Pfeiffer & L. Reddy (Eds.), *Innovative mental health programs for children* (pp. 15–29). Binghamton, NY: Haworth.

Olds, D. L., Sadler, L., & Kitzman, H. (2007). Programs for parents of infants and toddlers: Recent evidence from randomized trials. *Journal of Child Psychology and Psychiatry, 48*, 355–391.

Patterson, G. R. (1982). *Coercive family process.* Eugene, OR: Castalia.

Patterson, G. R., Reid, J. B., & Dishion, T. J. (1992). *Antisocial boys.* Eugene, OR: Castalia.

Petrie, J., Bunn, F., & Byrne, G. (2007). Parenting programmes for preventing tobacco, alcohol or drug misuse in children under 18: A systematic review. *Health Education Research, 22*, 177–191.

Polster, R. A., Dangel, R. F., & Rasp, R. R. (1987). Research in behavioral parent training in social work: Parent training in social work, a review. *Journal of Social Service Research, 10*, 37–51.

Prinz, R. J. (2007). Parenting and the prevention of childhood injuries. In L. S. Doll, S. E. Bonzo, J. A. Mercy, & D. A. Sleet (Eds.), *Handbook of injury and violence prevention* (pp. 333–346). New York: Springer.

Prinz, R. J., & Connell, C. (1997). Prevention of conduct disorders and antisocial behavior. In R. T. Ammerman & M. Hersen (Eds.), *Handbook of prevention and treatment with children and adolescents: Intervention in the real world context* (pp. 238–258). New York: Wiley.

Prinz, R. J., & Dumas, J. E. (2004). Prevention of oppositional defiant disorder and conduct disorder in children and adolescents. In P. M. Barrett & T. H. Ollendick (Eds.), *Handbook of interventions that work with children and adolescents: Prevention and treatment* (pp. 475–488). Hoboken, NJ: Wiley.

Prinz, R. J., & Jones, T. L. (2003). Family-based interventions. In C. A. Essau (Ed.), *Conduct and oppositional defiant disorders: Epidemiology, risk factors, and treatment* (pp. 279–298). Mahwah, NJ: Erlbaum.

Prinz, R. J., & Sanders, M. R. (2007). Adopting a population-level approach to parenting and family support interventions. *Clinical Psychology Review, 27*, 739–749.

Prinz, R. J., Sanders, M. R., Shapiro, C. J., Whitaker, D. J., & Lutzker, J. R. (2009). Population-based prevention of child maltreatment: The U.S. Triple P System Population Trial. *Prevention Science, 10*, 1–13.

Sanders, M. R. (2004). *Every parent: A positive approach to children's behavior* (Rev. ed.). Brisbane, Australia: Penguin.

Sanders, M. R. (2008). The Triple P—Positive Parenting Program as a public health approach to strengthening parenting. *Journal of Family Psychology, 22*(3), 506–517.

Sanders, M. R., Calam, R., Durand, M., Liversidge, T., & Carmont, S. A. (2008). Does self-directed and Web-based support for parents enhance the effects of viewing a reality television series based on the Triple P—Positive Parenting Program? *Journal of Child Psychology and Psychiatry, 49*(9), 924–932.

Sanders, M. R., Montgomery, D., & Brechman-Toussaint, M. (2000). The mass media and the prevention of child behavior problems: The evaluation of a television series to promote positive outcomes for parents and their children. *Journal of Child Psychology and Psychiatry, 41*, 939–948.

Sanders, M. R., & Prinz, R. J. (2008). Using the mass media as a population level strategy to strengthen parenting skills. *Journal of Clinical Child & Adolescent Psychology, 37,* 609–621.

Sanders, M. R., Turner, K. M. T., & Markie-Dadds, C. (2002). The development and dissemination of the Triple P—Positive Parenting Program: A multi-level, evidence-based system of parenting and family support. *Prevention Science, 3,* 173–198.

Spoth, R., Randall, G. K., Shin, C., & Redmond, C. (2005). Randomized study of combined universal family and school preventive interventions: Patterns of long-term effects on initiation, regular use, and weekly drunkenness. *Psychology of Addictive Behaviors, 19,* 372–381.

Sutton, J. M. (2007). Prevention of depression in youth: A qualitative review and future suggestions. *Clinical Psychology Review, 27,* 552–571.

Taylor, T. K., & Biglan, A. (1998). Behavioral family interventions for improving child-rearing: A review of the literature for clinicians and policy makers. *Clinical Child and Family Psychology Review, 1,* 41–60.

Webster-Stratton, C. (2006). *The Incredible Years: A trouble-shooting guide for parents of children aged 2–8 years.* Seattle, WA: Incredible Years.

Webster-Stratton, C., & Reid, J. M. (2003). The Incredible Years parents, teachers and child training series: A multifaceted treatment approach for young children with conduct problems. In A. E. Kazdin & J. R. Weisz (Eds.), *Evidence-based psychotherapies for children and adolescents* (pp. 224–240). New York: Guilford.

Wolchik, S., Sandler, I., Weiss, L., & Winslow, E. (2007). New Beginnings: An empirically-based program to help divorced mothers promote resilience in their children. In J. M. Briesmeister & C. E. Schaefer (Eds.), *Handbook of parent training: Helping parents prevent and solve problem behaviors* (pp. 25–62). New York: Wiley.

Wolery, M., Bailey, D. B., & Sugai, G. M. (1988). *Effective teaching: Principles and procedures of applied behavior analysis with exceptional students.* New York: Wiley.

Zubrick, S. R., Ward, K. A., Silburn, S. R., Lawrence, D., Williams, A. A., Blair, E., et al. (2005). Prevention of child behavior problems through universal implementation of a group behavioral family intervention. *Prevention Science, 6,* 287–304.

# 29

# Family Time in Consumer Culture
## Implications for Transformative Consumer Research

Amber M. Epp and Linda L. Price

Family time is not only a descriptive term that offers a perspective on some aspect of family togetherness, it is a prescriptive term that directs families to act in certain ways.

Kerry J. Daly
*(2001b, p. 284)*

Across numerous interviews with multiple members and generations of families, across contexts that include children's after-school activities such as soccer and family activities such as dinners, holidays, and vacations, and across family objects and spaces such as homes, farms, food, heirlooms, and technologies, we hear again and again the importance of time with family. However, we also hear how despite the idealized status and presumed centrality to the real meaning of life, family time easily gives way, displaced by minor obstacles, individual projects, and daily demands. Family time is often measured and written about quite literally as time spent when the family is copresent, meaning when multiple family members are together (Bianchi, Robinson, & Milkie, 2006). There has been much debate about whether family time has increased or decreased over the past decades and how it is socioeconomically and culturally distributed (Mestdag & Vandeweyer, 2005). However, our own and other research has suggested that for families, not all time together counts as family time, and what counts varies by class and culture (DeVault, 2000; Kremer-Sadlick, Fatigante, & Fasulo, 2008). When family members talk about scarcity, they are concerned with not just copresence but also the quality of time together, and this idea is a "major organizing principle across as well as within all modern societies" (Gillis, 2001, p. 22).

Consumption practices are implicated both as heroes and villains, but without question, they are central to how contemporary families go about the collective project of family time and are consequential in whether and how families gather and interact. For example, family meals, watching television, and traveling together on family outings constitute a significant portion of total family time in modern societies (DeVault, 2000; Mestdag & Vandeweyer, 2005). Consumer technologies have been criticized for diminishing the amount and quality of time families spend together, but also heralded as ways to enhance family time and reconnect across space and distances (English-Lueck, 1998; Morley, 2003; Venkatesh, 2006). Why is family time perceived as so central to well-being and vital to life meaning but paradoxically so fragile and scarce in daily life? How do consumption practices facilitate and inhibit the experience of family time, and what are the implications for consumer researchers and policy makers?

The purpose of this chapter is to bring clarity to the complex and culturally and socially embedded interplay of consumption and family time to uncover implications for enhancing consumer well-being. This chapter is organized around idealizations and metaphors that shape how families, especially in Western cultures, think about family time (Cotte, Ratneshwar, & Mick, 2004; Daly, 1996; Shore, 2003). We draw on our own research and that of others to unfold how these idealizations and metaphors structure both family and policy meanings and practices regarding family time. We begin with a brief introduction to the history and debate surrounding the meaning and nature of family time. Next, we discuss how the idealization of family life and the metanarrative of a middle-class, nuclear family have shaped "doing family" for a diversity of household types (e.g., low-income, single, divorced, gay; Nelson, 2006; Tubbs, Roy, & Burton, 2005). Once we have an overview of idealized family time, we theoretically integrate prior research on individual consumer time metaphors (Cotte et al., 2004) with family theory (Daly, 1996, 2003; Epp & Price, 2008) to develop policy and research directions motivated by several different ways that consuming families may think about and use time.

We use the family time metaphors adapted from Cotte et al. (2004) as an organizing framework to provide an explicit cultural, social, and temporal frame for understanding contemporary families' experience of family time (Daly, 1996; Gillis, 2001). We posit that families, like individuals, employ a range of metaphors for thinking about time, and in turn, these metaphors empower, constrain, and frame the role of consumption in pursuit of family time and well-being. Similar to how black-and-white photographs portray objects differently than color photographs, the metaphors we live by shape our experiences of family time and how we draw on and depart from our idealizations in our everyday practices. For example, these metaphors help us understand why so many U.S. families view it as difficult, laborious, or impossible to create family time, whereas in other parts of the world, dual-earner households view it as easy, natural, or expected (Kremer-Sadlik et al., 2008). As we unfold how these metaphors organize family life, we tack between meanings and practices to uncover tensions that can be addressed through Transformative Consumer Research (TCR).

## A BRIEF HISTORY OF FAMILY TIME

Family time is a recent notion, first appearing in the mid–19th century (Gillis, 1996, 2001; L. J. Miller, 1995). For the United States in particular, family time has become a symbolic locus, a special time set aside for connection and experiencing each other as a relational unit (Kremer-Sadlick et al., 2008). The current salience of family time is linked to the increase in dual-earner families and escalating work hours perceived as threatening parents' and children's time together (Bianchi et al., 2006; Hertz & Marshall, 2001; Hochschild, 1997, 2003; Jacobs & Gerson, 2004; Schor, 1991). However, a myriad of other factors have also been implicated in the harried, hurried, and disconnected experience of contemporary American families, including the changing character and boundaries of work and home, structural changes in families and communities, the push and pull of consumer culture, burgeoning expectations for parenting, and myths about the way families used to be (Darrah, Freeman, & English-Lueck, 2007; Douglas & Michaels, 2004; Heyman & Beem, 2005; Hochschild, 2005; Schor, 2005; Southerton & Tomlinson, 2005). Family time is idealized as precious, scarce, fleeting, and at risk (Daly, 1996, 2001c) and is remembered, practiced, planned, and prescribed (Daly 2001c, 2003). Parents feel obligated to give their children memories of family time and believe that spending time with children is necessary for their proper growth and development (Bianchi et al., 2006; Daly, 2001a).

Although ideologically revered, family time is freeing and constraining, in that individual members escape to it and from it. Inextricably bundled with spaces, material objects, and relationships, family time is carved out, left over, squeezed against, competed for, conflicted, and divided. Paradoxically, although both men and women have reported the desire for more time as a family (Milke, Mattingly, Nomaguchi, Bianchi, & Robinson, 2004), most research suggests that family time, particularly the number of hours parents spend caring for and doing things with their children, has actually increased over the past 20 years. Surprisingly, based on national studies of the changing workforce conducted by the Families and Work Institute, working mothers spend equivalent time with their children as compared to nonworking mothers and spend more time with their children than nonworking mothers did 20 years ago. Moreover, fathers spend more time with children than in the past (Barnett, 2005; Bond, Galinsky, & Swanberg, 1998; Bond, Thompson, Galinsky, & Prottas, 2003).

At the same time, research also demonstrates a gap between reported and observed family time, with families simultaneously overreporting time spent with children and yearning for more and higher quality time (Gillis, 1996). In addition, arguments have raged about the character and distribution of family time. For example, working parents may feel their family time is too fragmented to be quality time (Southerton, 2006). A major conclusion from the plethora of research is that "time not only takes place on the two dimensional plane of linear chronological time" (Adam, 1994, p. 513), but far more important is how a diversity of families experience time and the implications for transformative public policy (Daly, 1996, 2003). Ironically, although consumer culture has been directly implicated as a cause of the time squeeze, and consumption to facilitate and enhance family time is a major expenditure category for many families, consumer researchers have largely ignored the role of consumption in work–life balance (cf. Kaufman-Scarborough, 2006; Thompson, 1996). This chapter synthesizes existing literature on family time with a perspective on how consumption mediates and moderates the experience of it, and with attention to the meanings and practices of it in daily life.

## IDEALIZED FAMILY TIME

Idealized notions of family time are constituted in the dominant narratives that stream through our media representations of family. These cultural templates are accentuated and negotiated in our institutions (e.g., government, religion, education) and come to life in our interactions with other families. Idealizations contribute to taken-for-granted assumptions about proper consumption practices and public policy initiatives related to family time. For example, leisure, meal, and technology practices are all shaped by these idealizations of family time (DeVault, 2000; Epp, Frias-Gutierrez, & Price, 2009; Epp & Price, 2008; Hallman & Benbow, 2007; Kaufman-Scarborough, 2006). These idealizations are in constant, paradoxical tension with the practices and meanings of doing family in daily life and contribute to the politicized, gendered discourses that characterize policy debates surrounding family time (Daly, 2003; Douglas & Michaels, 2004; Gillis, 1996). It is imperative to deconstruct the cultural frames that underlie our theoretical assumptions about time to recognize how they structure our experiences (Daly, 2001b).

Although what is considered ideal necessarily evolves over time and is historically situated, common threads run through the writings of family researchers and help us build a composite of what constitutes contemporary, idealized family time. Invariably, family time is nearly always associated with nostalgia, even for an imagined past that may never have existed. This nostalgia is evidenced in families' continuous pursuits of the "social production of memories" (Daly, 2001b, p. 288). One of Daly's respondents described family time as an "experience library for the kids" (p. 288), and not just any memories will do. Only happy memories contribute to this catalog of family experiences; there is no room for conflict or negative valence in the ideal. Empirical research from our own work supports the nostalgic efforts linked to family time. In a study of family vacation experiences, participants in our study articulated a goal of securing idealized memories (Epp & Price, 2011):

> The goal of every trip is to make memories.... I want them to count on that. (Horton family, mother)

[The vacation] gives us a memory, because it gives us a history and a specific memory together. (Metcalf family, mother)

I mean to have … continuity of all doing one thing, one time.… Bringing up something and everybody remembers it … spend just that quality time. (Samson family, father)

Just being able to create memories for the boys, so it's something that they have, would have. (Tanner family, mother)

This sense of a need to make memories of family time is connected to the second assumption we encountered: Family time is sacred. Prior to the industrial revolution, the model of family time as being distinct from any other time was absent (Gillis 1996). That families would carve out specific, designated time for family was simply unnecessary. Family time did not require a label; it just was. However, when clock time emerged, leading to quantified measurements and paid wage labor, concern over a lack of interaction with family members and the decline of family togetherness emerged (Daly, 2001b; Kremer-Sadlik et al., 2008). Once this concept took hold in society, family time acquired sacred status as uninterrupted time set apart from work (Kremer-Sadlik et al., 2008). Given the contrast between family and work time, spontaneity is highly valued in idealized family time, because it indicates a departure from the scheduled nature of life, "a desire to strip away all activity … and be with their family" (Daly, 2001b, p. 289).

With its sacred standing came rules about which activities and parameters of these actually constitute family time. In comparison with other counties, the U.S. conception is rather rigid, with certain activities capturing the essence of family time better than others (Kremer-Sadlik et al., 2008). For example, activities oriented around children often fall within the definition (Daly, 2001b), but families may vary on whether certain activities count. Commonly identified activities include family meals, bedtimes, protecting downtime on the weekends (Daly, 2001b, p. 288), and Sundays, holidays, and vacations (Gillis, 1996). Along with the aforementioned positive valence, this time should be unstressed and relaxed (Daly, 2001b; Kremer-Sadlik et al., 2008). In addition, there are no shortcuts or replacements for idealized family time, so buying children material things or attempting to blend work and family time leads to guilt and normative judgment from others (Kremer-Sadlik et al., 2008).

A final condition of family time is that it is marked by the whole family doing something with everyone together (Daly, 2001b), often a difficult task to achieve as family members' commitments pile up outside the home. To further complicate matters, even as the most common family forms and structures shift, "the two-parent heterosexual family remains the yardstick" (Hertz, 2006, p. 798; see also Nelson, 2006). From this perspective, single-parent families, particularly mothers, often define only activities that include another adult as family time (Nelson, 2006), and their conception of family is perpetually "in motion" as various adults move in and out of family practices (Hertz, 2006, p. 799). For example, following a divorce, single-parent households find it difficult to achieve family dinner and will often recruit other adults to more closely fit the idealized form of family (Epp et al., 2009).

Not surprisingly, the experience of family time rarely lives up to these ideals (Daly, 2001b). In her book *The Commercialization of Intimate Life: Notes From Home and Work*, Arlie Hochschild (2003) cries out for change, recognizing that families need a new ideal, one that honors diversity, supports family-friendly reforms with shared responsibility among sexes and institutions, and reduces the isolation of the elderly. This begs the question, what does well-being actually look like for post-modern families? Family experiences are better captured in diverse metaphors of time that highlight and contrast with the template described above and more fully elucidate the contradictions inherent in everyday family life. Each metaphor of time (e.g., pressure cooker, map, mirror, river, feast) mediates how families enlist consumption in relation to idealized family time. It is important to stress that we use these metaphors theoretically as etic frames for organizing the diverse ways that families think about time. Although families may rely more on some metaphors than others, across varying contextual circumstances, families are likely to engage many, if not all, of these metaphors. For example, the metaphors families use for framing vacations or even weekends might be quite different from the ones they use to frame weekday evenings. We address these metaphors next and offer future research and policy implications.

## TIME AS A PRESSURE COOKER

A common metaphor for family time is time as a pressure cooker (Cotte et al., 2004; Daly, 1996; Thompson, 1996). Families feel pressed for time, squeezed, and time impoverished, and this feeling stems from the gnawing view of time as finite. Similar to a pot covered by a lid with no way to let the steam out, our lives are overflowing with events, and limited time often increases feelings of pressure, as we continually attempt to fit more and more activities into our already busy lives. There is no time left over; nothing else can fit. Although some research shows a general increase in family time (Galinsky, Aumann, & Bond, 2009), the presence of this metaphor may actually be a result of a *perceived* loss of family time: "The coordination of time has become more problematic because people nowadays are increasingly mobile and because institutions have become less rigid in their temporalities" (Ronka & Korvela, 2009, p. 92). The lack of structure and rigidity across contexts contributes to the complexity of coordinating time that engenders a sense of being harried. Prior work has indicated that those who live by the pressure cooker metaphor tend to be highly scheduled, analytic, and monochronic, meaning they typically focus on one activity at a time (Cotte et al., 2004). The guiding tenets of this metaphor often result in families struggling to keep it all together as they attempt to live up to idealized family time. In particular, this metaphor invites sentiments of continuous strife and guilt that accompanies the failure to set aside enough quality time for family. We systematically examine how this is linked to a diversity of family identities and roles and how families strategize to create a family work–life balance with this as their organizing metaphor. Further, our goal is to provide marketing and policy implications for addressing time-poor, overbooked families to enhance family well-being.

### Guilt and Stress for the Time Poor

In stark contrast to the relaxed, stress-free ideal of family time, in practice, time-poor families find this time crammed with activities, marred by a sense of moral obligation to ensure it is prioritized, and therefore loaded with tension and conflict. The late afternoon and early evening time commonly referred to as the family rush hour (Bittman & Wajcman, 2004; Schulz, Cowan, Cowan, & Brennan, 2004) or 6:00 crash (Larson & Richards, 1994) is loaded with negative emotions that seep in from the frustrations of a harried day. Piled on top of parents' work stresses are the multiple car pools, after-school activities, and sports of their children, followed by the ongoing challenges of scrounging up dinner and completing all of the nighttime routines before the day's end. Dual-earner families, such as that of 42-year-old Kim, have acknowledged the pressure to "fit it all in" in the evenings, a clear mark of the zero-sum view of time (as cited in Daly, 2001b, p. 291). Thus, even though many families plan to have dinner together each night, these plans regularly collapse under the weight of an emergency. Families reconcile the gap between plans for and actual experiences of family time with a series of weekly emergencies that collectively represent the daily reality of contemporary life (Frias-Gutierrez & Price, 2007).

Rising Expectations for Family Time

Families recognize that if left to spontaneity as in the ideal, family time would never occur, as daily tensions of work, school, and competing activities take over (Daly, 2001b). Thus, family time in actuality is purposeful and sometimes even "measured based on the amount of effort" put in to ensure that it happens (Kremer-Sadlik et al., 2008, p. 300). Through a great deal of planning and effort to coordinate schedules, families attempt to find family time where little is evident. Unfortunately, as time-saving solutions, such as ready-made foods, trip planners, online grocery stores, all-in-one floor cleaners, and dishwashers that scour dishes for you, have increased, society expects higher levels of output (Kaufman-Scarborough, 2006). Thus, rather than free up time for more relaxing, leisurely interactions with family, solutions have paradoxically raised expectations instead.

This burden of rising expectations may fuel families to take on more and more activities not only at the family level but also among individuals and smaller groupings (e.g. children, parents) within the family. This prompts new questions related to family well-being that existing literature has largely neglected. For example, we know that in order to build individual and relational identities among coalitions, carving out time for each is important (Epp & Price, 2008). However, parents in particular feel guilty when they prioritize self or couple time over family time (Daly, 2001a). The mantra of "family first" emerged as a central theme among participants in a study about how they manage competing loyalties in the context of family dinner (Epp et al., 2009). Jane, a 42-year-old professor and mother in a dual-earner family, explained the difficulties of managing the activities of multiple family members:

> To me, I've always had very clear in my mind the idea that you've got a few balls in the air that you can just never ever drop, and family is my ball that I never ever drop. It was much more difficult for me when I had small children to take care of. Now that I've got children that have more autonomy, you know, the youngest one being 12, that's a little bit easier, but it's a constant balancing act where you're always thinking about, well, who did I shortchange last, I don't want to shortchange them this time. And really, family, as much as I try to keep that sacrosanct, sometimes gets shortchanged a little bit, but I tend to prioritize around that. Family comes first. My personal goals—I'm a person who gets short-changed, so I tend to put things off until the summer or a holiday including even health-related issues. So I'm the person who gets shortchanged. I don't think I do a very good job on that.

Aligned with the ideal of ensuring that we prioritize collective family time over all else, future research should examine how families think about the relative importance of practices, sometimes referred to as the hierarchy of practices (Warde, 2005). Given that consumption is often embedded in family practices (e.g. Nintendo in family gaming, McDonald's in family dinner, Disney in family vacations), consumer researchers are uniquely positioned to uncover solutions to how families manage the interplay of collective, relational, and individual time (Epp & Price, 2011). Some families have turned to voluntary simplicity, a movement that focuses on "reducing material consumption and removing the 'clutter' from one's life" (Ballantine & Creery, 2010, p. 45) as a means of controlling the juggling act and socializing their children to reject a continuously escalating, consumption-driven lifestyle (Walther & Sandlin, 2008). Future research could focus on the effects this trend has on family well-being. Is this just a nostalgic longing for a life that never was, or a real change in consumption practices with positive implications for family well-being? Although critics have blamed consumer culture generally and technologies such as television in particular for the plummeting levels of family engagement and other societal ills (Schor, 2004, 2005), the empirical evidence is far from clear. Our own evidence suggests that more important than whether the family engages in a consumption-driven lifestyle is how the family engages with consumption. For example, families may use television shows to engage actively and vigorously in family identity practices replete with cuddling, joking behavior, and rituals. Moreover, when asked to reflect on family identity, consumption practices figure unprompted and prominently in childhood recollections of experiences that define family (Price & Epp, 2005).

## Balancing Work and Family Time

One major challenge to families trying to live up to the ideal is that new technologies have invaded the home and made the boundaries between work and family time much more porous (Gillis, 2001; Kaufman-Scarborough, 2006). This trend is in sharp contrast with the model of family time being kept separate and sacred. Although the trend of bringing work home may contribute to the increase in time parents are able to spend with their children, the nature of this time changes (e.g., level of involvement, types of activities), and attempting to hold it all together while juggling multiple tasks at once may only increase the pressure for those with a monochronic orientation.

An abundance of research has started to address consumer and policy issues that relate to balancing work and family. Given that, in the United States in particular, family matters are considered private and outside the scope of government, families are left to find their own solutions to issues of work–family conflict and time shortage, as opposed to profamily legislation that would increase paid family leave, for example (Kremer-Sadlik et al., 2008; Swindler, 2002). Setting aside quality family time is often viewed as the family's solution to managing work–family conflicts (Kremer-Sadlik & Paugh, 2007). However, they will likely need to turn to the marketplace to outsource other activities (e.g. cleaning, yard work, meals, eldercare) to carve out this time. Emerging studies in consumer research offer clues to how the marketplace may contribute to family time, as we search for a better understanding of where the boundaries are for outsourcing family practices.

For example, recent studies have examined how families care for elderly loved ones using a consumption ensemble that includes collaborations among paid in-home care providers, family members, and other service providers (Barnhart & Peñaloza, 2008). Similarly, Bradford and Sullivan (2010) offer insight into the decisions families make about daycare options. Preliminary findings indicate that families strive to convert typically profane relationships with commercial service providers into sacred relationships that allow them to think of the daycare providers as kin and avoid the stigma of contaminating family time by outsourcing it to the marketplace. Questions of family well-being and the potential role of the marketplace readily emerge in this context. Which activities do families view as acceptable to outsource? This question returns us to thinking about the hierarchy of practices that we previously introduced. How do we value and prioritize practices? Guilt also emerges as families try to outsource certain activities (e.g., child care, babysitting) in an attempt to find time for other activities (Daly, 2001b), so it is clear that not all practices are up for negotiation.

Another avenue for future research relates to the potentially collaborative roles of the marketplace and policy makers. Much debate has surrounded how intimately the government should be involved in family affairs. Comparisons of U.S. policies with those of other countries reveal that other countries are much more profamily with regard to parental leave, child support, and tax policies (Gentry, Epp, & Baker, 2005). Despite the popular call for improving family policies in the United States to relieve families of the tensions between work and family obligations, some resist government intervention. Sociologist David Popenoe "thinks the pro-family state actually has weakened the Swedish family ... by usurping functions traditionally located within the family" (as cited in Hochschild, 2003, p. 166), such as caregiving. However, Hochschild points to evidence that Sweden actually has stronger families, based on comparisons of marital breakup and teen pregnancy rates, than in the United States, where modest profamily legislation exists, except the Family and Medical Leave Act.

Along with others, Hochschild argues that governmental aid alone will not solve work–family tensions. Instead, we need a change in societal norms with regard to the division of labor between men and women. "The real solutions, like the real causes, lie somewhere else ... the cause of time famine is not just the scarcity of the thing itself, but inequitable systems of time production and distribution" (Gillis, 1996, p. 17). Solutions that involve changes in culture, governmental policies, and marketplace offerings become even more important when considering the well-being of low-income families, a topic we turn to next.

### Time Poor and Poor

The sense of time scarcity is heightened for low-income families whose unpredictable second- and third-shift work schedules coupled with limited resources make it difficult for them to outsource tasks such as day care, home maintenance, and meals. Poor mothers have described their lives as "more than simply hectic" (Roy, Tubbs, & Burton, 2004, p. 173). Many have articulated their frustration with time lost waiting for public transportation, meeting with various public-service institutions, and traveling to higher quality grocery and department stores located outside their neighborhoods (Crockett & Wallendorf, 2004). The issues that arise from incongruent timetables are often mistaken for a disorganized parenting style among low-income families, which has been associated with lasting effects on children's mental health and potential for substance abuse (see Prinz, Chapter 28 of this volume).

Due to the many activities necessary for family well-being, poor families must make real choices about whether to abandon family time, healthy meals, employment opportunities, or public aid, despite the fact that losing any one of these is painful (Roy et al., 2004). In addition, as institutions and norms set the pace of time, working mothers whose schedules deviate, especially in the context of poverty, are constantly striving and failing to live up to expectations as both caregivers and providers for their families (Roy et al., 2004). Some have recommended public policy changes that include offering more flexible social institutions and market solutions (e.g. longer daycare hours, extended transportation services, more flexible appointments with social service agencies) and encourage more dependence on support networks (Roy et al., 2004). Another option is better coordination between private and governmental support systems to lighten the burden, such as vouchers for child care and housing, expanded health care coverage, and high-quality grocery stores in low-income neighborhoods.

## TIME AS A MAP

Families also draw on the metaphor of time as a map: "A map gives people a sense of direction, and it helps situate where they are now in relation to where they wish to go" (Cotte et al., 2004, p. 337). This organizing metaphor treats time both as something necessary for achieving families' goals and a corrective that ensures they stay on the right path. In this way, idealized family time specifies what families should do at certain stages of life, such as when we should get married, focus on a career, have children, and retire. Thus, family goals are, in many ways, directed by cultural templates. Like individuals who enlist this metaphor, we speculate that families who adopt this view may be analytic, future oriented, and polychronic, meaning multitaskers or hoppers, as referred to in prior work (Cotte et al., 2004). Considering these characteristics, family research may study more explicitly how families form, strive for, and accomplish collective-level goals and the outcomes this has for well-being.

In a culture of competition, families make comparisons to their neighbors and others included in the familial gaze that is built from media images and convention (Hirsch, 1997). Thus, families frequently are defined and judged by their activities. Goal-driven families find it difficult to relax, as "there is nothing leisurely about today's family time ... every activity must have a purpose" (Gillis, 2001, p. 30). Status games often referred to in the literature and the popular press point to experiences and brands as symbols that communicate success in achieving these goals. When competitiveness among families drives members to escalate their commitments to different activities, little time is left to achieve collective goals (Ronka & Korvela, 2009). Despite this, we recognize that families do articulate specific collective goals, consult time repeatedly, and note discrepancies between what they have achieved and the ideal.

### Family Time and Goal Striving

Although family goals orient diverse consumption decisions related to time, such as household budgeting, health care planning, and college and retirement saving, this domain has received surprisingly little attention in consumer research. Prior work introduced the concept of we-intentions to better understand planned behavior and group action (Bagozzi, 2000; Bagozzi & Dholakia, 2006). However, substantive family research has generally neglected the idea of collective goals until recently. "For Searle and Bratman, it is the individual intention that we act jointly in some way. But is it possible to investigate group action where actions of members entail intentional acting by a collectivity?" (as cited in Bagozzi, 2000, p. 393). Ethnographic studies that use depth interviews and participant observation have taken on these questions in a family context. For instance, in their study of couples using assisted reproductive technologies to pursue parenthood, Fischer, Otnes, and Tuncay (2007) found that cultural discourses of scientific rationalism, self-management, and fatalism guided families' decisions to maintain, revise, or abandon the collective goal of starting a family. Each of these is also informed by a discourse of pursuing biological parenthood as the ideal.

Some of our current research also examines collective family goals. We find that the choices that families make about which products or services to purchase while on vacation are shaped by the goals they are trying to accomplish and how they manage the interplay among family, relational, and individual goals in this context (Epp & Price, 2011). Indisputably, families passionately strive for goals such as legitimizing particular family forms (e.g., adoptive, gay, single parent) or preserving unique parent–child identities amid divorce; they think of themselves in relation to a cultural ideal in which the timing and course of family life are already prescribed. In what ways might the marketplace help families who depart from cultural ideals achieve their goals? Considering that unpredictable schedules and lack of consistent resources for low-income families make setting, much less achieving, family goals challenging (Roy et al., 2004), what types of market solutions would best serve these families? Further, how might changes in family policies linked to marriage, access to benefits, and so forth ultimately change families' goals and the consumption practices that accompany them? Groups such as the New Beginnings Program (See Prinz, Chapter 28 of this volume) that focus on rebuilding mother–child relationships following a divorce, reducing interparental conflict, and helping the family adjust offer a way to define a new normal for families.

### Integrating Family Time and Work Goals

Goals may be propelled or thwarted as the lines between work and home are blurred. In contrast with the ideal that maintains these as separate spheres, the trend for families to blend work and family life within the context of the household raises new issues. Although in comparison to others, those who enlist the metaphor of time as a map tend to be multitaskers. As household activities become integrated with work goals (e.g., starting a load of laundry while completing a work report), conflicts can occur when home and work time regimes differ (Kaufman-Scarborough, 2006). Technology companies are already thinking about how to seamlessly incorporate integrated technologies into family life. Within the home, technologies have transformed the landscape of family relationships, especially as related to how they integrate work and family practices. In fact, home has been studied as the intersection of physical, social, and technological spaces (Venkatesh, 2006). It is important for us to consider how these spaces may affect one another. Specifically, main concerns might focus on how new technologies such as family gaming systems transform the social interactions that take place between family members in potentially transformed physical spaces, such as living rooms and family rooms, that must accommodate these new behaviors.

Thinking of time as a map necessarily orients us toward future destinations. When families contemplate their futures, they articulate a range of ideas about who they want to be or avoid becoming. We might label these identity projects as possible families in homage to the possible selves term coined for individuals (Markus & Nurius, 1986). Ideas about who we want to be as a family are likely to directly influence the goals we set and the consumption behaviors used to achieve them. This untapped topic is rich as an area of TCR. For example, families express genuine concern over avoiding a feared family reality when moving to a new place:

> They're not under your feet anymore. They're separated in different rooms! And so you can't interact all the time, and you don't interact all the time ... physically you don't have to be in the same room, and I worry about that just a little bit. Moving to a bigger house, I don't want us to lose that togetherness, and I don't want us to feel like we're not a unit anymore. (Megan Erikson, family mother; Epp & Price, 2010, p. 827)

Megan's anxiety reveals the tensions in being caught up in the idealized course of family time that comes with having more space for family practices, being able to entertain neighbors and friends, and continuing on a traditional trajectory. Families recognize that they must be vigilant (i.e., consult the map) regularly to ensure they do not become the kind of family they fear: disconnected, separate, and fragmented.

Possible families may also be those we hope will come to fruition and that we actively work to secure. Families let themselves imagine being the kind of family who volunteers in the community, or an active and outdoorsy family instead of the couch potatoes that currently take up residence in their living room, or an artistic and culturally informed family who goes to galleries and museums on the weekends. In some cases, these wishes are realized through careful planning and by enlisting the marketplace. For example, returning to our study of family vacations, the Hardy-Harrisons, a newly blended family of five, were adamant about realizing their visions of being a skiing family in the future:

> I think [the vacation] was geared more towards getting the kids involved in skiing, 'cause we wanted them to learn how to ski.... We wanted them to get excited about it, because we're (*points to wife Kendra*) going to go ski.... They're going with us, so.... (*Kendra smiles.*) (Hardy-Harrison father; Epp & Price, 2011, p. 22)

Research on possible families is in its infancy, and although the case above reveals how these may be achieved, many factors may hamper this goal and require further study. For example, multiple voices of coalitions and individual family members may conflict (Ronka & Korvela, 2009), resulting in potentially different visions of who we want to be as a family and/or our collective commitment and goals for achieving particular identities (Epp & Price, 2008). However, we lack an understanding of how these voices get disentangled and the outcomes for collective identity goals. Further, we may envision being a particular type of family, but a lack of resources, a lack of access to products and services, and/or commitments to different identities may stand in the way. How do we become the kind of family we want to be? Future TCR could investigate how hope and hopefulness interplay with conflicting demands in the collective goal progress (MacInnis & de Mello, 2005) and examine how consumption of products, services, and activities are recruited to achieve a hoped-for family and avoid a feared one (Patrick, MacInnis, & Folkes, 2002).

## TIME AS A MIRROR

Time is also a mirror: "time as self-reflection and personal assessment" (Cotte et al., 2004, p. 338). This metaphor encompasses how families reflect on who we are, who we have been, and who we want to be (Epp & Price, 2008). Much of consumer research inherently promotes the view of time as a mirror through evidence that we continually construct and reflect on our identities in our consumption choices (Belk, 1988; Schouten, 1991). Thus, how we choose to spend our time directly portrays who we are both within the family and to outsiders. Further, our actions are powerfully shaped by how quality time is defined in culture (e.g., the perfect family meal, vacation) and by comparisons of actual family time in relation to the ideal practices of family time (i.e., engaging in the "right" activities). Coupled with ideals of family time, families who live by this metaphor also draw on the cultural norm of continuous self-improvement. Just as looking in a mirror might reveal our flaws, comparisons to idealized family time prompts us to monitor discrepancies between the ideal and what is reflected in our own activities.

Consider the proliferation of self-help books about how to improve family well-being and better allocate time to make it count. These materials reflect the idea that collective activities should be purposeful (Kremer-Sadlik et al., 2008). In fact, in our study of family vacations (Epp & Price, 2011), families clearly and pervasively adopted this perspective as they articulated identity goals of building, reasserting, preserving, and transforming family identity in the activities they selected. The assumption that family activities carry with them the power of collective identity is evident in the following participant excerpt from a study of family practices. This family equates spending quality time together with the pure act of being a family, to the extent that if particular activities were lost, the family itself would atrophy:

*David (father):* We have board games.
*Maggie (mother):* Yeah. We have a slew, yeah. Umhum.
*David:* And that's like an extension that's been consistent since you were kids. Uh, we will, we always played board games a lot....
*Interviewer:* Okay. What do you think would be lost if all of a sudden your family stopped playing games?
*Venessa (daughter):* I think, I think we would not interact with each other as much, and we'd start focusing on external things.... Or, disbursing, and not doing anything together after dinner.
*David:* Exactly. We would segregate, you know. And, and that's one of the things I think we consciously try to avoid with family get-togethers, is where everybody segregates. You know, the men go here, the women go there. Everybody kind of like gets into their own little clique, and that to me is the start of, uh, you know, an atri—you know, atrophy of the family. (Keller family; Epp, Schau, & Price, 2010, p. 28)

Given the importance of these activities in reflecting identity, families focus on optimizing quality time and make consumption choices that allow them to maximize it. That is, they work toward continuous self-improvement to achieve a better reflection. Future TCR could address families' strategies for change and well-being. How do we improve our family's reflection both internally and to the outside world? How does this structure the way families actually manage and organize family time? Finally, how do we hold on to practices that define us in positive ways? This is a topic we turn to next.

### Building and Preserving Traditions

When families are living by the "time as a mirror" metaphor, they are likely to be past-oriented and analytic (Cotte et al., 2004), as a mirror reflects traces of the history that led to this point. As such, they focus on building traditions through family rituals, narratives, and preservation of intergenerational ties (Bradford, 2009). Each of these practices delineates boundaries of family membership (Rook, 1985; Wallendorf & Arnould, 1991), maintains continuity of identity over time (Curasi, Price, & Arnould, 2004; Moisio, Arnould, & Price, 2004), patterns consumption meanings and behaviors (Otnes & Pleck, 2003), allows families to negotiate the relative roles of members (Wallendorf & Arnould, 1991), and offers simplifying procedures during times of crisis (Gentry, Kennedy, Paul, & Hill, 1995).

For example, family narratives help create, structure, and preserve family time from generation to generation, as narratives are our way of making sense of the world and situating us within contexts and time. Consumer researchers have investigated family stories as a way to better understand how brands, products, and services get caught up and embedded in family activities (Epp & Price, 2011). These studies have practical implications for understanding how behaviors that cast us in a positive light are replicated over time and what the consequences might be for loyalty to what some call fortress brands (i.e., those embedded in daily rituals; Brady, 2007). Still, more work is needed from a macroperspective to understand how rituals and myths are implicated in the reproduction of inequitable division of labor and of age, class, and gender structures within the home (Gillis, 1996).

With a focus on building traditions comes attention to nostalgia. In the opening of this chapter, we pointed to it as one of the hallmarks of idealized family time. This focus on reminiscence leads to what might be called a paradox of documenting: Parents are often so preoccupied with capturing and creating memories to enact this nostalgic ideal that they feel disconnected from the actual experience as an onlooker who is absent from the intimacy of the moment. This speaks to the "illusiveness of family time … they somehow got lost between their future oriented investment in the memories of their children and the relatively unfulfilling playback of experiences that they were busy orchestrating" (Daly, 2001b, pp. 291–292). If we take a moment to reflect on the proliferation of new technologies that enable this documentation, from camera phones that instantly upload photos on social-networking sites to family websites maintained across members and distances, the paradox of documenting is likely to be exacerbated in the future, and with it come questions of how this will impact family well-being (Mick & Fournier, 1998).

### TIME AS A RIVER

Families may adopt the metaphor of time as a river:

> We may not have too much power over where the river might take us, but we can either attempt to try and control our direction and journey in the river or we can simply float along and go with the flow. (Cotte et al., 2004, p. 340)

From this perspective, although idealized family time may serve as a benchmark or an anchor point, families may view the template of family time that is nostalgic, happy, set apart from work, inclusive of all members, and narrowly defined by only certain activities as unrealistic and unachievable. Instead, these families are spontaneous and present-oriented; they "live in the moment … either by choice or default" (Cotte et al., 2004, p. 341). We examine how this metaphor shapes both dominant and resistant discourses for family empowerment and management with implications for policy.

In some cases, family members recognize that systemic constraints are inevitable, and trying to live up to the ideal is impossible. Daly (2001b) argues that because there is such discord between the real and the ideal of family time, families are resigned to guilt as "an expression of powerlessness to do anything to narrow the gap between the high standards of what family time should be and the demanding realities that routinely sabotage those ideals" (p. 292). For low-income families, restricted access to resources emphasizes the daily agency struggles that emerge in the river metaphor. Daily routines are driven by forces outside of their control. Institutional constraints, such as a 9-to-5 public timetable that reflects the collective rhythms of society, navigating and waiting on public transportation, and interacting with inflexible public aid offices, complicate families' ability to gain control. These families routinely improvise family time around unpredictable schedules, but many yearn for more certainty. Marie aptly framed market solutions as empowering when she said, "A car means that time is yours, that time doesn't belong to the bus," even as she lamented that this option is out of reach for some in her situation (as cited in Roy et al., 2004, p. 173). Like placing a boulder in a river, these types of solutions offer pockets of control but do not attempt to change the normative systems that sometimes lead to feelings of futility.

## Consumption Opportunities and Constraints

Although little family consumer research has adopted an agency perspective, scholars have much to learn about how the marketplace presents both opportunities and constraints. For example, we conducted a study that examines agency granted by a network of objects, spaces, and family practices that propels some objects into active participation in family activities and expels others to the market (Epp & Price, 2010). This study suggests that the fate of a family's objects and practices is both empowered and constrained by its own biography and the overlapping and competing biographies of other objects, practices, and spaces in the network. Just as time may be viewed as a river with many obstacles and currents, the network also draws objects into its flow and shapes outcomes for other objects and practices. Family time is, in part, contingent on how objects flow in and out of the network. For example, Megan Erikson talked about the narrative that accompanied a table that she recently inherited from her grandmother, Bea, that she intends to use in her home:

> That table has stories. It's not a happy story, but it's a story … my dad's dad was a very abusive man.… When Bea went into the [nursing] home, those five siblings [dad's] all said, "We would not want that table." We have horrible memories about it … nothing good. It's very expensive, but we don't want to see it.… I had nothing but good memories around it.… On Christmas Eve, my mom and dad and all us kids would go over and have this big, elaborate dinner around this Duncan Phyfe table. Bea had these gorgeous silver candlesticks.… He [my grandfather] also put a silver dollar under everybody's folded, linen napkin.… Those are my memories of the table—all happy. (Erikson family, mother; Epp & Price, 2010, p. 829)

The family time that occurred around this table, and other tables vying for a place in the Eriksons' dining room, helps determine whether it is used or not. In this case, the Eriksons inherited the table based on the constraints its biography posed to other family members and the positive associations it had for this family. Thus, the historicity of possessions (e.g., home, clothing, keepsakes) can impose constraints to action (D. Miller, 2001, 2005), especially with regard to how we enlist objects to facilitate family time.

Not only do the objects' biographies determine their use in family time activities, but also the dominant ideologies about these activities subject families to constraints and feelings of futility.

For some, we observe acceptance that they are part of a flow of time that includes challenges, and the families' best attempts to navigate are sufficient. Quests to navigate family dinnertime offer useful illustrations. Discourses on family dinner have presented the ideal as "home-cooked food, planned and prepared most often by a woman, eaten at a regular time, according to prescribed etiquette regarding behaviors such as manners and assigned seating of family members" (Larson, Branscomb, & Wiley, 2006, p. 4; see also Valentine, 1999). In addition, media depictions of family dinner, such as the recent campaign initiated by the National Center on Addiction and Substance Abuse, clearly endorse the traditional family dinner ideology. Specifically, the National Center on Addiction and Substance Abuse promotes regularity of family dinner, with high standards of five or more times per week; suggests its enemies are the "laziness and leniency" of family members; and touts the benefits of eating together, such that kids will stay away from drugs, perform better in school, and learn healthy eating habits (Gibbs, 2006, p. 3).

In response to this ideal, many of the families in our study (Epp et al., 2009), particularly mothers, rarely questioned the media's depiction or script for family dinner. Despite this, women experienced it as a barrage of obstacles that included competing with family members' outside obligations, responding to never-ending emergencies, and dealing with a lack of resources. Although realizations about how these practical obstacles stack up against ideal depictions of family dinner may inspire a sense of hopelessness, these families seek options that empower them as a way to manage this tension. Participants talked about a few ways that they try to make up for some of the gaps they experience between ideal and realized family dinners. One of the defenses common in the study was reliance on market solutions. However, the most common reflection about accessing market solutions was that these options were inadequate. Consider the following dialogue of Lydia and Adrian Gonzales, parents of a dual-earner family:

*Lydia:* Friday, Saturday, I usually cook. Or we grab something—um, we grab something or go out to eat.... I don't prefer processed food, fast food. Fast food's fattening and unhealthy.
*Adrian:* And expensive. (Gonzales family; Epp et al., 2009)

The consistent indictment that the market is not an adequate substitute for the family meal may reveal just how deeply entrenched the family dinner ideology is with regard to the template that meals should be home-cooked, balanced, prepared by mom, and so on. This has important implications for service providers in that market solutions such as fast-food or meal assembly services (e.g., Dream Dinners, Super Suppers) must pay attention to lived experiences of family dinner as they interplay with idealized versions (Arnould & Price, 2006). In addition, the responsibility of making family dinner happen continues to fall heavily on mothers. However, in other practices of family time, such as vacations, orchestration is more widely distributed among family members, indicating that we-discourses are more prevalent outside of the family dinner ideology. Thus, one public policy question that surfaces might be, how can shifts in media campaigns that adopt broader scripts shape mothering discourses related to family dinner? There is a desperate need for alternative discourses.

### Alternative Discourses for Family Time

Some examples of resistant discourses are emerging in consumer research in which rather than trying to live up to templates of idealized family time, families are articulating new discourses. Families who do not fit into the preformed categories of a canonical two-parent, heterosexual family with biological children seek legitimacy through both alternate discourses and collective consumption behaviors that define them as distinct. To illustrate, a recent study examined how stay-at-home dads legitimize unconventional gender identities within a maternally oriented discourse of parenthood

(Coskuner-Balli & Thompson, 2009). These fathers engage in collective consumption strategies that help combat the social isolation and stigma they experience as stay-at-home dads. This research paid explicit attention to the ways that cultural expectations and the scarcity of appropriate marketplace resources act as significant hurdles to performing a masculine social identity as fathers. Collectively, these fathers drive the market to provide resources that legitimate their identities as primary caregivers and contest prior expectations of parenting discourses. Considerable opportunities exist to further explore how unconventional families react to cultural templates of family and forge their own identities using marketplace resources and collective action.

In our own research, we have uncovered that while family time together in shared activities represents the idealized discourse for family time, the time spent in symbiotic sociality offers a vital, rewarding alternative (Epp & Price, 2011). Time spent in the same space but involved in different activities may provide many if not all of the same benefits as more intense family engagement. Yet, symbiotic sociality is rarely supported in marketplace alternatives or promoted in policy as an alternative way of doing family. Families may underreport time together doing different things as family time, yet such time is likely to contribute to family identity and consumer well-being. More research is needed to capture these types of family time and measure their relative impact. Such research could uncover market and policy alternatives to current cultural templates of family.

## TIME AS A FEAST

For some families, time is a feast. This metaphor is inextricably linked to consumption and suggests both the wealth of possibilities and the limits in our abilities to choose and consume. Some have argued that the wealth of consumption possibilities and burgeoning consumption responsibilities are the exact reason that families feel so time-poor (Hochschild, 2005; Southerton & Tomlinson, 2005). Paradoxically, when families live by the time as a feast metaphor, they embrace these possibilities rather than feel constrained by them. New outlets for participating in consumer culture have surfaced with increased globalization, access to credit, and sharing (Belk, 2010; Belk & Llamas, Chapter 30 of this volume), so the pressures that may be felt as time is compressed are slightly alleviated with broader access to diverse markets. These families do not acknowledge many of the tensions, such as asynchronous or harried time, present in other metaphors. Instead, their most prominent concerns are the opportunity costs of options not chosen. Here, we organize across diverse literatures to identify policy implications for helping families engage this feast without feeling like they are overcooked.

### Collective Variety-Seeking

We might describe these families as "omnivorous … which refers to preferences for a variety of cultural activities that draw from a diverse range of cultural genres" (Southerton, 2006, p. 449). Some studies have suggested that those with high cultural capital and incomes are more likely to seek variety (Holt, 1998; Southerton, 2006). In addition, these individuals also report a broader range of network ties that place them in diverse cultural contexts (Southerton, 2006). This conclusion is given credence by some of our data that exemplify the same pattern. One informant family, the Dodges, took a trip to China as part of the mother's work on a collaborative team that studies violence against women. This family of three would be considered upper middle class and boasts a wide social circle and a broad range of experiences. In line with prior research, this family was determined to try new things and be exposed to diverse circumstances:

*Mary (mother):* I think it's an incredible experience to be able to travel, but not just to be the tourist. To be open to hearing and seeing what people's lives are like, not just what the temple is or the art museum or whatever it is that they're willing to show you. So for me, I really did have a goal of Madeline [daughter] being exposed to another culture in a way that was not scary and opened her up to be able to do more of that. I was very conscious of that (*She looks to husband Matt for confirmation, and he nods in agreement.*) ... So, for us, when we think about—when I think about family vacations, I really am not so hesitant to take Madeline into something that's not just all child-oriented. I mean, she's a bright young woman (*looks at Madeline as she speaks about her*) that asks wonderful questions and comes back with all kinds of different perspectives, and I think she and her friends are—they are our hope that we can get past some of these problems with pollution and global warming and war and all this kind of stuff. I think that being not afraid of people who are different than you is so important, and that's just one of the things that happens. You're just not afraid! I mean, Madeline's a very reserved person, but she's just not afraid to come along and try new things....

*Interviewer:* What parts of this vacation reflect who you are as a family?

*Madeline:* Our ability to try new things and kind of learn (*smiles*). Our whole family just loves to learn, so I think that just going there and exposing yourself to all those things is kind of a reflection of our sense of adventure and that we're all willing to try new things and learn about different people and places.... The whole trip was like that ... even things like eating the food or something (*both parents listening intently, nodding in agreement, and smiling at her as she speaks*)—you don't even know, sometimes you don't even know what you're getting, because sometimes you think it's something and then it's just completely different from what we thought we ordered.... Then, I think, just walking around the city—it's a lot different than America, so it was kind of—well, different. (Dodge family; Epp, 2008, p. 63)

In this decision context, our informant family seems to implicitly embrace a feast metaphor for time. This extended excerpt captures many of the ways families who engage a feast metaphor experience time. When this metaphor frames time, families are present oriented and seek variety and possibilities (Cotte et al., 2004). At the same time, they realize that indulging in the feast requires effort; one must plan ahead to ensure that the benefits are realized.

Commonly, those who feast seek hedonic experiences, but little family consumer research has investigated this domain. Rather, the literature on family choice and decision making has been dominated by studies of relative influence that uncover how family members persuade one another to align their preferences (e.g., Belch, Belch, & Ceresino, 1985; Corfman & Lehmann, 1987; Cotte & Wood, 2004; Filiatrault & Ritchie, 1980; Palan & Wilkes, 1997; Su, Fern, & Ye, 2003). Adopting the time as feast metaphor for thinking about family choice could open up the field. For instance, research could focus on collective variety-seeking. What conditions lead families to unlatch from repetitive practices, as in the mirror metaphor, and seek out different experiences? In what ways do the desire for and evaluation of hedonic experiences link to high versus low cultural capital?

### Emotional Spillover Among Family Members

Although absent from consumer research, links among emotion, well-being, and family time have been the subject of many studies across disciplines (Daly, 2003; Westman, 2005). At the family level, this refers to the emotional life, atmosphere, or climate of the family (Daly, 2003). Given the proclivity of families with a feast orientation to try out new experiences, one promising area of future research would be to investigate emotional contagion or crossover that explains the spillover of emotions among family members (Ronka & Korvela, 2009) and contributes to the emotional atmosphere of the family. Consider the grumpy teenager who ruins Disney for younger siblings or the passionate father who sparks a family's interest in history. Understanding this phenomenon could have direct implications for how families collectively evaluate new consumption experiences. Further, when we consider the research on emotional work and regulation, it is clear that "the transmission of emotions is not, however, automatic" (Ronka & Korvela, 2009, p. 91; see also Erickson, 2005), which suggests that families and marketers alike may devise strategies that encourage or prevent emotional contagion as it relates to the evaluation of experiences and to family well-being.

## FINAL THOUGHTS

Family time and togetherness are primary determinants of consumer well-being, yet they have been the focus of little consumer policy or research. We have provided a review of the literature on family time that is firmly situated in consumer culture, and focused on the meanings and practices of contemporary family time. We examined how consumption both enhances and inhibits the experience of family togetherness and uncovered gaps in our understanding that offer rich opportunities for TCR. Finally, within the context of each metaphor, we explicitly developed a public policy and research agenda to improve family well-being.

We posit that families, like individuals, employ a range of metaphors for thinking about time, and in turn, these metaphors empower, constrain, and frame the role of consumption in pursuit of family time and well-being. Although we have depicted these metaphors as independent, it is far more likely that all families draw on this repertoire in different ways at different times. For example, during the peak career and family phase of mid-30s to mid-40s, the metaphor of time as a pressure cooker may frame family time more than at other points. It is during this period that family time may seem the most fragile and scarce. Similarly, time as a feast may be more salient when the family is planning a vacation than when it is trying to grapple with competing demands and exhaustion on a weekday evening. In addition, socioeconomic and other circumstances may lead families to frame time using one metaphor more than another. For example, low-income families or families in crisis or transition may feel time is a river that leaves them helpless and out of control. New families may engage time as a map for planning who and how they want to be, whereas older families may engage more with time as a mirror, taking comfort in the enactment of long-held rituals and everyday routines.

By contrasting the metaphors as they implicate consumption practices, we can see how the role of consumption is altered with broad implications for TCR and public policy. Table 29.1 offers a summary comparison of metaphors with regard to the view of time supported, the relationship to idealized family time, the role of consumption in well-being, and potential questions for future research. Elements of Table 29.1 are discussed below.

### Provide Realistic Alternatives to Time as a Constraint

Across metaphors, we see that time acts in three distinct ways. First, in both the pressure cooker and river metaphors, families view time as a constraint. In the former, time bears down on us, and the requirements of idealized family time serve only to exacerbate the pressure. Outsourcing some activities to the marketplace to keep the lid on offers only temporary relief, as guilt and increased expectations for productivity loom. In the latter, although incompatible cultural timetables and images of idealized family time constrain, those who think with a river metaphor escape the pressure to conform and instead accept that they will never live up to the ideal. This simple, freeing act empowers these families to view consumption as one parameter they can control; it offers reprieve from time constraints and motivates collective action to change institutional structures. When time is a river, policy and consumption opportunities are tools for managing uncertainty, chaos, and lack of control.

**Table 29.1** Comparison of Time Metaphors

| Metaphor | View of Time | Relationship to Idealized Family Time | Role of Consumption in Consumer Well-Being | Future Transformative Consumer Research Questions |
|---|---|---|---|---|
| Pressure cooker | Is finite, bears down, and constrains | Ideal exacerbates pressure, as experienced family time is mingled with work, not spontaneous, and filled with tension. | Outsource activities to the marketplace in an attempt to generate more family time | • How do families determine which practices to prioritize over others?<br>• How does voluntary simplicity (e.g., downsizing) affect family well-being?<br>• Where are the boundaries for outsourcing family practices?<br>• How should private and governmental support systems coordinate to lighten the burden for time-poor, especially low-income, families? |
| Map | Orients, grounds, and facilitates the tracking of progress | Ideal specifies what families should do over the life course. | Can either facilitate or hinder achievement of family goals | • How do families form and achieve collective goals, and what are the outcomes of this for well-being?<br>• In what ways might marketplace or public policy solutions aid families who depart from cultural ideals to achieve their goals?<br>• What are the conditions for achieving possible families? |
| Mirror | Reflects, orients, and encourages us to monitor for discrepancies | Ideal designates the "right" activities for achieving family time. | Portrays who we are both within and outside of the family | • How might families improve their reflections both internally and to the outside world?<br>• How do motivations for improvement structure the way families actually manage and organize family time?<br>• How do families hold on to practices that define them in positive ways?<br>• How are rituals and myths implicated in the reproduction of inequitable division of labor and of age, class, and gender structures? |
| River | Guides and constrains | Ideal is viewed as unrealistic and unachievable. | Empowers families to participate in collective action to change institutions | • How can shifts in media campaigns that adopt broader scripts shape family discourses?<br>• How do unconventional families react to cultural templates of family and forge alternate discourses that prompt collective action?<br>• In what ways does symbiotic sociality contribute to family identity and consumer well-being? |
| Feast | Indulges and provides endless possibilities | Ideals are in line with many aspects of how time is experienced, but families also boldly chart their own paths. | Offers a palette of positive choices | • What conditions lead to collective variety-seeking?<br>• In what ways do the desire for and evaluation of hedonic experiences link to high versus low cultural capital?<br>• How might families encourage or prevent emotional contagion to improve family well-being? |

Rather than casting family time as a hurdle that families should strive to attain, it could be framed as a resource to draw on and seek sanctuary in. Rather than family time being another impossible task, family can and should be a way of being that nurtures and restores. For example, soccer families may stop having dinner together but may find that preparing and traveling to tournaments is also meaningful family time. Rather than focusing on how families historically spent time together, TCR could focus on identifying new avenues for spending time together that are more consistent with contemporary life. Further, rather than trying to get families to live up to the ideal, which promotes guilt more than well-being, policy makers should focus on providing realistic options for closing the gap.

### Provide Consumption Options That Are Positive Partners in Family Time

Second, for families who adopt the map and mirror metaphors, time orients or ground them. Idealized family time specifies what we should do, stipulates which are the "right" activities, and gives us a place to turn to to track our progress. According to these metaphors, consumption aids in accomplishing our goals and signals when we have been successful. Unfortunately, consumption practices also produce negative reflections and may hinder our progress toward collective goals. Consulting the map or the mirror uncovers discrepancies between who we are and who we want to be just as readily as it captures positive images. A challenge for TCR is to frame consumption as a positive partner in family time rather than a weapon for the demise of family.

Both policy and consumption opportunities could fruitfully engage these metaphors by helping families find the path between their multiple goals and consumption choices. As a mundane example, home remodeling would first uncover the individual, relational, and collective goals of the family, then help them build spaces and arrange objects and technologies in these spaces to manage their array of goals. Family space would be oriented around where family members actually gather and interact rather than conventional designations of family rooms or living rooms. Policy and consumption opportunities would also help consumers represent and preserve family identity.

### Help Families Tailor Consumption Options to Collective Goals

Third, in the feast metaphor, families view time as an indulgence. These families may be more willing to buck the idealized version of family time in the interest of harnessing a better experience. They have a much broader range of activities that are considered acceptable family time, such that these do not always need to be child-centered activities. In fact, exposing children to more grown-up activities is one way of ensuring the social reproduction of cultural capital across generations. In short, consumption gives access to manifold opportunities. Here, families may need chances to opt out or "change portion size" to reach their collective goals. For example, our research suggests that family vacations may sometimes be a feast that leaves families scurrying to consume everything but failing to accomplish their most important collective and relational goals (Epp & Price, 2011). Further, feast families do not make apologies for mixing work and family time, but rather, they view work experiences as an additional opportunity to expose family members to wider social and experiential networks.

Despite this, living up to the ideal of family time may come more easily to feast families than to others, given that some of their behaviors are naturally aligned with the ideal, such as behaviors that are spontaneous, variety-seeking, relaxed, and unstressed. Of the metaphors we live by, when families adopt a feast orientation, they seem to have the most positive outlook and view consumption behavior as providing direct access to the hedonic and playful aspects of family life. Unlike those in the river metaphor, who engage in collective action from a place of stigma and unconventionality, feast families are likely to have high cultural capital and, consequently, are granted the power to effect change with fewer obstacles. As such, social marketers and public policy makers interested in pushing a TCR agenda will find strong advocates here.

Each of these metaphors reveals new questions and agendas for TCR scholars interested in family issues. Three broad conclusions emerge from considering the overlaps among these perspectives and from our review of existing work. First, family time is revered as a fundamental source of life meaning and, in contemporary society, is inextricably intertwined with consumption. Much social science research has implied that families must choose between consumption practices and family time rather than theoretically and empirically examining how consumption and family time can be linked in positive ways. Because consumer research has focused far more on individual than collective or family consumption and well-being, policy makers and marketers interested in promoting well-being are left with few guidelines for action.

Next, discourses and measures of family time borrowed from a different era leave families unable to attain the idealized cultural template and unarmed with constructive alternatives. Although change is slow, implementing policies and consumer solutions that encourage a broader and more flexible definition of family time—who should be included, which activities "count," and how the labor for orchestrating it should be divided among family members—would be a positive start. Also, policy and consumption opportunities that help families integrate individual, relational, and collective goals are sorely needed. For example, in the case of family dinner, policy might encourage families to gather in symbiotic sociality rather than imposing a membership ideal of everyone and a meal ideal of home-cooked entrées and sides that leads families to give up and scurry to their separate rooms with cereal bowls. Similarly, research would seek to uncover a more nuanced view of the role of consumption in how families do and do not spend time together. For example, research might explore conditions for television viewing that contribute to family identity and consumer well-being, or more broadly explore how technologies can be designed to facilitate family interactions.

Finally, more explicit partnerships between consumer researchers, the private market, and policy makers are in order for alleviating the constraints imposed on families, as exemplified in the pressure cooker and river metaphors, and for reframing various institutions as positive collaborators in producing family time, as illustrated in the map and mirror metaphors. These partnerships also may motivate families who live by the feast metaphor to engage in proactive consumption behaviors. For example, alignment of governmental and corporate policies on issues such as recycling, sustainability, healthy eating, and environmental conservation may inspire feast families to use their positive outlooks to incite social change.

## REFERENCES

Adam, B. (1994). *Time and social theory*. Philadelphia: Polity Press.

Arnould, E. J., & Price, L. L. (2006). Market-oriented ethnography revisited. *Journal of Advertising Research, 46*(3), 251–262.

Bagozzi, R. P. (2000). On the concept of intentional social action in consumer behavior. *Journal of Consumer Research, 27*, 388–396.

Bagozzi, R. P., & Dholakia, U. M. (2006). Antecedents and purchase consequences of customer participation in small group brand communities. *International Journal of Research in Marketing, 23*, 45–61.

Ballantine, P. W., & Creery, S. (2010). The consumption and disposition behaviour of voluntary simplifiers. *Journal of Consumer Behavior, 9*(1), 45–56.

Barnett, R. C. (2005). Dual-earner couples: Good/bad for her and/or him? In D. F. Halpern & S. E. Murphy (Eds.), *Work–family balance to work–family interaction: Changing the metaphor* (pp. 151–171). Mahwah, NJ: Erlbaum.

Barnhart, M., & Peñaloza, L. (2008). Negotiating agency in the elderly consumption ensemble. In A. L. McGill & S. Shavitt (Eds.), *Advances in consumer research* (Vol. 36, pp. 53–55). Duluth, MN: Association for Consumer Research.

Belch, G., Belch, M., & Ceresino, G. (1985). Parental and teenage child influences in family decision making. *Journal of Business Research, 13*, 163–176.

Belk, R. W. (1988). Possessions and the extended self. *Journal of Consumer Research, 15*, 139–168.

Belk, R. W. (2010). Sharing. *Journal of Consumer Research, 36*, 715–734.

Bianchi, S. M., Robinson, J. P., & Milkie, M. A. (2006). *Changing rhythms of American family life.* New York: Russell Sage Foundation.

Bittman, M., & Wajcman, J. (2004). The rush hour: The quality of leisure time and gender equity. In N. Folbre & M. Bittman (Eds.), *Family time: The social organization of care* (pp. 171–194). New York: Routledge.

Bond, J. T., Galinsky, E., & Swanberg, J. (1998). *The 1997 National Study of the Changing Workforce.* New York: Families and Work Institute.

Bond, J. T., Thompson, C., Galinsky, E., & Prottas, D. (2003). *Highlights of the National Study of the Changing Workforce, 2002* (No. 3). New York: Families and Work Institute.

Bradford, T. W. (2009). Intergenerationally gifted asset dispositions. *Journal of Consumer Research, 36*, 93–111.

Bradford, T. W., & Sullivan, T. (2010). *Creating extended family through daycare choices: Exploring an emotional consumption experience.* Unpublished manuscript, University of Notre Dame, IN.

Brady, D. (2007, May 10). Daily rituals of the world. *BusinessWeek.* Available: http://www.businessweek.com/bwdaily/dnflash/content/may2007/db20070510_522420.htm

Corfman, K. P., & Lehmann, D. R. (1987). Models of cooperative group decision-making and relative influence: An experimental investigation of family purchase decisions. *Journal of Consumer Research, 14*, 1–13.

Coskuner-Balli, G., & Thompson, C. (2009). Legitimatizing an emergent social identity through marketplace performances. In A. L. McGill & S. Shavitt (Eds.), *Advances in consumer research* (Vol. 36, pp. 135–138). Duluth, MN: Association for Consumer Research.

Cotte, J., Ratneshwar, S., & Mick, D. G. (2004). The times of their lives: Phenomenological and metaphorical characteristics of consumer timestyles. *Journal of Consumer Research, 31*, 333–345.

Cotte, J., & Wood, S. (2004). Families and innovative consumer behavior: Atriadic analysis of sibling and parental influence. *Journal of Consumer Research, 31*, 78–86.

Crockett, D., & Wallendorf, M. (2004). The role of normative political ideology in consumer behavior. *Journal of Consumer Research, 13*, 511–528.

Curasi, C. F., Price, L. L., & Arnould, E. J. (2004). Things that should be kept: How individuals' cherished possessions become families' inalienable wealth. *Journal of Consumer Research, 31*(3), 609–622.

Daly, K. J. (1996). *Families and time: Keeping pace in a hurried culture.* Thousand Oaks, CA: Sage.

Daly, K. J. (2001a). Controlling time in families: Patterns that sustain gendered work in the home. In K. J. Daly (Ed.), *Minding the time in family experience: Emerging perspectives and issues* (pp. 227–249). New York: JAI Press.

Daly, K. J. (2001b). Deconstructing family time: From ideology to lived experience. *Journal of Marriage and Family, 63*(2), 283–294.

Daly, K. J. (2001c). Minding the time: Toward a theoretical expansion of time in families. In K. J. Daly (Ed.), *Minding the time in family experience: Emerging perspectives and issues* (pp. 1–16). New York: JAI Press.

Daly, K. J. (2003). Family theory versus the theories families live by. *Journal of Marriage and Family, 65*, 771–784.

Darrah, C. N., Freeman, J. M., & English-Lueck, J. A. (2007). *Busier than ever! Why American families can't slow down.* Stanford, CA: Stanford University Press.

DeVault, M. L. (2000). Producing family time: Practices of leisure activity beyond the home. *Qualitative Sociology, 23*(4), 485–503.

Douglas, S. J., & Michaels, M. W. (2004). *The mommy myth: The idealization of motherhood and how it has undermined women.* New York: Free Press.

English-Lueck, J. (1998, June). *The impact on families.* Paper presented at the second congressional seminar of the Consortium of Social Science Associations, Washington, DC.

Epp, A. M. (2008). *Yours, mine, and ours: How families manage collective, relational, and individual identity goals in consumption.* ETD collection for University of Nebraska-Lincoln, Paper AAI3297655. Available: http://digitalcommons.unl.edu/dissertations/AAI3297655

Epp, A. M., Frias-Gutierrez, K., & Price, L. L. (2009, June). *The idealization of family dinner and post-feminist strivings.* Paper presented at the fourth Consumer Culture Theory Conference, Ann Arbor, MI.

Epp, A. M., & Price, L. L. (2008). Family identity: A framework of identity interplay in consumption practices. *Journal of Consumer Research, 35*, 50–70.

Epp, A. M., & Price, L. L. (2010). The storied life of singularized objects: Forces of agency and network transformation. *Journal of Consumer Research, 36*, 820–837.

Epp, A. M., & Price, L. L. (2011). Designing solutions around customer network identity goals. *Journal of Marketing, 75*(2), 36–54.

Epp, A. M., Schau, H. J., & Price, L. L. (2010). *Technologies as platforms for family identity.* Unpublished manuscript, University of Wisconsin, Madison.

Erickson, R. J. (2005). Why emotion work matters: Sex, gender, and the division of household labor. *Journal of Marriage and Family, 67,* 337–351.

Filiatrault, P., & Ritchie, J. R. B. (1980). Joint purchasing decisions: A comparison of influence structure in family and couple decision-making units. *Journal of Consumer Research, 7,* 131–140.

Fischer, E., Otnes, C. C., & Tuncay, L. (2007). Pursuing parenthood: Integrating cultural and cognitive perspectives on persistent goal striving. *Journal of Consumer Research, 34,* 425–440.

Frias-Gutierrez, K., & Price, L. L. (2007, July). *Consuming family dinnertime: Is family dinner a recipe for success?* Paper presented at the Transformative Consumer Research Conference, Hanover, NH.

Galinsky, E., Aumann, K., & Bond, J. T. (2009). *Times are changing: Gender and generation at work and at home.* New York: Families and Work Institute.

Gentry, J. W., Epp, A. M., & Baker, S. K. (2005). Senses of family as judged from cross-country comparisons of family public policies [Abstract]. *Journal of Macromarketing, 25,* 263.

Gentry, J. W., Kennedy, P. F., Paul, C., & Hill, R. P. (1995). Family transitions during grief: Discontinuities in household consumption patterns. *Journal of Business Research, 34,* 67–79.

Gibbs, N. (2006, June 4). The magic of the family meal. *Time.* Available: http://www.time.com/time/magazine/article/0,9171,1200760,00.html

Gillis, J. R. (1996). Making time for family: The invention of family time(s) and the reinvention of family history. *Journal of Family History, 21,* 4–21.

Gillis, J. R. (2001). Never enough time: Some paradoxes of modern family time(s). In K. J. Daly (Ed.), *Minding the time in family experience: Emerging perspectives and issues* (pp. 19–36). New York: JAI Press.

Hallman, B. C., & Benbow, S. M. P. (2007). Family leisure, family photography and zoos: Exploring the emotional geographies of families. *Social & Cultural Geography, 8,* 871–918.

Hertz, R. (2006). Talking about "doing" family. *Journal of Marriage and Family, 68,* 796–799.

Hertz, R., & Marshall, N. L. (2001). *Working families: The transformation of the American home.* Berkeley: University of California Press.

Heyman, J., & Beem, C. (2005). *Unfinished work: Building equality and democracy in an era of working families.* New York: New Press.

Hirsch, M. (1997). *Family frames: Photography, narrative and postmemory.* Cambridge, MA: Harvard University Press.

Hochschild, A. R. (1997). *The time bind: When work becomes home and home becomes work.* New York: Henry Holt.

Hochschild, A. R. (2003). *The commercialization of intimate life: Notes from home and work.* Berkeley: University of California Press.

Hochschild, A. R. (2005). On the edge of the time bind: Time and market culture. *Social Research, 72,* 339–354.

Holt, D. B. (1998). Does cultural capital structure American consumption? *Journal of Consumer Research, 25,* 1–25.

Jacobs, J. A., & Gerson, K. (2004). Understanding changes in American working time: A synthesis. In C. Fuchs & A. L. Kalleberg (Eds.), *Epstein, fighting for time: Shifting boundaries of work and social life* (pp. 25–45). New York: Russell Sage Foundation.

Kaufman-Scarborough, C. (2006). Time use and the impact of technology: Examining workspaces in the home. *Time & Society, 15*(1), 57–80.

Kremer-Sadlik, T., Fatigante, M., & Fasulo A. (2008). Discourses on family time: The cultural interpretation of family togetherness in Los Angeles and Rome. *Ethos, 36*(3), 283–309.

Kremer-Sadlik, T., & Paugh, A. (2007). Everyday moments: Finding "quality time" in working families. *Time & Society, 16*(2/3), 287–308.

Larson, R. W., Branscomb, K. R., & Wiley, A. R. (2006). Forms and functions of family mealtimes: Multidisciplinary perspectives. *New Directions for Child and Adolescent Development, 111,* 1–15.

Larson, R. W., & Richards, M. H. (1994). *Divergent realities: The emotional lives of mothers, fathers and adolescents.* New York: Basic Books.

MacInnis, D. J., & de Mello, G. E. (2005). The concept of hope and its relevance to product evaluation and choice. *Journal of Marketing, 69,* 1–14.

Markus, H., & Nurius, P. (1986). Possible selves. *American Psychologist, 41*(9), 954–969.

Mestdag, I., & Vandeweyer, J. (2005). Where has family time gone? In search of joint family activities and the role of the family meal in 1966 and 1999. *Journal of Family History, 30*(3), 304–323.

Mick, D. G., & Fournier, S. (1998). Paradoxes of technology: Consumer cognizance, emotions, and coping strategies. *Journal of Consumer Research, 25,* 123–147.

Milke, M. A., Mattingly, M. J., Nomaguchi, K. M., Bianchi, S. M., & Robinson, J. P. (2004). The time squeeze: Parental statuses and feelings about time with children. *Journal of Marriage and Family*, 66, 739–761.

Miller, D. (2001). Possessions. In D. Miller (Ed.), *Home possessions* (pp. 107–121). Oxford, England: Berg Press.

Miller, D. (2005). *Materiality*. Durham, NC: Duke University Press.

Miller, L. J. (1995). Family togetherness and the suburban ideal. *Sociological Forum*, 10, 393–418.

Moisio, R., Arnould, E. J., & Price, L. L. (2004). Between mothers and markets. *Journal of Consumer Culture*, 4(3), 361–385.

Morley, D. (2003). What's "home" got to do with it? Contradictory dynamics in the domestication of technology and the dislocation of domesticity. *European Journal of Cultural Studies*, 6(4), 435–458.

Nelson, M. K. (2006). Single mothers "do" family. *Journal of Marriage and Family*, 68, 781–795.

Otnes, C., & Pleck, E. H. (2003). *Cinderella dreams: The allure of the lavish wedding*. Berkeley: University of California Press.

Palan, K. M., & Wilkes, R. E. (1997). Adolescent–parent interaction in family decision making. *Journal of Consumer Research*, 24, 159–169.

Patrick, V. M., MacInnis, D. J., & Folkes, V. S. (2002). Approaching what we hope for and avoiding what we fear: The role of possible selves in consumer behavior. In S. M. Broniarczyk & K. Nakamoto (Eds.), *Advances in consumer research* (Vol. 29, pp. 270–276). Valdosta, GA: Association for Consumer Research.

Price, L. L., & Epp, A. M. (2005). Finding families: Family identity in consumption venues. In G. Menon & A. R. Rao (Eds.), *Advances in consumer research* (Vol. 32, pp. 9–13). Duluth, MN: Association for Consumer Research.

Ronka, A., & Korvela, P. (2009). Everyday family life: Dimensions, approaches, and current challenges. *Journal of Family Theory & Review*, 1(2), 87–102.

Rook, D. W. (1985). The ritual dimension of consumer behavior. *Journal of Consumer Research*, 12(3), 251–264.

Roy, K., Tubbs, C., & Burton, L. (2004). Don't have no time: Daily rhythms and the organization of time for low-income families. *Family Relations*, 53, 168–178.

Schor, J. B. (1991). *The overworked American*. New York: Basic Books.

Schor, J. B. (2004). *Born to buy*. New York: Scribner Press.

Schor, J. B. (2005). Work, family and children's consumer culture. In J. Heymann & C. Beem (Eds.), *Unfinished work: Building equality and democracy in an era of working families* (pp. 285–305). New York: New Press.

Schouten, J. W. (1991). Selves in transition: Symbolic consumption in personal rites of passage and identity reconstruction. *Journal of Consumer Research*, 17, 412–425.

Schulz, M. S., Cowan, P. A., Cowan, C. P., & Brennan, R. T. (2004). Coming home upset: Gender, marital satisfaction, and the daily spillover of workday experience into couple interactions. *Journal of Family Psychology*, 18, 250–263.

Shore, B. (2003). *Family time: Studying myth and ritual in working families* (Working Paper No. 27). Atlanta, GA: Emory Center for Myth and Ritual in American Life.

Southerton, D. (2006). Analyzing the temporal organization of daily life: Social constraints, practices and their allocation. *Sociology*, 40(3), 435–454.

Southerton, D., & Tomlinson, M. (2005). "Pressed for time"—the differential impacts of a "time squeeze." *Sociological Review*, 20, 215–239.

Su, C., Fern, E. F., & Ye, K. (2003). A temporal dynamic model of spousal family purchase-decision behavior. *Journal of Marketing Research*, 40, 268–281.

Swindler, A. (2002). Saving the self: Endowment versus depletion in American institutions. In R. Madsen, W. M. Sullivan, A. Swindler, & S. M. Tipton (Eds.), *Meaning and modernity: Religion, polity, and self* (pp. 41–55). Berkeley: University of California Press.

Thompson, C. J. (1996). Caring consumers: Gendered consumption meanings and the juggling lifestyle. *Journal of Consumer Research*, 22, 388–407.

Tubbs, C. Y., Roy, K. M., & Burton, L. M. (2005). Family ties: Constructing family time in low-income families. *Family Process*, 44(1), 77–91.

Valentine, G. (1999). Eating in: Home, consumption and identity. *Sociological Review*, 47, 491–524.

Venkatesh, A. (2006). Introduction to the special issue on "ICT in everyday life: Home and personal environments." *Information Society*, 22, 191–194.

Wallendorf, M., & Arnould, E. J. (1991). "We gather together": Consumption rituals of Thanksgiving Day. *Journal of Consumer Research*, 18(1), 13–31.

Walther, C., & Sandlin, J. (2008, July). *Family and social reproduction within families practicing voluntary simplicity.* Paper presented at the annual meeting of the American Sociological Association, Boston. Available: http://www.allacademic.com/meta/p241107_index.html

Warde, A. (2005). Consumption and theories of practice. *Journal of Consumer Culture, 5*(2), 131–153.

Westman, M. (2005). Cross-cultural difference in crossover research. In S. Poelmans (Ed.), *Work and family: An international research perspective* (pp. 241–260). Mahwah, NJ: Erlbaum.

# IX

*ENRICHING BEHAVIORS*
*AND VIRTUES*

# 30

# *The Nature and Effects of Sharing in Consumer Behavior*

## Russell Belk and Rosa Llamas

Thousands of candles can be lit from a single candle, and the life of the candle will not be shortened. Happiness never decreases by being shared.

Buddha

Sharing is a diverse, prehistoric, and increasingly significant contemporary consumer behavior, as suggested by a few examples:

- In most foraging hunter-gatherer societies, everyone in the village of a successful hunter is free to claim a piece of meat.
- In *The Republic*, Plato proposed an ideal society in which private property has a limited role, and a culture of public sharing prevails.
- Napster was the first successful large-scale system of file sharing in which users freely shared music, films, and digital copies of other documents.
- Car-sharing services like Zipcar work because they are more affordable, environmentally responsible, and convenient than private car ownership.
- The Robin Hood flour company encourages children, with the help of their parents, to bake cookies and share them with neighbors.
- Hundreds of thousands of people contribute advice, facts, opinions, photos, videos, and software code online each day.
- Because of such information, as well as online support groups, it is possible for medical patients to know more about their illnesses than their doctors do.
- Our public parks, libraries, roads, fire departments, museums, and recreational facilities are freely available for all.

The list could go on, but it suggests that sharing is a remarkably promising topic that has largely been overlooked in consumer research.

At the same time that sharing grows in significance, it is also threatened by several antisharing phenomena:

- Intellectual property rights legislation is rapidly expanding.
- Bioprospecting and securing patent rights to human and nonhuman genes have replaced the shared cooperation of the Human Genome Project.

- We are privatizing former family possessions and activities, including televisions, radios, telephones, cars, stereos, dinners, computers, incomes, and recreations.
- As global affluence grows, consumers increasingly privatize their transportation, education, health care, entertainments, housing, and finances.
- Social Security in the United States is actually impersonal financial security rather than the true social security of helping one another in times of difficulty.
- Growing materialism and possessive individualism discourage sharing and are negatively related to feelings of well-being.
- Free resources like smiles, directions, common courtesies, and even the time of day seem harder to come by in our anonymous urban landscape.
- Although academic researchers continue to share their research in the open model of science, prepublication academic sharing is increasingly scarce.

As these countersharing examples suggest, the topic of sharing is vital because of the battles taking place between open sharing and closed proprietary ownership. At stake is not only access to resources but also direct effects on the environment, science, sustainability, communal values, and human well-being.

A recent conceptual paper by Belk (2010) distinguishes sharing from commodity exchange and gift-giving and offers a distinction between the inclusive phenomenon of sharing in, in which those with whom we share are made a part of our extended selves, and the more charity-like phenomenon of sharing out, in which this incorporation into the extended self does not take place. In this chapter, we consider the basic nature of sharing and why it has become so contentious. We outline the implications of various practical issues involving sharing and not sharing. We draw on a multicultural exploratory study of sharing during the crucial life junctures of childhood and when forming a couple or family. By examining these data, we gain some understanding of the critical influences on sharing and nonsharing tendencies.

## WHAT IS SHARING?

Of the three fundamental ways of acquiring goods and services—by purchasing marketplace commodities, receiving gifts, and sharing—sharing is likely the most common and certainly the most neglected. We share our possessions and resources with other household members. In offering and receiving hospitality, donations, and charity outside of our households, we expand the sphere of intimates with whom we share. When we participate in various Internet forums, we share with a virtual community of strangers that may be vast. On a smaller scale, if we respond to requests for directions, the time of day, or spare change, these are also sharing activities. On a grander scale, we share a variety of public goods, including parks, water, and roads, as well as public services, such as government, fire protection, and police. Yet, with a few exceptions (Belk, 2007, 2010; Rose & Poynor, 2007; Tinson & Nuttall, 2008), little consumer research has addressed sharing behavior.

Even though working in employee-owned companies, participating in profit sharing plans, owning corporate stocks and bonds, and sharing laundry, cleaning, and cooking responsibilities at home are forms of sharing, they involve production rather than consumption. What concerns us here is shared consumption. Sometimes both production and consumption may occur simultaneously, as when we share information online or jointly prepare and consume a meal with friends. Yet, the conceptual distinction between sharing in consumption and sharing in production remains clear.

Both sharing and bartering can be traced back to ancient times and involve the circulation of resources. One key distinction between sharing and exchange phenomena is that exchange involves a transfer of ownership; what is mine becomes yours. Sooner, in the case of marketplace commodity exchange, or later, in the case of gift-giving, what is yours becomes mine to complete the reciprocal interchange. In sharing, however, either possession or ownership is joint. The shared object is effectively ours rather than mine or yours, or at least it appears so from within contemporary Western understandings of ownership, self, and bilateral exchange. Although there are instances when misunderstandings of the yours/mine/ours distinction between sharing and exchange may occur (e.g., "Oh, did you expect me to return that? I thought it was a gift"), even such claims of confusion recognize the basic distinctions.

Belk (2010) suggests that two key prototypes of sharing are mothering and the pooling and allocation of resources within the family. Neither involves the expectation of reciprocity or exchange, even though some scholars have treated them as reciprocity-inducing gift-giving (e.g., Godbout & Caillé, 1998; Vaughan, 1997) or even commodity exchange (e.g., Becker, 2005; Ruskola, 2005). The pooling and allocation of resources within the family in affluent societies are ideally a close approximation of the precept of "from each according to his or her abilities and to each according to his or her needs." On the one hand, children may either ask for food, a request that parents generally cannot deny (i.e., demand sharing), or help themselves to the contents of the family pantry (i.e., open sharing). They do not need to ask permission to enter their family home or use most of the facilities and possessions they find there, which are effectively joint possessions. They may also learn that they must use these joint possessions responsibly, as with cleaning up after they use the bathroom or kitchen. On the other hand, to use the personal possessions of others in the family, we normally ask permission and offer thanks. Such borrowing and lending are only quasi-sharing, because they involve individual rather than joint ownership and use.

A further characteristic of sharing is that it usually involves or expresses caring. Paid institutional caregiving may seem impersonal. Yet, D. Stone (2005) found that professional caregivers often become like family to their clients and frequently disregard administrative rules in order to help their clients, treating them as putative relatives by sharing their personal time and money.

## SHARING IN CULTURAL AND HISTORICAL PERSPECTIVES

### An Example of a Sharing Society

Nomadic hunter-gatherers reject the accumulation of material possessions, because they become an unnecessary burden to transport and care for. The mobility-based lifestyle relies on sociability and sharing. In recent decades, the last of the nomadic Australian Aborigines have settled in fixed communities, but a strongly ingrained sharing ethos often continues even with such possessions as televisions, VCRs, and automobiles (e.g., Belk, Groves, & Østergaard, 2000; Gerrard, 1989). Their sharing transcends home boundaries and helps assure the well-being of the community. Generosity is a highly valued ethic, and sharing shelter is an essential source of self-esteem (Hiatt, 1982; Schwab, 1995). Refusal to share brings shame to the person and the family and involves stigma and loss of face (Schwab, 1995). Although some analyses conclude that this is reciprocity with strict sanctions against nonreciprocity (e.g., Thompson, 1949), more recent analyses suggest that this may be a projection by those who expect to see reciprocity, and the sharing model is more apt (e.g., Altman, 1987; Stanner, 1979). Still, European influences, including private property and legal systems, have begun to alter these indigenous sharing patterns and conflicts about property, and instances of alcohol bingeing and bludging (i.e., demand sharing of others' cash and alcohol) are severe problems in many Aboriginal communities (Groves & Belk, 2001; Groves & Pettigrew, 2002; McKnight, 2002). Such potentially negative outcomes caution against an overly romanticized treatment of sharing as necessarily being good.

Once people become settled, especially in small-scale band societies, there remains a strong tendency to share food, tools, labor, and land (Price, 1975), but a small-scale band society does not guarantee pervasive systems of sharing. Reciprocity is one alternative, which Price (1975) argues misled Malinowski due to his selection of the Trobriands as his focus of study: "Malinowski was describing a relatively complex society without a strong sharing ethic. If he had lived among the Bushmen instead he probably would have perceived primitive society as operating by sharing rather than reciprocity" (p. 18). Indeed, sharing societies appear common and continue on various scales today.

There have been further theoretical issues raised by sharing in traditional societies. Foster (1972) proposes that a key problem for all human societies is how to deal with envy of those who have more. Besides concealment, denial, and offering a "sop"—a token form of sharing one's fortune—we may avoid others' envy by true sharing. In Foster's view, true sharing is most often a result of either institutional mechanisms like income taxes or strong moral or legal sanctions so that we have little choice but to share. Yet, Foster (1969) offers a way out of such a dismal view of sharing in another paper, in which he proposes the notions of limited good and unlimited good societies. In a limited good society, resources are perceived as scarce, and life is seen as a zero-sum game. There is only so much good to go around, and one person's gain is everyone else's loss. In contrast, a society that views good as unlimited sees nature as bountiful and views one person's gain as having no effect on others. In Cohen's (1961) account, members of such a society know "that there is always food to be gotten" (p. 325). Bird-David (1990) calls this view that of a giving environment as opposed to a reciprocating environment. This is likely an idealized view, and there are surely economies of scarcity, but sharing is by no means limited to economies of abundance.

### The Commons and Its Vestiges

Besides hunter-gatherer and band societies, pastoral societies are the other context in which sharing has often been examined. When we think of the pastoral commons today, we almost inevitably think of Hardin's (1968) "tragedy of the commons." Using a hypothetical common pasture shared by a number of animal herders, he suggests that each herder succumbs to the temptation to increase his or her herd by one more animal until the commons is ruined by overgrazing. In this view, sharing is the road to ruin. It thus offers a logical rationale for the enclosing and privatizing of European commons between the 15th and 19th centuries, supposedly resulting in saving these pastures and providing unparalleled production efficiency (Boyle, 2005).

This argument has also been widely adopted and applied to a number of subsequent environmental, economic, and public policy problems (e.g., Frischmann, 2005; O'Toole, 1998; Shultz & Holbrook, 1999). Yet, as appealing as Hardin's (1968) metaphor has been to economists and other advocates of both privatization and government management of public resources, it has flaws. Stevenson (1991) points out that Hardin's model is not that of a commons, which is a resource jointly managed by those who use it, but rather a model of free-for-all open access to resources with no management. If Hardin had chosen a true commons like the Swiss alpine grazing commons (Stevenson, 1991), Hutterite agricultural commons (Baden, 1998), or Canadian Ojibway wild rice commons (*The Ecologist*, 1993), he might have seen that commons can work quite well for sustaining resources and balancing individual and group desires. Moreover, the enclosure of the commons had the social effects of not only concentrating economic power in the hands of a few but also leading to "the loss of a form of life, and the relentless power of market logic to migrate to new areas, disrupting traditional social relationships, views of the self, and even the relationship of human beings to their environment" (Boyle, 2005, p. 236).

Boyle's (2005) reference to the migration of market logic to new areas resonates in a number of contemporary contestations between sharing and newly marketized private property, including human genes, organs, semen, eggs, wombs, and babies (e.g., Scheper-Hughes & Wacquant, 2002); music and film (e.g., Giesler, 2006); household labor, child care, and sex (e.g., Ertman & Williams, 2005); Internet images, advice, information, and software (e.g., Benkler, 2006); brand designs, colors, names, and trademarks (e.g., Phillips, 2005); and cultural heritage, artifacts, myths, and rites (e.g., Brown, 2004). Many of these contested spheres involve, on the one hand, that which has traditionally either been jointly owned and shared or regarded as operating outside the logic of the market and, on the other hand, the growing realm of trademarks, copyrights, and intellectual property rights. According to many critics, the tendency to provide legal property rights to more and more types of things and extend these rights for longer periods of time is an attempt to enclose the information commons, which is being extended to such invisible or virtual realms as cells, DNA, bits and bytes, and even dreams.

Barnes (2006) suggests that rather than commoners now exploiting these new commons for their private gain, it is increasingly corporations that are privatizing and exploiting formerly shared domains for their private gain. He offers these examples:

- *Disney stories taken from the public domain*—Aladdin, Atlantis, Beauty and the Beast, Cinderella, Davy Crockett, The Legend of Sleepy Hollow, Hercules, The Hunchback of Notre Dame, The Jungle Book, Oliver Twist, Pinocchio, Robin Hood, Snow White, Sleeping Beauty, The Three Musketeers, Treasure Island, The Wind in the Willows
- *Disney stories added to the public domain*—None (p. 120)

As this example and the contexts just noted strongly suggest, the consequences of sharing or not sharing can be profound, both economically and culturally. But before we can reasonably consider such broad issues, it is well to begin with some data closer to home.

## SHARING EXPERIENCES AS CHILDREN AND YOUNG ADULTS: A RETROSPECTIVE STUDY

### Methods

An interpretive study was undertaken based on verbal accounts by college students and other young adults in three cultures. The aim was to look at recollections of childhood sharing and ownership as well as how these patterns and outlooks seemed to change among young adults who were either single, married, or cohabiting. The initial informants were 24 graduate students (13 males, 11 females) in an interpretive consumer behavior class in the Western United States. After agreeing on a topical outline of sharing topics, each student wrote a personal essay about sharing experiences and inclinations. Topics included sharing during childhood while at home and at school, parental sharing lessons and behaviors, contemporary sharing, and feelings about sharing things on a list of 16 items ranging from books and videos to vacation homes and automobiles. The informants described childhood experiences and sharing, Internet posting, and file sharing, as well as positive and negative experiences with sharing.

After completing their personal sharing narratives and being trained in qualitative data collection, these students each conducted and transcribed two depth interviews, one with a man and one with a woman. The interview topic guide was approximately the same as that used for the personal sharing narrative. Most of these interviews were with peers of about the same age. This resulted in 72 U.S. self-narratives and interview transcriptions averaging 10 double-spaced pages each. Of the 72 U.S. informants, 86% were in their 20s or 30s, with a mean age of 28.2. The study was also carried out with 102 Eastern Canadian and 24 Northwestern Spanish participants, all with similar demographics to the U.S. participants.

After immersion in the data set, we began by distinguishing positive and negative aspects of sharing and attitudes toward sharing during childhood and among those who were currently in various types of relationships (e.g., living with roommates, cohabiting with a partner, married). Since the general pattern described was one of prosharing experiences and lessons as a child and a decline in sharing as a young adult, we became particularly interested in critical incidents cited as being influential in shaping or accounting for current tendencies to share or not share. We also paid attention to differences in sharing inclinations over different types of relationships and possessions. After several iterations of coding the material, some distinct patterns emerged that helped us understand factors that were cited as critical to current sharing tendencies. These patterns were interrogated in light of prior sharing literature.

## Findings

### The Couple

By far the strongest incentive for sharing reported by these young adults was finding a life partner or likely life partner:

> I share just about everything with my girlfriend; we even have shared toothbrushes.... I often share a bed at night, I share clothes with my girlfriend; yes, I even borrow some of her clothes from time to time, just not underwear! (20-year-old U.S. male)

According to our informants, sharing strengthens ties and binds people together. Not only is such sharing based on love and trust, but also it fosters these same feelings:

> Sharing everything with my wife has kept us closer than I believe we would be if we said, "This is mine and that is yours." I think the more sharing there is in marriage, the longer the relationship is likely to last, and the better the quality will be. (34-year-old U.S. male)

Computers, for example, were most commonly regarded as individual property by the couples studied, but most were nevertheless willing to share their computers with their partners. This included sharing personal passwords, which involves total transparency rather than privacy. However, negative experiences like a partner deleting personal files or using too much hard drive space made some informants refrain from sharing. Joint bank accounts, credit cards, and telephone calling plans were common among married couples, but this was not always the case either. Even with joint bank accounts, use of these funds was not necessarily expected to be free and equal, as one man explained:

> With my wife, sure, I'd have a joint bank account.... But I think you should still keep track of your bank account and how much you spend, because it can get confusing on who spent what in a joint account. (25-year-old U.S. male)

The concern here seems to be loss of financial control and added economic uncertainty. Although there is a tendency for couples to report and actually believe that they are pooling their money and sharing it equally, equal access to funds is the exception rather the rule. It is usually women in relationships who have less access to joint funds (e.g., Burgoyne, 1990; Marshall & Woolley, 1993; Wilson, 1987).

Sharing among couples was not universal, complete, or necessarily pleasing. One woman complained that she hated sharing a car with her husband, because he leaves his trash and clothes in the car. This example foreshadows concerns with contagion as well as loss of control of visible self-extending possessions, which are concerns that we will see in childhood sharing experiences as well, and shows that sharing can be a source of marital stress. Another woman complained that in sharing food with her husband, he had not learned moderation and took more than "his share." So, fairness and respect toward the other partner are key aspects for sharing within couples.

Marital vows to "share and share alike" seem to have an influence, since we found that there was greater resistance to sharing among boyfriends and girlfriends than among spouses. However, several couples who felt more committed demonstrated their joint involvement through sharing a possession like a dog or furniture to signal commitment, anticipate a future together, and express an emerging joint sense of self (Belk, 1988).

## The Family

The family is considered a moral economy rather than a market economy, gift economy, or political economy. Cheal (1989) distinguishes moral economies from political ones based on their valuation of social relationships and ritual interactions above rational self-interest. Sharing is one of the basic tenets of the family, and the extended family is where we experience the greatest amount of sharing, as these accounts suggest:

> With family, you have that trust and love no matter what. With that, you feel compelled to share what you have if it makes them and their lives feel better.
>
> I also think family is different. We have a duty to take care of our families, and that often means making sacrifices. I said before that our families are the most important thing within our [Indian] culture, and that a strong and healthy and successful family leads to everyone being very happy ... if I am unemployed and cannot feed my children while the rest of my brothers and sisters are doing well and are successful ... the rest of the family one way or another feels the pain of our hunger. So, doesn't it make sense to share your resources with your family and make sure everyone is doing well? (30-year-old Canadian male)

> It's great to share with the family. If I won the lottery, I wouldn't keep all the money, some of it would go to my family, that's for sure. The family means everything to me. (21-year-old Spanish female)

Family meals at the kitchen or dining room table entail two kinds of sharing: tangible (i.e., food) and intangible (e.g., experiences, plans, ideas, worries, aspirations). Fraser (1994) observed that "meal tables were the sites for confession, laughter, revelations of catastrophes, for rites of passage and initiation" (p. 15). Nevertheless, a tendency toward more individualistic lifestyles, along with the decrease in the number of family members and a fast-paced, time-impoverished life, drive us to share less in the family in terms of space and time and, consequently, also in terms of everyday life, meals, conversations, and entertainments. This is the argument of B. Stone (2009), who observes how the "high touch family breakfast" in the United States has been replaced by "high tech mornings" when laptops, iPhones, video games, Facebook, Twitter, and text messages receive the most attention (p. A1). A Canadian woman saw such changes even without technological competition:

> As a child, we share whatever we discover. We share our candies, our toys, and our experiences (usually involving friends that we bring home). As teens, we share long conversations with our parents, where we hear their stories and experiences and realize their intention is to teach us from those experiences. We also share moments and daily conversations at the table for breakfast, lunch, and dinner. As we start to grow, we still share with our family; however, the instances for sharing start to decrease as we move out from our home. Those sharing moments at breakfast, lunch, and dinner decrease to a couple of dinners or lunches during the week. (30-year-old Canadian female)

Besides changing social ecology, increased affluence and fewer members per family may be factors precipitating this decline in familial sharing:

> We had to share everything growing up. I had 12 brothers and sisters, and our house was only five bedrooms and one bathroom. It was really nice, though, so much love and good times we shared and memories. We had to sleep three to a bed sometimes. Now I have four bedrooms and only one child still living at home, four TVs and four phones, and three bathrooms. (59-year-old U.S. male)

There are some differences in Spain, where children leave their parents' house at a later age. With less atomized families, Spanish students also reported greater familial sharing than their counterparts in North America. The norms for sharing are also more relaxed within the family in Spain. Sharing without asking the owner for permission is one of the traits of the spontaneous and improvised character, when a high level of trust and familiarity shape the sharing. It could be that these patterns have been learned of necessity where multiple bedrooms and bathrooms are lacking. Whatever the cause, the familial sharing ethos appears stronger in Europe:

> We (my siblings and I) usually ask before taking something that belongs to one of the others, but sometimes we forget it. If it is something important, sometimes the owner gets angry, but usually it works. My parents want us to ask for permission before sharing something, but as I just said, sometimes we forget it. (24-year-old Spanish female)

There is some indication that early family sharing patterns may continue into adulthood. A Spanish man recalled that sharing was always part of his family life, ranging from his childhood when he used to share bikes and toys and inherit clothes from his older brother to nowadays when they share traveling, experiences, and computers.

Resources in moral economies are distributed and mobilized through social processes that define the meaning of the family rather than through market mechanisms of supply, demand, and prices. We found three key features of sharing within family boundaries. First, sharing with parents and adult siblings was seen to result from previously established love and trust. Second, sharing inside the family has a nonreciprocal nature unlike the need for reciprocity reported when sharing outside the family. Third, familial sharing lacks a strictly egalitarian character; redistribution of resources responds to needs:

> In our family, we have always shared everything. Everything belongs to everyone. My parents never give the same to every sibling; they give to every one of us what we need. My eldest brother practices motocross, which is a quite expensive sport, so he requires more money from the family budget than we do—my youngest brother and me—but we never complain about that. (22-year-old Spanish female)

This idyllic situation regarding distribution of family resources is not always the norm. One woman from France who was studying in Spain cited a controversial aspect of sharing in distributing goods among the family members when a person passes away:

> When a person dies, normally, the resources are distributed equally among children, but in some cases, the main recipient should be the child who took care of the parents (in the case that they suffered from some illnesses, for example). This distribution is sometimes the source of many conflicts in families. (22-year-old French female)

Zelizer (2005) also found that inheritance distributions are often problematic occasions when greed and envy of other family members' portions of the inheritance can overcome sharing tendencies within families. To a lesser degree and over a narrower range of possessions than in the case of sharing with life partners and immediate family, informants also said they currently shared the quasi-family of roommates and friends. In this narrowing of the sphere and intensity of sharing, we can begin to examine some of the justifications that people used to account for not sharing or not sharing outside their nuclear families.

## Friends

The American TV series *Friends* (Crane, Kauffman, & Bright, 1994–2004) cast the lives, loves, and laughs of six young friends who share life together in Manhattan. Like Rachel, Ross, Chandler, Phoebe, Joey, and Monica, many of our informants share daily life with friends and roommates. Sharing space and possessions makes boundaries vanish, fosters interpersonal relations, and opens us up to former strangers, while sharing nontangible issues and personal pieces of information involves strengthening emotional ties between people. One man expressed it this way:

> First of all, I share things because of confidence in the others; maybe it is not enough to share anything else, but then, when you really want to know these people, when you really want these people to be part of your life, you need to share different issues such as feelings, thoughts, worries, and so on. (22-year-old Canadian male)

A 25-year old U.S. student from France was living with three other students, and they all shared the same common room. He reported that they shared many other things also, including a television, photos, music, local travel, meals, food, an Internet connection, and a computer. He learned, however, that he could rely on some of his roommates more than others:

> I am sharing my living room and everything with Pui, my roommate—everything I can, I mean. I told her my things are your things, and she told me her things are my things. We used to leave [our] doors open, and whenever we need something, even if the other is not there, we can go ahead and take it, without asking.... [But] I am sharing my bathroom with Kate, and I am not really happy about that, because she never cleans it. I mean, we've been here for ... two months and a half, and I've cleaned the bathroom four or five times, I think, and she has not cleaned it at all.... A bathroom needs to be cleaned from time to time, you know. And she doesn't. The other day I was cleaning it after she took a shower, and she came and asked me, "Can I dry my hair, do you mind?" And I was like "No, go ahead," thinking that after drying her hair, she would come and help me. But she didn't, she didn't say anything, went to her room, closed the door and just forgot about it. (25-year-old U.S. male)

Here, open and closed doors represent corresponding attitudes toward sharing, trust, and open self boundaries. While Pui followed the tacit norms behind sharing of building trust and a sense of joint possessions ("my things are your things"), Kate adopted opportunistic behaviors that crossed the line defining responsible sharing.

A common condition for establishing trust among nonfamily members is that sharing has to be reciprocal in some way. If one person feels that he or she is doing all the giving, one is apt to feel that he or she is being taken advantage of. The opportunistic behavior of one person is one of the main threats to sharing in this nonfamilial context: "I wouldn't share with people who don't deserve it, because 'All lay loads on a willing horse'" (21-year-old Spanish female). Sometimes this reciprocity can be quite simple, as another informant put it: "In my view, sharing is very easy when I get a 'thank you' in return. I would be able to share everything with thankful people who like sharing. Instead, ungrateful and opportunistic people make it very difficult to share" (25-year-old Spanish male).

The codes for sharing—asking for permission and offering thanks—play an important role when sharing with friends and roommates. Gratitude is an important part of sharing outside of the family (Emmons & McCullough, 2004), but for the gratitude to be most effective, it should be perceived as a sincerely felt emotion rather than merely a ritual expression (Visser, 2008). Most participants also found that minimal reciprocity is a must in sharing with nonkin, and negative experiences were cited as one of the main barriers to such sharing. Trust is at the heart of sharing, so if one of the parties undermines the trust or fails to reciprocate, this can create a reluctance to share with that person. Trust can be built in other ways, but reciprocity is a demonstrative way of building it. Even though some degree of reciprocity is a key aspect to perpetuating sharing, when asked about the distinction between sharing and lending, most participants mentioned reciprocity as the line which differentiates them: "I think that sharing is giving without expecting anything in return, whereas lending is with the assumption that something will be given back or paid back" (34-year-old Canadian male).

Informants also told stories of inconvenience resulting from lending something like a snowboard and then not having it when they wanted it. Experiences like this were offered to justify not lending more. There was also reluctance to lend things that were valuable either financially or in terms of emotional attachment. The fear in such cases was not so much that the item would not be returned as that it would be treated badly:

> I think people tend to think that people need to earn the right to be shared with (similar to respect). Sharing involves trust (e.g., you need to trust that your neighbor won't break your snow blower if you lend it to him). (25-year-old Canadian female)

While couched in terms of financial worries, another feared injury here seems to be the one that might be inflicted on the extended self. We take care of our stuff well, because it is seen to be a part of us, but extended self is also involved in another way. As Belk (2010) argues, when people engage in "sharing in," they make those with whom they share a part of their extended self. But when someone engages in "sharing out," it is more like charity, and there is no lingering feeling of connection between those involved.

Besides possessions, sharing intangibles like feelings and secrets is another way to build or fail to build trust among friends: "On an emotional level, people might decide not to share their feelings, secrets, frustrations due to the fear of others' opinions or to preserve their intimacy, to keep a 'secret garden,' to protect themselves, or just because of shyness" (23-year-old Spanish female). Sentiments, thoughts, and personal information were placed by our informants in the sphere of highly valued possessions and, consequently, were often considered off-limits for sharing.

The fear of being exposed to the judgment of others, bothering people with one's problems, or feeling vulnerable were the reasons they pointed to as barriers to sharing. Female informants particularly mentioned their reluctance to share these:

> I'm more willing to share tangible things, objects, material possessions. But when it comes to intangibles like personal feelings or problems, I don't often share them, so I don't trouble anyone with my problems. (22-year-old Spanish female)

> I would not be willing to share secrets or things of great importance with anyone excluding my best friend. Things that are very personal and important with high emotional involvement would classify at these secrets. (22-year-old U.S. female)

> I think that it is difficult to share everything related with emotions and sentiments, particularly with love feelings. Revealing them is like "getting naked." You don't know what the other person thinks, and that makes it risky and difficult to share. (22-year-old French female)

In the same vein, some informants reported their unwillingness to share highly treasured goods like gifts or family heirlooms:

> I would never share personal objects with sentimental value, but besides those, I'm willing to share everything. (25-year-old Spanish male)

> I am pretty much open to sharing everything. I do not like sharing my pen because it has sentimental values, because I have been using the same pen for over 8 years. (42-year-old Canadian female)

There is also an important distinction among adults outside the family between joint use, as with borrowing something or feeling that it is free for another person to use, and joint ownership in a more formal sense. Joint ownership was seen as riskier outside of family, as one woman explained: "Books, videos, and clothing, I jointly own those things with my sister. It's hard to own something jointly with a group of friends, though, because when you go your separate ways, it'll be hard to tell who gets what" (21-year-old U.S. female). Aside from the practical concern expressed here, the formality of joint ownership takes things outside of the realm of sharing for some participants and makes it more like a market transaction: "I do not like joint ownership, because it is too materialistic. It takes the emotions out of the sharing process and makes it a business transaction. The positive feeling associated with sharing is lost in joint ownership" (30-year-old U.S. female). Our informants also expressed concern that there was less freedom in jointly owning possessions, whose use would have to be negotiated or planned rather than spontaneous. Nevertheless, some informants did go in with friends to jointly purchase occasionally used durables like ski boats, vacation homes, and all-terrain vehicles, but this was generally seen as a practical way to minimize costs rather than something done to build a sense of sharing in.

The counterpart of willingness to lend is willingness to borrow from other people. Reluctance to borrow was common, especially in the United States:

> I don't really borrow anything. I don't really like borrowing anything. I'll be honest, I do use things that someone has a lot of and that is not something special. Like, I'll use someone's coffee sometimes. I'll use little things that everyone uses as community anyway. (30-year-old U.S. male)

> I am having trouble thinking of things that I borrow from others, because I do not do it very often. I was brought up to be independent, which makes it difficult for me now to borrow things from others. Some say I need to let others help me. I don't look at it that way—I just like to be self-sufficient. (23-year-old U.S. female)

In part, this fear of borrowing was justified by fears of damaging an item, but there is also an American ethic of self-sufficiency evident here and a fear of intimacy (Aron, Aron, Tudor, & Nelson, 1991) that leads to unwillingness to either impose or feel dependent on others. There was also awareness that a breach of borrowing etiquette is likely a breach of a relationship:

> I am generally open with my personal items and don't mind lending things out to others. However, I am more hesitant about borrowing from others, as I don't want to put anyone out or take something they might need. Also, I remember once borrowing $20 from a friend while out to dinner, and she stopped talking to me, because I didn't pay her back right away. I had forgotten that I had borrowed and had no idea why she was mad at me until someone else told me. I wished she'd just reminded me, but we lost the friendship instead. I think this … made me more hesitant to borrow in the future. (31-year-old U.S. female)

When relationships are more secure, there is less chance of this happening, but one American woman did report a rough period in her relationship with her boyfriend after she broke a CD he had lent her. Thus, failure to take care of lent possessions may weaken, damage, and jeopardize relationships.

Some people also felt, as with joint ownership, that borrowing things can be more like a business transaction and less like sharing. Yet, this was not necessarily the case, as one man explained:

> In my opinion, lending or borrowing is not sharing, and this can be categorized as a business transaction where both the parties have a mutual material gain (like borrowing money from a bank), although the words lending and borrowing are commonly used to imply sharing, for example, lending a pen or book to someone. When the consideration of such a transaction cannot be materially justified, in my opinion, it is sharing—not lending or borrowing. (41-year-old Canadian male)

Among those who reported sharing outside their immediate families, the two most commonly invoked rationales were that it made financial sense to borrow or jointly own, and it was the friendly, neighborly, or godly thing to do. One man explained how interwoven sharing experiences with neighbors made them rely on one another:

> Today, my wife baked a bunch of cookies, and we are about to go share them with the neighbors. We often share food like this and in social situations. For example, we have our friends over and share our board games and snack food. Our friends have returned such favors. There is a friend of ours who has regular game nights with other friends, and they came to borrow a game we had several times. It was interesting, because they bought the expansion to the game but not the actual game. They relied on borrowing it from us. Lending, borrowing, and sharing have cut costs, saved time, and expanded our experiences for us as well as others we have shared with. It has contributed to the building of better relationships. (24-year-old U.S. male)

Unlike those who avoided borrowing to remain independent and free, the mutual dependency here was seen as a positive outcome of sharing, but others resisted this. Asked how he felt about sharing a lawn mower with neighbors, one man said,

> First of all, nowadays, people hardly make an effort to get to know the neighbor they've lived next to for 10 years let alone make the necessary communications to share a lawn mower with them. Second of all, who is going to be the one to own the lawn mower to be shared in the neighborhood? If everyone pitches in to buy a neighborhood lawn mower, who has to store it? And who pays for the gas it runs on? What about Mr. Johnson who mows his 13 acres versus Mr. Smith who mows his 10×10-foot patch of grass? How do you compensate for the wear and tear? I think that's a major issue—letting someone borrow items that receive wear and tear every time it's used. It's like letting someone drive your car for 500 miles. Even if they pay for gas, it still decreases the life of the car. (45-year-old U.S. male)

Nevertheless, it is clear that some of these reasons given for not sharing are imagined excuses and justifications rather than being based on actual negative experiences.

Possessiveness, attachment to things, and materialism are also behind an antisharing behavior according to a young Spaniard:

> The excessive attachment to things that we have nowadays makes it more difficult to share. Years ago, people had very few things and used to share them, but today we have more and more things and more expensive ones, so we feel afraid of losing those if we share them. (21-year-old Spanish male)

This suggests that when people share from necessity, they may feel a greater sense of sharing in. Yet, when sharing becomes a discretionary choice, a less personal sharing out may occur as well as a more possessive individual attachment to these things.

*Sharing During Childhood*

Having a life partner and having children are key events that dramatically expand sharing. Nevertheless, the first experiences related to sharing take place during childhood:

> Sharing with the family is the first step that one person takes in his/her process of integration in the society. In my view, the family is the first social group in which the person develops, so most of the attitudes learned in the family will be extrapolated to the rest of social relationships. With the family, we share not only possessions but also immaterial issues such as values, sorrows, joyful moments. (21-year-old Spanish female)

One of the first things children must learn to share is their parents:

> As a middle child (the fifth of seven), I suffer from the stereotypical and unending pursuit of my parents' attention. I suppose my first memorable experience with sharing highlights this fact clearly. I was in the first grade (5 years old), and after much pleading on my part, my mother had agreed to volunteer to supervise a class excursion to the Toronto Zoo with my grade 1 class.... Each parent was assigned two children to supervise for the day. My best friend and I were assigned to my mother. I was so looking forward to this trip, not because of the destination but because my mother was going to be there. However, it ended up being one of the worst trips I have ever participated in. My mother, trying to make my best friend feel comfortable, paid so much time focusing on her, I felt completely neglected. Even though, looking back on it, my mother was not ignoring me at all. I suppose I had accepted the fact that I had to share my mother's attention with my other siblings, but I definitely was not prepared to share her with my friends—not even my very best friend! Needless to say, I felt horrible that day and never asked my mother to come on another class trip. (32-year-old Canadian female)

Childhood sharing tendencies and attitudes were influenced by conscious lessons taught by parents, church leaders, and teachers; by unconscious parental modeling; and in interactions with and observations of siblings and friends. Parents and teachers offered maxims like "Share your toys, not your germs," "Sharing is caring," and "Share with others if you want them to share with you":

> When we were children, my brother and I used to fight for toys many times. Our mom used to bring peace to our conflicts, and she used to teach sharing lessons and commitments like "If you want to play with your brother's toys, then you must allow him to play with yours." (24-year-old Spanish female)

Some perceived cultural differences that they believe shaped their sharing tendencies:

> Although I was born and brought up in Canada, I have grown up in a traditional "Indian" home. This has meant numerous family gatherings, where I had to share my toys and overall living space, and the inherent lack of privacy stemming from such gatherings from childhood. I was told to partake in such activities without the promise of personal gain. For example, every time my "relatives" dropped by, I did not look for a toy/chocolate as a gift in return for my generosity to my cousins. I think that if you grow up in a culture that does not promote sharing from a young age, then sharing as an adult becomes especially difficult. In the Indian culture, socializing is a big part of it. We are not "individualistic," and as such, there are constant opportunities to share, and as part of the culture, it's not a choice but expected. (28-year-old Canadian male)

Teachers were also remembered for enforcing sharing by such tactics as putting out a box of crayons for a group of students to share. Parents taught similar lessons, usually framed in terms of sharing with siblings:

> I have one brother and one sister, so I'm used to sharing everything since I was a child. For example, my father used to go to buy bread for lunch on Sundays, and he would bring also some candies. We used to count them and divide them into three parts, regardless [of where] the three of us were at the moment. If one of us was not there, we would keep his/her candies in a safe place. Now that we are adults, we still do that, even though it might sound ridiculous. (21-year-old Spanish female)

Almost all the informants from Spain regarded their sharing experiences during childhood, whether with siblings or classmates, as positive. Only one woman mentioned that sometimes sharing with the family is more difficult than sharing with friends, because we choose friends but not family. She highlighted, however, that family ties are so strong that they are difficult to ignore. Yet, in North America, many informants described either resentment at having to share with siblings or relief at being an only child or a child with no siblings near their age to share with:

> A few short years later, I was graced with a stepsister with whom I hated sharing. Everyday was a battle for the both of us. We would never share anything even if it meant physically fighting over it. It didn't matter what the item was. (22-year-old U.S. female)

Several of those who reported not sharing with siblings as a child found it strange when their college roommates expected them to share possessions within a quasi-family group. Sometimes having to share with relatives was resented to such an extent that the informant became less generous with others:

> I didn't share much with my school friends. I think since I was a twin and was constantly sharing at home, I was very protective of things that were mine or that I didn't have to share with my twin. I didn't share many physical objects, such as clothes or movies or CDs, with school friends. (22-year-old U.S. female)

> One time a cousin of mine came from America, and her mom brought gifts for all of us. Her mom gave me a doll, a very cute doll, and my cousin was so mean that she wanted the doll back from me. She was spoiled and had no manners. I had to give her my brand new doll, because she would not listen to anyone. My mom forced me to give my brand new doll to her. I hated her for that. (37-year-old U.S. female from Pakistan)

Even in instances in which sharing with siblings was more positive, disagreements arose:

> I shared a bedroom with my brother until I was about 10 years old, then I got my own room. I liked sharing a room, because we would talk a lot at night, and I thought that was cool, but my brother likes to be very organized, and as you know, I am not very organized, so we would clash. We did the whole draw the line down the middle of the room thing. We shared a closet, and that caused problems, because I would always leave it dirty, and my brother liked it clean.... We had to share a bathroom. My brother would shower at night before school [the next morning], and I would shower in the morning. One time my brother decided that he was going to shower in the morning, so he got up and got in the bathroom before me and showered and threw the whole system off, so I ended up being late to school, and my mom was late to work, because she was sorting out the fight. We had a big fight and couldn't figure out who should be first. (26-year-old U.S. male)

The difference in organization of joint space here reflects different preferences for control and order. Such differences made it difficult to share and disrupted the sense of extended identity imposed on these spaces. It also reveals the unwelcome and contaminating overflow of the sibling's extended self.

In several cases in the United States, parents were reported to have provided each of their children with identical possessions to preclude such sharing squabbles, even if doing so reinforced a nonsharing ethos:

> They [his sisters] hated sharing. They couldn't share anything. If they got one thing, everybody had to have the same thing…. They each had to have one of their own. They all had to be the same thing, because otherwise someone would say, "You know the other one was better." (34-year-old U.S. male)

This is something that some parenting experts began to recommend in the 1920s in the United States (Matt, 2003). These feelings are bound up with feelings of sibling rivalry, individual identity formation, and desire for control. Issues of control and identity through the extension of self into possessions often translated into feelings of possessiveness and sometimes into abnormal fears of contagion from others' contact with "my things":

> I am a person that likes to be in control of things that I own. I also think that I take better care of my things than most people, so things that could get damaged, like my laptop, I don't like to share. I am also kind of obsessive-compulsive about germs, so I don't like to share food or clothes either. (22-year-old U.S. male)

In addition to material possessions, another thing that informants appreciated or missed in childhood was a private area of the home to which they could retreat and regard as a sanctuary from other family members. One woman recalled fighting so often with her sister, with whom she shared a bedroom, that their parents gave them their own rooms.

Despite childhood lessons that sharing is good, many informants reported learning the hard way that sharing with friends could lead to having possessions damaged or not returned at all. Six informants also recollected that their parents admonished them not to share clothes and other objects with schoolmates for these same reasons. Just as some traditional groups eat in private to avoid having to share with others, some parents of those studied were reported to have done something similar: "I do also remember my mom putting certain prized and fragile toys away when certain friends came over so that we wouldn't play with it and ruin it" (31-year-old U.S. female). Tinson and Nuttall (2008) also found that some sisters hid their possessions, so they would not be borrowed.

Besides lessons in sharing, adults were also cited as teaching potentially conflicting lessons about responsible ownership. Typically, lessons about sharing were based on the presumption that children owned their toys, clothes, and other possessions:

> Well, I always remember being somewhat selfish, you know, like every other kid. The famous words "it's mine, it's mine" I am positive rang out from my mouth. But, I think when the real principle of ownership struck me is when my parents gave me my first real, big bike when I was 13 years old. I then knew that I had to take care of it and put it away when I was not riding it, so it would not get stolen. It was an expensive item, and I did not want to lose it. (26-year-old U.S. male)

In a small number of cases, parents instead either suggested that their children's possessions were really group possessions belonging to the entire family or were possessions of the parents that their children were merely using.

Informants also recognized that parental lessons about sharing were conveyed by example. Parental examples of generosity include sharing with neighbors, donations to charity, and fairness and balance in sharing money and possessions with their children. Sometimes, deeper lessons were gained via examples than through platitudes and explicit teaching. Most recalled that as children, their parents showed no favoritism toward them or their siblings. If one was given something, then the other children in the family were usually also given something. Some informants even received gifts on their siblings' birthdays. Some parental sharing examples were pivotal in the recollections of informants:

> The most prominent story … while I was growing up was a time that my Dad and I stopped at a fast-food place to buy lunch for the both of us and some other friends. As we pulled out of the drive-thru, there stood a homeless woman. My Dad put the car in park, got out, and handed over all of the food we had just ordered. Situations like this have occurred a lot in my life, and seeing how generous and giving my Dad is has made me more apt to share. (22-year-old U.S. female)

Many childhood lessons about sharing were learned from sharing experiences with siblings and friends:

> As a child, my parents always stressed the importance of sharing. I shared a bedroom with my sister for 7 years. Objects such as toys, computers, and videos were considered "community" items in my family, where everyone had access to mostly everything. There is one instance in particular where I convinced my young sister that we should share money, because she had more than I did. My parents were quick to inform me that this was not an appropriate means of sharing and that I was taking advantage of my sister's innocence. (22-year-old U.S. female)

> We (cousins) would eat together always. We would share food, take bites out of each other's dinners, share dinner plates, etc. School friends were also like cousins, and there was nothing off-limits for them. We would share lunch and books, we would do homework for each other, sometimes help (cheat) each other in exams as well. In fact, it was not considered cheating among friends; we felt obligated to show our answers to friends if they were having a hard time. (44-year-old U.S. male)

The first example here is a case of trying to put limits on socially inappropriate sharing, whereas the second is a case of failing to put limits on socially undesirable sharing.

The sense of sharing in cheating also meant that it must be through mutual consensus:

> Cheating off someone without their knowledge is a violation; they are not choosing to share with you, you are taking from them. (25-year-old Canadian female)

> Cheating off is only sharing when there is a mutual consent; otherwise, it is opportunistic behavior. Personally, I prefer to share my knowledge and resources before the exam, lending my class notes and helping with doubts and avoiding the risk of getting caught. (26-year-old Spanish male)

If peer pressure could bring about socially undesirable sharing like cheating on exams, it could also bring about socially desirable sharing in the service of friendship:

> I can remember vividly the day I learned to share. After many times of my family nagging me to have a bite of my ice cream or a sip of my Sprite, how much I hated to have someone else's slobber on my straw or in my ice cream. I would always say "no" to my family, because I did not care what my family thought. All this was really the building up to my deciding factor. It really came down to peer pressure from my friends…. I was in the 7th grade, so about 12 or 13 years old. It took place in the school cafeteria at lunch. We were all drinking our own smoothies, and all of my friends decided to try each other's smoothies to see which one was the best. I realized at that moment that if I wanted to be accepted, I couldn't be selfish and tell them no that I did not want your spit like I could to my family. So I bit my lip and passed around my drink, and the worst part was re-drinking it. But after that, I realized that sharing was cool. (*laughs*) It was the "in thing" to do, and I fitted in. (22-year-old U.S. female)

Here, fear of contagion was overcome by the desire to bond with friends and not be a social outcast.

Another reason to share with schoolmates was the positive affirmation of extended self in having possessions that others wanted to borrow: "I would always share my toys with other kids after school, because I always had the coolest toys, and they all wanted to play with my toys" (21-year-old U.S. female). In this case, sharing of extended self through possessions was an affirmation of self-worth.

Others were never in such a position and instead saw that their sharing in childhood was born of necessity due to poverty. Yet, even without such an economic imperative, the overall sense in the accounts by these young adults was that there are more important things than having the most or best possessions and jealously guarding them against use or damage by others. Facing a choice between being a giver and being a taker, most people preferred the former role. One 23-year-old American man recounted a story of his high school friend who had a reputation of borrowing from others and never paying them back. Nevertheless, he agreed to loan his friend money:

> I agreed to front him some money for a road trip right after high school. He agreed to pay me back as soon as he had the money. Well, needless to say, he still doesn't have the money, and I don't really care about it anymore. At the time, the money was a big deal, but at this point, I could care less if I ever get it. It bothered me for a while, but I have now gotten over it and realized that no amount of money that I was willing to give up then was worth ruining our friendship, and if he absolutely needed money, I would probably do it again. (28-year-old U.S. male)

The trade-off here is friendship and caring support versus monetary advantage; that is, social security was preferred to financial security. Although in different circumstances this could potentially become an attempt to buy friendship, the recognition here that friendship is worth more than money suggests that the moral economy of sharing operates by rules that may conflict with the monetary or marketplace economy.

## DISCUSSION AND CONCLUSIONS

The other is essential to sharing. Sharing is bound up with ideas about property, ownership, and self and also notions of solidarity and generosity. It breaks barriers, removes interpersonal distance, creates bonds, and strengthens relationships. Asymmetries, lack of fairness, and transgressing social norms impede sharing. One of the main incentives for sharing is the desire for connection. According to Durkheim (1964), the desire for intimacy with others is the most important determinant of human behavior. It follows that fear of intimacy, not just fear of loss, is a major barrier to sharing. Although this was not directly expressed by informants, it can be seen masquerading as independence in the unwillingness to borrow from others, but social bonds in committed relationships are germane to experiencing well-being (Diener & Seligman, 2004). The findings presented here provide a glimpse of the role of intimacy in sharing behavior.

Children receive early lessons about the goodness of sharing. Their integration into society both at school and in the family involves sharing, beginning with crayons, games, toys, bedrooms, or food. Children learn not only that it is good to share but also that they should take care of their possessions. Inside the family, sharing is mutual, usually nonegalitarian, and rooted in the love among the family members. It can be spontaneous and altruistic, but it is more apt to be forced by parents and teachers. Even though sharing is sometimes a source of tension and fights between siblings, it is the glue cementing the family together (see also Epp & Price, Chapter 29 of this volume; Prinz,

Chapter 28 of this volume). At the same time, smaller families, rising affluence, and individualistic and fast-paced lifestyles all threaten sharing. With increased privatization of possessions within the family, some parents giving duplicate possessions to their children, and practices like giving gifts to siblings when one child has a birthday, there is not as much sharing in the middle-class family as there might be. Instead, there is a tendency toward individualization and claiming private space even when living in a common house. This trend is sharper in North America compared to Spain. Living in apartments instead of spacious houses, children leaving their parents' homes much later, and a more gregarious culture, in contrast to the more individualistic and autonomous ethos in North America, shape two different styles of sharing.

Despite the prevalent childhood lesson that sharing is good, among the young adults studied, sharing is not so open outside the family; some participants observed that sharing ends at the family front door, while others showed more extensive generosity although restricted to certain goods and certain others. Here, sharing is not forced or compulsory, as it might be during childhood; instead, adulthood brings independence to decide to share or not.

The sharing lessons learned in childhood, along with previous negative experiences when sharing, reportedly led to dilemmas about what to share and where to draw the line for sharing. Abusive and opportunistic behavior, asymmetries, violating the social norms of sharing, lack of gratitude, and selfish behavior all drain the opportunities to share and lead people to a less sharing-oriented behavior. There is reluctance to share expensive (e.g., jewelry), easily damaged (e.g., CDs), and symbolic possessions (e.g., gifts). Intimate pieces of information like personal secrets and feelings or personal diaries are not shared or are reserved for very best friends and partners. Fear of becoming vulnerable or being judged are the main barriers to sharing sensitive information, even though these emotional possessions are the ones that create engagement and meaningful relationships when shared. It seems that social media like Twitter and Facebook tend to have a disinhibiting effect on sharing personal information (Nissenbaum, 2010), which could either be because of an illusionary feeling of anonymity online or because the Internet fosters a true sharing community, as some have suggested (e.g., Benkler, 2006).

We also observed a tension between sharing as a means of social connectivity and the desire for material independence that resists sharing possessions with either siblings or friends. On the one hand, belongingness and building a sense of community act as drivers for sharing, whereas on the other hand, possessiveness, attachment, and independence inhibit and limit sharing. There also appears to be some gender bias, with females being more likely to be givers in sharing relationships.

Sharing nourishes the relationships between people and brings togetherness and belongingness, but it also has the power to make social ties evaporate. Differences of opinion about sharing and fair distribution of certain resources even within the families (e.g., wills) may lead to acrimony and resentment among the family members, fueling confrontations and tearing families apart (e.g., Sussman, Cates, & Smith, 1970; Titus, Rosenblatt, & Anderson, 1979). Furthermore, some family members who are writing wills may engage in either predeath coercing (e.g., "I can write you out of my will") or even postmortem control (e.g., "only on the condition that he marries within the faith").

In an era in which overconsumption seems to be the norm, reducing ownership and increasing sharing would benefit both individuals and society. At a macrolevel, sharing has economic, social, and environmental consequences. One of our informants from Spain explained that she shares clothes with her sister: "We love it, because this way, we don't need to buy so much" (24-year-old Spanish female). Sharing more means consuming less, which leads to a more sustainable way of life. By giving priority to sharing the use of things instead of sharing the ownership of things, we promote socially and environmentally conscious consumption. An example with an additional incentive is in the San Francisco Bay area, where freeways have special areas for those seeking rides. Lone drivers are apt to pick up these passengers, because it allows them to drive in the faster high-occupancy vehicle lanes.

It has been forecasted that in 40 years, 70% of the world's population will be living in cities, which is likely to lead to inequalities and a more dehumanized society (Zabalbeascoa, 2010). Sharing builds up communities, makes people feel engaged in groups, redistributes resources, and brings a more human touch to everyday life. According to Fiske (2004), unity, solidarity, and understanding the community as a "natural kind" of human coexistence are some of the outcomes of communal sharing (p. 69). When we share, we relate to others. Cova (1997) argues that links (i.e., social relationships) are more important than things (e.g., brands, products, experiences, ideas). People have reported greater happiness and life satisfaction when they experience relatedness and belongingness (e.g., Baumeister & Leary, 1995; Myers, 2000).

At a personal level, sharing goods frees up resources (e.g., time, money, space) that can be used for other purposes. If we are what we have, and we share what we have, then we feel an expanded aggregate sense of self. Sharing reaches the highest degree of intensity and intimacy when it takes place with a significant other and covers material and emotional issues, ranging from daily life objects to a joint life project, from bills to dreams, from home tasks to life aspirations, and from financial and emotional crises to blissfully happy moments.

As one of the aphorisms offered by a quoted informant has it, "sharing is caring." For the most part, the sharing reported by informants involved demonstrations of caring for another person. Parental sharing with children is quintessentially nurturing. Sharing a pleasing meal is an act of caring as well as nurturing. In this sense, there is a key distinction between compulsory sharing as a social norm and heartfelt sharing. While the latter is the most rewarding, the former can be experienced as forced, unnatural, and even unpleasant. Charity in this context does not necessarily connote either sacrifice or altruism. Rather, as Bajde (2006) found, "an absolute merger between self and other (leaving only 'us') annihilates the very foundation of concepts such as altruism and egoism" (p. 57). Here, too, we see the importance of the aggregate sense of self. With Bajde's charitable donors as well as D. Stone's (2005) emotionally involved personal care workers, we see strong evidence that sharing and caring need not end at the front door. Well-being is often related to prosocial motivation and the ability to make positive contributions to the lives of others. It entails less emphasis on *I* and *mine* and more appreciation of *we* and *ours*. From this perspective, the altruistic aspects of sharing and the positive impact on others' lives that it entails drive us to the highest level of both individual and collective well-being.

Sharing is a contemporary hotbed topic. As Leadbeater (2008) has put it, "In the 20th century we were identified by what we owned; in the 21st century we will be defined by how we share and what we give away" (p. 26). Choosing sharing instead of monopolizing influences our personal well-being, tightens bonds, enhances social connection, and builds a sense of macroaggregate self, minimizing repercussions on the environment and improving collective well-being.

Current models of consumer behavior are steeped in assumptions of egoistic individuals competing for limited resources and making independent decisions (Commuri & Gentry, 2005). Models of the family make assumptions that are not too different from these and emphasize conflict resolution and bargaining in decision making within the family. These models fail to recognize the factors identified here that may facilitate sharing. Under a sharing scenario, the individualistic ownership and the egoistic assumptions pitting people against one another in a zero-sum game evaporate. A growing number of models of sharing are ripe for investigation by scholars of Transformative Consumer Research. One is the growing number of bicycle- and car-sharing organizations (see, e.g., Jonsson, 2006; Katsev, 2003; Meijkamp, 1998). Another is the online organization CouchSurfing, which focuses on facilitating staying in a local host's home throughout most of the world. At a more general level, there are several online organizations that facilitate sharing various things with neighbors, such as The Sharehood and Sharability.

Digital file sharing and open source software like Linux are other examples (see, e.g., Giesler, 2006; Hemetsberger, 2006). Flickr, Wikipedia, Facebook, Twitter, YouTube, and millions of blogs, forums, and chat rooms provide ample evidence that sharing is alive, well, and growing, in spite of, and perhaps because of, increased privatization and intellectual property rights. Such sharing is by no means restricted to the more affluent world, and there are no doubt many more as yet uncharted opportunities for sharing globally. Examining and facilitating these opportunities is an immense opportunity for influencing well-being through Transformative Consumer Research.

## REFERENCES

Altman, J. C. (1987). *Hunter-gatherers today: An Aboriginal economy in North Australia.* Canberra, Australia: Australian Institute of Aboriginal Studies.

Aron, A., Aron, E. N., Tudor, M., & Nelson, G. (1991). Close relationships as including the other in the self. *Journal of Personality and Social Psychology, 60,* 241–253.

Baden, J. A. (1998). Communitarianism and the logic of the commons. In J. A. Baden & D. S. Noonan (Eds.), *Managing the commons* (2nd ed., pp. 135–153). Bloomington: Indiana University Press.

Badje, D. (2006). *Altruism and its relevance to consumer behavior and marketing: Exploring the meaning of donation to charity.* Unpublished doctoral dissertation, University of Ljubljana, Slovenia.

Barnes, P. (2006). *Capitalism 3.0: A guide to reclaiming the commons.* San Francisco: Berret-Koehler.

Baumeister, R. F., & Leary, M. R. (1995). The need to belong: Desire for interpersonal attachments as a fundamental human motivation. *Psychological Bulletin, 117,* 497–529.

Becker, G. (2005). *A treatise on the family* (Enlarged ed.). Cambridge, MA: Harvard University Press.

Belk, R. W. (1988). Possessions and the extended self. *Journal of Consumer Research, 15,* 139–168.

Belk, R. W. (2007). Why not share rather than own? *Annals of the American Academy of Political and Social Science, 611,* 126–140.

Belk, R. W. (2010). Sharing. *Journal of Consumer Research, 40,* 715–734.

Belk, R. W., Groves, R., & Østergaard, P. (2000). Aboriginal consumer culture. In R. Belk, J. Costa, & J. Schouten (Eds.), *Research in consumer behavior* (Vol. 9, pp. 1–45). Stamford, CT: JAI Press.

Benkler, Y. (2006). *The wealth of networks: How social production transforms markets and freedom.* New Haven, CT: Yale University Press.

Bird-David, N. (1990). The giving environment: Another perspective on the economic system of gatherer-hunters. *Current Anthropology, 31,* 189–196.

Boyle, J. (2005). Fencing off ideas: Enclosure and the disappearance of the public domain. In R. A. Ghosh (Ed.), *CODE: Collaborative ownership and the digital economy* (pp. 235–258). Cambridge, MA: MIT Press.

Brown, M. A. (2004). Heritage as property. In K. Verdery & C. Humphrey (Eds.), *Property in question: Value transformation in the global economy* (pp. 49–68). New York: Berg.

Burgoyne, C. B. (1990). Money in marriage: How patterns of allocation both reflect and conceal power. *Sociological Review, 38,* 634–665.

Cheal, D. (1989). Strategies of resource management in household economies: Moral economy or political economy? In R. R. Wilk (Ed.), *The household economy: Reconsidering the domestic mode of production* (pp. 11–22). Boulder, CO: Westview Press.

Cohen, Y. A. (1961). Food and its vicissitudes: A cross-cultural study of sharing and nonsharing. In Y. A. Cohen (Ed.), *Social structure and personality: A casebook* (pp. 313–350). New York: Holt, Rinehart and Winston.

Commuri, S., & Gentry, J. W. (2005). Resource allocation in households with women as chief wage earners. *Journal of Consumer Research, 32,* 185–195.

Cova, B. (1997). Community and consumption: Towards a definition of the linking value of products or services. *European Journal of Marketing, 31,* 297–316.

Crane, D., Kauffman, M., & Bright, K. S. (Producers). (1994–2004). *Friends* [Television series]. New York: NBC.

Diener, E., & Seligman, M. E. P. (2004). Beyond money: Toward an economy of well-being. *Psychological Science in the Public Interest, 5,* 1–31.

Diener, E., & Suh, E. M. (Eds.). (2003). *Culture and subjective well-being.* Cambridge, MA: MIT Press.

Durkheim, E. (1964). *The rules of sociological method*. London: Free Press.

*The Ecologist*. (1993). *Whose common future? Reclaiming the commons*. Philadelphia: New Society.

Emmons, R. A., & McCullough, M. E. (Eds.). (2004). *The psychology of gratitude*. New York: Oxford University Press.

Ertman, M. M., & Williams, J. C. (Eds.). (2005). *Rethinking commodification: Cases and readings in law and culture*. New York: Free Press.

Fiske, A. P. (2004). Four modes of constituting relationships: Consubstantial assimilation; space, magnitude, time, and force; concrete procedures; abstract symbolism. In N. Haslam (Ed.), *Relational models theory: A contemporary overview* (pp. 61–146). Mahwah, NJ: Erlbaum.

Foster, G. M. (1969). Peasant society and the image of limited good. *American Anthropologist, 67*, 293–315.

Foster, G. M. (1972). The anatomy of envy: A study in symbolic behavior. *Current Anthropology, 13*, 165–202.

Fraser, M. (1994, December 31). Australia makes a meal of the family duels. *Sydney Morning Herald*, p. 15.

Frischmann, B. M. (2005). An economic theory of infrastructure and commons management. *Minnesota Law Review, 89*, 917–1030.

Gerrard, G. (1989). Everyone will be jealous for that mutika. *Mankind, 19*, 95–111.

Giesler, M. (2006). Consumer gift system: Netnographic insights from Napster. *Journal of Consumer Research, 33*, 283–290.

Godbout, J. T., & Caillé, A. (1998). *The world of the gift* (D. Winkler, Trans.). Montreal: McGill-Queen's University Press.

Groves, R., & Belk, R. W. (2001). "Look at them blokes! Got no bloody control see": Alcohol consumption and the Australian Aborigine. In P. M. Tidwell & T. E. Muller (Eds.), *Asia Pacific advances in consumer research* (Vol. 4, pp. 310–317). Provo, UT: Association for Consumer Research.

Groves, R., & Pettigrew, S. (2002). Australia, alcohol, and the Aborigine: Alcohol consumption differences between non-indigenous and indigenous Australians. In R. Zwick & T. Ping (Eds.), *Asia Pacific advances in consumer research* (Vol. 5, pp. 148–153). Valdosta, GA: Association for Consumer Research.

Hardin, G. (1968). The tragedy of the commons. *Science, 162*, 1243–1248.

Hemetsberger, A. (2006). When David becomes Goliath: Ideological discourse in new online consumer movements. In C. Pechmann & L. Price (Eds.), *Advances in consumer research* (Vol. 33, pp. 494–500). Duluth, MN: Association for Consumer Research.

Hiatt, L. (1982). Traditional attitudes to land resources. In R. M. Berndt (Ed.), *Aboriginal sites, rites and resource development*. Perth: University of Western Australia Press.

Jonsson, P. (2007). A tale of a car sharing organization (CSO) monster. In H. Brembeck, K. M. Ekström, & M. Mörck (Eds.), *Little monsters: (De)coupling assemblages of consumption* (pp. 149–164). Berlin: Lit Verlag.

Katsev, R. (2003). Car sharing: A new approach to urban transportation problems. *Analyses of Social Issues and Public Policy, 3*, 65–86.

Leadbeater, C. (2008). *We-think: Mass innovation, not mass production: The power of mass creativity*. London: Profile Books.

Marshall, J. J., & Woolley, F. (1993). What's mine is mine and what's yours is ours: Challenging the income pooling assumption. In L. McAlister & M. L. Rothschild (Eds.), *Advances in consumer research* (Vol. 20, pp. 541–545). Provo, UT: Association for Consumer Research.

Matt, S. J. (2003). *Keeping up with the Joneses: Envy in American consumer society, 1890–1930*. Philadelphia: University of Pennsylvania Press.

McKnight, D. (2002). *From hunting to drinking: The devastating effects of alcohol on an Australian Aboriginal community*. London: Routledge.

Meijkamp, R. (1998). Changing consumer behavior through eco-efficient services: An empirical study of car sharing in the Netherlands. *Business Strategy and the Environment, 7*, 234–244.

Myers, D. G. (2000). The funds, friends, and faith of happy people. *American Psychologist, 55*, 56–67.

Nissenbaum, H. (2010). *Privacy in context: Technology, policy, and the integrity of social life*. Stanford, CA: Stanford Law Books.

O'Toole, R. (1998). The tragedy of the scenic commons. In J. A. Baden & D. S. Noonan (Eds.), *Managing the commons* (2nd ed., pp. 181–187). Bloomington: Indiana University Press.

Phillips, T. (2005). *Knockoff: The deadly trade in counterfeit goods*. London: Kogan Page.

Price, J. A. (1975). Sharing: The integration of intimate economics. *Anthropologica, 17*, 3–27.

Rose, R., & Poynor, C. (2007). Mi casa es whose casa? An experimental investigation of consumers' propensity to participate in a multilateral sharing system. In G. Fitzsimons & V. Morwitz (Eds.), *Advances in consumer research* (Vol. 34, pp. 342–344). Duluth, MN: Association for Consumer Research.

Rosen, F. (2003). *Classical utilitarianism from Hume to Mill*. London: Routledge.

Ruskola, T. (2005). Home economics: What is the difference between a family and a corporation? In M. M. Ertman & J. C. Williams (Eds.), *Rethinking commodification: Cases and readings in law and culture* (pp. 324–344). New York: New York University Press.

Sahlins, M. (1972). *Stone Age economics*. Chicago: Aldine-Atherton.

Scheper-Hughes, N., & Wacquant, L. (Eds.). (2002). *Commodifying bodies*. London: Sage.

Schwab, R. G. (1995). *The calculus of reciprocity: Principles and implications of Aboriginal sharing* (Discussion Paper No. 100). Canberra, Australia: Center for Applied Economics and Policy Research.

Shultz, C. J., & Holbrook, M. B. (1999). Marketing and the tragedy of the commons: A synthesis, commentary, and analysis for action. *Journal of Public Policy & Marketing, 18*, 218–229.

Stanner, W. E. H. (1979). *White man got no dreaming: Essays 1938–1973*. Canberra, Australia: Australian National University Press.

Stevenson, G. G. (1991). *Common property economics: A general theory and land use applications*. New York: Cambridge University Press.

Stone, B. (2009, August 10). Breakfast can wait: The day's first stop is online. *The New York Times*, p. A1.

Stone, D. (2005). For love nor money: The commodification of care. In M. M. Ertman & J. C. Williams (Eds.), *Rethinking commodification: Cases and readings in law and culture* (pp. 271–290). New York: New York University Press.

Sussman, M. B., Cates, J. N., & Smith, D. L. (1970). *The family and inheritance*. New York: Russell Sage Foundation.

Thompson, D. (1949). *Economic structure and the ceremonial exchange cycle in Arnhem Land*. Melbourne, Australia: Macmillan.

Tinson, J., & Nuttall, P. (2008). Insider trading? Exploring familial intra-generational borrowing and sharing. In S. Borghini, M. A. McGrath, & C. Otnes (Eds.), *European advances in consumer research* (Vol. 8, pp. 41–42). Duluth, MN: Association for Consumer Research.

Titus, S. L., Rosenblatt, P. C., & Anderson, R. M. (1979). Family conflict over inheritance of property. *Family Coordinator, 28*, 337–346.

Vaughan, G. (1997). *For-giving: A feminist critique of exchange*. Austin, TX: Plain View Press.

Visser, M. (2008). *The gift of thanks: The roots, persistence, and paradoxical meanings of a social ritual*. New York: HarperCollins.

Wilson, G. (1987). Money: Patterns of responsibility and irresponsibility in marriage. In J. Brannen & G. Wilson (Eds.), *Give and take in families* (pp. 136–154). London: Allen & Unwin.

Zabalbeascoa, A. (2010, February 5). *El desafío de la convivencia* [The challenge of coexistence]. *El País.com*. Available: http://www.elpais.com/articulo/portada/desafio/convivencia/elpepusoceps/20100502elpepspor_9/Tes

Zelizer, V. A. (2005). *The purchase of intimacy*. Princeton, NJ: Princeton University Press.

# 31

# *Resilience and Consumer Behavior for Higher Quality of Life*

Salvatore R. Maddi

Resilience involves not only surviving but also thriving despite stressful circumstances, a phenomenon that has substantial effects on one's emotions, convictions, and actions. Accumulated research has shown that some people are generally more resilient than others (Bonanno, 2004; Maddi & Khoshaba, 2001). Especially in our turbulent and, therefore, especially stressful times, it is essential to understand what makes some people more resilient than others and how this might guide developmental training for those who are less resilient. Important in this understanding is the research showing that a particular personality pattern of attitudes and strategies that has been called hardiness is a major pathway to resilience (Bonanno, 2004; Maddi, 1986, 1997, 1998a, 2002, 2004; Maddi, Harvey, Khoshaba, Fazel, & Resurreccion, 2009b; Maddi et al., 2006; Maddi & Khoshaba, 1994). This chapter emphasizes hardiness as the pathway to resilience, and the particular, ongoing effects of this on consumer behavior, other performance, perceived quality of life, and health.

## LIFE AS A STRESSFUL PHENOMENON

The conceptual framework for hardiness as the pathway to resilience derives mainly from existential psychology (Frankl, 1960; May, Angel, & Ellenberger, 1958). In this approach, life is presumed to be an ongoing stressful phenomenon due to the continually changing and unpredictable developmental process (Cannon, 1929; Frankl, 1960; Kierkegaard, 1843/1954; Maddi, 1988; May, 1950; Sartre, 1943/1956; Selye, 1976). This process begins with our being pushed out of our mother's womb and forced to begin breathing for ourselves in the cold, bright, noisy environment we had never anticipated. Rank (1929) called this experience the trauma of birth. As part of this developmental period, you try to understand and interact with other people and the environment without being mystified or hurting oneself. Yet, you fail frequently, as you crawl around and bang into things, feel too cold or warm, and experience being overwhelmed or alone, all of which are examples of the many ways you may feel uncomfortable. Then, if these experiences make you cry or express anger, you may be silenced or chastened by others.

No sooner do you make some progress in dealing with this early pattern of trauma, than you have to leave what has hopefully, through what you have learned, become your safe house to go to school (Maddi, 1988; Rank, 1929). You cry when your mother leaves you at kindergarten, and you have to somehow interact with other children who do not have your interests at heart, with a teacher who imposes rules and regulations on you, and with a curriculum that requires that you keep learning new things all the time. Even if you are fortunate to find some friends, interact cooperatively with teachers, and get at least reasonably good grades, as soon as you feel you have learned something, the situation changes again. If you fail to choose the right clothes to wear, brands to use, and/or activities to engage in, or if your family cannot afford these items, you may be ridiculed by peers (Wooten, 2006). Even if your family happens to be prosperous and continues to live in the same place, you will go from school to school, changing teachers, friends, and curricula in the process.

The stressful school experiences continue into college and become even harder to deal with, because by then, you have reached the age at which you are expected to begin considering what your adult life will be like (Maddi & Kobasa, 1984). Whether or not you are in college, you must seriously consider what kind of career, new family, and role in society you will have. Shall you have sex with anyone who is attractive, or should you be using all your resources, including sex, to find the right person to marry? Should you take whatever job is available to you or struggle to find the career that best expresses your skills, values, and preferences? By this time, you are responsible for your own consumer behavior. What brands of clothing, cars, food, beverages, and equipment should you buy, and what are the justifiable prices? Should you go into debt to try to progress socially and/or economically (e.g., to buy an expensive business suit, get an MBA) or live within your means (Nenkov, Inman, & Hulland, 2008)? Also, how should you feel about the reactions of your parents in all this?

Needless to say, the period of early adulthood is undoubtedly stressful, and as time goes on, the period of middle adulthood does not become less stressful. If you marry someone and start a family, before you know it you are struggling to help your children and spouse with their stressful circumstances (Maddi, 2004; Prinz, Chapter 28 of this volume). How can you be a good parent and spouse and still keep trying to find your own place in life? How do you and your spouse handle financial and consumer affairs, such as dividing up paychecks, shopping, and domestic tasks? How do you decide on large purchases (e.g., home, car), particularly if there are disagreements, and should you go into debt to get higher quality products (see, e.g., Loewenstein, Cryder, Benartzi, & Previtero, Chapter 19 of this volume; Soman, Cheema, & Chan, Chapter 20 of this volume)? How do you maintain your standard of consumption if you lose your job? If you have difficulties in your marriage, should you divorce, or have affairs, or is there a more constructive alternative? If you have not married, how do you face all the issues of adulthood alone?

Moving on to later adulthood is hardly less stressful (Bonanno, 2004; Maddi, 1980). By then, your peers and members of your family of origin are showing signs of deteriorating health or actually dying, to say nothing about the health problems you may be having. You begin looking back on your life and wondering if it was a sufficient expression of your wishes, values, and capabilities. You retire and wonder what you should do with yourself, whether there really is an afterlife, and whether your life was all worth it. You may also need to make heart-wrenching decisions about moving out of your home and giving up your life's most precious consumer possessions to relatives or friends (Pettigrew & Mochis, Chapter 27 of this volume; Price, Arnould, & Curasi, 2000).

As if the ongoing stressfulness of the natural developmental process were not enough, the period of time and society in which we live may well impose additional stresses (Maddi, 2002). At the present time, there are several megatrends increasing the stressfulness of everyday living (Maddi, 1998a). For example, we have experienced breathtakingly fast technological advance, starting with computers and progressing through the Internet and the telecommunications industry. Whereas the upside of this megatrend has been much greater ability to communicate, solve problems, and bring about new areas of functioning, the downside is the difficulty for many people of participating in, much less contributing to, this technological advance (see Hoffman, Chapter 9 of this volume). This stressful circumstance has been deemed the *digital divide*. An additional stressor resulting from this technological advance is the enormous pressure for social networking on the Internet. Yet, another aspect of this technological advance is the ever-increasing range of consumer products. The upside of this is the amazing range of goods, but the downside is the overwhelming difficulty of deciding which are best to buy and affordable, to say nothing about what marketing efforts to believe (see Mick, 2008; Mick, Broniarczyk, & Haidt, 2004; Mick & Schwartz, Chapter 32 of this volume).

Another ongoing megatrend of our time is globalization (Maddi, 1998a). Its upside is our greater knowledge of and interaction with people all around the world, but the downside is the threat constituted by globalization to the sense in societies and communities of their values, sense of what is right and wrong, and stability. Terrorism is one expression of this sense of threat, as some societies feel that the only way they can protect themselves from imposition by more powerful societies is to undermine them in subtle and not so subtle ways. Less powerful members of the powerful societies may also be undermined, as globalization encourages companies to outsource jobs to other countries where pay is lower. For that matter, even relatively powerful members of the powerful societies may increase in stress. Global business executives may feel increasingly stressed and anxious at having to do business with people in other countries, whose values and aims they do not know and whom they may never even meet.

In our time, another downside of rapid technological advance and emerging globalization is the megatrend of mounting, worldwide competition. The days are over when we could carry on work within our own country and its economy. Now, there is worldwide competition for the best products at the best prices. The upside of this is that many foreign countries are participating further in our economy, not only by buying our products but also by contributing technological advances to our production system. Ireland, India, and China, for example, have improved their economies significantly in recent years by having their young workers become expert in writing computer software programs and selling them to us at reduced prices. The downside of all this is that some of our companies and workers are floundering, as they cannot lower their prices and salaries enough to compete. All this is happening in our wonderfully democratic country at just the time when the pressure for equal opportunities for women and minorities in the workplace has mounted. The upside of this is less discrimination in the job market, but the downside is decreased job security. An additional factor in increasing job insecurity is our aging population. As people live longer, they are retiring from work at later ages than before, which is making it harder for younger people to find the jobs they want (Maddi, 1998a, 1998b).

Another megatrend being experienced now on a worldwide basis is economic downturn. Crucial companies in this country are being subsidized, but there is still an increasing number of job losses and company foreclosures going on. This has led to less money being spent by consumers and the resulting further slowdown of businesses. Needless to say, the trickle-down effect of these megatrends is imposing stresses on individuals, which adds to the more natural stress of the developmental process (Maddi, 1998a; May, 1950). These days, companies are constantly reorganizing, merging, closing down, and even starting up. As jobs and job security are decreasing, company loyalty is down, and employers are hard pressed to keep and attract the best staff and bring out the best in their ongoing staff.

In summary, the combination of ongoing developmental requirements and imposed megatrends have made our lives a continual experience of stressful changes that is quite consistent with the existential assumption that life is by its nature a stressful phenomenon. As depicted in Figure 31.1, the overall level of stress that impacts you determines your level of strain, which is your body's general arousal level. The evolutionary basis for this phenomenon harks back to when our immediate stresses tended to be larger and more vicious animals confronting us, so we needed to immediately increase the sugar in our bloodstream so that we could have the mental and muscular capability

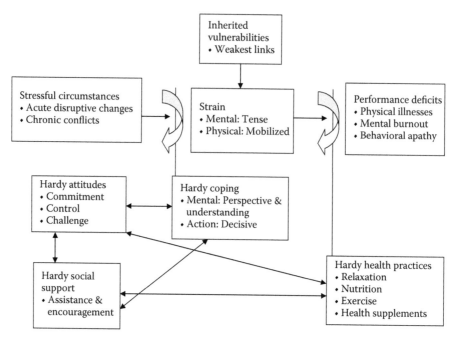

**Figure 31.1** The hardiness model. (From Maddi, S. R., & Kobasa, S. C., *The Hardy Executive: Health Under Stress*, Dow Jones-Irwin, Homewood, IL, 1984. Copyright Hardiness Institute, Irvine, CA. With permission.)

to fight or run away (Cannon, 1929). Now, even though our stresses tend to be more subtle and psychosocial than that, the strain response remains the same in nature. Typical signs of mounting strain are rapid heartbeat, stomach upset, muscular aches and pains, headaches, irritability, impatience, depression, anxiety, and memory and concentration loss. Also depicted in Figure 31.1 is the breakdown process that takes place when strain levels are too intense and prolonged, a phenomenon shown in the award-winning research of Selye (1976). In humans, this breakdown process can undermine performance, health, and consumer behavior. Figure 31.1 further indicates that these signs of breakdown will tend to take place along the lines of our genetic weaknesses.

Fortunately, there is also evidence that the degree of performance and health deterioration under stress varies among individuals. This phenomenon of resilience involves at least surviving, but perhaps also thriving, under stress (Binswanger, 1963; Bonanno, 2004; Maddi, 2002; May, 1950). Important as a pathway to resilience is the pattern of attitudes and strategies constituting hardiness that is emphasized in this chapter and depicted in the rest of Figure 31.1. The overall emphasis of hardiness is that trying to avoid and deny the stresses one is experiencing leads nowhere. Instead, it is incumbent on people to recognize stresses clearly and have the courage and strategies to turn them from potential disasters into personal growth opportunities.

## HARDY ATTITUDES AS EXISTENTIAL COURAGE

As depicted in Figure 31.1, the three hardy attitudes are commitment, control, and challenge (3Cs), which together constitute existential courage (Maddi, 2002, 2004). If you are strong in commitment, you believe that however stressful things get, it is important to stay involved with the people and events in your experience. It seems wasteful to let yourself shrink into isolation and alienation. If you are strong in control, you believe that however stressful things get, it is important to keep trying to have an influence on the outcomes going on around you. It seems wasteful to let yourself sink into passivity and powerlessness. If you are strong in challenge, you believe that stressful circumstances are normal in living and constitute an opportunity to learn from your experiences, whether they are positive or negative. It seems naive to you to think that you are entitled to easy comfort and security if your life is to be considered worthwhile.

These 3Cs of hardiness are considered to interact with each other to produce the existential courage and motivation to do the hard work of turning stressful circumstances to your advantage (Maddi, 2002, 2004; Sinclair & Tetrick, 2000). You do not consider life to be easy and recognize that there are both successes and failures along the way. Your emphasis is what you can do to facilitate your progress and learn from what you do. Engaging in this facilitative process leads you to be continually more convinced that life's successes and failures are what you make of them, and in this process, you continue to grow in wisdom and fulfillment (Maddi, 2002).

## HARDY STRATEGIES AS FACILITATORS OF DEVELOPMENT

Figure 31.1 summarizes three hardy strategies that are useful in turning stressful circumstances from potential disasters into growth opportunities. All of them involve hard work, which is why the courage and motivation constituted by the hardy attitudes is important in bringing these strategies about (Maddi, 2002, 2004). Further, as depicted in Figure 31.1, the most basic and direct of the hardy strategies is hardy coping (i.e., problem-solving; Khoshaba & Maddi, 2004), which involves perceiving stresses accurately and fully, figuring out what is the most advantageous thing to do under the circumstances, and carrying out the resulting, decisive plan of action to resolve the stress and improve one's performance, consumerism, health, and wisdom in the process. This hardy coping is the most direct and effective way of decreasing stress and strain levels and, hence, encouraging enhancement of performance and health. In this manner, hardy coping is dramatically at variance with the more regressive coping efforts that involve either denial or avoidance, or seeing oneself as the victim and then striking out. At the mental level, neither denial nor victimization leads to learning and wisdom, and at the action level, neither avoidance nor striking out improves one's living.

Also important, although somewhat less direct, is the practice of hardy, or healthy, self-care, which moderates strain levels without directly resolving the stressful circumstances that produced them (Khoshaba & Maddi, 2004). As shown in Figure 31.1, this involves engaging in a healthy pattern of consumer behaviors as related to relaxation, eating, and exercise that is most likely to keep strain levels low enough to facilitate the hard work of hardy, rather than regressive, coping and help in avoiding breakdowns in performance, other consumer behaviors, and health. The opposite pattern of unhealthy mental preoccupation with stresses and strain, rather than trying to relax, engagement in stress eating of sweet and fatty foods, and avoiding physical exercise continues strain levels that are excessive enough to discourage problem-solving coping efforts.

The other important hardy strategy shown in Figure 31.1 is socially supportive interactions with significant others (Khoshaba & Maddi, 2004). To continue to deepen your relationships with people important in your life, such as family members, friends, coworkers, neighbors, and fellow members of community organizations, you need to engage with them in a mutual pattern of giving and receiving assistance as well as encouragement in solving the stressful circumstances of living. This socially supportive pattern of interaction is quite different from interacting with significant others by being either destructively competitive, overtly or covertly, or stultifyingly overprotective. After all, the message to significant others, if you are competitive or overprotective, is that you are better than them. In contrast, trying to be mutually assisting and encouraging sends the message that you are together in dealing with life's stresses.

## IMPLICATIONS OF HARDINESS FOR CONSUMER BEHAVIOR AND QUALITY OF LIFE

There are many implications of resilience through hardiness in consumer behaviors (Maddi, 2002; Maddi, Khoshaba, Persico, Bleecker, & VanArsdall, 1997; Maddi, Wadhwa, & Haier, 1996) that have been implied in the previous emphases but need to be specified here. Once again, the overall implication of hardiness is that life is by its nature a continually stressful phenomenon. To be resilient, by turning ongoing stresses from potential disasters into fulfilling and growth-producing experiences instead, one needs high levels of the pattern of attitudes and strategies of hardiness that have already been elaborated. High hardy attitudes constitute existential courage and motivation, and high hardy strategies direct the hard work that fosters resilience under stress (Maddi, 2002).

In contrast, low hardiness levels will lead to reacting to stressful circumstances by denial (i.e., attempts to avoid recognizing stresses and strain levels) and avoidance (i.e., engaging in what seem like exciting and distracting activities; see also Albright, Chapter 24 of this volume; Faber & Vohs, Chapter 22 of this volume). Nonetheless, if and when the stresses and strain surface, people with low hardiness levels are likely to engage in exaggeration (e.g., they feel victimized by an uncaring world) and striking back (e.g., engaging in destructive competition to prove their point). The self-indulgence that these nonhardy reactions connote has many expressions in consumer behavior (Maddi, 2002).

It is helpful at this point to consider some of the actual tendencies in consumer behavior produced by having low levels of hardiness. Specifically, for such people, there is neither the existential courage and motivation to do the hard work of turning stresses to growth advantage nor the skills that would be needed to carry this out. Hence, as the ongoing stresses that are a natural part of living are not dealt with resiliently, people low in hardiness will experience continuously excessive and prolonged levels of bodily arousal, or strain, and the concomitant mental and physical symptoms of anxiety, anger, depression, meaninglessness, and self-pity.

In such low hardiness people, the resulting pattern of trying to overcome these mental and physical symptoms will vacillate between denial and avoidance, and victimization and striking back. There are many problematic consumer behaviors expressive of these tendencies. A common example of denying and avoiding the unresolved, mounting stresses that one is under is the distracting excitement of buying personal belongings, and even gifts that are not really needed, just for the fun of it (see Burroughs & Rindfleisch, Chapter 12 of this volume). As this process continues, it is easy for people to spend excessively, even beyond what they can afford (see Faber & Vohs, Chapter 22 of this volume; Soman, Cheema, & Chan, Chapter 20 of this volume). This excessive spending and resulting inability to pay one's bills may well have been a factor in the current economic downturn in our society. Another consumer behavior that is similar, as to denial and avoidance of stresses and strain, is overeating. In this, people low in hardiness will emphasize fatty and sweet foods, not because they are truly hungry but to blank out the underlying, painful thoughts and feelings (Maddi et al., 1997; see also Grier & Moore, Chapter 15 of this volume). This current ongoing tendency may well have been a factor resulting in the current obesity epidemic in our society.

There are also lots of other stress-distracting activities with an influence on consumer behavior that would appear to involve not only denial and avoidance but also some exaggeration and striking back. An example is the sexual promiscuity involved in provoking sexuality in most, or even all, of one's relationships for the fun of it, not as a search for the right partner (see also Fishbein & Middlestadt, Chapter 18 of this volume). The excessive consumer behavior involved may involve "partying," and lavishing gifts on the potential sexual partners. Indeed, one may even get into paying for sexual experiences with escorts and prostitutes, a form of consumer behavior that in some states may actually involve breaking the law, which may even increase the excitement and be justified by a sense of striking out against what seems like an unjustifiable society. This promiscuous consumer behavior may be a factor in the majority of marriages in our society ending in divorce, and in the large number of people who never marry. Another consumer activity that combines denial and avoidance with exaggeration and striking out is alcohol and drug abuse (Maddi et al., 1996). These potentially illegal behaviors, however distracting from the unresolved stresses they may be, are injurious not only to the person who does it but also to those around him or her. What also fits here is dangerously adventurous activities, such as driving too fast on crowded streets, risking too much on problematic investments, and gambling with the aim of taking everyone else's money (see also Cotte & LaTour, Chapter 23 of this volume). The kinds of activities mentioned here are consumer behaviors that are problematic not only for oneself but also for family, friends, and society.

In contrast, people high in hardy attitudes and hardy strategies are much more likely to avoid such distracting, exciting, and destructive behaviors by engaging instead in the resilient pattern of learning and developing from the positive and negative experiences resulting from the continuing process of working on the ongoing stresses of living (Maddi, 1998a, 2002). These people are open to clear recognition of the stressful circumstances they experience and rely on their courage and strategies to turn them from potential disasters into growth opportunities. They continually learn from these experiences, as they deal with them successfully and feel wise and fulfilled as a result (see Mick & Schwartz, Chapter 32 of this volume). Needless to say, these people also engage in consumer behaviors, but are not reckless, overindulgent, and destructive toward others in that process.

## WHERE DOES HARDINESS COME FROM?

Although it is possible that the attitudes and strategies of hardiness have some biological underpinning, it is much more likely that they are learned (Khoshaba & Maddi, 1999; Maddi, 2002). When you are a youngster, what is important in hardiness development is how your parents and other significant adults (e.g., teachers, relatives) interact with you. Specifically, it is important that your parents and significant adults encourage you to recognize that life is an ongoing stressful phenomenon, and what is important is what you learn from your efforts to turn the stresses to your advantage. In this, you must be encouraged to learn not only from your successes but your failures as well. Parents need to persist in this process of giving assistance and encouragement to their children, rather than overprotecting or punishing them (Khoshaba & Maddi, 1999; Maddi, 2002; Prinz, Chapter 28 of this volume).

This consistent parental approach of assisting and encouraging children to stay involved, try to turn stresses to their advantage, and grow in the process will lead to hardiness in the youngsters. As time goes on, these courageous attitudes and effective strategies will help them continue to grow and develop. This is depicted in Figure 31.1 by the arrows that link the hardy attitudes to the hardy strategies going in both directions. By constituting courage and motivation, the hardy attitudes facilitate the hard work of problem-solving coping, healthy self-care, and supportive social interactions. Yet, it is also likely that once you engage in this hard work, the feedback that you get from these effective activities will also enhance your hardy attitudes.

## RESEARCH ON HARDINESS ATTITUDES AND STRATEGIES

The first demonstration of the power of hardiness was our 12-year natural experiment at Illinois Bell Telephone (IBT) that began in 1975 and continued through 1987 (Maddi, 2002; Maddi & Kobasa, 1984). Each year in this study, extensive psychological data (e.g., interviews, questionnaires) and medical data (e.g., yearly physical examinations) were collected on 450 managers. At the beginning of the study, the telephone industry was a federally regulated monopoly, because cheap and reliable telephone service was considered in the national interest. However, the U.S. government decided in 1981 to deregulate telephone service to encourage the competition that has led to the present, highly competitive telecommunications and computer industries. The upheaval produced by the deregulation on the companies, one of which was IBT, is still regarded as among the greatest in corporate history. Examples of this stressful disruption included a downsizing of close to 50% from 1981 to 1982, the major and continual redefinition of job characteristics, and a virtual collapse of job security. As one manager interviewed in 1982 put it, "I have had 10 different supervisors in 12 months. They are in and out the door and don't know what they're doing, and I don't know what I'm doing."

In the 6 years of the study following deregulation, roughly two thirds of the managers in the research sample were severely disrupted, disoriented, and demoralized, and showed health deterioration. These problems showed up in increased wear-and-tear diseases (e.g., heart attacks, strokes), mental disorders (e.g., anxiety, depression), and performance problems (e.g., violence in the workplace, divorces). In contrast, the other third of the managers showed resilience by not only surviving but also thriving, with enhanced performance (e.g., rising to the top of the heap, starting their own competitive companies) and health (e.g., feeling greater enthusiasm and energy).

Scrutiny of the psychological data prior to the upheaval that differentiated the managers who survived and thrived from those who were undermined by the upheaval supported the hypotheses concerning hardiness as a pathway to this resiliency under stress. For example, prior to the upheaval, all managers in the sample were asked, "What is it like to be a manager in this company?" One manager who was subsequently resilient answered, "To be an accepted manager in this company, you have to have a bell-shaped head." When asked what that meant, he pointed to a multivolume work on his bookshelf that was published by the parent company, AT&T. Then he said,

> When a problem arises, you don't think it through on your own. Instead, you go to the index of these books by Ma Bell, and you are directed to the part of the books you need to read, which reading tells you exactly what to do. That's what I mean by needing to have a bell-shaped head.

Interestingly enough, this manager felt much more energetic after the upheaval, immersed himself in using his talent to figure out what needed to be done in the chaotic environment, and rose to the top of his reorganizing company.

The manager used as an example above was characteristic of those who survived and thrived despite the upheaval. Specifically, the research measures showed that following the deregulation, they were higher than those who deteriorated in the 3Cs of hardy attitudes, and the hardy strategies of problem-solving coping, socially supportive interactions, and effective self-care (Maddi, 2002; Maddi & Kobasa, 1984). Clearly, the IBT data were quite supportive of hardiness theorizing.

Since the IBT project, much research has been done on hardiness all around the world (see Maddi, 2002; Maddi & Khoshaba, 2001). One set of studies had to do with emerging measurement problems concerning the hardy attitudes (Funk, 1992). In particular, the first hardy attitudes measure that was developed on working adults (Kobasa, Maddi, & Kahn, 1982), when used with undergraduates, sometimes showed insufficient intercorrelations of the 3Cs to warrant considering a total score (Funk & Houston, 1987; Hull, Van Treuren, & Virnelli, 1987). However, later versions of the hardy attitudes measure seem to have corrected this problem (e.g., Maddi, 1997; Maddi, 2002, 2004; Sinclair & Tetrick, 2000).

Another problem is that the first hardy attitudes measure, which was heavily loaded with negatively worded items, appeared from its correlates that it might be getting at little more than negative affectivity (Hull et al., 1987). Later hardy attitudes measures have balanced negatively worded items with positively worded ones. Although these later measures still correlate negatively with indexes of negative affectivity, the magnitudes are lower, and several findings showing their construct validity as measures of existential courage are available (e.g., Maddi, 2002, 2004; Sinclair & Tetrick, 2000). Further, Maddi and Khoshaba (1994) have shown that the pattern of negative relationships between the latest hardy attitudes measure and the Minnesota Multiphasic Personality Inventory scales of psychopathology persists after negative affectivity has been controlled. This study further showed that although the hardy attitudes measure is negatively correlated with neuroticism on the NEO-FFI (Neuroticism-Extroversion-Openness Five-Factor Inventory) measure of the five-factor model of personality, it is also positively correlated with all four of the other factors (i.e., extroversion, agreeableness, conscientiousness, openness to experience). Thus, recent hardy attitudes measures are likely to be more than merely negative affectivity. Interestingly enough, all five factors together only predicted about 25% of the variance of hardiness, suggesting that the latter is not just a combination of the five factors as a depiction of personality.

The most recent hardy attitudes measure, the revised third edition of the Personal Views Survey (PVS III–R), is an 18-item questionnaire showing adequate reliability and validity (Maddi et al., 2009; Maddi, Harvey, et al., 2006; Maddi & Khoshaba, 2001). This test has been translated into several foreign languages. All the test items use a 4-point rating scale regarding their personal relevance. Commitment, control, and challenge are each measured by three positively and three negatively worded items. Examples for commitment are, "I often wake up eager to take on life wherever it left off" (positive indicator), and "It's hard to imagine anyone getting excited about working" (negative indicator); for control, "When I make plans, I'm certain I can make them work" (positive indicator), and "Most of what happens in life is just meant to be" (negative indicator); and for challenge, "Changes in routine provoke me to learn" (positive indicator), and "I am not equipped to handle the unexpected problems of life" (negative indicator). Although copies of the PVS III–R are available to researchers, the Hardiness Institute, which publishes the test, does not release its scoring algorithm. Hence, when the researchers administer the test, they send the resulting item scores to the Hardiness Institute for scoring and for scale scores for commitment, control, challenge, and total hardiness, along with relevant reliabilities. There is a nominal fee for this work.

Since the completion of the IBT project, there have also been many construct validation studies of the role of hardy attitudes in various aspects of functioning. As expected, there is evidence that commitment, control, and challenge are intercorrelated but not redundant with each other (Maddi, 1994, 1997; Maddi & Khoshaba, 2001; Sinclair & Tetrick, 2000). In an experiential sampling study (Maddi, 1999), participants were paged at random and asked to report the nature of their ongoing activities. Results showed a positive relationship between hardy attitudes measured earlier with the experiential sampling reportage of (a) involvement with others and ongoing activities (i.e., commitment), (b) the sense that experiences had been chosen and were influenced by the participants (i.e., control), and (c) the positive process of learning from the circumstances (i.e., challenge). In further studies, the expected positive correlations have been found between hardy attitudes and (a) problem-solving coping, rather than denial and avoidance (e.g., Maddi, 1999; Maddi et al., 2006; Maddi & Hightower, 1999); (b) socially supportive, rather than competitive or overprotective, interactions with others (e.g., Maddi et al., 2006; Maddi & Kobasa, 1984); and (c) facilitative, rather than undermining, self-care (e.g., Allred & Smith, 1989; Contrada, 1989; Khoshaba & Maddi, 2004; Maddi et al., 1996; Weibe & McCallum, 1986).

There are also accumulated findings indicating that hardiness renders self-confidence and resiliency to people experiencing stressful changes. For example, hardy attitudes have a buffering effect on both strain and illness symptoms (e.g., Bartone, Ursano, Wright, & Ingraham, 1989; Harvey,

2005; Kobasa et al., 1982; Kuo & Tsai, 1986). Under stress, hardy attitudes also have an enhancing effect on performance. For instance, positive relationships have been found between hardy attitudes and, subsequently, the following:

- Effective sports performance among, for example, high school varsity basketball players (Maddi, & Hess, 1992) and women's synchronized swimming competitors in the Olympics (Lancer, 2000)
- Success rates in intentionally stressful military officer training and firefighter training programs (e.g., Florian, Milkulincer, & Taubman, 1995; Maddi, Harvey, Resurreccion, Giatras, & Raganold, 2007; Westman, 1990)
- Retention rates, grade point averages, and innovativeness among college students (Lifton, Seay, & Bushke, 2000; Maddi, Harvey, et al., 2006)
- Leadership in military officer training school students (Bartone & Snook, 1999)
- Speed of recovery of baseline functioning following the disruption of culture shock (Atella, 1989; Kuo & Tsai, 1986)
- Protection against posttraumatic stress and depression disorders when military personnel encounter life threats while serving abroad (Bartone, 1999)
- Success in entrepreneurial functioning among professionals (Maddi, Harvey, et al., 2006)

The emerging research support for hardiness provokes consideration of its relative effectiveness in enhancing performance and health by comparison with other variables that are also conceptually relevant. Actually, some of the studies cited above permitted comparison of the effects of hardiness and other potentially predictive variables, and hardiness tended to be more powerful. For example, Lifton et al. (2000) found that hardiness is a better predictor of retention in college than either scholastic aptitude test scores or high school academic achievement rank. Also, Bartone and Snook (1999) found that in a cohort of West Point military cadets, hardiness was the best predictor of leadership behavior over the 4 years of training than were other available measures.

There have also been two studies done so far with the express purpose of comparing hardiness and other relevant factors in their relative effects on performance and health. One study (Maddi & Hightower, 1999) showed that in samples of students and working adults, hardiness is a better positive predictor of problem-solving coping, and negative predictor of avoidance coping, than is optimism. These findings suggest that optimism may be laced with complacency, whereas hardiness emphasizes the importance of facing stresses and doing the hard work of turning them to advantage. In another study (Maddi, Brow, Khoshaba, & Vaitkus, 2006), hardiness was a better protection against depression and anger among U.S. Army officers than was religiosity. The results showed that when hardiness is strong, religiosity does little to protect against those negative emotions that connote failure. With regard to anger, religiosity does have some protective effect, but only when hardiness is low. Perhaps the problem with religiosity is its strong emphasis on an ancient God figure and unchangeable credo, rather than encouraging one to be open to stressful experiences and learning from trying to turn them to advantage. Needless to say, there needs to be additional studies comparing the effectiveness of hardiness and other variables conceptualized as useful in living well (for additional information, visit the Hardiness Institute website at http://www.hardinessinstitute.com).

## RESEARCH AND PRACTICE ON HARDINESS TRAINING

As indicated earlier, the conceptualization of hardiness indicates that it can be learned, not only in childhood through interaction with one's parents but also in adolescence and adulthood through specific training procedures (Khoshaba & Maddi, 1999; Maddi et al., 2002, 2009; Maddi & Kobasa, 1984). This position was supported by the IBT study (Khoshaba & Maddi, 1999), which found that those managers high in hardiness remembered having had a stressful early life in which they were supported and encouraged by their parents. In this, they were identified as the family's hope and accepted that role.

That hardiness can be learned in adulthood was empirically supported by the early form of hardiness training that was developed and tested at IBT after the upheaval had occurred (Maddi, 1987). Utilizing 1-hour weekly group sessions for 10 weeks, hardiness trainers helped managers engage in the hardy strategy of problem-solving coping with each of their specific stressors in turn and use the feedback from their efforts to deepen their hardy attitudes. Guided by the trainer, the group members provided social support by assisting and encouraging their peers in this process. This first evaluation of the effectiveness of this procedure compared the hardiness training group to a waiting list control group of managers who also wanted to receive the training. This comparison showed that the hardiness training group had a greater increase in hardiness attitudes, job satisfaction, and feelings of social support, and a greater decrease in anxiety, depression, suspiciousness, and blood pressure, than did their peers in the waiting list control group. These findings persisted in a follow-up testing 6 months later. A second study with IBT managers (Maddi, Kahn, & Maddi, 1998) compared the effectiveness of hardiness training to a standard relaxation procedure and a social support placebo procedure. All trainers conducted all three procedures and showed no differences in competence. Results indicated that managers in the hardiness training group showed a greater increase in hardy attitudes and job satisfaction, and a greater decrease in anxiety, depression, and suspiciousness, than did managers in either of the other two groups.

Since that time, the hardiness training procedure has expanded to include exercises that entail not only hardy attitudes and problem-solving coping but also socially supportive interactions and effective self-care (Khoshaba & Maddi, 2001). Recently, a study evaluated the effectiveness of this comprehensive HardiTraining program on the academic performance of high-risk undergraduates (Maddi et al., 2002). In this study, two counselors offered hardiness training as a semester credit course to small freshman classes. The effectiveness of HardiTraining was compared to that of another semester credit course emphasizing other facilitative procedures, such as time management and study skills. Results showed that by comparison with the control course, the HardiTraining course led to not only greater increases in hardy attitudes and strategies but also retention in college, rather than leaving.

The HardiTraining procedure has also been researched when offered as a one-quarter credit course taught by qualified instructors at a large university (Maddi, Harvey, Khoshaba, Fazel, & Resurreccion, 2009a). The 349 undergraduates taking this course were compared to a control group of 378 undergraduates who took another course taught by the same instructors. Results obtained before the courses began showed that the experimental and control groups did not differ in demographics, time in school, grade point averages, or hardiness attitudes and strategies. By comparison with the control courses, the HardiTraining course led to an increase in hardiness attitudes and strategies, and a decrease in anxiety, depression, and strain. Further, at graduation, 6–24 months later, the students who had taken the HardiTraining course showed higher increases in their grade point averages than did those who had taken the control courses. Taken together, the studies completed thus far indicate that HardiTraining is effective in enhancing not only hardiness attitudes and strategies but performance and satisfaction as well.

The courses mentioned above were based on our HardiTraining workbook (Khoshaba & Maddi, 2004). This workbook includes narratives on hardiness, inspirational and troubling examples, specific exercises, and periodic checkpoints. Its emphasis is on exercising and developing the hardy strategies of problem-solving coping, socially supportive interactions, and effective self-care, and using the feedback obtained through these efforts to deepen the 3Cs of hardy attitudes.

The first step in problem-solving coping is for the trainees to make a list of all the stressful circumstances that are currently being experienced and have not yet been solved. Then, they engage in the following pattern for each of the stressful circumstances. First, they use situational reconstruction (Khoshaba & Maddi, 2004), which is an imaginative procedure designed to develop a broader perspective and deeper understanding of the stressful circumstance. That information then facilitates developing an action plan that can make a decisive difference in turning the stressful circumstance to advantage and carrying it out.

If situational reconstruction does not facilitate successful completion of these steps, then the trainees are faced with the possibility that they are suppressing strong negative emotions raised by the stressor in a way that is stifling imagination. To check out this possibility, trainees are taught to engage in focusing (Gendlin, 1978), a procedure for reflecting on signs of emotional upset or strain in one's body (e.g., chest tension, stomach upset) and listening to whatever insights emerge. If emotional insights are obtained through focusing, this will free up the imagination necessary for obtaining a broader perspective and deeper understanding when one tries situational reconstruction again, which will then permit planning and taking decisive actions to solve the stressful problem.

If neither situational reconstruction nor focusing works, trainees are permitted to conclude that they have encountered an unchangeable situation. The training emphasis then shifts to compensatory self-improvement (Khoshaba & Maddi, 2004), through which trainees protect their hardy attitudes by avoiding self-pity and bitterness about the world. They do this compensatory task by finding some other stressful circumstance that is related in their minds to the unchangeable one, and working on this other stressor instead with situational reconstruction and, if needed, focusing. The conclusion they reach is that although they cannot change all stressful circumstances, they are working on the ones they can change, which moderates self-pity and bitterness.

In working on each of their stressful circumstances through this overall process, trainees are also taught how to use the feedback they get from their efforts at problem-solving coping to deepen their hardy attitudes of commitment, control, and challenge. The three sources of this feedback are (1) observations of oneself in action, (2) observations made by others of one's actions, and (3) the effects of the actions one takes. Even if not all the action plans are completely successful, the feedback may well be enough to deepen the hardy attitudes.

In the social support component of HardiTraining (Khoshaba & Maddi, 2004), trainees evaluate, and improve as necessary, the effectiveness and value of their interaction networks with such significant others as family members, other loved ones, and coworkers. After making a list of significant others, trainees apply exercises as to pinpointing conflicts that may exist with these others, and then the task becomes resolution of the interactional problems. They learn to do this by practicing ways of improving communication and listening approaches. In this, the hardy coping process is helpful in facilitating a mutual pattern of giving and receiving assistance and encouragement, rather than continuing with damaging competition or overprotection. In this process, trainees are also taught how to use the feedback from their efforts to strengthen their 3Cs of hardy attitudes.

The final aspect of HardiTraining is beneficial self-care (Khoshaba & Maddi, 2004), which emphasizes maintaining organismic arousal at an optimal level for carrying out problem-solving coping and socially supportive interactions. The exercises they go through help trainees (a) identify whether their arousal is too high or too low, and (b) take the necessary relaxation, nutrition, and exercise steps to rectify these problems. Once again, as trainees engage in these steps, they are shown how to use the feedback they receive to deepen their hardy attitudes of commitment, control, and challenge.

In summary, the overall effect of HardiTraining is the involvement of the trainees in their process of interacting with others and the environment in a manner that recognizes the stressfulness of living but turns it from a potential disaster into a growth process instead. The training makes it difficult for them to deny and avoid stresses, as if they are entitled to easy comfort and security, or exaggerate and strike out against them, as if they are victimized by others and the world. Instead, they turn stresses to their advantage and grow in wisdom and fulfillment in the process. As to hardiness assessment, the HardiSurvey III-R is available at http://www.HardinessInstitute.com. Hardiness training is also available at http://www.HardiTraining.coursehost.com.

## CONCLUSIONS

There is accumulating research evidence for the role of hardiness in enhancing performance, health, and quality of life under stresses. Hardiness appears to be a pathway to resilience by facilitating the process of turning stressful circumstances from potential disasters into growth opportunities, but there is little research concerning hardiness and the specifics of consumer behavior. Studies are needed to determine whether there is empirical support for the hypotheses established in this chapter that high levels of hardiness (i.e., existential courage, hard work skills) are associated with more conscientious and positive consumer behaviors that promote well-being, especially when life is especially stressful for whatever reasons. In contrast, low levels of hardiness (i.e., absence of existential courage and hard work skills) lead to responding to overall life stresses by denial, avoidance, victimization beliefs, and aggressive responding. Thus, low hardiness is likely to be associated with excessive, adventurous, competitive, and progressively undermining consumer behaviors that thwart well-being. These behaviors likely include compulsive and impulsive buying, overspending, gambling, and dependencies and addictions that cover a wide gamut, from alcohol, drugs, and foods of certain types to television, video games, and pornography, among others.

There are some enlightening studies already conducted on the reaction of people to stresses that are specific to consumer pressures, and many more are needed. One relevant study (Duhachek, 2005) emphasized coping behaviors in response to stressful consumer episodes, such as lapses in service, and rude or negligent treatment by an employee. A factor analysis approach to the responses of subjects to questionnaire items covering a range of coping reactions to consumer stresses yielded evidence of both what has been structured in this chapter as hardy problem-solving coping, and denial and avoidance coping. However, this study did not address whether hardy attitudes (i.e., existential courage) influenced whether a person emphasized problem-solving coping rather than denial and avoidance. Another qualitative study emphasized whether informants reported excessive drinking or not (Piacentini & Banister, 2009). The study emphasized the stresses resulting from the informants existing in an excessive drinking culture, and the difficulty this imposes on individuals who may not want to conform. In considering why individuals may not want to drink excessively, several possible sociocultural reasons were emphasized, but there was no consideration of the possible importance of existential courage or hardiness per se. Several other studies (e.g., MacInnis & de Mello, 2005; Menon & Dube, 2007; Otnes, Lowrey, & Shrum, 1997) considered various coping strategies, emotional conflicts, hope, and emotional provider support in people's efforts to engage in consumer behaviors that affect quality of life. Although some of the findings of these various studies are compatible with the hardiness position of this chapter, none of them specifically tested and expanded on the principal hypothesis summarized here, namely, that hardy attitudes and skills can lead to beneficial consumer behaviors through more effective management of the overall stresses of living. Transformative Consumer Research can lead the way in exploring and enhancing this promising perspective to a much greater degree for the benefit of consumers across societies worldwide.

## REFERENCES

Allred, K. D., & Smith, T. W. (1989). The hardy personality: Cognitive and psychological responses to evaluative threat. *Journal of Personality and Social Psychology, 56*, 257–266.

Atella, M. (1989). *Crossing boundaries: Effectiveness and health among Western managers living in China.* Unpublished doctoral dissertation, University of Chicago.

Bartone, P. T. (1999). Hardiness protects against war-related stress in Army reserve forces. *Consulting Psychology Journal, 51*, 72–82.

Bartone, P. T., & Snook, T. (1999, May). *Cognitive and personality factors predict leader development in U.S. Army cadets.* Paper presented at the 35th annual meeting of the International Applied Military Psychology Symposium, Florence, Italy.

Bartone, P. T., Ursano, R. J., Wright, K. M., & Ingraham, L. H. (1989). The impact of a military air disaster on the health of assistance workers: A prospective study. *Journal of Nervous and Mental Disease, 177*, 317–328.

Binswanger, L. (1963). *Being-in-the-world: Selected papers of Ludwig Binswanger* (J. Needleman, Trans.). New York: Basic Books.

Bonanno, G. (2004). Loss, trauma, and human resilience: Have we underestimated the human capacity to thrive after extremely aversive events? *American Psychologist, 51*, 72–78.

Cannon, W. B. (1929). *Bodily changes in pain, hunger, fear, and rage.* New York: Appleton.

Contrada, R. J. (1989). Type A behavior, personality hardiness, and cardiovascular responses to stress. *Journal of Personality and Social Psychology, 57*, 895–903.

Duhachek, A. (2005). Coping: A multidimensional, hierarchical framework of responses to stressful consumption episodes. *Journal of Consumer Research, 32*, 41–53.

Florian, V., Milkulincer, M., & Taubman, O. (1995). Does hardiness contribute to mental health during a stressful real life situation: The roles of appraisal and coping. *Journal of Personality and Social Psychology, 68*, 687–695.

Frankl, V. (1960). *The doctor and the soul.* New York: Knopf.

Funk, S. C. (1992). Hardiness: A review of theory and research. *Health Psychology, 11*, 335–345.

Funk, S. C., & Houston, B. K. (1987). A critical analysis of the hardiness scale's validity and utility. *Journal of Personality and Social Psychology, 53*, 572–578.

Gendlin, E. T. (1978). *Focusing* (2nd ed.). New York: Bantam.

Harvey, R. H. (2005). *Hardiness at work: Psychophysiological indicators of everyday courage under stress.* Unpublished doctoral dissertation, University of California, Irvine.

Hull, J. G., Van Treuren, R. R., & Virnelli, S. (1987). Hardiness and health: A critique and alternative approach. *Journal of Personality and Social Psychology, 53*, 518–530.

Khoshaba, D. M., & Maddi, S. R. (1999). Early experiences in hardiness development. *Consulting Psychology Journal, 51*, 106–116.

Khoshaba, D. M., & Maddi, S. R. (2004). *HardiTraining: Managing stressful change* (5th ed.). Irvine, CA: Hardiness Institute.

Khoshaba, D. M., & Maddi, S. R. (2005). *Resilience at work: How to succeed no matter what life throws at you.* New York: Amacom.

Kierkegaard, S. (1954). *Fear and trembling, and the sickness unto death* (W. Lowrie, Trans.). Garden City, NY: Doubleday Anchor. (Original work published 1843)

Kobasa, S. C., Maddi, S. R., & Kahn, D. (1982). Hardiness and health: A prospective study. *Journal of Personality and Social Psychology, 42*, 168–177.

Kuo, W. H., & Tsai, Y. (1986). Social networking, hardiness, and immigrant's mental health. *Journal of Health and Social Behavior, 27*, 133–149.

Lancer, K. (2000). *Hardiness and Olympic women's synchronized swimming team.* Paper presented at the Conference on Improving Performance in Sports, Las Vegas, NV.

Lifton, D. E., Seay, S., & Bushke, A. (2000, Summer). Can student "hardiness" serve as an indicator of likely persistence to graduation? Baseline results from a longitudinal study. *Academic Exchange Quarterly*, 73–81.

MacInnis, D. J., & de Mello, G. (2005). The concept of hope and its relevance to product evaluation and choice. *Journal of Marketing, 69*, 1–14.

Maddi, S. R. (1980). Developmental value of fear of death. *Journal of Mind and Behavior, 1*, 85–92.

Maddi, S. R. (1986). Existential psychotherapy. In J. Garske & S. Lynn (Eds.), *Contemporary psychotherapy* (pp. 191–215). New York: Merrill.

Maddi, S. R. (1987). Hardiness training at Illinois Bell Telephone. In J. P. Opatz (Ed.), *Health promotion evaluation* (pp. 101–115). Stephens Point, WI: National Wellness Institute.

Maddi, S. R. (1988). On the problem of accepting facticity and pursuing possibility. In S. B. Messer, L. A. Sass, & R. L. Woolfolk (Eds.), *Hermeneutics and psychological theory: Interpretive perspectives on personality, psychotherapy, and psychopathology* (pp. 182–209). New Brunswick, NJ: Rutgers University Press.

Maddi, S. R. (1994). The Hardiness Enhancing Lifestyle Program (HELP) for improving physical, mental, and social wellness. In C. Hopper (Ed.), *Wellness lecture series*. Oakland, CA.: University of California/Health Net.

Maddi, S. R. (1997). Personal Views Survey II: A measure of dispositional hardiness. In C. P. Zalaquett & R. J. Woods (Eds.), *Evaluating stress: A book of resources* (pp. 293–310). New York: University Press.

Maddi, S. R. (1998a). Creating meaning through making decisions. In P. T. P. Wong & P. S. Fry (Eds.), *The human quest for meaning: A handbook of psychological research and clinical applications* (pp. 3–26). Mahwah, NJ: Erlbaum.

Maddi, S. R. (1998b). Dispositional hardiness in health and effectiveness. In H. S. Friedman (Ed.), *Encyclopedia of mental health* (pp. 323–335). San Diego, CA: Academic Press.

Maddi, S. R. (1999). The personality construct of hardiness, I: Effect on experiencing coping and strain. *Consulting Psychology Journal, 51*, 83–94.

Maddi, S. R. (2002). The story of hardiness: Twenty years of theorizing, research, and practice. *Consulting Psychology Journal, 54*, 173–185.

Maddi, S. R. (2004). Hardiness: An operationalization of existential courage. *Journal of Humanistic Psychology, 44*, 279–298.

Maddi, S. R., Brow, M., Khoshaba, D. M., & Vaitkus, M. (2006). The relationship of hardiness and religiosity in depression and anger. *Consulting Psychology Journal, 58*, 148–161.

Maddi, S. R., Harvey, R. H., Khoshaba, D. M., Fazel, M., & Resurreccion, N. (2009a). Hardiness facilitates performance in college. *Journal of Positive Psychology, 4*, 566–577.

Maddi, S. R., Harvey, R. H., Khoshaba, D. M., Fazel, M., & Resurreccion, N. (2009b). The personality construct of hardiness, IV: Expressed in positive cognitions and emotions concerning oneself and developmentally-relevant activities. *Journal of Humanistic Psychology, 49*, 292–305.

Maddi, S. R., Harvey, R. H., Khoshaba, D. M., Lu, J. H., Persico, M., & Brow, M. (2006). The personality construct of hardiness, III: Relationships with repression, innovativeness, authoritarianism, and performance. *Journal of Personality, 74*, 575–598.

Maddi, S. R., Harvey, R. H., Resurreccion, R., Giatras, C. D., & Raganold, S. (2007). Hardiness as a performance enhancer in firefighters. *International Journal of Fire Service Leadership and Management, 1*, 3–9.

Maddi, S. R., & Hess, M. (1992). Hardiness and success in basketball. *International Journal of Sports Psychology, 23*, 360–368.

Maddi, S. R., & Hightower, M. (1999). Hardiness and optimism as expressed in coping patterns. *Consulting Psychology Journal, 51*, 95–105.

Maddi, S. R., Kahn, S., & Maddi, K. L. (1998). The effectiveness of hardiness training. *Consulting Psychology Journal, 50*, 78–86.

Maddi, S. R., & Khoshaba, D. M. (1994). Hardiness and mental health. *Journal of Personality Assessment, 63*, 265–274.

Maddi, S. R., & Khoshaba, D. M. (2001). *Personal Views Survey*. Irvine, CA: Hardiness Institute.

Maddi, S. R., Khoshaba, D. M., Jensen, K., Carter, E., Lu, J., & Harvey, R. H. (2002). Hardiness training for high risk undergraduates. *NACADA Journal, 22*, 45–55.

Maddi, S. R., Khoshaba, D. M., Persico, M., Bleecker, F., & VanArsdall, G. (1997). Psychological correlates of psychopathology in a national sample of the morbidly obese. *Obesity Surgery, 7*, 397–404.

Maddi, S. R., & Kobasa, S. C. (1984). *The hardy executive: Health under stress*. Homewood, IL: Dow Jones-Irwin.

Maddi, S. R., Wadhwa, P., & Haier, R. J. (1996). Relationship of hardiness to alcohol and drug use in adolescents. *American Journal of Drug and Alcohol Abuse, 22*, 247–257.

May, R. (1950). *The meaning of anxiety*. New York: Ronald Press.

May, R., Angel, E., & Ellenberger, H. F. (1958). *Existence: A new dimension in psychiatry and psychology*. New York: Basic Books.

Menon, K., & Dube, L. (2007). The effect of emotional provider support on angry versus anxious consumers. *International Journal of Research in Marketing, 24*, 268–275.

Mick, D. G. (2008). Degrees of freedom of will: An essential endless question in consumer behavior. *Journal of Consumer Psychology, 18*(1), 17–21.

Mick, D. G., Broniarczyk, S., & Haidt, J. (2004). Choose, choose, choose, choose, choose, choose, choose: Emerging and prospective research on the deleterious effects of living in consumer hyperchoice. *Journal of Business Ethics, 52*(2), 207–211.

Nenkov, G. Y., Inman, J. J., & Hulland, J. (2008). Considering the future: The conceptualization and measurement of elaboration on potential outcomes. *Journal of Consumer Research, 35*(1), 126–141.

Otnes, C., Lowrey, T. M., & Shrum, L. J. (1997). Toward an understanding of consumer ambivalence. *Journal of Consumer Research, 24*, 80–93.

Piacentini, M. G., & Banister, E. N. (2009). Managing anti-consumption in an excessive drinking culture. *Journal of Business Research, 62*, 279–288.

Price, L. P., Arnould, E. J., & Curasi, C. F. (2000). Older consumers' disposition of special possessions. *Journal of Consumer Research, 27*, 179–201.

Rank, O. (1929). *The trauma of birth*. New York: Harcourt, Brace.

Sartre, J. (1956). *Being and nothingness: An essay on phenomenological ontology* (H. Barnes, Trans.). New York: Philosophical Library. (Original work published 1943)

Selye, H. (1976). *Stress in health and disease*. Reading, MA: Butterworth.

Sinclair, R. R., & Tetrick, L. E. (2000). Implications of item wording for hardiness structure, relations with neuroticism, and stress buffering. *Journal of Research in Personality, 34*, 1–25.

Weibe, D. J., & McCallum, D. M. (1986). Health practices and hardiness as mediators in the stress–illness relationship. *Health Psychology, 5*, 435–438.

Westman, M. (1990). The relationship between stress and performance: The moderating effect of hardiness. *Human Performance, 3*, 141–155.

Wooten, D. B. (2006). From labeling possessions to possessing labels: Ridicule and socialization among adolescents. *Journal of Consumer Research, 33*(2), 188–198.

# 32

## Can Consumers Be Wise?
### Aristotle Speaks to the 21st Century

DAVID GLEN MICK AND BARRY SCHWARTZ

What does it mean to be a wise consumer? We suspect that for most people, *wise* in this context means shrewd; that is, someone who is not taken in by marketing hype, who negotiates good deals, and who gets what he or she wants. In this chapter, we seek to develop a much needed and richer understanding of the wise consumer.

The origins of modern consumer behaviors have been debated by historians, whereas there has been little disagreement over the varieties and magnitude of acquiring, consuming, and disposing (Schor & Holt, 2000). Many analysts have noted that the proliferation of these practices, fostered by international organizations, governments, businesses, and consumers themselves, has harbored a general assumption that more products, possessions, and consumption translate into greater economic welfare and greater human satisfaction (Borgmann, 2001). However, the flaws underlying this supposition have been well exposed in recent years by distressing global and regional trends, including poor nutrition and rising obesity rates, thousands of annual vehicular deaths, wide-scale substance abuse (e.g., tobacco, alcohol, drugs), ecological degradation, credit card misuse and dwindling saving rates, heightened materialism and status aspirations, and declines in overall happiness (see, e.g., Andreasen, Goldberg, & Sirgy, Chapter 2 of this volume; Burroughs & Rindfleisch, Chapter 12 of this volume; Csikszentmihalyi, Foreword of this volume; Diener & Seligman, 2004; Grier & Moore, Chapter 15 of this volume; Kilbourne & Mittelstaedt, Chapter 14 of this volume; Markus & Schwartz, 2010; McDonagh, Dobscha, & Prothero, Chapter 13 of this volume; Pechmann, Biglan, Grube, & Cody, Chapter 17 of this volume; Schwartz, 2004; Scitovsky, 1976; Soman, Cheema, & Chan, Chapter 20 of this volume; Speth, 2008). According to some observers, many of these developments and their chilling and killing effects are due to foolish personal choices (e.g., Keeney, 2008).

These trends reveal just how much consumer behavior is a moral activity and how much all of us as consumers have underestimated, if not shirked, that responsibility (Borgmann, 2001; Brinkmann, 2004; Mick, 2005). Morality concerns how humans should live their lives, particularly in cases in which their actions can be assessed as essentially right or wrong. Consumer behavior has moral dimensions, because all consumer choices involve a combination of spoken and unspoken values directed toward living things (e.g., our selves; our loved ones; the people who harvest, mine, and combine the raw materials; the animals sacrificed or otherwise affected by production and consumption) and toward the environment (e.g., natural resources, the biodegradability of ingredients and packaging, the impact of fossil fuels in making and transporting products). The rippling of moral waves from our ongoing consumer behaviors means, in a most daunting and humbling way, that "there is always something at stake" (O'Dea, 2004, p. 9).

Yet, making excellent, or at least better, consumer choices seems to be getting harder and harder. Many factors, such as technology and information overload, are contributing to increased complexity and stress in modern life (Levey & Levey, 1999). To add to this dismaying condition, researchers in behavioral economics have catalogued numerous unconscious biases in human judgments that regularly lead people to make decisions that are contrary to their chief preferences or best interests (Ariely, 2008; Thaler & Sunstein, 2008). It seems we have limited control of ourselves as consumers. Lacking control, there is diminished potential for goodness and quality of life in our spirits, minds, bodies, families, societies, and ecologies.

Is it possible for consumers to be wise, to do the right thing more often, when they make consumption decisions? In this chapter, we put that question to Aristotle. The question itself, and his response, are both timely and timeless. For Aristotle, there are hope and direction through practical wisdom, which he called *phronesis*. No other virtue in his philosophy is more simultaneously linked to morality and human well-being. The foundation of Aristotle's practical wisdom is "the capacity to recognize the essentials of what we encounter and to respond well and fittingly to those circumstances" (Fowers, 2003, p. 415). However, being a wise consumer is not just knowing one's preferences well, adding more dimensions to one's multiattribute utility function, or being savvy at cost–benefit analysis. Wisdom is a metafunctional and integrative process that balances multiple and often conflicting factors. Rather than being a mixture of relevant expertise and useful decision rules, practical wisdom is about perceptive, context-sensitive judgments with a mission to maintain or enhance well-being.

In the next section, we review Aristotle's conception of practical wisdom in more detail, and then we turn to recent research from social science on wisdom. Next, we pull these insights together and apply them in the analysis of four consumer-behavior vignettes. We close with a discussion on the prospects of educating and encouraging consumers about practical wisdom and suggest future paths of scholarly research to understand and promote practical consumer wisdom.

## PRACTICAL WISDOM FROM THE ARISTOTELIAN PERSPECTIVE

Wisdom has been addressed for hundreds of years in theological, philosophical, and literary works as the epitome of human virtues (Assmann, 1994; Hall, 2010). Across these sources, wisdom has been viewed as a superior, complex, and desirable form of knowledge that reflects a keen understanding and experience of the fundamental nature of reality and humankind's relationship to it (Clayton & Birren, 1980). Eventually, in less ornate terms and more readily linked to everyday actions, *wisdom* came to be defined in *The Compact Oxford English Dictionary* (*COED*; 1991) as "the capacity of judging rightly in matters relating to life and conduct; soundness of judgment in the choice of means and ends" (p. 2325).

Aristotle (ca. 350 BCE/1999) was among the first to distinguish between different kinds of wisdom, dividing the philosophical from the practical. On the one hand, he equated the former with metaphysics, or the study of the definitive principles and causes of reality. Practical wisdom, on the other hand, he associated with searching for the ultimate good of human endeavors, and it is the wellspring of the *COED* definition above. Practical wisdom is also distinguished by its orientation to action; it is more about know-how (i.e., the pragmatics of life) rather than know-that (i.e., factual expertise). Practical wisdom also departs from practical intelligence by its specific concern with human actions that have moral consequences and implications.

Aristotle's moral theory is a virtue theory, which differentiates it from later theories like Kant's, which depends on universal principles, or John Stuart Mill's utilitarianism, which depends solely on rational decision procedures. The aim of life, Aristotle wrote in his book *Nichomachean Ethics*, is eudaimonia, which is akin to Seligman's (2002) notion of authentic happiness and has been also translated as well-being or flourishing. To achieve this aim requires the cultivation of the virtues—all of them. A parent or a judge who is strong in kindness and generosity but weak in justice and perspective would be a disastrous parent or judge—and not very happy. Further, Aristotle noted that more is not necessarily better when considering specific virtues for a given situation. Rather, we need to know how courageous, kind, honest, empathic, or loyal to be. The virtues need to exist in the right proportions, and they need to be developed and deployed to the right degree. In general, an excess of a virtue can be as counterproductive to eudaimonia as too little.

The need to choose among the virtues, calibrate our well-meaning actions, and balance virtues in conflict were central issues for Aristotle. In a well-known passage in *Nicomachean Ethics*, he warned that there can be too much of a good thing. Consider the virtue of courage so critical to a warrior. A good soldier needs to be brave enough to risk death, but taking himself, or his troops, into a battle in which he would be certain to be massacred is reckless, not courageous. Yet, if a soldier is never willing to put himself or his troops at risk, that is cowardice. Hence, courage lies somewhere between cowardice and recklessness. That point, in Aristotle's words, is the mean between cowardice and recklessness. Similarly, many consumer behaviors require, for instance, balances between needs and desires, frugality and indulgence, and short- and long-term preferences.

Aristotle's mean, however, is not a simple average of two extremes. Instead, it is just the right mix of caution and boldness, or thrift and lavishness, that is appropriate to the particular circumstance. Practical wisdom figures out what the mean or balance is for each situation.

Aristotle used several compelling metaphors to illustrate how to determine the mean. For example, a person who evokes a predetermined formula to find the mean, or a set of rules to identify which virtue should prevail in a situation of conflict, is like a builder who tries to use a straight ruler to make the curves of a molding. Instead, Aristotle suggested using the flexible lead rule in which the soft metal can be bent to conform to the shape of the molding. Thus, rather than forcing a situation to fit the formula or tool, a wise person knows when and how to adapt the formula or tool to fit the situation.

Furthermore, Aristotle argued that the right amount of any of the virtues is context specific. Is caution a strength? Yes. Remember to "Look before you leap," but change the context and remember that "He who hesitates is lost." The balance between caution and decisiveness is not the midpoint on some underlying scale. Where the balance or mean lies exactly will vary from circumstance to circumstance.

Practical wisdom, the master virtue, is Aristotle's solution to managing all the remaining virtues, including the judgment of which ones and in which degrees a specific context requires. Practical wisdom is essential for orchestrating the other virtues into an effective, moral, and happy life. From Aristotle's perspective, rules—whether Kantian, utilitarian, or of any other kind—are inadequate to the moral tasks of everyday life (see also Johnson, 1993; Nussbaum, 1995; Wallace, 1988). Rules have their place in our deliberations. Following rules is the best people can do if they do not know the context well enough to discern a pattern or its resemblance to other contexts they know. Thus, rules that consumers have learned directly or indirectly, such as do not discard unused paint in a garbage dump, give gift cards at holidays and celebrations when you do not know the recipient well, buy a higher priced item if you want better quality, and shop at store X if you want the lowest prices, make reasonable sense as best policies when a situation is full of ambiguity or ignorance. Following a good rule can often make the best of a difficult or perplexing situation. However, rules are like a road map that gets a driver to the right city but not necessarily to the right street. To find the right street, or know the right thing to do, Aristotle argued that practical wisdom is needed to improve on the mere application of a rule, however respectable or logical the rule might seem.

People need practical wisdom, because in order to decide how to act in any concrete situation, people must solve three problems. First, real-life situations do not always come labeled with the applicable rules or virtues attached. There is, thus, the problem of relevance. Second, real-life situations often put rules or virtues in conflict with one another. Finally, virtues and rules lack the specificity required for translation into action. Suppose two given situations necessitate, respectively, the virtue of kindness and the virtue of frugality. Then, it must be determined what exactly it would mean to be kind or frugal in those situations. It is in resolving these three issues—relevance, conflict, and specificity—that the Aristotelian philosophy of practical wisdom becomes essential (Wallace, 1988).

It is important to make clear that practical wisdom is not the same as practical intelligence. Practical intelligence, what Aristotle called *techne*, is what enables a person to know the right thing to do to achieve his or her goals. It is an important part of practical wisdom, but it is only one component. Practical intelligence is silent on the question of what human goals should be; it does not tell a person what to aim for. To have practical wisdom is to know what to aim for, to know the purpose of being a friend, a parent, a teacher, or a conscientious consumer. Also, practical intelligence does not make a person want to do the right thing. It is purely cognitive not motivational. Someone with practical wisdom not only knows the right thing to do but also wants to do it.

In terms of acquiring wisdom, Aristotle believed that wisdom is learned from experiences but cannot be taught, at least not didactically. One becomes wise by confronting difficult and ambiguous situations, using one's judgment to decide what to do, doing it, and getting feedback. Wisdom may thus be domain specific (e.g., the wise manager may not be a wise parent or a wise consumer). One becomes wiser in a given domain by developing the propensity for striving to be wise in that domain. In discussing the development of wisdom, Aristotle emphasized the importance of well-trained habit. People learn what wisdom is in the way they learn how to keep their balance when riding a bike: by practicing, falling, and trying again, until the moment-by-moment adjustments needed to stay upright eventually occur automatically and effortlessly. To be sure, many wise decisions require deliberation, but many require swift intuition honed by experience. Even the decisions that require deliberation are aided by experience-based intuition.

Aristotle thought of virtues such as courage, loyalty, and responsibility as enduring character traits of people. In other words, he wrote about courageous people, not just courageous acts. In the modern lexicon of social and behavioral science, these traits would be most usually labeled as personality traits or dispositions rather than character traits. The key difference, however, between personality traits and character traits is that the idea of personality is purely descriptive (e.g., you are outgoing, I am introverted). Character, in contrast, is also evaluative. Virtues are not just characteristics of people; they are excellent characteristics of people that are cultivated over time through repeated consideration and vigilant application.

## PARADIGMS OF WISDOM IN RECENT PSYCHOLGICAL SCIENCE

Compared to its Aristotelian heritage, the study of wisdom in the social sciences is young. The most prominent paradigms have variously drawn from Aristotle and include those headed by Clayton (Clayton & Birren, 1980), Baltes (Baltes & Smith, 2008; Baltes & Staudinger, 2000; Kunzmann & Baltes, 2005), Sternberg (1998, 2001), and Ardelt (2004). We focus on Baltes and Sternberg, as we are constrained by page limitations, and their paradigms have been the most influential thus far. Following Aristotle, Baltes and Sternberg both associate wisdom with certain types of knowledge and the application of knowledge, in pursuit of well-being and the common good. They regularly use the word *wisdom* without the modifier *practical*, but it is apparent they are most directly concerned with practical wisdom.

Baltes and his colleagues have mainly studied wisdom as an existential expertise that develops over the life span, known as the Berlin wisdom paradigm. They characterize wisdom as excellence in mind and virtue, specifically as an expert knowledge system, known as fundamental life pragmatics, for planning, managing, and understanding a good life (Baltes & Smith, 2008). Included in this system are knowledge of life's obligations and goals, knowledge of oneself and the limits of one's own knowledge, knowledge of translating knowledge into behavior (i.e., synergizing mind, virtue, and action), and understanding the socially and contextually intertwined nature of human life (Baltes & Staudinger, 2000). The measures of wisdom in action that Baltes and his colleagues have used include attentive listening, outstanding advice, insightful comments on challenging and ambiguous matters in life, affect regulation, and empathy in interpersonal settings. Some of the newest work in the Berlin wisdom paradigm is now examining the role of emotions as input into wise judgments and actions (Kunzmann & Baltes, 2005).

Sternberg's (2001) paradigm builds on his earlier work on intelligence. He defines *wisdom* as

> the application of tacit and explicit knowledge as mediated by values toward the achievement of a common good through a balance among (a) intrapersonal, (b) interpersonal, and (c) extrapersonal interests over (a) short and (b) long terms, to achieve a balance among (a) adaption to existing environments, (b) shaping of existing environments, and (c) selection of new environments. (p. 231)

Adapting means changing oneself to fit the existing environment or situation, shaping means modifying aspects of the environment or situation to fit one's interests, and selecting a new environment means abandoning the existing one for something else. Based on research he completed on people's implicit theories of wisdom among U.S. laypersons and experts, Sternberg (1985) uncovered six dimensions of wisdom: (1) reasoning ability (e.g., logical mind, makes connections and distinctions), (2) sagacity (e.g., displays concern for others, knows self best, unafraid to make mistakes and correct them), (3) learning from ideas and environment (e.g., attaches importance to ideas, learns from mistakes), (4) judgment (e.g., thinks before deciding or acting, is able to take long views), (5) expeditious use of information (e.g., is experienced, seeks out information, changes mind on basis of experience), and (6) perspicacity (e.g., can offer solutions that are on the side of right and truth, has intuition, is able to see through things and read between the lines).

Balancing is a key metaphor in Sternberg's paradigm, as it is in Aristotle's, the Berlin group's, and others'. Balancing is not just another word or manner for standard trade-off analyses. It reflects Aristotle's emphasis on the mean in terms of finding wise solutions and behaviors that are not extreme. Balancing also does not signify that all interests, consequences, or responses must be equally weighted. The weightings may vary depending on the degree to which a specific alternative contributes to a common good. Selecting the right balance depends on one's system of values, which serves to establish the person's vision of a common good and the relative weightings of various interests, consequences, and responses.

Tacit knowledge is another crucial component in Sternberg's paradigm. He argues that tacit knowledge (i.e., gained from prior relevant experiences) permits people to perceive intuitively and/or deliberately the exclusive complexities of the situation being faced and utilize the comprehension of those complexities in a tailored fashion to attain the desired objectives. Unlike some other wisdom theorists, Sternberg maintains that wisdom has aspects that can be taught or at least encouraged (Sternberg, 2001). Recently, he has developed a wisdom-oriented curriculum for precollege classrooms and is now engaged in tracking the results (see Reznitskaya & Sternberg, 2004).

There is an emergent fund of empirical findings from the social science of wisdom, including the burgeoning domain of neuroscience. Among the intriguing findings across research streams, wisdom has been found to be (a) correlated with, but distinct from, general intelligence; (b) positively associated with open-mindedness, mastery, maturity, autonomy, emotional regulation, compassion, humility, altruism, patience, creativity, effective stress management, self-actualization, tolerance for ambiguity, psychological and physical well-being, and successful aging; and (c) negatively related to depressive symptoms, feelings of economic pressure, and fear of death (Ardelt, 2004; Baltes & Smith, 2008; Hall, 2010; Peterson & Seligman, 2004; Sternberg, 1998, 2001).

## SUMMARY OF ARISTOTLE'S PRACTICAL WISDOM AND RECENT PSYCHOLOGICAL RESEARCH

Our overview of Aristotle's concept of practical wisdom and subsequent social science has been inevitably concise, and we hesitate to condense its kaleidoscopic qualities even further. However, for purposes of understanding its potential role in consumer behavior, we summarize as follows the facets of practical wisdom to which we want to draw particular attention:

- Practical wisdom is focused on producing judgments, decisions, and behaviors intended to attain or improve eudaimonia (e.g., well-being, flourishing, happiness); thereby, it is a morally oriented process insofar as such judgments, decisions, and behaviors can often be deemed right or wrong for achieving eudaimonia.
- Practical wisdom is transcendent and metafunctional, meaning that it is metacognitive, reflective, deliberative, and mindful of one's motives, thoughts, and feelings in the process of judging, deciding, and taking actions.
- Practical wisdom balances personal, interpersonal, and extrapersonal concerns, and in doing so, it seeks to balance particular virtues or values in many cases and finds the mean rather than extremes.
- Practical wisdom regularly adopts both short- and long-term perspectives.
- Practical wisdom regularly adopts a wide perspective, considering multiple stakeholders affected by or implicated in the decision options and consequences.
- Practical wisdom integrates values, goals, and behaviors.
- Practical wisdom is sensitive to and perceptive about the context in which a judgment, decision, or behavior occurs; it proceeds accordingly as a process and set of outcomes that are contingent on or relative to the given context.
- Practical wisdom often requires improvisation and does not rely solely on rules or algorithmic decision procedures.
- Practical wisdom often draws on learning from prior mistakes as a matter of self-knowledge and continual improvement.
- Practical wisdom often requires intuition, not just logic or rationality, to understand situations of importance that require moral judgments, decisions, and behaviors.
- Practical wisdom uses emotions, not just cognitions, as instructive input to how humans respond to situations and improve decisions and behaviors accordingly.
- Practical wisdom develops according to habits of being mindful, reflective, sagacious, perspicacious, and so forth; without habits of this sort, a person cannot develop a wise character for facing life's many challenging decisions.

With this foundation in place, we now use the qualities of practical wisdom to elucidate four consumer behavior scenarios that reflect everyday occurrences in which varied degrees of practical wisdom are evinced.

## APPLICATIONS OF PRACTICAL WISDOM TO CONSUMPTION CASES

Consider the following vignette involving a couple who faced a problematic decision about discarding an outdated, poorly performing television set:

---

Richard and Carol have been married for 16 years, over which time they have developed mutual interests in environmentalism, including recycling and donating. They are also not avid television viewers. But after 10 years of ownership, their current cathode ray television seemed small, and the picture quality had worsened. Repairing the set would cost more than its resale value. So, they searched television retailers in their area and found a good deal on a 42-inch, flat screen, high-definition television. Delivery and setup of the new set are scheduled for later this week.

With this new purchase completed, Richard and Carol now faced the decision of what to do with their older set. They are short on storage space in both their house and garage. One of their neighbors told them how he recently put out a broken-down television for the garbage service to pick up, and the next day, it was gone with the trash. That seemed the most convenient option, and he opined that the garbage service people probably know what to do with these older sets. The neighbor also mentioned that it seemed the sensible thing to do, because after all, he pays a monthly fee for trash removal, and it makes sense to use the service accordingly. Richard and Carol understand their neighbor's position, but they have private qualms about it. They have both read that throwing electronic devices into landfills poses hazards to the soil and groundwater, and it ignores the possible value of the set and some of its components for other purposes.

The next day, Carol talked about the television disposal decision with some coworkers. One of them, Alice, told Carol that there are definitely other options, based on what one of Alice's relatives did with their defunct television. Alice suggested that Carol should call some local appliance repair shops and do some searching on the Internet. Carol was thankful for the advice and determined that afternoon that a recycling center exists in the next county. It accepts old televisions for a $12 handling fee and then passes the sets on to appliance and electronics stores where parts and materials are salvaged, and the remaining materials are sent to an electronic-waste recycling facility in a nearby state. Two days later, Richard and Carol drove the round trip of 38 miles to drop off their old set, and they returned home that afternoon for the installation of their new one.

---

As is evident in this case, Richard and Carol wanted to dispose of their old television in a manner that made it more likely that as little as possible would be dumped into a landfill. Many, but far from all, consumers are aware that lead, copper, and plastic components in electronic equipment are not readily biodegradable. Careless disposal can increase earth and groundwater contamination, which is an unmistakable moral issue that affects quality of life for future generations of human and nonhuman beings. Rather than quickly following a neighbor's well-intended but expedience- and expense-driven advice, Carol showed the moral will to find an alternative option that emphasized recycling of key components. Richard and Carol thought about long-term issues and other stakeholders and balanced their interests with those of others and the environment for the common good. Without perhaps realizing it, they consciously sought an Aristotelian mean between a trouble-free versus onerous disposal of their old television set and between immediate removal and indefinite storage at home. They accepted the relatively moderate sacrifice of delivering the old set themselves to a recycling organization 38 miles away. In making their disposal decision, they reflected on and lined up their values, goals, and behavior in a meaningful way by asking important questions and seeking new information to do what seemed most right to them in this situation.

But, how much time should Richard and Carol have spent researching the alternatives? How much inconvenience should they have been willing to sustain to dispose of the television as safely as possible? What other useful things might they have done with their time if they had just left their old television at the curbside for garbage pickup? These are not easy questions to answer, but as it is so often the case in the assessment of practical wisdom, many of us, as *post factum* observers, would call Richard and Carol's actions admirable and wise. According to the qualities discussed above, their process evoked a substantial degree of practical wisdom.

Now, consider a woman named Beth who, like many contemporary parents, has children who have developed a keen interest in electronic games. Here are the details of her case:

---

Beth is a single mother with two sons, Ryan and Andy, ages 7 and 13, respectively. Like a lot of kids in their age groups, they are fond of electronic devices, particularly those that play video games. Andy recently had a birthday and has been unrelenting in asking his mother to allow him to use the money to purchase a new Apple iTouch; he does not have his own computer as yet. The iTouch uses WiFi to search the Web, send e-mails, and download music and games, among other activities. When Beth and the boys stopped at an electronics store to get a music CD for a friend, the boys gravitated immediately to the electronic devices. Andy was impatient with his mom, as she showed continuing hesitation to agree to let him buy an iTouch. At the same time, Ryan was playing with an iTouch as they stood in the aisle discussing the device. Ryan reminded his mom that he also had some Christmas money left over to buy his own iTouch. After all, if Andy was going to get one, he said, why couldn't he have one, too? Both Ryan and Andy pleaded with their mom, pointing out that some of their friends have an iTouch or something similar.

Beth felt stressed and under significant pressure from the boys. She didn't want the boys feeling left out or backward among their friends, but then she also knows that kids can be prone to playing video games too much, to the detriment of other worthwhile activities. With the purchase price of the iTouch being around $200 at the time, Beth asked the boys if they had enough money in their individual savings accounts at the bank, and both said yes, although it turned out that Ryan was wrong and had only $110 in his account. Beth agreed to let them each buy an iTouch. The boys were elated, and Beth wondered as they drove home whether this was a purchase decision she would soon second-guess or defend.

---

From the outline of this consumer decision, it seems that Beth did not think much about the context and appropriateness of the new electronic device for each son. Also, she rushed this decision in certain respects, when there seemed no reason to have done so, aside from getting her sons to stop whining. The older son is age-appropriate for the iTouch, but the younger is arguably not. Beth could have told the boys that she wanted to sit down in quiet with them at home, in advance of buying any device, to discuss the buying of new electronic devices. If the meeting was productive and cooperative, she could consider agreeing to the purchase of the devices. This short delay would have allowed her to find out more about the iTouch (e.g., via Internet and other parents) and determine whether a less sophisticated device would be available and satisfactory for her younger son for the foreseeable future (e.g., a Nintendo DS). She could also use the meeting to discuss guidelines for the use of the devices (e.g., when to use or not, how long each day they can play, her intentions to activate parental controls on the devices) and the consequences of going against those guidelines. The meeting would also allow her to discuss how some children get too attached to electronics and ask them to imagine and discuss what those problems might be. Once Beth knew more and had the parameters of device use established, she could return to the store and help the boys make the right purchases for them and their family situation.

This is obviously not what Beth did. She did not link up her values, goals, and behavior well, she did not try to consider short- and long-term perspectives on the purchases, and she did not trust her moral intuitions about the appropriateness of the product for both boys. Simply put, she did not read the situation well. Or, did she? This device decision is just one in a series of decisions Beth must make in raising her sons. She may have learned that parents must pick their battles if they are to avoid unending conflicts with their kids as the kids enter adolescence and struggle for independence. Should Beth hold the line here or save being tough for other things? How should she balance her desire to treat her kids equally with her desire to give each boy what he needs? Beth knows more about parenting her children than we do, and in this context, her decision may have been the right one. Yet, by the qualities of practical wisdom established above and the facts given about this case, Beth's practical wisdom in buying the same device for both boys, in the emotional buzz of an imposing electronic retail environment, without setting a baseline of family policies as to usage of the devices, seems less wise than it could have been. In general, she was not as metafunctional in the overall situation as she could have been, had she taken the time and effort to step back, rise above, and more thoroughly process the range of issues and implications that were in play for the nearer and longer terms.

Next, consider the following case that centers around a father's thorny decision about riflery training for his son:

---

Phil is married and has two sons, one of whom is 16 and the other 12. As a matter of his own beliefs, throughout his life, Phil has been critical of gun laws that he sees as too lenient and contributing to high rates of violent crime. In raising his sons, he has not owned a gun in his home and has limited their exposure to toy guns and other guns, such as BB guns and airsoft guns. Recently, however, his younger son attended a weeklong 4-H camp where one of the adult-supervised activities for kids 12 and over was training at a rifle range, with practice using bull's-eye targets in a remote side lot of the 4-H camp.

After returning home from the camp, his son expressed a strong wish to learn more about riflery. He showed his dad the paper targets he shot at, which had several hits near the middle of the target. His son sheepishly bragged that he was told that he had a real good eye and technique for shooting a rifle. His son also mentioned that one of the adult supervisors at the camp talked about a local gun club where rifles could be rented or purchased and classes and a rifle range are provided.

In light of the past, Phil naturally felt quite reluctant to give any prompt feedback that might indicate he could agree to his son's request. Phil thought more about his role as a father in protecting his sons, but also in building their skills and respect in things that matter to them, provided such related activities could be performed safely. He did some searching online, including on message boards and through chat rooms, to learn more about riflery. He shared these insights with his wife. Phil also called the local rifle range to get information on classes and costs, and then discussed the situation with his wife. They decided that it was worth the effort for Phil and the younger son to visit the range. Afterward, Phil and his wife decided to sign up both their son and Phil for classes in rifle use.

---

Phil approached this situation with much considered, well-articulated values, but he did not strictly or uniformly enforce his prior values as unbending rules. He also did not let his emotions (e.g., anger, frustration, fear) get control of him in this decision. His son had a growing interest in riflery. Phil balanced his feelings about weapons against his son's enthusiasm, and he strove to balance a number of other personal, interpersonal, and extrapersonal matters. He sought to make sure that safety would be maintained, and his son would learn to appreciate the need for protocols and practice in performing a dangerous activity well. Phil hoped that his son would learn to respect guns and respect the need to ensure the safety of those around him. Phil balanced his conflicted values, fitting them to the situation as best he could, and thought about the short- and long-term consequences for his son. In a sense, Phil sought an Aristotelian mean between authoritarianism and democracy or anarchy in the family. Going further into the realm of practical wisdom, Phil might also have taken into account the importance of his son's self-confidence in learning to shoot well. Phil might have thought further about the way in which the training involved would enhance perseverance and self-discipline. In addition, he might have contemplated how this training could develop in his son an appreciation for dedication and expertise in life. Finally, he might have also realized that denying his son access to guns via a rifle range could, as a boomerang effect, intensify the son's interest and lead the boy to use a gun in the future in a less respectful and unsafe manner.

Guns are almost certainly not the medium Phil would have chosen to teach his son certain lessons that Phil hoped the boy would learn in growing up. Yet, there it was. Phil could not deny his son's access to or interest in guns for the son's entire life. Overall, Phil approached the situation as one needing more than the unreflective application of a prior value rule (i.e., no guns). Instead, it required a strong dose of metafunctionality and an integration of thoughts, feelings, and values, plus flexibility and improvisation.

In the final vignette, a consumer named Chris buys some ground beef, which is typically a routine, low-involvement purchase:

---

Chris is running errands on a summer afternoon and needs to pick up some items for dinner that night with her husband and 6-year-old daughter. Like millions of other families in the United States, they enjoy cooking on their backyard grill. Chris stops at a large, regional grocery store and buys two pounds of packaged ground beef for $7, plus hamburger buns, pickles, and two tubs of coleslaw and potato salad.

---

In what sense might this decision be practically wise or not? The answer partly surrounds the response to a second question, namely, what are the true costs of a pound of beef? In a perceptive *New York Times Magazine* article, Pollan (2002) notes that we know what we pay for the beef in the market. But what about other costs—what economists call externalities—that are not reflected in the market price? Beef costs what it does, in part, because the growing of the corn that is used to feed the cows is subsidized by the U.S. federal government. So, we pay for beef with our taxes. Cows eat corn rather than grass, because it is cheaper to feed them corn than it is to have them graze on grass. However, the cow's digestive system cannot handle corn, so cows must be dosed prophylactically with antibiotics to keep them healthy long enough to get them to market. The cost to the farmer of the antibiotics is reflected in the market price of beef, but we also pay for this antibiotic prophylaxis in drug-resistant strains of bacteria that make human illnesses harder and more costly to treat. This cost is not reflected in a pound of beef.

Corn feed also changes the acidity of the cow's digestive environment, making it compatible with the human digestive system, so that microbes—some of them potentially lethal—can survive the trip from cow to person intact, and then make people sick. Corn-fed beef is fattier than grass-fed beef, and it is a kind of fat that is considered less conducive to human health. Growing the corn that feeds the cows also depends on heavy doses of fertilizer, which depends on petrochemicals. Thus, if one framed the price of a pound of beef broadly, to include all these externalities, the cost of a pound of beef would have to include some fraction of the cost of bacterial infection and cardiovascular disease. That, in turn, would have to include the costs of treatment, the costs in mortality and morbidity, workdays lost, and decreases in quality of life. Also, it would have to include some fraction of the cost, in money and lives, of a U.S. foreign policy partly driven by the need for reliable access to petrochemicals. Where does this accounting for the price of a pound of beef stop?

This case sounds like a situation in which the consideration of multiple stakeholders as well as short- and long-term effects could be overwhelming. In fact, as Kahneman (2003) points out, people tend to frame the options they face and the possible consequences of their choices very narrowly. They trudge up the hill, looking down at their feet, and fail to appreciate adequately the long-term consequences for themselves and others. This can lead to decisions that are incoherent when examined against a broader canvas, and decisions that poorly serve people's and society's long-term interests. But how broadly should decisions be framed?

For example, what should a person do with a $1,000 year-end bonus? We can, perhaps easily, see the foolishness of the individual running out and spending it on an item of clothing recently seen on display in an elegant neighborhood shop, but what is the sensible alternative to this impulsiveness? Should the consumer sit down and think about all the ways that money can be spent? If so, that $1,000 will not be worth much by the time the exhaustive, and exhausting, examination of possibilities is over.

"Frame your decisions more broadly" may be good advice for most people most of the time, but one of the benefits of narrow framing is that it gives people the opportunity to do less contemplating and more deciding. Narrow framing may lead to dubious judgments, but extremely broad framing can induce paralysis. Thus, narrow framing may lead to bad decisions, but the solution to this problem is not to frame decisions as broadly as possible in all situations. Clearly, a measure of balance, an Aristotelian mean, is called for, guided in large part by an assessment of what breadth of framing allows people to make good decisions in the context of a particular practice.

In the case of Chris's beef purchase, the decision was framed quite quickly and narrowly, without any consideration for personal health, the sentient animals involved, or the environment. There was no wider or more reflective perspective, even if only momentary. At one important level, the decision indicates an unquestioned inclination for certain habits or cultural routines. Although it seems harsh to say so, the argument can be made that Chris's purchase of the beef, based on a number of dimensions, was relatively unwise. Yet, to do the kind of analysis that Pollan did, not just in purchasing beef but also in purchasing any food, poses challenges that few ordinary people can meet during the flux of everyday decision making. Practical wisdom, therefore, is also about producing an appropriate amount of reflection relative to the web of interactions, moral issues, and consequences that inhere or result from the considered action.

What, then, is an appropriate amount of reflection? In the context of a wisdom framework for decision making that disdains hard-set rules, it is frustrating, but hardly surprising, that there is no formulaic answer to this central question. The answer is, it depends. It depends on the magnitude of the decision. It also depends on whether there are well-established social norms or institutional practices that will make elaborate reflection unnecessary. Sunstein (1996; Sunstein &

Ullmann-Margalit, 2000) has written extensively about the role of rules, laws, policies, and social norms in aiding individual decisions. Societies make what he calls second-order decisions about where to allow discretion for first-order decisions. Much cognitive effort and deliberation may go into formulating a rule or policy regarding, say, recycling, after which individual decision making becomes effortless. In this view, the appropriate amount of reflection in a given situation depends on one's assessment of how much reflection society has already done in setting down rules, policies, and guidelines. Wise judgment is still required to determine whether a given amount of what might be called collective reflection is enough, but at least the individual decision maker does not have to face each new situation from scratch.

## HELPING CONSUMERS BE WISER MORE OFTEN

Wisdom is an intricate concept and an intimidating goal. In fact, philosophers and social scientists have sometimes asserted that, as the pinnacle of human achievement, wisdom is relatively rare. Nonetheless, nearly all of these same analysts emphasize the significance of practical wisdom to decision making and quality of life. If nothing else, practical wisdom is a vision of human character that asks the most and best of people.

In the challenging era of human and earthly evolution we inhabit, which is pervaded by consumer behaviors, it would seem dangerously premature to give up on wisdom just because it demands a lot of us. These are times when practical wisdom deserves the most thoughtful analysis and research we can provide. Confronting practical wisdom, as we have done in this chapter, is not for creating or realizing algorithms that will definitively tell consumers what they should think, feel, or do in any given situation. Rather, our purpose has been to outline Aristotelian philosophy and recent social science for suggesting how practical wisdom can be evoked by consumers for implementing better judgments, decisions, and behaviors

Behavioral economists of the last few decades would likely say that practical wisdom requires too much of people in everyday situations. Humans, as these behavioral economists have maintained, have unavoidable, unconscious frailties for processing information, which lead them into consistently flawed decisions. These frailties include overconfidence, myopia, favoring the status quo, susceptibility to framing, and anchoring and adjustment (for others, see Thaler & Sunstein, 2008). Yet, as we have implied throughout, practical wisdom is directly concerned with recognizing and overcoming simple and mindless human inclinations, especially in decision contexts that have sensitive moral issues in play.

Practical wisdom is not all or none. It is a matter of more or less, according to the qualities discussed earlier. Importantly, it has long been believed in Western and Eastern philosophies that wisdom can be nurtured with practice. The next critical question becomes, how can such nurturing be facilitated among consumers?

### Consumer Education

Given the substantial role of consumption in daily life, it is clear that children, young adults, and older adults could benefit from increased instruction and guidance on practical wisdom in consumer behavior. Sternberg (2001) has outlined a number of strategies for teaching wisdom in school settings, and many of these could be developed specifically for the area of consumption. Depending on their educational level, students could read articles or watch films that inform them about current trends in economics, lifestyles, and ecologies that involve wise or unwise consumption behaviors, and then discuss their reactions and possible solutions within society and their own lives. One example is through documentary films, such as *Fresh* and *Food, Inc.*, which raise serious questions and dilemmas about contemporary food production and consumption in American society. New consumer cases can be written for class discussions, with the derivation of personal and societal solutions to be evaluated according to practical wisdom criteria (e.g., recognizing self-interests and balancing those with other interests; taking short- and long-term perspectives; using emotions and intuitions of moral issues as triggers to deeper thought and analysis of the situation at hand to be metafunctional; linking values, goals, and behaviors).

Consumption situations and decisions vary widely and occur persistently across daily life, from health decisions, food consumption, and the purchase of household furnishings, automobiles, and real estate, to credit card use and saving behavior and the discarding of garbage, packaging, and unused possessions. Books, newsletters, radio and television programs, community seminars, and online forums can be created to make adults more aware of the scope, processes, and consequences of their consumer decisions and behaviors and provide them with tools for being wiser and more fulfilled in their consumption activities. Ideas from other insightful books on decision making that dovetail with aspects of practical wisdom could be consulted to develop such programs and materials.

For instance, Keeney (1992) and Hammond, Keeney, and Raiffa (1999) emphasize the importance of people clarifying their values and objectives before making important and difficult decisions. These techniques need to be extended to a wider range of life's decisions. The authors also stress the merits of clarifying uncertainties and understanding consequences (e.g., how an imminent decision links with others that will be necessary later as a result). When possible, writing down values, objectives, uncertainties, and consequences during a calm moment can be quite beneficial. Focusing particularly on values, they argue, fosters more innovative thinking about decision alternatives and, potentially, stakeholders who could be affected by the decision. Keeney's and Hammond et al.'s perspectives exclude some aspects of practical wisdom (e.g., not recognizing the use of emotions and intuitions as resources for better decisions), but they express many worthy ideas that are concordant with aspects of practical wisdom.

Consumer education of the sorts we have pointed to is not a panacea and will not be successful for all consumers in engendering practical wisdom. For those who desire help and for whom such materials and programs fit with their learning abilities and styles, consumer education focused on practical wisdom could have some large and lasting effects on well-being. The greatest need may exist in elementary grades to begin planting the seeds of practical wisdom as children grow into full-fledged consumers. But to be true to the spirit of Aristotle, if wisdom depends on experience, on doing, then didactic efforts will be informative but only partially effective. People must act, sometimes mistakenly, and learn from their mistakes. The power of learning through trial and error is now, after a century of research, a truism in learning theory. It is also a prominent agent in the development and tuning of the architecture of the cognitive networks that have long been thought to play a major role in our ability to make sense of the world (McClelland, Rumelhart, & the PDP Research Group, 1986).

More recently, Churchland (1996) and others (e.g., Flanagan, 1996; Johnson, 1996) have illustrated how network theory applies to moral judgments in general and practical wisdom in particular. If we are mindful of the importance of mistakes, especially trial and error, we can seek to organize pedagogical experiences, especially among young people, and improve parenting perspectives so that mistakes are not too costly, and their role in building a life of greater practical wisdom is realized (see also Prinz, Chapter 28 of this volume). Among the most important topics under this broad approach include spending and saving, credit cards, gambling, and food consumption (Cotte & LaTour, Chapter 23 of this volume; Faber & Vohs, Chapter 22 of this volume; Grier & Moore, Chapter 15 of this volume; Loewenstein, Cryder, Benartzi, & Previtero, Chapter 19 of this volume; Soman et al., Chapter 20 of this volume).

### The Internet

Many insights and tools for wiser consumption exist via the Internet, although many consumers remain unaware of them or, worse, cannot access them (Hoffman, Chapter 9 of this volume). New websites, such as GoodGuide and Ethical Consumer, are appearing with general and specific advice on companies and products that seem more likely to assist consumers in making wiser decisions. The next step would be for an organization to serve as a locator, consolidator, and evaluator of such sites to ensure that the knowledge and guidance offered are as credible and valuable as possible for wiser consumption decisions. Such a development would be valuable for consumers across the world who have Internet access.

There is also the opportunity to make greater and better use of social media (e.g., Facebook, Twitter) to promote wiser consumption decisions. See Kozinets, Belz, and McDonagh (Chapter 10 of this volume) for specific insights and recommendations on the use of social media for facilitating consumer democracy and empowerment. This general approach could be particularly effective if organized and implemented by individuals versed in group discussion moderation as well as the literature on practical wisdom.

### Better Business Practices

Businesses themselves could begin to take an even higher road of corporate social responsibility by asking how they can facilitate consumer wisdom (see also Mick, Bateman, & Lutz, 2009). Retailers, for instance, have broad authority over their point-of-purchase displays, return policies, service departments, consumer help lines, and so forth. Each could be evolved in ways that reflect encouragement of wisdom, by asking key questions about needs, intended product uses, and past experiences with similar products; cautioning about debt that cannot be unquestionably repaid in a timely manner; making return policies more lenient; training service personnel to help consumers understand their values and goals before buying, and so forth. Such strategies may sound lofty and could be patronizing if not implemented effectively, but companies that genuinely take their customers' best interests to heart are likely to reap new levels of customer trust, loyalty, and positive word-of-mouth recommendations (Fournier, Dobscha, & Mick, 1998). The time has come for companies to not just satisfy consumers but also help them be as wise as possible. Some may say this is not business's job, but in today's world, no business can survive, let alone thrive, if it does not live up to its role as a steward of society and quality of life.

### Government Policies via Libertarian Paternalism

In their admirable book *Nudge: Improving Decisions About Health, Wealth, and Happiness,* Thaler and Sunstein (2008) use findings from behavioral economics to develop a philosophy of libertarian paternalism to guide public policies and consumers toward smarter decisions. Their suggestions are founded on the idea of structuring choice environments, so natural human biases in decision making can unfold in due course and still result in favorable outcomes for the individual and society. Their examples span from health care decisions and financial investing to education and marriage. For instance, many people profess to want to be organ donors upon their death, to aid society's medical needs, but they often do not sign up for such programs when offered the opportunity while obtaining or renewing a driver's license. It takes a deliberate effort to check off a box indicating that the individual is joining the program. The status quo or default option of not checking the box means that the individual is not volunteering as an organ donor. Thaler and Sunstein (2008) discuss research that reverses this choice situation, whereby the default is an assumption of being an organ donor, with the requirement to check a box if the person wishes to opt out of the program. Not surprisingly, the result of this change in one state was a near doubling of organ donors to over 80%.

This is arguably a valuable route to encouraging people to make wiser choices, insofar as wider and longer term considerations are taken into account, the common good is taken into account, and so forth. The trouble is, however, that the taking into account is not done by the consumer chooser but by someone else, namely the choice architect. In the example above, a large share of consumers who leave the box unchecked, and then become potential donors, never faces the given societal moral issue, are never reflective of their values and goals as linking to behaviors, and so forth. That is, the qualities of practical wisdom are hardly to be found in their decision processes.

Thaler and Sunstein (2008) argue that libertarian paternalism and choice architecture do not alter freedom of choice, which is true insofar as the decision maker is not restricted to only one option or compelled to pick an option from two or more. Nonetheless, in the example of the default option in organ donations, we would contend that the societal outcome can be subjectively judged to be wise, but the process internal to the consumer is rendered rather fallow in terms of practical wisdom. This is reminiscent of the age-old aphorism embedded in the question surrounding a situation in which there is a starving person who lives near a lake: Is it better to give him a fish to eat or teach him or her how to catch fish?

In sum, we admire many of Thaler and Sunstein's (2008) suggestions for guiding choices that improve quality of life. What remains to be more thoroughly considered is the extent to which the research and presumptions underlying their approach can lead not only to free choices but also to wise choices, either through the alteration of the choice architecture and/or the addition of questions and information to consumers before they decide. This is not a minor or hair-splitting concern. As Csikszentmihalyi (1995) has argued, evoking wisdom can be a joyful and rewarding experience unto itself. As Aristotle emphasized, wisdom is a character trait developed through good habits of thoughtfulness and behavior. If we can help people make decisions that are both free and wise, with the assistance of libertarian paternalism, then the decision outcomes will be beneficial not only to society but also to consumer decision makers. This should be an important priority for new research and policy consideration.

Present and Future Research

Research on practical consumer wisdom is just beginning, and the potential topics are many and varied. One approach would be the study of specific consumer behaviors in everyday settings and learning from the ground up how consumers evoke or do not evoke practical wisdom. Important areas include product safety and maintenance, parenting young consumers, disposing of hazardous materials, finding and using product information online and buying online, knowing when and how to use consumer credit, and so forth. Such studies can be used to compare and interpret actual consumer tactics in terms of wisdom theory and research, for the purpose of expanding knowledge about wisdom as well as consumer behavior.

For instance, using purchase diaries and interviews, Mick, Spiller, and Baglioni (in press) found that several of their participants perceived promotional deals (e.g., buy one and then get a second one at half the price) as encouraging excessive consumption that they felt was wrong. Promotions invited unwise purchases when the consumers became distracted by the pricing lure and, thereby, became less mindful of their emotional reactions and realistic product needs. Some participants also reported a conscious focus on regret minimization as their chief manner of increasing the wisdom of their purchases. To do this, they deliberated on their values and goals as well as they could and did not rush the final decision. More research insights such as these need to be developed and shared with consumers for encouraging wiser decision making.

Future research should focus particularly on when and why the qualities of practical wisdom are evoked or not in different consumption situations by different types of consumers. In other words, research should determine which wisdom qualities seem most crucial for which types of decisions and consumption situations, which dimensions of situations (e.g., physical, social, time) encourage or discourage practical consumer wisdom, and which types of consumers are more or less prone to be practically wise in specific situations, such as consumers who vary on life span stage, cognitive traits such as need for cognition or need for closure, and personality traits such as egoism. More basic research is needed to understand how and when consumers take multiple interests into account and how they balance those as best they can before deciding and acting.

Another major frontier surrounds the matter of learning from past mistakes, as this is crucial to the development of practical consumer wisdom; however, little is known in the consumer research field about this phenomenon. Questions abound, such as, what sorts of mistakes are consumers most prone to in their purchasing, using, and disposing of products? Why do consumers sometimes learn from mistakes and make wisdom-oriented corrections, and why at other times do they not? Also, which types of consumers are more likely to learn from and correct mistakes, and which are not?

The neuropsychology of practical wisdom is a resource-laden frontier waiting for further explorers (Hall, 2010; see also Litt, Pirouz, & Shiv, Chapter 25 of this volume). Topics could include the use of simulated purchase decision making, including the use of loans or credit cards, cognitive efforts at mental accounting, experiences in online gambling, the consumption of pornography, the construction of virtual lives through computers, sharing behaviors, and family consumption events (Albright, Chapter 24 of this volume; Belk & Llamas, Chapter 30 of this volume; Cotte & LaTour, Chapter 23 of this volume; Epp & Price, Chapter 29 of this volume; Loewenstein et al., Chapter 19 of this volume; Novak, Chapter 11 of this volume; Soman et al., Chapter 20 of this volume). Finally, the meaning and processes of practical wisdom are unstable across human history (Assmann, 1994) and probably not homogeneous across contemporary cultures and societies. Future research is needed to flesh out the similarities and differences, including the implications for guiding practical consumer wisdom in different settings in a manner that is locally respectful but still aiming to maximize the common global good.

Individuals, families, and societies need more wisdom. We have drawn from Aristotle and social science to sketch out the nature of practical consumer wisdom as it ensues from Western perspectives and research. We have discussed the role of consumer choices and morals, offered guidance on future wisdom research, and suggested how people could become more committed to and more capable of being wiser consumers.

## REFERENCES

Ardelt, M. (2004). Wisdom as expert knowledge system: A critical review of a contemporary operationalization of an ancient concept. *Human Development, 47*, 257–285.

Ariely, D. (2008). *Predictably irrational: The hidden forces that shape our decisions.* New York: HarperCollins.

Aristotle. (1999). *Nicomachean ethics* (M. Ostwald, Trans.). Upper Saddle River, NJ: Prentice Hall. (Original work ca. 350 BCE)

Assmann, A. (1994). Wholesome knowledge: Concepts of wisdom in a historical and cross-cultural perspective. In D. L. Featherman, R. M. Lerner, & M. Perlmutter (Eds.), *Life-span development and behavior* (pp. 187–224). Hillsdale, NJ: Erlbaum,

Baltes, P. B., & Smith, J. (2008). The fascination of wisdom: Its nature, ontogeny, and function. *Perspectives on Psychological Science, 3*(1), 56–64.

Baltes, P. B., & Staudinger, U. M. (2000). Wisdom: A metaheuristic (pragmatic) to orchestrate mind and virtue toward excellence. *American Psychologist, 55*, 122–136.

Borgmann, A. (2001). The moral complexion of consumption. *Journal of Consumer Research, 26*(4), 418–422.

Brinkmann, J. (2004). Looking at consumer behavior in a moral perspective. *Journal of Business Ethics, 51*, 129–141.

Churchland, P. M. (1996). The neural representation of the social world. In L. May, M. Friedman, & A. Clark (Eds.), *Mind and morals: Essays on ethics and cognitive science* (pp. 91–108). Cambridge, MA: MIT Press.

Clayton, V. P., & Birren, J. E. (1980). The development of wisdom across the life-span: A reexamination of an ancient topic. In P. B. Baltes & O. G. Brim (Eds.), *Life-span development and behavior* (Vol. 3, pp. 103–135). New York: Academic Press.

*Compact Oxford English Dictionary* (2nd ed.). (1991). Oxford, England: Oxford University Press. (1995). *Poetic justice*. Boston: Beacon Press.

Csikszentmihalyi, M. (1995). Toward an evolutionary hermeneutics: The case of wisdom. In R. F. Goodman & W. R. Fisher (Eds.), *Rethinking knowledge: Reflections across the disciplines* (pp. 123–143). New York: University of New York Press.

Diener, E., & Seligman, M. E. P. (2004). Beyond money: Toward an economy of well-being. *Psychological Science in the Public Interest, 5*, 1–31.

Flanagan, O. (1996). Ethics naturalized: Ethics as human ecology. In L. May, M. Friedman, & A. Clark (Eds.), *Mind and morals: Essays on ethics and cognitive science* (pp. 19–44). Cambridge, MA: MIT Press.

Fournier, S., Dobscha, S., & Mick, D. G. (1998). Preventing the premature death of relationship marketing. *Harvard Business Review, 76*(January/February), 42–51.

Fowers, B. J. (2003). Reason and finitude: In praise of practical wisdom. *American Behavioral Scientist, 47*(4), 415–426.

Hall, S. S. (2010). *Wisdom: From philosophy to neuroscience.* New York: Knopf.

Hammond, J. S., Keeney, R. L., & Raiffa, H. (1999). *Smart choices: A practical guide to making better life decisions.* New York: Broadway Books.

Johnson, M. L. (1993). *Moral imagination.* Chicago: University of Chicago Press.

Johnson, M. L. (1996). How moral psychology changes moral theory. In L. May, M. Friedman, & A. Clark (Eds.), *Mind and morals: Essays on ethics and cognitive science* (pp. 45–68). Cambridge, MA: MIT Press.

Kahneman, D. (2003). A perspective on judgment and choice. *American Psychologist, 58*, 697–720.

Keeney, R. L. (1992). *Valued-focused thinking.* Cambridge, MA: Harvard University Press.

Keeney, R. L. (2008). Personal decisions are the leading cause of death. *Operations Research, 56*(6), 1335–1347.

Kunzmann, U., & Baltes, P. B. (2005). The psychology of wisdom: Theoretical and empirical challenges. In R. J. Sternberg & J. Jordan (Eds.), *A handbook of wisdom* (pp. 110–135). New York: Cambridge University Press.

Levey, J., & Levey, M. (1999). *Wisdom at work: A treasury of tools for cultivating clarity, kindness, and resilience.* Berkeley, CA: Conari Press.

Markus, H. R., & Schwartz, B. (2010). Does choice mean freedom and well-being? *Journal of Consumer Research, 37*(2), 344–355.

McClelland, J., Rumelhart, D., & the PDP Research Group. (1986). *Parallel distributed processing: Explorations in the microstructure of cognition.* Vol. 2: Psychological and biological models. Cambridge, MA: MIT Press.

Mick, D. G. (2005, Fall). Choice writ larger. *Newsletter of the Association for Consumer Research.* Available: http://www.acrwebsite.org/topic.asp?artID=316

Mick, D. G., Bateman, T. S., & Lutz, R. (2009). Wisdom: Exploring the pinnacle of human virtues as a central link from micromarketing to macromarketing. *Journal of Macromarketing, 29*(2), 198–218.

Mick, D. G., Spiller, S. A., & Baglioni, A. J. (in press). A systematic self-observation study of consumers' conceptions of practical wisdom in everyday purchase events. *Journal of Business Research.*

Nussbaum, M. C. (1995). *Poetic justice.* Boston: Beacon Press.

O'Dea, J. (2004, September–November). Choice and consequence. *Shift: At the Frontiers of Consciousness,* 8–10.

Peterson, C., & Seligman, M. E. P. (2004). *Character strengths and virtues: A handbook and classification.* New York: Oxford University Press.

Pollan, M. (2002, March 31). Power steer. *The New York Times Magazine.* Available: http://www.nytimes.com/2002/03/31/magazine/power-steer.html?scp=2&sq=michael+pollan&st=nyt

Reznitskaya, A., & Sternberg, R. J. (2004). Teaching students to make wise judgments: The "teaching for wisdom" program. In P. A. Linley & S. Joseph (Eds.), *Positive psychology in practice* (pp. 181–196). New York: Wiley.

Schor, J. B., & Holt, D. (Eds.). (2000). *The consumer society: A reader.* New York: New Press.

Schwartz, B. (2004). *The paradox of choice: Why more is less.* New York: HarperCollins.

Scitovsky, T. (1976). *The joyless economy: The psychology of human satisfaction.* New York: Oxford University Press.

Seligman, M. E. P. (2002). *Authentic happiness*. New York: Free Press.

Speth, J. G. (2008). *The bridge at the edge of the earth: Capitalism, the environment, and crossing from crisis to sustainability*. New Haven, CT: Yale University Press.

Sternberg, R. J. (1985). Implicit theories of intelligence, creativity, and wisdom. *Journal of Personality and Social Psychology, 49*, 607–627.

Sternberg, R. J. (1998). A balance theory of wisdom. *Review of General Psychology, 2*, 347–365.

Sternberg, R. J. (2001). Why schools should teach for wisdom: The balance theory of wisdom in educational settings. *Educational Psychologist, 36*(4), 227–245.

Sunstein, C. R. (1996). Social norms and social roles. *Columbia Law Review, 96*, 903–968.

Sunstein, C. R., & Ullmann-Margalit, E. (2000). Second-order decisions. In C. R. Sunstein (Ed.), *Behavioral law and economics* (pp.187–209). New York: Cambridge University Press.

Thaler, R. H., & Sunstein, C. R. (2008). *Nudge: Improving decisions about health, wealth, and happiness*. New York: Penguin.

Wallace, J. D. (1988). *Moral relevance and moral conflict*. Ithaca, NY: Cornell University Press.

# *Epilogue*

## Suggestions for the Future

This volume begins with Mick, Pettigrew, Pechmann, and Ozanne's (Chapter 1) welcome historical perspective on what has become known as Transformative Consumer Research (TCR). There are in fact many precursors to TCR, including the public policy–style research element within the American Marketing Association and among professors like Lee Preston in the 1970s at the State University of New York at Buffalo. One of us also remembers using kindergarten teachers to interview 2–6-year-olds to assess the impact of television advertising on children, a popular 1970s topic. Interestingly, one 2½-year-old referred to himself in the third person and was unimpressed by cartoon character endorsements. When asked why a certain cereal was his favorite, he said, "Baby ah ha [Arthur] likes chocolate." This toddler's response suggested that the cumulative effect of advertising was more critical than any impact on specific brands, a result which, when reported to the Federal Trade Commission had a less than resounding impact.

Importantly, support for concern about consumers and nonfinancial aspects of business in general has been expressed for a long time by the heroes of capitalism. For example, Adam "Invisible Hand" Smith, whose *The Wealth of Nations* is a staple of free-market advocates, also wrote *The Theory of Moral Sentiments* (1759/2002), in which he noted that "gratitude and resentment, therefore, are the sentiments which most immediately and directly prompt to reward and to punish" (p. 81). Similarly John Maynard Keynes, known primarily for his influence on economic policy, also wrote, "The day is not far off when the economic problem will take the back seat where it belongs, and the arena of the heart and the head will be occupied or reoccupied, by our real problems—the problems of life and of human relations, of creation and behavior and religion" (as cited in McCann, 1998, p. 6). Thus, balancing economic activity, competition, and growth with concern for human sentiments and conditions has a long and distinguished history.

Of course, the term *Transformative Consumer Research* is a bit of a misnomer. In principle, understanding consumers (i.e., consumer/customer insight) is the basis for marketing decisions, and hence, all consumer research has the potential to change the behavior of firms and subsequently impact customers, or for customers to use the information to change their thoughts and behaviors on their own. Further, the transformation need not be positive (i.e., insights can be used to manipulate consumers in undesirable ways). In practice, the TCR term is being used to describe research designed for the purpose of improving consumer welfare. Because RDPICW (research designed for the purpose of improving consumer welfare) is a foreboding acronym, rather than quibble about the name, we treat TCR as a simpler name for RDPICW.

As we prepared this Epilogue, we were struck by the diversity of topics studied and approaches followed in this volume. To some extent, it matches the difference between the two of us, one of whom has committed an extensive amount of research and personal effort to such issues, and the other who has only dabbled in the area.

## CHAPTER-SPECIFIC COMMENTS

We enjoyed the chapters in this volume and appreciate the effort that went into them as well as the obvious concern the authors have for consumer welfare. We also had some brief observations on them. These thoughts are presented in the order of the major subheadings in the volume.

Part I, "Declaring and Projecting Transformative Consumer Research," provides an extensive summary of the literature related to the topic of transformation (Andreasen, Goldberg, & Sirgy, Chapter 2), a different perspective that captures the essence of transformative contributions within the scholarly domain (Wansink, Chapter 3), and a unique frame that helps position our research in the larger social science arena (Ozanne & Fischer, Chapter 4). Read together, we recommend starting with Wansink, since he provides an understanding of how to orient your career if you are interested in TCR as a life pursuit, and how best to accomplish meaningful research that remains within the parameters of rigorous scholarship. Andreasen et al. take work on impoverishment, social marketing, and quality of life and blend it into a cohesive whole, leaving the reader with a solid understanding of a large portion of the field. Ozanne and Fischer round out the contributions of Part I and reveal how to conduct compassionate research that is both personally and professionally meaningful.

Part II is simply titled "Economic and Social Issues," and its reach is as broad as its heading. Although the diverse nature of these issues makes it difficult for readers to grasp the full contribution of these chapters, nonetheless, their order herein serves the interests of scholars well. Part II begins with an orientation to subsistence markets from personal research experiences and revelations by Viswanathan (Chapter 5), followed by Shultz and Shapiro's (Chapter 6) look at one developing nation's efforts (i.e., Vietnam) to advance its goals in a complex global environment, and then a description of insightful research on subsistence and creativity by Rosa, Geiger-Oneto, and Fajardo (Chapter 7). The chapter by Williams and Henderson (Chapter 8) stands alone, but it can be integrated into the others if the reader views it from the perspective of how restriction plays out across demographic profiles.

Part III, "Technological Edges," may seem out of place to some, especially given the focus of the other contributions. However, in combination, these chapters reveal an essential aspect of life satisfaction and overall well-being that is playing out in cyberspace. For example, Hoffman (Chapter 9) describes the development of social capital online and the problems faced by those consumers on the wrong side of the digital divide. Although including consideration of the less developed and developing world may have enhanced the contribution, bringing together social capital and Internet resources is an important advancement. Kozinets, Belz, and McDonagh (Chapter 10) go one step further in their discussion of avatars and becoming part of online communities that transform participants and allow them to rise above physical and emotional limitations. Novak (Chapter 11) closes out Part III by emphasizing the importance of capturing an old construct in a new setting: quality of virtual life. Altogether, these authors demonstrate the necessity of allowing our most vulnerable consumers fuller cyber access to resources and communities if they are to improve their well-being in the age of the Internet.

Part IV, "Materialism and the Environment," seems most appropriate for a conversation on TCR, especially as it relates to over- and underconsumption. The chapters tend to focus on the former, which is no surprise given the orientation of this material in the consumer-behavior literature. McDonagh, Dobscha, and Prothero (Chapter 13) set a torrid pace, criticizing marketing and placing the problems of overconsumption squarely in the laps of a large portion of the profession, especially the practitioners. Although their discussion of the production–consumption linkage and societal well-being is somewhat one-dimensional, especially given inequities around the world, they provide a powerful challenge when they advance the concept of sustainable consumption. Kilbourne and Mittelstaedt (Chapter 14) add more fuel to this debate, using a historical perspective that opens our eyes to unique solutions. Part IV is perhaps best concluded by a reader focusing on the materialism review by Burroughs and Rindfleisch (Chapter 12), who boldly posit that materialism is the centerpiece of any conversation on TCR. Here again, a somewhat balanced discussion of how materialism plays out in affluent as well as impoverished marketplaces and communities would be helpful, but their description of the field is very useful in any case.

Part V, "Enhancing Health," is an eclectic mix of topics and perspectives that discuss some of the most vexing social issues of our time. Grier and Moore (Chapter 15), who are noted experts in this area, open Part V by examining childhood obesity. Although they spend considerable time, possibly more than may be necessary, describing why the problem exists, their examination of internal and external factors that contribute to the epidemic is enlightening, as are their approaches to prevention. Grunert, Bolton, and Raats (Chapter 16) look at the important topic of nutritional labeling, which ties nicely to the work on obesity. Once again, the background discussion is fairly long, but the meat of the material serves readers well, especially the portion that looks at theoretical and methodological challenges. Pechmann, Biglan, Grube, and Cody (Chapter 17) discuss the link of TCR and public policy to marketing research on tobacco and alcohol. The chapter's major contribution is a lengthy history of debates involving both products and their outcomes for consumer protection. Finally, Fishbein and Middlestadt (Chapter 18) provide a very thoughtful look at why risky sexual behaviors occur and a theoretical frame that may be effective in other consumer-behavior domains. Although it would have been useful had the authors more fully integrated relevant literature from the marketing and consumer field, the case studies and conclusions they provide are important, especially in a social marketing context.

Part VI, "Consumer Finances," covers some intriguing terrain. Loewenstein, Cryder, Benartzi, and Previtero (Chapter 19) reveal how mental accounting captures ordinary consumer behavior better than utility theory. Their list of problems and solutions that result from poor saving habits gives readers much to think about, especially with regard to middle-class lifestyles. Next up is Soman, Cheema, and Chan (Chapter 20), who provide an excellent discussion of the credit card mess that too many consumers find themselves in over time. Although this chapter tends to be oriented to the reasons why more affluent users run into trouble, the studies and theories advanced make for interesting reading. In the closing chapter to Part VI, Keller and Lusardi (Chapter 21) challenge our lay assumptions about retirement, often noting that our society is ill prepared to meet the challenges of the retiring baby boomers. Although the chapter does not address the fact that many people live paycheck to paycheck and never have the luxury of retiring, for many of us, their words need to be heeded.

Although the catch-all nature of Part VII's title, "Other Risky Behaviors and At-Risk Consumers," suggests a possible lack of cohesion and overlap with other segments, the individual chapters are uniformly appealing. The contribution of Baker and Mason (Chapter 26) is an excellent case in point. These two scholars have done some of the most impressive work on consumer vulnerability in the larger field, and we urge readers to examine their other contributions after enjoying this summary. Pettigrew and Moschis (Chapter 27) also discuss an important but neglected topic of consumer well-being, namely, aging. Although this chapter might be better placed elsewhere in this volume, it provides essential information that will serve marketers and policy makers as our society experiences an unprecedented and increasingly elderly subpopulation. The four chapters on gambling (Cotte & LaTour, Chapter 23), addiction (Litt, Pirouz, & Shiv,

Chapter 25), impulsive eating and spending (Faber & Vohs, Chapter 22), and pornography (Albright, Chapter 24) come together agreeably as a set of major societal issues that require more attention from TCR scholars, particularly in the developed world.

Part VIII, "Family Matters," seems regrettably short for a topic of such significance, especially given the different manifestations of what makes up family in the modern world. Nonetheless, Prinz (Chapter 28), a renowned parenting scholar, offers an intriguing discussion of effective child rearing. Although it would have been useful if he had been teamed up with someone familiar with related issues from the consumer behavior field, the ideas that he reviews from psychology provide TCR scholars an opportunity to find their own valuable linkages. Epp and Price (Chapter 29) discuss time, an extremely important topic for families within the developed and developing world. Although their examples are generally limited to more advanced economies, the topic of family time transcends geography, lifestyle, and development status.

Finally, Part IX, "Enriching Behaviors and Virtues," brings readers some closing contributions. Belk and Llamas (Chapter 30) review and extend Belk's recent contributions on sharing. The implications of this concept are extensive and profound, with implications for all peoples and societies. Maddi (Chapter 31), a social psychologist, follows this conversation with a look at resiliency and quality of life, a topic that surfaces in several other chapters in this volume. His descriptions of how stress negatively impacts our lives are convincing, although this chapter could also have been improved by adding a consumer scholar's perspective. Finally, Mick and Schwartz (Chapter 32) ask the question, "Can consumers be wise?" and take a decidedly philosophical slant on the topic. They provide an excellent template for understanding the moral dimensions of consumer decision making, at least in those portions of the world where we have the luxury of such thinking.

## OPPORTUNITIES FOR TCR

### Types of TCR and Separating Research From Advocacy and Action

In terms of consumer research in the arena of well-being, we believe there are three main types. The first is problem and solution identification, which Mick et al. (Chapter 1) call revelatory research. Basically, this is descriptive work indicating the existence or extent of a consumer problem as well as its consequences and what helps reduce it. This can be done at relatively arm's length or as a participant observer.

The second main type is policy experiments and interventions. When a researcher has an idea that something will improve consumer welfare, it makes great sense to see if it does. Both positive (i.e., please do X) and negative (i.e., please do not do X) objectives can be effective, although evidence has suggested that some direct approaches (e.g., fear appeals, recommendations) can actually backfire. Tests of reasonable interventions are certainly appropriate, often interesting, and occasionally impactful.

The third chief type is behavior explanation. Many behaviors that consumers pursue seem not to be in their best interests (e.g., overeating, compulsive gambling). Understanding this type of behavior is potentially directly beneficial, and linked to basic human behavior processes drawn from psychology, economics, sociology, and so forth. Of the three types mentioned here, this is the one most consistent with the apparent thrust of major outlets such as the *Journal of Consumer Research*.

It seems perfectly reasonable to conduct research when the results have the potential to be dramatic as well as influential, which Mick et al. (Chapter 1) call incendiary research. It also is perfectly reasonable for someone who feels strongly about an issue to advocate for their point of view. However, a person who approaches research with a preconceived view of the right answer has an increased risk of succumbing to researcher bias, which suggests that authors should indicate any such opinions during the discussion section of their papers, if not up front. However, mixing research and advocacy can have negative consequences, much of which, as many would argue, exists in the blurring between news articles and editorials in newspapers, talk radio, and blogs.

Some of the other methods discussed by Mick et al. (Chapter 1) also seem to combine either method- or solution-oriented action with research. For example, coalition research combines participant-observer research with laudable activities. Although advocacy and research can each inform the other, keeping them largely separate in written material increases academic and public credibility and forces an often useful thought process on the researcher/activist.

## Is Theory Critical?

The TCR movement seems to have an ambivalent attitude toward the role of theory. Mick et al. (Chapter 1) suggest that theory is essential. It is true that having a coherent explanation of a phenomenon and why it occurs (i.e., process) is a goal of science and generally desirable. It is also clear that many journal review processes today value, or perhaps overvalue, theory. Nonetheless, before something becomes sanctified as theory, it generally was a hunch, speculation, or story someone concocted to help others, and perhaps themselves, understand something. De facto, *theory* is operationally defined as a story someone else, preferably famous and/or from a basic discipline, managed to get published, which makes publishing something new quite difficult if it must be justified based on something old. In other words, although minor modifications are valued or at least easier to publish (e.g., by including additional moderators, mediators, and/or covariates), radically new conceptions are not readily accepted.

This problem is compounded when the goal of the research is primarily substantive, as seems to be the focus of TCR. If you view knowledge development as an ongoing process that continually cycles among thinking, confronting theory with data (i.e., hypothesis testing), and constructing theory from data, then developing good data and results, or stylized facts, is as crucial as developing or testing theory. Mick et al. (Chapter 1) also imply this viewpoint.

From a more practical perspective, consider the following. A researcher, perhaps one doing revelatory research, finds that a certain behavior exists that is harmful or helpful. This seems like a contribution even if we do not know exactly why it exists (e.g., which DNA element relates to it) or why it is harmful or helpful (i.e., the psychological, biological, or chemical process involved). Moreover, assume a researcher discovers a simple intervention that either (a) discourages or encourages the behavior or (b) reduces and minimizes or enhances the impacts (e.g., music at 70 beats per minute, eating beets). This, too, seems like a contribution, even if it does not wow reviewers. We thus offer a modest proposal. Why not let those who are good at discovering phenomena and ways to alter them focus on that and give them credit for it? In other words, why not think of TCR as battlefield engineering rather than theory development? If it happens to conform to popular theories (e.g., regulatory focus, fluency, construal, social networks), that's wonderful, and clearly that outcome is a plus.

Of course, we are not arguing for sloppiness. In fact, theory-lite research may require more rigor and attention to detail than first seems apparent. When going in with a strong theory, it is fairly clear what to do and expect. Absent this, however, there is a major burden on the researcher to meticulously document and follow procedures and actively surface, consider, and try to rule out alternative explanations for what he or she finds. For example, if you think or find that eating beets has a positive effect, then it is important to rule out that it is not eating per se, seeing red, chewing per se, or something about the participants (e.g., students in a lab) that causes the result. Although ideally this would be done logically and empirically, at a minimum, it would be helpful to consider and mention such alternative explanations. In summary, understanding (i.e., theory) is a desirable goal, if for no other reason than to increase confidence in a course of action. Given the choice between a theory-driven study that leads to a small potential improvement in consumer welfare and a less theoretical finding that has the potential for a large improvement in consumer welfare, the latter seems more appealing.

### Implementation: Confrontation Versus Co-Option

For better or worse, and fairly or unfairly, concern about consumers and their welfare is often portrayed as antithetical to corporate interests. At the extreme margin, this is clearly true; if a company charges $10 instead of $9 for a product the consumer has to have, then the consumer is $1 worse off and the company $1 better. (This assumes, for example, that the product is beneficial to the consumer, the consumption rate is independent of price paid, the benefit is positively related to amount consumed, etc.). A question that arises, therefore, is whether the best interests of consumers are served by going after corporations, either directly or through regulations. Or, does it make sense to look for common ground, including profit-making opportunities? Proverbs aside about catching flies better with honey than vinegar, it seems appropriate to consider corporate utility functions, which at some level include keeping workers gainfully employed and not just elevating short-term stock prices. For example, some companies have focused increased attention on green behavior; whether this is to do good or get positive public relations exposure is pragmatically not very important. Reports have suggested that initiatives such as General Electric's Ecoimagination are actually meeting revenue goals, which reveals a fascinating avenue for TCR. Why not, once a well-being problem has been identified, try to think up a business solution to it? This seems like a useful way to avoid the appearance of being, or being labeled, as simply anti, and it may well generate entrepreneurial ideas.

### Highlights and Shadows

This volume covers a wide variety of important substantive, conceptual, and methodological issues. Yet, like any output, it tends to emphasize some more than others. Therefore, we highlight some topics that received less attention here and have real potential for future work in TCR.

In terms of the substantive topics covered, many significant ones are explicitly addressed, including such obvious topics as poor and/or illiterate consumers, young and old consumers, discrimination, sustainability, compulsive behavior, and online behavior. In addition, some less obvious and potentially important ones are raised, including innovative businesses developed by subsistence consumers and the general topic of sharing. Clearly, there are other relevant topics. Here, we suggest five worthy of study:

1. *Consumption of education and learning*—How and why people learn, both in school and outside of it, have major consequences for the economic status of both individuals and societies, and for personal enrichment and satisfaction.
2. *Self-confidence and persistence*—At the root of many bad behaviors is the lack of sufficient self-esteem to make an independent judgment or "just say no."
3. *Medical consumption and exercise*—It was somewhat surprising that although several chapters focused on specific ailments (e.g., gambling, sexually transmitted diseases), general health behaviors such as exercise were not an explicit focus.
4. *Corporate decision making*—Understanding how consumer welfare is factored into decisions is an interesting topic, as is assessing the profit impact of doing so.
5. *Political and governmental decision making*—Similar to corporate decision making, the resulting decisions of those in politics and government have major impacts on consumers. The view that public policy makers have of consumers (i.e., whether they are viewed

as rational, helpless, overburdened, etc.) plays a role in TCR and is an interesting area for research. It is very possible that public policy makers, companies, and consumers have different views of how consumers behave, none of which may match how they actually do.

Methodologically, several approaches were in evidence in the book, including participant observation, surveys, experiments, and conceptual development. Obviously, these have much to contribute to TCR. Nonetheless, other approaches can also be useful, including:

- *Evolutionary biology*—The interplay between environment and heredity is a major influence on behavior.
- *Modeling*—This includes algebraic models of the economic or operations research variety. For example, it can be shown analytically that when both parties positively value the other's welfare, they reach agreements that leave them both better off and happier (Lehmann, 2001). Modeling also includes agent-based simulations in which the consequences of various behaviors can be extrapolated over time (e.g., Hill & Watkins, 2009).
- *Literary and media analysis*—How people are portrayed in books, television shows, commercials, and so forth reflects information and stereotypes and also influences future behavior. Thus, they provide a different vantage point from which to examine and influence behavior.

Some Final Questions and Observations

A number of topics come to mind as a result of reading the enclosed chapters. First, it is curious as to why proposals for simplifying the lives of all consumers, such as a flat tax with a substantial amount exempted, do not draw more enthusiastic support from consumer advocates, as opposed to accountants and lawyers who benefit from the system. Also, what are we doing personally? Do we still print rough drafts on one side on new paper, eat too much, and exercise too little? Are we willing to be that annoying person who reminds others to pick up their trash, turn the car off, raise the thermostat in the summer, and lower it in the winter? Do we simply throw out old clothes, furniture, and other recyclable or reusable consumables?

As researchers, are we willing to explain things in normal terms and common words? Is it really necessary to use all the many technical code words that appear throughout marketing and consumer research, including the chapters in this volume? Consumers are readers and vice versa; neither should need a dictionary to understand the basics of what we research and write. We are all biased in many ways. Disclosing the results we would have preferred to find provides some truth in reporting and allows readers, or listeners, to make whatever adjustments they deem appropriate in interpreting our findings.

Another crucial and perhaps obvious issue is whether it is best to establish a movement to confront issues or work within the capitalist structure. After all, the basic premise of marketing is that everything starts with the customer, which is evident in the American Marketing Association's (2007) latest definition of *marketing* as "the activity, set of institutions, and processes for creating, communicating, delivering, and exchanging offerings that have value for customers, clients, partners, and society at large" (para. 2). Simply implementing these tenets could go a long way toward helping consumers. Further, for better or for worse, it is probably easier and more likely to be successful by appealing to self-interest (e.g., regarding diet and exercise) or social pressure or using context effects or the availability of "good" options to motivate behavior, rather than attempting to ban "bad" actions; Prohibition did not work, and banning cigarette advertising on television two generations ago still has not ended smoking in the United States. This is especially true when the economic resources available are strained by a recession and massive government deficits. Put differently, bashing companies is likely to be no more effective than ignoring problems; rather, a third way is needed to ensure the welfare of both companies and consumers. Building on this lengthy and groundbreaking volume on TCR, we hope our comments can assist researchers further in conducting beneficial scholarship on well-being across its many contexts and dimensions.

## REFERENCES

American Marketing Association. (2007). Definition of marketing. *Marketing Power*. Available: http://www.marketingpower.com/AboutAMA/Pages/DefinitionofMarketing.aspx

Hill, R. P., & Watkins, A. (2009). The profit implications of altruistic versus egoistic orientations for business-to-business exchanges. *International Journal of Research in Marketing, 26*(March), 52–59.

Lehmann, D. R. (2001). The impact of altruism and envy on competitive behavior and satisfaction. *International Journal of Research in Marketing, 18*, 5–17.

McCann, C. R. (1998). *John Maynard Keynes: Critical responses*. London: Routledge.

Smith, A. (2002). *The theory of moral sentiments* (K. Haakonssen, Ed.). New York: Cambridge University Press. (Original work published 1759)

**Donald R. Lehmann**
*Columbia University*

**Ronald Paul Hill**
*Villanova University*

# Author Index

## A

Aaker, D. A., 69
Aakre, K., 198
Aaro, L. E., 361, 362
Aboujaoude, E., 477
Abraham, C., 400, 404
Abrams, D. B., 533
Abramson, L. Y., 470
Abramson, P. R., 392
Acemoglu, D., 566
Ackerman, J. M., 472
Adair, L. S., 313
Adam, B., 601
Addison, T., 512
Addy, C. L., 313
Adkins, N. R., 6, 19, 101
Adler, P., 195
Aero, L. F., 362
Agger, B., 17
Aghazadeh, F., 363
Agins, T., 507
Agras, W. S., 307
Agrawal, Y., 568
Ahmed, S. E., 534
Ahn, H., 433
Ahuvia, A., 254, 257
Ainscough, T., 50, 176, 186
Ainslie, G., 425–427, 447
Airhihenbuwa, C. O., 316, 317
Ajzen, I., 34, 35, 393, 396, 397, 449
Akyuz, Y., 132
Alba, J. W., 158
Alba, S., 309
Albarracin, D., 401
Albers, A., 364
Alberto, P., 586
Alday, C. S., 320
Alexis, M., 28, 29, 30
Allen, A. C., 570
Allen, C. T., 500
Allen, M., 512
Allred, K. D., 655
Allyn, D., 504
Almeida, D. M., 38
Aloise-Young, P. A., 41

Altchiler, L., 46
Altman, D. G., 364, 365
Altman, J. C., 627
Alwitt, L. F., 28, 175, 289
Amabile, T., 153, 164
Amaro, H., 404
Amber, J., 333
Ambler, G., 317
Ambler, T., 534
Ambrose, S. E., 80, 85
Ameriks, J., 418
Amir, O., 255
Ammerman, A. S., 322
An, V. K., 140, 147
Anand, P., 445, 450, 451, 453
Anderson, G., 487, 489, 494
Anderson, J. Q., 225, 226, 240, 241
Anderson, L., 7, 8, 16, 93, 101, 102
Anderson, P. F., 7, 8, 16, 367
Anderson, R. M., 392, 642
Anderson, S., 309, 528
Anderson, T. W., 269
Ando, A., 424
Andorfer, G., 85
Andreasen, A. R., 25–32, 90, 101, 172, 175, 178, 249, 252, 308, 313, 316, 321, 545
Andrews, G., 575
Andrews, J. C., 12, 363
Andrews, R. L., 358
Andriaanse, H., 362
Anes, M. D., 365
Anesbury, T., 314
Angel, D. P., 270
Angel, E., 647
Angus, K., 367, 370
Annison, J. E., 52
Antil, J. H., 269
Aral, S., 392
Arden, M. A., 401
Ardrey, W., 141
Ariely, D., 250, 253, 255, 429, 448, 450, 451, 454, 460, 530, 664
Aristotle, 663–668, 675, 677, 678
Arkes, H., 413, 420
Armitage, C. J., 401
Armstrong, G. M., 37, 308

# Subject Index